Essentials of Development Economics

Problems, programs, and data sets are available
at rebeltext.org/development.

Essentials of
Development Economics

Second Edition

J. Edward Taylor and
Travis J. Lybbert

UNIVERSITY OF CALIFORNIA PRESS

To Peri, Sebastian, and Julian

• • •

To Heather, Hannah, and Rockwell

University of California Press, one of the most distinguished university presses in
the United States, enriches lives around the world by advancing scholarship in the
humanities, social sciences, and natural sciences. Its activities are supported by
the UC Press Foundation and by philanthropic contributions from individuals
and institutions. For more information, visit www.ucpress.edu.

University of California Press
Oakland, California

First edition published 2012 by Arc Light Books/RebelText, Berkeley,
California. © 2012, 2013 by J. Edward Taylor. RebelText logo by Peri Fletcher.

www.rebeltext.org

Library of Congress Cataloging-in-Publication Data

Taylor, J. Edward, author.
   Essentials of development economics / J. Edward Taylor and Travis
J. Lybbert. — Second edition.
      pages cm
   Includes bibliographical references and index.
   ISBN 978-0-520-28316-9 (cloth : alk. paper) — ISBN 978-0-520-28317-6
(pbk. : alk. paper) — ISBN 978-0-520-95905-7 (ebook)
   1. Development economics.   2. Economic development.   3. Developing
countries—Economic policy.   I. Lybbert, Travis J., author.   II. Title.
   HD75.T39 2015
   338.9—dc23   2014044821

24 23 22 21 20 19 18 17 16 15
10 9 8 7 6 5 4 3 2 1

Contents

Sidebars

Figures and Tables

FIGURES

TABLES

Preface

The RebelText alternative textbook project was launched at the Taylor dinner table one night in fall 2012. Ed had just told the campus bookstore to order up 125 copies of an undergraduate econometrics textbook at $150 a shot. (That's a gross of $18,750 just from one class.) Over dinner that night, Ed's twenty-year-old son, Sebastian, announced that he had spent $180 (of his parents' money) on a new edition calculus text required for his course. Sebastian's little brother, Julian, exclaimed, "That's obscene!" Sebastian responded, "You're right. Basic calculus hasn't changed in decades. You don't need new editions to learn calculus."

Before dinner was over, Ed's two kids had ambushed him and made him promise never, ever, to assign an expensive textbook to his students again.

"So, what do you want me to do then, write one?" Ed asked them.

"Exactly," they answered in unison.

"And get a good title for it," Ed's wife, Peri, added.

The first RebelText creation was *Essentials of Econometrics,* with Aaron Smith and Abbie Turiansky. That seemed like a big enough project, but then Ed was assigned to teach a 350-student undergraduate development economics course. Naturally, he felt he had to write a book for that one, too. Travis climbed on board. That's how *Essentials of Development Economics* became the second member of the RebelText line.

What's RebelText? It's a textbook series designed to be affordable, compact, and concisely written for a new generation that is more at ease "Googling" than wading through big textbooks. Being both more affordable and compact, it's easier to carry around. Write in it. Don't worry about keeping the pages clean or whether there will be a market for your edition later, because at this price there's no need to resell it after the class is through. RebelText will naturally evolve as needed to keep pace with the field, but there will never, ever, be a new edition just for profits' sake.

In 2014, RebelText and UC Press struck an alliance. This UC Press edition offers readers a more complete coverage of what we see as the essentials of development economics than the original print-on-demand edition, while keeping the book affordable and compact. Through our new partnership with UC Press, we hope to turn RebelText into a better and higher impact alternative textbook initiative in a world that we all believe is in desperate need of textbook reform.

There is particularly a need for a new undergraduate development economics textbook. The books out there seem more interested in summarizing a bunch of topics than in teaching people what they really need to know in order to do development economics. This book is different.

WHO SHOULD USE THIS BOOK AND HOW

When we sat down to write *Essentials of Development Economics,* we wanted a compact book for an upper-division undergraduate development economics class. That is primarily what this is. The knowledge in this book should poise any undergraduate to engage in further study or to venture out into the real world with an appreciation for the essential concepts and tools of economic development. More than a textbook, this can be a helpful basic reference for any graduate student, researcher, or development practitioner.

There's a striking disconnect between development textbooks and journal articles. Specialized journal articles really are what shape the way we think about development economics problems and research. Sadly, they are not written for undergraduate courses. Nevertheless, the topics they cover, research approaches they use, and critical findings they present are essential to understanding development economics, and they *can* be made accessible. Journal article synopses are highlighted in sidebars throughout this book.

RebelText is intended to be used interactively with online content. QR (Quick Reference) codes at the end of each chapter link readers with online materials, including images, animations, video clips, and interviews with some influential development economists. You can access all of the URLs behind the QR codes on the website rebeltext .org, or by clicking on links in the e-version of this book. We encourage you to explore the multimedia material as a way to make the concepts come to life. On the website you'll also find the data sets included in this book, homework problems, study questions, and supplementary appendixes. When we use RebelText, the website becomes a center of class activity.

RebelText was created to make learning and teaching as efficient as possible. Students need to learn the essentials of the subject. They do not want to wade through thick textbooks in order to locate what they need, constantly wondering what will and won't be on the next test. Because it is concise, there is no reason *not* to read and study every word of *Essentials of Development Economics*. All of it could be on the test. Master it, and you will be conversant enough to strike up a conversation with any development economist and may even be able to get directly involved with development economics projects. You can think of this book as presenting the "best practices" and state-of-the-art methods for doing development economics. By mastering it, you'll also have the conceptual and intuitive grounding you need in order to move on to higher level development economics courses. You'll probably find yourself referring back to it from time to time, so keep it on your shelf!

If you are teaching or learning with RebelText, consider contributing your ideas about novel uses of the book and website, interesting data sets, programs, and projects. To find out how, visit rebeltext.org and click on "contributing to RebelText." Some of our best links have come from our students!

ABOUT THE AUTHORS

Ed loves teaching economics, especially microeconomics, econometrics, and economic development. He's been doing it for about twenty-five years now at UC Davis, where he is a professor in the Department of Agricultural and Resource Economics. He's also done a lot of economics research; he has published more than one hundred articles, book chapters, and books on topics ranging from international trade reforms to ecotourism, immigration, and rural poverty. He's in *Who's Who in*

Economics, the list of the world's most cited economists, and he has been editor of the *American Journal of Agricultural Economics*. He has worked on projects with the United Nations, the World Bank, the Organization for Economic Cooperation and Development, and the Inter-American Development Bank, as well as with foreign governments, including those of Mexico, Honduras, Canada, and China. His new book, *Beyond Experiments in Development Economics: Local Economy-Wide Impact Evaluation* (Oxford University Press, 2014), presents a new approach to doing impact evaluation and cost-benefit analysis. You can learn more about Ed at his website: jetaylor.ucdavis.edu.

Travis Lybbert was initially torn between environmental studies and landscape architecture as an undergraduate major at Utah State University. A class on environmental and resource economics demonstrated the power of economics as a way to size up social problems and evaluate potential solutions. After graduating with an economics major (and French and environmental studies minors), he and his wife, Heather, lived in Morocco for a year on a Fulbright fellowship. The experience prompted him to pursue graduate work in economic development at Cornell University. After teaching for two years at the Honors College at Florida Atlantic University, he arrived at UC Davis, where he is currently Associate Professor in the Department of Agricultural and Resource Economics. Travis has worked in North Africa (Morocco, Tunisia, Syria), sub-Saharan Africa (Burkina Faso, Niger, Ghana, Ethiopia, Kenya), India, and Haiti. As a visiting researcher, he has spent time at the World Trade Organization and the World Intellectual Property Organization in Geneva, the University of Cape Coast in Ghana, and the Max Planck Institute in Munich. His current projects cover a range of topics, including drought risk and vulnerability, asset and poverty dynamics, technology adoption and markets, childhood and maternal nutrition, and intellectual property and international technology transfer. Travis teaches graduate and undergraduate courses in economic development, applied economics, and econometrics. To learn more about him, visit his faculty website: tlybbert.ucdavis.edu.

ACKNOWLEDGMENTS

RebelText would not exist if it weren't for our families and students. Special thanks go to Sebastian and Julian, who shamed Ed into launching RebelText; to Peri, who has supported this project from the start; to Heather, Hannah, and Rockwell, who fully embraced the adventurous sabbatical year in Ghana that gave Travis the professional breathing room to work on this book; to colleagues at the Economics Department of the University of Cape Coast who made Travis's sabbatical year possible; to Steve Boucher and Michael Carter for providing many thoughts, inputs, and field tests of our book in the classroom; and to our cutting-edge team of graduate student assistants, including Anil Barghava, Isabel Call, Michael Castelhano, Diane Charlton, Mateusz Filipski, Justin Kagin, Dale Manning, Karen Thome, and Abbie Turiansky, all of whom provided valuable research assistance and advice at various stages of this project. Finally, we thank the many undergraduate students who kept us going by repeatedly telling us how "awesome" RebelText was and for catching errors and typos. They, too, are part of this project.

J. Edward Taylor and Travis J. Lybbert
Davis and Berkeley, California

What Development Economics Is All About

Suppose you were blindfolded and airlifted abroad. After you arrive in a small town and remove the blindfold, your job is to determine the income level of the place based only on sixty seconds of observation. What would you look for? If you have traveled or lived in a developing country, you might have a head start on this assignment: Is it hot and humid? What are people wearing? Eating? How are people getting around? What do the streets and buildings look like? Do the animals look pampered? Do you see trash or trash cans? And the smells! Most people, when exposed to living standards far below their own, want to help in some way. Economists (yes, even economists!) feel this impulse and wonder: Why are some places rich and others poor? What can be done to reduce poverty and encourage economic growth? In this chapter, we introduce development economics and describe the emergence and evolution of this field.

ESSENTIALS

- Description of development economics
- Evolution of development economics
- Import substitution and export promotion
- Market failures
- Inseparability of efficiency and equity
- Millennium Development Goals

Malawi is one of the poorest countries in the world. The average person living there had an annual income of $330 in 2010. That is not even a dollar a day. Even when we adjust for a low cost of living, the average Malawian lived off what in the United States would be the equivalent of around $850 per year.[1]

What is the solution to Malawi's pervasive poverty?

Like other least-developed countries (LDCs),[2] Malawi has tried a number of different strategies to stimulate development and raise the welfare of its people. It made the growth of smallholder production a cornerstone of its development and poverty-alleviation strategy by focusing on improving smallholders' access to agricultural input and output markets. Eighty-one percent of Malawi's population is rural, and smallholders make up about 90% of the poor. Food production is a major source of livelihood for most rural households. Productivity and, in particular, fertilizer use are low. Only 67% of agricultural households used fertilizer in 2004.[3]

Before 1998, Malawi relied on market price supports to transfer income to farm households. (Next door in Zambia, where per capita income was $1,400 in 2010, the government continues to pay farmers prices well above market levels for their maize.)[4] In recent years, fertilizer subsidies were the primary method of transferring income to rural Malawi households. Paying for farmers' inputs is expensive and controversial. More than 50% of the Ministry of Agriculture's budget has gone toward paying for input subsidies.[5]

Most recently, the country has taken a new line of attack by introducing a social cash transfer (SCT) scheme that targets ultra-poor households (those living on less than $0.10 per day) whose members are unable to work due to disability, age, illness, or a high dependency ratio (too many people to take care of at home). Rather than specifically targeting agricultural production, like the price supports or fertilizer subsidies, cash transfers raise incomes directly, allowing households to increase consumption or to invest in production activities. The government and researchers hope these transfers will stimulate production in other ways while creating positive spillovers that benefit other households in the economy.

Field research to test the effectiveness of SCT programs is ongoing. SCT programs are being implemented throughout the continent, in Ethiopia, Ghana, Kenya, Zambia, Zimbabwe, Lesotho, and other poor countries. The United Nations Children's Fund (UNICEF) and the UN's Food and Agricultural Organization (FAO), in conjunction with several universities and agencies, have launched an ambitious project to document the impacts of these transfer programs on a range of outcomes, from crop production to HIV/AIDS prevention.[6]

Development economists are on the front line of this effort, helping to design and evaluate SCT programs. On a micro level, this is a good example of the sorts of things development economists do. A whole chapter in this book (chapter 2, "What Works and What Doesn't?") is dedicated to project impact evaluation.

Development economics involves much more than this, though.

WHAT IS DEVELOPMENT ECONOMICS?

Usually, a development economics class is a potpourri of special topics. It's hard for it not to be, because economic development involves so many different things:

- It's income growth (how can we have development without growth in countries whose per capita incomes now hover around $1–$2 per day?).
- It's welfare economics, including the study of poverty and inequality.
- It's agricultural economics. How to make agriculture more productive is a big question in countries where most of the population—particularly the *poor* population—is rural and agricultural.
- It's economic demography, the study of population growth in a world with more than 7 billion people, and population distribution in a world with more than a quarter of a billion international migrants and many more internal ones. (China will have about that many internal migrants in the near future, if it doesn't already.)
- It's labor economics: education, health, conditions in the workplace.
- It's the study of markets for goods, services, inputs, outputs, credit, and insurance, without which whole economies can grind to a standstill.
- It's public economics, including the provision of public goods from roads and communications to utilities and waste treatment, and it's about managing the macroeconomy, too.
- It's about natural resources and the environment: energy, water, deforestation, pollution, climate change, sustainability.

What is development economics *not* about, you might ask?

Lurking behind this question is another one, which lies at the heart of why we wrote this book: Why is there even a field of development economics? After all, most economics departments have courses in each one of the above areas—and more.

Development economics seeks to understand the economic aspects of the development process in low-income countries. This implies that there must be something different about studying economics in low-income countries.

Clearly there is. Economic development entails far-reaching changes in the structure of economies, technologies, societies, and political systems. Development economics is the study of economies that do not fit many of the basic assumptions underpinning economic analysis in high-income countries, including well-functioning markets, perfect information, and low transaction costs. When these assumptions break down, so do the most basic welfare and policy conclusions of economics.

This book, like other development economics texts, touches on many different topics. However, its focus is on the fundamental things that distinguish rich and poor countries and the methods we use to analyze critical development economics issues. After reading and studying it, you'll be familiar with the basic tool kit development economists use to do research, begin to understand what makes rich and poor countries different, and have an appreciation for the theory and practice of development economics.

THE EVOLUTION OF DEVELOPMENT ECONOMICS

Economics classes rarely spend much time on history. But the brief history of development economics is instructive. Appreciating how economists have come to understand economic development helps *us* understand the various development approaches people have taken over time and how we got to the ideas that are popular now. What economists *thought* development meant at the beginnings of our field's history is quite different from the way we see it today.

The origins of modern development economics are not found in low-income countries, but rather in relatively developed countries devastated by war.[7] In the aftermath of World War II, there was a need for economic theories and policies to support the rebuilding of war-torn Europe and Japan. The United States adopted the Marshall Plan to help rebuild European economies. This was a massive program: $13 billion over four years was a lot of money back then!

In the wake of the success of the Marshall Plan, economists shifted their attention in the 1950s and 1960s from Europe to the economic problems of Africa, Asia, and Latin America. Lessons learned in Europe did not transfer easily to those settings; it quickly became clear that poor countries faced fundamentally different challenges.

Early development economists focused on income growth, often blurring the lines between growth and development. In poor countries, major structural transformations were needed to achieve growth. By comparing different countries' growth experiences (including the past experiences of the more developed countries), economists tried to uncover the conditions that determine successful development and economic growth.

Taking Off

Seminal work during this early period of development economics includes Walter Rostow's treatise on the stages of economic growth: the traditional society, the preconditions for takeoff, the takeoff, the drive to maturity, and the age of high mass consumption.[8] Nobel laureate Simon Kuznets (whom we shall revisit later in this chapter) countered this simplistic view that all countries go through a similar linear set of stages in their economic history. He argued instead that key characteristics of today's poor countries are fundamentally different from those of high-income countries before they developed.

The Anatomy of Growth

Economists recognized the need to understand how the growth process works. Growth is important enough to get its own chapter in this book (chapter 7). There, we'll focus on modern growth theory, but growth models have played an important role since the start of development economics.

A simple aggregate growth model developed by Sir Roy F. Harrod and Evsey Domar became part of the basic creed of development economists in the 1950s and 1960s.[9] The Harrod-Domar model's main implication was that investment is the key driver of economic growth. It focused economists' and policy makers' attention on generating the savings required to support higher growth rates in poor countries. Although simplistic, this was a precursor to models used to analyze economic growth in developing countries today.

Nobel laureate W. Arthur Lewis viewed growth through a higher resolution lens. His famed work, "Economic Development with Unlimited

Supplies of Labor," shifted attention from aggregate growth to structural transformation.[10] Lewis introduced the dual-sector model, demonstrating that the expansion of the modern (industrial or capitalist) sector depends on drawing labor from the traditional (agricultural or subsistence) sector. He focused on poor, labor-rich countries, in which a labor surplus in the subsistence sector could be a valuable resource for industrial growth: industry could expand without putting upward pressure on wages. Implicit in the Lewis model is a simple, demand-driven model of migration: as urban industry expands, people move off the farm to fill the new jobs. Whether or not workers really can be moved out of agriculture without losing crop production is an empirical question that some economists still try to answer today.

Lewis was criticized for largely ignoring agriculture. His work was extended and formalized by Gustav Ranis and John Fei, who demonstrated that industrial growth depends on agricultural growth as well as industrial profits.[11] If agricultural production does not keep up, food prices rise, and this forces urban wages up, squeezing profits and investment in industry. The growth of industry, then, depends on agriculture in a way that is easy to miss. Recognition that different sectors of the economy are linked in critical ways was an important contribution of dual-economy models and is a basis for more sophisticated economy-wide models today. We look at these models in chapter 10 ("Structural Transformation").

The assumption that there is surplus labor in the traditional sector (i.e., that the marginal product of labor there is zero) was questioned by another Nobel laureate, Theodore Schultz.[12] He pointed out evidence of labor shortages during peak harvest periods even in economies like India and China, where a labor surplus existed at other times of the year. Thus, he argued, one cannot assume that countries can move labor out of agriculture without suffering a drop in crop production—unless they adopt new agricultural technologies. Schultz emphasized the importance of technological innovation and revolutionized economists' thinking by putting forth the thesis that farmers in LDCs are "efficient but poor." That is, while they might appear to be inefficient (compared, say, to commercial farmers in rich countries), poor farmers actually optimize given the severe resource constraints they face, including traditional technologies and limited human capital. The efficient-but-poor hypothesis continues to shape the way development economists think about and model poor rural economies, as we see in chapter 9 ("Agriculture"). Nevertheless, recent work questions whether production, land tenancy (e.g., sharecropping), and other institutions in poor countries really are efficient in an economic sense.

The burgeoning early development economics literature produced far too many works to catalogue here, but two others deserve special mention because of the far-reaching impact they had on economic thinking and, more importantly, policies.

Import-Substitution Industrialization

In 1950, Raúl Prebisch and Hans Singer independently observed that the terms of trade, or the ratio of prices, between primary (agricultural, resource extraction) and manufactured products erodes over time.[13] As people's income increases, the share of income they spend on manufactures increases, while the share spent on primary goods falls. This happens globally as well as locally. Prebisch and Singer argued that this drives up the prices of manufactured goods relative to primary goods. Poor countries that continue to specialize in primary-goods production lose out compared to countries that protect and promote their industries. The way Prebisch and Singer saw it, sticking with primary-goods production is like investing in a waning industry—the opposite of what good investors do.

Prebisch and Singer's work was enormously influential in promoting protectionist trade policies, shielding infant industries in poor countries from international competition. Its policy prescriptions ran soundly against the doctrine that countries should follow their comparative advantage in trade. In retrospect, countries that followed this advice did not fare as well as countries like the "Asian Tigers" (Hong Kong, Singapore, South Korea, and Taiwan), which followed more outward (trade)-oriented development models, as we shall see in chapter 13 ("International Trade and Globalization").

Linkages

Albert Hirschman, another early pioneer in development economics, put forth the interesting and influential argument that imbalances between demand and supply in LDC economies can be good: they create pressures that stimulate economic growth.[14] Hirschman was instrumental in creating a focus on economic linkages, which pervade economy-wide modeling, a staple of development policy analysis today (chapter 10, "Structural Transformation") as well as of some recent project impact evaluation models (chapter 2, "What Works and What Doesn't?"). By promoting investments in industries with many linkages to other firms, governments can have a multiplier effect on economic growth; the effects of a policy spread to industries linked to the targeted industry. Backward linkages transmit growth effects from an input-demanding activity (e.g., textiles) to input suppliers (cotton mills or wool producers). Forward linkages stimulate the growth of activities ahead of firms, as when investment in an electricity generator facilitates the growth of electricity-using industries.

Hirschman argued that agriculture generated few linkages with the rest of the economy. This, particularly when combined with the Prebisch-Singer hypothesis, contributed to the sense among policy makers that agriculture is unimportant and countries ought to use their scarce resources to promote industrial, not agricultural, growth. John Mellor countered this argument in his seminal work, *The New Economics of Growth,* which documented the importance of consumption linkages between rural households and urban industries.[15] If most of a country's population is rural, where will the demand for new industrial production be if not in rural households? Rising agricultural incomes, then, provide a critical market for manufactures, thereby stimulating industrial growth.

Development economists had begun to take more of a systems view of poor economies, recognizing the linkages among production sectors and between firms and households that are important in shaping economic growth. They would soon rethink their emphasis on growth, though.

Rethinking Growth: Inequality and Poverty

The United Nations declared the 1960s to be the decade of development. In 1961, it "called on all member states to intensify their efforts to mobilize support for measures required to accelerate progress toward self-sustaining economic growth and social advancement in the developing countries." Each developing country set its own target, but the overall goal was to achieve a minimum annual growth rate of 5% in aggregate national income by the end of the decade.[16] The world came close to realizing the UN's goal. LDCs achieved an average annual growth rate of 4.6% from 1960 to 1967. However, their population also increased. As a result, their per capita gross domestic product (income divided by population) rose only about 2%.

When the UN Development Decade ended in 1970, the gap between rich and poor countries had widened: two-thirds of the world's population had less than one-sixth of the world's income. This raised new questions about the meaning of development. Evidently, a tide of rising world income did not lift all—or even most—boats. The UN General Assembly concluded that one of the reasons for the slow progress was the absence of a clear international development strategy.

The problem of rising inequality made development economists rethink their focus on growth. Before then, the key work linking growth and inequality was Simon Kuznets's "inverted U" hypothesis. It stated that economic growth decreases inequality in rich countries but increases it in poor countries.[17] It tended to create a sense of complacency about inequality: sure, inequality increases for a while as poor countries grow, but eventually countries "outgrow" it and become more equal. At least, that's what Kuznets saw when he used cross-section data to compare rich and poor countries. (Cross-section data are data on different countries at the same point in time. It would have been nice to track the same countries over time to see if inequality first increases then decreases as economies grow, but we didn't have the data to do that back when Kuznets put forth his novel theory.)

As panel data have became available to track individual countries' growth and inequality, the inverted-U theory has been challenged repeatedly in the development economics literature, though it seems to fit some countries well. (Panel data provide information on the same units [here, countries] over time.) Today, China is growing fast, and inequality there is increasing. Brazil and Mexico have much higher per capita incomes than China, and inequality there is going down. Then there's the United States, where inequality fell through the 1970s but is rising again now.

Development economics shifted its attention from income growth to income inequality (chapter 5, "Inequality"). In 1974, Hollis Chenery, head of the World Bank's economic research department, and colleagues published an influential book called *Redistribution with Growth*.[18] It demonstrated that when assets (such as land) are distributed unequally, economic growth creates an unequal distribution of benefits. Around the same time (1973), Irma Adelman and Cynthia Taft Morris published a book called *Economic Growth and Social Equity in Developing Countries*.[19] They found that as incomes grew, not only did inequality increase, but the *absolute* position of the poor *worsened*. At the early stages of a country's economic growth, the poorest segment of society may be harmed, as traditional economic relationships in subsistence economies are displaced by emerging commercial ones. Growth was more equitable in countries that redistributed assets, like land and human capital (education), *before* the growth happened.

Robert McNamara, the World Bank's president, put the world spotlight on inequality at a 1972 UN conference in Santiago, Chile.[20] This staked out a new position for the World Bank and the development economics profession more broadly that growth alone is not enough. McNamara and many development economists recommended redistribution before growth; for example, land reforms and other measures to raise the productivity of small farmers and widespread rural education programs. The development economics mantra had shifted from income growth (chapters 3 and 7) to poverty (chapter 4) and inequality (chapter 5). The work of Amartya Sen expanded the scope of economic development yet further to include dimensions of human development such as health, nutrition, education, and even freedom (chapter 6).

National planning offices cropped up around the world, often with "five-year plans" inspired by the Soviet Union's planning models but not necessarily socialistic in nature. (While Ed was an undergraduate student he worked for a year with the National Planning Office in Costa Rica, which had five-year plans but was hardly a communist state!) This period saw the advent of economy-wide models as a tool for development planning and policy. These models were designed to simulate the complex impacts that policies have on whole economies as well as on particular social groups. They continue to be a staple of development economics research and policy design and are often at the crossfire of a lively debate about the role of planning and markets in economic development.

The 1970s marked the beginning of what has become an ongoing friction between direct government involvement in the development process and market-led development—a tension we will address throughout this book because it stems from essential ideas in development economics. The traditional neoclassical economic view, inspired by Adam Smith's "invisible hand," is that individuals and firms, in the pursuit of their self-interest, are led as if by an invisible hand to economic efficiency. For example, competition among profit-maximizing firms drives down prices for selfish, utility-maximizing consumers. However, the invisible hand does not typically lead to fair outcomes, so government intervention can often play a role in promoting social objectives other than efficiency, such as equality or protection of domestic industries.

The 1960s and 1970s witnessed increasing government involvement in markets: setting prices, controlling trade, and creating "parastatal" enterprises that did everything from buying and selling crops to drilling for oil.

Much of the focus of these efforts was on stimulating industrial growth; however, most of the population in poor countries—especially the very poor—depended heavily on agriculture. In many countries, import-substitution industrialization policies created severe biases against agriculture, in three ways:

1. "Cheap food policies" directly harmed agriculture while helping to keep urban wages low.
2. Steep tariffs and quotas on imported industrial goods and direct subsidies were used to promote industrialization. This increased the profitability of industrial compared to agricultural production.
3. Macroeconomic policies like overvalued exchange rates made imported industrial inputs and technologies (as well as food) cheaper. This created yet another bias against agriculture by making traded goods (food) less profitable than nontraded goods (manufactures, which were protected from trade competition).

Trusting Markets

The 1980s saw the beginning of a backlash against too much state involvement in the economy. This was the era of Ronald Reagan and Margaret Thatcher, in which we recognized the inefficiencies of state-planned economic systems such as those in the Soviet Union and China compared with the more laissez-faire political systems in the west. Meanwhile, it became clear that the countries that were experiencing the most rapid and broad-based growth were *not* the inward-oriented countries following import-substitution industrialization, like Kenya, Mexico, and Brazil. Instead, they were the outward export-oriented economies, particularly the Asian Tigers. In those countries, governments were involved, sometimes heavily, in the economy, but opening up to market competition made it possible to become competitive on a world scale.

Another part of the impetus for shifting away from state involvement and toward markets came in the 1970s and 1980s as the world economy went into recession with soaring oil prices. This sparked debt crises in many LDCs (particularly in Latin America), forcing them to rethink their development policies—often as part of "structural adjustment" programs required by the International Monetary Fund (IMF) as a condition for restructuring their debt. These adjustments invariably reduced the direct involvement of the state in the troubled economies.

The World Bank's 1984 World Development Report endorsed many of these dominant promarket positions. It called for removing distortions created by governments' overinvolvement in agricultural markets. Almost overnight, governments began to withdraw from markets, dismantling import-substitution industrialization policies and opening up to trade. Less-developed countries around the world entered into free-trade agreements (see chapter 13).

Not (Quite) Trusting Markets

The market liberalization movement continued into the 1990s; however, the enthusiasm for free trade became tempered by a realization that market liberalization does not necessarily improve people's economic welfare if markets do not work properly. This produced a surge of research documenting market failures in LDCs as well as their underlying causes. (Market failures are a focus of chapter 11.)

Broadly speaking, a free market fails if it does not work efficiently—that is, if there is another scenario in which a market participant could be made better off without making others worse off. Often, markets fail so miserably that they do not exist at all for many people. Most poor people do not have access to credit, most farmers in Africa do not sell their crops, and almost nobody in poor countries has access to formal insurance.

Joseph Stiglitz, who received the 2001 Nobel Prize in economics, along with other economists, demonstrated that markets are rarely efficient. He attributed this largely to imperfect information, which creates high transaction costs that lead to widespread market failures, particularly in poor countries. Since understanding market failures is fundamental to development economics, we will learn about several sources of market failures in this book.

When markets do not work well, government involvement in the economy can often improve welfare. Development economists have been careful to warn that market failures do not necessarily warrant broad state intervention in the economy: government failures can be worse than market failures. However, the scope for the state to improve welfare by intervening in markets, it seems, is much larger than previously thought.

The Experimental Revolution

Today, much of the focus of development economics has shifted to the micro-level and to project evaluation. Increasingly, development economics research involves using experiments to learn about people's economic behavior and evaluate the impacts of policy interventions on welfare outcomes. When experiments are not possible, economists use other methods, including econometrics and simulation modeling, to try to identify the impacts of policies and programs. The social cash transfer programs mentioned at the start of this chapter are an example. Today, if you work for a nongovernmental organization (NGO), an international development agency, or even an LDC government, there is a good chance you'll be dealing with experimental economics. Experiments have become such an important part of development economics that we devote an entire chapter to them in this book (chapter 2).

WHAT IS ECONOMIC DEVELOPMENT, THEN?

Economic development has different meanings in different contexts. In rich countries, it is pretty much equated with growth. Picture the urban developer who makes skyscrapers sprout from vacant lots in a blighted city core. Politically, development projects in high-income countries often are motivated by some of the same goals that inspire development projects in poor countries, particularly the creation of new jobs, incomes, and tax revenues. Their ultimate aim, however, is likely to be growth.

Most development economists today would say that economic development is not equivalent to growth, although it is difficult to achieve development goals without growth. Development projects around the world focus on concrete outcomes related to poverty, malnutrition, inequality, and health. Development is about satisfying basic physical needs like nutrition, shelter, and clothing, and about the development of the mind (and of course people's earnings potential) through education. Projects also focus on the environment, conservation, and sustainable resource use; on human rights, gender and ethnic equity, and even government corruption (a topic we take up in chapter 8, "Institutions").

All of these questions can be vital not only to determining who reaps the benefits of economic growth, but also to understanding growth itself. Herein lies a fundamental difference in the way we tend to look at economics and politics in rich and poor countries. In high-income countries (not to mention our microeconomics courses), economic efficiency and equity tend to be viewed as separate questions. The efficient allocation of resources is critical to ensure that economies produce the biggest possible economic pie, given the constraints they face (i.e., limited resources and technologies). Efficiency is the primary focus of the vast majority of our economics classes.

What about equity? How the pie gets distributed is usually an afterthought in economics—something more in the domain of politics than economics. Think about the economics courses you've taken. The textbook view is that efficiency and equity are sequential, or recursive, problems: first grow the pie, then, once that's done, think about how it gets distributed (or step back and let the market decide).

Clearly, there's an important separability assumption here: that efficiency can be achieved regardless of how income is distributed. Is this a reasonable assumption? In a competitive market equilibrium, there will be different outcomes depending upon what the initial distribution of wealth looks like. But provided the basic assumptions of the competitive model (which you learned in your introductory economics courses) hold, all will be efficient in the Pareto sense: you cannot make anyone better off without making someone else worse off. If you ever studied an Edgeworth box, you've seen how economists show this.

The separability of equity and efficiency was reinforced by the Nobel laureate Ronald Coase, who argued that bargaining will lead to an efficient outcome regardless of the initial allocation of property rights, even in the case of externalities (a cost or benefit not reflected in prices, like pollution). According to Coase, as long as we can costlessly negotiate it doesn't matter whether you have the right to smoke or I have the right to breathe clean air. Once we have finished bargaining with each other, the amount of smoke in the air will be the same. This view has achieved the status of a theorem: Coase's Theorem.

If efficiency and equity are truly separate issues, then there is not much room for economic policy, nor much reason for efficiency-minded economists to worry about equity. (Of course, even economists might worry about equity for other [i.e., humanitarian] reasons.)

If only things were that simple! Alas, negotiation is never costless (and often prohibitively expensive). For this and many other reasons, a great deal of development economists' effort goes into discovering how equity and efficiency are intertwined, especially in poor countries. How assets are distributed clearly affects efficiency if the following conditions hold:

- Banks are unwilling to loan money to small farmers.
- Poor people cannot get insurance to protect themselves against crop loss or sickness.

- Poverty and malnutrition prevent kids from growing up to become productive adults.

- Access to markets for the stuff people produce, the inputs they use, and the goods they demand is different for the poor and rich.

- The ability to get a job depends on who you are, not on how productive you are.

In these and many other cases, the separability of equity and efficiency breaks down. A person's capacity to produce (or even consume) efficiently depends upon how wealth is distributed to start out with because the basic assumptions of competitive markets often don't hold for the poorest members of society. A rich farmer can produce where the market price equals the marginal cost of producing a crop, the basic requirement for profit maximization and efficiency. But if a poor farmer lacks the cash to buy fertilizer, and no bank will lend to her, she will not be able to produce as efficiently as the large farmer. This implies that efficiency depends on how income is distributed to begin with, which is an important departure from standard assumptions in economics.

The conditions under which equity affects efficiency are many, and they permeate the economies and societies of poor countries. Development economics, more than anything else perhaps, is the study of economies in which equity and efficiency are closely interrelated. This opens up a whole realm of possibilities for policy and project interventions to increase economic efficiency as well as equity. More often than not, equity and efficiency are not only complementary; they are inseparable.

THE MILLENNIUM DEVELOPMENT GOALS (MDGS)

Eradicating extreme poverty continues to be one of the main challenges of our time, and is a major concern of the international community. Ending this scourge will require the combined efforts of all—governments, civil society organizations and the private sector—in the context of a stronger and more effective global partnership for development. The Millennium Development Goals set timebound targets, by which progress in reducing income poverty, hunger, disease, lack of adequate shelter and exclusion—while promoting gender equality, health, education and environmental sustainability—can be measured. They also embody basic human rights—the rights of each person on the planet to health, education, shelter and security. The Goals are ambitious but feasible and, together with the comprehensive United Nations development agenda, set the course for the world's efforts to alleviate extreme poverty by 2015. (United Nations Secretary-General Ban Ki-moon)

In September 2000, 189 nations came together at United Nations Headquarters in New York and adopted the United Nations Millennium Declaration. In it, they committed to creating a new global partnership to reduce extreme poverty and achieve a set of specific development targets by 2015. These targets (see appendix at the end of this chapter), which range from health to environment to gender equality, have become known as the Millennium Development Goals (MDGs).[21] Setting goals like these and monitoring our progress toward achieving them requires tremendous amounts of data, measurement methods, and above all, commitment.

If you attend almost any international development meeting, you almost certainly will hear the MDGs come up. The MDGs are often used by governments and international development agencies to motivate and justify specific development projects. They have galvanized efforts to meet the needs of people in the world's poorest countries, but they are not without their detractors. There is ongoing debate among economists about whether this kind of formal, "technocratic" approach, in which scientists and experts are in control, is beneficial or harmful. It may help the poor by funneling funds and expertise to areas of urgent need. However, it could do the opposite by imposing external power and plans that do not reflect local context.[22]

THE ORGANIZATION OF THIS BOOK

This book was written to provide students with the essential tools and concepts of development economics. Most development texts are written around topics: money, labor, population, and so on. The chapters in this book are less about topics than about providing a window into how developing economies are different and how this shapes the way we study them. Most of the cutting-edge research by economists is found in journal articles that are beyond the reach of most undergraduate students. Sidebars scattered throughout the book try to make this research accessible, summarizing the questions it asks, the methods it uses, key findings, and why they are important. Our hope is that by the end of this book, students will have a new understanding of what economists bring to development research and policy and be conversant in many of the approaches they employ.

The rest of this book is all about seeking answers to big questions.

As households and individuals seek out livelihoods in increasingly complex and global economies, governments, international development agencies, and development banks carry out a wide diversity of development projects. Evaluating the impacts of these programs is the focus of a new generation of development economists, inspired largely by experimental methods. Chapter 2 ("What Works and What Doesn't?") looks at why economists do experiments, what the limitations of experiments are, how to evaluate impacts when there is no experiment, cost-benefit analysis of development projects, and how projects and policies may affect non-beneficiaries as well as beneficiaries.

Chapters 3 through 6 are about understanding, measuring, and analyzing the four key elements of economic development: income (chapter 3), poverty (chapter 4), inequality (chapter 5), and human development (chapter 6).

A theme that emerges from the first six chapters is that income growth is an important, though by no means sufficient, condition for achieving economic development. How can countries, regions, and households make their incomes grow? Chapter 7 ("Growth") gives an introduction to aggregate (national) growth theory and concludes by asking whether poor countries, regions, and households are "catching up," and whether income growth alone will enable countries to reach the Millennium Development Goals.

Institutions are like the operating systems for economies and societies. When they don't work well, even the best-designed development policies and projects can fail to meet their objectives. We dedicate a whole chapter (chapter 8) to institutions, what they mean to a development economist, and how they shape economic development outcomes.

Agriculture still dominates the economies of many countries in terms of income and employment. Chapter 9 ("Agriculture") presents the key tools economists have come up with to analyze agricultural economies, with an eye toward understanding a wide array of impacts, from agricultural policies to trade and climate change. This chapter begins with the agricultural household model, the staple of microeconomic analysis of agricultural and rural economies. It concludes with village and rural economy-wide models, which let us see how households are connected with each other and transmit impacts of policy, market, and environmental shocks.

Most of the world's poverty is in rural areas. Rural economies, though, are becoming less agricultural over time, as households get an increasing share of their income from non-agricultural activities. For a growing number of people, getting out of poverty means moving off the farm. Chapter 10 ("Structural Transformation") looks at the far-reaching transformations of rural and national economies that accompany economic growth and what this means for how we do economic analysis and design development policies.

Markets and trade are vital for countries to grow and spread the benefits of this growth across a broad population. However, markets fail for many people, and others find themselves unable to compete in an increasingly global economy. In chapters 11 ("Information and Markets"), 12 ("Credit and Insurance"), and 13 ("International Trade and Globalization"), we see why economists think markets are so important to economic development, why markets fail for many people, how globalization creates both winners and losers, and what this all means for development policies. Two markets, those for credit and insurance, are particularly important—and more often than not conspicuously missing—for poor people in LDCs. Chapter 12 looks at how credit and insurance markets are important, why they fail, and what development researchers and practitioners are doing about it.

The epilogue (chapter 14) is about where you will go from here and how the tools and skills in this book prepare you for new adventures in development—and life.

At the end of each chapter you will find a link to multimedia resources that you can explore to enrich your learning, meet experts, and bring the real world into the textbook and classroom.

www.rebeltext.org/development/qr1.html
Enrich your appreciation of what development economics is about by exploring multimedia resources while you read.

APPENDIX

The Eight Millennium Development Goals (MDGs)

MDG 1: Eradicate Extreme Poverty and Hunger
  Target 1.A: Halve, between 1990 and 2015, the proportion of people whose income is less than $1.25 a day

Target 1.B: Achieve full and productive employment and decent work for all, including women and young people

Target 1.C: Halve, between 1990 and 2015, the proportion of people who suffer from hunger

MDG 2: Achieve Universal Primary Education

Ensure that, by 2015, children everywhere, boys and girls alike, will be able to complete a full course of primary schooling

MDG 3: Gender Equity

Eliminate gender disparity in primary and secondary education, preferably by 2005, and in all levels of education no later than 2015

MDG 4: Reduce Child Mortality

Reduce by two-thirds, between 1990 and 2015, the under-five mortality rate

MDG 5: Improve Maternal Health

Target 5.A: Reduce by three-quarters, between 1990 and 2015, the maternal mortality ratio

Target 5.B: Achieve, by 2015, universal access to reproductive health

MDG 6: Combat HIV/AIDS, Malaria, and Other Diseases

Target 6.A: Halt by 2015 and begin to reverse the spread of HIV/AIDS

Target 6.B: Achieve by 2010 universal access to treatment for HIV/AIDS for all those who need it

Target 6.C: Halt by 2015 and begin to reverse the incidence of malaria and other major diseases

MGD 7: Ensure Environmental Sustainability

Target 7.A: Integrate the principles of sustainable development into country policies and programmes and reverse the loss of environmental resources

Target 7.B: Reduce biodiversity loss, achieving, by 2010, a significant reduction in the rate of loss

Target 7.C: Halve, by 2015, the proportion of the population without sustainable access to safe drinking water and basic sanitation

Target 7.D: Achieve, by 2020, a significant improvement in the lives of at least 100 million slum dwellers

MDG 8: Develop a Global Partnership for Development

Target 8.A: Develop further an open, rule-based, predictable, non-discriminatory trading and financial system

Target 8.B: Address the special needs of least-developed countries

Target 8.C: Address the special needs of landlocked developing countries and small island developing states

Target 8.D: Deal comprehensively with the debt problems of developing countries

Target 8.E: In cooperation with pharmaceutical companies, provide access to affordable essential drugs in developing countries

Target 8.F: In cooperation with the private sector, make available benefits of new technologies, especially information and communications

Learn more about the Millennium Development Goals at www.un.org /millenniumgoals/global.shtml.

ADDITIONAL READING

Each year, the World Bank publishes its World Development Report with its own special topic (not to mention a lot of data on an array of development indicators). As you can see, they cover an enormous array of topics. These reports are available online at http://go.worldbank.org/LOTTGBE9I0. The following are summaries taken from the World Bank website.

World Development Reports, 2000–(Upcoming) 2016

Upcoming WDR 2016: The Internet and Development. Will assemble the best available evidence on the Internet's potential impact on economic growth, on equity, and on the efficiency of public service provision. Will analyze what factors have allowed some governments, firms, and households to benefit from the Internet, and identify the barriers that limit gains elsewhere.

Upcoming WDR 2015: Mind and Society. Will be based on three main ideas: *bounds on rationality*, which limit individuals' ability to process information and lead them to rely on rules of thumb; *social interdependence*, which leads people to care about other people as well as the social norms of their communities; and *culture*, which provides mental models that influence what individuals pay attention to, perceive, and understand (or misunderstand).

WDR 2014: Risk and Opportunity: Managing Risk for Development. Examines how improving risk management can lead to larger gains in development and poverty reduction. This report argues that improving risk management is crucial to reduce the negative impacts of shocks and hazards, but also to enable people to pursue new opportunities for growth.

WDR 2013: Jobs. Stresses the role of strong, private-sector-led growth in creating jobs and outlines how jobs that do the most for development can spur a virtuous cycle. The report finds that poverty falls as people work their way out of hardship and as jobs empower women to invest more in their children. Efficiency increases as workers get better at what they do, as more productive jobs appear, and as less productive ones disappear. Societies flourish as jobs foster diversity and provide alternatives to conflict.

WDR 2012: Gender Equality and Development. Finds that women's lives around the world have improved dramatically, but gaps remain in many areas. The authors use a conceptual framework to examine progress to date, and then recommend policy actions.

WDR 2011: Conflict, Security, and Development. Conflict causes human misery, destroys communities and infrastructure, and can cripple economic prospects. The goal of this World Development Report is to contribute concrete, practical suggestions to the debate on how to address and overcome violent conflict and fragility.

WDR 2010: Development and Climate Change. The main message of this report is that a "climate-smart" world is possible if we act now, act together, and act differently.

WDR 2009: Reshaping Economic Geography. Places do well when they promote transformations along the dimensions of economic geography: higher densities as cities grow; shorter distances as workers and businesses migrate closer to density; and fewer divisions as nations lower their economic borders and enter world markets to take advantage of scale and trade in specialized products. WDR 2009 concludes that the transformations along these three dimensions of density, distance, and division are essential for development and should be encouraged.

WDR 2008: Agriculture for Development. In the twenty-first century, agriculture continues to be a fundamental instrument for sustainable development and poverty reduction. WDR 2008 concludes that agriculture alone will not be enough to massively reduce poverty, but it is an essential component of effective development strategies for most developing countries.

WDR 2007: Development and the Next Generation. Developing countries that invest in better education, health care, and job training for their record numbers of young people between the ages of twelve and twenty-four years of age could produce surging economic growth and sharply reduced poverty, according to this report.

WDR 2006: Equity and Development. Inequality of opportunity, both within and among nations, sustains extreme deprivation, results in wasted human potential, and often weakens prospects for overall prosperity and economic growth, concludes this report.

WDR 2005: A Better Investment Climate for Everyone. Accelerating growth and poverty reduction requires governments to reduce the policy risks, costs, and barriers to competition facing firms of all types—from farmers and microentrepreneurs to local manufacturing companies and multinationals—concludes this report.

WDR 2004: Making Services Work for Poor People. This report warns that broad improvements in human welfare will not occur unless poor people receive wider access to affordable, better quality services in health, education, water, sanitation, and electricity. Without such improvements, freedom from illness and from illiteracy—two of the most important ways poor people can escape poverty—will remain elusive to many.

WDR 2003: Sustainable Development in a Dynamic World. Without better policies and institutions, social and environmental strains may derail development progress, leading to higher poverty levels and a decline in the quality of life for everybody, according to this report.

WDR 2002: Building Institutions for Markets. Weak institutions—tangled laws, corrupt courts, deeply biased credit systems, and elaborate business registration requirements—hurt poor people and hinder development, according to this report.

WDR 2000–2001: Attacking Poverty. This report focuses on the dimensions of poverty, and how to create a better world, free of poverty. The analysis explores the nature and evolution of poverty, and its causes, to present a framework for action.

2

What Works and What Doesn't?

Beginning with Adam Smith, economists have long tried to understand why some people and countries are rich while others are desperately poor—typically in the hopes of alleviating poverty. Historically, this work was mostly heavy on theory and light on data. Much of the work introduced in chapter 1, for example, was focused on abstract growth and trade models. By contrast, in recent decades development economists have become decidedly more empirical and more reliant on data to understand what works in practice and what doesn't—typically with a strong microeconomic focus. Today, experiments of different forms are a basic tool in the development economist's kit. Taking a development economics class without learning about experiments and the selection problems they solve is like graduating from medical school without knowing CPR. This chapter will introduce you to randomized control trials (RCTs) and other experimental methods we use to understand the impacts of projects and policies on development outcomes.

ESSENTIALS

- Randomized control trials (RCTs)
- The selection problem
- The reflection problem
- Cost-benefit analysis
- Lab and natural experiments
- Market interlinkages

Ed has allergies. Not the dangerous kind some people get from peanuts or bee stings, but the hay fever kind: sneezing, itchy eyes, congestion, and on bad pollen days, a grueling sinus headache. Fortunately, there is a spray he can shoot up his nose that really helps. He's sure of it. Well, he thinks so. Maybe. Alright, there are days when he uses it and still feels pretty messed up, and other days when he doesn't use it but feels just fine.

The problem is, on spring days when puffballs of pollen float through the air like in a Fellini film, Ed doesn't know what *would* have happened if he *hadn't* sniffed the stuff. Those are the days he almost always uses it. When he forgets to, he can't be sure what would have happened if he *had* taken it.

To complicate matters, once he uses that spray, he acts differently. He feels like he can take on any allergen out there! Students observe Ed bicycling through the Davis countryside with the crops in full bloom. He sneezes from time to time, but that's because he's really putting the sniffer to the test and it isn't supposed to work all the time. Right?

In 2011, international development agencies spent an estimated $US147.74 billion to solve problems far more serious than Ed's allergies.[1] Trying to evaluate whether or not development programs work is a lot like figuring out whether allergy medication works. Development programs are a treatment, and the problems they try to solve are like an allergic reaction to pollen.

Donors must have better ways of knowing whether their programs work than Ed has for nose spray, right?

Sadly, until fairly recently they did not. Development agencies' shelves and hard disks are filled with final reports concluding that the projects they funded were successful (usually) at achieving their stated goals. But it can be extremely difficult to show whether a treatment is successful or unsuccessful. That is, unless you've got an experiment.

The people who make nose spray know all about experiments. That's what drug trials are all about. Before they can market a new drug, they have to perform a *randomized control trial,* or RCT. The formula to do an RCT is simple: (1) devise a treatment; (2) identify your target population and from it randomly select a sample of people to run your experiment on; (3) split the sample randomly into two groups, a treatment group and a control group; (4) give the treatment group the treatment and the control group a "placebo" that looks like the treatment but isn't; (5) after enough time has elapsed for the treatment to take effect, gather new information on your treatment and control groups; and (6) compare outcomes of interest between the treatment and control groups.

In 1997, Mexico did something similar to a drug experiment, but it was to test an entirely different sort of treatment: a new welfare program. PROGRESA (Programa de Educación, Salud, y Alimentación) was designed to combat rural poverty from two angles. First, it gave cash to poor people. A number of studies have shown that women are more likely than men to spend income on food and other goods that benefit their families, so women were the target of the program. Second, in order to get the cash, a poor woman had to follow some rules to improve her family's nutrition, health, and education. Kids had to be enrolled in school and in the local medical clinic. These behavioral requirements made PROGRESA what is called a "conditional cash-transfer program," or "CCT."

The theory behind this CCT was simple. In the short run, cash is what poor people need most in order to feed and clothe their families and satisfy their basic needs and wants. In the long run, the best way to break the intergenerational transfer of poverty is to give kids the human capital they need to lead productive lives; hence the two C's.

So far, we've got most of the first two elements of an RCT: the treatment (the CCT) and a target population (poor rural women). Mexico had to find out who was in this target population, so it carried out a nationwide survey. It identified 2.6 million families in fifty thousand rural communities who were eligible to receive PROGRESA benefits. That's about 40% of all rural families. The plan was to give the PROGRESA treatment to all eligible women.

If all eligible women get the treatment, how can we test whether the treatment works? We could compare everyone before and after the program starts. But if we saw differences, say, in school attendance or family nutrition, could we be sure it was because of PROGRESA? Many other things were happening in Mexico at the same time as PROGRESA. NAFTA (the North American Free Trade Agreement) had just gone into effect. In Mexico, as in many other countries, the mid-1990s saw far-reaching agricultural reforms that included eliminating subsidies for small farmers, with big impacts on rural incomes. New rural schools were being built. People were migrating. The weather was changing. There was lots of pollen in the air.

If you give everyone an allergy spray, they might still sneeze if the pollen count rises—or they might not sneeze at all if it doesn't. When you can't control for everything else, you can't figure out whether your treatment worked. Something else might have changed. This has been the curse of development-program evaluations over the years. We need a control group of similar, randomly chosen people who did *not* get the treatment but experienced, on average, the same changes in all those other variables that the treated people did. If treatment and control groups go into the pollen together, we should be able to determine whether the drug works.

Fortunately, the way PROGRESA was rolled out created a random control group for evaluating the program's impacts. There was no way to roll out the program to all eligible families in rural Mexico at the same time, so the government had to choose which poor villages to "treat" first. It could have gone for the villages closest to Mexico City, near where powerful politicians lived, or where poverty was highest, but it didn't. Instead, it rolled out the program randomly. All eligible women in randomly chosen villages got PROGRESA payments the first year of the program. They were the treatment group. In the rest of the villages, none of the eligible women got PROGRESA right away. They were the control group.

Randomization ensured that the treatment and control villages, households, and women, on average, were identical except for the treatment, just like the treatment and control groups in a drug trial. Researchers could compare any outcome they wanted—school attendance, nutrition, whatever—between the eligible households in these two groups of villages. All you had to do was compare averages. The difference could be attributed to PROGRESA.

Within three years, all 2.6 million eligible families were getting PROGRESA, so the experiment vanished. But for a short period of time, Mexico had given the world the gift of a randomized "social experiment" in the form of an RCT (see sidebar 2.1). PROGRESA became the model for both designing and evaluating anti-poverty programs in many other developing countries and even in New York City.[2]

RANDOMIZATION AND THE SELECTION PROBLEM

Over the years we've noticed that people who use nose sprays sneeze more than people who don't. Could it be that nose spray *makes* you sneeze?

That's a silly question, you say. People who use nose spray sneeze more because they had more allergies to begin with; that's why they chose the nose spray treatment. That's probably true, but you can see the problem here. We cannot determine whether the nose spray is effective by comparing people who use it with people who don't. If we do that, we might well conclude that the drug makes people sneeze! This is what experimentalists call *selection bias*. Selection bias confounds all sorts of studies. Here are three illustrations:

The economists Joshua Angrist and Jörn-Steffen Pischke took people who were hospitalized (the treatment group) and people who were not

Sidebar 2.1   Progressing with PROGRESA

Mexico's PROGRESA data have spawned more development economics research (not to mention PhD student theses) than almost any other micro data set in the world. Here are some key findings on PROGRESA's impacts, all made possible by the way in which the program was randomly implemented across rural Mexico.

Nutrition: PROGRESA improved both calorie consumption and the quality of beneficiaries' diets. Eligible households in treatment localities consumed 6.4% more calories than comparable households in the control localities. When it comes to nutrition, the quality of calories also matters. The study found that PROGRESA's biggest impact was on calories from vegetable and animal products. PROGRESA made people eat not only more, but better.

J. Hoddinott and E. Skoufias, "The Impact of PROGRESA on Food Consumption," *Economic Development and Cultural Change* (October 2004):37–61.

Schooling: PROGRESA had a significant positive effect on school enrollment. Many kids drop out of school after grade 6, when often they must leave their village to continue on in school. The largest difference between PROGRESA and control households was for kids who had already completed grade 6; the PROGRESA kids' enrollment rate was 11.1% higher, reaching 69%, and the program's impact was disproportionately concentrated among girls. Exposure to PROGRESA for 8 years, starting at age 6, increases children's educational attainment by an average of 0.7 years, and 21% more children attend secondary school.

T. Paul Schultz, "School Subsidies for the Poor: Evaluating the Mexican Progresa Poverty Program," *Journal of Development Economics* 74, no. 2 (2004):199–250.

Jere R. Behrman, Piyali Sengupta, and Petra Todd, "Progressing through PROGRESA: An Impact Assessment of a School Subsidy Experiment," *Economic Development and Cultural Change* 54, no. 1 (2005):237–75.

Health: PROGRESA significantly increased preventive care, including prenatal care, child nutrition monitoring, and adult checkups. It reduced inpatient hospitalizations, suggesting a positive effect on major illness. PROGRESA children age 0–5 had a 12% lower incidence of illness, and prime age adults (18–50) had 19% fewer days of difficulty due to illness than did non-PROGRESA individuals.

Paul Guertler, "Final Report: The Impact of PROGRESA on Health" (Washington, DC: International Food Policy Research Institute, 2002 (www.ifpri.org/sites/default/files/publications/gertler_health.pdf)

(the control group) and compared their health status a year later.[3] The people who had been hospitalized were less healthy. Do hospitals make people sick?

Governments around the world offer job training programs. Many studies find that a year or two later the people who chose to be in these programs are more likely to be employed than the people who chose not to do the job training. Are job training programs successful, or is it the kind of person who chooses to go for job training?

Economic studies consistently show that people with more education have higher earnings. Is this because schools make people more productive, or do higher ability people go to school?

In these (and countless other) cases, the outcomes we see after the treatment reflect two things: first, who chooses to get the treatment (the selection effect), and second, the effect of the treatment, itself. Because of this, simply comparing outcomes for people who did and did not get a treatment may tell us nothing at all about whether the treatment was effective. We've got to untangle the two.

What we'd really like to do is compare the same person's outcome with and without the treatment. We can't do that, though, because once a person gets treated, we can't see what would have happened to her without the treatment. And if the person does not get the treatment, we'll never know what would have happened if she had been treated.

The selection problem arises when things that determine whether or not someone gets treated are correlated with the outcome we want to measure. Sick people (whether they go to hospital or not) are likely to be less healthy in the future. Motivated people choose to participate in a training program, but they are more likely to get a job with or without the program. High-ability people are more likely to have higher earnings, regardless of how much more productive schools make them.

Randomization solves the selection problem. By randomly choosing who gets the treatment and who does not, RCTs create treatment and control groups that on average are the same except for the treatment. Any differences we observe between the two, then, must be the result of the treatment. You can find a formal presentation of the selection problem and how randomization solves it in the appendix to this chapter, "The Math of Selection."

Theoretically, in a perfectly designed experiment, we could test whether or not the treatment is successful simply by comparing outcomes between treatment and control groups. Randomization would ensure that everything but the treatment is identical, on average, between the two groups. Real life rarely gives us something approaching perfect randomization, though. Thus, we usually need baseline (pretreatment) information to make sure the treatment and control groups really are the same except for the treatment. Baseline surveys are costly, but tests showing there are no significant differences between the treatment and control group prior to the treatment are important to validate RCTs.

Baseline surveys are important for other reasons. We saw previously that Mexico's PROGRESA had to carry out a baseline survey in order to find out who would be in its target population, that is, which women met the criteria for receiving PROGRESA payments.

Baseline information can help researchers control for other variables that affect the outcome of interest. For example, while treatments are carried out, other things in the economy are changing, like the weather, macroeconomic policies, and recessions. With good baseline data, we can compare *changes* in outcomes for the treated and control groups before and after the treatment. For example, we might hope that cash transfers raise crop production in poor households. Meanwhile, if the economy is growing, poor households might increase their crop production with or without the program. If the transfers really do increase crop production, though, *the change in crop production should be larger in the households that got transfers*. Instead of comparing crop production between treated and nontreated households, then, we can learn more about the program's impacts if we compare *differences* in crop production between the two groups. This is called the "difference in difference" method. We first calculate the difference in the outcome variable (crop production) before and after the treatment for both the treatment and control groups. Then we calculate the difference between these differences. If it's positive, we conclude that the treatment had a positive effect on the outcome. This useful method requires having data on the treated and control groups before as well as after the treatment.

THE EXPERIMENTAL REVOLUTION IN DEVELOPMENT ECONOMICS

The chief architect behind PROGRESA was an economist named Santiago Levy who got his PhD from Boston University in 1980. By the time Mexican president Ernesto Zedillo (an economist with a PhD from Yale in 1974) asked him to lead a team to address extreme poverty in Mexico, Santiago had done enough data analysis to appreciate how selection bias can make it tough to know whether any program actually works in practice.

The program he and his team launched was the first large-scale randomized policy experiment in a developing country. The RCT approach to evaluating its impact was inspired by the work of economists studying policies in developed countries (especially related to labor markets). This, in turn, set the stage for a revolution in how development economists try to learn what works and what doesn't. The essence of this methodological revolution is quite simple: the less choice people have about whether to be "treated," the easier it is to test what works and what doesn't.

Many development economists see RCTs as the impact-evaluation gold standard, because in their purest form RCTs do not permit people to have any choice about whether or not they are treated. In 2003, Esther Duflo cofounded the Poverty Action Lab, which is dedicated to the use of RCTs.[4] She writes: "Creating a culture in which rigorous randomized evaluations are promoted, encouraged, and financed has the potential to revolutionize social policy during the 21st century, just as randomized trials revolutionized medicine during the 20th."[5] The J-PAL website states: "Randomized evaluations are often deemed the gold standard of impact evaluation, because they consistently produce the most accurate results . . . to determine whether a program has an impact, and more specifically, to quantify how large that impact is."[6]

Today, RCTs are being used to evaluate a wide array of development programs, from a new generation of social cash transfer (SCT) programs in sub-Saharan Africa to microcredit, HIV/AIDS prevention, immunization, and even "hope." Here are a few examples of the kinds of questions RCTs address.

RCTs for African SCTs

African countries are different from Mexico in ways that could shape the outcome of cash transfer programs. They are poorer and characterized by a greater level of risk and vulnerability. African SCT programs typically target households that are labor-poor as well as being in extreme poverty and containing vulnerable children. HIV/AIDS has its global epicenter in Southern Africa. The region has less developed markets and greater political instability. People's livelihoods and ability to escape from poverty are more linked to small-holder agriculture and the informal economy than to the formal wage economy. Public institutions tend to be weaker, and governments have fewer resources to invest in poverty programs; thus international donors play a much more significant role in financing social programs in sub-Saharan Africa. Competing donors often have conflicting ideas as to the types of social protection interventions to pursue. There is a lack of consensus among governments, too, along with a weaker capacity to implement and evaluate programs, and fewer complementary services like health, education, and nutrition. All these considerations make sub-Saharan Africa both an important laboratory for impact evaluation and a challenging place to do it.[7]

Another fundamental difference between the African and Mexican programs is that, for the most part, the African programs are not conditional. Often, behavioral changes like better nutritional practices and keeping kids in school are encouraged, but with few exceptions they are not required as a condition of getting the transfer. That is why these programs are often referred to as SCT instead of CCT programs. Is conditionality really needed, or, given the cash and information, will people choose to do the right thing? These questions loom in the debate and evaluation of SCTs in sub-Saharan Africa. There are exceptions that involve some sort of conditionality. Ethiopia's Productive Safety Net Program (PSNP) pays people from eligible households in chronically food-insecure *woredas* (districts) to work on labor-intensive projects. It is conditional in the sense that people have to work in order to get benefits. The idea behind this project is to give cash and food to the poor while building up the country's infrastructure, particularly irrigation, via work projects in which the beneficiaries participate.

A number of evaluations have come out of pilot programs designed to test the effectiveness of SCTs before the programs are "scaled up" to the larger population. Sidebar 2.2 summarizes what some of the key African SCT evaluations have been finding. Randomizing the "SCT treatment" is the key to being able to make statements like these about causality.

Credit

Access to credit is vital to people in poor as well as rich countries, as we shall see in chapter 12. There is strong theoretical reason to think that people will invest in new activities and technologies when they get access to credit. But how big is the impact? Do microcredit projects really make people more productive, and if so, how much?

Sidebar 2.2 Impacts of SCTs in Sub-Saharan Africa

An evaluation of a pilot SCT program in Malawi showed a significant reduction in child morbidity, gains in school enrollment, and increases in food consumption and diet diversity. Agricultural investments increased. The SCT also reduced child labor outside the home.

C. Miller, M. Tsoka, and K. Reichert, "Impacts on Children of Cash Transfers in Malawi," in *Social Protection for Africa's Children*, edited by S. Handa, S. Devereux, and D. Webb (London: Routledge, 2011), 96–116.

Katia Covarrubias, Benjamin Davis, and Paul Winters, "From Protection to Production: Productive Impacts of the Malawi Social Cash Transfer Scheme," *Journal of Development Effectiveness* 4, no. 1 (2012):50–77.

Ethiopia's Productive Safety Net Program caused an increase in school attendance for some groups, particularly younger children, and a reduction in child labor for some activities among boys, but an increase in girls' labor time.

J. Hoddinott, D. O. Gilligan, and A. S. Taffesse, "The Impact of Ethiopia's Productive Safety Net Program on Schooling and Child Labor," *Social Protection for Africa's Children*, edited by S. Handa, S. Devereux, and D. Webb (London: Routledge, 2011), 71–95.

South Africa's Child Support Grant decreased school absences, illnesses, and hunger and increased height-for-age scores among children receiving the grant. It increased access to cell phone use and supported the sustainability of agricultural activities in households with children receiving the grant. It also significantly reduced risky behaviors among adolescents, including sexual activity, pregnancy, alcohol use, drug use, criminal activity, and gang membership.

DSD, SASSA, and UNICEF, *The South African Child Support Grant Impact Assessment: Evidence from a Survey of Children, Adolescents and Their Households* (Pretoria: UNICEF South Africa, 2012; www.unicef.org /evaldatabase/files/CSG_QUANTITATIVE_STUDY_FULL_REPORT_2012 .pdf).

Kenya's Cash Transfers for Orphans and Vulnerable Children (CT-OVC) increased children's secondary enrollment on par with what has been found from *conditional* cash transfer programs in other parts of the world. Participating households had significantly higher expenditures than control households in food, health, and clothing and significantly less spending on alcohol and tobacco. They shifted from tubers to cereals, meat and fish, and dairy.

The Kenya CT-OVC Evaluation Team, "The Impact of Kenya's Cash Transfer for Orphans and Vulnerable Children on Human Capital," *Journal of Development Effectiveness* 4, no. 1 (2012):38–49.

Testing the effect of credit on investments and other outcomes is difficult, because the kinds of people who get loans (i.e., who apply and are accepted) are different from the kinds that do not, so we cannot simply compare the two. How can you make an experiment out of credit?

Dean Karlan and Jonathan Zinman figured out a way.[8] They convinced a lender in South Africa to grant loans to a random sample of applicants with low credit scores. These were people who applied for credit but had been deemed not credit worthy. Giving credit to people who do not qualify for it might raise some ethical concerns (see "The Ethics of Experiments" later on in this chapter), but by randomly giving credit to some people in this group, Karlan and Zinman avoided the problem that more credit-worthy people get loans and might do well with or without credit. It was an RCT because only some randomly chosen people with low credit scores were given loans, while others were not.

The researchers compared those who got credit to those who did not in terms of "economic self-sufficiency" (employment and income), food consumption, and other outcomes six to twelve months after the treatment. They found that economic self-sufficiency and food consumption were higher for the treated group. They also found that depression and stress were higher for the people who won this loan lottery, perhaps due to anxiety from being in debt.

People didn't randomly incur debt in the RCT that Suresh de Mel, David McKenzie, and Christopher Woodruff did in Sri Lanka—they just got money or machines.[9] The entrepreneurs who got chosen for this "Santa Claus treatment" ended up with a significantly larger capital stock, which is not so surprising for the ones that got the machines but not predictable for the ones that got the cash. However, the effect of this treatment on the profitability of enterprises was small or insignificant. These results suggest that some businesses are constrained by a lack of capital while others are not.

Insurance

Evaluating how insurance affects poor households is challenging because almost no rural households have access to insurance, and those that do have insurance tend to be very different from those that do not. Characteristics of households that are correlated with whether or not they have insurance are also likely to explain outcomes like crop production, income, or nutrition. Because of this selection problem, comparing outcomes between households that get insurance and those that do not generally tells us little.

We know from past research (see chapter 12) that poor households diversify their activities more than rich households to protect themselves against uncertainty. By not "putting all their eggs in one basket," though, they forfeit the potential income gains from specializing in what they do best. Access to insurance could bring substantial economic benefits to rural households, because if harvests are insured, banks might be more willing to lend to farmers, and farmers might be better able to specialize. To test this, though, we need a treatment group of households that have access to insurance and a control group that does not. We also need to avoid the problems of *adverse selection* and *moral hazard,* which we'll learn about in chapter 12; otherwise, insurance companies will not be willing to offer insurance to small farmers. Where can we find all of this?

Sarah Janzen and Michael Carter came up with a way.[10] They offered a new kind of insurance to a random group of pastoralists in the Marsabit District of northern Kenya: index-based livestock insurance (IBLI). Satellite measures of vegetative cover are used to predict average livestock mortality from drought in local communities. The payout households get from this insurance has nothing to do with their behavior; this insurance pays if the average livestock mortality predicted from satellite images reaches 15%. This avoids the problem of moral hazard (people changing their behavior once they have insurance). Janzen and Carter convinced an insurance company in Kenya to make this insurance randomly available to some small farmers but not others. This helped solve the problem of adverse selection (higher risk people taking out insurance).

A drought hit in 2011, after the insurance was made available. Insured households got an average payout of $150. It is too soon to assess the impact of this insurance, but we can ask what people *think* it will be. Janzen and Carter asked both the insured and uninsured households how they plan to deal with the drought. Many responded that they'll eat fewer meals, but a significantly smaller percentage of those with insurance said this. The number who anticipated selling additional livestock to cope with the drought was 50% lower for the insured households. The insured households also said they will rely less on food aid and assistance from others.

If what households end up doing is anything like what they say they'll do, this project will have succeeded in helping pastoralists deal with drought risk and avoid some of the worst impacts of the drought, while demonstrating the importance of insurance in risky environments.

Hope and Optimism

Most people care about their future. But what if, when they look there, what they see are dim economic prospects? Psychologists call the uncomfortable tension people feel from simultaneously holding conflicting thoughts "cognitive dissonance." Could it be that the poor, by closing their eyes on the future, reduce their psychological distress at the cost of worsening their future economic well-being? If poor people close their eyes on the future, they will have no reason to save and invest for it. This can create a "psychological poverty trap."

In November–December 2010, a team of researchers in Mozambique ran a lottery in which the winners got a free input subsidy for 70% of the cost of a seed and fertilizer package.[11] Winners of this lottery could expect to get a larger harvest. In April–May 2011 both the winners and losers of the lottery were asked the question, "How much time ahead do you plan your future expenditures?" On average, winning the lottery increased an individual's time horizon by more than a month, from 198 days to 235 days. It seems that the farmers who won the lottery became more forward looking.

Another RCT, in India, found evidence that helping desperately poor people invest gave far better results than expected, consistent with breaking out of a psychological poverty trap (see sidebar 2.3).

You will find many other RCTs scattered throughout this book. They test the impacts of a wide variety of programs, from immunizations to HIV/AIDS and government corruption.

RCTS AND THE PRACTICE OF DEVELOPMENT

The introduction to this chapter alluded to a methodological progression in development economics. The core questions about why some people and societies are poor and what might help alleviate this poverty have stayed essentially the same, but the methods economists use to try to address these questions have changed markedly. The approach of Adam Smith and his contemporaries was largely qualitative and even

Sidebar 2.3 Hope

In the Indian state of West Bengal, a microfinance institution, Bandhan, tried something different. Instead of giving loans to extremely poor people, who they thought would be unlikely to repay, they gave out assets: a few chickens, a cow, a pair of goats. They also taught people in this treatment group how to take care of their animals and manage their households. Just to make sure they wouldn't eat the animals right away, they also gave them a little cash to spend.

The theory behind this RCT was that people would learn how to manage their finances better and make a little income selling the products their farm animals would provide. To test the results of this project, researchers compared these treated households with a random control group of poor households, which did not get any of these things.

The results? The treatment worked better than anyone had hoped for. Long after the treatment had ended, the treated households ate 15% more, earned 20% more, and skipped meals less often than households in the control group. They were saving more, too. The improvements were far too big to be explained by the direct effects of the grants. That is, the treated households could not have sold enough eggs, milk, or meat to explain these big outcomes.

The project gave the treated households more than it had expected. The research team, headed by economist Esther Duflo, called it hope. The project gave people a reason to work harder—28% more hours, to be precise. The incidence of depression fell. In addition to a few animals and a bit of advice, it seemed, Bandhan had succeeded in administering a healthy dose of optimism. Could it be that the hope for escaping from poverty traps is hope, itself?

"Hope Springs a Trap: An Absence of Optimism Plays a Large Role in Keeping People Trapped in Poverty," *Economist* (May 12, 2012; www.economist.com/node/21554506).

philosophical. As economics became more formalized and mathematical, development economists focused mostly on theoretical models to shed light on these questions. When international development assistance expanded rapidly after World War II, there was a substantial rift between the abstract modeling of ivory tower economists and the emerging ranks of "boots on the ground" development practitioners who designed and managed development projects. These were two different worlds that, at best, shared only poverty questions as a raison d'être.

The availability of data and computing power in the 1970s and 1980s shifted many development economists away from purely theoretical models toward serious empirical analysis—and enticed them to spend more time in the field collecting data. The 1990s brought additional empirical advances to development economics. During these decades development economists tended to interact more and more with development practitioners, but there remained a persistent gap between applied development research and the practice of development.

The experimental revolution of the 2000s has shrunk this gap noticeably and increasingly brought practitioners and economists together as collaborators. In a typical collaboration, an implementing practitioner organization (e.g., an NGO, agency, or company) that intends to launch or expand a project relies on a team of research economists to design an RCT to rigorously evaluate the intervention and conduct the analysis. Success demands careful coordination and close interaction between practitioners and development economists.

These new models of collaboration have shaped both development economics and the practice of development. Greater integration of the two has brought development economists into earlier stages of project design and evaluation. Aligning research and programmatic objectives often also leads economists to analyze more directly the costs and benefits of specific development programs and interventions. (We will learn about how to do a cost-benefit analysis later on in this chapter.) Cost-benefit analysis can build directly on RCTs, which can help quantify impacts and associated benefits.[12] Close collaboration with the implementing partner makes it easier to incorporate program costs into this analysis and determine whether the carefully measured benefits justify the costs required to reap these benefits. Ideally, more rigorous cost-benefit analysis of this sort improves development policy and programs by distinguishing good projects from bad ones.

RCT-based research has also shaped the practice of development in important ways. Development organizations of all sorts now feel pressure to rigorously evaluate their projects. While this presents new opportunities to learn what works and what doesn't, it also brings new risks. The prospect of establishing very clearly and cleanly that something works sounds great, but establishing with equal clarity the opposite looks and feels like failure. This can be a threat, perceived or real, to both reputation and future funding. In contrast, less rigorous impact evaluation methods can be more forgiving, allow organizations to use selection bias to their advantage, and leave plenty of room for casting evidence in a more favorable light (glossy annual reports often do exactly this).[13]

WHEN EXPERIMENTS CAN GO AWRY

For all their promise, RCTs have many potential pitfalls. We have high-lighted a collection of well-executed experiments, but in practice, the ideal experiment is exceedingly hard to find. In general, the best experiments are those in which the question asked lends itself neatly to experimental methods, and the researchers have control over how the experiment is designed and executed. This usually is not the case with large-scale government programs, in which many things can go wrong, from politics to poor administration of treatments and research. Anyone reading about or designing RCTs had better be aware of these pitfalls.

There are two types of pitfalls that are worth noting: technical pitfalls that may undermine what we are able to learn from an RCT, and ethical pitfalls that arise in experimenting with people. We focus initially on the technical pitfalls of RCTs and discuss the ethical considerations, of RCTs in particular and experiments more broadly, later in the chapter.

The following subsections describe a few of the technical pitfalls that may beset an RCT.

Creating Treatment and Control Groups

An RCT requires treating one randomly selected group and denying treatment to another. Before we can conduct an experiment, we need to have valid treatment and control groups. Creating treatment groups is not as easy as it may at first seem. Why not? Because it is often difficult to ensure that the people who are randomly assigned to treatment are actually treated. For example, if you wanted to test the impact of a new crop variety on household income, you could offer incentives to adopt the new variety to the farmers in the treatment group, but you cannot ensure complete compliance. That is, farmers still must choose to plant the new variety—and this choice threatens to introduce the selection bias described above. As we will discuss later in this chapter, economists have devised ways for careful experimental design and data analysis to remedy this potential pitfall.

There are yet deeper potential problems surrounding the creation of control groups, which sometimes simply may not be possible. Take tourism, for example. Ecotourism development projects are among the fastest-growing parts of development bank loan portfolios. Many countries see tourism as a way to stimulate economic growth and fight poverty. Suppose we are interested in quantifying the impacts of a tourism-development project. The treatment is the project. The treatment group is effectively the entire population at the tourist destination, and the control group is the same population without the project. It is not possible to make this project happen for one group of people but not for others at the tourist destination. One might argue that the project could be implemented at some randomly chosen tourist sites but not others. However, almost by definition tourist destinations are unique (hence the reasons tourists want to go there). This makes it difficult to come up with reasonable alternative locations as a control, that is, sites identical to the "treated" site except without the treatment. They simply do not represent the region without the project. There is no counterfactual for the Galápagos Islands.

There are many other cases in which problems arise in the construction of treatment and control groups. Irrigation and other infrastructure projects create public goods that potentially affect everyone in the zone in which the projects are carried out. Staple price supports frequently have been used as a mechanism to transfer income to farmers (with dubious welfare benefits). However, it is generally not feasible to offer a high price to some randomly selected farmers but not others.

It may be politically infeasible to randomly create a treatment group, or it may be considered unethical to deny benefits to a control group (see "The Ethics of Experiments," below). In theory, input subsidies could be implemented randomly through targeted vouchers. In practice, though, it may not be politically feasible to deny benefits to a control group while offering them to a treatment group.[14] Even in a country like Malawi, where fertilizer vouchers targeted poor farmers, they were not given out randomly. If subsidies are given to all qualifying farmers, there is no control group.[15] It is not uncommon for researchers to be called upon to conduct impact evaluations after a project has already been implemented. In this case, we can see who got the treatment and who did not, but we might not have the pretreatment data we need to do a clean RCT, and there might be concerns over whether the creation of the treatment and control groups was truly random.

Control Group Contamination

Measuring a project's impact on the treated requires isolating the control group from the project's effects. This is often not so easy to do in practice. Even in a medical experiment it may be difficult to isolate the control group from the treatment group, for example, if the treatment involves curing a communicable disease. The effects of treatments on control groups frequently confound experimental research in the social sciences.

A well-known RCT in Kenya illustrates this point. It was designed to treat school children with worms in an effort to keep them in school. But treating kids in some schools caused the incidence of worms among kids in *control* schools to go down (see sidebar 2.4). When the treatment affects the control group as well as the treatment group, it can be difficult or impossible to reliably estimate the impact of the treatment, because both groups change. We call this problem "control group contamination."

Economic linkages can transmit impacts from treatment groups to others inside and outside the local economy. Take a cash transfer program. The household that gets the cash spends it. In the process, it transmits the impacts of the program to others inside and outside the village. Ed spoke with a shopkeeper in an Ethiopian village who loved the cash transfer program there. "You get transfers?" Ed asked. "No, but the people who get money come here to spend it!" he answered.

This shopkeeper was not eligible for the treatment, but he benefited from it just the same. If treated households buy more food, local farmers can benefit. If they fix up their house, so can the local bricklayer. These people, in turn, may hire more workers and buy more inputs. This can lead to a village version of Keynesian economics, in which the infusion of new cash into the economy has a multiplier effect on village income.[16] If we only look at the treated households, we are likely to underestimate the overall effects of the treatment.

Economic spillovers do not necessarily result in control group contamination, but they may. If the control households are in another village, economic linkages from the treated villages might not reach them. However, all around Africa, periodic markets bring people together from many different villages to buy and sell. If households from treated and control villages interact in these markets, the result can be control group contamination.

Treatment spillover effects raise challenges for RCTs, and they can be good or bad for people. If the treatment positively affects the control

Sidebar 2.4 Worms

Worms are bad (unless they're the garden variety). Hookworm and roundworm each infect approximately 1.3 billion people around the world; whipworm affects 900 million, and 200 million are infected with schistosomiasi. Intense worm infections keep kids from going to school and reduce their educational achievement. Could it be that a key to literacy is (getting rid of) worms?

Edward Miguel and Michael Kremer analyzed an RCT experiment to raise school attendance in Kenya by treating children for worms. A clearly defined treatment for worms was administered to children in a randomly selected sample of schools (the treatment group) but not in other schools (the control group). This project had a simple and easily measured outcome: school attendance. The ex-post research question was whether or not children in the treated schools were more likely to attend school after the treatment.

It seemed to be a squeaky clean experimental design. What could go wrong with it?

Actually, something went too right, from an analytical point of view. The treated schools treated the control schools. Maybe treated kids played with control kids after school or had contact with others who, in turn, had contact with control kids. The study could not tell us why, but for whatever reason, kids in the control schools got better, too.

Miguel and Kremer call this an *externality* of the treatment. (We'll learn about externalities in chapters 6 and 11.) In experimental jargon, it is called control group contamination. Really, it is a linkage—in this case, an epidemiological one—that transmitted the benefits of the project from those directly affected (the kids in the treatment school) to others in the project's zone of influence. Not surprisingly, the authors found that the farther a treated school was from a control school, the bigger the measured impact of the treatment.

Since kids in control schools got better, it was hard to find a positive effect on school attendance by comparing the treatment and control groups. It is ironic that a treatment potentially can be so successful that you cannot show it has any effect at all.

Edward Miguel and Michael Kremer, "Worms: Identifying Impacts on Education and Health in the Presence of Treatment Externalities," *Econometrica* 72, no. 1 (January 2004):159–217.

group, we might conclude that the treatment was not effective when in fact it was—both the treatment and control group benefit from it. It is also possible that the spillover is negative. For example, some villagers complain that cash transfers push up food prices. Giving cash to people might lead them to work less, in which case wages could go up. This in turn creates a cost for those who hire workers. If a project negatively affects the control group, we run the risk of concluding that the treatment was effective when really it was not: the treatment appears to make the treated better off when really it makes the control group worse off.

Under ideal circumstances, randomization can ensure that the expected outcome for the control households equals the expected outcome of the treated households had they not gotten the treatment. This ideal randomization relies in fact on two conditions. The first is having a "clean" control group that is isolated from the treatment. That is, it must be absolutely unaffected by the presence or absence of the treatment. The second is that the control group needs to be so similar to the treatment group on average that, had there been no treatment, the two groups would have displayed the same outcome.

Can Development Be Studied Like a Pill?

There is no question that the widespread use of RCTs in international development that started with PROGRESA has profoundly changed the way economists, NGOs, aid agencies, and governments approach development problems. RCTs are a major—perhaps the major—focus of development economics today. It is hard to find a development student PhD thesis that does not include some kind of randomized treatment. The strongest proponents of RCTs argue that randomized evaluations are "the gold standard of impact evaluation."[17] A big lesson from RCTs is that there is no single solution or explanation for underdevelopment. Different kinds of action are needed in different settings.

Others, we have seen, question whether RCTs are the end-all tool they claim to be and whether the most pressing development questions can be answered using a randomized experiment. For example, one of the most ambitious development interventions of recent decades—the Millennium Village Project—is a grand social experiment, but it was not designed as an RCT. In the minds of many development economists, this limits our ability to evaluate the project's impact. Jeffrey

Sachs—the architect of this project—dismisses these concerns, saying, "Millennium Villages don't advance the way that one tests a new pill."[18] His view, which is shared by some other researchers, is that restricting ourselves to a single methodological approach will severely hamper our ability to understand the complexities of the development process. What do you think?

IF NOT RCTS, THEN WHAT?

Although RCTs have become its poster child, the experimental revolution in development economics extends beyond this method. Recall that the essence of this methodological revolution is that the less choice people have to opt in or out of a treatment, the easier it is to test the treatment effect. RCTs offer a clean and direct way to introduce random treatment (albeit not as cleanly and simply as it might seem, as discussed above), but there are experimental alternatives, specifically (1) laboratory experiments and (2) natural experiments. Let's look at each of these in turn.

Laboratory Experiments

In a laboratory experiment, subjects make economic decisions in a contrived setting that is designed by researchers to elicit a specific kind of response from them. Travis has designed and conducted economic experiments like this in India, Morocco, Bolivia, and in several sub-Saharan African countries to learn how people make decisions. Individuals' responses in these controlled settings help us measure things that are otherwise difficult to measure: aversion to risk, patience, trust, concerns about fairness, and willingness to cooperate, to name just a few.

These "laboratory experiments" rarely take place in a laboratory when development economists do them. Instead, trained teams (often consisting of local university students or recent graduates) conduct these experiments in places where people tend to gather: under trees, in health clinics, near village schools, and so on. The structure of the experiments is carefully crafted to ensure that participants fully understand their tasks and to get a very specific kind of response from them. To encourage participants to formulate their decisions thoughtfully and to do the best they can, they are rewarded (typically paid in cash) according to their performance in the experiment.

The earliest experiments in development economics sought to understand how farmers in India make risky decisions in order to know whether risk aversion among poor farmers might prevent them from trying new seeds. As we'll describe in chapter 12, World Bank economist Hans Binswanger[19] implemented simple risk "games" in which farmers were given money and had to decide how much they were comfortable risking on defined gambles. By presenting all farmers with the same series of gambles and putting real money on the table, economists can measure each farmer's degree of risk aversion, which can influence many real-world decisions and thereby inform the design of development policy and interventions.

Natural Experiments

The international migration of labor is an important component of globalization and economic development in many LDCs. The number of international migrants, or people residing in a country other than their country of birth, has increased at an increasing rate over the past forty years, from an estimated 76 million in 1965 to 215 million in 2010. According to the World Bank, migrants sent US$325 billion home to LDCs in 2010, far more than official development assistance programs did: for each dollar of aid rich countries give poor countries, migrants send home more than $2.50. The flow of international migrant remittances to LDCs is increasing—faster than the number of migrants, in fact.

How do these remittances affect migrant-sending economies? This is an important question in development economics. Unfortunately, the selection problem makes it very hard to answer. Migration is not like a random treatment; households and individuals decide whether or not to migrate. There is a huge selection problem. The households that send family members off as migrants are different from the households that do not, in ways that are likely to affect almost any outcome we want to study.

We could imagine a hypothetical thought experiment in which we randomly plucked some people out of some households and made them migrate (the "migration-treatment" group), while keeping everyone else at home (the control group). Then we could go back at some future date and compare outcomes of interest, like remittance income, kids' schooling attendance, and productive investments, between the two groups.

With a randomized "migration treatment," households with and without migrants would be the same, on average, except for migration. There would be no selection problem.

Such an experiment, of course, is unrealistic, and even if it weren't, it would be unethical to make some people migrate (even if they didn't want to) while preventing others from migrating (even if they wanted to). It would violate the "do no harm" axiom, which we'll learn about later in this chapter. There is no RCT to study the impacts of migration on migrant-sending economies.

Is evaluating migration's impacts hopeless, then? Dean Yang, an economist at the University of Michigan, found a way (see sidebar 2.5).

Sidebar 2.5   A Remittance "Natural Experiment" from the Philippines

It's hard to imagine designing a randomized control trial to evaluate the impacts of migrant remittances, but Dean Yang came up with what might be the next best thing. He noticed that, at the moment of the Asian financial crisis of 1997, Philippine households had migrants in many different Asian countries. In some cases, the same household had migrants in more than one country. When the crisis hit, the Philippine peso devaluated more against some Asian countries than others. When the peso devalues, the value of remittances in pesos increases. For example, each Hong Kong dollar a migrant sent home turned into more Philippine pesos than before the crisis.

Nobody expected the crisis to happen. The impact on each household's remittances depended on where its migrants happened to be at the time of the crisis. That, Dean argued, makes the changes in remittances almost as good as random.

He found that a 1% peso devaluation increased remittances by 0.6%. These positive remittance shocks caused households to invest more time and money in human capital as well as in local businesses. Child schooling rose, while child labor decreased.

This study was important because of its "natural-experiment" approach to measure remittance impacts and its finding that remittances have a positive impact on investments in migrant-sending households.

Dean Yang, "International Migration, Remittances and Household Investment: Evidence from Philippine Migrants' Exchange Rate Shocks," *Economic Journal* 118 (April 2008):591–630.

Whereas with laboratory experiments researchers have direct control over the experiment and with RCTs researchers typically have indirect control over the experiment (because a partner NGO or agency typically administers the "treatment"), with natural experiments researchers have no control whatsoever. Instead, they take what history, legislation, or nature serves up and try to uncover circumstances in which people had little choice about being "treated" with something of interest. Used in the right way, such circumstances can remedy what is known as a "reflection problem." Often, we want to know how some "treatment" X (like remittances, in the example we just saw) affects some outcome Y (like poverty), but Y may also affect X. Poor households might be more likely to migrate in search of higher incomes, or they might be less likely to migrate if migration involves high costs and risks. If X reflects Y in this way, it becomes very difficult to disentangle the effect of X on Y from the effect of Y on X. The selection problem is related to this reflection problem.

Hollywood gives us a nice illustration of the reflection problem. Some famous movie scenes with villains have a hall of mirrors. Every time the villain moves, so does his reflection in a bunch of different mirrors. That's what happened to James Bond in *The Man with the Golden Gun*. This is a classic identification problem. You see the outcome (all those reflections of the bad guy raising his gun), but you don't know the cause (how can you identify the *real* bad guy who makes all the reflections move?).

That's how it often is with identifying cause and effect in economics. We see the outcome, but usually we don't have a neat RCT, so we need more information to figure out the cause. For example, if the villain coughs or steps on a twig, James can isolate him from the reflections and take him down. The sound is associated with the real bad guy but not his reflections, so it lets Bond figure out which is which. Basically, that's the strategy we have to follow in order to establish cause and effect in economics when we don't have a good RCT.

Economists are always on the lookout for variables that are correlated with treatments but not with the outcomes they study. These are called "instrumental variables." An example is the Asian economic crisis in Dean Yang's study (sidebar 2.5). Many of the most important development economics questions cannot be studied with the aid of well-designed RCTs. Econometric methods are then used, along with carefully chosen instruments, in an effort to isolate cause and effect. In the rest of this book we will learn about a number of different studies in which economists came up with novel ways to identify impacts without the benefit of an RCT.

James Bond found a more straightforward solution to his identification problem. He quickly shot out all the mirrors until the only thing left was the bad guy, Francisco Scaramanga!

THE ETHICS OF EXPERIMENTS

Experimenting on people raises ethical considerations. History gives us extreme and frightening examples of incidents in which people have been harmed by research, particularly in the medical and psychological areas. They include deliberate infection with serious diseases, exposure to biological or chemical weapons, human radiation, and many other atrocities. Some are less obviously harmful. A Stanford University study funded by the US Office of Naval Research in 1971 used students as guinea pigs to investigate the causes of conflict between military guards and prisoners. Students participated voluntarily for $15 per day. They were randomly assigned to play the roles of prisoners and guards in a mock prison in the basement of the psychology building, but they internalized their roles too well. By the time the experiment was terminated, the guards were subjecting their prisoners to physical and psychological abuse. The Stanford Prison Experiment often is held up as an example of unethical scientific research.

Today, any time human subjects are part of research, careful measures are required. Institutional review boards (IRBs) have to approve, monitor, and review biomedical as well as behavioral research involving humans. IRB approval is even required in order to carry out most kinds of economic surveys, because when you ask people questions in a survey, the respondents are your research subjects. It is important to remember this anytime you engage in social science research involving people. Guidance on complying with human subjects requirements is available at most universities and from the US Department of Health and Human Services (HHS; www.hhs.gov/ohrp/archive/irb/irb_guidebook .htm).

Despite IRB reviews, as RCTs have become a dominant methodology in development economics, they have raised considerable controversy, including with regard to ethics. Economists Chris Barrett and Michael Carter point out four classes of ethical considerations that arise in experiments by development economists.[20] These are discussed in the following four subsections.

Adverse Consequences of Experiments

The first rule in studies involving humans is the "do no harm" principle. Experiments manipulate people's environment in an effort to learn about their behavior. If in doing so they harm people, they are unethical and should not be implemented. This is the primary focus of IRBs.

Often, adverse effects of experiments are predictable and clear-cut. For example, if an RCT would encourage people to do something illegal or would put them in harm's way, it is definitely not ethical. An RCT in India created incentives for people to get driver's licenses without necessarily successfully completing the required training and testing. This potentially put innocent people at risk on the roads.

Other experiments are less blatant but still raise concerns. For example, researchers in China studied the impact of treating kids for iron deficiency (anemia) on school performance. Some children known to have anemia were given iron pills, and others were not. This study would not be approved in the United States because withholding treatment for something like anemia would not be considered ethical.

Barrett and Carter listed a number of cases in which experiments are likely to produce adverse consequences. One experiment tested whether large grants of money to women's organizations change them in ways that lead to the exclusion of poor women, potentially harming poor women. The study's finding that it did lead to exclusion seems to confirm that poor women may have been harmed by the experiment.

Think about the credit experiment we looked at previously, in which some people with low credit scores were given loans. Does it comply with the "do no harm" rule? Fannie Mae (the Federal National Mortgage Association), a US government–sponsored enterprise, made many home loans to people who should not have gotten them. This was a major cause of the "Great Recession" beginning in 2008. Needless to say, it was not a good thing for the people who shouldn't have gotten loans and ended up going into default. Giving loans to people who do not qualify for them can put their property and reputation at risk.

It is hard to imagine doing any harm by giving people good stuff like goats, chickens, or cash. Yet as we have seen, cash transfer programs can potentially harm some nonparticipants, for example, by pushing up local prices for food and other items they buy. This is not to say that these programs should not be implemented—they almost certainly do considerably more good than harm. Nevertheless, when we implement experiments or other programs, we have a responsibility to anticipate possible negative impacts on participants or nonparticipants and do whatever we can to mitigate them. This is part of the "do no harm by doing good" maxim.

Informed Consent

There is a difference between people being willful participants in experiments and people as subjects manipulated for research ends. The right of informed consent is well accepted; everyone who participates in a drug trial does so voluntarily. In RCTs, people often are unaware that they are (or are not) part of an experiment. IRBs require that participation in research studies, including simply being surveyed as part of an RCT, be strictly voluntary. The question, then, is how much information researchers should give their human subjects before they decide whether or not to be part of an RCT.

Blindedness

In medical research, people can know they are in an experiment without knowing whether they get treated. The use of a placebo makes this possible: the placebo pill looks the same as the real thing, so no one except the researcher knows who's being treated. Very few RCTs attempt to use a placebo. (For an interesting exception see sidebar 2.6.)

When you give someone an economic treatment, it's hard to keep it a secret. If a person knows she is in an RCT but ends up in the control group, she knows it. Keeping who gets the treatment and who doesn't a secret is a basic tenet of medical research, but it generally is not possible in economic RCTs.

The most important ethical rule, we have seen, is to do no harm. If people know they are in the control group, might they suffer emotional distress because they are not getting the benefits of the treatment? Imagine that you are desperately poor and malnourished. Could there be adverse emotional, psychological, even health consequences of knowing that you have been excluded from a treatment that could significantly improve your situation?

If so, there could be not only ethical but also research concerns. If you know you're in the control group and lose hope as a result, you could end up doing worse than you would have done without the experiment. Thus, the treatment group might look better off compared to you, making it seem like the treatment worked better than it did.

Sidebar 2.6   What? An Economic Placebo?

Using a placebo is basic in medical research. Treatment and control groups take an identical pill, but no one (except the researcher) knows which pill is the real thing. That's important, because if you know you are (or aren't) getting the treatment, the experiment is likely to get contaminated; for example, your behavior might change (like taking an antihistamine and then riding off into the pollen on your bicycle).

Economic RCTs are different, though. For example, people know whether or not they're getting a cash transfer. It's impossible to give people an "economic placebo."

. . . or is it? Four researchers ran an RCT in which farmers didn't know whether or not they were getting the real treatment. In randomly chosen treatment villages, farmers got a modern high-yielding variety (HYV) of cowpea seed. In control villages, they got the placebo: a traditional variety (TV). None of the farmers knew which seed they were planting. The result? Yields were the same between the treatment and control groups.

In another set of treatment villages, the farmers ran a normal RCT: the farmers knew whether they were getting the HYV or the TV. When farmers knew they were getting the TV, their yields were much lower than when they did not know. Their behavior changed. That is a placebo effect.

High-yielding seeds are designed to produce a bigger harvest when combined with the right combination of inputs: fertilizer, water, and so forth. The experimenters could have given farmers a package of inputs to use along with the seeds. That way, the only difference between treatment and control farmers would have been the seed, itself. Scientists frequently run experiments in which they control all inputs on experiment station plots. They are left with the question: Do experiment station results reflect what really happens out on farmers' fields? If we want to find out how a new seed affects crop yields in the real world, we have to recognize that farmers' input choices will be a key factor shaping the outcome—and those choices will depend on knowing which seed they're planting.

Erwin Bulte, Gonne Beekman, Salvatore Di Falco, Joseph Hella, Pan Lei, "Behavioral Responses and the Impact of New Agricultural Technologies: Evidence from a Double-Blind Field Experiment in Tanzania," *American Journal of Agricultural Economics* 96, no. 3 (2014): 813–30.

Is it ethical to involve people in experiments without their knowledge? If you answer "no" to this question, then you immediately hit another one: Can you reliably measure the impact of a social treatment if people *know* whether or not they are in the experiment? Will people—even people in the control group—change their behavior in ways that tarnish the RCT?

Targeting

Development organizations and governments have scarce resources to carry out development projects. It might seem logical (and ethical), then, to efficiently target these resources. Community knowledge can be used to make sure help goes to those most in need. RCTs routinely treat individuals who are not most in need of the treatment, while denying treatment to those who are. Strict randomization thus is viewed by many as being both wasteful and unfair. This can—rightly—be a stumbling block to convincing governments and communities to participate in RCTs.

An additional concern in experiments is the Treat-and-Run Syndrome. PROGRESA left Mexico with one of the world's most comprehensive social welfare programs, one that continues to this day. However, most RCTs are not conducted as part of large-scale government programs; many researchers abandon their research sites once the results of their RCTs are in. What are the long-term impacts of this "treat-and-run" way of doing research? If providing benefits to a treatment group does no harm during an experiment, does ceasing those benefits do no harm in the long run? What are the effects of leaving people behind after an RCT is over?

However you might answer these ethics questions, on one thing we can all agree: anytime we use human beings as research subjects, we have a special responsibility to make sure that we do them no harm, not only during the experiment, but afterward, as well.

THE INVARIANCE ASSUMPTION

Experiments, in order to be valid, must satisfy the *invariance assumption,* which states that the actual program will act like the experimental version of the program. Often, the purpose of RCTs is to test interventions that, if deemed successful, will be scaled up to a larger—or perhaps the entire—population. Will the large-scale program have the same kinds of impacts as the small-scale RCT? Or is there something about ramping up a project that creates new impacts not captured in experiments?

Actually, there may be. Once the program gets scaled up, the control group disappears. Linkages can transmit impacts of the program through the whole economy. Now everyone is likely to be affected, directly or indirectly, by the treatment. We call the total effect on the economy the "general equilibrium (GE) effect." We look at GE effects of projects at the end of this chapter. GE effects are a major reason why the invariance assumption may be violated. An intervention does not have to be particularly large in order to unleash GE effects; it only has to be important relative to the size of the economy in which it happens. In a poor region, a small project can have a large GE impact.

MULTIPLE TREATMENTS AND INTERRELATED OUTCOMES

In the worms experiment there was a clearly defined treatment (for worms) and outcome of interest (children's school attendance). Often, programs have multiple instruments (e.g., a cash transfer plus conditionality and eligibility requirements, or cash transfers and input subsidies or crop-price supports) and interrelated outcomes. In these cases, it quickly becomes difficult to connect specific components of the program with specific outcomes of interest.

Consider the social cash transfer (SCT) program initiated in 2011 in Tigray, Ethiopia. Many of the households eligible to receive the SCT already participated in a different transfer program: the Productive Safety Net Program (PSNP) had been offering them the opportunity to work a limited number of days on public projects in return for food or cash. When a household gets the SCT treatment, it stops getting the PSNP one. The new program crowds out the old, and both coexist within the same (treatment and control) localities. Disentangling the effects of these two programs is essential if we wish to evaluate the SCT's impacts. Some of the best experiments involve multiple treatments, but when there are many different interventions happening simultaneously, RCTs may not be up to the task of sorting out the impacts.

The impacts of most projects and policies are almost certain to be heterogeneous, with both winners and losers. Few experimental studies consider the ways in which some people may gain while others may lose as a result of a policy or program.

"WHETHER," "WHY," AND "HOW"

Consumer theory gives us a familiar equation relating a household's demand for a good *(D)* with its income *(Y)* and the market prices of this and other goods *(P)*:

$$D = \beta_0 + \beta_1 Y + \beta_2 P$$

This is what we call a structural equation. It is structural because it is derived from a theory of how the household economy works. Thanks to consumer theory, we know why income and prices are in this equation, and we even know what signs to expect on the parameters (for example, $\beta_1 > 0$ if we are dealing with a normal good, and $\beta_2 < 0$ if P is the price of the good in question).

When it comes to estimating this equation, though, we have a problem. Current income is endogenous. It is the result of work and other choices people make, and those choices might be related to consumption decisions in ways other than through income. Thus, when we compare demands among people at different income levels, there is likely to be a selection problem.

In chapter 6 we'll learn about Jacob Mincer, who argued that people's permanent income depends on their schooling *(S)* and work experience *(E)*, which we can treat as given at any point in time:

$$Y = \alpha_0 + \alpha_1 S + \alpha_2 E + \alpha_3 E^2$$

We could substitute this equation into our consumer demand model, eliminating the problem income variable and expressing demand as a function of schooling, experience, and prices:

$$D = \gamma_0 + \gamma_1 S + \gamma_2 E + \gamma_3 E^2 + \gamma_4 P$$

This is what we call a "reduced-form model." In economics, a reduced-form model is what you get once you've solved for the endogenous variables (here, income). In the reduced-form model, the variable of interest (here, D) is a function only of exogenous variables. If you do the algebra, you'll find that its parameters are functions of the parameters in the other two equations.

We might use econometrics to estimate this reduced-form model with survey data. We might find, for example, that the demand for smartphones increases with people's schooling. However, we would not be able to interpret the economic meaning of this result without knowing the underlying structural model. There are many reasons why schooling might influence the demand for smartphones. According to the structural model, schooling increases income, which in turn increases cell phone demand. A finding that schooling positively affects cell phone demand would be support for the hypothesis that cell phones are normal goods, based on the structural model.

A common rap against experimental methods is that they are reduced form. In a well-designed experiment, the treatment is exogenous. We estimate its impact on an outcome of interest. Experiments are a good way to test whether a treatment has an effect, but like other reduced-form methods, they do not tell us why. The economist Angus Deaton wrote: "In ideal circumstances, randomized evaluations of projects are useful for obtaining a convincing estimate of the average effect of a program or project. The price for this success is a focus that is too narrow to tell us 'what works' in development, to design policy, or to advance scientific knowledge about development processes."[21]

Designing good policies depends on understanding "why" as well as "whether." It also requires focusing our research on the highest-priority questions.

The best experimental studies not only test program impacts but also try to offer glimpses into the structural reasons why a treatment produces the outcomes it does. For example, in a clever experimental study in Kenya, some farmers were offered free fertilizer delivery early in the season and others not, while still others were offered a fertilizer subsidy. The study found that offering delivery early was more effective at increasing fertilizer use than was a subsidy.[22]

In general, though, it is far more difficult to answer the question of *why* a treatment has the effect it does than *whether or not* there is an effect and *how big* the effect is.

OPPORTUNITY COSTS

So your RCT finds that a program is effective at achieving its goals. Should the program be scaled up? The answer implicit in most experimental studies seems to be "yes." But is it the best way? Economists often talk about "opportunity costs." The opportunity cost of doing one thing is the value of what you could have done instead. When doing RCTs, it is easy to forget that every project and every way of carrying out a project has an opportunity cost. Finding that a treatment has a significant effect on an outcome of interest does not necessarily mean that the treatment is the best use of scarce public resources. A cash transfer, output price support, technology policy, or fertilizer voucher all might raise incomes in the beneficiary households, but they are unlikely to be equally effective at transforming a dollar of public expenditure into an increase in income in the treatment (or nontreatment) households.

COST-BENEFIT ANALYSIS

Economics offers a methodology to choose among different actions. It is called cost-benefit analysis (CBA, for short). You probably use CBA all the time without even thinking about it, like when you picked up this development economics book! CBA is the basic tool that development banks use to determine whether a development project is viable before it gets funded, and it can be used to compare the viability of different projects, as well—provided that the costs and benefits of projects can be quantified.

The basic idea behind CBA for development projects is simple: add up all the benefits and costs of the development project and take the difference. If this difference is positive, the project is viable; if not, then there is not an economic basis for undertaking the project. If it is positive for two or more different projects but you can only afford to carry out one of them, pick the project in which the difference between the benefits and costs is greatest.

In practice (like everything in life, it seems), CBA gets complicated. For one thing, most projects involve heavy start-up costs in the short run and benefits that are in the future. A dollar in the future is not worth the same as a dollar today—that's why banks have to pay interest in order to get us to save.

Discounting and Net Present Value

CBA has a straightforward way to deal with the timing problem: use the interest rate to discount future values and express them in present value (PV). If i is the interest rate, the PV of $100 of income a year from now is $100/(1 + i)$. If the interest rate is 5% (that is, .05), we get $100/1.05 = $95.24. If you had $95.24 today, you could turn it into $100 a year from now by putting it in the bank at 5% interest—and waiting.

What is the PV of $100 two years from now? In other words, how much would you need to put in the bank today to end up with $100 after two years? The answer is $100/(1 + i)^2$. At a 5% interest rate, the PV of $100 two years from now is $100/(1.05)^2 = $90.70. When doing CBA, we convert all future benefits and costs to PV by dividing them by $(1 + i)^t$, where t is the time period: $t = 1$ in year 1, $t = 2$ in year 2, and so on.

Once we have discounted all future benefits and costs of a project, we sum their differences to get the project's net present value (NPV):

$$NPV = \sum_{t=0}^{T}\left(\frac{Benefits^t - Costs^t}{(1 + i)^t}\right)$$

The capital Greek sigma (Σ) denotes the sum; our formula adds up the discounted difference between benefits and costs from the start of the project ($t = 0$) until the end of the time period over which we wish to perform the cost-benefit analysis ($t = T$).[23]

The NPV formula is the basis for carrying out any CBA. If NPV > 0, the project passes the economic cost-benefit test. If you can only fund one project, on purely economic grounds choose the one with the highest NPV.

Determining Benefits and Costs

The trick always is in figuring out what the benefits and costs are. Often, a project's costs are immediate and known. For example, it is not hard to determine the cost of running an extension program to train one hundred farmers on how to use a new technology and giving each farmer a technology start-up package (for example, high-yielding seed and fertilizer to plant one acre). Or the cost of building a new school room and staffing it with a teacher. Or of carrying out an immunization program in one hundred villages.

Calculating benefits can be a different matter, though. If you carry out the extension program, how much higher will the farmers' incomes be? If you build the school, will students attend? How many parents will bring their kids to the clinic to get the immunization? If more kids attend school or get immunized, will their future incomes go up because they become more productive?

This is where experiments and the other evaluation methods in this chapter can help. Cleverly designed RCTs can provide estimates of how many farmers will adopt a new technology and how much their yields are likely to increase if they do. The PROGRESA and African cash transfer RCT studies described earlier in this chapter estimate impacts on school attendance. Chapter 6 includes an RCT to evaluate the demand for immunizations.

TABLE 2.1   PRESENT VALUE OF COSTS AND
BENEFITS OF A HYPOTHETICAL PROJECT

t	Cost(t)	Benefit(t)	Benefit(t)–Cost(t)
1	100		–100
2		18.18	18.18
3		16.53	16.53
4		15.03	15.03
5		13.66	13.66
6		12.42	12.42
7		11.29	11.29
8		10.26	10.26
9		9.33	9.33
10		8.48	8.48

NPV: 15.18

Here's a simple illustration of the mechanics of CBA: imagine a project that would cost $100 to carry out, with all of those costs occurring in year 1. Beginning in year 2, based on our experimental or other estimates, we expect the project to produce benefits of $20 per year. Your funding agency requires that the project break even within ten years—that is, the project's NPV, evaluated over a ten-year period, must be positive. Is it?

Using a fairly conservative (10%) discount rate, we can construct a table showing the PV of this project's costs and projected benefits (table 2.1).

The balance of annual benefits and costs starts out negative, because there are only costs in year 1. It turns positive once the project begins to yield the $20 benefit per year. The $20 number doesn't appear in this table, though. Benefits have to be discounted: the PV of $20 after one year is $18.18; after two years it is $16.53, and so on. (If there were costs in years 2–10, they would have to be discounted, too.)

Adding up all of the discounted benefits and costs over the ten-year period, we get an NPV of $15.18. It is greater than zero; thus, the project is economically viable. Whether it is economically optimal will require comparing this to the NPVs of competing projects.

You might want to experiment using the CBA worksheet posted online for this chapter. You would find that this project would not pass the economic cost-benefit test if the benefits were $17 per year, if the interest rate were 14%, or if there were an annual cost of $2 to keep the project going.

In chapter 6 we carry out a simple cost-benefit analysis of going to school for a child in a poor Lesotho village. It is not unlike the CBA you might have carried out while deciding whether or not to study development economics.

Non-Economic Benefits and Costs

Many benefits and costs cannot be quantified. CBA can be a good tool for evaluating economic costs and benefits and selecting projects on economic grounds. Clearly, there are reasons to carry out projects on other grounds, as well. How can one deny a child education or good health if it is at all possible to provide her with these basic human rights? Non-economic benefits strengthen the argument for carrying out some development projects. Non-economic costs can do the opposite. An example of the latter is an activity that produces negative externalities, for example, a negative environmental impact. Positive externalities, on the other hand, can strengthen the case for a project. For example, "treating" some farmers with information about better cultivation practices could have positive externalities if the "treated" farmers share this information with others. In short, CBA is a useful economic tool, but it may not be the sole criterion for implementing a development project.

BEYOND EXPERIMENTS: LOCAL ECONOMY-WIDE IMPACTS OF DEVELOPMENT PROGRAMS

Suppose we wish to evaluate the impact of an income transfer program on rural poverty. Poor households receive the transfer, which might entail some sort of conditionality (for example, PROGRESA's requirement that children attend school) or not (the case in almost all of the SCT programs in Africa). Figure 2.1 illustrates the pathways by which this project might impact a local economy. Arrow (a) represents the transfer's direct effect on the income of a recipient (poor) household. This is equal to the amount of the transfer. With higher income, the household's demand for normal goods and services increases. The transfer can affect the household's production activities in a number of different ways. By raising the household's income, it can stimulate consumption demand, including the demand for leisure and goods produced by the household.[24]

For example, an increased demand for food could encourage a subsistence household to grow more food crops, while an increased demand

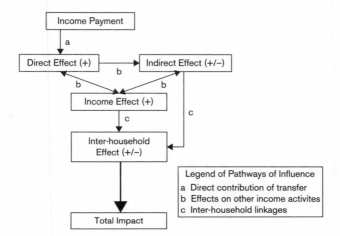

FIGURE 2.1. An income transfer project creates both direct and indirect income effects in the treated economy.

for leisure could do the opposite. If leisure demand increases, the household's wage income could fall. The transfer could loosen liquidity constraints on crop production, enabling the household to purchase more fertilizer and other inputs or shift into input-intensive cash crops.[25] Finally, it could reduce income risk, and this might encourage the household to invest more of its scanty resources in risky activities. (We'll learn about agricultural household behavior in chapter 9.) Conditionality could create still other impacts in recipient households. For example, the requirement that children attend school could decrease the family's labor available for crop production.

Arrow (b) depicts these myriad indirect effects of the transfer on the treated household's income from production and labor activities. Experimental methods, when feasible and carefully executed, can provide insights into the net influences represented by arrows (a) and (b).

As the recipient households demand more consumption goods and change their allocation of resources to production and wage activities, others in the local economy invariably are affected. Local markets transmit impacts of the transfer from the recipient to nonrecipient households, as represented by arrow (c) in the figure. Households and businesses supplying goods and services to the recipient households benefit. If the transfer alters the recipient household's wage labor supply, this could drive up wages, or as consumption demand rises, so might local prices. These will affect nonrecipient households in other (possibly negative) ways. As local activities adjust, a new round of changes in input demands, incomes, and household expenditures follows, creating additional rounds of changes in incomes and expenditures. Given income leakages, successive rounds of impacts become smaller and smaller, and the total (direct plus indirect) effect of the program eventually converges to an income multiplier. To the extent the goods demanded by the recipient households are supplied locally, the income transfer could create a multiplier considerably greater than one. On the other hand, if the recipient households purchase goods from outside the local economy, some or perhaps most of the multiplier will go elsewhere. Clearly, the behavior of the households that get the transfer to begin with is critical in shaping the impacts that result from the program, but so is the behavior of the nontreated groups and the structure of the local markets connecting them with each other.

The economic linkages that transmit impacts through economies are called "general-equilibrium feedback effects." In a few cases, RCTs have collected data on ineligible households and found evidence that they are affected by treatments. One such study was done on the effects of Mexico's PROGRESA on the households that did not get PRO-GRESA transfers. The impact was found to be positive, implying that only focusing on the treated underestimates the program's impact.[26]

To understand the ways in which a treatment affects both treated and nontreated households, we generally have to go beyond RCTs and try to model economic linkages. As the diagram in figure 2.1 illustrates, the direct and indirect impacts of an intervention are shaped by how households change their supply and demand decisions and by the structure of local markets, which in turn reflect various constraints (technology, transaction costs, liquidity, risk). Performing project evaluations in such environments may require integrating models of heterogeneous households into a model of the whole local economy, a local general-equilibrium (GE) model. A model for the economy targeted by the project (village, region, rural sector) can provide a laboratory in which the project is designed and its impacts assessed, using a simulation approach.

There are fundamental differences—some might call these philosophical differences—between RCTs and simulation models. An RCT, we've seen, is like a drug experiment; it can tell us whether something works, but not why. An advantage of experiments is that statistical significance can be attached to RCT findings; for example, "with 95% certainty we can say that the transfer increased food consumption by between $10 and $15 per month." The validity of an RCT depends on getting the experiment right; otherwise, the findings, however significant statistically, may be biased. At conferences where researchers present studies using RCTs, much of the discussion centers around what might have gone wrong in the experiment and how this might have affected the results. This illustrates how much more difficult it can be to run "clean" economic experiments than drug trials. Often, one is left with questions about why a treatment had the effect that it did on those who got the treatment.

Simulation models try to answer the question "why" while capturing complex interactions that shape project outcomes, in ways that often are beyond the reach of experiments. The validity of a simulation model depends on getting the model right. Imagine a flight simulator. Schools do not teach pilots how to fly by hitting them with dangerous real-world situations in mid-air. Pilots can step into a flight simulator. The simulator is programmed with equations representing the physics of flight. It becomes a laboratory in which flight experiments are conducted. If you've ever played a computer game, you know what simulations are all about. If the flight simulator is programmed wrong, well, you won't want to fly with that pilot!

A simulation approach to project impact evaluation highlights the interactions within the local economy that transmit impacts, good or bad, from directly affected actors to others in the economy. We can construct simulation models using data from the same surveys that are used to do RCT research. If our simulation model represents the way in which the local economy works, it can be a valuable tool to understand the full, economy-wide impacts of cash transfers and many other programs and policies.

There are two main knocks against simulation models. One is that they depend on getting the model right, especially how agents behave and how markets transmit impacts from one agent to another (like getting the flight simulator equations right). Another is that it is more difficult (though not impossible) to attach statistical significance to simulation results.

A new method, local economy-wide impact evaluation (LEWIE), uses data from RCT surveys to estimate simulation models and construct confidence bounds around their results. This is a step in the direction of bringing together the best of RCT and simulation methods.

A LEWIE simulation model was used to evaluate the local GE effects of a cash transfer program in the southern African country of Lesotho.

Sidebar 2.7   Impacts of a Treatment on the Nontreated in Lesotho

When poor people get cash transfers, they spend them. This transmits impacts of cash transfer programs from treated to nontreated households. Lesotho's Child Grants Program (CGP) seeks to improve the living conditions, nutrition, health, and schooling of orphans and vulnerable children. It seeks to accomplish this via an unconditional cash transfer targeted to poor and vulnerable households.

A local economy-wide impact evaluation (LEWIE) found that each $1 transferred to a poor household raises total village income by $2.23, with a 90% confidence interval (CI) of $2.08 to $2.44. Even though all of the cash transfers go to poor eligible households, nearly half of the benefits they create ($1.18) go to ineligible households.

If there are constraints that limit the local supply response, though, higher local demand may push up prices instead of stimulating production. Price inflation reduces the multiplier in real (price-adjusted) terms. (We'll learn how to adjust income for inflation in chapter 3.) It raises consumption costs for everyone in the local economy. If supply constraints are severe, the *real* income multiplier may be as low as $1.36 (CI: $1.25–$1.45). The study found that loosening capital constraints, say, through effective microcredit programs that enable households to buy more crop inputs, can be a key to avoiding inflation and raising the real transfer multiplier.

This study is important because it reveals potential impacts of cash transfer programs that are unlikely to be picked up by RCTs—including impacts on households that do not get the cash. Large local income multipliers suggest that social cash transfer programs promote income growth in poor villages. That's good news for both social welfare ministers and finance ministers in LDCs.

J. Edward Taylor, Mateusz Filipski, Karen Thome, and Benjamin Davis, "Spillover Effects of Social Cash Transfers: Lesotho's Child Grants Program," in *Beyond Experiments in Development Economics: Local Economy-Wide Impact Evaluation,* edited by J. Edward Taylor and Mateusz Filipski (Oxford: Oxford University Press, 2014), 181–202.

It uncovered import spillover effects, including effects on the households that did not get the transfer (see sidebar 2.7).

www.rebeltext.org/development/qr2.html
Learn more about what works and what doesn't by
exploring multimedia resources while you read.

APPENDIX

The Math of Selection

The math behind RCTs is not very hard, but it takes most people some time to wrap their minds around it because it involves some "what ifs." Here's how it works:

We want to know whether a treatment (like a development project) affects some outcome of interest (say, income or health). Let's call person i's outcome Y_i. If a person gets treated, the outcome is Y_{1i}, and if she does not get treated, it is Y_{0i}. Each person has both a Y_{1i} and a Y_{0i}, but there's a catch: we can only see one of them. If i gets treated, we see Y_{1i} but not Y_{0i}. If she doesn't get treated, we see Y_{0i} but not Y_{1i}.

Let's make a variable D_i that equals 1 if person i gets treated and 0 otherwise. A concise way to represent the outcomes is:

$$Y_i = \begin{cases} Y_{1i} \ if \ D_i = 1 \\ Y_{0i} \ if \ D_i = 0 \end{cases}$$

The outcome we "see" for person i is whatever it would be without the treatment, Y_{0i}, plus whatever effect the treatment has, which is $(Y_{1i} - Y_{0i})D_i$. For short, let's call the actual effect of the treatment ρ:

$$Y_i = Y_{0i} + \underbrace{(Y_{1i} - Y_{0i})}_{\rho} D_i$$

The treatment effect, ρ, is what we want to find out. It is the change in the outcome that is *caused* by the treatment. (If the person does not get treated, $D_i = 0$, so this second term is zero.)

Now suppose we simply compare expected or average outcomes for people who do and do not get the treatment. In stats talk, the expected or average outcome given that a person gets the treatment is $E[Y_i|D_i = 1]$, and the expected outcome for people who don't get the treatment is $E[Y_i|D_i = 0]$. ("E" means "the expected value of," and the slash marks mean "given that.") The average difference we see between the people who are treated and the people who are not, then, is

$$E[Y_i|D_i = 1] - E[Y_i|D_i = 0]$$

This difference is not the average effect of the treatment on the treated, because it includes selection bias. The average effect of the treatment on the treated is the difference between (1) the expected outcome for people with the treatment, given that they got it ($E[Y_{1i}|D_i = 1]$), and (2) the expected outcome for these same treated people *if they had not been treated* (which we can call $E[Y_{0i}|D_i = 1]$). In other words, the average treatment effect on the treated, which is what we want to know, is

$$E[Y_{1i}|D_i = 1] - E[Y_{0i}|D_i = 1]$$

Imagine the people who get the treatment (that's the first term). If, after they get the treatment, we could put them into an Orwellian time machine, send them back in time, and then not treat them, we'd have the second term. If that person did not change in any other way, the difference would be the true average effect of the treatment on the treated.

Obviously, we cannot both treat and not treat the same people. We have to compare people who get treated to people who don't. This leaves us with selection bias. Selection bias is the difference between (1) the expected outcome for those who got treated, if they hadn't gotten treated (same as the second term in the expression above: $E[Y_{0i}|D_i = 1]$), and (2) the expected outcome without the treatment for the people who didn't get treated ($E[Y_{0i}|D_i = 0]$). In other words:

$$E[Y_{0i}|D_i = 1] - E[Y_{0i}|D_i = 0]$$

In the hospital example, the selection bias is negative, because the people who get the "hospital treatment" (the first term above) are less healthy, on average, than the people who don't get the treatment (the second term). It is reasonable to expect that, on average, the people who went to hospital would have had poorer health without going ($E[Y_{0i}|D_i = 1]$) than the people who didn't go got by not going ($E[Y_{0i}|D_i = 0]$). The people in this last group probably didn't go because they didn't need to.

To sum it all up:

$$\underbrace{E[Y_i|D_i = 1] - E[Y_i|D_i = 0]}_{\textit{Observed difference in average health}}$$

$$= \underbrace{E[Y_{1i}|D_i = 1] - E[Y_{0i}|D_i = 1]}_{\textit{Average treatment effect on treated (positive—we hope!)}}$$

$$+ \underbrace{E[Y_{0i}|D_i = 1] - E[Y_{0i}|D_i = 0]}_{\textit{Selection bias}}$$

What makes this challenging to understand is that the repeated term on the right-hand side of the equation above, $E[Y_{0i}|D_i = 1]$, is hypothetical. We cannot see what did not happen.

Randomization solves the day. If the treatment is truly random, then on average the people who get it are identical to those who do not, so their outcomes without the treatment, on average, are the same: $E[Y_{0i}|D_i = 1] = E[Y_{0i}|D_i = 0]$. The selection bias term disappears, leaving only the average treatment effect on the treated. That's why, in a well-designed RCT, we can estimate the average effect of the treatment on the treated simply by comparing average outcomes for the random treatment and control groups.

3

Income

Economic development entails many different sorts of outcomes: income growth, poverty, inequality, human welfare. These outcomes are obviously interrelated. Understanding these interrelationships is a central theme in development economics. As we shall see, these economic outcomes can shape one another in complex and important ways. Before we learn how to study these interactions and outcomes and before we consider ways to influence them with policies and projects, we need to know how to measure them. In this chapter, we focus on measuring income. That might sound boring and straightforward, but read on—you may be surprised by how interesting, challenging, and controversial income can be. It is often consequential as well, because a country's measured income level can determine whether it gets special privileges or preferential treatment in international organizations and negotiations.

ESSENTIALS

- GDP and GNP
- Subsistence goods and shadow values
- Market failures: externalities and public goods
- Development classifications and categories
- Input-output analysis and income multipliers
- Purchasing power parity and price deflators
- Creating and using indexes

MEASURING INCOME

Income is a basic development indicator. Indeed, it provides the most obvious distinction between the rich and the poor. It is also an important input in the economic development process, since investments of all kinds—in people, in society, in innovation, in nature—require resources.

Poor countries have low income and therefore fewer resources available to accomplish their development goals.

Before going any further, we should agree on how to measure income. The most basic measure of a country's income is its gross domestic product (GDP). This concept is based on a fundamental identity (i.e., relationship) in economics: in all economic activities, total income must always equal total expenditures. Every dollar of sales by a shirt factory (income) either goes toward purchasing the inputs used to produce the shirts or gets paid out to the factory's owners as profit (expenditures). Based on this identity, we can calculate a country's GDP in one of two ways.

First, we can add up the value of all *final* goods and services *produced within the country and then sold*. By "final," we mean goods and services that are *not* inputs into the production of some other good. For example, cotton is rarely a final good; it is an input into the production of cloth. Cloth, in turn, is an input into producing clothes. Clothes are almost always a final good—we buy and wear them, rather than using them to produce something else.

You can see the potential for double-counting here. The price of a shirt includes the cost of the cotton fabric to the garment factory as well as the cost of the cotton to the textile mill. If we added the value of the cotton, fabric, and shirt together to calculate GDP, we would significantly overstate the value of what was produced in our economy. We also want to be careful not to count the value of inputs produced in foreign countries. If the buttons on shirts sold in the United States were produced in Mexico, they are part of the GDP of Mexico, not the US. The US-Mexico border really matters in this case, because GDP is meant to capture the geography of economic activity. In short, calculating national income is a lot harder than it sounds.

After we determine which goods to include, we have to add them all together to get a measure of total production. We do this by putting a value on each of the goods. What value do we use for all of these final goods? Economists tend to trust markets to indicate what goods are worth, so, not surprisingly, we use market prices. This gives us the GDP at market prices.

The second way to estimate GDP is to focus on inputs instead of final goods and to add up the cost of all factor inputs (capital, labor, land). Any economic activity takes intermediate inputs (cotton fabric, thread, buttons) and uses factors of production (labor and capital) to turn these inputs into a product (shirts). The income the shirt factory creates is called its "value-added" and consists of the difference between the value of the shirts it sells and the cost of the cotton fabric, thread, buttons, and other intermediate inputs it buys to produce the shirts. This is the value that the shirt factory adds to the cotton fabric and other intermediate inputs once it has turned them into shirts. Value-added is the factory's payments to labor and capital. While adding up all this value-added gives us the GDP at factor cost without running the risk of double-counting, determining value-added, as you might guess, is also not without its complications!

Input-Output Analysis

To make the difference between these two approaches crystal clear, let's introduce a new concept: input-output analysis. To be introduced properly to this concept, you should really meet Russian American economist Wassily Leontief, who founded input-output analysis and picked up a Nobel Prize in 1973 for his contribution. Table 3.1 is a Leontief input-output table for a simple economy consisting of only three production sectors: agriculture, industry, and services. In this simple economy, agriculture produces a total output of $920, and industry and services produce $1,425 and $567, respectively. You'll notice that these numbers appear twice, as both the row and column total for each sector.

The columns show the expenditures of each sector, that is, where all the money went. In order to produce its output, agriculture bought $225 in intermediate inputs from itself (e.g., seed), $320 from the industrial sector (e.g., chemical fertilizer), and $75 from services (e.g., contractors and accountants). It spent $100 in wages and purchased $50 in imported inputs. Finally, the agricultural sector generated $150 in profits, for an expenditure total of $920.

The total expenditures must equal the total value of agricultural production. The Agriculture row tells us where this production went, or in other words, who paid money to farms. Reading across the first row you can see that $225 of the value of agricultural output was sold back to agriculture, as intermediate inputs (e.g., seeds), $75 to industry (e.g., as wheat to flour mills), and $2 to services (e.g., food to schools). The difference between the total agricultural production ($920) and these intermediate uses of agricultural goods ($225 + $75 + $2 = $302) is the final demand for agricultural output ($618).

You can interpret the industry and service accounts in exactly the same way.

TABLE 3.1 AN INPUT-OUTPUT TABLE (IN USD)

Income Account	Agriculture	Industry	Services	Final	TOTAL
Production Sectors					
Agriculture	225	75	2	618	920
Industry	320	200	85	820	1,425
Services	75	150	30	312	567
Factors					
Labor	100	400	275	n/a	775
Capital (Profits)	150	300	125		575
Imports	50	300	50		400
TOTAL	920	1,425	567	1,750	

$775 + 575 = 1,350$
(GDP at factor cost)

$1,750 - (50 + 300 + 50) = 1,350$
(GDP at market prices)

It is easy to calculate GDP from the input-output table, using either of the two methods. GDP at market prices is the sum of the total final demand ($618 + $820 + $312 = $1,750) minus imported inputs ($50 + $300 + $50), or $1,350. GDP at factor cost is just the sum of payments to factors (labor and capital), or value-added: $775 + $575 = $1,350. As you can see, it doesn't matter which way we do it—we end up with the same GDP.

This basic method can be used to calculate the GDP for any economy—a country, state or province, even a village. If the state of California were a country, it would have the eighth largest GDP in the world, just behind Brazil and in a near tie with Italy and the Russian Federation.[1] Some economic surveys of rural households gather all of the data needed to calculate a village's GDP. This can be quite complicated, because many rural households both produce and consume agricultural goods, as we will learn in chapter 9.

Multiplier Analysis

In the prior exercise, you not only learned how to calculate GDP, but picked up a little bit about input-output (IO) accounting along the way. As it developed in the twentieth century, IO analysis became the conceptual foundation for socialist planning. From an IO table like this one, it is not hard to derive a Leontief multiplier matrix, which tells us how much each sector in an economy has to produce in order to (1)

TABLE 3.2 LEONTIEF MULTIPLIERS

a. Production

Production Sectors	Agriculture	Industry	Services
Agriculture	1.365	0.086	0.019
Industry	0.584	1.223	0.196
Services	0.182	0.143	1.079

b. Factor Value-Added and GDP

Factor	Agriculture	Industry	Services
Labor	0.401	0.422	0.580
Capital	0.386	0.303	0.282
GDP	0.787	0.725	0.863

satisfy all final demand and (2) supply all the intermediate inputs that are needed by all the production sectors. That's a big part of the central planner's resource allocation problem—and it is no easy task, which is why market economies, which let markets do all this work, have largely outperformed planners.

While masterminding whole economies using IO analysis is no longer in vogue, we've learned that the basic exercise can be very insightful for budding development economists. The appendix to this chapter shows how to derive production, factor value-added (wage and profit), and GDP multipliers from this IO table in three steps, using Excel. The result is shown as table 3.2.

The entries in a Leontief production multiplier matrix are the outputs each row (sector) has to produce in order to satisfy a $1 increase in the column's (sector's) final demand. For example, to meet a $1 increase in final demand for agricultural goods, agriculture must produce an additional $1.36 in output, industry must produce an additional $0.58 in output, and services, $0.18. To produce an additional $1 of industrial output, agriculture must produce $0.09, industry, $1.22, and so on through the table.

From this matrix you can see that in order for production to increase in *any* sector, *all* sectors have to produce more, because each sector demands inputs from other sectors. Only in the extreme case where a sector is an enclave, that is, not connected in any way with other sectors in the economy, would the diagonal element for that sector be 1 and the off-diagonal elements all be 0. Otherwise, economic linkages will transmit impacts from a shock in one sector to all of the other sectors in the economy.

They will also affect wages and profits in the economy. The $1 increase in final demand for agriculture, industry, and services boosts payments to labor by $0.40, $0.42, and $0.58, respectively. Profits increase by $0.39, $0.30, and $0.28, respectively. Adding the wage and profit multipliers together, we get GDP multipliers of $0.79, $0.72, and $0.86, respectively, as a result of the $1 increases in final demands, assuming that all sectors are able to expand their production to meet the new demand.

In addition to providing insights for budding development economists, Leontief IO analysis continues to influence some of the frontiers of development economics. IO analysis inspired Albert Hirschman (chapter 1) to appreciate how economic linkages across sectors can be exploited to help grow whole economies (i.e., by investing in one carefully chosen sector, governments can stimulate growth in other sectors), and these linkages continue to be important to both development economics and development policy. Extensions of IO analysis—for example, the inclusion of households and government, investment, and trade in the form of a social accounting matrix (SAM)—are the starting point for doing almost any kind of economy-wide analysis. Computable general-equilibrium (CGE) models and other types of economy-wide analysis are largely beyond the scope of this book, but we will refer to them from time to time, and when we do, you can remember this simple IO example.

IO tables can be constructed for any economy or activity, from countries or groups of countries (even the entire world!) to villages and agricultural households. With the right data, you could make one for your university, student union, or student farm.

Other Measures of Income

You will run across a couple of other names for national income. The gross national product (GNP), also known as gross national income (GNI), is the same as GDP, but it includes the value of goods and services produced by citizens abroad. For example, Mexican migrant workers in the United States send home, or remit, more than $25 billion annually. This is value produced by Mexicans abroad, so it is counted in Mexico's GNP (but not in its GDP). It is removed from the US GDP for calculating the US GNP. For the most part, there is little difference between GNP and GDP, so the two are often used almost interchangeably. This is not technically correct, though, and in a few cases it matters. For example, in a Mexican village, counting the remittances that flow in makes a big difference in the calculation of village income (the gross village product).

WHAT'S NOT IN GDP

Now that we know what's in GDP, let's explore what isn't. This might seem technical, but it really matters, especially in poor countries where a lot of what's produced never gets sold and a lot of what people use is never actually purchased in a market.

Look back at our IO table. Everything is in value terms. The GDP at market prices is the value of all *final* goods and services *produced* in a country then *sold*. The GDP at factor cost also was calculated based on goods sold and inputs purchased.

Much of the staple production in poor countries, particularly by the poorest farmers, is for subsistence: it isn't sold. We'll discuss subsistence production and its ramifications in detail in chapter 9. For now, what matters is that, unless a crop is sold, it may not be counted as part of national income. To count subsistence production, we would need not only to expand our definition of national income to include it, but also to find a way to place an economic value on a nonmarketed good. Some countries try to do this more than others.

Since much of the economic interaction and exchange in poor countries is not formalized and documented the way it tends to be in rich countries, several similar complications arise. Many poor households rely heavily on home-produced goods such as agricultural production or small-scale retail shops and roadside stands. Almost none of the family inputs provided to these operations involve a market transaction. Labor on small farms or in small shops is not hired but supplied by the family members themselves. No wage is paid for this labor, yet clearly it is part of the value-added produced by an economy. What about barter or labor exchanges? Transactions that involve informal trades of one good or service for another are similarly difficult to track and count. Generally, these complications of the informal economy, which account for a bigger share of total economic activity in poorer countries, mean that portions of the value-added that should be part of GDP may simply be missed—and that this missing portion is likely to be bigger the poorer the country.

We can take special steps to count these nonmarket activities in our income calculations, but it won't be easy. For starters, how do we value a subsistence crop? Family labor? Labor exchanged? In a village where most farmers are subsistence producers there might be a few who sell their harvests. Could we use the price they get to value other farmers' subsistence production? This would imply that subsistence farmers value their crops at a market price that they do not—and likely cannot—receive. In chapter 9, we'll see how households are driven into subsistence production when it is too expensive for them to buy and sell on the market. As a result, subsistence producers value their crops at a price that is different—and possibly very different—from the market price. The price of a traditional variety of maize grown by an indigenous farmer in Oaxaca is not the same as the price of corn in a market (it turns out to be higher). To distinguish it from the market price, economists use the term "shadow value" to describe the value of nontraded goods like subsistence crops. Just as you can characterize some features of a tree based only on the shadow it casts in the morning or afternoon sun, so we can sometimes characterize the value a poor farmer places on his maize crop even if he doesn't sell it in the market. His shadow value for the maize he grows cannot be seen directly, but the trade-offs he makes when managing his maize can imply a specific shadow value. With the right data, we can estimate shadow values even though we cannot see them.

What about family labor? Do we look around the village for someone who worked for a wage or hired a wage worker, and use that wage to value family labor? In some cases, households use both family and hired labor to grow crops. Can we assume the two are interchangeable and value both at the same market wage? I might have to monitor my hired workers to make sure they give me the same value product per day as my own (or my family members') labor does (see chapter 11, "Information and Markets"). You can bet that I have know-how about my farming operation that hired workers do not. A day of my labor is likely to be more productive than a day of hired or exchanged labor, and therefore worth more than the market wage. I might be able to squeeze more work out of my family members than I can out of a hired worker.

What if I cannot hire workers, say, because I do not have enough cash to pay them? The labor I have available to work on my farm, then, will be limited by my family's size. Unless I have a big family, I might experience a labor shortage and value family time above the market wage. What if other farmers don't hire? A shortage of work opportunities on other people's farms might trap my family's labor on my farm—

I might have too much labor, and it might be worth less than the market wage. Either way, it is not at all clear that the market wage is the right way to value family labor. In fact, the shadow value of labor is likely to be quite different from the market wage. While we cannot directly observe a farmer's shadow value of family labor, how he manages these labor trade-offs casts a "shadow" that can be used to characterize his underlying shadow value of family labor.

Estimating shadow values for nontraded goods is complicated, so these goods are typically just dropped from national income accounting. Even in rich countries that tend to rely more on market transactions, real goods and services are often missed in income accounting. The same work may or may not contribute to national income, depending on who does it. Last night, Ed and his wife made a nice teriyaki chicken dinner. The value of this home-cooked meal obviously didn't get counted in GDP. However, if we had hired a cook to do the same thing, it would have. Travis can hire a carpenter to fix his house or do it himself (that's what Home Depot is for). In the first case, GDP goes up; in the second, it does not. All the time we spend raising our children doesn't count in the US GDP. If we hired a nanny, the nanny's time would.

You may have noticed a pattern across these examples: often the distinction between what is and what isn't counted in GDP reflects that some things are formalized in market transactions while others involve traditional divisions of labor within the home. In many settings, women are more involved in nonmarket activities than men are, and the many contributions women make are consequently undercounted in GDP. The technical details in national income accounting may seem pretty dry, but some of them strike at the heart of some fundamental development questions, including gender and gender roles.

Then there is the underground economy, which generally does not get counted in the GDP yet in some cases might include a significant part of the economy. In 2012, the US states of Colorado and Washington voted to legalize marijuana. Both states' GDPs increased as a result. Part of this increase may be due to expanded marijuana use, but a sizable portion is due to existing use suddenly being measured as a formal (legal) market transaction.

In 2014, the United Kingdom decided to include the sale of illicit drugs and prostitution in its GDP. This proved to be controversial, but it made the UK's GDP calculations compatible with those of the rest of the European Union, which includes some countries in which narcotics and prostitution are legal (and thus counted in the GDP). Drugs and sex added $16.7 billion to the UK's GDP![2]

You probably never thought measuring national income could be so interesting . . . and controversial!

PER CAPITA INCOME

Once we know gross national income, we can convert it to per capita income simply by dividing by the country's population. This is very important if we wish to compare standards of living across countries. China's gross GDP was $5.8 trillion in 2010. The US GDP was $14.6 trillion. Yet with a little more than 1.3 billion people (compared to 308 million in the US), China's per capita income was $4,260, while that in the US was $47,140.

Of course, just because we generally use these kinds of comparisons to contrast the standard of living in two different countries does not mean that country-level analysis is always very useful. Both the US and China have rich regions and poor regions. Average differences between two countries can be useful, but they can also be misleading. Thankfully, as we have already mentioned, the same concepts of income accounting apply to other scales of analysis, which enables comparisons of regions or cities within a given country. We explore this kind of inequality in chapter 5.

EXCHANGE RATES AND PURCHASING POWER PARITY

In the process of making this comparison between China and the US, we confess to using a sleight of hand that we should reveal in the interest of full disclosure. Because all economists use this same trick anytime they make cross-country income comparisons, it is one you should understand. How did we come up with this income figure in dollars for China? After all, they don't use dollars much over there; the currency in China is the renminbi (its basic unit is the yuan). To convert to dollars, we divided the China GDP in renminbi by the nominal exchange rate, which in 2010 was 6.62 renminbi per dollar.

But wait, there's more to the trick. This isn't a fair comparison, you might say, because $4,260 goes a lot further in China than in the US, where the cost of living is higher. You're right—about 78% further, according to the World Bank.[3] If we add this additional "purchasing power" to the per capita income of China, we get 1.78 * $4,260 = $7,570. We call this the purchasing power parity (PPP)—adjusted per capita income. PPP adjustments are essential if we wish to compare incomes and understand differences in standards of living across countries.

How do we make a PPP adjuster? In principle it is not hard: define a basket of goods and services, price it in different countries, and you've got a way to adjust for costs of living. In practice, of course, things are harder. We have to decide what to include in the basket, and in what proportions. Some goods and services are easier to price than others. For example, what is the value of a food crop produced for a family's own subsistence? Prices vary within countries, as well as among them. Do we price our basket in the capital city or in a rural hinterland? The answer to this question will result in vastly differently priced baskets in some cases.

The World Bank does it in three steps. First, it calculates PPP for individual products. For example, a liter of Coca-Cola might cost 2.3 euros in France and $2 in the US, so the PPP for Coke between France and the US is 1.15 (= 2.3/2). Then it averages the PPPs for all goods within a product category. Coca-Cola is in the category of "beverages and concentrates." This gives the PPP for the product category. Finally, it averages the PPPs across product categories to get an overall PPP for each country.

If that sounds hard, you can use a Big Mac to do essentially the same thing (sidebar 3.1).

PRICE DEFLATING

Besides comparing incomes across countries, we also want to compare incomes in the same countries over time. This is central to studying income growth, the subject of chapter 7. When we do that, we need to adjust for changes in prices over time. Here's an example: between 2009 and 2010, the GDP of the Democratic Republic of the Congo (DRC) rose a hefty 31%, from $12.2 billion to $16.1 billion. But it didn't really grow that much (that is, not in *real* terms). Inflation in 2010 was 22%, which makes the 2010 GDP look higher than it really was. To get the real (inflation-adjusted) GDP growth, we have to take the 2010 GDP and divide it by one plus the rate of inflation: GDP(real) = GDP(nominal)/ (1.22). This gives us a 2010 real GDP of $13.1 billion and a (still respectable) real GDP growth rate of (13.1/12.2) − 1 = 0.07, or 7%. The DRC had an unusually high inflation rate by international standards. In all countries, though, when comparing incomes over time, you have to adjust for inflation.

Sidebar 3.1   PPP and the Big Mac Index

Ng Yat-chiu, the man who introduced McDonald's hamburgers to Hong Kong, came up with a simple way to compare the cost of living across countries: just look at the price of Big Macs! In 1986 the *Economist* magazine ran an article about the Big Mac Index. It was meant to be a parody of the PPP, but the idea caught on like, well, hamburgers and french fries! The Big Mac Index has been calculated and published every year since then.

For example, in July 2008, the price of a Big Mac was $3.57 in the US and 2.29 pounds, or $4.58 at the current exchange rate, in the UK. That implies a PPP rate of 1.56. By comparison, in Germany a Big Mac traded at 2.99 euros, which at the dollar-euro exchange rate was $3.66; thus, the Big Mac PPP rate between the US and Germany was 1.11.

Is the Big Mac a good basis for constructing a cost-of-living index? In one respect it would seem to be: Big Macs are ubiquitous—what country doesn't have them? How representative Big Macs are of people's expenditures generally is another question, though. The poorer the society, the more Big Macs are a luxury good to which the majority of the population does not have access. Nevertheless, its simplicity and wit have made the Big Mac Index a subject of academic debate as well as a comical analogue to the PPP.

Jiawen Yang, "Nontradables and the Valuation of RMB—An Evaluation of the Big Mac Index," *China Economic Review* 15, no. 3 (2004):353–59.

GREEN ACCOUNTING AND EXTERNALITIES

Yet another thing missing from national accounts is the environmental cost of producing countries' incomes. Remember that anything not bought and sold in an economy is not counted as part of GDP. This includes the clean air and water that get "used up" when factories belch smoke into the atmosphere and sludge into a river. We call these "environmental externalities." The GDP may miss the depletion of natural resources if the cost of these resources is not properly reflected in market prices. Does the rising world price of oil reflect the fact that we are nearing "peak production?" It can be argued that the cost of natural resource depletion is already factored into rising resource prices. Climate change takes the stakes of not considering environmental costs to a whole new, global, level.

To the extent environmental costs are not reflected in the GDP, the methods described above may overstate income. The economist Robert

TABLE 3.3 AN INPUT-OUTPUT TABLE WITH GREEN ACCOUNTING

Income Account	Agriculture	Industry	Services	Final	TOTAL
Production Sector					
Agriculture	225	75	2	618	920
Industry	320	200	85	820	1,425
Services	75	150	30	312	567
Factor					
Labor	90	360	247.5	n/a	697.5
Capital (Profits)	135	270	112.5	n/a	517.5
Imports	50	300	50	n/a	400
Environment	25	70	40	n/a	135
TOTAL	920	1,425	567	1,750	

Repetto and co-authors wrote that ignoring environmental costs in our GDP calculations "reinforces the false dichotomy between the economy and 'the environment' that leads policy makers to ignore or destroy the latter in the name of economic development."[4] The economist Peter Wood proposed a way to deal with environmental costs in GDP calculations. He called it "green accounting." If we know what the environmental costs of production are, we can include them in our input-output table by adding an "environment account," as in table 3.3.

Notice the new row, labeled "Environment." Think of it as environmental inputs (like clean air) that get used to produce stuff. Now, producing $920 in agricultural output incurs a $25 environmental cost. The environmental costs associated with industrial and service production are $70 and $40, respectively. These environmental costs decrease our GDP from $1,350 to $1,215.

To include this environmental account in our table, we assumed that 10% of value-added in each activity was at the expense of "using up" environmental inputs for which there are no market transactions. This might seem arbitrary, and indeed it is: we do not really know what the true environmental costs of production are (though they're not likely to be zero). This is the greatest challenge to green accounting, though substantial research is going into estimating the environmental costs of various economic activities. If we can figure out a way to create markets for environmental goods, our green accounting problem will be solved (see sidebar 3.2).

Environmental costs are not the only externalities we might want to think about. Obesity, for example, increases the GDP: the more food

Sidebar 3.2   Green Accounting and the Pollution Drag on GDP

How much does pollution cost an economy? The Environment and Planning Institute of China's Ministry of Environmental Protection decided to use green accounting to find out. It reported that ecological and environmental degradation cost China US$83.5 billion in 2004 and $248 billion in 2010. That's more than 3% of the country's entire GDP up in smoke.

China's efforts have been lauded as one of the most ambitious attempts to do green accounting in any country. However, the approach China uses is not without controversy, which highlights the challenges of doing green accounting. It focuses on three sources of pollution (air, water, and solid waste), calculates the costs of abating them, and adds these up to get an estimate of the total cost of environmental degradation. China did not include tough-to-quantify items like the effect of pollution on public health and workers' productivity, the depletion of aquifers, or the loss of agricultural productivity to soil erosion. If these were counted, the environmental costs of China's rapid economic growth would be even higher.

Vic Li and Graeme Lang, "China's 'Green GDP' Experiment and the Struggle for Ecological Modernisation," *Journal of Contemporary Asia* 40, no. 1 (2010):44–62.

Fergus O'Rorke, "China's Revived Green GDP Program Still Faces Challenges," *CleanBiz.Asia* (March 28, 2013; www.cleanbiz.asia/news/chinas-revived-green-gdp-program-still-faces-challenges#. UvBI5fldWSr).

people consume, the higher GDP becomes. Overconsumption comes at a cost, though: the World Health Organization estimates that 1.5 billion adults twenty and older were overweight in 2008. Sixty-five percent of the world's population lived in countries where being overweight killed more people than being underweight.[5] The health consequences of overconsumption are not reflected in our GDP calculations except, ironically, as a benefit: higher value-added in the health industry! So should we include the negative health consequences of obesity as externalities in our GDP calculations? If so, then where do we stop and call it a day?

WHERE DO WE STACK UP? MAKING AN INDEX

Earlier in this chapter we considered how to compare economies in terms of income. In coming chapters we will also compare countries with respect to other outcomes, including poverty, inequality, and human welfare. With 196 countries in the world, that's a lot of outcomes. It gets more complex still when we look at data from surveys of thousands of households within countries. We need efficient, easy-to-understand ways of making sense of all those data. Often, a good way to start is to make an index.

To make an index, we take a variable of interest (say, income, poverty, inequality, or even a composite of different things) and normalize it to have a common starting point or range. You will run across a wide variety of indexes in this book. For most of these indexes, we will take the variable of interest, which typically takes on a wide range of values, and transform it into a measure that ranges from zero to one. This can be an incredibly useful tool to make sense of complex data, as we shall see.

Here's a simple example of how to make an index of country per capita income. It will convey the intuition behind an index, and is the basis for constructing part of the Human Development Index that we will explore in chapter 6. Let Y_i be the PPP-adjusted per capita income of country i, Y_{min} be the lowest per capita income of all countries, and Y_{max} be the highest. In 2010, PPP-adjusted per capita incomes in the world ranged from US$409 (Burundi) to $86,899 (Luxembourg).[6] Egypt had a PPP-adjusted per capita income of $6,180. Is this high or low? Clearly, it is a lot lower than Luxembourg's, which other countries could never aspire to. Yet it is considerably higher than Burundi's.

One way of comparing country incomes would be to rank them from poorest to richest. An income ranking would place Egypt sixtieth from the poorest among the 167 countries for which per capita income was available from the World Bank in 2010. We could divide Egypt's rank by the total number of countries, and we would have the share of countries with income at or below Egypt's. This turns out to be 60/167 = 0.359.

Doing this for all countries gives us the cumulative distribution function of per capita incomes. We shall use this to calculate the Gini index of inequality in chapter 5.

A drawback of an index based on rankings instead of actual incomes is that it does not tell us *how much* higher or lower one country's income is than that of other countries. Being the sixtieth from the poorest country doesn't tell us much if we don't know what the distribution of incomes looks like. We can make an index sensitive to income levels for any country i as follows: take the difference between country i's income and that of the poorest country (Burundi), and divide this by the difference between the highest (Luxembourg) and lowest (Burundi) income:

$$I_Y(i) = \frac{Y_i - Y_{min}}{Y_{max} - Y_{min}}$$

This index will range from zero (for the poorest country, the numerator is zero) to one (for the richest country, the numerator is the same as the denominator). It has other nice properties. For example, if country i's income stays the same, while the richest country's income increases, country i's income position as measured by this index will decrease. It turns out that the same thing will happen if country i stays put, but the poorest country's income increases.

For Egypt, the value of our index is

$$I_Y (Egypt) = (6{,}180 - 409)/(86{,}899 - 409) = 0.067$$

As you can see, Egypt looks much worse off with this index than the one based only on rankings (0.067, compared with 0.359). Many countries are much richer than Egypt. It turns out that Egypt's income makes it more similar to the countries below it than to those above it in terms of income. The last index gives us a better sense of where Egypt finds itself on the global income spectrum.

The average per capita income is one way of measuring welfare. In a microeconomics course we measure consumer welfare using a utility function in which utility depends on consumption. Consumption, in turn, is constrained by income. Thus, rising income translates into higher utility for consumers. Nevertheless, the average per capita income does not tell us anything about how income is distributed: a very equal or unequal income distribution can have the same average per capita income. In chapter 5 we will see how to consider income inequality when we are measuring social welfare.

DEVELOPMENT TYPOLOGIES AND CLASSIFYING COUNTRIES

Many different terms have been used over the years to classify countries in terms of their income levels. The introduction of the term "development" goes back to the extensive European colonization of Africa that occurred during the nineteenth century. By this time, disparities in living standards between Europe and Africa were becoming obvious (and growing rapidly). Europeans often understood these differences as being different points on a continuum of economic development and indeed invoked this notion as grounds for continued ambitious colonization of Africa, which was fueled by other, less altruistic, motives as well. Europe not only could but *should* help move Africa closer to the European end of the development spectrum—it was commonly argued—and it had a moral duty to colonize Africa as a means to achieve this development, as well as to compensate for four centuries of enslaving Africans: "The merit of a colonizing people is to place the young society it has brought forth in the most suitable conditions for the development of its natural faculties."[7]

For well over a century now, differences in income have generally been framed as differences in "development," even though, as we'll see in subsequent chapters, development involves many things besides income. Within this development framing, though, the specific terms used to classify and contrast countries have changed over the years.

"Third World" has been used to refer to low-income countries, but it is now an unfashionable and rarely used term. It was a product of the Cold War years, in which the world was divvied up into three geopolitical-economic groups of countries: the "First World" (high-income western countries: Western Europe, the United States and Canada, and Japan); the "Second World" (a little-used label referring to the USSR, China, and Eastern Europe); and the "Third World" (low- and middle-income countries, which sadly were often the theater in which conflicts between First and Second World countries played out).

"North" and "South" sometimes are used as synonyms for "developed" and "less developed." This simple typology is rather imprecise, though, because there are relatively high-income countries in the South (e.g., Australia and New Zealand) and relatively low-income countries in the North (e.g., Afghanistan and Haiti), depending upon where the line between "North" and "South" is drawn. (Indeed, most of the world's land mass is "North" if one uses the Equator as the geographic delineator.)

"Less developed," "underdeveloped," "developing," and "least-developed countries" (LDCs) are terms often heard at international forums. The first, being comparative, is a broad classification containing any country not included among the "more developed" or "developed" countries. The second has a somewhat pessimistic connotation, implying that the country is less developed than it ought to be, while the third has a more optimistic twist, implying that countries in this group are, indeed, developing. The fourth term, LDCs, is based on an official UN list of countries having the lowest income (GNI per capita [averaged over three years] of less than US$992) and Human Development Index (HDI) ratings in the world. (We will learn about the HDI in chapter 6.) The LDC classification is often used to grant countries preferential status within UN organizations. For example, World Trade Organization (WTO) agreements often grant special exemptions and more flexible terms to WTO members officially recognized by the UN as LDCs.[8]

High-income economies sometimes are called "industrialized"; however, this term is antiquated given that rich countries exist in a postindustrial world in which the biggest share of the economy is services, not industry.

"Transitional economies" are those that once were in the "Second World" but are transitioning toward becoming open-market economies. This term most often is used in reference to Eastern Europe and the former Soviet republics.

The rapidly growing economies of Asia, Latin America, and Eastern Europe are sometimes referred to as "emerging economies." China is a clear example from this group in Asia, Brazil in Latin America. In international policy arenas, five of the most influential emerging economies often coordinate their efforts under an association and refer to themselves as BRICS countries: Brazil, Russia, India, China, and South Africa. With almost 3 billion people and rapidly growing economies, these countries are exerting greater influence in policy circles and negotiations with each passing year.

As you can see, these are broad, imprecise, and somewhat value-laden categories. Moreover, they seem to shift with the shifting sands of political correctness. We need a more objective typology to work with. The World Bank's country classification is based on an objective measure, the income measures we have described in this chapter, and includes four broad categories: low, lower middle, upper middle, and high income. More than simply a descriptive typology, this designation is used in World Bank operations to determine which countries are entitled to receive assistance under different lending terms and which are entitled to different programs. The low- and middle-income economies are also classified by region. The World Bank recognizes that a country's income classification does not necessarily reflect its development status. Nevertheless, its classification is widely used. In 2012, the per capita gross national incomes (defined below) defining each group were as follows:

Low income	$1,025 or less
Lower middle income	$1,026–$4,035
Upper middle income	$4,036–$12,475
High income	$12,476 or more

There are clear geographic patterns. African countries dominate the "low-income" category. Haiti is the only country from the Americas in this category.. Asian countries in this group include Afghanistan, Bangladesh, Cambodia, Democratic Republic of Korea, Kyrgyzstan, Myanmar, Nepal, and Tajikistan.

As we move up to the "lower-middle-income" group, we see Central American countries and three South American ones: Bolivia, Guyana, and Paraguay. India, Iraq, the Philippines, Pakistan, and Vietnam are in this category, along with a few African countries, including Egypt, Morocco, Sudan, Ghana, and Zambia.

By the time we get to the "upper-middle-income" countries, Africa is barely represented. Here we find Algeria, Angola, Botswana, Libya, Namibia, South Africa, and Tunisia. A number of Eastern European and Middle Eastern countries are found here, along with most of South America, including Brazil, Chile, and Argentina. Mexico straddles the line between "upper-middle income" and "high income." China, Malaysia, and Thailand are the major Asian countries in this category.

At the top tier we find one African country—Equatorial Guinea, an oil producer. There are no Latin American countries. Western Europe dominates this category, along with Canada, the United States, the "Asian Tigers," and a few Middle Eastern oil exporters, including Kuwait, Oman, Qatar, Saudi Arabia, and the United Arab Emirates.[9]

MEASURING INCOME AT THE HOUSEHOLD LEVEL

From a practical perspective, the World Bank's classification is useful because it gives us precise definitions of which countries belong in which group. These classifications are useful for policy makers and researchers, but they are too coarse for microeconomic analysis in development economics. Many of the questions development economists study require that we track income at the individual level or, more often, the household level.

As we saw in chapter 2, most of the research development economists do to evaluate what works requires data on household-level outcomes. These data are collected in structured and detailed household surveys. The World Bank and other international organizations fund many household data collection efforts throughout the developing world. Very often, researchers collect their own household data to ensure that they get the right information from the right households. With greater detail about household production, assets, expenditure, and livelihoods, development economists can get a much more complete picture of a household's standard of living—one that can include the shadow values of all the nontraded goods and services a household produces or consumes. Getting all these data is not easy. As graduate students quickly learn, research in development economics—especially development *microeconomics*—often requires fieldwork and data collection, which can be extremely demanding but also rewarding.

POVERTY, INCOME INEQUALITY, AND HUMAN WELFARE

Consider these three statements:

- In 2010, just under 1.3 billion people—22.4% of the world's population—lived on less than $1.25 a day (PPP adjusted).[10]
- In 2010, the low-income countries contained 12.5% of the world's population but controlled less than 1% of its income, while the high-income countries had a little over 16% of its population and 72% of its income.[11]
- In the poorest 10% of countries in 2010, those with GDP per capita less than $1,123, life expectancy averaged 54.4 years (compared to 80 in the richest 10%), and years of schooling averaged 3.2 years (compared to 10.5 years).[12]

These statements present a lot of striking numbers, but they tell us very different things. The first sentence is about poverty, the second is about inequality, and the third is about human welfare. How are they related to one another and to what constitutes economic development? Are they just different sides of the same story? Does inequality imply poverty? Is it sufficient to focus our attention on poverty if our ultimate goal is to improve human welfare? Is income growth sufficient to deal with all these concerns?

In the next three chapters we'll learn how development economists study poverty, inequality, and human welfare and their relationship to income.

www.rebeltext.org/development/qr3.html
Enrich your appreciation of income by exploring multimedia resources while you read.

APPENDIX

Deriving a Leontief Multiplier Matrix in Excel in Three Easy Steps

Here's how we derived the Leontief multiplier matrix (table 3.2) using Excel:

1. Convert the Leontief input-output matrix into a matrix of coefficients for the three production activities by dividing each element in the original (3 × 3) production matrix by its corresponding column total. For example, the first element in the new matrix is 225/920 = .245. Let's call this new matrix "A" (table 3.A1).

2. Now subtract the A matrix from the identity matrix, which has all zeroes except for ones along its diagonal (table 3.A2). The result is shown in table 3.A3.

TABLE 3.A1   THE LEONTIEF COEFFICIENT (A) MATRIX

Production Sector	Agriculture	Industry	Services
Agriculture	0.245	0.053	0.004
Industry	0.348	0.140	0.150
Services	0.082	0.105	0.053

TABLE 3.A2   THE IDENTITY (I) MATRIX

Production Sector	Agriculture	Industry	Services
Agriculture	1	0	0
Industry	0	1	0
Services	0	0	1

TABLE 3.A3   THE *I − A* MATRIX

A	B	C	D
1 Production Sector	Agriculture	Industry	Services
2 Agriculture	0.755	−0.053	−0.004
3 Industry	−0.348	0.860	−0.150
4 Services	−0.082	−0.105	0.947

TABLE 3.A4   THE LEONTIEF MULTIPLIER MATRIX
$M = (I − A)^{-1}$

Production Sector	Agriculture	Industry	Services
Agriculture	1.365	0.086	0.019
Industry	0.584	1.223	0.196
Services	0.182	0.143	1.079

The Leontief multiplier matrix, M, is the inverse of this $I − A$ matrix. In Excel, we calculate the inverse of a matrix by making a new matrix and in the top left cell with a number in it, enter " = MINVERSE(B2:D5)." Then drag your cursor to select this and the other eight cells, push the F2 key, and hold down "CTRL+SHIFT+ENTER." This completes our construction of the Leontief multiplier matrix. The result is shown in table 3.A4.

Where It Comes From

Now that we've got a recipe to make a Leontief multiplier matrix, you might be wondering where it came from. It isn't hard to see if you can imagine the simplest economy in the world, with only one sector, say, corn. Suppose that by planting 5 kilograms of seed you could expect to harvest 100 kilograms of corn. There is only one input-output coefficient in this tiny economy, which we can call a_c, and it equals .05. Farmers have to grow a quantity of corn, y_c, to meet the final (e.g., households') demand, which we can call f_c, plus the seed they'll need to plant in the next period, which is $a_c y_c$:

$$y_c = a_c y_c + f_c$$

Solving this for y_c, we can immediately see the multiplier for this economy:

$$(1 − a_c) \, y_c = f_c$$

$$y_c = \frac{1}{1 − a_c} f_c = (1 − a_c)^{-1} f_c$$

This equation tells us that to meet a one-unit increase in final demand, f_c, farmers will have to produce an additional amount of corn equal to $(1 − a_c)^{-1}$. As

TABLE 3.A5   FACTOR INPUT-OUTPUT VECTOR A_F

Factor	Agriculture	Industry	Services
Labor	0.109	0.281	0.485
Capital	0.163	0.211	0.220

TABLE 3.A6   FACTOR VALUE-ADDED MULTIPLIER MATRIX
$M_F = A_F M = A_F (I - A)^{-1}$

Factor	Agriculture	Industry	Services
Labor	0.401	0.422	0.580
Capital	0.386	0.303	0.282
GDP ·	0.787	0.725	0.862

long as a_c is positive and less than one, as an input-output coefficient should be, this multiplier will be greater than one.

Compare this to the formula for our Leontief multiplier matrix, $(I - A)^{-1}$. The only difference between the two is that the second is for an economy with more than one production sector, so we have to use matrices. Instead of y_c, we need a vector with the three sectors' output in it:

$$Y = \begin{vmatrix} y_1 \\ y_2 \\ y_3 \end{vmatrix}$$

We need a vector with three final demands, too:

$$F = \begin{vmatrix} f_1 \\ f_2 \\ f_3 \end{vmatrix}$$

. . . and a matrix of input-output coefficients, which is matrix A, above:

$$A = \begin{vmatrix} a_{11} & a_{12} & a_{13} \\ a_{21} & a_{22} & a_{23} \\ a_{31} & a_{32} & a_{33} \end{vmatrix}$$

Completely analogous to our corn model, the vector of total outputs required to meet the final demand is

$$Y = AY + F$$
$$(I - A)^{-1}Y = F$$
$$Y = (I - A)^{-1}F = MF$$

That's why $M = (I - A)^{-1}$ is the Leontief multiplier matrix. The method is the same no matter how many production sectors there are in the economy—the I and A matrices simply get bigger the more sectors you have.

Once we know the Leontief output multipliers, we can easily calculate a matrix of labor and capital value-added multipliers (M_F) by pre-multiplying the multiplier matrix by the input-output coefficients for labor and capital, which we can arrange in a (2×3) matrix called A_F:

$$M_F = A_F M = A_F (I - A)^{-1}$$

To get the input-output coefficients for the two factors, we divide payments to factors by their respective column totals in the original input-output matrix (table 3.A5).

The matrix of factor value-added multipliers is shown in table 3.A6. The last row in this table gives the sums of the factor value-added multipliers, which are the GDP multipliers of changes in each sector's final demand.

4

Poverty

If you really want to understand something, you must begin by measuring it. For poverty, this is true not only because we must have reliable measures of it before we can compare poverty in different places or track changes in it from one year to the next, but also because deciding how to measure poverty challenges us to understand its key dimensions and complexities. In this chapter, we describe how development economists measure poverty and some prickly dilemmas we encounter along the way. We explore how poverty changes over time and why this dynamic perspective on poverty matters to poor households and therefore to anyone hoping to alleviate poverty.

ESSENTIALS

- Poverty lines
- Headcount poverty index
- Poverty gap
- Foster-Greer-Thorbecke poverty index
- Risk and uncertainty
- Vulnerability
- Wealth dynamics
- Poverty traps
- "Big push" interventions

Alleviating poverty is the single biggest concern confronting development economics. Before we can tackle the challenges of addressing poverty, we have to agree on how to measure it.

On the surface, measuring the poverty rate in a population may seem straightforward. Count how many people are below the poverty line, divide this number by the total population, and you've got the share of people in poverty. If there are q people with income below the per capita poverty level and N people in the total population, this share of people in poverty is

$$P_H = \frac{q}{N}$$

We call this the "poverty headcount index." In chapter 3, we learned how to make an index for a variable (there it was income) by dividing by the largest value the variable can take on. N is the largest number of poor people there can be—that is, if everyone in the population were poor. Because N is always greater than q, the headcount measure will always be less than one, and it will be zero only if nobody is below the poverty line. In other words, it is simply the percentage of the population in poverty. This makes it a good index because it is independent of the size of the population, which gives us a common metric for comparing poverty in big and small countries.

The poverty headcount index is also convenient because it is easy to construct: counting heads is all you need to do to make the headcount index . . . or is it? Suppose you had to construct a poverty index for a remote region of Thailand starting from scratch. This kind of problem comes up a lot in development economics. To make your job easier, suppose that Thailand recently conducted a population census in this region, so you have a good estimate of the region's population. What next? As you might have already realized, before you can go any further you have to answer this question: "Where's the poverty line?"

FINDING THE POVERTY LINE

Every country has its own poverty line—typically, a level of income that separates the poor from the non-poor. Often there are different poverty lines for urban and rural populations, because it often costs more to survive in a big city than in a rural village. Where exactly do these lines come from? Politics invariably play some role in deciding where the poverty line *is* drawn, but where the poverty line *should be* drawn is fundamentally an economics problem.

Establishing a poverty line requires some careful thinking about the nature of poverty. For starters, let's think about food poverty. How much does it cost to meet a person's minimum food requirements? A nutritionist's answer would be "It depends." There are online calorie calculators by gender, weight, height, and activity level. The World Health Organization (WHO) establishes nutritional guidelines for different countries. As this passage from the WHO website suggests, it is not an easy task: "The [WHO] Department of Nutrition for Health and

Development . . . continually reviews new research and information from around the world on human nutrient requirements and recommended nutrient intakes. This is a vast and never-ending task, given the large number of essential human nutrients. These nutrients include protein, energy, carbohydrates, fats and lipids, a range of vitamins, and a host of minerals and trace elements."[1]

Suppose we agree on the minimum nutrient intake for an average individual in our study area. We could then find all the baskets of foods available that can give us this nutrient level, price each one, choose the cheapest basket, and call this the food poverty line. This food poverty line would be the minimum amount of money needed for a person to meet his or her nutrient requirements.[2]

The trouble is that people do not live on food alone. We have other essential needs: clothing, shelter, cooking fuel and other energy, health care, and, if we want our children to escape from poverty someday, education, too. Where we draw the poverty line will depend on the costs of these things as well as food. Now our job is getting more complicated. But fortunately people are constantly making these kinds of consumption choices—choices that implicitly take these trade-offs into account and that might help us determine where to draw the poverty line so it reflects this more complete consumption context.

Suppose we survey a large sample of people in the population, asking them what foods they consume (a one- or two-week recall is commonly used for this), how much they consume, the prices they pay for each food item, and what their income is. Surveys like this have been done for nearly every country, thanks largely to the Living Standards Measurement Survey (LSMS) initiative by the World Bank.[3] We could take all the food combinations from the survey and convert them into the amounts of nutrients consumed, using conversion coefficients available from the WHO. Then we could graph nutrient demand ($C(Y)$, on the vertical axis) against income (Y, on the horizontal axis), as in figure 4.1.

Once we have this graph, we can find c^*, the minimum nutrient requirement, and bounce a line off our nutrient demand curve to get the minimum level of income needed to meet the food requirement. This minimum income (z in our figure) would take into account the fact that people spend income on things other than food, so it can be our poverty line.[4] Taking into account how households actually choose to spend their money, both on food and things other than food, leverages a fundamental concept in economics called "revealed preference": observed

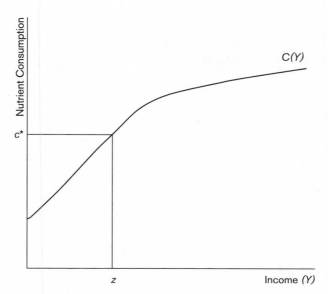

FIGURE 4.1. The poverty line, z, is the income required to reach the minimum level of nutrient consumption, given households' spending patterns.

patterns of behavior reveal something about an individual's underlying preferences, which are difficult to observe directly.

You might argue that z is too high, because some people spend too much of their income on non-nutritious stuff. For example, if people spend money on alcohol, cigarettes, or fancy clothes instead of food, their income will have to be higher in order to reach a nutrient intake of c^*. On the other hand, one also can argue that at very low incomes people do not spend *enough* income on essentials like health, shelter, or education. In that case z will be too low; people really need more money to satisfy their nonfood basic needs. On balance, our figure probably gives a reasonable approximation to the poverty line. In practice, economists construct poverty lines in different ways, but the basic theory that guides the process is essentially captured in this figure. Development economists are constantly building on this logic in an attempt to improve or otherwise enhance our ability to measure poverty. A recent approach proposed by Robert Jensen and Nolan Miller, for example, pushes the "revealed preference" logic even further in order to create poverty measures that are better able to reflect individual or household-level differences in nutritional needs (see sidebar 4.1).

Sidebar 4.1 The "Hunger Hurts—Need Cheap Calories" Approach to Poverty Measurement

A few limitations of a caloric threshold-based poverty line (i.e., c^* in figure 4.1) stand out as especially problematic. First, there is no clear consensus about what the threshold, if it exists at all, ought to be. Second, the caloric intake threshold for a strapping young man who works ten hours a day on the farm is vastly different than the intake threshold for his grandmother. Third, the background health status of an individual or her household can dramatically shape her ability to absorb and benefit from nutrients. This implies that achieving a minimal caloric *intake* may not be sufficient to make some people healthy. Finally, poor people—just like all of us—are constantly making choices about what foods to consume, and often they will change the composition of their diets drastically if their income changes. These changes typically involve substituting cheap calories with tastier and pricier ones (e.g., fruits, vegetables and animal products) as incomes rise.

Robert Jensen and Nolan Miller use these limitations to motivate an approach to measuring hunger and malnutrition (i.e., food poverty) that is based squarely on peoples' food consumption choices and therefore on "revealed preferences." Their basic idea can be summed up as follows:

When people are below their minimal nutrition threshold, the body protests, which doesn't feel good. Maximizing utility means consuming calories; the marginal utility of calories is extremely high. The cheapest source of calories typically is a staple like cassava, rice, or wheat. Beyond subsistence, though, the marginal utility of calories falls. People start substituting foods that are more expensive calorie sources but provide non-nutritional benefits, like taste.

We cannot "see" people's actual subsistence threshold, but by looking at the choices people make we can figure it out (analogous to inferring a farmer's shadow value of family labor, as described in chapter 3). When people are switching away from staples, they are telling us that their calorie threshold has been met. Thus, "the percent of calories consumed from the staple food source, or the staple calorie share (SCS), can be used as an indicator for nutritional sufficiency."

Jensen and Miller apply their approach to detailed household data from China and find that there is a well-defined SCS threshold at just over 75%. Staples constitute about three-quarters of total calories for very poor people, and this doesn't change much as income rises until a critical income level is reached, at which point SCS falls rapidly because people replace cheap calories with tasty calories.

Robert Jensen and Nolan Miller, "A Revealed Preference Approach to Measuring Hunger and Undernutrition" (working paper no. 16555, National Bureau of Economic Research, Cambridge, MA, November 2010).

At some point in the past decade, you have probably come across headlines that use a $1-a-day poverty line to characterize global poverty. This simple metric emerged from essentially the process described above, along with a bit of "public relations" spin. In the late 1980s, a group of World Bank economists noticed that several developing countries drew their poverty lines at about $370 a year, PPP adjusted. Martin Ravallion, a member of this group and leading expert on poverty measurement, realized that this worked out to roughly $1 a day and that this simple poverty line might be catchy enough to get some real traction in the media and with potential donors. Martin was certainly right about it being catchy: for more than two decades now, this kind of poverty line has shaped the international poverty discourse—including the MDGs described in chapter 1. Of course, these lines have been updated as economic conditions and prices have changed over the years. The average poverty line in developing countries, PPP adjusted, was $2 a day in 2010.[5] Since 2008, the World Bank has set the extreme poverty line at $1.25 in PPP-adjusted 2005 dollars. The official poverty line is much higher in rich than poor countries. For example, the US poverty income for a family of four in 2012 was $23,050 per year, or $15.79 per person per day.[6]

On the other hand, not everyone is enamored by such $1-a-day poverty measures. They are "average averages" (averages over a year averaged across several developing countries). They gloss over individual and regional variation in nutritional needs and the critical fluctuations in income and well-being within the year that make poor households particularly vulnerable.

Lant Pritchett, a development economist at Harvard University, worries that these simple measures have put too much focus on philanthropy and not enough on long-run development: "Instead of promoting prosperous economies, it's about 'how do we identify and target and get transfers to the few people under this penurious line?' which just isn't the way, historically, anybody has ever eliminated poverty."[7] Development economists must often try to strike a balance between the rigor and richness of their methods and the ability to communicate their results in ways that resonate with a broad policy and donor community.

MORE THAN COUNTING HEADS

Most people think of the incidence of poverty, or headcount index, when they think about quantifying "poverty." The headcount measure is useful, but it doesn't tell us all we need to know in order to analyze poverty and design policies to alleviate it. In practice, we need to know *how poor* people are, not just *whether* they are poor. That is, we need to know the depth of poverty. We could easily imagine two countries with the same poverty headcount but with the poor clustered just below the poverty line in one country and far below the poverty line in the other. A cash transfer to eliminate poverty would have to be larger in the second country, where poor people tend to be very poor instead of a little poor.

The difference between a person's income and the per capita poverty line is called the "poverty gap." If we know poor person i's income (Y_i) and the poverty line (z), we can easily calculate the person's poverty gap; it is

$$z - Y_i$$

The total cost of eliminating poverty is the sum of all poor people's poverty gaps. Summing the gap across all q poor people in our population, we get the total poverty gap:

$$\sum_{i=1}^{q} (z - Y_i)$$

The total poverty gap is critical to know for poverty alleviation programs because it is the cost of bringing everyone up to the poverty line at a given point in time.

The poverty gap gives us more information than the headcount, allowing us to measure the impacts of programs on poverty more accurately. For example, a program might raise a poor person's income but not by enough to get her above the poverty line. A reasonable person would say the program reduced poverty. The poverty gap would decrease as a result of the program, even though the headcount measure would not change.

The Severity of Poverty

Does the poverty gap give us all the information we need? Consider this scenario: program A reduces the total poverty gap by providing a cash transfer to people just below the poverty line. Program B reduces the poverty gap by the same amount, but it does this by targeting the transfer to the very poorest people in society, that is, people in extreme poverty. The poverty gap does not let us distinguish between the effects of these two programs because it changes by the same amount no matter which poor person gets the cash.

How can we make our poverty measure sensitive to who gets the cash, that is, the severity of poverty?

The easiest way is to square the poverty gap. If we measure poverty using

$$(z - Y_i)^2$$

our index will increase disproportionately as the poverty gap increases. For example, if the gap is $2, the gap squared is $4, but if the gap is $4, the gap squared is $16. Based on this index, a program is more effective at reducing poverty if it raises the income of extremely poor households.

The economists Erik Thorbecke and his students Joel Greer and James Foster proposed a single index that embodies all three of these measures as special cases.[8] The Foster-Greer-Thorbecke (FGT) measure is the most widely used poverty index in economics. Its formula is

$$FGT_\alpha = \frac{1}{Nz^\alpha} \sum_{i=1}^{q} (z - Y_i)^\alpha$$

Where we set α depends on the kind of index we want. You can see the poverty gap, $z - y_i$, to the right of the summation. You can think of α as the weight we attach to this poverty gap while calculating our poverty index. When $\alpha = 0$, the term in the summation equals one for every poor person, since anything raised to the zeroth power is one. We sum up the ones over the q poor people and divide by N (since z^α also equals 1 when $\alpha = 0$). This yields the headcount measure. That is,

$$FGT_{\alpha=0} = \frac{q}{N}$$

It is a useful index because

$$0 \leq FGT_{\alpha=0} \leq 1$$

When $\alpha = 1$, the index equals

$$FGT_{\alpha=1} = \frac{1}{Nz} \sum_{i=1}^{q} (z - Y_i)$$

The right-most term,

$$\sum_{i=1}^{q} (z - Y_i)$$

is the total poverty gap, or the cost of bringing all poor people just up to the poverty line. To make an index, we have to divide this by the largest value the total poverty gap could have. Nz, the total population times the poverty line, is what the total poverty gap would be if everyone in the population had zero income. The total poverty gap divided by Nz, like the headcount index, lies between zero (nobody is in poverty) and one (everyone is in poverty and no one has any income at all).

To analyze the severity of poverty, we set $\alpha = 2$. In this case, the index becomes

$$FGT_{\alpha=2} = \frac{1}{Nz^2} \sum_{i=1}^{q} (z - Y_i)^2$$

In this version of the FGT index, we weight people in extreme poverty more than people who are just below the poverty line. You can see that this, too, is bounded by zero (nobody is in poverty) and one (everybody is in poverty and no one has any income at all). In the latter case, the term in parentheses is just z. It is summed $q = N$ times, and the numerator is Nz^2, so the quotient becomes one.

Often, when we perform poverty analyses we report all three versions of the FGT index. The second ($\alpha = 1$) and third ($\alpha = 2$) versions decrease whenever the income of a poor person increases. The third version decreases more if the poor person whose income goes up is extremely poor. The first ($\alpha = 0$) version decreases only if the income gain pops the poor person above the poverty line. Together, the three versions of the FGT provide a comprehensive picture of changes in poverty due to a policy or some other exogenous shock.

Calculating an FGT Index: A Simple Example

Suppose we survey a small village consisting of only ten people, with a poverty line of $z = 28$. We find their incomes to be as shown in table 4.1.

TABLE 4.1   INCOMES AND POVERTY MEASURES FOR A HYPOTHETICAL VILLAGE

Person	Income	1 if in Poverty, 0 Otherwise	Poverty Gap	Poverty Gap-Squared
1	5	1	23	529
2	12	1	16	256
3	22	1	6	36
4	24	1	4	16
5	30·	0	0	0
6	40	0	0	0
7	50	0	0	0
8	70	0	0	0
9	80	0	0	0
10	100	0	0	0
SUM		4	49	837
z	28			

Using the data in the table, we can calculate the three versions of the FGT index:

$$FGT_{\alpha=0} = 4/10 = 0.40$$

$$FGT_{\alpha=1} = \frac{49}{10(28)} = 0.18$$

$$FGT_{\alpha=2} = \frac{837}{10(28^2)} = 0.11$$

Now let's check the sensitivity of our measures to different cash transfers. Suppose we transfer $5 to person 3, bringing her income up to $27. This is still (just) below the poverty line, so the headcount doesn't change. The poverty gap measure falls by 2 points, from .18 to .16. The gap-squared falls less, from 0.11 to 0.10.

Now what if we gave the $5 to the poorest household instead? The change in the poverty gap is the same as before, because it is insensitive to which poor person gets the cash. However, the gap-squared measure falls all the way to 0.08—a 24% decrease in the severity of poverty!

Because of its sensitivity to changes in extreme poverty, the third measure is the one Mexico uses to measure poverty impacts. In fact, $\alpha = 2$ is in the Mexican constitution, which explains why PROGRESA (chapter 2) targeted the poorest of the poor.

VULNERABILITY AND POVERTY DYNAMICS

Suppose you're a poor family farmer in the Sahel, with kids to feed. In a normal year, you can get enough out of your grain crop to cover your family's needs, provided you sell an animal or two to supplement your farm income. With a herd of six, including some decent breeding stock, you can do this every year (see sidebar 4.2).

But one year the rains don't come. Your crop fails. You've got six months until you can try your luck planting again and a few months after that until you can even hope to harvest something. How do you keep food on your family's table during this "hungry season?"

You decide to sell one of your animals. Then another, and another. As you plant your next crop, you're down to three animals. The seeds begin to germinate, the rain comes, but your money runs out. You sell another animal, and now you're down to two. With two months to go before harvest, your money runs out again.

What do you do? If you sell your last two animals, your breeding stock, how will you ever rebuild your herd?

Recent research by Travis and colleagues Michael Carter at UC Davis and Chris Barrett at Cornell suggests that, in all likelihood, you won't sell those last few animals. If you do, you know you might never get out of poverty—you'll be caught in a "poverty trap" without a herd and without respect or status among your peers.

But not selling your last two animals brings its own cost: you and your family will have no choice but to skip meals and go hungry. You might survive alright, and so might your spouse and oldest kids. But what about your two-year-old girl? Your newborn baby boy, still unweaned? By preserving your herd in the short run, are you stunting your children's growth and jeopardizing their potential to lead a productive life in the future?[9]

Poor people around the world face these sorts of cruel choices daily. This highlights a very important point about poverty: it is not just that some people are poor and others are not. In our discussion of poverty lines and poverty measurement above, we glossed over a crucial dimension of poverty, namely, that poverty is dynamic, meaning that it changes over time. Some people are never poor. Others always seem to be poor, caught in a "poverty trap." Still others find themselves on the very cusp of poverty, and all it takes is a single shock event to tip them into a poverty from which there may be no coming back.

For decades, development economists have appreciated how important it is to take into account not just static measures of poverty (like the

Sidebar 4.2   Drought, Poverty, and Inequality: The Sahel

The Sahel is a ribbon of land running east-west across Africa and separating the Sahara desert to the north from the savannas in the south. The contrast between it and the sands of the Sahara are what give this zone its name, which means "coast" in Arabic.

As a transition zone, the Sahel is also a high-risk zone from an agro-ecological point of view. In 1984 a severe drought struck the Sahelian zone of Burkina Faso in West Africa. It was a human tragedy, but its timing was a researcher's dream, because it hit during a multi-year household survey being carried out by the International Food Policy Research Institute (IFPRI). IFPRI had just finished surveying households in a normal year, 1983–84. They surveyed the same households again the next year, after the drought struck. Households in this region practice rain-fed agro pastoralism. The Sahel has extremely variable rainfall, a fragile environment, and poor agro climate. The people living there have learned how to adapt to their environment, doing their best to diversify their incomes beyond crop production.

Nothing prepared them for this drought, though.

The IFPRI data give us a unique insight into the impacts of agro-climatic shocks on poor households. Crop income was by far the largest source of income for households in the normal year, constituting 53% of the total. It fell 64% when the drought hit. All of the other income sources increased during the drought, though, as households scrambled to make up for their lost crop income. They sold off livestock: livestock accounted for just 14% of the normal year's income, but animal sales increased 154% during the drought. Local non-farm income, mostly from wages, rose 26%; remittances from migrant work increased 54%; and transfers among households, while very small (1% in the base year), increased 58%.

It comes as no surprise that poverty rose sharply in the drought year. The headcount index shows that the poverty rate more than doubled, from .20 to .51. The severity of poverty increased by a factor of more than 8, from 0.02 to 0.19. The FGT index paints a stark picture of the human toll of drought in the Sahel.

Thomas Reardon and J. Edward Taylor, "Agroclimatic Shock, Income Inequality, and Poverty: Evidence from Burkina Faso," *World Development* 24, no. 5 (1996):901–14.

Sidebar 4.3 Poverty and Witch Killing in Rural Tanzania

Witch killings are frequent in western Tanzania. Most of the victims are poor, elderly women, and most of the perpetrators are relatives of the victims.

Ted Miguel tested two theories of why these killings occur. The *income shock theory* posits that big negative income shocks associated with extreme weather are the culprit. Most witch killings happen in the pre-harvest period, when households' food stores from the previous harvest are depleted, the next harvest is known, and people realize they'll need food and energy to bring in the next harvest. The *scapegoat theory* predicts that *any* adverse shock witches are believed to control, including disease, should lead to more witch murders, as households eliminate the "cause" of their suffering.

Miguel found that extreme local rainfall shocks (but not disease) negatively impact income. If the income shock theory is correct, then, rainfall shocks—but not disease—should explain witch killings. That is just what Miguel found: "Only the shock that leads to lower income (extreme rainfall) results in more witch murders, while disease epidemics lead neither to lower income nor to witch murders."

This study is important because of the novel identification strategy employed to solve the reflection problem, using random weather shocks to uncover a link between poverty and crime. It has potential policy implications as well. To reduce crime induced by weather shocks, governments might do well to provide poor households with crop insurance, so that when harvests fail they will not have to make the cruel choice of which mouths to feed. Cash transfers, ideally targeted at elderly women (to empower them), also might be effective at reducing witch killings.

Edward Miguel, "Poverty and Witch Killing," *Review of Economic Studies* 72 (2005):1153–72.

headcount measure) but also dynamic poverty measures—measures that capture household vulnerability. There is a large body of work developing concepts and measures of vulnerability. While this research is important and typically covered in advanced development economics courses, our focus here is more conceptual: a household with income just above the poverty line may not be counted as poor, but may be threatened constantly by poverty and destitution. This threat of poverty, this risk of destitution, can be a major source of anxiety and stress and can change the choices people make. Vulnerability and the sense of desperation that can come from seeing future prospects shriveling up before your very eyes can led to desperate—even unthinkable—measures (see sidebar 4.3).

Out of Poverty—Then Back in Again

The 2003 Mexico National Rural Household Survey (Spanish acronym ENHRUM) found that 47% of the rural population had income below the poverty line. In 2008, the same households were surveyed again. This made it possible to look at the dynamics of poverty by tracking the same households' poverty status over time. In the five years between these two surveys, poverty in rural Mexico fell. The Mexican government has three different poverty lines, one for food (the food poverty line), another that adds in the cost of health and basic education (the capacities poverty line), and a third that adds in clothing, housing, and energy costs (the asset poverty line). By all three measures, the headcount rate fell by between 3.6% and 4.0%. The other two components of the FGT measure, the poverty gap and severity (gap-squared), also fell, as shown in table 4.2.

This seems like good news—and it is. But it masks the fact that many rural Mexicans were worse off in 2008 than in 2003. Table 4.3 takes all the rural Mexicans who were in poverty in 2003 and shows what percentage were still in poverty in 2008. It does the same for those who were *not* in poverty in 2003. The table reveals some interesting—and troubling—poverty dynamics.

TABLE 4.2   POVERTY DYNAMICS IN RURAL MEXICO

FGT Index	Food Poverty Line			Capacities Poverty Line (Adds Health, Basic Education)			Asset Poverty Line (Adds Clothes, Housing, Energy)		
	2002	*2007*	*Change*	*2002*	*2007*	*Change*	*2002*	*2007*	*Change*
Headcount[a] ($\alpha = 0$)	0.47	0.44	−3.6%	0.54	0.50	−3.9%	0.70	0.66	−4.0%
Depth[b] ($\alpha = 1$)	0.24	0.21	−2.2%	0.27	0.25	−2.5%	0.39	0.35	−3.4%
Severity[c] ($\alpha = 2$)	0.16	0.15	−1.3%	0.19	0.17	−1.6%	0.27	0.25	−2.4%

[a] Share of population in households with income below the poverty line
[b] Also reflects how far below the poverty line poor individuals find themselves
[c] Places greater weight on the poorest of the poor when calculating the poverty index
SOURCE: Analysis of Mexico National Rural Household Survey data, 2003–2008.

TABLE 4.3 A TRANSITION MATRIX OF POVERTY DYNAMICS IN
RURAL MEXICO

	Poor in 2008	Not Poor in 2008
Poor in 2003 (47%)	51%	49%
Not Poor in 2003 (53%)	30%	70%

SOURCE: Analysis of Mexico National Rural Household Survey Data, 2003–2008.

Of the people who were in poverty in 2003, 51% were still in poverty in 2008. Let's call this "group A." These people—around 24% (47% * 51%) of the rural Mexican population—seem to be in a state of persistent poverty (though we would need to track them longer to be sure). At the other extreme, 70% of those who were *not* in poverty in 2003 were still not in poverty in 2008. This group, which we can call "group B," seems to be persistently *out* of poverty.

The good news is that 49% of the people who were *in* poverty in 2003 were *above* the poverty line in 2008. These people transitioned out of poverty during the five-year period, which is the reason why poverty in rural Mexico fell.

The bad news is that 30% of those who were *not* poor in 2003 *were* poor in 2008. These people transitioned *into* poverty.

Let's call these two transitional poverty groups "group C." They might not be so different from one another.

Why are poverty dynamics important? First, just because people transition out of poverty doesn't mean their poverty problem is solved. Our challenge is not simply to get people out of poverty; it is also to keep them there, as well as to keep others from slipping into poverty.

Second, it is almost certain that different anti-poverty policies are needed for each one of these groups. For group A, we need to have policies to enable people to extricate themselves from what might be poverty traps. For group B, we need policies that will create opportunities to stay out of poverty.

For group C, those at the margins of poverty, for whom things can go either way, we need policies that can prevent adverse shocks from pushing them into potential poverty traps, and keep them out. The Sahelian farmer-pastoralist in our previous example is a good illustration of the kinds of people likely found in this group. If we somehow could devise an insurance scheme that could enable people at the fringes of poverty to feed their children *and* preserve their productive assets at times of adversity, we might have a big impact on poverty and on preventing people from falling into poverty traps over time.

As economists, we can do better than just characterize and measure vulnerability. We can study the underlying processes that determine where a household can reasonably expect to end up in the future. That is, we can try to understand how a household's context, productive activities, and assets interact to shape its wealth dynamics.

To illustrate this idea, consider the total poverty gap defined above. As we mentioned there, for a given country this gap is literally the total cost of lifting every poor person in the country out of poverty. But if we could implement such an income transfer, what effect would it actually have on poverty? In the short run, a transfer that perfectly targets each poor household with just enough income to lift it above the poverty line would indeed eliminate poverty. In the longer run, however, all bets are off. Why? Because unless the transfer actually changes the wealth dynamics of these households and allows them to create enough wealth to stay out of poverty, they may well slip back into the same poverty they experienced before the transfer.

Rigorous research into poverty dynamics can be tricky, but understanding the underlying concepts is an essential of development economics. Economists typically use recursion function graphs like that shown at the top of figure 4.2 to depict these dynamic forces (we borrow the idea of recursion functions from mathematics and the natural sciences). Be patient as we describe how to understand this figure; we are confident it is worth the effort.

In this recursion function graph, the assets a household owns this year (horizontal axis) determine its assets next year (vertical axis) because assets produce income, which can be invested in more assets. To be more concrete, let's pick up our livestock example again. If the asset in question is livestock, the relationship between your herd size this year and next year is quite clear: the larger your herd, the more income you can make from it by selling animals and milk. It's also true for human capital: the healthier you are and the more education and skills you have, the more productive you can be and thus the higher your earnings. As we saw in the example above, families can "consume" their assets, selling them off to get through a hard time, but that leaves them with less in the next period. They can also lose human capital if, for example, kids go hungry or don't go to school. Human capital can go down if malnutrition impairs children's development and learning. This, too, leaves households with less income in the future.

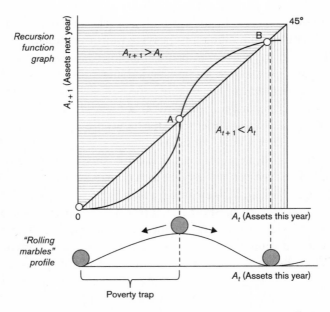

FIGURE 4.2. An asset recursion function with a poverty trap. To the right of point A assets grow larger in the next period, driving the household to a favorable steady state at point B. To the left of point A assets decrease, driving the household into a poverty trap.

The 45° diagonal line in this graph plays an important role: it indicates points at which assets next year are expected to be the same as assets this year. In other words, these points represent points of "equilibrium" where we expect assets (e.g., herd size) to remain constant. The S-shaped curve in this figure is the function that maps current assets into expected future assets, which is the recursion function. At each point where the function crosses the 45° line, this relationship is in equilibrium. The recursion function graph in this figure has three equilibria, each denoted by a small white dot (0, A, and B). Whenever there is a gap between the 45° line and the recursion function, we expect assets to be changing over time. Whether assets are increasing or decreasing depends on the direction of the gap. Whenever the function is *above* the diagonal, assets are increasing (i.e., next-period assets are expected to be greater than this period's assets), but when the function is *below* the diagonal, assets are decreasing.

To help you visualize the dynamics that are captured in the recursion function, we have added a "rolling marbles" profile at the bottom of figure 4.2. The three marbles in this profile are each at a different equilibrium asset level. As long as no one bumps the profile, this is where the three marbles will stay (i.e., assets do not change over time). What happens if someone bumps the profile? Can you see that any small bump will cause the marble at A to roll downhill to the right or left? This means that the equilibrium at asset level A is "unstable" because it is not self-reinforcing. In contrast, equilibrium asset levels 0 and B are stable: bumping the profile may cause these marbles to roll around but they will eventually return to their original position.

Now that you understand how this figure is constructed, let's walk through the story it tells. The S-shaped curve roughly captures the herd dynamics for the Borana pastoralists of southern Ethiopia,[10] so we'll tell the story in that context. Suppose a pastoralist has a herd of size A this year. Because this is an equilibrium point, he expects that his herd will have A animals next year as well. Now suppose that a bandit sneaks into the camp one night and steals two animals, which is actually not uncommon. This is like bumping the marble a bit to the left. How does this affect the dynamics of his herd? Next year, he will expect his herd to shrink; same for the year after that. If figure 4.2 is an accurate depiction of herd dynamics in this context, losing two animals puts the herder on a downhill path to the left that ends with him losing his entire herd (i.e., marble ends up at 0).

How does this collapse happen? The dynamics depicted in the figure reflect key features of the underlying production context. In the case of the pastoralist, the collapse is driven by the fact that the only profitable way to manage a herd of livestock on arid rangeland is to migrate with the herd, because this is the only way to take advantage of the best pastures and watering holes. If you can't move your livestock around, you can't survive in this setting as a pastoralist—at which point you must either choose to migrate to the slums of a big city or settle down in a small town with a few chickens. Pastoralists always prefer to stay on the range with their livestock, but their ability to migrate with their animals is a function of their herd size, because you must have enough animals in the herd to sustain a herder (usually a young son) with milk and blood[11] during the migration. This is the key twist in the production context that drives the collapse: with a herd of size A or larger, the herd can sustain a young herder and therefore migrate around to take advantage of greener pastures; but below A the herd is too small to sustain a herder. Thus, it misses out on greener pastures and slowly dwindles.

Our figure thus has two *steady states*, which should be obvious in the "rolling marbles" profile. One of them is at point B. If a pastoralist gets knocked off point B, the asset dynamics will take him right back to it. The other steady state point is zero, the poverty trap. Adverse shocks like theft or a drought can take a household that is near point A and knock it into a poverty trap, possibly driving its assets all the way to zero, from which it cannot easily recover. Adverse shocks can also knock households off point B, but if we've got the dynamics right, they will on average recover and return to the favorable steady state.

BIG POVERTY TRAPS AND THE "BIG PUSH"

The poverty traps we have described thus far have been microtraps that affect single households. In the pastoralist communities in southern Ethiopia we discussed, different households with different herd sizes are subject to different herd dynamics. The notion of poverty traps is often writ much larger than this. In theory, entire regions or countries could get trapped in poverty.

Some economists argue, for example, that unfavorable geography (e.g., being land-locked) can constrain a country's productive capacity and effectively trap an entire country in poverty. Others argue that cycles of violence, corruption, and weak governance can create big poverty traps that ensnare entire regions or nations. While evidence of micro poverty traps in some contexts seems quite compelling, whether big traps like this exist in practice remains a hot and often contested area of research in development economics. If entire countries were actually trapped in poverty, the policy implications might seem straightforward: the country clearly needs a push from the outside to break free. At this scale, however, things are rarely this simple.

Jeffrey Sachs, a high-profile development economist we will encounter repeatedly in this book, is convinced that big poverty traps exist and should be taken seriously by the development community. Indeed, Sachs sees these big traps as the primary argument in favor of international aid and has succeeded in shaping aid flows in impressive ways in recent decades. This is precisely the motivation behind the United Nations Millennium Villages Project, which Sachs directs and which we will learn more about in chapter 7.

The logic here is simple (much simpler than the research required to test it). If poor countries are effectively trapped in poverty, what they need is a big push from rich countries. This big push—in the form of target investments in infrastructure and education, for example—can catalyze a virtuous cycle of increasing productivity that puts poor countries on a path of economic growth and development. Notice that this is conceptually identical to giving our pastoralist in figure 4.2 enough additional livestock to make his herd larger than *A*, then letting him keep growing his herd to the high equilibrium. The need for this big push should be easy to visualize in the "rolling marbles" profile in this figure.

While the essence of this kind of big push model was developed in the 1940s,[12] Sachs is its contemporary champion. As we encounter him again in later chapters, we'll also learn about some of his detractors, who claim that ambitious external plans are at best ineffective, because they ignore much of the richness and nuance of local context, and at worst destructive, because they can put the rights of autocratic states ahead of the rights of the poor.

www.rebeltext.org/development/qr4.html
Learn more about poverty by exploring multimedia
resources while you read.

5

Inequality

As humans, we often feel an irresistible impulse to compare ourselves to others. Sometimes these comparisons are vain and superficial, but they can often be much more consequential. Disparities in income can have real economic consequences by shaping the opportunities and well-being of individuals and affecting more broadly the way markets and governments function. As we have already seen, efficiency and equity objectives are often difficult to achieve separately because they are interrelated in important ways in developing countries. In this chapter, we focus on how economists measure inequality and how different forms of inequality matter in development economics, including gender inequality within households.

ESSENTIALS

- Distinction between poverty and inequality
- Inseparability of efficiency and equity
- Gini coefficient
- Social welfare analysis
- Definition of a household
- Gender inequality

Inequality matters to people everywhere. It was inequality that fueled the passion of the Occupy Movement, which struck cities around the world in the fall of 2011 with the rallying call "We are the 99 percent!" There are several reasons why inequality is important from an economic (or political-economic) point of view:

- *Social justice.* Many people believe it is unfair for the benefits of economic growth to be concentrated among a select few.
- *Relative deprivation.* Economists usually assume people optimize: firms maximize profits, households maximize utility from con-

suming more goods. But sociologists have long recognized that being deprived of goods that others have can make people unhappy. Suppose you live in a poor village and your income does not change while your neighbor's does. You see him remodel his house, his kids start dressing well, and a parabolic TV dish sprouts from his rooftop. Do you feel as well off as before?

- *The structure of economies.* Different income groups have different spending patterns, and how income gets spent can help shape the structure of economies. (This is less the case in countries that open up to trade, as we shall see in chapter 13.) Research from India, Mexico, and other countries reveals that poor and middle-income households are more likely to spend their income on goods and services that were produced within their country and that stimulate local employment. Rich households are more likely to use their income to buy imports, to buy goods produced in more capital-intensive industries, or to save abroad. Changes in the distribution of income can thus have important effects on production and employment in poor—as well as rich—countries.

- *Economic efficiency.* Economic efficiency is likely to depend on how income is distributed—particularly in poor countries where assumptions about perfectly functioning markets break down. If there is no bank willing to loan money to the poor, then their ability to buy fertilizer probably depends on whether or not they have the liquidity (cash) to "self-finance" their production. If you have the cash, you use the optimal amount of fertilizer. If you don't, you don't and your productivity (efficiency) will suffer. The inseparability of efficiency from equity is an ongoing theme in this book.

- *Growth and poverty alleviation.* Inequality can directly shape how overall economic growth of an economy translates into poverty alleviation. Because it can affect both the efficiency and the structure of any economy in ways that disadvantage the poor, inequality can channel the benefits of growth away from the lower socioeconomic classes. Ensuring that growth reduces poverty in practice requires policies that explicitly take inequality into account—either by countering the effects of inequality on economic structure and inefficiency or through targeted transfers and other redistribution programs. Improving human development outcomes without growth in poor countries requires redistribution.

INEQUALITY IS NOT POVERTY

You might think inequality matters in development economics because the more unequally income is distributed the more poor people there are. But that's not true: inequality is different from poverty. A society could have an unequal distribution of income with no one living below the poverty line, or a very equal distribution with everyone living in poverty. Poverty, as we explored in chapter 4, is about individuals' well-being relative to a set standard of living. Inequality is about individuals' well-being relative to each other.

To reinforce this idea, consider a situation in which changes in inequality and poverty are related. Imagine an egalitarian society (i.e., there is no inequality) with enough income to maintain everyone in the population *just above* the poverty line. In this fictitious society, everybody gets the per capita income, which in turn is just above the poverty line. In this case, the introduction of *any* inequality would also bring poverty to the society. This implies that, in general, the richer a country is, the more inequality can increase without increasing poverty.

Most countries in the world have per capita incomes well above the poverty line, which makes this *theoretical* and mechanical connection from increasing inequality to increasing poverty irrelevant in practice. This does not imply that there is no relationship between inequality and poverty. Indeed, characterizing and understanding this relationship is an important area of research in development economics. What it does imply, instead, is that the relationship is *empirical* and context dependent: it is positive in some cases, negative in others, and apparently nonexistent in still others.

To illustrate how this important relationship between the distinct concepts of inequality and poverty depends on context, we'll return to the drought in Burkina Faso described in chapter 4 later in this chapter and see that it simultaneously increased poverty and decreased inequality. But first we need to establish ways to measure inequality empirically. Exploring these measures requires us to carefully define inequality and—just like the poverty measures we discussed in the last chapter—this provides a natural opportunity to learn more about this essential concept of development economics.

MEASURING INEQUALITY

When we compared the index of per capita income with income rankings in chapter 3, we saw that the distribution of global income is very unequal. Can we use what we learned there to construct a useful index of income inequality? Inequality can be measured in different ways. Some of these measures make eye-catching headlines. The Occupy Movement slogan "We are the 99%" is a good example of such a measure: the richest 1% of Americans owned about a third of the country's wealth. Measures that make headlines, however, do not always prove useful for comparing inequality across countries or in the same country over time. The workhorse measures of inequality in the development economists' tool kit are based on frequency distributions of income.

Frequency Distributions

Often, just eyeballing the distribution of income in a country is illuminating. This is precisely what frequency distributions allow us to do (in addition to serving as the basis of the most common inequality index). To construct such a graphical depiction, you simply rank everyone in the country from poorest to richest, group them into income groups, and make a bar chart showing the percentage of the population in each income group. You just created a frequency distribution for income.

Figure 5.1 shows frequency distributions for Albania, Nicaragua, Tanzania, and Vietnam. Looking at frequency distributions of different countries like the ones shown in the graph can give you a sense of differences in income inequality, but we typically want a more precise way to compare income inequality across countries. We want an index measure of inequality.

A first step toward creating such an index and comparing income distributions is to group the population into equal parts along the horizontal axis. This allows us to turn income frequency distributions measured in dollars (figure 5.1) to income frequency distributions measured in *percentiles*. These percentile frequency distributions allow for more direct comparisons of inequality within countries with different income levels. Figure 5.2 compares frequency distributions of income for Mexico (left) and Sweden (right), in which the population has been divided into ten equal parts, or *deciles*.[1]

You can see in the picture that the poorest decile of Mexico's population received a small fraction of the income: the height of the smallest

Frequency Distributions of Income

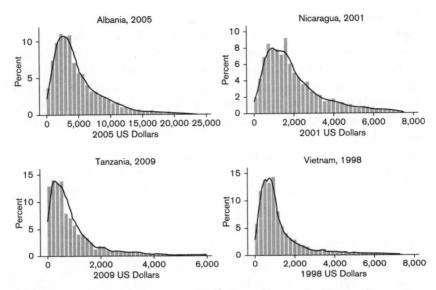

FIGURE 5.1. Comparison of frequency distributions of income for Albania, Nicaragua, Tanzania, and Vietnam.

bar is 1.2, telling us that the poorest 10% of the population gets 1.2% of the income. None of the bottom seven deciles gets anywhere near its proportional share (10%) of income. At the other extreme, the richest 10% get 42.2% of the income.

When we know what to look for in frequency distributions, they give us a convenient snapshot of inequality. In a perfectly equal income distribution, all the bars would be the same height. This clearly is not anywhere near the case in Mexico. It is not even the case in Sweden, which has the world's most equal income distribution.

Sweden's distribution seems more equal than Mexico's, but how much more equal is it? Is Mexico's more or less equal than, say, Tanzania's? How can we track changes in income inequality in the same countries over time? This is why we need an index of inequality.

If you've taken statistics you might already know some measures of dispersion that could be applied to income: the variance, standard deviation, or coefficient of variation. It turns out that these are not very good indexes. The variance has no bounds and is sensitive to the units we use to measure income. For example, suppose we calculated the

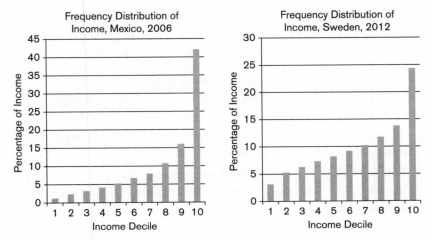

FIGURE 5.2. Decile frequency distributions of income for Mexico and Sweden.

variance of China's income. We could do this either in yuan or, using the 2013 exchange rate of a little more than 6 yuan per US dollar, in dollars. Either way, it would be a huge number. If we calculated the variance of China's income in yuan instead of dollars, it would come out 6^2 (or 36 times) larger!

The standard deviation (SD) is the square root of the variance. It has the same problems as the variance for comparing dispersion or inequality across countries. Sometimes we try to normalize the SD of a variable like income by dividing by the variable's mean. This gives us the coefficient of variation (CV). It doesn't solve the problem, either: the CV of income for a country can take on any positive value.

In short, these conventional statistical measures of variance don't help us compare inequality across countries (or in the same country over time).

Gini in a Nutshell

The most commonly used measure of inequality is the Gini coefficient. Not only is it a neat index, with values between zero and one, but it satisfies all five properties that an inequality index should have. These properties, incidentally, were established by economists to provide guidelines for how a measure of inequality should and should not behave in order for it to be useful. As you'll see, these properties—often called axioms or "self-evident truths"—are intended to be so uncontroversial that they are essentially impossible to reject as guidelines.

1. Pigou-Dalton transfer principle: Inequality, as measured by the index, should increase when income is transferred from a low-income household to a high-income household.

2. Symmetry: The measured level of inequality does not change when individuals trade places in the income distribution.

3. Independence of income scale: A proportional change in all incomes (like measuring income in dollars instead of yuan) does not alter inequality.

4. Homogeneity: A change in the size of the population will not affect measured inequality.

5. Decomposability: We would like to be able to use our index to understand how income from different sources (wages, profits) affects inequality. This means we should be able to decompose it with respect to income sources.

Several measures of inequality satisfy these given assumptions. The Gini coefficient is the most intuitive among them, as we shall see. It is also a measure of dispersion, like the variance. In fact, it has been argued that we should use it instead of the variance for portfolio analysis and other types of research.[2] That doesn't mean that the Gini coefficient is perfect; it is an aggregate measure, and there are some important dimensions of income inequality that it does not pick up, as we shall see below.

RECIPE FOR MAKING A GINI COEFFICIENT

Here's how to make a Gini coefficient: First, remember in chapter 3 when we lined everyone in the country up from poorest to richest? Let's do that again and make everyone stand on top of a horizontal axis (specially designed to support their weight!), as in figure 5.3.

Pick a person—say, person i. Starting at the far left, add up how many people are to the left of person i. That's how many people are poorer than person i. Add one and divide by the country's total population and you get the share of people with income at or below that of person i. Do this for every person and you have the cumulative popula-

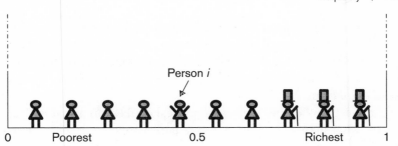

FIGURE 5.3. Ranking of population from poorest to richest.

tion share from poorest to richest. For person *i* in our figure you can see that the share is 0.5, and for the far-right (richest) person it is 1.0.

Now figure out what share of the country's income each of these people has. To get the cumulative income shares, add up the income shares, starting at the far left, for each person in the population. Plot the cumulative income shares above each person, as in figure 5.4.

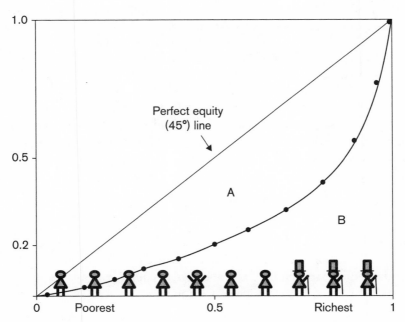

FIGURE 5.4. The Lorenz curve relates population shares (horizontal axis) to cumulative income shares (vertical axis). The Gini coefficient of income inequality is the area between the perfect equity (45°) line and the Lorenz curve (area A) divided by the area of the triangle below the perfect equity line (area A + B).

For person i, the cumulative income share is 0.2. In other words, one-half of the population has income at or below person i's, but those people control only 20% of the country's total income. By the time we get to the very richest person, we have 100% of the country's population and income.

Connecting the dots, we get what is called the Lorenz curve (LC). It shows what share of income each cumulative population share controls, from poorest to richest. The more unequal the country's income distribution, the more bowed the LC will be toward the southeast corner of the unit box. The possibilities are bracketed by two extremes:

Perfect Equity. No society has it, but perfect equity means that each population share would have an equal share of total income: the poorest 20% would have 20% of the income, the poorest 50% would have 50%, and so on. (Really, they wouldn't be the poorest 50%, because everyone would have the same income.) The "perfect equity line" is just the diagonal running from the origin to the top right corner of the box.

Perfect Inequality. No society has this, either, because all but one person would starve to death. In a world of perfect inequality, no one has anything except for the richest person, who has it all. The "line of perfect inequality" is just the outside border running across the horizontal axis and up the right-hand side of our box.

Now look at the area in between the LC and the perfect equity line (area A) and the area between the LC and the perfect inequality line (area B). Add them together and you get a triangle forming the southeast half of the box. The ratio

$$\frac{A}{A + B}$$

is the Gini index (or coefficient) of inequality. As a good index, the Gini index always lies between zero and one. It equals zero only if there is perfect equity, so that the LC is the perfect-equity line (area A is nil). It equals 1.0 only if there is perfect inequality, so the LC is the outside border of the box (area B is zero).

Because $0 \leq G \leq 1$, the Gini coefficient is a useful way of measuring inequality, not only of income but of other things, as well, including wealth and assets. For example, a high Gini coefficient of land tells us

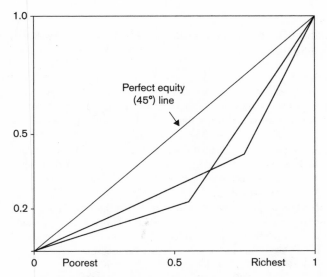

FIGURE 5.5. With intersecting Lorenz curves, different income distributions can give the same Gini coefficient.

that land is unequally distributed, and a low Gini for land indicates the opposite.

Still, it is important to keep in mind that, like per capita income, the Gini coefficient is an aggregate measure, a summary statistic. It does not tell us everything we might want to know about the distribution of whatever it measures. Many different distributions can give the same Gini coefficient. In fact, the same Gini can come from an infinite number of different Lorenz curves! To illustrate this, look at figure 5.5. Low-income households have a smaller share of total income in the economy depicted by the Lorenz curve that starts out lower. Yet the two Lorenz curves in this figure give the same Gini coefficient: the ratio $A/(A + B)$ is the same for both. The Gini coefficient could go down because income rises in a very poor or middle-income household, or because the income of a rich household drops. Looking only at the Gini coefficient, we do not know which. We also do not know how *polarized* a society is; income inequality and income polarization are two different concepts (sidebar 5.1).

Nevertheless, with Gini coefficients we can get a pretty good sense of how different countries stack up in terms of inequality. It might seem hard to calculate the area between the Lorenz curve and perfect equity line, but

Sidebar 5.1 Income Polarization Is Not Income Inequality— and Why It Matters

To be precise, the Occupy Movement we describe was motivated at least as much by income polarization as it was by income inequality. You might think these two concepts are one and the same, but they are not. And since we are focusing on how economists measure income inequality, it is worth taking a minute to understand why the Gini coefficient picks up income inequality but not income polarization.

Much of Marx's thinking about society and economics hinged on the idea of polarization—a process by which society breaks up into hostile, antagonistic classes: the bourgeoisie and the proletariat. These classes become progressively more internally homogeneous while also becoming more distinct as separate camps. This is income polarization.

Economists Joan-María Esteban and Debraj Ray have studied the measurement of income polarization. To understand why polarization is not income inequality, let's return to figure 5.3. Suppose we numbered each of the 10 individuals depicted in this figure 1, 2, 3, . . . , 10 from poorest (left) to richest (right) and assigned each individual an income that was proportional to his number—for simplicity, $1, $2, $3, . . . , $10. This society obviously is not polarized into income groups. Now suppose that we wanted to polarize the income in this society by redistributing income. Specifically, we create a proletariat class from individuals 1–5 by taking from the rich (4 and 5) and giving to the poor (1 and 2) so that everyone in this class has $3, and we create a bourgeoisie class by doing the same with individuals 6–10 so each of their incomes is $7.

Esteban and Ray point out that while the polarized society we have created certainly "feels" quite different from the one we started with— it may even appear to have higher income inequality—in the process of polarizing this society we actually made the Gini coefficient go down! To see why, notice that our redistribution satisfies the Pigou-Dalton transfer principle, because every transfer involved the richer giving to the poorer. Have they convinced you that income inequality is different from income *polarization*?

Lest this sound like a very technical distinction, it is worth pointing out that highly polarized societies with clear concentrations of money and power function very differently than less polarized societies, even if their Gini coefficients are identical! In addition to the (Marxian) risks of social and political conflict, Tewodaj Mogues and Michael Carter, for example, show how polarization in social norms and networks can create feedback loops that in turn dial up income inequality.

J.-M. Esteban and D. Ray, "On the Measurement of Polarization," *Econometrica* 62, no. 4 (1994):819–51.

T. Mogues and M. R. Carter, "Social Capital and the Reproduction of Economic Inequality in Polarized Societies," *Journal of Economic Inequality* 3, no. 3 (2005):193–219.

TABLE 5.1 A HYPOTHETICAL
INCOME DISTRIBUTION

Person	Income (Y_i)	$F(Y_i)$
1	79.6	0.1
2	128.7	0.2
3	153.1	0.3
4	177.8	0.4
5	200.3	0.5
6	223.6	0.6
7	249.4	0.7
8	284.2	0.8
9	332.8	0.9
10	587.9	1
	$Cov(Y,F(Y))$	34.48
	Mean Income	241.74
	Gini Coefficient	0.28

there's an easy way: after ranking everyone in the economy, just take the covariance between their income (Y_i) and the cumulative distribution of income $(F(Y_i))$, double it, and divide by mean income (μ). That is,

$$G = \frac{2\,Cov(Y_i, F(Y_i))}{\mu}$$

For example, take a little economy with ten people and incomes, as in table 5.1. The first column ranks people from poorest (1) to richest (10). The second column gives each person i's income, Y_i. The third gives the cumulative distribution of income, or share of people with income at or below Y_i, which we denote $F(Y_i)$. If we take the covariance between the last two columns (34.48), double it, then divide by mean income (241.74), we get the Gini coefficient.[3]

WHAT'S UNEQUAL? INTERNATIONAL COMPARISON OF INEQUALITY

In our little example, the Gini coefficient is very low: 0.28. That's around where the Gini for Sweden is, which is not surprising, because for our example we took the income deciles for Sweden and pretended they were people. This actually gives us a rough approximation of the Swedish income Gini. It isn't a very efficient use of our formula, though, because we lose a lot of information by lumping everybody into deciles.

TABLE 5.2   GINI COEFFICIENTS FOR SELECTED COUNTRIES

Country	Source	Year	Gini Index	Country	Source	Year	Gini Index
Very Low Inequality				Medium Inequality			
Serbia	WB	2008	0.28	Thailand	WB	2009	0.40
Kazakhstan	WB	2009	0.29	Russian Federation	WB	2009	0.40
Pakistan	WB	2008	0.30	Philippines	WB	2009	0.43
Egypt, Arab Rep.	WB	2008	0.31	Argentina	WB	2010	0.44
Bangladesh	WB	2010	0.32	United States	CIA	2007	0.45
Low Inequality				High Inequality			
Poland	WB	2009	0.34	Mexico	WB	2008	0.48
Niger	WB	2008	0.35	Costa Rica	WB	2009	0.51
Sudan	WB	2009	0.35	Chile	WB	2009	0.52
Vietnam	WB	2008	0.36	Brazil	WB	2009	0.55
Japan	CIA	2008	0.38	Very High Inequality			
Turkey	WB	2008	0.39	South Africa	WB	2009	0.63
Burkina Faso	WB	2009	0.40	Namibia	CIA	2003	0.71

Source: World Bank (http://data.worldbank.org/indicator/SI.POV.GINI); Central Intelligence Agency (www.cia.gov/library/publications/the-world-factbook/fields/2172.html).

We'd be better off having a row in our data table for every single Swede. (A random sample of Swedes would do.)

Sweden is pretty much the lower bound on the world's Gini coefficients, because it has about the most equal income distribution on the planet. The US Gini is a lot higher—around 0.45. If we grew the Swedish economy by one-third and gave *all* the new income to the richest decile, we'd get a Gini coefficient like that of the United States. (To do this in our example, just increase the top decile's income by 798.) Or we could grow the economy by 50% and split it between the top two deciles. Or we could just take away 70% of the poorest three deciles' income and give it *all* to the richest decile. There are many ways to transform Sweden's income distribution and end up with the same Gini as the United States has, but any one of them would be a huge redistribution in favor of the rich.

Table 5.2 lists some Gini coefficients from other countries. It shows a wide range of Gini coefficients around the world, from below 0.30 for the most equitable countries to as high as 0.71 for the countries with the most unequal income distributions.

You might wonder what the Gini coefficient for *the whole world* is. Would it be higher or lower than most country Ginis? Think about it:

world income inequality includes both inequality within countries (which is what we have in our table) and inequality among countries, which is big: just look at the range of average per capita incomes we saw in chapter 3. A recent study put the global income Gini coefficient at around 0.62, which would put the world in our "very high inequality" category.[4] The good news, however, is that this global Gini has been falling in recent decades. In what might seem like a contradiction, global inequality has fallen even as income gaps between countries have widened.[5]

INEQUALITY AND POVERTY

In the last chapter we saw how a severe drought in the Sahel affected poverty. The poverty rate increased significantly, regardless of whether we measure it using the headcount or the severity measure. What happened to inequality? Was rising poverty in the Sahel accompanied by rising inequality?

Table 5.3 compares the impacts of the drought on poverty, as measured by two variants of the FGT measure, and on income inequality, using the Gini index. It might come as a surprise that the drought had an equalizing impact on household incomes. The Gini coefficient for this region fell slightly, from 0.34 to 0.31. Virtually all households were hard hit by the drought. As the headcount shows, many households fell into poverty, while the severity index reveals that many poor people became much poorer. In relative terms, though, high-income households took a bigger hit. This explains why the Gini coefficient fell.

These findings illustrate the lack of a mechanical relationship between poverty and inequality. When poverty increases, inequality may either

TABLE 5.3   IMPACTS OF DROUGHT ON HOUSEHOLD
INCOME INEQUALITY AND POVERTY IN BURKINA FASO

	Poverty		
Year	Headcount	Severity	Gini
Normal Year	0.20	0.02	0.34
Drought Year	0.51	0.19	0.31

SOURCE: Thomas Reardon and J. Edward Taylor, "Agroclimatic Shock, Income Inequality, and Poverty: Evidence from Burkina Faso," *World Development* 24, no. 5 (1996):901–14.

increase or decrease depending on the context. As we mentioned earlier, however, one thing about the context that conceptually matters in this relationship is the rate and severity of poverty before a shock like a drought hits. In the Sahel, desperately poor households may have simply had little income to lose—even if the little they lost really hurt. Less poor households, by contrast, had more to lose and still lacked any real protection from the drought. By contrast, imagine the same drought hitting a richer country with fewer people at subsistence levels and drought insurance for richer households. Can you see how the same drought could both increase poverty *and* increase inequality in such a context?

INEQUALITY AND SOCIAL WELFARE

At the end of chapter 3 we noted that the average per capita income often is used as an indicator of social welfare. This is true, but it is only a rough indicator because it does not take into account how income is distributed. Now that we have a convenient measure of inequality, we can do better. One way to bring income inequality into a social welfare function is to use the Gini coefficient of income inequality (G):

$$W = y(1 - G)$$

. . . where W represents social welfare and y is the average per capita income in the economy (country, region, village, or whatever level we want to carry out the welfare analysis on).[6] This social welfare function has the properties that either an increase in income of any member of society or a transfer of income from a rich to a less-rich person will increase social welfare, no matter what the original income distribution looks like.[7] Of course, there are lots of other ways to combine income and inequality in a social welfare function. One of the critical features of any of these functions is how much "weight" we put on income relative to inequality. Differences in political opinion and philosophy can translate into very different weights, but for our purposes let's run with this simple welfare function.

Using this welfare function instead of per capita income makes a big difference in measuring the impacts of income changes on welfare. For example, let's take the economy in table 5.1 and give thirty units of income (an amount equal to 5% of the richest decile's income) first to the poorest and then to the richest decile (leaving all other deciles

TABLE 5.4 IMPACTS OF AN INCOME INCREASE ON PER CAPITA INCOME,
INEQUALITY, AND WELFARE IN A HYPOTHETICAL ECONOMY

Impact on Per Capita Income, Inequality, and Welfare	Transfer of $30 (5% of Richest Decile's Income) to	
	the Poorest Decile	*the Richest Decile*
Change in Average Per Capita Income	1.2%	1.2%
Change in Gini	−5.0%	2.6%
Change in Welfare ($W = y(1 - G)$)	3.2%	0.2%

unchanged). The results are shown in table 5.4. In both cases, adding an amount equal to 5% of the richest decile's income raises average household income by 1.2%. However, the Gini coefficient falls when this income goes to the poorest decile, and it increases if the cash goes to the richest decile. Welfare increases 3.2%—more than the percentage increase in average income—if the cash goes to the poorest decile. It goes up by only 0.2% if the same income goes to the richest decile. With this welfare measure, adding new income to an economy will not make welfare decrease, even if there is a negative effect on inequality; however, a negative effect on inequality drags down the measured welfare impact.

WHAT IS A HOUSEHOLD?

Because households are the basic unit of society, they also tend to be a useful unit of analysis for understanding income and income inequality. Even though we often use per capita income—the average income per *person*—to compare the income levels of different countries, the income level of the average or median *household* can be easier to interpret. In the case of income inequality, the household is almost always the unit of analysis, which consequently requires that we clearly define what constitutes a household.

Development economists typically define a household as a group of people who share a common pot of food or who otherwise share or pool productive resources. In many developing countries, particularly in rural areas, households by this definition can be quite large and include several nuclear families residing in the same compound. As you can imagine, this can really complicate the process of filling out detailed household survey questionnaires!

To illustrate how important the definition of a household can be for measuring inequality, consider a place like Niger (Gini coefficient of 0.35; table 5.2), which typically has large households that include several family units (usually, brothers and their families). What would happen if richer households suddenly got smaller (i.e., had fewer kids)? If we computed the Gini coefficient based on the average income per household member, would this change raise or lower the Gini? The answer is that it would raise measured inequality. In contrast, average per capita income for Niger (shockingly low at $246 in 2012) is impervious to how individuals group into households.

In the past forty years, the composition of households has changed dramatically in the US and other developed countries. You won't be surprised to learn that this can have big effects on measured inequality. Since 1970, the Gini coefficient in the US has increased from 0.39 to 0.48, but part of this increase reflects a steady evolution in the composition of US households. We have many more single-mother households and many more dual-income households today than we did in 1970. Since these two types of households are overwhelmingly low and high income, respectively, the change in household composition pushes up the US Gini coefficient.

In developing countries, household structure has changed less in recent years, but there are changes brewing that could have important implications for how we measure inequality. In many cities, the structure of households is beginning to change. In rural areas, out-migration has reshaped many households. In the next decade or two, it will become increasingly important for development economists to take these demographic changes into account when computing inequality measures and comparing them over time.

THE SOURCES OF INCOME INEQUALITY

Earlier in this chapter we said that one of the properties we would like our inequality index to have is decomposability. If we want to know what explains income inequality, we had better be able to represent inequality as a function of income from different sources, like profits, wages, cash transfers, or a new development project. It turns out that this is easy to do in the case of the Gini coefficient. The appendix to this chapter shows how to decompose the Gini coefficient by income sources. Here's what we end up with:

$$G = \sum_{k=1}^{K} S_k G_k R_k$$

The interpretation of this formula gives us insight into what determines income inequality.

- S_k is the share of income from source k in total income in the economy. The larger the income source is relative to total income, the bigger the impact it can potentially have on inequality.
- G_k is the Gini coefficient of inequality for income source k. It tells how unequally income from a source is distributed. In order for an income source to have a big effect on income inequality, it has to be unequally distributed. If income from a particular source is perfectly equally distributed, its Gini coefficient is zero and it cannot affect income inequality.

  You might think that an income source that is large and unequally distributed would increase inequality. But what about welfare payments? Consider social cash transfers, like Mexico's PROGRESA (chapter 2). They are large relative to total income in many poor villages. They are unequally distributed, because only the poorest of the poor get the transfers; thus, the Gini coefficient for social cash transfers is high. Yet we would expect welfare programs to decrease income inequality because of who gets the payments. Social cash transfers target the poorest.
- R_k tells us who gets income from source k. It is the Gini correlation between income from source k and total income. It ranges from -1 (income from source k has a perfect negative correlation with households' total-income rankings) to 1 (a perfect positive correlation). For k = profits, we'd expect R_k to be positive, because profits tend to flow disproportionately to richer households. For k = welfare income, R_k should be negative—provided the right households get the cash.

When does a development project reduce income inequality in an economy—say, in a village? When it has a large positive effect on village income, when this effect is unequally distributed across village households, and when it favors those at the bottom and middle of the village income distribution. The same is true for migration (see sidebar 5.2).

Sidebar 5.2 Remittances and Inequality

The migration of labor off the farm is a universal feature of economic growth, as we'll see in chapter 10. Each day thousands of people throughout the developing world migrate out of their villages seeking work in other parts of the country (internal migration) or abroad (international migration). If they are successful at finding a job, they are likely to send home part of their earnings as migrant remittances.

How do migrant remittances affect rural income inequality? If remittances increase across the board, does the rural income Gini coefficient increase or decrease? There is a long-standing debate on this question. Ed teamed up with two other economists, Oded Stark and Shlomo Yitzhaki, to provide an answer using a Gini decomposition of village incomes. They hypothesized that remittances affect inequality differently at different stages of a village's migration history. Migration—especially international migration—entails high costs and risks. The first migrants are likely to come from relatively well off village households; when they send back remittances, inequality in the village is likely to increase. Over time, though, the pioneer migrants can help others migrate by providing information and assistance. If access to migrant labor markets eventually spreads to other households in the village, remittances could become less unequalizing—or even equalizing—over time.

To test this migration diffusion hypothesis, household survey data were used to perform a Gini decomposition of income in two Mexican villages, one with a long history of sending migrants to the United States, and the other a relative newcomer to international migration. The study found that remittances increased income inequality in the village that was just beginning to send migrants abroad, but they reduced inequality in the village that had a long history of US migration. In the first village, remittances from migrants in the US constituted 16% of village income ($S = 0.16$). They were unequally distributed, with a Gini coefficient of 0.90, and they were highly correlated with total income ($R = 0.86$). In the village with a long US migration history, remittances represented a larger share of village income ($S = 0.21$), but the Gini coefficient was lower ($G = 0.68$), and the correlation with total income was much lower ($R = 0.33$). The authors showed that a percentage increase in remittances from the US, due for example to a peso devaluation or an improvement in US labor markets, would increase the Gini coefficient of income inequality in the first village while decreasing it in the second.

O. Stark, J. E. Taylor, and S. Yitzhaki, "Remittances and Inequality," *Economic Journal* 96 (1986):722–40.

INTRA-HOUSEHOLD INEQUALITY AND GENDER

Income inequality at different scales matters for different reasons. By far, countries are the most common unit of analysis for inequality measurement, but inequality analyses at subnational levels can also be instructive. Do you think the Gini coefficient for your hometown is higher or lower than for New York City? If you guessed lower, you are almost certainly right: New York City has the highest income inequality of any major city in the US, with a Gini of 0.504. Which city has the lowest inequality? Salt Lake City, with a Gini of 0.417.

But why stop at cities? There is a yet deeper level that is a common unit of analysis for inequality research in development economics: the household. One of the greatest sources of inequality in poor countries is not between households but within them: gender inequality between men and women living in the same household.

Women are less likely to go to school, less likely to work, less likely to earn the same wage for comparable work, more likely to be in poverty, and less likely to hold political positions. In many countries, they lack basic legal rights, like the right to own property or even travel without their husband's permission.

And then there are the millions of women who are missing. What do we mean by "missing"? The female share of the world's population is lower than it would be if women had access to the same resources as men and if parents did not practice selective abortion. Amartya Sen coined the term "missing women," and Esther Duflo called it "the starkest manifestation of the lack of gender equality . . . Most of these missing women are not actively killed," she writes. "They die from cumulative neglect."[8]

Understanding and addressing the inequality between men and women is a major concern in development economics. Gender inequality both is affected by economic development and can directly hinder development. For example, if poor couples are less likely to value girls, rising incomes should favor more gender equality. But discrimination against women can hinder development in the first place. When women lack the same legal protections and access to resources as men, they are not as productive as they otherwise could be. But the missed opportunity is deeper than just underutilized resources. Women tend to have greater influence over future generations than men, through their effect on families and, by extension, societies.

A key theme of this book is that it generally is not possible to separate issues of equity and efficiency in poor countries. This inseparability of efficiency and equity is perhaps easiest to see within the household, where continued suppression of women makes households less productive and less efficient. Gender inequality thus hinders economic development, as well as being exacerbated by underdevelopment.

www.rebeltext.org/development/qr5.html
Learn more about inequality by exploring
multimedia resources while you read.

APPENDIX

Deriving the Gini Decomposition

Here's how we derived the Gini decomposition by income sources.
    First, take our formula for calculating the Gini coefficient:

$$G = \frac{2Cov(Y_i, F(Y_i))}{\mu}$$

Second, represent household income, Y_i, as the sum of income from K different income sources:

$$Y_i = \sum_{k=1}^{K} y_{ki}$$

For example, $k = 1$ could be wages; 2 could be profits; 3, welfare income; and so forth. We add these up over all K sources to get a household's total income.
    Now substitute this for Y_i in the formula for the Gini coefficient:

$$G = \frac{2Cov(\sum_{k=1}^{K} y_{ki}, F(Y_i))}{\mu}$$

Now we're taking the covariance between a sum of things (the y_{ki}) and something else ($F(Y_i)$). This equals the sum of covariances between each income source and the cumulative income distribution:[9]

$$G = \frac{2\sum_{k=1}^{K} Cov(y_{ki}, F(Y_i))}{\mu}$$

In a mathematical sleight-of-hand, we multiply this by a couple of rather interesting names for one, namely:

$$\frac{\mu_k}{\mu_k}$$

and

$$\frac{Cov(y_{ki}, F(y_{ki}))}{Cov(y_{ki}, F(y_{ki}))}$$

where μ_k is the mean income from source k, and $F(y_{ki})$ is the share of households with source-k income at or below y_{ki}. If we do this we get a crazy plateful:

$$G = \frac{2 \sum_{k=1}^{K} Cov(y_{ki}, F(Y_i))}{\mu} \cdot \frac{\mu_k}{\mu_k} \cdot \frac{Cov(y_{ki}, F(y_{ki}))}{Cov(y_{ki}, F(y_{ki}))}$$

But after regrouping terms we get a new formula, which decomposes the Gini coefficient into each of its K income sources:

$$G = \sum_{k=1}^{K} S_k G_k R_k$$

where

$$S_k = \frac{\mu_k}{\mu}, 0 \le S_k \le 1$$

$$G_k = \frac{2 Cov(y_{ik}, F(y_{ik}))}{\mu_k}, \ 0 \le G_k \le 1$$

$$R_k = \frac{Cov(y_{ki}, F(y_i))}{Cov(y_{ki}, F(y_{ki}))}, \ -1 \le R_k \le 1$$

6

Human Development

If this book had ended with the previous chapter, we might be accused of seeing income as an end, instead of a means to an end. This would be misleading. There is a rich, decades-long record of work in development economics that distinguishes between income and the deeper dimensions of human development that ultimately matter most. Nobel laureate Amartya Sen has led this charge to consider "development as freedom." As he has forcefully argued, income may be a potent predictor of individuals' quality of life, but we misunderstand key aspects of economic development if we focus exclusively on income. Sen inspired the creation of a measure of human development—the Human Development Index—which has been a centerpiece of international development since its launch in 1990. We describe the construction of the Human Development Index in this chapter as a way to explore how development economists think about development as deeper than just income.

ESSENTIALS

- Human Development Index (HDI)
- Human capital
- Market failures: Externalities and public goods
- Opportunity cost
- Conditional cash transfers
- Cost-benefit analysis
- "Development as freedom"

Poverty is about income. Economic development ultimately is about people. In 1990, the Pakistani economist Mahbub ul Haq began urging the United Nations Development Program (UNDP) to create a broader measure of development that focused on human outcomes. He felt this was necessary in order "to shift the focus of development economics from national income accounting to people-centered policies" (p. 9).[1]

The measure Haq proposed had to be simple to understand, and it had to encompass both economics and human well-being. Above all, it had to be an *index* which would make it possible to compare improvements in well-being across countries. The Nobel laureate Amartya Sen provided the conceptual framework for this project. Actually, Sen initially opposed the idea, worrying that it would be too difficult to capture the full complexity of human development in a single index. In the end, Haq swayed Sen by persuading him that only a holistic development index could shift policy makers' and researchers' attention from economics to human well-being. Only a concept that confronts GDP head-to-head, as a single number, could get real traction in the policy process. That is how the Human Development Index (HDI) was born.

After considerable discussion and debate, the UNDP decided on an index that included the following economic and human outcomes:

Life expectancy at birth (years; LE). Because it is measured at birth, this index is affected by high infant mortality rates in some countries.

Education, composed of two separate measures: expected years of schooling for children (EYSC), and mean years of schooling for adults (MYSA). By having a separate measure for expected education of children, this index can reflect improvements in low-education countries that invest in expanding educational opportunities for kids. Mean years of schooling for adults would reflect such improvements only after many years have elapsed.

Income (GNI), measured as the gross national income per capita, PPP adjusted to take into account cost-of-living differences among countries.

Table 6.1 shows the highest and lowest outcomes for each of these variables across the globe in 2010. It reveals massive disparities in human development indicators. People in the highest-ranked countries live more than 75% longer, have more than ten times more schooling, and make more than 350 times more income, on average, than people in the lowest-ranked countries.

We can argue about whether these variables are sufficient to capture the most critical differences across countries in terms of their human development. Surely, you can think of other variables that might be included in an HDI. A good index does not have to include every human outcome we can think of, though. A few well-chosen ones should do, as long as they are correlated with the other important outcomes that get

TABLE 6.1   THE TWO ENDS OF THE HUMAN DEVELOPMENT SPECTRUM

Min/Max and Country	Life Expectancy at Birth (LE, Years)	Expected Years of Schooling (of Children) (EYSC, Years)	Mean Years of Schooling (of Adults) (MYSA, Years)	GNI Per Capita in PPP Terms (Constant 2005 International $)
Minimum	47.4	2.4	1.2	260
Country	Sierra Leone	Somalia	Mozambique	Liberia
Maximum	83.2	18	12.6	93,383
Country	Japan	Australia	Norway	Qatar

SOURCE: Data from United Nations Development Program (http://hdr.undp.org/en/statistics/data/).

left out. For example, access to health care is an essential part of development. But because life expectancy is closely related to health care, we do not necessarily have to include both life expectancy and health care in our index.

There is a difference between having a long life and a healthy life, though. Other measures have been proposed to capture both the length and quality of life. One is the disability-adjusted life year (DALY). People with disabilities lose time to premature death and spend time disabled by disease. One DALY is equal to one year of healthy life lost, due either to death or disability. Health research based on DALY highlights the importance of psychiatric and neurological conditions as well as physical disabilities that take away healthy life years. In some cases, the health of countries with a long life expectancy does not look as impressive when researchers adjust for DALY. DALYs have not been included in the HDI.

One variable that has been added to the HDI is inequality. The Inequality Adjusted Human Development Index (IHDI) discounts each dimension of the HDI (income, health, and education) by the degree of inequality in that dimension. When there is no inequality in any dimension, the IHDI is equal to the HDI; otherwise, it is lower. Wide variability in per capita incomes, life expectancy, and education across a population can substantially reduce the population's HDI.[2] Countries with low human development tend to have high levels of inequality in more dimensions.

CONSTRUCTING THE HDI

Creating the HDI raised a challenging technical question: How do you construct an index from such qualitatively different outcomes as income, education, and life expectancy? The HDI is an index of indexes, one for each outcome. The outcomes in it are diverse, are measured in different units, and take on a very wide range of values.

Actually, we've already learned pretty much everything we need to make the HDI. At the end of chapter 2 we constructed an income index. We calculate our gross national income index to include in the HDI for each country i, which we can call $I(GNI_i)$, as follows:

$$I(GNI_i) = \frac{Ln(GNI_i) - Ln(GNI_{min})}{Ln(GNI_{max}) - Ln(GNI_{min})}$$

This is just like the income index in chapter 2 except that it takes the natural log of each GNI. There is a good reason to do this. We just saw that the country per capita incomes for the 2010 HDI ranged from $260 (Liberia) to $93,383 (Qatar). That's a big range. We would expect that an increase in income in rich countries won't affect human development as much as the same increase in poor countries. Taking the natural log of each country's income accomplishes this. It compresses the income range, since $Ln(260) = 5.56$ and $Ln(93,383) = 11.44$.

Notice how we've used the highest and lowest GNIs to construct this index. The UN uses the highest and lowest incomes any country had between 1980 and 2010 ($163 and $108,211, respectively). We can use the same method to construct indexes for life expectancy at birth and the two education variables. For life expectancy, the UN uses a minimum value of 20, which from a practical point of view is about the lowest a society could have and still reproduce itself. The maximum LE is 83.2 (Japan in 2010). For the mean years of schooling for adults, it uses a maximum of 13.2 (the United States in 2002), and a minimum of zero (since, in theory, a society could survive with zero schooling). For expected years of schooling for children, the maximum is 20.6 (Australia in 2002), and the minimum, as for the other education variable, is zero.

In all these indexes, a country with an outcome equal to the minimum gets a value of zero, while a country with an outcome equal to the maximum gets a value of one. All other countries have values between zero and one.

The last step is to combine these four indexes to make the HDI. We could just take the average of the four. The problem with that approach is that a country could do well on one component but miserably fail on another and still come out looking alright. If a country really fails on one human development dimension, we want our index to reflect this.

TABLE 6.2 COUNTRY HDIS BY
PER CAPITA INCOME QUINTILE

Quintile		HDI Range	
		Low	*High*
Richer ↓	1	0.22	0.44
	2	0.45	0.61
	3	0.61	0.69
	4	0.70	0.78
	5	0.78	0.91

The UN opted for using geometric means. The geometric mean of N variables is the Nth root of the product of the N variables. This sounds pretty mathematical, but the math we choose depends on what we want our index to say about society.[3]

Here's how to make the HDI: first, the two educational indexes are combined, using a geometric mean, to make a single educational index, which we can call $I(E_i)$. It is computed as

$$I(E_i) = \sqrt{I(EYSC_i)*I(MYSA_i)}$$

The HDI is calculated by taking the geometric mean of the three indexes, $I(GNI_i)$, $I(LE_i)$, and $I(E_i)$:

$$HDI_i = \sqrt[3]{I(GNI_i)*I(LE_i)*I(E_i)}$$

(Notice that this is the cubed root, since we are dealing with three indexes.) The HDI, like each of its components, ranges from zero to one. It is zero if a country has a zero for any of the three component indexes. It can only equal one if a country maxes out on all three indexes. We can take all 187 countries for which we have data, sort them from lowest to highest HDI, and divide them into quintiles (fifths). Table 6.2 shows the HDI ranges for each quintile; the HDI and its components for selected countries appear in table 6.3. Among all countries (click on the QR code at the end of this chapter), the lowest quintile is dominated by African countries; in fact, with only a handful of exceptions (Afghanistan, Haiti, Nepal), all of the countries in the lowest quintile are African. With the exception of a couple of oil-producing and Asian countries, all in the top quintile are European or North American. In between is a diverse group of countries, including some that do well on one or two HDI components but not on the other one or two.

TABLE 6.3   OVER- AND UNDERPERFORMERS IN HUMAN DEVELOPMENT

Country	LE[a] Level	LE[a] Index	EYSC[b] Level	EYSC[b] Index	MYSA[c] Level	MYSA[c] Index	GNI[d] Level	GNI[d] Index	HDI	GNI Rank (Lowest to Highest)	HDI Rank (Lowest to Highest)	GNI Rank −HDI Rank
Worst Performers												
Equatorial Guinea	50.8	0.49	7.7	0.37	5.4	0.41	16,908	0.71	0.51	143	54	89
Kuwait	74.5	0.86	12.3	0.60	6.1	0.46	46,428	0.87	0.73	181	129	52
Botswana	53.3	0.53	12.2	0.59	8.9	0.67	12,479	0.67	0.61	124	74	50
Oman	72.8	0.84	11.8	0.57	5.5	0.42	22,633	0.76	0.68	150	100	50
South Africa	52.2	0.51	13.1	0.64	8.5	0.64	9,257	0.62	0.59	109	66	43
Angola	50.7	0.49	9.1	0.44	4.4	0.33	4,659	0.52	0.46	79	40	39
Gabon	62.3	0.67	13.1	0.64	7.5	0.57	11,771	0.66	0.64	121	83	38
Qatar	78.2	0.92	12	0.58	7.3	0.55	93,383	0.98	0.80	187	153	34
Bhutan	66.8	0.74	11	0.53	2.3	0.17	5,060	0.53	0.49	82	49	33
United Arab Emirates	76.4	0.89	13.3	0.65	9.3	0.70	59,819	0.91	0.82	185	158	27
Trinidad and Tobago	69.9	0.79	12.3	0.60	9.2	0.70	22,979	0.76	0.73	151	125	26
Average	64.35	0.70	11.63	0.56	6.76	0.51	27,761	0.73	0.64	137	94	44
Best Performers												
Cuba	79	0.93	17.5	0.85	9.9	0.75	5,253	0.53	0.74	84	131	−47
Georgia	73.5	0.85	13.1	0.64	12.1	0.92	4,535	0.51	0.69	76	111	−35
Grenada	75.8	0.88	16	0.78	8.6	0.65	6,914	0.58	0.71	93	121	−28
Palau	71.5	0.81	14.7	0.71	12.1	0.92	9,617	0.63	0.75	110	138	−28
New Zealand	80.5	0.96	18	0.87	12.5	0.95	23,776	0.77	0.87	153	180	−27
Madagascar	66.5	0.74	10.7	0.52	5.2	0.39	840	0.25	0.44	11	37	−26
Average	74.47	0.86	15.00	0.73	10.07	0.76	8,489	0.54	0.70	88	120	−32

[a] Life expectancy at birth (years).
[b] Expected years of schooling (of children; years).
[c] Mean years of schooling (of adults; years).
[d] Per capita GNI in PPP terms (constant 2005 international $).

SOURCE: Analysis of data from the UNDP Human Development Report (http://hdr.undp.org/en/statistics/data/).

INCOME AND HUMAN DEVELOPMENT

As we emphasized at the outset of this chapter, income is important because it is a means to an end—to meaningful, healthy, and empowered existence. But just *how* potent a means to human development is income? With only income, can we predict human development, or do countries at similar income levels often have different human development outcomes? There is clearly a built-in relationship between income and the HDI because one of the HDI's components is income. There is also almost certainly a relationship between income and both life expectancy and educational attainment. We can see evidence for this in figure 6.1, which graphs different countries' HDIs (vertical axis) against their per capita gross national incomes (horizontal axis).

It is clear that the HDI rises sharply with per capita income, but it tapers off sharply at higher income levels, which is precisely the motivation for using log transformations of income. Nevertheless, there are some wide variations in human development outcomes among countries even at the same income levels.

Let's dig more deeply into the UNDP data and look for countries in which the connection between income and human development is not so clear. This might offer us some insights into why some countries have managed to do a better job of meeting their human development challenges than others. One way to do this is to rank countries first in terms of per capita GNI, then in terms of HDI, and then take the difference between the two rankings. A positive difference means that a country was ranked relatively high in terms of income but low in terms of the HDI. You can think of these as the underperformers: they seem to have gotten disproportionately little human development out of their incomes. If the rank difference is negative, a country overperformed: it was ranked higher in HDI than income.

Table 6.3 shows the countries with the biggest rank differences, positive or negative. You could draw the line on what "biggest" means wherever you wish; we chose countries that have a rank difference of more than 25 (positive in the top panel, negative in the bottom).

Look at Equatorial Guinea. Its income rank is very high: it had the forty-fourth highest income among the 187 countries in our data. It is the richest country in Africa in terms of per capita income, with a PPP-adjusted per capita income of $16,908. You'd think it would score high on life expectancy and education, the other two components of the HDI, but it doesn't. Its average life expectancy is a dismal 50.8 years, and the average adult has only 5.4 years of schooling.

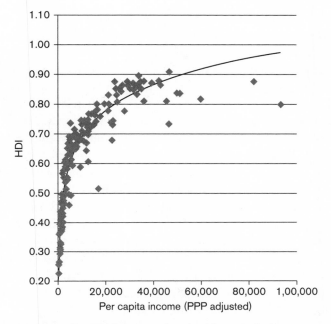

FIGURE 6.1. The HDI increases sharply with per capita income and then tapers off.

What's the story in Equatorial Guinea? It is one of the largest oil producers in Africa, but its considerable oil wealth is in the hands of relatively few people. Most of the population lives in rural areas, where subsistence production predominates. (We will look at subsistence production in chapter 9.) Getting quality data on Equatorial Guinea is problematic. A Gini coefficient for income is not available from the World Bank or the CIA. However, the Vision of Humanity's Global Peace Index estimates a Gini coefficient of 0.65, making Equatorial Guinea one of the most unequal countries in the world.[4]

It might seem surprising that a country with so much oil wealth would have a relatively poor record in terms of the HDI, but Equatorial Guinea is not the only one. The United Arab Emirates, Kuwait, Angola, and Qatar are among the top twenty oil exporters in the world, and all of them are on our "underperformers" list. So are Gabon and Trinidad and Tobago, two other oil exporters. Oil riches do not seem to buy human development—or, perhaps more accurately, having easy oil money can shape the structure of an economy and society in ways that slow human development gains.

Another standout on the worst performers' list is South Africa. It has the largest economy in Africa, and the World Bank ranks it as an upper-middle-income country. But it also has one of the world's most unequal income distributions (a Gini coefficient of 0.63, according to the World Bank), and an alarmingly high HIV infection rate (on the order of 20%). You can see in the table that South Africa does relatively well in terms of education, but its life expectancy at birth is only 52.2 years.

It is harder to find countries that significantly overperform in terms of human development. The world's greatest overperformer is Cuba, ranking forty-seven places higher in terms of human development than income. This is a country where the PPP-adjusted per capita income is $5,253, about half of South Africa's and less than a third of Equatorial Guinea's. Yet Cuba has one of the highest life expectancies in the world (79 years). The average Cuban child can expect to end up with 17.5 years of schooling, more than the average US child (16 years). Overall, there are only six countries whose HDI ranking beats their GNI ranking by more than twenty-five places, but there are eleven in which the HDI ranking is twenty-five places lower than the GNI ranking.

In short, there are large variations in human development outcomes among countries. There are also large discrepancies within countries. In particular, human development outcomes tend to be most dismal in rural areas of poor countries, where most of the world's poverty is found. Still, there's no denying that income appears to be a key correlate of human development. Income growth is a key for improving human well-being in the world's poorest countries.

Income growth is the topic of our next chapter. The rest of this chapter will focus on the two other components of the HDI: education and health. We will learn why each is important, not only in and of itself but also in *determining* other development outcomes. We'll also learn how development economists think about the role of government in providing people with education and health, and how economists study the determinants of education and health as well as the impacts of each on economic development.

EDUCATING A COUNTRY

Why are you here? We don't mean the big cosmological question—we mean here, as in this school, taking this class, reading this book. You would probably answer something like: "to learn development economics," or "to get a good job someday," by which you might mean a high-paying job or perhaps a fulfilling one, or both. No one to whom we've asked this question ever answered "to make other people more productive." Yet from a societal point of view, that's one of the important things education does. By becoming more educated, we become more productive, which is why we can hope to get paid more. But people become more productive when they have other educated people to work with, too.

This is what we call a positive externality, a social benefit that your private decision creates. When people decide how much schooling to get, they do a sort of cost-benefit analysis, as we shall see later on in this chapter. But we only consider the private costs and benefits in our calculation—how much it costs us to have another year of school, and what we can expect to get out of it. We do not normally consider the social benefit that our schooling investment creates by making other people more productive. Because people do not take the social benefits into account, left to their own devices they will tend to underinvest in education.

In the presence of externalities, there is a compelling case for governments to get involved in the market with policies designed to make people take social benefits and costs into account, or at least nudge them closer to the social optimum. If we were rewarded for the social good our schooling creates, we might be willing to invest more in schooling. Economists call this *internalizing the externality*. That essentially is what public education does by making the cost of getting schooled lower than it would be in a private school system. Public investment in education is the principal way in which countries try to solve the education externality. But there are other ways, as we shall see. Simply building new classrooms and putting teachers in them might not be sufficient to make the students come, especially if their families are poor.

When deciding whether or not to send their kids to school, parents weigh the costs and benefits. To achieve the millennium development goal of universal primary education and beyond, policy makers need to understand what kinds of interventions will get kids into the classroom and make them learn. That means getting the costs and benefits right.

The True Cost of Going to School

How much does it cost to send a kid to school? You might be imagining the costs of books, supplies, uniforms, transportation to and from school, meals, and tuition. These costs can easily be prohibitive for poor people, but they are only part of the cost of sending kids to school. They are what we would call the *direct costs* of education. There's also an *opportunity cost* of spending time in the classroom and studying. In economics, the opportunity cost of going to school is the benefit foregone by not doing the next best thing. If you weren't studying economics, you might be playing a sport or engaging in a hobby that you enjoy, in which case your opportunity cost would include the utility loss from having less leisure. Maybe you would have a job, in which case the opportunity cost of going to school would include your lost wages.

For a poor family in an African village, the opportunity cost of sending kids to school almost certainly includes the value of the labor that kids would provide at home—helping in the fields, watching animals, taking care of siblings, and so forth—if they were not studying. Even attending a school that is free has its costs. For a very poor household, the opportunity cost of sending kids to school might be insurmountable.

The Benefits of Going to School

At any moment in your education, you could stop going to school and get a job. You continue studying because, as you perceive it, the benefits outweigh the opportunity cost of not working plus the "hard costs" of going to school. What are the benefits of going to school?

Human capital theory provides a useful framework for understanding the benefits of going to school. Human capital is the set of knowledge and skills that make workers productive. To these we can also add health, without which it is hard for even highly skilled people to be productive, and less tangible things like the values we hold that make us work hard, take risks, and embrace new ideas (or not).

If schools impart useful knowledge, skills, and values, then we accumulate human capital by going to school. By making people more productive, schooling raises their wages. This basic tenet of human capital theory comes straight out of the microeconomics of the firm. A firm will not hire a worker unless the additional value he produces (his marginal value product of labor, or MVPL) is at least as large as what it will have to pay the worker (that is, the wage, w). Figure 6.2 illustrates this classic "MVPL = w" rule. It shows the MVPL curve, which is downward sloping due to diminishing marginal productivity of labor. The firm hires labor up to the point where the market wage just equals the MVPL. Characteristics that raise workers' productivity, like schooling and work experience, therefore, should bring higher wages.

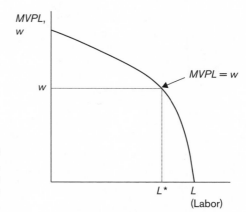

FIGURE 6.2. Firms optimize by hiring labor up to the point where, at the margin, the value of the marginal product just equals the market wage.

Jacob Mincer, a labor economist, invented what has become one of the most famous empirical models in all of economics. The Mincer model posits that people's wages are a function of their human capital, in particular their years of schooling and work experience. Econometric studies consistently find that, on average, more highly educated people have significantly higher earnings. Schooling raises earnings proportionately *more* in poor than rich countries, because human capital is scarcer in poor countries.

This gives us a way to understand schooling decisions. Once we know the costs of going to school, including the opportunity costs, we can compare them with the private benefits, which are the future stream of earnings gains that will result, discounted to reflect the fact that income in the future is worth less to people than income earned now. That is, we can perform a cost-benefit analysis, similar to what we did for project evaluation in chapter 2. Knowing how to apply cost-benefit analysis to different situations is an essential of development economics. The basic method of cost-benefit analysis is the same no matter what the analysis is for: a new airport, road, irrigation system, tourism project, or going to school. Applying this method to schooling can give us insights into the challenges to achieving educational goals in poor countries.

A Cost-Benefit Analysis of Going to School

The appendix to this chapter takes us through a cost-benefit analysis for the following case: consider a twelve-year-old child in a poor country (we picked Lesotho because we have good data from a recent survey Ed helped carry out there).[5] She has just finished primary school and is deciding whether or not to continue on and do three years of secondary (middle) school.

If children are not in school, often they work, especially if their family is poor. Our data show that the average annual wage for a working child (younger than sixteen years of age) in rural Lesotho in 2012 was 487 maloti (around US$64) per year for boys and 279 maloti (US$52) for girls. We use these as the opportunity costs of going to school.

We estimated a Mincer wage equation for the whole sample of working-age adults. (We control for the fact that many people do not work for a wage.) It found that each additional year of schooling raises the wage by 9.8% for males and by much more—18.6%—for females. Three additional years of schooling thus translate into a 29% increase in the wage for males and a 56% increase for females. That turns out to be an annual wage gain of 142 maloti for males and 218 for females, compared to the adult wage for someone with only primary schooling.

Unfortunately, we do not see these wage gains until after the student finishes secondary school—that is, until the fourth year and after. To perform a cost-benefit analysis, future benefits and costs must be discounted back to the present, using a discount factor that reflects how much weight people place on the future compared to the present. Our survey does not provide information on how heavily people discount the future. In real life, as we shall see in chapter 12, different people have different ways of thinking about the future, and thus different discount rates. Poor people with pressing, life-and-death needs today may put little weight on costs and benefits that are off in the future—that is, they may discount the future using a personal discount rate that is very high.

It is common practice in cost-benefit analysis to use the prevailing interest rate to discount future benefits and costs. That's because the interest rate is the economy's price for waiting. It is what a bank has to pay us to keep our money for a year, and it is what consumers have to pay for their impatience when they take out a loan. To keep things simple in our example, we'll use an interest rate of 4.4%, which was the real (inflation-adjusted) interest rate in Lesotho in 2012 according to the World Bank's Indicators.[6] We can use this rate to discount future costs and earnings.

Under the best of circumstances there is a public secondary school nearby, and the direct costs of going to school might be small. But remember, the individual (and her household) lose the wage earnings during the three years she is in secondary school.

Should she do it?

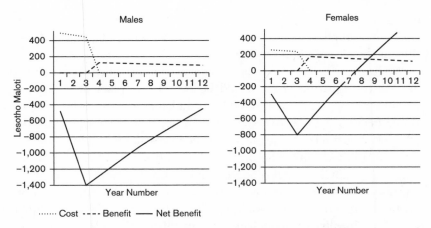

FIGURE 6.3. Students incur opportunity costs during the three years they are in secondary school. Girls recoup these costs by year 8, while boys still have not recouped the costs in year 12.

Our cost-benefit analysis concludes that secondary schooling is worth the opportunity cost for both boys and girls (see appendix). The net present value of investing in secondary schooling, or difference between total discounted future benefits and opportunity costs, is 958 maloti for boys. It is considerably larger (2,816 maloti) for girls, who have a higher estimated wage gain from schooling and a lower opportunity cost of going to school.

Even though secondary school passes our cost-benefit test, it takes a while—quite a while in the case of boys. We can calculate the break-even point, or the year in which the net benefits turn positive. Figure 6.3 shows that for a girl, the break-even point on investing in a three-year secondary education is not until five years after she leaves school. For boys, it is much later. The figure shows that in year 12, boys still do not reach the break-even point. In fact, it takes fifteen years from the time they graduate for males to recoup the opportunity cost of completing secondary school. That's a long time to wait—too long for many poor families. It's no wonder that secondary school enrollment rates are low for children in rural Lesotho (28.0%), especially for boys (21.3%; the rate for girls is 35.5%).[7]

Some Caveats

Bear in mind that we assumed a discount rate of 4.4%. If poor people in rural Lesotho discount the future more heavily than that, which is likely, the break-even points will shift farther out. Having to pay for books and supplies, school uniforms, and other school items would also shift the break-even point rightward.

We further assumed that schooling is exogenous when we estimated the Mincer equation. That would be the case if years of completed schooling were somehow randomly sprinkled across the population of young people, as in an RCT (chapter 2), but that obviously is not the case. There is a selection problem: the people who go to school are different from the people who do not in ways that we cannot see in our data. If high-ability people choose to go to school, we cannot say with certainty whether the economic returns we estimated are from schooling or ability. High ability could lead to high earnings with or without schooling. Ideally, we would like to control for ability in the Mincer regression.

Our cost-benefit analysis was for a sample of rural households in Lesotho. Its findings would not necessarily apply to other countries or to urban areas in Lesotho, like the capital of Maseru. There, wages as well as the economic returns to schooling are considerably higher than in the remote rural villages from which most of our sample was drawn. Factory jobs create a demand for educated workers that is apparent to urban children as well as to their parents. Poor rural households have a demand for labor on the farm that does not have an analogue in most urban households, and lower poverty might make parents in urban areas more amenable to investing today in order to reap gains in the future.

On the other hand, it is possible that the true economic returns to rural education are higher than what we could capture in our analysis, because those who are most successful after leaving school might not stick around for us to survey. We shall see in chapter 9 that schooling significantly raises the odds of young people migrating out of rural areas. People (logically) tend to take their human capital to the labor market where it is likely to bring them the greatest economic rewards. This usually is in urban areas rather than on the farm, and for some people it is in foreign lands. The schooling-then-migrate decision might well yield higher economic returns than schooling alone.

Policy Options: Building Schools and Beyond

If the opportunity cost of sending kids to school is high and the rewards from doing so are in a future that seems far away from the immediate demands of feeding a family, how can poor countries hope to signifi-

Sidebar 6.1 Do More Schools Mean More Education?

Indonesia launched a huge school-building campaign between 1973 and 1978, adding more than sixty-one thousand new schools. What effect did this have on educational attainment and earnings? That is a hard question to answer, because the number of schools increased for *everyone* in Indonesia. It's like the reflections in a hall of mirrors; we can't separate cause from effect. To determine the effect of the new schools, we'd need a treatment group of people who got more schools and a control group that didn't. But we don't have that, right?

Actually, we do. It occurred to economist Esther Duflo that new schools wouldn't affect schooling for people who were too old to go to school, but they would have an effect on kids who were just the right age to benefit from them. She looked at children 2 to 6 years old in 1974 and found that they got significantly more schooling than people who were older at the time the new schools were built. It's pretty random how old a person was at the time of the school-building craze. That's what made it possible to isolate cause and effect. Nature provided the randomization. Duflo also found that the new schools had a big effect on wages.

This study not only answered an important development question but also provided an imaginative way to identify impacts of school construction without the benefit of a randomized controlled trial.

Esther Duflo, "Schooling and Labor Market Consequences of School Construction in Indonesia: Evidence from an Unusual Policy Experiment," *American Economic Review* 91, no. 4 (September 2001), 795–813.

cantly raise educational attainment? Our cost-benefit analysis offers some insights.

First, since people do not factor the social benefits of schooling into their cost-benefit analysis, and the hard costs of schooling easily can tip the scales against sending kids to school for poor, cash-constrained households, countries need to provide universal and free education. Building schools and staffing them is a necessary first step. An imaginative study by Esther Duflo found that the expansion of schools in Indonesia significantly increased educational attainment—as well as wages—for the people who were young enough at the time to benefit from it (see sidebar 6.1).

Second, governments need to ensure that there is a high economic return to schooling. That means growing the nonfarm sectors of the economy, where the productivity gains from schooling are highest, as well as creating an infrastructure—transportation, information, communications—that will get people to jobs there.

Third, governments need to ensure that people do not discount their futures so heavily as to diminish the present value of future income gains from going to school. This means following sound macroeconomic policies that reduce economic uncertainties—and build hope—in people's futures. High unemployment and inflation environments tend to do the opposite. So does poverty. Desperately poor people naturally tend to be preoccupied with keeping food on the table now, which leaves little room to think about investing in a better future.

Finally, governments need to consider the opportunity cost of going to school. That is what pushes the break-even point out so far in our cost-benefit analysis. Child labor and school attendance laws, if effectively enforced, can reduce the opportunity cost of sending kids to school by denying parents the option of working their children on the farm. However, such laws do not change the fact that very poor households depend on their children to make ends meet. When parents depend on their children's labor to survive, laws prohibiting child labor and requiring school attendance can be very difficult to enforce.

How can governments reduce or eliminate the opportunity cost of sending children to school? Mexico's PROGRESA, which we learned about in chapter 2, tried to do just that. By giving ultra-poor women cash payments conditional upon their children being enrolled in school, PROGRESA turned what would have been an opportunity cost into an economic gain for poor households. Social cash transfer programs in Lesotho and other African countries hope to accomplish the same end, but without conditions. Lesotho's Child Grants Program gives poor households with children a transfer of 360 maloti (US$48) per quarter. This is three to four times greater than the opportunity costs we calculated from our survey data and used in our cost-benefit calculation. It seems that conditions matter for some things (see sidebar 6.2), but RCTs are already showing significant and positive impacts of unconditional cash transfers on school attendance in poor African countries.

MAKING A COUNTRY HEALTHY

The architects of the HDI recognized that human development is all about enabling people to lead productive and healthy lives. The "life expectancy at birth" component of the HDI is intended to capture health as broadly

Sidebar 6.2 Do Conditions Matter?

If a government program gives cash—enough to compensate for the opportunity cost of sending kids to school—will it be enough to get the kids into the classroom? Or does the cash have to come with strings attached, in the form of a requirement that the kids go to school in order for the poor parents to get the cash? That's a big question, because monitoring people's behavior is costly, and there is always a potential for corruption when some local official, like a school administrator, has to sign off before a poor person can get her cash.

Two research teams carried out RCTs to answer this question. In each one, a randomly selected treatment group of poor people were given cash without conditions, while a second treatment group received cash, but receipt was conditional upon kids being in school. Both were later compared to a random control group that did not get any cash.

In Burkina Faso researchers found that conditionality didn't matter when it comes to kids with high ability or whom parents tend to prioritize anyway, including boys and older children. However, attaching conditions did make transfers more effective at improving the enrollment of children who are less likely to go to school, including girls and younger or lower-ability children.

A cash transfer program in Malawi found that when poor people were given cash unconditionally, fewer of their children dropped out of school than in a control group that got no cash. However, this effect was much smaller than for those who got cash conditional upon their children being in school. There was a surprise, though: teenage pregnancy and marriage rates were substantially *lower* in the group that got the cash without any conditions, compared with the control group. There's a logical explanation for this. When girls in the conditional group dropped out of school, the payments stopped. The girls in the unconditional group who dropped out of school continued to benefit from the cash payments. Apparently, continuing to get cash transfers made girls significantly less likely to marry or become pregnant.

These interesting findings suggest that there is no simple answer to the question of whether to attach conditions to cash transfer programs. It depends in part on what the objectives of the programs are.

Sarah Baird, Craig McIntosh, and Berk Ozler, "Cash or Condition? Evidence from a Cash Transfer Experiment," *Quarterly Journal of Economics* 126, no. 4:1709–53.

Richard Akresh, Damien de Walque, and Harounan Kazianga, "Cash Transfers and Child Schooling: Evidence from a Randomized Evaluation of the Role of Conditionality" (policy research working paper no. 6340, World Bank, Washington, DC, 2013).

as possible in a single indicator. The Millennium Development Goals (chapter 1), not surprisingly, place more emphasis on health outcomes than on any other goal, including child health (MDG 4), maternal health (MDG 5), and combating HIV/AIDS and other diseases (MDG 6).

We saw earlier in this chapter that life expectancy at birth ranges from a high of more than eighty-three years in Japan to a low of just over forty-seven years in Sierra Leone. What explains this huge disparity in health outcomes? How directly involved should governments become in managing their people's health? And most importantly, how do you make a poor country healthier?

The Market for Health

Everybody wants to be healthy. Nevertheless, left to their own devices, people are likely to invest less in health than is optimal from society's point of view, for two reasons. First, there are externalities in health, just as there are in education. If you are healthy, the people you live, work, and study with are more likely to be healthy, too (and vice versa). Health, like schooling, is a key component of human capital. Indeed the two are strong complements: even an educated person will find it hard to be productive if she is in poor health. Thus, when you are healthy, you and the people you work with are more productive. When you are not, you can make others sick by going to work and interacting with them in other ways. When deciding how much to invest in health, will individuals consider the benefits and costs for the rest of society? Not likely—we often take into account how our health affects those closest to us, but rarely does this extend to society at large.

A second reason why people underinvest in health is because making people healthy requires some large-scale investments with big fixed costs followed by low or negligible marginal costs of service use. An example is a potable water system. The big cost is tapping into the water source—a distant river, maybe, or a subterranean aquifer—and delivering clean water to a village. Once this investment is made, people can collect water from the system at little, or virtually no, marginal cost. All they have to do is turn the tap of the public spigot. A public sanitation system is another example: once the treatment plant is constructed and the sewers are laid, the cost of treating an additional family's waste is small. These are examples of increasing returns to scale. The greater the use, the lower the average cost of providing the service, because the large fixed cost gets spread across more and more users.

Potable water and sanitation systems are like bridges. Once a bridge is built, it costs virtually nothing to let another car cross it. This means that the standard rule of profit maximization—equating the market price with the marginal cost—does not work here. Moreover, you might be able to keep a car off the bridge, but once the water system is in place, anyone can turn the spigot, so it may be hard (and unethical) to exclude people from it. This creates a free-rider problem, similar to what happens in firefighting. If you could choose whether or not to pay for fire protection, you might decide not to, knowing that if your house catches fire, the fire will have to be put out to keep it from spreading to other houses. If asked to contribute toward a public works project, you might choose not to on the assumption that others will. If everyone thinks that way, of course, the project doesn't happen.

A similar problem arises with respect to disease. If a communicable disease hits some part of the population and is not contained, it is likely to spread, much like a fire. Will the first people who become ill do what is necessary to keep the disease from spreading? (Probably not.) If a new immunization becomes available to keep people from getting a disease, will people choose to be inoculated? If I know others around me are inoculated, it is highly unlikely that I will contract the disease from them. So will I get inoculated, too? What if it costs me money and time (and maybe a little pain) to get the vaccine?

Free-rider problems crop up when it comes to public licensing and health inspections of food establishments, food processors, and phytosanitary control of food imports. Clearly, when it comes to health, market failures abound. Most of us make our health decisions without considering their ramifications for the rest of society, and it is hard for private investors to make a profit supplying public health services. This is a fundamental reason why countries have health departments, public disease treatment, and immunization programs.

Figuring out how to improve health outcomes in poor countries is one of the highest priorities in development. It is hard to imagine anything as central to people's welfare, or to economic growth. Health is human capital; healthier people have the potential to be more productive and to earn more income, which enhances human development even more.

The Economic Benefits of Good Health

Some researchers have tried to estimate the effect of health on earnings and compare this to the effect of schooling on earnings for individuals.

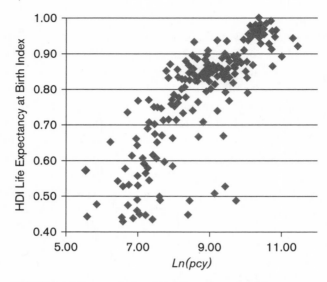

FIGURE 6.4. Life expectancy at birth in various countries (vertical axis) rises sharply with per capita income (horizontal axis). Source: Analysis of HDI data.

Others have taken a more aggregate view and tried to test whether country-wide health outcomes (typically, life expectancy at birth) explain income growth.

There is no question that life expectancy and other measures of good health correlate positively with per capita incomes; poor populations are less healthy than rich ones. Figure 6.4 shows that the component of the HDI that measures countries' life expectancy at birth increases sharply with per capita income. Even within rich countries, life expectancy is not the same everywhere. A recent study by the US Centers for Disease Control (CDC) found that people who live in southern US states, where poverty is relatively high, can expect to live fewer years—and more importantly, fewer healthy years—than people who live in other parts of the country.[8] It seems that the best predictor of your life expectancy in the United States is your zip code of residence.

This raises a question that is crucial for development policy: does poor health *cause* low incomes, or do low incomes cause poor health, or is the truth some combination of the two? There is a classic reflection problem (chapter 2): each of these two variables affects the other in ways that are difficult to isolate. Poor countries spend less on public health than rich countries do. Poor households have less access to good nutrition, health services, and information about how to stay healthy. Many lack access to clean water and sanitation and face environmental risks, for example, the use of traditional fuels like firewood that can have negative health consequences. Places with high poverty rates tend to be the kinds of places where life expectancy is shorter, populations are less healthy, and health services are less available. We can imagine many variables that influence both health and income, as well. How can we identify the health-income relationship?

There is no RCT here: we cannot do an experiment in which one group of people is randomly treated with good health while another is not. We can, however, randomly increase some people's income and not the income of others, as in the social cash transfer projects described in chapter 2. Moreover, health experiments offer some insights into how policies can be effective at improving health and nutritional outcomes. RCTs are commonly used by health scientists to test the effectiveness of specific health treatments, including spillover effects on people who do not get the treatment (see sidebar 6.3).

It's hard to design an experiment to test whether measures to improve people's health lead to higher incomes, but Edward Miguel and Michael Kremer's worms study (chapter 2) found a health intervention that increased school attendance, which we have seen is a key to increasing people's productivity and incomes down the road.

If people underinvest in health, then economic incentives may be required to nudge them toward making a more socially optimal level of health investment. "Investment" here means not only investing money (which poor people lack) in health (e.g., medical services), but also making the effort to get family members to public health services (e.g., free immunizations) if they are available, using bednets provided by an aid program, feeding children and pregnant and lactating mothers the most nutritious diet possible subject to a family's budget, and practicing good sanitation at home. Malaria once covered the world. In rich countries, development got rid of it.

Researchers have carried out a variety of experiments to test how various kinds of economic incentive structures can encourage people to invest in health. Two examples of health-related RCTs follow.

Immunizations

Immunizations are one of the most effective ways to save lives, yet the World Health Organization reports that 27 million children don't get

Sidebar 6.3 Bednet Spillovers

Malaria is a fact of life—and a taker of lives—in tropical Africa. Bednets treated with insecticide can provide protection to the people who use them as well as to people around them (by killing off malaria-carrying mosquitoes and depriving them of access to people's blood). But if a development program gives people bednets for free, will they use them? If people have to share in the cost—paying a subsidized price for getting a bednet—will the program be less wasteful, because only those who really need and will use a bednet will buy one? These are big questions, given the scarce resources development programs have to work with.

Two economists decided to find out, by running a randomized controlled trial in Kenya. Prenatal clinics sold bednets treated with anti-malarial insecticide to pregnant women at randomized prices. The study found no evidence that getting a bednet for free made women less likely to use it. There was no evidence that women who needed a bednet more were more likely to purchase one. However, cost-sharing significantly reduced the demand for bednets. The researchers found that free distribution could save many more lives. Not only that, more widespread use of treated bednets would create a positive externality by reducing the likelihood that others contract malaria. Once this externality is taken into account, it appears that free distribution would actually be a *more* economical way to save lives; it would result in a lower cost of bednets per life saved.

Jessica Cohen and Pascaline Dupas, "Free Distribution or Cost-Sharing? Evidence from a Malaria Prevention Experiment," *Quarterly Journal of Economics* 125, no. 1 (2010):1–45.

essential immunizations each year. Immunizations are a centerpiece of work by the wealthiest foundation in the world (the Bill and Melinda Gates Foundation), and governments as well as donors invest considerable resources in them. So why do so many poor children not get immunized? Is it that parents do not believe in immunizations, or is it something else?

It could be what Esther Duflo calls "the last mile." Parents procrastinate, health centers usually are a good walk away, and once people get there, lines are long and the health center is certain to be understaffed and may not even be open when it is supposed to be. The cost (including time) of getting to immunization centers and unreliable service there create disincentives for parents to get their children immunized. Researchers at J-PAL designed an RCT to test this (see sidebar 6.4).

Sidebar 6.4   The Last Mile?

Researchers Abhijit Banerjee and Esther Duflo hypothesized that eliminating disincentives would make the difference between children getting or not getting immunized. In Udaipur, Rajasthan, India, a new
project set up monthly "vaccination camps" in randomly selected
treatment villages. These camps were well publicized and sure to be
open rain or shine. The idea was to replicate an ideal health-delivery
system. It also gave some randomly chosen people an extra incentive:
a kilo of lentils. Then researchers compared immunization rates
between the treated villages and a randomly selected group of control
villages where there were no vaccination camps.

The percentage of vaccinated kids tripled, from 6% to 18%, in the
villages with camps. When lentils were thrown in, the percentage rose
by a factor of more than six, to 39%. An unexpected benefit of the
program was that the cost of immunizations fell by half, as the same
number of nurses was able to immunize many children. That is, the
researchers found increasing returns to scale in this health-care intervention.

This project's research contribution was not so much to show that
economic incentives work; we already knew that from PROGRESA
and other CCT programs. It was to demonstrate that a small incentive,
like a few lentils, can have a big effect on people's demand for crucial
health services like immunization.

Abhijit Banerjee and Esther Duflo, "A New Look at an Old Problem: Why
Do So Many Poor Children Miss out on Essential Immunizations?" UNICEF,
Child Poverty Insights (June 2011; (www.povertyactionlab.org/sites/default/
files/ChildPovertyInsights_June2011_EN%281%29.pdf).

HIV/AIDS

In 2010 an estimated 22.9 million people in sub-Saharan Africa were
living with HIV and 1.2 million died of AIDS, leaving 16.6 million children orphaned. Rates of HIV infection among adults 15–49 years old
were 17.8% in South Africa, where 5.6 million adults were infected,
and reached as high as 23.6% in Lesotho, 24.8% in Botswana, and
25.9% in Swaziland.[9] Besides being a human tragedy of epic proportions, AIDS can have a major impact on countries' economic prospects
because it strikes at the heart of the working-age population and thus
takes a particularly heavy toll on human capital. A study in Mozambique concluded that the disease reduced total economic growth by as

much as 1% per year. Estimates for other sub-Saharan African countries range from 0.56% to 1.47% lost income growth per year, and these estimates may be low.[10]

RCTs are giving us important insights into how to fight HIV/AIDS in poor countries. Lack of education and economic dependence on men ("transactional sex") are believed to be important causes of HIV infection among young women. An RCT tested whether cash transfers to young women reduced infections among school-age girls in Malawi, where 11% of the adult population has HIV/AIDS. It found strong evidence that they did, if they target young unmarried women still in school (see sidebar 6.5).

PUBLIC WORKS PROJECTS TO IMPROVE HEALTH

The impacts of large-scale health projects with big fixed costs can be challenging to evaluate. It is rare to find such projects rolled out in a random fashion, like social cash transfers often are, so that their impacts can be evaluated without running into the selection problem. Take water, for instance. Intestinal diseases traceable to unsafe drinking water supplies and a lack of sanitation systems are a major cause of death in poor countries, especially among children. There is little doubt that governments and international aid agencies should invest in tube wells, hand pumps, and village taps to provide people with access to groundwater protected from the contaminants found in surface water, including lakes and streams. The problems of increasing returns to scale and public goods make these kinds of investments unlikely unless governments or aid agencies step up and do them. But will a public works project solve the problem?

Surprisingly, evaluations find mixed impacts of water projects on illnesses linked to waterborne pathogens. Some find large impacts on morbidity, while others find little impact at all. Katrina Jessoe wanted to find out why. The answer, she hypothesized, lies in what people do to the water once it is inside their homes (see sidebar 6.6). Simply providing people with clean groundwater, it seems, may not be enough to keep them safe.

NUTRITION AND HEALTH

It is difficult to imagine anything as fundamental to health and economic development as people's nutrition. The American economic historian and Nobel laureate Robert Fogel showed that over time, people's

Sidebar 6.5 A Cash Transfer Program for AIDS

It is widely believed that poverty and a lack of education increase the risk of HIV infection among school-age women by making them economically dependent on older sex partners. This is often referred to as the "sugar daddy" phenomenon. If it is true, then giving cash to young women who are enrolled in school should reduce their incidence of HIV and other sexually transmitted diseases (STDs).

A team of researchers from US universities and the World Bank set out to test this hypothesis in Malawi. They took a sample of 1,289 females aged 13–22 years who were enrolled in school and never married, randomly assigning some to get cash payments (the treatment group) and the others (the control group) to get nothing. Women in the treatment group, in turn, were randomly divided into two subgroups, one getting the cash unconditionally and the other conditional upon staying in school. The payments ranged from US$1 to $5 monthly, and the women's parents were also given $4 to $10 per month.

After eighteen months, 1.2% of the treatment group and 3.0% of the control group tested positive for HIV or herpes simplex virus 2 (HSV-2). The difference between the two groups was statistically significant. Among the women who got cash, the study found no significant difference in HIV infection between those required to continue in school to get the cash and those who got the cash regardless of school attendance.

You might conclude from these findings that only the cash matters—not school attendance. To test whether that is true, the study also followed 417 women in the same age group who already had dropped out of school before the experiment. Among those women, the cash transfer had no significant effect at all, revealing that school enrollment does, indeed, matter.

These findings show that cash transfer programs, which do not directly target sexual behavior, can reduce HIV and HSV-2 infections among adolescent schoolgirls in a poor country. To be effective, however, the cash transfer program must target adolescent women while they are still in school. Once they have dropped out, it is too late.

Are cash transfers and education enough? Almost certainly not. For one thing, the "sugar daddies" are still out there. If cash transfers and school attendance take some poor young women out of the transactional sex market, what will happen to the rest?

This study is important in showing that a cash transfer program, not targeted at sexual behavior, can be an important complement to other interventions to reduce the spread of STDs.

Do findings from a small research experiment like this one hold up in a large-scale government cash transfer program? In chapter 2

(continued)

(sidebar 2.2) we learned about the Kenyan government's large scale Cash Transfers for Orphans and Vulnerable Children (CT-OVC) program, which gives cash to ultra-poor households. Four researchers at the University of North Carolina found that the CT-OVC transfers lowered the odds of sexual debut among men and women 15–25 years old by a significant 31%. Thus, large-scale cash transfer programs with poverty alleviation objectives may reduce HIV risk among young people.

Sarah J. Baird, Richard S. Garfein, Craig T. McIntosh, and Berk Özler, "Impact of a Cash Transfer Program for Schooling on Prevalence of HIV and HSV-2 in Malawi: A Cluster Randomized Trial," *Lancet* 379, no. 9823 (April 2012):1320–29 (www.thelancet.com/journals/lancet/article/PIIS0140-6736%2811%2961709-1/abstract).

Sudhanshu Handa, Carolyn Tucker Halpern, Audrey Pettifor, and Harsha Thirumurthy, "The Government of Kenya's Cash Transfer Program Reduces the Risk of Sexual Debut among Young People Age 15–25," *PloS one* 9, no. 1 (2014): e85473.

average height is linked to changes in standards of living, mortality, and perhaps even morbidity. As nations' incomes grow, people get taller! The average height of mature people in the United States, Côte d'Ivoire, Brazil, and Vietnam rose by between .75 and 1.5 centimeters per decade during the twentieth century.[11] Fogel argued that height is a useful index of a population's well-being, both between and within countries. When there are large variations in adult height within countries, he claimed, we learn something about how the benefits of economic growth have been distributed across the country's population. In the poorest regions, people tend to be less healthy—and shorter.

Not only that, history shows that taller people earn more. In Brazil, for example, a 1% increase in height is associated with an 8% increase in people's wages, according to two development and health economists, John Strauss and Duncan Thomas. Taller people also are better educated, and we have already seen that education increases earnings. In Brazil, for example, these economists found that a ten-centimeter difference in height corresponds to a 25% increase in completed schooling.[12]

If these findings are correct, then improving people's—especially children's—nutrition could have multiple benefits. By improving health, better diets make people happier and more productive. Higher productivity, in turn, can provide people with the income they need to eat healthy diets. On

Sidebar 6.6 Keeping the Water Safe

Jessoe hypothesized that when people get access to cleaner water, they feel less of a need to treat their water at home, and this reduces health benefits from water projects. She compared in-home treatment of water, including boiling (the most effective way to kill pathogens), between households with and without access to improved water sources in rural India.

Ideally, this study would have used an RCT. You can imagine an experiment in which projects to deliver clean groundwater are carried out in a random group of treatment villages. Changes in at-home treatment and health outcomes before and after the projects could be compared to changes in a random sample of control villages that did not get water projects. Unfortunately, no such experiments are available in rural India. To complicate matters, water projects in rural India tend to target disadvantaged places with few health services. These are likely to be the kinds of places with poor health outcomes with or without new water projects. Because of this selection problem, it might not be surprising to find poor health outcomes in places that get water projects!

Without an RCT, the trick is to find an instrumental variable that is highly correlated with households' drinking water source but not with health outcomes or water treatment behavior except through the source. Jessoe found an unusual instrument: the type of rock underneath the communities she studied. Substratum rock types determine what type of water source a community has. However, there is little reason to think that it affects people's water-treatment behavior or health outcomes except through the drinking water source effect.

Using this instrument to predict water source, this study found that households are 25%–27% less likely to treat their water at home when they get the water from an improved source. Apparently, they feel that they don't have to. The practice of boiling water falls by 18%. These changes in treatment at home offset a large part of the gains from public investment in water projects; the improvement in water quality at home is smaller than would be the case if people did not change their water-treatment behavior.

This study is important because it teaches us that public investments in water projects may not be enough to combat waterborne disease. Information campaigns and other economic inducements to get people to practice safe water treatment at home also may be required.

Katrina Jessoe, "Improved Source, Improved Quality? Demand for Drinking Water Quality in Rural India," *Journal of Environmental Economics and Management* 66, no. 3 (2013):460–75.

the other hand, low incomes lead to poor nutrition, health, productivity—and thus low incomes in the future. That sounds suspiciously like a health poverty trap, akin to the poverty trap we learned about in chapter 4.

Econometric studies have estimated the impact of people's income on their nutrient intake (which economists call "nutrient demand"). In China, Ed and World Bank economist Xiao Ye found that as income rises, people's calorie intake also rises—although more slowly. A 1% rise in income increased total calorie demand by 0.45% in the poorest household group. (By contrast, it had almost no effect on calorie intake in the highest-income rural households.)[13]

The big impact was on *where* people get their calories. Calories from meat jumped 1.43%, while calories from grain rose only 0.28%. As people shift from grain to animal products, the average cost of the calories they consume goes up. The United Nations considers the share of people's energy provided by animal products as a key indicator of diet quality, because calories from animal products come with an almost complete package of vitamins and minerals essential to a good diet.

Some RCTs are beginning to confirm these findings in other contexts. For example, the Malawi study cited in sidebar 6.2 found that dietary diversity increased in the households that got cash transfers.

THE BIG PICTURE: HEALTH AND INCOME GROWTH

Whether better health causes higher incomes, or whether it is the reverse that explains most of the positive association we see between health and income, is very hard to determine. Nevertheless, we saw in chapter 2 that programs that randomly give cash to poor households improve children's nutrition (as well as their schooling). We can see the impacts on people's diets fairly quickly—within the one or two years of the start of a cash transfer program. Impacts on morbidity and mortality are likely to take more time to materialize, and impacts on child growth stunting and adult height take considerably more time than evaluations usually cover. Nevertheless, there is some early evidence that cash transfers to poor households reduce children's illness in some countries.

When it comes to the big question of how health affects economic development and vice versa, researchers have tried to find econometric strategies to try to identify causal impacts. One way is to see whether periods of rapid income growth are followed by improvements in health outcomes in countries. For example, we can calculate changes in income (that is, income growth) over a given period and changes in mortality rates over a following period for a sample of countries, then test whether one explains the other. This is called a "difference in difference" approach. We can also find instruments that explain income growth but arguably do not directly affect health except through income.

Two World Bank economists, Lant Pritchett and Lawrence Summers, used both these strategies to get an estimate of how much income affects child mortality.[14] One of the instruments they employ is the ratio of countries' investment to GDP. They find that this variable significantly explains income growth. And when they use it as an instrument for income growth, they find that income growth significantly decreases child mortality. In chapter 8 we'll see how two other economists, Daron Acemoglu and James Robinson, considered the opposite direction of causation, arguing that mortality resulting from malaria in colonial settlements affected countries' economic performance in the very long term.

In chapter 2 we learned that natural experiments can offer a way to identify impacts. If a health shock strikes some people but not others— or some people more than others—we might be able to compare people's economic outcomes later in time and gain insights into how health affects incomes. That's what two teams of development and health economists did, using China's great famine to evaluate the long-term impacts of malnourishment in utero on people's economic outcomes (see sidebar 6.7). Their findings underline the importance of nutrition in shaping economic outcomes in the long run.

SEN'S "CAPABILITIES APPROACH" AND "DEVELOPMENT AS FREEDOM"

We started this chapter with a hat tip to Amartya Sen, whose work inspired the creation of the HDI and now three generations of development economists. Sen worried about development economists' "overarching preoccupation with the growth of real income per capita."[15] In the 1980s, he and several collaborators proposed an alternative framework for understanding development in distinctly human terms—a framework that has come to be known as the "capabilities approach." We alluded to this framework at the beginning of this chapter. To conclude the chapter, we describe the capabilities approach in greater detail and evaluate how well the HDI captures its essence.

Sen's framework has three key elements. *Functionings* are the *actual* "beings and doings" of life, what a particular individual chooses to do with her life. *Capabilities* are the *possible* "beings and doings" of life,

Sidebar 6.7   The Long-Term Effects of Famine

Documenting the long-term effects of famine is challenging because it requires tracking individuals over long periods of time. This has not deterred development and health economists from teaming up to test how much of an impact childhood malnutrition has on adult outcomes in poor countries, though.

China's Great Leap Forward policies (1958–1961), including the abolition of land ownership and diversion of peasant labor to industry, created the worst famine in history: between 16.5 and 30 million people perished. What human capital legacy did the famine—and the ill-designed policies that caused it—leave behind?

One study tested the effect of being exposed to the famine in utero on people's economic and health outcomes. The famine was widespread, and it was not random. However, whether or not an individual happened to be in her mother's womb at the time of the famine, one could argue, was random. The researchers followed cohorts of children born during the famine (1956–1964) into their adulthood, using data from the 2000 Chinese population census.

The results show that there are long-term economic and health consequences when mothers are exposed to famine. Males exposed to famine in utero were significantly more likely to be illiterate, less likely to work, and less likely to be married four decades later. Females were also more likely to be illiterate and less likely to work, and they tended to marry men with less education. Fetal exposure to famine also substantially reduced the sex ratio; males are more vulnerable to maternal malnutrition, so fewer males survived.

The adverse impacts of famine did not end with the generation exposed in utero. The authors uncovered what they call an "echo effect" of the famine on the *next* generation. Women who had been exposed to famine in utero, once they became mothers, were more likely to give birth to daughters.

In Zimbabwe, three development economists used a more direct approach. They followed siblings who faced different civil war and drought shocks that led to different nutritional outcomes during their preschool years. Children who, because of these shocks, had lower height-for-age as preschoolers also had lower height as young adults, and they completed fewer years of school. If preschool Zimbabwe children in this study had had the same stature as an average developed-country child, they would have been 3.4 centimeters taller as adolescents, completed an additional 0.85 grades of school, and started school six months earlier.

Maternal malnutrition is a major problem throughout the developing world. These studies provide insights into some of the long-term consequences not only of famine, but of maternal malnutrition in general.

Yuyu Chen and Li-An Zhou, "The Long-Term Health and Economic Consequences of the 1959–1961 Famine in China," *Journal of Health Economics* 26, no. 4 (2007):659–81.

Harold Alderman, John Hoddinott, and Bill Kinsey, "Long Term Consequences of Early Childhood Malnutrition," *Oxford Economic Papers* 58, no. 3 (2006):450–47.

everything an individual realistically could choose to do with her life. *Agency* is an individual's *freedom to choose* what to be or to do according to what she considers to be meaningful or valuable in life. True development enriches lives by building agency and expanding capabilities so that individuals can be and do what they want to be and do. Clearly, income can only be a means to an end in this approach.

The difference between voluntary and involuntary fasting illustrates this approach. A person who fasts (skips meals) because he has no food is obviously in very different circumstances from those of a person who fasts because of a deeply held personal conviction. Many religions encourage adherents to fast periodically for spiritual or religious purposes. Protesters often use hunger strikes to achieve social or political objectives. When fasting is a choice—an expression of a person's agency—we see it as empowering and enriching. But when fasting is imposed by one's circumstances, we rightly see it as degrading, deplorable, and disturbing.

Sen's framework sees freedom as being both instrumentally and inherently valuable. If you only cared about having greater freedom because it allowed you to be or do more (because it expanded your functionings), there would be little need for capabilities and agency in the framework. But freedom is valuable in and of itself, too. A bit of introspection will surely confirm to you that having greater freedom just plain feels good. Having options and being empowered to choose among those options based on what you think makes life meaningful feels good, because freedom is inherently valuable.

In 1996 and 1997, Amartya Sen gave a series of lectures at the World Bank on "development as freedom" and described this perspective on development:

Viewing development in terms of expanding substantive freedoms directs attention to the ends that make development important, rather than merely to some of the means that, inter alia, play a prominent part in the process . . . Development requires the removal of major sources of unfreedom: poverty as well as tyranny, poor economic opportunities as well as systematic social deprivation, neglect of public facilities as well as intolerance or overactivity of repressive states. . . . Freedom is central to the process of development for two distinct reasons. (1) The evaluative reason: assessment of progress has to be done primarily in terms of whether the freedoms that people have are enhanced. (2) The effectiveness reason: achievement of development is thoroughly dependent on the free agency of people.[16]

Now let's return to the HDI. With Sen's broader thinking about development as freedom in mind, can you see why he initially resisted the idea of a crude index composed of only income, life expectancy, and educational outcomes? Although the HDI certainly sacrifices some important dimensions of human development, it has the virtue of being easy to communicate, which in large part explains how it has successfully shaped the international development dialogue since 1990. And because so many other dimensions of human empowerment and freedom are correlated with the HDI, the index seems to strike about the right balance between simplicity and usefulness.

As we'll see in the next chapter, a good model—like a good index—must strike a balance between simplicity and usefulness. An index like the HDI necessarily glosses over some of the richness of reality, but it does so to achieve a clear purpose. The same holds for model building.

www.rebeltext.org/development/qr6.html
Learn more about human development by
exploring multimedia resources while you read.

APPENDIX

A Cost-Benefit Analysis of Getting a Secondary Education

These are the critical numbers we need in order to perform our cost-benefit analysis of getting a secondary education in rural Lesotho:

Opportunity costs: According to our data, average wages for kids fifteen and under are 487 maloti for boys and 279 for girls.

Direct schooling costs: To keep things simple, we assume these are zero. In real life, parents may have to pay costs of school supplies, books, and uniforms to attend public schools, so our assumption here may give an overly optimistic cost-benefit result.

Returns to schooling: The Mincer model we estimated showed expected returns to an additional year of schooling equal to 9.8% for boys and 18.6% for girls.

Wages without secondary schooling: Average wages for adults (eighteen and older) with primary schooling (5–6 years) are 549 for males and 307 for females. These, along with the percentage returns to schooling, permit us to estimate the gains from an additional year of schooling as 9.8% * 549 for boys and 18.6% * 307 for girls.

The discount rate: We use the real interest rate for Lesotho, which according to the World Bank was 4.4% in 2012. If poor people discount the future more heavily than this, our analysis will be overly optimistic about the benefits of going to secondary school.

Now we are ready to do our cost-benefit analysis of completing secondary school. We will do this separately for boys and girls, since they have different opportunity costs as well as different expected returns from going to school. In the abbreviated table 6.A1, the analysis for boys is in columns B–E, and for girls, columns B′–E′. (This table is also available as an Excel file in an online appendix for this chapter. You can use it to explore how sensitive the results of this cost-benefit analysis are to the interest rate, secondary schooling costs, and the economic returns to schooling.)

During the first three years, parents incur the opportunity cost of sending their kids to school in the form of lost children's wages. We calculate the present value (PV) of these lost wages by dividing them by $(1 + i)^{t-1}$, where i is the discount rate and t is the year number. So the PV of the year 1 opportunity cost of sending a boy to secondary school is $487/(1+.044)^{1-1} = 487$, whereas in year 2 it is $487/(1+.044)^{2-1} = 467$, and in year 3 it is 447. For girls, the discounted opportunity costs are 279, 267, and 256, respectively, over the first three years. The discounted opportunity costs appear in columns B and B′.

The discounted wage gains from the three years of secondary schooling appear in columns C and C′ of the table. For a male the gain is $142/(1+.044)^{4-1} = 125$ in year 4, the first year out of secondary school. It is $142/(1+.044)^{5-1} = 120$ in year 5, and so on. The discounted future wage gains for girls are 191, 183, 176, and so on.

Columns D and D′ report the net benefit of going to secondary school each year, or the difference between that year's benefit and cost. You can see that these are all negative (equal to the discounted opportunity cost) for the years the child is enrolled in secondary school and assumed not to work. They turn positive, equal to the PV of the wage gain from secondary schooling, after that.

To create figure 6.3, we need to keep a running account of the discounted costs and benefits year by year. Columns E and E′ report this. For boys, the cumulative gain from three years of secondary school is negative until year 18, fifteen years after secondary school graduation. For girls it turns positive by year 8.

TABLE 6A.1   RESULTS OF A COST-BENEFIT ANALYSIS OF SECONDARY SCHOOLING IN LESOTHO

	Males				Females			
Year (A)	Opportu- nity Cost (B)	Benefit (C)	Benefit Minus Cost (D)	Cumula- tive Net Benefit (E)	Opportu- nity Cost (B')	Benefit (C')	Benefit Minus Cost (D')	Cumulative Net Benefit (E')
1	487	0	−487	−487	279	0	−279	−279
2	467	0	−467	−954	267	0	−267	−546
3	447	0	−447	−1,401	256	0	−256	−802
4	0	125	125	−1,276	0	191	191	−611
5	0	120	120	−1,157	0	183	183	−428
6	0	114	114	−1,042	0	176	176	−252
7	0	110	110	−932	0	168	168	−84
8	0	105	105	−827	0	161	161	77
9	0	101	101	−727	0	154	154	232
10	0	96	96	−630	0	148	148	379
11	0	92	92	−538	0	142	142	521
12	0	88	88	−450	0	136	136	657
13	0	85	85	−365	0	130	130	787
14	0	81	81	−284	0	124	124	911
15	0	78	78	−206	0	119	119	1,030
16	0	74	74	−132	0	114	114	1,144
17	0	71	71	−61	0	109	109	1,254
18	0	68	68	8	0	105	105	1,359
40	0	26	26	958	0	41	41	2,816

We can sum up the net benefits over a child's working life to see whether secondary schooling is worthwhile. The sum of columns D and D' is the Net Present Value (NPV) of completing the three years of secondary school. (It is also the bottom number in the running total in columns E and E'.) If it is positive, secondary schooling passes the cost-benefit test, and if it is negative, it does not. The cost-benefit analysis comes out favorable for both boys and girls. The NPV for boys is 958 maloti. For girls, it is 2,816.

7

Growth

If we could trace the history of modern economic thought to a single question, it would almost certainly be the one implied by Adam Smith in the title of his magnum opus, *An Inquiry into the Nature and Causes of the Wealth of Nations*. The Industrial Revolution brought profound changes to production systems and lifestyles that have created ever-growing disparities between rich and poor countries. Obviously, since these countries were essentially the same not so many centuries ago, this gap is explained by rich countries growing faster than poor countries over many, many years. But how did they do it? In the words of Nobel laureate economist Robert Lucas (p. 5), "The consequences for human welfare involved in questions like these are simply staggering: once one starts to think about them, it is hard to think about anything else."[1] This chapter explores the models economists use to identify and understand the determinants of economic growth. Since the drive to find these determinants is commonly motivated by the desire to improve human welfare, growth models are often used as the basis for policy action—and debates about policy action can get contentious and controversial!

ESSENTIALS

- Value and use of models
- Production functions
- Neoclassical (Solow) growth model
- Regression
- Innovation and technology adoption
- Spillovers and agglomeration effects
- "Big push" interventions
- "Planners vs. searchers"
- Endogenous growth theory
- Incentives

The average per capita GDP in 2000 was $35,082 in the United States, $450 in India, and $256 in Uganda. Where do such vast differences in economic performance come from? For one thing, workers were a lot more productive in the United States than in India, and they were more productive in India than in Uganda. The average worker in the United States produced $70,102 of income (GDP) in 2000. By contrast, the average worker in India produced $1,211, and in Uganda, $611.

But why was worker productivity so different? For one thing, US workers had a lot more capital to work with (i.e., equipment, machinery, tools, etc.) than Indian workers, and Indian workers had a lot more than Ugandan workers. The average US worker had about $146,640 worth of capital to work with. The average worker in India had $6,848, and in Uganda, $536.[2] There is no question that capital makes workers more productive.

Does this mean that capital is the key to development?

As we saw in chapter 1, many early development economists thought so. They saw investment in capital as the key to growth. We have seen that income is an important ingredient in what we think of as economic development (though not the only one). Without economic growth, making real development progress and improving household outcomes becomes very difficult. If countries could accumulate capital through investments in equipment and machinery that enhance productivity— investments that are perhaps partly provided by big infusions of international aid—would their economies grow faster?

In this chapter, we'll learn what the best-known growth economist, Nobel laureate Robert Solow, thinks. ("No.") We'll explore the basics of neoclassical growth theory, which Solow pioneered in the 1950s; the relatively recent field of endogenous growth; and theoretical versus empirical growth models. The big questions we want to answer here are these: "What makes economic growth happen?" and "Why do some countries grow so much faster than others?"

Lurking behind these questions is another, perhaps bigger one. If the economic returns to capital are as high as they seem based on comparisons of places like the US, India, and Uganda, why don't poor countries with so much opportunity to grow attract investors in droves? Why do some economies invest so much in capital, while others invest so little?

WHAT A DIFFERENCE A CENTURY MAKES

Imagine a country where the life expectancy at birth is 47.8 years. Out of every 1,000 babies born, 150 die within their first year of life. Ten percent of the population is completely illiterate, and only 7% ever graduate from high school. One-third of homes have running water, 15% have flush toilets, and only 3% are lit by electricity. Women comprise only 18% of the paid workforce. Flu and pneumonia are common causes of death. The average per capita income is around $18.15 per day.

Is this country real? It might strike you as bizarre. For one thing, a per capita income of $18.15 per day (about like Egypt's) is high for a country with such poor human development outcomes.

It is real, though—or more accurately, was. The country described above is the United States in the year 1900.[3]

What happened during the twenty-first century that catapulted the US economy into a completely different realm? As Robert Lucas pointed out, the vast consequences of questions like this can make them irresistible. Providing answers to them is the great challenge of modern growth theory.

THE NEOCLASSICAL GROWTH MODEL

You may have noticed that economists often rely on models to help them make sense of how markets work, how individuals make decisions, and how markets and people interact to create outcomes that shape society. Of course, models are fundamental to just about any human endeavor. Trying to recognize and interpret patterns in order to make sense of the world is a fundamental human impulse. Most of the time, the resulting models remain loose mental constructs. When they are formalized, however, models can provide a very useful platform for exploring and understanding the complexity of our world.

Many economic models look and feel like models from the hard sciences, especially physics. Yet, because economics is a social science, things are inherently less precise than in physics. Thus, economic models cannot predict the future the way a model of gravity can predict an object's terminal velocity. They can, however, help us understand which factors shape future outcomes and why.

As we explore growth models in this chapter, beginning with the neoclassical growth model, keep in mind that, as development economists (like economists generally), we use models like these to generate insights about complex patterns in the world. Like the famous statistician George Box, we acknowledge that "essentially, all models are wrong, but some are useful."[4] The usefulness of models of economic growth ultimately hinges on whether they point us to effective policy tools to stimulate growth.

The Production Function

To analyze why incomes grow over time, we need a model of how income gets "produced." In other words, we need an *income production function*. Income production functions take many forms and are estimated on different levels, from countries to households. Here we'll learn about the aggregate growth model, which is what most people think about when they hear the word "growth." First, though, let's go out to the farm and learn what a production function is.

A *production function* in economics summarizes the technological relationship between inputs and outputs. You can think of it as taking different combinations of inputs and determining the maximum level of output attainable with those inputs. Alternatively, you can think of it as telling us the minimum combinations of inputs required to produce a given level of output.

Figure 7.1 shows a simple production function for a firm (e.g., a farm) that produces an output, Q (say, kilograms of corn), using only two inputs: days of labor (L) and hectares of land (K). That is, the production function illustrated in the figure looks like this: $Q = F(L,K)$. The function itself $(F(\cdot))$ represents the technology that turns inputs into output. To make things even simpler, let's assume land is fixed; the farmer cannot change how much land she plants in corn, at least not in the short run. The assumption of fixed land (or other capital) is often reasonable; for example, most crops have to be planted at a certain time of year, and once you plant the crop, you're stuck with it until after the harvest. We can show land is fixed by putting a bar over the K.

This figure illustrates two important things about production functions. First, the production function slopes upward, indicating that it is increasing in the inputs. Land is fixed, but you can see that as labor increases, so does output. The slope at any point (say, at L' days of labor) gives the change in output from a small change in the input, or the marginal product of the input (here, the marginal product of labor, or MP_L). If you're math-minded, you'll recognize this as the derivative of output with respect to the input, and it's positive.

The other important thing to notice is that the marginal product of labor is not the same for all input levels; it decreases as the amount of

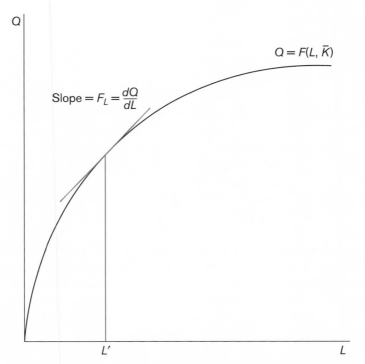

Q

$$\text{Slope} = F_L = \frac{dQ}{dL}$$

$Q = F(L, \bar{K})$

L'   L

FIGURE 7.1. The firm's output (Q) increases with labor inputs (L) but at a decreasing rate.

labor increases. In math speak, this is a *concave* function: join any two points along the curve with a line segment, and all the combinations of labor and income on the segment will be feasible—they will lie below the curve. Think of a fixed plot of land, say, one hectare large. Without any labor, you cannot produce anything on it. Add a little labor, and you start getting output; you can till the land, plant seeds, add fertilizer, weed, and harvest. After a point, though, each hour of labor you add to this single hectare of land will get you less of an increase in output than the previous hour of labor you added. Geometrically, the slope gets flatter as we move out to the right in our diagram. We call this *decreasing marginal returns* to inputs. (Mathematically speaking, the second derivative is negative.) Off to the right of our picture the curve flattens out completely. At that point, the MP_L is zero. Beyond it, the MP_L could even become negative: more labor, less output (as when too many workers get into each other's way or trample the crops).

An Aggregate Production Function

Imagine adding up the value of everything produced in the whole economy (that is, the GDP), as well as all the labor and capital used to produce it. This gives you an *aggregate production function*. Just as farms, industries, and service firms take labor, capital, and other inputs to produce a quantity of output (tons of corn, millions of motherboards, or billions of Facebook messages), so entire economies combine their labor and capital to produce a GDP. Aggregate production functions are used to describe the relationship between inputs and income in national economies. Neoclassical growth theory is all about how aggregate production grows over time, and where it will end up if a policy or other event (say, war or earthquake) shocks it in one direction or another.

We will use the simplest aggregate production function, which is the staple of the neoclassical growth model. It relates aggregate income (Y) to labor (L) and capital (K): $Y = F(L,K)$. Under certain conditions, you could increase all inputs by the same factor and output will increase by that factor. Double all inputs, and output will double. This is called "constant returns to scale" (CRS). (There are also *decreasing returns to scale* [DRS] and *increasing returns to scale* [IRS], but as in neoclassical growth theory, we'll assume CRS here.)

If there are CRS, we could multiply all the inputs by any number, for example $1/L$. Output would increase by a factor of $1/L$, so our aggregate production function would become $Y/L = F(L/L, K/L)$, or just $y = f(k)$, where y is the output-to-labor ratio (Y/L) and k is the capital-to-labor ratio (K/L). In an economy with constant returns to scale, output per worker depends on capital per worker. We could do the same thing to the production function of our individual farm, above, as long as it also exhibits CRS. (We'll revisit farm production functions in chapter 9, "Agriculture.")

It's important to keep the distinction between returns to scale and returns to one of the factors of production clear. When we talk about returns to scale, we're talking about increasing *all* of the inputs by the same multiple, for example, doubling both labor and capital in our simple two-input case. Even if we have constant (or increasing) returns to scale, we typically have decreasing returns to any single input. Suppose doubling your labor and your capital allows you to double your output. Then imagine doubling only your labor: without also increasing your capital, you won't be able to double your output. It's like increasing the number of

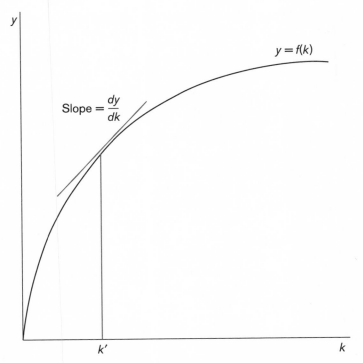

FIGURE 7.2. Aggregate production per worker *(y)* increases with capital per worker *(k)* but at a decreasing rate.

cooks in a crowded kitchen; eventually they won't have enough pots and pans to go around and they'll start getting in each other's way.

We can draw a picture of an aggregate production function (figure 7.2). Given the two properties of production functions we discussed earlier (output is increasing in inputs, but at a decreasing rate), this aggregate production function will look a lot like the individual firm's production function shown in figure 7.1.

Figure 7.2 shows output per worker increasing with capital per worker. At any point along the curve, the slope is the change in output per worker that results from a small increase in the amount of capital available per worker in the economy. More capital/worker means more output/worker. But as was the case for an individual farm, for the whole economy, there are diminishing marginal returns to *k*, that is, to capital/worker.

You can see how important capital is in this model. With no capital per worker, there's no GDP! Since neoclassical growth models share the basic structure we've laid out thus far, the factors that explain the amount of capital per worker in an economy become the main focus of these models. These factors include the following:

- the amount of investment per worker, which is what creates capital
- the population growth rate, which adds workers and dilutes the amount of capital per worker
- the capital depreciation rate (how quickly capital wears out during the production process), which steadily erodes the capital stock and implies that economies have to keep investing in new capital just to stay in the same place—as if they were on a treadmill of sorts

We need a way to represent these factors in our model. Investment comes from savings. In national accounting, total investment always equals total savings (which could include some foreign savings or investment, but let's set that aside for now). Let's use s to represent the savings rate in the economy. Thus, for every dollar/worker that gets created in the economy, $\$s$ gets saved and turns into investment, or capital. Savings per worker, then, is just $s * y$. We can show savings per worker on our graph, as in figure 7.3.

Next we have to add the population growth rate and the rate of depreciation. Let's call the population growth rate n, and the rate of depreciation d. Suppose we start the year with 2,000 units of capital and 20 workers, so $k = 2000/20 = 100$ units of capital per worker. By the end of the year, 200 units wear out ($d = .10$). That leaves a total of 1,800 units of capital, or 90 per worker. Meanwhile, the labor force grows by one worker ($n = .05$), so now there are 21 workers sharing 90 units of capital. Depreciation of capital and growth of the workforce thus results in the capital/worker ratio falling to 85.7 (1800/21).

The economy will need a minimum of $(n + d)k$ in savings per worker just to stay in the same place. We can put this in our graph, too. It's a straight line with a slope equal to $(n + d)$, as shown in figure 7.4.

Nothing catches an economist's eye like two lines crossing in a graph. You can see a crossover at point A, where the savings per worker *(sy)* just equals what's needed to keep the capital/worker ratio stable $((n + d)k)$. This point, at the capital/labor ratio of k^*, is the economy's steady state. When the economy is at this point, output per worker is constant over time.

To the left of the steady state point, savings *exceeds* what is needed to keep up with depreciation and labor force growth (the savings line *sy*

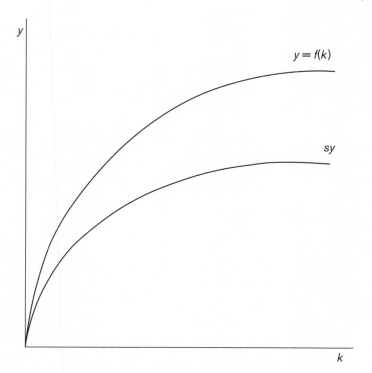

FIGURE 7.3. Savings per worker is output per worker times the savings rate, s. Since the savings rate is less than 1, the sy curve lies below the y curve.

is above $(n + d)k$), so the capital per worker will increase until we get to k^*. To the right of the steady state, there is not enough savings to keep up with depreciation and labor-force growth, so the capital per worker will fall back to k^*.

In short, once the economy is at k^*, there is no reason for it to go anywhere else in this simple model, and if something throws the economy off of k^*, the economic forces at work in our diagram will always bring it back to the steady state. This is the famous Solow growth model, named after its cofounder, the Nobel laureate Robert Solow. (It is also called the Solow-Swan model after T. W. Swan, who independently came up with a similar model at the same time.)

The big question we want to take on now—indeed the question that became an obsession to Robert Lucas—is how to make growth happen. What does the Solow model have to say about this?

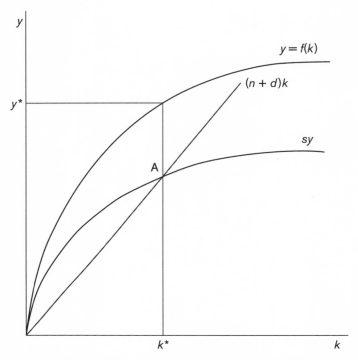

FIGURE 7.4. To the left of point A, savings per worker exceeds what is needed to keep up with labor force growth *(n)* and depreciation *(d)*, so capital per worker increases. The opposite is true to the right of A. Thus, A is the steady-state income and capital per worker in the economy.

At the steady state in our picture the economy is growing just enough to keep up with depreciation and labor force growth. Income per worker is y^*. How can we make it increase?

One thing we can try is raising the savings rate, say, from s to s'. This pivots the savings-per-worker curve upward, from sy to $s'y$, as in figure 7.5.

At the existing capital-worker ratio k^*, the amount of savings in the economy jumps from point A to point B. Point B is not a steady state, though, because savings is higher than what is needed to keep up with depreciation and labor force growth. Capital per worker thus goes up, and with it, so does income per worker. The economy moves up the $s'y$ curve to point C. The new capital-labor ratio is k'^*, and output per worker is now y'^*.

Notice that increases in the labor force growth rate or depreciation rate have the opposite effect. If n or d goes up, say, to n'' or d'' (see figure 7.6),

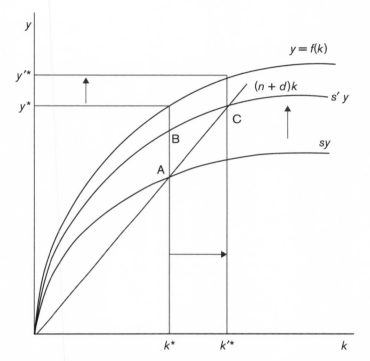

FIGURE 7.5. An increase in the savings rate leads the economy to a higher steady-state capital-labor ratio and income per worker.

the $(n + d)k$ line gets steeper. This shifts the steady state from point A to D, driving down both output and capital per worker. This does not mean that labor doesn't make the economy grow—it does. The aggregate production function is increasing in labor. But if the workforce is growing faster than total income, income *per worker* will decrease. It should come as no surprise that income per worker is lower in countries where the workforce is growing rapidly.

Technological Change in the Solow Model

We opened the chapter with a snapshot of the US in 1900 to contrast how much life has changed in just over a century. What one word best explains these dramatic changes? Our pick: technology. Since technology clearly matters in practice, it must show up somewhere in growth models. What does technology change do to our Solow diagram?

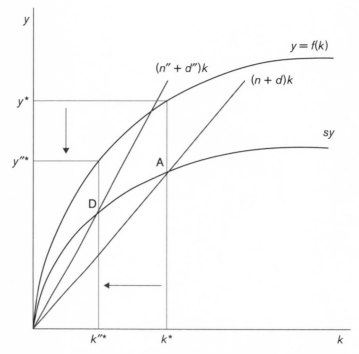

FIGURE 7.6. An increase in the labor-force growth or depreciation rate takes the economy to a lower steady-state income and capital per worker.

Assume as before that, at any point in time, there are diminishing marginal returns to capital per worker, so the basic shape of the *y* and *sy* curves does not change. However, technological change and the accumulation of human capital increase productivity, shifting the income per worker *(y)* curve upward over time. Assuming a constant savings rate, the *sy* curve follows the *y* curve upward, as illustrated in figure 7.7. The figure shows how the economy's steady state shifts up toward the northeast, raising both *k* and *y* as the productivity of labor and capital in the economy increases.

TESTING THE NEOCLASSICAL GROWTH MODEL: FROM THEORY TO EMPIRICS

As we warned earlier, this model—like all models—is essentially wrong because it abstracts from the richness of the real world. The right question

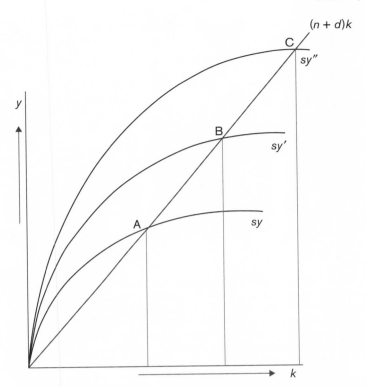

FIGURE 7.7. As productivity in the economy increases, the steady-state capital and output per worker rise from point A to B to C.

to ask is whether it is useful. A useful growth model should provide insights that are tough to see without the model, and it should hold up well enough to real-world tests that these insights might inspire sensible action.

The Solow model does offer some important insights. In order to grow, countries need both capital and labor. A poor, labor-abundant country is unlikely to increase its income per capita without increasing its capital per worker. "Capital" includes physical capital (e.g., machines) as well as human capital (education and skills). And don't forget public capital like roads, irrigation, and the Internet. These are known as *public goods* because they typically benefit everyone. Governments usually have to make investments in public goods, because private firms cannot capture and profit from many of their benefits; thus, left to the private sector, there will not be enough investment in them.

If you look around the world, you'll find that the major success stories, like the Asian Tigers and now China, involved substantial investments

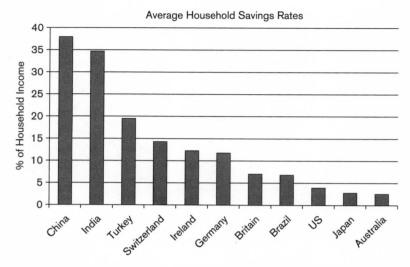

FIGURE 7.8. Average household savings rates vary widely across countries. Source: "Savers and Spenders: How Household Savings Stack Up in Asia, the West, and Latin America," *BloombergBusinessweek* (June 10, 2010; www .businessweek.com/magazine/content/10_25/b4183010451928.htm; compiled from data provided by OECD, World Bank, Standard Chartered, Turkish State Planning Office, and British Office for National Statistics).

providing workers with capital that they did not have before. These investments were financed, at least in part, by domestic savings. Savings rates vary widely across countries, as shown in figure 7.8. China, one of the fastest-growing economies in the world, also has a very high savings rate: in 2010, households in China saved an average of 38 cents out of every dollar of income they received!

Increases in capital per worker lead to higher wages, because with more capital, workers produce more value, and employers will not pay a worker a wage that exceeds the value she produces. It's telling that real wages are rising so fast in China (about 10% a year) that they are nearly as high as Mexico's now, as you can see in figure 7.9.

Where population is growing rapidly, more investment is needed just to keep pace; otherwise, income per worker may stagnate or even decline. You can't deny that labor is a key input into the production of GDP, but without capital, there are diminishing returns to labor in the production process. It's no surprise that high-population-growth countries tend to have low per capita incomes.

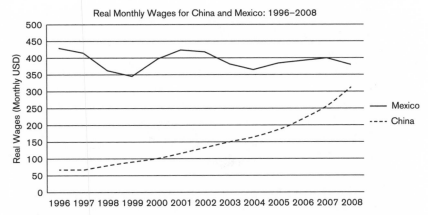

FIGURE 7.9. Real monthly wages in China and Mexico converged between 1996 and 2008. Source: Compiled from the International Labor Office (ILO), *International Labor Statistics* (http://laborsta.ilo.org/).

Now what about real-world tests of the neoclassical growth model? We test models by taking their predictions and seeing whether they hold up in the real world. A number of key predictions come out of the Solow model.

One prediction is that when major shocks like war or natural disasters strike, economies will return to their steady state. Rich country economies tend to bounce back quickly from natural disasters. Post–World War II Europe is a good example (with a little help from the Marshall Plan). There is some evidence that this is true even in poor developing countries (see sidebar 7.1). However, the long-term impact of disaster is challenging to identify, the data to do this are hard to come by, and largely because of this it is a little-researched area in development economics. Recovering from disaster in other ways (e.g., psychologically) is an entirely different matter.

Other predictions of the Solow growth model do not hold up so well. For example, look at the aggregate production function again. It implies that growth in aggregate income can be explained by growth in labor and growth in capital. In the real world, do changes in labor and capital explain all or most of the differences in economic growth we see among countries and in the same countries over time?

The empirical growth economist Xavier Sala-i-Martin says no. By running nearly 2 million econometric regressions, he found twenty-two different variables that appear to be significant in explaining differences in income growth among countries! These variables include capital

Sidebar 7.1 The Growth Legacy of the Vietnam War

The Vietnam War involved the heaviest aerial bombardment of any war in human history. War destroys capital. Neoclassical growth theory predicts that when exogenous events destroy physical and human capital, countries will recover, with no long-term impact on their steady-state equilibrium. Of course, the horrors of war include more than the destruction of capital. War impacts psychology, technology, social institutions, and other outcomes in complex and possibly long-term ways.

A unique study by Edward Miguel and Gérard Roland tested the long-term impact of US bombing in Vietnam. The authors used actual US military data on bombing intensities in different districts in Vietnam. (The data were provided by the Vietnam Veterans of America Foundation and the Vietnam Ministry of Defense Technology Center for Bomb and Mine Disposal.) The study tested whether districts that were more heavily bombed during the war had higher poverty rates, lower consumption, poorer infrastructure, more illiteracy, or lower population densities three decades later.

The econometric results showed no significant difference in growth outcomes between heavily bombed districts and the country's other districts. The legacy of war did not prevent Vietnam from recovering and experiencing rapid economic growth. Such findings are consistent with a return to the steady state following a major economic shock, as predicted by the neoclassical growth model. The authors warn, however, that Vietnam may have unique features that help explain its postwar economic success, and they advise caution in generalizing their results to other countries.

Edward Miguel and Gérard Roland, "The Long-Run Impact of Bombing Vietnam," *Journal of Development Economics* 96, no. 1 (September 2011):1–15.

investment, but they also include a diverse list of other things, from openness to trade to political rights, black markets, colonial legacy, war, and religion (see sidebar 7.2).

Another key prediction of neoclassical growth models is that the income levels of poor countries will tend to catch up, or *converge*, with the income levels of rich countries over time. For this to happen, poor countries would have to be growing faster than rich ones. Are they?

In figure 7.11, we plot countries' annual change in per capita GNI between 1990 and 2010 (vertical axis) against their initial (1990) per

Sidebar 7.2   The Man Who Ran 2 Million Regressions

Econometricians use real-world data to model relationships among variables and test key hypotheses that come out of their theories. For example, if some variable such as capital investment *(X)* increases income growth *(Y)*, we should be able to take data on these two variables, make a scatter plot, and fit a line (or curve) to the data, as in figure 7.10.

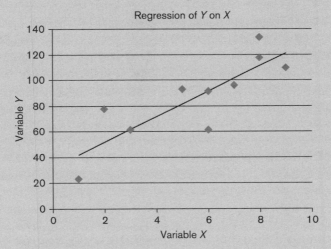

FIGURE 7.10. Illustration of a regression of variable *Y* on *X*; we can use the values of *X* to predict values of *Y*. *X* might be capital investment, and *Y* income growth.

Econometrics is about finding the best way to model relationships, which usually involve not just two but many variables. (You can learn about econometrics in *RebelText: Essentials of Econometrics* or any number of expensive econometrics textbooks.)

Empirical growth economists have found many variables that seem to correlate with countries' economic growth, but often correlations lose their statistical significance when new variables are included in the growth model.

Xavier Sala-i-Martin's big contribution was to come up with a way to estimate many different models, with every conceivable combination of variables, and find the variables that come out significant most often in explaining economic growth. Here's the list he came up with and the sign of the correlation between each variable and economic

(continued)

growth (you can learn more about these variables and how he measured them by reading his article, cited below):

Equipment investment (+)	Black-market premium (–)
Number of years open economy (+)	Primary exports in 1970 (–)
Fraction Confucian (+)	Degree of capitalism (+)
Rule of law (+)	War (–)
Fraction Muslim (+)	Non-equipment investment (+)
Political rights (–)	Absolute latitude (+)
Latin America (–)	Exchange-rate distortions (–)
Sub-Saharan Africa (–)	Fraction Protestant (–)
Civil liberties (–)	Fraction Buddhist (+)
Revolutions and coups (–)	Fraction Catholic (–)
Fraction of GDP in mining (+)	Spanish colony (–)

Xavier Sala-i-Martin, "I Just Ran Two Million Regressions," *American Economic Review* 87, no. 2 (May 1997):178–83.

capita income (horizontal axis). If the convergence hypothesis is
correct, the points in this graph should form a clear downward-sloping
line.

But that is not what the figure shows. Growth rates are all over the
place, especially for poor countries. An econometric regression of
1990–2010 growth against 1990 income shows no significant relationship between the two. There is, however, one important caveat to this
interpretation of the data. The graph in figure 7.11 uses countries as the
unit of analysis and therefore implicitly weights China and Chad
equally, even though China is more than one hundred times bigger in
population. If we resized the dots in this figure so they reflected the
population of the country they represent, your eye would likely pick up
a downward sloping tendency because the two biggest countries in the
world—China and India—were poor in 1990 and grew faster than the
average in the subsequent two decades.[5]

Although empirical growth studies focus on differences in economic
performance across countries, there are tremendous disparities in
income growth within countries, too. Almost every country in the world
has its "left-behind" regions, from western China to southern Mexico

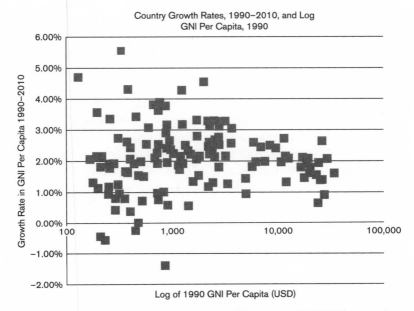

FIGURE 7.11. There is no significant relationship between initial (1900) per capita income and country growth rates between 1990 and 2010. Source: Constructed from World Bank data (http://data.worldbank.org/indicator/NY.GNP.PCAP.CD).

to, as remarkable as it sounds, California's Central Valley, the richest agricultural land in the world, where many towns have per capita incomes lower than Mexico's! Economists have not done much work on why we do not see economic convergence within countries. As in the case of intercountry comparisons, it seems that the facts are inconsistent with the predictions of neoclassical growth models.

REVISITING THE ASSUMPTIONS

Why doesn't the neoclassical growth model describe what actually happened in terms of economic growth? The model is internally consistent: the math behind it all works. If its predictions do not hold up, we have to look at the model's assumptions. Incidentally, this is another benefit of using models: they force us to make our assumptions transparent. Perhaps our model left out something that stimulates income growth in relatively high-income countries and/or impedes it in poor countries, thereby preventing convergence from happening.

To check on the model's assumptions, let's go back to where we started. We had an aggregate production function describing a CRS technology in which output depends on labor and capital (the $F(L,K)$ function). One assumption behind the convergence theory is that countries share the same or similar technologies. Another is that the production function does not change. If rich and poor countries have different production functions, or if technologies are changing in ways that favor rich countries, convergence may not occur. Still another assumption is CRS. What if the returns to scale are increasing instead of constant? Could it be that the more an economy grows, the faster it is able to grow in the future? Economies of scale describe a situation in which the larger the economy becomes, the more efficiently it is able to turn inputs into outputs.

Rich countries give us plenty of examples where "game-changing" technologies transformed the relationship between inputs and outputs and created enormous production and income gains. Between 1908 and 1915, the Ford Motor Company introduced the assembly line, which transformed the production function for making cars. Suddenly, the same labor and capital investment could turn out vastly greater numbers of cars, and mass production made automobiles available to middle-class consumers. In the 1980s and 1990s the Internet transformed all facets of production and consumption, laying the foundation for new production activities never even imagined before. New startups sprouted up where information and technology production already was concentrated, as in California's Silicon Valley.

Today, social networking is transforming the production landscape of the city of San Francisco. Where else in the world could a company like Facebook become a hundred-billion-dollar-plus company within eight years? Facebook produces social networking. Down the road sits Google, which produces searches. How much labor and capital are required to create an additional hundred messages or searches? An additional million? With a gross income of $38 billion in 2011, Google would rank eighty-third among countries, above Ghana and about the same as Costa Rica. (Apple would rank fifty-fifth, just ahead of Vietnam.) What country in the world has an income production function that looks anything at all like Google's?

It is indeed hard to argue that the technologies that combine inputs to create outputs are similar in rich and poor countries, or that they stay the same over time. Even though we can represent technological change as improvements in labor productivity in a Solow growth model, as we did above, this is clearly too constraining a depiction of technology and its impact. Thus, the far-reaching technological advances in high-income countries that have transformed lives and lifestyles do not really seem to have a place in the neoclassical growth model. This shortcoming was not lost on economists, who appreciate the depth of these technological transformations as much as anyone.

ENDOGENOUS GROWTH THEORY

A new generation of growth theory, endogenous growth theory, emphasizes technological change and "knowledge spillovers" while explaining differences in income growth over time and among different countries. The economist Paul Romer, who along with Robert Lucas helped found the new growth theory, describes what he did this way: "Robert Lucas . . . and I . . . cited the failure of cross-country convergence to motivate models of growth that drop the two central assumptions of the neoclassical model: that technological change is exogenous and that the same technological opportunities are available in all countries of the world." He goes on to argue: "Each unit of capital investment not only increases the stock of physical capital but also increases the level of the technology for all firms in the economy through knowledge spillovers" (p. 4).[6]

This is a good example of how new theories build upon old ones that do not stand up to tests against real-world data and events. In the Solow model, investment raises the stock of capital. In endogenous growth theory, it also raises the level of technology for all firms by creating knowledge spillovers, new ideas that make people more productive. Just think of the knowledge spillovers the Internet created! When there are significant knowledge spillovers, the whole production function changes when capital investment goes up. There are incentives for new activities to set up around existing ones, as in California's Silicon Valley, where Internet start-ups are drawn together like iron to magnets. The benefits of setting up where other successful firms already operate are called "economies of agglomeration."

Neoclassical and endogenous growth theory stress different determinants of economic development. In neoclassical theory, as Romer (p. 543) writes, "nations are poor because they lack valuable objects like factories, roads, and raw materials." In endogenous growth theory, "nations are poor because their citizens do not have access to the ideas that are used in industrial nations to generate economic value." Romer calls the first explanation an "object gap" and the second an "idea gap."[7] Closing the object gap requires savings and investment, as emphasized by the Solow model. Closing the idea gap requires focusing attention on "the patterns of interaction and communication between a developing country and the rest of the world." Some measures, including good macroeconomic policies, educational investments, and the development of well-functioning legal institutions, can help close both gaps. In Romer's view, closing both the idea and object gaps is the key to achieving the upward shifts in productivity illustrated in figure 7.7.

Endogenous growth theory builds upon neoclassical growth theory by incorporating new elements of economies of scale, technology change, and agglomeration. In the neoclassical growth model, an increase in capital per worker raises output per worker, which in turn generates savings that are used to invest in new capital. Endogenous growth theory adds a new "technology loop." New investments in capital, including human capital, lead to technological change and create spillover and agglomeration effects, which in turn stimulate new increases in incomes. This is the way most economists think about economic growth today. We've noted that countries with rapid population growth have lower growth in per capita incomes. Endogenous growth theory explains why this is true. Rapid labor force growth retards income growth because it creates *negative* spillover effects. When there is plenty of labor, producers don't have an incentive to invest in labor-saving innovations that can generate positive spillover effects in the economy. Without a good reason to invest in labor-saving capital and technologies, productivity per worker stagnates.

In practice, endogenous growth models have directly shaped development policy. Because these models hinge on spillovers and agglomeration effects, they suggest that location can really matter. Based on evidence of these location effects during the 1980s and 1990s—particularly in sectors that depend heavily on knowledge and technology—economist Michael Porter formalized the study of clusters and cluster development. This work has strongly influenced the way countries around the world and across the income spectrum approach economic development.

Silicon Valley, the standard example for illustrating how these locational effects play out, has come to epitomize cluster development. Pick just about any industry (e.g., food processing, biotechnology, call centers, etc.) and you can probably find a country with an explicit strategy to create the next "Silicon Valley" of it by providing infrastructure, other public goods, and industry-specific incentives to attract a critical mass of firms in the industry to a specific cluster. Once this critical mass is achieved, it is hoped that spillovers and agglomeration effects will kick in and catalyze sustained regional growth.

Some places in some countries have seen spectacular success using this strategy, including regions of Japan, South Korea, Singapore, China, and India. What about the rest? When we think "endogenous growth," will Zimbabwe ever come to mind? Is there any hope for countries that are not likely to become tech leaders anytime in the foreseeable future? Can they still manage to raise their living standards and be a productive part of the global economy?

GROWTH MODELS AND THE PRACTICE OF DEVELOPMENT

The growth models we have encountered throughout this chapter and the economists behind them hope ultimately to improve policy and development outcomes. How much of an influence have they actually had on development policy and on the practice of development? Has this influence led to improved outcomes? The first question is easier to address than the second for the reasons we described in chapter 2, but both are worth some attention as we conclude this chapter.

Many of the growth models we have described have had important effects on development policy and practice. In the decades after World War II, the neoclassical growth model directly shaped the emergence of international aid. In more recent decades, endogenous growth models and their basic insights have had enormous impact on national and regional development strategies. But the process of influencing policy and practice and evaluating this impact can be both controversial and contentious. To make this point, let's revisit economist Jeffrey Sachs, whom we met in chapter 4, now that we've had the benefit of studying growth models.

Go back and look at figure 4.2 in chapter 4, which describes Sachs's poverty trap model. It looks different from the curve in the Solow model. It is an S instead of a nice convex growth curve. To the left of point A in that figure, the curve is not convex. Join any two points along it with a line segment and you get outcomes that are not feasible (assets next year that are not possible given assets this year). Assets—and thus, income—don't grow to a favorable steady state unless we somehow get the country past point A in the poverty trap diagram. Big push growth models—which, in contrast to the models we covered in this chapter, are characterized by poverty traps—influenced development policy and practice before the 1980s, but they then fell out of favor because big push recommendations didn't seem to work. But Sachs is convinced that entire countries in sub-Saharan Africa are trapped, and he is the current champion of big push development approaches to help villages, regions, and entire countries escape these traps.

Specifically, with the right policies and carefully targeted aid interventions—including the diffusion of technologies from rich to poor countries—Sachs believes it is possible to eliminate extreme poverty within a couple of decades. He points to China, where the number of people living on less than $1.25 per day plummeted from 85% of the population in 1981 to 16% in 2005. To Sachs, a key to eradicating extreme poverty is to dramatically increase foreign aid, with a focus on providing subsistence farmers with improved seeds, irrigation, and fertilizer, as well as supporting microcredit and health programs.

To make the point, Sachs founded the United Nations Millennium Villages Project (MVP). The project started by setting up twelve "research villages" in ten African countries. Each village gets a flood of assistance equivalent to US$250 per villager per year based on the MVP motto: "No single intervention is enough . . . we must improve them all." Here's how the MVP website describes the project's goals:[8] "The Millennium Villages are based on a single powerful idea: impoverished villages can transform themselves and meet the Millennium Development Goals if they are empowered with proven, powerful, practical technologies. By investing in health, food production, education, access to clean water, and essential infrastructure, these community-led interventions will enable impoverished villages to escape extreme poverty, something that currently confines over one billion people worldwide."

William Easterly, an economics professor at New York University, disagrees vehemently with this orchestrated approach to development. Instead, he favors focusing on incentives and taking into account who has power and how they wield it. In his book *The Elusive Quest for Growth* he writes:[9]

> Many times over the past fifty years, we economists thought we had found the right answer to economic growth. It started with foreign aid to fill the gap between "necessary" investment and saving . . . [we] thought investment

in machines was the key to growth . . . education was a form of "human machinery" that would bring growth . . . population control . . . loans to induce countries to do policy reforms. Finally . . . debt forgiveness.

None of these elixirs has worked as promised, because not all the participants in the creation of economic growth had the right incentives. (p. 23)

Easterly argues that without the right incentives for people to work hard, be creative, and invent and adopt new technologies, development won't happen. He is a harsh critic of foreign aid, arguing that the billions of dollars spent on it have little to show for themselves and certainly have failed to foster sustainable growth. Aid, he argues, often operates from a "do-good" mentality instead of trying to create an environment in which markets provide people with the incentives needed to make growth happen.

Who's right, Sachs or Easterly? This question is much deeper than two bickering, high-profile economists. The question is deeply rooted in development economics and, indeed, in economics, political science and philosophy more broadly.

Let's first consider this question as it applies to the MVP. Has the project been successful? For a variety of reasons, it is remarkably hard to tell. The project was intentionally not designed as an RCT (see chapter 2) because, according to Sachs, the idea "that one can randomize villages like one randomizes individuals [is] extraordinarily misguided."[10] This makes it difficult for any analysis to provide conclusive evidence of success. We are instead left with a growing collection of mixed reports of limited success at best, the possibility of negative effects, and the standard implementation challenges that beset many big push attempts. Not surprisingly, Sachs is confident that his project is succeeding and that there will be enough empirical evidence in the coming years to convincingly document this success. For now, however, the jury is still out when it comes to the MVP.

More broadly, the debate about the MVP underscores two very different philosophical approaches, which Easterly characterizes as "planners vs. searchers." According to Easterly, big plans like the MVP are destined to fail—they always have been and they always will be. Among other reasons, planners fail because they lack sufficient knowledge about complex local processes and don't have enough skin in the game (i.e., they lack the right incentives). Searchers, on Easterly's other hand, are locals who have a potent combination of local knowledge and incentives. We will take up the "knowledge problem" that lurks behind the failure of many big plans in a future chapter. But let's take up his concern about incentives here.

Is getting the incentives right the key to making development happen, as Easterly argues? China's remarkable progress in combating poverty would be unimaginable without the far-reaching economic reforms that unleashed markets throughout the country and gave people powerful economic incentives that they did not have before. Yet, China also made major top-down investments in its rural areas, with new roads, communications, schools, marketing infrastructure, and productivity-increasing agricultural research—and hundreds of billions of dollars of foreign investment didn't hurt. It even had its own "model villages" along the way. Even with that, massive disparities persist. Shanghai is a developed global city, with per capita income similar to Italy's, while some rural areas in China still have per capita incomes on par with Ghana's, as illustrated brilliantly by Hans Rosling (to see the Rosling clip, use the QR code or URL at the end of this chapter).

In reality, most economies today rely on some degree of planning and government intervention, because markets that function well often require a supporting infrastructure (more on this in the next chapter). Where countries have successfully developed clusters of innovative firms, planning, public investment, and government action commonly have played a role in this success. But Easterly's concerns about big plans are certainly important to keep in mind: the history of international development is riddled with plans and projects that failed spectacularly owing precisely to the concerns he raises.

In a more recent book,[11] Easterly argues that the problem with big plans is not only that they rarely work but also that they tend to ignore or even trammel fundamental rights of the poor to govern their own lives. That is, they put states' rights ahead of individual freedom. The classic state-versus-market dichotomy cannot easily accommodate this critique, he claims, because many autocratic rulers embrace market reforms in order to stimulate growth, while simultaneously disregarding the political and economic freedom of individuals, especially the poor, who have little or no connection to the ruling elite. Instead of state-versus-market, Easterly proposes a continuum of total state power at one extreme and full individual freedom at the other. Framed in this way, it is easy to see just how deeply the roots of the planners-versus-searchers debate run—and how they ultimately tap into political and even philosophical positions.

With some introspection, you may be able to see the fingerprints of your own political views and your own philosophical leanings on the lens through which you perceive this debate in development practice.

www.rebeltext.org/development/qr7.html
Learn more about growth by exploring multimedia
resources while you read.

8

Institutions

Our lives are largely governed and heavily influenced by
things we don't often see or appreciate. As you learned in
elementary school, the persistent contractions of the involuntary muscles of your vital organs keep you alive. All of your
favorite electronic devices require mountains of complex code
to function. As you live your life—working, playing, studying, engaging in markets, and interacting with others—there
is a largely hidden set of norms and rules of engagement that
help you function. In this chapter, we explore the influence of
these "institutions" on economic development. Their
influence on developing countries and your own little world
is likely to be far greater than you have previously appreciated. And woe is the development economist who underestimates how fundamentally they shape the process of economic
development!

ESSENTIALS

- Corruption
- Institutions and transaction costs
- Incentives
- Dynamics
- Instrumental variables
- Entrepreneurship
- Innovation and technology adoption

If you have ever had to park your car on the streets of New York City,
you know how bewildering it can be. Driving in Manhattan is hard, but
parking in Manhattan can be almost impossible. In addition to being
exorbitantly expensive, it is complicated: there are layers of parking
laws that govern where you can park, when, and for how long.

Now, imagine that you were living and working in Manhattan and
were granted blanket immunity from parking citations. You could park

anywhere you wanted on any public street at any time for as long as you'd like. If you parked illegally, you could still get a parking ticket—but you could safely ignore any tickets you got because of your "immunity status." How many parking tickets do you think you'd rack up in your first month of immunity?

This kind of parking citation immunity may seem far-fetched (a bit like the remote control Travis always wanted that would turn any traffic light green), but until 2002 UN diplomats enjoyed precisely these parking privileges as part of their diplomatic immunity. Raymond Fisman and Edward Miguel spotted a cool research opportunity. Even though the NYC police issued parking citations to these diplomats, they didn't have to pay them, so cultural norms were the only thing keeping the diplomats in line. Because the NYC police kept a record of these violations, it was possible to know how many citations each diplomat received.

Which diplomats abused this privilege? Fisman and Miguel wanted to know whether the parking behavior of a country's diplomats reflected its "corruption culture" as measured by Transparency International's Corruption Perceptions Index, which ranks countries from least to most corrupt. In the 2013 rankings, for example, Denmark and New Zealand came in first place as least corrupt, the United States tied with Uruguay in 19th place, Mexico was 106th, Egypt 114th, and Somalia, North Korea, and Afghanistan were in a dead heat for most corrupt among the 175 countries evaluated.

Using this index, Fisman and Miguel discovered that diplomats from highly corrupt countries were much more likely to rack up parking citations than those from less corrupt countries.[1] In London, where diplomats also have immunity, one Egyptian diplomat, who drove a Mercedes C Class, racked up £10,000 in fines.[2] In contrast, if Swedish diplomats get tickets (they don't, according to Fisman and Miguel's data), their government requires them to pay the fine.[3]

Corruption is an example of what economists call "institutions." When you hear the word "institution" it might conjure up something more concrete than corruption. We call universities "institutions of higher learning." There are research institutions, banking institutions, philanthropic institutions. When we hear someone got institutionalized we often think of a mental health facility, or maybe a prison.

If you have taken a political science course, you know all about political institutions. Democracy is one: popular voting, parliamentary procedures, government checks and balances—these are institutions. You may even have bumped into institutions in a zoology course; animal behaviorists sometimes speak of animal institutions in the wild.

Anthropologists study many kinds of informal institutions. Here's an example: "Human social life is . . . guided by less formally codified institutions in the forms of symbolically mediated practices. These include, for instance, codes of dress, modes of greeting people, and symbolic communication systems such as spoken language. Central to both legally codified and uncodified modes of coordination are their normative quality . . . Social conventions and institutions do not specify what 'is done,' but rather what 'ought to be done.'"[4]

Institutions act like operating systems for societies and economies: they provide a platform of rules, conventions, norms, and processes that enable people to know what they can reasonably expect as outcomes from their decisions and interactions with others. They can have a profound effect on how individuals and groups make decisions, how their decisions affect others, and how all these decisions and interactions work together to create markets and the broader society. They often function in the background of our lives and go underappreciated—that is, until they get buggy and crash.

Now, let's return to corruption, which can be a pervasive institution because it creates norms and expectations about what are acceptable courses of action for oneself and for others. In this sense, the Egyptian diplomat was simply reflecting norms of conduct that he had internalized from "cutting his teeth" in a context where corruption was prevalent.

The institution of corruption bends the rules of the game in favor of some people and to the detriment of others—and ultimately to the disadvantage of society as a whole. It can create serious obstacles to economic development by diverting the energy of clever people into corrupt instead of productive pursuits, and by turning laws and law enforcement into opportunities for personal gain instead of broader social benefit. In their book *Economic Gangsters,* Fisman and Miguel write: "The concurrence of violence, corruption, and persistent poverty is so pervasive that it is almost impossible to separate the study of poverty from these other social ills" (p. 15).[5]

You might think that once people realize an institution is bad, they'll change it. After all, it's people who create institutions in the first place, right? In reality, though, it can be tough to change a norm that has become "institutionalized," even if it is not the best way to do things (see sidebar 8.1). In the case of corruption, for example, those who

Sidebar 8.1 Typing, Eating, and "Path Dependency"

One example of an institution is literally shaping what I am doing right now: typing this sentence. The layout of the keys on this keyboard conforms to the dominant QWERTY convention, which emerged in a curious manner. (If you haven't noticed, the first six letter keys on your keyboard are Q-W-E-R-T-Y.)

As the US Civil War was ending, a tinkerer in Milwaukee named Christopher Latham Sholes was inventing the first typewriter. An early prototype had a mechanical problem that Sholes solved by arranging the keys in a specific way. The problem was that the typebars (metal rods with letters mounted on them, which hit the paper when the corresponding key was pressed) would clash if two neighboring keys were pressed in rapid succession. Sholes realized he could remedy this problem by configuring the keyboard in a way that put a safe distance between letters that commonly appear in pairs (like *T* and *H*). With some help from a local educator, QWERTY was born. QWERTY keyboards were popular on early mechanical typewriters because they reduced clashing and thereby made for faster typing.

The original motivation for QWERTY keyboards has long since faded, but we stick to this convention. Overlapping generations (i.e., our kids) learn to type on such keyboards. Several "better" alternative configurations have been developed in the past decades, but none have dethroned QWERTY.

Here's a second, equally tangible example: how we eat. You may have noticed that Europeans and Americans follow different conventions. Most Europeans hold the fork in their left hand and knife in their right. Many Americans start this way, holding the knife in their right hand to cut, then switch the fork from left to right hand before eating a bite. When Ed was a kid growing up in California, he thought that was inefficient, so without even knowing how Europeans ate he taught himself to eat like one. Ed's American friends have made fun of him ever since!

Travis came across an explanation for this American "zig-zag." Archeologist James Deetz claimed that it stemmed from the belated arrival of the table fork in American colonies. Americans had to use a spoon instead of a fork to pin down food while cutting with a knife. Once a piece was cut, eating it required more dexterity with a spoon than a fork, so Americans took to switching the spoon from the left to the right hand between cutting and eating. What explains forks arriving late in the colonies? It seems that British mercantilist policies are to blame for table forks being a luxury in the colonies, long after they were ordinary utensils in Europe. Curiously, even though forks are

(continued)

now as common and cheap in America as in Europe, table manner differences persist.

There are conventions that govern both how we type and how we eat. They are a type of "institution" in the way economists use this term. They help us formulate expectations and make decisions—albeit not consequential decisions that can shape the growth of an economy. They are also prone to "path dependency." A particular set of conditions that prevail at a given moment in history may explain the emergence of an institution, but it can persist long after these conditions fade because conformity pays dividends in social and economic interaction. As Karl Marx observed, "Men make their own history, but not of their own free will . . . The tradition of the dead generations weighs like a nightmare on the minds of the living."

Paul A. David, "Clio and the Economics of QWERTY," *American Economic Review* 75, no. 2 (1985):332–37.

Travis J. Lybbert, "The Economic Roots of the American 'Zigzag': Knives, Forks, and British Mercantilism," *Economic Inquiry* 48, no. 3 (2010):810–15.

Karl Marx, "The Eighteenth Brumaire of Louis Bonaparte," in *Karl Marx: Surveys from Exile*, edited by David Fernbach (New York: Vintage Books), 146.

benefit most are typically powerful, and they resist changes that would erode their control and ability to profit from continued corruption.

In this chapter, we explore development economics as seen from the profound perspective of institutions. As we shall see, institutions matter enormously to development. Perhaps the most concise explanation about why institutions matter to the development process comes from a famous bank robber named Willie Sutton, who had a reputation of being a real gentleman during his robberies.[6] When a reporter asked him why he robbed banks, Sutton said, "Because that's where the money is." Institutions determine "where the money is" in a given society—they shape the incentives individuals and organizations face and can have profound effects on development outcomes.

HOW MUCH DO INSTITUTIONS MATTER TO DEVELOPMENT?

For centuries, many economists—beginning with Adam Smith—have appreciated how fundamentally institutions affect the way individuals and organizations interact in markets and how these interactions translate into economic performance. More recent insights from several economists, including four Nobel laureates (Ronald Coase, Douglass North, Elinor Ostrom, and Oliver Williamson), led to the emergence in the 1970s of "New Institutional Economics" as an influential field of study. The New Institutional Economics encompasses a broad range of topics. Several directly relate to contemporary development issues, including property rights, social norms, governance and transparency, corruption and rent seeking, enforcement of contracts, and transaction costs.

Institutions seem to be so fundamental to development that the success of just about any development policy, project, or intervention is shaped by them. Development economists broadly agree that institutions matter. But just how much they matter, compared with other potential factors, is a point of contention. It is difficult to settle by relying on empirical evidence because of the challenges described in chapter 2. Confounding factors and selection bias can undermine even careful attempts to estimate how much institutions *cause* economic growth—and therefore how much they explain about differences in development outcomes across different countries or time periods. Institutions shape economic development, but economic development can enable countries to invest in stronger institutions (like better law enforcement). It's a chicken-and-egg problem.

Take crime and corruption. They can undermine economic development; how can a country hope to eliminate poverty if government officials skim development assistance to Swiss bank accounts, or if the threat of theft—or worse, death—plagues the countryside? It's easy to imagine why crime keeps poor countries from developing. But poor countries also tend to have more crime. Poverty and weak legal institutions tend to go hand in hand. The nonprofit Transparency International found that in Liberia, with a per capita income of $1.16 per day, more than 95% of the people say their police are corrupt. In eight of the nine most corrupt nations, more than four out of five people say the police are corrupt.[7]

So do corruption and crime cause underdevelopment, or does underdevelopment cause corruption and crime? We dare you to design an RCT to answer this question! What about randomly sprinkling different districts or villages in a country with criminals or corrupt police officers and then measuring what happens to poverty?

Is isolating the impact of poverty on crime or corruption a Sisyphean task, then?[8] This empirical challenge has sparked vigorous debate among some of today's best economists and other social scientists.

Institutions Matter Big Time

Over the course of fifteen years of research, Daron Acemoglu (MIT) and James Robinson (Harvard) have wrestled with historical data on economic growth from around the world to try to understand what explains the patterns of economic development we see today (sidebar 8.2). They recently assembled much of this evidence into a book entitled *Why Nations Fail.*[9] As the title suggests, the authors do not shy away from claiming to know why some countries are rich and others are poor. They argue that differences in economic and political institutions are *the* dominant explanation for these patterns. There are several strands in this argument that are worth appreciating—strands that in our judgment qualify as essentials of development economics.

First, much of Acemoglu and Robinson's argument hangs on the distinction between "inclusive" and "extractive" institutions. Inclusive institutions begin with political systems that are pluralistic, protect individual rights, and create the conditions that reward innovation and entrepreneurship, including secure private property and competitive markets. In contrast, extractive institutions (as you might guess) are characterized by concentrated political power and economic institutions that reinforce and often enrich the powerful few. Such institutions are extractive, like mining: gold mining extracts but does not create gold. In a similar manner, the governing elite of extractive institutions opportunistically extract value from the resources they control (land, minerals, monopoly rights, public coffers, people, foreign aid, etc.), with little regard for making investments that create value and improve welfare for the broader society. To be sure, societies with inclusive institutions also have governing elites who try to cash in on their power and influence for personal profit. However, this impulse is constrained by the checks and balances of an "operating system" that limits such opportunities and provides incentives for productive and creative investments.

A second strand of Acemoglu and Robinson's argument is that institutions can be a potent economic force because of the positive or negative dynamics they trigger. For example, inclusive institutions are much better at fostering and encouraging innovation than are extractive institutions. In Acemoglu and Robinson's argument, this innovation dynamic is precisely what makes institutions the dominant development factor. As with any dynamic process, small differences today often become big differences tomorrow. If a ship sailing out of the San Fran-

Sidebar 8.2　How Malaria Became Central to the Institutions Debate

When trying to use data to make sense of the world, economists sometimes rely on seemingly strange connections between events. A connection between malaria (and other tropical diseases) and colonization plays a pivotal role in the debate over how important institutions are to economic growth and development.

It is relatively easy to show that institutions *correlate* with economic growth. It is much harder to show that they *cause* it. Acemoglu and Robinson teamed up with colleague Simon Johnson to figure out how institutions *cause* economic growth. They used an instrumental variables identification approach (see chapter 2). Their challenge was to find a variable, or instrument, that affects growth *only through its effect on institutions*.

The crux of their approach is the observation that as European powers were colonizing much of the world in the seventeenth, eighteenth, and nineteenth centuries, the kinds of institutions they imported to a given place depended on how pleasant they found the place to be. If Europeans could live in a place without a constant threat of tropical diseases or other hazards, they tended to import more inclusive institutions (after all, Europeans would expect nothing less). If, instead, mortality risks kept Europeans from settling en masse in a location, they opted for more extractive institutions, putting a few colonial masters in place to maintain (heavy-handed) order.

Could "settler mortality risk" be a good instrument for extractive institutions? Acemoglu, Robinson, and Johnson argued that it could be. They found that higher settler mortality caused Europeans to put extractive colonial institutions in place. Places that had extractive colonial institutions, in turn, had lower income per capita in 1995. This is the central tenet of their strong claim about institutions *causing* economic growth.

Recall from chapter 2 that in order for settler mortality risk to be a valid instrument, it must be correlated with extractive institutions (which it is) *and* not have a direct effect on 1995 income. In the case of malaria, a major determinant of mortality risk, this means that malaria-prone places were more likely to have extractive institutions, but malaria cannot directly affect present-day income.

Since this paper was published in 2001, several critics have claimed that mortality risk is not a valid instrument because it can directly affect current income levels. Many places that had high malaria risks two hundred years ago continue to have malaria risks today, and current disease pressure in a society can directly affect current income through lost productivity. Thus, it is not clear whether extractive institutions or malaria caused the lower incomes.

(continued)

> So what does this all mean? The analysis shows conclusively that nineteenth-century mortality is correlated with income levels in 1995, but it is less clear whether this effect comes from the institutions European powers left behind or the current disease ecology.
>
> Daron Acemoglu, Simon Johnson, and James A. Robinson, "The Colonial Origins of Comparative Development: An Empirical Investigation," *American Economic Review* 91, no. 5 (2001):1369–1401.

cisco Bay changes its course by only a few degrees, it might well end up in Sydney instead of Shanghai!

Third, some policies are widely recognized to be "bad" in the sense that they hamper the economy and keep people poor. Often there are known remedies to these bad policies. "If only" policy makers and leaders knew how to fix bad policies, the power of the market would be unleashed and economic development would take off. While some elites may simply not know how to improve things, Acemoglu and Robinson point to a more basic problem: elites may not *want* things to improve, since genuine improvements may deteriorate their power. Almost by definition, the status quo "rules of the game" benefit the elites (that is how they became elite!). Recognize, however, that the "elite" in this sense includes everyone with enough power or influence in society to potentially undermine the control of the ruling party or family, who often have to shower rival elites with financial and other goodies in order to retain their grip on power. For much of the past fifty years, the risk of being overthrown in a coup has been high enough that the top priority of the ruling elite in many developing countries was to keep their rivals either fat and happy or silent (dead or in jail). Either approach reinforces harmful institutions and hampers economic growth.[10] The fact that changes to these existing institutions may threaten their status and influence does not, however, mean that the ruling elite can get away with doing nothing. They often have to *pretend* to want to change and even *publicly advocate* it—while privately ensuring that little actually gets done.

The Dissenting View: Institutions Aren't Everything

The strong position staked out by Acemoglu and Robinson is not without its critics. You'll remember Jeffrey Sachs from the last chapter. He argued that massive aid is needed to promote development in poor countries. Aid is not likely to be the answer if institutions are the cause of underdevelopment. In a lively debate that started as a formal review of *Why Nations Fail* and then morphed into something like an academic street brawl in the blogosphere, Sachs offered a counterargument to Acemoglu and Robinson.

First, he argued that they "incorrectly assume that authoritarian elites are necessarily hostile to economic progress" (p. 142).[11] He cites several examples of dictators who launched economic and political reforms that made institutions more inclusive—albeit typically as a response to threats to their power. These threats come from inside a country (e.g., instability), as well as pressures from other countries.

Second, while inclusive institutions do encourage innovation much more effectively than extractive ones, Sachs argues that the diffusion of technology from other countries sometimes matters more than innovation, particularly at early stages of development. In fact, most recent episodes of dramatic economic development, like South Korea, began with the adoption and reverse-engineering of existing technologies rather than new inventions. And dictators sometimes speed rather than impede the diffusion of new technologies.

Finally, Sachs agrees that corrupt politicians might not want things to change, but he sees other big constraints on development and economic growth. Even if we could magically turn institutions from extractive to inclusive, unfavorable geography and other factors may continue to constrain growth and development. His Millennium Village Project, as we saw, aims to relax the constraints that Sachs believes are the root causes of poverty traps: lack of access to practical technologies, health, food production, education, clean water, and other essential infrastructure. Sachs accuses Acemoglu and Robinson of acting "like doctors trying to confront many different illnesses with only one diagnosis" and argues that "the key to troubleshooting complex systems is to perform what physicians call a 'differential diagnosis': a determination of what has led to the system failure in a particular place and time" (p. 145).

WHERE DO INSTITUTIONS COME FROM?

Even Sachs agrees that, at a fundamental level, institutions matter to economic development. So why is there continued debate over whether they are *the* driver or only *one* of the drivers of development? And, if there is general agreement, can't we use our basic appreciation for the importance of institutions in development to help the poor in some way? The answer to both of these questions hinges on deeply rooted political and even philosophical differences—differences that can entrench positions, fuel passionate disagreement, and lead to marked differences in policy recommendations to help the poor. This rift largely traces its origins to the question: "Where do institutions come from?"

In the last chapter we met William Easterly, who left the World Bank because he was critical of what he thought were its misguided efforts to aid poor countries. Where institutions come from is at the foundation of his critique and frustration with international aid.

Easterly provides a caricature of two opposing views on the origins of institutions, but acknowledges that most thoughtful viewpoints lie somewhere in between these extremes. (After we describe the views, decide where your views lie on this spectrum!) He calls these opposing views "top down" and "bottom up."

The top-down view maintains that institutions are created by leaders and legislators who govern and establish laws. The bottom-up view, in contrast, sees institutions as emerging and constantly evolving, based on the social norms, traditions, values, and beliefs of individuals as they interact and exchange with each other in a society. In this view, laws are codified and accepted as laws after (and because) they seem reasonable and useful to people. The political and philosophical differences between these viewpoints were prominently on display during the eighteenth century Enlightenment, when French philosophers Jean-Jacques Rousseau and Nicolas de Condorcet advocated the top-down view and Irish philosopher Edmund Burke espoused the bottom-up view.

These two views on the origins of institutions lead to dramatically different positions on how to solve problems and improve society—differences that continue to generate an endless stream of political commentary in the media. According to the top-down view, leaders and legislators can directly and decisively determine a society's institutional path. In extreme cases, they even get "do-overs," in which they scrap the existing laws and start afresh with new and improved ones. We call such episodes revolutions.

According to the bottom-up view, institutions only change gradually, as individuals change their values or beliefs. Astute leaders and legislators formalize these institutions into laws and regulations, perhaps attempting to nudge them in one direction or another. In Easterly's words, bottom-up institutions are "evolutionary rather than revolutionary." Adam Smith emphasized a similar process of institutional evolution that is directly shaped by the size of the market. As the volume of goods and services traded in a market expands, specialization and division of labor emerge and raise productivity. This more sophisticated economy both enables and is enabled by the emergence of institutions that help to govern market transactions.

INSTITUTIONS AND THE PRACTICE OF DEVELOPMENT

These opposing views have direct implications for what we do professionally as development economists. The top-down view implies that experts are needed to help craft and refine institutions. The bottom-up view suggests that there is little that experts can do to create institutions. Much like Acemoglu and Robinson's argument that dictators know what changes would help their country as a whole but resist them because these changes would also undermine their own power, the bottom-up view sees little room for experts to engineer institutions to solve social or economic problems.

As Easterly points out, the extreme version of either view may not provide a useful description of reality. In practice, effective policy making often borrows insights from both positions. Nevertheless, the distinction between these opposing viewpoints raises a couple of important implications for development economists.

First, imposing institutions from the top down in the form of laws and regulations may be effective in some circumstances, but only with an appreciation for the richness and complexity of preexisting bottom-up norms, values, and beliefs. They may not be formally codified and may be difficult to see, but bottom-up institutions govern individual behavior and social interaction in profound ways—and they exist for specific reasons. Woe unto the policy maker who thinks the legislative pen is mightier than these foundational institutions! The emergent bottom-up norms that exist in a society often determine what kinds of top-down institutions can realistically be imposed by leaders and legislators. If a law strays too far from preexisting norms, it is likely to be either unenforced and ignored or disruptive and ultimately ineffective. As Easterly says, "Even if the bottom up economists can think of NO reason why a particular institution exists, they are still cautious about changing existing institutions abruptly . . . with the knowledge that there is SOME reason, not yet understood and perhaps never to be understood, for their existence. As Richard Dawkins said about the analogous exercise in evolutionary biology of trying to understand the rationale for the anatomy of each species, 'evolution is smarter than you are'"[12] (p. 96).

Second, the distinction between bottom-up and top-down origins of institutions—combined with an appreciation for how importantly institutions shape economic outcomes—can inform how we use and what we mean by the term "development." President Harry Truman first introduced the metaphor of a development continuum in his post–World War II "Four Point Plan." This continuum ranged from undeveloped countries on one side to developed countries on the other and implied a linear development process from one side to the other, similar to Rostow's stages of economic growth, which we learned about in chapter 1. This is consistent with a top-down view of institutions, in which developed countries look alike and the development process consists of adopting developed-world institutions. By contrast, "The bottom up view of institutions is more open to the possibility that societies evolve different institutions even in the long run" (p. 96). Diverse informal institutions arise when formal institutions are missing (sidebar 8.3). The rapid rise of China since 1990, with its unique mix of political and economic institutions, seems to fit better into this latter view. The combination of China's ever-expanding influence and its unique institutional makeup ensures that there will continue to be lively debates on these issues.

LAND OWNERSHIP INSTITUTIONS AND ECONOMIC DEVELOPMENT

Thus far, we've mainly discussed institutions in the abstract. Let's get more concrete. Since many of the world's poor live in rural settings and rely on agricultural production, economists have thought long and hard about land and land ownership. In many places, complex institutions govern who has access to land, when, and what bundle of rights comes with the land, for example, to buy and sell, rent in or out, use as collateral for a loan, keep or share the harvest, or simply decide what gets cultivated, and how. Many economists see reforming land institutions as a prerequisite to spur productivity growth in agriculture and encourage soil conservation, because security of land ownership has such an important effect on people's incentives to invest in the land—or not. Figuring out how land rights affect investments is not easy, though (see sidebar 8.4).

Even as poor countries become more urbanized, these land issues remain crucial, not least because a family's home and the land it occupies

Sidebar 8.3   How Market Institutions Make It
Tough to Do Business in Sub-Saharan Africa

Imagine for a moment how it might be to run a T-shirt factory in Ghana. You might first think about where to locate your factory, how to hire workers, and how to manufacture your T-shirts. While these and a thousand other decisions would be part of running a successful factory, there are some critical, deeper dilemmas that are easy to overlook if you have not spent time in places like Ghana—dilemmas that arise because of the institutions that govern markets and market transactions. Marcel Fafchamps, a leading development economist, has shed more light on this topic in countries throughout sub-Saharan Africa than anyone else.

Which supplier will you turn to for cotton fabric? How will you pay for your supplies? What will you do if a supplier cheats you by mixing inferior cloth in with your more expensive roll of cloth? How many workers will you hire? These questions raise serious dilemmas in Ghana.

Legal contracts are rarely used and difficult to enforce, which means that firms often look only for suppliers from their own "social networks"—from people they trust because of a shared ethnicity or tribe. This introduces frictions and inefficiencies. When your first priority is finding a supplier who is unlikely to cheat you because you have no legal recourse, it is tough to select suppliers based on standard features such as price, quality, and service. Without the competitive forces of the market, deliveries are often late, quality is often bad, and customer service is often lacking. So-called crony capitalism can emerge naturally in such a setting. Connections can matter more than competition.

Missing or purely informal market institutions make it difficult to find access to loans to cover inventory, which leads to a host of inefficiencies. They also make it difficult to decide who and how many workers to hire. For example, Fafchamps finds that many manufacturing firms hire fewer workers than would be optimal because that's how they reduce the risk of theft. Fewer workers are easier to monitor.

Fafchamps's work has challenged development economists to look more carefully at the diverse informal institutions that emerge to regulate market transactions when the formal institutions of well-developed markets are missing. These market institutions profoundly shape how businesses are run and whether and how they respond to opportunities. Fortunately, some of these insights are starting to filter into intervention and policy design.

Marcel Fafchamps, *Market Institutions in Sub-Saharan Africa: Theory and Evidence* (Cambridge, MA: MIT Press, 2004).

Sidebar 8.4   Do Land Rights Make People More Productive?

Where people have secure rights to their land, are they more productive? That turns out to be a hard question to answer because of the *selection problem* (chapter 2). We could compare how productive farmers are in places where land rights are secure and in places where land rights are insecure. The trouble is, if land institutions are different between two places, chances are that a lot of other things are different, too—things that might affect productivity. We might look for a place where institutions changed. After the Mexican Revolution (1910–1920), Mexico created a communal land-holding system called the *ejido*. People could not own *ejido* lands. This changed in the 1990s—but so did a lot of other things in Mexico. If we see a change in productivity, how can we know it's because of the *ejido* reform and not some other change in agricultural policy that happened at the same time?

Three researchers spotted an opportunity to learn about land tenure insecurity and productivity in rural China. At the time of their study, local leaders periodically redistributed lands from some farmers to others in the same villages. Decisions to expropriate (take away) some farmers' lands varied across villages and, the authors argued, they were largely exogenous from the farmers' point of view. A farmer doesn't know if or when his land will be taken away.

Farmers can invest in making their land more productive by applying organic fertilizer—some combination of manure, dredged soil, decayed vegetable matter, and other wastes from the farm yard. The benefits of doing this (unlike chemical fertilizer application) can last several years. Are farmers who live in places with a low threat of expropriation more likely to make this investment?

The answer, it seems, is yes. The authors used an econometric model to estimate the risk of expropriation in a sample of villages in China. They found that farmers invest more intensively in organic fertilizer where their threat of expropriation is low. This confirms that land tenure security affects productive investments. However, the authors also found that eliminating the risk of exploitation is not enough to raise productive efficiency in a big way. Public investments, like irrigation, drainage, and terracing, are critical, and these do not depend on individuals' plot rights in rural China.

Hanan G. Jacoby, Guo Li, and Scott Rozelle, "Hazards of Expropriation: Tenure Insecurity and Investment in Rural China," *American Economic Review* 92, no. 5 (2002):1420–47.

constitute one of its most valuable assets and can provide a potent source of financial leverage. Without a formal title of ownership, the family is unlikely to be able to use property as collateral to get a loan, which can make it hard to start or expand a small business, for example.

For much of the past century, increasing land tenure security through land titling has been a policy priority. The logic is simple: better security provides an incentive for people to make productive investments in their land. Yet, despite decades of devoted effort to impose land titles from above, only a tiny fraction of land in Africa is registered under a formal system. Moreover, even where titling has happened, the anticipated boost in investment has largely been absent. Does this mean the simple logic is flawed? Not likely. Instead, it probably says something about the complexity of land ownership institutions.

In Europe and North America, we have a relatively simple concept of land ownership: a plot of land either belongs to an individual or organization or it belongs to the state. In much of the developing world, land ownership concepts are much more complex. In the argan forests of southwestern Morocco, for example, the land is formally "owned" by the government, but locals have usufruct (use) rights to collect fruit and dead wood from the forest and to graze their livestock in the forest. These usufruct rights change from one season to the next, however, so determining who has the right to do what on a given plot of land depends not only on the location of the plot but also the month of the year. These usufruct rights can be bought or sold, but they are also passed down through inheritance.

Generations of inheritance transfers add further complexity to land rights. In the argan forests, use rights to a given tract of forest land can be shared between several different families, and the sharing arrangement can change from one season to the next. Nearly all of the informal ownership institutions that govern locals' use of the argan forest have emerged from the bottom up, based on local norms and religious (Islamic) notions of ownership and inheritance.

In contexts with rich bottom-up institutions governing land rights, what happens when top-down land titles are imposed by the state? One common outcome is local resistance and even conflict. Many a land-titling program has failed to formalize land ownership or has fallen far short of its intended coverage because of frictions with preexisting informal ownership institutions. Even when a program succeeds in titling land, these land titles—which to the outsider seem to offer much greater tenure security—do not seem to induce much additional investment. In practice, these titles can introduce confusion and uncertainty into land ownership because it is often unclear how they will change local informal norms in practice.

ENTREPRENEURSHIP, INSTITUTIONS, AND INSTITUTIONAL INNOVATION

For several years, Travis has asked the students in his Introduction to International Economic Development class the question, "How entrepreneurial are Americans?" After collecting their responses on a scale of 1 to 10, he asks them the same question for Europeans and then for Africans. The answers for a recent class are shown in figure 8.1.

Are Americans really more entrepreneurial than Europeans? Are both really that much more entrepreneurial than Africans? While this is clearly not a rigorous survey, the pattern of perceptions is consistent across classes and offers an interesting perspective on how institutions shape economic development.

The word "entrepreneur" traces its origins to seventeenth-century France, where the term described a government subcontractor who supplied specified goods or services (from "entre," between, and "preneur," taker). The payment to the subcontractor was fixed and determined by the contract, so he had to find creative ways to keep his own costs low in order to make a profit. The risk of making or losing money on the proposition was borne by the entrepreneur, which provided strong incentives for him to lower costs as much as possible. Those who study entrepreneurship often point out that this ability to solve problems by exerting ingenuity and making connections in order to earn a profit is an ever-present aspect of human activity, an innate impulse.[13] Some people are simply better entrepreneurs than others, but just as with innate math or music skills, the concentration of this trait is no greater on one continent than another. But if this is true, what explains the patterns in figure 8.1? Perhaps they are simply misperceptions of reality, but let's dig deeper than that.

To address this question, recognize that while human nature changes very little from one continent to another, institutions can change dramatically—and institutions direct human ingenuity and impulses in specific directions. In Willie Sutton's language, institutions determine "where the money is" in a society and thereby channel the entrepreneurial capacity of a people. Local norms and values can also powerfully shape whether people recognize entrepreneurial opportunities, as well as whether and how they respond.

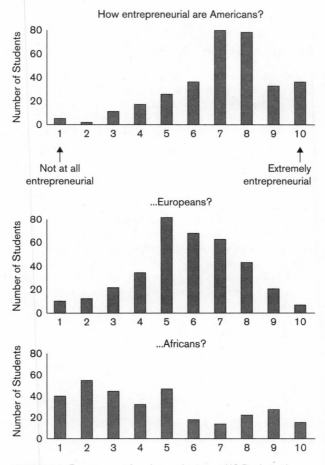

FIGURE 8.1. Responses of undergraduates at UC Davis to the question, "How entrepreneurial are ____?"

In part, the patterns in figure 8.1 reflect the way we sometimes romanticize entrepreneurship. Entrepreneurs innovate and create new products and jobs. They connect people to goods, services, and other people in new and cheaper ways. They may get rich, but they improve or contribute to society in the process. While capitalism reveres entrepreneurs as a result, their incentives are not always aligned with those of the broader society. Indeed, some institutional configurations encourage entrepreneurs to focus all their energies on creating new rent-seeking procedures. In this sense, bad institutions like cronyism and corruption can spawn impressive and genuinely innovative entrepreneurship.

Sidebar 8.5 Entrepreneurial Monks and the "Innovation Machine"

Thinking about differences in entrepreneurship in America, Europe, and Africa generates some useful insights into what entrepreneurship entails and what influences it. In a similar way, looking over time at different forms of entrepreneurship can be very enlightening. One of the most influential modern economists, William Baumol of New York University, did precisely that in an entertaining article and insightful book.

Baumol compares different historical episodes of entrepreneurship—including Ancient Rome, Medieval China, and Middle Age Europe—and tells some intriguing stories. For example, monks may not strike you as entrepreneurs, but the Cistercian monks of the Late Middle Ages in Europe were as entrepreneurial as any of their contemporaries and were "the spearhead of technological advance."

How did this happen? Baumol explains that the rules of the game offered large economic rewards to the exercise of Cistercian entrepreneurship. Specifically, instead of getting direct support from royal coffers, these monks received exemptions from the ruling elite from all river and road tolls and from payment of tithes. This raised marginal returns to investment and led the order of monks to operate and develop new water mills, among other productive pursuits.

In related work, Baumol characterizes capitalism as an "innovation machine" that, while imperfect, is better at encouraging innovation and productive entrepreneurship than any other economic system. In order to function, capitalism requires institutions such as rule of law, property rights, and market exchange. Economists have long recognized the efficiency of markets to allocate goods and services. Baumol argues convincingly that these institutions have an even more potent dynamic virtue: they channel entrepreneurial effort into, and reward, innovation, which is the basis of long-run economic growth.

W. J. Baumol, "Entrepreneurship: Productive, Unproductive, and Destructive," *Journal of Political Economy* 98, no. 5, part 1 (October 1990):893–921.

W. J. Baumol, *The Free-Market Innovation Machine: Analyzing the Growth Miracle of Capitalism* (Princeton: Princeton University Press, 2002).

The problem, of course, is that creative rent seeking is not only unproductive; it can undermine legitimate productive economic activity.

If we perceive Americans to be more entrepreneurial than Africans, perhaps it is because we restrict our definition of entrepreneurship to productive pursuits—and one can make a compelling case that there is more productive entrepreneurship in the US than in most African countries. (Wall Street's creative concealment of subprime mortgages in innovative securities, which triggered the 2008 financial crisis, weakens this case!) Our mistake, then, is to exclude innovative rent seeking from our definition of "entrepreneurship" and thereby overlook the substantial share of African entrepreneurial effort that is unproductive for society as a whole but lucrative for the entrepreneur. History also teaches us about how the "rules of the game" help define entrepreneurship (sidebar 8.5).

Innovation and entrepreneurship are in many ways the lifeblood of the global economy. Sustained economic growth and genuine economic development require healthy institutions, because innovation and entrepreneurship are shaped so fundamentally by these rules of the game. Whether one agrees with Acemoglu and Robinson that institutions are *the* dominant determinant of economic growth or not, inclusive institutions are clearly better than extractive ones at encouraging productive, dynamic entrepreneurship and innovation. The best inclusive institutions not only resist capture by special interests and the elite, they also have built-in mechanisms to adapt to new economic forces and technological opportunities in resiliently inclusive ways.

www.rebeltext.org/development/qr8.html
Learn more about institutions by exploring
multimedia resources while you read.

9

Agriculture

In 1979, development economist Theodore W. Schultz won the Nobel Prize. The opening lines of his Nobel Prize lecture provide the perfect springboard for this chapter: "Most of the people in the world are poor, so if we knew the economics of being poor, we would know much of the economics that really matters. Most of the world's poor people earn their living from agriculture, so if we knew the economics of agriculture, we would know much of the economics of being poor."[1] The 1960s and 1970s brought unprecedented agricultural productivity gains thanks largely to investments in international aid. In the 1980s and 1990s, the role agriculture plays in economic development was frequently ignored—but it was remembered anew in the 2000s. Throughout these cycles, poor farmers kept farming. These agricultural households have some important economic features that are worth understanding. They face distinct constraints that shape the way they farm and how they are affected by markets and government programs.

ESSENTIALS

- Structural transformation
- Production functions
- Risk and uncertainty
- Green Revolution
- Innovation and technology adoption
- Food security versus self-sufficiency
- Agricultural household model
- Subsistence goods and shadow values
- Gender inequality
- Inseparability of efficiency and equity
- Market interlinkages

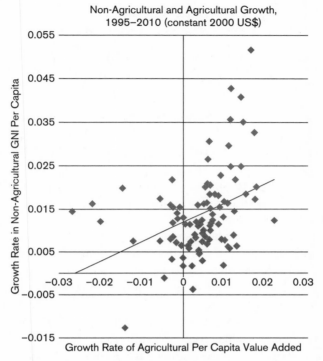

FIGURE 9.1. There is a positive association between countries' agricultural and non-agricultural economic growth. Source: Analysis of World Bank data (data.worldbank.org).

Seventy percent of the world's poor live in rural areas, and in the poorest countries most rural households are involved in agriculture. Agriculture is a fascinating and crucial sector of the economy. Virtually all countries start out with economies based primarily on agriculture, but agriculture's shares of GNI and national employment fall as economies grow. It would seem, then, that agriculture starts out being important, but becomes less so over time.

There is, however, an important connection between agriculture and economic growth. You can see it in figure 9.1, which relates countries' growth in agricultural GDP with growth in non-agricultural GNI over time. There is wide variation in both agricultural and non-agricultural growth rates across countries, but the figure shows a significant positive relationship between the two. Agricultural and non-agricultural growth seem to go hand in hand; the countries that had the highest agricultural GDP growth also tended to have the highest non-agricultural GNI growth. If we do an econometric regression using the data in this picture, we find that a 1% increase in agricultural growth is associated with nearly a half (0.45) percentage point increase in non-agricultural growth.[2]

This does not necessarily mean that agricultural growth *causes* total income growth. In fact, it could be the reverse: countries that do well overall might be better at growing their agricultural sector. More likely, it is some combination of the two. Increases in agricultural production facilitate growth in other sectors of the economy, and this, in turn, has a positive feedback effect on agricultural growth. In addition, there may be other factors, like technological change or—as we learned in the last chapter—healthy institutions such as clear and stable rule of law, that make both sectors grow.

Decades of experience have shown that most countries need to grow their agriculture if they want to grow their economy as a whole. Agriculture continues to be the main source of income and employment for many people in the world today, making agricultural households an important market for manufactured goods. Agriculture is the principal source of food and labor to fuel expanding urban economies. It provides essential intermediate inputs such as fruits, vegetables, and grain to food processors. When a large part of the economy is agricultural, where else are the savings to invest in industry going to come from? As evidence of the crucial cash that can be generated by the agricultural sector, countries around the globe have devised a variety of means to "tax" agricultural income as a way to support industrial sectors. Japan, in the Meiji period (1868–1912), taxed its farmers directly. The former USSR taxed farmers indirectly by paying them prices below the world price for their crops. This model of state enterprises ("parastatals") paying farmers low prices (and selling at high prices) in order to fund other activities has since been followed by many developing countries.

This chapter is an introduction to how economists study agriculture as it relates to economic development. The first thing we'll learn is that agriculture is different from other parts of the economy, and agricultural producers in poor countries are also households. They are neither pure firms nor pure consumers, but rather a combination of the two. The microeconomic theory of the firm does not describe their behavior, but neither does the theory of the consumer. We will learn how to model the dual nature of agricultural households as producers and consumers, and what this means for designing policies to address rural poverty and food security.

Next, we'll look inside the household. Building on our discussion in chapter 4 on intra-household inequality, we'll see how unequal access to resources can affect not only how the household's economic pie gets divvied up among household members (equity), but also how big the pie is (efficiency). We'll see that gender divisions within households can result in significant losses in agricultural productivity. Similar losses of economic efficiency and income can occur in other domains as well, which can create unintended consequences for development projects in both agricultural and non-agricultural settings.

Finally, we'll look beyond the household and see how diverse households interact within rural economies. We'll see how economic linkages transmit impacts of policy and market shocks among households, often with surprising outcomes.

HOW AGRICULTURE IS DIFFERENT

Agriculture is different from other sectors of the economy in ways that have far-reaching ramifications for both development policy and economic analysis.

To start with, let's think about the production function. In most sectors of the economy, the production function represents a knowable engineering relationship between inputs and outputs, like how many copies of RebelText can be produced from a given amount of paper, ink, capital (printing machines), labor, and so on. The agricultural production process is biological and filled with uncertainty. Farmers rely heavily on inputs from nature, including weather. The good news is that nature provides inputs like sunshine and rainfall for free. The bad news is that you never know when the rains won't come, the sun won't shine, or a swarm of locusts will devastate your crop. Adverse shocks break the engineering relationship between inputs and outputs. Agricultural economists pay a great deal of attention to incorporating risk into the production function. In agriculture, the production function is random, or stochastic (from the Greek word "στόχος" [stóchos], meaning "guess" or "target"). Stochastic production analysis is beyond the scope of this book, but as you read on it is important to bear in mind this critical difference between agriculture and other sectors. We will introduce some dimensions of risk in this chapter and save the details of the topic for chapter 12.

Agricultural production involves long time lags—often many months—between purchasing and applying inputs and harvesting outputs. Neither the size of the harvest nor (usually) the output price is known at planting time. Farming requires land, so agriculture is spread out over wide geographic areas. Because agricultural production is spread out, seasonal, risky, and involves long time lags, reliable and timely access to markets is critical. These include markets for inputs such as seeds and fertilizer, crop outputs produced by farmers, and financial markets for savings and credit to finance input purchases, as well as insurance to protect against crop failures. Imagine, then, the challenges farmers face in poor countries, where markets don't work well (coming in chapter 11), banks won't lend money to small farmers, and formal insurance is nonexistent (coming in chapter 12).

Some sectors, like energy, steel, or automobiles, are dominated by a few large producers. The minister of industry might be able to get key industry players to sit down around a table and discuss industrial development policies. Agricultural production is carried out by large numbers of farmers with unequal access to resources, from large agribusinesses (sometimes referred to as "factories in the fields") to smallholder farmers with tiny plots. To get agricultural policies right, we have to understand the behavior of thousands, millions, or (in China and India) hundreds of millions of heterogeneous actors whom the minister of agriculture couldn't possibly get around a table! Influencing agricultural outcomes thus requires having good economic models of diverse agricultural producers and knowing how they are likely to respond to different kinds of policies. To complicate matters, as we shall see, what's good for big farmers can be bad for small ones.

Perhaps the biggest difference between agriculture and other sectors in poor countries is that agricultural production decisions are almost always made within economic units that also function as households. That is, unlike firms that are focused exclusively on production decisions, agricultural households jointly and simultaneously make both production and consumption decisions. This may seem like a technical distinction, but as we'll see it is actually a real "game changer" when it comes to economic analysis.

THE AGRICULTURAL HOUSEHOLD MODEL

In rich countries, most agricultural producers are firms that produce for the market. Agricultural households in poor countries are different from rich-country farmers as well as from their non-agricultural counterparts, because they consume part or all of what they produce. They also supply many of their own inputs, particularly land and labor. You can think of them as a hybrid of firm and household. Our models therefore have to reflect agricultural households' dual nature as both producer and consumer to provide a reliable basis for understanding the agricultural economy and offer guidance for designing policies.

The analysis of agriculture and development in this way leads to surprises, because what is good for agricultural households as producers often is not good for them as consumers. When the price of food goes up, most crop producers in poor countries are *not* better off, because they also face higher prices as food consumers. Failure to understand the workings of agricultural households has been a source of many ill-fated development policies.

The Household as Consumer

The agricultural household model is the staple for any kind of microeconomic analysis of agriculture in poor countries. Let's start with consumer theory. Figure 9.2 shows the famous indifference curve and budget constraint in the consumer model, which you'll remember from your microeconomics classes. The axes measure the quantities of food (horizontal axis) and other stuff (vertical axis) the household demands. We could have more categories of goods, but each new good adds a dimension to our figure, which makes it hard—or impossible—to draw, so let's keep it at two. Our findings will generalize to more than two goods.

The straight line represents the household's budget constraint. In a standard consumer model, we almost always assume the household's income is fixed. In an agricultural household model, though, it includes profits from producing food. Remember this—it's an essential part of the household-farm model.

The point where the budget constraint hits an axis (the intercept) is the maximum amount of the good on the axis that the household could consume if it spent all its available income, Y^*, on that good. To see where the budget constraint hits the two axes, just divide income by the price per unit of each good. The maximum amount of food this household could consume, which we'll call X_a^{max}, is the household's income divided by the price of food. For example, if your income is $100 and food costs $2 per kilo, the most food you can consume if you don't buy anything else is 50 kilos. The line between those two points shows all the combinations of food and other stuff the household can afford if it spends all of its money.

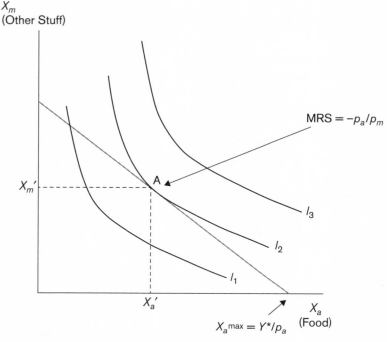

FIGURE 9.2. The household as consumer optimizes at the point of tangency between the indifference curve and budget constraint. At point A, its marginal rate of substitution between goods equals the (negative) ratio of market prices.

The budget constraint has a slope equal to the (negative of the) price of food (or whatever's on the horizontal axis) divided by the price of other stuff (or whatever's on the vertical axis). You can see that this line tells us the rate at which the market trades off food for other stuff. Its slope tells us how much other stuff we could buy if we gave up one unit of food (and vice versa).

The basic precept of consumer economics is that at the optimum, every household consumes at the point where its own personal (subjective) trade-off between food and other stuff equals the rate at which the *market* trades off the two goods. The market's rate of trading off food for other stuff is just the slope of the budget line, or the (negative of the) ratio of market prices.

How should we depict the household's preferences, or rate of trade-off in terms of satisfaction (what economists call "utility")? Should it be a line, like the budget constraint? Probably not. Your trade-off in preferences will almost surely not be constant because of the law of diminishing marginal utility. The more you have of something, the less utility you get from having one more unit; thus, the more you'd be willing to trade to get an additional unit of something else. That's why you'll almost never end up consuming at either end of your budget constraint. You won't spend your whole budget on food (unless you face a very severe nutritional constraint that forces you to do so in order to survive). And you'll never end up at the other end of the budget line, either, because you obviously need to spend some of your budget on food.

Given diminishing marginal utility, we need a curve, not a line, to depict consumer preferences. An indifference curve (I_1, I_2, or I_3 in the figure) depicts all the combinations of food and other stuff that leave the household equally well off; that is, along each indifference curve, the household's utility is constant. There are many (really, an infinite number of) indifference curves. As we move from the origin up to the northeast in the diagram, we hop onto indifference curves providing higher levels of utility. Most, like curve I_3, describe bundles of food and other stuff that the household cannot afford given its budget constraint. Others, like I_1, describe bundles of goods the household can afford, with money left over.

Point A in the figure is the bundle that gives the highest utility the household can attain given its budget constraint. That's the point where the household's marginal rate of substitution (MRS) between food and other stuff just equals the (negative of the) price ratio. It is where the household's trade-off in preferences equals the market trade-off. Every household will set its trade-off in preferences equal to the ratio of prices. In an economy where every household faces the same market prices, everyone will consume at the same MRS between food and other stuff. When that happens, consumption is said to be Pareto efficient: no household can be made better off without making another one worse off.

What happens if the price of food increases? Modeling how an outcome changes when some exogenous variable (here, the price of food) changes is called "comparative statics." If the household allocated its whole budget to food, it would be able to buy less than before. However, if it spent all its income on other stuff, it could still buy the same amount as before, so the vertical intercept does not change. As a result, the budget line pivots inward, as in figure 9.3.

You may remember that the comparative statics of a price change from microeconomics. Faced with a higher food price, the household substitutes other stuff for food. If it could stay on the same indifference curve as before, the new ratio of prices would drive it from A to B in the

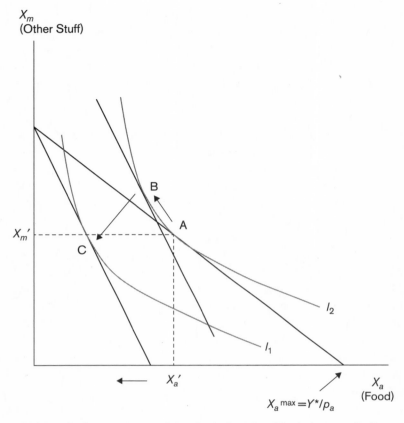

FIGURE 9.3. In the consumer model, a rise in the price of food triggers substitution (A → B) and real income (B → C) effects that reinforce one another; the quantity of food demanded decreases.

diagram. This is called the "substitution effect," because consumers substitute away from the good that has gotten more expensive in favor of other goods, which have become less expensive relative to food. In our figure, the substitution effect decreases food demand.

The household cannot afford to consume at point B, though. With the higher food price, its real income falls, forcing it down to a lower indifference curve (point C). A negative real-income effect reinforces the negative substitution effect. That's why demand curves slope downward: as the price of food (or pretty much any good) increases, consumers demand less of it.

That's the end of the comparative statics of an own-price change in the consumer model—but not in the household-farm model. Remember,

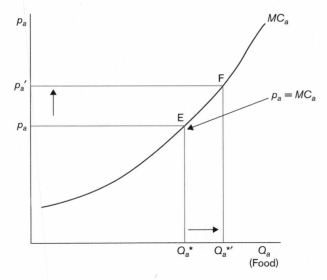

FIGURE 9.4. The farm household produces at the point where the food price equals the marginal cost of producing food. When the food price rises, so does food production.

agricultural households also produce food. How does this change things? An increase in the price of food hurts consumers, but it makes producers better off, because farm profit goes up.

The Household as Producer

To show the production-side effect of the price change, we need to borrow a curve from producer theory. You'll recognize the one in figure 9.4. The marginal cost (MC) gives the cost of producing an additional unit of food. A profit-maximizing firm produces where the MC equals the market price. At different prices (vertical axis) we can determine the supply response (horizontal axis) from the MC curve. Thus, the MC curve is also the firm's supply curve.

The $p = MC$ rule makes good sense. The price is the reward the firm gets for producing one more unit. If the price is higher than the MC, the firm will want to produce more. If the MC is higher than the price, it will cut back on production until it brings MC down to the market price. As a producer, our agricultural household will have the same incentive to do this as a firm would.

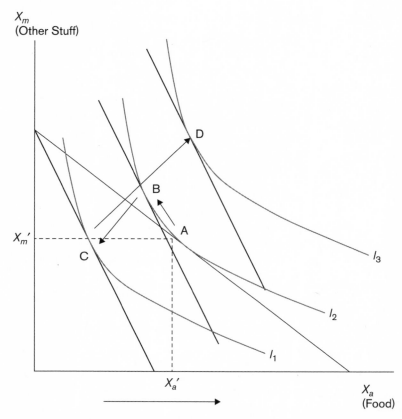

FIGURE 9.5. The farm profit effect shifts out the budget constraint, possibly resulting in a positive effect of food prices on the household's food demand.

At the food price p_a, our household farm maximizes its profit from food production at point E, producing a level of output equal to Q^*_a. Its profit, $\Pi = p_a Q^*_a - MC_a$, is the more-or-less triangular area above the marginal cost curve but below the price in our figure.

What happens when the price of food goes up? At the higher price, p_a', price equals MC at point F. Output jumps to $Q^*_a{'}$ and profit increases (you can see that the triangle below the new price line is bigger).

This is not the end of the story either, because remember: profit is part of the household's income. When the price of food goes up, the household's income goes up because of the profit effect. To see what that does to our comparative statics, we have to go back to our indifference curves.

Before we considered the profit effect, the household was at point C in figure 9.5. We show an increase in income as a parallel outward shift in the budget constraint (an increase in income changes the point where the budget constraint intersects the axes because the household can afford more of either good). This increases the demand for both food and other stuff, as long as both are normal goods.

To determine the overall effect of a price change on demand we need to know how much the budget constraint shifts due to the profit effect. If the increase in profits only shifted the budget constraint a little, food demand would remain lower than before the price increase. But it could shift the budget constraint out farther, maybe all the way to where it's tangent to indifference curve I_3. At point D, the household consumes a bundle that is actually to the right of where it started, at point A. That means its food demand increased when the price of food went up. An agricultural household's food demand curve can slope upward if the profit effect is big enough! In fact, often when economists estimate household-farm models with real-world data, they find that it does slope upward (see sidebar 9.1).

THE AGRICULTURAL HOUSEHOLD MODEL AND DEVELOPMENT POLICY

The agricultural household model changes the way we think about most of the agricultural producers in the world. It also has some important lessons for agricultural development policy.

First, if a government wants to increase the supply of food for its urban consumers, raising the price of food will not necessarily help. The amount of food available from domestic producers to the market, or marketed surplus *(MS_a)*, is the difference between what the farm household produces and what it consumes; that is, $MS_a = Q_a - X_a$. Assuming the household does not face serious production constraints, production increases when the price goes up. This would increase the marketed surplus if the farm household's demand stayed the same—but it doesn't. The more the household farm's consumption increases because of the profit effect, the smaller the marketed surplus effect. Governments often are disappointed when they offer farmers expensive price supports but the market supply doesn't change much.

Second, most people—including economists—assume that if the price of food goes up, that's bad news for urban consumers but good for farmers. The agricultural household model shows that this might not be the case. If a household is to benefit from higher food prices, the positive profit effect has to outweigh the negative consumption effect. In order for that to happen, the household has to be a net seller of food—that is, its marketed surplus must be positive.

Sidebar 9.1 Upward-Sloping Demand Curves?

A generation or two of graduate students in development economics learned how to understand and use the agricultural household model from economists Inderjit Singh, Lyn Squire, and John Strauss. In their classic book on the topic, they demonstrated the importance of taking into account the relationship between production and consumption decisions with a comparison of findings from agricultural household models for Taiwan, Malaysia, Korea, Japan, Thailand, Sierra Leone, and Northern Nigeria. Four of the seven studies found a positive own-price elasticity of demand for agricultural goods. In those cases, the positive profit effect was stronger than the negative real income and substitution effects. In all seven cases, the profit effect substantially lowered the effect of a food-price increase on the marketed surplus of food.

This may not be the first time you've heard of upward-sloping demand curves. Most introductory microeconomics textbooks mention the possibility of "Giffin" goods that also have upward-sloping demand curves—although for a distinctly different reason. Understanding the distinction may help reinforce the logic behind the agricultural household model.

Until recently, such Giffin goods were treated a bit like the Loch Ness monster because no one had ever actually *seen* them in the real world. In 2008, economists Robert Jensen and Nolan Miller, who devised the revealed preference measure of poverty (Staple Calorie Share) we encountered in chapter 4, provided convincing evidence of Giffin behavior using data from 1,300 poor households in China. They found that as the price of rice increased, extremely poor households actually consumed *more* rice.

What's the explanation? The agricultural household model cannot explain this result for one simple reason: these were *urban* poor who did not reap a profit benefit from higher rice prices. Instead, this appears to be driven by subsistence concerns: as the price of rice—their main source of calories—increases, the food budgets of these poor households tighten, and they start cutting back on other food purchases. But to survive, they must make up the calories somehow and choose the cheapest calories available: rice!

Inderjit Singh, Lyn Squire, and John Strauss, eds., *Agricultural Household Models, Extensions, Applications and Policy* (Baltimore: Johns Hopkins University Press, 1986).

Robert T. Jensen and Nolan H. Miller, "Giffen Behavior and Subsistence Consumption," *American Economic Review* 98, no. 4 (2008):1553–77.

TABLE 9.1 NET BENEFIT RATIOS BY RURAL HOUSEHOLD GROUP IN FOUR
CENTRAL AMERICAN COUNTRIES

Household Group	Country			
	El Salvador	Guatemala	Honduras	Nicaragua
Landless	−0.16	−0.36	−0.63	−0.49
Subsistence	−0.01	−0.32	−0.78	0
Small Commercial	0.31	−0.12	−0.13	0.39
Medium Commercial	1.2	0.07	1.01	0.62
Large Commercial	3.88	0.64	1.71	1.79

SOURCE: J. Edward Taylor, Antonio Yúnez-Naude, and Nancy Jesurun-Clements, "Does Agricultural Trade Liberalization Reduce Rural Welfare in Developing Countries? The Case of CAFTA," *Applied Economic Perspectives and Policy* 32, no. 1 (2010):95–116.

It might surprise you to learn that most of the world's farmers produce less food than they consume. The development economist Chris Barrett compared findings from twenty-three agricultural household surveys in eastern and southern Africa. He found no case in which most farmers were net sellers. The percentage of agricultural households that sold their crops ranged from a high of 45% (maize in Zimbabwe) to lows of 10%–12% (barley, sorghum, and wheat in Ethiopia). This means that most farmers—those who produce less than they consume— lose if the price of the crops they grow goes up.[3]

Another development economist, Angus Deaton, came up with a handy way to determine how much welfare increases if the price of food crops goes up: the ratio of net agricultural sales, or marketed surplus (MS), to the household's total expenditures on all goods (E). He called this the net benefit ratio (NBR):

$$NBR = \frac{MS}{E}$$

The NBR can be interpreted as the percentage change in welfare resulting from a 1% change in the crop's price. Table 9.1 gives the NBR for different rural household groups in El Salvador, Guatemala, Honduras, and Nicaragua.

The NBR is almost always negative for small-farm households. For subsistence producers in Honduras, a 1% increase in food prices *reduces* welfare by 0.78%. An important implication of these findings is that trade agreements that lower import tariffs on food actually benefit most food producers in these Central American countries.

A third lesson from agricultural household models is the importance of the production response. When we talk about agricultural households we mean small farmers. Big corn farms in the United States are family operated, but for all practical purposes they are pure firms because they consume a negligible part of their harvest. Farm households, in order to survive and help feed the burgeoning urban population in their countries, have to be able to increase their production in response to price changes.

Feeding the World: The Elasticity of Agricultural Supply

The MC curve is the household's supply curve. The flatter (more *elastic*) it is, the more it will respond to an increase in price by producing more. In the extreme case where the supply curve is vertical (perfectly *inelastic*), no change in price will lead to an increase in output.

Why would an agricultural household ever have a vertical, or nearly vertical, supply curve? In the real world, small farmers face many different kinds of production constraints that large farmers in rich countries typically do not face. A few of the most common ones are as follows:

· limited access to land, and especially irrigated land
· poor land quality
· technological limitations, including lack of access to high-productivity seeds
· limited access to modern inputs like fertilizer
· a lack of cash to purchase inputs, and limited or no access to credit
· limited or no access to insurance to protect against crop failure
· labor constraints

Typically, a constellation of constraints restrict small farmers' capacity and willingness to increase production and shift into higher value crop activities. Small landholdings mean high administrative costs for banks and limited collateral to offer them as security against loans to pay for inputs, as we'll see in chapter 12. High production risks and a lack of crop insurance make banks even more unwilling to lend to small farmers. All of these constraints can also make small farmers unwilling to "risk the farm" and take out loans, even if banks are willing. Households that lack the cash to hire workers from their village, or who face a limited supply of potential workers, have to farm their land themselves; families with few, old, or unhealthy members often then have little choice but to leave land fallow. The result can be a vicious cycle between poverty and production, leading to a poverty trap.

Our agricultural household models need to include these constraints if we want them to reflect the way agricultural economies work. This is necessary for our models to be a useful basis for designing policies to increase food production and combat poverty in agricultural areas. In fact, there have been many extensions of the agricultural household model to incorporate these constraints.

Agricultural Technology: Improving Production Potential of Crops

Let's begin with the most fundamental constraint on agricultural production: technology. Technology is reflected in the production function, which specifies the maximum output obtainable from a given set of inputs. Graphically, it is reflected in the shape and position of the supply curve. When new technologies come along enabling farmers to get more output from the same set of inputs (or use fewer inputs to get the same output), an inelastic supply curve can shift outward, as illustrated in figure 9.6.

Agricultural production technologies took a great leap forward with the advent of the Green Revolution. The Green Revolution began as a series of agricultural research initiatives started in 1943 by Norman Borlaug, an agronomist and eventual winner of the Nobel Peace Prize who has been credited with saving more than a billion lives.[4] Borlaug set out to breed new varieties of plants—especially rice and wheat—that could produce more food. Most plant breeders aspire to doing something like this, but Borlaug succeeded like no one before him ever had. His work began in Mexico, but his ideas were put to the test in India, which in 1961 was on the brink of mass famine. Its rice yields at the time were only around two tons per hectare. By the mid-1990s, Indian rice yields had tripled, rice prices had fallen (despite continuing population growth), and India had become a rice exporter.

How did this huge technological change happen? New rice varieties developed at IRRI (the International Rice Research Institute in Los Baños, Philippines) were bred to more efficiently exploit soil nutrients. This, together with an expanded use of fertilizer and irrigation, vastly increased the world's ability to feed itself—and then some. Rice isn't the only crop that experienced a Green Revolution. Between 1950 and

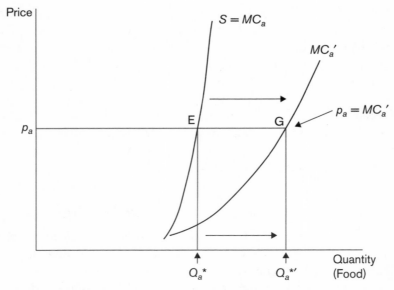

FIGURE 9.6. Productivity-enhancing technological change shifts the agricultural supply (marginal cost) curve outward to the right, increasing the quantity supplied at a given price.

2005, wheat yields in the world rose from around 750 kilograms per hectare to more than 2,500.[5] Today, a network of international crop research institutes, called the CGIAR (www.cgiar.org), continues to seek new solutions to feeding the world's still growing population. The CGIAR's main job is to continue shifting out the agricultural supply curve. Today, in an era of climate change, this means taking on environmental as well as biological challenges.

AGRICULTURAL TECHNOLOGY ADOPTION

Once crop scientists have succeeded in breeding high-yielding varieties that are well suited for a given location, it might seem like farmers would be drawn quickly to these new technologies. Such a "build it and they will come" approach to agricultural technology may work with rich farmers, but things aren't so simple with poor farmers. Even after high-yielding varieties are available, there are several constraints that can prevent small-holder farmers from adopting them. One of the most active research areas in development economics—agricultural technology adoption—seeks to understand these other constraints.

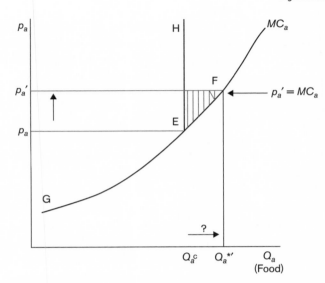

FIGURE 9.7. A liquidity constraint (segment EH) can result in suboptimal production and a welfare loss.

Financial Adoption Constraints

Let's consider a liquidity (cash) constraint in our comparative statics example above. Suppose that at the initial food price, the household is spending all the cash it has to buy inputs. It faces a liquidity constraint. A basic problem in agricultural production is that inputs have to be purchased many months before the harvest comes in. Unless the household can borrow against the harvest, which poor small households cannot, its input demand is constrained by its available cash. In figure 9.7, the food price goes up, but the liquidity constraint prevents the household from increasing production. The liquidity constraint is represented by the vertical line in the diagram. The MC curve is the same as before, but because the household cannot expand production beyond the constrained level, its supply curve effectively is "kinked," so it is given by GEH. The shaded triangle is the welfare loss to the household from not being able to adjust its production to the higher level. The only way to increase production and raise the household's welfare in this case is to loosen the liquidity constraint.

A lack of access to credit, insurance, or hired labor may reflect market failures due to information and other problems, which we will look at in chapters 11 and 12. The household also may face high transaction costs in selling its output or purchasing inputs, for example, if transportation to markets is very expensive. If transaction costs are high enough, the household's best bet may be to withdraw from the market completely and become a subsistence producer.

Information Adoption Constraints

In addition to these financial and economic constraints, there are several potential information and even cognitive constraints to technology adoption. Obviously, a farmer must learn about new technologies or new production practices before she can adopt them. How do poor farmers learn about new seeds? In some places, they may first hear about a new technology from an official agricultural "extension agent," but they typically are only willing to adopt it after seeing someone else's experience or testing it out on a small piece of their own land. Social learning and learning by doing are therefore important topics in this area of development economics and often shape the design of farmer training and extension programs (see sidebar 9.2).

We opened the chapter with a quote from Theodore Schultz's 1979 Nobel Prize lecture. In that lecture and indeed throughout his career, he emphasized how critical it was that farmers be able to learn and adapt to changing circumstances. As he saw it, "While land *per se* is not a critical factor in being poor, the human agent is," because smarter farmers who have learned how to learn, and who look for new ways to enhance their productivity, can take advantage of new opportunities.[6]

What makes the economics of technology adoption complicated and challenging is how the various constraints on technology development and adoption interact. Here, we have presented these constraints in an order that seems logical: first, new and improved technologies must be developed. Then, the constraints keeping small farmers from adopting these new technologies need to be addressed. But in practice, things are more complex: the presence of farm-level constraints discourages investments in the development of new technologies. Why would any profit-minded company invest in creating new seed varieties and other technologies, knowing that small farmers are too constrained to adopt them? This is why investments in international agricultural research are unpopular as private-sector investments. They are more likely to be provided as a form of development assistance. Indeed, agricultural research and development are among the most cost-effective ways of reducing rural poverty.

Sidebar 9.2   Learning from Others

The Green Revolution brought new high-yielding seeds to India's farmers, whose production technology had changed little for decades. Many did not adopt the new seeds, even though agronomic field tests had shown them to be significantly more productive than traditional seed varieties. Andrew Foster and Mark Rosenzweig, using data that tracked farmers over time, found that a lack of knowledge about how to manage new seeds was a significant deterrent to adoption. The profitability of the new seeds for farmers increased as their neighbors gained experience growing them. Because of this, farmers whose neighbors had experience growing the new seeds planted more of their own land in high-yielding varieties. Thus, the authors concluded, farmers who adopted the new technology created benefits not only for themselves but also for others, by providing important "knowledge spillovers."

In a more recent study, Timothy Conley and Chris Udry investigate the role of social learning among pineapple farmers in Ghana. Many of these farmers began growing pineapple in the 1990s, learning through trial and error how much fertilizer to use to maximize their profit. By analyzing data on social networks and this trial-and-error process, they found that farmers do indeed learn from their "information neighbors," but only when their neighbors get a surprisingly good or bad result from trying a particular fertilizer dosage rate.

These studies have documented how the spread of information about new technologies can be critical in making farmers in poor countries more productive. They have influenced the design of agricultural extension programs—and sparked several follow-up studies by development economists seeking a yet deeper understanding of the information and cognitive constraints that impede technology adoption.

Andrew D. Foster and Mark R. Rosenzweig, "Learning by Doing and Learning from Others: Human Capital and Technical Change in Agriculture." *Journal of Political Economy* 103, no. 6 (1995):1176–1209.

Timothy G. Conley and Christopher R. Udry, "Learning about a New Technology: Pineapple in Ghana," *American Economic Review* 100, no. 1 (2010):35–69.

FOOD SECURITY AND SELF-SUFFICIENCY

Food security is the most fundamental of all human rights and the most basic objective of economic development. Food self-sufficiency is not. The two have nothing to do with each other—as long as markets exist, that is. Ed has a measly garden that yields a few organic greens and herbs, along with an orange or lemon from time to time. Ed is certainly not self-sufficient in food, but he is not food insecure. If something happens that keeps markets from working, however, food security and food self-sufficiency have everything to do with each other.

The point that food security and self-sufficiency are different concepts might seem obvious, but over the years many countries have confused one with the other and launched expensive programs in an effort to achieve self-sufficiency in food production. Japan has strived to achieve self-sufficiency in rice by offering farmers up to ten times the price farmers in other countries get. In 1980, Mexico launched an expensive program called SAM (Sistema Alimentario Mexicano) to reduce its dependence on corn imports. It became so expensive that it was aborted in 2002.

We can use our agricultural household model to learn why self-sufficiency is normally a bad idea. The *Oxford Dictionary* defines self-sufficiency as "needing no outside help in satisfying one's basic needs, especially with regard to the production of food." What happens when our agricultural household has to be self-sufficient?

To explore this question, suppose the household can allocate its fixed resources (for example, land) between two production activities. When Ed conducted surveys in China's Jiangsu Province, he saw many family farms converting some of their rice fields into fish ponds, so let's consider rice cultivation and fish ponds as an example. Land is not perfectly transformable between these two activities; there are likely to be decreasing returns to scale in each one. (If you're smart, you'll dig out your least productive rice land for fish ponds.) The various combinations of rice and fish production the households in a region can produce are given not by a straight line, but instead by a concave production possibilities frontier (PPF), as in figure 9.8. Where the PPF touches the axes, it tells us how much of each good the region could produce if it produced only that good. If we start where it crosses the x-axis (the economy is producing only rice) and move along the PPF, we see how much fish could be produced as less rice is produced. The PPF is curved due to diminishing marginal returns: each subsequent unit of fish requires the economy to give up more rice as land more suited to rice cultivation is converted to fish ponds.

Where along the PPF will our households produce? If they are self-sufficient, they will produce exactly as much as they consume. We'll need to bring in an indifference curve to figure out where the optimal production (which equals consumption) choice will be.

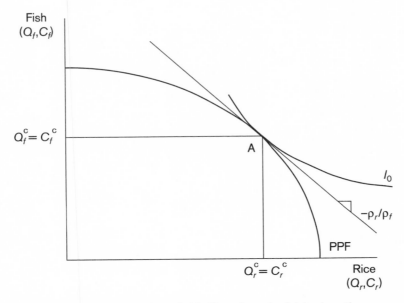

FIGURE 9.8. A self-sufficient household will produce at point A, where the marginal rate of transformation in production equals the marginal rate of substitution in consumption. Notice that the production possibility frontier (PPF) takes the place of a household budget constraint.

The slope of the indifference curve I_0 in this figure describes the households' trade-off in preferences between rice and fish: how much of one it would *be willing to give up* to get one more unit of the other. The slope of the PPF is its technological trade-off: how much of one good it would *have to give up* in order to *produce* an additional unit of the other. The point of tangency between the two is the optimal solution to the households' problem given self-sufficiency. It is where the slope of the PPF, the marginal rate of transformation (MRT) of rice into fish, equals the MRS of rice for fish. There are no market prices; however, the slope at this optimum equals the (negative of the) ratio of household shadow values, or subjective valuations of rice (ρ_r) and fish (ρ_f).

Suppose now that the households can trade rice and fish at the going market prices of p_r and p_f, respectively. The market trade-off between rice and fish is the ratio of these two prices, represented by the price line in figure 9.9.

With a market to trade in, the households no longer have to be self-sufficient in rice or fish. They can sell one and buy the other. The market makes it possible to decouple production from demand, just like you do

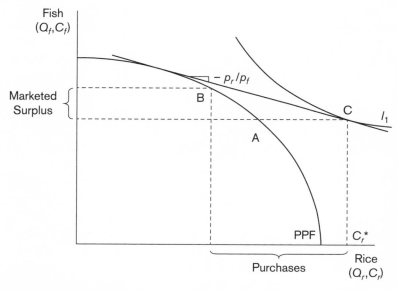

FIGURE 9.9. Markets enable the household to increase its welfare by separating its production and consumption decisions.

and just like we do (we being professors who pay other people to grow our food).

On the production side, the households will now equate their MRT with the ratio of market prices. They'll produce at point B. Notice that at point B they produce more fish and less rice than when they have to be self-sufficient. Then they can trade along the price line and climb onto the highest indifference curve they can reach. On the consumption side, they'll end up at point C. They've produced more fish than they demand and traded fish for rice. As a result, they consume more rice than they could possibly produce: C_r^* is to the right of where the PPF hits the rice axis.

The moral of this story is clear: markets let our household farms trade up to a higher indifference curve (I_1) than they could reach if they were constrained to be self-sufficient. In other words, markets improve welfare. This, in a nutshell, is the argument for free trade. We'll come back to this argument (as well as its limitations) in chapter 11. For now, think about how important food markets are to you in your everyday life.

Protective trade policies, like import tariffs and quotas, prevent countries from trading. For agricultural households, prohibitive costs of buying and selling prevent trade. In Tigray in the 1980s, the cost of trading was that you'd likely be shot on sight if you walked the highway. For most agricultural households, it's far less dramatic than that. Poor roads, communications, and information make it too expensive to get produce to or from the market, which might be tens of kilometers away over roads that are impassible part of the year. As Adam Smith wrote, "The division of labor is limited by the extent of the market."[7] The gains to specialization and trade are significant, but they must be preceded by infrastructure and institutions that expand the "extent of the market."

When it comes to food, it turns out that very few households are truly self-sufficient; everyone seems to buy and sell little bits here and there in their village, in weekly markets or through "door-step trade." However, many villages and regions are largely cut off from outside markets. When droughts strike, instead of markets drawing in food from other places, local prices skyrocket, food stocks dwindle, and families' nutrient intake falls. The consequences can be dire and long term, especially for children, as we saw in chapter 6.

Food aid may rush in to try to fill the vacuum. As we'll explore in greater detail in chapter 13, emergency food relief, while of course necessary to keep famines in check, can set back local farming by driving prices to zero. Development practitioners can labor for years helping to develop more vibrant local farm production systems, only to see their efforts set back when drought hits and food aid rushes in.

Imagine an alternative world in which farmers have access to crop insurance and agricultural households are integrated with outside markets. A drought hits, insurance pays off, and the payoff is used to buy food that the market brings in the minute prices begin to rise. At most, the local price of, say, rice, would rise to whatever the world price is at the nearest port, plus the cost of getting the rice out to the village.

In short, food insecurity and its extreme form, famine, are not just a production problem. They are a problem with markets, and ultimately, governments. Amartya Sen, whom we encountered in chapters 1 and 6, focused much of his research on this topic—and earned a Nobel Prize for his work. Oxfam, one of the world's major aid and development organizations, explains it this way:[8] "Famine is the 'triple failure' of (1) food production, (2) people's ability to access food and, finally and most crucially (3) in the political response by governments and international donors. Crop failure and poverty leave people vulnerable to starvation—but famine only occurs with political failure. In Somalia years of internal violence and conflict have been highly significant in creating the conditions for famine."

INSIDE THE HOUSEHOLD

So far we've been considering households as if they were single, homogeneous units. But in real life, they are a composite of individuals, each with different access to resources and with their own preferences and needs. Human development depends on the distribution of food and other resources within as well as among households. Households bring together groups of individuals, usually family members, who can share in production and consumption. But power asymmetries within households can profoundly influence how resources get allocated. They not only determine who gets to consume what; they also can determine whether households act in ways that can make the pie as big as it can be. In other words, household dynamics can affect efficiency as well as equity.

Nutritionists focus on individuals, not households. A new generation of agricultural household models has emerged that takes into account conflict within households and its ramifications for efficiency as well as equity.

Nash-Bargained Household Models

In the agricultural household model we just learned about, income was pooled, and consumption decisions were made as though the household acted as a single unit. That model works if the household members share the same preferences. Alternatively, in the "dictator model," one person has all the power, and his or her preferences determine expenditures. We call these "unitary households."

In the Nash-bargained household model, in contrast, different members have different preferences and access to income. (This model is named after Nobel laureate mathematician John Nash, subject of the Hollywood film *A Beautiful Mind,* who invented the game-theoretic model on which it is based.) Household members naturally influence expenditures in ways that reflect their preferences.

How do we model such a household? Two people, person m and person f, decide whether to stay single or form a household. Let v_m be person m's utility or welfare if they do not form a household, and let v_f be person f's. If they form a household, they'll combine their income and spend it on things either or both care about. Person m's welfare will be U_m and f's will be U_f. Neither one will want to form a household unless there's a positive welfare gain in it, so both $U_m - v_m$ and $U_f - v_f$ must be positive (that is, unless it's a forced marriage).

Once the household is formed, v_m and v_f are "threat points," the utilities that each person would have if they were single. The higher a person's threat point, the more bargaining power he or she has in the Nash-bargained household. Thus, anything that affects a person's threat point can help explain what the household spends its income on. If my threat point is high, I should be able to influence my household's spending in a big way.

What's in a threat point? Lots of things, potentially, but one of them certainly is unearned income. Earned income, like wages, might be affected by what one's spouse earns, but unearned income (from assets, for example) is the same regardless of whether or not a person is part of the household. If I'm independently wealthy, my threat point will be high. If I'm penniless, it will be low.

In a unitary household model it wouldn't matter who had the unearned income because all the income would get pooled. In a Nash-bargained household, it would matter. Who controls the unearned income determines who has the most bargaining power within the household, and therefore how much money gets spent on what. Tests for whether we've got a unitary or Nash-bargained household boil down to this question: Does who controls the non-earned income explain household expenditures? Or is total household income the only thing that matters—that is, a rupee is a rupee, no matter who controls it?

A number of studies find that it does matter who controls the income (see sidebar 9.3). Their findings demonstrate that power asymmetries within households can profoundly affect spending and equity.

Are Households Efficient?

Does who has control within the household also affect efficiency? When economic power within households is unequal, does this affect the size of the economic pie as well as its distribution?

The Nash-bargained model described above assumes there is no reason why households would not maximize their incomes, even if power relations within households affect expenditures. If I exert a large influence on how my household's income gets spent, shouldn't I try to make that income as large as possible? And if I do not, wouldn't I still want my household's income to be large? Having a little influence over a larger pie is better than having a little influence over a little pie.

Sidebar 9.3   Who Controls the Cash?

A number of studies find that it matters who in the household controls income. Using data from a household survey in Brazil, Duncan Thomas tested whether unearned income controlled by fathers and mothers had the same effect on how households spent their money. He found significant differences between the two. Income controlled by mothers had a much bigger positive effect on children's health than income controlled by fathers. The effect of mother's income on child survival probabilities was almost twenty times larger. This is one reason why cash transfer programs in developing countries often give the money to poor women instead of men. (We learned about cash transfer programs in chapter 2). The study also found that mothers are more likely to spend their income on daughters and fathers on sons.

A study from Thailand found that the more property income males had, the more likely they were to marry. But for women, unearned income had the opposite effect. It seems marriage is an "inferior good" for Thai women!

Both of these studies were influential in showing that, at least for some types of research, the assumption of unitary households may not be appropriate.

Duncan Thomas, "Intra-Household Resource Allocation: An Inferential Approach," *Journal of Human Resources* 25, no. 4 (1990):635–64.

T. Paul Schultz, "Testing the Neoclassical Model of Family Labor Supply and Fertility," *Journal of Human Resources* 25, no. 4 (1990):599–634.

This is an important question. If someone in the household could be made better off without making others worse off, the household economy is said to be not Pareto efficient.

Testing whether who controls income and wealth within households affects expenditures is easier than testing whether it affects efficiency. A pioneering study in the African country of Burkina Faso found a way, though. It concluded that power asymmetries within households reduce efficiency. The economic pie in such a context would be larger if women controlled more of the assets (see sidebar 9.4).

BEYOND HOUSEHOLDS

Households do not exist in isolation from one another. Diverse, heterogeneous households interact within rural economies, like individual

Sidebar 9.4   Bad to Be a Female Plot

In many African countries, crops are produced on plots controlled by different members of the household. Pareto efficiency implies that these plots are managed so as to maximize income—that is, make the pie as big as it can be, however it might end up being divvied up. Are household economies Pareto efficient? Chris Udry explored this question using data on male and female plots in Burkina Faso households. If the household is efficient, it will allocate its fertilizer such that the benefit of the last bit of fertilizer (the marginal product) is the same on all plots. Udry's econometric analysis refuted this. It found that plots controlled by women were farmed much less intensively than the male-controlled plots; yields were 30% lower on female plots within the same household. This study was influential because it demonstrated that heterogeneous preferences and access to resources within households affect not only equity, but also efficiency.

Christopher Udry, "Gender, Agricultural Production, and the Theory of the Household," *Journal of Political Economy* 104, no. 5 (October 1996):1010–46.

cells that together make up a complex organism. When a policy, market, environmental, or some other shock strikes one household, its effects reverberate through the economy, like ripples in a pond. The models we have looked at so far in this chapter focus on individual households; they ignore linkages among households.

To illustrate the importance of these linkages, suppose a poor household receives a 100-peso transfer from a government welfare program like the ones we looked at in chapter 2. The immediate effect of the transfer is to raise the poor household's income by the amount of the transfer. But that is not the end of the story, because the poor household spends the money. Suppose it spends 50 pesos to buy meat from a herder in the same village. The herder's income goes up by 50 pesos. So far, the 100-peso transfer has increased village income by 150 pesos. Now suppose that the herder spends half of her new income in the village, hiring a mason to fix her house. The mason now has 25 pesos. As the money circulates through the village, it creates more income. Some of the money leaves the village along the way, contributing to income somewhere else in the country (or world). But the money that stays in the village has a multiplier effect on income in the village. Most people spend most of their income closer to home. If people spend half of their income in the

Sidebar 9.5 The Mystery of Maize in Mexico

In 1995, Mexico did away with policies that guaranteed farmers high prices for their maize and other basic crops. The producer price of maize in Mexico immediately fell by around 40%, but this was followed by a record-high maize harvest that couldn't be explained by the weather. Why would maize production increase after the price fell?

A study by three UC Davis economists offered an answer. Most maize producers do not sell their crop; they are subsistence farmers. When the price of maize fell, farmers who were not in the market were not directly affected.

Typically, villages have many subsistence farmers and a few commercial ones. They interact with each other in local labor markets, as subsistence households hire out labor to commercial farms.

When the price shock hit, commercial maize farmers cut back their production and hired less labor. This transmitted a negative impact to the subsistence households, even though they did not sell maize. Unable to find employment, subsistence farmers had to find another use for their labor. Their solution? Grow more maize for home consumption!

The result seemed paradoxical: the price of maize fell, but maize production on subsistence farms increased. The authors refer to this as a "retreat into subsistence." Across Mexico, maize production went up on rain-fed lands, where subsistence farmers are concentrated. Despite higher maize production, though, Mexico's maize farmers were worse off after the price plunge.

George A. Dyer, Steve Boucher, and J. Edward Taylor, "Subsistence Response to Market Shocks," *American Journal of Agricultural Economics* 88, no. 2 (2006):279–91.

village, it can be shown that every peso of income transferred to a poor household ends up creating two pesos of income in the village.

If you have taken a macroeconomics class, you might recognize this story. It is just like the Keynesian income multiplier, which became an important part of economic policies in rich countries following the Great Depression and, most recently in the United States, "Obamanomics."

A relatively new area of research in development economics takes models of individual households and "nests" them within models of the larger economies of which these households are part: villages, regions, or nations. Economy-wide impacts created by interactions among economic agents, like income multipliers, are called "general equilibrium effects." General equilibrium effects can take many forms, and they can dramatically alter the ways development policies affect incomes, employment, and welfare in poor economies (see sidebar 9.5). We'll look at general equilibrium effects again in chapter 10.

www.rebeltext.org/development/qr9.html
Learn more about agriculture by exploring
multimedia resources while you read.

10

Structural Transformation

Poverty and wealth dynamics are fundamental to development economics. In prior chapters, we described how a household's wealth today can shape its wealth trajectory into the future. The same can be true for villages or even countries. The dominant driver of these large-scale dynamics is the transformation of an economy from agriculture to manufacturing and services. Today's developed countries underwent this transformation in the past century or so. Developing countries are undergoing this transformation before our eyes—some at an incredible pace. As a result, for the first time in human history more people now live in cities than on farms. This raises new challenges in the form of strain on already weak infrastructure, environmental pressures and congestion of different forms, but also opens new opportunities for leveraging economies of scale, spillovers, and agglomeration effects. In this chapter, we explore the insights development economists have gained on this fundamental economic transformation process.

ESSENTIALS

- Elements of structural transformation
- Dual-economy (Lewis) model
- Migration
- Human capital
- Specialization and diversification
- "Supermarket revolution"
- Market interlinkages

In January 2006 the United Nations Food and Agricultural Organization (FAO) held a workshop called "Beyond Agriculture." To appreciate how striking this is as a title of an FAO conference, consider the FAO's mandate: "to raise levels of nutrition, improve agricultural productivity, better the lives of rural populations and contribute to the growth of the world economy."[1]

For years, with most of the developing world's population living on farms, one could assume these were compatible objectives. For example, high-yielding seeds could raise agricultural productivity, reduce poverty, and provide people with more secure access to food.

The FAO was telling us that wasn't the case anymore.

On May 23, 2007, the world became more urban than rural.[2] That's the day that, according to the United Nations, more than half of the globe's population was living in towns and cities—for the first time ever.[3]

Not only is the world becoming less rural; rural populations are becoming less agricultural. Rural households in Malawi and Ghana still get 55%–56% of their income from crop production, but the crop share is 41% in Vietnam, 21% in Nicaragua, and only 15% in Bangladesh.[4] In Mexico, the share of agriculture in rural household income was 14% in 2002 and 11% in 2007; only around 2% came from corn.[5] In these settings, substantial gains in agricultural productivity may benefit poor households that rely more heavily on agricultural production, but these gains are unlikely to raise the average income for rural households very much when most income is non-agricultural.

The FAO found itself grappling with the question of how to achieve multiple objectives that, in the modern world, are less and less related to one another.

How did we get here?

The growth models in chapter 7 give an aggregate, bird's-eye view of income growth and why some countries grow faster than others. The empirical growth model of Sala-i-Martin suggests that growth involves a complex array of variables, and there may be more than one way to make growth happen. As endogenous growth theorists point out, there are important feedbacks that shape growth in different countries. Economic incentives are important in shaping these feedbacks. Poverty trap models suggest that exogenous "big push" interventions like Jeffrey Sachs's Millennium Village Project are required to kick-start asset accumulation and income growth.

Unfortunately, aggregate models mask far-reaching transformations that have to occur within economies in order to make growth possible and that are themselves a product of growth. Countries start out being mostly agricultural in terms of where people derive their income and where they are employed, with most people living in rural villages. As economies grow, they morph into manufacturing-and-service economies. That is, the structure of the economy changes.

The structural transformation from largely agricultural to non-agricultural societies is one of the most fundamental features of economic development. The Nobel laureate W. Arthur Lewis (whom we will learn about below) called it the heart of the development process. Whatever nostalgia you might have for picturesque farming villages and the rural way of life, you'd better get over it, because economic development leads inescapably to people leaving the farm. (Of course, a society can invest in trying to keep picturesque villages alive, as France has, but it will not be cheap, and not very many people will live in them.)

Figure 10.1 drives home the point. It shows a scatterplot of countries at different levels of per capita income (PPP adjusted, measured on the horizontal axis) and shares of the workforce employed in agriculture (vertical axis). Each country is represented by a ray whose starting point tells us where the country was in 1990 and whose tip shows where it was in 2005. The very top arrow belongs to Burundi, with a per capita income of $620 per year and 94% of the workforce in agriculture. The right-most rays correspond to countries with very high per capita incomes and almost none of their workforces in agriculture. There you would find the United States and even France and Japan, which have expensive government programs to support farmers and rural villages.

As country per capita incomes rise, the share of the workforce in agriculture doesn't just decrease—it drops off a cliff. First, look at how the arrows line up. With no exceptions, the countries with low per capita GDPs have high shares of their workforces employed in agriculture. As per capita incomes rise, the arrows fall sharply, forming a hyperbolic curve. Not only that—almost all the arrows slope toward the southeast. (If you see an exception, there is a unique story behind it, like a resource-extracting country without agriculture, or a former Soviet republic struggling to adjust to a postsocialist existence.)

The sloping arrows tell us that between 1990 and 2005, per capita incomes increased while farm labor shares fell. At high per capita incomes, the arrows converge toward the horizontal axis, where agriculture's share of the workforce is zero. No country ever reaches zero— you can't grow crops without *any* workers. However, some rich countries have agricultural labor shares of 2% or less. Some of the smallest farm workforce shares in the world are in countries with expensive gov-

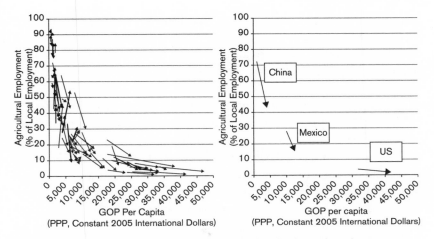

FIGURE 10.1. Changes in per capita GDP and agriculture's share of employment, 1990–2005. As countries' per capita incomes increase, the share of the labor force doing farm work decreases. Source: World Development Indicators (WDI), World Bank (http://data.worldbank.org/data-catalog/world-development-indicators).

ernment programs to support agriculture, like the US, the EU countries, or Japan, whose domestic price of rice is as high as seven times the world price.

The right-hand diagram removes all but three of the countries on the graph: China, Mexico, and the United States. China is the economic miracle, with income growth exceeding 10% in some years. You can see that it starts out in 1990 with over 75% of its workforce in agriculture. In 2010, 49% of Chinese workers had farm jobs—and the farm share was falling fast. Mexico began the period with a higher income and a much smaller workforce share in agriculture than China. Its income continued to grow and its farm employment share fell, though at a slower rate than China's. The United States began the period with one of the world's highest per capita incomes and around 2% of its workforce in agriculture. Most hired farmworkers in the United States are from Mexico.[6]

MODELING THE TRANSFORMATION

In order to understand what drives this economic transformation, we need to dig underneath the aggregate growth numbers we looked at in chapter 7. Multisector models allow us to study the interactions between agriculture and the non-agricultural sectors in an economy, including the movement of people between them. They offer insights into what has to happen to get growth going and how economic growth transforms poor economies. We'll see what development economists have to say about how the transformation from agricultural to industry-and-service economies unfolds and the ramifications for economic development research and policy.

The simplest multisector models involve only agriculture (often called the "traditional sector") and the non-agricultural sectors (the "modern sector"). Because they have only two sectors, these are called dual-economy models. They are a good starting point for learning about interactions between sectors. Today, though, almost all multisector models used in development economics have many different sectors as well as many different actors: households, governments, and others. After learning about two-sector models we'll take a look at multisector models and how they are being used for development policy and research.

Leaving the Farm

Francisco is a farmer in a village in southern Mexico.[7] He and his wife Alde have a three-hectare (about 7.5 acre) plot of good land, three sons, and two daughters. A horse, a team of oxen, and some goats and chickens fill out the family.

A construction job opens up in the city of Oaxaca fifty miles away, and a contractor comes to the village to recruit able-bodied villagers willing to work. Francisco and Alde's seventeen-year-old son, Alejandro, asks if he can go. His best friend migrated to Oaxaca a few months earlier. Alejandro reminds his parents that his friend sends home $50 a month to help his family. "I could do the same thing," he assures them.

Should they let him go? Alejandro's fifteen-year-old brother, Ramiro, says he can fill in for Alejandro on the farm. "There isn't enough work for all of us here, anyway," he says.

The next morning Alejandro hops on the bus for Oaxaca.

A month later, Francisco and Alde's daughter Alicia's friend heads off to work in an electronics plant in Tijuana. Alicia says she's already sending back $25 a month to her parents. "I could do that, too," she tells them.

"But if you go, who will watch the animals and help me around the house?" her mom asks.

"I will," her little sister, Silvia, assures her.

The next week, Alicia is gone. Within a month, Francisco and Alde get $75 a month in migrant remittances, the income sent home by their two kids. Not only that, they now have fewer mouths to feed. Ramiro and his dad have no trouble bringing in the harvest, with a little help from the younger daughter, Norma, and her little brother Tomás. The extra income from Alejandro and Alicia helps pay for Norma and Tomás to go to school.

A year later, Alejandro comes back to visit for the fiesta of the virgen de Guadalupe. "The work's good," he tells Ramiro. "Ever think of going to the city?"

"Don't think of it!" Alde tells them. "Who will help your father in the field?"

"I will!" little Tomás and Norma exclaim in unison. "I'm *never* leaving home!" Norma insists.

Their father shakes his head, knowing all too well that kids with schooling don't stick around the village. "I'm not getting any younger, Ramiro. If you go, I fear there will be no harvest," Francisco sighs.

Ramiro stays, gets married, and his new wife moves into Francisco and Alde's house. Little by little Ramiro takes over the farm, with some financial help from his migrant siblings when there's an investment to be made or when the harvest isn't good. Tomás and Norma both migrate to the city the summer after their high school graduation.

This story is a composite of families all over rural Mexico, and indeed, the world. It's so universal that there's a well-known economic model that describes precisely this story.

The Lewis Model

The economist W. Arthur Lewis, a Nobel laureate, wrote a famous paper called "Economic Development with Unlimited Supplies of Labor."[8] Lewis looked at the surplus labor in rural areas and recognized its tremendous potential for economic development. He argued that the marginal product of labor in the subsistence sector (agriculture) is virtually zero—or at least very low compared to the "subsistence wage," or what it takes to keep a person alive in the rural economy. This means that, at the margin, agricultural workers produce next to nothing, yet naturally everyone has to consume enough food to survive (a "subsistence bundle"). Think of the subsistence wage, w_s, as the cost of this subsistence bundle.

An employer in the city, in theory, only has to offer a wage equal to the cost of subsistence—plus maybe a little extra for the bus fare and the higher urban cost of living—in order to induce a worker to move off the farm and migrate to a modern-sector job.

The power of Lewis's argument is this: workers can move out of the subsistence sector without the economy suffering any loss in agricultural output. In effect, the movement of labor off the farm could provide a seemingly endless supply of labor to the expanding modern (industrial and service) sectors, and farms would still be able to produce the food to feed them (as long as there are good markets to get the food to the city; see chapter 11). As the urban economy expands, urban employers do not have to offer higher wages to get more workers to come, as long as there is a surplus of labor ready to move off the farm. The supply of labor to urban jobs, therefore, is perfectly elastic: the urban labor supply curve is horizontal. If urban capitalists create jobs, the workers will come—from the farm to the city. And if urban wages stay low, this is precisely what capitalists will do. Low wages mean high profits, which in turn can be reinvested to make the urban economy grow even more.

Figure 10.2 illustrates the Lewis model. The horizontal axis in each graph represents labor. The economy starts out with an amount of labor equal to $\bar{L}$, all of it in the traditional (or agricultural) sector. Since the economy starts out with virtually all its labor in the traditional sector, any gain in labor to the modern sector implies a loss of labor from the traditional sector.

The top figure represents agriculture. You should start out at its southeast corner and read from right to left. The curve depicts the marginal value product of labor (MVPL) in agriculture, given the other inputs (land, capital) available to farms. This curve is drawn steeply to reflect sharply decreasing marginal returns to labor under traditional technologies. For the first few workers, the MVPL in agriculture is high. These workers would include Francisco and Ramiro. As more and more people work the land, the contribution of the last worker becomes smaller. Eventually, Lewis argues, it bottoms out at zero; there is surplus labor, and the agricultural MVPL curve flattens out along the horizontal axis. Over the flat range of the MVPL curve, workers can leave the farm without having any adverse effect on agricultural output.

The bottom graph is about the modern (industrial and service) sector. We have to read it from left to right because any gain to the modern-sector workforce implies a loss for the traditional-sector workforce. This figure shows three MVPL curves in the modern sector, each cor-

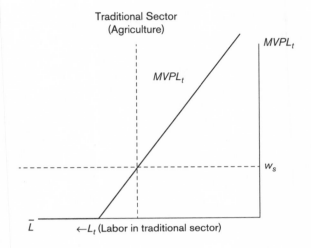

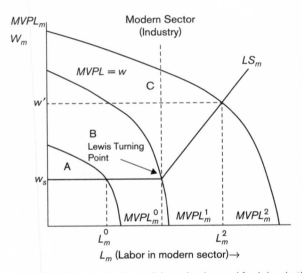

FIGURE 10.2. In the Lewis model, as the demand for labor in the modern sector increases (bottom), surplus labor is drawn from the traditional sector (top) without putting upward pressure on wages until the Lewis turning point is reached.

responding to a different level of capital investment. As more capital is invested in new plants and equipment, the MVPL shifts out to the right. Like the MVPL curve in agriculture, each modern-sector MVPL curve is decreasing with labor: an additional worker adds less and less to output at a given level of capital. New investments increase this MVPL, though.

In addition, the bottom graph shows the labor supply (LS) curve for the modern sector. You can also think of it as the wage curve: for each wage (vertical axis), we can read off this curve the amount of labor the traditional sector is willing to supply to the modern sector. It will not supply any labor if the wage is less than subsistence.

Lining the bottom graph up with the top graph, you can see that the modern-sector LS curve is horizontal until the traditional-sector MVPL exceeds the subsistence wage. Over this range, the traditional sector will supply all the labor the modern sector demands—that is, until the labor surplus dries up and the agricultural MVPL rises above the subsistence wage. This is called the "Lewis turning point."

Beyond the Lewis turning point, if more workers leave the farm, the value of agricultural production goes down by more than the subsistence wage. Modern-sector employers will have to pay higher wages to induce more workers to move off the farm. They'll have to convince people like Ramiro. That's why the LS curve turns upward beyond the Lewis turning point.

How much labor will the modern sector hire? The MVPL for the modern sector tells us how much revenue will increase if another worker is hired. The wage line tells us how much industries will have to pay for that additional worker. Modern-sector firms will hire additional workers up to the point where their MVPL just equals the wage they have to pay. The modern sector starts out with a low level of capital, at $MVPL_m^0$, paying a wage equal to w_s; thus, it demands L_m^0 workers.

The difference between the MVPL and the wage at each level of labor use is the marginal worker's contribution to profit. Cheap labor creates high profits.

For any MVPL curve, profits are the area underneath the curve but above the wage (or labor supply) curve, and wages are the area underneath the wage line. At $MVPL_m^0$, the modern sector's profit is given by area A, and wages are the area of the box defined by $w_s * L_m^0$. Part of this profit is invested in new plant and equipment, which shifts the MVPL curve out to $MVPL_m^1$. You can see that the new profit, depicted by areas A + B, is much larger than the original profit (A). Modern-sector growth, then, is self-perpetuating, as long as a large part of the profit is reinvested.

Eventually, the surplus labor in the traditional sector becomes exhausted. Once the MVPL in agriculture exceeds the subsistence wage, the modern sector has to offer higher wages to attract new workers. At that point, the income distribution begins to shift in favor of labor. At

$MVPL_m^2$, total modern-sector wages are the box given by $w'* L_m^2$, and profits are given by the area above the w' line (C).

With this brief description of the Lewis model under your belt, let's take some time to digest the model, which has been very influential in development economics, policy, and practice. Why exactly was this model important? The Lewis model gets us inside the "black box" of the aggregate growth models we presented in chapter 7. It illustrates what has to happen in order for incomes to grow: the economy has to transition from a traditional, agricultural one to a modern, industrial-and-service one. Growth in the modern sector cannot be understood in isolation from the traditional sector. Lewis pioneered what is known as "dual-economy" or "two-sector" economic models. As income grows, the workforce shifts out of the traditional sector.

The Lewis model is not without its critics or limitations. Theodore Schultz, an economist we met in chapter 9 who shared the Nobel Prize with Lewis, questioned the assumption of a zero marginal value product of labor in agriculture. More generally, Lewis largely ignored the importance of agriculture in his model. An influential study by Gustav Ranis and John C.H. Fei pointed out that agricultural production has to be sufficient to support the whole economy with food and raw materials—otherwise, rising food and raw-materials prices will choke off the expansion of the modern sector.[9] Their work shows the importance of investing in *agriculture* if a country wants its *modern* sector to grow. Agricultural investments can make it possible to produce more with fewer workers, thereby freeing up labor for the growing modern sector.

Although dual-economy models offer new insights into the economic and social transformations accompanying growth in poor economies, they are still aggregate models (though less so than the models in chapter 7). They do not tell us much about what has to happen on a micro level to enable people to move up economically by moving off the farm, or how to feed them once they are in the city. For food to be available to urban workers, markets have to work. Market failures are a quintessential feature of poor countries, especially in rural areas (chapters 11 and 12).

Can countries continue feeding themselves as people leave the farm? The answer to this question depends on farmers' ability to produce more food more efficiently—to raise productivity. Limited access to credit, insurance, and markets for inputs and output severely constrains small farmers' capacity to invest in new technologies and production

Sidebar 10.1   Can China Feed Itself as People Leave the Farm?

If agriculture is past the Lewis turning point, farm households cannot sacrifice labor to the nonfarm sector without losing production. A study of agricultural households in the northeast of China found that crop yields fell sharply when family members migrated from farm to nonfarm jobs. However, the study also found that those who left the farm sent home remittances, and remittances, in turn, raised crop yields. This finding suggests that the income family members send home loosens financial constraints on investing in fertilizer and other inputs that raise crop production. This study concluded that, on balance, the migration of labor off the farm has only a small effect on the aggregate supply of food in China.

Scott Rozelle, J. Edward Taylor, and Alan deBrauw, "Migration, Remittances, and Agricultural Productivity in China," *American Economic Review* 89, no. 2 (May 1999):287–91.

activities. Via remittances, family members who migrate can provide farmers with capital they need to raise productivity.There's no place for this kind of feedback of migration on agricultural investment in Lewis's or Fei and Ranis's models.

How does the Lewis model hold up when tested against hard data? Finding data to test how off-farm labor affects crop production is not easy, because few household surveys provide good information on both migration and crop production. The studies that do, though, almost unanimously reject the Lewis hypothesis of zero marginal value product of labor in agriculture. However, they also find that off-farm work may help farmers overcome the lost-labor effect and raise productivity (see sidebar 10.1).

FROM FARMER TO FACTORY WORKER

The skill demands of modern-sector jobs are different from those of subsistence production. The Lewis model leaves us with big questions in this regard. There's no human capital in the Lewis model—only hands. (This stands in stark contrast to Schultz, who believed human capital was as important for farmers as it was for anyone else.) Lewis does not offer insights into who leaves the farm and who does not. Do countries have to invest in preparing people to enter nonfarm jobs? Without investments in education, people will not be prepared to work in the modern sector. China had an unusual situation when its market reforms happened: a massive workforce with secondary education, ideal to fill factories with skilled workers and make China the world's workshop. Ireland had a similar situation but at a higher skill level. Its policy of free university education created a very highly trained workforce, and it became the headquarters for many corporations positioning themselves to supply the European Union's markets.

Research shows that the people who migrate off the farm look different from those who stay behind. These differences teach us about the things people—and countries—need in order to make the transition from an agricultural to a manufacturing-and-service economy.

Who Leaves, Who Stays, and Who Succeeds?

In a happy world, there would be jobs for people wherever they wanted to work, and people would have whatever skills they needed to fill those jobs. Reality is not much like that, even in the best of worlds. A student may love Davis, but the chances of finding a job in a small college town after graduation are low. In poor countries, millions of people leave their villages to work in the city and end up unemployed because they do not have the right skills, the jobs aren't there, or they just aren't in the right place at the right time. The transition from agricultural to industrial-and-service economies involves huge dislocations and wrenching adjustments. Hundreds of millions of people move off the farm and have to compete and live in a very different, urban, world. As populations shift from rural- to urban-based activities, pressures on food production and public services in urban areas increase. Many people—though a tiny minority of the world's population—migrate to other countries.

Industry and service jobs may not materialize because investors do not believe that workers with the right skills will be available. In the 1989 Hollywood movie *Field of Dreams,* an Iowa corn farmer (Kevin Costner), hearing voices, interprets them as a command to build a baseball diamond in his fields; he does, and the players come. Good players. If you build a factory, will the right workers come?

In the story of Francisco and Alde, Alejandro and Alicia both migrate to nonfarm jobs, one in construction, the other in an electronics factory. In real life, can *any* kid raised for farm work simply shift over to a nonfarm job? How did Francisco know that his two youngest kids would migrate away as soon as they finished school?

The Lewis model doesn't answer the questions of who migrates and who does not, or whether factories in the city can get the quantity as well as the quality of labor they need. Instead, it treats workers as homogeneous and ignores human capital.

Human capital theory (see chapter 6) can help us answer these questions. Econometric evidence confirms that there are significant and high economic returns to education in the modern sector—higher than in farmwork. At the very least, basic literacy, and possibly schooling beyond the primary level, may be required for a person to become a productive factory worker.

If this is true, then a human capital migration model would predict that people with more schooling are more likely to migrate from the traditional to the modern sector. Empirical studies consistently find this to be the case (for example, see sidebar 10.2).

THE "DE-AGRICULTURALIZATION" OF RURAL ECONOMIES

As people move off the farm, rural households diversify their income sources. A poor rural household in Burundi is likely to get most or all of its income from farming. But in Latin America, Asia, and increasingly even sub-Saharan Africa, it is hard to find households that specialize in farming. Most are income diversifiers. Table 10.1 illustrates this for several countries in Africa, Asia, and Latin America.

It is clear from these data that when we think "rural" we should not automatically think "agricultural." To end up with average shares as high as these, many households must have nonfarm income shares that are very high indeed.

High shares of non-agricultural income in rural households have important implications for development policies as well as for research. The following sections discuss two of the most important ones.

Productivity and Poverty

If poor rural households get a large share of their income from agricultural production, raising agricultural productivity could have a big effect on poverty. In general, poor rural households get a larger share of their income from agriculture the poorer a country is. However, in a transforming rural economy, raising agricultural productivity and raising rural incomes become different policy goals—even when it comes to poor households. For example, take a poor household that gets

Sidebar 10.2   Who Migrates and Who Doesn't?

A study using survey data from rural Mexico found that migration is highly selective: the characteristics of those who migrate off the farm are different from those who stay, in ways consistent with human capital theory. As in the story of Francisco and Alde, migration seems to be a household strategy. Household heads are significantly less likely to migrate to the city than their children. Each year of additional schooling raises the likelihood that a child migrates by 0.6%. This is not a small effect considering that 7% of all rural Mexicans were found to be internal migrants. (Another 6.7% were international migrants, working in the United States.) An additional year of work experience also increases the likelihood of migration. Thus, a child with ten years of schooling and work experience is more than 11% more likely to migrate to the city than a person without any schooling or experience. The probability of migrating is lower for women than men, and it is lower the more land the family has (why?). If one family member migrates, the likelihood of another family member migrating rises. Each family migrant raises the odds that another family member will migrate by 3.5%. Thus, migration is a network-driven process.

Human capital theory would predict that schooling would have the largest effect on migration to jobs where it raises workers' productivity the most. The study found that higher schooling *decreased* the likelihood of migrating to farm jobs. Schooling was found to have *no significant effect* on the likelihood of migrating to the United States. Most people who migrate from rural Mexico to the United States do so illegally, and education does not help much if you're working abroad as an undocumented immigrant. Schooling significantly *increased* the likelihood of migrating to urban areas within Mexico, however.

Jorge Mora and J. Edward Taylor, "Determinants of Migration, Destination, and Sector Choice: Disentangling Individual, Household, and Community Effects," in *International Migration, Remittances, and the Brain Drain*, edited by Çağlar Özden and Maurice Schiff (New York: Palgrave Macmillan, 2005), 21–52.

20% of its income from growing and selling staples. Suppose a new technology (say, a Green Revolution seed variety) raises staple productivity by 10% for this poor household. How much will its income go up? The immediate effect of the new technology will be to raise this household's income by 10% * 20% = 2%. In other words, the income

TABLE 10.1 NONFARM INCOME SHARES OF SELECTED LDCS

Country	Year of Survey	Nonfarm Income Share
Mozambique	1991	15
Gambia	1985–86	23
Malawi	2004	23
Tanzania	1980	25
Nigeria	1974/75	30
Rwanda	1990	30
Vietnam	2002	37.7
Sudan	1988	38
Ghana	1998	39.1
Nicaragua	2005	43.1
Guatemala	2000	50
Mozambique'	1988-89	59
Bangladesh	2000	63.1
South Africa (former homelands)	1982/86	75
Botswana	1985/86	77
Lesotho	1976	78
Kenya	1987/89	80

SOURCES: Thomas Reardon, "Using Evidence of Household Income Diversification to Inform Study of the Rural Nonfarm Labor Market in Africa," *World Development* 25, no. 5 (1997):735–47; Erik Jonasson, Mateusz Filipski, Jonathan Brooks, and J. Edward Taylor, "Modeling the Welfare Implications of Agricultural Policies in Developing Countries," *Journal of Policy Modeling* 36, no. 1 (2014): 63–82.

effect is much smaller than the production effect. In time, the household might be able to put more effort into staple production and get a higher return from the new seeds. But the point is clear: in a rural economy where a large share of income does not come from growing staples, raising productivity in staples might not be the best way to move households out of poverty.[10]

In a diversified economy, households' income sources can span different activities as well as different locations. The key to moving out of poverty might well be to move out of agriculture and into higher paying non-agricultural jobs. Policies that stimulate non-agricultural activities inside rural areas, or that encourage kids to go to school so they can grow up to have nonfarm jobs, can play an important role in combating rural poverty. So can employment growth in urban areas, which may benefit poor urban households as well as rural households, through migration. Keeping ties with rural households might be an important form of livelihood insurance for migrants in distant labor markets.

Consumers versus Producers

Some countries try to support their rural households by offering farmers artificially high prices for their crops. In many cases, this means that crop producers get higher prices, but consumers pay more for food. Agricultural households are both producers and consumers of food. We saw in chapter 9 that when the price of food goes up, these households win as producers but lose as consumers. If only a small share of income comes from food production, the consumption effect will outweigh the production effect, and higher food prices will hurt rural (as well as urban) households. Many rural households do not have land and do not grow crops at all. For them, like urban consumers, higher food prices are almost certainly welfare-reducing. Never assume that higher food prices are necessarily good for rural households, particularly the rural poor.

Another implication of diversification away from agriculture concerns the benefits of technological change. Consider a new technology, like a high-yielding seed, that raises crop productivity. If everyone is a farmer, the main benefits of this new technology will be on farms. As more and more people move away from farming, they benefit indirectly, through lower food prices.

Who Diversifies and Who Doesn't?

Economists often talk about the gains from specializing. The economist David Ricardo advised countries to specialize in producing goods in which they enjoy a "comparative advantage" and trading to get whatever else they wish to buy. As rural economies diversify, it is natural to ask whether the same advice applies to rural households. Mark Twain once said: "Put all your eggs in one basket—and watch the basket." Clearly, most rural households do not follow Twain's advice. Should they?

An economist would look at diversification and conclude that it is welfare-maximizing. Otherwise, why would households diversify? Or maybe households would like to specialize wherever their comparative advantage lies, but for some reason they cannot. Perhaps there is a market failure or some other barrier to maximizing income. (Market failures will be a topic of chapters 11 and 12.)

An action can be welfare (or constrained-welfare) maximizing even if it does not maximize income. For example, a household might be willing to sacrifice income in order to reduce income risk. In that case, its welfare depends not only on expected income but also on income uncertainty, which might be measured by the variance of income or the probability that income will fall below some minimum subsistence threshold. Does aversion to risk prevent poor households from making the investments needed to lift themselves out of poverty? This is an important question in development economics.

What is the relationship between diversification and income? The answer to this question depends on why households diversify. Are they "pushed" into diversifying for some reason other than to increase their income? Or are they "pulled" into diversifying because they can get higher income by investing in non-agricultural activities?

The "diversity push" view mostly emphasizes risk. A poor farmer could put all his effort and cash into crop production, but if the crop fails, he will not be able to put food on the table for his family. Poor farmers around the world lack any access to crop insurance. If the crop fails, that's it. Diversification allows a poor household to fall back on its other income sources should the crop fail.

The "diversity pull" view stresses diminishing marginal returns in crop production or intra-household considerations. Beyond a point, the more you invest in crop production, the smaller the marginal returns to that investment—whether it is cash spent on fertilizer or family labor. If a farmer could earn more by working an additional day for a wage or in some noncrop production activity than in his own fields, it makes sense for her to diversify into wage work, or noncrop production. The same applies to different family members. A strong son with little schooling might be a productive crop producer but have few prospects as a factory worker, whereas his sibling (sister, perhaps) with secondary schooling would be ill-placed in the fields.

These two theories of why households diversify provide different hypotheses, which might be testable using survey data. If the diversity push view is right, we would expect that households most vulnerable to risk (and with the least access to other forms of income security) would

Sidebar 10.3   Do Nonfarm Activities Increase Inequality?

A survey of findings from several African countries found that many rural households diversify into nonfarm activities, including nonfarm rural enterprises like food processing that rely on agriculture for inputs. In most areas, nonfarm wage work and nonfarm production generate higher income than agricultural work, and they constitute an important part of rural household incomes. However, poor households face severe barriers to entry into these nonfarm activities. Taking a chance on a nonfarm investment entails risks and requires capital, both financial and human. Getting access to a nonfarm wage job requires schooling and skills. These are all things that the poorest households generally cannot afford. Thus, most of the gains from diversifying into nonfarm activities bypass the poor, and as a result, off-farm income increases inequalities in rural areas.

Thomas Reardon, "Using Evidence of Household Income Diversification to Inform Study of the Rural Nonfarm Labor Market in Africa," *World Development* 25, no. 5 (1997):735–47.

diversify, and this would lead to lower incomes relative to households less vulnerable to risk. If the diversity pull view is correct, we would expect diversification into noncrop activities to be associated with higher incomes. That's what a survey of research findings from African countries found—but not everyone can diversify into nonfarm activities (see sidebar 10.3).

The Transformation of Agriculture and the National Economy

The economist Peter Timmer identified four stages of the transformation of agriculture and its role in national economies.[11] First, agricultural productivity per agricultural worker begins to rise, creating an economic surplus. Second, this surplus is tapped in ways discussed in chapter 9 (taxes, surplus labor migrating to the city, or government price policies). The second stage is the main focus of the dual-economy models, like the Lewis model. In stage 3, the agricultural sector becomes increasingly integrated with other sectors of the economy. This happens as markets develop, linking agriculture with the urban economy, and also as the rural economy diversifies into non-agricultural activities, as

Sidebar 10.4   The Supermarket Revolution

Supermarkets used to be the rich country consumer's place to shop, but not any longer. In Asia, Latin America, and Africa, the spread of supermarkets is transforming food markets within and across countries. And the transformation is happening fast. The supermarket growth that took five decades in the United States happened in a single decade in Latin America; by 2000, supermarkets there accounted for 50%–60% of total retail food sales. In East and Southeast Asia it is happening even faster. It is just beginning to unfold in some African countries.

The supermarket transformation of agricultural markets has big implications for economic development and development policy. Can small farmers compete in a world dominated by Walmart and other big players with centralized procurement, for whom quality and timing are paramount? How can development projects help small producers, processors, and traders succeed in this new world instead of being excluded from new market opportunities? As the leading economist studying supermarkets and development, Thomas Reardon and his colleagues write: "Development models, policies, and programs need to adapt to this radical change. Development agencies must understand that 'product markets' will mean 'supermarkets'" (p. 1140). "Market oriented programs and policies" will in fact be "supermarket-oriented" (p. 1146).

Thomas Reardon, C. Peter Timmer, Christopher B. Barrett, and Julio Berdegué, "The Rise of Supermarkets in Africa, Asia, and Latin America," *American Journal of Agricultural Economics* 85, no. 5 (2003): 1140–46.

discussed earlier in this chapter. Eventually, in stage 4, agriculture is just another sector of the economy. As Timmer writes: "The role of agriculture in industrialized economies is little different from the role of the steel, housing, or insurance sectors" (p. 6).

Even in poor countries, it is important to view agriculture in the context of an increasingly diversified and integrated national economy. Perhaps the most concrete way to appreciate the transformation of agriculture in developing countries is through a place you have likely patronized at least once in the past month: a supermarket (see sidebar 10.4).

As we shall see next, viewing agriculture as one of many interacting sectors in a complex economic system changes the way we think about, and model, developing economies.

RURAL-URBAN LINKAGES

In chapter 9 we learned about the how important agricultural development is to the urban economy. In this chapter we met W. Arthur Lewis, who demonstrated agriculture's importance as a source of labor to the expanding urban industrial sector. Then we met Gustav Ranis and John Fei, who used a dual-economy model to show how agricultural production has to keep up with the demand for food and raw materials in the rest of the economy. In 1976, John Mellor—then an economics professor at Cornell University—showed that the rural economy was critical in another respect: poor countries depend on demand in rural households to provide a market for the goods produced in the urban sector.[12]

From these and other studies a new picture of developing economies emerged. Economists began to recognize that the rural and urban economies of developing countries become integrated in complex ways. Each sector depends upon the other. A shock in one sector gets transmitted to the other. A poor harvest adversely affects urban households through high food prices. An expansion in urban employment affects agricultural households by drawing workers off the farm; these workers, in turn, share part of their urban earnings with rural households, through migrant remittances.

Market linkages between sectors play a useful role in economies by diffusing the impacts of shocks through the whole economy. To give an example, in chapter 5 we saw that when a drought hit agricultural households in Burkina Faso, remittances from migrants increased sharply to help compensate for the rural income loss. In chapters 11, 12, and 13 we'll learn about the important role markets and international trade can play in helping people adjust to adverse shocks.

Connections between rural and urban households do not always lead to beneficial outcomes, however. For example, you would think that people would not migrate to cities if work was not available there—but in practice many choose to migrate despite high urban unemployment. In the 1950s and 1960s, governments became overwhelmed by rising urban unemployment and, at the same time, urban population growth fed by increasing streams of rural-to-urban migrants. Urban slums proliferated. Government revenues could not keep up with the demand for public services, from sanitation to schools. By the end of the 1990s, one slum in Mumbai, India, covered 175 acres with a population density of an astounding 1,200 people per acre![13] By 2003, nearly a third of the world's urban population—almost 1 billion people—lived in slums, according to the United Nations.[14] In many of the world's slums, most people live in makeshift dwellings on land they are not authorized to occupy.[15]

Increasing rural-to-urban migration in the face of rising urban unemployment does not make any sense in the models of Lewis and Ranis and Fei. Why leave the farm and migrate to a city in search of jobs that aren't there?

In 1970, economists John Harris at MIT and Michael Todaro at the University College of Nairobi came up with an explanation for this seemingly irrational behavior.[16] When deciding whether or not to migrate, people compare their expected wage in the city to their marginal value product on the farm. The expected wage is the actual wage times the probability of finding a job. For example, if the going wage for a migrant worker in the city is $6 per day, and a new migrant has a 50-50 chance of getting a job at that wage, her expected wage is 50% × $6 = $3. If the income she could generate on the farm is less than $3, she will migrate; otherwise, she will stay on the farm. (In real life, other considerations factor into the migration decision, including the economic and psychic costs of moving.) That's why migration happens even if the urban unemployment rate is high.

The Harris-Todaro model shows how a rational decision by an individual to migrate to the city can lead to an outcome that is inefficient for society. If a person can produce something on the farm but migrates to a crowded city slum and ends up unemployed, society obviously would be better off if he had not migrated.

It also has big policy implications. What should governments do to reduce urban unemployment? Create new jobs in the city? That will raise the probability of employment and bring more migrants in, driving the unemployment rate back up again. A country would be better off creating jobs for people in rural areas.

Many topics in the development economics literature fall under the "rural-urban linkages" area. They include the functioning of labor markets, the role of the informal economy, entrepreneurship and microenterprises, slums, the creation of infrastructure, migrant remittances and their impacts, and the sustainability of cities. New approaches that make creative use of technology and people will be critical if poor countries hope to accommodate their expanding urban populations (sidebar 10.5).

Sidebar 10.5 Smart Cities

Cities in developing countries will have to absorb enormous new populations in the next two decades, including an additional 350 million people in China, 250 million in India, and 380 million in Africa. How they do that will shape how people interact in their urban environments, how livable cities will be (and for whom), the competitiveness of cities and nations, and the environment—80% of global carbon emissions now come from cities. Anyone who has breathed the air in Cairo or Beijing or sat in a São Paulo or Nairobi traffic jam understands how daunting the challenge is.

Making cities "smart" is the key to responding to this challenge. In rich countries the term "smart cities" conjures up images of intelligent buildings, thousands of networked devices gathering real-time information, even sensors in trash cans to tell garbage collectors where to go. In poor countries, smart development means delivering more services to more people in a more efficient and effective way, using whatever technology is available at the moment. Invariably, this means involving citizens in planning, managing, and collaborating with local governments to provide better services. For example, the touch of a smartphone app can take the place of a remote sensor to provide information that is fed into systems to improve the design and delivery of urban services.

World Bank, "Building Smarter Cities" (https://blogs.worldbank.org/ic4d/building-smarter-cities).

World Bank, "Urban Development" (www.worldbank.org/en/topic/urbandevelopment).

BEYOND THE DUAL ECONOMY: ECONOMY-WIDE MODELS IN DEVELOPMENT

Empirical research using survey data finds that rural households engage in an array of farm and nonfarm activities as well as rural-to-urban migration. Urban economies are more complex, with a large number of interacting production sectors, factors, labor types, and households. An economy is really a complex organism, a vast marketplace in which millions and millions of decisions by a diversity of actors lead to both aggregate (for example, national) and micro (for example, household-level) economic outcomes. The interplay of demand and supply determines both prices and quantities of goods as well as factors of production.

Both aggregate growth models and dual-economy models miss these complex interactions, which are the essence of modern economies. Over the past quarter-century, a new breed of economy-wide models has emerged to enable researchers to simulate the ways in which development policies impact whole economies and the actors within them. These models are called "computable general equilibrium" (CGE) models, and they have become a staple of development policy analysis.

CGE models are complex, and building one is beyond the scope of this text.[17] Like climate models and even computer games, constructing CGE models requires having an understanding of the system being modeled (in this case, the workings of the economy) and the mathematical and programming skills to create the simulation model.

Nevertheless, development economics students, researchers, and practitioners are likely to come across them at some time or another, so having a basic understanding of how they work has become an essential of development economics. Mary Burfischer, in the preface to her "how-to" book on CGE modeling, writes: "A CGE model is a powerful analytical tool that can help you to gain a better understanding of real-world economic issues. . . . Economists today are using these models to systematically analyze some of the most important policy challenges and economic 'shocks' of the twenty-first century, including global climate change, the spread of human diseases, and international labor migration" (p. xiii).

The Anatomy of a CGE Model

So what is a CGE model? Actually, we already saw a miniature one in chapter 9. An agricultural household model, estimated with real-world data, is a CGE model for a very small economy: that of a household farm. It includes both supply and demand. If agricultural households are involved in many different kinds of activities, both farm and non-farm, the household-farm model can be expanded to include these activities. Then it is a multisector model. A household-farm model can be used to simulate the impacts of policies and other shocks on the agricultural economy.

Now imagine combining a household-farm model with similar models of *all* producers and consumers in the national economy. There would be models for urban as well as rural households, and urban firms as well as rural household farms. Most CGE models are national. Some even link models of several nations into an international CGE model.

They commonly include several different household groups and scores of different production sectors.

To a non-expert, CGE models are likely to seem like complex black boxes. In this sense, they are like any simulator, from flight simulators to *World of Warcraft* (or whatever your favorite computer game is). All involve a set of equations describing the behavior of the system they are simulating. For example, a flight simulator contains equations describing the physics of flight and aerodynamics. As long as these equations are correct, the simulator can teach pilots how to fly. Similarly, a CGE model with equations describing the behavior of an economy can teach us how economies function, how they evolve over time, and how they adjust when "shocked" by a policy, market, or environmental change. Of course, in many ways an economy with millions of consumers and producers is more complex than flying an airplane, so these simulations—like all models—are not perfect. But even imperfect simulators can be quite useful.

A CGE model is an "economy-wide model" because it is created to represent the economic behavior and interactions among *all* of the actors in an economy, producers as well as consumers.

Let's take a brief tour through a typical CGE model to see how it works, using the tools we already know from microeconomics courses and previous chapters of this book.

Producers (Firms or Farms)

The behavior of producers in a CGE model is represented by production functions describing the technologies that combine inputs to produce output (for example, Cobb-Douglas production functions), as well as the classic conditions for profit maximization: that firms demand inputs at the point where their marginal value products just equal their prices. Each sector in the economy has its own set of equations in the model.

To produce output, firms purchase inputs. Payments for intermediate inputs become demands for the output of other firms. The income firms generate, above and beyond these intermediate input costs, is the firms' value-added, which we saw in chapter 3 adds up to a country's GDP. Firms also pay taxes, for example, sales taxes, also called "indirect taxes." They also may save (retained earnings). At the end of the day, each firm's total revenue must equal its total expenditures; all of the money has to go somewhere.

Households

The value-added generated by firms gets channeled into households, in the CGE model as in the real world. It, along with any other income households might receive, determines households' budget constraints. Expenditure functions in a CGE model describe how households spend their income, as a function of their income as well as prices. The equations describing households' expenditures are derived from the maximization of household utility functions, subject to the budget constraint. In addition to demanding goods and services, households save and pay taxes (called "direct taxes"). At the end of the day, households' total expenditures must equal their total income (plus borrowing). Each household group in the economy has its own set of expenditure equations in a CGE model, and sometimes there are many different groups, depending on the model's focus. Households can be grouped using many different criteria, for example, by their main economic activities, demographic makeup, ethnicity, location, or poverty status.

Governments

The taxes paid by firms and households determine the government's budget constraint. Governments use their income (often supplemented by borrowing) for many purposes, most of which involve demanding goods and services in the economy or transferring income back to households.

Investors

Savings by households and firms (perhaps supplemented by other sources, including foreigners) turn into investments. Investments, in turn, create a demand for goods and services in the economy. For example, construction investment involves the purchase of materials as well as labor and capital.

For every economic agent, total income must equal total expenditures. This fundamental identity of economics is critical in building CGE models, just like the input-output model in chapter 3.

When incomes increase, so do the demands by households, government, and investors, and this stimulates the production of goods and services in the larger economy, which in turn creates new incomes, and so on. Everyone is part of the circular flow of goods, income, and spending in an economy. As in any ecosystem, an exogenous shock to any

Sidebar 10.6   Climate Change and Poverty

A team of economists and climatologists at Purdue and Stanford Universities used a CGE model to study the effects of climate change on poor households in fifteen different developing countries. Climate change alters crop yields. This can affect poor households directly, if they grow crops, as well as indirectly, by changing food prices. Even poor urban households, which are not involved in crop production, may suffer if food prices rise.

Understanding the impacts of climate change on poverty requires a systems approach that integrates climate science with CGE modeling. Climate simulation models give us predictions of the effects of climate change on key variables affecting crop yields, particularly temperatures and rainfall. These climate predictions are used as inputs into CGE models, which then simulate the impacts of the resulting crop production changes on the incomes of different household groups as well as the prices they must pay for food and related products.

Under one climate change and food production scenario, prices for major staples rise 10% to 60% by 2030. The effects of these higher food prices on poverty are different in different countries. In some non-agricultural household groups, the poverty rate rises by 20% to 50% in parts of Africa and Asia. Meanwhile, in other parts of Asia and in Latin America, some households specializing in agriculture actually gain as a result of climate change. Climate change, like most everything else in life, creates winners as well as losers.

This study was unique in bringing together experts in CGE modeling and climate science. Its findings have been influential in alerting policy makers to the adverse effects climate change is likely to have on poverty. The CGE findings also offer insights into where government policies might focus their efforts to protect the most vulnerable households from the negative effects of climate change.

Thomas W. Hertel, Marshall B. Burke, and David B. Lobell, "The Poverty Implications of Climate-Induced Crop Yield Changes by 2030," *Global Environmental Change* 20, no. 4 (2010):577–85.

part of the economy reverberates through the economic system, carrying impacts from one actor to another.

A CGE model "solves" to find the set of prices and quantities at which the economy is in equilibrium. This is the point at which the quantity supplied equals the quantity demanded for all goods and factors, like at an enormous auction.

Once we have a CGE "base model," we can use it to run experiments. For example, we can ask what is likely to happen if the government implements a particular policy, if there is a change in world food prices, or if climate change reduces crop production. Each of these policies "shocks" the CGE model and throws it out of equilibrium, but the model adjusts, through a series of iterations, to find a new equilibrium set of prices, quantities, and incomes. If the model is detailed enough, it can show us how different shocks are likely to affect different production sectors and household groups, as well as the overall economy (see sidebar 10.6).

www.rebeltext.org/development/qr10.html
Learn more about transformation by exploring
multimedia resources while you read.

11

Information and Markets

International development debates, just like domestic policy debates in most countries, often reveal how much we trust markets, on the one hand, and governments, on the other, to improve society. Framing these debates as either–or may be good political strategy, but it is often a false dichotomy that is ultimately not very helpful. To function efficiently, markets rely on a host of institutions, many of which require some form of government intervention to offset basic market failures. Conditions in developing countries frequently magnify these market failures. Development economists must appreciate how markets function in practice in poor countries and where they fail to function well, because these market failures can prevent the poor from reaping the big benefits markets can bring—benefits that planning without markets could never match.

ESSENTIALS

- Specialization and diversification
- Market integration and efficiency
- Institutions and transaction costs
- Market failures: asymmetric information
- Subsistence goods and shadow values
- Market failures: externalities and public goods
- The "knowledge problem"

Imagine you wake up one day and there are no markets. Not for food or other stuff. No credit, either—not that it would matter, without access to goods to spend money on. You'd eat whatever your plot of land gave you—no more, no less. You would be *your own* market; your internal balance of supply and demand would determine how much you consume and produce.

It also would determine how much you value things. If you're running low on food, you'd value it highly. In economics jargon, your

Sidebar 11.1   Famine and Missing Markets in Tigray

Between 1983 and 1985 a widespread famine took more than four hundred thousand lives in northern Ethiopia. The blame for the famine often is put on drought. However, the drought did not strike until months after the famine was already under way. In fact, as northern Ethiopia suffered famine, record harvests were reported in other parts of the country. Civil conflict against the Derg government and repressive policies shut down rural markets, forcing peasant households into self-sufficiency. When record low rainfall hit, markets could not function to fill the region's food deficit, and the rural population was left without access to food.

In January 2012 Ed visited a village in Tigray, the hardest hit province. The village had only a few hundred inhabitants, but this was market day. Thirty thousand people filed in from smaller villages as far away as twenty miles, all on foot. The line of people coming and going stretched off into the distance as far as he could see. Some hoisted bags of grain over their shoulders, others carried bags of produce or bunches of live chickens bound at their feet, and a few led goats on leashes fashioned from rope.

Ed asked his guide, an official in the state government, what this market looked like during the famine years. He sighed and said, "You do not understand. The soldiers would not let anyone walk the roads then. There was no market."

Alex de Waal, *Evil Days: Thirty Years of War and Famine in Ethiopia* (New York and London: Human Rights Watch, 1991), and personal interviews in Tigray province.

"shadow price" of food would be high. If your plot produces too many tomatoes, your shadow price of tomatoes will be low.

I don't know about you, but I'd be in serious trouble without a food market. When people in Tigray province, Ethiopia, lost their access to food markets in 1983, the result was catastrophic (see sidebar 11.1).

Things would be better if we could get everyone in town together and form a market. You grow food, we do something else (like teach economics!). Someone else could make us candles, and others could bake us bread (assuming there's wax and wheat around), fire bricks, or carve furniture (assuming there's wood to be had). Having a local market, we could all begin to specialize.

With more far-flung markets, we'd get access to stuff we couldn't possibly produce locally and be able to sell stuff we produce best or have too much of. Tomatoes could be rotting on the vine in your yard, but in a mill town in the next valley over there might be a tomato short-age. They'd pay dearly for your tomatoes and you for their wood, if only the two of you could discover one another, get together, and trade.

These insights about how the size of a market shapes incentives to specialize is a fundamental economic truth, but markets demand more than just buyers and sellers. Markets are based on specialization and trade, which require coordination and information. Buyers and sellers need to know about each other. If your "thing" is doing carpentry, you need to know where your buyers are and, in turn, where to get the food you'll need to eat.

One way to coordinate production across space is through central-ized planning, as in the former Soviet Union and pre-reform China. Central planners faced an enormous task: coordinating production and demand across millions of producers and consumers and typically very large spaces (those countries were big!). They turned out not to be very good at it, as evidenced by their persistent use of rationing (exemplified by the long bread lines in Moscow in the 1960s), their inefficiency, and ultimately the demise of large centrally planned economies altogether.

Interestingly, large corporations in the world today face serious coor-dination challenges reminiscent in some ways of the ones faced by cen-trally planned economies. (Imagine the coordination it takes to make a Boeing 747!) Over the years, corporations have tended to oscillate between having highly centralized and decentralized decision models. They have come up with innovations to deal with their information and coordination demands, including structures that mimic markets and, of course, extensive use of computers and the Internet to track and coordi-nate activities.

Since ancient times, markets have been the answer to overcoming local resource constraints and gaining access to new goods. Archeolo-gists have uncovered prolific evidence of ancient trade. For example, ceramic pottery and silver coins from fifth-century Athens are still being unearthed all around the Mediterranean Sea, from Egypt to Sicily. In ancient Athens, the Long Walls connected the city to its port, Pireaus, so that citizens would never be cut off from trade by sea, which provided most of the Athenians' food supplies. When Athens did lose control of the sea in the Peloponnesian War (404 BC), it quickly fell to Sparta and its allies—a vivid illustration of how critical access to markets is.

Today, markets are seen as the key to economic efficiency even in the world's former centrally planned economies. Why is this?

The Nobel laureate economist Friedrich August von Hayek had a simple answer to this question. He argued that markets effectively pool information from many different sources—more than any single person could easily understand—into a convenient measure of market conditions: a price (see sidebar 11.2). To most people, a price is nothing more than what you pay to buy something or what you get from selling it. To an economist, prices aggregate and convey information more effectively than any one person (or computer for that matter) could. A high price tells producers there is excess demand for their good, so they should produce more, and it tells consumers to cut back and seek out consumption substitutes. High input prices tell producers to seek out input substitutes while creating incentives for others to develop these substitutes. As we will see, this insight about markets has important implications for development policy and practice.

Markets are critical to economic welfare because they bring together sellers and buyers, integrate vast amounts of information, and distill that information into prices. In rich countries life would be unimaginable without access to a wide array of reasonably well functioning markets, from food to credit and insurance. It is almost never the case that a rich-country household has to produce something in order to consume it, or that its members cannot sell their labor for a salary or wage. Credit markets function for small businesses and farms to finance their investment projects. People pop out credit cards for convenience, to get through a tough time, or to buy things they can't afford at the moment. Insurance markets help protect people from unexpected income and health shocks. Every day more and more people interact in "virtual marketplaces," where buyers and sellers find each other and transact online, like on eBay and Amazon.com.

Missing markets create inefficiency. When markets don't work, prices vary from one place to another. Wages are high in my town but low in yours; food prices are low in my town but outrageously high in yours; I lack a forest but you have cheap wood. Almost nothing catches an economist's eye more quickly than price differences across space, because of the obvious efficiency implications. Widely varying prices for the same goods suggest that there is poor market integration and an opportunity to increase the economic pie for everyone.

Access to markets is just as compelling for a poor rural household in Rwanda, India, or Peru as for someone in a high-income country. With-

Sidebar 11.2 All in One Price

As a number of countries were experimenting with centrally planned economies, Friedrich von Hayek was looking "inside" prices. What he found there can tell us a lot about why centrally planned economies failed and why, without well-functioning markets, the economic prospects for poor societies are dim.

Think of anything that can shift around a supply or demand curve: changing technology, population, ethnicity of consumers, people's expectations, government policies, the weather, a war, the Internet, whatever. So many things that it's impossible to keep track of them all. Yet in a market, the intersection of supply and demand determines the price. If any of the multitude of things affecting supply or demand changes, we see it in the price. The Beatles said, "All you need is love." Economists say, "All you need is price." That's why market economies are better coordinated than centrally planned economies.

The price system, Hayek argued, is a "communications network" and the most efficient means of making use of economic information. It transmits information from one part of the market to another. For example, a drought might cause a grain-crop failure in one region, pushing up the grain price there. The higher price immediately communicates information to *other* regions where prices are lower. Astute traders see an opportunity to *arbitrage* (buy cheaply in one region and sell dearly in the other). In so doing, they resolve the excess-demand problem in the drought region while driving down prices there. If the market works very efficiently, a local drought will have almost no effect at all on local grain prices—the minute the price goes up, grain will rush in from other regions, driving it back down again. All because of the way prices convey information. The key to making prices play this valuable economic role is the rough-and-tumble process of market agitation that Hayek called "market competition."

Even well-developed market economies sometimes experience system-wide coordination failures leading to artificial booms and busts and even collapse into economic depression. These failures, Hayek argued, stem from coordination problems. Coordinating activities over time is more difficult than coordinating them at a given point in time. For example, producers have to make decisions today anticipating what other producers and consumers will do in the future. It turns out that prices are better at conveying information at a single point in time than through time. We'll see an example of this when we learn about credit and insurance in chapter 12.

Hayek's work changed the way we think about prices and the critical role that markets play in both developing and developed economies.

Roger W. Garrison and Israel Kirzner, "Friedrich August von Hayek," in *The New Palgrave: A Dictionary of Economics* (London: Macmillan, 1987), 609–14 (www.auburn.edu/~garriro/e4hayek.htm).

Friedrich A. von Hayek, "The Use of Knowledge in Society," *American Economic Review* 35 (September 1945):519–30 (www.econlib.org/library/Essays/hykKnw1.html).

out good access to markets, a poor household cannot market its produce, obtain inputs, sell labor, obtain credit, learn about or adopt new technologies, insure against risks, or obtain consumption goods at low prices. Equally important, it cannot use its scarce resources like land and labor efficiently. Its decision making is constrained.

TRADABLES, NONTRADABLES, AND SHADOW PRICES

When an economy does not have access to outside markets for a good, the good is called a "nontradable" for that economy, and the economy is called a "closed economy" for that good. The economy in question could be of a country, village, or even a household. The price of a nontradable is determined by the intersection of demand and supply within the economy, as in an Econ 1 graph of market equilibrium; that is, it is *endogenous* to the economy.

When the economy is integrated with outside markets for a good, the good is said to be a "tradable," and the economy is called "open" for that good. The price of a tradable is determined outside the economy; that is, it is *exogenous*. At that price, if there is excess demand for the tradable, the difference is purchased in outside markets (imported). If there is excess supply, the surplus is sold in those markets (exported).

The notions of tradables, nontradables, and where prices come from apply to *any* economy—whether of a country, region, village, or household.

> *For a nation:* The minute a country opens up to international trade, world prices replace internal equilibrium prices for tradables. The world price is what people must pay for what they buy, or what they get for what they sell, on the world market.

> *For a village:* When a new road or communications network links a remote village up with a regional commercial center, goods that once were nontradable can become tradable. Village prices get replaced by prices determined in the outside market.

> *For a household:* A subsistence household—one that consumes what it produces and has to produce what it consumes—is a very small closed economy with respect to the subsistence good. The subsistence good has a price, which we call a "shadow price." You can think of it as being what the subsistence household would be willing to pay in order to have a little more of the subsistence good. We cannot see this price, because there is no market to show it to us, but it is there, and we can see its shadow (hence the name) and infer something

Sidebar 11.3   Estimating the Shadow Price of Corn

You know what a shadow price is—you've surely "felt" one before. Imagine you're backpacking in a remote part of the Sierras and a bear gets your food. (That happened to one of us once, sad to say.) What you would pay for a freeze-dried pack of lasagna then! That's a shadow price. If you were standing in a backpacking shop, your shadow price would be the same as the price on the shelf. Hungry, isolated, and foodless in the mountains, *where there is no market,* you'd almost certainly be willing to pay more.

We can't see shadow prices, but sometimes we can estimate them. Consider a subsistence corn farmer in a remote village in southern Mexico. Assuming he follows basic economic precepts of optimizing behavior, he will produce at the point where the price just equals the marginal cost, as we saw in chapter 7. If we can estimate the marginal cost, then, we'll know what price the farmer is using to value his crop, whether it's for the market or for his family's own consumption.

A recent study used this approach to estimate the shadow price of maize for Mexican farmers. For commercial farmers, who are integrated with markets, the shadow price was found to be not significantly different from the market price. For subsistence farmers growing traditional maize varieties, though, it was significantly higher. The more remote the farmer was from markets, the higher his shadow price. Indigenous farmers were found to place a particularly high value on their traditional corn varieties.

This study showed how to estimate the shadow price of a subsistence crop, and it offered an explanation for why small farmers seem to produce corn at a loss: they put a higher value on their corn than the market does. Friedrich von Hayek would not be happy about that!

Aslihan Arslan and J. Edward Taylor, "Farmers' Subjective Valuation of Subsistence Crops: The Case of Traditional Maize in Mexico," *American Journal of Agricultural Economics* 91, no. 4 (2009):895–909.

about it if the right data are available (see sidebar 11.3). Keep this in mind as you read this chapter; it is fundamental to understanding trade and economic development. This shadow price gets replaced by an exogenous market price if the subsistence household becomes connected with village markets or markets outside the village.

Some goods by their very nature tend to be nontradables. Haircuts are an example: it's hard to buy them from somewhere else unless you travel to wherever the hairdresser is. (Ed "imported" a pretty good haircut from Paris last year, but that's because he happened to be there for a workshop.) Lodging and restaurant food are other examples of nontradables. Sometimes, goods that are nontradable can become tradable. Highly perishable foods, like fish, are nontradables if they have to be carried by hand or on a donkey's back over long distances in the heat. They can become tradables if traders have trucks and ice boxes, public transport becomes available, or the fisherman gets a motorcycle.

When goods and services that *could* be tradable *are not,* two important questions arise. First, "Why not?" And second, "What are the consequences for economic welfare, particularly of the poor?"

WHAT MAKES TRADABLES NONTRADABLES?

The explanations for why things that *could* be tradable are *not* tradable fall mostly into two categories: transaction costs and trade policies. High transaction costs can inhibit trade within as well as among countries. Trade policies almost always have to do with trade among countries; it is rare for a country to regulate trade within its own borders. In the rest of this chapter we will learn the essentials of understanding transaction costs and how they can limit or shut down markets within countries. In the next chapter we will learn about international trade and trade policies.

Transaction Costs

Usually government policies do not limit trade within countries. However, *transaction costs* can turn tradables into nontradables within countries in much the same way that restrictive trade policies cut countries off from international markets.

The market price is what a buyer pays or a seller receives as a result of a transaction, like the ones that happen billions of times a day in marketplaces and stores around the globe. Transacting is not free, though. Buyers and sellers have to know where to find one another. Both have to know the specifics of what is being transacted, including its quality. When you sell something to me, property rights change hands. What was yours becomes mine. We both need to be convinced that you had the right to sell it and I have secure rights to the thing once I buy it. All of these things have to happen every time we buy or sell anything: a potato, a day's work, a piece of property, a loan, or an insurance policy.

Simply put, there are three kinds of transaction costs:

1. The costs of searching out buyers or sellers and discovering or signaling the quality of the good or service being bought or sold.
2. The costs of negotiating deals and setting up contracts.
3. The costs of enforcing contracts once the deal has been made.

For a potato, (2) and (3) would probably be too small to even think about, but (1) might be important. For property, credit, insurance, labor, and many other goods and services, all three are likely to be considerable. In developed countries, institutions (chapter 8) evolve to deal with these, but in poor economies, the institutions needed to lower these costs enough so that transactions actually occur are often weak or nonexistent. The result is market failure.

Many of the institutions we described in chapter 8 have big economic effects because they determine the transaction costs involved in these market transactions. For many transactions, like buying a lemon, transaction costs might be trivial. But what if the lemon is an old car?

The Power of Information

In 1970, UC Berkeley economist George Akerlof published a revolutionary paper called "The Market for 'Lemons.'"[1] The paper was so novel that it got rejected by three top economics journals before eventually winning Akerlof the Nobel Prize. It was about the power of information to make—or break—markets. Its argument goes something like this:

You want to sell your used car. After taking good care of it all these years, you know it's in top shape, and you want to get a good price for it. But what do the potential buyers know? Only what they can see. There is *asymmetric information*: you know more about your car's quality than they do. Unless you can persuade them otherwise, the most they'll be willing to pay will be the price of the average-quality car out there.

So what do you do? Unless you can figure out a way to resolve this information asymmetry, you either sell below what you know your car is worth, or else you pull your car off the market. If you decide not to offer your car for sale, the average quality of cars on the market falls. Over time, this lowers used car prices. Other people with high-quality used cars leave the market, quality and prices fall further, and before you know it, only low-quality cars are left. This is what Akerlof calls "The Market for Lemons."[2] In the extreme case, the market collapses.

When the *Journal of Political Economy* rejected this paper, the editor informed Akerlof that "if this paper was correct, economics would be different."

It was correct, and economics is different.

Today we understand that information is the lubricant that makes markets work. Yet information asymmetries abound, especially in poor countries. Because of them, markets can fail. Surrounded by market failures, poor people's prospects of escaping from poverty are grim.

Food export markets provide a classic example of information asymmetries that make markets fail—for small producers, at least. Diversifying into high-value export crops is critical if poor countries wish to increase their foreign exchange and raise farm incomes. Some African countries, such as Ethiopia, Kenya, and Uganda, are well positioned to supply crops year-round to developed countries, particularly in Europe. However, without the right information this trade cannot happen.

Take food safety, for example. High-income countries have stringent food safety standards. The United States inspects food imports to make sure they comply with food safety rules, even inspecting foreign food facilities.[3] The European Union, the world's biggest food importer, requires that all imported food meet the same level of food safety as food produced within the EU.[4]

Food safety concerns are understandable, of course. But even if a small African farmer can meet the EU's food safety requirements, how will she convince the EU that she has done so? The cost of many small producers complying with these requirements is likely to be significantly higher than the cost for a few big producers. Certifying food safety is a transaction cost of selling food to high-income countries, and it can impose high costs on poor countries (sidebar 11.4).

Another example involving certification is titling, which we discussed in chapter 8. A formal title provides security that the seller really owns the property being sold. Without it, a potential buyer would face risks that easily could kill the deal. Around the globe, governments keep public records of land and building titles and histories of sales, which permits "title searches." In the United States, you cannot get a loan to buy a house without a title search; this information creates the credit. That's why land titling has been a focus of development projects by international development banks.

Information is critical to making other markets work. Without the certification that a fruit or vegetable was organically grown, who would

Sidebar 11.4 The High Cost of Saving Two in a Billion

If countries wish to export food to developed countries, they have to meet food safety standards concerning pesticide residues, harvesting and packing operations, and a means to trace back to their source any food safety problems that do arise. In 1997, the European Union set new, stringent limits on aflatoxins, which are toxic compounds that contaminate certain foods and can result in the production of acute liver carcinogens. The proposed limits were far below the limits that some individual EU countries had previously adopted. A number of food-exporting countries, including Bolivia, Brazil, Peru, India, Argentina, Canada, Mexico, Uruguay, Australia, and Pakistan, raised concerns that the new standards were unnecessary and overly restrictive.

What effect would this new food safety standard have on developing countries? Three World Bank economists estimated the impact on African food exports, using a gravity model (chapter 13). They found that the new standard would reduce health risk by approximately 1.4 deaths per billion a year, but it would cut African exports by 64%, or US$ 670 million, compared with existing international food safety standards. Their findings illustrate the trade-off between health risks and the high transaction costs rich-country food standards impose on poor-country producers.

Tsunehiro Otsuki, John S. Wilson, and Mirvat Sewadeh, "Saving Two in a Billion: Quantifying the Trade Effect of European Food Safety Standards on African Exports," *Food Policy* 26, no. 5 (2001):495–514.

pay the price to "buy organic"? Certification is the key to green, eco-friendly labeling. The same goes for any quality standard. The US Department of Agriculture enforces quality standards for agricultural products; no meat packing plant is without its USDA inspector and inspection stamps. These activities not only protect consumer health but also create information vital to making markets work.

In a striking example of the power of information and uncertainty, beef consumption in Japan fell 60% after the first case of mad cow disease was reported there in 2001. The vast majority of beef in Japan was free of the disease, of course, but without access to information about *which* meat was mad-cow free, the market reeled. The Japanese beef market recovered once the country began testing *all* of its cows.

HOW MARKETS CAN LOWER TRANSACTION COSTS

What exactly is a market? When you think of a market you might conjure up images of a grocery store or a mall, or perhaps a marketplace like the one in Tigray, Ethiopia, to which we linked up earlier in this chapter. Markets do not have to be physical places, though. If you bought this book, there's a good chance you did it online, without going to a bookstore. More and more, commerce within and among countries is conducted online, thanks to the likes of Amazon, eBay, and many other companies. eBay is a prime example of a virtual marketplace. It brings buyers and sellers together without ever having them at the same location. People use it for one simple reason: it dramatically lowers transaction costs. Sellers can easily make their wares available for the whole world to see, and buyers can search these goods out effortlessly. The transaction can happen with the click of a mouse. What's someone else's becomes yours instantly. There are still transaction costs. Sellers have to make an effort to list their goods and describe them adequately so that prospective buyers can learn about them. Buyers have to sit down and search out what is available online. And information asymmetries have to be dealt with. Buyers need assurances that they will get what they think they are paying for, and sellers have to be sure that the buyer's money is good. Online marketplaces have solutions for these information problems. They track the reputation of buyers and sellers, facilitate the transaction by letting people pay with secure electronic wallets (like PayPal), and even provide quality guarantees and easy returns should a transaction not turn out right. These services are all about reducing transaction costs in online markets.

So what is a market, then? Here are some definitions taken from well-known dictionaries:

mar·ket \'märkət\

An open place or a covered building where buyers and sellers convene for the sale of goods. (Dictionary.com)

A meeting together of people for the purpose of trade . . . a public place where a market is held. *(Merriam-Webster)*[5]

A regular gathering of people for the purchase and sale of provisions, livestock, and other commodities. *(Oxford)*[6]

None of these captures what economists really mean when they talk about markets. Here's a more comprehensive definition, which encompasses virtual as well as physical markets:

A market is where

- buyers and sellers find one another and their wares,
- price discovery happens, and
- an infrastructure and set of institutions facilitate the transfer of property rights from one person to another.

The third function of markets above—facilitating the transfer of property rights—is fairly simple for a persimmon or laptop. However, it can be very complicated indeed for a loan or an insurance policy, which is why we have a special chapter in this book dedicated to credit and risk. The notion of information is central to all three aspects of our definition of markets. Buyers and sellers have to learn about each other and the true nature of the goods or services to be transacted. Prices have to convey information in order for the market to work properly, as we saw in sidebar 11.2. Buyers and sellers have to be reasonably sure of who holds the property rights before and after a transaction is made— and how these rights will be protected. If any bit of this information is missing, the transaction is likely to fall apart.

Information asymmetries can easily shut small farmers out of domestic as well as international markets. Consider a poor farmer who can produce high-quality berries at a low price. In town, exporters are willing to pay 20 cents a basket for berries like the ones he can grow. Poor roads and communications, however, cut the farmer off from information about buyers: where to sell, when to sell, how to ensure quality, and the price the farmer might get once he transports his berries to the market. This makes marketing a perishable crop too expensive and risky. So the farmer produces a few baskets for his family's and maybe a few neighbors' consumption, and he spends the rest of his time doing low-wage work, when available, on a nearby ranch. A basket of berries costs him 10 cents to produce (including the cost of his time). Implicitly, then, this is his decision price, or the price at which he is willing to produce berries. If he could become part of the export supply chain, his decision price would instantly rise to the market price. He could be more efficient, shifting some or all of his time from low-wage work to berry production, and he would have an incentive to invest in his farm. Most importantly, he could generate badly needed cash for his family.

We can illustrate the welfare loss from high transaction costs using the concepts of producer and consumer surplus. Let's begin by seeing what the producer and consumer surplus are without village-town trade, and then we'll see what trade does to them.

Producer Surplus

Without trade, village supply and demand determine the village equilibrium price and quantity of berries, as shown in figure 11.1. Following the basic rule for profit maximization, the quantity of berries supplied in the village is given by the point where p_v = MC, that is, where the village price line hits the supply curve. You can see in figure 11.1 that, at the equilibrium price, the optimal output is Q_v. Producers make no profit on the last unit supplied (because its MC just equals the price). However, they *do* make a profit on all the other units $(Q < Q_v)$, because on those units the price exceeds the MC. Total profits are given by the area of triangle B, which is the sum of the difference between price and MC for all of the units supplied, up to Q_v. (In calculus terms, in case that's how you like to think, it's the integral from zero to Q_v of the function $p - MC(Q)$.)

This is the *producer surplus*. For all units from zero to Q_v, producers get a price higher than the minimum they would require in order to supply the goods. The producer surplus is our measure of producers' economic welfare.

Consumer Surplus

There is an analogue to the producer surplus for consumers. Not surprisingly, it is called the "consumer surplus." Have you ever paid less for something than you would have been willing to pay? Maybe picked up what you want on sale, surprised by how cheap it was, and then asked yourself what you'll do with all the money you saved? That difference between what you would have been willing to pay and what you did pay is your consumer surplus.

Look at the market demand curve in figure 11.1. It represents consumers' willingness to pay for each quantity of the good. The quantity demanded in the market is given by the point where the village price line hits this demand curve; in this figure it is Q_v. For all the quantities from zero to Q_v, consumers would have been willing to pay more than the village price. The sum of differences between consumers' willingness to pay and the village price, then, is the total consumer surplus in this market. It is shown as triangle A in the figure. It will be our measure of consumers' economic welfare.

Total economic welfare is the sum of producer surplus and consumer surplus. It is the sum of these two triangles.

Village Berry Market

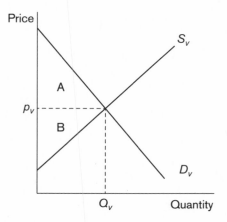

FIGURE 11.1. Equilibrium in the village berry market without trade.

Trade and Economic Welfare

What does village-town trade in berries do to villagers' economic welfare? Suppose that in town, our berry producer could sell his berries at a regional price equal to p_r. This price might be determined by supply and demand in the regional berry market, or it might even come from the world market, if town traders export the berries they buy from local farmers. The right side of figure 11.2 illustrates the case in which the price is determined by equilibrium in the regional berry market.

On the left side of figure 11.2 we see the village berry market again. The way we drew this figure, the regional price, p_r, is higher than the village equilibrium price, p_v. Naturally, given the choice, our berry farmer will choose to sell in the town, at the higher price. That's the price village consumers will have to pay the farmer if they want him to sell berries to them instead of to the town.

In this particular example, farmers gain from trade, but consumers lose. Consumer surplus falls by an amount equal to the trapezoidal area A in figure 11.2. That's the decrease in the size of the triangle underneath the demand curve when the price rises from p_v to p_r. Producer surplus, however, increases by an amount equal to areas A plus B. The gain to farmers exceeds the loss to consumers, and total economic welfare increases. In theory, producers could fully compensate consumers and still have higher profits than without trade. (Whether they will or not is another question. It underlies controversies about free trade, which we will consider in chapter 12.)

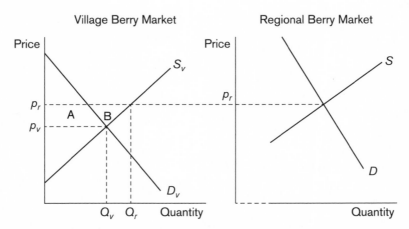

FIGURE 11.2. If the regional price is higher than the village price, trade increases the producer surplus more than it decreases the consumer surplus. Thus, the total economic surplus rises.

You might wonder what happens if the regional price is *lower* than the village price. We leave it as an exercise to show that the total economic surplus still increases from trade. If $p_r < p_v$, producer surplus decreases, but consumer surplus rises more than enough to compensate.

How Transaction Costs Can Kill Trade

In order to sell in the regional market, though, the farmer will have to incur a transaction cost equivalent to $t per unit sold. You can imagine the high cost of transporting the berries over bad roads, and before that, whatever costs in money and time she has to incur to travel to town, find out about prices there, and arrange the sale (a cell phone might help). Then there's always a risk that, once she delivers the berries to the market, the buyer will change his mind and decide not to buy (an enforceable contract would help). Market uncertainty adds what economists call a "risk premium" to t. You can think of it as the amount the farmer would be willing to pay to insure against the possibility of the sale falling through. When you talk to farmers in poor villages, these are the sorts of things they mention when explaining why they do not sell in outside markets.

Given these transaction costs, the farmer's net price will be $(1 - t)p_r$. Figure 11.3 shows the case where the price the farmer gets by selling in town, net of transaction costs, is less than the village price. Faced by high transaction costs, the farmer is better off selling only in the village, at the village price p_v. In doing so, he produces less and loses profit

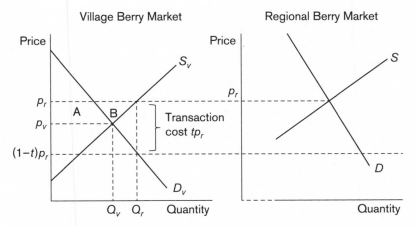

FIGURE 11.3. When transaction costs cut producers off from higher prices in outside markets, producer surplus falls (area A + B). Consumer surplus increases (area A), but not by enough to compensate for the fall in producer surplus.

(producer's surplus) equal to the areas A + B in figure 11.3. Consumers gain by being able to buy berries at the lower village price, but their gain (area A) is not enough to make up for the producer's loss.

In this age of the supermarket revolution, getting small farmers into the Walmart supply chain can be the key to raising agricultural incomes and reducing poverty. But transaction costs can make Walmart shut its doors to small farmers (see sidebar 11.5).

Microeconomics courses teach us that firms optimize by producing where their marginal cost (MC) equals the output price, or equivalently, where each input is used at the point where its marginal value product just equals its price. Consumers do something similar by demanding goods at the level where their marginal rate of substitution (MRS, the slope of the indifference curve or ratio of marginal utilities any two goods create) just equals the ratio of prices.

If everyone bases decisions on the same prices, things cannot be any more efficient. The MC will be the same for all producers (and equal to the output price). The marginal rate of substitution will be the same for all consumers (equal to the ratio of prices).

As you can see in figure 11.3, though, when there are high transaction costs, different producers (for example, near or far from markets) may face different prices and thus produce at different MCs. Recall that the supply curve *is* the marginal cost curve. The farmers who supply the regional market produce at an MC equal to p_r, whereas the village farmer produces at an MC equal to p_v. The same thing happens to consumers:

Sidebar 11.5   Walmart in Nicaragua

Many people think of supermarkets as the rich world's place to shop, but the rapid rise of supermarkets is transforming agricultural supply chains in Africa, Asia, and Latin America. The supermarket explosion leaves development economists with big new questions. Can poor farmers make their way into the supply chains of Walmart and other major players in the supermarket space, given the exacting standards they face? Or will the supermarket revolution pass them by and possibly leave them more marginalized than before?

An economist at Columbia University's Earth Institute set out to answer these questions by asking what determines whether small farmers become suppliers of food to Walmart in Nicaragua. This is a tricky question, because as in program evaluation (chapter 2), unobservable variables may determine whether farmers participate in the Walmart supply chain, and they can easily confound estimates of how other things affect participation.

This study followed the same farmers over time. It found that only farmers with advantageous access to roads and water are likely to participate in the Walmart supply chain. The study is important because it identifies obstacles to small-farmer participation in the Walmart supply chain, including factors related to transaction costs.

Hope C. Michelson, "Small Farmers, NGOs, and a Walmart World: Welfare Effects of Supermarkets Operating in Nicaragua," *American Journal of Agricultural Economics* 95, no. 3 (2013).

they equate their marginal rates of substitution with the ratio of the prices they face, which may be very different from the prices others face.

When this happens, efficiency could be increased—dramatically, perhaps—by reducing or eliminating transaction costs, so that trade can equalize prices across markets. Remember this—it is the fundamental problem that high transaction costs create in poor economies: market failure occurs when economic actors are unable to get together to make efficiency-enhancing trades. Transaction costs resulting from imperfect information are a major reason why this happens. (Another is civil strife, as in the example from Tigray at the start of this chapter.) In fact, billions of people—particularly poor people—opt out of markets, apparently because the transaction costs of using markets are too high.

When transaction costs cause prices to vary across space, a cell phone can literally keep food from rotting on the vine—or fish from rotting on the beach (see sidebar 11.6).

Sidebar 11.6 Saving Fish with Cell Phones

People need price information in order to trade efficiently. In Kerala, India, more than 1 million people fish. While at sea, fishermen can't observe prices at markets along the coast. Transportation costs are high, and fish are perishable. This keeps fishermen from moving from port to port looking for the best price once their boats are full. Thus, almost all fishermen sell their catch locally, and this can create a surplus of fish in some places—in fact, the price of fish can drop all the way to zero. When that happens, fish literally are left to rot. Meanwhile, just down the coast, people in other towns might be happy to pay a good price for this fish. If only the fishermen had known—they could have chosen to put in their boats down the coast, instead.

Between 1997 and 2001, mobile phone service was introduced in Kerala. Robert Jensen hypothesized that this could be very good for fishermen and consumers—not to mention the fish. He gathered data on the ups and downs of fish prices along the coast both before and after the introduction of cell phones. His analysis found that mobile phones dramatically reduced price variability and waste and raised fishermen's profits as well as consumers' welfare. Since improvements in market efficiency can benefit all market participants, even fishermen without cell phones were better off when some of their fellow fishermen started using them.

This study is a dramatic illustration of how the exchange of information via cell phones enabled fishermen to sell their catch where prices are high, leveling out price variability along the Kerala coast. Cell phones made the fish market work, and the market made people better off—while saving a whole lot of fish. And obviously, this effect is not unique to fish markets: development economists have found similar dramatic market effects due to the introduction of cell phones. Jenny Aker, for example, found that the arrival of mobile phones in Niger between 2001 and 2006 substantially reduced the variation in grain prices across rural markets, bringing big benefits to the hardest-to-reach markets.

Robert Jensen, "The Digital Provide: Information (Technology), Market Performance, and Welfare in the South Indian Fisheries Sector," *Quarterly Journal of Economics* 122, no. 3 (August 2007):879–924.

Jenny C. Aker, "Information from Markets Near and Far: Mobile Phones and Agricultural Markets in Niger," *American Economic Journal: Applied Economics* 2, no. 3 (July 2010):46–59.

TRANSACTION COSTS IN INPUT MARKETS

So far we've focused on the effects of transaction costs in output markets. Asymmetric information and high transaction costs can also shut farmers out of input markets. When a farmer cannot get fertilizer or hire labor at the times needed, or cannot be sure of input quality, he may sow less land or not adopt more productive technologies, and his output may fall as a result. Efficiency is critical because even a small income gain can make a huge difference for an impoverished household—particularly if that gain can be sustained month after month, year after year.

Labor Markets

Anyone who has taken microeconomics knows the textbook solution to the labor-hiring problem: employers should hire workers up to the point where their marginal value product (MVP) just equals the wage. The MVP is how much value (gross revenue) the last (marginal) worker will create. The wage is how much it will cost to hire him.

But how can we be sure that that last worker will really produce that MVP? Or the worker before him, for that matter? What if you hire him and he doesn't work hard, generating less revenue than the wage you have to pay him? This is called "shirking," and it is a form of moral hazard. Employers can deal with this problem by monitoring the workers they hire, just like a bank can monitor borrowers, but that's expensive.

There is also the possibility of adverse selection. Some workers are more productive than others. How do you know you'll end up with a "good" one—that is, a worker who produces an MVP higher than the wage? If the worker is a member of your own family, you'll have good information about him. If not, information may be asymmetric—the worker knows how good he is, but you do not. It might be possible to overcome adverse selection by offering a wage higher than the going market wage in order to attract more productive workers. But this, like monitoring, is costly.

The costs of monitoring and screening workers are transaction costs in labor markets. The true cost of hiring a worker is the wage plus these transaction costs. If the transaction costs are high enough, the labor market will fail: no workers will be hired. Then producers are forced to use their own labor. If you can hire workers, it doesn't matter how big your family's labor endowment is—you simply hire up to the point where the MVP equals the market wage. If you can't, then how much you produce depends on how much family labor you have.

In a labor-constrained household, the "family shadow wage," or opportunity cost of family time, is high. (The family shadow wage is the wage you would be willing to pay if you could hire workers.) In a labor-abundant household, the family wage is low; the market failure traps labor in the household. In that case, you would be willing to work for a relatively low wage, but no one will hire you because of the asymmetric information problem: employers are not sure how productive you'll be.

If my shadow wage is low and yours is high, we might both be better off if I worked for you. You'd pay a wage lower than your reservation wage, and I'd get a wage higher than my reservation wage. If transaction costs in the labor market are too high, though, the labor exchange won't take place.

There is a simple solution to the adverse selection and moral hazard problems in labor markets: pay workers a piece rate. It is common in both poor and rich countries to pay farmworkers a flat cash amount per unit harvested: box, kilo, bundle, and so forth. Harvest workers in Mexico often are paid a share of the corn crop. Fishermen often pay their crew a share of the catch. California farmers pay strawberry pickers a piece rate per twelve-pint tray during peak harvest periods.[7]

Piece rates have advantages and disadvantages. From the producer's point of view, they have the advantage of shifting all the risk associated with adverse selection and moral hazard onto the workers. Farmers know exactly how much it will cost to pick, say, a ton of peaches if they pay a piece rate, but not if they pay a wage. Piece rates have the disadvantage of encouraging workers to focus on quantity, not quality, for example, to pick as many peaches as possible but not worry about bruising them. Employers who pay piece rates thus have to be extra careful about monitoring quality, for example, by checking the fruit and docking workers for poor quality.

The piece-rate system ensures that workers get paid according to their productivity. Pick fast and your day's pay will be higher. Pick too slowly and you might not have enough food to eat. This is good news for highly productive workers, but it obviously is a disadvantage for less-productive ones. Less-productive workers may not be able to pick enough to cover their subsistence (or the minimum wage, if there is one). In California, farmers are required by law to pay all workers at least the minimum wage, even if they are not productive enough to "pick" the minimum wage. This shifts some of the risk associated with adverse selection and moral hazard back onto employers. While some kinds of work lend themselves to piece rates, others do not. It's easy to pay a piece rate to strawberry pickers, but what about workers in soil preparation, planting, or weeding?

Other Inputs

When people face transaction costs in input markets, the price they pay for their inputs includes the cost of making the transaction. Adverse selection and moral hazard are not so much problems in the case of purchased inputs; the quality of fertilizer usually is pretty much known by everyone, and fertilizer—unlike workers—does not have a mind of its own or need to be monitored.

Other problems can create transaction costs and make input markets fail, though. Foremost among them is timing. Not having an input at the time it is needed often is as bad as not having it at all. Seed, fertilizer, insecticides, and herbicides all must be applied at just the right time or the farmer will risk losing his crop. Input markets have to work efficiently to make sure this happens, yet often they do not.

Poorly functioning input markets can even keep people from adopting more productive technologies. The Green Revolution (high-yielding) seeds we encountered in chapter 9 were engineered to give high yields as long as complementary inputs, particularly fertilizer, are applied in a timely fashion. If a farmer is unsure that he'll be able to buy fertilizer at the moment it has to be applied, he may be better off not planting the high-yielding variety.

People could take measures to ensure that they have the inputs they need at the time they need them. For example, instead of investing their scarce cash in more productive activities, they could use it to stockpile fertilizer when they can get it, then let the fertilizer sit there until the time comes to apply it. Or they could invest time and money into searching out sources of inputs, from distant cities if needed. By taking steps like these, farmers could make sure they have the inputs they need at the time they are needed, but obviously these steps are costly. In the end, the effective price of fertilizer is the market price plus the transaction cost the farmer incurs to make sure he has the fertilizer when he needs it. That transaction cost may make all the difference (see sidebar 11.7).

Sidebar 11.7   Nudging Poor Farmers to Use Fertilizer

Poor farmers in Africa do not use nearly enough fertilizer. For example, fertilizer use in sub-Saharan Africa was only 8 kg/ha in 2002, compared with 101 kg/ha in South Asia. Such massive disparities in fertilizer use between Africa and the rest of the world suggest that there are structural impediments limiting fertilizer availability and demand. It is very unlikely that African farmers are applying fertilizer at a level that equates its marginal value product with the world price. They act as though the price of fertilizer is much higher than the price in the market. Why the disparity?

One possibility is that poor farmers simply don't have the cash. Three economists offered a different explanation: timing. Even poor farmers who are willing to pay the market price for fertilizer cannot be sure they'll be able to get the fertilizer they need when they need it.

In a clever experimental study in Kenya, some farmers were offered free fertilizer delivery early in the season and others not, while still others were offered a fertilizer subsidy. The study found that offering delivery early was more effective at increasing fertilizer use than was a subsidy—not to mention cheaper.

Esther Duflo, Michael Kremer, and Jonathan Robinson, "Nudging Farmers to Use Fertilizer: Evidence from Kenya," *American Economic Review* 101, no. 6 (2011):2350–90.

TRANSACTION COSTS AND SPATIAL MARKET INTEGRATION

So far, we have discussed participation in either output or input markets as a binary variable. That is, a given farm household either sells its maize in the local market or it does not; it either hires labor or it does not. As we've already explored, transaction costs can have a big influence on this decision, and the decision can, in turn, have a big effect on household efficiency and welfare. Because they affect these decisions, transaction costs can have a big impact on how markets in one location are related to other markets. This is what economists call "spatial market integration," which is often a key determinant of how and how well markets in developing countries function.

While potential buyers and sellers typically face a binary decision to participate in a market or not, spatial market integration is measured as a continuous variable. If a wheat market in Meknès, Morocco, is unintegrated with the other wheat markets in Morocco (much less international wheat markets), then wheat prices in Meknès will be completely determined by local supply and demand. In the case of drought, wheat prices will skyrocket. If instead the Meknès wheat market is fully integrated with the world wheat market, a local drought will not affect local prices because any local shortfall will be filled by the world wheat supply.

Most input and output markets in developing countries fall somewhere between these two market integration extremes. Whether a given market is poorly integrated or well integrated depends on many of the sources of transaction costs we have already encountered: information, transportation, contracts, tariffs and other barriers to trade, and so on. This degree of market integration can directly affect welfare outcomes.

In addition to subjecting households to greater price volatility—and, in the case of food markets, greater vulnerability to food insecurity—poor market integration can constrain local productivity by directly affecting production decisions. For example, a few years ago Travis was conducting focus group discussions with wheat farmers in Meknès. It was March, and it was shaping up to be a perfect rainfall year—the wheat looked beautiful. But the farmers were intentionally getting lower yields than they could have. Why? Because nearly all the farmers had decided not to use fertilizer once they realized how good the rainfall would be. This was especially perplexing to agronomists because fertilizer dramatically increases yields when rainfall is good. What then was holding back these farmers?

As the farmers explained (with impressive economic intuition), "We know fertilizer could really increase our yields this year because of the rainfall, but even without fertilizer everyone's yield will be high and wheat prices will collapse at harvest. With lower prices, we might not even cover the cost of the fertilizer!" This is what poorly integrated markets look like to poor farmers.

THE ROLE OF GOVERNMENT

We conclude this chapter with some thoughts about the role of government in a world of asymmetric information and market failures.

Economists almost uniformly agree that markets are crucial to people's welfare. Free-market economists believe that the free functioning of markets, without government intervention, leads to the greatest common good, often citing Adam Smith's reference to "an invisible hand." This belief is an underpinning of free-trade agreements among nations and market reforms within them. The Fundamental Theorem of Welfare Economics states that competitive markets lead to a "first best" allocation of resources that is *Pareto efficient;* that is, nobody can be made better off without someone else being made worse off.

The fundamental theorem does not necessarily hold when markets are incomplete or information is imperfect—two common features of poor economies. We have seen that there are many cases in which there is no market, and we will see still others in the chapter on credit and risk. In such an environment, there is no first-best outcome, and a government hands-off or laissez-faire approach to markets is not likely to be optimal. As the Nobel laureate economist Joseph Stiglitz explained it, "The theories that said that markets work perfectly were all based on very simplistic models of perfect competition, perfect markets, and perfect information . . . The reason that the invisible hand often seemed invisible was that it wasn't there."[8]

The question today is no longer whether governments should be involved in markets, but how much—that is, finding the right balance between the market and government.

Grounds for Government Intervention in Markets

One does not have to reject market economics to recognize situations in which governments should become involved in markets. One of these is the provision of information, which can lower transaction costs for everyone. Governments around the world have statistical bureaus that gather information and make it publicly available.

There are other instances in which a strong case can be made for government intervention in markets:

Externalities: The actions of an individual have bad (or good) impacts on others for which the individual doesn't pay (or get compensated). Externalities are crucial in environmental economics, from pollution to biodiversity. Markets, left to themselves, produce too much air and water pollution (which harms people who breathe the air or drink the water), too little research (which creates public benefits), too little education (my education can make other workers more productive), too few beehives (bees pollinate peach orchards), too much global warming (how much carbon did you put into the atmosphere today?), too little information (how do you turn a profit selling information in a poor village?), and too little biodiversity (sidebar 11.8). Yet another negative externality is trash, which sadly is a pervasive feature of developing-country landscapes.

Public goods: Roads, marketing infrastructure, communications, police, and firefighting are public goods that create benefits for society that are difficult for private investors to capture; thus, there are not likely to be enough of them unless governments get involved. A classic case is firefighting. If fire departments were private, I might pay for fire protection but my neighbor might not. Yet if her house catches fire, the firefighters will have to put it out in order to save my house—a classic free-rider problem.

Market power: The welfare gains from markets depend on competition. When someone gains too much market power, either as a seller or buyer, the fundamental theorem breaks down. This is the justification for antitrust legislation.

Resolving the information problems and providing the infrastructure needed to make markets function properly involves classic problems of increasing returns to scale and public goods. These are familiar to you from chapter 6, where we learned about the public goods nature of health and education investments. Let's review them here.

Creating an information system involves high (fixed) setup costs of gathering the information and making it available in a form that people can use. However, once an information system is in place, the cost of providing the information to an additional person is negligible or zero. Marginal cost pricing is not feasible, as in the case of a bridge. You can put information online and it can spread like wildfire. It's difficult to exclude people from having information once it is available. There's a natural free-rider problem here. Once new information gets out, no one can control where it goes, particularly in a world of online news, social media, and e-mail. Information creates important externalities, too. The positive spillovers from information were central to the endogenous growth model we learned about in chapter 7.

These characteristics of information have advantages and disadvantages. A big advantage is that once information gets out there, it can spread and create benefits widely. A disadvantage, though, is that there is little or no private incentive to invest in information systems, because it is hard for private investors to make money by producing something over which they have little control. These are problems similar to what we

Sidebar 11.8 Which Seeds to Save?

Plant breeders have been remarkably successful at creating new high-yielding seeds to meet the growing global food demand. Green Revolution seed varieties were engineered from traditional varieties with the characteristics agronomists wish to breed into the new varieties. But what if the traditional varieties weren't there anymore?

To reap the benefits of high-yielding varieties, farmers have to plant them. But to create new seed varieties in the future, scientists need the genetic diversity found in traditional seed varieties. What if the new seeds are so superior that farmers stop growing traditional varieties altogether? What if other forces at work, like the spread of markets, lead farmers to stop growing traditional varieties, which then go extinct? How would scientists get the genetic resources they need to continue breeding new crop varieties—whether to increase yields or to breed in resistance to new diseases and pests?

There is not a market for biodiversity, so when farmers decide to stop growing traditional varieties, they do not take into account the costs to society of losing valuable crop genetic resources. Researchers have found evidence that traditional seed varieties are disappearing, a process called "genetic erosion."

Some research suggests that high transaction costs and marginal environments may slow crop genetic erosion. Studies of wheat in Turkey, potatoes in Peru, and maize in Mexico find that isolation from markets limits the spread of high-yielding varieties. When people face high transaction costs and must produce what they consume, they are much more likely to plant traditional varieties—because they taste better. Most high-yielding varieties were engineered to outperform traditional varieties, but only in high-quality environments with fertile, level land and access to water. Farmers are more likely to plant traditional seeds on marginal lands. Transaction costs and marginal environments, then, seem to be friends of crop genetic diversity.

This raises an important question: As rural markets become better integrated with national markets and new seeds are engineered to do well in marginal environments, how will we make sure that we have the genetic resources we need for agricultural research?

Stephen B. Brush and Erika Meng, "Farmers' Valuation and Conservation of Crop Genetic Resources," *Genetic Resources and Crop Evolution* 45, no. 2 (1998):139–50.

Stephen B. Brush, J. Edward Taylor, and Mauricio Bellon, "Technology Adoption and Biological Diversity in Andean Potato Agriculture," *Journal of Development Economics* 39, no. 2 (1992):365–87.

M. Van Dusen and J. E. Taylor, "Missing Markets and Crop Diversity: Evidence from Mexico," *Environment and Development Economics* 10, no. 4 (2005):513–31.

came across with regard to education and health investments. Left to their own devices, people will underinvest in information—and health and education, and roads and bridges. The same arguments apply to communications and marketing systems.

This is why Cornell economist Chris Barrett writes: "The institutional and physical infrastructure necessary to ensure broad-based, low-cost access to competitive, well-functioning markets" requires "significant investment, typically by the public sector, paid for out of tax revenues or aid flows. One has to get institutions and endowments, as well as prices, 'right' in order to induce market-based development" (p. 300).[9]

But, just because a market doesn't work well does not mean the government should fix it. There are many problems out there competing for scarce public funds. Is fixing a particular market failure the best use of scarce public resources? Picture a poor isolated village facing high transaction costs. The government could build a new road there and put in a cell phone tower, but the same money could be used to provide credit to poor farmers or schools or health care for their children. Policy makers, like poor people, often face cruel trade-offs.

Markets and the "Knowledge Problem"

Understanding how markets work and where they work well can provide a yet deeper perspective on the role of governments in economic development. Hayek, who—as we learned at the beginning of this chapter—thought a lot about how markets work, was convinced that despite their potential flaws markets do something no individual, no committee, no team of experts, and no government agency could. Markets collect little bits of information from those choosing to transact in markets as well as from those choosing not to participate in markets. When they are able to adjust to changing conditions, prices convey extremely valuable information about the underlying conditions as experienced by individuals.

Hayek's insights about markets set the stage for what he called the "knowledge problem": we are quick to formulate big plans to directly improve society, but rarely possess the knowledge of current circumstances required to make these big plans succeed. No one person or committee possesses this knowledge because it "is not given to anyone in its totality" (p. 76).[10] But markets can aggregate this diffused knowledge—that is, if they function well enough.

As we have already seen throughout this book, this "knowledge problem" appears often in international development dilemmas. Big development plans and projects often fall far short of expectations because of this problem. According to Hayek, appreciating the nature of this knowledge problem and what it implies for program and policy design is fundamental to economics because it relates directly to markets: "The curious task of economics is to demonstrate to men [and women] how little they really know about what they imagine they can design" (p. 76).[11]

www.rebeltext.org/development/qr11.html
Learn more about information and markets by
exploring multimedia resources while you read.

APPENDIX

The Math of Lemons

In his award-winning paper, George Akerlof gave a simple example to show how asymmetric information can lead to a market failure. Here's how it goes:

Everyone knows that used cars vary in quality. Imagine an index of quality such that the worst quality car gets a "0" and the best quality car gets a "1." We do not know how the quality of used cars out there is distributed across the [0,1] quality interval, so we'll assume it's even, or uniform. That means the average quality equals ½.

Sellers and buyers both value cars based on their quality. Again, to make things simple, suppose sellers value cars identically to their quality, so that a car with quality equal to q is worth $\$q$. This might sound strange, since q is always between 0 and 1, but if you're thinking in, say, tens of thousands of dollars, a car worth $1/2 on the q scale would cost $5,000, and so on.

To make this example interesting, buyers have to value cars differently than sellers. It makes sense to imagine that cars are worth more to buyers than sellers in terms of the utility or satisfaction an additional car would bring. Akerlof assumed that a car of quality q is worth $\$3/2q$ to a buyer. (Actually, buyers routinely seem willing to spend more than sellers are willing to accept. Farmgate prices are far lower than what consumers pay for food at a grocery store, and anyone who buys something at auction has to pay a buyer's fee, which makes the price paid higher than the price received by the seller.)

In theory, then, it seems like the price for a used car will end up somewhere between $\$q$ and $\$3/2q$, depending on the bargaining power of the buyer and seller. Both buyer and seller would be better off if a transaction in this price range happened.

Now here's the catch: Only sellers know the quality of their car; in other words, information about car quality is asymmetric. The buyer's best guess is that a given car's quality is average—that is, q = ½. If this is the case, the buyer won't be willing to pay $\$3/2q$; she'll only be willing to pay half that, or ½ × 3/2$\$q$ =

3/4$q. But the seller won't sell a car of quality q at a price less than $q. The market fails; the high-quality cars get pulled off the market, and only the worst cars ("lemons") are left.

The "market for lemons" problem can arise in any situation in which sellers have better information about the quality of a good or service than buyers do. The thing being traded (or not) could be a commodity. (Does your produce meet food safety standards? Is it organic?). As we'll see in the next chapter, it could also be a service. (Will you be a productive worker if I hire you? Will you pay me back if I loan you some money?)

12

Credit and Insurance

By definition, economic development is a process that takes
time. Things that take time are risky because we don't know
what the future has in store for us. At the global or regional
level, we know something about these risks, which include
weather shocks and climate change, financial and commodity
market volatility, and sociopolitical instability. At the
household level, time and risk have very personal effects.
They determine a household's livelihood options, its level of
food security, and its ability to invest in its own future. We
have seen in prior chapters how time and risk can directly
shape development outcomes. In this chapter, we focus more
explicitly on these essentials of development economics
through the lens of credit and insurance—which, for poor
households, can take formal and informal forms.

ESSENTIALS

- Credit
- Market failures: asymmetric information
- Adverse selection and moral hazard
- Microfinance
- Risk and uncertainty
- Risk aversion
- Dynamics
- Insurance

There is a good chance that you bought this book with a credit card and
that you have a savings account, an ATM card, and maybe a student
loan. Yet well over half of the world's population does not participate
in financial markets at all. Nearly all of the world's financially unserved
adults live in Africa, Asia, or Latin America. In Kenya, Pakistan, and
Nicaragua, fewer than one in five people used financial services of any
kind, either as savers or borrowers, as of 2009.[1]

Sidebar 12.1 Saving for a Rainless Day

In the West African semi-arid tropics, poor households engage in rainfed agriculture in a drought-prone environment. Most lack access to credit or insurance to see them through when the rains don't come. Without other alternatives, animals are both the bank and the insurance policy. In good years, households invest in animals, and in bad years they sell off animals in an effort to keep food on the table, like taking money out of the bank.

But a study by three development economists found that this is a far-from-perfect way of insuring against income shocks. The return to "livestock savings" is low if many people have to sell off animals at the same time to get through a drought. This study followed 631 Burkina Faso households over a period of four years that included a severe drought. It found that livestock sales play less of a consumption-smoothing role than expected. On average, sales of animals made up for 15%–30% of income shortfalls due to drought and other adverse shocks. Low prices from distress sales of livestock may make animals a poor way to save for a rainless day.

Marcel Fafchamps, Christopher Udry, and Katherine Czukas, "Drought and Saving in West Africa: Are Livestock a Buffer Stock?" *Journal of Development Economics* 55, no. 2 (April 1998):273–305.

Without access to financial markets, people can still save and insure themselves against adverse economic shocks, but they have to find ways to do it that don't involve banks, insurance companies, or other formal institutions. For example, instead of putting their savings into an account that will give them a sure return, they might just buy a goat (see sidebar 12.1).

Understanding the importance of credit and insurance, why credit and insurance markets fail, and what can be done about it is essential to development economics. These topics trace their roots to two of the deepest dimensions of the human experience: time and risk. Most of the big decisions we make in life directly involve both time and risk. While this is as true for you as it is for someone your age living in rural Pakistan, the welfare implications of risky decisions that play out over time are likely to be quite different in rural Pakistan. As evidence of how central these dimensions are to development economics, the World Bank's 2014 World Development Report is entitled "Risk and Opportunity: Managing Risk for Development."[2]

In several places throughout this book, we've seen how time and risk shape development outcomes, including vulnerability and poverty dynamics (chapter 4), educational investment decisions (chapter 6), capital investments over time (chapter 7), and agricultural technology adoption (chapter 9). In this chapter, we provide a distinctly microeconomic perspective on time and risk by learning about credit and insurance markets. As we shall see, the two are closely related. The same duo of problems, adverse selection and moral hazard, is likely to thwart both, particularly in poor and risky environments. These problems stem from the economics of information and market failures we learned about in chapter 11.

CREDIT

As we will learn, credit fundamentally involves both time and risk dimensions. Before we turn to that topic, consider the three basic roles credit plays in modern economies.

First, it allows you to get ahead (credit for investment). Borrowing money enables people with good ideas, skills, and other assets who lack liquidity to make productive investments and raise income. Without credit, a farmer cannot purchase inputs ahead of the harvest (which she must do to get a good harvest) unless she has other sources of cash (like savings). A poor household usually cannot borrow money to set up a small business—even if all this means is buying a simple sewing machine.

Second, it prevents you from falling behind (credit for consumption). Borrowing allows households that experience a negative income shock to maintain their consumption levels and assets, preserving their ability to produce income in the future. If the crop fails or a breadwinner becomes sick or injured, there is cash to see the family through. Credit is insurance, as anyone who has lost his job and used his credit card to get through can attest.

Third, credit shifts risk from borrowers to lenders (credit as risk sharing). Default clauses and liability rules define the conditions under which a borrower does not have to repay a loan. Because default is an option, loans shift risks from borrowers to lenders. Defaulting on a loan doesn't sound very nice, but actually default and bankruptcy play an important role in modern economies. By shifting risk from borrowers to lenders, credit can induce people to take out loans and make high-return, but risky, investments that otherwise they would not make. Any investor knows that high-return investments entail risk, and the higher the return, the more risk there is likely to be. Without making risky investments, people are likely doomed to live in a low-return, low-income society.

Already you can see that credit and risk are related. In fact, in poor villages, it can be hard to tell where one ends and the other begins, as one development economist discovered in Nigeria (see sidebar 12.2).

Considering how important credit is, why don't more people have access to it? The answer to this question boils down to the information asymmetries we learned about in chapter 11. It's easy to buy a potato, but it's a lot harder to take out a loan. Credit is one of the most striking examples of how asymmetric information creates market failures.

Why Credit Is Different from a Potato

When you buy a potato, the transaction is simultaneous: you pull the cash out of your purse or pocket, and the vender hands you the potato.[3] Usually, you and the seller agree on what you're getting. You can examine the potato and make sure it is fresh and firm. At the Davis farmers' market, summer peach vendors offer samples just to make sure we know how good their fruit is before we buy some.

Credit is not like that, for several different reasons. In a potato transaction, you pay and walk away with the potato, and after that, you and the vendor can forget about each other. Credit involves an *intertemporal* exchange. You loan me the money today; I pay it back to you (with interest) sometime in the future. You give up the use of the money in return for a promise to get the money back. I get the money today in return for a promise to pay you back the money tomorrow.

So, what's being transacted here? Promises, actually. The borrower is "selling" a promise that he will give the lender resources to use in the future. In return, he gets to use the resources today. The lender is "buying" this promise that the borrower will repay the loan in the future. In return, he gives up the use of the resources today.

If what's promised always happened, things would be simple and there would be a lot more credit in the world. In real life, though, repayment is uncertain. Borrowers face a variety of risks. Projects are risky: loans are used to create businesses that may or may not succeed or to plant crops that may fail if the rains don't come. A borrower might be unable to repay due to any number of adverse shocks. Bad weather, a

Sidebar 12.2   Is It Credit or Insurance?

If you considered only loans from banks, private companies, or projects, you'd conclude that the credit market is more or less nonexistent in the four villages in northern Nigeria that economist Christopher Udry studied. But Chris uncovered a thriving informal credit market. Most—65% of all households—in Chris's random sample of village households borrowed money from other households, mostly members of the same kinship group. Even more—75%—lent money out to other households. More surprisingly, most of the households in the sample were both borrowers and lenders: two-thirds of all of the households that lent money also borrowed money. Households with more wealth lent more, but they also borrowed more. Could households be "hedging their bets" by borrowing and lending at the same time?

You might think that if you borrow a *naira,* that's what you'll pay back, if you can. In the Nigerian villages, how much people paid back on their loans depended upon how big their harvest was. That makes sense; if things go badly people repay less; even in the formal sector, banks sometimes adjust people's loan terms when they are not able to make their payments. But Udry's study found that lenders' harvests affected loan repayments, too: the larger the harvest a lender got, the less his borrowers paid back. To put this in more familiar terms, this would be like Citibank telling its borrowers that they don't have to repay as much of their loan this year because its profits are good!

This is a vivid example of how lines can blur between credit and insurance. By lending, borrowing, and making repayment depend on how each party's harvest turned out, people in these villages insured one another against crop yield risk.

Christopher Udry, "Credit Markets in Northern Nigeria: Credit as Insurance in a Rural Economy," *World Bank Economic Review* 4, no. 3 (1990):251–69.

recession, illness, or an injury can keep him from turning the loan into the income he'll need in order to repay it.

These kinds of uncertainties pose challenges to credit transactions, but they don't necessarily kill the deal. If lenders can correctly evaluate the risk of each borrower, they can cover for this risk by charging higher interest rates. High-risk borrowers would pay a higher interest rate than low-risk ones. The credit market could work just fine; borrowers, on average, could make a profit off their loans.

Credit and Asymmetric Information

Unfortunately, evaluating credit risk is hard to do. Take you, for instance. There's a good chance you're reading this book because you're a student. Suppose you want to take out a student loan. You promise you'll pay it back once you're out of school and working. Should the bank say "here, take some money"?

Not so quick. From the bank's point of view, your repayment risk is unknown, because of things it cannot even see (maybe because you don't want it to!).

First, the risk depends on who you are, that is, your intrinsic characteristics. The bank can observe some of these. For example, it can verify that you're a student in good standing—a proof of enrollment and transcript will do. It can't see other things about you, though. How smart are you, really? And how driven to succeed? Making it to college is a good signal about your innate abilities, but how will that translate into labor market success, which is what you'll have to have in order to repay a student loan?

Strike 1 against getting a student loan.

Then there's the nature of the investment, itself. Your investment is in human capital. Is it a good investment? The bank would like to know that. It knows (from studies economists have done) that, on average, education translates into higher earnings for people in the workforce. (If you've ever taken an econometrics class, you may have estimated the economic returns to schooling, which usually come in at around a 7% earnings gain per year of additional schooling.)[4]

That's an average, though. Does it represent you? Maybe the field you decide to invest in won't be so marketable once you get out of school. In 2012, there was such a glut of lawyers that recent law graduates sued their law schools for fraudulently marketing the profession as a secure source of employment. (The New York Supreme Court ruled against the grads.)[5]

Strike 2 against getting your loan.

Then there's the question of whether you'll behave or not once you get the loan. The actions you take in life will determine the likelihood of paying back your loan. What choices will you make? Will you study hard and wisely use your loan to position yourself for labor-market success? Will you work hard once you are out of school? And if there is, indeed, a life after graduation, will you choose to repay the loan when you are able? These are definite concerns to lenders.

That's strike 3. You're out!

You're a lot like a poor farmer in this respect: who you are and what you do will shape your likelihood of repayment, and information about you is asymmetric. There are many intrinsic things about you that the bank *can't* see but you *can,* things that might well affect your ability to repay, positively or negatively. You probably know yourself pretty well, but the bank doesn't. You know more about your human capital investment project, too. And you can decide your own behavior, but the bank can't observe it until it might be too late.

Actually, the bank could get a lot of this information if it really wanted to. It could find out more about you and learn more about how your major and college are likely to affect your job prospects. It could even hire a private investigator to follow you around and make sure you study hard. Besides being kind of creepy, that would be expensive—so expensive that the bank would never do it. So the problem with asymmetric information is not that the bank can't get the information; it would simply cost a lot of money to get it. This is an example of a transaction cost: the cost of getting the information the bank requires before it will give you a loan. Transaction costs tend to be very high in credit markets (and even higher in insurance markets, as we'll see below).

If you've got a student loan, it's almost certainly government guaranteed. That means the government has agreed to repay your loan if you fail to. That's what the banks demand in order to take on an investment as risky as you! If you didn't know before why student loans are government backed, now you do.

Time, uncertainty, and information asymmetries imply that credit transactions require contracts—not necessarily written ones, as many villagers around the world know, but contracts nonetheless. You don't need a contract to buy a potato! Information flow is critical. So is legal enforcement of the contract. Without the ability to enforce the loan contract, the loan won't happen.

This means that *institutions* (chapter 8) play a *key* role in making credit markets work: the legal system, to enforce contracts; credit bureaus, to provide lenders with information about people's credit worthiness; and property registries, to verify that the owners of property purchased with (or used to secure) credit are who they say they are.

In 2001, three economists—George Akerlof (whom we met in chapter 11), Joseph Stiglitz, and Michael Spence—won the Nobel Prize for their roles in creating the field of information economics. They and others have given us a powerful framework for understanding imperfections and failures in many markets where contracts are critical. Their work centers around two notions: adverse selection and moral hazard. Both are intimately related to asymmetric information. They explain why credit markets (and often other markets) don't work for most people in poor countries, and also why insurance markets are almost nonexistent. To understand why credit markets fail to meet the needs of poor people, we need to understand these notions of adverse selection and moral hazard.

Adverse Selection

Adverse selection occurs when "bad" outcomes happen because the seller knows more than the buyer about the product being sold—and exploits this advantage in some way. In Akerlof's market for lemons (chapter 11), the seller is the used-car owner, who knows more about the car's quality than any buyer could. I'm more likely to try to sell my car if I know it is crummy and unreliable, especially if these problems can be hidden under a coat of wax. (Buyer, beware!)

The same thing can happen with crummy promises. In credit markets, the seller is the borrower; she sells the promise of future repayment. This seller of promises knows more about her likelihood of default than the lender does. Since the quality of her promise depends on this default probability, she may try to make herself look more financially responsible than she knows herself to be.

This has a critical implication for credit availability. If the demand for potatoes exceeds the supply, the vender raises the price of the potato. If there really isn't enough credit in poor countries (i.e., demand for credit exceeds the supply), why don't banks raise the price of credit (the interest rate), and lend money until demand equals supply? Then, there would be equilibrium in the credit market, and the equilibrium "price of promises" would be the interest rate.

Adverse selection keeps banks from doing this. By increasing the interest rate, lenders may adversely affect the quality of their applicant pool, and this would lower their profits. Think about it: suppose you're totally credit worthy. You should be able to get a loan at a low interest rate because your promise is good (that is, your risk of default is low). You are willing to take out a loan at a low interest rate, but not at a high one—those high-interest loans are for high-risk people, not you.

So what happens if banks raise their interest rate? High-quality borrowers like you "select themselves" out of the market. You're the seller of promises. If you've got good ones to sell, then having to pay a high interest rate means you're selling your promises too cheaply. It's just like what happens in Akerlof's used-car market model. There, high-quality used cars leave the market when the price of used cars goes down. Because of asymmetric information, there is adverse selection; only low-quality cars (lemons) are left.

If the interest rate goes up high enough, only low-quality (high-risk) borrowers will be left in the credit market. You can see how the credit market, like the used-car market, can easily fail when there is adverse selection. You can find a numerical example that leads to this result in appendix 12.A.

Moral Hazard

The second big reason why credit markets fail is moral hazard, which is closely related to adverse selection: where adverse selection is about hidden information about quality, moral hazard is about hidden *actions* that affect quality (appendix 12.B).

In the market for lemons, if I plan to sell my car in the next few months, I might not bother to change the transmission fluid even if I was supposed to change it five thousand miles ago because it's unlikely the buyer will know. (That's why some people demand to see service records for the used cars they buy.)

In the world of credit, borrowers take actions that affect the quality of the promises they make, but the bank cannot see these actions. Credit shifts risk from borrowers to lenders. Consider this agricultural loan contract: "Repay if the harvest is successful and default (pay nothing) if the harvest fails."

This contract creates a disincentive for borrowers to take on "safe" projects, that is, ones with a high probability of success. A safe project might mean working hard and using seeds I'm pretty sure will give me a decent harvest, even if the weather is not great. An unsafe one might use a seed that *could* perform *really well* but only if the weather is perfect, which is unlikely in my village.

If my project fails, the worst that can happen to me is that I'll default on the loan, so I'll go for the unsafe project, knowing that if it does succeed I'll make a killing. The bank hopes a farmer who takes out a loan will buy seed, fertilizer, and other inputs that (weather permitting) will enable her to repay the loan after the harvest. But it knows the farmer *could* gamble on a risky seed. She could even use the money for something else, like playing the lottery. (You could do that with your student loan, too.)

The higher the interest rate, the more profit the borrower has to make in order to cover the loan and come out ahead, so the more likely he'll go for the high-risk, high-payoff investment. Thus, moral hazard, like adverse selection, can make lenders unwilling to raise interest rates and make loans even if there is excess demand for credit.

In short, when it comes to credit markets, adverse selection means that people who aren't credit worthy get the loan. Moral hazard means that once they get it, they don't do what they need to do in order to pay it back. Both happen because of asymmetric information: borrowers have greater information than lenders—information that affects the probability of involuntary as well as voluntary default. Borrowers know themselves, their projects, and the actions they take. If lenders raise the interest rate, they cause good types of borrowers to drop out of the market (adverse selection). They also can cause borrowers to take actions that the lender doesn't like, for example, choosing a risky technique (moral hazard). Lenders would have to charge a high interest rate in order to cover the risks of default caused by adverse selection and moral hazard, but if the interest rate is too high, the most credit worthy people leave and the market collapses.

In economics we're accustomed to thinking that the quantity of a product depends on its price. When it comes to credit, though, the quality of the customers and their actions depends on the price (the interest rate), too. When credit markets fail, profitable investments don't happen, and poor people stay poor. Research by development economists documents how big a difference credit can make (see sidebar 12.3).

SOLVING ADVERSE SELECTION AND MORAL HAZARD IN CREDIT MARKETS

History provides frightening examples of illegitimate measures taken to overcome the problems of moral hazard and adverse selection, as anyone who has seen the Hollywood film *The Godfather* knows. (Even today, mafias and loan sharks have effective ways to make borrowers make good on their loans.)

There are two kinds of *legitimate* mechanisms that lenders can use to try to resolve the problems of adverse selection and moral hazard. Indirect mechanisms involve the terms of contracts. Direct mechanisms are actions lenders can take that address information asymmetries.

Sidebar 12.3 Credit and Productivity in Peru

Estimating how credit affects production is tricky because the kinds of people who get credit are different from the people who do not. For example, more productive farmers are probably more likely to succeed in getting credit. So if we find that farmers with credit are more productive, is it because of the credit or because productive farmers are the ones who get credit in the first place?

There are two main ways to get at this question using econometrics: first, control for the characteristics that determine whether farmers are credit constrained or not, and second, track the same farmers over time. Catherine Guirkinger and Steve Boucher did both, using what is called "switching regression" and data from a survey of farmers they carried out in northern Peru. Their analysis found that credit constraints lowered the value of agricultural output in the study area by 26%. This study was important because it documented the importance of credit for productivity while controlling for who gets credit and who doesn't.

Catherine Guirkinger and Stephen R. Boucher, "Credit Constraints and Productivity in Peruvian Agriculture," *Agricultural Economics* 39, no. 3 (November 2008):295–308.

Indirect Mechanisms

Credit contracts can include many different terms.

The Interest Rate. The most obvious term in loan contracts is the interest rate. We've already seen that if lenders set the interest rate too high they may lose quality borrowers and encourage borrowers to take riskier actions. By carefully adjusting the interest rate, a lender can partially control both adverse selection and moral hazard.

Progressive Loan Size. A second indirect mechanism involves the loan size. A lender could start out by offering a borrower a small loan. If it is repaid, he can offer the borrower larger and larger loans—like when the bank raises the limit on your credit card. This is called progressive lending. It addresses adverse selection by enabling the lender to cheaply identify really bad types (they default on the small loans). It addresses moral hazard because the promise of larger future loans gives the borrower an incentive to behave well (repay). An obvious problem here is that the larger the loan, the greater the incentive to misbehave (moral hazard). A bad guy could behave well, maximize his credit line, and then "cash out" by defaulting.

The Threat of Termination. If a borrower defaults, the bank denies future access to loans. This addresses moral hazard by providing incentives for borrowers to behave well or else risk termination. A problem with this mechanism is that you probably do not have access to information from other lenders who may have terminated someone who applies for a loan from you. That's why credit agencies were created: to provide lenders with credit information about you before they give you a loan. You won't find many of them in poor rural areas, though. Another problem is that default may be legitimate: even quality borrowers make investments that fail sometimes. That's what business bankruptcy laws were created for, but you will not find this institutional development in most parts of the world, either.

Collateral. Collateral requires borrowers to secure the loan with personal property like land or a house, which the lender can foreclose upon in the event of default. Collateral addresses adverse selection: risky types won't apply for a loan because the probability of losing their collateral will be too high. It addresses moral hazard: the threat of foreclosure creates incentives for borrowers to behave well so they can repay their loans and keep their house.

Collateral requirements create other problems, though, particularly in poor societies. Many people do not have the collateral required to secure a loan. The institutions described in chapter 8 can directly affect the feasibility and enforceability of collateral requirements. For example, as we described in that chapter, many small farmers do not have formal title to their land. For collateral to work, property rights must be well defined and easily transferable. Titled land, a house, a business, jewelry, machines, vehicles, or a standing crop (harvest) are good candidates for use as collateral. The value of the collateral must not be subject to moral hazard. (I could trash my house or run off with my jewels before the bank takes them.) The property must be immobile (like a house) or else really small, so that the lender can hold it (a diamond ring). By design, collateral also shifts some risk back onto the borrowers, which can create "risk rationing": people with good projects may not undertake them because collateral-based contracts force them to bear too much risk. I want to invest in a business, but I won't risk my house for it.

In short, collateral requirements are generally not a good way to get credit to poor people, who do not have many assets. The assets poor people have may be unacceptable to banks. The transaction costs of posting collateral are high. Even if they have some assets that banks accept, poor people may be unwilling to risk using them as collateral. Collateral requirements affect the demand for credit as well as the supply. A poor person may not have credit because she tried to get it but was denied (supply rationing), she was unwilling to pay the high interest rate (price rationing), or she didn't apply because she was unwilling to put her collateral at risk (risk [demand] rationing).

Direct Mechanisms

Contractual terms to deal with adverse selection and moral hazard are what we call "indirect mechanisms." They are indirect because they try to influence what kinds of people apply for loans (selection) and their behavior once they get a loan (moral hazard). Lenders can also try to deal with adverse selection and moral hazard *directly, by screening applicants ex-ante and monitoring them ex-post.* Direct mechanisms, like indirect ones, can take many forms.

> *Ex-ante Actions.* Before a loan is made, loan officers can require would-be borrowers to fill out loan application forms, documenting their income and assets and providing other information critical to screening. They can require loan applicants to submit investment plans demonstrating that the project for which the loan will be used is viable. They can directly inspect applicants' farms, businesses, and assets to make sure they are good enough to use as collateral. A loan officer might interview family members and neighbors to learn about the applicant's integrity, work ethic, reliability, and other personal characteristics. If a credit bureau exists, the loan officer almost certainly will buy information about the applicant's credit history. This last step can be crucial because it provides information on the applicant's performance on loans from other lenders.
>
> This all sounds like a lot of snooping around, and it is. But borrowers put up with this sort of thing all the time in order to get a loan. Lenders incur the costs of screening in order to get the best applicants.
>
> These ex-ante measures deal mostly with the adverse selection problem. However, they also can address moral hazard, for example, by screening out the applicants who are most likely to shirk or misbehave once they have a loan.

Ex-Post Actions. After making a loan, lenders can take direct actions to increase the likelihood of repayment. They can visit borrowers and their farms or businesses to make sure the loan funds are being used properly and check on the progress of the project. Is the business being run efficiently? Are the fields being carefully tended? If the loan is for crop production, a loan officer might well show up just before the harvest—not a bad strategy given that the loan repayment is sitting out in the field! (Pretending your harvest is smaller than it is in order to avoid repayment is a great example of moral hazard.)

Direct and indirect measures like those outlined above can go a long way toward resolving the problems of adverse selection and moral hazard. However, they are costly; information is not free. The value of the time loan officers invest in screening applicants and monitoring borrowers can add considerably to the cost of loans. These are classic examples of transaction costs. They make the transaction more expensive, and if they are high enough, they keep the transaction from happening. Without them, though, information asymmetries may shut down the market altogether.

Given the high transaction costs of overcoming information problems in credit markets, it is little wonder that formal lenders do not serve poor people or, for that matter, farmers or entrepreneurs who are not poor but small. If you're a lender, and you have to incur these transaction costs no matter who you lend to, clearly you're better off making a few big loans than many little ones.

THE MICROFINANCE REVOLUTION

That's where microfinance comes in. Microfinance, also called microcredit, is the provision of very small (micro) loans, typically less than US$100, by lending institutions. Microfinance institutions focus on people near or below the poverty line who have been excluded from the formal credit market (that is, banks). They also lend to micro-entrepreneurs, people with small-scale (typically informal) businesses. Microloans usually are made without collateral.

Wait a minute, you might say. Isn't this a setup for failure? Banks don't loan to poor people and small businesses because of the high transaction costs of overcoming adverse selection and moral hazard. Demanding collateral is a critical tool to ensure repayment. Why would a microfinance institution think it could pull off something that well-staffed banks—not to mention well-funded government credit programs—have failed miserably at?

Actually, making small loans to low-income people and microbusinesses is not new. Informal village moneylenders have been doing it profitably for centuries, usually at very high interest rates. What do they know that we don't?

Seeing local moneylenders thrive in villages that banks will not touch seems puzzling. But clearly there's a lesson here, and in the past couple of decades economists, microfinance institutions, and governments have begun to catch on. If banks won't make small loans to poor people, the transaction costs of doing so must be high for banks. If local moneylenders *do* make small loans to poor people, they must have figured out a way to overcome the problems of adverse selection and moral hazard, and at a low enough cost to turn a profit.

In 1976, the Bangladeshi economist Muhammad Yunus, third of nine children and son of a jeweler, began working with poor women who made bamboo furniture with usurious loans in the village of Jobra, near the university where he lectured. Three decades later, in 2006, he (together with the Grammeen Bank he founded) received the Nobel Peace Prize. The Nobel Committee declared: "Muhammad Yunus . . . managed to translate visions into practical action for the benefit of millions of people, not only in Bangladesh, but also in many other countries. Loans to poor people without any financial security had appeared to be an impossible idea. From modest beginnings three decades ago, Yunus has, first and foremost through Grameen Bank, developed micro-credit into an ever more important instrument in the struggle against poverty."[6]

Yunus figured out how to solve the asymmetric-information problem (see sidebar 12.4).

By 2010 the Grameen Bank had a total loan portfolio of $939 million—8.3 million active borrowers with an average loan of $113. The vast majority of its borrowers are women. Repayment rates are claimed to be 95%.

The Grameen Bank's methodology has been replicated and spread throughout the world, including the United States. Yunus became an international microfinance phenomenon, appearing on *The Daily Show with Jon Stewart* (2006), *The Oprah Winfrey Show* (2006), *The Colbert Report* (2008), and *The Simpsons* (2010). Texas named a holiday after him. The United Nations declared 2005 the "International Year of Microcredit."

Sidebar 12.4   Muhammad Yunus and the Grameen Bank

The Bangladeshi economist Muhammad Yunus had an answer to the problems of adverse selection *and* moral hazard: design a system in which local information and monitoring could make loans viable. While visiting some of the poorest village households in India, he realized that very small loans could make a big difference. In the village of Jobra, women made bamboo furniture but had to pay usurious interest rates on loans to buy bamboo. Yunus's first loan, out of his own pocket in 1976, was for US$27, but it wasn't to a single individual; it was to forty-two women!

What was Yunus's secret to solving the moral hazard and adverse selection problems?

Informal groups of women apply for loans. They know each other. The group's members act as coguarantors of repayment. If one member fails to do what she needs to do to pay back her part of the loan, the rest of the group has to pay or else loses the chance to get loans in the future. The group, therefore, has a vested interest in seeing to it that every member of the group succeeds. That means monitoring and supporting one another—just what is needed to overcome moral hazard. What about adverse selection? Well, who would *you* choose to have in your group?

Yunus turned microfinance into a viable business model, which has spread around the world. That's why the Nobel Committee recognized his contribution to humanity by awarding him the Nobel Peace Prize in 2006.

Muhammad Yunus, *Banker to the Poor* (New Delhi: Penguin, 1998).

Microfinance in Theory and Practice

Grameen-style microfinance addresses asymmetric-information problems in two ways.

First, through self-selection into borrower groups. To take out a Grameen loan, people have to get together and form a borrower group. The loan goes to the borrower group, and then it is dispersed to individuals within the group. Loan repayments are made jointly by the group, and with high frequency. If one member does not repay, the entire group is denied access to loans in the future. This is called "joint liability." Thus, the group has to make sure each of its members pays back her loan—the rest of the group must cover for any members who do not repay.

Who, then, will you choose to have in your group? Clearly, you'll admit only good types of borrowers into your group. Since you live in the same village, you probably have pretty good information about who those people are; information asymmetries will be small. This addresses the adverse selection problem. Group monitoring to make sure each member repays addresses the moral hazard problem. Together, these make the group loan a low-risk investment for the microfinance institution, which thus can charge an interest rate low enough to keep the good types in the market. Microfinance solves the adverse selection and moral hazard problems by taking advantage of borrowers' information about each other, and also by designing contracts to give borrowers incentives to overcome the asymmetric information problems that banks cannot overcome.

As we've explored in several places in this book so far, however, development is not easy, and there are plenty of challenges and critiques when it comes to microfinance. Thus, some observers feel that the promise of microfinance is overblown.

First, it's hard to implement a successful microfinance scheme. For every Grameen-style success, there are ten failures! A lack of human capital, limited administrative expertise to build a microfinance institution, and corruption all are major obstacles to successful microfinance programs.

Second, microfinance may be better than loan sharks charging exorbitant interest rates, but it is still expensive by formal-sector standards. Average annual interest rates on microcredit loans are in the 30% to 40% range.

Third, most successful microfinance programs have had subsidies—sometimes large ones—to help them get started. The cost of these subsidies, which may be paid by governments or NGOs, often is not factored in when people guage the success of microfinance programs.

Fourth, microfinance programs are vulnerable to *covariate shocks*. When unexpected events like droughts or floods affect many people in a locality at the same time, the group can default. Large banks and insurance companies cover themselves for multivariate shocks by making loans over a large geographic area instead of focusing on individual locations. Even so, covariate risks can kill a deal even in rich economies, as anyone who's tried to get flood, earthquake, or hurricane insurance can attest.

Fifth, microfinance programs have a built-in problem of borrower "graduation." Good types of borrowers often don't need further micro-credit once they've succeeded in "getting ahead." This tends to drain credit groups of their lowest-risk members over time, which can make it hard for groups to remain viable and repay future loans.

Finally, as with any development project, microfinance raises the big question: Is this the *best* use of scarce development resources—not only money but also the effort and creative energy of international development agencies and local governments? Does it address the deeper, structural causes of poverty? Inequality, lack of infrastructure, poor educational systems, poor health-care systems—these are all critical issues that need to be addressed by development policies. Microfinance obviously is not a cure-all for these problems, but it has become an essential part of the development economist's tool kit.

RISK AND RISK AVERSION

To understand the economics of insurance markets, you must first understand some essential details about risk and risk aversion. We've touched on related topics in many places in this book. In this section, we discuss risk and risk aversion as essentials in development economics and as prerequisites to understanding how insurance works in developing countries.

No matter who you are or where you live, risk and uncertainty are part of your daily routine—and the feelings they induce in you and in others are fundamental to the human experience. Great literature often offers compelling descriptions of characters confronting or taking great risks. *Les Misérables* epitomizes great literature of this sort and, through the confrontation of characters and circumstances, leads us to wonder how we would hold up in the face of such overwhelming risk and calamity.

While risk is part of life everywhere, some people in some places obviously face much greater and more consequential risks than others. In developed countries, most folks pay a premium to reduce their exposure to risk. Sometimes, people actually choose to literally pay a premium to avoid risk in the form of life, health, or property insurance. Other times, we choose to pay extra for safety features in cars or houses. Often, developed countries make public investments or require individuals to make investments to reduce risk in the workplace, in the environment, and at home. Entrepreneurs and others often willingly take great risks in the hopes of success, and indeed this willingness to take risks and try new things fuels much of the innovation machine we introduced in chapter 8. An individual is much more likely to take these kinds of commercial risks if she is protected from personal and property risks.

The average person living in Africa or India lives with a lot more risk in her life than does her counterpart in North America or Europe. This fact was immediately apparent to Travis's ten- and twelve-year-old kids during a recent sabbatical year in Ghana. They quickly noticed and commented on small risks like whether you have water or electricity, larger risks like traffic hazards and serious illnesses, and even (perhaps especially) the risks animals face when they are not coddled and pampered as pets.

Measuring Risk Aversion

While people in developing countries generally face greater risks, the impulse to avoid or reduce consequential risks where possible is an innate human survival instinct. But some people care more about risk—and are willing to do or spend more to reduce their exposure to risk—than others. Economists call such people "risk averse" and attribute these differences from one person to another to "risk preferences."

Because individuals' level of risk aversion can directly influence the decisions they make and can even shape market outcomes, risk preferences often play an important role in the theoretical models economists use to understand economic development processes. Since these preferences can really matter in practice, development economists have also developed experimental methods to measure individual risk aversion.

Suppose for a moment that you are a maize farmer in Malawi. If you are generally willing to take risks when potential returns are high, you will likely manage your farm differently than a more risk averse neighbor farmer. You may manage other dimensions of your household and livelihood activities differently as well. Because these differences can be important, any economist who comes to your village trying to better understand local development issues and opportunities will want to try to discern these differences in risk aversion.

The economist has three basic options for estimating your degree of risk aversion and that of your neighbors. First, she can ask you directly, "How willing are you to take risks?" Second, she can collect detailed information about you and your household and try to infer something about your risk preferences from this information. Third, she can create risk "games" and offer real money based on your performance in these "games." In the past decade, the third option, originally adapted from experimental psychology techniques, has emerged as a favorite tool of development economists.

Experimental economics has grown rapidly as a methodological tool for studying individual decision making. As mentioned in chapter 2, these methods are part of the recent experimental revolution in development economics. Development economists have made some important contributions to the field of experimental economics along the way. In the late 1970s, a development economist named Hans Binswanger was the first to take experimental economics out of university laboratories and classrooms and into the field—among Indian farmers no less.[7]

Binswanger wanted to understand how much risk aversion varied from farmer to farmer and how much it mattered to their adoption of high-yielding new seed varieties. He decided to create a risk experiment. Over the course of several visits to these farm households, he and his research team presented farmers with seventeen different risk "games." In each game, farmers would choose between essentially the following six payoff pairs (note that we've converted the original rupee payoffs into rough current dollar equivalents):

Choice	Low payoff for "heads"	High payoff for "tails"
O	$50	$50
A	$45	$95
B	$40	$120
C	$30	$150
D	$20	$160
E	$10	$190
F	$0	$200

As you might have guessed from this list, after a farmer made his choice, the research team would flip a coin to determine which payoff the farmer would earn. You might also notice that these payoff pairs entail a basic risk-return trade-off: After choice "O," each pair is riskier than the one before it, but also provides a potentially higher payoff. Using this clever experiment, which is "incentive compatible" because there is real money on the table, Binswanger had a way of discerning the risk aversion of the farmers in his study. He found that roughly 75% of farmers were risk averse at moderate or intermediate levels and about 8% were severely or extremely risk averse.

Since Binswanger conducted this risk experiment in India, development economists have refined their use of experimental economics in the field. A more recent risk experiment used by Laura Schechter is even simpler than Binswanger's.[8] She gave farmers in Paraguay roughly $1.25 (two-thirds of the daily wage rate) and asked them how much they were willing to wager on the roll of a die where rolling a 1, 2, 3, 4, 5, or 6 multiplied the wager by 0 (losing the wager), 0.5, 1.0, 1.5, 2.0, or 2.5, respectively.

Development economists now have several experimental options for eliciting risky decisions from individuals, which can only be a good thing given how fundamentally these risk preferences shape individual and household decision making.

Risk and Poverty

Risk really matters in development economics because it really matters to the poor and it can really shape development outcomes. We discussed how risk affects poverty in chapter 4 when we introduced vulnerability and poverty dynamics. There we used the "rolling marbles" profile to depict the dynamic forces that can expand or erode a household's assets over time. To distinguish between stable and unstable equilibria, we had you visualize what would happen to the marbles in the profile if we "bumped" the profile. Introducing risk into this kind of system is exactly like unpredictably bumping the profile.

Poor households routinely endure negative shocks to their assets. Sickness can sap individuals' strength and compromise their ability to work on the farm or work for wages. Storms can wash away land and crops. Drought can weaken and kill livestock. Theft or extortion can wipe out months of savings. But good things can unexpectedly happen, too. Bumper crops and high prices can provide extra income. A new road can bring new work opportunities. Better access to technology and information can improve productive decisions and increase profit margins. If the household is subject to anything like the dynamic forces described in figure 4.2, these positive and negative shocks ("bumps") can shape welfare outcomes for a long time to come and shift the household to a higher or lower equilibrium asset level.

Much of the work of economists on risk and poverty aims to understand the impact of shocks like these on poverty. Obviously, these shocks can be painful and, as we just described, they can have long-run implications if there are asset dynamics at work. But these shocks are not the only effect risk can have on poverty—indeed, they may not even be the most important effect. In many settings, the biggest impact risk has on poverty is much harder to see.

Consider the effect drought risk has on the maize farmer and his family in Ethiopia. How exactly does drought risk affect this household? First, if a drought happens to occur, the household clearly suffers. This is the obvious ex-post burden of drought. But a drought doesn't actually have to happen for drought risk to hurt the household. The threat of drought may be enough to hurt the household. Just as a sixth-grade bully causes some kids to change how they get to school and where they hang out at recess, so the threat of drought at the beginning of the maize season causes many households to make very conservative maize farming decisions. This is the *ex ante* effect of risk on poverty: it can make poor households exposed to risk so cautious and conservative that they miss out on better livelihood strategies.

INSURANCE AND ASYMMETRIC INFORMATION

Output and credit markets illustrate how information problems can lead to market failure. Asymmetric information can also shut down insurance markets, and this can lead to efficiency losses that keep poor people poor.

The Importance of Insurance

There is nothing more important to poor people than the security of putting food on the table—today, this week, and next month. Without any way to smooth consumption, income shocks would translate directly into consumption shocks. We illustrate this in figure 12.1 by graphing the hypothetical ups and downs of a family's income and consumption. You can see that the variation in income around its mean is high. In many years (six, to be exact), income is lower than the subsistence minimum needed for the family to survive. If consumption followed income exactly, this family would be in trouble.

How can a household decouple its consumption from its income enough to keep from falling below the subsistence minimum? Decoupling consumption from income is called "consumption smoothing." There are two ways to smooth consumption—ways that correspond to the two effects of risk we just described: ex-ante and ex-post.

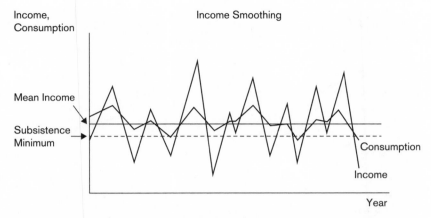

FIGURE 12.1. Consumption smoothing seeks to break the connection between consumption and income and keep households above their subsistence minimum even in bad years.

Ex-ante, a household can take steps to smooth out its income. For example, instead of specializing in a single source of income (say, a single cash crop), it can diversify its activities. It can put some land in cash crops, some in staples; some labor in crop production, some in wage work or migration. Ex-ante risk coping tries to compress the income profile in this figure, pulling the troughs up, but in the process almost certainly pushing the spikes downward (see sidebar 12.5).

Ex-post, households can try to smooth their consumption given income swings like the ones shown in the figure. If households had access to formal insurance, this would be easy. They'd pay a premium (the price one pays to buy an insurance contract), which would bring down their income in good years. However, in bad years the policy would pay out, providing cash for consumption. Formal income insurance is virtually nonexistent in poor societies, though, for reasons we'll look at below.

How else can you smooth your consumption when income is so volatile? You might use your credit card, but that isn't an option for a poor household in rural Malawi for the reasons described above. Poor people could save in good years and dis-save in bad ones, but that's easier said than done when there is no access to savings institutions.

In ancient times there were no banks, and people kept their savings for a rainy day in silver and gold coins, hidden away in a metal box. This was called "hoarding." Today ancient coin hoards are still found from time to time around the Mediterranean Sea. Behind every one of

Sidebar 12.5   Why Poor People Pay a High Price for (Ex-Ante) Insurance

A study of rural Indian households by Mark Rosenzweig and Hans Binswanger found that in order to protect themselves against income uncertainty, poor households diversify their activities more than rich households. That way, for example, if the rains don't come and the crop fails, they'll have other activities to fall back upon. The authors found that in places with high climate risk, poor households diversify more.

By diversifying, though, poor households forfeit the income gains from specializing in what they do best. The authors concluded that access to insurance could bring substantial economic benefits to rural households, especially the poor. A crop insurance policy guarantees that poor families will have food on their table even if the rains don't come, and this should make them more willing to plant crops, if that's what they do best.

Mark Rosenzweig and Hans Binswanger, "Wealth, Weather Risk, and the Consumption and Profitability of Agricultural Investments," *Economic Journal* 103 (1994):56–78.

these uncovered hoards is a story, long lost, that no doubt would illustrate why hoarding is not a very good insurance strategy.

Without markets, households could use their money in good times to buy things they can sell off in hard times. Many poor people in rural areas use livestock as a bank. Distress sales of animals are a common feature of people trying to make it through an adverse shock, for example, a severe drought.

There are problems with selling off assets, though. One is the price: if you're selling because of a drought, there's a good chance other people are, too, so the price is likely to be low at just the wrong time. In a poor economy facing high transaction costs, cut off from outside markets, there's the question of whom to sell your assets to. The biggest problem is that once you sell off your assets you've lost the chance to use them to recover from the shock. Knowing that makes it hard to sell off that last animal (see sidebar 12.6).

Credit and insurance often come up in the same breath when we talk about risk. The possibility of using credit or savings ("borrowing from yourself") to get through hard times makes credit and insurance close relatives when it comes to survival in poor societies.

Sidebar 12.6   Holding On to the Last Cow (or Two)

When a covariate shock (for example, drought) or an idiosyncratic one (illness) strikes, one way to pull through is to sell off some assets—say, your animals—to keep up your consumption. We saw in sidebar 12.1 that economists used data from Burkina Faso to show that on average households only offset 15%–30% of the income shortfall due to drought with livestock sales. This seems like very little consumption smoothing, but there's more to the story.

As is often the case, it is useful to look beneath this "average" response. What does this limited consumption smoothing response on average imply about how different kinds of households responded to drought? Exploring this question sheds new light on consumption smoothing.

Using the same panel data from Burkina Faso as described in sidebar 12.1, Travis and Michael Carter discovered that the average response is composed of two very different types of households: a small group that completely smooth their consumption by selling livestock and a large group that don't sell livestock at all. The small group of consumption smoothers have much bigger herds than the large group of "asset smoothers" who resist selling livestock. By holding on to their last few animals, poor households cling to the chance of being able to recover from the drought instead of falling into an "asset poverty trap" they might not be able to get out of. Remember the "rolling marbles" profile in chapter 4? Asset smoothers have small herds that are close to the unstable equilibrium on top of the middle hill: the slightest bump—in this case selling off an extra animal to smooth consumption in the short run—can cause the marble to roll down the hill to the left and into the poverty trap.

But there's a big catch. If holding onto those last few animals means your family doesn't have enough food to eat, you are effectively drawing down your future human capital (the bodies and brains of your children, who cannot develop properly without food and thus may be less productive in the future) in order to avoid drawing down your tiny herd and ending up in the likely poverty trap that comes with it. A lack of insurance to protect assets leaves poor households with this cruel intertemporal choice.

Michael R. Carter and J. Travis Lybbert, "Consumption versus Asset Smoothing: Testing the Implications of Poverty Trap Theory in Burkina Faso," *Journal of Development Economics* 99, no. 2 (2012):255–64.

IDIOSYNCRATIC VERSUS COVARIATE SHOCKS

Broadly speaking, people face two kinds of shocks in life: idiosyncratic and covariate.

> *Idiosyncratic shocks* affect specific individuals but not others around them. If a farmer has an accident in his field and is injured, for example, he has experienced an idiosyncratic shock. The kinds of policies that are widely available to people in high-income countries primarily insure against idiosyncratic shocks: fire, theft, death, and so on.
>
> *Covariate shocks* affect many people at once. If the rains don't come to your farm, they won't come to your neighbors' farms, either. Examples of covariate shocks are weather, earthquakes, and epidemics. The fine print in insurance policies frequently contains exclusions associated with covariate shocks, like floods and earthquakes in homeowners' insurance policies.

Within an economy, it is easier to insure against idiosyncratic shocks than against covariate shocks. If I become ill, my fellow villagers might be able to help me out (informal insurance). If I have insurance from a private company, it can pay me if I suffer an idiosyncratic shock covered by the policy, knowing that it can cover this loss with premiums paid by others around me.

A private company will be loath to issue protection against covariate shocks, like a storm or earthquake, knowing that if such a shock hits it will have to pay out on many claims simultaneously. After the 1994 earthquake centered in Northridge, California, insurance companies stopped issuing policies covering earthquake damages. The state of California had to step in and create its own earthquake insurance for homeowners.

Insuring against covariate shocks usually requires having access to resources outside the economy in which the shocks might occur. Insurance companies recognize this. They buy insurance policies from other insurers—that is, outside their own companies—to protect themselves in the event many claims hit at the same time. Some global "reinsurance" companies specialize in insuring insurers.

WHY INSURANCE MARKETS FAIL

The same problems of adverse selection and moral hazard that constrain credit markets virtually prevent the formation of insurance markets in poor areas.

Adverse Selection

When a person takes out life or crop insurance, he buys a promise from the insurance company to "pay off" if he dies or the crop fails. He pays the insurance company the price of the policy (the policy premium) in return for this promise. The insurance company sells him the policy if his risk of death (or crop failure) is low enough that, on average, the company will make a profit. The higher the risk of death (or crop failure), the higher the premiums the insurance company will have to charge.

That's where adverse selection and moral hazard come in. People with a high risk of death or crop failure have more of an incentive to get insurance than people with a low risk. Often, the high-risk people know who they are, but the insurer does not. If I have a terminal disease, I will want life insurance. If I farm in a risky environment, I will want crop insurance. There's no reason to buy earthquake insurance on your house if you live in Kansas, but a big reason to if you live in San Francisco. In short, the kinds of people with the greatest incentive to get insurance are the worst bets for the insurance company. This drives the price of insurance upward. But as the insurance premium rises, low-risk people no longer find it advantageous to buy insurance. Only the high-risk types stay in the market.

Adverse selection is a big reason why insurance markets function the way they do. It also explains why insurance companies test people and look at their medical records before selling them a life insurance policy, why "Obamacare" requires everyone to have health insurance, and why private health insurance is hard to get and often has exclusion clauses for "preexisting conditions" (a practice not permitted under the new US health reform law).

Moral Hazard

Once a person gets insurance, the moral hazard problem of hidden action comes in. Knowing the insurer will pay off in the case of my crop failure, what incentive do I have to work hard in my field? Armed with a good life and health insurance policy, am I more inclined to take on risky behavior, like smoking or flying over the Himalayas in a hot-air balloon? With a good theft policy, I could sell my bike, declare it stolen, collect on insurance, and double my money (and hope no one catches me!).

As in the case of credit, insurers could invest in screening (getting information about how risky I am) and monitoring (making sure I work hard on my land); however, this is expensive. Screening and monitoring are part of the transaction cost of insurance. The rarity of insurance suggests that this cost is simply too high for formal insurance markets to form in most parts of the world.

In short, when it comes to insurance markets, adverse selection means that high-risk people get insured. Moral hazard means that once they get insured, they engage in risky behavior. Sometimes the line between these two concepts can be a bit thin. For example, Travis is a risk taker. That's a characteristic that the insurance company can't see. Once he gets his life insurance policy, he starts taking hot-air balloon rides over the Himalayas, knowing his family's needs will be covered if he goes down. Anyone who really knows him wouldn't be surprised, but the insurance company doesn't know Travis.

Here, as in the case of credit markets, both adverse selection and moral hazard happen because of asymmetric information: those seeking insurance have greater information than the insurers do—information that affects the probability of an insurance policy having to pay out. If insurers raise their premiums to cover these risks, they drive the good risk types out of the market (adverse selection). They also cause the insured to take actions that the insurer doesn't like, for example, going for a risky investment (or taking hot-air balloon rides over the Himalayas). That is moral hazard. If premiums are too high, the "best-bet" people leave the insurance market, and the market collapses.

INDEX INSURANCE

There is, in theory, a simple solution to both adverse selection and moral hazard in insurance: design the insurance policy so that its payout is completely independent of who demands insurance and how he behaves. That's what *index insurance* does. An index insurance policy pays out if some trigger goes off that has nothing to do with what the insured people do.

An example of an index trigger is a drop in the average yield for a whole region, the water level in a reservoir, or rainfall measured at a local weather station. Even if you choose a risky action or fail to work hard, you won't affect any of these indexes, so your riskiness to the insurance company will not depend on who you are or what you do. If your yields tend to move up and down with the yields of others around you, though, index insurance can be valuable to you. It can also be profitable for an insurance company: knowing what the probability of

Sidebar 12.7   Insuring with Satellites

A big challenge in index insurance is how to come up with a good index. If there is no irrigation, you can't draw a line on the side of the irrigation reservoir. You could base the index on local rainfall data, but crop yields depend on when the rains come as well as how much rain there is. Ideally, the index would be based on whether overall yields, say, in a valley, drop enough to trigger an index insurance payout. But that would require annual yield surveys in the valley, which would be costly.

That's where satellites can help.

Satellite pictures provide a way to measure vegetation density, using the Normalized Difference Vegetation Index (NDVI). Every ten days NDVI is measured and freely available on the Family Early Warning System Network website, at a resolution of 8 × 8 kilometers. Rachid Laajaj and Michael Carter showed that the NDVI can be used to make an effective insurance index. In the region they studied in Burkina Faso, they showed that a satellite-based index captured 89% of the variance of village yields—much better than an index based on rainfall.

Rachid Laajaj and Michael Carter, "Using Satellite Imagery as the Basis for Index Insurance Contracts in West Africa" (draft, 2009; www. agriskmanagementforum.org/doc/using-satellite-imagery-basis-index-insurance-contracts-west-africa).

the trigger event is, the company can price its product to make a profit, on average.

Access to index insurance might enable farmers to get bank credit and achieve higher crop yields. Imagine two farmers soliciting a loan, both farmers identical except that one has index insurance and the other does not. Which one would you give the loan to if you were the bank?

The big drawback to index insurance is that it cannot insure people against risks associated with idiosyncratic shocks, or with covariate shocks that are not related to the index. If a farmer has an accident and is injured, or if a disease sweeps through everyone's herds, the water level in the local reservoir obviously is not affected, so an index policy linked to the water level will not pay out. Nevertheless, if the index chosen is both easily measured and highly correlated with a key income source, like farming, index insurance has the potential to contribute toward reducing—though not eliminating—income risk.

A trick is coming up with a good index. Satellites can help (see sidebar 12.7).

GOVERNMENT, CREDIT, AND RISK

In light of the problems of adverse selection and moral hazard that we have looked at in this chapter, it is little wonder that governments have had a poor record of solving credit market failures. India gives us a striking example: in 2008, the finance ministry had to forgive government loans to 40 million small and marginal farmers, at a cost of over US$15 billion. What went wrong? Asymmetric information. The government did not know the people it was lending to. This resulted in both moral hazard and adverse selection. In trying to address a credit market failure, India ended up with a big-time policy failure on its hands.

That doesn't mean there isn't anything governments can do to address credit and insurance market failures. We have seen the importance of public goods to the functioning of credit markets, including titling of collateral, legal institutions to enforce credit contracts, and credit market information. These are likely to fall into the domain of the public sector. So is investment in public education to increase "financial human capital," including poor people's awareness of, and ability to use, financial institutions.

There may also be a role for subsidies to give poor people better access to financial institutions, particularly in rural areas. In Mexico, a relatively high income developing country, 74% of all counties *(municipios)* had no bank branches in them at all in 2007. Not surprisingly, these are mostly rural counties in which the transaction costs of offering banking services tend to be high. It might make sense to have government subsidies that encourage banks to locate branches in these rural counties by partly offsetting these transaction costs. Alternatively, governments could attack the transaction costs at their roots by investing in new rural infrastructure.

Public provision of weather and other geographic information system (GIS) information, not to mention satellite imagery, is critical to the functioning of index insurance schemes. Providing critical public goods can have positive repercussions that go well beyond credit and insurance markets.

Whatever policies are considered to provide credit and income security to poor people, it is important to keep in mind that the same problems that make markets fail in the first place are likely to hamper government efforts to correct market failures.

www.rebeltext.org/development/qr12.html
Learn more about credit and insurance by
exploring multimedia resources while you read.

APPENDIX 12.A

Adverse Selection: A Tale of Two Types

You're a loan officer. A man walks in the door and says: "I'm Honest Abe. I've got a 'sure thing' that will yield a 50% rate of return. I need $1,000 to finance it."

You know there are two *types* of borrowers in the world:

"Honest Abe" always repays the loan.

"Slick Willy" takes the money and runs (defaults).

Suppose you also know that the population is equally split between these two types. That is, if you randomly pick someone from the population, there's a 50% chance you'll get an Abe and a 50% chance you'll get a Willy. Your problem is that you can't observe a borrower's true type. Slick Willy may pretend to be Honest Abe.

To set up our problem, let's define the following variables:

i = the interest rate (.05 → 5% interest rate)

R = the loan repayment (this is the lender's revenue)

L = the loan principal; assume it is $1,000 (this is the lender's cost)

π = the lender's profit

Our first objective is to find the interest rate, i, that allows the lender to earn zero *expected* profit. That is what we would expect the lender to get in a competitive credit market, in which the interest rate is the normal rate of return on loans. The lender's profit is $\pi = R - L$. R is the amount he gets repaid, or his revenue. L is the opportunity cost of the money he lent out, or simply his cost.

π is a random variable. When the creditor loans out the money, he doesn't know if he will get the money back. The value of repayment, R, is a random variable, and this makes π a random variable, too. The expected value of π, $E(\pi)$, equals expected revenue, $E(R)$, minus the cost of the loan, L. So we need to figure out what $E(R)$ is.

$$E(R) = Pr(\text{Borrower is Abe}) * (\text{Repayment if Abe}) + Pr(\text{Borrower is Willy}) * (\text{Repayment if Willy})$$

... where $Pr(\cdot)$ means "the probability that what is in the parentheses happens." There's a 50-50 chance the borrower is an Honest Abe, in which case the lender gets back the \$1,000 with interest. However, there's also a 50-50 chance he's a Slick Willie, in which case he gets nothing back at all. In math:

$$E(R) = (\tfrac{1}{2}) * [(1 + i) * 1,000] + (\tfrac{1}{2}) * \$0$$
$$E(R) = (\tfrac{1}{2}) * [(1 + i) * 1,000]$$

This makes sense: expected revenue is the total amount repaid when the borrower is an "Abe" times the probability that the borrower is an "Abe." Since $L = 1,000$, the lender's expected profit is:

$$E(\pi) = E(R) - L = (\tfrac{1}{2}) * [(1 + i) * 1,000] - 1,000$$

When does this expected profit just equal zero? When

$$E(\pi) = (\tfrac{1}{2}) * [(1 + i) * 1,000] - 1,000 = 0$$

Let's solve this for i to find out what the equilibrium interest rate must be in this world of Slick Willies and Honest Abes:

$$0 = (\tfrac{1}{2}) * [(1 + i) * 1,000] - 1,000$$
$$500 * (1 + i) = 1,000$$
$$1 + i = 2$$
$$i = 1$$

Thus, the interest rate must be 100% in order for the lender to break even on average. That's a problem: Abe's rate of return on the investment is only 50%. It would not make sense for him to pay 100% interest on a loan to make an investment that yields only 50%.

Abe won't take this loan.

Willy will, though! The lender will be left with only "Slick Willy" types in the market. The only way to get Abe back is to lower the interest rate.

APPENDIX 12.B

Moral Hazard: A Tale of Two Actions

Again, you're a loan officer. Suppose there's only one type of borrower: Farmer Jimmy. But now there are two possible *actions* that Jimmy can take: he can choose either of two techniques.

Technique 1: Grow safe *regular peanuts* (RP). Jimmy invests \$1,000 and gets \$1,200 in revenues with certainty. His profit is $\pi = 1,200 - 1,000 = \$200$.

Technique 2: Grow risky *salted peanuts* (SP). Again, Jimmy invests \$1,000, but with this technique, 20% of the time he is successful, earning \$2,000 in revenues. The other 80% of the time he fails, with \$0 revenues.

The loan contract requires Jimmy to repay the loan if the harvest is successful, but if the harvest fails, Jimmy defaults (pays nothing). As a loan officer, you think: "If I charge i, what will Jimmy do?"

What *does* Jimmy do? Jimmy compares his expected profit under the two techniques.

Recall that, in general, *E(Profit)* is given by the following equation:

$$E(\text{Profit}) = Pr(\text{Success}) * (\text{Profit if success}) + Pr(\text{Fail}) * (\text{Profit if fail})$$

His expected profit given that he chooses regular peanuts (RP), which we call $E(\text{Profit}|RP)$, is

$$E(\text{Profit}|RP) = 1,200 - (1 + i) * 1,000 = 200 - 1,000i$$

If he chooses salted peanuts (SP) his expected profit is

$$E(\text{Profit}|SP) = .2 * [2,000 - (1 + i) * 1,000] + .8 * 0 = 400 - (1 + i) * 200 = 200 - 200i$$

The expected profit growing the riskier salted peanuts, $200 - 200i$, clearly is greater than the expected profit growing regular peanuts, $200 - 1,000i$. So Jimmy will always choose SP!

Now, the lender is smart, so he knows that Jimmy will choose SP. What does he do, then? Let's see what the lender's profit looks like given that Jimmy plants SP:

$$E(\pi|SP) = E(\text{Repayment}|SP) - 1,000$$
$$E(\pi|SP) = .2 * (1 + i) * 1,000 + .8 * 0 - 1,000$$
$$E(\pi|SP) = 200 * (1 + i) - 1,000$$

We can set this equal to zero and see what interest rate the lender must charge to break even:

$$200 * (1 + i) - 1,000 = 0$$
$$1 + i = 5$$
$$i = 4$$

Knowing Jimmy will plant SP, the lender must charge 400% to break even. Would Jimmy want this loan? Let's see what his expected profit growing SP would be if he had to pay a 400% interest rate:

$$E(\text{Profit}|SP) = .2 * [2,000 - (1 + 4) * 1,000] = -600$$

At $i = 4$, Jimmy's expected profit growing SP is negative. That's a problem. Jimmy would never agree to take such a loan. The loan market collapses.

International Trade and Globalization

The efficiency gains a country can reap from specializing and trading with other countries can be huge. It is no wonder, then, that the most spectacular episodes of economic growth in recent decades have happened as countries traded more and more internationally. Yet, it is often politically difficult to open one's borders to international trade. Separating efficiency from equity is especially hard when it comes to trade because the distribution of gains and losses straddles international borders: some groups in some countries appear to gain in the short run while other groups in other countries appear to lose. This chapter provides an overview of the role of international trade in economic development. We begin with trade in goods, services, and factors of production—including foreign direct investment and international migration—and we conclude by asking whether international aid—a particular type of "free trade"—is good or bad for development.

ESSENTIALS

- Inseparability of efficiency and equity
- Import substitution and export promotion
- Specialization and diversification
- Comparative advantage
- Neoclassical trade theory
- Gravity trade models
- New trade theory
- Globalization and free-trade agreements
- Migration
- Social welfare analysis

Massive protests rocked the streets outside the Washington State Convention and Trade Center in November 1999. It was the largest demonstration ever in US history against an organization dedicated to free trade. It came to be known as the "Battle of Seattle." Afterward, the Seattle police chief said the protesters had won, and he resigned.

In the fall of 2013, Ukraine president Viktor Yanukovych refused to sign a free-trade agreement with the European Union, and massive protests *in favor of* trade integration shook the nation's capital, Kiev.

Why is international trade so contentious? Does free trade promote or hinder economic development? Understanding international trade is essential to development economics. Some developing countries see international trade as a major threat; others see it as an unparalleled opportunity to boost their economies. Several—most recently, China— have tapped this opportunity with spectacular success.

Trade is a big topic, the subject of whole courses, PhD theses, and dedicated journals. Our goal is to cover the basics of how development economists think about the role of trade in economic development, building upon what we learned about markets in chapter 11. As we shall see, there are strong similarities between how trade within and among countries affects people's welfare.

THE THEORY OF COMPARATIVE ADVANTAGE

Ed's wife, Peri, is a great cook—way better than Ed. She's also faster at cleaning the kitchen. You might think she ought to do both, then. But that isn't what Ed and Peri do. Peri cooks; Ed cleans up. Both agree they are better off that way.

Peri and Ed are just following David Ricardo's Theory of Comparative Advantage, laid out in his classic 1817 book *The Principles of Political Economy and Taxation*.[1] Ricardo presented a remarkably simple model with only two countries and two goods. Here's how it works:

Take two countries—country A and country B. (In Ricardo's famous example, country A was England and country B was Portugal.) Table 13.1 gives each country's cost of producing one unit of cloth and wine. As you can see, country B is better at producing both. Country A would love to get cloth *and* wine at the cost of producing them in country B, but why would country B ever want to trade with country A?

You might think trade isn't going to happen, but Ricardo says it will. Country A will specialize in producing only cloth and country B only wine. Then they will trade.

Here's the logic: suppose wine and cloth have the same price, so one unit (say, a bolt) of cloth trades for one unit (a case) of wine.[2] If country

TABLE 13.1   DAVID RICARDO'S
ILLUSTRATION OF COMPARATIVE
ADVANTAGE

	Unit Labor Costs	
Country	*Cloth*	*Wine*
A	100	110
B	90	80

SOURCE: David Ricardo, *On the Principles of Political Economy and Taxation* (reprint, 1965; London: J. M. Dent and Son, 1817).

A produces only cloth, then each unit of cloth it makes will cost it 100. By trading with country B, it can buy one unit of wine with one unit of cloth. So through trade it can get a unit of wine for 100 (the cost of producing the cloth to export). If it produced the wine at home it would cost 110. Thus, country A is better off specializing in cloth and trading for wine. (Besides, who would doubt that Portuguese wine is better than British wine?)

What about country B? After all, it takes two to tango. If country B produces the thing it makes comparatively efficiently—wine—and then trades for cloth, it can get a unit of cloth at a cost of 80. Producing cloth at home would cost 90. So country B is better off specializing in wine and trading for cloth.

Ricardo's genius was in recognizing that country B doesn't really pay country A its cost of producing cloth (100). Instead, it produces wine (at 80) then exchanges the wine for cloth, which it would have to pay 90 to make itself. Trade lets it do that.

Both countries, then, are better off because of trade. A country might not have an *absolute* advantage in *anything,* but *all countries have a comparative advantage in something.* Ricardo's advice is to follow your comparative advantage, specialize, and trade. Everyone will be better off because of it.

By exploiting comparative advantage, trade can offer huge advantages by letting people specialize. This is true for nations as well as for individuals, households, villages, and regions. But as the "Battle of Seattle" attests, moving from a conceptual appreciation of comparative advantage to actually trading stuff between countries can be controversial. This is because in practice international trade can be simultaneously good for some people and bad for others—at least in the short run.

International Trade Can Be Good

International trade opens up potentially vast markets for the goods countries produce and consume. Without it, a country would have to satisfy all of its own demand for goods and services. When a country can export and import, the whole world becomes its market! It can follow Ricardo's advice and specialize in what it produces best. Then it can import a diversity of goods that simply would not available if all the country's demand had to be met by its own producers. International trade can make countries more food secure, too. If a drought strikes, a bad harvest can raise food costs and even lead to famines, but food prices will not rise at all if the country can import food at world prices. Bad weather in any one country is unlikely to have much—if any— impact on world food prices, so trade can provide food security—if countries let it.

By producing for the world market, poor countries can put large numbers of low-skilled workers to work earning wages that, although low by rich-country standards, are typically much higher than what workers would earn without trade. As the demand for labor in export production expands, eventually wages rise. We see this in China, where the average wage for a factory worker nearly quadrupled in real terms, from US$67 to $312 per month, between 1996 and 2008 (see figure 7.9 in chapter 7). Rising wages and employment can have a big impact on reducing poverty—including in the poor villages from which many factory workers migrate and to which they send remittances, as we saw in chapter 10.

Opening up to global capital markets can give countries access to investment funds far beyond what domestic savings could provide, enabling them to invest in capital. Trade gives countries access to new technologies and ideas as well as goods and services. Imported technologies and ideas can make domestic firms more productive and raise people's incomes. In chapter 7 we saw how important both capital and ideas are to promoting economic growth.

International Trade Can Raise Concerns

The case against free trade rests largely on how the benefits of trade are distributed, worries about whether poor countries can compete in global markets, and fears of becoming vulnerable to global economic shocks.

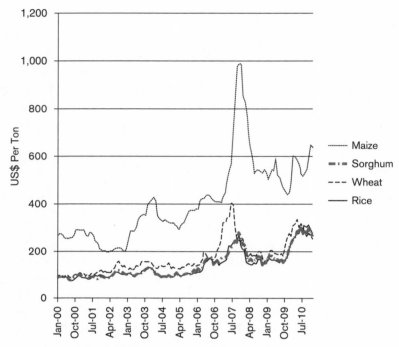

FIGURE 13.1. World food prices are increasing and becoming more volatile.
Source: UN FAOSTAT (http://faostat.fao.org/).

Small open economies are vulnerable to global trade shocks. It might feel unsettling to think that at any moment world prices might change and prices on your country's store shelves will follow. When the prices of commodities like iron ore, copper, rare-earth metals, or other raw materials are booming in the world market, a country that exports those commodities (like many African countries do) can prosper. If global commodity prices suddenly plunge, though, the negative impacts can reverberate through the whole domestic economy. Many poor countries depend on food grain imports. The prices of grains have become increasingly volatile as the world's population and income have risen and as competition over the use of grain for food, feed, and fuel has intensified (figure 13.1).

Countries worry about having to compete with other countries' producers, who might undercut them in the global marketplace. If a country opens its borders to trade, not everyone in it will be able to compete. Look at Ricardo's example (table 13.1) again. If country A specializes in cloth, its cloth producers will be happy, but its wine production will evaporate. Conversely, country B's wine producers will be toasting to their own success, but its cloth industry will fold. That's under the best of circumstances.

Technology can flip countries' comparative advantage. Most Mexican farmers grow corn, often with labor-intensive ox-and-plow technology. Iowa grows corn with the most capital-intensive technology in the world. It is way cheaper to grow corn in Iowa than in Mexico.

Economic crises can spread fast, like a contagion, when countries are connected through trade. The collapse of several major US banks in September 2008 triggered an economic crisis that almost instantly went global, thanks to world capital markets. Free trade in capital means that investors can buy stocks in foreign companies, banks in capital-rich countries make loans to private individuals or governments in poor countries, and multinational corporations build factories around the globe (and repatriate their profits wherever they wish). Countries that borrowed heavily on global capital markets—like Greece—were particularly hard hit by the 2008 crisis. The idea that bad home loans in the US could spark a severe global recession testifies to how quickly things—bad and good—can spread across an interconnected world, and how vulnerable everyone is to market shocks.

Political economy—that is, how political forces affect the choice of economic policies—always plays a central role in free-trade discussions. Even if the overall gains from trade are positive, the losers may block a free-trade agreement unless they can be convinced that there is something in it for them.

MODELING THE GAINS FROM TRADE: NEOCLASSICAL TRADE THEORY

In chapter 11 we saw how a household or village can increase its welfare by trading on markets within a country. The measure of welfare we used there was the economic surplus. We saw in figure 11.2 that when berry producers got access to an outside market with high berry prices instead of having to sell all their berries in the village, their producer surplus (profit) went up. Consumer surplus fell, but the gain in producer surplus increased more than the drop in consumer surplus. Producers could easily compensate consumers, and everybody could be better off with trade. If the outside market price had been lower than the village price, consumers would have gained more than enough to compensate producers for lower profits.

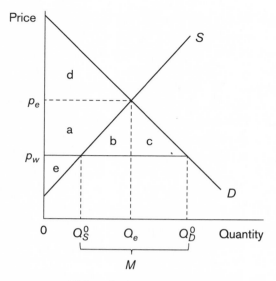

FIGURE 13.2. With trade, the consumer surplus equals the sum of areas a + b + c + d. The producer surplus is area e.

This same basic argument applies to free trade among countries. Figure 13.2 illustrates a country's supply and demand for some good, say, rice. If the country could not trade with the rest of the world, its equilibrium price and quantity of rice would be given by the intersection of the supply and demand curves: the country would consume an amount Q_e of rice at a domestic price equal to p_e. We can call this domestic price without trade the "autarkic" price. ("Autarky" means economic independence or self-sufficiency—in this case, for a country.) Without the possibility for trade, rice would be a nontradable.

Rice is a globally traded commodity, so if the country's policies permit it, there most certainly will be trade. When there is trade, the world price, p_w, replaces the equilibrium price, p_e. The world price could be higher or lower than p_e, depending on whether the country is an efficient or inefficient rice producer (the position of its supply curve) and whether it is a large or small demander of rice (the position of the demand curve). If $p_w > p_e$ the country will supply more rice than it produces and export the difference; if $p_w < p_e$ (as in this diagram) it will do the opposite. The country in our figure imports an amount M of rice from the rest of the world.

Trade in this case makes consumers happy: they can pay the lower world price for rice. The country's rice producers are not so happy, though. They have to sell at the low world price; if they charge the higher equilibrium price, no one will buy from them. Given that there are winners and losers from international trade, how do we know whether opening up to trade is good or bad for a country? We need a way to measure countries' total welfare.

In chapter 11 we learned about consumer and producer surplus, the basic tools of economic welfare analysis. We can use those same tools to demonstrate that economic welfare is higher with trade than without it, as well as to show how restrictionist trade policies reduce economic efficiency as well as welfare.

Trade and Welfare

To understand how trade affects economic welfare, we have to start by agreeing on what we mean by "economic welfare." Economic welfare is the sum of producer and consumer surplus. Figure 13.2 shows the consumer and producer surplus with trade. The consumer surplus is given by the triangle under the demand curve and above the world price, which has an area equal to a + b + c + d in the figure. The producer surplus is the triangle below the world price and above the supply curve, which has an area equal to e. Total economic surplus with trade, then, equals the sum of all these areas.

You can do exactly the same thing as in chapter 11 to demonstrate that the economic welfare with trade is larger than the economic welfare without trade. Without trade, at an equilibrium price higher than the world price, as in figure 13.2, the producer surplus will increase, but the consumer surplus will fall by a greater amount. If we had drawn the same figure but with the world price above the equilibrium price, the reverse would happen: without trade, the consumer surplus would increase, but the producer surplus would fall by more. In either case, total economic surplus is lower without trade.

In short, if a country opens up to trade, its economic pie will be larger, and the winners (consumers, in figure 13.2) could compensate the losers (producers). Whether compensation actually happens depends on the political process in the country and on the influence producers and consumers have over policy and trade agreements. To complicate matters, the same people may win and lose from trade. A farmer might gain, by being able to buy cheap imported fertilizer, and lose, because the world price for his crop is lower than the domestic price. Households might gain, as consumers of goods that are cheaply imported, but lose with respect to other goods, or maybe even with respect to income if workers in the household find themselves competing with workers in low-wage countries.

The power of the theory, though, is that in any market, total economic surplus is higher with trade than without it (or at least never lower), regardless of who benefits. The worst that can happen is no change in economic surplus, and that only occurs if the world price happens to be the same as the equilibrium price without trade.

What Restrictive Trade Policies Do to Economic Welfare

Based on what we have just learned, you might imagine that trade restrictions lower economic welfare. Many countries impose taxes (tariffs) on the goods they import and/or export. The main justification for import tariffs is to protect domestic producers from foreign competition. A justification for both import and export tariffs is to collect tax revenue, which is easy for the government to do at the port. (Collecting sales tax from thousands of businesses or income tax from millions of households is much harder.) Both of these policies create what economists call a "deadweight" welfare loss to the country because they divert the economy away from what it does best.

An import tariff distorts trade by protecting domestic producers from foreign competition. In the process, it creates winners and losers while reducing overall economic welfare. By imposing an import tariff, a country hurts consumers, but producers of the protected good will thank the government all the way to the bank. That's what rice farmers do in Japan, where the price of rice is often seven times the world price because of trade policies! But if you add up the economic welfare of producers and consumers, it will be lower than without the tariff. That's because import tariffs, like other distortionary trade policies, create what is called a "deadweight loss."

Import Tariffs and Deadweight Loss

Import tariffs raise the price people in the country have to pay for imports by the per-unit amount of the tariff. That is, instead of paying p_w per ton of imported rice, consumers have to pay $p_w(1 + t_{im})$, where t_{im} is the per-ton tariff. Export taxes lower the price the country's producers get for selling their goods abroad; instead of p_w they get paid $p_w(1 - t_{ex})$, where t_{ex} is the export tariff per ton.

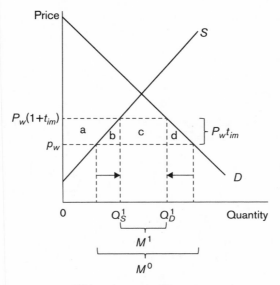

FIGURE 13.3. With an import tariff, consumers lose a + b + c + d, government gains c, producers gain a, and there is a deadweight loss of b + d.

The case of an import tariff is illustrated in figure 13.3.

With an import tariff of $t per unit of the good, the relevant price (everyone's *decision price*) is now $p_w(1 + t)$, as shown in figure 13.3. Before the tariff, the country's consumers demanded Q_D^0, and producers supplied Q_S^0. The country imported the difference, $M^0 = Q_D^0 - Q_S^0$ (see figure 13.2). After the tariff is imposed, the country imports a smaller amount because consumers demand less and producers supply more. The new level of imports, shown in figure 13.3, is $M^1 = Q_D^1 - Q_S^1$.

Let's see what this does to economic welfare. First, it raises the producer surplus by an amount equal to the area of the trapezoid with area a in the figure. Producers now sell at the higher price, so they make more profits than before. Producers' welfare goes up as a result of the tariff. Second, it generates tax revenue for the government. The government's tax gain is given by the area of the rectangle c. It is the tariff, t, times the level of imports after the tariff is in place, $Q_D^1 - Q_S^1$. The government, like producers, is better off with the tariff than without it.

What happens to consumer surplus? Consumers have to pay a higher price than before, so their surplus falls. Remember that the consumer surplus is the difference between the price line and the demand curve.

Thus, the fall in consumer surplus is given by the area (a + b + c + d). That's how much the economic welfare of consumers falls when the tariff is imposed.

Let's take stock of what happened here. Producer surplus went up by a. Government revenue went up by c. But consumer surplus *fell* by a + b + c + d. That's b + d more than the gains to producers and government. Where did that consumer loss go? Whose gain did it become?

The answer is: nobody's. The tariff distorted the economy and led to an efficiency loss equal to the areas of the two triangles, b + d. That's what economists call a *deadweight loss*. Avoiding deadweight losses is the core of the argument for free trade. Eliminating the tariff makes total economic welfare increase because the economic pie becomes bigger. If a tariff is eliminated, producers and government lose, but consumers gain more. In short, everyone could be made better off if the government didn't charge the tariff and then taxed consumers and handed some of the proceeds to producers.

Of course, this means the government must have the administrative capacity to efficiently collect taxes from consumers and make transfers to producers. Some taxes are easier to collect than others. Import tariffs are easy to levy at the port. Income taxes are notoriously difficult to levy because they require having information on incomes of large numbers of people. Sales taxes and value-added taxes are levied on businesses and are easier to collect than income taxes but more difficult than import tariffs. In countries lacking the administrative expertise to levy taxes efficiently, there may be large deadweight losses from tax collection.

Tariffs create a wedge between the import and export price. If the tariffs are large enough, it becomes too expensive for the country to import or export rice. In figure 13.4, the import price (including tariff) is above the autarkic (equilibrium) price, and the export price is below it. (Assuming there's no export tariff, the export price is the world price.) If you want to buy rice, you are better off paying the autarkic price p_e than the import price plus tariff. If you are selling, you'll get a better price selling to local consumers, at the autarkic price, than exporting at the world price. (All the more if there is an export tariff, too!) Thus, in our example, consumers will buy from domestic producers, and producers will sell to domestic consumers. There will be no trade. The country will be self-sufficient in rice. This self-sufficiency will come at a cost, though. Producers will be happy, gaining a surplus equal to area a in the figure, but consumers will lose more—areas a + b + c. That means total economic surplus will fall by areas b + c, which represent

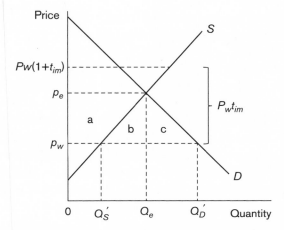

FIGURE 13.4. A very high tariff can drive an economy into self-sufficiency, producing a deadweight loss of b + c.

the deadweight loss in this case. (The government gets no benefit from a policy that drives the country into self-sufficiency.)

This example illustrates how you can use trade policy to take a tradable and turn it into a nontradable—that is, force the economy to become self-sufficient, or autarkic, with respect to a particular good. A more direct way is simply to restrict imports by imposing a *trade quota*. There is bound to be a welfare loss, though. That makes sense: if someone else can make something more cheaply than I can, I should buy it instead of making it myself. That's what we do every time we go to a farmers' market or grocery store. Countries, it seems, should do the same.

STRATEGIES FOR TRADE-BASED GROWTH

There is no conclusive experiment to help us determine whether and how much free trade promotes economic growth. Over the years, different countries have followed different trade strategies, but not randomly. Countries decide which trade strategies to follow concurrently with many other decisions that, along with trade, shape economic development outcomes. Other policies influence the impacts of trade on income growth. For example, a country that opens up to trade and also invests heavily in public education, roads, ports, and communications is likely to see different outcomes from those of a country that opens to trade without making the investments required to be competitive. Institutions affect policy choices as well as growth outcomes. In countries with inclusive institutions (chapter 8), we might expect to find greater and more broad-based benefits from trade than in countries with extractive institutions. When economists try to figure out how free trade affects economic development, they are haunted by questions like, "Is it trade, or is it institutions, that led to the outcomes we see?" Things can get pretty complex.

That said, history gives us the opportunity to compare the development records of countries that did and did not open themselves up to trade. Trade strategies fall broadly into two categories: import-substitution industrialization and export-led growth. Let's see what these strategies entail and then compare the records of countries that followed each one.

Import-Substitution Industrialization

In chapter 1 we briefly met Raúl Prebisch and Hans Singer, who argued that developing countries should shift from producing primary goods, like crops and raw materials, to manufactured goods. They based their argument on a simple observation: as people's and countries' incomes rise, the share of income spent on manufactured goods increases. This puts upward pressure on the prices of manufactured goods compared to primary goods. In other words, the prices of primary goods relative to manufactured goods—what economists call the "terms of trade for primary goods"—decrease as incomes rise around the world. Thus, if a poor country specializes in producing, say, food crops, it will find itself paying ever higher prices for the imported manufactured goods its consumers and industries demand.

Wouldn't a poor country be better off developing its own capacity to produce manufactured goods, for its own population or, better yet, exports? Doing so would require, among other measures, imposing high tariffs or even limits (quotas) on imported manufactured goods to ensure that domestic "infant industries" are profitable until they are able to stand on their own feet. Such measures are part of what is called "import-substitution industrialization."

Prebisch and Singer found support from others in political science and economics who argued that poor countries lose by virtue of the way in which they are integrated into the "world system."[3] Proponents of dependency theory claimed that, through trade, a "core" of rich countries extract resources from a "periphery" of weaker, poor countries. Thus, trade results in the economic exploitation of poor countries and the transfer of economic surplus (production beyond subsistence) from poor to rich countries. The idea that poor countries (the periphery) have to sell what they produce at low prices while buying from rich countries (the center) at relatively high prices is central to dependency theory.

Dependency theory influenced trade policies in many countries. A major dependency theorist, Fernando Henrique Cardoso, was president of Brazil from 1995 to 2002. Singer was an Argentine economist who worked for the United Nations Economic Commission on Latin America. Both argued that developing countries needed to impose at least some protective trade policies if they wished to achieve self-sustaining economic growth. In a number of Latin American countries, including Argentina, Brazil, and Mexico, arguments against free trade were reinforced by a strong sense of nationalism and political sovereignty. Some dependency theorists, inspired by Marxist theory, believed that socialist revolution would be required in order to eliminate economic disparities in the world system.

Countries that followed Prebisch and Singer's advice used a number of different policy levers to promote import-substitution industrialization, including the following:

- Protective trade policies: Tariffs or quotas on imports of manufactured goods that might compete with local industries.

- Exchange-rate policies: Artificial overvaluation of the country's currency made imported inputs and technology needed by infant industries cheaper. It also made imported food cheaper—a way to keep food prices and thus wages low in order to make new industries more profitable.

- Sectoral policies: Governments combined these trade policies with subsidies, preferential credit, and investments in infrastructure (electricity, transportation, communications) targeting infant industries.

- Parastatals: The creation of government-controlled companies was the most extreme measure countries took to create new industries.

It is important to bear in mind that all of these policies, by making industrial production more profitable, also made agriculture and other primary-goods production relatively less profitable. Thus, they discriminated against some sectors in order to encourage the movement of labor, capital, and other resources into the protected industries.

Although these distortions in the economy were strategic, they nonetheless created deadweight loss, as in the case of the trade barriers described above.

Export Promotion: Learning from Tigers

In contrast to the countries that followed import-substitution industrialization, exports were the centerpiece of economic development strategies in some Asian countries, like the Asian Tiger economies (Hong Kong, Singapore, South Korea, and Taiwan) and more recently, China. They based their development model largely on "export-led growth."

Proponents of export-led growth point to a number of problems with import-substitution industrialization. Corruption (chapter 8) is one. Control over the economy, particularly through the creation of parastatals, concentrates economic power in the hands of government officials, who are not subject to the same controls that market competition places on private companies' behavior. Once measures are in place to protect and subsidize favored industries, those industries tend to become politically powerful, and this makes it difficult to eventually wean them off of subsidies and force them to compete in a global marketplace. Better, say the Asian Tigers, to make domestic industries compete with foreign industries from the get-go.

Companies that have to compete in world markets have an incentive to be efficient, to innovate, and to produce high-quality products. Subsidies to infant industries are expensive and divert scarce public resources from other uses, including the sorts of poverty programs we learned about in chapters 2, 4, and 6. This becomes even more of a concern once countries find themselves saddled with inefficient industries exerting political power to maintain their preferential treatment.

Exchange-rate policies that make imported technology and inputs cheaper also make exports more expensive to the rest of the world. This can lead to ongoing trade imbalances. Protected industries and governments easily can get into trouble by borrowing heavily from foreign banks to finance inefficient industries that might never become competitive enough to generate the income and foreign exchange (from exports) to pay back their loans. If an economic crisis hits, companies and governments may default on foreign loans.

When countries lack the political will to move beyond import substitution, history shows that major economic crises often are required before governments choose—or else are forced by international devel-

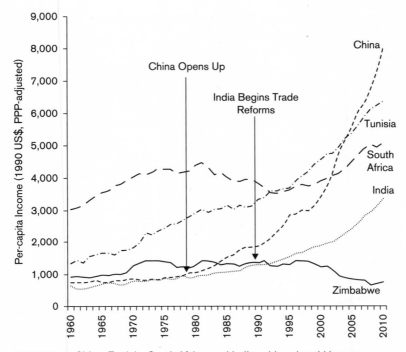

FIGURE 13.5. China, Tunisia, South Africa, and India achieved rapid income growth after opening up to trade. Zimbabwe, which followed import-substitution policies, saw its per capita income decline. (This figure and fig. 13.6 use Geary-Khamis dollars, which are real values in 1990 US dollars adjusted for purchasing power parity throughout the time-series range.) Source: Maddison Project (www.ggdc.net/maddison/maddison-project/home.htm).

opment agencies like the International Monetary Fund (IMF)—to dismantle their costly import-substitution policies.[4]

Overall, countries that followed export-led growth policies fared better than countries that adhered to import-substitution industrialization policies. There are plenty of examples of this—most clearly the Asian Tigers, but there are others (see figure 13.5). China's economic growth skyrocketed—and poverty there plummeted—after the country opened up to trade and enacted internal market reforms, led by Deng Xiaoping in 1978. India broke out of economic stagnation and began to grow once it started opening up to trade in 1990; its per capita income nearly tripled between 1990 and 2010. Outsourcing of tech jobs to India played an important role in this growth. In Africa, Zimbabwe has followed import-substitution industrialization, and it is one of the worst performers on

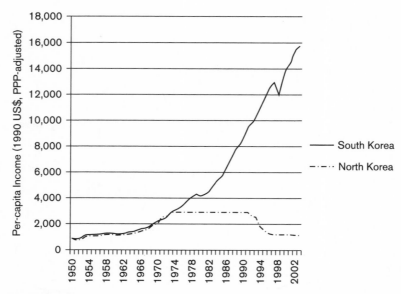

FIGURE 13.6. Per capita income growth in South and North Korea, 1950–2002.
Source: Maddison Project (www.ggdc.net/maddison/maddison-project/home.htm).

that continent. South Africa and Tunisia, on the other hand, emphasized more export-led growth, and their performance has been impressive.

The two Koreas provide us with an interesting experiment. In 1953, after the armistice that ended the Korean War, North and South Korea had similar per capita incomes, populations, and resource endowments. From that point onward, South Korea followed an export-led development strategy, while North Korea isolated itself from world markets and pursued an import-substitution strategy. Today, South Korea is the sixth largest exporter and the seventh largest importer in the world. North Korea describes itself as a *Juche* (self-reliant) state, which sounds a lot like autarky. It ranks 111th and 132nd among countries in exports and imports, respectively (most of the trade it has is with China).[5] South Korea's average per capita income exploded after 1974, while North Korea's fell (see figure 13.6). Today, South Korea's per capita income is US$39,950. That's twenty-two times North Korea's per capita income, which to the best of our ability to measure it is around $1,800, lower than that of Bangladesh. The disparities between these two countries show up in other measures as well. For example, average life expectancy at birth is sixty in North Korea and eighty-one in South Korea.

Does the huge difference in economic growth and development between South and North Korea prove that export-led growth is superior? Not exactly. We could debate how other policies and institutions shaped these two countries' growth performance, but one thing is clear: South Korea could not have accomplished what it did *without* trade.

There is more general evidence that trade promotes growth. In chapter 7 we met the empirical growth economist Xavier Sala-i-Martin, who conducted a systematic analysis of what determines economic growth. You might recall that Sala-i-Martin found a positive and statistically significant association between countries' outward orientation and their rates of income growth.

In short, empirical evidence suggests that trade is beneficial for economic growth and development. It does not tell us much about why, though. For that, we need some more theory.

WHERE DOES COMPARATIVE ADVANTAGE COME FROM? THE HECKSCHER-OHLIN MODEL

Ricardo doesn't tell us where a country's comparative advantage comes from. In 1931, two Swedish economists, Eli Heckscher and his student, Bertil Ohlin, gave an answer: factor endowments. Some countries are labor rich and capital poor; others are the opposite. Factors produce output. It makes sense, then, that countries rich in labor would have a comparative advantage in producing labor-intensive goods. Those rich in capital (including human capital) have a comparative advantage in producing more capital-intensive goods. Logically, then, labor-rich countries should trade with capital-rich countries.

Factors are not limited to labor and physical capital. Natural resources can be considered a factor of production. A country rich in oil (Saudi Arabia) naturally has a comparative advantage in oil, one rich in gorgeous beaches (Tahiti) or historical sites (Italy) has a comparative advantage in tourism, and so forth. In today's world, the most important factor shaping economic growth is human capital. Countries rich in human capital (like the United States) have a comparative advantage in creating new technologies and exporting them around the globe.

The Heckscher-Ohlin model builds upon Ricardo's model in a simple way, with two countries, two goods, and two factors (labor and capital). Its insights can be generalized to situations involving more countries, goods, and factors, though.

This view of trade has important implications for world income inequality. If a labor-rich country follows its comparative advantage and produces more and more labor-intensive goods, what will happen to wages? Paul Samuelson, who won the Nobel Prize in 1970, proved that, under general conditions, trade causes factor prices to equalize across countries. This theoretical finding was considered so important that it became a theorem in economics: the Factor Price Equalization Theorem (FPET). As labor-abundant countries rev up their production of labor-intensive goods, they demand more labor, and their wages converge toward wages in labor-scarce countries. According to the FPET, low-skilled workers' wages should rise in China and Mexico—and they may fall in the United States—as these countries trade with each other and jobs for low-skilled workers shift across borders. The FPET predicts that trade will equalize the prices of other factors over time, including the rental rate on capital, in other words, the profit rate.

PUTTING RICARDO AND HECKSCHER-OHLIN TO THE TEST

Ricardo and Heckscher-Ohlin give us to two clear predictions. First, countries should specialize in goods whose production is intensive in the factors they possess in greatest abundance. Second, we would expect to find that most of the world's trade is between countries with different factor endowments. Samuelson's FPET adds another hypothesis: that wages and other factor prices equalize across countries over time as a result of trade in commodities.

It is relatively easy to come up with examples of countries that export goods in which they have a comparative advantage. Guatemala exports handpicked berries and tropical fruits to the United States, while the United States exports high-tech products to Guatemala. China exports labor-intensive manufactured goods to everyone. Saudi Arabia exports oil. Tourism is the main source of foreign exchange in Tahiti—in effect, Tahiti "exports" its beaches by letting us go there and lie on them.

But the prediction that most trade is between countries with different factor endowments just doesn't hold up. Most of the trade we see is between countries with similar factor endowments. Take the United Kingdom, for example (table 13.2). With one exception—China—all of the UK's top trading partners are other high-income countries, arguably with similar kinds of factor endowments: lots of capital and human capital, not much labor. If we exclude China from the list, 60% of the UK's exports go to high-income, capital-rich countries, and 54% of its imports come from such countries. China is the one clear example that seems to fit the Heckscher-Ohlin predictions. Having become the workshop of the world, it features highly on pretty much every country's import list.

TABLE 13.2 THE LARGEST TRADING PARTNERS OF THE UNITED
KINGDOM (2011)

	Exports		Imports	
Rank	*Country*	*%*	*Country*	*%*
1	United States	13	Germany	12.6
2	Germany	11.3	United States	7.7
3	France	7.8	China	7.6
4	Netherlands	7.7	Netherlands	7.1
5	Irish Republic	5.8	Norway	6.1
6	Belgium	5.3	France	5.9
7	Italy	3.4	Belgium	4.8
8	Spain	3.3	Italy	3.6
9	China	2.9	Irish Republic	3.2
10	Sweden	2.1	Spain	2.8
TOTAL		62.6		61.4

SOURCE: HM Revenue and Customs, Overseas Trade Statistics (www.uktradeinfo.com /Statistics/Pages/Statistics.aspx).

What if we look at a poor country? Table 13.3 shows Zambia's top ten trading partners. Most of its major trading partners are its neighbors, with two big exceptions: China is Zambia's largest supplier of imports, and Switzerland and China are its largest markets for exports (75% of which are copper or copper related). Almost all of its other top ten trading partners are African countries.

Uganda's top trading partners for exports and imports are, respectively, Sudan and Kenya; Bolivia's are Brazil and Chile; Paraguay's are Uruguay and Argentina on the export side and China and Brazil on the import side. South African Customs Union countries are Zimbabwe's major partners on both the import and export sides. Some high-income countries appear on these top-ten lists; the farther north we go in Africa, the more western European countries feature in African countries' lists of top trading partners, and the US appears on the lists of many Latin American countries. China seems to be on everyone's list of top import suppliers, and it is a major buyer of raw material exports from many countries. Nevertheless, what we see does not seem to support the hypothesis that most trade happens between countries with vastly different factor endowments.

What about the factor price equalization theorem's prediction that wages and profit rates equalize between countries that trade with each other? We have seen that low-skilled workers' wages increased sharply in

TABLE 13.3 ZAMBIA'S MAJOR TRADING PARTNERS

	Exports		Imports	
Rank	*Country*	%	*Country*	%
1	Switzerland	37.3	China	18.6
2	China	30.9	Nigeria	11.1
3	So. African Customs Union	5.6	Uganda	7.2
4	Korea, Rep.	3.6	Cameroon	6.8
5	Congo, Dem. Rep.	3.4	Kenya	6.3
6	Saudi Arabia	2.5	Tanzania	6.1
7	Zimbabwe	2.3	Zambia	5.2
8	Egypt	2.1	So. African Customs Union	5.2
9	United Arab Emirates	1.8	Netherlands	4.9
10	Malawi	1.2	Germany	4.8
TOTAL		62.6		61.4

SOURCE: Massachusetts Institute of Technology, *The Observatory of Economic Complexity* (http://atlas.media.mit.edu/).

China between 1996 and 2008. A recent study found that real wages for high school graduates in the US fell more than 10% between 1965 and 2013.[6] China-US trade may have closed the wage gap for workers without a college education; however, the wage gap between rich and poor countries is enormous, despite a tremendous expansion in global trade.

What Do the Econometric Models Show?

Applied trade economists routinely crunch through gigabytes of data on international trade flows. In fact, there is an extensive literature in empirical trade modeling alongside the theoretical trade models. It probably won't surprise you to learn that their findings generally do not support the hypothesis that trade takes place mostly between countries with contrasting factor endowments, and studies do not find consistent evidence in support of the FPET hypothesis that wages and returns to capital converge as countries at different levels of development trade with each other.

There is one model that gives pretty good results when predicting trade between countries, but it looks nothing like the neoclassical trade models we've been learning about. In fact, it's straight out of astrophysics! The gravity trade model posits that trade between any two countries—call them country i and country j—depends on how big the two countries' economies are (that is, their economic masses) and on the distance between them. This is the same kind of model used to calculate the gravitational attraction between celestial bodies. Big celestial bodies have a lot of attraction—that is, unless they are very far away from each other. Smaller bodies, like the earth and moon, can attract each other a lot if they are close to each other. When it comes to trade, economies seem to be connected in the same way that gravity connects stars, planets, and moons.

The main difference between the way applied trade economists think of trade and the way physicists think about gravity is that to an economist's mind, "distance" is a fairly abstract concept. It is only partly about space. Two countries can be far apart yet easily accessible to one another by sea (like China and the United States). They can have special agreements that make trade easier—or not. Historical (colonial, cultural, language) ties also can facilitate trade. All of these things figure in what economists think of as "distance," which really is more like "trade friction."

Gravity models overwhelmingly find that larger countries trade with each other. Consumers in high-income countries buy a huge diversity of goods from other high-income countries. A lot of this trade is in what seem to be similar products. Germans buy Volvos from Sweden, and Swedes buy BMWs from Germany. Gravity models are pretty good at predicting how much trade happens between countries, but not so good at predicting trade in BMWs versus Volvos.

Proximity matters, too, though not as much as size. The United States's first and third largest trading partners are Canada and Mexico (China is number two). Malawi and Lesotho's top trading partner is South Africa. Some gravity models find that history matters. Reflecting colonial history, Morocco's major trading partner is France, while Ghana trades more with the UK. Free-trade agreements reduce trade frictions and stimulate trade among members of the agreement. For example, Mexico's imports to and exports from the United States increased sharply after NAFTA took effect (figure 13.7).

Theoretical trade economists have criticized the gravity model because it does not seem to have much connection with the theory of comparative advantage. It almost seems to have just dropped out of the sky! In many ways, what happened with trade is similar to what happened with growth (chapter 7). In both cases, empirical models failed to confirm key predictions from theoretical models. Theorists had to go back to the drawing board.

That's what the theoretical trade economist Paul Krugman did, and the New Trade Theory was born.

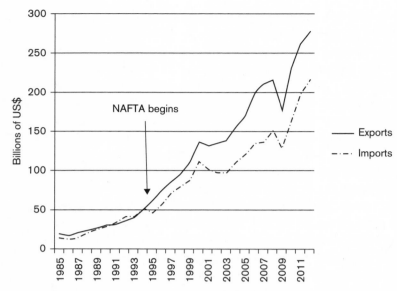

FIGURE 13.7. Mexico's trade with the United States increased after NAFTA took effect on January 1, 1994. Source: US Department of Commerce, Bureau of Census, Foreign Trade (www.census.gov/foreign-trade/balance/).

THE NEW TRADE THEORY

Back in chapter 7 we learned about the new (endogenous) growth model. Increasing returns to scale take center stage in that model. As economies grow, they not only invest in capital but also become more productive because of technological change, which in turn stimulates more growth. Basically, the faster an economy grows, the more productive it becomes. The cost of production falls as production rises. Double all inputs and output more than doubles, because the production function itself changes.

Paul Krugman argued that something similar happens when countries engage in trade.

Over the years, Germans have gotten very good at making BMWs, as well as a lot of other finely engineered machinery. The United States became dominant in computer technology, then the Internet, and now social networking. In fact, it seems like the more a country does of something, the better it gets at doing it and the more dominant it becomes in global markets. That sounds a lot like increasing returns to scale.

Thanks to trade, countries build up a comparative advantage that feeds on itself. They become globally dominant. There are few limits to how dominant a country can become in a particular production sector, as long as the world is its market.

Increasing returns to scale reshape comparative advantage. Once a country begins to grow a sector, like automobile production, the economy changes in ways that actually reduce production costs, making the country ever more competitive in international trade.

An often-cited example is the enormously successful automobile industry in Japan. After World War II, Japan experienced record economic growth, which included the birth of a globally dominant auto industry. What raw materials did it take to make automobiles? Oil and coal for energy, iron ore, and other metals. Japan had none of those—it had to import them. But it more than paid for these imports by exporting manufactured goods, and it built the most productive auto industry in the world.

Japan wasn't only about cars. When Ed was little, "Made in Japan" meant about the same thing that "Made in China" means today. Almost all of Ed's wind-up toys were made in Japan! Japan started out by using its abundant labor to export cheap manufactured goods. Then it began innovating. On his sixth birthday Ed got a monkey that clashed two cymbals together, like a musician in an orchestra, and you didn't even have to wind it up! Japan had created the first battery-powered toys. You can think of Ed's monkey as a crude robot. Pretty soon Japan was making much better robots, and robots were making cars. As Japan's exports became more diverse and expanded, its industries innovated and became more productive, and they became increasingly dominant in global trade. The population benefited: Japan's per capita income more than quadrupled between 1955 and 1973. The country's transformation through trade was dubbed "the Japanese economic miracle."

When most people think of the Japanese miracle, they think "export-led growth." In reality, though, the key to Japan's success was more complicated than simply following an export-promotion development strategy. It was a mixed model. Japan succeeded through close cooperation between government, on one hand, and manufacturers, suppliers, distributors, and banks, joined in closely knit groups called *keiretsu*. Japanese companies were given preferential access to foreign exchange and other government support to import needed foreign inputs and technologies, but they were required by law to produce 90% of their parts domestically within a short period of time. Meanwhile, protectionist measures limited consumers' access to foreign-produced goods like cars. Basically, Japanese consumers had to buy Japanese. That doesn't sound exactly like free trade. Japan's development strategy included *both* import-substitution industrialization *and* export promotion.

It worked, though. Households in Japan benefited as their incomes rose dramatically during the miracle years. As consumers, they suffered in the short run by not being able to purchase cheaper and higher quality goods from abroad, but in the long run they thrived. Of course, today Japan's consumers, like those in California and South Africa, can buy vehicles and other goods made in Japan that are among the most economical and high quality in the world. Japan illustrates how a combination of export promotion with strategic deviations from free trade ended up creating world-dominant industries and stimulated tremendous economic growth in the process.

The New Trade Theory offers an explanation for the findings from gravity models that large economies trade with each other. Increasing returns to scale (IRS), superimposed upon comparative advantage, enable countries to become increasingly globally dominant in particular production niches over time. Dominance in international trade makes countries rich. Rich consumers demand diversity, which they import from other dominant players—Ed has a Volvo, his wife has an Audi, and his neighbor has a Mitsubishi.

IRS also explains the failure of international trade to diminish income inequality over time. Global dominance means there's a lot of money to be made. Factors—labor, land, capital, human capital—create income. Increasing returns to scale plus free trade enable factors in a given country and sector to produce income at an increasing—and sometimes astonishing—rate. Samuelson's theoretical prediction that trade causes factor prices to converge across countries over time does not necessarily hold in a world where increasing returns to scale permit a country to increase its global dominance in product areas over time. The more productive you are, the more productive you become in the future. Comparative advantage is not a given. It changes over time, and carefully crafted trade policies may be able to help countries attain a comparative advantage in new product areas.

THE NEW TRADE THEORY AND DEVELOPMENT PRACTICE

We saw that, historically, countries that followed an export-promotion strategy grew faster than countries that followed an import-substitution strategy. New trade theory suggests that there might be a reason to revisit import substitution industrialization—or perhaps combine export promotion and import substitution in new and strategic ways. If a country can protect an infant industry by limiting import competition, if it can make sure the industry "grows up" to become internationally competitive, and if increasing returns to scale eventually take hold to make the growth self-perpetuating, there might be a case for including an element of import-substitution industrialization in a country's development strategy. Those are a lot of "ifs," but there is no question that the New Trade Theory adds a new dynamic dimension to the way we think about comparative advantage in international trade.

Cambridge University economist Ha-Joon Chang argues that rich countries, including Britain and the United States, historically used heavy government subsidies, import tariffs, and weak (or no) respect for others' intellectual property to help promote their economic development. By urging poor countries to embrace free trade, he claims, "rich countries are trying to kick away the ladder that allowed them to climb where they are."[7] The implications of this argument for poor countries are clear. In Chang's words, when it comes to trade and other development policies, "there can be no 'best practice' policies that everyone should use."

Today, most developing countries in the world appear to be convinced that international trade and trade policy are an important component of successful development strategies. This requires forming trade agreements that give member countries access to one another's markets. Making trade agreements and enforcing them once they are in effect is not easy, though. Where does a country begin? If it enters into a free-trade agreement, but then its trade partners employ unfair trade practices like giving export firms an unfair advantage through subsidies and other means, what redress does it have? Countries face high transaction costs when it comes to making international trade agreements and enforcing their provisions.

Enter the World Trade Organization, or WTO.

The WTO is a place where governments can get together to negotiate trade agreements and settle trade disputes, where member governments try to sort out the trade problems they face with each other. In effect, it tries to lower the transaction costs of making and enforcing international trade agreements. While its motto is "free trade," it does not impose trade agreements upon unwilling parties. Countries have to choose to be members of the WTO. This is how the WTO describes what it does: "The *rules* of the WTO system are agreements resulting from negotiations among member governments, the rules are *ratified* by

TABLE 13.4   MAJOR FREE-TRADE AGREEMENTS BY YEAR

Agreement	Year Established
Greater Arab Free Trade Area (GAFTA)	1957
European Economic Community (EEC)	1957
Asia-Pacific Trade Agreement (APTA)	1975
Gulf Cooperation Council (GCC)	1981
Southern Common Market (MERCOSUR)	1991
ASEAN Free Trade Area (AFTA)	1992
Southern African Development Community (SADC)	1992
Central American Integration System (SICA)	1993
Common Market for Eastern and Southern Africa (COMESA)	1994
G-3 Free Trade Agreement (G-3)	1995
North American Free Trade Agreement (NAFTA)	1994
South Asian Free Trade Area (SAFTA)	2004
Trans-Pacific Partnership (TPP)	2005 (proposed)
Central European Free Trade Agreement (CEFTA)	1992
Central American Free-Trade Agreement (CAFTA)	2004

members' parliaments, and *decisions* taken in the WTO are virtually all made by consensus among all members. In other words, decisions taken in the WTO are negotiated, accountable and democratic."[8]

Members can bring trade disputes before the WTO's Dispute Settlement Body (which consists of all country members); this body determines whether a country has broken a trade accord of which it is part. If so, it has to change what it does in order to conform to the accord.

Even with the WTO's help, attempts to craft global free-trade agreements have faltered. Instead, most of the success in recent decades has been in creating *regional* trading blocks, many of which include less-developed countries. The European Economic Community was a pioneer in this area; it combined European countries into a common market beginning in 1958. The North American Free Trade Agreement (NAFTA, 1995) was unusual in bringing together countries at very different levels of per capita income and development (Canada and the United States, on one side, and Mexico, on the other). It was extended southward into Central America and the Caribbean through the Central American Free-Trade Agreement (CAFTA, 2006). Table 13.4 lists major regional trade agreements around the world.

Regional trading blocks are somewhat of a mixed bag from the point of view of people advocating free trade. On one hand, they have proven good at stimulating trade between members of the blocks. On the other hand, they tend to divert trade away from the rest of the world, shifting it inside the block (that is, discouraging trade between the block and the rest of the world). In the long run, though, one might see regional trade blocks as a step along the way toward global free trade. It might well be easier for a few blocks to enter into a global trade agreement than for many diverse countries to do so. That, someday, could make the WTO's job easier.

The great challenge for poor countries and those assisting them is how to harness new trade opportunities while designing economic development programs and policies. As one group of international development agencies wrote in its joint report: "[Trade] has created many new opportunities, but also new questions regarding the roles, functions and core capacities of the various key players. Deep-rooted principles and paradigms have been cut down in a short period. It is sometimes like mixing an Italian basketball team with Nigerian soccer players, and trying to play in a volleyball tournament. The new situation raises many questions about how the game is played, and who are the winners and losers."[9]

TRADE IN CAPITAL, PEOPLE, AND BRAINS

Goods aren't the only things that flow between nations. Factors—capital, people, and brains (human capital)—do, too. Capital, people, and brains are pretty different from goods and services. Yet many of the lessons we learned from models of trade in goods and services are relevant here, as well. For example, there are deadweight losses associated with restrictions on trade in factors, much like what we see with restrictions on trade in goods and services.

Trade in Capital

Foreign direct investment is a capital flow. Instead of producing a capital-intensive good in a capital-rich country, someone can invest in a factory to produce the good in a capital-poor (but labor-rich) country. In fact, there is a basic economic incentive to do that, because where capital is scarce, the economic returns to capital (rents) often are high, just as where labor is scarce, wages are high.

Global capital markets make it possible for poor countries to invest more in new capital than would be possible from domestic savings alone.

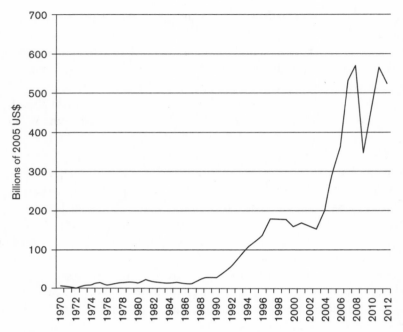

FIGURE 13.8. Foreign direct investment inflows to low- and middle-income countries have increased sharply in the new millennium. Source: World Bank (http://data.worldbank.org/indicator/BX.KLT.DINV.CD.WD).

Each year, vast amounts of capital flow from rich to poor countries in the form of foreign direct investment (FDI), often bringing new technologies along with it (see figure 13.8). Jobs shift from high- to low-wage countries, a process called "offshoring" or "outsourcing." Offshoring can include highly skilled work, like computer programming, as well as low-skilled work, like garment and other "sweatshop" production.

Enormous advances in shipping and communications allow large firms to fragment their operations, moving more unskilled, labor-intensive stages of production to countries where unskilled wages are low. Sweatshops employ millions of workers in poor countries to produce goods that are immediately exported to rich countries. The wages these workers earn are low by the standards of high-income countries, yet they are clearly high enough to lure workers to the factory floor.

Labor standards, including worker safety, as well as their enforcement, also tend to be more lax in poor countries. Ensuring safe and comfortable working conditions costs money; not doing so can enhance an industry's international advantage when it comes to producing labor-intensive goods. The results can be tragic. In 2012, a fire and collapse of clothing factories killed more than 1,100 workers in Bangladesh. Growing consumer awareness in rich countries puts pressure on global companies to certify that the factories to which they outsource follow acceptable labor standards.

How can they be sure? You'll recognize an asymmetric information problem here, similar to what we learned about in chapter 11. The Fair Labor Association, a nonprofit consortium of universities, civil service organizations, and private companies, certifies that its member companies and their suppliers comply with national and international labor laws.[10] Its monitoring includes independent and unannounced audits of factories abroad. Its efforts are not without controversy, but without independent monitoring and certification, the information needed to create a "market for fair labor practices" would not exist.

Trade in Labor

In addition to capital flowing across the globe to where the workers are, workers can move to where the capital is. Trade in labor across international borders is called "labor migration," and the payment countries receive for "exporting workers" is called "migrant remittances."

There is no question that international migration is increasing, and so are remittances—to the point of being a major source of both income and foreign exchange for many countries. In some countries, migrant remittances exceed the value of all merchandise exports combined. In those countries, it can be said that people are the major export, in terms of the income they provide.

In 2013, the United Nations estimates that more than 231.5 million people in the world were immigrants, that is, people living outside their country of birth.[11] That was 51% more than in 1990. The world's total population grew by 33% over that same period (from 5.3 to 7 billion). In other words, international migration is growing faster than world population. If one could take all of these people and bring them together into a single country, that nation of immigrants would be the sixth largest on earth, with a population about the size of Indonesia's.

Migrant remittances are rising more rapidly than the number of migrants (figure 13.9). Globally, the World Bank's data show that

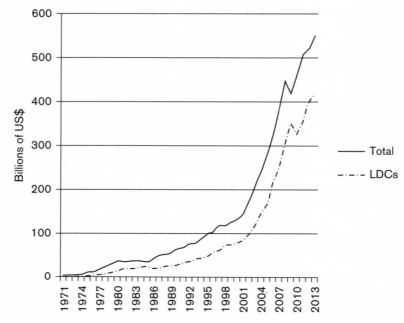

FIGURE 13.9. Total world remittance receipts have increased sharply since 1970. Source: World Bank (http://go.worldbank.org/092X1CHHD0).

remittances to less-developed countries surpassed $400 billion in 2013. That's a whopping thirteen times higher than the estimate for 1990. To put remittances into perspective, we could compare them to international aid as a source of support for less-developed countries. If we added up all of the development assistance provided by all of the countries in the world, migrant remittances would be 3¼ times greater.

Remittances have captured the imagination of international development agencies, including the United Nations and the World Bank, for several reasons. First, they are big. Second, unlike aid, they happen without using rich countries' taxpayer money. Third, much of this money flows to relatively low-income households, including households in poor rural areas. In short, migrant remittances could be an important resource to help countries develop.

They also have costs, though. In order to get remittances, a country has to sacrifice workers. In the process, it may lose skills and other human capital, like enterprising spirit, to other countries. Poor countries bear the cost of educating children who grow up and migrate abroad, taking their human capital with them. The human capital, then, is put to work creating value-added for the foreign country. The loss of human capital to migration is called the "brain drain."

The remittances migrants send home might compensate for the loss of human capital, but this won't necessarily be the case. It depends, in part, on how much value the migrant would contribute to the economy by not migrating abroad. Here you'll immediately notice that we have a selection problem, like the ones we studied in chapter 2. Once an individual migrates, we can see the remittances she sends home, but we cannot see how much income she would have created by not migrating. Conversely, we see income produced at home only for the people who do not migrate. This selection problem arises regardless of whether it is countries, households, or individuals we are looking at. With countries, since people tend to emigrate from (and send remittances to) poor countries, it might look like remittances increase poverty, even if poor countries would be poorer without them.

Suppose we wish to evaluate the impacts of migration and remittances on a poor migrant-sending economy. Think of the households with migrants as a treatment group—they get the "migration treatment" by sending family members abroad and receiving remittances. The households without migrants, then, are the control group. If migration were a random process, we could simply compare outcomes like poverty or crop productivity between these two groups.

But migration is not random, you might say. It is selective, and as we saw in the case of internal migration (chapter 10), it may select people with high levels of human capital. The kinds of people who migrate are different from the kinds of people who don't.

You'd be absolutely right—unless, maybe, you are in Tonga (see sidebar 13.1).

Tonga might not be representative of other migrant-sending countries, but to our knowledge, there is no other case in the world in which international migration can be treated as being random (or more accurately, nearly random, because people chose whether or not to apply for the Tonga migration lottery to begin with). That leaves us with two other alternatives to evaluate migration's impacts on development outcomes: natural experiments and econometrics. We can also use simulation methods to explore how migration impacts local economies.

In chapter 2 we met Dean Yang, a development economist at the University of Michigan who spotted a natural experiment opportunity to study the impacts of migration on poverty and investment in the Philippines (sidebar 2.5). He found strong evidence that migration and

Sidebar 13.1 A Migration Lottery

What would be the ideal experiment to test the impacts of international migration on migrant-sending households? Randomly plucking migrants out of some households but not others, sending those migrants abroad, then after some time elapses going back and comparing development outcomes in the households with and without migrants? Sounds unrealistic, doesn't it?

Not in the case of migration from the Tonga Islands, a poor country, to New Zealand, a rich country. Each year, New Zealand runs a lottery allowing up to 250 Tongan Islanders the chance to immigrate as permanent residents. Three economists spotted a research opportunity here. Think of a treatment group consisting of households with a member lucky enough to win the lottery and emigrate to New Zealand. Those households get the "migration treatment" of losing a member to New Zealand but gaining remittance income. The control group is households with members who were in the lottery but not chosen. The only thing separating these two groups is the "luck of the draw," making this migration treatment almost as good as random.

The researchers found that the households whose members won the lottery ended up *worse off* than those that lost. The remittances their migrants sent home did not make up for the migrants' lost earnings in the Tonga Islands; thus, per capita incomes in their households fell—even though household size (the denominator in per capita income) was smaller without the migrants. The study also found evidence of less food intake among the family members left behind.

David McKenzie, Steven Stillman, and John Gibson, "How Important Is Selection? Experimental vs Non-Experimental Measures of the Income Gains from Migration," *Journal of the European Economic Association* 8, no. 4 (2010):913-45.

remittances have favorable development impacts in Philippine households, increasing investments and children's schooling.

Two economists from the University of California, San Diego, used an econometric approach to study the impacts of Mexico-to-US migration on business investments in Mexico.[12] They had to come up with a convincing instrument to deal with a selection problem resulting from the fact that entrepreneurial people might be more likely to migrate as well as to have businesses in Mexico. That is, they needed a variable correlated with migration but not with business investments, except through migration. History gave them one (see sidebar 13.2).

Sidebar 13.2 Migrants on Rails

Before Mexico had a road system, railroads were the main way to get migrants from Mexico to the United States. The authors of one study found that the location of railroads in the early 1900s is closely associated with migration today. They used states' distance to the nearest stop on a north-south railroad line in the early 1900s as their instrument for migration. This strategy allowed them to estimate the impacts of migration on microenterprise investments while dealing with the selection problem. The authors found evidence that migration increases investments and capital-output ratios in Mexico's microenterprises. They also found higher levels of profits and sales by microenterprises in states with strong migration networks with the United States. These findings suggest that Mexico-US migration may be an important source of knowledge and funds for microenterprise investments in Mexico.

C. Woodruff and R. Zenteno, "Migration Networks and Microenterprises in Mexico," *Journal of Development Economics* 82, no. 2 (2007):509–28.

The pessimistic findings from Tonga (sidebar 13.1) seem to contrast with those from Mexico (sidebar 13.2). An explanation for this might lie in the differences between the two countries' economies. The Mexican economy is far larger and more diverse than that of Tonga. In fact, migrant remittances were equivalent to 12.6% of Tonga's GDP in 2012, compared with 2% of Mexico's.[13] A large, complex economy might have more possibilities to substitute for emigrants' labor. Remittances flowing into such an economy might be better able to stimulate income growth by loosening liquidity constraints on production activities and raising the local demand for goods and services produced within the country. Not surprisingly, Tonga relies heavily on imports to meet local demands; its imports are equivalent to 63% of GDP, while Mexico's are equivalent to only 34%.[14]

Trade in Brains (Human Capital)

When a person migrates, she takes her human capital with her. The "brain drain" is poor countries' biggest worry when it comes to international migration. Home countries invest in educating their youth, but when educated people emigrate, they take this schooling with them. The destination-country economy benefits when highly skilled and motivated immigrants arrive on their shores. The history of the United States—a nation of immigrants—clearly attests to this.

Data on poor countries' loss of highly skilled workers to emigration highlight the brain drain problem. For example, here are some striking examples from news reports:

- Ghana's official statistics institute reported that between 1999 and 2004, 448 doctors, or 54% of those trained in the period, left to work abroad.[15]
- Over 80% of Jamaicans with higher education live abroad.[16]
- Ethiopia, according to one study, lost 75% of its skilled professionals over ten years.[17]

Of course, many of these skilled emigrants send home remittances, which may exceed the income they would earn by staying home. In fact, some countries actively train people to emigrate in the expectation that the remittances they send home will exceed the cost of training them. The Philippines is an example of this. At the end of 2012, over 10 million Filipinos were living overseas.[18] Nevertheless, human capital that emigrates cannot be put to work for development at home.

Not all economists agree that the brain drain is a serious problem for poor countries as a whole, though. The concept of the brain drain has a major limitation: it is static. If a country has a fixed amount of human capital in it, and emigration takes it away, logically there is less human capital than before in the migrant-sending country.

The dynamics of real life can turn this static picture on its head. Human capital is the result of investments people make. Economist Oded Stark and coauthors posited that skilled emigration actually may increase the amount of human capital in migrant-sending countries.[19] People in poor countries can see the benefits of education followed by migration. This creates an incentive for them to invest in their own and their children's schooling. Schooling investments increase human capital. If not all of the increase in human capital emigrates, there is a possibility that a static brain drain creates a dynamic brain gain.

Something similar, it seems, happens with baseball (see sidebar 13.3).

In theory, whether emigration results in a brain drain or a brain gain depends on two key questions. First, does the possibility of migrating to work abroad create incentives for people to invest in schooling? Second,

Sidebar 13.3   Bat Drain or Bat Gain?

The Dominican Republic is the biggest exporter of major league base-ball players in the world. The baseball commissioner's office reports that 28.1% of all US major league baseball players in 2013 were born outside the United States. Of those, 37% were *dominicanos*.

While Ed was in the Dominican Republic doing research a few years back, he hired a taxi to drive him around the island. Every time they passed through a town the driver proudly listed off the names of people from the town who had become major league baseball players in the United States. It sounded a lot like a bat drain.

"All those baseball players leaving your country—isn't that really bad for baseball here?" Ed asked.

"No, it's the best thing that could happen," the driver responded.

"But you're losing a lot of players," Ed protested.

"You don't understand," said the driver. "Every kid in my country dreams of playing big league baseball. Many become great, but only a few get to play in the United States. The rest play here. We've got the best baseball in Latin America."

But what would happen if the Dominican Republic actually played a baseball game against the United States? That happened in 2013 at the World Baseball Classic—baseball's equivalent of soccer's World Cup—held in San Francisco, California. The US team had a major league all-star in every position. The Dominican Republic won, 3 to 1. It went on to become the first team ever to win the Classic without losing a single game.

It seems that the taxi driver's "bat gain" hypothesis had won the day.

"2013 Major League Baseball Racial and Gender Report Card," *Sports Business News*, May 15, 2013 (www.sportsbusinessnews.com /content/2013-major-league-baseball-racial-and-gender-report-card).

do enough of the people who get schooling in the hopes of someday emigrating end up staying at home?

The answer to the first question seems to be "yes" for children in India who want to grow up to be computer engineers in California's Silicon Valley, but probably "no" for kids in rural Mexico expecting someday to take low-skilled jobs as unauthorized immigrant farm-workers in California's Central Valley.

The answer to the second question depends on a number of things, including immigration policies in migrant-destination countries, migration costs, and probably most importantly, what kind of future educated people see for themselves in their home countries.

At the very least, it is safe to say that the question of whether the emigration of educated people leaves poor countries less educated than before does not have a clear answer. In the best of cases, as economists Oded Stark and Yong Wang argue, the hope of someday emigrating could be a catalyst for poor people to invest in schooling. In this way, it could help solve the problem we learned about in chapter 6 that left to their own devices, people tend to underinvest in education.[20] Then there is the possibility that people who emigrate eventually return home, bringing new skills with them.

Empirical economists have put the brain gain hypothesis to the test by comparing educational attainment in countries with and without high levels of emigration. One study found that average education levels were higher in countries from which large numbers of educated people emigrated.[21] That seems to suggest a brain gain. But looking at it from a different angle, you also could say that more educated people leave countries with high average schooling levels. That sounds more like a brain drain. There is a classic reflection problem here. Average schooling and emigration of educated people seem to move up or down together, and it is not clear which causes which. There is no way to run an experiment that plucks educated people randomly out of some countries but not others and then compares schooling investments. Using instrumental variables, this study found evidence that high-skilled emigration does promote schooling investment back home.

This does not mean that countries shouldn't worry about the brain drain. Perhaps a more nuanced and proactive view is in order: that countries need to invest in education and reap the benefits of remittances from highly skilled emigrants, while at the same time creating incentives for skilled workers to stay home—and for emigrants to return once they've gotten new skills abroad. After all, most people seem to be home—97% of the people in the world live in the country in which they were born.

Interconnections among Trade and Migration

If you're thinking that trade in goods and services, capital, and people are not unrelated, you are right. In the new global economy they are interconnected in ways that can have far-reaching ramifications for economic development.

Mexico's President Salinas, while negotiating the North American Free Trade Agreement (NAFTA) in the early 1990s, came up with a now-famous quote: "We want NAFTA because we want to export goods, not people."[22] Salinas, a Harvard-trained economist, knew about trade models. His quote comes straight out of the Factor Price Equalization Theorem. Salinas knew that without trade, Mexico, a labor-abundant country, would continue having low wages, but with free trade, the price of the abundant factor eventually will rise. That means NAFTA will increase wages in Mexico. Econometric models show that people migrate from low- to high-wage economies. In short, rather than migrating to pick tomatoes in California, Mexican workers can pick tomatoes in Mexico, and then Mexico can export the tomatoes to the United States. Their children can go to school and get jobs in factories that are financed by foreign capital and export automobiles to showrooms in the United States. Without trade, this would not be possible, and migration pressures would be higher.

United Nations secretary-general Kofi Annan sees linkages among migration, capital flows, and trade that go beyond any trade model we've considered in this chapter:

> Today's international migrants are, more than ever before, a dynamic human link between cultures, economies and societies . . . just a few seconds are needed for the global financial system to transmit their earnings to remote corners of the developing world, where they buy food, clothing, shelter, pay for education or health care, and can relieve debt . . . The skills and knowhow they accumulate are also instrumental in transferring technology and institutional knowledge. They inspire new ways of thinking, both socially and politically. India's software industry has emerged, in large part, from the intensive networking among expatriates, returning migrants and Indian entrepreneurs at home and abroad. After working in Greece, Albanians bring home new agricultural skills that enable them to increase production . . . It should be no surprise that countries once associated exclusively with emigration, including Ireland, the Republic of Korea, Spain and many others, now boast thriving economies, which themselves attract large numbers of migrants.[23]

"FREE TRADE" AND INTERNATIONAL AID

As we described in the introduction to this chapter, international trade can be very contentious. While planet Earth would almost certainly be richer if it were integrated through international trade into a single giant market, the distribution of these gains would just as certainly be uneven. In the short run, some people would win big; others would lose. Perhaps the most common "national interest" concern about international trade is that it pushes down the price of some goods and factors of production. Even though consumers may be better off, for those producing and selling these goods or earning a living from these factors of production (e.g., their own labor), lower prices hurt. Lower prices are simultaneously a boon to consumers and a bane to producers. What do you think might happen, then, if trade pushed prices for some goods all the way to zero in some places? In addition to who is helped and who is hurt, how do you think free goods and services would impact an economy?

These might seem like purely rhetorical questions since competitive markets normally do not push prices lower than marginal cost (firms that incur costs to produce something must charge a price that at least covers their cost of producing the good). International aid, however, makes these questions very real—particularly from the perspective of recipient countries. International aid effectively pushes the price of some goods at specific times and places to zero. To the ultimate recipients, aid can look like free trade of a literal sort: rich countries sending free stuff to poor countries. Throughout this book we have touched on aid and on the ongoing debate about whether it works or not. We conclude this chapter by looking at international aid through the lens of international trade.

While private investment in and trade with developing countries now far outstrip international aid to these countries, aid continues to play an important role—for better or for worse—in many countries. International aid can take many forms. It can be "official development assistance" (ODA)[24] that is provided from one government directly to another (bilateral) or from a coalition of governments to a particular government through an international organization (multilateral). Some of this ODA aims explicitly to induce greater private investment and trade by providing subsidized loans and insurance for businesses to engage with firms and markets in developing countries. For example, the US government's development finance arm, the Overseas Private Investment Corporation (OPIC), has mobilized over $200 billion in private capital to "help U.S. businesses gain footholds in emerging markets, catalyzing revenues, job and growth opportunities both at home and abroad."[25]

Aid can also come from private foundations or nongovernmental organizations (NGOs). While such "private" aid has been around a long time, the Bill and Melinda Gates Foundation has recently put this form of aid on par with many ODA donors. Whatever its form, aid is typically earmarked for a particular use, such as specific projects or interventions (e.g., building schools and roads, supporting health programs), technical assistance, training and capacity building (e.g., agricultural research, medical training), subsidized loans (e.g., for building dams or power plants), or emergency and humanitarian response (e.g., relief from famine, natural disaster, or conflict). A goal, explicit or implicit, of many current public and private aid projects is to enable poor people and nations to engage with local and global markets more effectively. The International Fund for Agricultural Development (IFAD) calls for "a new approach . . . that is both market-oriented and sustainable." Its president writes: "It is time to look at poor smallholder farmers and rural entrepreneurs in a completely new way—not as charity cases but as people whose innovation, dynamism and hard work will bring prosperity to their communities and greater food security to the world in the decades ahead."[26]

Not surprisingly, international aid is not as free as it may appear. Obviously, the goods and services transferred from a rich country to a poor one cost something, and someone must ultimately pay this bill. Those paying these bills may be concerned purely with the well-being of the poor and the future prosperity of poor countries, but they are also likely to have ulterior motives related to political or military support or their own economic interests. Such motives are apparent not only in bilateral aid but also in the pressure rich countries often exert on the multilateral organizations to which they contribute. While the goods and services transferred as aid are clearly not free from the perspective of the donor, they are typically not free from the perspective of the recipient, either, because they often come with strings attached. In addition to the political support that the recipient must provide to keep bilateral ODA flowing from the US, for example, US funds earmarked for constructing a new road may stipulate that the work be done by an American construction company. Since 2000, China has become a major player in Africa using a distinct and rather opaque version of this model of international aid (see sidebar 13.4). Overall, then, we can understand the flows of ODA from rich to poor countries around the world as simply a manifestation of familiar concepts of comparative advantage—albeit broadened to include political and strategic elements.

Food Aid

From the perspective of both donor and recipient governments, international aid is not as free as it may appear, but at some point in the deliv-

Sidebar 13.4 "The Dragon's Gift," "The New Scramble for Africa," and "Aid 2.0"

For a development economist, conversations with taxi drivers do not normally qualify as "data collection," but they can be insightful and interesting (e.g., see sidebar 13.3). For several years now, one of Travis's favorite topics to raise with taxi drivers in Africa is the role China plays in their country. This is a natural taxi topic because China has been investing heavily in African infrastructure: roads, bridges, and especially oil pipelines.

Reactions from taxi drivers to this Chinese aid generally fall into two quite different categories. Many complain about Chinese reliance on Chinese companies and workers, the quality of the work, and a perceived disregard for environmental impacts of the work (especially in mining). Others praise the Chinese for focusing primarily on what Africa needs most: infrastructure. A similar range of opinions appear almost daily in African newspapers and have spurred a flurry of books and international media coverage on the topic.

Many claim that China's generosity to African countries is driven by its appetite for natural resources: oil from Sudan and Angola and copper from Zambia and the Democratic Republic of Congo, for example. Others see this as a strategic "soft power" "charm offensive" with a broader geopolitical agenda and, as evidence, cite China's widespread investment in Chinese culture and language centers and in sports stadiums throughout the continent. China does not condition its aid on human rights performance or governance outcomes, and it seems to pay less attention to labor and environmental standards than traditional donor countries do, which is often cited as a potential threat to conventional ODA. As *Foreign Policy* editor-in-chief Moisés Naím wrote in 2007, China is "effectively pricing responsible and well-meaning aid organizations out of the market in the very places where they are needed the most. If they continue to succeed in pushing their alternative development model, they will succeed in underwriting a world that is more corrupt, chaotic, and authoritarian" (www .foreignpolicy.com/articles/2007/02/14/rogue_aid).

Investigating any of these claims has been difficult, because Chinese aid flows are opaque, even secretive (which naturally raises popular suspicions). Recently, a team of economists from William and Mary College compiled a database of Chinese aid to Africa using media reports. This new database provides some interesting insights.

China committed roughly $75 billion to Africa between 2000 and 2011. (US aid to Africa was $90 billion during this same period.) Of this Chinese aid, $20 billion went to two countries that didn't appear in the top-ten list of recipients of US aid: Ghana and Nigeria. The vast majority of these aid commitments indeed target oil pipelines, mining, energy, and roads. Chinese aid also looks different from aid from traditional donors because the heavy involvement of state-owned enterprises makes it difficult to distinguish between official assistance and private investment flows, and often it raises additional suspicions during the bidding process for new construction and mining projects.

Other emerging powers, including India and Brazil, are ramping up their international aid programs. In 2011, the *Economist* magazine described this shift as "Aid 2.0" and called it encouraging: "Like trade, aid benefits from specialization and comparative advantage. Emerging countries, with recent experience to draw from, might do a better job of infrastructure spending" (www.economist.com/node /21525899).

Deborah Brautigam, *The Dragon's Gift: The Real Story of China in Africa* (Oxford: Oxford University Press, 2009).

Padraig Carmody, *The New Scramble for Africa* (Cambridge: Polity Press, 2011).

Andy Sumner and Richard Mallett, *The Future of Foreign Aid: Development Cooperation and the New Geography of Global Poverty* (Basingstoke, UK: Palgrave Macmillan, 2012).

ery process these transfers effectively become free stuff. And at this point, the questions we asked at the beginning of this section become quite important. To answer these questions, consider first what is arguably the highest profile and most tangible form of ODA: food aid.

The largest food aid donor in the world is the US, which launched its food aid program in 1954. Over its sixty-year history, it is estimated that US food aid has benefited over 3 million people around the world.[27] While the political and strategic goals of US food aid—both domestic and international—have changed over the years, the basic model has remained essentially the same: the US government buys food commodities from US farmers and pays to ship the food to countries in crisis or with chronic food shortages. Chris Barrett, a development economist at Cornell University, is a leading expert on US food aid—and a vocal critic of this model.[28] Among its flaws, two stand out as especially disturbing. First, it is extremely inefficient, with more than half of each food aid dollar going to transportation and overhead. Second, flooding local markets with free food can hurt local producers and discourage investments in productivity.

Notice that this second flaw of US food aid is a manifestation of essentially the same concerns that international trade triggers when it lowers the price received by producers in a given country—albeit a more extreme version in which local producers compete against imported goods that are not just cheap but free.[29] To illustrate this point, imagine how Starbucks would have felt about the "Battle in Seattle" if the WTO negotiations included distributing free coffee outside all its coffee shops. It might well have joined the demonstration!

Of course, Sudan is not Seattle. During times of emergency response—in the wake of an earthquake, hurricane, or tsunami that destroys or disrupts local food supply chains—there may be few local food alternatives, and food delivery could be well justified. But much of US food aid is delivered into markets where local farmers and traders have food to sell. The arrival of US food in such a market not only reduces local food purchases but also can directly suppress local food prices because much of this food is "monetized" (sold) by governments to raise money they can allocate to local needs as they see fit. Local farmers and local food supply chains risk being severely undercut precisely during years when market prices would normally be high, and this can discourage investments in productivity, storage, and transportation technologies. Development practitioners know that administering emergency food relief is not as hard as figuring out what to do afterward.

After decades of pressure from economists like Chris Barrett, NGOs, and even other governments to change this system—to untie food aid from food—there are finally signs of hope. The 2008 US Farm Bill authorized pilot programs to purchase food aid on local and regional markets, something most other countries started doing a long time ago. The 2014 farm bill allows USAID to spend just over 5% of its food aid budget on these local food purchases, much less than the 40% the Obama administration wanted but seemingly a move in the right direction.

Other Kinds of Aid and "Free" Trade

What about international aid that delivers free or heavily subsidized malaria or tuberculosis treatments to poor countries? Or what about Doctors without Borders offering free medical services in such countries? Even though such transfers are akin to free food flooding a local market, there is an obvious and important difference: many of these countries lack the capacity to procure, much less produce, such pharmaceutical products or lack qualified medical technicians to provide these services. Although the local market effects of "free" trade of this sort are therefore negligible—especially compared to the urgency of pressing health threats—such transfers can impose a longer term dynamic opportunity cost that is not unlike some of the concerns that make international trade contentious. In short, chronic dependence on free medical supplies and services imported from abroad may in the long run discourage the creation of local medical capacity and competency.

To appreciate this dynamic opportunity cost, consider what might have happened to that shirt you recently gave to Goodwill, the Salvation Army, or other charity. If you are anything like us, you may have felt a bit of "warm glow" after donating a box of old clothes or shoes to charity and imagining that someone needy will benefit from your generosity. Many of these clothing donations end up in giant bails that are shipped to Africa and eventually make their way to fascinating and chaotic "second-hand" clothing markets. While a flood of cheap used clothes can drive down prices in local markets (good for consumers), this would seem to pose no real threat to local producers because without much of an apparel industry most African countries would seem to have no or few producers to be hurt. But this ignores the dynamic opportunity cost that cheap clothes impose on these economies, namely, that a thriving textile and apparel industry may never emerge because the steady flow of cheap, donated used clothes keeps prices low and thereby discourages entrepreneurs from being the first to start such a factory.[30]

www.rebeltext.org/development/qr13.html
Learn more about international trade and globalization by exploring multimedia resources while you read.

14

Choose Your Own Epilogue

In chapter 1 we wrote that the goal of this book is to cover "the fundamental things that distinguish rich and poor countries and the methods we use to analyze critical development economic issues." Identifying the essentials is not an easy thing; one of the biggest challenges in writing *Essentials of Development Economics* was deciding what to put in the book and what to leave out. At every step of the way, we had to ask ourselves what the *essentials* of development economics are, as opposed to topics—however important—whose study requires fluency with the essentials. Along the way, we have touched on many different topics—in fact, nearly all of the topics in a conventional textbook can be found somewhere on these pages. Mostly we have emphasized microeconomic development, because we believe that's the logical place to start; it is where most of the cutting-edge work in development economics today is happening, and it reflects our own areas of expertise.

In addition to distilling the essentials of development economics, we've aimed to highlight in this book what development economists actually do and how they do it. Now obviously, everyone cannot grow up to be a development economist. Although we can't understand why everyone wouldn't *aspire* to become one, even Ed and Peri's kids do not harbor this aspiration (sigh; on the other hand, there may still be hope for Travis and Heather's). We are convinced, however, that no matter what kind of future you envision for yourself, appreciating the essentials of development economics can enrich your career as well as your life more broadly. In true economist form, this conviction has an empirical basis. Combined, we have taught these essentials to thousands of students over many, many years. On the basis of interactions with friends, colleagues, and students (many of whom keep in touch for years after taking the final exam), we are convinced that some of the essentials we have covered can have a significant effect on your view of the world and perhaps even shape your career choices.

The conviction that there is truly something for everyone in the study of development economics has shaped our parting words in this epilogue. Some of you may have read (or at least heard of people reading in the 1980s and 1990s) *Choose Your Own Adventure* books. We've opted for a similar structure here and have written three separate epilogues—one for budding development economists, a second for aspiring "internationalists," and a third that showcases deep truths that are relevant for everybody. And don't worry: you can read all three epilogues without spoiling the ending.

EPILOGUE FOR BUDDING DEVELOPMENT ECONOMISTS

Development economists have always been more likely to do fieldwork than other kinds of economists (many of whom experience spectacular professional success without leaving their offices). Many students end up in graduate programs in development economics precisely because they want to experience—and perhaps change—the wider world. This is perhaps truer now than it ever has been because of the push for rigorous empirical methods in development economics.

As we've described along the way, one of the biggest recent developments in development economics is that researchers are collaborating closely with practitioners from a wide range of fields. This creates some fascinating and sometimes challenging fieldwork opportunities. Over the past three years Ed has found himself designing and analyzing the evaluation component of social cash transfer programs set up by UNICEF specialists in child protection and health, in conjunction with African social welfare ministries, and he has advised the president of Mexico on rural development options. Travis has collaborated closely to design and evaluate the impact of agricultural projects in Haiti, Kenya, and India and of nutrition interventions in Ghana, Burkina Faso, and Malawi. Partners in these projects range from small NGOs to large multilateral development organizations and from private companies to large foundations and government ministries. In many of these projects, it is hard to draw a line between research and practice because the two are so closely intertwined.

In the best of circumstances, the evaluations development economists carry out as part of these projects involve a randomized treatment to deal with the selection problem. However, the analytical tools economists use run the gamut presented in chapter 2, from straightforward randomized controlled trials to econometric models to impact simulations. They include ways to measure economic outcomes like income, poverty, inequality, and human development (chapters 3–7). They have to grapple with challenging institutional environments (chapter 8). The diversity of the development economist's tool kit reflects the programs, contexts, and outcomes of development projects, which are becoming more varied over time.

Development practitioners usually want to know not only whether a program has an impact, but why. Understanding why is crucial in order to design and carry out effective development interventions. This requires having a firm grounding in theories of how economic actors behave, how markets work (and don't work), and how to design interventions that address the challenges of working in places where the basic assumptions of the economic theories we're accustomed to break down. Chapters 8–13 provide some of the theoretical foundations needed to make impact evaluations make sense. In recent years, many research economists—worried that simple experiments are displacing economic theory—have pushed for greater theoretical rigor. As RCTs did over the past decade, this push is now shaping development economics. Economics is defined by a set of disciplinary tools, and development economists must know how to use multiple tools in order to make contributions as economists.

Finally, measuring and having impact are two entirely different things in development economics. Having an impact requires asking the right questions, doing a convincing analysis, and conveying findings to people for whom they can make a difference. "Conveying findings" means getting people's ears (and eyes) *and* crafting presentations so that the findings resonate with those we wish to reach—many or most of whom probably are not economists. Our theories, models, and empirical findings together give us a compelling story to tell. Effectively packaged in narratives and PowerPoint images, they can empower development economists to have an impact on development practice and policies. Sadly, we often do not make the effort required to have an impact beyond the journals in which we publish. The institutional environment (chapter 8) in which we work all too often does not reward it.

Few students ever take a course on how to make economic findings come to life in a PowerPoint presentation or a policy briefing flyer. In the end, though, we know who our main clients are—they are the poor—and having an impact on them is the reason we do development economics.

EPILOGUE FOR ASPIRING "INTERNATIONALISTS"

If you envision yourself in an international career more broadly, the insights and essentials of development economics may help you appreciate the complexity of the world in new and useful ways. As you develop and deepen your expertise along your chosen path, we believe these insights will also enable you to engage with projects and people more effectively.

In several chapters, we encountered important intersections between development economics and other disciplines. These interdisciplinary boundaries are often the most important and rewarding places for researchers to explore and decision makers to understand. Regardless of your plans for an international career, you are likely to share a broad frontier with economics that is worth appreciating, and you're almost certain to encounter development economists with whom you'll have to communicate along the way. Here are a few examples—there are many more—that illustrate how development economics interfaces with other fields of study.

Climate Change, Natural Resources, and Environmental Sustainability

Are you a globally focused environmentalist, ecologist, or climatologist? Environmental economics is all about market failures of the sorts covered in this book. Households and firms extract natural resources and pollute the environment without considering the costs this creates for society. Poor farmers take down forests to plant crops without considering the impact on climate change and biodiversity. They decide which seeds to plant without thinking about the importance of conserving crop genetic resources for future agricultural research. Environmental externalities create a classic justification for public action to internalize the externality—that is, make individual actors take into account the social impacts of their actions.

Climate change takes environmental externalities to a whole new, global, level. Ultimately, though, it all boils down to the decisions of firms and households. Firms "use up" clean air and water when they pollute. Households extract and consume firewood and other natural resources, much as they produce and consume crops, but without considering the impacts on carbon loads in the atmosphere, erosion, or other adverse social consequences of their actions.

Resource extraction and other activities are connected with each other in complex ways. A rich and rapidly growing literature in economics, environmental studies, and development journals examines resource extraction and environmental impacts from the perspective of agricultural households in imperfect-market environments, and development economists are commonly brought in to help evaluate environmental programs in poor countries. Much of this work involves development economists teaming up with environmental scientists. The skills and concepts in this book are a prerequisite for studying development-environment interactions.

Nutrition and Public Health

Is international health or nutrition your thing? Collaborations among nutritionists, agronomists, and development economists have become commonplace as foundations and development agencies spearhead large-scale interventions to enable farmers to grow more nutritious crops and to make nutritional supplements available to poor and malnourished children. Nutritionists have come up with ways to provide a developing child with all the essential nutrients she needs in small, low-cost packets.[1] Yet, to provide a sustainable solution, there needs to be an effective demand for these food supplements and crops among poor households. Is there? Methods in this book are instrumental in providing answers to questions like this, as well offering insights into how nutritional programs raise productivity, educational attainment, and other outcomes needed to enable people to escape from poverty over time.

Migration

Ed has done more work on migration and development than perhaps any other topic. He was the lone economist on a team of demographers and sociologists that wrote the 1999 book *Worlds in Motion*—the most cited thing he ever did.[2] It should come as no surprise, then, that Ed drafted a chapter on migration. We decided not to put it in this book, because it is more of a topic than an essential of development economics. Without a doubt, migration and development is one of the most important topics in development economics. It is poised to become even more important in the future as people continue moving off the farm and across borders. To understand it, we need the essential skill and idea sets in this book as well as insights from population studies. We need trade, because migration and remittances involve trade in labor, as we learned in chapter 13. We need agricultural household modeling, because migrants come from households, and households are where the immediate impacts of migration and remittances are evident. We also need to understand markets, because the impacts of migration and remittances are different in an environment with missing markets for goods, factors, insurance, and credit, and migration decisions are partly a response to market failures. And we need the tools of impact evaluation to understand migration's impacts and how to harness them for development.

Population and Fertility

Are you a population scientist? We also drafted a chapter on population and economic development but in the end decided that it was more of a topic than an essential. Population growth is the outcome of fertility, mortality, and migration. These are the basic components of the field of demography, and all three involve decisions by households—to have children, to invest in health, and to emigrate or not. Parents make fertility decisions without taking into account the implications for society at large; in other words, fertility generates externalities. This is the rationale for government actions to curb fertility in poor countries, the most extreme of which was China's famous one-child-per-couple policy. We saw in chapter 6 that health and life expectancy are affected in complex ways by household and public investments, and they involve externalities, public goods, and scale economies that commonly lead to a divergence of the private from the public good.

Psychology

Psychology—say what? Actually, some of the most interesting and important advances in thinking about development have come when psychologists team up with economists and even brain physiologists to study poverty. The "Hope" sidebar in chapter 2 is an example in which a development program might have changed the way people think about their futures.

Economists Sendhil Mullainathan, Eldar Shafir, and others have brought together new methods in psychology and behavioral economics to test basic propositions about people's behavior, including the behavior of the poor. One explanation for why people are trapped in poverty might be that the very condition of being poor keeps people from "thinking" their way out of poverty. As the title of one article states, "poverty impedes cognitive function."[3] People under economic stress have little mental room to think about the optimal strategy to get out of poverty, like investing in schooling or a new crop technology. If this is true, then cash transfers and other programs that reduce the mental as well as physical stress of poverty might have the added benefit of making strategies to become more productive "top of mind," instead of being buried deep below the immediacy of where the next meal will come from. Many development projects try to change people's behavior, for example, getting them to send their kids to school and spend more of their scarce income on nutritious foods and health care. We cannot assume that the underlying parameters shaping people's decisions are given, yet in almost every undergraduate economics class—not to mention most of our economic models—we do precisely that! Instead, behavior and cognition may be endogenous, influenced by, as well as influencing, development outcomes.

Business Management

Thinking of business? It is easy to slip into a mind-set that confounds international development with international aid. Most of the real development gains the world has witnessed in the past fifty years are attributable to the functioning of markets and private-sector firms. Small-scale entrepreneurs create value and tap opportunities at a local level. Small and medium enterprises are engines of job growth in cities around the world. Even large multinational corporations, which are popular targets for protests of all sorts, contribute in important ways to local economies. Development economists have studied these impacts, but so have business consultants. Many business schools have programs devoted to international business, and many of these relate to doing business with the poor—so called Bottom of the Pyramid strategies. Social impact investing that often aims at a "triple bottom line" (economic, environmental, and social impact) has similarly expanded rapidly in the past decade. Development economists are currently using the tools we described in this book to evaluate these impacts in collaboration with social impact investing firms.

Politics and International Relations

There's a reasonably good chance you have a background in international relations or political science—many of the students who take our courses do. What in this book *doesn't* relate in some way to politics and international relations? Development policy, poverty, inequality, human development, institutions, corruption, crime, globalization, aid. It is difficult for a foreign relations expert to do anything without thinking about development economics, just as it is unrealistic for a development economist to ignore politics and institutional environments. If you walk the halls of the United Nations, the Organization for Economic Cooperation and Development (OECD), the Carnegie Endowment for International Peace, or any other organization with a focus on global politics, as we often do, you are guaranteed to find a potpourri of experts with development economists mixed in—all of whom will be interacting and collaborating with one another, trying to make their distinct disciplines merge and make sense to one another.

EPILOGUE FOR EVERYBODY: DEEP TRUTHS FROM DEVELOPMENT ECONOMICS

This epilogue really is intended for everybody. You may have no desire to even visit Africa, Asia, or Latin America, much less work there, but there are nevertheless deep truths we draw from development economics that might just enrich your life and expand your worldview. These deep truths stem from several of the essentials we have discussed in this book. Four such deep truths stand out in our minds.

Deep Truth One: "What is, is for a reason"

If there is any single lesson that emerges from this book, it's that context matters. Economists, like any scientists, seek to identify patterns amidst the complexity of the world. While there are many patterns to be found in development economics—otherwise there would be no "essentials"—universal truths are highly elusive in social science research. When we are new to a place, it is easy to wonder why on earth people do the things they do; it is easy to see perplexing behaviors as fundamentally irrational or inefficient. Often, this is because the context creates constraints that we don't fully understand or appreciate—because the people we are observing understand the richness of their economic environment better than we do as outsiders. These contextual constraints may or may not serve a clear social or cultural purpose and may have emerged simply by accident, but they often impose real constraints on the behavior of individuals and households. This implies that humility beats hubris when it comes to achieving real impact. The knowledge problem implies that we often know less than we think we know, which can undermine our best-laid plans.

Deep Truth Two: "True development expands freedom"

Money buys a lot of things, but anytime money becomes the end rather than a means to an end we get in trouble—at both personal and societal levels. Development economists have focused increasingly on broader measures of human development in developing countries to reflect this fact. But the objective of expanding human agency and freedom is relevant for every country. For rich or for poor, true development enriches lives by building agency and enabling individuals to be and do what they want to be and do. True development expands freedom and opportunities—opportunities that come from having a healthy body and brain, an education and intellectual stimulation for cognitive development, and access to markets to secure a livelihood and contribute to society in the process. Freedom is not just about having more choices, but must also build accountability, because when accountability breaks down—whether it is the elite abusing their power or common individuals being denied the fruits of their labor—having more choices means very little.

Deep Truth Three: "Markets that work are powerful,
but they are not free"

When markets work well, they can dramatically improve individual lives and social outcomes. They not only allow individuals to enjoy the greater freedoms that true development brings but can also harness enhanced choice and accountability for the broader social good. In order to work well, though, markets require a basic infrastructure of political, social, and cultural institutions—norms, rules, and processes that govern our interactions with others. While it is true in rich and poor countries alike that governments rarely improve things by tinkering directly with markets, this does not mean that governments don't have a role to play. Markets that function well—that adjust freely as underlying conditions change—do not come free. They require major public investments and targeted government action. They also require deeply rooted supporting institutions that, whether they emerge from the bottom up or are imposed from the top down, are shaped importantly by government action.

Deep Truth Four: "Be self-seeking and fellow-feeling"

Adam Smith's insight that an invisible hand leads people, through market interactions, to outcomes that were not part of their intention is one of the most important ideas in modern social thought.[4] In these pages, we have repeatedly seen how critically markets and the efficiency gains they bring can shape economic development. The invisible hand that makes markets so powerful works through a basic human instinct to promote one's own well-being and interests—through our "self-seeking" nature. We've also seen that conditions in developing countries often make it important to consider efficiency and equity at the same time. In a similar vein, Adam Smith insisted that markets could improve society most when market interactions between people reflect their instincts to be both self-seeking and fellow-feeling. This fellow-feeling impulse—a sense of sympathy for others' circumstances—provides the most basic motivation for doing development economics. The way we address fundamental questions of human development and social welfare as economists, the way we seek to harness markets to achieve both efficiency and equity objectives, and indeed, the way we each try to fill our lives with meaning and purpose must take both instincts into account: be self-seeking as well as fellow-feeling.

www.rebeltext.org/development/qr14.html
Explore multimedia resources while you read this epilogue.

Notes

CHAPTER 1

1. The true cost of living is difficult to compare across countries. Here we use the purchasing power parity method. Even income can be hard to measure in a country where most crop production is for home consumption. These issues will be addressed later in this book.

2. A least-developed country, according to the United Nations, is a country that has the lowest indicators of socioeconomic development and the lowest Human Development Index (HDI; see chapter 6) levels of all countries in the world. We'll learn about country-development typologies in more detail at the end of chapter 2.

3. Mateusz Filipski and J. Edward Taylor, "A Simulation Impact Evaluation of Rural Income Transfers in Malawi and Ghana," *Journal of Development Effectiveness* 4, no. 1 (2012):109–29.

4. Chewe Nkonde, Nicole M. Mason, Nicholas J. Sitko, and T. S. Jayne, "Who Gained and Who Lost from Zambia's 2010 Maize Marketing Policies?" (working paper no. 49, Food Security Rresearch Project, Lusaka, Zambia, January 2011; www.aec.msu.edu/fs2/zambia/wp49.pdf).

5. http://web.worldbank.org/wbsite/external/countries/africaext/malawiextn /0,,contentMDK:21575335~pagePK:141137~piPK:141127~theSitePK: 355870,00.html.

6. You can read about some of these programs at the Transfer Project website, housed at the University of North Carolina, Chapel Hill (www.cpc .unc.edu/projects/transfer).

7. Economist William Easterly provocatively argues that the real origins of development economics trace further back, to the 1920s and 1930s, and that the "technocratic" approach to development that continues to shape high-level discussions and plans about development was born of a general disregard for

the rights of the poor as individuals during these early decades. See William Easterly, *The Tyranny of Experts: Economists, Dictators, and the Forgotten Rights of the Poor* (New York: Basic Books, 2014).

8. Walter W. Rostow, *The Stages of Economic Growth: A Non-Communist Manifesto* (Cambridge: Cambridge University Press, 1960).

9. Roy F. Harrod, "An Essay in Dynamic Theory," *Economic Journal* 49 (1939):14–33; Evsey Domar, "Capital Expansion, Rate of Growth, and Employment," *Econometrica* 14, no. 2 (1946):137–47.

10. W. Arthur Lewis, "Economic Development with Unlimited Supplies of Labor," *Manchester School of Economic and Social Studies* 22 (1954): 139–91.

11. Gustav Ranis and John C. Fei, "A Theory of Economic Development," *American Economic Review* 51 (September 1961):533–58.

12. Theodore W. Schultz, *Transforming Traditional Agriculture* (New Haven: Yale University Press, 1964).

13. Raúl Prebisch, "Commercial Policy in the Underdeveloped Countries," *American Economic Review* 49 (May 1959):251–73; Hans Singer, "The Distributions of Gains between Investing and Borrowing Countries," *American Economic Review: Papers and Proceedings* 40 (1950):473–85.

14. A. Hirschman, "A Generalized Linkage Approach to Development with Special Reference to Staples," *Economic Development and Cultural Change* 25 (1977):67–98.

15. John W. Mellor, *The New Economics of Growth: A Strategy for India and the Developing World* (Ithaca, NY: Cornell University Press, 1976).

16. United Nations, *Encyclopedia of the Nations* (www.nationsencyclopedia .com/United-Nations/Economic-and-Social-Development-first-un-development-decade.html).

17. Simon Kuznets, "Economic Growth and Income Inequality," *American Economic Review* 45 (March 1955):1–28.

18. H. B. Chenery, M. S. Ahluwalia, C. L. G. Bell, J. H. Duloy, and R. Jolly, *Redistribution with Growth* (London: Oxford University Press, 1974).

19. I. Adelman and C. T. Morris, *Economic Growth and Social Equity in Developing Countries* (Stanford, CA: Stanford University Press, 1973).

20. World Bank archives (http://web.worldbank.org/wbsite/external/extaboutus /extarchives/0,,contentMDK:20502974~pagePK:36726~piPK:437378~theSit ePK:29506,00.html).

21. See www.un.org/millenniumgoals/bkgd.shtml.

22. Later in this book we will encounter one of the lead detractors of the MDGs, economist William Easterly, and explore his arguments.

CHAPTER 2

1. This is the amount reported by the twenty-four members of the Organization for Economic Cooperation and Development's (OECD) Development Assistance Committee for 2011 (http://stats.oecd.org/Index.aspx?DatasetCode = ODA_DONOR). About 80%–85% of developmental aid comes from government sources as official development assistance (ODA). The remaining 15%–

20% comes from private organizations such as nongovernmental organizations (NGOs), foundations, and other development charities (e.g., Oxfam).

2. Opportunity NYC, an experimental CCT, was launched in New York City with support from the Rockefeller Foundation, the Robin Hood Foundation, the Open Society Institute, the Starr Foundation, AIG, and Mayor Bloomberg's personal foundation. It ended on August 31, 2010.

3. J. Angrist and S. Pischke, *Mostly Harmless Econometrics: An Empiricists' Companion* (Princeton: Princeton University Press, 2008).

4. Now called the Abdul Latif Jameel Poverty Action Lab (J-PAL).

5. www.povertyactionlab.org/news/randomized-evaluations-interventions-social-science-delivery.

6. Poverty Action Lab, "What Is Randomization?" (www.povertyactionlab .org/methodology/what-randomization).

7. For an excellent discussion see Benjamin Davis, Marie Gaarder, Sudhanshu Handa, and Jenn Yablonski, "Evaluating the Impact of Cash Transfer Programmes in Sub-Saharan Africa: An Introduction to the Special Issue," *Journal of Development Effectiveness* 4, no. 1 (2012):1–8.

8. Dean Karlan and Jonathan Zinman, "Expanding Credit Access: Using Randomized Supply Decisions to Estimate the Impacts," *Review of Financial Studies* 23, no. 1 (2010): 433–64, doi:10.1093/rfs/hhp092.

9. Suresh de Mel, David McKenzie, and Christopher Woodruff, "Returns to Capital in Microenterprises: Evidence from a Field Experiment," *Quarterly Journal of Economics* 123, no. 4 (2008): 1329–72.

10. Sarah A. Janzen and Michael R. Carter, "After the Shock: The Impact of Microinsurance on Consumption Smoothing and Asset Protection" (Working paper no. 19702, National Bureau of Economic Research, Washington, DC, 2013).

11. Rachid Laajaj, "Closing the Eyes on a Gloomy Future: Psychological Causes and Economic Consequences" (working paper, University of Wisconsin, Madison, and Paris School of Economics, December 7, 2011; http://agecon .ucdavis.edu/research/seminars/files/laajaj-closing-the-eyes-on-a-gloomy-future .pdf).

12. Measuring impact and putting a value on it are often two different things. For example, measuring the impact of a literacy program on literacy test outcomes is straightforward, but valuing these literacy gains can be very difficult. In such cases, a good alternative to cost-benefit analysis is cost-effectiveness analysis, which measures how costly it is to achieve a specific impact (e.g., an increase in literacy of one standard deviation).

13. For more discussion, see http://marcfbellemare.com/wordpress/2013/11 /impact-evaluation-and-nimby-comments-and-discussion/.

14. An excellent discussion appears in Christopher B. Barrett and Michael R. Carter, "The Power and Pitfalls of Experiments in Development Economics: Some Non-random Reflections," *Applied Economic Perspectives and Policy* 32, no. 4 (2010):515–48.

15. A next-best strategy might be to use the same farmers prior to the subsidy as a control group, provided that before-and-after data are available. This effectively is what Sadoulet, de Janvry, and Davis did in their fixed-effects analysis of

the income effects of Mexico's PROCAMPO crop subsidy program. This strategy can be confounded by the inability to adequately control for time-varying variables, however. For example, changes in the economy at large might coincide with the timing of the transfers and affect the outcomes of interest. See E. Sadoulet, A. de Janvry, and B. Davis, "Cash Transfer Programs with Income Multipliers: PROCAMPO in Mexico," *World Development* 29, no. 6 (2001):1043–56.

16. In Keynesian economics, government spending can increase income by more than the amount of the spending. This is the idea behind economic stimulus programs in the US and other countries in response to the economic crisis beginning in 2007–2008.

17. Poverty Action Lab, "What Is Randomization?" (www.povertyaction lab.org/methodology/what-randomization).

18. www.millenniumvillages.org/uploads/ReportPaper/MP-2010-Annual-Report---Complete---FINAL.pdf.

19. His experiment and results are presented in Hans Binswanger, "Attitudes toward Risk: Experimental Measurement in Rural India," *American Journal of Agricultural Economics* 62, no. 3 (1980):395–407.

20. Christopher B. Barrett and Michael R. Carter, "The Power and Pitfalls of Experiments in Development Economics: Some Non-random Reflections, *Applied Economic Perspectives and Policy* 32, no. 4 (2010):515–48.

21. Angus S. Deaton, "Instruments of Development: Randomization in the Tropics, and the Search for the Elusive Keys to Economic Development" (working paper, no. 14690, National Bureau of Economic Research, January 2009; www.nber.org/papers/w14690).

22. Esther Duflo, Michael Kremer, and Jonathan Robinson, "Nudging Farmers to Use Fertilizer: Evidence from Kenya," *American Economic Review* 101, no. 6 (2011):2350–90.

23. Development banks often evaluate the costs and benefits of a new project over a fifteen- to twenty-year period, depending on the nature of the project. They also tend to use conservative (that is, high) discount rates—typically on the order of 10% or higher. Risk plays a role here: The riskier you think the future is, the sooner you'll want your money back and the higher the discount rate you'll use in your CBA.

24. Dwayne Benjamin, "Household Composition, Labor Markets and Labor Demand: Testing for Separation in Agricultural Household Models," *Econometrica* 60, no. 2 (March 1992):287–322; H. Jacoby, "Shadow Wages and Peasant Family Labor Supply: An Econometric Application to the Peruvian Sierra," *Review of Economic Studies* 60 (1993): 903–21; A. de Janvry, M. Fafchamps, and E. Sadoulet, "Peasant Household Behavior with Missing Markets: Some Paradoxes Explained," *Economic Journal* 101 (1991):1400–1417.

25. E. Sadoulet, A. de Janvry, and B. Davis, "Cash Transfer Programs with Income Multipliers: PROCAMPO in Mexico," *World Development* 29, no. 6 (2001):1043–56.

26. M. Angelucci and G. De Giorgi, "Indirect Effects of an Aid Program: How Do Cash Transfers Affect Ineligibles' Consumption?" *American Economic Review* 99(2009):486–508.

CHAPTER 3

1. Center for the Continuing Study of the California Economy, "California Poised to Move up in World Economy Rankings in 2013," *Numbers in the News* (July 2013; www.ccsce.com/PDF/Numbers-July-2013-CA-Economy-Rankings-2012.pdf).

2. Melvin Backman, "Britain, Italy Add Drugs and Sex to GDP," *CNN Money,* May 30, 2014, http://money.cnn.com/2014/05/29/news/economy/uk-italy-prostitution-gdp/.

3. http://siteresources.worldbank.org/datastatistics/Resources/gnipc.pdf.

4. R. Repetto, W. Magrath, M. Wells, C. Beer, and F. Rossini, *Wasting Assets: Natural Resources in the National Accounts* (Washington, DC: World Resources Institute, 1989).

5. www.who.int/mediacentre/factsheets/fs311/en/.

6. You can see all the countries' PPP-adjusted GDPs at the World Bank website, http://data.worldbank.org/indicator/NY.GDP.PCAP.PP.CD.

7. Paul Leroy-Beaulieu, *De la colonisation chez les peuples modernes* (Paris, 1874). See also the discussion in chapter 2 of G. Rist, *The History of Development: From Western Origins to Global Faith* (London: Zed Books, 2002).

8. Interestingly, some WTO agreements also grant privileges to "developing countries" (e.g., the original Agreement on Trade Related Intellectual Property Rights) without clearly defining which countries can qualify by this definition. In such cases, member countries of the WTO designate themselves as developing countries, but there are obvious bounds on which countries can get away with this self-designation!

9. Source: World Bank. For a complete listing, see http://data.worldbank.org/about/country-classifications/country-and-lending-groups#Low_income.

10. http://povertydata.worldbank.org/poverty/home/. Unless otherwise specified, you can assume that per capita incomes mentioned in this chapter are PPP adjusted.

11. World Bank, *2011 World Development Report* (http://web.worldbank.org/wbsite/external/extdec/extresearch/extwdrs/0,,contentMDK:23256432~pagePK:478093~piPK:477627~theSitePK:477624,00.html).

12. *United Nations Human Development Report* (2011; http://hdr.undp.org/en/statistics/hdi/).

CHAPTER 4

1. See www.who.int/nutrition/topics/nutrecomm/en/index.html.

2. Some nutrients are easier to get from cheap foods than others. The most costly essential nutrients would have a relatively large impact on the cost of this poverty food basket.

3. The Development Research Group at the World Bank established the LSMS in order "to facilitate the use of household survey data for evidence-based policy-making." See http://go.worldbank.org/IPLXWMCNJ0.

4. This is the approach proposed by Joel Greer and Erik Thorbecke, "Food Poverty Profile Applied to Kenyan Smallholders," *Economic Development and Cultural Change* 35 (1986):115-41.

5. World Bank, "Poverty Overview" (www.worldbank.org/en/topic/poverty /overview).

6. This figure is for the forty-eight contiguous states plus the District of Columbia. The poverty lines are higher in Alaska and Hawaii.

7. See www.bbc.co.uk/news/magazine-17312819.

8. J. Foster, J. Greer, and E. Thorbecke, "A Class of Decomposable Poverty Measures," *Econometrica* 52, no. 3 (1984):761–66.

9. The seminal article on poverty and asset dynamics is Travis J. Lybbert, Christopher B. Barrett, Solomon Desta, and D. Layne Coppock, "Stochastic Wealth Dynamics and Risk Management among a Poor Population," *Economic Journal* 114 (October 2002):750–77. A more recent article directly addresses the dilemma described here: Michael Carter and Travis J. Lybbert, "Consumption versus Asset Smoothing: Testing the Implications of Poverty Trap Theory in Burkina Faso," *Journal of Development Economics* 99 (2012): 255–64.

10. Travis J. Lybbert, Christopher B. Barrett, Solomon Desta, and D. Layne Coppock, "Stochastic Wealth Dynamics and Risk Management among a Poor Population," *Economic Journal* 114 (October 2002):750–77.

11. In much of East Africa, the herder relies as much or more on the blood of the cattle as he does their milk.

12. Paul Rosenstein-Rodan first outlined this model in 1943. Paul Rosenstein-Rodan, "Problems of Industrialization of Eastern and South-Eastern Europe," *Economic Journal* 53, no. 210/211 (1943):202–11.

CHAPTER 5

1. The frequency distribution for Mexico was constructed from data in Gerardo Esquivel, "The Dynamics of Income Inequality in Mexico since NAFTA" (El Colegio de México, December 2008; www.cid.harvard.edu/Economia /GEsquivel.pdf). Swedish disposable income data are from Statistics Sweden (www.scb.se/Pages/TableAndChart___226030.aspx).

2. H. Shalit and S. Yitzhaki, "The Mean-Gini Efficient Portfolio Frontier," *Journal of Financial Research* 28, no. 1 (2005):59–75.

3. If you aren't statistically inclined, don't worry: Excel will take the covariance for you. Just pick a cell and insert "= covar(array1, array2)" where array1 is the data in the second column and array2 is the data in the third column.

4. Postscript to Bob Sutcliffe, "World Inequality and Globalization," *Oxford Review of Economic Policy* (Spring 2004; http://siteresources.worldbank.org /INTDECINEQ/Resources/PSBSutcliffe.pdf).

5. Some of the fastest-growing countries in recent decades have been poor countries with very large populations, especially China and India. While this has dramatically raised the average income of nearly 40% of the world's population, these two countries account for barely 1% of all the countries in the world. Therefore, the effect on the global Gini is much greater than on the disparities between countries.

6. This social welfare function was proposed by Shlomo Yitzhaki, "Stochastic Dominance, Mean Variance and Gini's Mean Difference," *American Economic Review* 72 (1982):178–85.

7. In calculus terms, the derivative of W with respect to income is positive (since $G < 1$), and the derivative with respect to G is negative.

8. Esther Duflo, "Gender Equality in Development" (BREAD policy paper no. 011, December 2005; http://siteresources.worldbank.org/INTAFRREG TOPGENDER/Resources/EstherDufloGenderEqualityinDevelopment. pdf; Amartya Sen, "More Than 100 Million Women Are Missing," *New York Review of Books* 37, no. 20, 1999 (www.nybooks.com/articles/archives/1990/dec/20/more-than-100-million-women-are-missing/).

9. It is a property of covariances that $\text{Cov}(x + y, z) = \text{Cov}(x, z) + \text{Cov}(y, z)$.

CHAPTER 6

1. Mahbub ul Haq, *Reflections on Human Development* (New York: Oxford University Press, 1995).

2. You can learn more about the IHDI at the UNDP website, http://hdr.undp.org/en/statistics/ihdi.

3. Choosing between the average and geometric mean might seem technical, but really it's about what we care about in development. Should a country that does well on one dimension but poorly on another have the same HDI as a country that does reasonably well on both? If all three indexes are the same (say, ½), you can easily verify that the average and geometric mean will be the same:

$$\sqrt[3]{(1/2)^3} = 1/2$$

$$(1/2+1/2+1/2)/3 = 1/2$$

Otherwise, they will be different: for example if the indexes are ¼, ½, and ¾, the average is still ½, but the geometric mean is only 0.45. Suppose two countries have the same education level, but one has moderate income and moderate life expectancy, while the other has high income and low life expectancy. Even if the average of the three indexes is the same for the two countries, the second one will have a lower HDI according to the geometric mean. The geometric mean penalizes countries that do well on one component but poorly on another.

4. You can read about the Global Peace Index at www.visionofhumanity.org/gpi-data/#/2011/conf/.

5. We are grateful to the United Nations Children's Fund (UNICEF Lesotho) and the Food and Agricultural Organization (FAO) for allowing us to use these data to illustrate the costs and benefits of going to school.

6. You can find real interest rates for different countries at the World Bank's data website: http://data.worldbank.org/indicator/FR.INR.RINR.

7. These percentages are for children twelve to nineteen years of age.

8. Centers for Disease Control and Prevention, "State-Specific Healthy Life Expectancy at Age 65 Years—United States, 2007–2009," *Morbidity and*

Mortality Weekly Report 62, no. 28 (July 19, 2013):561–66 (www.cdc.gov/mmwr/preview/mmwrhtml/mm6228a1.htm).

9. These statistics are from the United Nations, "UNAIDS Report on the Global AIDS Epidemic" (2010; www.unaids.org/documents/20101123_Global Report_em.pdf) and "World AIDS Day Report 2011" (www.unaids.org/en/media/unaids/contentassets/documents/unaidspublication/2011/jc2216_worldaidsday_report_2011_en.pdf).

10. C. Bell, S. Devarajan, and H. Gersbach (2003) (PDF). *The Long-run Economic Costs of AIDS: Theory and an Application to South Africa* (working paper no. 3152, World Bank; http://siteresources.worldbank.org/INTPRH/Resources/Longrun_economic_costs_of_AIDS.pdf).

11. These estimates come from John Strauss and Duncan Thomas, "Health, Nutrition, and Economic Development," *Journal of Economic Literature* 36, no. 2 (1998):766–817.

12. Ibid.

13. Xiao Ye and J. Edward Taylor, "The Impact of Income Growth on Farm Household Nutrient Intake: A Case Study of a Prosperous Rural Area in Northern China," *Economic Development and Cultural Change* 43, no. 4 (1995): 805–19.

14. Lant Pritchett and Lawrence H. Summers, "Wealthier Is Healthier," *Journal of Human Resources* 31, no. 4 (1996):841–68.

15. Jean Dreze and Amartya Sen, *India: Economic Development and Social Opportunity* (Oxford: Clarendon Press, 1999).

16. Amartya Sen, *Development as Freedom* (New York: Anchor Books, 1999), pp. 3–4.

CHAPTER 7

1. Robert Lucas, "On the Mechanics of Economic Development," *Journal of Monetary Economics* 22 (1988):5–42.

2. Marcelo Mello, "Decomposing the International Variation in Capital per Worker," *Economics Letters* 113 (2011): 189–91.

3. The data for life expectancy are from the Department of Health and Human Services, National Center for Health Statistics, *National Vital Statistics Reports* 54, no. 19 (June 28, 2006; www.dhhs.gov; http://americandigest.org/mt-archives/american_studies/america_in_1900.php); Richard H. Steckel, *A History of the Standard of Living in the United States* (http://eh.net/?s=A+History+of+the+Standard+of+Living+in+the+United+States). The data for US GDP in 1900 were compiled by GAPMINDER (www.gapminder.org/data/documentation/gd001/#.U--qoGMY6EA), using estimates from Angus Maddison, *The World Economy: Historical Statistics* (www.ggdc.net/maddison/maddison-project/data.htm), and converting them to 2002 dollars.

4. George E. P. Box and Norman R. Draper, *Empirical Model-Building and Response Surfaces* (New York: Wiley, 1987).

5. For a discussion of this adjustment and why it may matter, see "Global Economic Inequality: More or Less Equal?" *Economist* (March 2004; www.economist.com/node/2498851).

6. Paul M. Romer, "The Origins of Endogenous Growth," *Journal of Economic Perspectives* 8, no. 1 (Winter 1994):3–22.

7. Paul M. Romer, "Idea Gaps and Object Gaps in Economic Development," *Journal of Monetary Economics* 32, no. 3 (1993): 543–73.

8. See the Millennium Villages Project website: www.unmillenniumproject .org/.

9. William Easterly, *The Elusive Quest for Growth* (Cambridge, MA: MIT Press, 2002).

10. See "Economics Focus: The Big Push Back," *Economist* (December 3, 2011; www.economist.com/node/21541001).

11. William Easterly, *The Tyranny of Experts: Economists, Dictators, and the Forgotten Rights of the Poor* (New York: Basic Books, 2014).

CHAPTER 8

1. Raymond Fisman and Edward Miguel, "Corruption, Norms, and Legal Enforcement: Evidence from Diplomatic Parking Tickets," *Journal of Political Economy* 115, no. 6 (December (2007):1020–48.

2. Yasmine Saleh, "Egypt Diplomats Worst Traffic Offenders, Says London Paper," *Daily News Egypt* (2008; http://emiguel.econ.berkeley.edu/assets /miguel_media/60/ParkingTicket_DNE20081210.pdf).

3. "Foreign Diplomats Owe Huge Parking Fine Debt," *The Local: Sweden's News in English* (August 17, 2012; www.thelocal.se/20120817/42678).

4. Emily Wyman and Hannes Rakoczy, "Social Conventions, Institutions, and Human Uniqueness: Lessons from Children and Chimpanzees," in *Interdisciplinary Anthropology* (Berlin, Heidelberg: Springer, 2011), 131–56.

5. R. Fisman and Edward Miguel, *Economic Gangsters: Corruption, Violence, and the Poverty of Nations* (Princeton: Princeton University Press, 2008).

6. One person who witnessed one of Sutton's robberies said that it was like being at the movies, except the usher had a gun.

7. The Corruption Perceptions Index data can be found at Transparency International's website: http://cpi.transparency.org/cpi2012/results/.

8. In ancient Greek mythology, Sisyphus was a cruel king condemned to spend eternity rolling a huge stone up a hill in Hades, only to have it roll back down as he neared the top.

9. D. Acemoglu and J. Robinson, *Why Nations Fail: The Origins of Power, Prosperity, and Poverty* (New York: Random House Digital, 2012).

10. For more of this institutional view of domestic violence and economic development, see D.C. North, J.J. Wallis, S.B. Webb, and B.R. Weingast, eds., *In the Shadow of Violence: Politics, Economics and the Problems of Development* (Cambridge: Cambridge University Press, 2012).

11. J. Sachs, "Review Essay: Government, Geography and Growth—The True Drivers of Economic Development," *Foreign Affairs* 91, no. 5 (2012): 142–50.

12. William Easterly, "Institutions: Top Down or Bottom Up?" *American Economic Review* 98, no. 2 (2008):95–99.

13. Peter J. Boettke and Christopher J. Coyne, "Entrepreneurship and Development: Cause or Consequence?" *Advances in Austrian Economics* 6 (2003):67–87.

CHAPTER 9

1. The full lecture is available at www.nobelprize.org/nobel_prizes /economic-sciences/laureates/1979/schultz-lecture.html.

2. This point was made by Peter Timmer in his paper, "The Agricultural Transformation," published as chapter 8 in the *Handbook of Development Economics,* vol. 1, edited by H. Chenery and T. N. Srinivasan (Amsterdam: Elsevier Science, 1988), 275–331.

3. Christopher B. Barrett, "Smallholder Market Participation: Concepts and Evidence from Eastern and Southern Africa," *Food Policy* 33 (2008):299–317.

4. Gregg Easterbrook, "Forgotten Benefactor of Humanity," *Atlantic,* January 1997 (www.theatlantic.com/magazine/archive/1997/01/forgotten-benefactor-of-humanity/306101/).

5. United Nations Food and Agricultural Organization (FAO).

6. Again, the full text of this lecture is available here: www.nobelprize.org /nobel_prizes/economic-sciences/laureates/1979/schultz-lecture.html.

7. Adam Smith, *An Inquiry into the Nature and Causes of the Wealth of Nations,* edited by Edwin Cannan (reprint, 1904; London: Methuen, 1776). The quotation is the title of book 1, sec. 3.

8. www.oxfam.org/en/emergencies/east-africa-food-crisis/famine-somalia-what-needs-be-done.

CHAPTER 10

1. www.fao.org/about/en/.

2. The terms "rural" and "urban" are problematic. At what population does a village become a town? (Many governments, including the US Bureau of the Census, use 2,500 as the cutoff.) As expanding roads, communications, and markets integrate town and country, the distinction becomes ever more blurred.

3. "Transition day," as this day has become known, is largely symbolic. The date was estimated from the UN's prediction that the world would be 51.3% urban by 2010. Researchers at North Carolina State University and the University of Georgia interpolated the transition date by using the average daily rural and urban population increases from 2005 to 2010.

4. E. Jonasson, M. Filipski, J. Brooks, and J. E. Taylor, "Modeling the Welfare Implications of Agricultural Policies in Developing Countries," *Journal of Policy Modeling* 36, no. 1 (2014):63–82.

5. Aslihan Arslan and J. Edward Taylor, "Transforming Rural Economies: Migration, Income Generation and Inequality in Rural Mexico," *Journal of Development Studies* 48, no. 8 (2011):1156–76.

6. US Department of Labor, National Agricultural Worker Survey (NAWS) (www.doleta.gov/agworker/naws.cfm).

7. Francisco and his family are a composite constructed from field surveys carried out by researchers at UC Davis and the Colegio de México in Mexico City.

8. W. Arthur Lewis, "Economic Development with Unlimited Supplies of Labour," *Manchester School* 22, no. 2 (1954):139–91.

9. Gustav Ranis and John C. H. Fei, "A Theory of Economic Development," *American Economic Review* 60 (September 1961):533–65.

10. In a subsistence household, on the other hand, raising productivity can free up family time for other activities, including wage work.

11. C. Peter Timmer, "The Agricultural Transformation," chapter 8 in *Handbook of Development Economics*, vol. 1, edited by H. Chenery and T. N. Srinivasan (Amsterdam: Elsevier Science, 1988).

12. J. Mellor, *The New Economics of Growth* (Ithaca, NY: Cornell University Press, 1976).

13. Jan Nijman, "A Study of Space in Mumbai's Slums," *Tijdschrift voor economische en sociale geografie* 101, no. 1 (February 2010):4–17.

14. United Nations Human Settlements Programme, *The Challenge of Slums: Global Report on Human Settlements 2003* (London and Sterling, VA: Earthscan, 2003).

15. The World Bank has a dedicated website on urban development: www.worldbank.org/en/topic/urbandevelopment.

16. John R. Harris and Michael P. Todaro, "Migration, Unemployment, and Development: A Two-Sector Analysis," *American Economic Review* 60 (1970):126–42.

17. The best introduction to building CGE models is Mary Burfischer, *Introduction to Computable General Equilibrium Models* (Cambridge: Cambridge University Press, 2011).

CHAPTER 11

1. George A. Akerlof, "The Market for 'Lemons': Quality Uncertainty and the Market Mechanism," *Quarterly Journal of Economics* 84, no. 3 (1970):488–500.

2. George A. Akerlof, "Writing the 'The Market for "Lemons"'": A Personal and Interpretive Essay" (www.nobelprize.org/nobel_prizes/economics/laureates/2001/akerlof-article.htm).

3. United States Food and Drug Administration (www.fda.gov/Food/InternationalInteragencyCoordination/default.htm).

4. European Commission, "Health and Consumers" (http://ec.europa.eu/food/food/chemicalsafety/residues/third_countries_en.htm).

5. www2.merriam-webster.com/cgi-bin/mwthesadu?book=Dictionary&va=market.

6. www.oxforddictionaries.com/us/definition/american_english/market.

7. "Labor: U.S. Fruits and Vegetables," *Rural Migration News* 17, no. 1 (January 2011) (http://migration.ucdavis.edu/rmn/more.php?id = 1596_0_5_0).

8. Joseph E. Stiglitz, "Smith's 'Invisible Hand' a Myth?" Address to the Commonwealth Club of San Francisco (February 22, 2010; www.youtube.com/watch?v=9qjvwQrZmpk).

9. Christopher B. Barrett, "Smallholder Market Participation: Concepts and Evidence from Eastern and Southern Africa," *Food Policy* 33, no. 4 (2008): 299–317.

10. Friedrich August Hayek, *The Fatal Conceit: The Errors of Socialism* (Chicago: University of Chicago Press, 2011).

11. Ibid.

CHAPTER 12

1. Alberto Chaia, Aparna Dalal, Tony Goland, Maria Jose Gonzalez, Jonathan Morduch, and Robert Schiff, "Half the World Is Unbanked" (Financial Access Initiative Framing Note, October 2009; http://financialaccess.org/sites/default/files/110109%20HalfUnbanked_0.pdf).

2. See http://go.worldbank.org/OSAT4FHFP0.

3. We are indebted to Steve Boucher for coming up with this intriguing comparison.

4. You can see a cool example in *RebelText: Essentials of Econometrics,* chapter 7 (rebeltext.org).

5. "Glut Leads Lawyers to (Surprise) Sue Law Schools," *Businessweek,* March 23, 2012 (www.businessweek.com/articles/2012-03-23/glut-leads-lawyers-to-surprise-sue-law-schools).

6. www.nobelprize.org/nobel_prizes/peace/laureates/2006/presentation-speech.html.

7. Hans P. Binswanger, "Attitudes toward Risk: Experimental Measurement in Rural India," *American Journal of Agricultural Economics* 62, no. 3 (August 1980):395–407.

8. Laura Schechter, "Risk Aversion and Expected-Utility Theory: A Calibration Exercise," *Journal of Risk and Uncertainty* 35, no. 1 (2007):67–76.

CHAPTER 13

1. David Ricardo, *The Principles of Political Economy and Taxation* (reprint, 1965; London: J. M. Dent and Son, 1817).

2. You can pretty much always make two things have the same price by redefining their units—like pricing beer in six-packs instead of bottles or chocolate in ounces instead of pounds.

3. Some of the major dependency texts include Paul A. Baran, "On the Political Economy of Backwardness," *Manchester School* 20, no. 1 (1952):66–84; Andre Gunder Frank, *The Development of Underdevelopment* (Boston: New England Free Press, 1966); Immanuel M. Wallerstein, *World-Systems Analysis: An Introduction* (Durham, NC: Duke University Press, 2004).

4. The IMF makes loans to bail out countries that cannot make good on their foreign debts, and it will not do this unless countries agree to enact policy changes that the IMF thinks are needed to make them more solvent.

5. The World Trade Organization, International Trade Statistics (www.wto.org/english/news_e/pres12_e/pr658_e.htm).

6. Pew Research Center, "The Rising Cost of Not Going to College" (February 2014; www.pewsocialtrends.org/2014/02/11/the-rising-cost-of-not-going-to-college/).

7. Ha-Joon Chang, "Kicking Away the Ladder," *Post-Autistic Economics Review* 15 (September 4, 2002) (www.paecon.net/PAEtexts/Chang1.htm).

8. World Trade Organization, "Understanding the WTO: Basics: What Is the World Trade Organization?" (www.wto.org/english/thewto_e/whatis_e /tif_e/fact1_e.htm).

9. The Royal Tropical Institute (KIT), Faida MaLi, the International Institute for Rural Reconstruction (IIRR), and L. Peppelenbos, eds., *Chain Empowerment: Supporting African Farmers to Develop Markets* (Amsterdam: KIT, 2006; www.kit.nl/kit/Publication?item=1952).

10. The Fair Labor Association's website is www.fairlabor.org/.

11. It is difficult to separate labor migration from migration for other motives, for example, accompanying a spouse or parents abroad.

12. C. Woodruff and R. Zenteno, "Migration Networks and Microenterprises in Mexico," *Journal of Development Economics* 82, no. 2 (2007): 509–28.

13. World Bank, data, personal remittances received (% of GDP) (http:// data.worldbank.org/indicator/BX.TRF.PWKR.DT.GD.ZS).

14. World Bank, data, imports of goods and services (% of GDP) (http:// data.worldbank.org/indicator/NE.IMP.GNFS.ZS).

15. Stuart Price, "Reversing the Brain Drain," *All Business.com* (November 1, 2004; http://archive.is/5orQF).

16. Onlineuniversities.com, "10 Countries Facing the Biggest Brain Drain" (www.onlineuniversities.com/blog/2011/07/10-countries-facing-the-biggest-brain-drain/).

17. Ibid.

18. Commission on Filipinos Overseas, "Stock Estimate of Overseas Filipinos as of Dec. 2012" (www.cfo.gov.ph/index.php?option=com_content&view =article&id=1340:stock-estimate-of-overseas-filipinos&catid=134).

19. Oded Stark, Christian Helmenstein, and Alexia Prskawetz, "A Brain Gain with a Brain Drain," *Economics Letters 55*, no. 2 (1997):227–34.

20. Oded Stark and Yong Wang, "Inducing Human Capital Formation: Migration as a Substitute for Subsidies," *Journal of Public Economics* 86 (2002):29–46.

21. Michel Beine, Frédéric Docquier, and Hillel Rapoport, "Brain Drain and Economic Growth: Theory and Evidence," *Journal of Development Economics* 64, no. 1 (2001):275–89.

22. http://archive.fortune.com/magazines/fortune/fortune_archive/1992/12 /28/77310/index.htm.

23. *International Migration and Development—Report of the Secretary-General* (United Nations General Assembly, Sixtieth Session, May 18, 2006; www.unhcr.org/44d711a82.html).

24. For simplicity, we refer to international aid from governments as ODA, but in practice there are other official aid flows that are classified separately.

25. See www.opic.gov/.

26. International Fund for Agricultural Development, *Rural Poverty Report 2011* (www.ifad.org/RPR2011/index_full.htm).

27. http://foodaid.org/resources/the-history-of-food-aid/.

28. See Christopher B. Barrett and Daniel G. Maxwell, *Food Aid after Fifty Years: Recasting Its Role* (London: Routledge, 2005); Christopher Barrett, "How to Get Food Aid Right," *CNNWorld* (http://globalpublicsquare.blogs.cnn.com/2013/05/06/how-to-get-food-aid-right/).

29. As economists like to point out, there is no free lunch. This conventional wisdom often applies even to food aid recipients. Long lines at distribution depots and other features that impose opportunity costs on recipients are often used in an attempt to ensure that those with the greatest need receive the food.

30. See G. Frazer, "Used-Clothing Donations and Apparel Production in Africa," *Economic Journal* 118, no. 532 (2008):1764–84. As you might expect, good data on used clothing donations and imports are tough to come by, and any rigorous analysis is fraught with potential data problems; see A. Brooks and D. Simon, "Unraveling the Relationships between Used-Clothing Imports and the Decline of African Clothing Industries," *Development and Change* 43, no. 6 (2012):1262–90.

CHAPTER 14

1. For example, see Pat Bailey, "Tiny Packets of Hope: UC Davis Leads Efforts against Malnutrition with a $16 Million Gates Foundation Grant," *UCDAVIS Magazine Online* 27, no. 2 (Winter 2010) (http://ucdavismagazine.ucdavis.edu/issues/win10/tiny_packets_of_hope.html).

2. Douglas S. Massey, Joaquin Arango, Graeme Hugo, Ali Kouaouci, Adela Pellegrino, and J. Edward Taylor, *Worlds in Motion: Understanding International Migration at the End of the Millennium* (Oxford: Oxford University Press, 1999).

3. A. Mani, S. Mullainathan, E. Shafir, and J. Zhao, "Poverty Impedes Cognitive Function," *Science* 341, no. 6149 (2013):976–80.

4. Adam Smith, *An Inquiry into the Nature and Causes of the Wealth of Nations,* edited by Edwin Cannan (reprint, 1904; London: Methuen, 1776); E. L. Khalil, "Beyond Natural Selection and Divine Intervention: The Lamarckian Implication of Adam Smith's Invisible Hand," *Journal of Evolutionary Economics* 10, no. 4 (2000):373–93.

Index

Photo Atlas of Nursing Procedures

Second Edition

Pamela L. Swearingen

SPECIAL PROJECTS EDITOR

in association with

Indiana University School of Nursing

Department of Nursing Services
Indiana University Hospitals

and the

Physical Therapy and Respiratory
Therapy Programs
Division of Allied Health Sciences
Indiana University School of Medicine
Indianapolis, Indiana

ADDISON-WESLEY NURSING

A Division of The Benjamin/Cummings Publishing Company, Inc.

Redwood City, California • Menlo Park, California
Reading, Massachusetts • New York
Don Mills, Ontario • Wokingham, U.K.
Amsterdam • Bonn • Sydney • Singapore
Tokyo • Madrid • San Juan

Sponsoring Editor: Mark McCormick
Executive Editor: Debra Hunter
Editorial Assistant: Michèle Mangelli
Production Supervisor: John Walker
Production Services: The Book Company
Text Designer: Janet Bollow, with revisions
  to the Second Edition by The Book Company
Text Photographer: Jeffry Collins
Cover Designer: Rodolphe M. Zehntner
Cover Photographer: Tom Ferentz
Copy Editor: Melissa Andrews
Composition and film: York Graphic Services

The author and publishers have exerted every effort to ensure that drug
selection, dosage, and composition of formulas set forth in this text are in accord
with current formulations, recommendations, and practice at the time of
publication. However, in view of ongoing research, changes in government
regulations, the reformulation of nutritional products, and the constant flow of
information relating to drug therapy and drug reactions, the reader is urged to
check product information or composition on the package insert for each drug for
any change in indications of dosage and for added warnings and precautions.
This is particularly important where the recommended agent is a new and/or
infrequently employed drug.

Library of Congress Cataloging-in-Publication Data

Swearingen, Pamela L.
    Photo atlas of nursing procedures/Pamela L. Swearingen; in
association with Indiana University School of Nursing . . . [et al.].
    —2nd ed.
        p.   cm.
    Rev. ed. of: The Addison-Wesley photo-atlas of nursing procedures.
c 1984.
    Includes index.
    ISBN 0-201-13239-7
    1. Nursing—Pictorial works.   I. Swearingen, Pamela L. Addison-
Wesley photo-atlas of nursing procedures.   II. Indiana University.
School of Nursing.   III. Title.
    [DNLM: 1. Nursing—atlases.   WY 17 S974a]
RT41.S96 1991
610.73′022′2—dc20
DNLM/DLC   90-14407
for Library of Congress   CIP

    345678910 -KE- 95 94 93 92 91

Addison-Wesley Nursing
A Division of The Benjamin/Cummings Publishing Company, Inc.
390 Bridge Parkway
Redwood City, California 94065

For
Muriel and
Arthur Olson
and
Jessamin
Swearingen

Preface

Do you remember the anxiety that surrounded your first performance of a new procedure in the hospital—an injection, a catheterization, suctioning an airway? Most nurses never forget.

Mastering the procedures—the psychomotor skills that underlie day-to-day nursing care—is one of the most important and most difficult educational experiences in nursing. Performed correctly, as part of an overall plan of nursing care, these procedures help promote comfort and recovery for clients. Performed less than competently, some procedures can be life-threatening.

Procedures usually are learned by watching a skilled demonstration and then performing a return demonstration. Because one on-site performance is seldom enough practice, methods and guidelines are needed to repeat the demonstrations until skills are mastered. The *Photo Atlas of Nursing Procedures, Second Edition,* offers you that extra assistance.

This single volume provides convenient access to realistic and detailed demonstrations of the procedures most frequently required of general duty staff nurses. It focuses on procedures directly involving a client; thus, such skills as bedmaking are not included. Critical care procedures are not included nor are those procedures that require a hands-on inservice demonstration to ensure safe client care. Because cardiopulmonary resuscitation is a basic technique taught to all hospital personnel, it is not in-

cluded here. Two procedures included in the first edition that have been deleted in the second edition are "Using Infusion Controllers and Pumps" (because of the ongoing equipment changes and refinements for controllers and pumps and the many variations from company to company) and "Setting up a Pleur-Evac (Closed Chest Drainage) System," also because of the variations in closed chest drainage systems from company to company.

Audience

Faculty, students, and practitioners alike will find this two-color atlas a highly effective supplemental text for use in teaching, learning, or practice. New graduates, staff nurses, and nurses returning to practice will welcome its comprehensive reference value. This new atlas uses more than 1500 black-and-white photographs taken in a clinical setting to graphically present more than 300 guidelines and procedures. It assumes the reader's understanding of basic sciences and nursing fundamentals.

Organization and Approach

The *Photo Atlas of Nursing Procedures, Second Edition,* is organized in two units: Unit One includes procedures basic to all nursing care; Unit Two includes procedures related to disorders of individual body systems. Since these are procedures that can be depicted by photography, psychosocial skills are not included.

Each body-system chapter begins with a review of anatomy and physiology, followed by a nursing assessment outline for that system. Where appropriate, variations of care throughout the life cycle are included in the narrative.

Every attempt has been made to include the necessary detail and rationale for each procedure while making each step easy to understand. The steps are within the nursing process framework, thus helping ensure optimal care of the client. The clear, professional tone of the presentation and the inclusion of rationale help establish an ideal climate for client teaching.

There are often several "correct" ways to perform a procedure based on agency practice and/or personal preference. This atlas depicts generic procedures that can be adapted to the materials and equipment available and to the method the reader has used successfully. Occasional use of identifiable commercial products in the photographs is not intended as product endorsement.

The photographs in this book represent the variety of nursing attire currently worn in hospitals and other health care settings around the nation. Thus, nurses are shown both with and without the traditional nursing cap and wearing many different styles of professional attire. For simplicity and to avoid referring to clients always as he or she, we have chosen instead to refer only to the gender of the client in each photograph.

Additions to the Second Edition

Sections added to the second edition include procedures for obtaining a throat culture, using the metered-dose inhaler, administering heparin, disposing of needles and sharp instruments, recapping needles using the one-hand method, initiating patient-controlled analgesia, managing the implantable subcutaneous port, performing external electronic fetal monitoring, obtaining a urine specimen from the neo-nate, managing the gastrostomy button, using small-bore feeding tubes, managing the ileoanal reservoir, performing mouth-to-mask ventilation, managing the CPAP mask, obtaining the ankle-brachial pressure ratio and paradoxical pulse, positioning electrodes for the 12-lead EKG, understanding the continent urinary diversion, managing clients with blood reinfusion systems and continuous passive motion, assessing clients with subarachnoid drains, and understanding beds that employ air fluidized therapy and pulsating air suspension therapy.

All procedures reflect 1988 Universal Body Substance Precautions from the Centers for Disease Control (CDC).

The *Photo Atlas of Nursing Procedures, Second Edition,* was created and developed to assist nurses at every level of practice as they learn, relearn, review, and update their hands-on skills in client care. Ultimately this will enhance the quality of that care—a goal we all share.

Acknowledgments

The journey from idea to bound book is never solitary. On a project of this magnitude, the author requires assistance, encouragement, and support from many. I am fortunate to have found an abundance of all three requisites at every step.

The *Photo Atlas of Nursing Procedures, Second Edition,* had its inception at one of the great teaching centers in nursing—Indiana University School of Nursing at Indianapolis. I am grateful to Dean Constance Baker for granting us permission to use the Learning Laboratory once again. Judith Halstead and Jean Hutton, current director and former coordinator of the Learning Laboratory at the School of Nursing, were wonderful and went out of their way to make sure our work there went smoothly. Sonna Ehrlich, Director of Nursing and Associate Director of Indiana University Hospitals, graciously allowed us use of Indiana University Hospitals and enabled us to work with the excellent and knowledgeable nurses.

As in the First Edition, we enjoyed working with Rebecca Porter, Director and Associate Professor of the Physical Therapy Program, School of Medicine, Indiana University, and Chuck Christoph, Acting Director, Respiratory Therapy, Indiana University and Indiana University Hospitals.

Four people in particular have earned special praise and appreciation for their second edition contributions. Jeffry Collins reprised his role as *photographer extraordinaire,* helping make the long hours and late nights shooting as fun and pleasant as possible. Cheri Howard, Unit Director at Indiana University Hospitals, was the on-site coordinator. She not only found the skilled nurses, scheduled *and* participated in many of the shoots, reviewed the nursing literature, and reviewed the manuscript, she did it all so graciously, alleviating for me much of the burden of managing the project from my Connecticut home. I would not want to write a book without the input of Marguerite Jackson, Director of Medical Center Epidemiology Unit and Assistant Clinical Professor of Community Medicine at University of California, San Diego. Her practical, no-nonsense approach to infection control obviates the "ritual and magic" that historically have been a part of techniques and fundamental books, and promotes instead an understanding of why and when nurses use gloves and other barrier devices to prevent the spread of infection. Michèle Mangelli, who, among other important tasks, functioned as my liaison with Addison-Wesley and all the reviewers, and was there for me from the planning stages to the project's end, even though she could have begun the job she was promoted to a month earlier than she did. You are all dear and valued friends.

Careful and thoughtful critiques from the following experts helped ensure the accuracy and clarity of the procedures depicted: Joan Kinniburgh, Product Manager of the Specialty Access Devices Division of Davol, Inc., of Cranston, Rhode Island; Jacqueline Jones Clibourn, Clinical Services Supervisor of Haemonetics Corporation in Braintree, Massachusetts; and Linda Nicholson, Nurse Specialist, Catheter Technology Corporation of Salt Lake City, Utah. The following reviewers from University of California Medical Center at San Diego helped us with the venous access device revision: Diana C. McPherson, RN, BSN, CIC; Margaret K. Grover, RN, CEIN; and Bertha J. Robles, RN, MSN. The following reviewers helped us plan the revision with the needs of the student in mind: Martha Thompson, RN, MSN, MAEd, Professor of Nursing, San Jose State, San Jose, California; Mary Cacace, RN, MSN, Director of Education, James Archer Hospital, Homestead, Florida; and Kathy Blais, RN, EdD, Professor of Nursing, Florida International University, North Miami, Florida.

P.L.S.

Second Edition On-Site Advisory Board

CONSULTANT BOARD

First Edition
On-Site Advisory Board

Phoebe, Alfke, ET
Enterostomal Therapist
Indiana University Hospitals

Cheryl K. Ashbaucher, RN, MSN
Assistant Professor
Indiana University School of
  Nursing

Janice S. Bruckner, RPT, MS
Assistant Professor
Division of Allied Sciences,
  Physical Therapy Program
Indiana University School of
  Medicine

Charles L. Christoph, RRT, BS
Clinical Instructor, Respiratory
  Therapy
Indiana University, Indiana
  University Hospitals

Ursula J. Easterday, RN, BSN,
  CCRN
Patient Care Coordinator
Indiana University Hospital

Noreen G. Feller, RN, BSN
Pediatric Orthopedic Coordinator
James Whitcomb Riley Hospital
  for Children
Indiana University Hospitals

Martha Greenwald, RN, BSN
Patient Care Coordinator
Indiana University Hospital

Carlene M. Grim, RN, MSN
Coordinator for State
  Hypertension Program
Indiana State Board of Health

Christina L. Harlett, RN, BS
Staff Development Coordinator
Indiana University Hospital

Cora D. Hartwell, RN, MSN
Staff Development Coordinator
Indiana University Hospital

Cheri Howard, RN, MSN, CCRN
Patient Care Coordinator
Indiana University Hospital

Damien Howell, RPT, MS
Associate Professor
Physical Therapy Program,
  Division of Allied Health
  Sciences
Indiana University School of
  Medicine

Marchusa A. Huff, RN, MSN,
  SCN
Associate Professor
Indiana University School of
  Nursing

Jean R. Hutten, RN, MSN
Associate Professor, Coordinator
  of Learning Lab
Indiana University School of
  Nursing

Mona L. Jacobs, RN, BSN
Staff Assistant for Continuing
  Education
Department of Materials
  Management
Indiana University Hospitals

Slobodanka Libby Jacobs, RN,
  BSN
Nurse Epidemiologist
Indiana University Hospitals

Christine M. Krejci, RRT, BS
Clinical Instructor, Respiratory
  Therapy
Indiana University Hospitals

Jane F. Marshall, RN, BSN
Staff Nurse
James Whitcomb Riley Hospital
  for Children
Indiana University Hospitals

Nancy Martin, RN
Unit Director
Indiana University Hospital

Frederick E. May, RN, MSN
Assistant Professor
Indiana University School of
  Nursing

Catherine Monken, RN, BSN
Patient Care Coordinator
Indiana University Hospital

Ann D. Nice, RN, MSN
Assistant Professor
Indiana University School of
  Nursing

Jody Obear, RN
Staff Nurse/Childbirth Educator
Indiana University Hospital

Patricia Pierce, RN, MSN
Staff Development Coordinator
Indiana University Hospital

Rebecca E. Porter, RPT, MS
Associate Professor, Director
Physical Therapy Program,
  Division of Allied Health
  Sciences
Indiana University School of
  Medicine

Sheryl L. Randolph, RN, ET
Enterostomal Therapist
Richard L. Roudebush Veterans
  Administration Hospital
Indianapolis

Mary Jane Shepherd, RN, MSN
Assistant Professor
Indiana University School of
  Nursing

Teresa J. Smith, RN, MSN
Assistant Professor
Indiana University School of
  Nursing

Joanne Sprinkle, RRT, MS
Assistant Professor, Staff
   Development Coordinator
Respiratory Therapy Program,
   Division of Allied Health
   Sciences
Indiana University School of
   Medicine

Lillian Stokes, RN, MSN
Associate Professor
Indiana University School of
   Nursing

Linda F. Strickland, RN
Neonatal Nurse Practitioner
Indiana University Hospital

Diana Sullivan, RN, MSN, CNOR
Staff Development Coordinator
Indiana University Hospital

Brief Contents

Contents

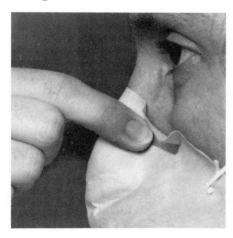
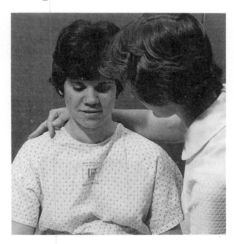

Chapter 3

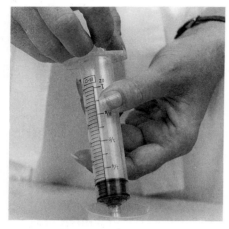

Administering Medications and Monitoring Fluids 81

UNIT II PERFORMING SPECIALIZED NURSING PROCEDURES 185

Chapter 4

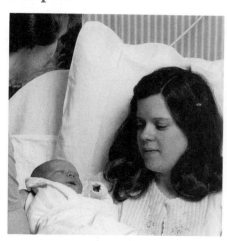

Managing Female Reproductive Procedures and Immediate Care of the Newborn 187

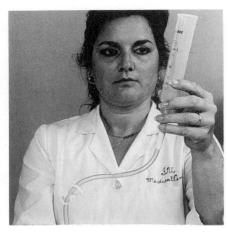
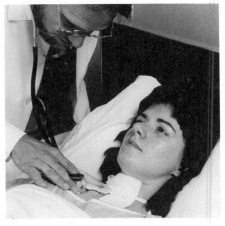

Chapter 7

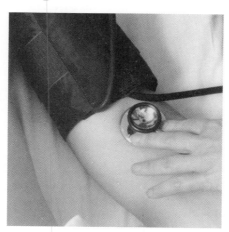

Managing Cardiovascular Procedures 397

Chapter 8

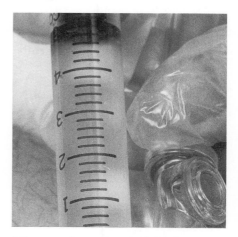

Managing Renal-Urinary Procedures 437

Chapter 9

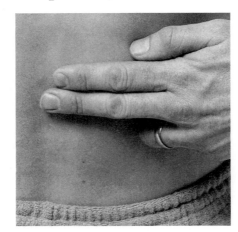

Managing Musculoskeletal Procedures   501

Chapter 10

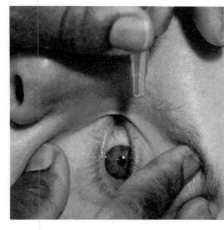

Managing Neurosensory Procedures   591

Unit I

Performing Basic Care Procedures

Chapter 1

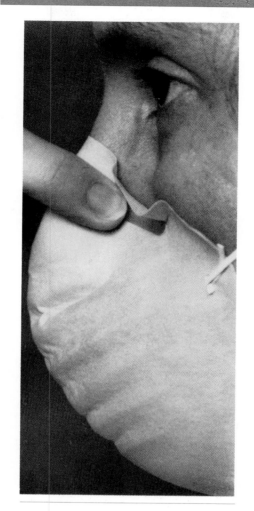

Employing Techniques for Infection Prevention and Control

CHAPTER OUTLINE

APPLYING BASIC INFECTION CONTROL MEASURES

Nursing Guidelines to Protocols for Handwashing and Cleansing Agents

    Handwashing
    Cleansing Agent
    Reviewing Basic
      Handwashing

Implementing Universal Body Substance Precautions

    Body Substance Isolation
    Using Protective Barriers
    Removing Protective
      Barriers

PREPARING FOR A STERILE PROCEDURE

Applying Sterile Gloves

Establishing a Sterile Field

    Opening a Sterile Pack
    Dropping Sterile Supplies
      onto a Sterile Field
    Placing a Sterile Bowl
      onto the Sterile Field
    Pouring Sterile Solutions

Putting on Sterile Attire (Including the Closed-Glove Technique)

OBTAINING A THROAT CULTURE

PACKING A WOUND (USING WET TO DRY DRESSINGS)

Applying Basic Infection Control Measures

NURSING GUIDELINES TO PROTOCOLS FOR HANDWASHING AND CLEANSING AGENTS

HANDWASHING

Handwashing is the single most important procedure for preventing nosocomial infections. According to the Centers for Disease Control (CDC), in clinical situations in which *superficial* contact has been made with a client, handwashing generally is not required. Superficial contact includes handshaking, measuring blood pressure, and handing medications or food to the individual. However, handwashing *is* indicated when one has had prolonged and intense client contact. In addition, handwashing is indicated before performing invasive procedures; before caring for susceptible individuals, such as newborns, individuals in intensive care units, or individuals who are immunocompromised; and before and after touching wounds. Handwashing is also indicated after situations in which microbial contamination of the hands is likely to have occurred, **even if gloves were worn.** These situations include contact with mucous membranes, blood, body fluids, secretions, and excretions as well as contact with inanimate objects likely to be contaminated (e.g., urine measuring device). The hands also should be washed between procedures for the same client (e.g., after touching the urinary drainage container and before changing a wound dressing). Finally, handwashing is encouraged *any time personnel are in doubt about its necessity!*

CLEANSING AGENT

Absolute indications for handwashing with plain soaps and detergents versus handwashing with products containing antimicrobial agents are unknown. However, for most routine patient care activities, the use of plain soap appears to be sufficient because the friction used with the soap allows most transient microorganisms to be washed off. Antimicrobial handwashing agents are used before caring for clients in high-risk areas, including newborns and severely immunocompromised individuals. Hands are also washed with antimicrobial agents between clients in high-risk areas. For more information, see Table 1-1.

Table 1-1   Recommended Agents for Preparing Hands and Cleaning Skin *Before** Nonsurgical and Surgical Procedures†

Procedure	Example	Handwashing	Gloves‡	Preparation of patient's skin	Comment
Nonsurgical					
Instruments used in procedure will come in contact with intact mucous membranes	Bronchoscopy, gastrointestinal endoscopy, and tracheal suction	Soap and water	Recommended	In general, none is required.	

*Hands should be washed *after* all procedures when microbial contamination of the operator is likely to occur, especially those involving contact with mucous membranes, whether or not gloves are worn. Soap and water are usually adequate for such handwashing.

†From Centers for Disease Control. Guideline for hospital environmental control: Antiseptics, handwashing, and handwashing facilities. In *Guidelines for the Prevention and Control of Nosocomial Infections.* Atlanta, GA: U.S. Department of Health and Human Services, 1981.
Centers for Disease Control. *Guideline for Handwashing and Hospital Environmental Control.* Atlanta, GA: U.S. Department of Health and Human Services, 1985.
U.S. Department of Health and Human Services, Public Health Service. Update: Universal precautions for prevention of transmission of human immunodeficiency virus, hepatitis B virus, and other bloodborne pathogens in health care settings. *MMWR* (June 24) 1988; 37:377–388.

‡Gloves protect the patient and the operator from potentially infectious microorganisms.

(Continues)

Table 1-1 *Continued*

Procedure	Example	Handwashing	Gloves‡	Preparation of patient's skin	Comment
	Cystoscopy, urinary tract catheterization	Soap and water	Sterile recommended	Antiseptics should be used to prepare urethral meatus.	
Insertion of peripheral intravenous or arterial cannula	Intravenous therapy, arterial pressure monitoring	Soap and water or antiseptic	Recommended	Antiseptics should be used; a fast-acting one is desirable. Tincture of iodine is preferred, but alcohol is adequate if it is applied liberally and allowed to act for 30 seconds.	Most epidemics of infection associated with arterial pressure-monitoring devices appear to be caused by hospital-associated contamination of components external to the skin, such as transducer heads or domes.
Percutaneous insertion of a central catheter or wire	Hyperalimentation, central venous and capillary wedge pressure monitoring, angiography, cardiac pacemaker insertion	Antiseptic	Sterile recommended	Antiseptics should be used; a fast-acting one is desirable. Tincture of iodine is preferred. "Defatting" agents, such as acetone, are not recommended.	"Defatting" agents do not appear to decrease infections but can cause skin irritation.
Insertion (and prompt removal) of a sterile needle in deep tissues or body fluids, usually to obtain specimens or instill therapeutic agent	Spinal tap, thoracentesis, abdominal paracentesis	Soap and water or antiseptic	Sterile recommended	Antiseptics should be used; a fast-acting one is desirable. Tincture of iodine is preferred.	
Surgical					
Insertion of a sterile tube or device through tissue into normally sterile tissue or fluid	Chest tube insertion, culdoscopy, laparoscopy, peritoneal catheter insertion	Antiseptic	Sterile recommended	Antiseptics should be used. Hair should be clipped with scissors if hair removal is considered necessary.	
Minor skin surgery	Skin biopsy, suturing of small cuts, lancing boils, mole removal	Soap and water	Sterile recommended	Antiseptics should be used.	Gloves are usually worn for a short time and thus antiseptic handwashing is not usually necessary to suppress resident flora for these superficial procedures.

Table 1-1 *Continued*

Procedure	Example	Handwashing	Gloves‡	Preparation of patient's skin	Comment
Other procedures (major and minor surgery) that enter tissue below skin	Hysterectomy, cholecystectomy, herniorrhaphy	Antiseptic	Sterile recommended	Antiseptics should be used after the site has been scrubbed with a detergent. The patient can be shaved immediately before the procedure although clipping hair or using a depilatory is preferred.	Handwashing before surgical procedures that enter deep tissue is usually prolonged to ensure that all areas that harbor bacteria are adequately cleaned.

REVIEWING BASIC HANDWASHING

According to the CDC, frequent handwashing is the single most important procedure for reducing the transmission of potentially infectious agents.

1 Before washing your hands, remove the rings from your fingers to facilitate thorough cleansing and drying. If your watch has an expansion band, slide it above your wrist. Adjust the water to a warm temperature, and rinse your hands.

2 Lather your hands thoroughly. The friction from rubbing your hands together removes potentially infectious organisms from the skin. A 10-second vigorous handwashing will remove most transient flora adequately.

(Continues)

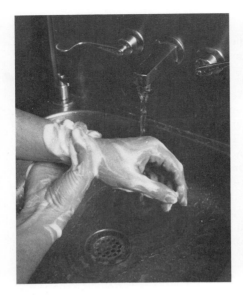

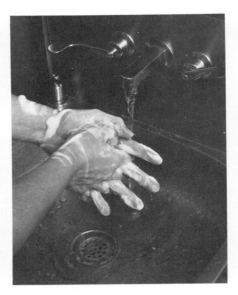

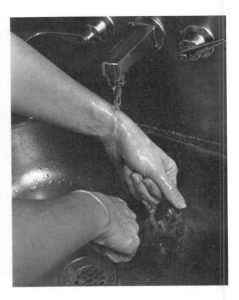

3   Wash each wrist by vigorously sliding the opposite hand around its surface area.

4   Interlace your fingers and thumbs, and slide them back and forth. Clean under your nails and around the nail beds with the fingertips and nails of the opposite hand.

5   Thoroughly rinse each hand from the wrist down. If your hands were grossly soiled, repeat steps 2–5 above.

6   Dry your hands with disposable towels.

7   To protect your hands from the contaminated surface of the faucet handle, turn off the faucet by placing a dry section of your used towel over the handle.

IMPLEMENTING UNIVERSAL BODY SUBSTANCE PRECAUTIONS

The CDC recommends universal blood and body fluid precautions in caring for *all* clients. These precautions (1988) pertain to blood and body fluids containing visible blood, as well as to semen, vaginal secretions, tissues, cerebrospinal fluid, synovial fluid, pleural fluid, peritoneal fluid, pericardial fluid, and amniotic fluid. In the health care setting, blood is the single most implicated source of human immunodeficiency virus (HIV), hepatitis B virus (HBV), and bloodborne pathogens. Penetrating injury caused by needlesticks or other sharp instruments following a procedure is the primary cause of infection, although nonintact skin and mucous membrane contact with blood are two other potential causes.

The 1988 CDC guidelines excluded the following body fluids from their universal precautions: feces, nasal secretions, sputum, sweat, tears, urine, and vomitus, unless they contain visible blood. However, they caution that exclusion of these body fluids does not eliminate the need for category-specific or disease-specific isolation precautions, for example, for instances in which enteric precautions for infectious diarrhea or isolation for pulmonary tuberculosis should apply. The CDC has told hospitals that they can choose either category-specific or disease-specific isolation precautions for isolation, or they can design their own system.

BODY SUBSTANCE ISOLATION

Body substance isolation (BSI) is an example of an alternative to category-specific or disease-specific isolation precautions. BSI was developed to serve two purposes: (1) *For clients,* BSI reduces the risk of cross-contamination of organisms, usually from the hands of personnel; and (2) *for health care workers,* BSI reduces the risk of infection from organisms harbored by clients. BSI is appropriate for the care of all clients, regardless of their diagnosis, because it calls for the use of protective barriers between the caregiver and all body substances, not just those body fluids implicated in the transmission of HIV and HBV. In this system for infection precautions, body substances are defined as blood, oral secretions, urine, stool, vomitus, and other body fluids. It has been well documented that infectious agents are transmitted via stool, urine, and oral secretions. At least one third of all nosocomial (hospital-associated) infections are potentially preventable, a portion of which are caused by cross-

contamination of organisms between clients via hands of personnel.

USING PROTECTIVE BARRIERS

Protective barriers include the following: gowns (or plastic aprons), masks, gloves, and appropriate roommate and caregiver selection. Roommate and caregiver selection involves avoiding roomsharing when one individual extensively soils articles with body substances, thereby placing the roommate at risk of contacting the soiled articles. Another example is avoiding roomsharing or client care for individuals whose infections are spread by the airborne route (e.g., chicken pox [herpes zoster]) by individuals who are not immune to these diseases; for example, a client with chicken pox or shingles should not be cared for by someone who has not had chicken pox.*

Applying a Gown

Gowns or plastic aprons are worn to prevent soilage of clothing when caring for clients. They are indicated when caring for any client if clothing is likely to be soiled with secretions or excretions, for example, when changing the bed of an incontinent client.

---

*Chicken pox is the clinical presentation for primary infection with the herpes zoster (varicella) virus. Once an individual has had chicken pox, the virus remains latent in the dorsal root ganglia of the spinal cord. Sometimes the virus becomes active, travels down the ganglion, and produces eruptions that are called shingles. In some clients, the virus disseminates and causes a clinical syndrome similar to primary chicken pox. Transmission of the virus from isolated shingles lesions is by contact; disseminated herpes zoster is also believed to be transmitted by the airborne route. Health care workers who have not had chicken pox can be infected with the herpes zoster virus from clients with either chicken pox or shingles.

1 To put on a gown, slip your arms into the sleeves and then tie the strings at the back of the neck.

2 Overlap the gown in the back so that it covers the back of your clothing, and tie the strings at the waistline.

Applying a Mask

Masks are needed when it is likely that the caregiver's oral and nasal mucous membranes will become splattered with the client's moist body substances or when the caregiver is working directly over large open skin lesions, such as an open wound or burn injury. *Note: Traditionally, masks have been worn while caring for clients with airborne communicable diseases, but there is no evidence that masks protect caregivers who are susceptible to chicken pox or measles and minimal or no evidence that they protect the individual from tuberculosis.*

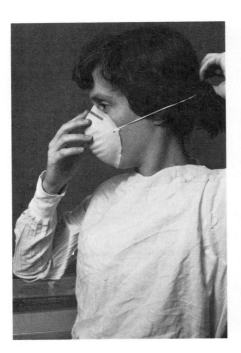 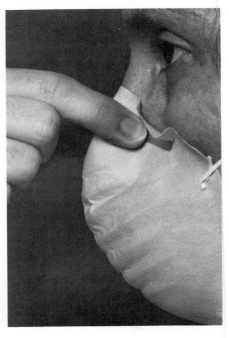

1 Generally, cup masks are worn. To apply the mask, position the elastic strap securely around the back of your head.

2 To minimize the gap between the mask and your nose, pinch the nose clip, as shown.

Applying Gloves

Gloves are worn for three reasons. First, they protect the wearer from contact with the client's microorganisms. Second, they minimize the potential for the wearer to transmit his or her own resident microbial flora to the client; and third, they minimize the risk of cross-contamination from one client to another. Gloves are indicated when touching blood, secretions, excretions, or body fluids.

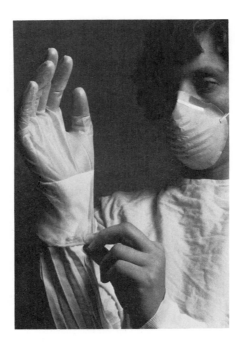

Put on the gloves, making sure they cover the cuffs of the gown if the gown is also worn.

REMOVING PROTECTIVE BARRIERS

When you have completed the care for your client, remove your contaminated attire before leaving the room.

1 If you are wearing a gown, untie its waist strings.

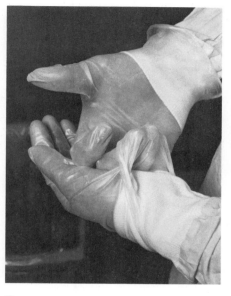

2 Remove your gloves: With your dominant hand, make a cuff by hooking gloved fingers into the lower outside edge of the other glove. Pull the glove inside out as you remove it, and then hold the glove in your gloved hand.

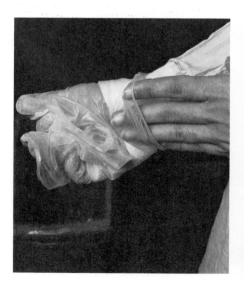

3 Tuck your ungloved fingers into the inside edge of the remaining glove. Remove that glove by pulling it inside out and encase the other glove as you do. Discard the gloves into the designated waste container. If you are wearing a gown, untie the neck strings next.

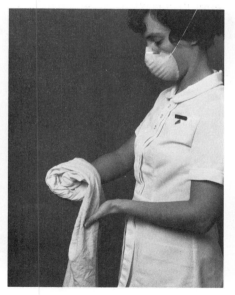

4 After untying the neck strings, remove the gown by turning it inside out during the process.

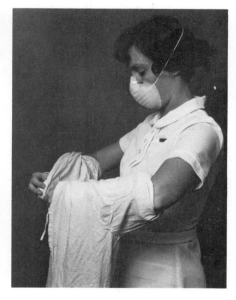

5 Hold the gown away from your body, and roll it up so that the contaminated side is innermost.

(Continues)

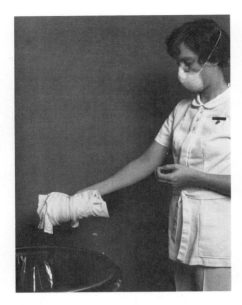

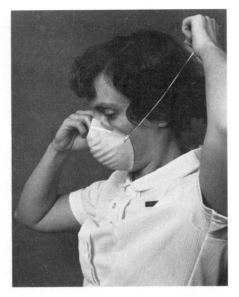

6   Place the gown in the designated laundry container.

7   Finally, remove the mask by grasping it by the elastic strap and pulling it off. Dispose of it in the waste container, and wash your hands before leaving the room.

Preparing for a Sterile Procedure

APPLYING STERILE GLOVES

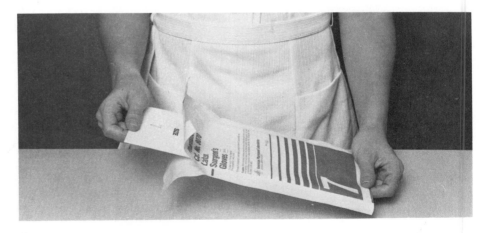

1   After washing your hands, open the outer wrap of the sterile glove pack and remove the inner wrap. Place the inner wrap on a clean, dry surface.

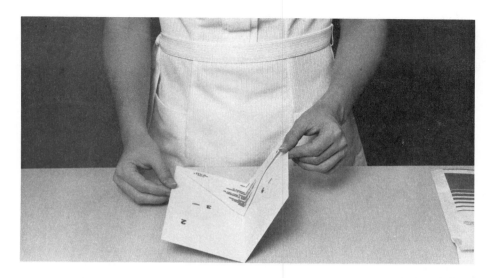

2 Carefully unfold the inner wrap, touching only the outside edges.

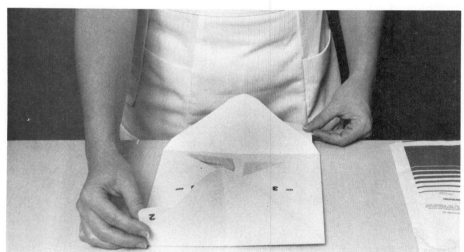

3 If the inner wrap has numbered flaps (as shown), open them numerically. Be sure to touch only the folded tabs. If the wrap is unnumbered, open the gloves by following the steps for opening a sterile pack on p. 16.

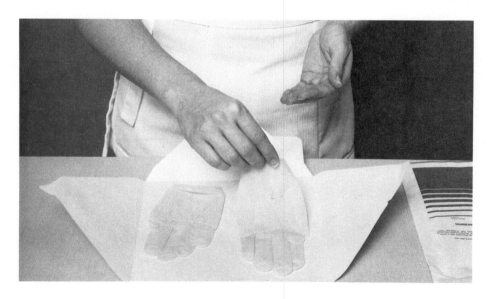

4 With your dominant hand, grasp the opposite glove at the inner edge of the folded cuff.

(Continues)

5 Carefully slip your hand into the glove.

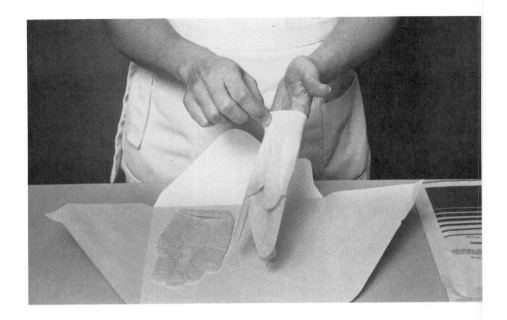

6 While still grasping the inner edge of the folded cuff, pull the glove over your hand.

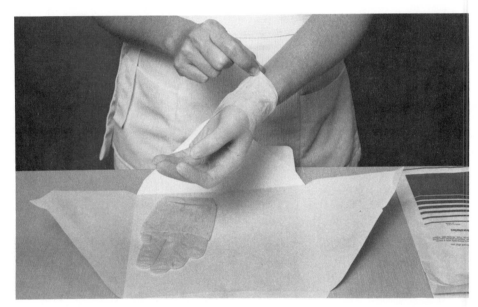

7 With your sterile gloved hand, slip your fingers into the folded cuff of the remaining glove.

8 Carefully slip the glove over your fingers.

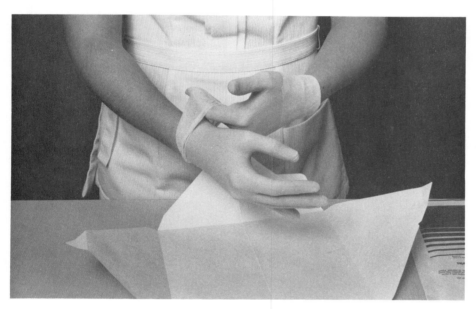

9 Pull the glove over your hand.

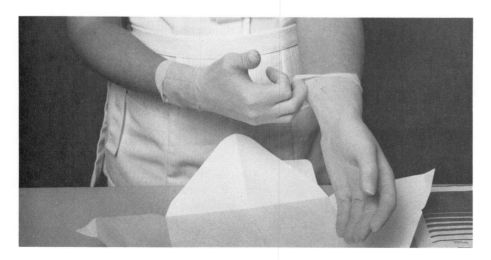

10 Adjust each glove to ensure a snug fit over your hands and fingers. Carefully slide your fingers under each cuff and pull it up.

ESTABLISHING A STERILE FIELD

OPENING A STERILE PACK

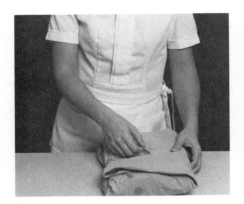  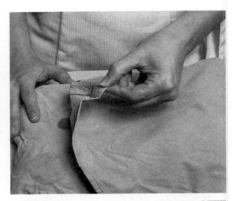

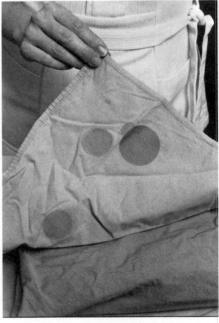

1 Wash your hands with an antimicrobial soap before opening the sterile pack. A sterile pack must be opened on a clean, dry surface. The outer wrap of commercially wrapped sterile packs should be inspected both for tears and for the sterility expiration date. Follow agency policy for returning outdated supplies. If the pack is agency-wrapped (as shown), ensure its sterility by inspecting the chemical indicator tape both for the integrity of its seal with the pack and for a change of colors, indicating it has been properly sterilized. Also check the sterility expiration date, which is written on the tape. Remove the indicator tape by pulling it from the center toward the outer edge of the pack.

2 Position the pack so that its outermost flap faces away from you. With your thumbs and index fingers, grasp the flap by small sections of its folded crease and lift it up and away from you. Hold your arms at the sides of the pack to avoid reaching over the sterile area.

3 Open the side flaps (top). Grasp the folded corner of the uppermost flap by touching a small section with your thumb and index finger; lay the flap to the side. Do the same with the opposite flap. Lift the remaining flap toward you (bottom), stepping back 12.5–25 cm (5–10 in.) as you do, so that you do not contaminate the wrap with your clothing. If the pack has an inner wrap, repeat the above procedure to open it.

DROPPING STERILE SUPPLIES ONTO A STERILE FIELD

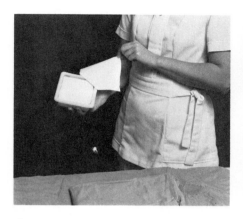

1 If your commercially wrapped sterile package is a peelback container (as shown), grasp the flap by its unsealed corner and pull the flap toward you. Position the pack so that its open end will face the sterile field.

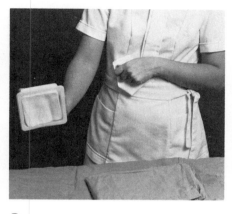

2 To prevent the container from contaminating the field, hold the opened pack approximately 15 cm (6 in.) above the sterile field, and allow the contents to drop well within the sterile area. Remember that the 2.5 cm (1 in.) border along the edge of the field is considered to be contaminated.

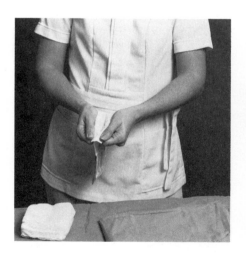

3 To open other types of commercially wrapped peelback containers such as glove packs or syringes (as shown), grasp both sides of the pack's unsealed edge and gently pull them apart.

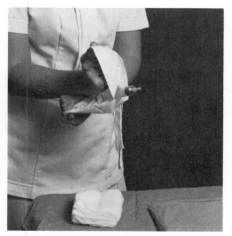

4 Hold the package so that its opened end is positioned away from your body and facing the sterile field. Carefully fold the sides back so that the outside wrap covers your hands and protects the contents. With the contents protected in this manner, allow it to drop onto the sterile field making sure it drops well within the sterile area.

PLACING A STERILE BOWL ONTO THE STERILE FIELD

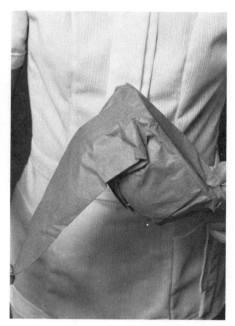

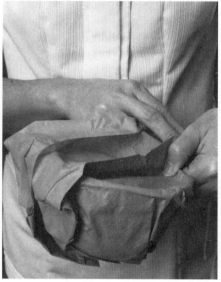

1 Hold a wrapped bowl at the rim with your thumb and index finger. Detach one of the corners (top) and bring it up and over the rim (bottom). Then hold the detached corner in place with your thumb and index finger.

(Continues)

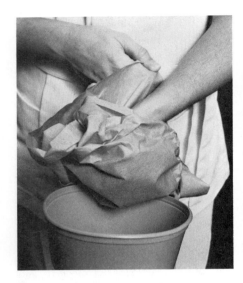

2 In the same manner, bring all the ends up to the rim; hold them in place with your thumb and index finger, confining the ends to a small area at the rim.

3 Place the bowl onto the sterile field. If it will be used to contain sterile solutions, place it near the edge of the field. This will enable you to pour the solution without reaching over a large section of the sterile area.

POURING STERILE SOLUTIONS

Because the sterility of a solution cannot be ensured once its container has been opened, try to obtain a container with an amount of solution appropriate to the procedure. As you pour the solution, hold the container to the side of, and at an angle to, the sterile field so that your hand and arm do not reach over the sterile area. To minimize the risk of contamination, hold the container approximately 10–15 cm (4–6 in.) above the bowl; pour slowly to avoid splashing the sterile drape and contaminating the sterile field.

PUTTING ON STERILE ATTIRE (INCLUDING THE CLOSED-GLOVE TECHNIQUE)

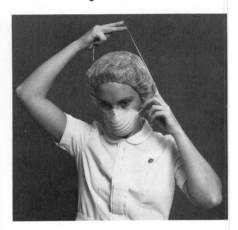

1 When you are required to wear sterile attire for procedures in which surgical asepsis is necessary, you must first wash your hands, put on a hair cover and face mask, and then open the sterile pack containing the sterile gown. (See steps on p. 16.)

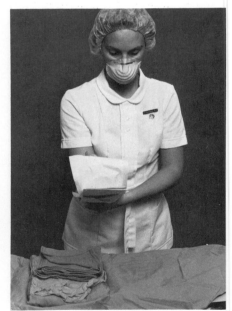

2 Remove the sterile gloves from their outer wrap and drop the inner wrap onto the sterile pack (as shown). Wash your hands with an antimicrobial soap and dry them thoroughly with the towel provided in the gown pack.

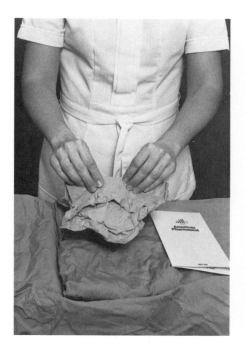

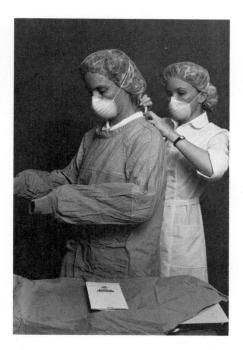

3 Grasp the sterile gown by its uppermost folded crease near the neckline.

4 Step into an area in which you will have space to open the gown without contaminating it, and hold it away from you to allow the gown to unfold. Place your hands inside the gown and work your arms through the shoulders, being certain to touch the inside of the gown only.

5 If you perform the closed-glove technique, advance your hands only as far as the proximal edge of the cuff (as shown). However, if you apply sterile gloves using the usual aseptic (open-glove) technique, extend your hands through the cuff, but do not touch the outside of the gown. Regardless of the gloving technique you use, a co-worker will be needed for assistance. The co-worker should first put on a mask and hair cover and then grasp the ties at the neckline area at the back of your gown and pull the gown up to cover the neckline of the front of your uniform. She will then tie the ties without touching the exterior of your gown.

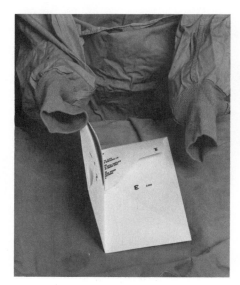

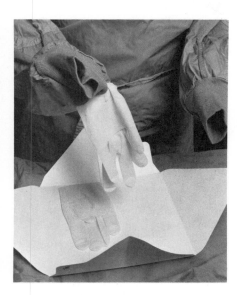

6 Unfold the inner wrap of the sterile gloves. If you are using the closed-glove technique, do this with your covered hands (as shown). Otherwise, follow the guidelines for applying sterile gloves using the technique described on pp. 12–15 and proceed to step 14.

7 Grasp the first glove by manipulating your thumb and index finger through the fabric of the sleeve or cuff.

(Continues)

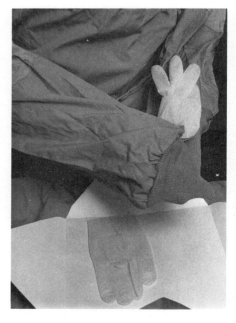

8 Place the glove palm down onto the cuff of your sterile gown. The fingers of the glove should point toward your elbow.

9 Manipulate your fingers within the cuff to anchor the glove. With your other covered hand, stretch the glove over the entire cuff.

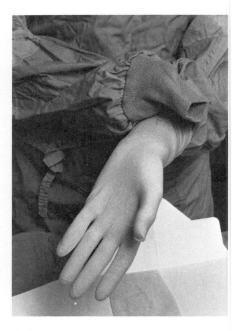

10 When the glove has been pulled successfully over the cuff, extend your fingers into the glove.

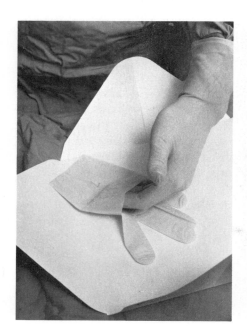

11 Place your gloved fingers within the folded cuff of the remaining glove.

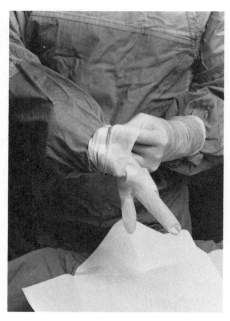

12 Position the glove over the closed cuff.

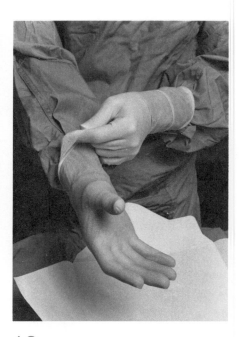

13 Pull the glove up over the gown's cuff as you extend your fingers through the glove. Adjust the glove to fit your fingers. Make sure both gloves cover the cuffs of the gown.

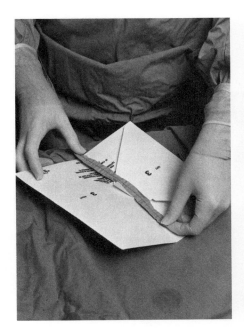

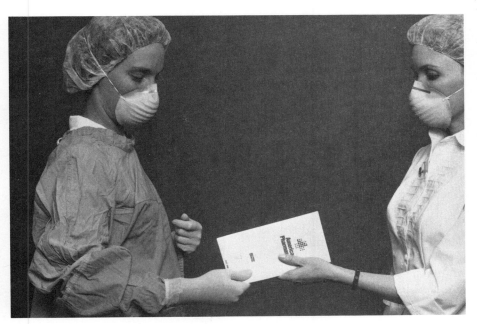

14 Place the back tie of the gown's waistband into the crease of the empty inner glove wrapper.

15 Close the wrapper and hand it to your co-worker. Instruct her to touch the outer wrap only.

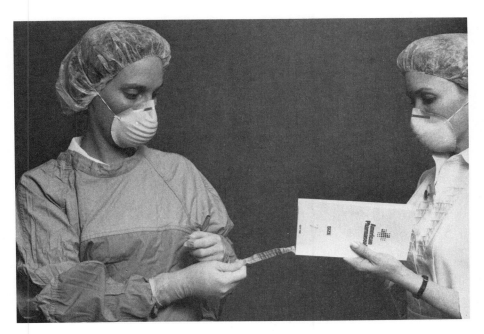

16 Make a three-quarter turn; then pull the tie from the wrapper and tie the gown at the front.

Note: If you prefer, your co-worker may instead put on a sterile glove and grasp the tie with her gloved hand while you make a three-quarter turn.

Obtaining a Throat Culture

1 If a throat culture has been
prescribed, obtain the culture
tube and applicator stick. Wash
your hands and remove the applicator stick from the culture tube.
With the client in Fowler's position, place her so that natural
light or a treatment light provides adequate visualization. Ask
the client to open her mouth.
Swab the back of her throat
along the tonsillar area, using a
tongue blade, if necessary, to depress her tongue.

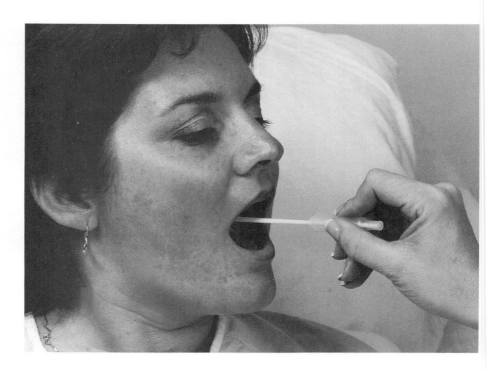

2 After obtaining the specimen,
replace the applicator stick in the
culture tube, pushing the stick
firmly until it punctures the compartment containing the culture
medium. Label the culture tube
and send it to the laboratory.
Wash your hands.

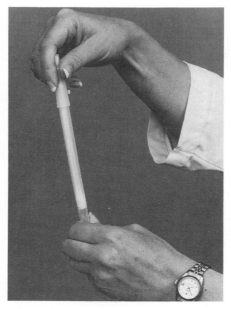

Packing a Wound (Using Wet to Dry Dressings)

Assessing and Planning

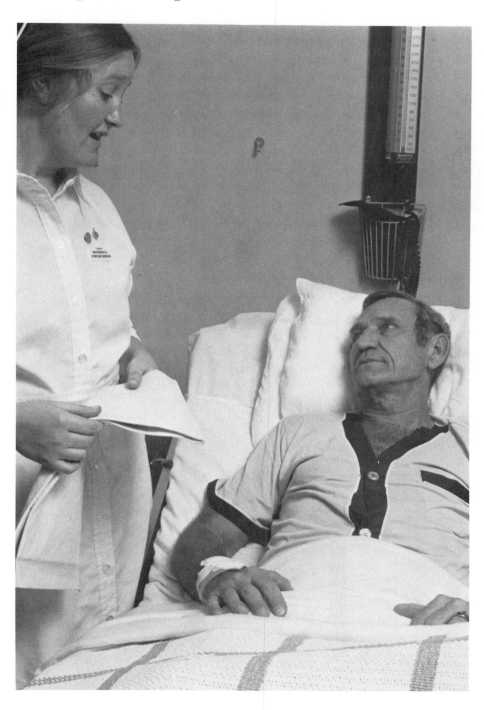

1 Check the client's chart and care plan or nursing Kardex for wound care information.

Explain the dressing change procedure to your client. Assess his level of comfort; if a pain medication has been prescribed, ask him whether he will need one for the procedure. If you do administer the medication, delay the procedure for 20 minutes until the medication takes effect. Position the bed at an optimal working height, provide privacy for the client, and place a bed-saver pad under the area of the wound to protect the bed linen. Inspect the dressing site and determine the approximate number of gauze pads you will need for the packing and outer dressing, as well as the need for either tape, fresh Montgomery straps, gauze roll, or surgical netting.

(Continues)

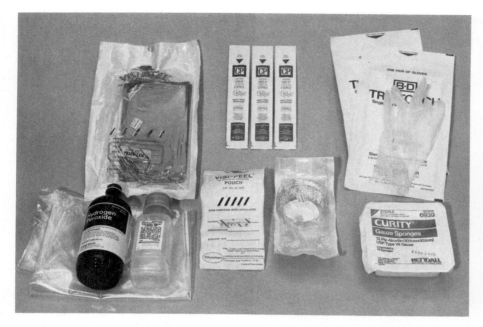

2 Assemble the following materials: sterile barrier, the prescribed cleansing/debriding and wetting solutions (hydrogen peroxide and normal saline are being used for this procedure), sterile basins, sterile cotton swabs, one pair of clean gloves, two pairs of sterile gloves, sterile gauze pads, and an impervious plastic bag for the disposal of used supplies. In addition, you will need paper or plastic tape if Montgomery straps are not used or a gauze roll if the wound is on an extremity. You also may use surgical netting in place of tape or Montgomery straps.

(It is important that the gauze pads be unfilled and made of a fine mesh. A filled gauze pad has cotton fiber filling that can get left behind in the wound, and fine mesh is necessary for optimal wound debridement because larger mesh gauze may remove the healing granulation tissue.)

3 Place the impervious plastic bag in a convenient place that is away from the dressing change site. Adjust the client's gown or remove it, and provide warmth and privacy. Wash your hands and prepare the sterile field at this time, following the steps on pp. 16–18. Carefully pour the prescribed solutions into the sterile basins. For this procedure, the nurse will use one basin for the cleansing and debriding solution (equal parts of normal saline and hydrogen peroxide) and the other basin for the wetting solution (normal saline).

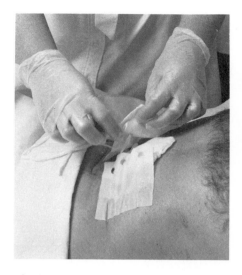

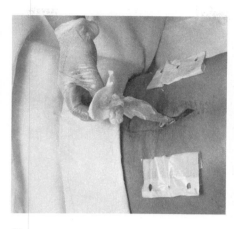

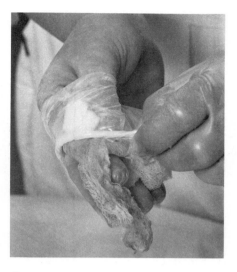

4   Put on the clean gloves and untie the Montgomery straps, move the netting away from the area of the wound, or remove the tape and outer cover dressing.

5   Grasp the gauze packing by securing it with the outer dressing that covers it. Pull gently to remove all the packing.
Caution: Use a sterile glove when removing the packing from a deeper wound.

6   Inspect the contaminated dressing to assess the amount and color of debris and drainage; note if it has an odor, which may be indicative of an infection. Encase the dressing in your gloves as you remove them, and dispose of both in the impervious plastic bag.

Implementing

7   Put on a pair of sterile gloves and soak a gauze pad in the cleansing solution. At this time, designate one hand contaminated for cleaning and rinsing and the other sterile for contact with the sterile field. Before cleaning the site, inspect the wound and assess for swelling, size, color, odor, and drainage. Estimate the amount of healing granulation tissue. Saturate the wound from top to bottom with the cleansing solution, and dispose of the contaminated pad.

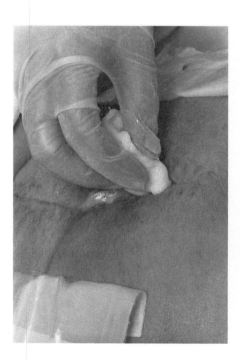

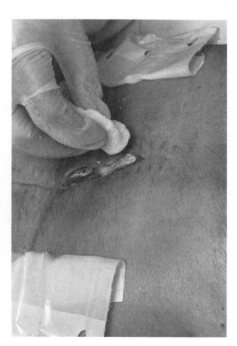

8   Soak another gauze pad in the cleansing solution and clean the area around the wound, beginning at the wound edge and working away from it in a circular motion.

(Continues)

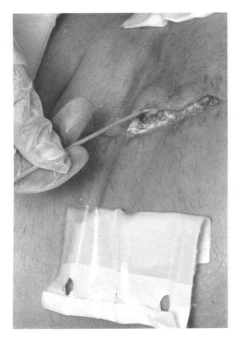

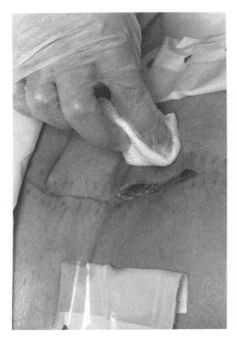

9 Moisten a cotton swab in the cleansing solution and clean the crevices of the wound. You may also use a fresh cotton swab to assess the depth of the crevice. This information will be important later when you pack the wound. Then, rinse the wound and surrounding area with the normal saline or designated wetting solution, following steps 7 and 8.

10 Use a dry gauze pad to blot the skin surrounding the wound. Remove your gloves and dispose of them along with the contaminated gauze and cotton swabs.

11 Apply a fresh pair of sterile gloves and prepare to pack the wound by moistening a gauze pad in the wetting solution. Be certain to wring out the excess moisture because packing that is too wet will not debride the wound effectively. In addition, saturated packing could moisten the outer dressing and draw potentially infectious organisms into the wound.

12 Unfold the moistened gauze pad to expand its surface area into a single layer.

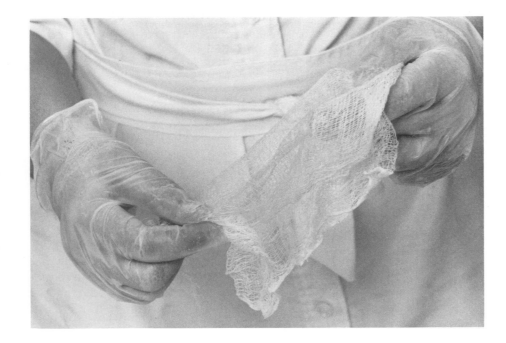

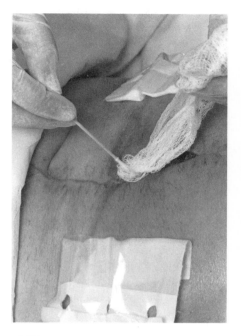

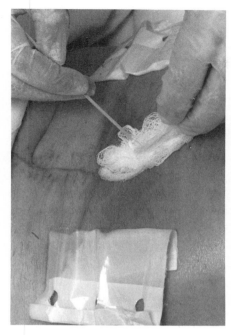

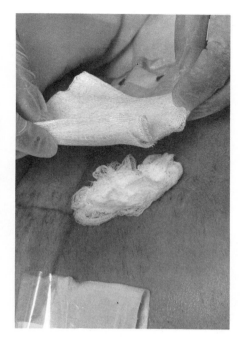

13 Use a cotton swab to place the gauze into the crevices of the wound.

14 Completely fill the wound, adding more gauze as necessary. Pack loosely and do not overpack.

15 Cover the wet gauze with a dry dressing.

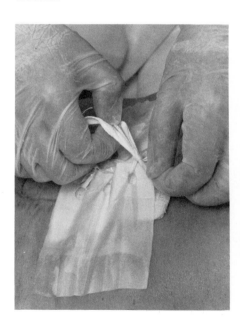

16 Tape the dressing in place. If the wound is on an extremity, wrap the dressing with a strip of gauze roll to secure it. If Montgomery straps are used, change them if they are soiled, and then tie them securely (as shown). If surgical netting is used, roll it back into place. Replace it if it is soiled.

Evaluating

17 Return the client to a position of comfort and assist him with his gown if he is unable to do it himself. Securely tie off the impervious plastic bag, remove it from the bedside, and dispose of it according to agency policy. Then, wash your hands. Finally, record the procedure in your nurse's notes. Document the appearance, size, and odor (if present) of the wound and describe the amount and quality of the drainage. Note the amount and appearance of the granulation tissue as well.

References

Centers for Disease Control: Guideline for isolation precautions in hospitals. In: *Guidelines for Prevention and Control of Nosocomial Infections*. Atlanta, GA: U.S. Department of Health and Human Services, 1983.

Centers for Disease Control: *Guideline for Handwashing and Hospital Environmental Control*. Atlanta, GA: U.S. Department of Health and Human Services, 1985.

Centers for Disease Control: Recommendations for prevention of HIV transmission in health care settings. *MMWR* (Aug 21) 1987; 36(Suppl 2S): 1S–18S.

Jackson MM: Implementing universal body substance precautions. *Occupational Medicine: State of the Art Reviews* 1989; 4(Special issue):39–44.

Jackson MM, Lynch P: An alternative to isolating patients. *Geriatr Nurs* (Nov/Dec) 1987; 7:308–311.

Jackson MM, Lynch PL: Infection prevention and control in the era of the AIDS/HIV epidemic. *Semin Oncol Nurs* 1989; 5(4):236–243.

Jackson MM, McPherson D: Infection control: Keeping current. *Nurse Educator* 1986; 11(4):38–40.

Jackson MM et al: Why not treat all body substances as infectious? *Am J Nurs* 1987; 87(9):1137–1139.

Jagger J et al: Rates of needle-stick injury caused by various devices in a university hospital. *N Engl J Med* (Aug 4) 1988; 319:284–288.

Kozier B et al: *Introduction to Nursing*. Redwood City, CA: Addison-Wesley, 1989.

Larson E: Hand washing: It's essential—even when you use gloves. *Am J Nurs* 1989; 89(7):934–939.

Lynch P, Jackson MM: Infection control: Medical asepsis. In: *Basic Nursing: A Psychophysiologic Approach*, 2d ed. Sorenson KC, Luckmann J (editors). Philadelphia: Saunders, 1986.

Lynch P et al: Rethinking the role of isolation practices in the prevention of nosocomial infections. *Ann Intern Med* 1987; 107(2):243–246.

Smith S, Duell D: *Clinical Nursing Skills*, 2d ed. Norwalk, CT and San Mateo, CA: Appleton & Lange, 1989.

U.S. Department of Health and Human Services, Public Health Service. Update: Universal precautions for prevention of transmission of human immunodeficiency virus, hepatitis B virus, and other bloodborne pathogens in health care settings. *MMWR* (June 24) 1988; 37: 377–388.

Chapter 2

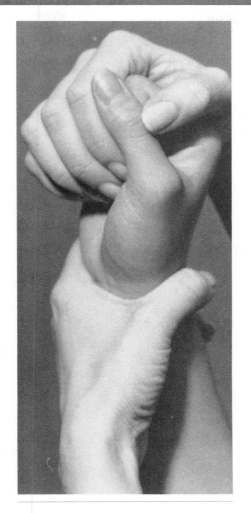

Using Proper Positioning, Mobilization, and Transferring Techniques

CHAPTER OUTLINE

ASSISTING THE CLIENT WITH POSITIONING AND MOBILIZATION

Performing Passive Range of Motion Exercises

   Performing Traditional ROM Exercises
   Performing Proprioceptive Neuromuscular Facilitation Exercises

Nursing Guidelines for Using Pressure-Relief Mattresses and Pads

   Sheepskin
   Eggcrate Mattress
   Flotation Pad
   Air Mattress
   Lapidus Airfloat System

Nursing Guidelines for Proper Client Positioning

   Supine
   Side-Lying
   Prone
   Positioning Aids

Assisting the Client with Crutches, Canes, and Walkers

   Checking the Correct Crutch Height
   Guarding the Client
   Assisting the Client with Crutches to Sit in a Chair

TRANSFERRING MOBILE AND IMMOBILE CLIENTS

Nursing Guidelines for Lifting and Transferring Clients

Moving the Client up in Bed

   Assisting the Mobile Client
   Lifting the Immobile Client

Dangling the Client's Extremities on the Side of the Bed

   Assisting the Mobile Client
   Moving the Immobile Client

Moving the Client from the Stretcher to the Bed

   Teaching the Segmental Transfer Technique
   Transferring the Immobile Client

Logrolling the Immobile Client

Assisting the Client from the Wheelchair (or Chair) to the Bed

Using a Mechanical Lifting Device

Assisting the Client with Positioning and Mobilization

PERFORMING PASSIVE RANGE OF MOTION EXERCISES

To prevent disuse syndrome caused by contractures (the shortening of soft tissues/muscles, ligaments, joint capsules, or fasciae) and ankylosis (the abnormal consolidation of a joint), nurses must ensure that range of motion (ROM) exercises are performed every day for all immobilized clients with *normal* joints. Modification may be necessary if the client has decreased tone (flaccidity), which is seen initially following spinal cord injury or cerebrovascular accident; if ROM is done incorrectly, the potential for subluxation increases. In addition, if the client has increased tone (spasticity), which may develop as the recovery sequence progresses in either of the above disorders, the use of routine exercise positions may actually enhance spasticity. If you lack experience with these disorders, consult with the educational staff, physician, physical therapist, or occupational therapist to assist you in modifying the exercise plan for these clients. ROM is contraindicated during the inflammatory phase of rheumatologic diseases and for joints that are dislocated or fractured. However, after assessment of the client, the need for initiation of ROM is an independent nursing judgment, and it should be incorporated into the daily care plan of the immobilized client. Many of the movement patterns can be performed concurrent with position changes and bed baths. In addition, the principles of ROM can be applied when getting a client on and off the bed pan or while changing the hospital gown.

Before initiating ROM, familiarize yourself with the following terms:

- *Passive Range of Motion:* These exercises are performed by the nurse, therapist, or significant other to help the client maintain full joint movement and to prevent contractures. Because the client's muscles are not used to perform the exercise, muscle strength is neither maintained nor augmented.
- *Active Range of Motion:* These exercises are performed by the client, helping to maintain full joint movement. They also assist in the maintenance of muscle strength.
- *Assisted Range of Motion:* The client moves the part through some portion of the range of motion, with the nurse, therapist, or significant other assisting in completing the movement. The degree of the client's participation in the exercise will determine the degree to which muscle strength will be maintained.
- *Abduction:* Moving a limb away from the body's midline.
- *Adduction:* Moving a limb toward the body's midline.
- *Extension:* Straightening of a bent part (increasing the angle between two bones at a joint).
- *Flexion:* Bending (decreasing the angle of two bones at a joint).
- *Hyperextension:* Moving a body part beyond the plane of the body.
- *Opposition:* Combination of abduction, rotation, and flexion of the thumb so that the tip of the thumb can touch the fingers.
- *Radial Deviation:* Moving the hand toward the radial (thumb) side of the wrist while the hand and forearm stay in the same plane.
- *Ulnar Deviation:* Moving the hand toward the ulnar (fifth-finger) side of the wrist while the hand and forearm stay in the same plane.
- *Rotation:* Turning of a body part on its vertical axis.

PERFORMING TRADITIONAL ROM EXERCISES

The exercises in the following procedures are passive and employed when the client is unable to move the specified body part. Adapt these exercises for situations in which the client has partial body movement and requires assisted ROM. When active ROM is desired, you can teach these exercises to the client. You may also teach these exercises to clients who are capable of exercising their paralyzed sides with the assistance of their stronger sides. Remember to include family members and significant others so that they, too, can help exercise the client.

Before starting the exercises, explain them to the client, and obtain a sheet or bath blanket for warmth and privacy. Remove the pillow to allow full movement of the client's head and shoulders.

Unless it is contraindicated, assist the client into a supine position. Perform the exercises from head to toe, completing them on one side of the body before moving to the other side of the body. Then assist the client into a prone position and perform the exercises that are indicated for that position. Never push a movement beyond the point at which the client complains of discomfort or at which you feel resistance to the movement. If possible, consult with a physical therapist or occupational therapist to assist you with modifying the exercise on a joint in which you have elicited pain, tremors, or spasms. To avoid straining your back, elevate the bed to an optimal working level; move the client to the right side of the bed before exercising the right side of the body (and vice versa). Be sure to allow room at the head of the bed for the neck and arm movements. To assist you with proper hand positioning, we have shown the neutral (start) position for the exercises. For convenience, all the exercises have been demonstrated on the right side of the client's body. Be certain that you practice correct body mechanics when performing all exercises. Repeat each exercise at least three to five times.

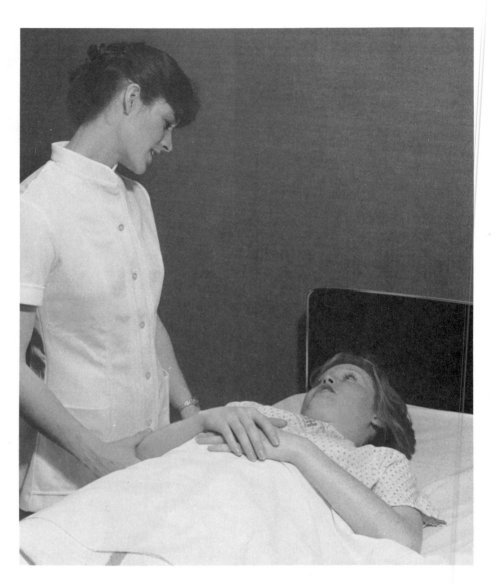

Exercising the Neck

1 To begin the neck exercises, cup the client's chin with your right hand and support the back of the head with your left hand. Be sure to position your right hand high enough on the chin to avoid putting pressure on the trachea during the flexion exercises. *Caution: Do not force any of the neck movements.*

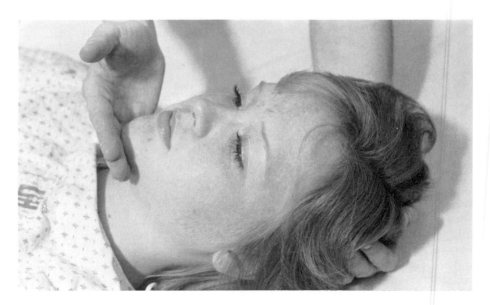

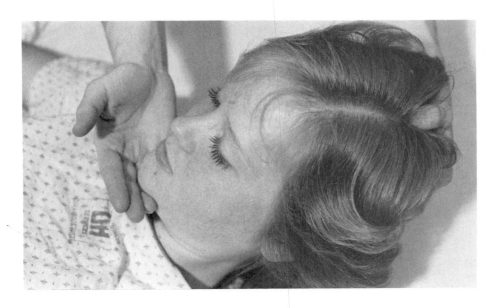

2 To flex the neck, gently tilt the back of the head forward and move the chin toward the chest, touching it if possible.

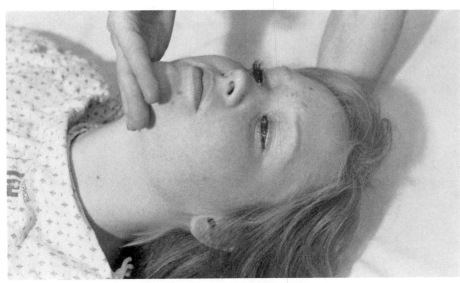

3 Extend the neck by gently tilting the chin upward and moving the head back as far as it will comfortably go without forcing the movement. Return to the neutral position.

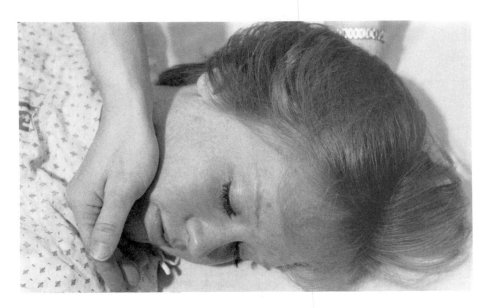

4 To rotate the neck, slowly and gently turn the head to the left (as shown), and touch the left ear to the mattress, if possible. Then rotate the neck to the right in the same manner.

(Continues)

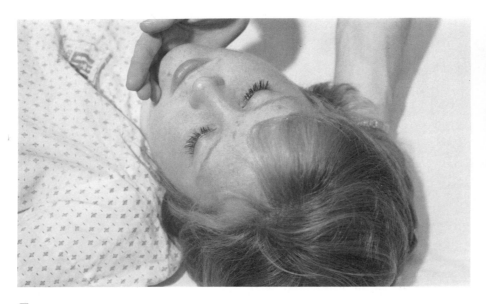

5 To flex the neck laterally, gently guide the ear toward the left shoulder, keeping the client's nose pointing toward the ceiling (as shown); then guide the ear toward the right shoulder.

6 When the client is prone, you may extend the neck by supporting the chin with your right hand and gently pushing back on the forehead with your left hand. Move the back of the head toward the spine as far as it will *comfortably go without forcing the movement.*

Exercising the Shoulders

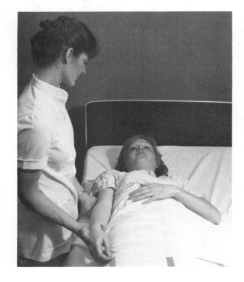

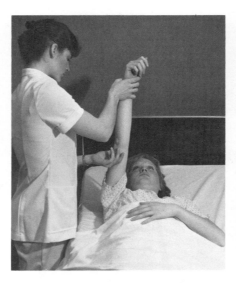

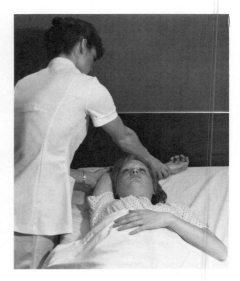

1 To achieve the neutral position for flexing and extending the shoulders, support the elbow with your left hand and the wrist and hand with your right hand. The arm should be in alignment with the body and flat on the bed.

2 As you elevate the arm, maintain the extension of the elbow. Move the arm toward the head of the bed.

3 At the point at which the arm touches the client's ear, allow the elbow to bend so the movement can be completed without hitting the headboard. From this flexed position, return the arm to the neutral position to extend the shoulder and elbow.

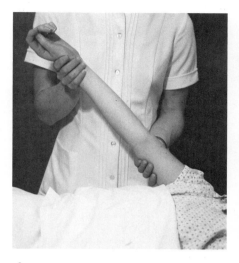

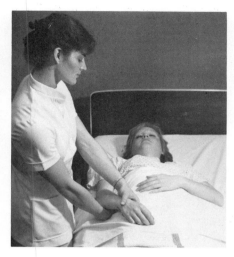

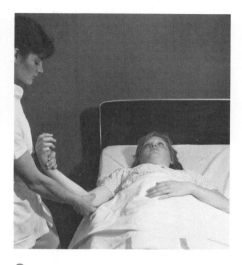

4 When the client is prone, you may extend the shoulder beyond the plane of the body (hyperextension) by supporting the upper arm above the elbow and lifting gently on the forearm.
Caution: Do not force the anterior aspect of the shoulder down into the bed.

5 To achieve the neutral position for shoulder abduction, support the wrist with your left hand and the elbow with your right hand.

6 As you abduct the arm, step back (as shown) and ensure that the humerus remains level with the bed. Note that the humerus must externally rotate as the nurse abducts the arm.

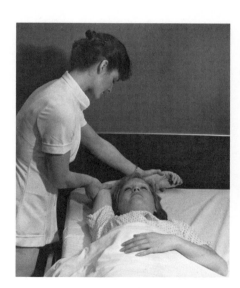

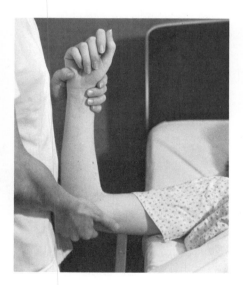

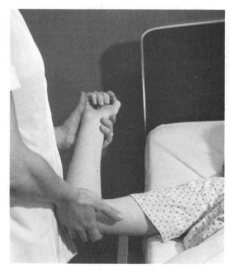

7 To complete the abduction, continue to move the arm laterally until it touches the side of her head. Bend the elbow (as shown) if the headboard prevents abduction with the elbow extended. To adduct the arm, return to the neutral position while maintaining support of the wrist and elbow.

8 To achieve the neutral position for internal and external shoulder rotation, abduct the arm to shoulder level at a 90-degree angle to the body. The humerus should be level with the bed. Flex the elbow to a 90-degree angle to the body. Support the wrist with your left hand and the upper arm with your right hand.

9 To rotate the shoulder externally, gently rotate the arm toward the head of the bed so that the forearm is moving toward the plane of the bed surface. Continue the movement as far as it will comfortably go without raising the client's back from the bed's surface. Return to the neutral position.

(Continues)

10 Internally rotate the shoulder by moving the forearm toward the foot of the bed as far as it will comfortably go (left). *Note: A common mistake with internal rotation is to force the rotation beyond the range of the shoulder joint (right). Notice how the proximal aspect of the humerus moves off its supporting surface.*

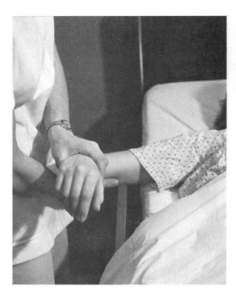 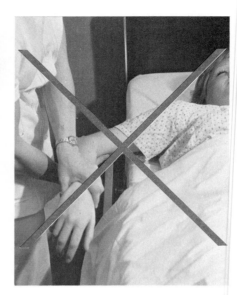

11 To achieve the neutral position for horizontal shoulder adduction, support the upper arm with your left hand and the hand and wrist with your right hand (left). Hold the arm with the elbow flexed at a 45–90-degree angle to the body. Slowly guide the arm across the body toward the left side of the bed (right).

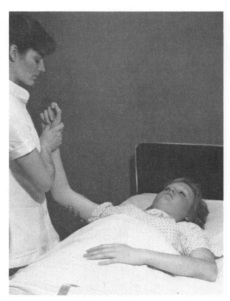 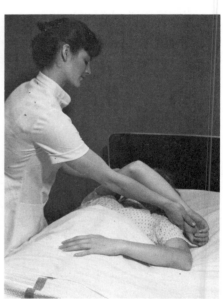

12 To complete the horizontal adduction, move the arm as far across the body as possible. Allow the elbow to extend slightly so that the contact of the hand with the bed does not block the motion of the humerus.

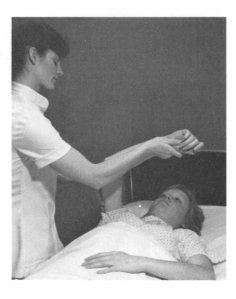

Exercising the Elbows

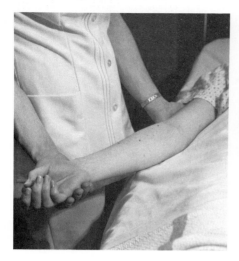 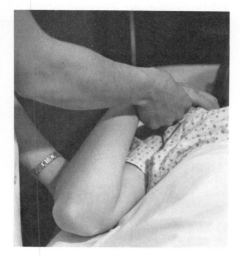 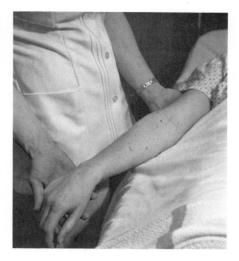

1 To achieve the neutral position for flexing the elbow with the forearm in supination, support the wrist with your right hand and the upper arm with your left hand. The arm should be slightly abducted from the body with the elbow extended and the palm turned up.

2 Guide the palm toward the shoulder. The degree of elbow flexion will be determined by the amount of upper arm musculature. (The greater the musculature, the less the degree of flexion.) Return to the neutral position while maintaining support of the upper arm and wrist.

3 To achieve the neutral position for flexing the elbow with the forearm in pronation, support the wrist with your right hand and the upper arm with your left hand. The arm should be slightly abducted from the body with the elbow extended and the palm turned down.

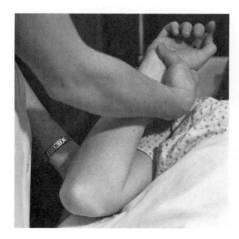

4 Flex the elbow and guide the dorsum of the hand toward the shoulder. Again, the degree of elbow flexion will be determined by the amount of upper arm musculature. Return to the neutral position. Alternating flexion with supination and flexion with pronation allows you to perform the elbow and forearm movements simultaneously.

Exercising the Wrists and Fingers

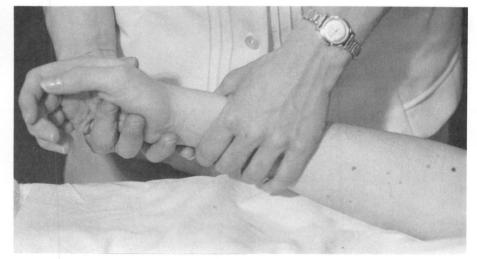

1 To achieve the neutral position for wrist flexion and extension, support the forearm proximal to the wrist with your left hand. Support the hand distal to the wrist with your right hand.

(Continues)

2   To flex the wrist (palmar-flexion), gently push down on the dorsum of the hand.

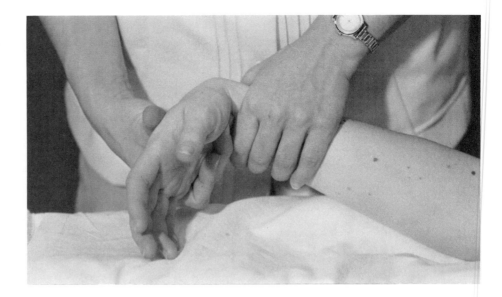

3   Extend the wrist (dorsiflexion) by gently pushing up on the palmar surface of the hand.

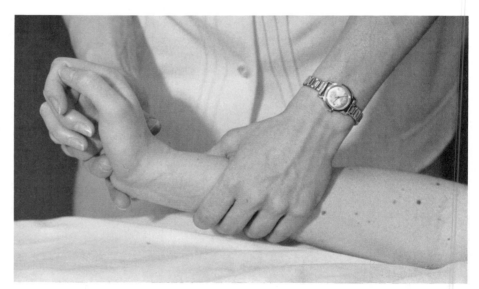

4   To achieve the neutral position for radial and ulnar deviation, support the hand with your right hand and the wrist with your left hand. The hand and wrist should be in the same plane.

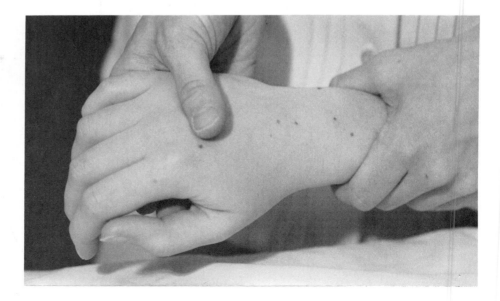

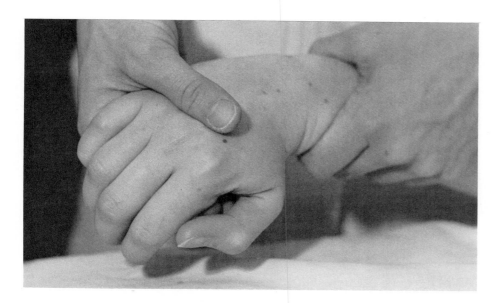

5 For radial deviation, gently guide the thumb side of the hand toward the wrist.

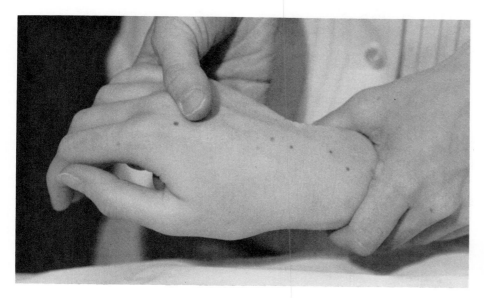

6 Gently guide the fifth-finger side of the hand toward the wrist for ulnar deviation.

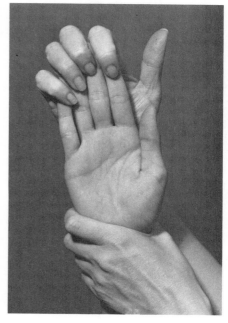

7 Extend the fingers by gently straightening them with your right hand while you support the wrist with your left hand. Do not pull the fingers beyond the plane of the hand.

(Continues)

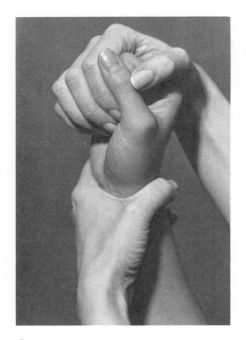

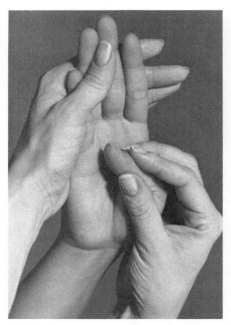

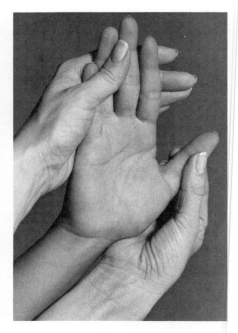

8 Flex the fingers by gently curling them with your fingers.

9 With the fingers extended, oppose the thumb to the base of the fifth finger.

10 Extend the thumb.

Exercising the Hips and Knees

1 To achieve the neutral position for hip and knee flexion and extension, place your left hand under the knee and your right hand under the ankle (as shown). Lift the leg so that it bends at the hip and knee, and move the thigh as close to the trunk as possible (bottom). To avoid blocking the flexion at the knee, place your left hand on top of the knee as you complete the movement.

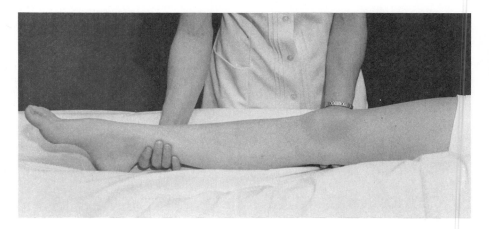

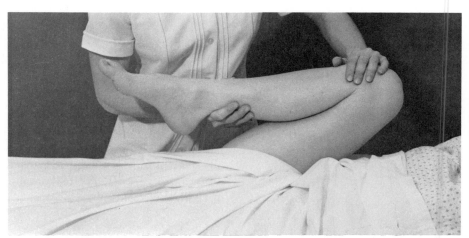

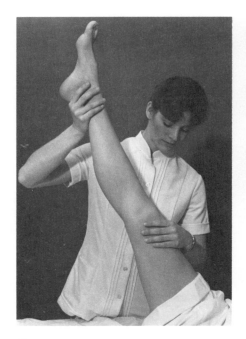

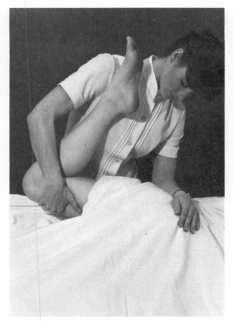

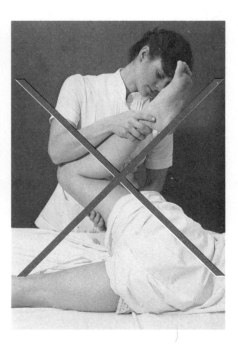

2   To flex the hip with the knee extended, return to the neutral position. Then gently lift up on the ankle with your right hand while keeping the knee straight with your left hand. You have reached the client's full range when you feel the knee begin to bend or when the client complains of a pulling sensation in the back of the knee.

3   When the client is prone, you may extend the hip while flexing the knee. To do this, stabilize the pelvis with your left hand and support the anterior thigh with your right hand. Lift gently on the anterior thigh, no more than 7.5–12.5 cm (3–5 in.), depending on the client's range.

Note: This photo depicts incorrect hip extension. The movement is occurring in the lumbar joints because the nurse is lifting the thigh too high.

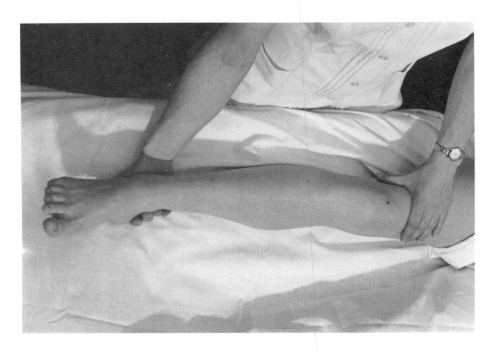

4   To achieve the neutral position for internal and external rotation of the hip with the hip and knee extended, support the ankle with your right hand and place your left hand proximal to the knee. The knee should point toward the ceiling.

(Continues)

5 To rotate the hip internally, gently turn the leg toward the midline of the client's body.

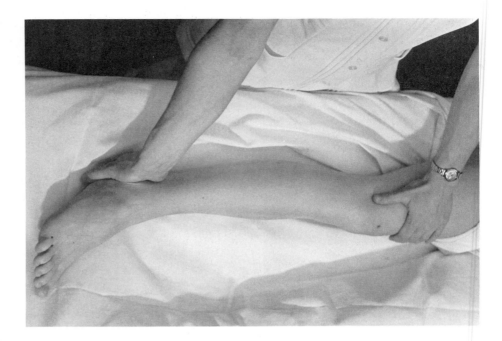

6 Turn the leg toward yourself (laterally) for external rotation.

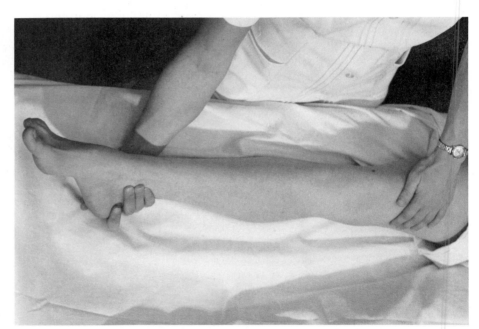

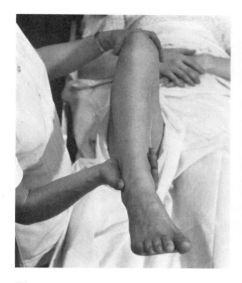

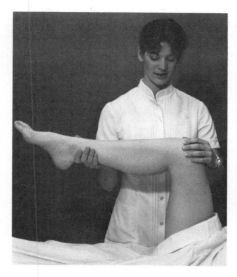

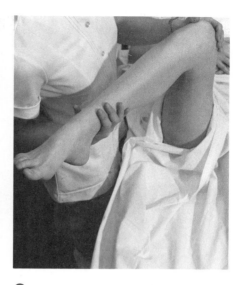

7 This photo depicts the neutral position for internal and external rotation of the hip with the hip and knee flexed. Position the femur at a 90-degree angle to

the body (see above), and flex the knee at a 90-degree angle to the femur. Place your left hand on the knee, and support the ankle with your right hand.

8 To rotate the hip externally, gently guide the client's foot toward yourself. Remember to keep the knee and dorsum of the foot pointing toward the ceiling to ensure that you do not change the vertical position of the femur.

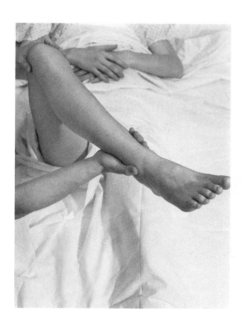

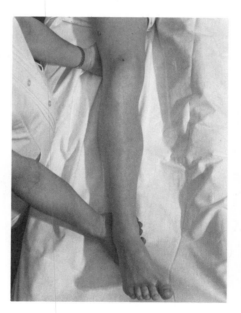

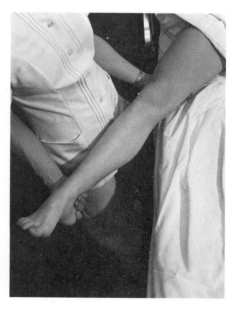

9 To rotate the hip internally, guide the foot toward the client's midline.

10 This photo depicts the neutral position for hip abduction and adduction. Position your left hand under the knee and your right hand under the ankle.

11 To abduct the hip, simultaneously move the leg off the bed as you step back with your right foot and pivot onto your left foot. Keep the client's toes and knee pointing toward the ceiling as you move the leg. Then, adduct the hip by returning the leg to the midline.

Exercising the Ankles and Toes

1 To achieve the neutral position for ankle dorsiflexion, place your left hand under the knee and cradle the foot with your right hand and forearm.

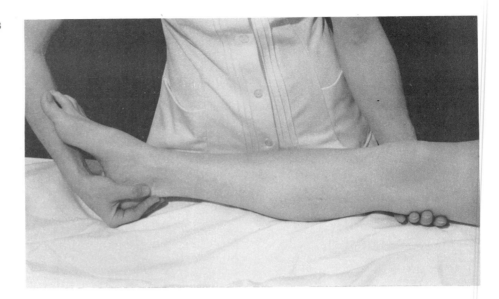

2 To dorsiflex the ankle, shift your weight onto your left leg and push against the ball of the client's foot with your right forearm. As you do this, pull the heel in the opposite direction with your right hand.

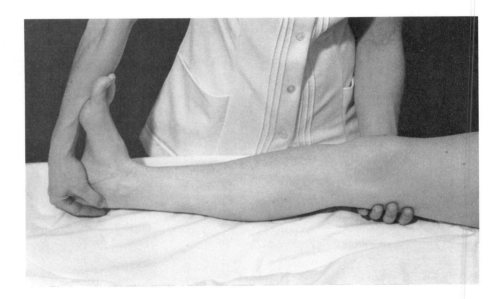

3 It is seldom necessary to plantarflex the ankles because in bed, feet posture naturally in this position. However, if the client can pull the toes up but cannot push them down, you must also plantarflex the ankles. To do this, cradle the heel with your right hand and press gently on the dorsum of the foot with your right hand.

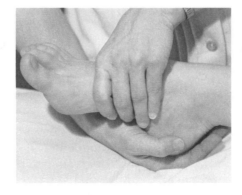

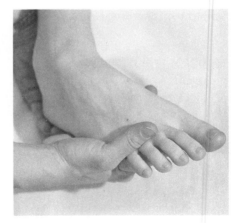

4 To invert the ankle, turn the client's foot toward the midline without changing the position of the heel.

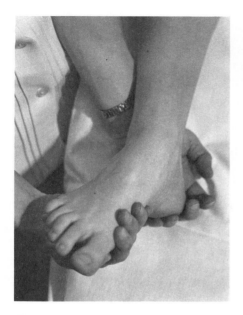

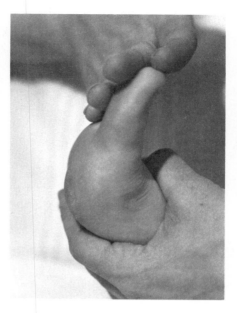

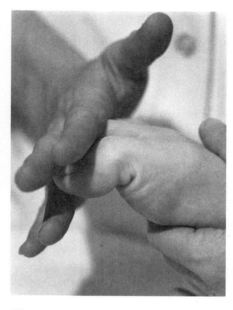

5 Evert the ankle by turning the foot laterally toward yourself. Normally, your client will have more range with inversion than with eversion.

6 To extend the toes, support the forefoot with your left hand and gently guide the toes toward the dorsum of the foot with your right hand.

7 Flex the toes by bending them toward the sole of the foot with your opened fingers.

PERFORMING PROPRIOCEPTIVE NEUROMUSCULAR FACILITATION EXERCISES

The movement patterns described below provide an alternative to the traditional passive ROM exercises. Their advantage over the latter is that they combine movements at several joints simultaneously, thereby reducing the amount of time necessary to complete the series. To achieve this end, each exercise is performed on the diagonal. For example, one movement pattern (diagonal) for the upper extremities combines components of flexion, abduction, and external rotation of the shoulder. To help you understand both the movement components occurring at each joint and the correct hand positioning for the involved joints, review the steps for the traditional ROM exercises (see pages 31–45). Consult with your agency's educational staff or occupational or physical therapist for added information if these exercises are new to you.

Explain the exercises to your client, and provide a drape for warmth and privacy. Elevate the bed to an optimal working level, remove the pillow (if your client can tolerate it), and position her so that she is flat on her back. If you will exercise her right side first, move her to the right side of the bed. Never push the movement beyond the client's range; and modify the exercise on a joint in which you elicit pain, spasms, or tremors. Remember to use proper body mechanics. Repeat each movement three to five times.

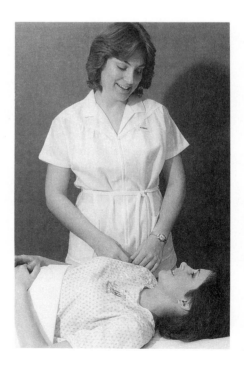

(Continues)

Exercising the Neck

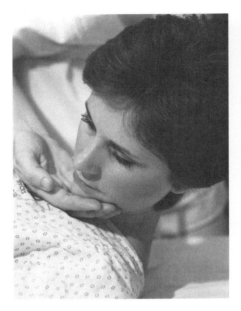

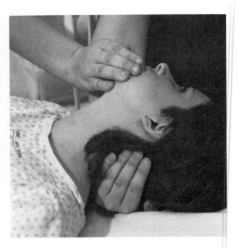

1 For the first diagonal movement, position the client's head so that her neck is flexed and rotated to the left as if she were looking down at her left elbow.

2 Extend the neck while you rotate it to the right so that she is looking up and over her right shoulder. The second diagonal is the direct opposite of the first. Position the client so that the neck is flexed and rotated to the right as if she were looking at her right elbow. Extend her neck while rotating it to the left so that she is looking up and over her left shoulder.

Exercising the Upper Extremities

1 To perform the Diagonal-One (D-1) movements, start with the arm extended, abducted, and internally rotated at the shoulder so that the client's thumb points toward the floor. If you are exercising the right upper extremity, your right hand will guide the movement of the client's hand while your left hand will support and guide the movement of the humerus.

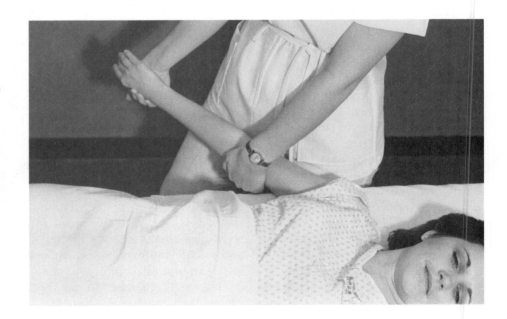

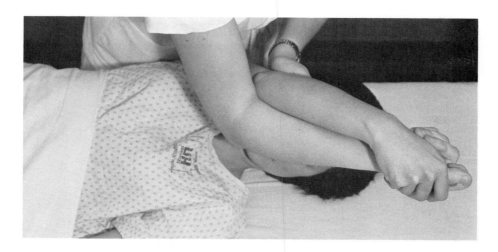

2 Move the arm diagonally up and across her nose as if she were reaching for the opposite corner of the bed. This movement results in shoulder flexion, adduction, and external rotation with the elbow extended.

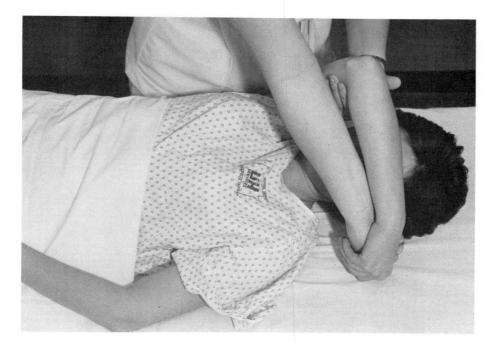

3 Return to the start position for D-1, and perform the same shoulder movements, but allow the elbow to flex as the shoulder flexes.

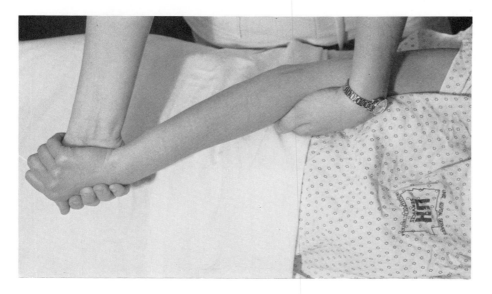

4 For Diagonal-Two (D-2) movements, start with the arm extended, adducted, and internally rotated at the shoulder. The client's thumb should be resting against her left anterior iliac crest.

(Continues)

5   Lift the arm up and across the client's body so that her hand points toward the opposite corner of the room and the thumb points downward. This completed diagonal flexes, abducts, and externally rotates the shoulder with the elbow extended.

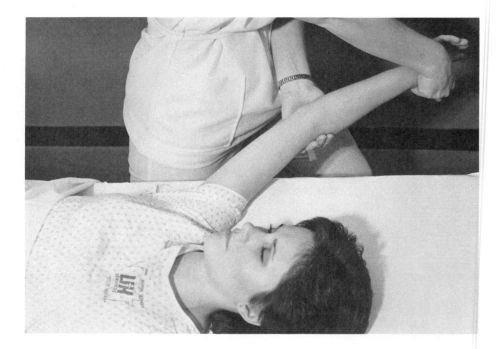

6   Return to the start position for D-2 and perform the same shoulder movements, but this time allow the elbow to flex as you flex the shoulder.

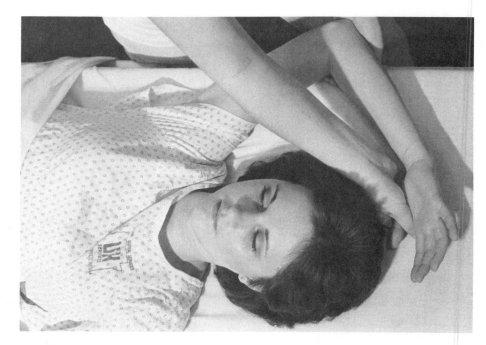

Exercising the Lower Extremities

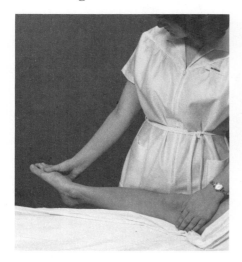

1 To perform D-1 movements, start with the hip extended, abducted, and internally rotated. The knee should be extended and the ankle plantarflexed (as shown). Your right hand will support and guide the movement of the lower leg while your left hand will guide the movement of the thigh.

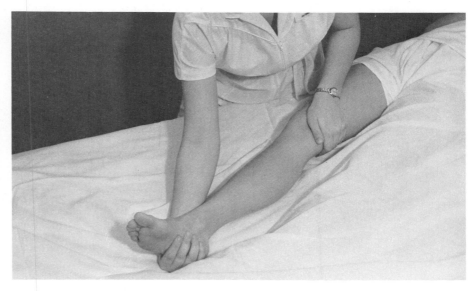

3 For D-2 movements, start with the client's hip extended, adducted, and externally rotated with the knee extended and the foot plantarflexed.

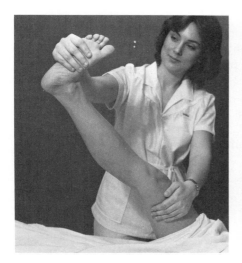

2 Lift up on the leg and move it along the diagonal into a position of hip flexion, adduction, and external rotation with the ankle moving into dorsiflexion and inversion. The completed diagonal is similar to a soccer kick in which the ball is kicked with the inner aspect of the foot. Return to the start position.

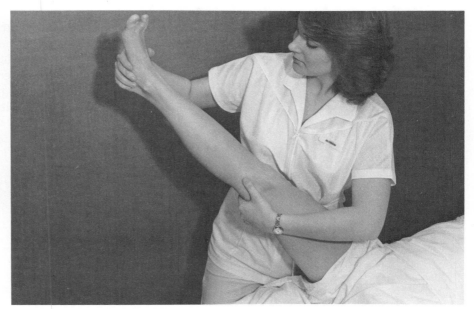

4 Move into a position in which the client's hip is flexed, abducted, and internally rotated with the knee extended and the foot moving into dorsiflexion. This diagonal can be compared to kicking a ball with the outer aspect of the foot. Return to the start position. Now assist the client to the left side of the bed and perform the exercises on her left side. *Note: Knee flexion also can be performed along with the hip flexion patterns, or it can be done separately.*

Nursing Guidelines for Using Pressure-Relief Mattresses and Pads

SHEEPSKIN

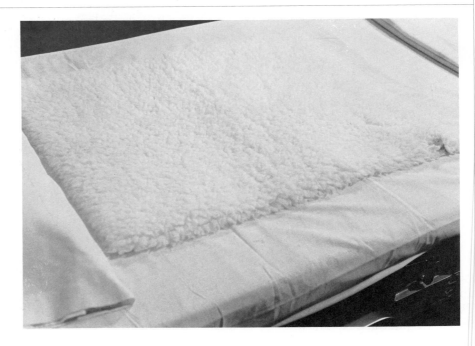

Use

The cushionlike fibers pad the body to distribute the pressure around the bony prominences and minimize the potential for skin breakdown. The sheepskin also improves air circulation and enhances the drying of perspiration to prevent skin maceration, potentially caused by continued exposure to moisture.

Nursing Considerations

- Change the pad whenever it becomes wet or soiled. Larger pads are impractical for the incontinent client. For incontinent clients, consider the use of smaller pads placed under heels or shoulders.
- Because the client buys the sheepskin, make sure it is properly labeled prior to each laundering.
- Pads made from synthetic fabrics launder better than natural sheepskin.
- Place the pad on top of the bottom sheet so that it has immediate contact with the client's skin.

EGGCRATE MATTRESS

Use

The corrugated surface minimizes the pressure points under the bony prominences. In addition, it promotes better air circulation to help prevent skin breakdown.

Nursing Considerations

- To keep the bottom sheet taut and wrinkle-free, knot each corner (see below).
- If the client is diaphoretic, consider using a thin bath blanket rather than a bottom sheet.
- If the mattress becomes soiled, wash the soiled area with soap and water. Let it dry thoroughly before replacing it on the client's bed.

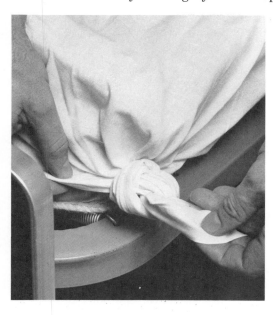

(Continues)

FLOTATION PAD

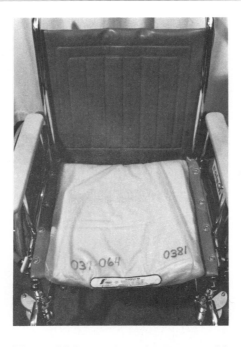

Use

The gel-like inner substance molds to the client's body to help minimize pressure over the bony prominences. The smaller pad (as shown) fits in a chair or wheelchair.

Nursing Considerations

- Keep pins, needles, and other sharp objects away from the pad.
- Cover the pad with nothing thicker than a sheet or pillow case so that you do not diminish its effectiveness.
- The pad's plastic outer surface may promote increased perspiration that could lead to skin maceration. Inspect the client's skin frequently.

AIR MATTRESS

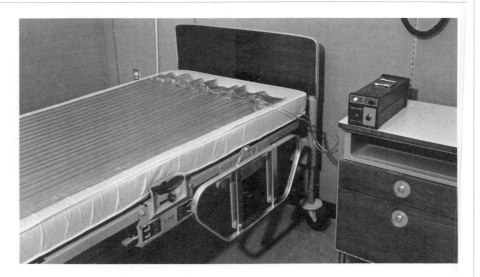

Use

The air in the mattress displaces the client's weight and minimizes pressure over the bony prominences.

Nursing Considerations

- To ensure adequate mattress inflation, indent the plastic surface with your fingertip. Adjust the pressure if you can indent more or less than 1.25 cm ($\frac{1}{2}$ in.). Remember that underinflation can promote hip flexion contractures and protraction of the shoulder girdle, and overinflation may cause pressure to the bony prominences.
- To prevent damage to the mattress, keep needles, pins, and other sharp objects away from its surface.
- The noise of the machine may become a sensory problem, especially for neurologic clients.
- Unless the manufacturer provides a sponge pad for covering the mattress, keep only a bottom sheet or a thin bath blanket between the client and the mattress.
- Keep the electrical cord out of the path of the client and agency personnel.
- Some units provide alternating pressure, which also enhances peripheral circulation while relieving pressure.
- Even though immobilized clients on these mattresses may require fewer position changes, it is important that ROM exercises are continued to prevent contractures and ankylosis.
- Assess the client's skin for increased perspiration and potential maceration caused by the plastic surface of the mattress.

LAPIDUS AIRFLOAT SYSTEM

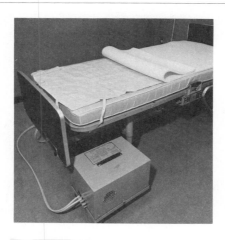

Use

This mattress changes its pressure points over the body every 15 seconds, aerates the skin through tiny air holes in the mattress, and rapidly circulates air in a wavelike fashion. These features prevent decubiti; absorb perspiration, thereby preventing skin maceration; and stimulate peripheral circulation.

Nursing Considerations

- Always use the system with its 2.5 cm (1 in.) foam pad that absorbs moisture. The foam pad dries spontaneously by means of the circulating air flow underneath it.
- A 50 × 50 cm (20 × 20 in.) pad can connect to the same power supply for use on a wheelchair or chair.
- Keep the power box and electric cord out of the path of the client and agency personnel.

Nursing Guidelines for Proper Client Positioning

In addition to ROM exercises, meticulous skin care, and frequent turning, the immobilized client also requires carefully planned positioning to prevent the complications of prolonged bed rest. Proper positioning will minimize pressure to the bony prominences, maintain correct body alignment to reduce stress and strain to the joints, ensure maximal chest expansion for proper breathing, and prevent the formation of contractures.

For most clients a good rule for positioning in bed is to try to achieve the proper standing alignment. The head should be neutral or slightly flexed on the neck, the hips extended, the knees extended or minimally flexed, and the feet at 90-degree angles to the legs. If pillows are unavailable for maintaining your client's position, consider substituting blankets, towels, or spreads. Review the following general procedures to assist you in positioning immobile clients.

SUPINE

Lower Body

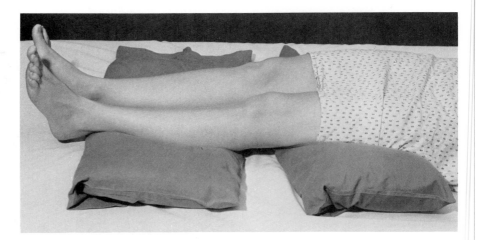

- To take pressure off the lower back, slightly flex the client's hips by placing a thin pillow under the thighs. The pillow should not extend into the popliteal area, nor should it be placed directly under the knees because it could occlude the popliteal arteries.
- To prevent hip flexion contractures, ensure that the client is side-lying or prone with the hips extended for the approximate amount of time she is supine.
- Placing a pillow under the thighs is contraindicated for clients with inflammatory joint diseases because they have a tendency to posture in flexion due to pain. It is important that you attempt to maintain their hips and knees in extension with every position change.
- Place a thin pillow under the client's ankles and lower legs to keep the heels off the bed's surface, thereby preventing pressure. As an alternative, use sheepskin or heal protectors; or, if possible, use a pressure-relief mattress or pad.

Upper Body

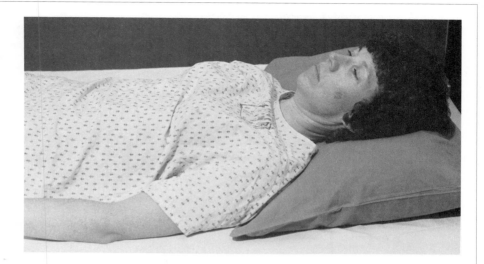

Unless a flat position is required (for example, for neck pain or neck injury), support the client's head and shoulders with a small pillow or foam wedge so that the head is neutral or slightly flexed on the neck.

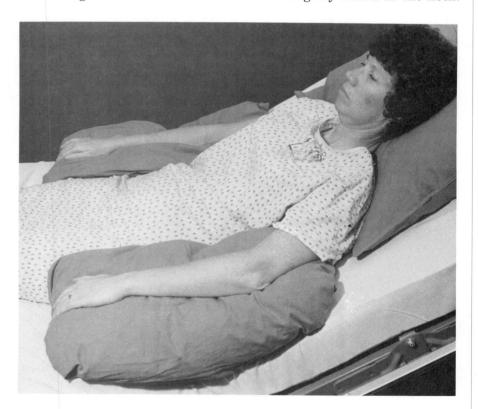

Semi-Fowler's Position (30-Degree Head Elevation) When the head must be elevated, extend the shoulders and support the arms on each side of the body with pillows. Allow the fingertips to extend over the edges of the pillows to maintain the normal arching of the hands. Because this position places the client in hip flexion, ensure that alternate positions, with the client's hips in extension, are also used.

(Continues)

SIDE-LYING

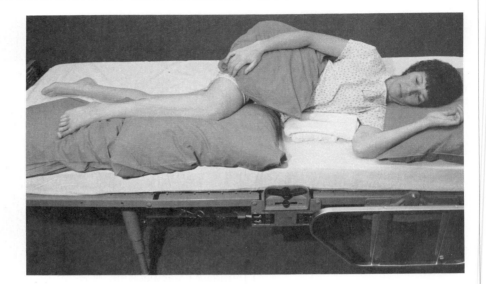

- Ensure that the client's spinal column is in straight alignment from the head to the coccyx.
- Place a pillow under the head to maintain its normal alignment with the body. The pillow should be just thick enough to accommodate the space between the bed and the head.
- For curvaceous clients, a pad positioned between the iliac crest and the axilla will help to maintain proper spine alignment. It should be thick enough to prevent the vertebral column from sagging into the bed and wide enough so that the pressure it may potentially produce in the soft tissues can be evenly distributed over the entire rib cage.
- Place a pillow under the upper arm to prevent shoulder adduction and internal rotation. To ensure optimal chest expansion for proper breathing, the weight of the upper arm and pillow should be centered over the pelvis rather than over the rib cage.
- The upper leg should be flexed at the hip and knee and supported by a thick pillow to prevent both internal rotation and adduction of the hip and pressure to the patella. Ensure that the thigh is well supported and that the pillow does not touch the lower leg.
- If necessary, place a second pillow under the upper foot to prevent its inversion and to maintain its alignment with the rest of the leg. This is an optimal time to position the lower leg in extension from the hip. You may slightly flex the knee for the client's comfort.
- It may be necessary to support the client's position by placing a pillow behind the back.

PRONE

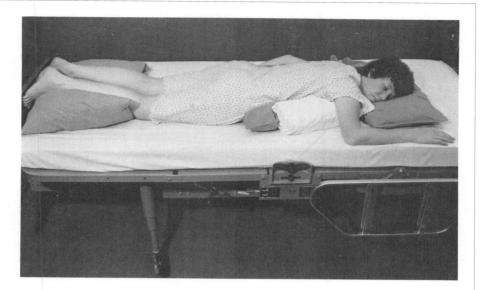

Caution: *This position is contraindicated for clients with tracheostomies, cervical injuries, or breathing difficulties.*

- Turn the client's head to the side and place a flat pillow under the head and shoulders to prevent hyperextension of the neck.
- Place thin pads under the angles of the axillae and the lateral aspects of the clavicles. This will prevent internal rotation of the shoulders, maintain the anatomic position of the shoulder girdle, and promote optimal chest expansion for breathing.
- Position one arm so that it is flexed at the shoulder and elbow and the other arm so that it is extended from the shoulder with the palm flat on the bed. Periodically reposition the arms to prevent joint stiffness.
- Place a flat pillow (the darker pillow in the photo) under the waistline so that it cushions the anterior superior iliac spines and prevents pressure to the area. It will also minimize strain to the lower back, promote chest expansion, allow room for breast tissue, and prevent a lordotic posture (swayback).
- To flex the knees minimally, position a thin pillow under the lower legs. This will minimize pressure to the patellae and keep the toes off the mattress as well. Be certain that the toes clear the pillow.
- To prevent plantarflexion and hip rotation and to prevent injury to the toes and heels, move the client to the end of the bed to allow her feet to recline between the edge of the mattress and the footboard. Position the feet so that they are as close to a 90-degree angle from the legs as possible.

(Continues)

POSITIONING AIDS

Trochanter Rolls

To prevent abduction and external rotation of the hip, position the client on a large towel or bath blanket that has been folded so that it extends from the client's waist to the midthigh (photo at left). The material should drape equally on either side of the body. Turn the fabric as the nurse is doing in the photo at right so that the roll is undermost.

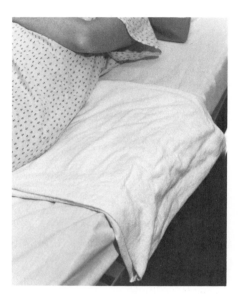
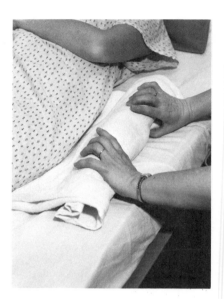

Tuck the roll tightly against the client's hips, and do the same on the opposite side. Ensure that the lower legs and feet internally rotate toward the client's midline.

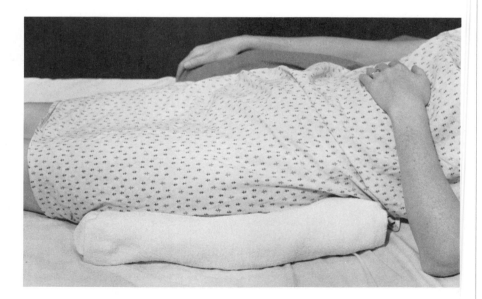

Sand Bags

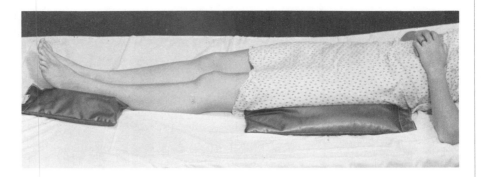

Sand bags are positioning aids that prevent abduction and external rotation of the hips. Although smaller clients might be properly supported by placing only the larger sand bags at the hip area, bigger or more flaccid clients requiring added support will benefit from two sets of sand bags (as shown). Place the larger bags from the waist to the midthighs and the smaller bags along the lower legs. The bags are positioned correctly if the legs and feet are rotated internally toward the midline. For client comfort, wrap the sand bags with pillow cases or towels.

Foot Supports

Caution: Foot supports might be contraindicated for clients who are hypertonic (spastic), for example those with head injuries, multiple sclerosis, or in the spastic recovery phase of a cerebrovascular accident. Experts contend that the contact of the foot's surface on the board may actually trigger spasticity and hence reinforce plantarflexion.

Your spastic clients might benefit instead from foot cradles, which keep bed linen off their feet, or from more frequent ROM exercises. Another option is to cut off a pair of high-top tennis shoes so that each shoe ends just proximal to the head of the client's metatarsals. These shoes will maintain dorsiflexion, yet prevent contact of the balls of the feet with a hard surface. However, clients without spasticity usually are helped with foot supports, such as the device in the photo. This foot support not only prevents plantarflexion, but prevents external rotation of the hips as well. Pad these devices with fleece, a blanket, or a towel to prevent the formation of decubiti on the soles of the feet.

(Continues)

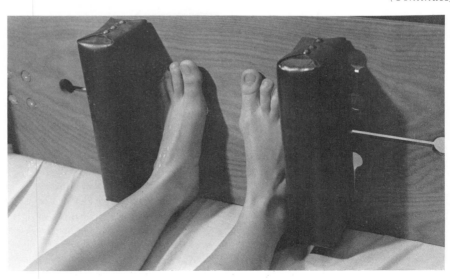

Hand Rolls

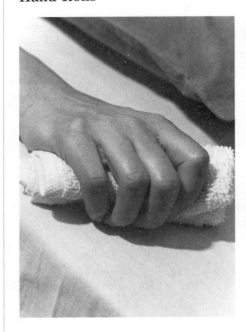 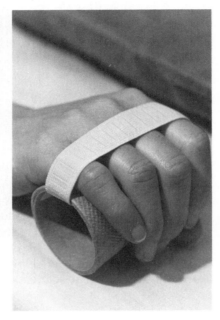

Hypotonic (flaccid) clients (for example, those with spinal cord injuries) may benefit from positioning devices such as a rolled washcloth (left) placed within their grasp. This will place the hand, wrist, and fingers in a position that maintains a functional grasp. The thumb is positioned so that it opposes the tip of the index finger. Spastic clients, on the other hand, may require the firm surface of a splint or a cone (right). The hard surface of these devices presses on the muscles to inhibit spasticity. In addition, the elastic band that secures the cone to the hand stimulates the extensor muscles, thus encouraging finger extension.

ASSISTING THE CLIENT WITH CRUTCHES, CANES, AND WALKERS

CHECKING FOR CORRECT CRUTCH HEIGHT

Before assisting your client with crutch walking, it is important to ensure that the crutches are the correct height. With the client's elbows flexed 20–30 degrees, the shoulders in a relaxed position, and the crutches placed approximately 15 cm (6 in.) anterolateral from the toes, you should be able to place two fingers comfortably between the axillae and the axillary bars (as shown). Adjust the crutches if you find either too much or too little space at the axillary area. Advise the client never to rest the axillae on the axillary bars because this could injure the brachial plexus (the nerves in the axillae that supply the arm and shoulder area). Terminate ambulation and recheck the crutch height if the client complains of numbness or tingling in the hands or arms.

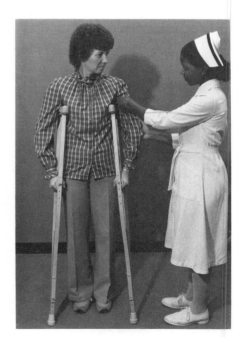

GUARDING THE CLIENT

Caution: For your client's safety, always inspect the rubber tips of the assistive device to make sure they are not worn; also ensure that the client wears appropriate shoes with nonslip soles.

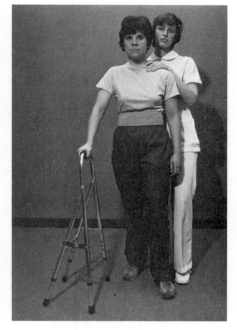

Canes: If your client is walking with a cane, stand at the affected side and guard her by grasping the security belt and positioning your free hand at the shoulder area. This is the same stance used in crutch walking. Remind the client to place the cane on the unaffected side so that the cane and the weaker leg can work together with each step. The top of the cane should reach the level of the greater trochanter of the client's femur.

Hemi or Quad Canes: Hemi canes are used for clients who have the use of only one upper extremity, and they give more security than a quad cane (below) can provide. Both canes give the client greater stability than a single-tipped cane. Either is positioned at the client's unaffected side, with the straight, nonangled side adjacent to the body. The canes should be positioned approximately 15 cm (6 in.) from the client's side, with the hand grips level with the greater trochanter of the femur. Guard the client as you would if she were using a single-tipped cane.

Crutches: When walking with clients who are using crutches, stand on the affected side and grasp the security belt in the midspine area at the small of the back (top). Position your free hand at the shoulder area so that you can pull the client toward you in the event that there is a forward fall. Make sure, however, that you do not obstruct the movement of the humerus. Instruct the client to look up and outward toward the destination rather than at her feet.

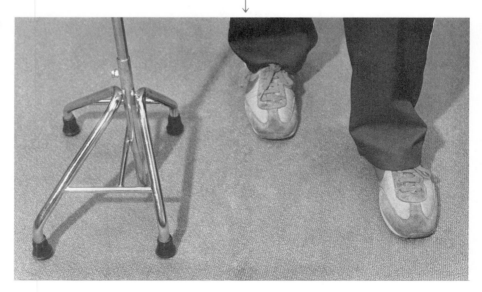

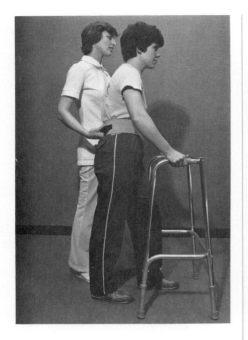

ASSISTING THE CLIENT WITH CRUTCHES TO SIT IN A CHAIR

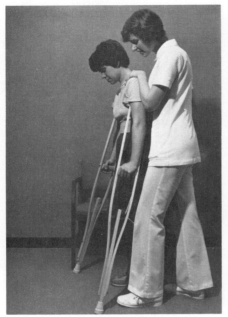

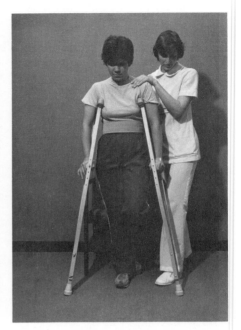

Walkers: If your client is using a walker, guard her as you would a client using a cane or crutches, and stand adjacent to her affected side. Instruct the client to put all four points of the walker flat on the floor before putting weight on the hand pieces. This will prevent stress cracks in the walker and help ensure the client's safety. Instruct her to move the walker forward and walk into it and then repeat the movement.

1 Before the client sits in a chair, you must first secure the chair by bracing it against a wall. Then instruct her to walk toward the chair and when she reaches it to begin her turn (as shown) so that ultimately the chair will be directly behind her.

2 She should place her unaffected leg against the front of the chair.

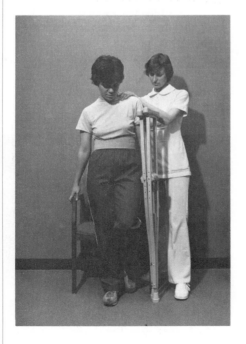

3 Instruct the client to move the crutches to her affected side and to grasp the chair's arm with the hand on the unaffected side.

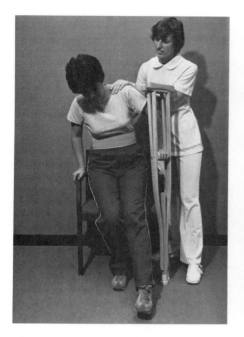

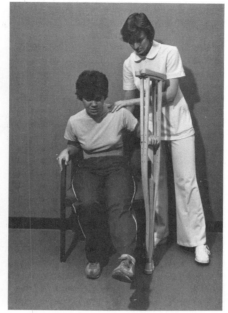

4 Tell her to flex the knee of her unaffected leg to lower herself into the chair. Advise the client to place her affected leg straight out in front of her to ensure that it remains nonweight bearing, if this is appropriate.

5 Once she has been seated, she should slide back into the chair so that she is in a good sitting posture. Place a support under the foot if the knee must remain extended while the client is sitting. Reverse these steps to assist her to stand from a sitting position.

Transferring Mobile and Immobile Clients

Nursing Guidelines for Lifting and Transferring Clients

- To promote your clients' independence and to help maintain their muscular strength, always encourage them to move themselves or to participate in the move as much as possible.
- Whenever possible, use mechanical lifting devices to transfer immobile clients, especially those who are obese.
- Always adjust the height of the bed to a level that enables you to maintain a vertical back while lifting and transferring.
- To avoid bending your back or stretching across the bed, position the client as close to you as possible.
- Instead of using the muscles in your upper body for lifting, flex your knees and use your larger leg and hip muscles; straighten your knees as you lift.
- Before initiating a lift or transfer, spread your feet apart to provide a wide base of support. One foot should be positioned slightly in front of the other.
- As you move the client from one position to another, shift your weight in the direction of the move.

MOVING THE CLIENT UP IN BED

ASSISTING THE MOBILE CLIENT

If your client is strong enough to lift up with her arms and push down on her feet, teach her how to move herself up in the bed. This is important because it will promote independence, help to maintain her physical strength, and minimize the strain on your own back as well.

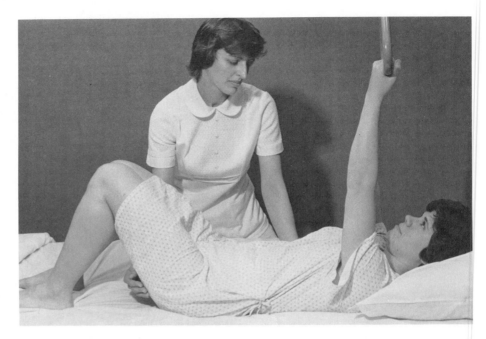

1   Flatten the bed, and adjust its height to an optimal working level. Instruct the client to bend her knees and to reach up and grasp the trapeze. (In most agencies, it is not necessary to obtain an order for a trapeze for the adult client.) Place your right hand under her buttocks so that you can guide her during the move.

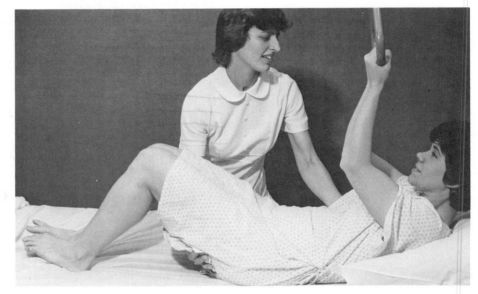

2   Instruct her to push down on her feet and to lift her upper body with her arms. As you guide her, face the direction of the move; shift your weight to the leg that is closer to the head of the bed.

LIFTING THE IMMOBILE CLIENT

1 If your client is immobile, ask one or more helpers to assist you with the lift. Position her on a draw sheet that extends from her head to her midthighs. Cross her arms across her chest to prevent them from dragging across the bed; then roll the draw sheet close to her body. With two movers, each would stand on opposite sides of the bed and grasp the sheet at the head and buttocks area. With three movers (as shown) the nurses on the same side will cross their adjacent arms to distribute the client's weight more evenly between them.

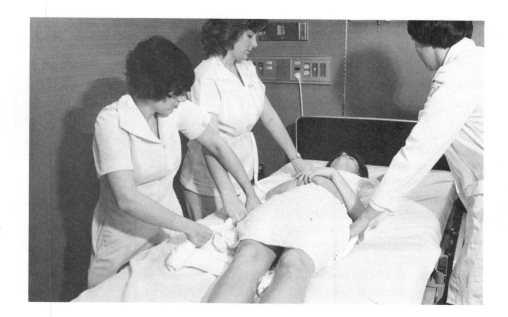

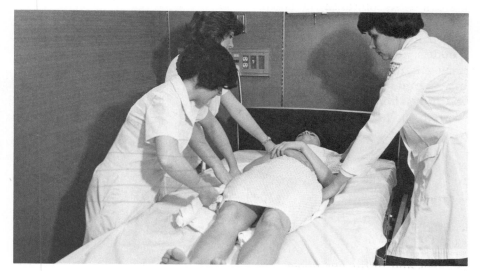

2 On a predetermined signal, shift your weight back and away from the client as if you were pulling the sheet apart. In this way, the taut sheet will elevate the client just enough to make the move to the head of the bed easier. To avoid injuring your back, it is important that you keep the natural curve in your back and avoid extending it as you pull back. As soon as the client has been elevated, shift your weight to the foot closer to the head of the bed and move the client forward.

Note: When the movers are of different heights, all will not be at an optimal working height with the bed.

DANGLING THE CLIENT'S EXTREMITIES ON THE SIDE OF THE BED

ASSISTING THE MOBILE CLIENT

1   On the day of surgery, most clients are required to sit on the side of the bed and dangle their legs before getting out of bed. If your client has mobility, encourage her to do most of the moving and lifting with your assistance. Explain the procedure to her and raise the height of the bed to a comfortable working level. The procedure described next will be performed in stages to protect the client's back, minimize the strain to an abdominal or perineal incision, and exercise her upper extremities. With the client flat on her back, place a hand on her far hip to guide her. Explain that she should roll toward you next (bottom).

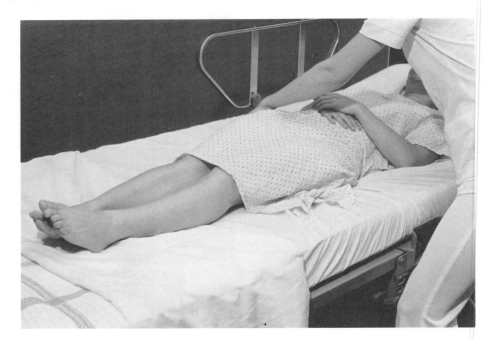

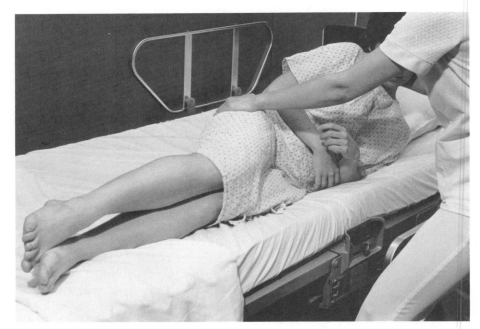

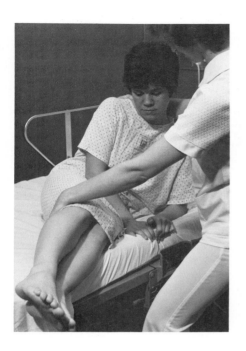

2 Once she is on her side, instruct her to flex her knees slightly and slide her legs off the side of the bed as she pushes up with her arms. You may assist her by guiding her legs and supporting her shoulders.

3 Support her at the edge of the bed until she feels comfortable and stable. Once she is secure, lower the bed so that her feet can dangle on the floor, or put a foot stool under her feet.

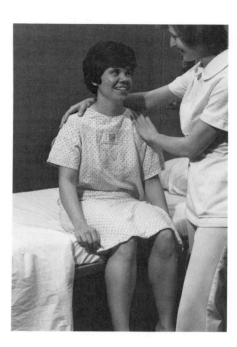

MOVING THE IMMOBILE CLIENT

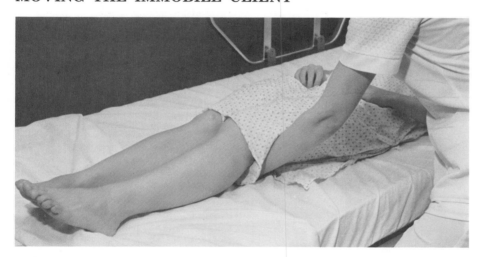

1 To dangle the extremities of the immobile client, you will need to do most of the lifting and moving yourself. Explain the procedure to the client and ask her to assist you as much as possible. Raise the bed to a comfortable working level, and place your hand under her knees so that you can flex them and lift her feet off the bed (bottom).

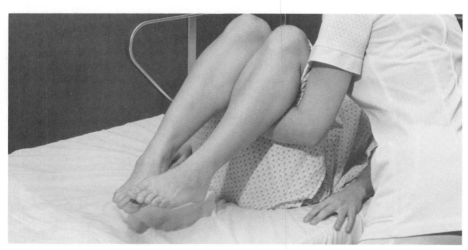

(Continues)

2 Place your right arm around her shoulders and pivot her upper body up and around as you lower her legs over the side of the bed. For your own stability and safety, place your feet apart and pivot your weight from your right foot to your left foot as you lower her legs over the side. *Note: As an alternative, you can raise the head of the bed 90 degrees and pivot the client to the side of the bed, using the same hand positioning depicted in this photo.* Because she may experience dizziness for a while, continue to support her until she is stable enough for you to rest her feet on a foot stool or to lower the bed for her feet to rest on the floor.

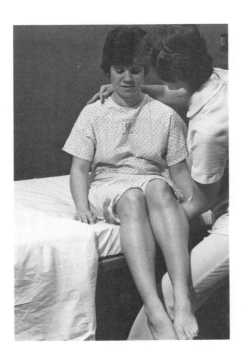

MOVING THE CLIENT FROM THE STRETCHER TO THE BED

TEACHING THE SEGMENTAL TRANSFER TECHNIQUE

1 If your client can assist in the transfer, you can instruct her to move onto the bed from the stretcher by employing the segmental transfer technique. Before she begins the move, ensure that both the bed and the stretcher are locked in place to prevent them from separating during the move; adjust the bed to a height as close to that of the stretcher as possible. Explain to the client that she will move her head, trunk, and feet in stages.

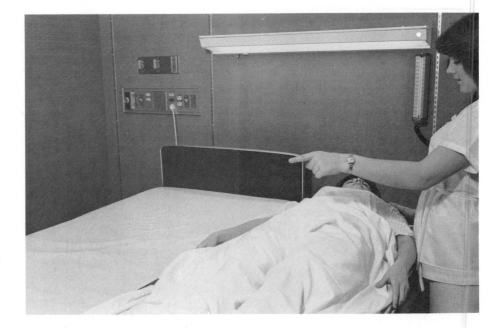

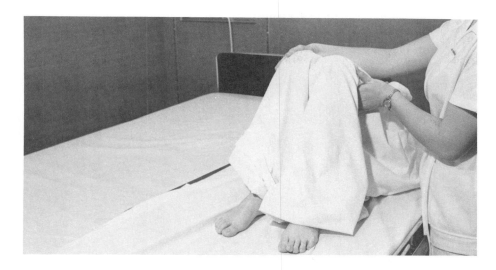

2 Ask her to flex her hips and knees so that her feet are flat on the stretcher.

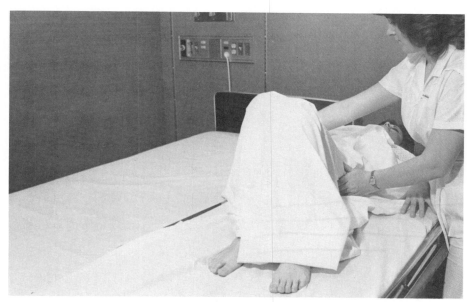

3 She should press down on her feet and slide her trunk, her buttocks, and then her head over to the side of the stretcher.

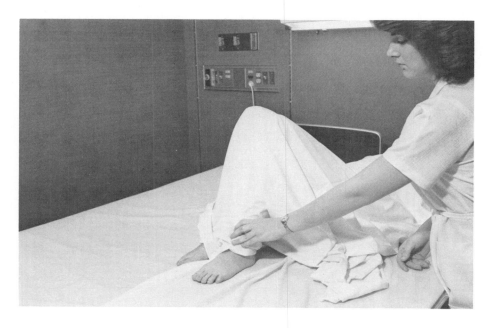

4 Instruct her to lift her feet and move them to the edge of the stretcher.

(Continues)

5 She should move her trunk and then her head as close to the edge of the stretcher as possible.

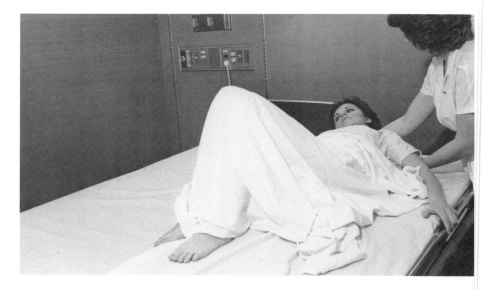

6 Tell her to place her feet on the side of the bed.

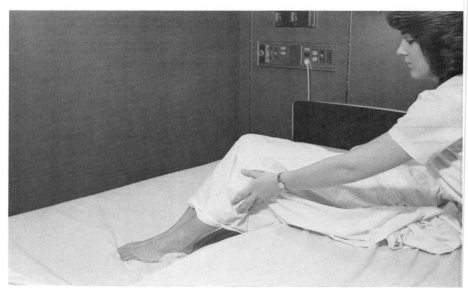

7 Instruct her to make a bridge with her trunk by lifting her pelvis off the stretcher.

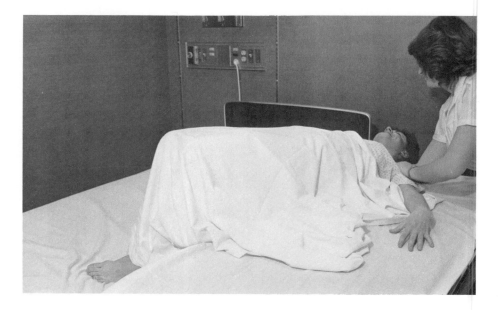

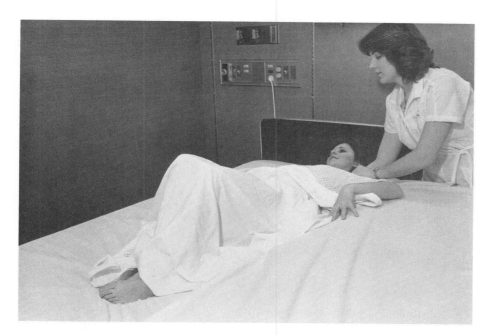

8 She will then move her pelvis and trunk onto the bed.

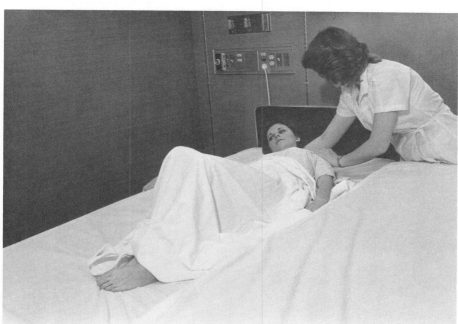

9 While her knees are still flexed, instruct her to press down on her feet to move her trunk and then her head to the center of the bed.

TRANSFERRING THE IMMOBILE CLIENT

1 If your client is immobile, seek the assistance of one or more helpers to transfer her from the stretcher to the bed. When three persons perform the move, two of the three movers should be on the side to which the client will be transferred (as shown). Explain the procedure to the client and then raise the bed to a height as close to that of the stretcher as possible and position her on a draw sheet that extends from the head to the midthighs. Lock the bed and stretcher in place to prevent their separation during the move. It is important to be close to the client during the lift, so the nurses who will do the initial lifting should get up onto the bed. (Nurses with slip-on shoes can remove them prior to getting up onto the bed. A towel or bed-saver pad can be placed under oxford-type shoes.) Roll the draw sheet close to the client's body, and cross her arms over her chest to prevent them from dragging on the bed during the transfer.

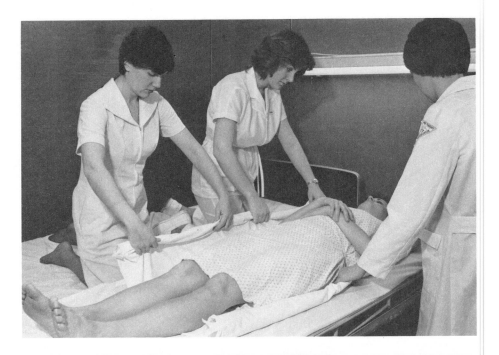

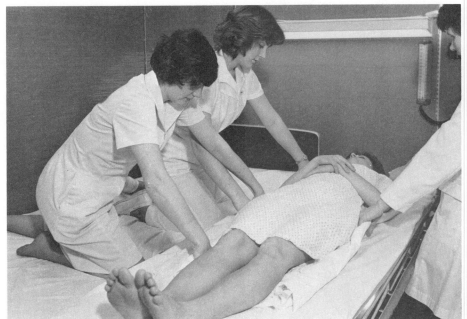

2 In preparation for lifting the client to the edge of the stretcher, the nurses on the bed will each place one knee behind the other to establish a wide base of support. They then cross their adjacent arms to distribute the client's weight evenly between them. The helper adjacent to the stretcher grasps the draw sheet, placing one hand at the level of the client's pelvis and the other hand at the level of the shoulder girdle.

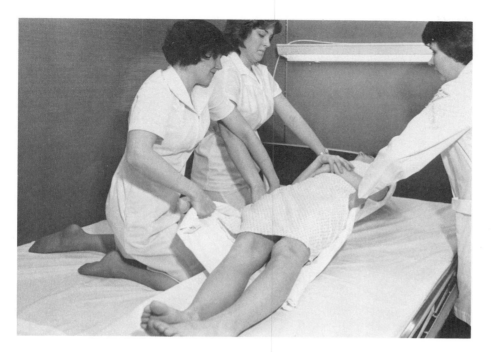

3 On a preestablished signal, the nurses on the bed will elevate and move the client by pulling back on the sheet. At the same time, the helper adjacent to the stretcher maintains tension on the sheet and follows the movement of the client by shifting her weight onto her forward leg. Note that as the client is moved to the edge of the stretcher, she is lifted only high enough to clear it.

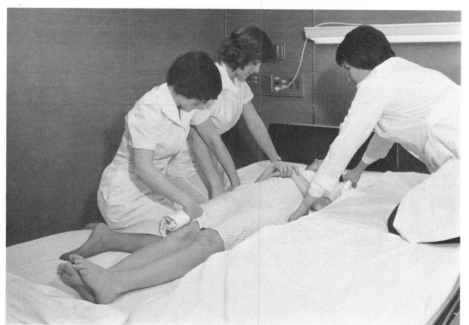

4 As the client is moved from the edge of the stretcher to the bed, the helper adjacent to the stretcher gets up onto its surface so that she can be as close to the client as possible, and the nurses on the bed move back toward the bed's edge. The client is then moved onto the bed using the same procedure that was employed to transfer her to the edge of the stretcher.

(Continues)

5 Remove the stretcher and move the client from the edge of the bed to the center of the bed following the same technique.

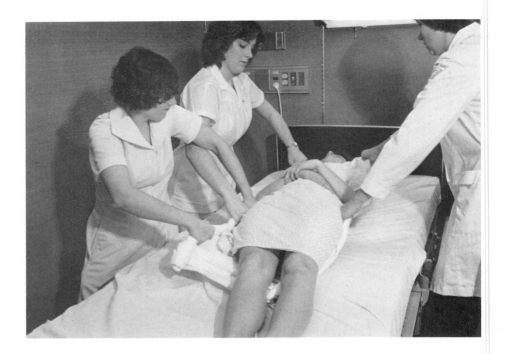

LOGROLLING THE IMMOBILE CLIENT

1 If your client has a neck injury or a spinal disorder, it will be necessary for you to logroll her when you change her position so that you maintain the alignment of her vertebral column during the turn. Logrolling is also indicated for clients with hip pinnings or hip prostheses to keep the hips in extension. Seek the assistance of a helper (find a third person if the client's head and neck require support), and explain the procedure to your client. Raise the bed to an optimal working level, and using a draw sheet, move the client to the edge of the bed opposite the side toward which she will be turned. (Review the steps in the preceding procedure.)

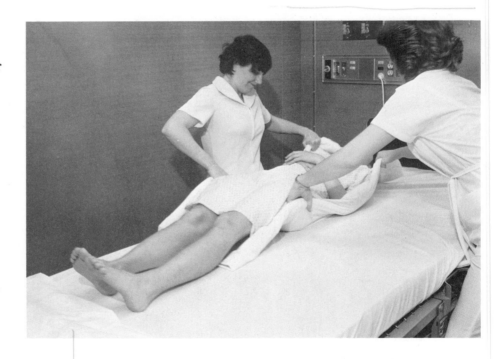

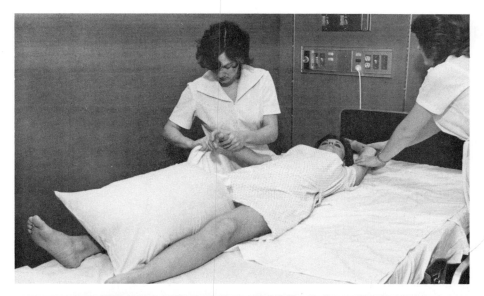

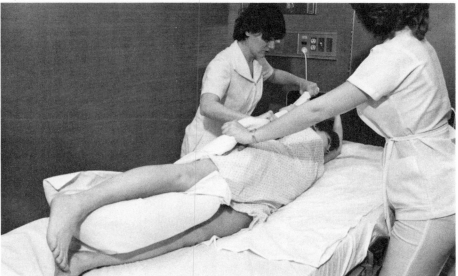

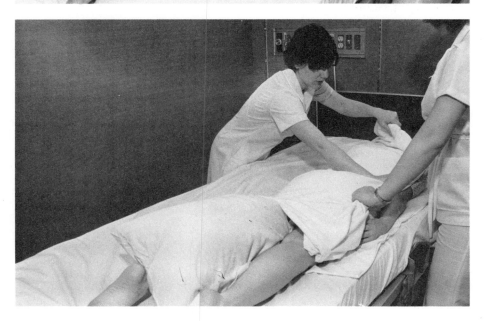

2 Straighten the draw sheet on the side to which the client will be turned, and place a pillow between her legs to maintain the position of the lower extremities. To roll the client toward the left side of the bed, you should first place her right arm beside her body; then flex her left arm over her head so that she will not roll over it during the turn. However, if your client has limited shoulder movement, keep the arm in extension next to the body. *Caution: If your client has a neck injury, you will need a second helper at this point to support the neck during the turn.*

3 The nurse on the left side of the bed will flex her knees, maintain a wide base of support with her feet, and then grasp and lift up on the rolled draw sheet to guide the client toward herself. The nurse on the right side of the bed will maintain tension on the sheet to ensure the client's proper alignment. Note that the nurses' hands are alternated on the sheet to distribute the client's weight evenly. Either support the client in a side-lying position (see steps, p. 56) or continue to the prone position (as shown in step 4).

4 Continue the turn with the nurse on the right side of the bed guiding the client onto her abdomen. Place the client in a proper prone position (see steps, p. 57).

ASSISTING THE CLIENT FROM THE WHEELCHAIR (OR CHAIR) TO THE BED

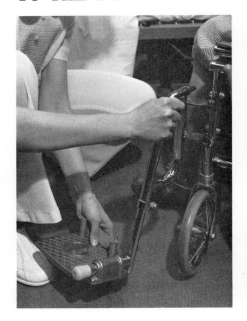

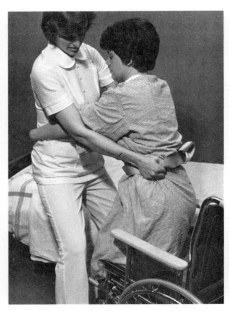

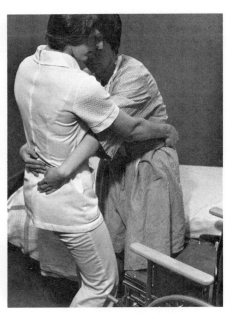

1 Clients who have enough mobility to help support themselves during the transfer may be assisted from the wheelchair or chair to the bed with the standing-pivot technique. Position the wheelchair at a 45-degree angle to the bed and lock both the wheelchair and the bed to ensure their stability. If the client will be transferred from a chair, make sure it is stable and will not slide on the floor. It is important either to remove the wheelchair's leg rests or to swing them out of the way so that they will not obstruct the move. Explain the procedure to the client and ensure that she understands each step and her role during the transfer. Encourage her to assume as much of the lifting and weight bearing as she can comfortably handle, using her stronger leg, if this is appropriate. Before starting, however, you must ensure that her transfer belt is fastened securely around her waist.

2 Flex your knees and position your feet into a wide base of support with one foot slightly in front of the other. Grasp the client's transfer belt, and instruct her to position her arms around your waist. On the cue to stand, the client will prepare to stand on her stronger leg as you assist her into the standing position by pulling her trunk forward and up. As you pull her forward, transfer your weight from your forward leg to your back leg.

3 To ensure the stability of your client's stronger leg, position the side of your knee against the side of her knee to maintain it in extension. Pivot the client and guide her until the backs of her legs are positioned against the bed. Keep your knees flexed and your back straight.

4 Assist the client in lowering herself to the sitting position by using a slow bending of your knees to control the rate of descent.

5 Support her until she is stable and comfortable. Then remove the transfer belt and robe and assist her into bed. Reverse the procedure to move her from the bed to the chair.

USING A MECHANICAL LIFTING DEVICE

Mechanical lifts, such as the Hoyer, are excellent devices for lifting and transferring the immobile client. They are, however, contraindicated for clients with certain types of spinal disorders that require the vertebral column to be maintained in static alignment.

1 Be sure to read the operating instructions for the mechanical lifting device your agency employs. Be certain that the client's weight does not exceed the device's weight limit. Although it is possible to use the lift alone, a helper will both facilitate the process and ensure the client's safety by guarding him during the lifting procedure. First, explain the procedure to the client and assure him that he will be safe and comfortable during the transfer. Then, adjust the bed to a comfortable working height and roll the client into a side-lying position. Place the canvas sling along the client's body, extending it from his head to no farther than the popliteal fossa of his knees. While your helper supports the client's position, fan-fold (accordian-pleat) the sling.

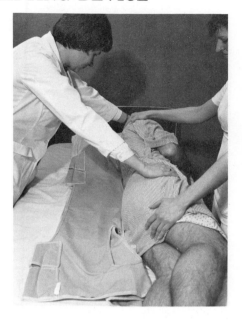

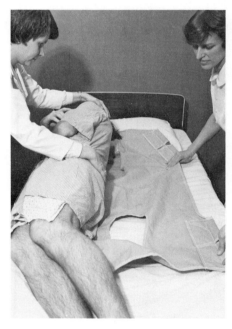

2 Roll the client to his opposite side and straighten the sling.

(Continues)

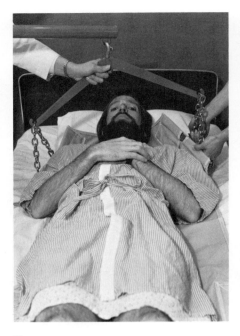

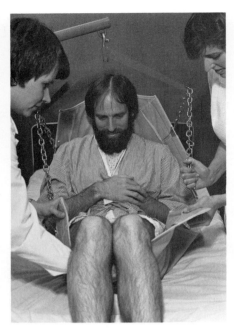

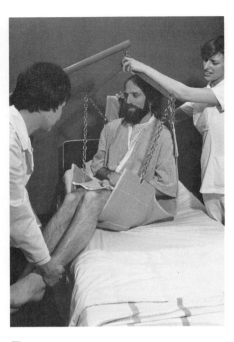

3 Return the client to his back, and cross his arms across his chest. Move the lift to the side of the bed. Center the boom over the sling so that the chains can be attached to its upper section.

4 Elevate the boom slightly so that the chains can be attached to the lower section of the sling. While one nurse attaches the chains, the other should support and flex the client's knees. Ensure that the client's weight is evenly distributed in the sling.

5 Either elevate the lift slightly, or lower the bed just enough so that you can clear the client of the bed and guide his legs over the side.

6 Move the client and the lift away from the bed and push a wheelchair or other transfer device under the client. Lock the wheelchair and then lower the lift so that the client is seated securely in the wheelchair. Protect his head as the boom is being lowered. Instruct the client to keep his arms folded during the transfer. This keeps the device balanced and prevents the client's arms from striking against the chair.

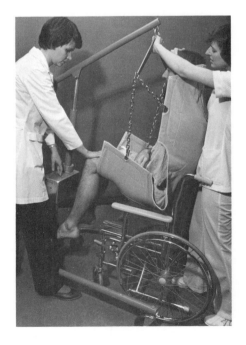

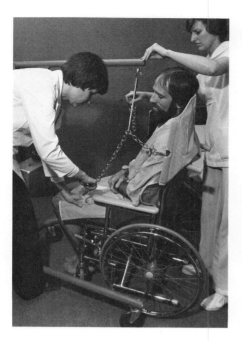

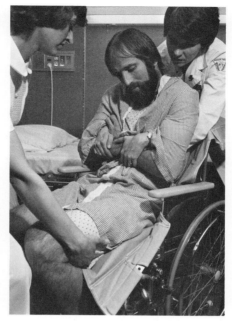

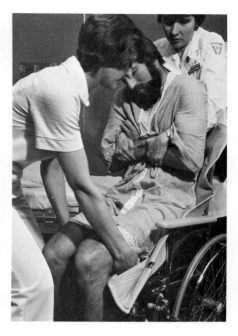

7 Unhook the chains, and either remove the sling if the client will be in the chair for an extended period of time or adjust it to remove the wrinkles. Place a security belt around the client's pelvis to ensure his stability in the chair.

8 If your client slides down in his chair and is sitting on his sacrum, it will be necessary for you to lift him up so that he is positioned correctly. To do this, first cross his arms across his chest. Then, while one nurse stabilizes his legs and feet and prepares to push his pelvis back into the chair, the other stands behind the chair and positions her arms under the client's axillae and grasps his forearms. By grasping the crossed forearms rather than under the axillae, you will avoid the application of a force that could potentially separate the humerus from the glenoid fossa.

9 On a predetermined signal, the person behind the wheelchair will pull the client back and up in the chair while the nurse in front pushes his legs toward the back of the wheelchair to slide his pelvis into the correct position.

References

Baas L, Ross D: Caring for patients on prolonged bedrest. In: *Manual of Nursing Therapeutics: Applying Nursing Diagnoses to Nursing Disorders*, 2d ed. Swearingen PL (editor). St. Louis: Mosby, 1990.

Cuzzell JZ, Willey T: Pressure relief perennials. *Am J Nurs* 1987; 87(9): 1157–1160.

Farber SD: *Neurorehabilitation: A Multisensory Approach*. Philadelphia: Saunders, 1982.

Kisner C, Colby LA: *Therapeutic Exercise: Foundations and Techniques*. Philadelphia: FA Davis, 1985.

Kozier B, Erb G: *Techniques in Clinical Nursing*, 3d ed. Redwood City, CA: Addison-Wesley, 1989.

Potter P, Perry AG: *Fundamentals of Nursing: Concepts, Process, and Practice*, 2d ed. St. Louis: Mosby, 1989.

Rantz MF, Courtial D: *Lifting, Moving, and Transferring Patients*, 2d ed. St. Louis: Mosby, 1981.

Sullivan PE, Markos PD: *Clinical Procedures in Therapeutic Exercise*. Norwalk, CT and Los Altos, CA: Appleton & Lange, 1987.

Voss DE et al: *Proprioceptive Neuromuscular Facilitation*, 3d ed. Philadelphia: Harper and Row, 1985.

Chapter 3

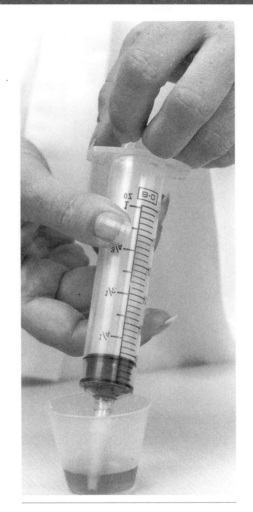

Administering Medications and Monitoring Fluids

CHAPTER OUTLINE

Administering Topical Medications

GIVING OPHTHALMIC MEDICATIONS

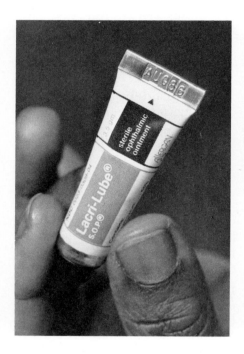

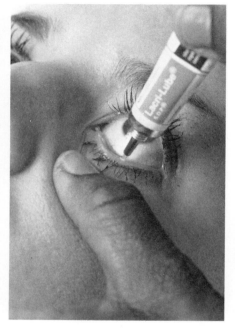

canthus and extend the medication outward toward the outer canthus. Generally, a 1–2 cm strip is adequate. If a small dose of medication has been prescribed, squeeze a small strip of ointment into the center of the sac.

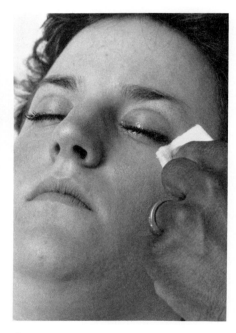

INSTILLING OINTMENT

1   Before instilling anything into the eye, ensure that the medication is a sterile ophthalmic solution and that the date for usage has not expired. Because sight is so valuable and the tissues are delicate, wash your hands thoroughly and use aseptic technique when you instill anything into the eye, even though the eye itself is not sterile.

2   With the client either sitting or lying flat, the head should be tilted back slightly. If secretions adhere to the lashes or corners of the eye, remove them with a sterile 2 × 2 gauze pad or a sterile cotton ball, wiping from the inner to the outer canthus. Instruct the client to look upward as you instill the medication. This will minimize the chance of stimulating the corneal reflex, which could potentially cause the client to jerk and injure the eye. Expose the lower conjunctival sac by exerting gentle traction on the area that is just distal to the center of the lower lashes. This will form a pocket into which you will instill the ointment. With your dominant hand, gently squeeze a strip of medication along the conjunctival border. Start at the inner

3   Release the lower lid and ask the client to close her eyelids and move her eye around gently to distribute the ointment. Remove the excess ointment by wiping gently across the lashes from the inner to the outer canthus with a sterile cotton ball or soft gauze pad.

INSTILLING EAR DROPS

INSTILLING DROPS

Review the preceding technique for instilling ointment. Follow the same guidelines, but dropper the medication into the center of the conjunctival sac (as shown). After administering the medication, instruct the client to close her eyelid and move her eye around to distribute the medication. At the same time, apply gentle pressure to the inner canthus for 30 seconds to 1 minute to minimize the potential for systemic absorption through the tear ducts.

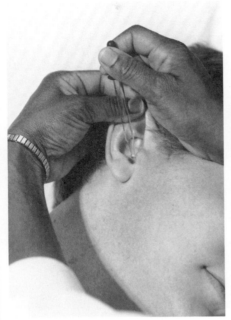

1   Wash your hands. For your client's comfort, make sure the medication has been warmed to body temperature; then fill the dropper with the prescribed amount of medication. Ask your client to turn his head to the side so that the affected ear is uppermost. With your nondominant hand, pull up and back on the auricle to straighten the auditory canal. For an infant, pull down and back on the earlobe instead. Rest the wrist of your dominant hand on the client's head. This will allow your hand to move with the client rather than potentially injure the ear with the dropper, should he jerk during the instillation. Administer the medication, aiming it toward the wall of the canal rather than directly onto the eardrum. This will make the instillation less startling and hence more comfortable and safe for the client.

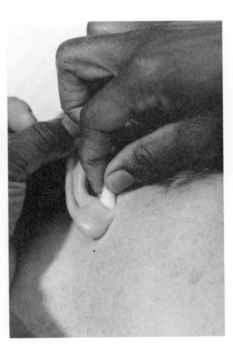

2   Unless the physician requests that the solution drain freely from the ear, you may insert a small piece of cotton loosely into the external auditory canal. Instruct the client to remain with the affected ear uppermost for 10–15 minutes to retain the solution.

INSTILLING NOSE DROPS

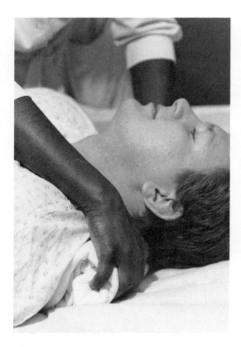

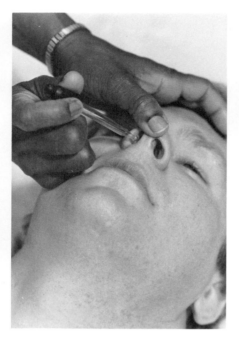

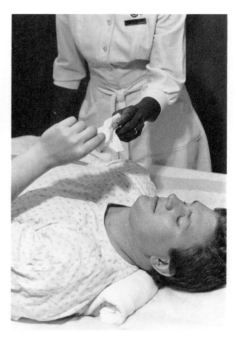

1 Wash your hands. Instruct your client to blow his nose gently. Assist him into a supine position with his head tilted back. It may be helpful to place a small pillow or a rolled towel under his shoulders to help maintain this position.

2 With your nondominant hand, press back gently on the tip of the nose to open the nares. Rest your dominant hand lightly on the face so that your hand will move along with the client should he move suddenly. This will prevent the dropper from accidently injuring the nasal mucosa. Insert the dropper just inside the naris and instill the prescribed medication.

3 To ensure that the medication has time to drain through the nasal passages, encourage the client to maintain this position for a few minutes. Provide him with tissues in which to expectorate the solution that drains into the throat and mouth.

GIVING INHALANT MEDICATIONS

USING A METERED-DOSE INHALER

Clients who require bronchodilator aerosol (e.g., for relief of bronchospasm in reversible obstructive airway disease or prevention of exercise-induced bronchospasm) may use metered-dose inhalants. Teach the client to follow these steps:

- Shake the inhaler immediately before use. Remove the protective cap, making sure the metal cannister is firmly inserted in the plastic case.
- Sit upright and exhale fully through the mouth.
- Position the mouthpiece 2.5–5.0 cm (1–2 in.) from the mouth, holding it in an upright position. Holding the mouthpiece away from the mouth

rather than in it will reduce the amount of aerosol hitting the oropharynx (Barnes, 1988:173). A 4-cm spacer to ensure appropriate distance of the mouthpiece to the mouth may be used by children or clients with coordination problems.

- While inhaling deeply and slowly through your mouth, depress the top of the metal

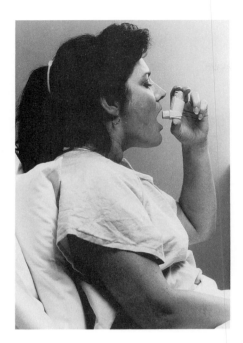

cannister with your fingers, as shown.

- Hold your breath as long as you can. Before exhaling, release your fingers from the cannister.
- Wait 1 minute. Repeat the steps above, as prescribed.

Instruct the client to cleanse the inhaler at least once a day. Demonstrate by removing the metal cannister from the plastic case and rinsing it thoroughly in warm running water. Dry thoroughly and replace the cannister in the plastic case. Finally, recap the case.

USING A NEBULIZER

If your client has a pulmonary disorder, it may be necessary for you to use a nebulizer to administer an inhalant solution. The prescribed amount of solution is poured or droppered into the nebulizer (in the client's left hand, as shown). The compressor (on the bedside table) is then plugged in. With the client sitting upright to enhance chest expansion, instruct her to hold the nebulizer 2.5–5 cm (1–2 in.) from her mouth. She should first exhale and then inhale as she closes off the finger valve (adjacent to the client's right index finger) to deliver the fine mist into the alveoli or other areas of the lung. Explain that she should hold her breath for 3 seconds and then repeat the process until all the medication has been delivered from the nebulizer. *Caution: Some bronchodilators, such as metaproterenol, significantly alter the heart rate. Monitor the client's pulse rate frequently throughout the therapy and record the pretreatment and posttreatment measurements. Be sure to stay with the client throughout the treatment.* Ensure that the nebulizer and tubing are thoroughly cleaned and dried daily, according to your agency's guidelines. This practice reduces the likelihood that the nebulizer will become a reservoir for bacteria.

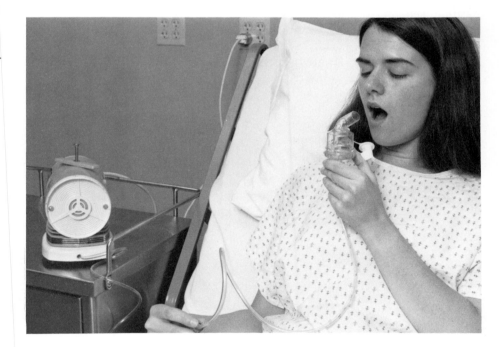

GIVING NITROGLYCERIN

APPLYING NITROGLYCERIN OINTMENT

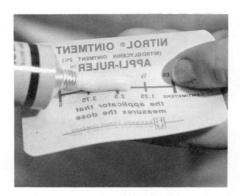

1 Nitroglycerin ointment is applied directly to the skin of clients with angina pectoris and cardiac ischemia to produce systemic vasodilation. This results in a decreased cardiac workload and improved myocardial tissue perfusion for a period of 4–6 hours. Before administering the medication, check your client's blood pressure and apical pulse to establish a baseline for subsequent comparison. Squeeze the prescribed dose directly onto the manufacturer's applicator paper. To ensure an accurate dosage, use an even pressure to produce a continuous column of medication. *Caution: Be sure to avoid direct contact with the nitroglycerin because it could give you a headache if it is absorbed through your skin. Wash your skin immediately with soap and water if this occurs.* Remove any residual ointment from previous applications prior to applying this dose.

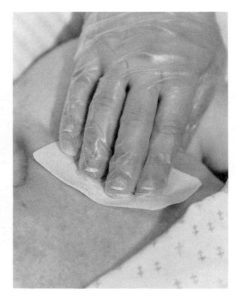

2 If desired, put on a clean glove to protect yourself from potential contact with the medication. Apply the ointment via the applicator paper directly to your client's skin. For optimal absorption, apply the ointment to skin that is hairless and dry. Application sites commonly used are the shoulders, anterior and posterior chest, abdomen, and legs. Be sure to rotate application sites to prevent sensitization and dermal inflammation.

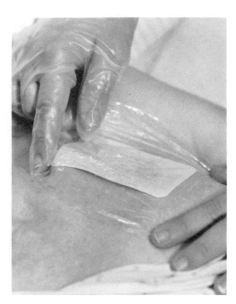

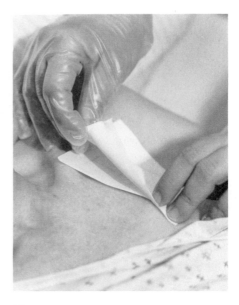

3 If the client is not receiving the desired effect from the medication, the physician may request that you cover the applicator paper with an occlusive plastic wrap (top) or with a wide strip of air-occlusive tape (bottom). Either will enhance absorption. However, if your client is achieving the desired effect without an air-occlusive dressing, avoid applying one because the increased absorption from the dressing could result in headache and dizziness.

4 Check your client's blood pressure a few minutes after applying the ointment. There should be a moderate decline in the systolic pressure. Continue to monitor your client for headaches, fainting, or dizziness. If these symptoms occur, alert the physician, who will probably decrease the dosage until the client develops a tolerance to the side effects of the drug.

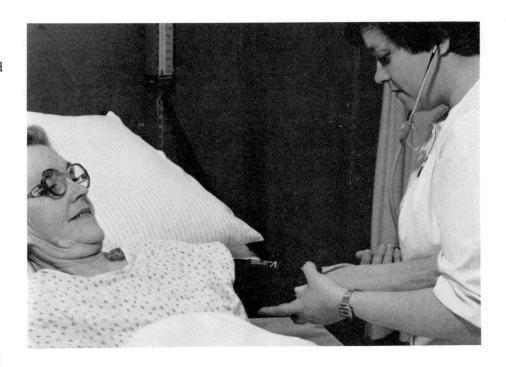

APPLYING A NITROGLYCERIN DISK

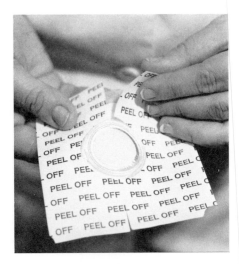

1 Review the previous steps for applying nitroglycerin ointment because the principles for application and usage are similar to the disk's. The advantages in using the disk are its neatness, its dose accuracy, and its known duration of action. In addition, it poses less of a hazard for the person administering the drug. Disks produce a continuous release of medication over approximately a 24-hour period, starting approximately 30 minutes after application. To apply the disk, peel off the strip of protective paper backing from one side of the disk.

2 Adhere that side of the disk to a dry, hairless area of your client's skin. Then remove the remaining protective paper strip.

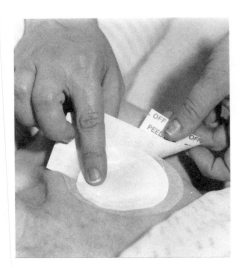

3 Securely adhere the disk's sticky surface to the client's skin.

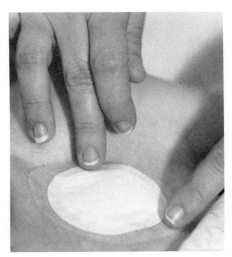

ADMINISTERING MEDICATIONS THROUGH A NASOGASTRIC TUBE

Have medications been prescribed that must be administered through your client's nasogastric tube? This can be done easily using a large bulb or piston syringe, an emesis basin and bed-saver pad (to protect the linen when confirming proper tube positioning), and ≥30 ml tap water.

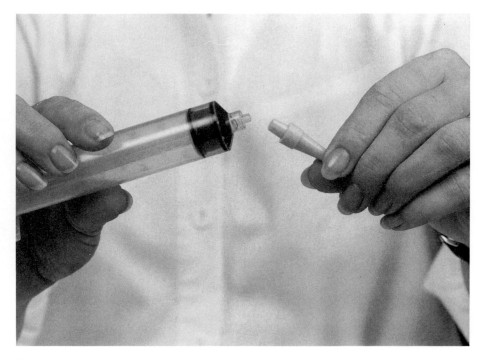

1   First, attach a Luer-type adaptor to the syringe you will use.

2   Then, draw up the prescribed amount of medication. *Note: Use liquid dosage forms when administering medications through a nasogastric tube. Crushing tablets or opening capsules changes the product form and may alter therapeutic effects.*

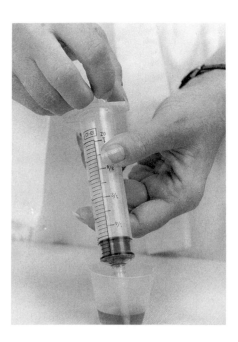

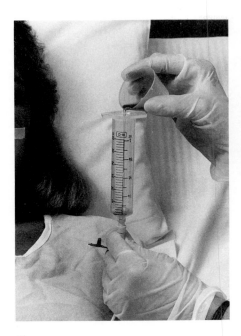 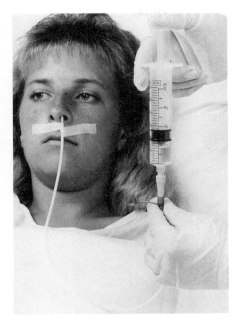 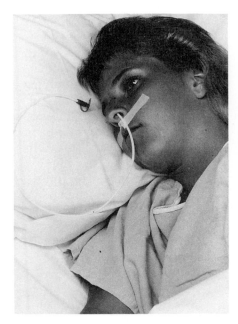

3 Next, put on clean gloves and confirm that the distal end of the tube is properly positioned in the stomach by aspirating for the presence of gastric contents (see procedure, p. 261). Reinstill the aspirate to prevent loss of electrolytes and gastric fluids. Before the aspirate completely drains from the syringe barrel, pour the medication into the barrel. Pouring the medication into the barrel before the aspirate completely drains will prevent the administration of air into your client's stomach.

4 Instill 20–30 ml tap water into the tube before the medication completely drains from the barrel. Instilling water will ensure that none of the medication adheres to the lumen of the tube. If your client has a small-bore feeding tube, as shown, use the plunger, applying gentle pressure to instill the water. If your client has a larger-bore nasogastric tube, allow the fluid to flow into the stomach via gravity.

5 When you have completed the instillation, close the tube by inserting the tube plug. Place the client in high-Fowler's or a slightly elevated right side-lying position, as shown, to facilitate absorption of the medication. Clean and return the syringe to the client's bedside. Finally, chart the medication and record the amount of instillation on the client's intake and output (I&O) record, if appropriate.

PERFORMING A VAGINAL IRRIGATION (DOUCHE)

Vaginal irrigations are prescribed for preoperative cleansing—for example, with a povidone-iodine solution—for soothing inflamed vaginal mucosa and for applying heat or medications to the vaginal mucosa and cervix. They are contraindicated in late pregnancy and during postpartum and menstruation. Use clean technique, and wear clean gloves for your own protection unless the client has an open wound. In that case, use sterile technique to protect the client from the potential spread of infection.

1 Prepare the prescribed solution, and check the solution's temperature with a thermometer to ensure that it is not too hot. Usually, 40.5°C (105°F) is the recommended temperature. Bring the solution and equipment to your client's room, and hang the container on an IV pole 30–45 cm (12–18 in.) above the level of the client's vagina. This height will provide an adequate gravity flow yet prevent the solution from entering the vagina with too great a force. Explain the procedure to the client and ask her to void if she hasn't recently done so. An empty bladder will make the procedure more comfortable and allow greater expansion of the vaginal canal. Provide privacy, and drape her with a bath blanket or bed sheet. Assist her into a dorsal recumbent position, and place a bed-saver pad and bed pan under her buttocks. Her knees should be flexed and separated (as shown). Remove the protective cap from the nozzle, and inspect the nozzle for cracks or other irregularities that potentially could harm the vaginal mucosa.

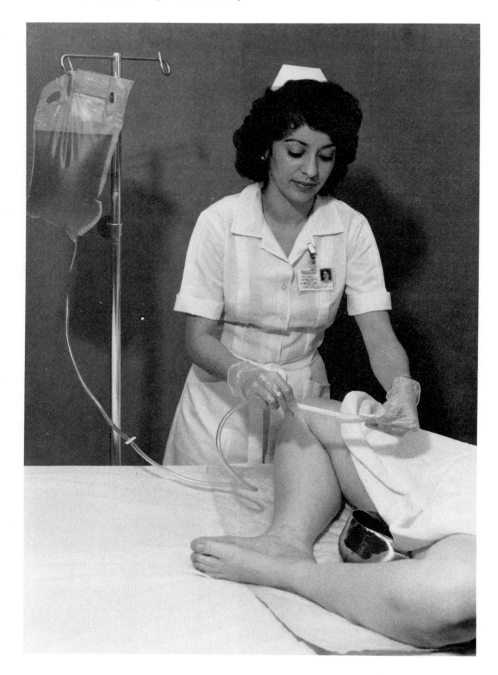

2   Direct the nozzle over the bed pan, and then open the tubing clamp to run the solution to the end of the nozzle. This will flush the tubing of air and lubricate the nozzle to facilitate its insertion into the vagina.

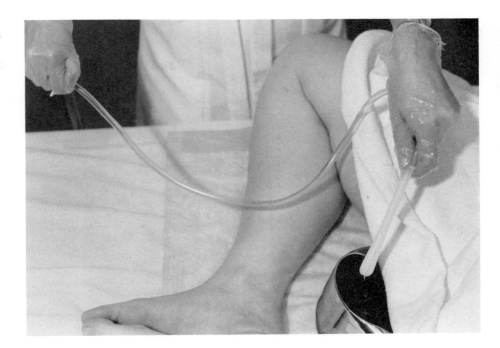

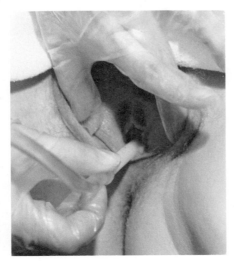

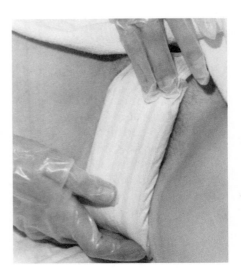

3   Separate the labia and allow the solution to flow over the external genitalia and vulva to prevent the introduction of contaminants into the vagina and uterus. Then close the clamp. *Note: If the client has copious discharge, cleanse the area with cotton balls soaked in a soapy solution. Use a fresh cotton ball for each single downward stroke.* Gently insert the nozzle into the vagina.

4   Direct the nozzle approximately 5.0–7.5 cm (2–3 in.) into the vagina, angling it toward the sacrum to follow the anatomic structure of the vagina. Open the clamp again and allow the solution to flow. Unless the client has had cervical or vaginal surgery, gently rotate the nozzle to irrigate all the vaginal surfaces. When the solution has drained from the container, clamp the tubing and remove the nozzle. Then raise the head of the bed to permit the solution to drain out into the bed pan.

5   Dry the perineum with tissues, wiping from the front toward the anus. Then apply a sterile peripad to the perineum to absorb the residual solution and protect the clothing or bed linen from the irrigant. Remove the equipment from the bedside, and either dispose of it or clean it according to agency procedure.

GIVING RECTAL MEDICATIONS

INSERTING A SUPPOSITORY

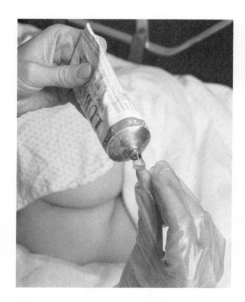

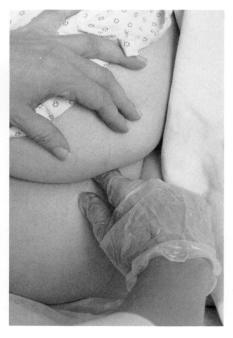

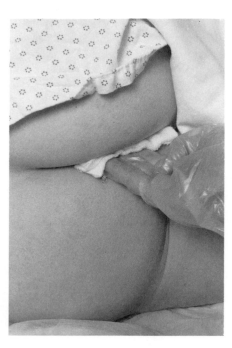

1   To insert a suppository, provide privacy and assist the client into a position in which the rectum is easily accessible, for example, a side-lying position with the upper leg flexed (Sims) as shown. Put on a clean glove, and generously lubricate the suppository with a water-soluble lubricant.

2   With your free hand, gently lift the uppermost buttock. With your index finger, guide the suppository into the anus, directing it along the rectal wall and away from fecal masses. To prevent immediate expulsion, be sure to insert the suppository beyond the internal sphincter.

3   With a tissue or gauze pad, press gently on the anus for a few moments to help the client retain the medication; then clean the rectal area with the tissue or pad. Encourage the client to retain the suppository for at least 20 minutes before using the bed pan or going to the bathroom, if it is appropriate for the suppository to be expelled.

INSTILLING OINTMENT

Review the preceding technique for inserting a rectal suppository. To lubricate the applicator, remove its protective cover and squeeze the tube (as shown). This will push the ointment through the small openings on the applicator and facilitate its insertion into the rectum. Insert the applicator gently to avoid injury to the rectal canal or to hemorrhoids. Squeeze the prescribed amount of ointment. Clean the rectal area with tissues, and assist your client to a comfortable position.

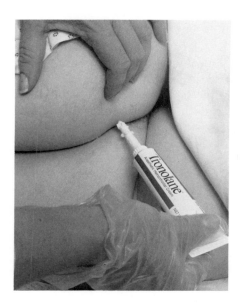

Administering Injectable Medications

GIVING INTRADERMAL INJECTIONS

LOCATING THE SITE

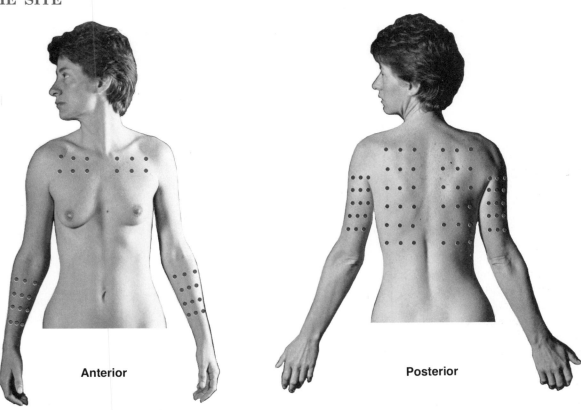

Anterior

Posterior

Review these anatomic overlays to assist you in locating the proper sites for intradermal injections. The most common uses for intradermal injections are tuberculin skin testing (Mantoux test) and allergy testing.

The most frequently injected site is the ventral aspect of the forearm. To locate an appropriate injection site for this area, measure a hand's breadth from the antecubital space and a hand's breadth from the wrist. You can safely inject into the ventral area bordered by your two hands, provided the site is not scarred, covered with hair follicles, or inflamed, because these conditions would interfere with the reading.

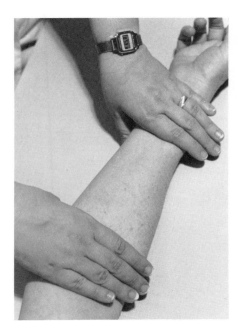

INJECTING THE MEDICATION

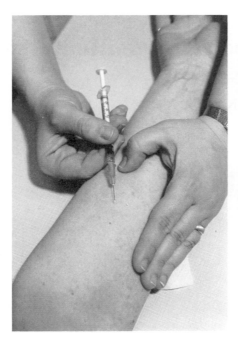

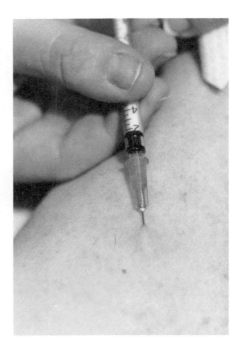

1 Prepare the medication and draw it up into a tuberculin syringe that has a ⅜-in. to ⅝-in., 26-gauge, short-beveled needle. Ask your client to sit facing you, flex the elbow, and rest the forearm on a flat surface. Prepare the skin with an alcohol sponge, starting at the injection site and working your way outward in a circular fashion to cover an area 5 cm (2 in.) in diameter. Allow it to dry. With one hand, stretch the skin at the injection site between your thumb and index finger to facilitate the needle's penetration into the area just underneath the skin's surface. Hold the syringe between your thumb and index finger with the needle positioned at a 10- to 15-degree angle to the skin with the bevel up.

2 Insert the needle just under the surface of the skin, and slowly inject the medication. *Note: If the needle is inserted correctly, you should feel some resistance as you inject the medication. You might have inserted the needle too deeply if the medication can be injected too easily.* While injecting the medication, observe for the development of a wheal approximately 0.5 cm in diameter. Withdraw the needle. Do not massage the site because this could distort the eventual reading. If appropriate, closely observe the client for signs of an anaphylactic reaction to the substance that was injected. Discard the syringe and needle unit uncapped into a puncture-resistant container (see procedure, p. 110). Be sure to document the type and amount of medication, the date, the exact time you administered it, and the injection site. In addition, document any reactions to the solution that was injected. Explain to the client that the reading of the test will be done in 2–3 days.

GIVING SUBCUTANEOUS INJECTIONS

LOCATING THE SITE

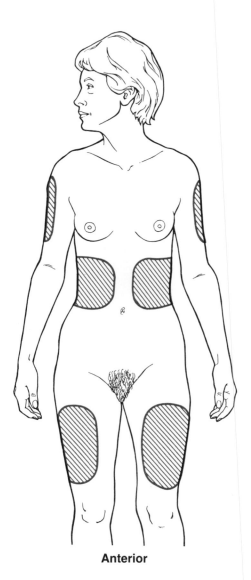

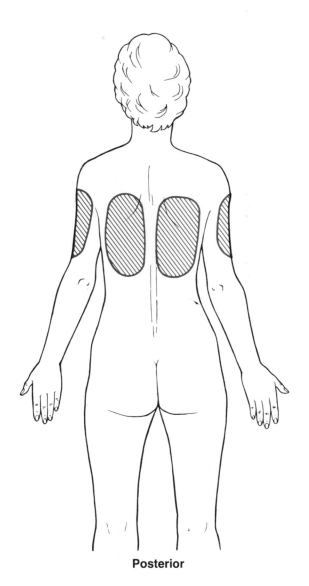

Anterior   **Posterior**

Review these diagrams to help you select a site for a subcutaneous injection. Rotate sites for medications that are administered repeatedly, for example, insulin or heparin.

INJECTING THE MEDICATION

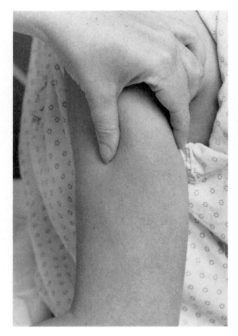

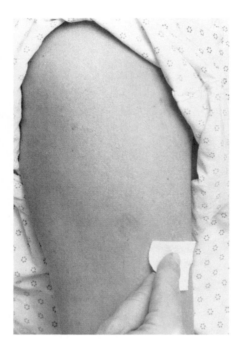

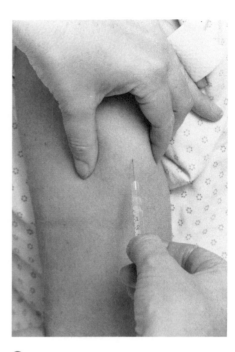

1 A subcutaneous injection is properly given into the layer of tissue that is above the muscle and below the skin and fat. To reach this layer effectively, you will need to assess each client to help determine the correct angle of insertion and, occasionally, the need for a longer or shorter needle. With a ⅝-in. needle you can usually vary the angle of insertion to penetrate the subcutaneous layer correctly. However, for very obese clients, a ⅝-in. needle may not be long enough to penetrate past the fatty layer. The same needle may be too long for children or very thin clients. Form a skin fold (as shown) to assess the amount of fat at the selected injection site and to determine the correct angle of insertion for reaching the subcutaneous tissue. If your client has an average build, a 45-degree angle is usually effective. An obese client may require a 90-degree angle, and a thin client may require an angle ranging from 15 to 45 degrees.

2 Draw up the prescribed medication into a 2- to 3-ml syringe with a 25-gauge, ⅝-in. (or the correct length) needle. The use of an air bubble should be determined by your agency's policy to ensure consistency in the amount of medication routinely delivered to each client. For example, if you use an air bubble and your co-worker does not, the amount of medication you deliver to your client will be slightly more than that delivered by your co-worker because the air will clear the needle of medication. Consistency is especially crucial for diabetic clients receiving insulin. Prepare the site with an alcohol sponge. Start at the insertion site and work your way outward from the center in a circular fashion to cover an area 5 cm (2 in.) in diameter. Allow the alcohol to dry.

3 Bunch the skin between your thumb and index finger. This will minimize your client's discomfort as the needle is inserted. Insert the needle with the bevel up, at the angle appropriate for your client.

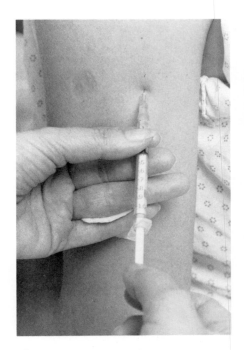

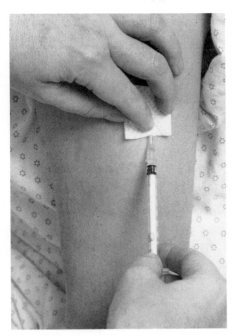

4 Release the skin and pull back on the plunger (as shown) to aspirate for blood. If you do aspirate blood, withdraw the needle because injecting a medication into a vascular area could result in a systemic reaction to the medication. Obtain a new syringe and needle, as well as new medication, and try again. When you are certain you are in a nonvascular layer of subcutaneous tissue, slowly inject the medication. *Caution: Do not aspirate if you are injecting heparin because it could cause a hematoma to form at the injection site (see next procedure).*

5 When the medication has been injected, withdraw the needle at the same angle in which it was inserted to minimize trauma to the tissues. Apply pressure with an alcohol sponge at the insertion site to avert bleeding. If massage has not been contraindicated, as it would be with heparin, it can be employed to facilitate absorption of the medication. Discard the syringe and needle unit uncapped into a puncture-resistant container (see procedure, p. 110).

ADMINISTERING HEPARIN

Heparin is administered subcutaneously because intramuscular injection can cause hemorrhage and hematoma formation. Heparin's effects are also longer lasting when administered subcutaneously rather than via the intramuscular route.

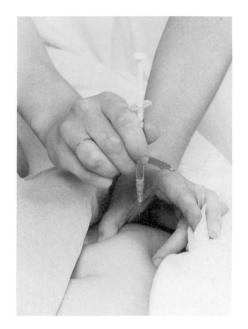 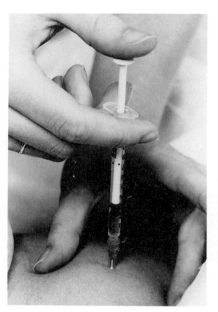 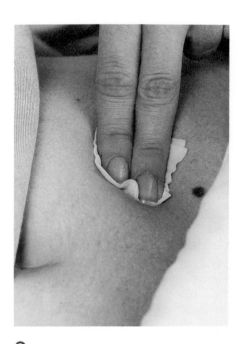

1 Use a 1-ml tuberculin syringe with a ⅝-in., 25-gauge needle. After drawing up the prescribed amount of medication, change needles to prevent bruising or tracking through the subcutaneous tissues. Form a fat roll on the iliac or abdominal tissue by grasping the tissue gently. Avoid any areas that are bruised, and avoid needle insertion within 2 inches of the umbilicus or any scar. Cleanse the site gently with an alcohol swab. Then insert the needle at a 90-degree angle, as shown, into the elevated fatty tissue.

2 Reduce finger pressure on the tissue slightly and slowly inject the heparin. When the medication has been injected, withdraw the needle at the angle in which it entered the tissue, releasing the skin roll as you do to minimize tissue damage.

3 Press an alcohol swab over the injection site for 2–3 minutes to prevent oozing or bruising. *Caution: Do not massage the injection site, as this could damage the tissue.* To prevent hematoma formation, rotate injection sites with each administration of heparin. Document the medication and the site used.

GIVING INTRAMUSCULAR (IM) INJECTIONS

MAPPING MUSCLE SITES FOR IM INJECTIONS

Dorsal Gluteal

1 Review this anatomic overlay of the posterior gluteal (dorsal gluteal) area to assist you in locating the correct site for IM injections. Although this site is commonly used, extreme caution must be employed to avoid the sciatic nerve and gluteal artery. Notice that the nerve and trunk of the artery are distal to the diagonal line that extends from the posterior superior iliac spine to the greater trochanter of the femur. *Caution: Do not use this site for children under the age of 2 who have not been walking long enough to have developed adequate musculature. This site also may be contraindicated for the older adult or immobile client whose gluteal muscle could be deteriorated.*

2 Ask the client to assume a prone, toe-in position. Internal rotation of the hips will relax the muscle and make the injection less painful.

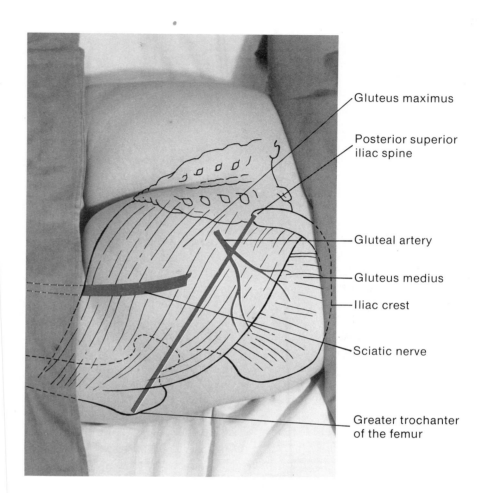

Gluteus maximus

Posterior superior iliac spine

Gluteal artery

Gluteus medius

Iliac crest

Sciatic nerve

Greater trochanter of the femur

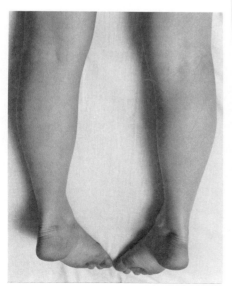

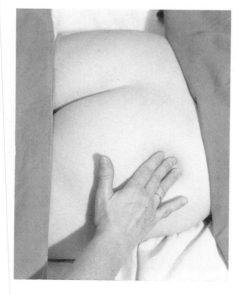

3 Although it is essential that you provide the client with as much privacy as possible, you must fully expose the buttocks to ensure complete visualization of the anatomic landmarks. Also, inspect and palpate the skin and tissue to assess for edema, fibrous areas, nodules, lesions, or draining wounds, which could either prevent adequate absorption or promote the spread of infection. *Note: Explain to the client what you are doing so that you do not cause unnecessary alarm.*

(Continues)

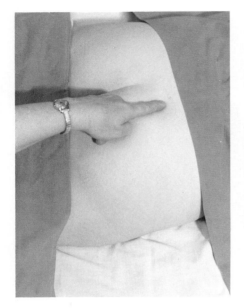

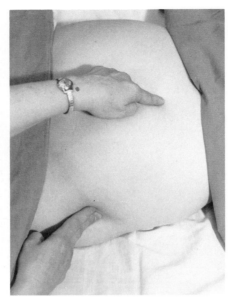

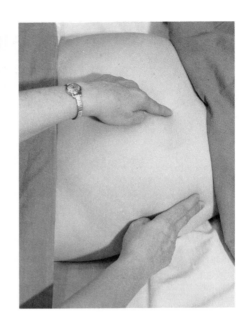

4 If the tissue is healthy, inspect and palpate the anatomic landmarks. Locate the posterior superior iliac spine. On many clients, this landmark can be identified as a dimpled area in the skin. It also can be palpated as a bony ridge approximately 2.5–5.0 cm (1–2 in.) lateral and slightly superior to the separation between the buttocks.

5 Locate the greater trochanter of the femur. You can locate this site visually on most clients by following the lower curve of the buttock outward toward the lateral hip. You can also palpate the indentation at the hip where the hip and thigh join. The greater trochanter is just distal to the indentation.

Note: If you are still unable to locate the landmark, press and slide your fingers from the waistline (as shown) downward until you feel the indentation.

6 The diagonal line that extends from the posterior superior iliac spine toward the greater trochanter of the femur, and the horizontal line extending from the posterior superior iliac spine to the lateral hip two fingers' breadth below the iliac crest, form the boundary for the area that is safe for IM injections.

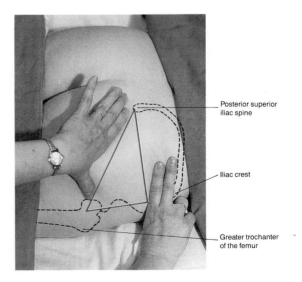

Posterior superior iliac spine

Iliac crest

Greater trochanter of the femur

Ventrogluteal

1 Review this anatomic overlay of the ventrogluteal area of the hip to assist you in locating the correct site for IM injections. Note that compared to the dorsal gluteal area, it is free of major nerves and blood vessels, and it is farther from the rectum, minimizing the risk of contamination. In addition, it has a dense muscle and minimal fat.

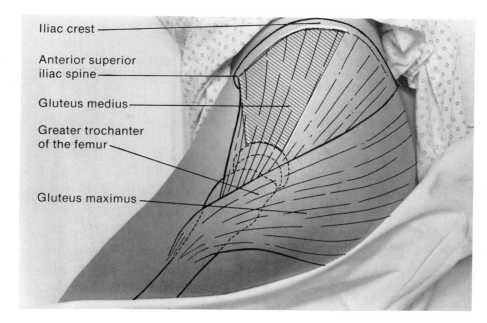

Iliac crest

Anterior superior iliac spine

Gluteus medius

Greater trochanter of the femur

Gluteus maximus

2 Although the client can be supine or prone for injections into this site, a side-lying position with the upper leg flexed and in front of the lower leg (as shown) will better expose the anatomic landmarks and relax the gluteal muscle.

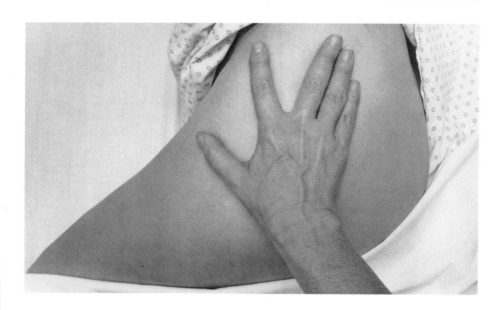

3 To inject the medication into the client's left hip (as shown), place your right palm over the greater trochanter (or use your left hand on the client's right hip). Position your index finger on the anterior superior iliac spine and form a "V" by placing your middle finger along the iliac crest. You may safely inject the medication into the center of the "V." Spread the tissue and angle the needle slightly, toward the client's head.

Vastus Lateralis

1 Review this anatomic overlay of the anterior lateral aspect of the thigh to locate the vastus lateralis muscle. This site is also free of major nerves and blood vessels, and it is usually well developed in both adults and children.

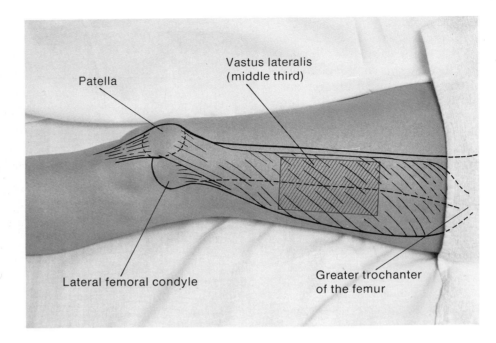

2 The preferred position for your client is supine with the hip internally rotated (toes pointing toward the midline) to better expose the lateral aspect of the thigh. The site then may be divided into thirds, beginning at the greater trochanter of the femur to the lateral femoral condyles at the knee. The middle third is the correct area. You may also measure a hand's breadth below the greater trochanter and a hand's breadth above the knee (as shown), and select the site central to this boundary.

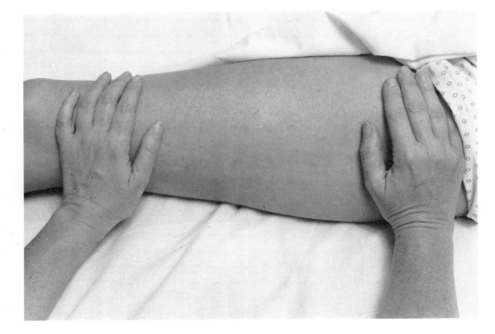

Mid-Deltoid

1   Review this anatomic overlay of the lateral aspect of the upper arm to help you locate the mid-deltoid muscle. Although an advantage of this site is its easy access, the muscle covers a relatively small area, and it is close to major bones, nerves, and arteries. In addition, this muscle cannot tolerate frequent injections or large doses of medication (not more than 1 ml in the average-sized adult). Thus you should limit your injections into this muscle to adults and teenagers with well-developed muscle mass.

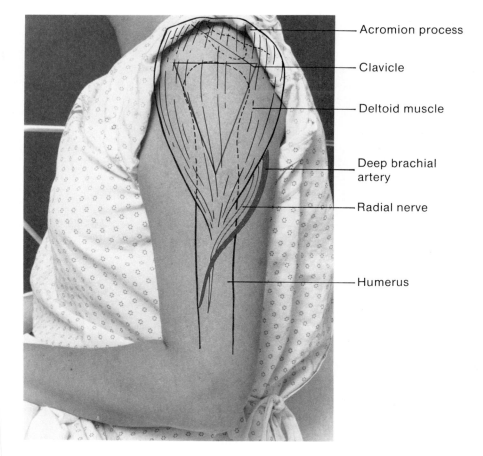

— Acromion process

— Clavicle

— Deltoid muscle

— Deep brachial artery

— Radial nerve

— Humerus

2   The client may sit, stand, or lie down to receive an injection in the mid-deltoid muscle, but it is important for the elbow to be flexed and supported so that the muscle can be relaxed. To map the muscle, locate the lower edge of the acromion process with one hand and then identify the area on the lateral aspect of the upper arm that is in a line with the axilla (as shown). Be certain that the gown or clothing does not interfere with your visualization of the site. The mid-deltoid muscle is bounded by an imaginary triangle that can be envisioned between the two hands (review top photo).

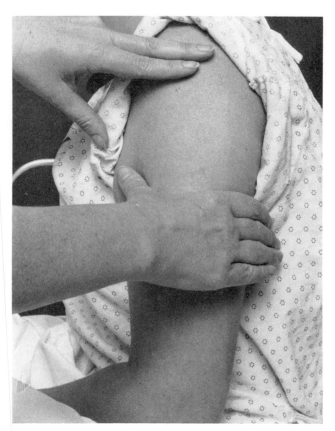

PROVIDING AN AIR LOCK

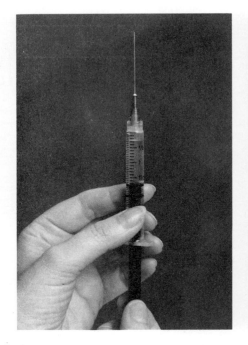

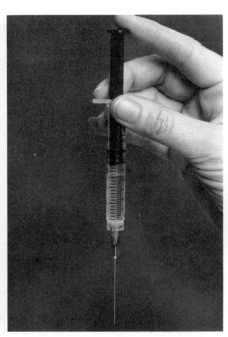

INJECTING THE MEDICATION

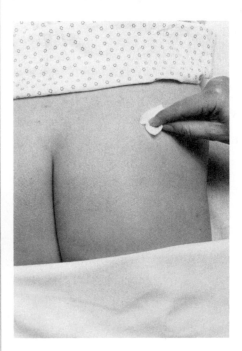

1 An air lock is used with an IM injection when the medication may be potentially harmful to the subcutaneous tissue. A bolus of air follows the administration of the medication to ensure that all the solution is ejected from the needle, thereby preventing tracking of the medication into the subcutaneous tissue after the needle has been withdrawn. After drawing up the prescribed amount of medication (and changing the needle, if appropriate), pull back on the plunger to aspirate approximately 0.5–1.0 ml of air into the syringe. Point the needle toward the ceiling (as shown) and **expel** all except 0.2–0.5 ml of air: The required amount of air will depend on the length and gauge of the needle. A 21-gauge, $1\frac{1}{2}$-in. needle, for example, will require 0.2–0.3 ml of air to provide an effective air lock.

2 Note that the air rises to the top of the barrel when the syringe is held perpendicular to the floor. If the syringe were positioned parallel to the floor, for example, to inject the mid-deltoid muscle with the client sitting, the air bubble would move to the side of the syringe and become ineffectual. So if you wish to use an air lock for ventrogluteal or deltoid sites, the client must be sidelying. Similarly, a prone position is necessary for dorsal gluteal injections, and supine or sitting positions are required for injections into the vastus lateralis muscle. ***Note:*** *Air locks are usually contraindicated for the pediatric population.*

1 After you have prepared the medication, identified the client, and selected the appropriate injection site, prepare the skin with an alcohol sponge. Start at the proposed injection site and work your way outward from the center in a circular motion. Be sure to cover an area at least 5 cm (2 in.) in diameter. Allow the alcohol to dry.

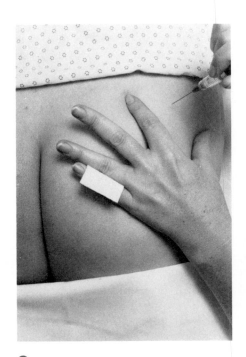

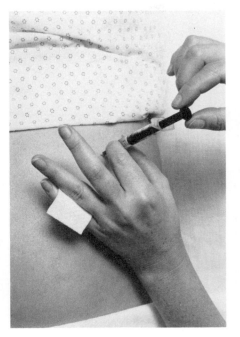

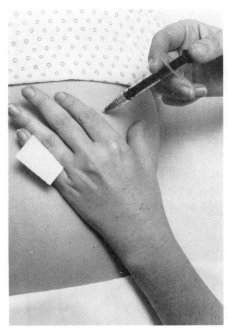

2 Spread the tissue between your thumb and index finger to make the skin taut, and then insert the needle in a quick dart-like motion. It is helpful to hold an alcohol swab between the last two fingers so that it is readily available after the needle has been withdrawn. *Note: For children and thin adults it may be necessary to bunch the tissue when injecting into the mid-deltoid or vastus lateralis muscle.*

3 Support the barrel with your nondominant hand and pull back on the plunger with your dominant hand to aspirate for blood. If blood is aspirated, withdraw the needle and replace the syringe, needle, and medication.

4 Inject the medication slowly to minimize your client's discomfort and distribute the solution evenly.

5 Withdraw the needle, place the alcohol swab at the injection site, and apply pressure. This will minimize the chance for the medication to seep into the subcutaneous tissues. If rapid absorption is desired, massage the site for 1–2 minutes with the swab. *Note: To minimize trauma to the tissues, withdraw the needle at the same angle in which it was inserted.* Discard the syringe and needle unit uncapped into a puncture-resistant container (see procedure, p. 110). Finally, document the procedure and the site that you used.

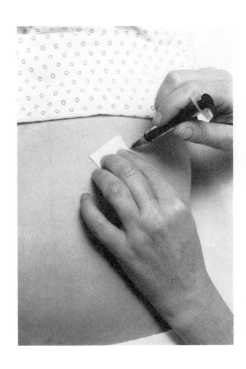

PERFORMING THE Z-TRACK TECHNIQUE

Z-track injections are indicated when complete absorption of the medication is crucial or when medications such as iron preparations may seep into the injection tract and stain the skin or surrounding tissues. Some agencies require the Z-track method for all injections into the gluteal muscle. The tissue is displaced downward and toward the median before, during, and after the injection so that when the tissue is released, the needle tract that normally would have formed becomes instead a broken, noncontinuous line. This method keeps the medication deep in the muscle by preventing its seepage up through the tissues.

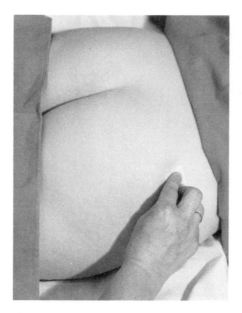

1 Draw up the medication, and then change the needle to one that is at least 5 cm (2 in.) long (for the average adult). Because you will need to inject deeply to reach the muscle, the size of the needle will depend on the size of the client. Draw up a 0.5-ml air bubble (or larger, depending on the length and gauge of the needle). This will enable you to clear all the medication from the needle as well as eject the residual medication from the needle's end to prevent tracking the solution as the needle is withdrawn. Now you are ready to prepare the site with an alcohol sponge (as shown). Prepare the skin before displacing the tissue because it is difficult to maintain the required traction on the tissue for the length of time it takes for the alcohol to dry. Cleanse an area that is at least 10 cm (4 in.) in diameter to ensure that you will have covered the injection site.

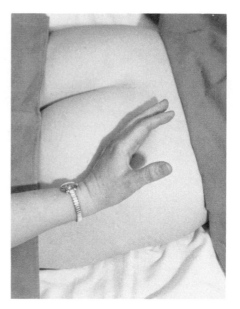

2 After preparing the skin, place the ulnar side of your nondominant hand along the diagonal that extends from the posterior superior iliac spine to the greater trochanter of the femur.

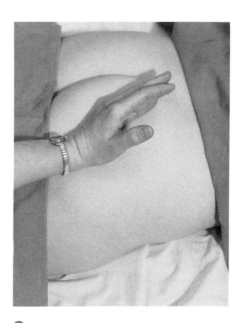

3 Displace the tissue downward and toward the median as far as you can and yet comfortably maintain the traction on the tissue.

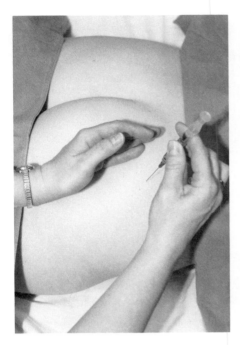

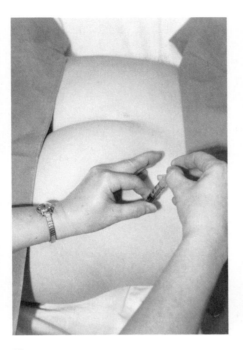

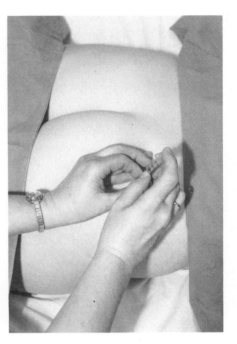

4 Continue to displace the tissue as you insert the needle.

5 Carefully extend the thumb and forefinger of the hand that is displacing the tissue to support the base of the syringe. Aspirate with your other hand. *Do not release the traction on the tissue.*

6 Continue to maintain the traction as you slowly inject the medication. When you have completed the injection, wait 10 seconds to provide the necessary time for the medication to disperse into the muscle and to give the muscle time to relax after having been stimulated by the needle and medication.

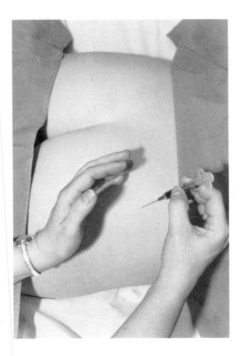

7 After waiting 10 seconds, remove the needle and immediately lift your other hand to release the tissue. Do not massage the injection site, and advise your client not to exercise or wear tight clothing following the injection. This will minimize the chance for the medication to spread into other layers of tissue. Discard the syringe and needle unit uncapped into a puncture-resistant container (see procedure, p. 110).

DISPOSING OF NEEDLES AND SHARP INSTRUMENTS

As often as possible place puncture-resistant containers in all work areas for the disposal of nonreusable needle-syringe units, scalpel blades, and other sharp items. These containers are intended for the disposal of needle-syringe units that are uncapped and unbroken (as shown).

RECAPPING NEEDLES USING THE ONE-HAND METHOD

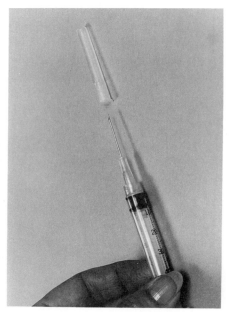

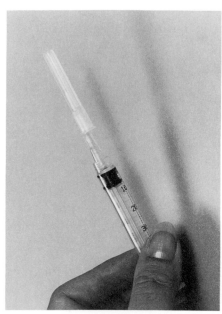

1 When it is necessary to recap needles following injection (e.g., in a psychiatric facility where needle disposal containers are not in the clients' rooms, or for recapping needles on IV lines used for intermittent infusions through heparin locks or other ports) use one hand only to prevent needle sticks. To do this, place the cap on a flat surface, and position the syringe-needle unit on the same plane as the cap.

2 Scoop the cap with the needle, as shown. Press the cap to the surface area to secure the cap to the syringe-needle unit, or grasp the cap at the base with the other hand to secure it.

Nursing Guidelines for Managing Insulin Pumps

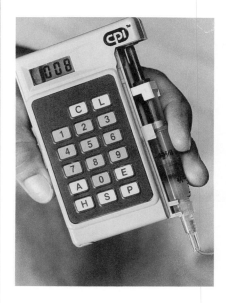

1 *An insulin pump* is a computerized device that delivers a constant insulin infusion throughout the day and night (called the basal delivery), with the capability of administering boluses manually at specified times, for example just prior to meals. Thus, unlike conventional insulin therapy, which relies on single or multiple daily injections, the insulin pump acts more like the client's own pancreas. However, unlike the pancreas, an insulin pump can only respond to the client's programming, based on frequent self-monitoring of blood glucose. There are several pumps available to the diabetic client, and each varies in method of operation and programming. Each pump has rechargeable batteries, a syringe, a programmable computer, and a motor and drive mechanism. Regular (short-acting) insulin is used, and it is contained by the syringe that inserts directly into the pump. A 60- to 105-cm (24- to 42-in.) length of plastic tubing attaches on one end to the syringe, and at the other end to a 27-gauge needle that is inserted into the subcutaneous tissue. The client may attach the pump to a leather belt, fabric belt, or shoulder strap or carry it in a purse or pocket.

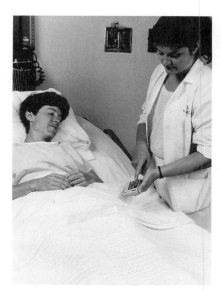

2 *If the physician* decides that your client is a good candidate for insulin-pump therapy, it may be your responsibility to explain the operational principles of the pump (each pump has a detailed manufacturer's manual), reinforce the client's knowledge about dietary management, and review self-monitoring of blood glucose (see steps, pp. 143–147). Initially, the basal rate and the meal boluses will be regulated by the physician, based on blood-glucose measurements. Frequent testing of the blood glucose must be performed, and it should become a part of the daily regimen of every client with an insulin pump. It is the client's best assessment tool for measuring the effectiveness of diabetes management.

(Continues)

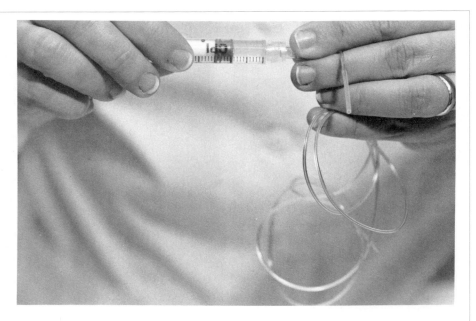

3 *To ensure a proper flow rate,* instruct the client to use only the syringe and tubing supplied by the manufacturer. It is also important to check the tubing periodically for kinks. With some pumps, the tubing may be primed manually; with others, the tubing is primed automatically by programming the pump. In either case, the syringe and battery generally are routinely changed every 24 hours. Many pumps have alarms that alert the user to a low battery, kinked tubing, or an empty syringe.

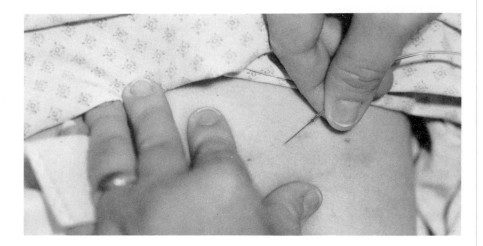

4 *Rotate the sites* for needle insertion as you would for conventional insulin therapy. However, because the needle will be indwelling, the choice for a potential site is limited by the length of the plastic tubing, the style and fit of the clothing, and the client's personal preference. Most clients choose the abdomen as an insertion site, but others occasionally use the upper thigh, hips, and arms. Prepare the skin with an alcohol sponge, and insert the needle at a 30- to 45-degree angle. If desired, povidone-iodine ointment may be applied to the insertion site.

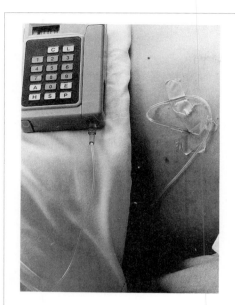

5 *The needle is anchored* with strips of hypoallergenic tape. A 10-cm (4-in.) loop of tubing just proximal to the needle is also taped to minimize the traction on the needle. Encourage the client to check the needle periodically to ensure that it has not become dislodged or disconnected from the tubing. With proper care, the same needle may be left indwelling for as long as 72 hours for some adult clients, depending on infusion set type and physician recommendation. However, it generally is recommended that the infusion set be changed every 24 hours to reduce the risk of infection, skin irritation, changes in the absorption of insulin, and infusion set obstruction. At the first sign of inflammation, however, the client should change both the site and the needle. With the physician, establish the protocol for intervention during insulin shock and acute hyperglycemia. In most cases, you will treat the hypoglycemia—for example, by giving orange juice, dextrose, or sugar—rather than altering or discontinuing the pump.

Administering Intravenous Fluids and Medications

PREPARING THE SOLUTION AND INFUSION SET

INSPECTING THE CONTAINER

1 Wash your hands and inspect the label to ensure that the solution and amount match the physician's order and that the date for usage has not expired. Hold a glass container against a light source and observe for discoloration, cloudiness, particulate matter, and cracks while you slowly rotate the bottle. Replace the container with a new one if you detect any of these irregularities.

(Continues)

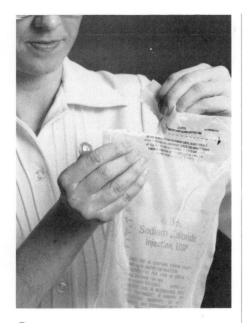

2 Will you administer a solution in a plastic container instead? Remove it from its overwrap after tearing along the broken line.

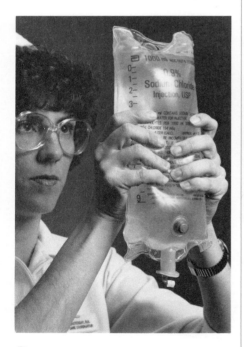

3 Inspect the plastic container in the same manner you would inspect a glass container, but, in addition, squeeze it gently and observe for leakage. Any irregularity, including leakage, necessitates replacement.

ASSEMBLING THE INFUSION SET

1 Inspect the package that contains the infusion set to ensure that it is intact, and then remove the tubing. If possible, slide the roller clamp directly under the drip chamber. If the tubing has a backcheck valve for the administration of piggyback fluids (as shown), slide the roller clamp up under the backcheck valve. By sliding the clamp up as high as possible, you will have quick access to the clamp for controlling the drip rate, and it will enable you to adjust the rate while closely monitoring the drip chamber. Then close the roller clamp.

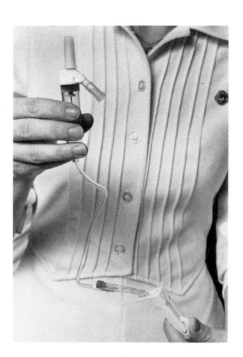

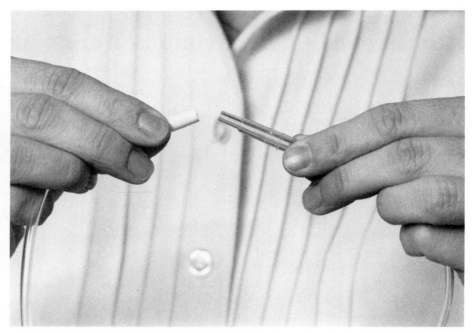

2 If you want to allow the client more mobility or to provide extra ports for the administration of medication, you can attach extension tubing to the distal end of the IV tubing. Then close its slide clamp. Ensure that all connections are securely attached.

SPIKING THE CONTAINER

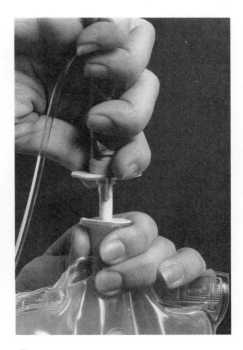

1 To ensure that contaminants have not entered the bottle, inspect the protective metal cap on a glass container to verify that it is intact. Then remove the cap. If the container also has a rubber diaphragm, remove it at this time. You should hear a swoosh of air as you remove it.

2 Place the container on a flat, secure surface. Remove the protective cap from the spike on the infusion set, squeeze the drip chamber, and insert the spike into the rubber port of the glass container. Vented tubing, such as this, is more often used with glass containers unless the container itself has a vent.

3 To spike a plastic container, hold the neck securely and remove the protective tab. Then slide the spike through the port. With plastic containers, nonvented tubing is used.

PRIMING THE INFUSION SET

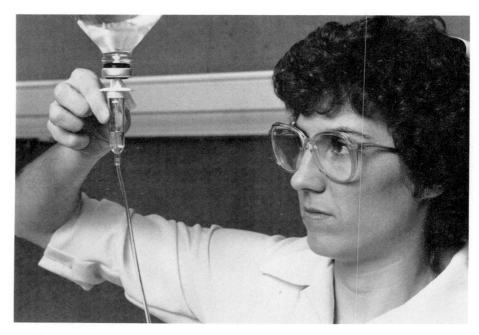

1 Hang the solution on an IV pole and, prior to opening the clamps and priming the tubing, squeeze the drip chamber and prime it with solution to the half-fill line. This will minimize the formation of air bubbles in the tubing when you prime the tubing.

2 Open the clamps and let the solution flow to the end of the tubing to clear it of air. Hold the distal end of the tubing over a waste container or emesis basin as you do this. If the tubing has a backcheck valve (as shown), invert the valve as you prime the tubing and snap it lightly to disintegrate the bubbles. Reclamp the tubing and perform a venipuncture, or attach the primed tubing to the indwelling needle or catheter.

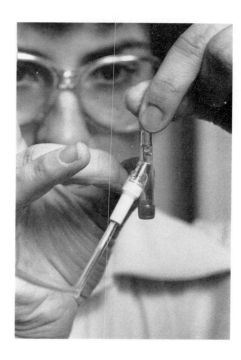

ATTACHING AND PRIMING A FILTER

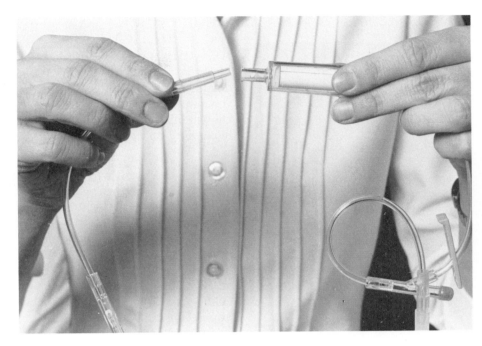

1 Filters are frequently built in or attached to infusion tubing to ensure that particulate matter does not enter the client's bloodstream. Very fine filters (0.22 μ) are the most effective in filtering particulate matter; however, they are so fine that they may become clogged by viscous solutions. Be sure to read the manufacturer's instructions to ensure that your filter is compatible with the prescribed solution. If your infusion set does not have a built-in filter, attach the male end of the infusion set to the female end of the filter. To ensure a secure connection, twist the ends together tightly. If the infusion set does not have Luer-lock connections, tape all connections securely.

2 Before priming the filter, open the slide clamps on either side. Invert the filter and allow the solution to flow into it from the bottom to the top. Tap it lightly to disintegrate the bubbles.

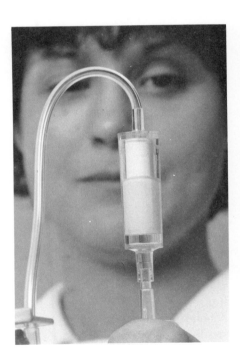

LABELING THE TUBING AND CONTAINER

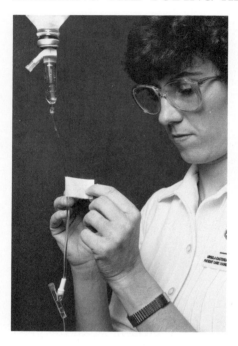

←

1 Attach a tape tab to the proximal end of the IV tubing, documenting the time and date the solution was hung. Change the tubing every 48–72 hours, depending on agency policy.

2 If the solution will be run slowly on a "keep vein open" (KVO) basis, label the container with the time and date it was hung. The container should be replaced at least every 24 hours. However, if it will be run more quickly, attach a timing label to enable you to gauge carefully the number of milliliters that must be infused hourly. *Note: In most agencies, KVO rate must be specified in ml/hr.*

→

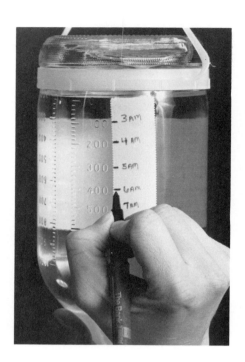

INSERTING A PERIPHERAL VASCULAR ACCESS DEVICE

ASSEMBLING THE MATERIALS

Before selecting the puncture site and assembling the materials, determine whether the client will receive short-term or long-term therapy, and note the viscosity of the prescribed solution. Clients with faster running infusions, viscous solutions, and presurgical and obstetric clients who may require blood transfusions all will require the use of larger needles, and hence, larger veins. Smaller wing-tipped needles are more often used for short-term therapy, children, older clients, or for clients with small, fragile veins. To insert a peripheral vascular access device, assemble the following (or variations of) materials, depending on agency routine: sterile gauze pads; tourniquet; air-occlusive 7.5-cm (3-in.) tape;

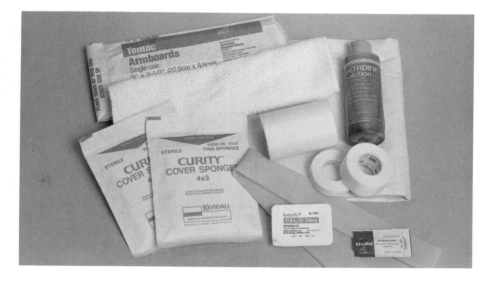

1.25-cm (½-in.) tape; 2.5-cm (1-in.) tape; bed-saver pad; arm board (optional); antimicrobial ointment (depending on agency policy), such as povidone-iodine; an antimicrobial skin preparation, such

as povidone-iodine; and the desired needle. We have chosen a wing-tipped (butterfly) needle for this procedure. In addition, you will need a pair of clean gloves.

CHOOSING A VENIPUNCTURE SITE

1 Review these anatomic overlays to assist you in locating the proper sites for a venipuncture.

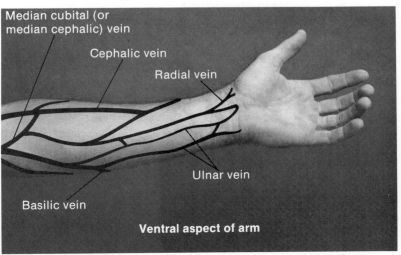

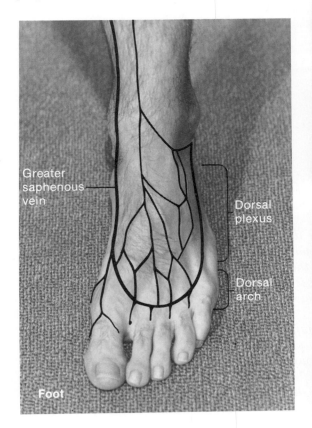

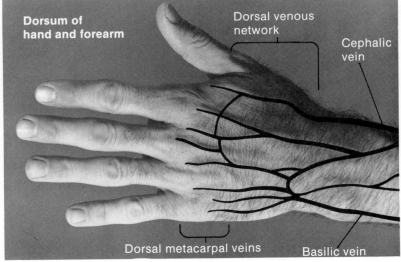

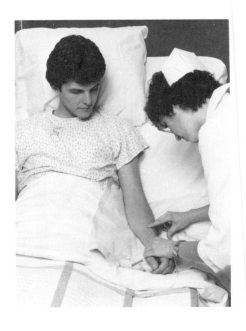

2 Wash your hands and explain the procedure to the client. Plan to use the nondominant arm if your client will have short-term therapy. Never use an arm with an arteriovenous fistula or the involved arm for a client who has had a radical mastectomy. Begin by inspecting the median, distal basilic, and cephalic veins in your client's hand and forearm. Observe for large, superficial, full veins in a site that is neither inflamed nor irritated. Palpate the site to ensure that the vein is soft, unscarred, and relatively straight. Always begin at the distal end of the vein, if possible, to preserve the proximal vein for future IV sites. If you can avoid it, stay away from joints such as the wrist and elbow because needles are easily dislodged in these areas.

DILATING THE VEIN

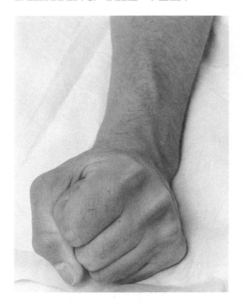

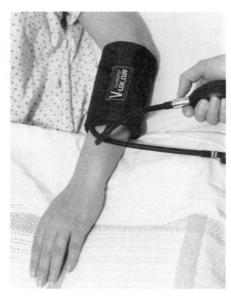

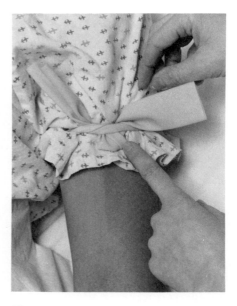

1 If the veins are not readily prominent, ask the client to open and close his fist. You may also apply manual pressure by wrapping your hands around the area just proximal to the potential insertion site and squeezing moderately to help dilate the vein. Applying hot, moist towels around the insertion site is also effective for many clients.

2 *Note: If you still have difficulty palpating the veins, wrap a blood pressure cuff below the antecubital fossa and inflate it to just below your client's systolic pressure (usually around 100 mm Hg). Deflate the cuff after palpating the veins. If you plan to use the cuff instead of a tourniquet to dilate the veins, deflate it to 40 mm Hg after having dilated the veins.*

3 When you have selected a viable site, wrap a tourniquet a few inches above it. To prevent pinching the skin, position the tourniquet over an article of clothing such as the sleeve of the hospital gown. The tourniquet should be tight enough to impede venous flow but not so tight that it occludes the arteries. You should still be able to palpate an arterial pulse distal to the tourniquet.

PREPARING THE SITE

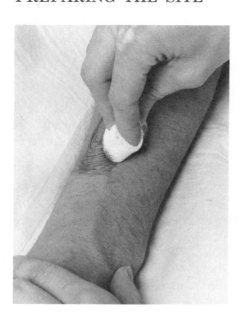

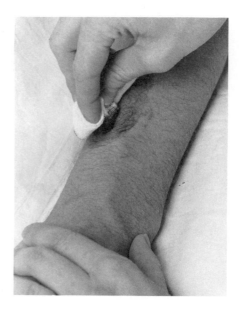

1 ← Prepare the insertion site by swabbing the skin with an antimicrobial solution, such as povidone-iodine. Apply the solution directly to the center of the site with a sterile applicator, such as a gauze pad.

2 Prepare the surrounding skin → using a circular motion and working outward to cover an area at least 5 cm (2 in.) in diameter. Allow the solution to dry thoroughly before inserting the needle.

INSERTING A WING-TIPPED (BUTTERFLY) NEEDLE

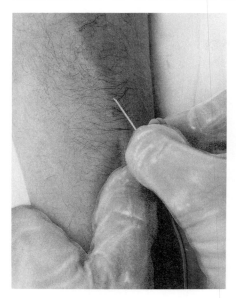

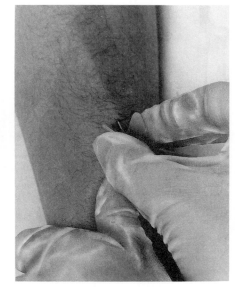

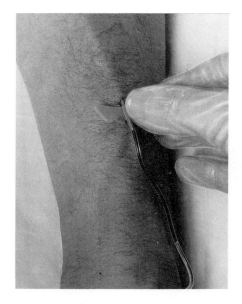

1 Apply gloves. With your free thumb, stabilize and anchor the vein distal to the insertion site. Ask the client to sustain a fist if his vein is not prominent. With the needle's bevel up, squeeze the wings together and position the needle at a 30- to 40-degree angle over the vein.

2 As you pierce the skin and enter the vein, decrease the angle to around 15 degrees. Advance the needle into the vein and continue to decrease the angle of the needle until it is parallel to your client's skin. You will feel a release or a gentle pop as the needle enters the vein. Then ask your client to open his fist. Release the tourniquet.

3 In most instances if you have inserted the needle properly, you will see a backflow of blood in the tubing. To prime the needle's tubing, allow the blood to fill its entire length. If the venipuncture has been unsuccessful, withdraw the needle; insert a new, sterile needle; and attempt the venipuncture again proximal to the initial site or in another vein.

4 If the needle is to be used for the infusion of IV fluids, carefully attach the adaptor of the primed infusion tubing to the needle's connector; slowly open the roller clamp (left) to start the infusion. Observe the drip chamber for an easy flow and inspect the insertion site for the presence of swelling, which would occur if the needle were positioned improperly. When you are certain that the venipuncture has been successful, decrease the flow and prepare to tape the needle and tubing.

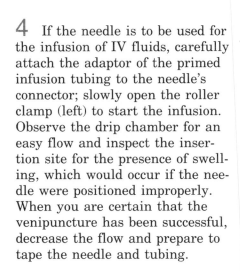

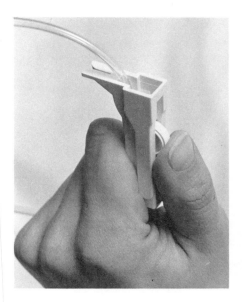

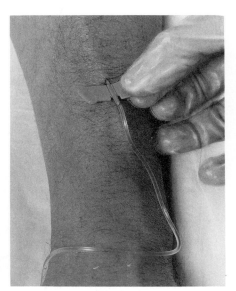

TAPING THE WING-TIPPED NEEDLE

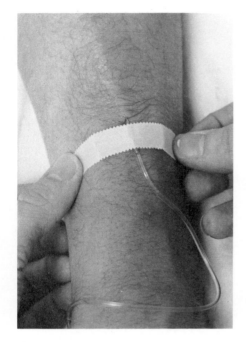

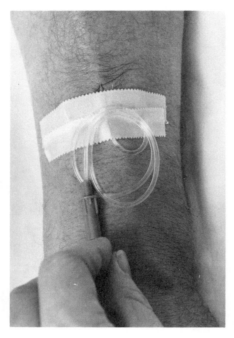

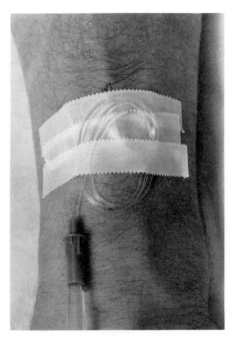

1 We recommend the following method for taping the wing-tipped needle. Cut three 7.5-cm (3-in.) strips of 1.25-cm (½-in.) tape. Place the first strip directly over the wings of the needle.

2 Attach the second strip of tape over the distal edge of the first strip. Then loop the tubing.

3 Place the third strip of tape over the looped tubing. Remember to keep the connector hub exposed so that you will have access to it for changing the tubing, for example, or for attaching an adaptor plug.

INSERTING AN OVER-THE-NEEDLE CATHETER (ANGIOCATH)

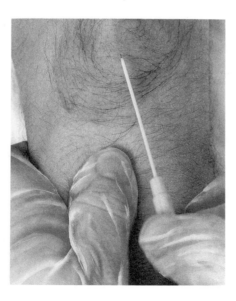

1 Review the preceding steps for preparing the skin and inserting a wing-tipped needle. Position the tip of the over-the-needle catheter over the selected vein at a 30- to 40-degree angle to the skin. With your free thumb, firmly anchor the vein distal to the insertion site.

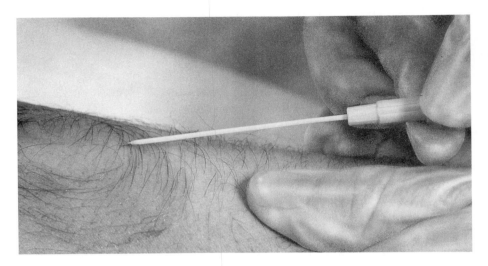

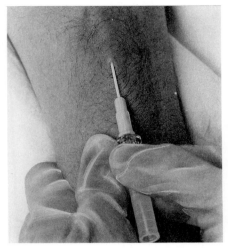

2 As you pierce the skin, reduce the angle of the needle to around 15 degrees (as shown).

3 Continue to advance the catheter into the vein and decrease the angle as you do until the needle is parallel to the skin. After the catheter has been inserted approximately 2.5 cm (1 in.), release the tourniquet. Remove the protective cap from the distal end of the infusion tubing and hold the tubing carefully between your last two fingers so that you are prepared for the next step.

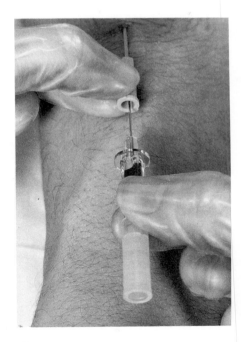

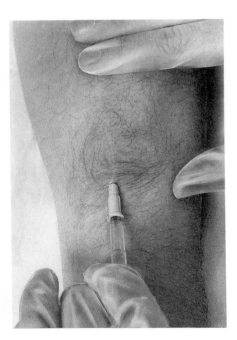

4 Firmly grasp the catheter hub with your thumb and index finger, and withdraw the needle with your free hand. If the catheter has been positioned properly, you should see a backflow of blood in the plastic hub of the needle.

5 After removing the needle, attach the distal end of the primed infusion tubing. Open the roller clamp slowly and observe for an easy flow of solution into the drip chamber. To double check, you can also apply pressure to the vein just proximal to the insertion site (as shown). If the dripping stops in the drip chamber at this time, you can be quite certain that the vein is patent and the needle has been positioned properly.

TAPING THE OVER-THE-NEEDLE CATHETER

1   An effective way to tape the over-the-needle catheter is to employ the "U" method. To do this, you will need three 7.5-cm (3-in.) strips of 1.25-cm (½-in.) tape. Place the first strip sticky side up under the needle's hub. Fold the end over (as shown) so that the sticky side adheres to the skin.

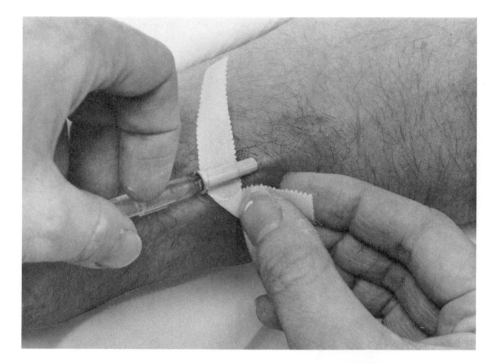

2   Fold the opposite end over and up in the same manner.

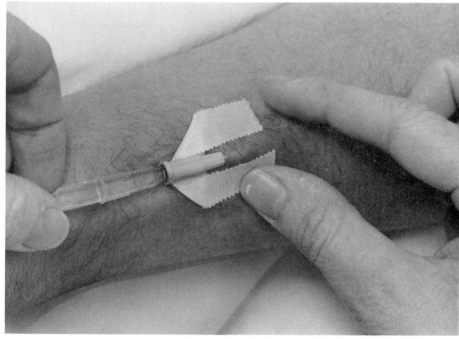

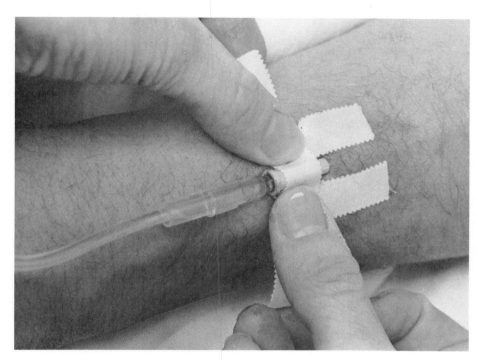

3 Place a second strip of tape sticky side down over the needle's hub.

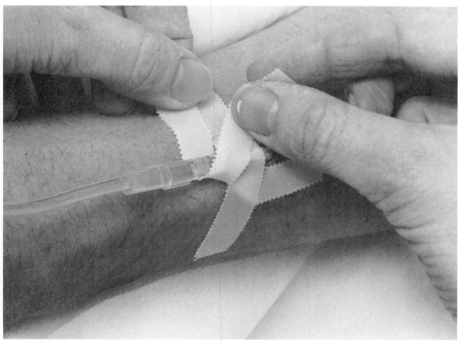

4 Place the third strip of tape sticky side up under the catheter hub and distal to the second strip. Then fold it diagonally across the hub sticky side down (as shown). Do the same for the opposite side of the tape.

APPLYING ANTIMICROBIAL OINTMENT AND A GAUZE DRESSING

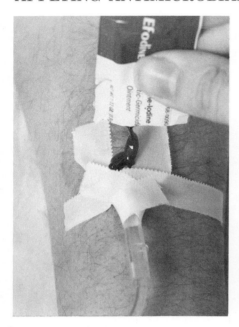

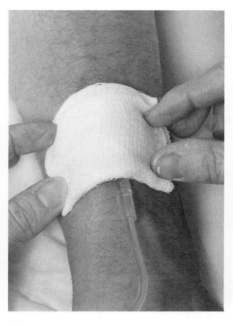

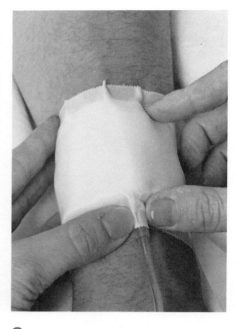

1 If antimicrobial ointment is used by your agency, apply it directly to the taped insertion site.

2 Cover the area with a sterile gauze pad. *Note: Dressings are often avoided in the neonate to ensure better site observation.*

3 Cover the gauze dressing with a 7.5 × 10-cm (3 × 4-in.) strip of tape. *Note: Transparent sterile dressings, such as Op-Site, are also used. These dressings allow close observation of the insertion site without the removal of the dressing (see procedure, pp. 166–167).*

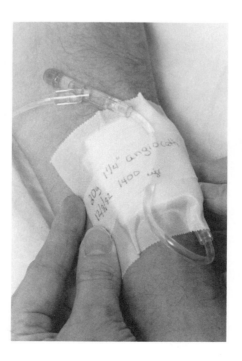

4 Loop the tubing over the tape. Secure it with a 2.5-cm (1-in.) strip of tape on which you have written the time and date of insertion, the type and gauge of needle, and your initials. At least daily, gently palpate the insertion site through the dressing to assess for tenderness. If the client has tenderness at the insertion site or an unexplained fever, you must visually inspect the site for redness or discharge. The needle or catheter should be changed every 48–72 hours unless another peripheral insertion site cannot be found at that time.

IMMOBILIZING THE EXTREMITY

USING AN ARMBOARD OR SPLINT

1   To prevent the needle or catheter from dislodging, it will be necessary for you to splint the extremity when a client is disoriented or combative or when the venipuncture site is at or near a joint, such as the wrist or elbow. For your client's comfort, be sure to pad the armboard or splint with a small towel or wash cloth. A short splint usually will be adequate if the venipuncture site is in the lower arm or hand, but use a long splint if the site is near the antecubital fossa. The hand should be prone (as shown) and well supported by the splint if the needle is in the hand or wrist. However, the fingers should be free to both extend and flex around the armboard.

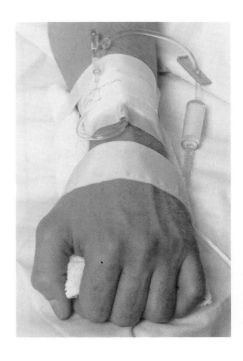

2   Secure the splint to the arm with two or three tape strips. To make a tape strip, you will need two pieces of tape of equal widths. Tear one piece long enough to encircle the arm and splint. The shorter piece should be just long enough to face the longer piece over the area that would otherwise cover the skin. Place the shorter piece of tape in the center of the longer piece with the sticky surfaces together (as shown). Then wrap the tape strip snugly around the arm and the splint. Be certain, however, that you do not impede circulation. Monitor the client frequently to ensure that color, sensation, and pulses are normal in the hand and arm.

APPLYING A COMMERCIAL WRIST RESTRAINT

1 If you have a physician's order (an order may not be necessary for the pediatric population), you can restrain the wrist of a disoriented or combative client who potentially may dislodge the needle or catheter in the opposite arm. Wrap a commercial restraint snugly (but not tightly) around the wrist to prevent the client from pulling the hand through the opening.

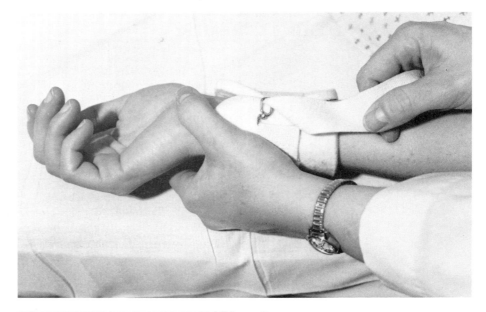

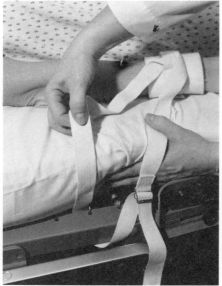

2 Attach the restraint to the bed frame. *Caution: Never attach the restraint to the side rails because this could result in injury to the arm when the side rails are lowered.* Allow enough slack in the restraint to provide the client adequate range of motion yet prevent contact with the opposite arm. Because the restraint will prevent normal movement, it is essential that you remove the restraint and change your client's position every 2 hours. Provide range of motion (ROM) exercises if the client must be restrained on a long-term basis. Also, ensure that color, sensation, and pulses are normal distal to the restraint, and provide skin care, such as massages with a moisturizer, if the skin under the restraint shows any sign of irritation.

3 As an alternative, a mitt restraint may be applied to prevent the client from removing the needle or catheter in the opposite arm. Ensure that it is tied snugly but not tightly around the wrist and that it is removed at least once per shift (or according to agency protocol) to provide skin care and perform ROM exercises on the wrist and fingers.

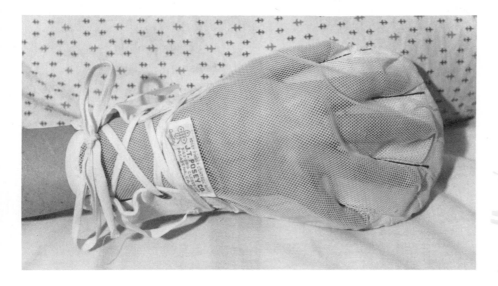

APPLYING A GAUZE RESTRAINT

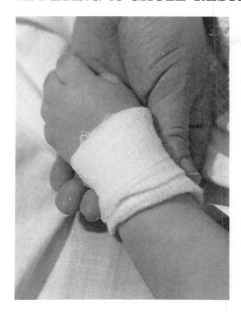

1 If commercially made restraints are unavailable, you can improvise with gauze pads and a strip of gauze roll at least 125 cm (50 in.) in length. First pad around the wrist with a double thickness of gauze padding.

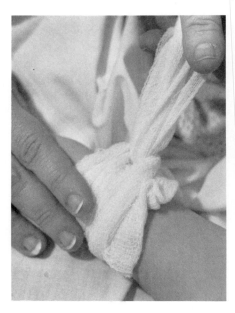

2 Tie the gauze roll around the gauze pad using a knot, such as a slip knot (as shown), that can be readily released in the event of an emergency.

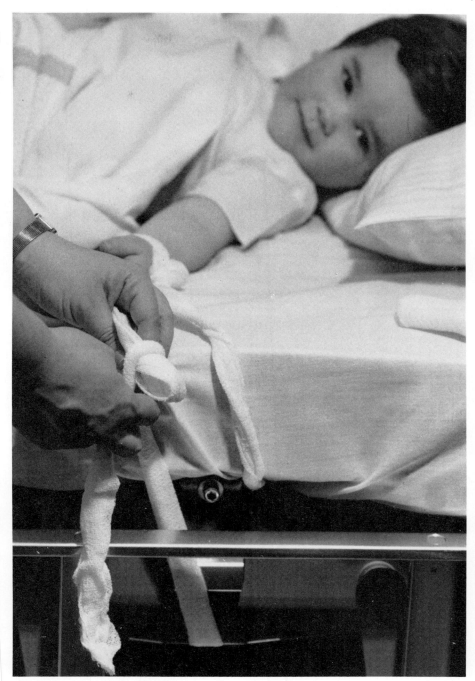

3 Wrap the gauze roll around the bed frame (not the side rails), and tie it in a bow so that you can easily release it in an emergency. When using gauze rather than a commercial restraint, it is especially important that you monitor the client frequently for signs of neurovascular impairment because of the difficulty in controlling the degree of tension on the wrist. Remove the restraint every 2 hours, and ensure that color, sensation, and pulse are normal. Provide skin care as necessary.

ADMINISTERING INTRAVENOUS (IV) MEDICATIONS

INJECTING MEDICATIONS INTO HANGING IV CONTAINERS

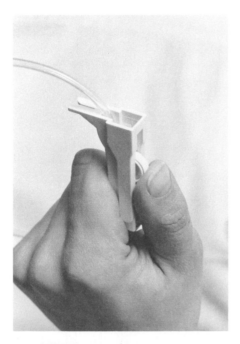

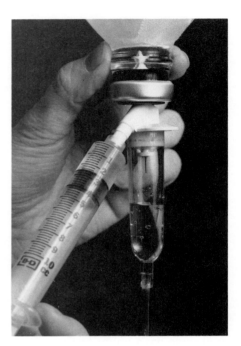

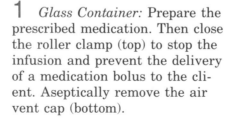

2   Remove the needle from the medication syringe and insert the syringe directly into the air vent. Inject the medication, and then gently rotate the bottle between your hands to mix the medication. Vigorous shaking would produce air bubbles. Replace the air vent cap and open the roller clamp. Adjust the rate of flow to the prescribed amount. Label the bottle with the type and amount of medication, the time and date it was added, and your initials. Document that medication was added to the IV infusion.

1   *Glass Container:* Prepare the prescribed medication. Then close the roller clamp (top) to stop the infusion and prevent the delivery of a medication bolus to the client. Aseptically remove the air vent cap (bottom).

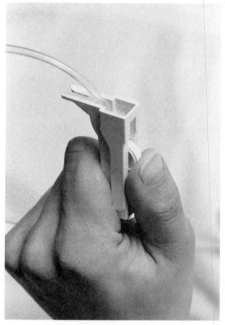

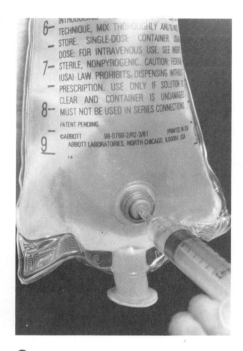

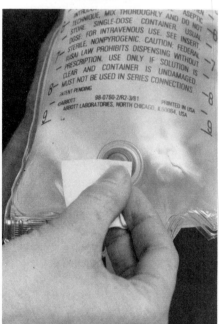

2 Insert the needle into the injection port and inject the medication. Gently rotate the bag between your hands to mix the medication; open the roller clamp to achieve the desired rate of flow. Make a medication label, noting the type and amount of medication, the time and date you added it, and your initials. Attach the label to the IV container, and document the medication.

1 *Plastic Container:* Prepare the prescribed medication, and close the roller clamp (top) to stop the flow of solution. This will prevent the delivery of a medication bolus to your client. Clean the injection port with an alcohol sponge (as shown).

GIVING MEDICATIONS BY IV BOLUS

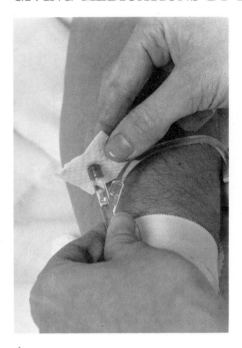

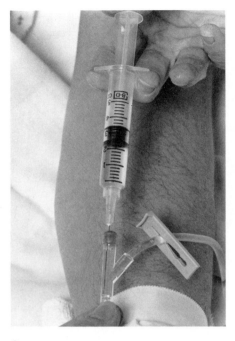

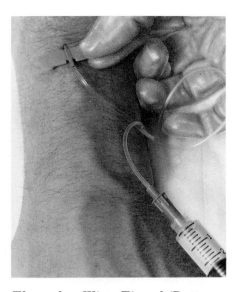

1 *Through a Primary Line:* After drawing up the prescribed medication, swab the injection port with an alcohol sponge.

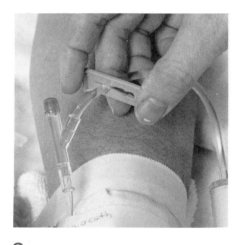

2 Close the roller clamp to stop the flow of the hanging solution; then close the slide clamp on the extension tubing (as shown), to ensure that the medication will be delivered directly into the client's vein.

3 If the hanging solution is compatible with the medication, insert the needle of the medication syringe into the injection port. To avoid dislodging the needle or catheter, stabilize the port between the thumb and index finger of your free hand; then aspirate for a blood return to ensure that the needle or catheter is safely in the vein. *Caution: Aspiration is usually contraindicated in infants and small children. Be especially alert to the signs of infiltration in this population.* Inject the medication at the prescribed rate. Stop the infusion immediately if the client exhibits a reaction to the drug. *Note: If the medication is incompatible with the IV solution, flush the tubing before and after the bolus with infusions of normal saline.* Open both clamps, and allow the hanging solution to flow again at the prescribed rate. Discard the syringe and needle unit uncapped into a puncture-resistant container (see procedure, p. 110). Document the medication.

Through a Wing-Tipped (Butterfly) Needle: If an intravenous medication has been prescribed for a client who does not have an indwelling catheter or needle, prepare the medication, and insert a wing-tipped needle (see steps, p. 121). A wing-tipped needle will be more stable than a needle that is attached to a syringe, and it will be less likely to become dislodged and traumatize the client's vein. After inserting the needle, remove the needle from the syringe, and attach the syringe to the administration port of the extension tubing. Anchor the wings of the needle with your free thumb and index finger as you aspirate for a backflow of blood. This will not only ensure that the needle is in the vein, it will also fill the extension tubing with blood so that you can inject the medication without forcing air into your client's vein. Then slowly inject the medication at the prescribed rate. This may take anywhere from a minute to several minutes. Stop the infusion immediately if your client shows any signs of an allergic reaction. When the medication has been infused, remove the needle and apply pressure at the insertion site with a sterile gauze pad. Maintain the pressure for a minute or until the client stops bleeding.

INSERTING A MALE ADAPTOR PLUG (HEPARIN LOCK) FOR INTERMITTENT INFUSION THERAPY

An intermittent infusion set (heparin lock) is an indwelling reservoir in the vein for intermittent infusion therapy when continuous infusion therapy is not indicated. Periodic injections of heparin into the device keep the needle or catheter patent. Be sure to follow your agency's protocol for injections of normal saline and heparin both before and after infusions into the lock. Indications for using either solution will vary from agency to agency.

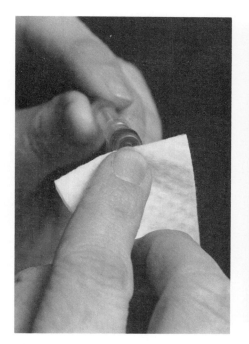

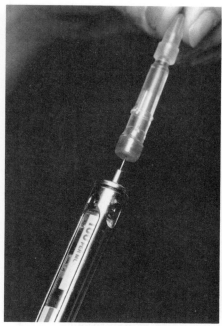

1 When continuous infusion therapy has been discontinued for your client who has an indwelling over-the-needle catheter, you can insert a male adaptor plug (MAP) into the catheter to convert it to a heparin lock. Before inserting the plug, swab the injection port with an alcohol sponge. Maintain asepsis by holding it by its protective cap (as shown).

2 Prime the MAP with the prescribed amount of heparinized solution both to keep it patent and to remove air from the chamber. *Note: Normal saline is used to prime the MAP in some agencies.*

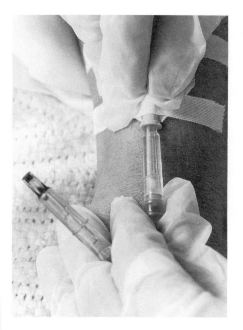

3 Close the roller clamp on the infusion set to stop the infusion. Put on clean gloves because there is the risk of contact with blood as you remove the IV tubing and insert the MAP. Aseptically remove the protective cap from the MAP. Detach the IV tubing, and insert the primed adaptor plug into the catheter hub. Apply a fresh dressing (see steps, p. 126) being certain to keep the injection port outside the air-occlusive tape for quick access.

(Continues)

4 To inject medications into the heparin lock, follow this general procedure. Remember to modify it according to your agency's protocol.

a. *In three separate syringes,* draw up the prescribed medication: 4 ml normal saline, or the prescribed amount, and 0.5 ml heparinized solution. The syringe needles should be no longer than 2.5 cm (1 in.), and the gauge should be small (25 gauge, for example) to avoid large puncture holes in the injection port.

b. *Swab the injection port* with an alcohol sponge.

c. *Insert the syringe* containing the normal saline and aspirate for a blood return to ensure that the catheter is in the vein.

d. *Inject* 2 ml of normal saline to flush the heparin from the catheter. (Some agencies advocate omitting this step and proceeding to the next step.)

e. *Remove the syringe* containing the normal saline, cap it to maintain the needle's asepsis (see procedure, p. 110), and attach the medication syringe. Inject the medication slowly, at the prescribed rate of infusion. Observe for adverse reactions to the medication.

f. *Remove the medication* syringe, and reattach the syringe containing the normal saline to flush the medication and prepare the lock for the heparin.

g. *Remove the normal saline* syringe, and insert the syringe with the heparinized solution to fill the lock and ensure patency for subsequent infusions.

h. *Every 8–12 hours* ensure patency by aspirating and flushing with 2–3 ml of normal saline. Then refill the lock with the heparinized solution. Unless another peripheral insertion site cannot be found, the heparin lock should be changed every 48–72 hours.

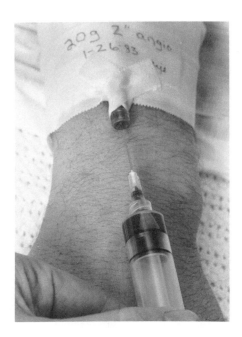

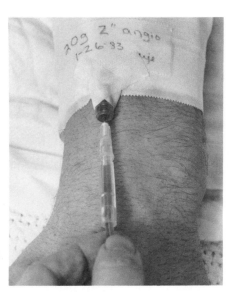

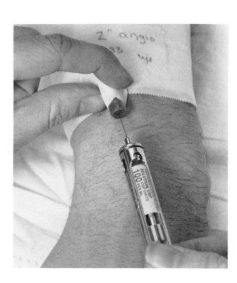

5 To administer intermittent infusions of a hanging solution, attach a 2.5-cm (1-in.) needle to the male end of the infusion tubing. Swab the injection port of the MAP with an alcohol sponge, and insert the infusion tubing (as shown). Adjust the roller clamp to achieve the desired rate of flow.

6 After discontinuing the hanging solution, clean the injection port with an alcohol sponge, and inject the prescribed amount of heparinized solution to ensure patency of the lock for subsequent infusions.

GIVING MEDICATIONS VIA A PARTIAL-FILL (PIGGYBACK) CONTAINER

Piggyback medications are administered through an established IV line via a secondary (piggyback) bottle, which attaches to the upper injection port on the primary line. The primary line must have a backcheck valve to prevent the tubing from running dry after the piggyback bottle empties. The backcheck valve allows the primary solution to run after the piggyback solution reaches the level of the drip chamber on the primary infusion tubing.

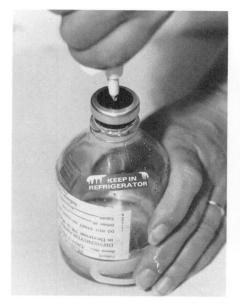

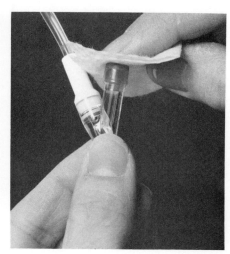

1 The piggyback infusion set may be primed by following the same general steps for priming a primary set (see pp. 116–117). However, the following steps for priming piggyback tubing will ensure that none of the medication is wasted during the priming. This is especially important when minute quantities of medication are to be infused. Close the slide clamp on the piggyback infusion set. On a flat surface, spike the piggyback bottle containing the medication.

2 Swab the upper injection port on the primary line with an alcohol sponge.

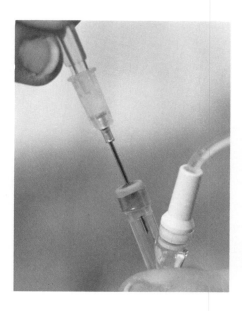

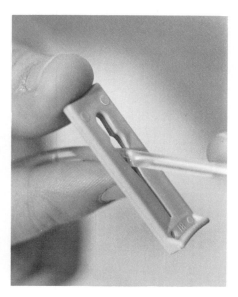

3 Close the roller clamp on the primary line to stop the infusion. Attach the piggyback needle to the end of the infusion tubing, and insert it into the upper injection port (left). Open the slide clamp on the piggyback infusion set (right). Solution from the primary container will run into the piggyback tubing, clearing out all the air. When the solution reaches the drip chamber on the piggyback tubing, close the slide clamp.

(Continues)

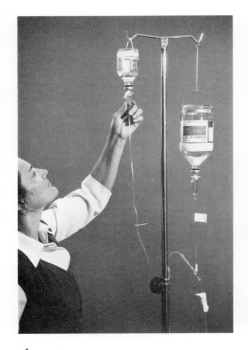

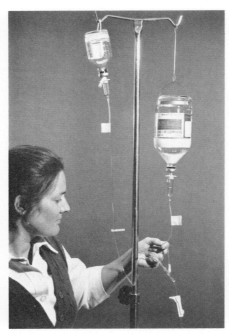

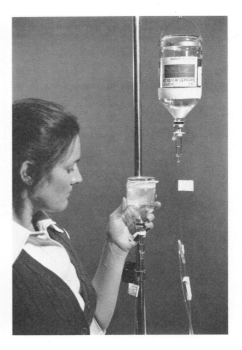

4 Hang the piggyback bottle on the IV pole. You will need an extension hook to rehang the primary set, making it lower than the piggyback container. This will activate the backcheck valve. Squeeze the drip chamber on the piggyback tubing and fill the drip chamber to the half-fill mark. Adjust the roller clamp on the primary tubing to regulate the rate of flow. Finally, label the piggyback's infusion tubing with the time and date. Document the medication.

5 *Note: When the piggyback container empties, you can administer the residual medication in the tubing by pinching the primary tubing just above the upper injection port until the fluid level reaches the needle at the upper injection port. When you release the pressure on the tubing, solution from the primary container may move into the piggyback tubing, but the backcheck valve will prevent it from entering the piggyback bottle.*

6 If you will need to hang a second piggyback bottle, close the roller clamp on the primary set and lower the empty bottle below the drip chamber on the primary set (as shown). Open the slide clamp on the piggyback tubing, and allow the primary solution to fill the piggyback tubing. Close the slide clamp on the piggyback tubing, remove the spike from the empty container, and aseptically insert it into the newly prepared piggyback container. Hang it on the IV pole, open the slide clamp, and adjust the flow rate with the roller clamp on the primary set.

ASSEMBLING A VOLUME-CONTROL IV SET

When it is necessary for you to administer precise doses of dilute medications to a child (or to an adult) over an extended period of time, a volume-control set will make this a safe and effective procedure for your client. Hang it as a primary line for a child. For an adult, it is most often used on a secondary line.

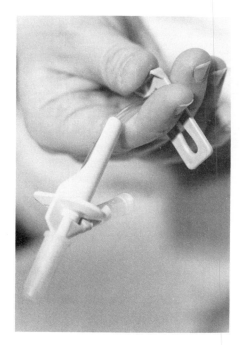

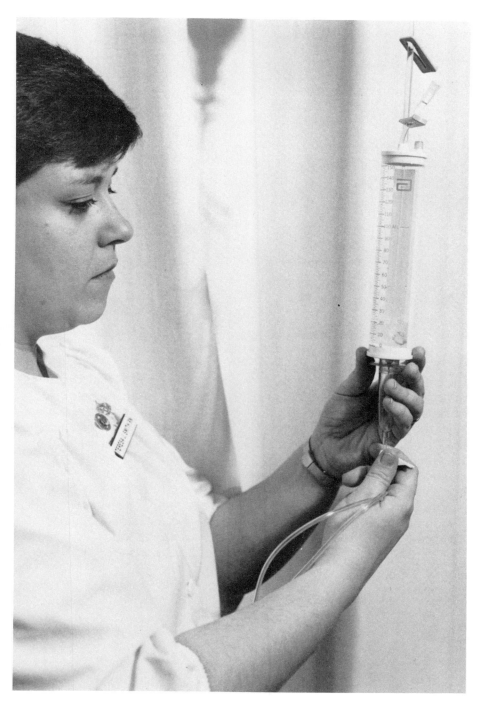

1 Prepare the IV container. Then slide the roller clamp up under the drip chamber and close it off. Close the main slide clamp under the spike (as shown). Remove the spike's protective cover, spike the container, and suspend it on an IV pole.

2 Open the main slide clamp and allow 25 ml of the solution to enter the burette (the fluid chamber). Close the main slide clamp.

(Continues)

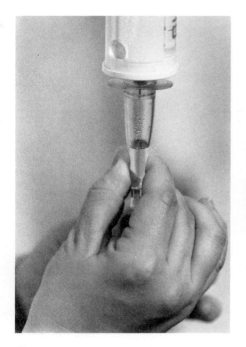

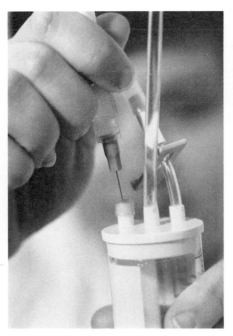

3 Squeeze the drip chamber to fill it to the half-fill line. This also should float the diaphragm at the base of the burette. Then open the roller clamp and allow the solution to flush the air from the tubing. Close the roller clamp. *Note: If the drip chamber becomes overfilled, close all the clamps and invert the burette. Squeeze the drip chamber to expel the excess fluid into the burette.*

4 To add medication to the burette, first ensure that the air filter (on the right in photo) is open. Then clean the medication port with an alcohol sponge, and inject the prescribed medication (as shown).

5 If the medication requires diluting, open the main slide clamp to add the desired amount of solution to the burette. Then close the slide clamp.

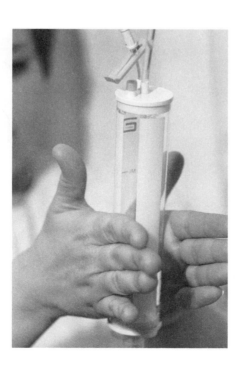

6 Gently roll the burette between your hands to mix the medication with the solution. Attach the distal end of the tubing either to your client's indwelling needle or catheter or to the injection port on the primary tubing. Open the roller clamp, and administer the medication at the prescribed rate. The flow will automatically shut off when the burette empties. To refill the burette, repeat steps 2 and 3 above. Be sure to label the burette with the name and dose of the medication and your initials. Document the medication.

ADMINISTERING IV FAT EMULSIONS

1 Fat emulsions are prescribed for clients who are deficient in essential fatty acids because of disorders such as severe burns, end-stage kidney diseases, ulcerative colitis, or malignancies. They may be administered via either peripheral or central veins, and they are usually delivered along with total parenteral nutrition solutions, which help restore the client's other nutritional deficiencies. It is important that you check vital signs prior to administering the fat emulsion so that you have a baseline for subsequent assessment during the infusion. If the solution has been refrigerated, let it stand for 30 minutes at room temperature so that the client will be more comfortable during the infusion. Liposyn, however, is stored at room temperature. Inspect the solution for signs of instability, such as discoloration or curdling, and discard the container if you note either of these irregularities. Your agency may specify a certain type of tubing for infusing fat emulsions because some plastic tubings may be incompatible with lipids. If you will deliver the solution via an infusion pump,

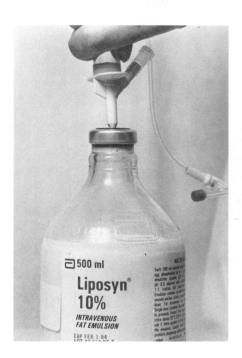

use the special tubing recommended by the manufacturer of the pump. For gravity infusions, however, a macrodrip tubing will more easily accommodate the fat globules. Spike the container (as shown), and hang it on an IV pole. Then prime the tubing, being certain to flush out all the air. To minimize the formation of air bubbles, prime the tubing more slowly than you would with a less viscous solution.

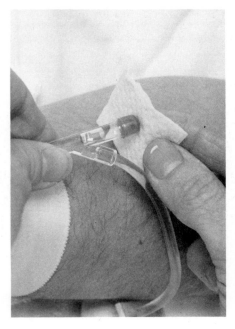

2 With an alcohol swab, clean the injection port that is closest to the insertion site. Using this port rather than others that may be farther up on the infusion tubing will minimize the amount of time during which the fat emulsion will mix with the primary solution and decrease the potential for the emulsion to break down.

(Continues)

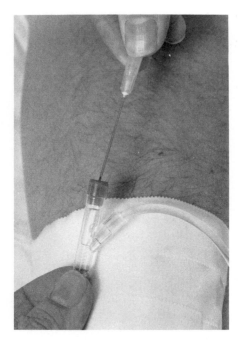

3   Attach a 20-gauge needle to the end of the infusion tubing and insert it into the port. Securely tape the connection. Remember that you must not connect a filter below the insertion of the fat emulsion because the density of the solution would clog the filter.

4   When gravity infusion is used, note that because of its viscosity, the fat emulsion is hung higher than the total parenteral nutrition solution. This prevents the solution from backing up into the infusion tubing. Be sure to label the container with the time and date the solution was hung. To minimize the chance for bacterial growth, the solution should be discarded if it has not infused within 12 hours. To prevent waste, smaller flasks should be hung if the unit of use required over a 12-hour period is considerably less than 500 ml. In most instances, the fat emulsion will be infused slowly at first to test the client's ability to tolerate the lipids. Guidelines for infusion will vary, depending on the manufac-

turer, the concentration of the fat emulsion, and the route of administration (either peripheral or central vein). Follow physician or agency guidelines carefully to ensure your client's comfort and safety. In many cases, no more than 1 ml/min should be delivered during the first 30 minutes, and vital signs should be taken every 10 minutes. For infants and children, you may be required to administer as little as 0.1 ml/min. Assess for adverse reactions to the fat emulsion, for example, chilling, fever, headache, nausea, vomiting, dyspnea, and chest pain. If these reactions occur, stop the infusion and notify the physician. If there is no reaction, increase the infusion to the prescribed rate. As a general guideline, the usual adult dosage is 500 ml/day, and it should never be delivered over a period of less than 4–6 hours. A child usually receives 250 ml/day. Continue to assess the client for an adverse reaction during the period of time the fat emulsion is being delivered. In addition, closely monitor the laboratory values for the serum triglycerides and liver function tests, which are indicators of your client's ability to metabolize the lipids. However, blood should not be drawn for 4–6 hours after the fat emulsion has been administered because the lipids would not have left the bloodstream and an incorrect blood value could result.

Collecting, Monitoring, and Administering Blood

COLLECTING A BLOOD SAMPLE WITH A VACUTAINER

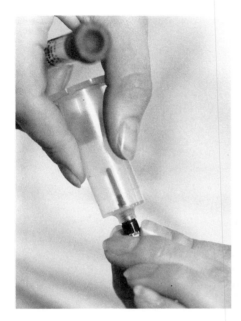

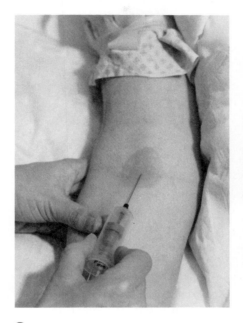

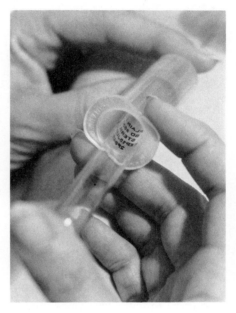

1   Aseptically screw the double-ended needle into the plastic outer container, with the shorter needle positioned inside the outer container (as shown). Then insert the vacuum tube into the outer container with the rubber stopper of the tube resting against the shorter needle.

2   Review the procedures earlier in this chapter for preparing the skin, dilating the vein, and performing a venipuncture, and proceed with the venipuncture at the antecubital space. *Caution: 1988 CDC guidelines state that nurses should wear clean gloves for venipuncture under the following circumstances: (1) if the nurse has cuts, scratches, or other skin breaks; (2) if the situation is one in which blood contamination may occur (e.g., pediatric or uncooperative client); and (3) if the nurse is learning venipuncture.*

3   After puncturing the vein, stabilize the plastic outer container, and gently yet firmly advance the vacuum tube to pierce the rubber stopper with the short needle.

(Continues)

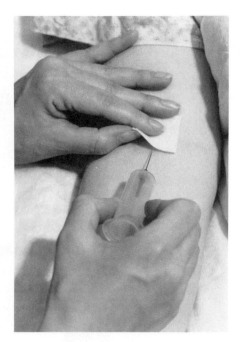

4 Because of the vacuum, blood immediately should begin spurting into the vacuum tube. As soon as it does, release the tourniquet to prevent the blood from seeping into the surrounding tissues. Remove the vacuum tube when it becomes full and set it aside. If required, insert another vacuum tube.

5 For your client's comfort be sure to remove the vacuum tube, thus preventing vacuum, before you remove the needle from the vein. Then gently remove the needle. Apply a sterile sponge to the site, and ask the client to press on the sponge for 1–3 minutes to stop the bleeding. Once the bleeding has ceased, place a bandage over the puncture site. Arrange for the delivery of the blood to the laboratory, and document the procedure.

TEACHING THE DIABETIC CLIENT SELF-MONITORING OF BLOOD GLUCOSE

Until a few years ago, urine testing was the only method available to the diabetic client for testing of glucose levels at home. Now, however, there are several blood-glucose testing products available that provide a much more accurate indicator of current glucose levels. In addition, they give greater control over the management of the disease and help in the prevention of such acute complications as hypoglycemia and hyperglycemia as well as chronic complications, such as

blindness, renal failure, and neuropathies. Of course, the client must continue to test the urine for ketones if he or she is ill or if blood-glucose levels are high. Blood glucose can be monitored both visually and with an electronic meter.

MONITORING BLOOD GLUCOSE VISUALLY

1 For visual monitoring of blood glucose, assemble facial tissue, reagent strips for showing glucose levels, and a watch with a second hand. In addition, you will also need a device for puncturing the skin (usually at the fingertip) to obtain the capillary blood. Either a manual device, such as a needle or lancet, or an automatic device (as shown) may be used.

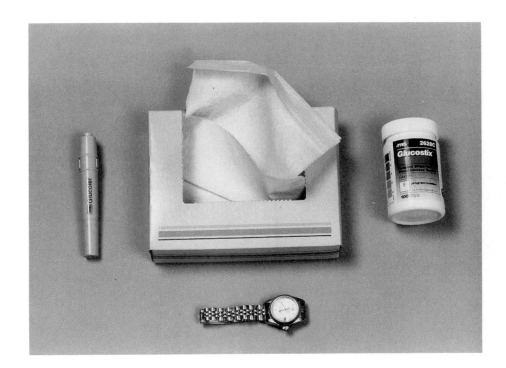

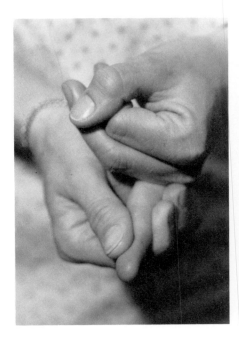

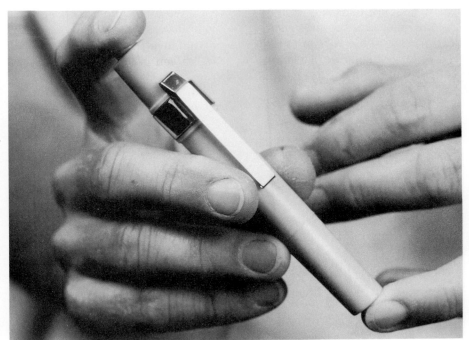

2 Have the client wash both hands with soap and warm water to remove surface bacteria and increase peripheral dilatation; the hands then should be dried thoroughly. Instruct the client to squeeze the fingertip while holding the arm below the level of the heart. This will well the blood at the puncture site.

3 The platform of the automatic puncturing device should be placed directly over the puncture site. The periphery of the fingertip should be used because it is less sensitive to pain, and, in many clients, it has fewer callouses than other areas of the finger. To lower the lance and puncture the skin, instruct the client to depress the button (under the client's right index finger).

(Continues)

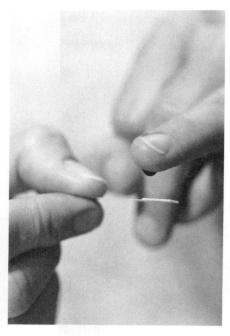

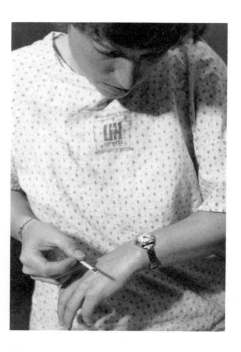

4 The client should then milk the finger by alternately squeezing and releasing the pressure until a drop of blood is produced that is large enough to cover the reagent pad on the test strip.

5 Have the client position the test strip just under the droplet of blood (as shown), and cover the entire surface area of the reagent pad with the blood. Smearing the blood onto the surface, however, could cause the blood to soak in unevenly and distort the reading.

6 The moment the blood touches the strip, the client must begin timing the strip for a period of 30 seconds (or the specified time).

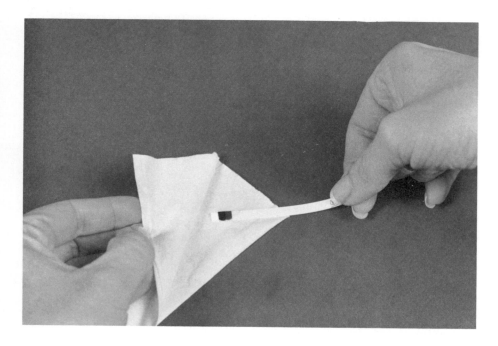

7 When 30 seconds have elapsed, instruct the client to blot the blood gently between the folds of the facial tissue. *Note: This step will vary, depending on the manufacturer of the test strip. Follow the instructions for the reagent strips your agency uses.* After blotting the blood, wait 90 seconds (or the specified time).

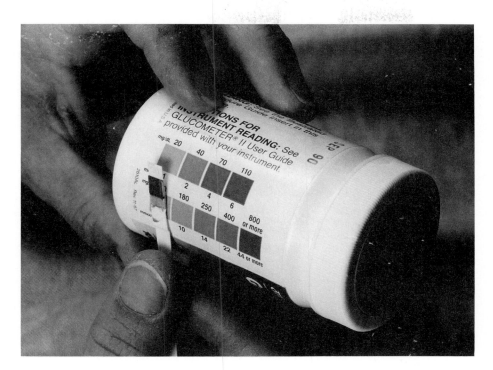

8 Compare the reagent pad to the colored blocks on the back of the container from which the strip was obtained. If the color of the reagent pad falls between two of the color blocks, instruct the client to take the average of the two values to estimate the glucose level. This is called interpolation. The client should then record the result in a log book, along with the time and date, the time and dose of the last insulin injection, and the amount of stress or activity currently being experienced. Blood glucose values for the client with diabetes will vary, depending on such conditions as food intake, exercise, or insulin dose. Capillary blood glucose values for the nonpregnant, nondiabetic adult are as follows: *fasting* <100 mg/dl (5.6 mmol/l); *2-hour glucose tolerance test* 140 mg/dl (7.8 mmol/l).

MONITORING BLOOD GLUCOSE WITH AN ELECTRONIC METER

1 Clients who desire a more precise method of blood-glucose monitoring than visual testing may be candidates for an electronic meter. The following is the procedure for using a Glucometer II®, a brand of electronic meter. Adapt this procedure for the meter used by your agency or client. In addition to the meter, assemble the following items: a skin-puncturing device, the reagent strip required by the meter manufacturer (Glucostix® for this meter), and facial tissues (or as required by the meter manufacturer).

(Continues)

2 Review steps 2–4 on pp. 143–144 for preparing and puncturing the skin and obtaining a large droplet of blood. Before puncturing the skin, turn the meter on (left arrow). Once the blood droplet has been obtained, instruct the client to press the "start" button (right arrow). Approximately 9 seconds will elapse before the first buzzer will sound.

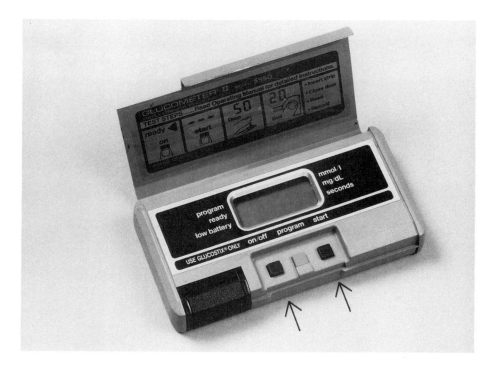

3 At the sound of the buzzer, the client quickly applies the droplet of blood to the reagent strip, as shown. Remind the client that smearing the blood too thinly may distort the test results because the blood could unevenly soak into the reagent pad or dry, making it difficult to remove the blood. When the first buzzer sounds, the meter will display 50 on the digital panel and begin its countdown from 50 to 0 seconds. During this countdown, the client must hold the reagent strip level with the table to prevent the blood droplet from falling off the reagent pad, potentially distorting the value.

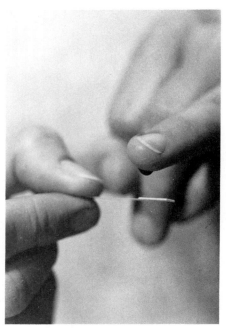

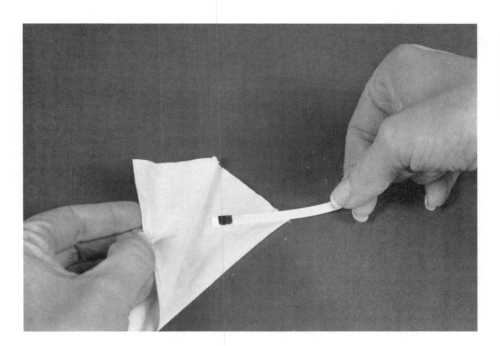

4 At 23 seconds the meter will beep. Instruct the client to blot the reagent pad on the facial tissue at 20 seconds and to repeat the blotting a second time on a clean portion of the tissue.

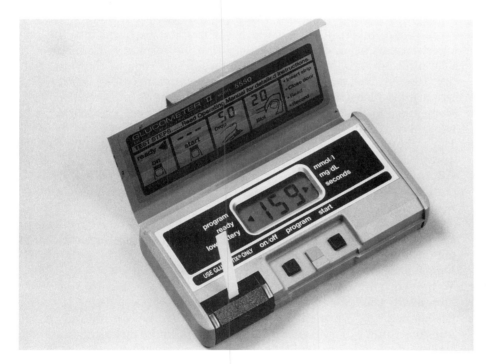

5 Once the reagent pad has been blotted (and before the meter counts down to 0), the client immediately inserts the strip into the strip guide of the meter. The digital panel will display the blood-glucose value automatically. Encourage the client to record the value while it is still illuminated on the digital panel, and then turn off the meter. The client should then continue to record other data in the record log, such as the time and date, number of hours since the last meal and insulin injection (unless an insulin pump is used), and the amount of activity or stress currently being experienced.

INITIATING AND MONITORING BLOOD TRANSFUSIONS

Nursing Guidelines for the Safe Administration of Blood

- To decrease the risk of potential bacterial growth, a blood infusion should be started within 30 minutes after it has been issued from the blood bank.
- For normal, healthy adults, use an 18- to 19-gauge needle or catheter to enhance the flow rate and to prevent injury to the red cells (hemolysis). Children and clients with small or thin-walled veins may require needles as small as 23 gauge: Monitor these clients carefully for adverse reactions and expect a much slower infusion rate.
- Use a special blood administration set with a filter specified by your agency for filtering out cellular debris.
- Hang only 0.9% normal saline with the blood. Dextrose, Ringer's solution, medications and other additives, and hyperalimentation solutions are incompatible and may result in hemolysis or clumping.
- To prevent incompatibilities with a primary solution, and for a more secure insertion site, avoid piggybacking the blood into the injection port of an existing primary line. Perform a venipuncture at a different site, or (with a physician's order) remove the infusion set from an existing indwelling 18- to 19-gauge needle and attach the primed blood infusion set directly to the indwelling needle. Remember to flush an existing needle with 50 ml of 0.9% normal saline before infusing the blood.
- Hang the blood and normal saline approximately 1 m (3–4 ft) above the client's heart for an optimal flow rate.
- Administer the blood at the rate of flow prescribed by the physician. Obtain an order for the administration rate if one has not been written.
- The maximum time for infusing a unit of blood is 4 hours (American Association of Blood Banks, 1987:54). There is an increased potential for bacterial growth in blood that is allowed to hang for a longer period of time.
- To prevent circulatory overload for clients with cardiac disorders, administer the transfusion slowly.
- Blood should be warmed *only* when large amounts are infused rapidly and could otherwise cause hypothermia and dysrhythmias. Rapid infusions more typically occur in the operating room, in the emergency room, or in the critical care setting.

ADMINISTERING BLOOD OR BLOOD COMPONENTS

Assessing and Planning

1 Prior to administering the blood, carefully compare the data on the crossmatch report and requisition form to the blood unit information. Check the following data with another health care professional: the client's name and hospital number, blood unit number, blood expiration date, blood group, and blood type. Inspect the blood for abnormalities, such as gas bubbles or black sediment, which are indicative of bacterial growth and necessitate returning the blood to the blood bank.

2 Explain the procedure to the client. Both you and a co-worker should then compare the blood unit information to the data on the client's wristband. Ensure that the client's name and hospital number positively match the data on the blood unit; then sign the blood transfusion form according to agency policy. Reconfirm data from the client history regarding known allergies or previous adverse reactions to blood transfusions. Be sure to take and record the vital signs to provide a baseline for subsequent assessments during the transfusion.

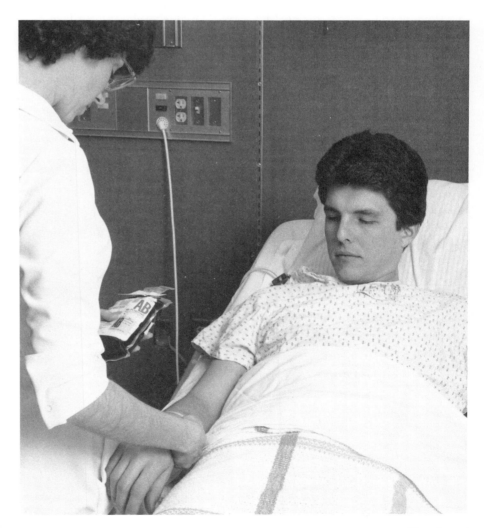

(Continues)

Implementing

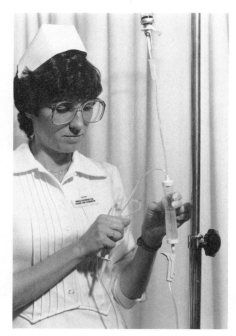

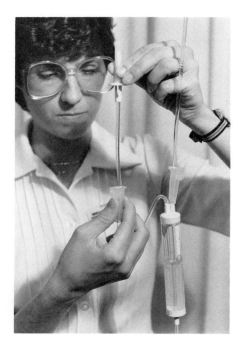

3 Review the procedures earlier in this chapter for inserting a peripheral access device and spiking and priming infusion sets. Obtain a "Y" infusion set for the administration of blood, as specified by your agency. Ensure that the attached blood filter is appropriate for the whole blood or blood components that will be transfused. Close all the clamps on the "Y" set (as shown), and spike a container of 0.9% normal saline with one of the "Y" spikes. Hang the container.

4 Open the clamp on the normal saline line and squeeze the drip chamber to prime the upper line and blood filter. Tap the chamber to remove any residual air.

5 Open the clamp on the empty line on which you will eventually hang the blood. The normal saline will flow up the blood line to prime that part of the "Y." Then close the clamp on the blood line, leaving the clamp on the normal saline line open.

6 Open the main roller clamp to prime the lower infusion tubing and flush out the air. Close the main roller clamp.

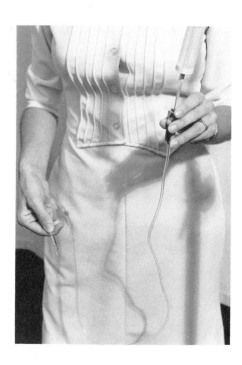

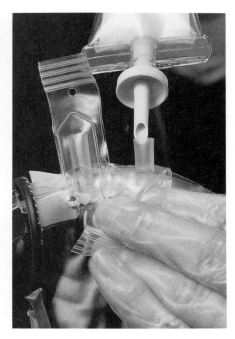

7 Wearing clean gloves, aseptically pull apart the plastic tabs on the blood container (as shown) to expose the blood port.

8 Insert the remaining "Y" spike into the blood port, and hang the blood at the same level (1 m) as the normal saline.

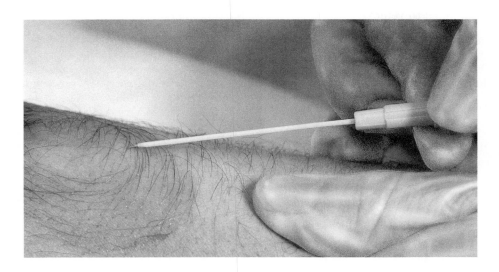

9 Perform a venipuncture with an 18- to 19-gauge needle or catheter, or, if the physician has ordered its discontinuation, remove the infusion tubing from an indwelling 18- to 19-gauge needle. Attach the primed infusion set to the needle, tape it securely, and, if necessary, secure a splint or armboard to the client's arm to ensure the needle's stability. If appropriate, run in 50 ml of the normal saline to flush a preexisting needle of an incompatible solution. Otherwise, close the upper roller clamp on the normal saline, and open the clamp to the blood. Adjust the main roller clamp to deliver approximately 10–25 ml over the next 15 minutes.

(Continues)

Evaluating

10 Assess the client frequently over the next 15–30 minutes, and monitor him for signs of an adverse reaction to the transfusion (Table 3-1). After the first 15 minutes of the transfusion, check the vital signs again and compare them to the baseline. Be especially alert to a sudden decrease in blood pressure or a rise in temperature. If the vital signs are stable, gradually increase the rate of flow to the prescribed rate. Continue to monitor the client and document the vital signs at least hourly, or more frequently, depending on agency guidelines. If your client has a cardiac disorder, or if large amounts of blood are being in-

fused over a short period of time, auscultate the lung bases for adventitious breath sounds such as crackles (rales) that could indicate circulatory overload. When the blood has been infused, flush the tubing and filter with 20–50 ml of the normal saline to deliver the residual blood. Then either run the normal saline at a KVO rate, or hang another solution as prescribed (after changing the blood administration set). Maintain the venipuncture site in case the client develops a delayed reaction to the blood. Document the procedure.

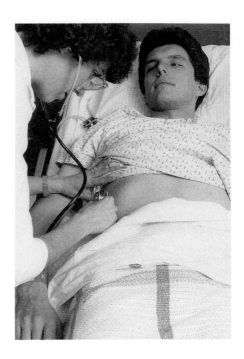

Table 3-1   Recognizing Transfusion Reactions

Reaction type	Clinical indications	Nursing interventions
Allergic: caused from a sensitivity to a plasma protein in the donor blood	*Mild:* rash, hives, itching *Severe:* wheezing, laryngeal edema, bronchial spasm, anaphylactic reaction	Stop the infusion, monitor client carefully, notify physician, and administer prescribed injections of antihistamines. *For severe symptoms:* stop transfusion; keep vein open with a slow infusion normal saline; notify physician; administer prescribed injections of antihistamines, or if more serious, epinephrine or corticosteroids; stay with client and monitor for potential anaphylaxis.
Septic: caused from bacterial contamination, improper storage or refrigeration of the blood, and other unknown factors	Chills, increased temperature, headache, hypotension, lumbar or leg pain, nausea, and vomiting	Maintain venipuncture site, but stop transfusion immediately; change infusion set as soon as possible; notify physician and blood bank; send used infusion set to lab for culturing; administer prescribed antibiotics, antipyretics, vasopressors, or steroids; stay with client; monitor vital signs; observe for anaphylaxis.
Hemolytic: caused from incompatibility of donor blood with recipient blood, improper storage or refrigeration, improper infusion with dextrose or any other additive or solution other than 0.9% normal saline	Anxiety, restlessness, chills, increase in temperature, chest pain, cyanosis, hematuria, hypotension, tachycardia, and tachypnea. If untreated, shock and anuria ensue.	Discontinue transfusion, maintain venipuncture site, change infusion set and keep vein open with normal saline or prescribed solution, notify physician, administer oxygen, obtain blood and urine samples and send them to blood bank with the suspect unit of blood, administer prescribed diuretic or vasopressor, stay with client and monitor vital signs and intake and output.
Circulatory Overload: caused from excessive infusion amounts or too rapid an infusion rate	Chest or lumbar pain, cyanosis, dyspnea, moist productive cough, crackles (rales) in lung bases, distended neck veins, increase in central venous pressure	Discontinue infusion, but keep vein open with dextrose, or as prescribed; raise head of bed and deliver oxygen; notify physician; administer diuretics and aminophylline as prescribed; stay with client and monitor vital signs; prepare for a phlebotomy if symptoms are severe.

Initiating Patient-Controlled Analgesia

Patient-controlled analgesia (PCA) involves the use of a programmed syringe pump that delivers predetermined amounts of analgesia at preset intervals. PCA enables the client to titrate analgesia to maintain a consistent serum level of narcotic rather than experience the peaks and troughs that occur with p.r.n. injections. Client populations for whom this device is indicated include those in need of parenteral analgesia, those willing to operate the device, and those mentally alert and able to follow instructions. Populations for whom the device is usually contraindicated include those with chronic pulmonary diseases, those with a history of allergies to morphine or meperidine, those with a history of drug abuse, and those with major psychiatric disorders.

The pump is programmed by the nursing staff as prescribed by the physician for the following: dose increment to be delivered, minimum time interval between delivered doses ("lockout" interval), and total doses available over a 4-hour period. Clients initiate infusions by pressing a handheld control button that is connected to the pump. The client has an IV infusion running to keep the vein open between analgesia infusions.

Client instruction is a critical part of this therapy. The client must verbalize understanding of how the PCA device works *before* the therapy is initiated. Provide the client with verbal instructions, and reinforce this information with reading materials, such as booklets about PCA therapy. In addition, instruct the client to notify staff for the following: pain relief not being obtained, change in the severity or location of pain, machine appearing to malfunction, alarms sounding, or any questions arising regarding the machine or pain relief.

Note: The following procedure applies to the Abbott pump. These guidelines will vary, depending on the manufacturer of the PCA equipment.

Assessing and Planning

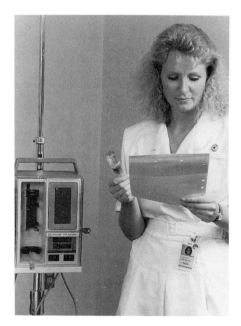

1 Verify physician prescription for the PCA, comparing it to the vial of analgesia that was obtained from the pharmacy and noting prescribed pump settings. *Note: If the pump is for a pediatric client, it is recommended that two nurses verify pump settings.* Morphine is supplied in 30-ml vial injectors with a concentration of 1 mg/ml, and meperidine (Demerol) is supplied in 30-ml vial injectors with a concentration of 10 mg/ml.

Be aware that administration of blood or any other medication incompatible with morphine or meperidine requires a second IV site. If a triple-lumen catheter is to be used for the infusion, the narcotic infusion is usually administered through the proximal port.

Perform a baseline assessment of your client's respiratory system (see Chapter 6) for ongoing comparison throughout the PCA therapy. Also verify that your client is not allergic to morphine or meperidine, whichever is prescribed. Reinforce client teaching information as described above. Assemble the PCA pump and infusion tubing.

(Continues)

Implementing

2 Snap off the caps from the injector (plunger) and prefilled vial, and connect the injector to the vial by screwing them together.

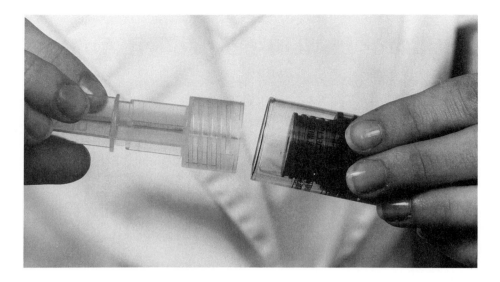

3 Prime the unit by pushing down on the injector to eject the air.

4 Next, attach the female connector on the long end of the PCA tubing to the male end of the injector in the vial.

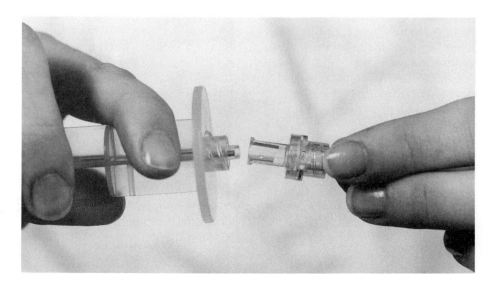

5 Flush the tubing *only* as far as the Y-branch (Y-injection site backcheck valve port). *Caution: Flushing all the tubing would administer more than the prescribed dose of IV narcotic when it is attached to the client.* Close the slide clamp on the PCA tubing, as shown.

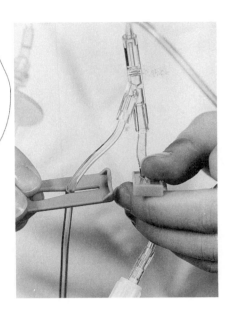

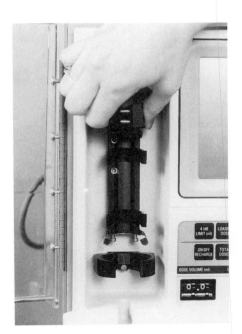

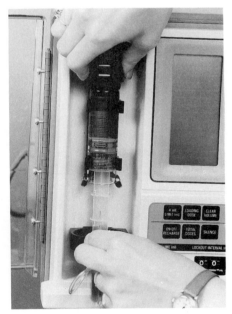

6 Open the machine door by turning the key. Activate the drive release mechanism on the pump by pinching the spring-loaded lever, as shown, and retracting the drive assembly (moving it all the way up).

7 Load the vial into the drive assembly and clamp it securely in place, with the graduations on the vial facing out. After the vial has been clamped in place, activate the drive release mechanism again by pinching the spring-loaded lever (as shown), and slide the drive assembly down until it securely locks the vial in place. The flange on the injector (behind the nurse's lower hand) must

"click" into its locked position in the holder. Then close the door on the pump and take it to the client's room. Plug the pump into an appropriate outlet unless battery operation is desired.

(Continues)

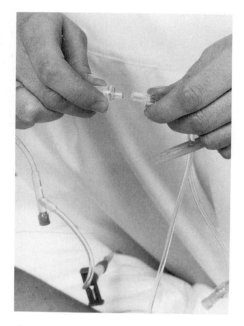

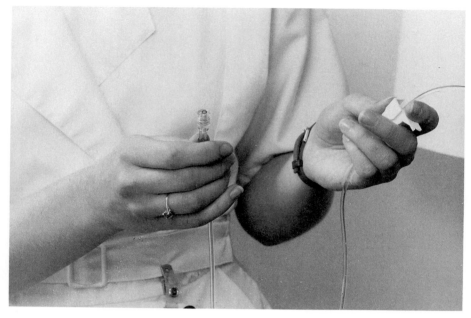

8 Remove the protective cap from the Y-site on the PCA tubing, and attach it to the distal end of the client's maintenance IV fluid tubing.

If the client already has maintenance fluids running, stop the infusion by clamping off the fluids using the roller clamp on the tubing. Disconnect the maintenance fluid tubing from the client's connector tubing, being certain to maintain sterility. Remove the protective cap from the Y-site on the PCA tubing, and attach the distal male connector of the maintenance IV tubing to the female connector of the PCA tubing.

9 Prime the remainder of the PCA tubing by adjusting the roller clamp on the maintenance infusion tubing.

10 Attach the male end of the PCA tubing to the female end of the client's connector tubing. Open the slide clamps on the main IV infusion tubing, the PCA tubing, and the client's connector tubing. Or, as another option, remove the client's connector tubing, and insert the PCA tubing directly into the hub of the angiocath.

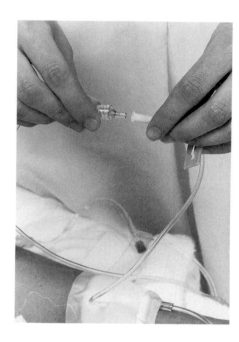

11 If appropriate at this time, press the ON/OFF button to turn on the machine. DOOR OPEN and VOLUME DELIVERED messages will appear once the machine is turned on. CHECK SYRINGE and ALARM messages also will appear if the injector is not positioned securely in the injector holder.

Adjust the pump dials according to the physician's prescribed limits. If a loading dose has been prescribed, establish this before setting the other limits. Set LOCKOUT LIMIT at 00 minutes, and then set the prescribed volume to be delivered, using the DOSE VOLUME control (set in tenths of a cc). Then press LOADING DOSE. The pump's screen

will reflect the volume delivered.

If a loading dose has not been prescribed (or after a loading dose has been delivered), establish the limits as follows: DOSE VOLUME: as prescribed for client delivery and given in tenths of a cc; LOCKOUT INTERVAL: the interval between allowable doses given in minutes (9 minutes will appear as 09; 15 minutes will appear as 15).

Set the FOUR-HOUR LIMIT as prescribed by the physician. This represents the maximum amount of medication the patient can receive in a 4-hour period, and it is prescribed in increments of 50 (e.g., 1 cc q10min with a 4-hr limit of 20 cc).

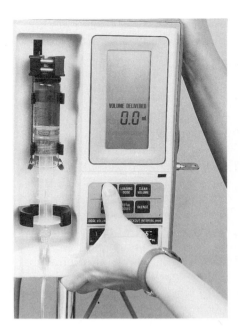

Evaluating

12 Close the pump's door, making sure it is locked securely. Remove the key and put it with the narcotics keys, or according to agency-established protocol. On a piece of tape, write the time and date when the vial was inserted and attach it to the pump. Usually the container is discarded after 24–48 hours of its having been placed in the pump, depending on agency policy. Any drug remaining in the pump after 24–48 hours or when the PCA is discontinued is wasted according to pharmacy protocol for narcotic waste.

Give the handheld button to the client or tie it to the side rail for easy access. Review instructions for the use of the machine and button with the client.

The READY message that appears indicates that the PCA infuser is now in the patient control mode, and the first dose is available to the client. When the client presses the handheld but-

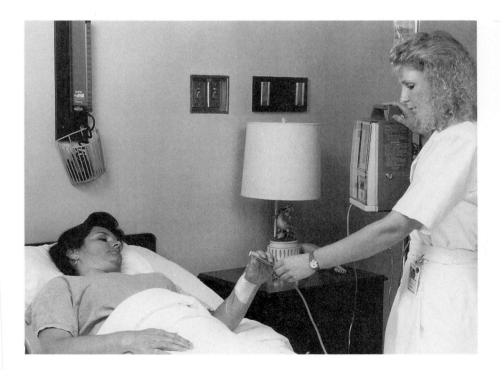

ton, a beep will acknowledge the request, the dose will be delivered, and READY will disappear.

VOLUME DELIVERED will display the increments of medication as the dose is delivered (as well as the loading dose that was given).

LOCKOUT INTERVAL message appears as the dose delivery is completed. When the allotted time has elapsed following the last delivered dose, the LOCKOUT INTERVAL message will disappear and READY will reappear. If the client desires, press-

(Continues)

ing the handheld button at this time will deliver another dose.

Adjust these dials accordingly if the physician changes the PCA prescription during the course of therapy.

Continue to assess the client throughout the therapy at frequent intervals (q2h during the first 24 hr; q4h thereafter). Compare each respiratory system assessment to the baseline for potential changes. Be alert to bradypnea (<12 breaths/min) as well as to hypotension, dizziness, nausea, and vomiting. Remember that the goal of PCA is relief of pain without sedation. Also check patency of the IV lines q2h. Change PCA and maintenance IV tubing q48h, or according to agency protocol.

Note: To change an injector vial: First close the manual slide clamp that is most proximal to the Luer-lock connector on the plunger. This will maintain the primed tubing and prevent entry of air. Assemble the replacement plunger and vial and remove air according to instructions in steps

2 and 3, above. Remove the empty vial from the clamping mechanism on the pump. Attach the male Luer-lock connector on the vial's plunger (injector) to the female end of the PCA tubing (see step 4). Load the vial and plunger device into the drive assembly, and lock it in place by following steps 6 and 7, above. Release the manual slide clamp when therapy is to be resumed. Affix a piece of tape to the pump, noting the date and time this and subsequent injector vials were placed in the pump.

To stop an infusion in progress: Close the slide clamp that is most proximal to the Luer-lock connector on the injector vial, unlock and open the security door, and press the "off" button to turn the unit off. This will stop the infusion automatically. *Note: The history of the infusion will be lost if the machine is turned off for more than 1 hour; therefore, record the amount of medication administered before turning the machine off.*

To discontinue the infusion: Close the slide clamp that is most

proximal to the Luer-lock connector on the injector vial, unlock and open the security door, remove the injector from the infuser, and disconnect the set. Press the "off" button to turn the unit off. Continue or discontinue the maintenance IV as prescribed.

Documentation: Document PCA infusion on proper chart forms, usually q8h or according to agency protocol. To determine the amount of morphine or meperidine given, press TOTAL DOSES and multiply by the number of "ccs" prescribed for the increment dose. For example, if the prescribed dose was 1 cc and the client administered 10 doses, multiply $10 \times 1 = 10$ cc. Pressing CLEAR VOLUME at the end of each 8-hour period will indicate the amount of analgesia used by the client. *Note: LOADING DOSES are usually charted separately on the medication record and are documented according to the exact time they were administered. Finally, remember to document the amount of pain relief obtained from the PCA medication.*

Managing Venous Access Devices (VADs)

Nursing Guidelines for Managing Venous Access Devices (VADs)

CHRONIC (LONG-TERM) CENTRAL VENOUS CATHETERS

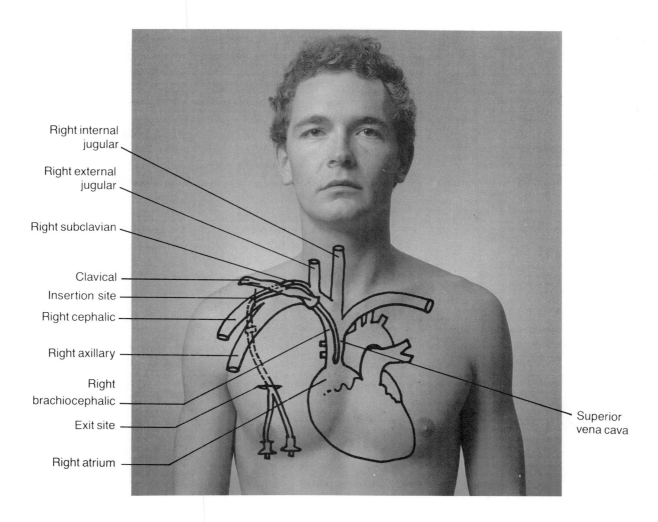

Right internal jugular
Right external jugular
Right subclavian
Clavical
Insertion site
Right cephalic
Right axillary
Right brachiocephalic
Exit site
Right atrium
Superior vena cava

Description

Long-term catheters that have single, double, or triple lumens. They are inserted either percutaneously into the subclavian vein or by cut-down into the external jugular vein. The catheter is tunneled subcutaneously and externalized at a convenient site on the chest wall. The catheter tip is positioned at the junction of the superior vena cava and right atrium and subcutaneously anchored with a Dacron cuff.

Uses

Provide long-term (i.e., 6 months to 2 years or more) venous access for blood drawing and administration of drugs, antibiotics, chemotherapy, total parenteral nutrition (TPN), blood, and blood products.

(Continues)

Nursing Considerations

■ Lower infection rate than the acute multi-lumen central venous catheters because (1) the entrance and exit sites are apart, and (2) the Dacron cuff forms a barrier against ingress of organisms.

■ More invasive insertion and removal than with the acute multi-lumen central venous catheters.

■ Catheter occlusion is usually the most common complication.

■ Mechanical problems (e.g., leakage in the external catheter) usually can be resolved with the line repair kits that are issued by the catheter manufacturer.

■ To prevent blood loss or air embolus in the presence of a damaged external line (e.g., cut, puncture, or leakage), clamp the catheter with a padded hemostat or smooth-edged clamp as close to the chest wall as possible (or proximal to the damaged lumen). If an air embolus is suspected, position the client in a left side-lying position with the head lower than the heart (see procedure, p. 182). Set up equipment for catheter repair.

■ The silicone material is biocompatible and makes the catheter more durable and comfortable than the polyurethane material used in most acute central venous catheters.

■ When the catheter lumens are not being used for infusion of IVs or medications, keep them sealed with Luer-lock caps or rubber injection caps.

■ Irrigation protocol varies according to manufacturer, client condition, and agency. Follow specific guidelines established for each client.

ACUTE (SHORT-TERM) MULTI-LUMEN CENTRAL VENOUS CATHETERS

INTERMEDIATE (MEDIUM-TERM) MULTI-LUMEN CENTRAL VENOUS CATHETERS

Description

Temporary venous access devices that have two or three separate polyurethane or silicone lines encased in one catheter. They are usually inserted into the subclavian vein by percutaneous stick and sutured in place.

Uses

Acute Catheters: Provide short-term (5 to 7 days) delivery of multiple infusions through one venipuncture, including continuous TPN, chemotherapy, antibiotics, blood, and blood products; simultaneous delivery of physically incompatible drugs; and frequent blood drawing for clients who require therapy for approximately a week. They also enable monitoring of central venous pressure (CVP).

Intermediate Catheters: Provide medium-term (6 to 8 weeks) delivery of multiple infusions as discussed above. These catheters are indicated for conditions that necessitate 6- to 8-week courses of antibiotics (e.g., with osteomyelitis) or nutrition (e.g., before and after gastrointestinal surgery or with Crohn's disease).

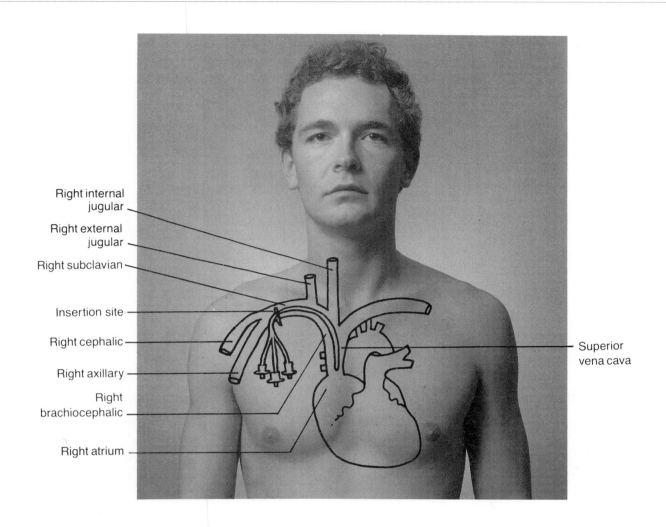

Right internal jugular
Right external jugular
Right subclavian
Insertion site
Right cephalic
Right axillary
Right brachiocephalic
Right atrium
Superior vena cava

Nursing Considerations

- Seen more frequently in critical care areas.
- Higher rate of infection and migration than with the chronic central venous catheters.
- Catheters made with silicone are more biocompatible than those made with polyurethane and can stay in place longer.
- These lumens are more likely to clog with fibrin sheaths than the lumens of the chronic central venous catheters because of the vessel injury that occurs with the percutaneous insertion. If this occurs, a dye study and x-ray usually reveal the location of the fibrin, which is then lysed with thrombolytic therapy. Urokinase is usually the drug of choice.
- Mechanical problems (i.e., leakage) usually necessitate line replacement.
- To prevent blood loss or air embolus in the presence of a damaged line (e.g., a cut, puncture, or leakage), clamp the catheter with a padded hemostat or smooth-edged clamp as close to the chest wall as possible (or proximal to the damaged lumen). If an air embolus is suspected, position the client in a left side-lying position with the head lower than the heart (see procedure, pp. 182–183). Set up equipment for line replacement.

IMPLANTABLE SUBCUTANEOUS PORTS

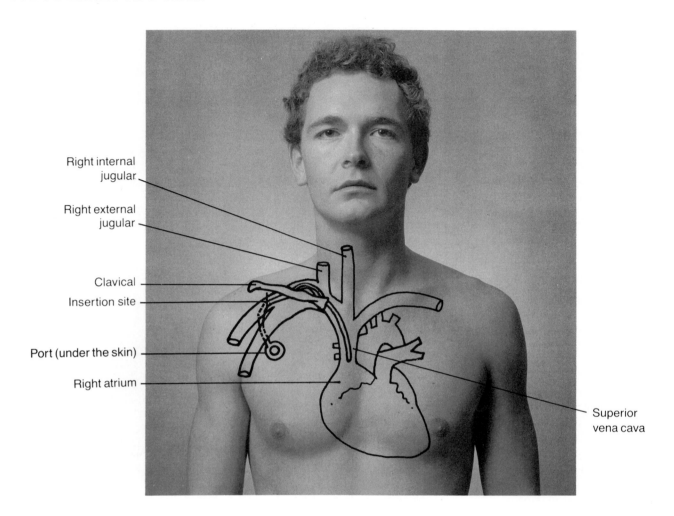

Right internal jugular

Right external jugular

Clavical

Insertion site

Port (under the skin)

Right atrium

Superior vena cava

Description	Totally implanted devices that enable repeated access to the central venous system without multiple venipunctures. These devices consist of a silicone catheter and port with a self-sealing silicone-rubber septum that allows 1,000 to 2,000 punctures (depending on the manufacturer). Using local anesthesia, the physician creates a subcutaneous pocket for portal implantation. The catheter's distal end is threaded into the appropriate blood vessel, with the proximal end positioned at the port site. The port is sutured in place.
Uses	Enable repeated blood drawing and infusions of TPN, blood and blood products, continuous fluid replacement, antibiotics, chemotherapy, and bolus medications.

Nursing Considerations

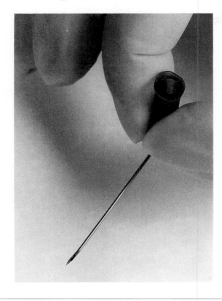

- Use only a special, noncoring (Huber) needle (left) to minimize trauma to the self-sealing septum.
- Advantages over the external central venous catheters include excellent client acceptance due to absence of external catheter, no dressing once the site has healed, minimal maintenance, and decreased risk of infection.
- Flush and fill the port with heparinized solution after every use.
- Observe the insertion site for wound hematoma, infection, and port rotation or extrusion.
- Before accessing the port, prepare the overlying skin using aseptic technique.
- Insert Huber needle firmly and perpendicular to the skin into the rubber septum until the needle tip reaches the bottom of the portal chamber.
- Generally, 90-degree Huber needles are used for long-term IV infusions, and the straight needles are used for blood samples or a single maintenance irrigation.
- Flush with normal saline or aspirate for blood to confirm catheter patency and proper needle placement prior to use.

CHANGING THE EXIT SITE DRESSING FOR A CHRONIC CENTRAL VENOUS CATHETER

Assessing and Planning

1 Assemble the following materials: clean gloves, an impervious bag for disposal of dressings and supplies, hydrogen peroxide or alcohol for cleansing the skin, antiseptic solution or swabsticks (e.g., alcohol, povidone-iodine, or chlorhexidine are commonly used antiseptic agents; check for client allergies before making your selection). Also assemble either a commercially prepared dressing change kit or a variation of the following sterile materials: an overwrap for a sterile field, cotton swabs, gauze pads, gauze or transparent occlusive dressing, antiseptic ointment, antiseptic wipes, tape, and basin(s) in which to pour the povidone-iodine, hydrogen peroxide, or alcohol if swabsticks are not used. The use of masks and caps is optional, depending on whether or not a clean or sterile procedure is to be used. Generally, a sterile procedure is used for the first week following catheter placement, and the dressing is changed daily if the client has increased risk for localized infection (e.g., with granulocytopenia or bleeding at the exit site). In addition, the dressing should be changed p.r.n. whenever it becomes contaminated (e.g., with excess drainage, perspiration, or blood). A clean technique is usually followed the week after catheter placement, and the dressing is changed three times a week if a gauze dressing is used and one to two times a week if a transparent dressing is used (or more frequently if the client has drainage at the exit site). Bring the materials to the bedside.

(Continues)

2 Explain the dressing change procedure to your client. Let him know that he either will wear a mask or will need to turn his head away from the insertion site during the dressing change so that he will not breathe on the site, potentially contaminating it. Adjust the height of the bed to facilitate the dressing application. If your client's catheter will be disconnected for an IV tubing change, flattening the bed helps to increase intrathoracic pressure, thereby minimizing the risk of an air embolism.

Wash your hands. Put on a cap and mask if they are required by your agency. As appropriate, ask your client to put on a mask also. Establish your sterile field on a clean and dry surface, using ei-ther a sterile towel or the sterile wrap from the commercially pre-pared dressing change kit (see technique, p. 16). Place the sterile basins on the sterile field (see technique, p. 17). If you will use pledgets or swabsticks, open the packages now so that you can pull them out of their packages with your sterile hand later in the procedure. If you are not using swabsticks, pour the anti-septic solution into one bowl and the hydrogen peroxide or alcohol into the other. Squeeze the anti-septic ointment into the center of a 2 × 2 sterile gauze pad. Then, lower the client's gown at the in-sertion site.

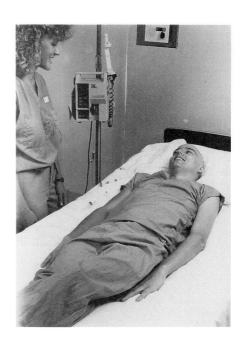

3 Put on clean gloves. If your client is not wearing a mask, in-struct him to turn his head away from the site. Gently remove the old dressing, assessing for the presence of redness, drainage, swelling, tenderness, and odor—signs that the client may have a localized infection. As appropri-ate, culture any drainage that appears to be purulent. *Note: For clients whose catheters have a VitaCuff® Antimicrobial Cuff,* a small darkened area may be noted at the insertion site for up to 6 weeks after catheter insertion. This is normal and is caused by discoloration from the silver that is used as a broad-spectrum anti-microbial agent.*

*VitaCuff® is a registered trademark of Vitaphore Corporation.

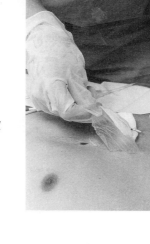

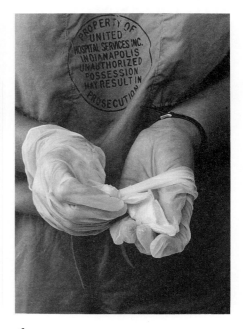

4 Encase the dressing in your gloves and deposit them in the impervious plastic bag.

Implementing

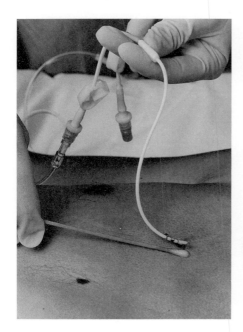

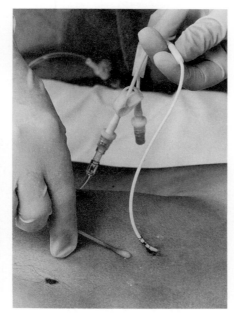

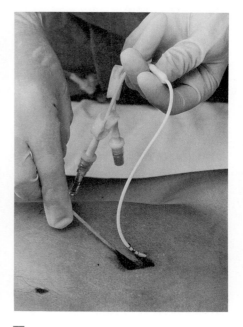

5 Wash your hands and put on the sterile gloves. Designate one hand sterile and the other clean. Using your sterile hand, cleanse the exit site with a sterile swab saturated with hydrogen peroxide or alcohol. Cleanse in a circular motion, starting at the exit site, as shown. Never return to the exit site with a used swab. Use your clean hand to lift the catheter up and out of your working area.

6 Continue to cleanse outward 2 inches in diameter away from the exit site, using a circular motion. Discard the swab. As necessary, repeat this procedure using fresh swabs until the site is free of encrustations and particles and the entire area has been cleansed.

Dry the site with a sterile cotton swab, using a circular, outward motion.

7 Next, prepare the skin with an antiseptic swabstick, again starting at the exit site.

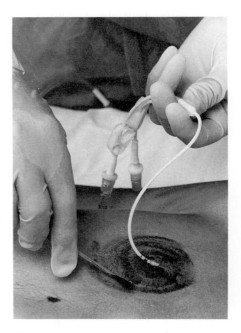

8 Continue to prepare the skin in a circular and outward motion, as shown, until you have covered an area 2 inches in diameter from the exit site.

(Continues)

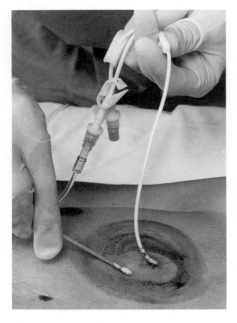

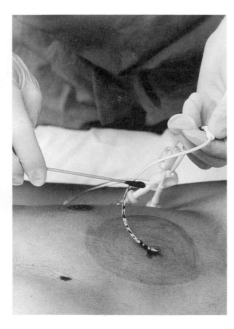

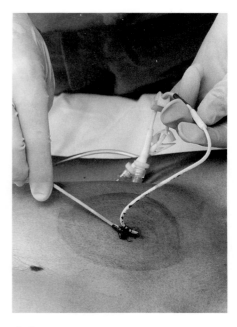

9   Wait 1 minute for the antiseptic solution to dry. If there is excess solution left on the skin, either pat the excess solution with a sterile gauze pad or encircle the area once again, using a dry, sterile swab (as shown).

10   Use another antiseptic swabstick to cleanse the proximal 3 inches of the catheter.

11   Saturate a sterile swab with the antiseptic ointment you squeezed onto the 2 × 2 gauze dressing when you prepared the sterile field (step 2), and apply it to the exit site.

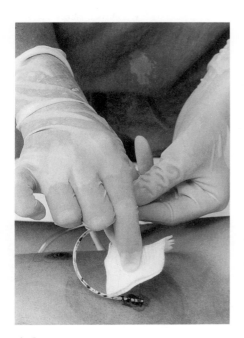

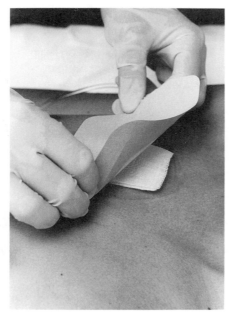

13   Or, use a transparent occlusive dressing as depicted in the following photos. ***Note: The following technique is used to demonstrate application of a transparent occlusive dressing. Do not use an occlusive dressing if you are also covering the exit site with a gauze pad as shown in the photo, since the gauze pad obstructs visualization of the exit site and thus defeats the purpose of the transparent dressing.***

12   If your client has drainage at the exit site, place the 2 × 2 gauze dressing over the exit site (as shown), and tape it in place.

14 If you are using a transparent occlusive dressing, remove the cover on the periphery of the dressing.

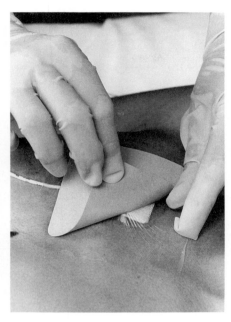

15 Then remove the backing on the dressing (as shown).

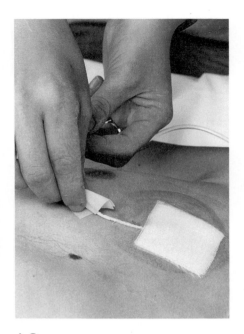

16 Cleanse the exposed catheter that is outside of the dressing with an alcohol wipe, wiping from its proximal to its distal end.

Evaluating

Remove your gloves. Initial and write the dates of both the catheter insertion and the dressing change on a label and adhere it to the dressing. Assist the client into a comfortable position. Remove the waste from the bedside and dispose of it according to agency policy. Wash your hands. Document the procedure in your nurses' notes, recording the date and time of dressing change, your assessment of the catheter exit site and adjacent skin, and the manner in which the client tolerated the procedure.

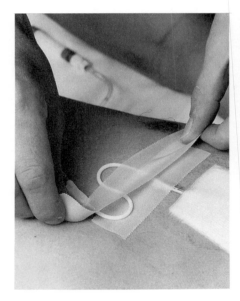

17 Then either coil the catheter and secure it to the dressing with one strip of tape, or use the following method. Cut three strips of tape and attach one strip of tape along the proximal end of the catheter. Then, loop the catheter and adhere the loop to the client's skin with a second strip of tape (as shown).

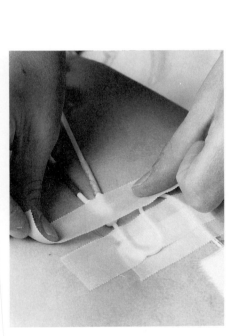

18 Attach a third strip of tape at the catheter's bifurcation.

DRAWING BLOOD FROM A CHRONIC (HICKMAN®-TYPE) CENTRAL VENOUS CATHETER AND FLUSHING THE CATHETER FOLLOWING BLOOD WITHDRAWAL

1 Wash your hands and assemble the following materials or as prescribed: antiseptic wipes, a syringe for blood discard and syringe(s) of the appropriate size for a blood sample (or obtain a Vacutainer adaptor), a vial of normal saline, a 10-ml syringe into which you will aspirate 5 ml (or the prescribed amount) of normal saline, a vial of heparinized solution if the line is to be capped and clamped following blood withdrawal, a capped needle, and an injection cap, if appropriate. In addition, you will need clean gloves (because of the possibility of coming in contact with blood) and vacuum tubes for the blood sample (the quantity determined by the amount of blood to be withdrawn).

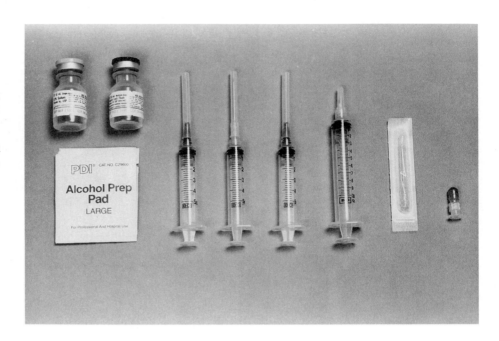

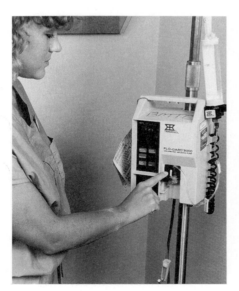

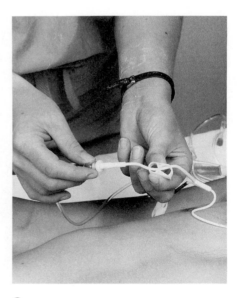

2 Describe the procedure to the client; explain that you will obtain venous blood for diagnostic laboratory work. If the client's catheter is attached to IV infusion(s), stop the infusion(s) at this time.

3 Clamp the catheter lumen (as shown). If the client has a double- or triple-lumen catheter, ensure that the other lumens are clamped as well.

4 Apply gloves. If the client has a single-lumen catheter through which an IV infusion is running, remove the needle and cap from one of the 5-ml syringes (as shown). Cleanse the catheter/tubing junction with an antiseptic wipe. Disconnect the infusion tubing from the catheter hub, attach the capped needle to the distal end of the infusion tubing to keep the tubing sterile, and set it aside.

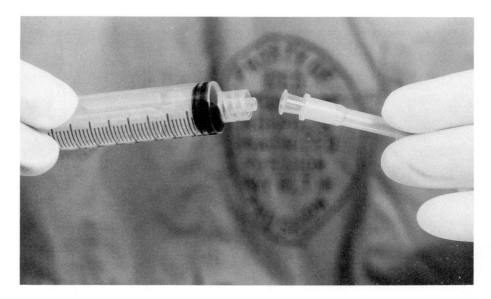

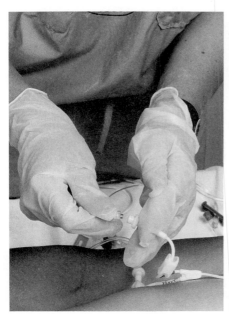

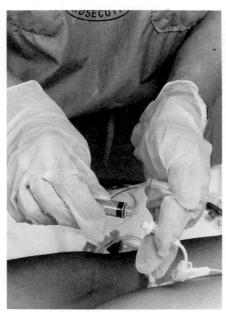

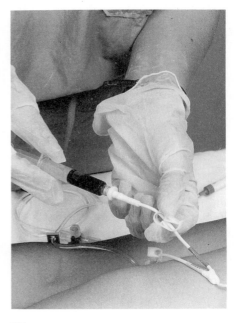

5 If the lumen through which you will withdraw the blood has an injection cap, you may remove the injection cap from the catheter (as shown). Or, as an alternative, you may scrub the injection cap with an antiseptic wipe and insert the needle of the syringe or Vacutainer adaptor into the center of the cap.

6 If you have removed either the injection cap or the infusion tubing from the catheter, attach the syringe to the catheter (as shown).

7 Unclamp the catheter and aspirate approximately 5 ml of blood, or as prescribed, for discard. Laboratory values may be altered if the infusion solution or solution used to flush the catheter is not cleared adequately from the catheter; but because the external line holds, on the average, no more than 1 ml, 5 ml is usually adequate for discard. Reclamp the catheter and remove the syringe. If you are using a Vacutainer adaptor, insert a new vacuum tube after withdrawing approximately 5 ml of blood.

(Continues)

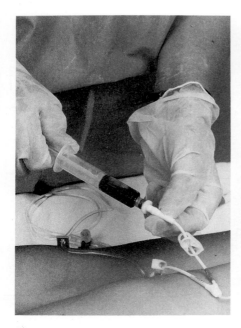
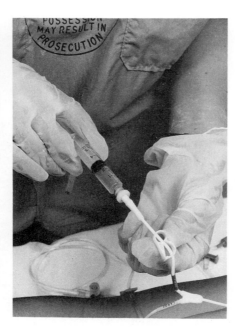
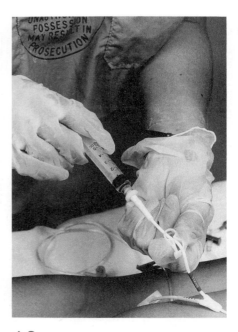

8   If you are not using a Vacutainer adaptor, remove the needle from the syringe that is to be used for a blood sample, and attach the syringe to the catheter hub (as shown). Or, insert the needle that is attached to the syringe to be used for a blood sample into the injection cap. Unclamp the catheter and aspirate the prescribed amount of blood. Reclamp the catheter and detach the syringe containing the blood for bloodwork. If you are not using a Vacutainer adaptor, attach a capped 20-gauge needle to the syringe to protect it from contamination.

9   If the catheter lumen will be attached to an IV infusion following this procedure, attach the syringe containing the normal saline to the catheter, unclamp the catheter (as shown), and inject all but 0.5 ml of the solution to flush the tubing of residual blood.

10   Then begin to clamp the catheter while simultaneously injecting the remaining 0.5 ml. Once the catheter has been clamped, however, stop injecting the solution. There may be a small amount of solution left in the syringe. *Caution: Do not inject solution against a clamped catheter because this could damage the catheter.* The simultaneous injection during the clamping procedure will provide enough positive pressure in the external line to prevent backflow of solution into the catheter tip.

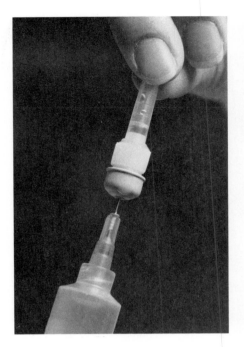

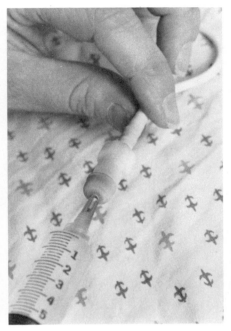

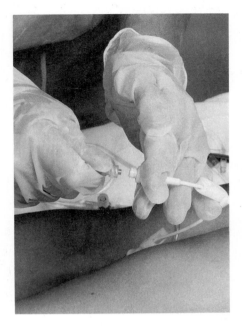

11 If the catheter will be capped and clamped following this procedure (rather than attached to an IV infusion), you will need to attach a new injection cap. First you will prime the injection cap to remove the air before attaching it to the catheter. Remove the cap from its sterile package and grasp it by its protective cap. Inject the irrigant through the rubber diaphragm until you see the return of the irrigant in the protective cap.

12 After priming the cap, aseptically attach the injection cap to the catheter's hub. Insert the needle of the syringe containing the irrigating solution into the injection cap, unclamp the catheter, and inject the prescribed amount of solution. To avoid aspirating any of the solution from the line and into the syringe, maintain positive injection pressure while simultaneously withdrawing the needle. *Caution: Some agencies advocate clamping the catheter before injecting the last 0.5 ml of the solution to produce positive pressure in the line and prevent backflow of blood into the line and thus deter clotting. However, pressures generated by small syringes when the catheter is clamped may damage the catheter, and therefore this procedure is not recommended.*

13 For clients whose catheter will be reconnected to an IV infusion, remove the protective capped needle and reattach the infusion tubing to the catheter junction (as shown). Open the catheter clamp and turn the solution on. Adjust the rate of flow, as appropriate.

(Continues)

14   If you have not used a Vacutainer, inject the blood into the appropriate tubes (as shown), if this procedure is used by your agency. Label blood sample tubes with the client's name and send them to the laboratory with the appropriate requisition slip. Remove your gloves and wash your hands. Dispose of the discarded blood following agency protocol for disposal of body fluids.

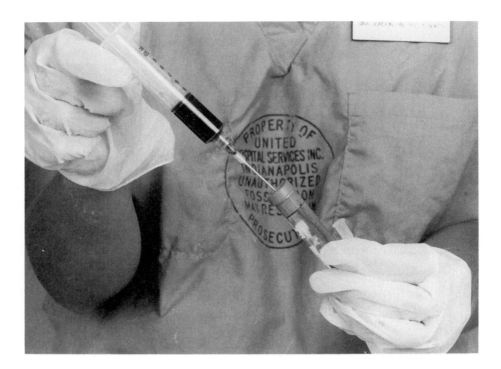

PERFORMING A ROUTINE IRRIGATION OF A CHRONIC CENTRAL VENOUS CATHETER

Chronic central venous catheters are flushed immediately following each infusion. Various concentrations of heparinized saline, from 10 to 1,000 USP units/ml, are commonly used for Hickman® and Broviac® catheters.* The Groshong™* catheter with the three-position Groshong valve eliminates the need for heparin and is flushed with normal saline only. For frequently (at least every 8 hours) accessed Hickman® and Broviac® catheters, flushing between infusions with 5 ml of normal saline without heparin has been shown to be effective. When the catheter has not been accessed in at least 8 hours, a periodic heparin flush is recommended to maintain catheter patency. Flushing frequencies

ranging from once a day to once a week have been found to be effective. Determination of the appropriate heparin concentration, volume, and flushing frequency is based on the client's medical condition, laboratory results, and prior clinical experience.

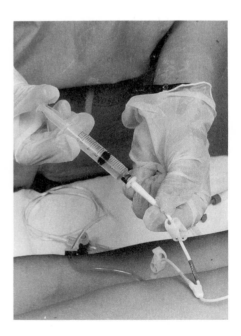

Prepare the prescribed amount of irrigant. Clamp the catheter and detach the infusion tubing. Cleanse the catheter hub with an antiseptic wipe and attach the syringe to the catheter hub. If the catheter has an injection cap, cleanse the injection cap and insert the needle attached to the syringe directly into the injection cap. Unclamp the catheter and inject the irrigant. For photo depiction of these steps, see the previous procedure. Wear gloves if this procedure follows either blood withdrawal or flushing that has been performed to prevent blood from backing up into the catheter.

*Hickman and Broviac are registered trademarks of C. R. Bard, Inc. Groshong is a trademark of C. R. Bard, Inc., or its subsidiaries.

CHANGING THE IV SOLUTION AND TUBING FOR A CHRONIC (HICKMAN®-TYPE) CENTRAL VENOUS CATHETER

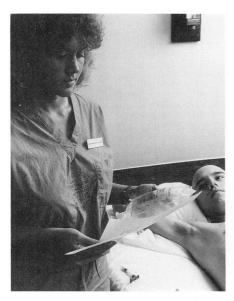

1 IV solution and tubing for a chronic central venous catheter are changed q48–72h, depending on agency protocol. Obtain the appropriate tubing and solution. Compare the prescribed infusion solution to the physician's prescription for your client.

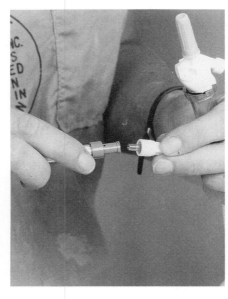

2 Attach extension tubing and filter (if appropriate) to the primary infusion set (as shown). Then spike the fresh solution container (see procedure, pp. 115–116), and prime the tubing (see procedure, pp. 115–116) to remove all the air. Turn off the infusion pump if the client has one, and clamp the client's central venous catheter.

3 If your client has an infusion pump, follow manufacturer's instructions for priming the line, threading the tubing through the infusion pump, and purging the tubing as described by the infusion pump manufacturer. Invert the cassette (as shown) that is used by your agency's infusion pump, and depress the button on the cassette (or per manufacturer's instructions) to purge air from the cassette chamber.

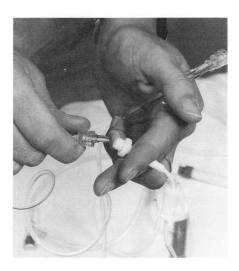

4 Clean the catheter/tubing junction with an antiseptic wipe, and detach the old infusion tubing from the catheter. Hold the hub of the catheter in such a way that you avoid contaminating it.

5 Remove the protective cap from the new infusion tubing, cleanse the catheter hub with an alcohol swab, and attach the new infusion tubing to the catheter hub. Unclamp the catheter. Then insert the new tubing into the infusion pump, following manufacturer's instructions. Clear the pump to determine the amount of fluids previously infused, and set the appropriate rate as needed. Unclamp the infusion tubing and turn the infusion pump on.

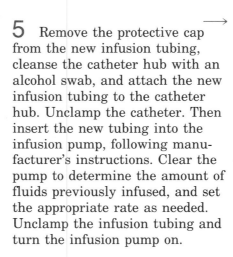

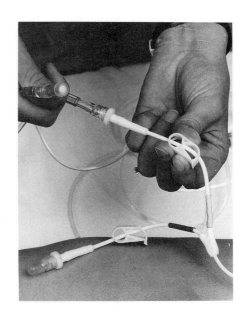

ACCESSING THE IMPLANTABLE SUBCUTANEOUS PORT

1   Assemble the following materials: two pairs of sterile gloves, antiseptic wipes, injectable normal saline, an 18–22 g ($\frac{5}{8}''$ to $1\frac{1}{2}''$) needle, 10-ml syringe, isopropyl alcohol, antiseptic (e.g., povidone-iodine) solution or presaturated swabsticks, sterile gauze pads or sterile cotton-tipped applicators, and a special access Huber point needle with extension tubing. In addition, you will need sterile basins for saturating the gauze or cotton-tipped applicators with the antiseptic and alcohol if you are not using presaturated swabsticks.

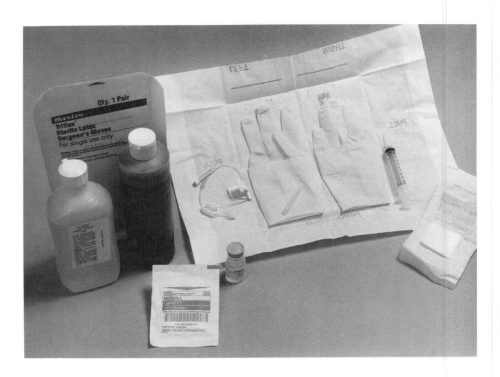

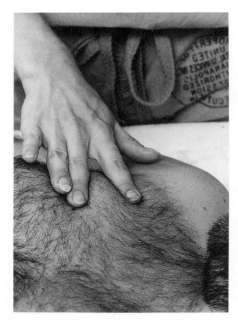

2   Explain the procedure to your client. Palpate over the site of the implanted device to locate the rubber septum. Identify this site visually with landmarks so that you can recall it later.

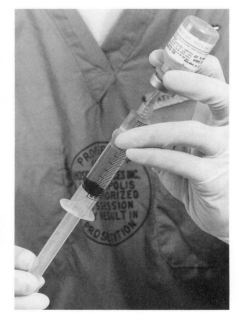

3   Establish your sterile field. If you will not be using presaturated swabsticks, pour isopropyl alcohol and antiseptic solution into two sterile basins and saturate the gauze pads. Drop the sterile syringe, cotton-tipped applicators (if they are to be used), and port access needle with extension tubing onto the sterile field (see procedure, p. 17). Put on sterile gloves and attach the sterile needle to the sterile syringe. Then aspirate 10 ml of normal saline from the vial (as shown) and place the filled syringe on the sterile field. Remove your gloves because they have become contaminated from the vial of saline.

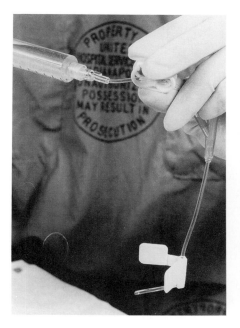

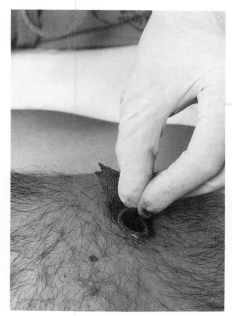

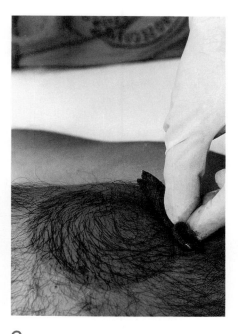

4 Apply the second pair of sterile gloves. Detach the needle from the syringe, and attach the syringe to the connector on the extension tubing. Release the clamp and prime the extension tubing with some of the normal saline. Clamp the extension tubing and return it to the sterile field along with the syringe.

5 Cleanse the skin over the port site with the antiseptic solution, starting in the center (as shown). If you are cleansing the site with gauze, designate your nondominant hand clean and use it for this task, since your hand will become contaminated if you are using this method. Use your dominant hand if you are using a presaturated swabstick or cotton-tipped applicator.

6 Continue to clean in a circular and outward motion until you have cleansed an area 2 to 3 inches in diameter. Repeat steps 5 and 6 using fresh gauze or a new cotton-tipped applicator or swabstick.

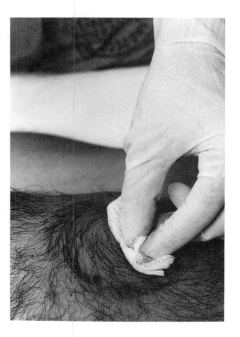

7 After allowing the antiseptic solution to dry, cleanse the skin with the gauze or cotton-tipped applicator saturated in the isopropyl alcohol. Start in the center and work your way outward in a circular motion. Repeat, using fresh gauze or applicator.

(Continues)

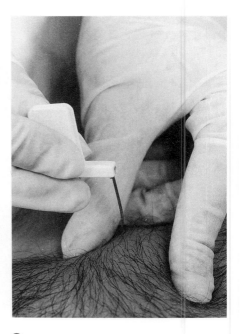

8   Using your sterile hand, remove the protective needle sheath that covers the needle attached to the extension tubing.

9   Recall the location of the rubber septum (the site you identified in step 2), and position your clean fingers so that they form a triangle over the septum (as shown). With your sterile hand, grasp the wings of the needle and hold the needle perpendicular to the client's skin.

10   Insert the needle until you feel it touch the metal bottom of the port. Unclamp the extension tubing and aspirate with the syringe for a blood return to confirm that you have properly accessed the port.

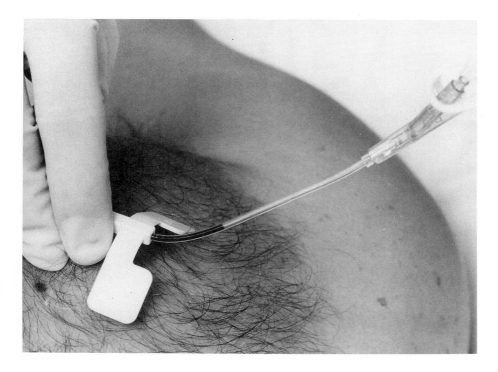

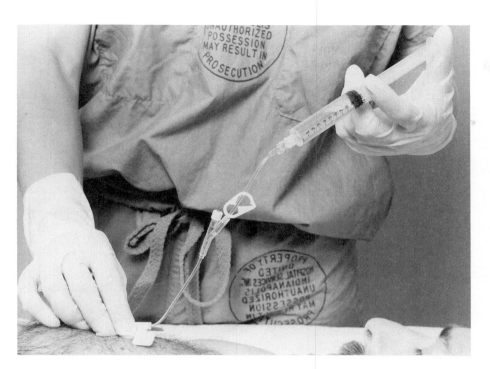

11 Inject the normal saline to clear out the heparin in the port. Attach another syringe for blood withdrawal (see next procedure) or attach infusion tubing if the client is to have an IV infusion through this port. When the necessary procedures have been completed, prepare a heparin lock (see procedure, p. 181). If a long-term infusion is to be established, fold a 2 × 2 gauze pad and position it under the needle. Cover with a dressing, tape the dressing, and secure the line (see procedure, pp. 166–167).

WITHDRAWING BLOOD FROM AN IMPLANTABLE SUBCUTANEOUS PORT

1 Assemble the following materials: three 10-ml syringes, two 18-gauge ($\frac{5}{8}''$ to $1\frac{1}{2}''$) needles, antiseptic swabs or wipes, clean gloves, and injectable normal saline.

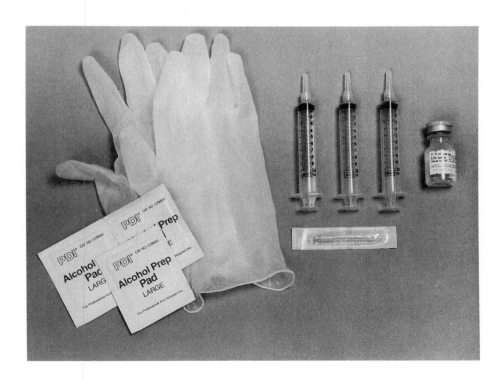

(Continues)

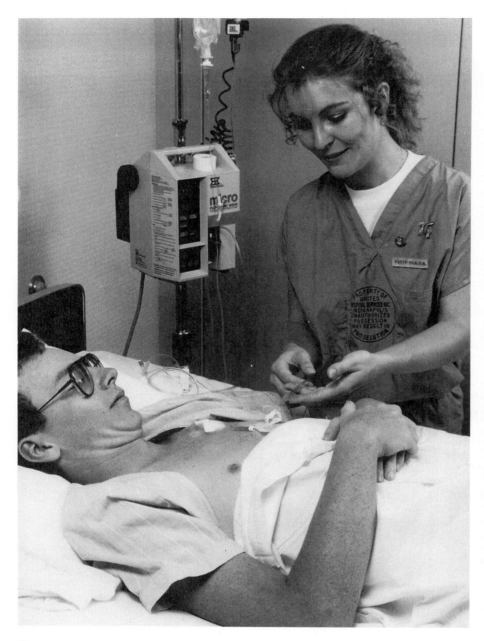

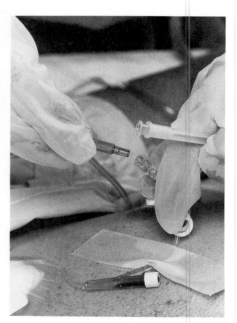

2 Explain the procedure to your client. Position him for comfort and to ensure that you have easy access to his implanted port.

3 Wash your hands. Attach a needle to one of the syringes and aspirate 5 to 10 ml, as prescribed, of the normal saline. Cap and remove the needle, and set the syringe aside in a clean area. Put on the clean gloves. If your client has an IV infusion running, stop the infusion, clamp the extension line, and detach the infusion tubing from the port's connector hub (as shown).

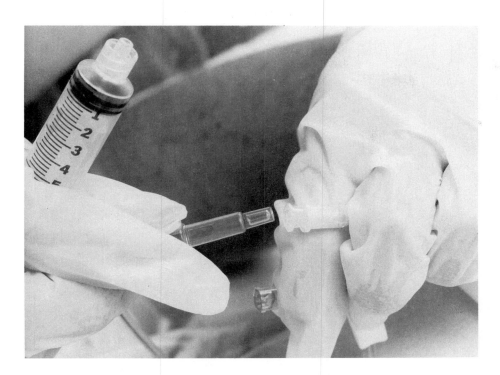

4   Attach the needle and cap to the end of the infusion tubing to keep the infusion tubing sterile.

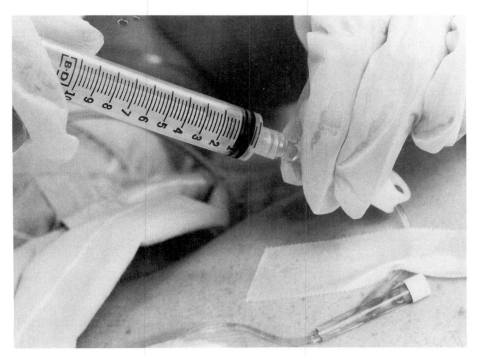

5   Cleanse the connector on the port's extension tubing with an antiseptic wipe. Then attach a 10-ml syringe to the connector (as shown).

(Continues)

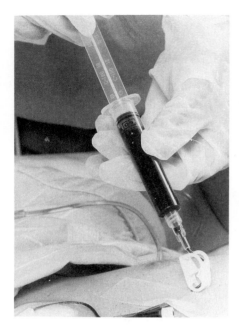

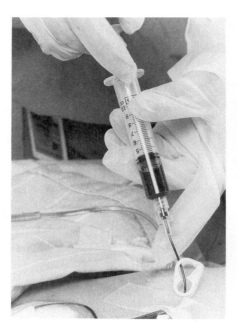

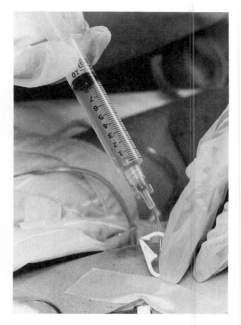

6 Unclamp the line and aspirate 10 ml of blood for discard. Reclamp the line and remove the syringe.

7 Attach the syringe that you will use for blood withdrawal. Unclamp and aspirate the prescribed amount. Reclamp the line and remove the syringe. *Note: Unless you contaminate the connections during the switching of the syringes, it is not necessary to clean the connection with antiseptic between syringe attachments.*

8 Remove the needle from the syringe containing the normal saline and attach the syringe to the port's connector. Inject 10 ml of the normal saline. Because of the small diameter of the tubing, it is important that you inject the saline vigorously to prevent clotting of the tubing. Clamp the extension line and remove the syringe.

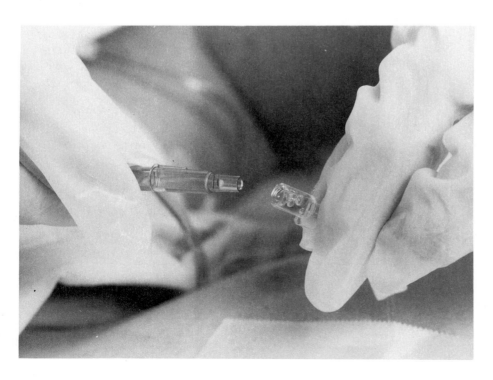

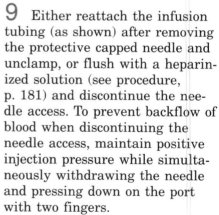

9 Either reattach the infusion tubing (as shown) after removing the protective capped needle and unclamp, or flush with a heparinized solution (see procedure, p. 181) and discontinue the needle access. To prevent backflow of blood when discontinuing the needle access, maintain positive injection pressure while simultaneously withdrawing the needle and pressing down on the port with two fingers.

If appropriate, inject the blood into the proper tube(s) (see procedure, p. 172), label, and send to the laboratory. Remove the gloves and wash your hands; document the procedure. Dispose of the blood obtained for discard following agency protocol for disposal of body fluids.

ESTABLISHING A HEPARIN LOCK IN AN IMPLANTABLE SUBCUTANEOUS PORT

1 After each use, it is necessary to fill the port with sterile heparinized solution to prevent clot formation and subsequent catheter blockage. If the port is not used for prolonged periods of time, it should be flushed at least once every 4 weeks. Assemble clean gloves (to prevent contact with blood), injectable normal saline solution, heparin (100 u/ml), gauze pad, antiseptic wipes, and two 10-ml syringes with needles. Fill one syringe with 10 ml normal saline and the other with 10 ml heparin (100 u/ml), or as prescribed. Clamp the extension tubing and cleanse the connector hub with an antiseptic wipe. Attach the syringe containing the normal saline to the connector. Unclamp the line and inject the normal saline into the port. Reclamp.

Remove the empty syringe and attach the syringe containing the heparin. Unclamp and inject the solution.

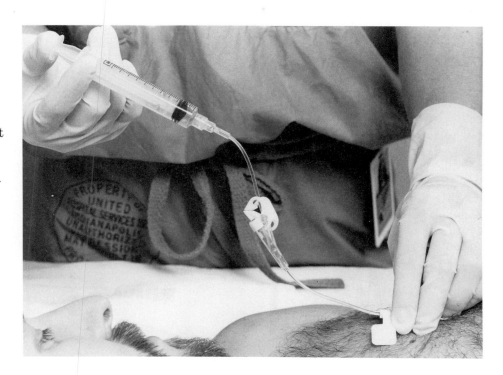

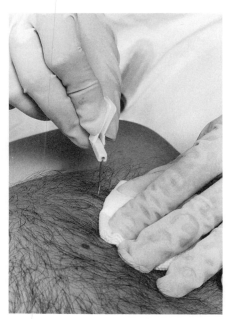

2 When you have injected the solution (and if you will reconnect IV infusion tubing), remove the syringe. Then, reattach the infusion tubing if appropriate.

Or, if you will be discontinuing the needle and extension tubing, squeeze the needle wings together and maintain positive injection pressure while simultaneously withdrawing the needle and pressing down on the port with two fingers. Maintaining positive pressure on the syringe barrel will prevent blood backflow into the catheter tip. Blot the needle's exit site with a sterile gauze pad (as shown). Bleeding should be absent or minimal.

ASSESSING AND INTERVENING FOR AN AIR EMBOLISM

1 All clients with IV lines are at risk for an air embolism. Rapid infusion rates compound the risk by producing high vascular pressure—for example, the administration of a unit of blood over a 10–15 minute period. Because an air embolism can be fatal, it is essential that you monitor and observe the client for the presence of chest pain, coughing, hypotension, cyanosis, and hypoxia. In addition, if the client does have an air embolism, auscultation over the right ventricle may reveal a churning "windmill" sound.

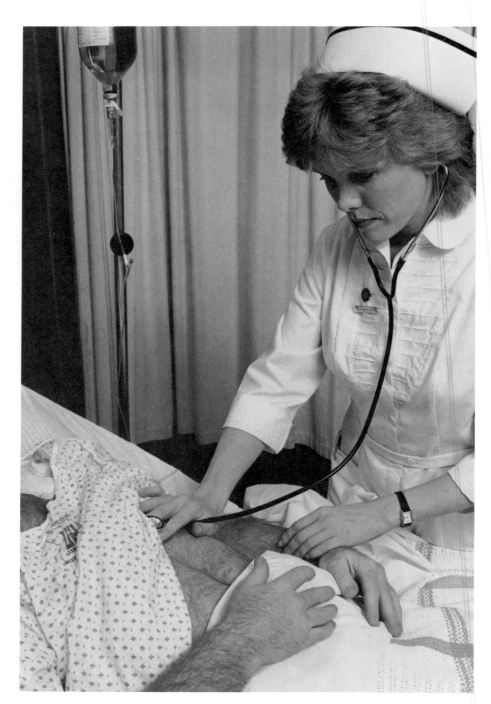

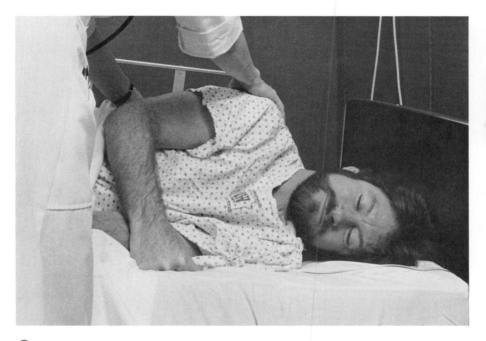

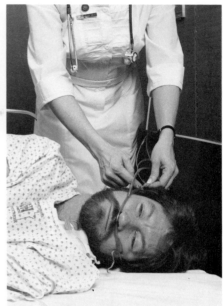

2 Any indication of an air embolism necessitates an immediate intervention. Turn the client to his left side to displace the air into the apex of the heart and to help prevent its rapid movement into the pulmonary artery. Then remove the pillow and lower the head of the bed into Trendelenburg's position. Lowering the head of the bed will increase intrathoracic pressure, decreasing the flow of air into the vein during inhalation.

3 Administer oxygen, if it is at the bedside, and notify the physician immediately. If the air has not slowly and safely dissipated into the pulmonary system, the physician may aspirate the air from the apical area. Stay with the client and continue to reassure him.

References

American Association of Diabetes Educators: Education for continuous subcutaneous insulin infusion pump users. *Diabetes Educator* 1986; 13(1):10.

Barnes T: *Respiratory Care Practice.* Chicago: Year Book Medical Publishers, 1988.

Centers for Disease Control: Recommendations for prevention of HIV transmission in health care settings. *MMWR* (Aug 21) 1987; 36(Suppl 2S):1S–18S.

Cyganski JM et al: The case for the heparin flush. *Am J Nurs* 1987; 87(6):796–797.

Dolorich M et al: Optimal delivery of aerosols from metered dose inhalers. *Chest 80* 1981; (Suppl):911–915.

Dunn D, Lenihan SF: The case for the saline flush. *Am J Nurs* 1987; 87(6):798–799.

Hagle ME: Implantable devices for chemotherapy: Access and delivery. *Sem Oncol Nurs* 1987; 3(2):96–105.

Hoffman KK et al: Bacterial colonization and phlebitis-associated risk with transparent polyurethane film for peripheral intravenous site dressings. *Am J Infection Control* 1988; 16(3):101–106.

Holland P et al: Standards for blood banks and transfusion services, 13th ed. Arlington, VA: American Association of Blood Banks, 1987.

Horne M, Swearingen PL: *Pocket Guide to Fluids and Electrolytes.* St Louis: Mosby, 1989.

Howser DM, Meade CD: Hickman catheter care: Developing organized teaching strategies. *Cancer Nurs* 1987; 10(2):70–76.

Jones PM: Indwelling central venous catheter—related infections and two different procedures of catheter care. *Cancer Nurs* 1987; 10(3):123–130.

Klass K: Troubleshooting central line complications. *Nurs 87* 1987; 17(11):58–61.

Kleiman RL et al: PCA vs. regular IM injections for severe postop pain. *Am J Nurs* 1987; 87(11):1491–1492.

Knox LS: Implantable venous access devices. *Crit Care Nurs* 1987; 7(1):70–73.

Kresl JS: Patient-controlled analgesia. *AORN J* 1988; 48(3):481–487.

Magdziak BJ: There's just no excuse for IV complications. *RN* (Feb) 1988; 30–31.

Millam DA: Tips for improving venipuncture techniques. *Nurs 87* (June) 1987; 46–49.

Newman LN: A side-by-side look at two venous access devices. *Am J Nurs* 1989; 89(6):826–833.

Panfilli R et al: Nursing implications of patient-controlled analgesia. *J Intravenous Nurs* 1988; 11(2):75–77.

Pedersen S: Aerosol treatment of bronchoconstriction in children with or without a tube spacer. *N Engl J Med* 1983; 308:1328–1330.

Reynolds A, Steckler D: Practical aspects of blood administration. Arlington, VA: American Association of Blood Banks, 1986.

Robertson C: The new challenges of insulin therapy. *RN* (May) 1989; 34–38.

Rutherford C: Insertion and care of multiple lumen peripherally inserted central line catheters. *J Intravenous Nurs* 1988; 11(1):16–19.

Swearingen PL: *Manual of Nursing Therapeutics: Applying Nursing Diagnoses to Medical Disorders,* 2d ed. St Louis: Mosby, 1990.

Tomky D: Tapping the full power of insulin pumps. *RN* (June) 1989; 46–48.

U.S. Department of Health and Human Services, Public Health Service. Update: Universal precautions for prevention of transmission of human immunodeficiency virus, hepatitis B virus, and other bloodborne pathogens in health care settings. *MMWR* (June 24) 1988; 37:377–382.

Wachs T et al: No more pokes: A review of parenteral access devices. *Nutritional Support Services* 1987; 7(6):12–17.

Weinstein S: Intravenous filters. *Infection Control* 1987; 8(5):220–221.

Unit II

Performing Specialized Nursing Procedures

Chapter 4

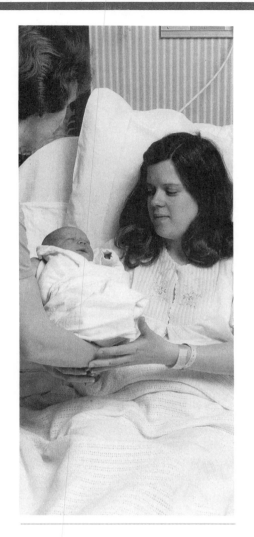

Managing Female Reproductive Procedures and Immediate Care of the Newborn

CHAPTER OUTLINE

PERFORMING ROUTINE GYNECOLOGIC TECHNIQUES

The Female Reproductive System

Nursing Assessment Guidelines

Teaching Breast Self-Examination

Assisting the Client with Postsurgical Mastectomy Exercises

    The Exercises

Providing Perineal Care

    Using a Squeeze Bottle
    Preparing a Sitz Bath
    Using a Surgi-gator

Providing Care for Clients with Cervical-Uterine Radiation Implants

PERFORMING PRENATAL TECHNIQUES

Assessing the Prenatal Abdomen

    Measuring Fundal Height
    Inspecting and Palpating Fetal Parts
    Auscultating Fetal Heart Tones

Performing External Electronic Fetal Monitoring

Assessing for Amniotic Fluid

Providing Comfort Measures

    Applying Counterpressure to Relieve Leg Cramps
    Applying Pressure to Relieve Back Pain

PERFORMING POSTPARTUM TECHNIQUES

Assessing the Mother

    Inspecting and Palpating the Breasts
    Palpating the Fundus and Bladder
    Evaluating the Lochia
    Inspecting the Perineum

Assisting with Infant Feeding

    Positioning the Infant
    Burping the Infant
    Massaging the Breasts for Manual Expression of Breast Milk

Using Breast Pumps

    Managing Hand Pumps
    Assisting with Electric Breast Pumps

CARING FOR THE NEWBORN

Admitting the Neonate to the Hospital

    Obtaining Footprints
    Instilling Erythromycin or Silver Nitrate
    Administering a Vitamin K Injection
    Obtaining a Blood Sample
    Obtaining a Urine Specimen

Assessing the Neonate

    Performing a General Inspection
    Auscultating
    Taking an Axillary Temperature
    Palpating
    Taking an Arterial Blood Pressure
    Measuring and Weighing the Infant

Providing Neonatal Care

    Giving Umbilical Cord Care
    Suctioning
    Using Bili-Lites (Phototherapy)

Performing Routine Gynecologic Techniques

THE FEMALE REPRODUCTIVE SYSTEM

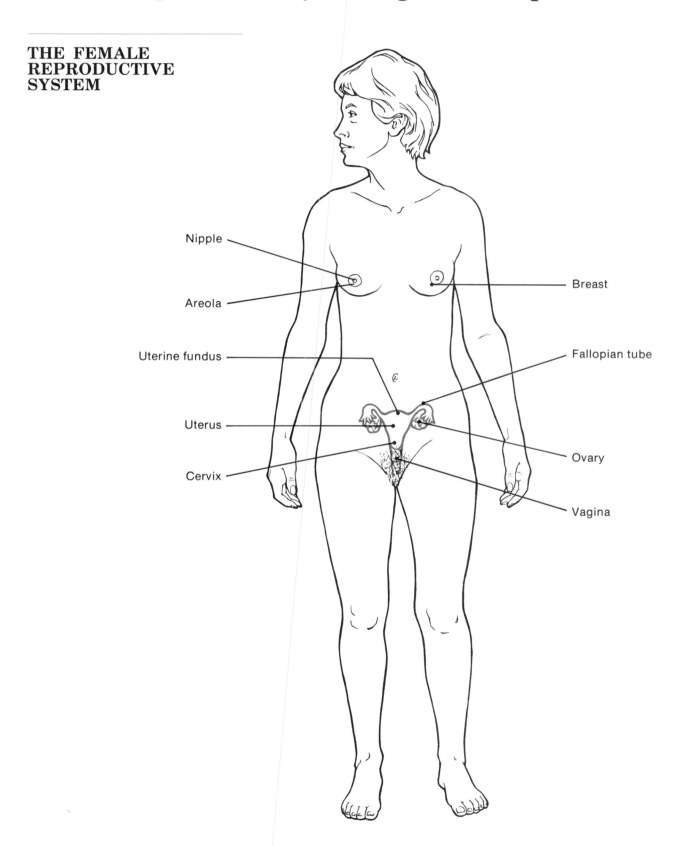

Nipple

Areola

Uterine fundus

Uterus

Cervix

Breast

Fallopian tube

Ovary

Vagina

Nursing Assessment Guidelines

Prior to teaching the examination, gather subjective data from the client. A comprehensive client history should include a complete evaluation for the following factors:

Risk Factors: client history of breast surgery, cancer, or fibrocystic disease; family history of cancer, fibroids, mother's taking of diethylstilbestrol (DES); history of smoking and/or exposure to carcinogens; history of obesity, diabetes mellitus, or hypertension; history of chronic psychological stress; use of estrogens; dietary intake high in animal fats.

Personal Factors: client's age—risk increases steadily after age 35, with the greatest risk occurring in clients over age 85; ages at which menstruation and menopause began—clients with early menstruation (11 years or younger) or late menopause (after 52 years) are at greater risk; age at first full-term pregnancy—clients over 30 years and nulliparous clients are at higher risk, and clients having their first child at age 20 or younger have decreased risk; discharge or secretions in nipples—color, amount, frequency; changes in breasts since adulthood—size, shape, color; mammography history and results; knowledge of breast self-examination, frequency of performance, and time of month it is performed.

TEACHING BREAST SELF-EXAMINATION

Assessing and Planning

The most common site for cancer in the adult woman is the breast, and the single most effective means for improving survival rates in breast cancer is early detection of breast tumors using breast self-examination. This important procedure should be incorporated into the discharge planning for *all* your adult female clients.

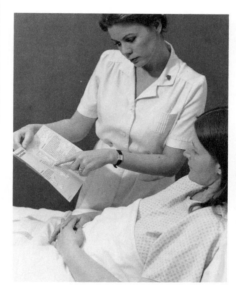

1 Provide a warm and private environment for your client, and arrange for her to sit facing away from the door. Explain that she should routinely perform breast self-examination about a week after her menstrual period has begun because at that time her breasts will have been the least swollen and a lump will be more readily detected. To ensure consistency, menopausal clients or those who have had hysterectomies or oophorectomies should perform the examination at the same time every month, for example on the first day of the month.

Take your time, encourage questions, and give the client literature on breast self-examination, such as the free pamphlets provided by the American Cancer Society. The goal of this procedure is to familiarize your client with the way her breasts normally look and feel. Optimally, the examination will give her confidence in her knowledge base and skill in assessing abnormalities so that should cancer be detected, she will have found it at its earliest, most treatable stage. In addition, teaching your client breast self-examination will enable you to assess for abnormalities at the same time.

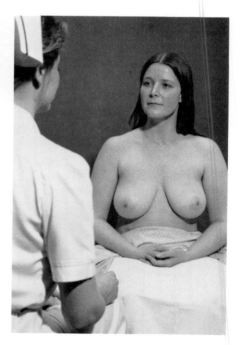

Implementing

2 The assessment consists of both inspection and palpation. To begin the inspection segment of the examination, instruct the client to sit on the side of the bed

and to lower her gown to the waist. Explain that she should relax her arms in her lap and inspect her breasts in a large mirror. If a mirror is unavailable, she should pretend that you are a mirror so that she can follow each step without losing the continuity of the examination. As she looks in the mirror, explain that each breast may normally deviate slightly from the other in size and symmetry, but she should be alert to any monthly *changes* in contour and appearance. Instruct her to look for swelling, puckering, dimpling of the skin, changes in texture and color, as well as a change in a mole. Striae (stretch marks) are normal, and symmetrical venous patterns are fairly common in fair-complexioned women. Explain, however, that diffuse, blue casts, suggestive of an increased blood supply to an area, should be followed up with a physician's examination. The areolae also may vary slightly in size and shape from one another, but differences in color, rashes, scaling, or ulcerations should be noted. Discharge from the nipple is usually abnormal in the mature, nonlactating woman; an inverted nipple also can signal a problem, especially if it was recently everted. Explain also that an inverted nipple that becomes everted during movement can occur with an underlying pathology. *Note: At this time, you also should be alert to peau d'orange, skin that is large-pored and edematous caused by a tumor obstructing the lymph glands. This is an advanced sign of breast cancer and generally is not necessary to include for client education.*

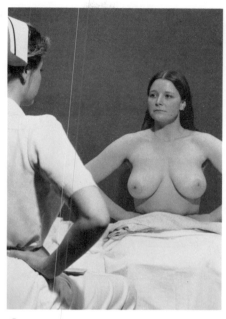

3 Instruct the client to tense her pectoral muscles by squeezing her waist. She should look again for asymmetry in size and contour, dimpling, puckering, or retractions of the skin.

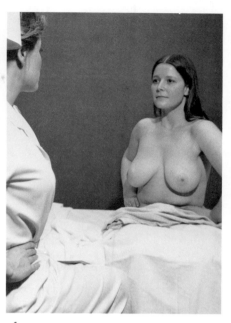

4 While continuing to squeeze her waist, she should turn from side to side so that she can view all of the breast tissue.

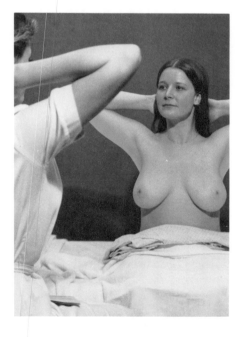

5 Demonstrate raising the arms by placing them behind the head. This will enable the client to look for unilateral changes in symmetry and contour of each breast.

(Continues)

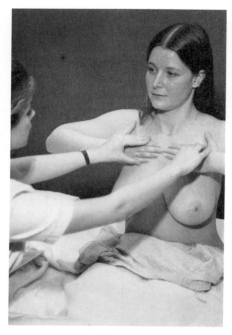

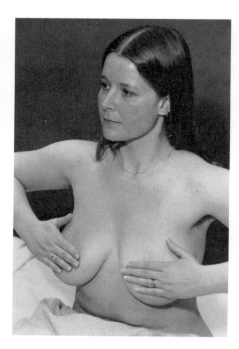

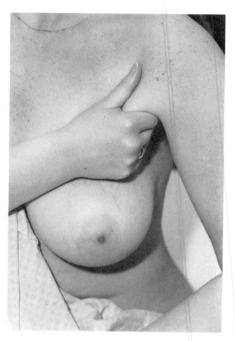

6 To begin the palpation segment of the examination, wash your hands; and then show your client how to sweep her breasts bilaterally. Explain that this is done to assess for lumps in the upper breast tissue, which begins just under the clavicles. Show her how to position her hands at the clavicles (as shown) and to sweep them downward onto the nipples (center photo). Occasionally, a hardened area will be palpated, and most often it is a rib. To ensure that it is, the client should be shown how to palpate across the area to feel for the underlying rib. If the hardened area is not contiguous, she should see a physician. This segment of the examination can be facilitated if it is performed in the shower. The wet skin will enhance the sensitivity of the fingertips.

7 Show the client how to assess the muscle and lymph tissue at the axillae. To relax the muscle, she should rest an arm in her lap, with the elbow slightly flexed. She should then grasp the tissue between the thumb and fingers of her opposite hand and gently squeeze the tissue in a rolling motion to palpate for lumps or swollen lymph glands.

8 While she is sitting, teach her the procedure for palpating each breast in concentric circles. This is the portion of the examination that the woman will regularly perform in a supine position. Show her how to find the 12:00 position at the periphery of the breast tissue, the uppermost and outermost section. Explain that she should palpate around the breast in a circular fashion, using flattened fingers, until she returns to 12:00. In this photo, the nurse is showing her client how to palpate with the right hand and guide the movement with the left hand. Explain that a ridge of firm tissue at the curve of the lower breast is normal. However, she should see a physician if she detects lumps, knots, or thickened tissue. Typically, a malignancy is painless, is attached to underlying tissue, and occurs most often in the upper outer quadrant.

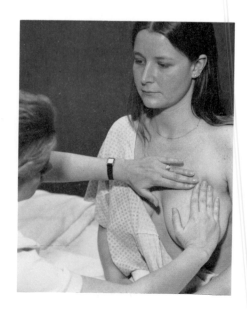

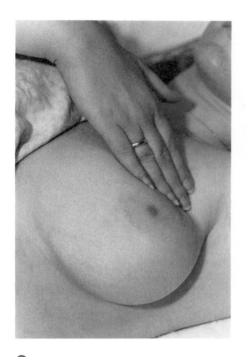

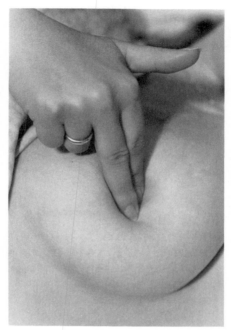

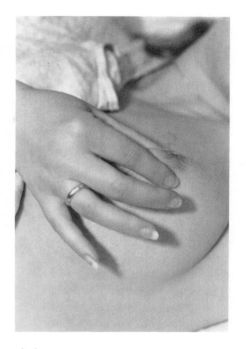

9 For self-examination, the client should lie down, and while supine, apply the above technique. To examine the left breast (as shown), a towel or a small pillow should be placed under the left side and shoulder, and her left hand should be positioned behind her head. This position will distribute the breast tissue over the chest wall more evenly. Explain that she can facilitate the gliding motion and increase the sensitivity of her fingertips by generously applying lotion to her fingertips. After palpating in a complete circle around the outer breast tissue, she should advance an inch toward the nipple and repeat the process until the *entire breast* has been examined in this manner.

10 After the client has examined the breast, she should next examine the nipple. She should depress the nipple with her index and middle fingers to palpate the area underneath, which is referred to as the *well*. This is a common location for tumors, and it too often is missed during a cursory examination.

11 Instruct her to squeeze and milk the nipple gently to assess for discharge. Any new discharge in an adult nonlactating female is significant, and it should be referred to a physician.

Evaluating

12 After completing the assessment of the left breast, the client should repeat the examination in the right breast while you observe and answer any questions she may have.

When the assessment has been completed, compare your observations with those of the client. Arrange for a physician referral if you have detected any abnormalities. Reassure her that most lumps and abnormalities (eight out of ten) are benign, but that only a physician can make a diagnosis and arrange for the appropriate treatment. For women with fibrocystic breasts, suggest that a graph be made, noting areas of lumps and thickened tissue. This will provide a comparison so they can quickly determine whether the lumps are preexisting or indicative of change.

ASSISTING THE CLIENT WITH POSTSURGICAL MASTECTOMY EXERCISES

Postsurgical arm and shoulder exercises are crucial to the full recovery of your clients who have had mastectomies because they help to maintain circulation in the involved arm, reduce edema, and promote maximum function. If your client is scheduled for a mastectomy, consult with her physician prior to the surgery to determine the type of mastectomy anticipated so that you can develop an individualized exercise plan that can be implemented as soon as the client arrives in the recovery room. In addition, with physician approval, you can arrange for a visit by a member of the American Cancer Society's "Reach to Recovery" support group or other similar groups in your community for the postsurgical period. To ensure that your client's progress warrants the increased range of movement, check with her physician before initiating each new exercise. The movements depicted in the following photographs range from the simple to the advanced. As appropriate, teach the following exercises to the client **before** surgery. Review them with her during her hospitalization and again just prior to hospital discharge. *The photos that follow demonstrate client teaching **before** surgery.*

THE EXERCISES

1 Passive range of motion (ROM) exercises can be initiated as soon as the client arrives in the recovery room; once she has returned to her room you can begin assisted ROM exercises on her involved shoulder (as shown). Review the procedures in Chapter 2 to assist you with the movements involved. Because the client may have both discomfort and apprehension about stretching the incisional site, be sure to explain the reason for the exercises and reassure her that the movements will be adapted to her level of tolerance. For maximal joint mobility, these exercises should be performed in sets of 10, three times a day.

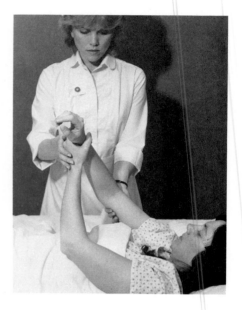

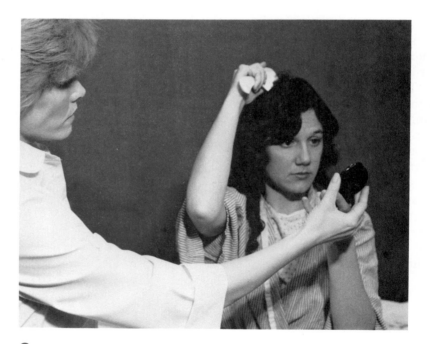

2 By the second postoperative day, activities of daily living using the involved arm should be encouraged as much as possible.

For example, combing the hair, putting on makeup, or washing the face are all activities that will exercise the involved arm.

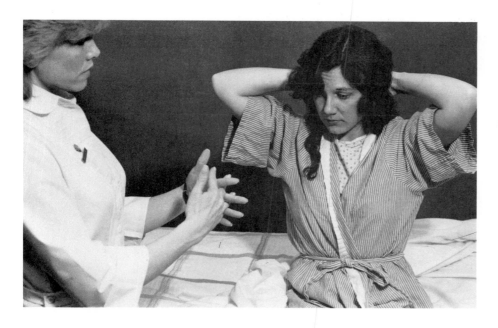

3 When your client is able to lift her involved arm actively without assistance, instruct her to clasp her hands behind her head (as shown).

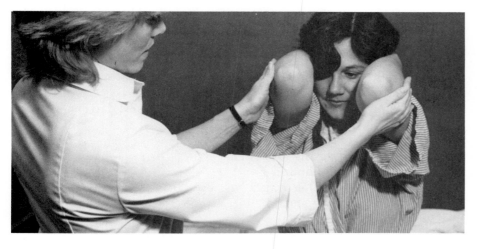

4 She should then attempt to touch her elbows together, or to bring them as close together as possible. This movement will flex, externally rotate, and adduct the involved shoulder.

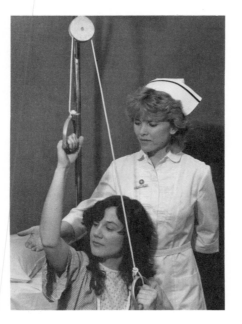

5 You also can use assistive devices to achieve shoulder flexion. With physician approval, assemble a rope and pulley system onto an overhead trapeze bar. The client should grasp the hand grips and begin the exercise with the involved arm in the lower position. Instruct her to pull down gently with the hand of the uninvolved arm, allowing the involved arm to be raised gradually (as shown). Explain to the client that some discomfort and a sensation of stretching the incision is normal, but that to achieve maximum shoulder range, she should flex the shoulder as much as possible. **Note:** *The client may adapt this exercise at home by placing a rope over a stable shower curtain rod or over a wall hook.*

(Continues)

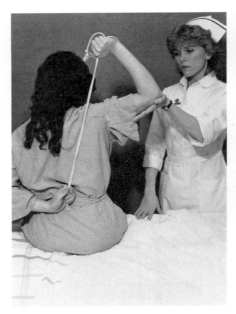

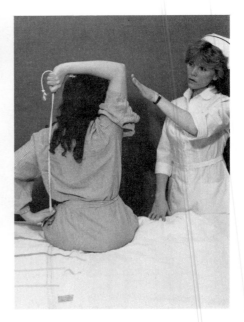

6   You also can teach the client how to "climb a wall," which will promote shoulder flexion without the use of an assistive device. The client should face the wall and position her involved arm at shoulder level. Gradually she will scale the wall by "walking" her fingertips upward (as shown). Encourage her to achieve maximum shoulder ROM. *Note: Place a tape marker on the wall to indicate her progress after each exercise. This will give her a goal to strive for with each new attempt.*

7   Around the second postoperative week, usually after the sutures have been removed, the client can begin exercises that will maximize external rotation and abduction of the shoulder. A 75-cm (30-in.) rope can be used to assist the client in achieving maximum range. Instruct her to grasp the rope, holding the lower end in her uninvolved hand in the back at the level of her waistline. The top of the rope should be held in the hand of her involved arm at about the level of her head.

8   She should very gently pull down on the rope with the hand of her uninvolved arm, guiding the involved arm through abduction and external rotation. This exercise should be performed at least three times daily in sets of 10 each.

9   For implementation **after** the incision and underlying tissue have healed, teach the client how she can achieve maximum shoulder flexion by touching her fingertips behind her back with the involved arm uppermost. This exercise simulates the range required for zipping back zippers and fastening brassieres.

PROVIDING PERINEAL CARE

USING A SQUEEZE BOTTLE

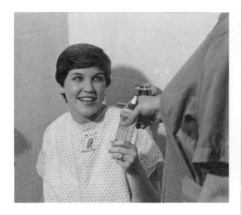

1 A very simple method for providing perineal care is the use of a squeeze bottle filled with tap water warmed to approximately 37.8°C (100°F). A postpartum client can use this method after every voiding to cleanse her perineum.

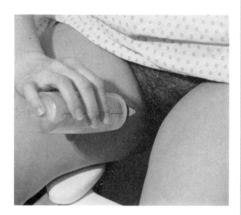

2 Instruct the client to insert the nozzle of the bottle between her legs and to squirt the bottle so that it sprays onto the perineum. Explain to the client that it will take several squirts to thoroughly cleanse the area. She should then blot her perineum from front to back when she has finished with the squeeze bottle, using either toilet paper or clean wipes provided by your agency.

PREPARING A SITZ BATH

1 A sitz bath is prepared for clients who have vulvar pain and swelling and who require warmth to heal the perineal area, for example after vaginal hysterectomies, vulvectomies, childbirth, or hemorrhoidectomies. Ensure that the basin has been thoroughly scrubbed with a disinfectant cleaning agent. Place towels around the seat to pad the area where the client will sit. This not only will promote comfort but it also will prevent the client from slipping on the wet, slick surface of the tub. Padding the basin prior to running the water will prevent the towels from floating out of place.

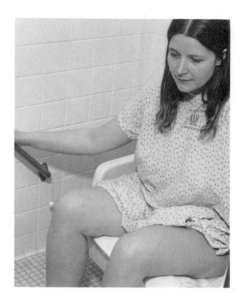

2 Adjust the temperature of the sitz bath so that it is in the range of 37.8°–40.5°C (100°–105°F). If the system does not have a built-in thermometer, use a bath thermometer to verify the temperature. The bath should fill from a third to a half of its capacity, and many models will drain continuously to provide a source of fresh water for the client. Assist the client into the sitting position. If you cannot stay with her during the prescribed treatment time, make sure the emergency call light is within her reach. Because of the warmth of the water, the client must be monitored periodically for potential fainting. Sitz baths are usually recommended for periods of 20–30 minutes.

USING A SURGI-GATOR

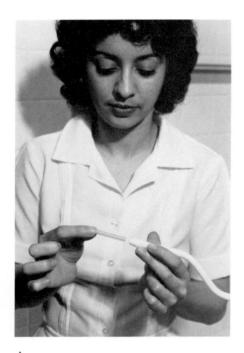

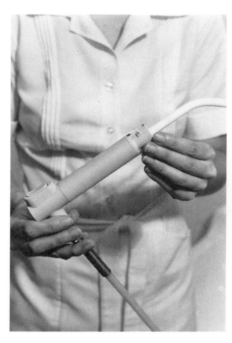

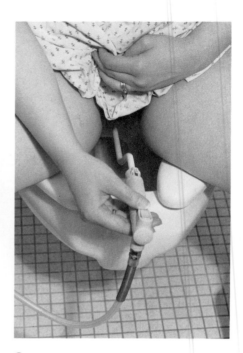

1   If your agency has a Surgi-gator perineal care system for cleansing and providing warmth to the perineum, you can teach your client how to use the system on her own for the times in which it is prescribed, as well as during the times she experiences perineal discomfort.

Every client is issued her own applicator. Explain to the client that she must first insert the soap cartridge into the proximal end of the applicator.

2   The proximal end is then inserted and snapped into the dispensing handle that connects to the wall-mounted unit. Explain that depressing the control button on the dispensing handle delivers both the cleansing cycle and the rinse cycle. Make sure the temperature is set at approximately 37.8°C (100°F).

3   Instruct the client to sit on the toilet, spread her legs apart, and insert the Surgi-gator applicator between her legs so that it is just distal to her perineum.

4   After depressing the control button, she can adjust the distance of the applicator to her perineum to achieve the desired force of spray. Remind her to return the applicator to the bedside for subsequent use.

PROVIDING CARE FOR CLIENTS WITH CERVICAL-UTERINE RADIATION IMPLANTS

If your client has gynecologic carcinoma, such as endometrial cancer, she may be treated with external radiation and/or sealed radioactive implants that are placed within her body. Because the implant is sealed within a metal capsule or supplied as a solid substance, the potential for contamination is negligible. The external radiation level associated with these implants is substantial, however, and necessitates that exposure to staff, other clients, and visitors be minimal. Therefore, clients undergoing internal radiation usually have private rooms. Women who are pregnant or who potentially may be pregnant should not enter the room. Visitation is restricted to individuals older than age 18 and often to the client's spouse or significant other only. Visitors under the age of 45, with the exception of the client's spouse, often are asked to limit their visits to 30 minutes a day. Clients with radiation implants must have warning signs posted on their closed doors and charts to alert staff and visitors that radiation therapy is in process.

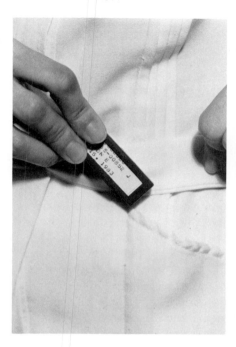

1 Before entering the client's room, attach a radiation badge to your clothing at about the level of the client's uterus. Monthly radiation levels, according to federal regulations, never should exceed 400 mrem. Nurses who care for these clients rarely receive monthly amounts this high.

2 Plan client care carefully so that you can accomplish as much as possible in the shortest amount of time. If the client is allowed to move from a supine position for brief periods of time, plan care around the scheduled position changes. Comfort measures, such as upper back care, the use of sheepskin pads, and on-time administration of pain medications, are essential for helping to minimize the client's discomfort. Because the client will have an indwelling urinary catheter to decompress the bladder, inspect the catheter and drainage system and assess the

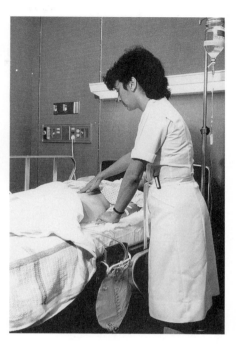

bladder to ensure that the system is draining effectively. An obstructed catheter, causing bladder distention, could result in radiation burns to the bladder. Whenever possible, stand at the head of the bed to maximize the distance between yourself and the client's uterus. Be sure to inspect the vaginal introitus to ensure that the gauze packing and implants are intact. If you do find metal in the bed, *do not touch it.* Notify the radiation department so that they can remove the implant with forceps. However, be assured that the client's excretions and secretions are *not* radioactive. **Caution:** *Avoid use of oil-based lotions or creams on the client's back, abdomen, or buttocks. When used in conjunction with radiation, these products may cause burning of the skin. Use water-soluble lubricants, instead.*

Performing Prenatal Techniques

ASSESSING THE PRENATAL ABDOMEN

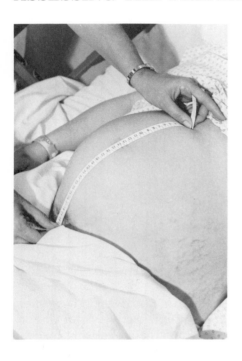

MEASURING FUNDAL HEIGHT

Assessing uterine size by measuring fundal height is often initiated in the client's second trimester. It is continued into the third trimester as a routine assessment tool for monitoring fetal growth. Although it is not a precise indicator of fetal development, it will alert you to sudden growth spurts found, for example, in multiple gestations, or to a lag in progression indicating intrauterine growth retardation. To measure the fundal height, obtain a nonstretchable tape measure; position one end at the fundus and measure the distance to the symphysis pubis in centimeters. Up until the third trimester, the measurement will, on average, correlate with the gestational age. For example, at 24 weeks' gestation, the fundus measures around 24 cm for the average woman, and it is usually at the level of the umbilicus.

Using McDonald's Rule

When the client is in her third trimester, apply McDonald's rule to estimate gestational age. For example, if your client measures 28 cm from the fundus to the symphysis pubis, you can estimate gestational age in lunar months by calculating in the following manner:

$$\frac{\text{Fundal height in cm}}{3.5} =$$

Gestational age in lunar months

$$\frac{28 \text{ cm}}{3.5} = 8 \text{ lunar months}$$

INSPECTING AND PALPATING FETAL PARTS

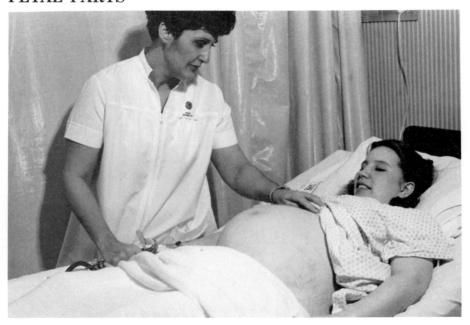

Palpate and locate fetal parts prior to auscultating for fetal heart tones (FHTs). Once you have identified the fetal back, you can readily elicit heart sounds because there is less bone and tissue through which to auscultate. Provide warmth and privacy for your client; for her comfort and to relax the abdominal wall, make sure she has recently voided. After explaining the procedure, elevate her head slightly and ask her to flex her knees, which will further relax the abdomen. Expose the abdomen from the xiphoid process to the symphysis pubis, and then inspect it to help you assess the position of the fetus. Does it appear to lie up and down in a longitudinal position or left and right in a transverse position?

Performing Leopold's Maneuvers

Leopold's maneuvers are performed to determine fetal position. Make sure your hands are warm, and perform the assessment between contractions, whether Braxton Hicks or labor contractions.

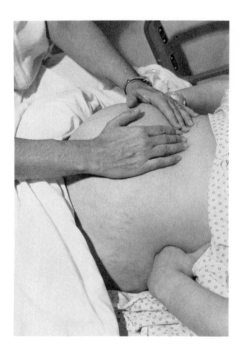

First Maneuver: Face the client and bilaterally palpate the upper abdomen. This will help you determine which of the fetal parts is in the uterine fundus. The breech is large, soft, and asymmetrical; the head is round, hard, and it moves more freely.

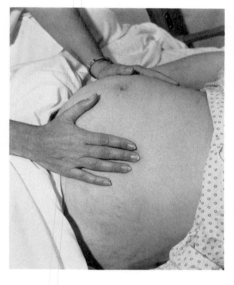

Second Maneuver: Continue facing the client, and place each hand along the sides of the abdomen. Gently but firmly palpate with your palms and fingers. Assess one side and then the other to determine the side on which the fetal back lies. One side should feel smooth and quite firm—the fetal back; the other side should be indentable and less resistant—the extremities on the opposite uterine wall.

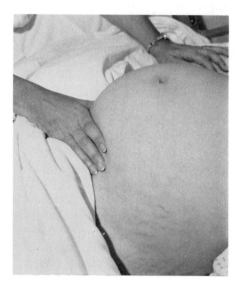

Third Maneuver: While still facing the client, position your dominant hand over the lower abdomen just proximal to the symphysis pubis, and firmly palpate with your thumb and index finger. Explain to the client that this maneuver may be uncomfortable. This maneuver helps to confirm the data gathered in the first maneuver. Again, the head will be round, hard, and ballotable (movable) if it has not already engaged. The breech will feel soft and asymmetrical. (This assessment will be much more difficult if the presenting part has already engaged.)

(Continues)

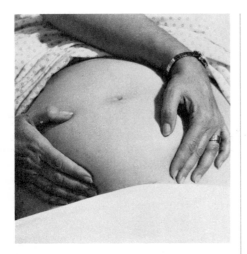

Fourth Maneuver: Face the client's feet and position your hands on both sides of the abdomen with your fingers curving downward toward, and immediately proximal to, the pubis. This maneuver will help you locate the cephalic prominence, which is the most prominent portion of the fetal head. Press deeply with your fingertips because you will need to palpate through several layers of tissue, muscle, and fluid. The cephalic prominence is located on the side in which your fingers meet the greatest resistance. If it is located on the side opposite the back, the head is flexed and a normal delivery will probably ensue. If it is located on the same side as the back, the head is extended and the face or brow will probably present. Again, the greater the engagement, the more difficult the assessment.

AUSCULTATING FETAL HEART TONES

Once you have located the fetal back using Leopold's maneuvers, you can readily auscultate FHTs. This assessment will also reconfirm your assessment of the location of the fetal parts. However, in an emergency, auscultate in the midline between the umbilicus and symphysis pubis, the site in which FHTs are the loudest in the more typical cephalic presentation. With a fetoscope, the FHTs will be inaudible until weeks 18–20 of gestation, and at that time the point of maximum intensity is just above the pubis. Thereafter, the point of maximum intensity varies depending on the fetal position and presentation. Most often it can be heard best over the fetal back.

Using a Fetoscope

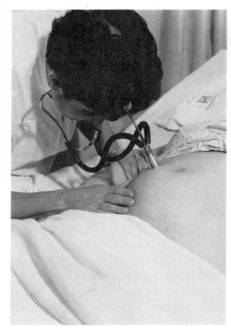

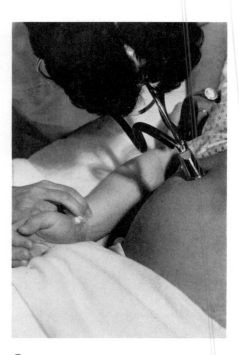

1 Position the warmed fetoscope over the palpated fetal back. Move the fetoscope around until you locate the point of maximum intensity. Generally, with cephalic presentations, the FHTs can be heard in the lower quadrant, toward the mother's flank. In breech presentations they can be heard closer to the midline around the level of the umbilicus. Apply slight pressure with the fetoscope bell to elicit the sounds.

2 When the heart tones are at their loudest, palpate the mother's radial pulse as you count the FHTs. This will ensure that you have not confused the mother's *souffle* with the fetal heart tones. This *souffle* is a soft, rushing sound produced by blood moving through the uterine arteries, and it is synchronous with the maternal heart rate. Count the FHTs for one full minute. They should range from 120 to 160 beats/minute.

Using Ultrasonic (Doppler) Auscultation

PERFORMING EXTERNAL ELECTRONIC FETAL MONITORING

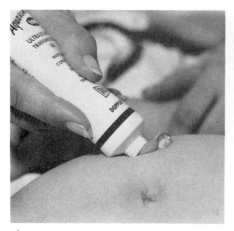

1   Review the procedure, p. 408, for a description of the Doppler. An ultrasonic transducer has the advantage of detecting FHTs by the 12th week, and occasionally as early as the 9th or 10th week. Lubricate an area over the fetal back using a thin layer of conducting jelly.

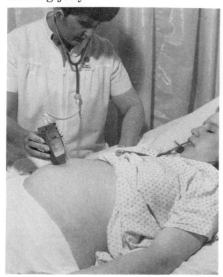

2   Position the transducer over the lubricated area. If the Doppler has an extra headset, allow the mother to listen simultaneously. Count the beats for a minute. You may also elicit a *bruit*, a hissing sound produced by blood moving through the umbilical arteries and other fetal vessels, as well as a *souffle*.

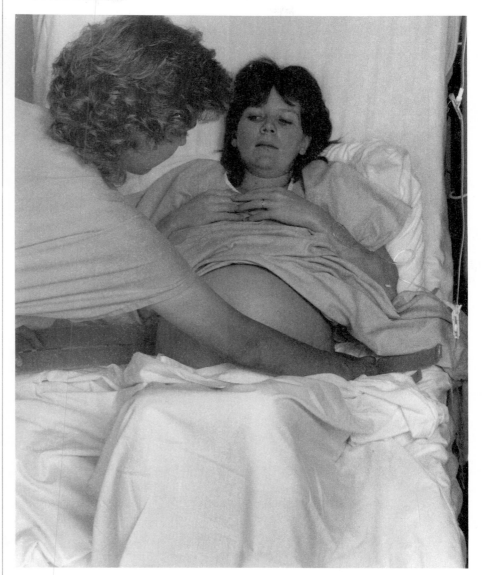

Electronic fetal monitoring is used in the clinical setting to monitor both fetal heart rate and uterine activity. This is accomplished by means of an ultrasonic transducer, which uses the sonar principle to detect continuous sound waves from the fetal heart, and a tocodynamometer, which is a pressure device that simultaneously transmits a signal that reveals frequency of uterine contractions. Both signals are recorded on the screen and graph paper.

1   Wash your hands. Identify the client and explain the procedure to her. Tell the client that the top belt will be secured snugly to ensure an accurate reading. Place the client in a position of comfort, usually semi-Fowler's position. Slide the transducer belts under the client's abdomen, as shown.

(Continues)

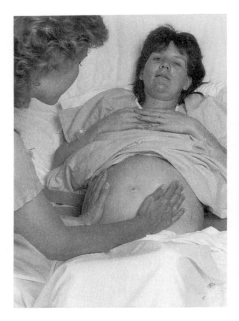

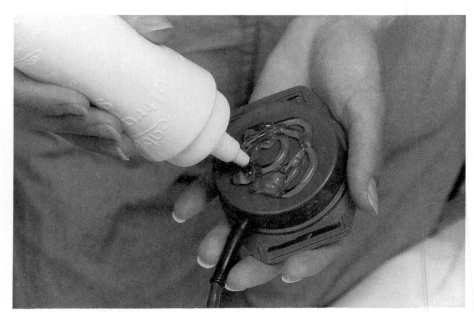

2   Identify fetal parts using Leopold's maneuver (see p. 201) to determine the position of the fetal back.

3   Apply conducting gel to the underside of the ultrasound transducer (as shown).

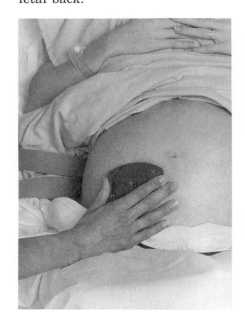

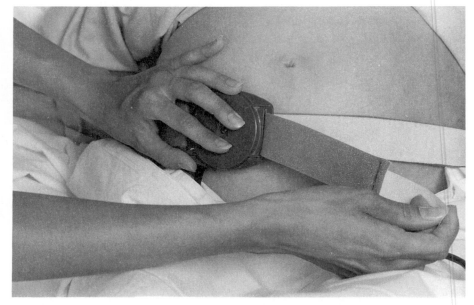

4   Caution the client that the transducer will be cold from the gel. Apply the transducer to the area over the fetal back proximal to the fetal head (as shown for this client). Start the tracing on the monitor and wait 3–5 seconds for the tracing to begin. If FHTs are not audible, reassess fetal position and repeat step 2.

5   If FHTs are audible, secure the transducer with the belt (as shown). Identify the graph tracing with client information, including client's name, medical record number, vital signs, date, time, and type of fetal monitor used.

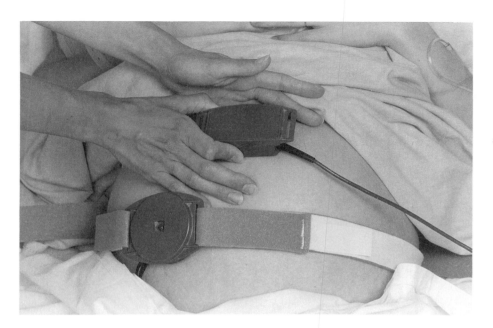

6 Next, position the tocotransducer over the fundus, where uterine contractions are most accurately assessed. Adjust the uterine activity on the monitor to the zero point. Secure the tocotransducer with the remaining abdominal belt, applying the belt snugly against the client's abdomen to ensure that uterine pressure against the tocotransducer is enough to record the contractions on the monitor.

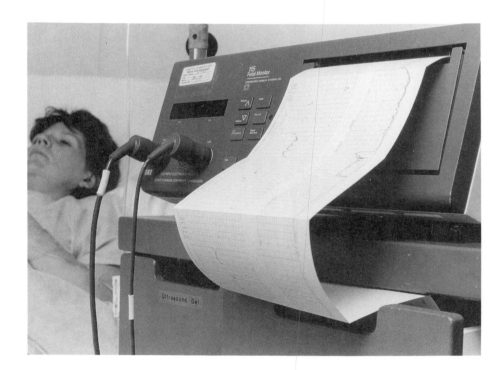

7 Let the monitor run for 20–30 minutes if checking fetal status. If the mother is in labor, let the monitor continue running as prescribed.

(Continues)

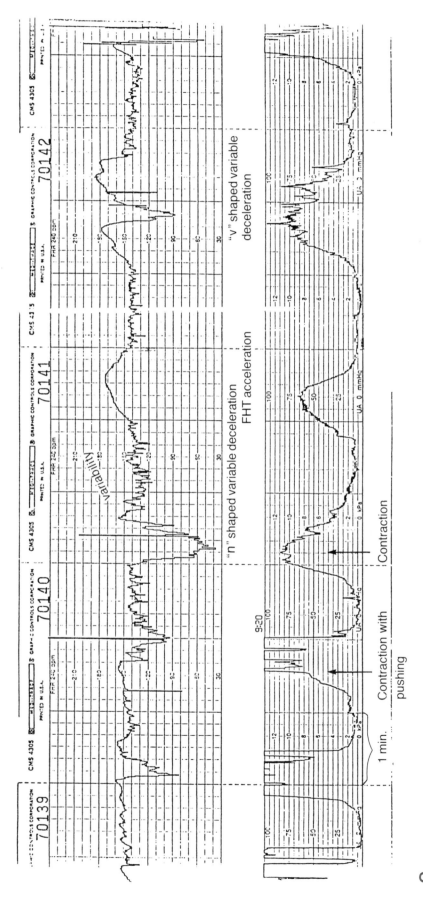

8 Inspect the strips to assess FHTs and uterine activity. Although it is not our purpose in this text to teach strip interpretation, the variable "n"-shaped segments in the FHT strip denote FHT acceleration. The variable "v"-shaped segments show FHT deceleration. The strip with uterine activity shows contractions with pushing and contractions without pushing. Note that the contractions are 1 minute apart.

ASSESSING FOR AMNIOTIC FLUID

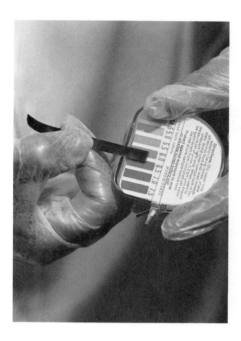

If you or your client notes the presence of clear fluid on her peripad or garment and you suspect that her membranes have ruptured, the first priority is to inspect the perineum and introitus to determine the presence or absence of a prolapsed cord. Next, monitor FHTs. If severe bradycardia ($\leq$100 bpm) is present, notify the physician at once. Then apply gloves and perform a vaginal examination to determine if the cord is being compressed by the presenting part. If you note cord compression, place the client immediately into Trendelenburg's position while pushing the presenting part upward to relieve the cord compression. Maintain this position while the physician evaluates the client further.

To determine if the fluid is amniotic, place a nitrazine test strip directly into the fluid and shake off any excess. ***Note: Avoid placing the test strip on the peripad or garment itself, as this may result in a false reading due to the presence of blood, mucus, or diluted urine.***

Immediately compare the results to the color chart on the nitrazine container (as shown). Amniotic fluid is alkaline with a 7.2 pH, and the darker the test strip, the more likely it is that the membranes have ruptured. ***Note: A false positive may result if the client has had a recent vaginal examination with a water-soluble lubricant or if the fluid contains blood.***

PROVIDING COMFORT MEASURES

APPLYING COUNTER-PRESSURE TO RELIEVE LEG CRAMPS

Your pregnant client may experience painful muscle spasms in her legs, especially during the third trimester when circulation is impaired in the lower extremities and the weighty uterus presses on the nerves in her legs. These cramps are often precipitated when the client is recumbent and extends her feet. They can be relieved by straightening the leg with one hand as you dorsiflex the foot with the other hand. Be sure to teach this technique to your client's partner.

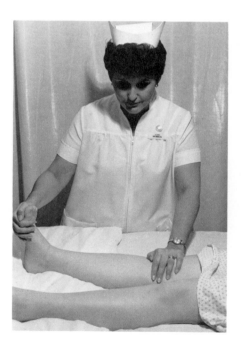

APPLYING PRESSURE TO RELIEVE BACK PAIN

If your client experiences back pain, which may be caused from increasing curvature of the back or a relaxation of the pelvic joints, assist her onto her side and apply firm pressure with the heel of your hand to the sacrococcygeal area. Continue to exert pressure until the discomfort is diminished or relieved.

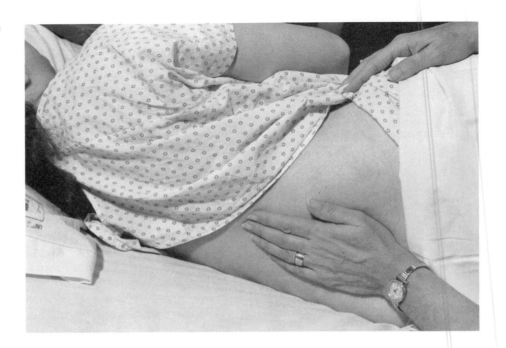

Performing Postpartum Techniques

ASSESSING THE MOTHER

Wash your hands and explain the procedure to your client. Be sure to provide privacy. To make the process as comfortable as possible, ensure that the client has recently voided. Begin the assessment by taking vital signs to ensure that they are within normal limits when compared to the baseline. Frequent assessment is essential, especially during the first 24 hours when the client is at the greatest risk for postpartum hemorrhage. Perform vital sign assessment before your hands-on assessment of the client because the discomfort of a fundal check could be reflected in an elevated blood pressure and pulse rate.

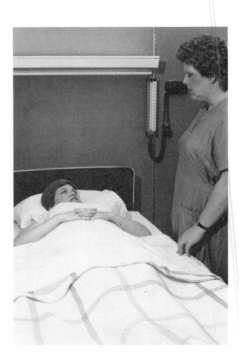

INSPECTING AND PALPATING THE BREASTS

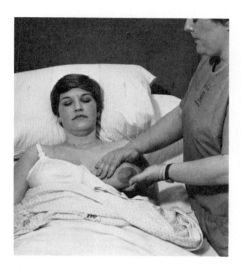

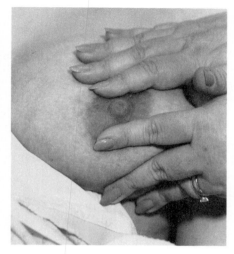

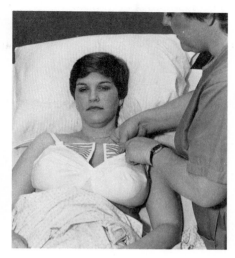

1   Raise the head of the bed, and ask your client to lower her gown so that you can examine her breasts. Inspect each breast, noting reddened areas or any irregularities such as asymmetry; and if present, assess the degree of engorgement. Palpate each breast, assessing for heat or nodules caused by occluded milk ducts. These occur most frequently in the upper outer quadrants.

2   Inspect and palpate the areolae and nipples. Gently spread the areola between your fingers, noting cracks, fissures, tenderness, blood, or a buildup of secretions. Also assess for erectility of the nipple by rolling the nipple between your thumb and index finger. If cracks or fissures are noted, encourage the client to keep the flaps of her bra unhooked and down to enhance air drying. Creams or ointments should be used only in instances of severe irritation because most require removal prior to breastfeeding, resulting in increased irritation to the area. It is acceptable to use pure hydrous lanolin, however, because it is more readily absorbed into the skin and does not require removal prior to breastfeeding.

3   Breast engorgement is usually indicative of inadequate feeding or expression frequency. In most cases, beginning breastfeeding immediately after birth and ensuring the infant's unlimited access to the breast as desired (usually every 1½ to 3 hours) will prevent engorgement. If engorgement occurs, the mother should nurse her baby more frequently or express the milk by pump (see procedures, p. 217) if the baby is unavailable. Using hot packs and massaging the breasts before feeding help promote milk ejection. In the nonnursing mother, ice packs, such as the chemical packs shown in the photo, and a supportive bra are recommended.

PALPATING THE FUNDUS AND BLADDER

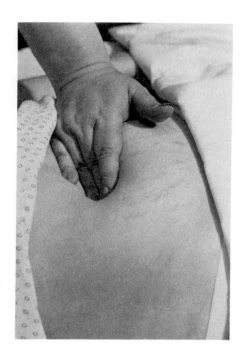

The fundus should be assessed for location and tone at frequent intervals, according to agency protocol, until around the 10th day postpartum when it is usually no longer palpable. Because most clients are discharged much earlier than this, instruct the client in self-examination so that she can be alert to changes in her uterus. To assess the fundus and bladder, lower the head of the bed so that the abdomen will be relaxed. Ensure that the client has recently voided because a full bladder will displace the fundus. Fundal height is measured in relationship to its distance in finger breadths from the umbilicus. To measure the distance, position your ring finger directly over the umbilicus so that your small finger is closest to the client's head. Using your ring finger as a fulcrum, roll your hand back and forth gently. If the fundus is more than a finger's breadth (FB) above the umbilicus (U) or more than two below, reposition your fingers in the appropriate direction. Document the measurement accordingly, for example:
1 FB ↑ U; or 1 FB ↓ U; or @U.
At the same time, note the fundal relationship to the midline. Displacement to either side of the midline is usually caused by a distended bladder. Normally the fundus will be at the midline. If it is displaced, palpate the bladder gently, following the procedure, p. 442. Also, describe the uterine tone. Optimally, it will feel firm and well contracted; it should not be excessively tender to the touch.

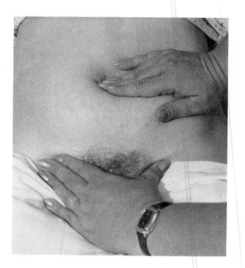

Performing Fundal Massage: If the uterus feels soft and boggy, perform a light massage in an attempt to contract and harden it. Ask the client to flex her knees to relax her abdomen, and to release the peripad so that you can clearly assess the amount, color, and consistency of the lochia expelled during the massage. Place the flattened fingertips of your dominant hand at the client's fundus. To prevent uterine prolapse, provide support with your other hand (as shown). Lightly massage the fundus in a circular motion. If the uterus does not respond to a light massage, repeat with more vigorous movements. If the client's uterus is nonresponsive and remains soft and boggy, and if this is accompanied by copious bleeding, contact the physician for immediate intervention. *Caution: Never massage a well-contracted uterus. Overstimulation can result in muscle fatigue and uterine relaxation.*

EVALUATING THE LOCHIA

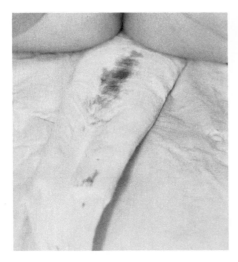

INSPECTING THE PERINEUM

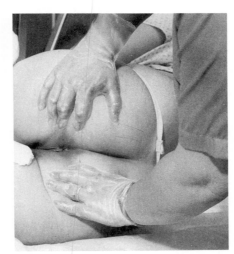

To assess the lochia, detach the peripad from the client's sanitary belt. Be sure to remove it from the front to the back to minimize the risk of contaminating the vagina with rectal discharge. Note the amount, character, and odor of the discharge. During the first few days, the lochia should resemble menstrual blood in that it should be dark and red (lochia rubra). After the third day it should appear more serous and brown in color (lochia serosa). Clots are usually abnormal and could mean that the client has retained placental tissue or inadequate uterine contraction. If clots are found, further investigation is indicated, and a referral may be necessary. Be sure to ask the client about her evaluation of the bleeding and the number of pads she has saturated. Four to eight saturated pads may be considered normal over a 24-hour period. However, if your client has had a cesarean delivery, that amount would be excessive. Also, foul-smelling lochia on a fresh pad could be indicative of an infection. Document the amount and character of the lochia, for example: lochia rubra, moderate amount with a few small clots; or lochia serosa, scant.

To inspect the perineum, instruct the client to assume a side-lying (Sim's) position. It is important that she flex the top leg to minimize the strain on the episiotomy. Apply gloves and gently separate the buttocks, which will enable you to fully inspect the perineum. Assess the area for stage of healing, presence of edema, bruising, dehiscence, and signs of infection, as well as for hemorrhoids. Document your observations. If indicated, apply ice packs to the perineum for the first 12 hours to minimize edema. After the first 12 hours, apply heat, such as chemical heat packs or perilights, or encourage the use of a sitz bath. If your client has had a cesarean delivery, it is still important to assess the perianal area for the presence of hemorrhoids.

ASSISTING WITH INFANT FEEDING

The infant should be nursed as often as he desires (approximately every 1½ to 3 hours) with unlimited feeding time. Provide time for the mother to prepare for infant feeding. For example, she may wish to void, and she should wash her hands and get into a comfortable position. To provide her with privacy, draw the curtain around her bed and shut her door. If the infant and mother are not rooming together, be sure to verify that the infant's name and identification numbers match those of the mother.

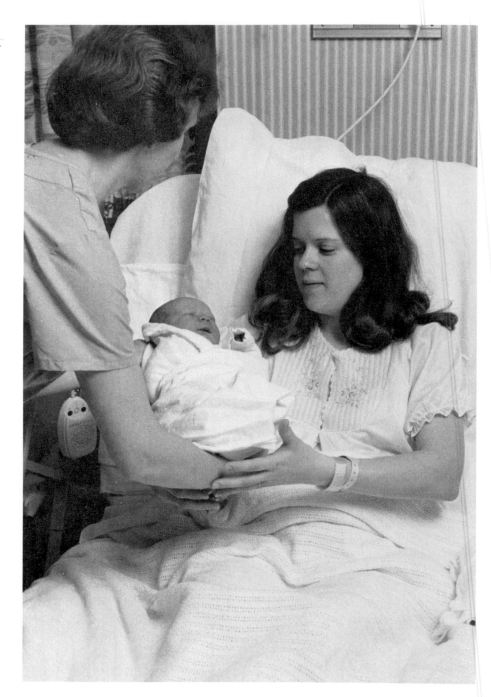

POSITIONING THE INFANT

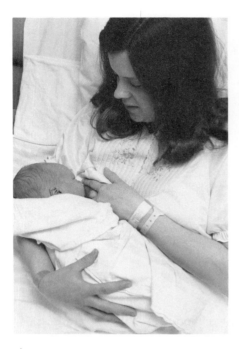

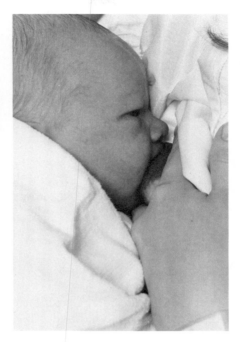

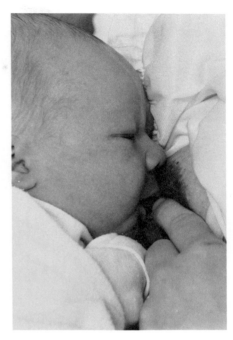

1 *The Cradle Hold:* A commonly used position for breast-feeding is the cradle hold in which the mother is sitting upright, with the infant's head held in the crook of her arm, its spine supported by her forearm and its buttocks cradled in her hand. Teach the mother to draw the infant close to her body to minimize traction on her nipple. Ensure that the infant's abdomen is against the mother's abdomen. Support her arm with pillows, as needed, to prevent maternal fatigue.

2 Note that the mother positions her index and middle fingers on both sides of the areola, squeezing gently. This encourages the infant to place his mouth around as much of the areola as possible, which in turn stimulates the milk ducts underneath the areola. This hand position also prevents the breast from obstructing the infant's nose. Teach the mother to elicit the rooting response (see p. 228) so that the infant will suck when placed at the breast.

3 When the mother desires to remove the infant from her breast, teach her to break the suction by inserting her finger into the corner of the infant's mouth (as shown).

(Continues)

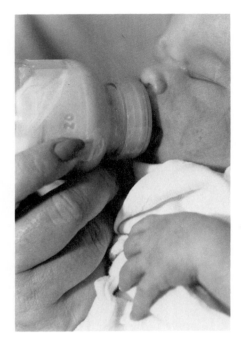

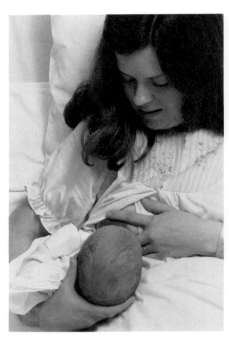

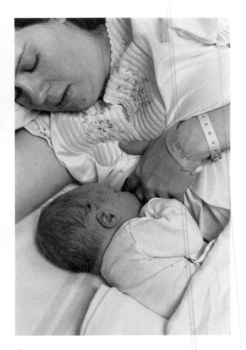

4 Bottle-fed infants are positioned in the cradle hold position because it enhances the warmth and physical closeness that occur with breastfeeding. The bottle *always* should be held rather than propped up, and the nipple must be full of milk to avoid introducing air into the infant's stomach.

5 *Football Hold:* This position is recommended for mothers who have had a cesarean delivery, because it enables them to support the infant's weight off their abdomens. The infant is held supine along the forearm with the head supported by the mother's hand. The infant's weight can be supported by a pillow.

6 *Side-Lying:* When the mother wishes to rest, a side-lying position will enable her to lie down with the infant at her side rather than in her arms. The infant can be supported in the side-lying position by placing a rolled blanket or towel behind his back. This position is also excellent after cesarean deliveries. Ensure that the infant's abdomen is positioned against his mother's abdomen.

BURPING THE INFANT

1 After feeding the infant at each breast, the mother should burp him gently by patting or rubbing his back to expel the air bubbles. She can hold the infant over her shoulder (as shown) with a diaper or towel placed under his mouth to absorb any fluid that potentially may be expelled.

MASSAGING THE BREASTS FOR MANUAL EXPRESSION OF BREAST MILK

2 In another burping position, the infant sits with his head flexed forward. The mother supports his chest and head with one hand and pats or rubs his back with the other.

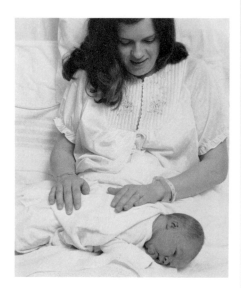

3 The infant also can be burped in a prone position over the mother's thighs. Positions 2 and 3 are recommended for newborns because either position allows the mother to see the infant's face, which will alert her to choking and aspiration.

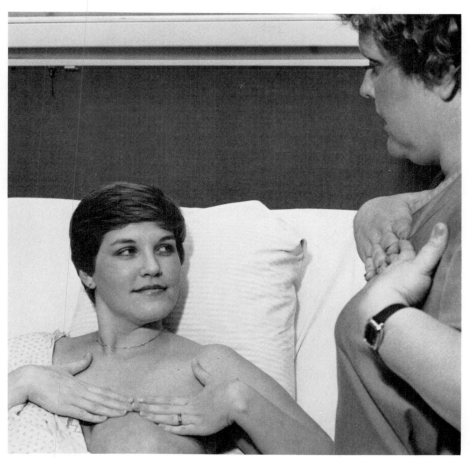

1 Teach your breastfeeding client how to massage her breasts to facilitate the manual expression of breast milk. This will enable her to produce a small amount of milk or colostrum, which will help entice a disinterested infant to eat. It also will allow her to relieve breast engorgement and to store milk for future feedings in her absence.

The mother should first wash her hands. Explain that breast massage will enhance the flow of milk through all the milk ducts. Show her how to sweep her fingers from the chest wall onto the upper surface of the breast.

(Continues)

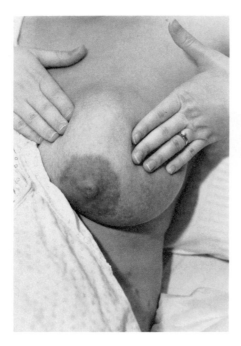

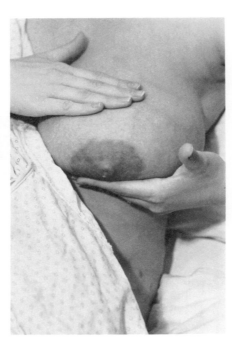

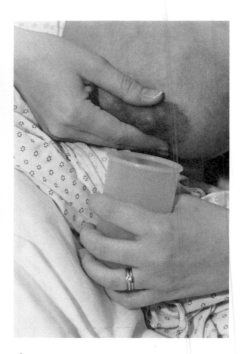

2 Next, she should slide her fingers down both sides of the breast.

3 Her hands should then be positioned on the top side and under side of the breast, sweeping toward the areola.

4 She can express the milk manually by grasping the areola between her thumb and index finger. As she presses the thumb and index finger together, the breast should be held against the chest wall to express the milk. She should then repeat the nipple compression as she repositions her thumb and index finger in a circular fashion around the breast. Instruct her to alternate massage with manual expression to facilitate complete emptying of each breast. Ensure that the expressed milk does not run over her fingers but rather runs directly into the sterile container.

USING BREAST PUMPS

Breast pumps are used to express milk for the relief of breast engorgement in the nursing mother, as a means of maintaining lactation, or as a method for milk storage when the mother must be absent from feedings. In the hospital, aseptic technique is used; after she is discharged, the mother can use clean technique.

MANAGING HAND PUMPS

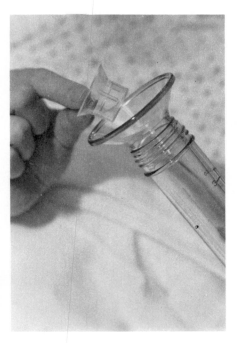

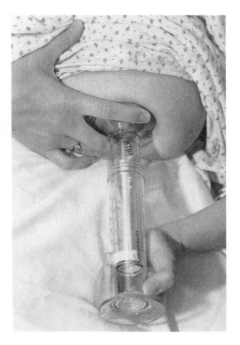

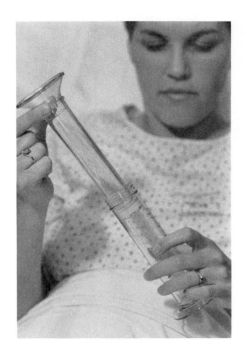

1 The manual breast pump is best used for the occasional expression of milk. The Marshall Kaneson breast pump is a popular brand of pump used for this purpose. After your client has washed her hands, teach her how to insert the inner cylinder into the outer cylinder (as shown), using aseptic technique.

2 She then can select and attach the flange that most closely accommodates her nipple and breast size. The flange screws into the inner cylinder. The flange is important because it provides tactile stimulation to the areolar skin, which is necessary for the milk ejection reflex (letdown).

3 Instruct the client to place the flange over the nipple or slightly off center if the nipple is too small to contact the flange. Teach the client to slide the outer cylinder in and out gently, using small movements until letdown has occurred and the milk is flowing. At that point the client can increase the in-and-out movements to fill the inner cylinder with the milk. When the cylinder is nearly full of milk, she should pour the milk into a sterile plastic bottle or plastic liner from a commercial nurser if she wishes to store the milk for later use. Glass containers should be avoided because leukocytes in breast milk have a tendency to adhere to the sides of these containers.

After each use the breast pump should be cleaned thoroughly according to agency protocol, dried, and stored in a closed container at the bedside.

ASSISTING WITH ELECTRIC BREAST PUMPS

Electric breast pumps, such as the Medela, are an efficient and time-saving method of initiating lactation without the suckling baby for obtaining breast milk on a long-term basis.

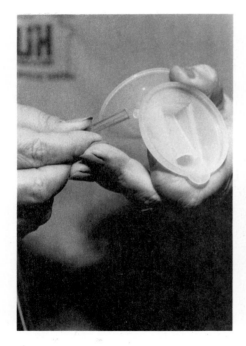

1 First, instruct the client to wash her hands and then select the breast shield with a bell size that provides the most contact with her areolar skin; this is necessary for the milk ejection reflex (letdown). To assemble the equipment she should begin by attaching the hose to the breast shield (as shown).

2 Then snap the breast shield onto the plastic container.

3 Attach the distal end of the hose to the container on the pump.

4 Instruct the mother to position the breast shield so that it is positioned slightly off center on the areolar skin to maximize contact for milk ejection.

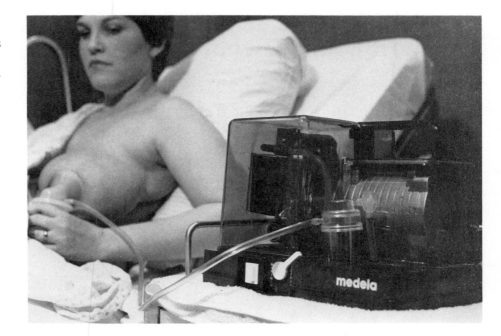

5 She can then adjust the control lever on the pump to the desired amount of suction. She can start expressing with the pressure level set at "minimum" and increase it if she desires by turning to "normal" to maximize maternal prolactin levels and milk supply. It is best to express the breasts simultaneously using a double-pump kit for 10–15 minutes at both breasts. If a single-pump kit is used (as shown), she should express for 5 minutes on the first side, turn off the power and gently remove the bell, and express for 5 minutes on the other breast. This should be repeated for 4 minutes on each side, followed by 3 minutes on each side, then 2 minutes, and then 1 minute. This alternating pattern will improve milk supply and hormone stimulation. *Note: To heal tender nipples, mother's milk is an excellent ointment to apply to them following milk expression.* Store the milk and cleanse the equipment according to the procedure for using hand pumps.

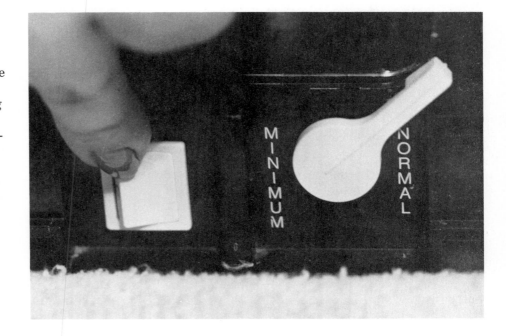

Caring for the Newborn

ADMITTING THE NEONATE TO THE HOSPITAL

OBTAINING FOOTPRINTS

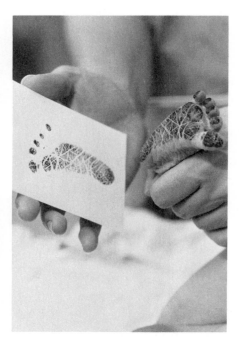

INSTILLING ERYTHROMYCIN OR SILVER NITRATE

The instillation of either a 1% silver nitrate solution or an antibiotic ophthalmic solution, such as erythromycin, is a procedure mandated by most states as a prophylaxis for gonococcal ophthalmia neonatorum. Although many agencies require the immediate instillation in the delivery room, others delay the process until the neonate's admission into the nursery to facilitate the newborn's bonding with the parents.

1 If your agency requires footprints and/or palm prints as a part of the permanent birth record, recording them may be the responsibility of the nurse who admits the newborn to the nursery. To obtain the footprints wipe any vernix off the sole of the foot and position the carbon plate over the entire length of the newborn's foot. Use moderate pressure as you ink the sole because too much ink can obscure the lines and creases.

2 After inking the foot, press the footprint sheet onto the inked sole. To stimulate the newborn to spread his toes, press the footprint sheet from the heel to the toes. Repeat the process on the other foot, and then file the prints in the infant's chart. After obtaining the footprints, rub the soles of the feet with baby oil and wipe the feet with a towel or cloth diaper to remove the ink. Your agency may also file the mother's fingerprint along with her newborn's footprints.

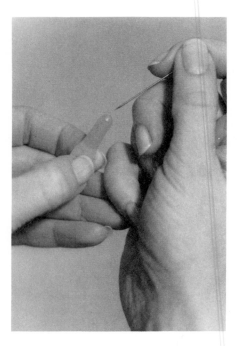

1 If administering silver nitrate solution, pierce the wax ampul with the needle that is usually provided with the ampuls.

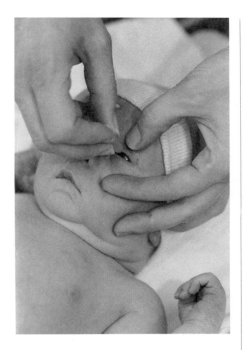

2 Lightly touch the upper lid, which will cause the neonate to open the eye, and then apply gentle pressure on the lower lid to expose the lower conjunctival sac. If administering silver nitrate, instill one or two drops (according to agency guidelines) into the sac. Avoid instilling the medication directly onto the cornea because this could cause corneal irritation. Allow the eye to close so that the medication can be spread over the surface of the eye. Repeat the procedure in the other eye. If you are administering an antibiotic ointment, instill the ointment into the conjunctival sac from the inner to outer canthus (review procedure, p. 84). Because either medication could result in a mild conjunctivitis, be sure to explain to the parents that this is a temporary condition.

ADMINISTERING A VITAMIN K INJECTION

A vitamin K injection is administered as a prophylaxis for transient coagulation deficiency in the neonate. It usually is given on the day of birth because the coagulation disorder potentially would appear between the second and fifth day after birth.

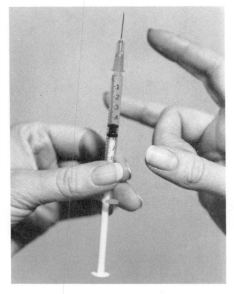

1 Wash your hands and draw up the prescribed dose of the medication into a tuberculin syringe that has a 25-gauge needle. Usually, 0.5–1.0 mg is administered.

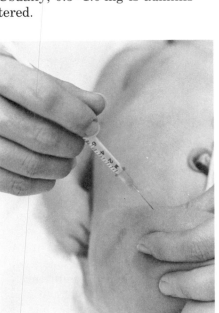

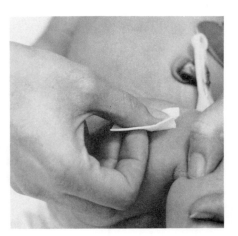

2 Swab the anterolateral segment of the upper thigh (the vastus lateralis muscle) with an alcohol sponge. Allow the alcohol to dry.

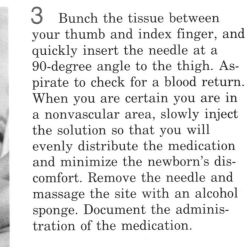

3 Bunch the tissue between your thumb and index finger, and quickly insert the needle at a 90-degree angle to the thigh. Aspirate to check for a blood return. When you are certain you are in a nonvascular area, slowly inject the solution so that you will evenly distribute the medication and minimize the newborn's discomfort. Remove the needle and massage the site with an alcohol sponge. Document the administration of the medication.

OBTAINING A BLOOD SAMPLE

Blood samples are obtained during the first few hours of birth as an assessment for hypoglycemia. Those at especially high risk include the following: infants of diabetic mothers, premature infants, infants small or large for gestational age, infants who are ill, and infants of prolonged or very stressful labor.

1 Apply gloves. To obtain the blood sample, dorsiflex the foot and prepare the lateral aspect of the heel with an alcohol sponge. When the alcohol has dried, firmly pierce the skin with the lancet, just deeply enough to elicit a large droplet of blood.

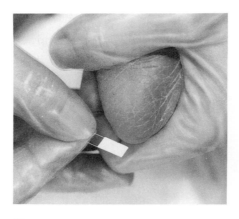

2 Position the pad of a reagent strip directly under the puncture site and collect a large droplet of blood onto the pad without smearing the blood. Review the steps, pp. 143–145, for visually monitoring blood glucose.

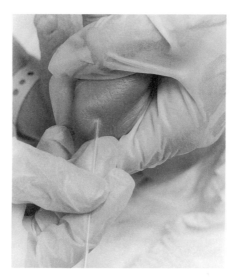

3 When a hematocrit has been ordered for evaluation of blood volume, prepare the heel and pierce the skin, according to step 1. Warming the heel prior to making the puncture will improve both the blood flow and the accuracy of the test. Place the capillary tube at the puncture site and allow it to become at least half full of blood.

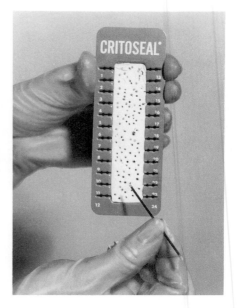

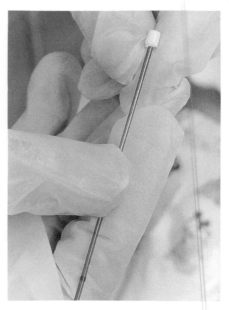

4 After obtaining the blood, place one end of the capillary tube into Critoseal (top) or cap the tube (bottom) to prevent specimen loss. Follow agency guidelines for spinning the tube in a centrifuge and reading the value.

OBTAINING A URINE SPECIMEN

Applying an External Urine Collection Device

If a urine specimen is required for routine urinalysis or assessment of latex agglutination for beta *Streptococcus,* a specimen can be obtained using an external urine collection device. If the infant is quiet, this procedure can be performed easily by one person. A crying or restless infant may require two people.

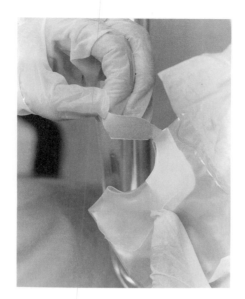

1   Apply clean gloves, remove the neonate's diaper, and cleanse the genitalia. Then detach the backing from the adhesive surface of the urine collection device (as shown).

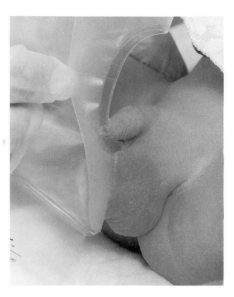

2   Abduct the neonate's legs and position the opening of the collection device over the perineum and along the labia for a female or under and around the penis for a male (as shown).

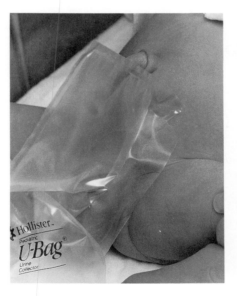

3   Gently smooth the adhesive sides around the groin to seal the contact with the baby's skin.

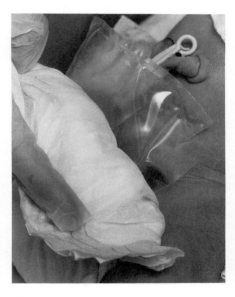

4   Cover with a diaper and recheck in 30–60 minutes.

Removing an External Urine Collection Device

1 After the infant has voided, apply gloves and gently peel the adhesive surface of the collection device from the top downward, exerting gentle pressure with your opposite hand (as shown) to break the seal of the adhesive surface to the infant's skin.

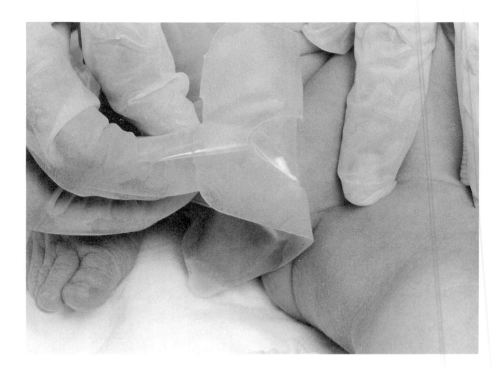

2 Once the collection device has been removed from the infant, adhere the two adhesive surfaces together (as shown), label with the infant's name and hospital number, and send to the laboratory.

ASSESSING THE NEONATE

PERFORMING A GENERAL INSPECTION

Wash your hands with an antimicrobial soap, and prepare to assess the infant in a warm environment such as the radiant warmer or at the mother's bedside. Remove the diaper and shirt, but keep the infant's stockinette cap on for as long as possible to minimize the heat loss through his head. The heart-shaped foam pad worn by the infant in these photos is holding a temperature probe in place.

Observe the resting posture. A normal-term infant's posture is flexed even when he is asleep. Also, note the color. In white infants, the color is normally ruddy or pink tinged. Darker-skinned infants can be assessed by inspecting the lips and mucous membranes, which are normally pink. A yellow cast may indicate jaundice; a blue tint at the feet, hands, and mouth is often indicative of sluggish peripheral circulation. This is usually transient and clears in several hours. However, cyanosis, along with restlessness and choking, necessitates immediate suctioning to remove esophageal mucus. Count the respirations for a full minute and note their quality. Normally, they range between 40 and 60 breaths per minute. Because neonates are diaphragmatic breathers, observe the abdomen rather than the chest for respirations. Respirations greater than 60 after the first 4 hours of birth or less than 30 per minute at any time, as well as substernal and subcostal retractions, are abnormal. With cyanosis, they could be indicative of aspiration or of disorders such as respiratory distress, transient tachypnea, or congenital heart disease. Slow respirations may be indicative of narcotic depression from drugs given to the mother during labor, central nervous system disorders, or deep sleep. These infants should be referred to the attending physician immediately.

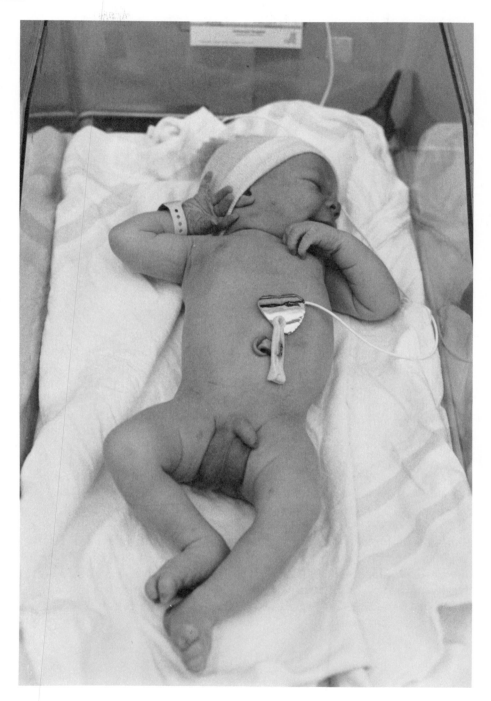

AUSCULTATING

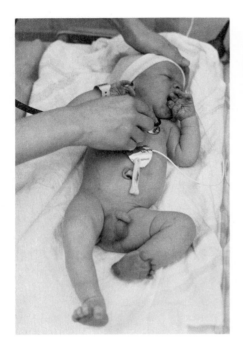

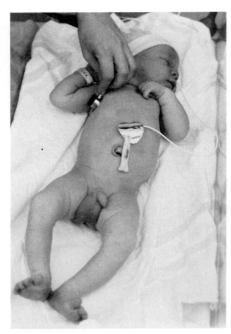

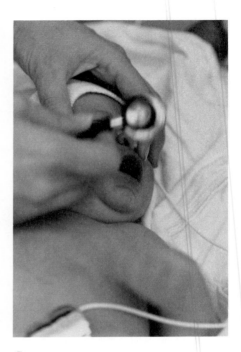

1 Auscultation, especially for heart sounds, should be performed when the infant is quiet. It is usually a good idea, therefore, to auscultate before initiating the hands-on assessment. Auscultate over the precordium for a full minute to assess apical pulse. Note the rate, rhythm, and intensity of the pulse. It should range from 130 to 160 beats/ minute. However, the pulse may be as low as 90 at rest or as high as 200 when the infant cries. Be alert to irregularities, such as dysrhythmias, or to murmurs, which are heard as slurs or clicks between lub and dub.

2 Auscultate over the lung fields to assess breath sounds. Review Chapter 6 to assist you with auscultation sites and breath sounds. Be alert to diminished breath sounds when comparing one side to the other, especially if breath sounds were normal immediately following birth. Crackles may be heard immediately following birth because of unabsorbed amniotic fluid. Within the next few hours, the breath sounds should become clear as the fetal lung fluid is absorbed and the alveoli open throughout the lungs.

3 Assess the patency of the nares by alternately obstructing each naris with an index finger. Listen with the stethoscope over the open naris to assess airflow. If the airflow is abnormal, either suction with a bulb syringe or attempt to pass a sterile catheter gently down the naris. Notify the physician if one or both nares are obstructed.

TAKING AN AXILLARY TEMPERATURE

PALPATING

While the infant is quiet, insert a thermometer into the axillary area; hold it in place for 3–5 minutes. An axillary temperature is often preferable to a rectal temperature because the rectum maintains the core temperature longer than the skin. Therefore, the axillary temperature will alert you more readily to rapid temperature changes that frequently occur in the newborn. The axillary temperature should register around 36.5°–37°C.

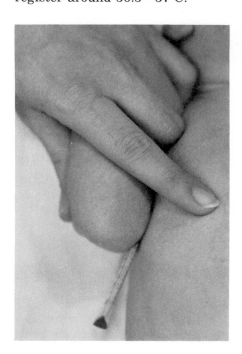

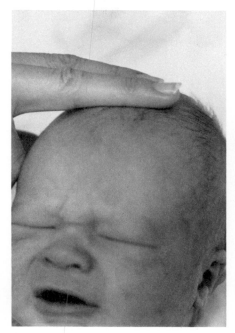

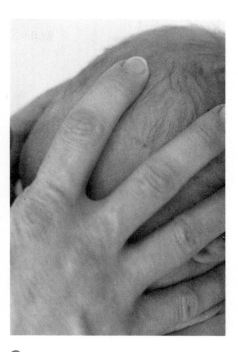

1 Begin your hands-on assessment of the neonate at the head by palpating the fontanelles (soft spots)—both the anterior fontanelle (as shown) and the posterior fontanelle at the occiput. It is a good idea to measure your own fingers in centimeters to give yourself a built-in tape measure. The anterior fontanelle is normally 2–3 cm in width, 3–4 cm in length, and diamondlike in shape. It can be described as soft, which is normal, or full or bulging, which could be indicative of increased intracranial pressure. Conversely, a depressed fontanelle could mean that the neonate is dehydrated. The posterior fontanelle is smaller and triangular in shape, and it closes within 6–12 weeks; or it may be closed at birth. The anterior fontanelle usually closes within 12–18 months.

2 Palpate the sutures, which are the junctions of the cranial bones and are normally movable. Overriding sutures are normal in the first week of life secondary to the molding of the head during birth. Fixed sutures are abnormal and should be called to the physician's attention.

(Continues)

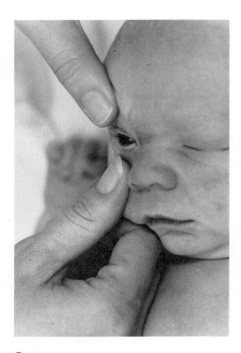

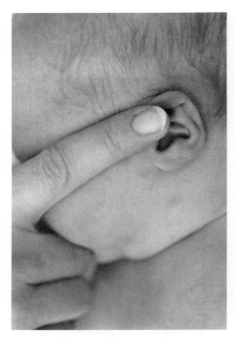

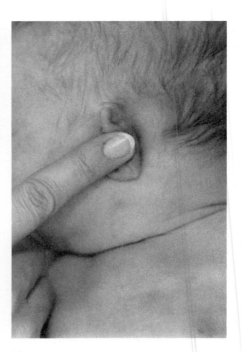

3   Inspect the eyes by gently separating the lids. Assess the pupillary reflex with an ophthalmoscope or penlight to ensure that the pupils react equally to light. Also observe for the equality of pupil size. Unequal pupils could suggest birth trauma. Note whether the corneas appear cloudy, which is indicative of a congenital infection, or hemorrhagic, which is usually transient and caused from pressure during delivery.

4   Assess the infant for low-set ears, which may be indicative of chromosomal abnormalities and are often associated with genitourinary disorders. Normally, the pinna of the ear is in a straight line with the outer canthus of the eye.

5   Assess the development of the ear cartilage next. If the auricle stays in the position in which it is pressed, or returns to its original position slowly, it usually means that the gestational age is less than 38 weeks. Also, inspect for preauricular skin tags, which are usually normal and often are removed for cosmetic reasons.

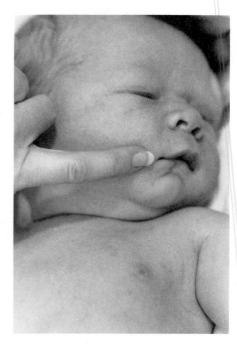

6   To assess the rooting reflex, lightly stimulate the cheek by stroking from the outer corner of the mouth toward the ear on the same side. The infant should turn toward the finger in an attempt to suck. Teach this technique to the breastfeeding mother.

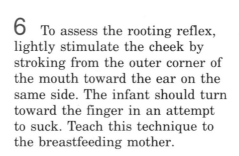

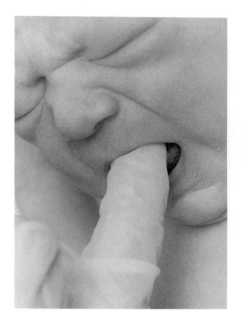

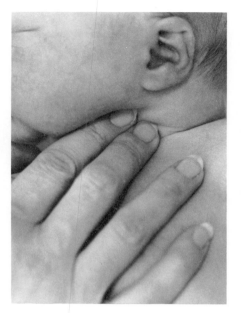

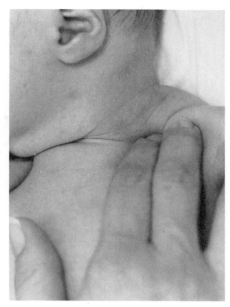

7 Assess the sucking reflex by donning a clean glove and inserting a finger in the neonate's mouth. In addition, inspect and palpate the hard and soft palates to assess for clefts as well as for Epstein's pearls, which are white specks occasionally found on the gums and hard palate and may be palpated as hardened areas. These are normal and usually disappear after several days. You also might palpate neonatal teeth on the gum line. Because there is a potential for aspiration, notify the physician that you have found them in the event that removal is indicated. Deciduous teeth, however, are not removed.

8 Bilaterally palpate the neck to assess for masses, trachial deviation, an enlarged thyroid, or swollen lymph glands. Although the trachea normally is slightly at the right of the midline, the other findings are abnormal and should be referred to the physician. Also, assess the sternocleidomastoid muscles for symmetry and the shoulder joints for full range of motion.

9 Palpate the clavicles to ensure that they are symmetric and contiguous. A lump along one of the clavicles could be a fracture site caused from a difficult delivery.

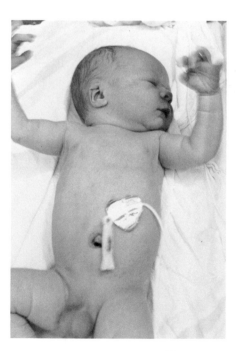

10 Elicit the startle reflex with a loud noise—for example, by clapping your hands together. Normally, the newborn will abduct and extend his arms. The fingers will extend and then flex into a "C." An asymmetric response suggests a fractured clavicle or an injury to the brachial plexus. Lack of a response is indicative of a hearing loss or brain damage.

(Continues)

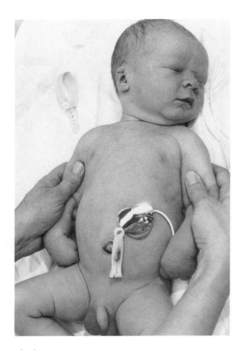

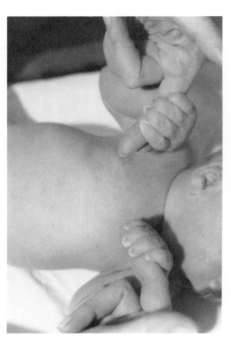

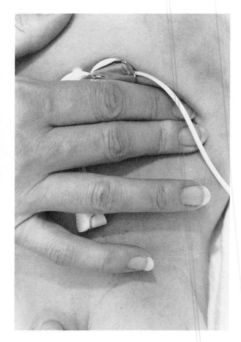

11 Continue your palpation of the upper extremities. Assess for adequate range of motion and bilateral symmetry of bones, muscles, and movement.

12 Assess the grasp reflex by stimulating the newborn's palms with your fingers. He should grasp your fingers tightly enough to be lifted up off the surface on which he is lying. An asymmetric or weak grasp suggests possible central nervous system damage. Also, assess the hands for extra digits. If present, a physician likely will tie them off, and they will usually drop off after 2–3 days.

13 While the infant is relaxed, palpate all four quadrants of the abdomen, noting masses and/or tenderness. Normally it feels soft to the touch. To feel the tip of the spleen, press down and sweep upward when palpating the left upper quadrant (as shown). To palpate the liver's edge, follow the same sweeping motion on the right upper quadrant. Palpate the suprapubic area to assess the bladder.

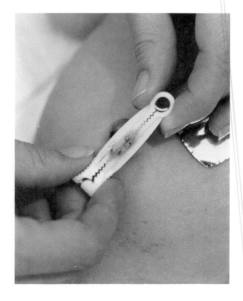

14 Inspect the umbilical cord for the presence of three vessels— a vein and two arteries. An absence of an artery may be associated with abnormalities of the genitourinary tract and should be noted on the chart.

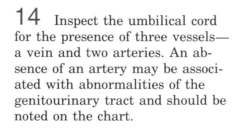

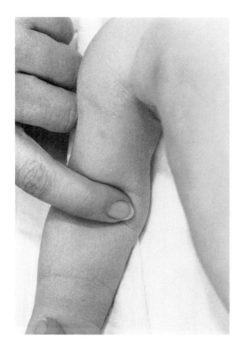

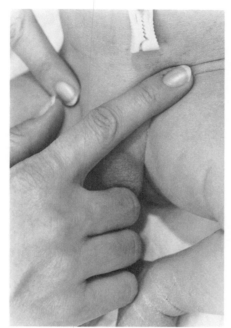

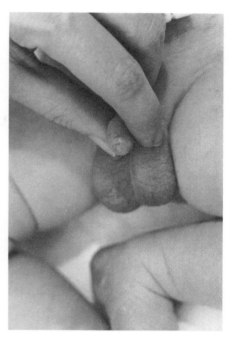

15 Assess the pulses, beginning with the brachial pulse. According to the American Heart Association's Standards and Guidelines for Cardiopulmonary Resuscitation (CPR) and Emergency Cardiac Care (ECC), the brachial pulse often is a more accurate indicator of true heart rate in the infant than the apical pulse because the precordium may transmit impulses rather than pulsations. Bilaterally assess the brachial pulses for equality in rate and intensity. Palpate for the brachial pulse above the antecubital fossa.

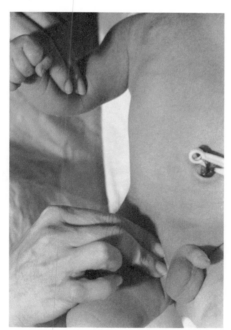

16 Bilaterally palpate the femoral arteries for rate and intensity of the pulses. Press each fingertip gently at the groin (top). Compare the femoral pulses to the brachial pulses by palpating the pulses simultaneously (bottom) for a comparison of rate and intensity. If the pulsations are less intense in the femoral arteries, the newborn may have a coarctation of the aorta.

17 Assess the genitalia next. In the female, examine the labia for appropriate size and symmetry and the clitoris for appropriate size. Assess for both a vaginal and urinary os, and observe for a vaginal discharge, which may be bloodtinged. This is normal, and it is caused by the presence of the mother's hormones in the neonate. In the male, examine the penis and assess for hypospadias, a condition in which the urethral meatus appears on the underside of the penis. Palpate the scrotum to assess both testes if they are not readily visible. The testes may be undescended, or they may be drawn up into the abdomen if the infant is chilled.

(Continues)

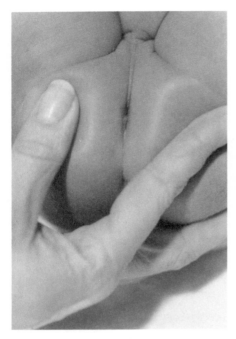

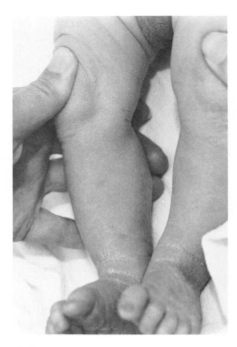

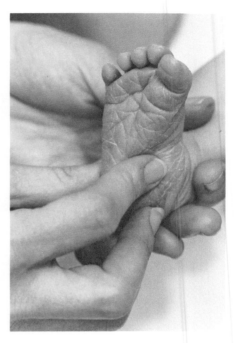

18 Spread the buttocks and assess the anus for patency and placement. If the anus appears to be either anteriorly or posteriorly positioned, the physician should be notified. In females, a rectal-vaginal fistula may be present, or this could represent a blind pouch with the true rectum correctly positioned but not patent. Patency is confirmed by the passage of the first meconium stool.

19 Continue to palpate the lower extremities for range of motion and bilateral symmetry of bones, muscles, and movement.

20 Inspect each foot to assess for clubfoot. Normally the foot is positioned at the midline of the tibia. A foot that is both inverted and plantarflexed and cannot be manipulated to midline necessitates a referral to the physician for further assessment. Also, inspect the soles of the feet for creases. If the creases do not cover the sole, the infant is probably less than 38 weeks' gestational age.

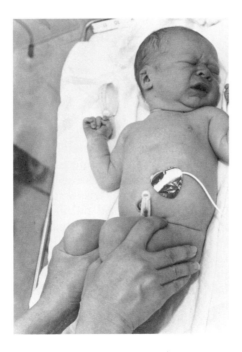

21 To assess for congenital hip dislocation, perform the Ortolani click test. Position your middle fingers over the greater trochanters and your thumbs along the medial thighs. Then flex the hips and knees.

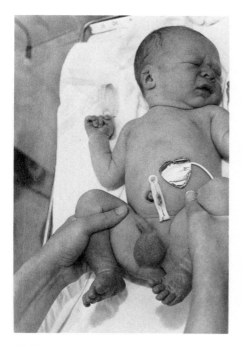

22 Gently abduct the hips and flex them to an even greater degree.

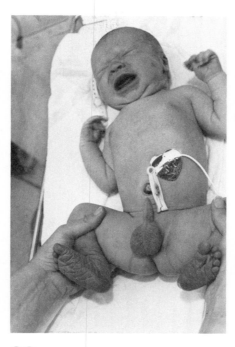

23 Externally rotate the hips. Unilateral or bilateral limitations in mobility, along with clicking, occur with hip dislocation or subluxation. Notify the physician for further evaluation.

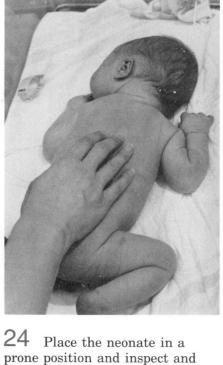

24 Place the neonate in a prone position and inspect and palpate the spine to assess for missing vertebrae and defects. Assess for dimples, sinuses, and tufts of hair, especially in the sacrococcygeal area, where a nevus pilosus (hairy nerve) is often indicative of spina bifida. Mongolian spots also may be present on the buttocks and in the dorsal lumbar area. These are bluish areas found usually in dark-skinned ethnic and racial groups. Be sure to explain to the parents that these spots are normal and that most fade within the first or second year.

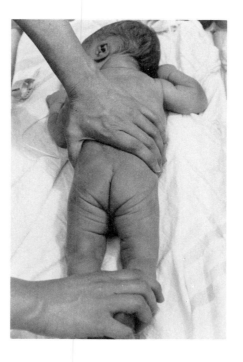

25 Straighten the legs and observe for symmetry in the creases of the buttocks and legs. Asymmetry could suggest a congenital hip dislocation.

TAKING AN ARTERIAL BLOOD PRESSURE

MEASURING AND WEIGHING THE INFANT

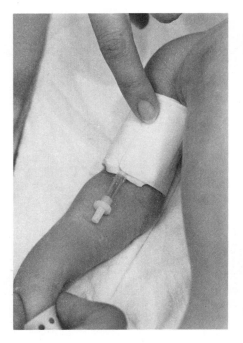

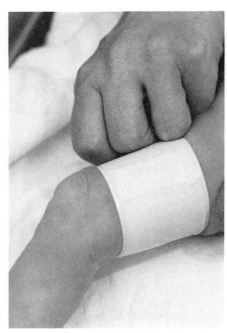

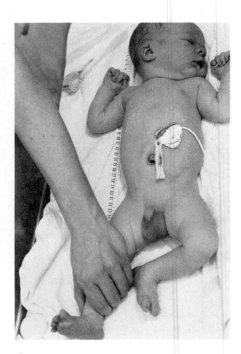

1   If your agency requires blood pressure monitoring for the neonate, you probably will use an ultrasonic device, such as the Doppler. Wrap a blood pressure cuff of the appropriate size around the newborn's upper arm (see procedure guidelines, Chapter 7). Attach the cuff to the Doppler device and obtain the pressure reading according to manufacturer's instructions. A diastolic pressure less than 40 and a systolic pressure greater than 100 require further investigation. If the newborn is crying, the reading may be falsely elevated.

2   If the femoral pulses are weak or absent, suggesting coarctation of the aorta, assess the blood pressure in the leg. Wrap the cuff around the upper thigh and obtain the pressure reading. The reading should be slightly higher in the leg than in the arm. A vast difference between the two, however, helps to confirm coarctation of the aorta, and you should obtain a pressure reading in all four extremities.

1   To measure the infant's length, place him in a supine position and extend one of his legs. The tape measure is then positioned from the top of the head to the heel.

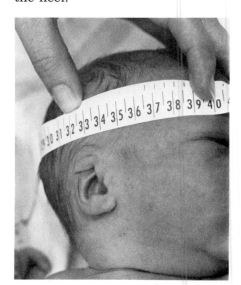

2   The head circumference is measured along the broadest part of the occiput with the tape positioned just slightly above the eyebrows. If the head is severely molded from the delivery, repeat the measurement daily.

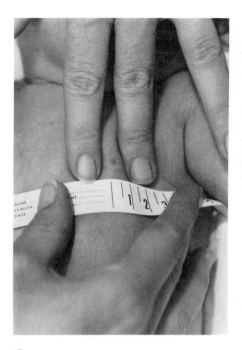

3 You also may measure the breast tissue to evaluate gestational age further. Compress the tissue between your thumb and index finger and measure the tissue in centimeters. At a normal gestational age, the tissue should measure between 0.5 and 1 cm. An absence of or decreased breast tissue is often indicative of prematurity or a newborn who is small for gestational age. Also observe for supernumerary nipples, which are not harmful and may be removed at a later date. Both female and male infants may have breast engorgement with actual milk production caused by the presence of maternal hormones. Be sure to explain to the parents that this is normal.

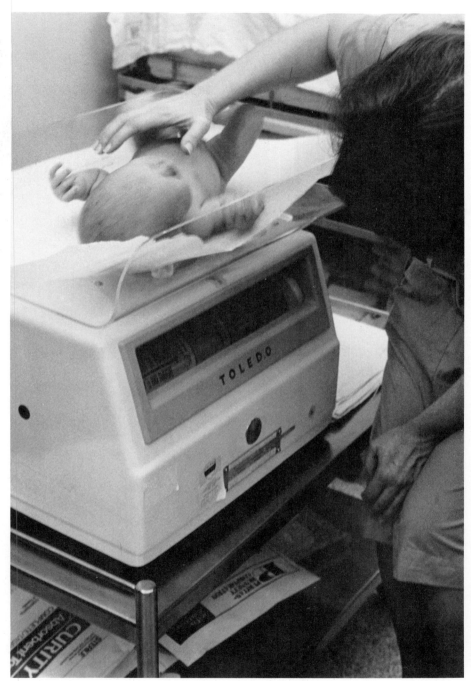

4 The neonate may lose 5%–10% of his body weight over the first 3–5 days because of normal fluid loss and low intake. Therefore, you must weigh the infant daily to monitor weight loss or gain. The scale should be balanced, cleaned, and covered with a fresh paper or pad before weighing each infant to prevent cross-contamination and to minimize heat loss. Always place your hand above the infant to prevent him from falling off the scale.

PROVIDING NEONATAL CARE

GIVING UMBILICAL CORD CARE

SUCTIONING

To help prevent infection and to promote drying of the umbilical cord, cleanse the cord daily with alcohol or antibiotic ointment, according to agency guidelines. Be sure to swab around the entire surface of the cord base. The cord will usually fall off on its own after 7–10 days. Observe for redness or discharge, which are signs of infection, and be certain to keep the diaper below the cord. Instruct the parents in cord care.

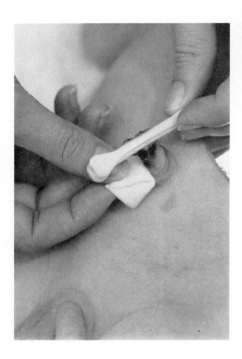

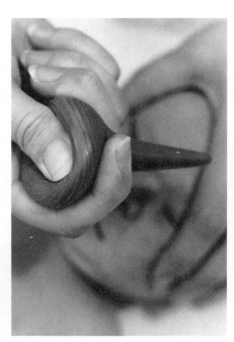

1   *Using a Bulb Syringe:* A bulb syringe is kept in the newborn's crib for removing secretions in the nose and mouth. To use the bulb syringe correctly, first depress the bulb with your thumb.

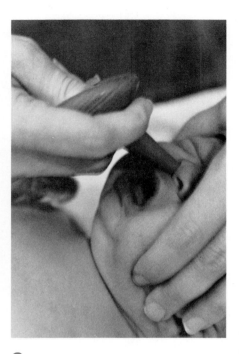

2   Insert the tip of the nozzle into each naris, and allow the bulb to expand slowly. Be sure to stabilize the infant's head with your free hand to minimize the risk of injuring the nasal mucosa. If indicated, suction the mouth as well. To remove the drainage from the bulb syringe, compress the bulb and point the nozzle over a tissue. Be sure to instruct the parents in the proper use of the bulb syringe. *Caution: Limit nasal suctioning to an "as-needed" basis. Frequent suctioning can irritate the mucous membrane and stimulate the vagal nerve.*

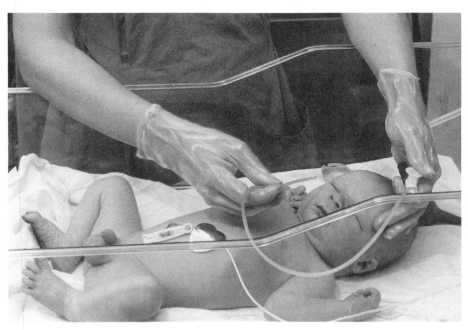

1 *Using Mechanical Suctioning:* Set the suction pressure gauge at or less than 80 cm H₂O.

2 Review the suctioning procedure on pp. 343–347. Suction no deeper than the infant's pharynx.

USING BILI-LITES (PHOTOTHERAPY)

1 Premature infants commonly experience jaundice due to increased serum bilirubin levels. To help prevent the bilirubin from reaching dangerous levels or to help decrease the bilirubin count, phototherapy, commonly called bili-lites, is used. The infant's entire skin surface is exposed to the light for prescribed time periods. Monitor serum bilirubin test results closely to assess the efficacy of the therapy. Be alert to potential side effects of the therapy: skin rash, loose green stools, increased water loss necessitating fluid replacement, and increased temperature. The infant's position should be changed every 2 hours to facilitate exposure of the light to all skin surfaces. ***Note:*** *The dose of phototherapy is determined*

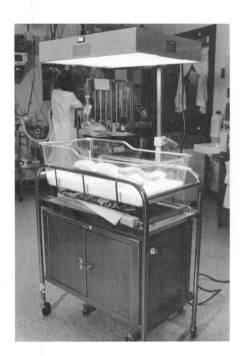

by the irradiance levels of the light bulbs and the infant's distance from the lights. The standard distance is 45 cm (18 in.).

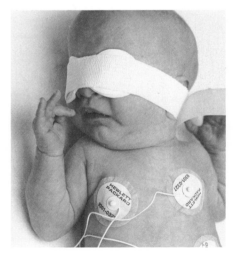

2 Always make sure the infant's eyes are well protected from the light. Eye patches or masks must be used with each treatment. To prevent corneal abrasion, make sure the infant's lids are closed before applying the patches. Some agencies suggest use of protective covering over the genitalia, as well. ***Note:*** *This infant's electrode patches are unrelated to his phototherapy.*

References

American Cancer Society: *Reach to Recovery.* New York: American Cancer Society, 1983.

American Cancer Society: *Breast Self-Exam.* New York: American Cancer Society, 1988.

American Heart Association: Standards and guidelines for cardiopulmonary resuscitation (CPR) and emergency cardiac care (ECC). *JAMA* 1986; 255(21):2841–3044.

Avery G: Neonatology pathophysiology and management of the newborn, 3d ed. Philadelphia: Lippincott, 1988.

Blank JJ: Electronic fetal monitoring: Nursing management defined. *JOGNN* (Nov–Dec) 1985; 463–467.

Boback IM et al: *Maternity and Gynecologic Care,* 4th ed. St. Louis: Mosby, 1989.

Bowers AC, Thompson JM: *Clinical Manual of Health Assessment,* 3d ed. St. Louis: Mosby, 1988.

Daze AM, Scanlon JW: *Neonatal Nursing: A Practical Guide.* Rockville, MD: Aspen, 1985.

Eyal FG, O'Neal W: *Neonatology: Basic Management.* Norwalk, CT and San Mateo, CA: Appleton and Lange, 1989.

Lawrence R: *Breastfeeding: A Guide for the Medical Profession,* 3d ed. St. Louis: Mosby, 1989.

Merenstein GB, Gardner SL: *Handbook of Neonatal Intensive Care,* 2d ed. St. Louis: Mosby, 1989.

Olds SB et al: *Maternal-Newborn Nursing: A Family-Centered Approach,* 3d ed. Menlo Park, CA: Addison-Wesley, 1988.

Pheigaru JL: Keeping staff up on electronic fetal monitoring. *Matern Child Nurs* (Sept/Oct) 1988; 13: 334–335.

Saunders S et al: *Breastfeeding: A Problem-Solving Manual.* Durant, OK: Creative Informatics Publishing, 1987.

Schreiner R, Bradburn N: *Care of the Newborn,* 2d ed. New York: Raven Press, 1987.

Spence A, Mason E: *Human Anatomy and Physiology,* 3d ed. Redwood City, CA: Benjamin/Cummings, 1987.

Streeter N: *High-Risk Neonatal Care.* Rockville, MD: Aspen, 1986.

Thompson JM et al: *Mosby's Manual of Clinical Nursing,* 2d ed. St. Louis: Mosby, 1989.

Tucker SM: *Pocket Nurse Guide to Fetal Monitoring.* St. Louis: Mosby, 1988.

Wardell DW: Reproductive disorders. In: *Manual of Nursing Therapeutics: Applying Nursing Diagnoses to Medical Disorders,* 2d ed., Swearingen PL (editor). St. Louis: Mosby, 1990.

Chapter 5

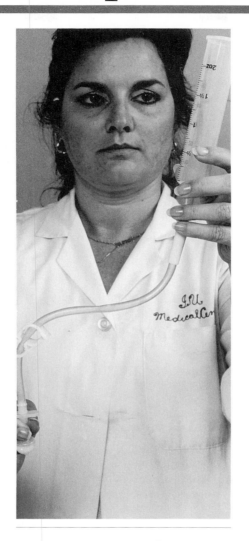

Managing Gastrointestinal Procedures

CHAPTER OUTLINE

ASSESSING THE GASTROINTESTINAL SYSTEM

The Gastrointestinal System

Nursing Assessment Guideline

Examining the Oral Cavity

Inspecting the Mouth
Inspecting the Tongue and Pharynx

Examining the Abdomen

Inspecting the Abdomen
Auscultating the Abdomen
Percussing the Abdomen
Palpating the Abdomen

Examining the Rectum

Inspecting the Rectum
Palpating the Rectum

MANAGING GASTRIC TUBES

Nursing Guidelines for Managing Gastric Tubes

Single-Lumen Tubes
Double-Lumen Tubes
Triple-Lumen Esophageal-Nasogastric (Blakemore) Tubes
Four-Lumen (Minnesota Sump) Tubes
Gastrostomy Tubes
Gastrostomy Button

Inserting a Nasogastric Tube

Inserting a Small-Bore Feeding Tube

Inserting an Orogastric Tube

Removing a Nasogastric Tube

Irrigating a Nasogastric Tube

Administering Nasogastric Tube Feedings

Giving an Intermittent Tube Feeding
Giving a Continuous-Drip Tube Feeding
Managing Feeding Pumps

Administering Gastric Lavage

Aspirating Stomach Contents for Gastric Analysis

Giving Gastrostomy Tube Feedings

MANAGING INTESTINAL TUBES

Nursing Guidelines for Managing Intestinal Tubes

Single-Lumen Tubes
Double-Lumen Tubes
Jejunostomy Tubes

Assisting with the Insertion of an Intestinal Tube

Removing an Intestinal Tube

MANAGING STOMA CARE

Nursing Guidelines for Managing Ostomies

Ascending Colostomy
Transverse Colostomies
Descending or Sigmoid Colostomy
Ileostomy
Continent Ileostomy (Kock Pouch)
Ileoanal Reservoir

Patch Testing Your Client's Skin

Applying a Drainable Pouch

Dilating a Stoma

Irrigating a Colostomy

Draining a Continent Ileostomy (Kock Pouch)

MANAGING RECTAL ELIMINATION AND DISTENTION

Administering a Nonretention Enema

Administering a Retention Enema

Inserting a Rectal Tube

Testing Stool for Occult Blood

Assessing the Gastrointestinal System

THE GASTROINTESTINAL SYSTEM

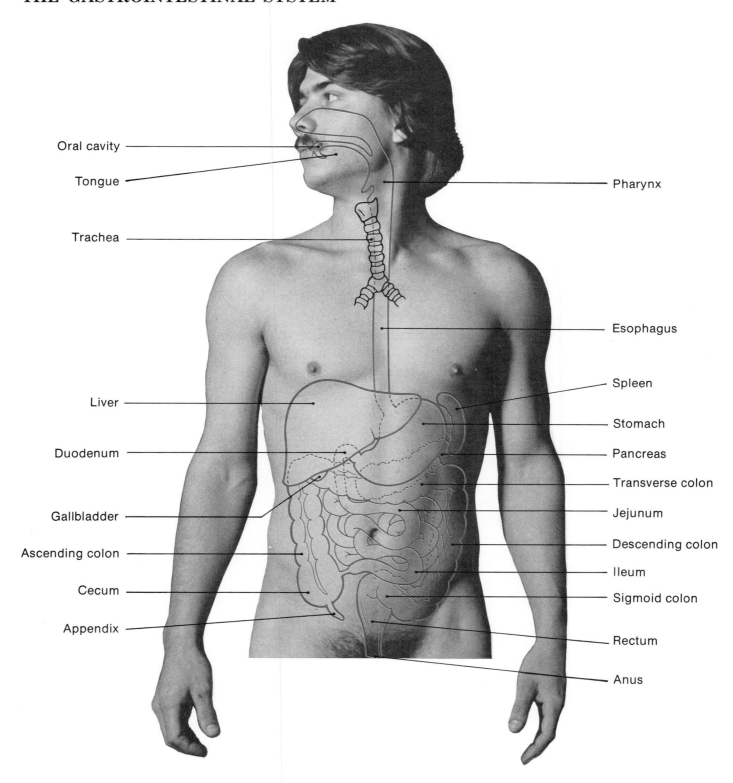

Oral cavity

Tongue

Trachea

Pharynx

Esophagus

Liver

Spleen

Stomach

Duodenum

Pancreas

Transverse colon

Gallbladder

Jejunum

Ascending colon

Descending colon

Cecum

Ileum

Sigmoid colon

Appendix

Rectum

Anus

Nursing Assessment Guideline

To assess your client's gastrointestinal system, you will need to interview him or her for subjective data; take vital signs; and examine the oral cavity, abdomen, rectum, and sacrum. A comprehensive nursing care plan will include a complete evaluation for the following subjective data:

Personal factors: age, occupation, marital status, cultural/religious/economic life-style indicators (for example, those that would affect diet)

History of medically related problems of nutrition: alcoholism, hyperlipidemia, obesity, diabetes mellitus, peptic ulcer disease, ulcerative colitis, Crohn's disease, malignancy, paralysis

History of: previous oral, nasal, abdominal, or intestinal surgery

Risk factors: psychologic stressors, smoking, environmental pollutants

Presence of: dentures, loose (or missing) teeth, ostomy, hemorrhoids

Medications: type; use of laxatives, enemas, vitamins

Pain: onset; location; intensity; radiation; intensified or relieved by food (type), change in position, activity

Appetite impairment: early satiety; compulsive-eating patterns; anorexia nervosa; precipitated by stress, depression, activity

Alterations in abdominal status: distention, rigidity, tenderness

Food intolerances/allergies: special diet

Recent weight gain/loss

Description of daily dietary intake: amount and type of food and fluid

Alterations in oral intake: anorexia, dysphagia, nausea, reflux, vomiting, eructation

Emesis: frequency, character, amount, hematemesis

Alterations in bowel elimination: diarrhea, constipation, incomplete evacuation, flatulence, anal discomfort

Stool: frequency, character, color, amount, presence of mucus or blood

EXAMINING THE ORAL CAVITY

A complete evaluation of your client's gastrointestinal system will include an assessment of the oral cavity. For adequate visualization, you will need a penlight and a tongue depressor.

INSPECTING THE MOUTH

INSPECTING THE TONGUE AND PHARYNX

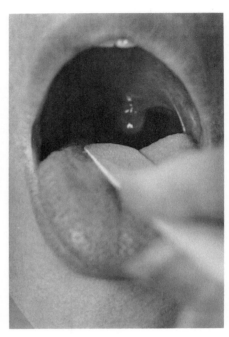

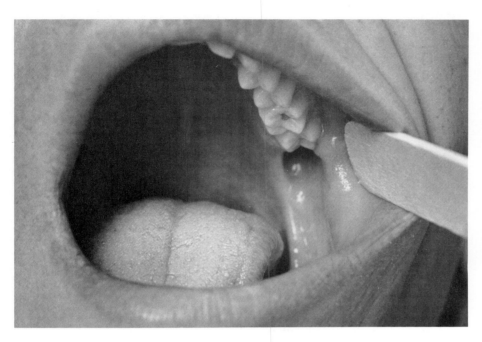

Wash your hands and explain the procedure to your client. Observe for drooping of the mouth and the presence of drooling. These are indications of paralysis, which can interfere with dietary intake. If your client wears dentures, check for optimal fit, and then remove them before initiating examination of the oral cavity. Assess the lips for color and lubrication. Note any bleeding, cracks, or lesions. Inspect the teeth for looseness, cracks, and gross caries and the gums for inflammation and bleeding, which occur with gingivitis or periodontitis. To visualize the buccal surface, retract the cheeks with a tongue depressor and use your penlight to examine the membranes. They should be reddish-pink, smooth, and moist. Abnormalities may include canker sores or inflammation, generally referred to as stomatitis. Bluish patches are considered normal in the black client. Also, be aware that halitosis can occur with such disorders as an infection, abscess, dehydration, or esophageal problems. *Note: Be sure to examine both sides of the mouth, because diseases can be manifested on one side only.*

Depress the tongue. Note the color and observe for the presence of edema or an abnormal, thick coating, which is an indicator of thrush. A thin, white coating is usually considered to be normal. Assess the tonsils for inflammation or exudate. Normally, they are small and pink. The uvula should rise with the soft palate when the client says "aah." The hard palate should be pale and moist, but a yellow hue is often indicative of jaundice. Stimulate the gag reflex by pressing the tongue depressor on the back of the tongue. You should be able to see the involuntary contraction at the oropharynx. Finally, ask your client to move his tongue from side to side. An inability to do so suggests a pathology of the 12th cranial nerve. Palpate the tongue with a gloved finger, noting any lumps or sores.

EXAMINING THE ABDOMEN

To examine the client's abdomen, provide a quiet, warm, and private environment. Explain the assessment procedure, and ensure that the client has recently voided. Assist the client into a supine position, and place pillows under his head and knees and ask him to position his arms at his side or across his chest to help relax the abdominal muscles. As you are preparing the client, observe his body alignment and facial expression for objective indicators of discomfort, such as grimacing or flexing the legs, which often occurs with acute appendicitis or peritonitis. Remember that your examination should begin with a visual inspection of the abdomen, followed by auscultation, and finally percussion and palpation. Because touching and temperature variations stimulate both peristalsis and muscle guarding, these reactions would alter the frequency and character of bowel sounds.

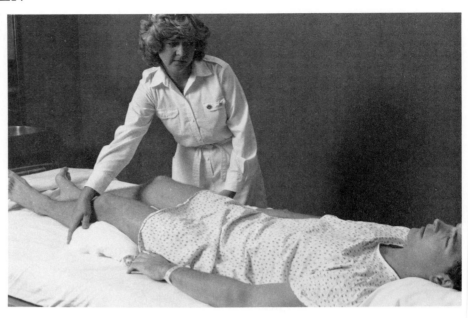

INSPECTING THE ABDOMEN

Expose the abdomen from the sternum to the pubis. Note the contour of the abdomen, which can be described as protuberant (e.g., with pregnancy or obesity), rounded, flat, or scaphoid (concave). Observe for distention; asymmetry, which could indicate the presence of a mass; or peristaltic waves, which although not often seen, are indicative of intestinal obstruction in the adult or pyloric stenosis in the infant. Also observe for unusual pigmentation; striae, which occur after a pregnancy or weight gain; and loose skin folds, which can occur with weight loss. Assess the umbilicus for infection in the neonate, for inversion, or for eversion in clients with umbilical hernias or extreme ascites, and make a note of any abdominal scars. Also, observe the epigastrium for the presence of pulsations. Mild pulsations normally may be seen

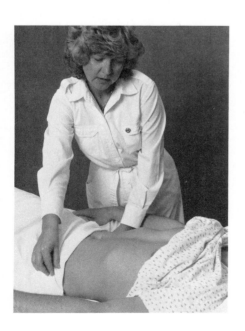

in very thin clients; however, vigorous pulsations occur in clients with right ventricular hypertrophy or with masses anterior to the aorta. Be alert to a pronounced venous network in the abdominal area. This is seen in adults with hepatic obstruction, portal hypertension, or ascites. However, it may be normal in infants and children. Note the presence of any ostomies, the color and character of the stoma, the appearance of the peristomal skin, and the amount and character of the effluent (fecal drainage) in the pouch. Question the client about the presence of scars, which may be indicative of previous surgery. Also be alert to abdominal breathing, which can signal thoracic problems in the client older than 6 or 7. Children younger than 6 or 7 normally breathe using their abdominal muscles.

AUSCULTATING THE ABDOMEN

Review this anatomic overlay to assist you in dividing your client's abdomen into quadrants. The epigastric, umbilical, and hypogastric areas are further delineated. For auscultation, palpation, and percussion, you should develop your own pattern of assessment—for example, a clockwise examination of each of the four quadrants—and follow the same pattern consistently.

To auscultate the abdomen, warm the diaphragm of the stethoscope and then place it in the center of each of the four quadrants, counting the frequency and character of the bowel sounds for a full minute. Move the stethoscope to various areas within the quadrant if you are unable to elicit sounds in the center. Generally, you will be able to hear 5–34 bowels sounds per minute. With hyperperistalsis you will hear more frequent, high-pitched gurgling. These sounds will occur with diarrhea, gastroenteritis, or intestinal hemorrhage. In a late obstructive process, paralytic ileus, or peritonitis, bowel sounds are typically absent. However, with a developing obstruction, bowel sounds may be absent in the quadrant in which the obstruction occurs, yet increase in frequency proximal to the point of

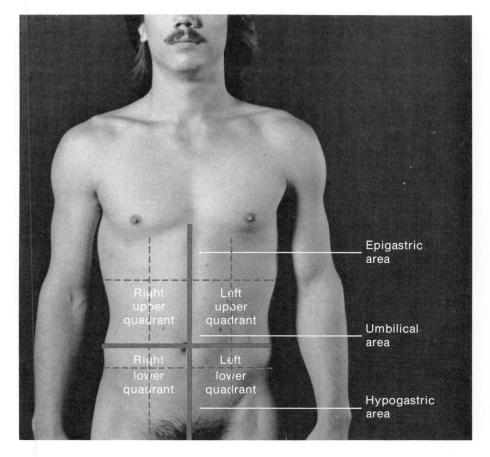

obstruction. Hypoactive bowel sounds may be heard in the postoperative client.

During auscultation you should be alert to circulatory sounds such as *bruits*. These are swishing sounds, which may be heard in the midepigastric area in clients with diseased aortas or over the renal or femoral arteries. *Venous hums* are softer and more

continuous than bruits and may be heard in the upper epigastric area and over the liver in clients with advanced cirrhosis. *Friction rubs* sound like sandpaper rubbing together, and they are heard best with the client taking deep respirations. They may be heard over diseased livers, spleens, and gall bladders.

PERCUSSING THE ABDOMEN

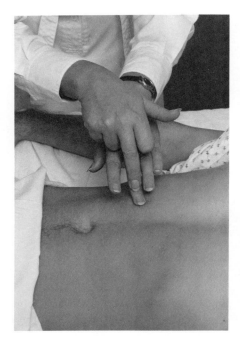

PALPATING THE ABDOMEN

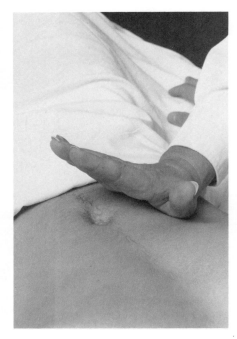

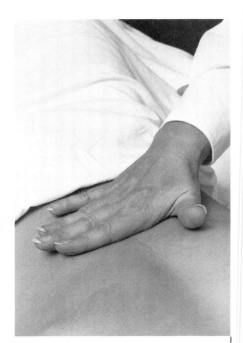

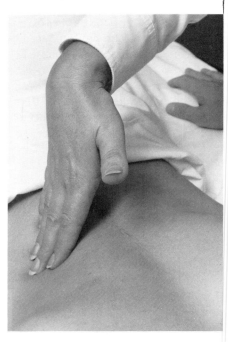

To percuss the abdomen, place your middle or index finger on the client's skin, and then strike that finger with the same finger on your opposite hand to elicit sounds. This assessment technique will reveal the density of the underlying structures. Hollow cavities, such as the empty intestine, will elicit high, tympanic sounds. Dull, flat sounds are heard over a distended bladder or over an organ, such as the liver in the right upper quadrant or the spleen in the left upper quadrant. You may also hear dullness while percussing the left lower quadrant over the sigmoid colon prior to the client's defecation. Dull sounds in other locations may be indicative of an abnormality, such as a mass.

Lightly palpate the abdomen to determine muscle tone, tenderness, distention, organ size, pulsations, or the presence of a mass. You might use your entire hand not only because it is more comfortable for the client and the process will produce less muscle guarding, but also because you will have a larger surface area from which to assess abnormalities. Roll the hand over an abdominal area starting with the heel of the hand, middle photo, above, progressing to the palm, top right photo, and finishing at the fingertips. If you prefer, palpate with flattened fingertips, as in the lower right photo. A healthy abdomen should feel soft and supple, but you will feel resistance with a distended abdomen and it will be less pliant. *Caution: Clients with peritonitis, who have boardlike abdomens, will find even light palpation extremely uncomfortable. Do not palpate the abdomen for an individual in whom Wilm's tumor is suspected.*

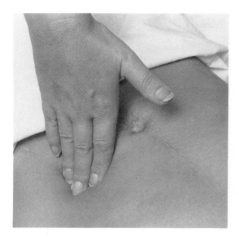

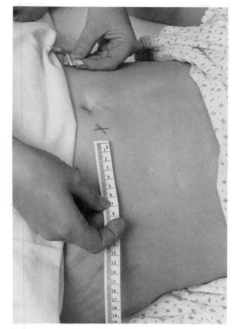

Deep Palpation: Deep palpation is employed after light palpation to assess for enlarged organs or for the presence of masses. In addition, if your client feels discomfort over a particular area during light palpation, you can use this technique to assess for rebound tenderness. This is found in clients with peritoneal inflammation or appendicitis. Gently and slowly press your flattened fingertips approximately 6–8 cm (2–3 cm in the neonate; 3–6 cm in the child) into the quadrant *opposite* that in which you elicited pain; then quickly release the pressure. Your client will feel a sudden, sharp pain over the original area of discomfort if rebound tenderness is present. *Caution: Never deeply palpate the right lower quadrant if appendicitis is suspected. Deep palpation is also contraindicated in clients with rigid abdomens, or in those who may have pancreatitis or ectopic pregnancy because the procedure can be very painful and it could also cause serious injury to the client.*

Measuring Abdominal Girth: To assess for increasing degrees of distention, including ascites, you will need to measure the abdominal girth daily and at the same time of day—for example, before breakfast. Mark a spot on the abdomen with indelible ink to ensure that you measure around the same circumferential site with each measurement. Measure the girth of the abdomen, using a nonstretchable tape measure, and record the result. Daily increases in girth are significant and should be reported to the attending physician. (Note the presence of striae on this client.)

EXAMINING THE RECTUM

INSPECTING THE RECTUM

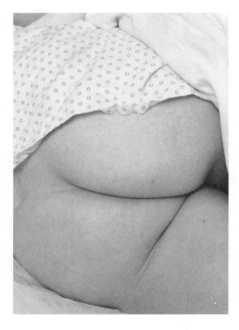

Before inspecting the rectum, provide your client with privacy, explain the procedure, and assist her into Sim's position. Expose the buttocks, and inspect the rectal and sacral areas for the presence of external hemorrhoids, alterations in the integrity of the skin, pilonidal cysts, and fissures.

PALPATING THE RECTUM

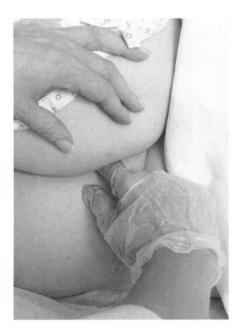

Put on a disposable examination glove, and lubricate your index finger with water-soluble lubricant. Ask the client to breathe deeply and to bear down. Gently and slowly insert your index finger 5–10 cm (2–4 in.) into the rectum, past the external and internal sphincters. Palpate along the circumference of the rectal wall to assess for the presence of masses, fistulae, or stool. Use special care if the client has external or internal hemorrhoids. Assess sphincter tone by asking the client to tighten the sphincter around your finger. After removing your finger, inspect the glove for the presence of stool, blood, or mucus. *Caution: If this procedure is performed for infants or small children, use the small finger rather than the index finger. Because of the risk of vagal stimulation with a rectal examination, this procedure may require a physician's order.*

Managing Gastric Tubes

Nursing Guidelines for Managing Gastric Tubes

SINGLE-LUMEN TUBES

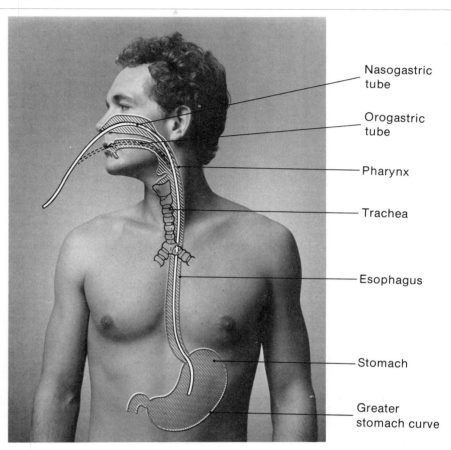

Nasogastric tube

Orogastric tube

Pharynx

Trachea

Esophagus

Stomach

Greater stomach curve

Description	76–125 cm (30–50 in.) in length, rubber or plastic material, may have radiopaque tips for x-ray film detection, smaller-lumen tubes may have insertion guides.

Levin-type tubes:	12–18 French (F) for adults
	8–12F for children
	5–8F for infants
Pediatric feeders:	5–8F
Oral tubes:	30–40F

Uses　　　　　　Gavage, administration of medications, lavage, diagnostic evaluation, decompression

Nursing Considerations

- Chill rubber tubes in icy water prior to insertion, if desired.
- Warm plastic tubes in hot water prior to insertion, if desired.
- Most tubes are inserted through the nose unless the nasal route is contraindicated.
- Larger-lumen tubes cause more irritation to the stomach, esophagus, and nose.

(Continues)

- For decompression, the tube should be connected to intermittent suction or placed to gravity drainage.
- Smaller tubes (8F) may require insertion guides (contraindicated for the neonate) for easier intubation.
- Check tube placement in stomach before *any* instillation.
- Provide oral and nasal hygiene at least three to four times a day.

DOUBLE-LUMEN TUBES

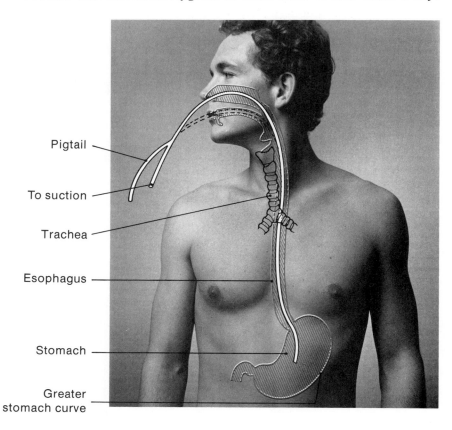

Pigtail

To suction

Trachea

Esophagus

Stomach

Greater
stomach curve

Description

85–125 cm (35–50 in.) in length, plastic or rubber material, may have radiopaque tips for x-ray film detection and mercury-weighted tips to facilitate movement to the stomach.

12–18F for adults
 8–12F for children
 5–10F for infants

Oral tubes: 30–40F

Uses

Decompression, lavage, gavage

Nursing Considerations

- Irrigate sump tubes through large port only.
- Inject *only* air into pigtail port of sump tubes, after reconnecting the large port to suction.
- For decompression, sump tubes work best when connected to continuous suction at 30 mm Hg.
- Check for correct stomach placement before *any* instillation.
- Provide oral and nasal hygiene at least three to four times daily.
- Remove tube only after an assessment that reveals active bowel sounds, the passing of flatus, and an undistended or minimally distended abdomen.

TRIPLE-LUMEN ESOPHAGEAL-NASOGASTRIC (BLAKEMORE) TUBES

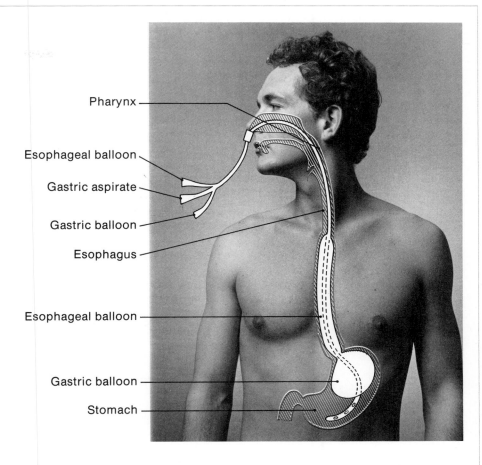

Pharynx

Esophageal balloon

Gastric aspirate

Gastric balloon

Esophagus

Esophageal balloon

Gastric balloon

Stomach

Description	86–98 cm (36–39 in.) in length; x-ray film opaque; latex rubber; has ports for gastric balloon, esophageal balloon, and gastric aspiration. 16–20F for adults 12F for children
Uses	Compression; as a tamponade for control of esophageal bleeding; decompression; lavage
Nursing Considerations	■ The tube is usually inserted by a physician. ■ The client requires constant observation while the balloons are inflated. ■ A Levin or sump tube is sometimes inserted into the opposite naris for aspiration of the esophagus. ■ Provide comfort measures while the tube is in place: blankets during lavage, backrubs and skin care, oral and nasal hygiene. ■ A football helmet may be positioned on client's head so that exterior traction on the tube can be achieved by taping the tube to the face guard. ■ The esophageal balloon is deflated for 5 minutes every 8–12 hours to prevent erosion to the esophagus. ■ Tape scissors to the head of the client's bed for emergency tube cutting (deflating both balloons) in the event of acute respiratory distress.

(Continues)

FOUR-LUMEN (MINNESOTA SUMP) TUBES

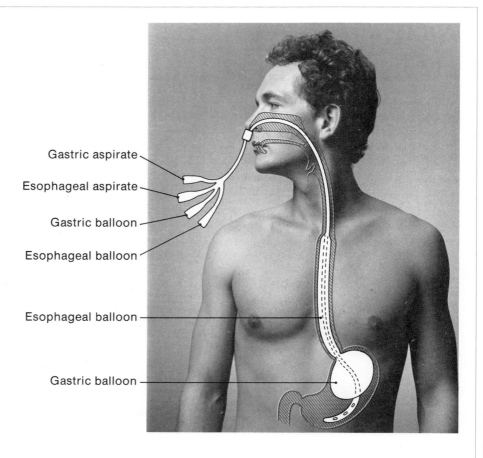

Gastric aspirate

Esophageal aspirate

Gastric balloon

Esophageal balloon

Esophageal balloon

Gastric balloon

Description   Has a fourth port for esophageal aspiration; thus, the need for a Levin or sump tube is eliminated.

Uses   See Blakemore tube, 251.

Nursing Considerations See Blakemore tube, 251.

GASTROSTOMY TUBES

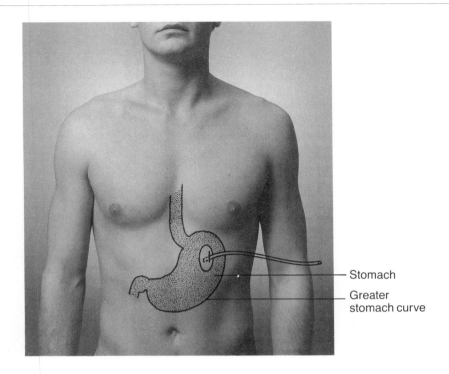

Stomach

Greater
stomach curve

Description

35 cm (14 in.) in length; 20–28F; rubber or latex material, often with an inflatable balloon (as shown).

Uses

Gavage, or it may be inserted during intestinal surgery for decompression.

Nursing Considerations

- The tube is surgically inserted into the stomach.
- Unless the client has nausea, discomfort, or distention, keep the tube plug attached to the tube when the tube is not being used for feedings.
- The skin at the abdominal exit site requires careful observation because leaking gastric contents can cause skin irritation. Use skin barriers or pouches as needed.
- Follow aseptic technique for dressing changes.
- Two weeks after surgery, the tube usually can be removed and inserted as needed for tube feedings.
- Clean the inside and outside of the feeding port with a cotton-tipped applicator.
- Clean around the stoma with a cotton-tipped applicator or a moist cloth. For the healthy stoma, soap and water are usually adequate cleansing agents.
- Irrigate the tube with 30–50 ml water (10–25 ml for the infant or child), or as recommended by the tube's manufacturer.

(Continues)

GASTROSTOMY BUTTON

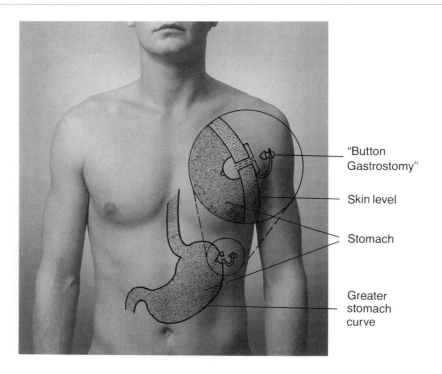

"Button Gastrostomy"

Skin level

Stomach

Greater stomach curve

Description

Flexible silicone device with a radiopaque dome on the distal end that secures the button in the stomach, two small wings at the proximal end that are flush with the abdominal skin, and an outer plug that is attached to the wings. Sizes include small (18F), medium (24F), and large (28F); and lengths range from 1.7 cm to 4.3 cm. An antireflux valve at the distal end helps prevent backflow and leakage of gastric contents. Each button comes with a kit that includes an obdurator for ease of insertion, a stoma-measuring device, and a special feeding apparatus.

Use

Long-term gavage of 6–8 months to 1 year.

Nursing Considerations

- Insertion requires a well-established gastrostomy site. Usually the site is dilated over a 3–4 week period with increasingly larger Foley catheters prior to the initial button insertion. Once positioned, the button can stay in place until malfunction occurs.
- Stoma depth is measured with a stoma-measuring device (top left photo p. 255) to facilitate button size selection.
- Because the button is flush with the skin, it has a more cosmetically pleasing appearance than a gastrostomy tube.
- Most clients experience greater mobility and independence with the button than with a tube.
- Be alert to gastric contents leakage, which can signal malfunction of the antireflux valve.
- If gastric contents leak, insert the obdurator gently into the button shaft (top right photo p. 255) to return the antireflux valve to its closed position. If this fails, it may be necessary to replace the button with a new one.

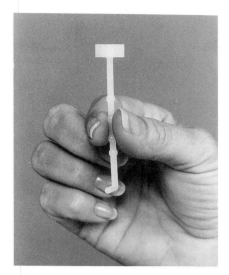

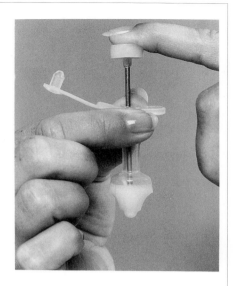

- Rotate the button in a full circle during site care to facilitate thorough cleaning.
- Use mild soap and water to clean around the stoma one to two times a day. This can be accomplished during the daily bath, since the button can be immersed safely in water. To ensure thorough drying, allow the stoma site to be exposed to air for 20 minutes before covering with clothing.
- If the peristomal skin becomes reddened and irritated when cleansing with soap and water, try cleaning the site with water alone, followed by povidone-iodine swabs or liquid. Another option for impaired skin integrity is the use of stomahesive powder or pectin wafer skin barrier on the peristomal skin.
- For bolus feedings, attach special feeding catheter and syringe (bottom left photo) to the proximal end of the button. This equipment comes as part of a special kit with each button. Check for residual from previous feedings (see p. 268) before administering new feeding.
- Continuous feedings also can be administered via gravity or infusion pump over a 16–24 hour period. Check residual from previous feedings q8h.
- To prevent clogging of the button with formula, rinse with water (10 ml for pediatric client, 30–50 ml for the adult) after every feeding or insertion of medication.
- Crush medication tablets and contents of capsules, and mix with water prior to instillation.
- Maintain client in Fowler's or slightly elevated right side-lying position for at least 30 minutes during and after feedings or medication instillation to reduce the risk of aspiration of stomach contents.
- Rinse feeding apparatus with water after every feeding. Once a day, wash the feeding apparatus in warm, soapy water, and rinse well. Soak in mild vinegar solution weekly and rinse well.

(Continues)

■ Weight gain and growth, especially in the pediatric population, will necessitate a larger and longer button.

■ Avoid using oily substances around the stoma, which would deteriorate the silicone button and make it difficult to keep the outer plug in place.

■ Insertion steps are as follows:

—Measure depth of the stoma with stoma-measuring device (p. 255) to ensure proper size selection of the button.

—Lubricate the tip of the obdurator with a water-soluble lubricant. Insert obdurator into the button's lumen (p. 255), and distend the button several times to ensure patency of the antireflux valve.

—Lubricate the button's dome and the client's stoma with water-soluble lubricant, and insert the button into the stoma to the stomach.

—Rotate the obdurator slightly on removal to prevent its adherence to the antireflux valve.

—After removing the obdurator, look through the button's lumen to ensure that the antireflux valve is in the closed position.

—Insert the outer plug into the button's lumen, keeping the plug in place between feedings.

INSERTING A NASOGASTRIC TUBE

Caution: *Nurses should not insert, withdraw, or irrigate nasogastric tubes for postoperative clients with gastric or esophageal resections. Hemorrhage could result from an injury to the suture line.*

Assessing and Planning

1 Wash your hands and assess the client to obtain her baseline gastrointestinal status (see pp. 242–248). Assess her knowledge of the procedure, and explain why the tube has been prescribed and how her assistance can facilitate the procedure. Evaluate the need for premedication, and obtain an order if appropriate. Together, agree on a signal she can use, such as tapping your arm, that will alert you to stop momentarily if the procedure becomes too uncomfortable. A thorough explanation, combined with a relaxed and empathetic manner, will help to ensure a successful and quick insertion.

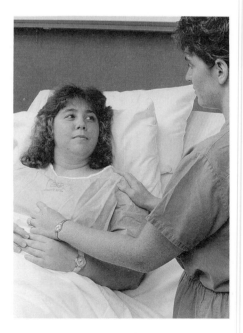

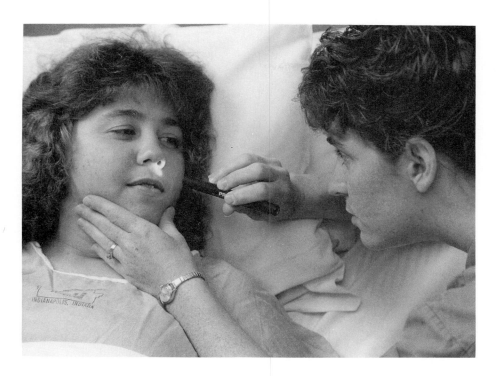

2 With your penlight, inspect both nares to determine which is more patent. Alternately close each naris to check airflow. Ask the client which nostril breathes more easily, and whether she has ever had a fractured nose, which could affect passage of the tube. If both nares are obstructed, you may need to intubate through her mouth (see procedure, p. 264).

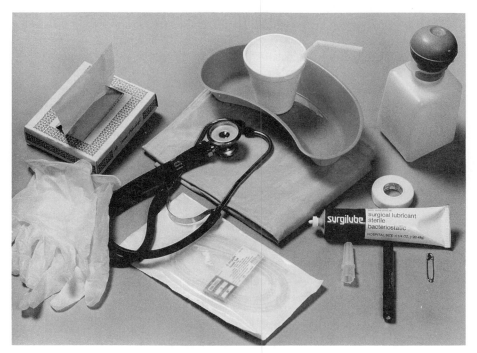

3 Gather the following materials: the prescribed nasogastric tube (a Levin, 16F, is shown here); irrigation set with a 50-ml bulb or piston syringe; tissues; glass and a straw; penlight; stethoscope; hypoallergic tape, 1.25 cm wide; bed-saver pad; emesis basin; water-soluble lubricant; and gloves. In addition, if the tube will be used for gavage rather than for decompression, you should also have a tube plug or a clamp and a safety pin.

(Continues)

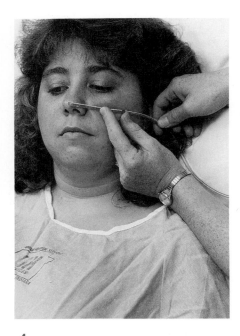

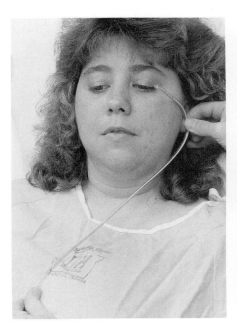

4 Measure the tube against the client to help ensure its proper placement into the stomach. Measure the distance from the tip of the nose to the ear.

5 Measure the distance from the ear to the xiphoid process. The total measurement, referred to as NEX (Nose-Ear-Xiphoid), should be either marked on the tube with tape or indelible ink or compared against the markings on the tube and remembered. Many tubes are marked at 45 and 55 cm, the average length to an adult's stomach. Compare these marks to your measurement. They should be within a comparable range.

6 Ensure patency of the tube by flushing it with water. Also, check for rough edges that could harm delicate mucosa. If you are inserting a rubber tube, you may need to chill it in icy water to firm it up. A stiff plastic tube can be made more pliant by immersing it in warm water.

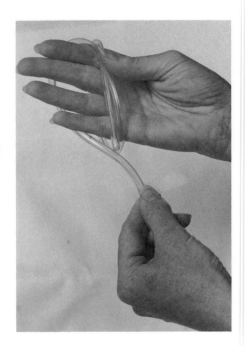

7 Find the natural curve of the tube, or wrap the tube around your fingers to establish a moderate curve that will accommodate the arc of the nasal passage.

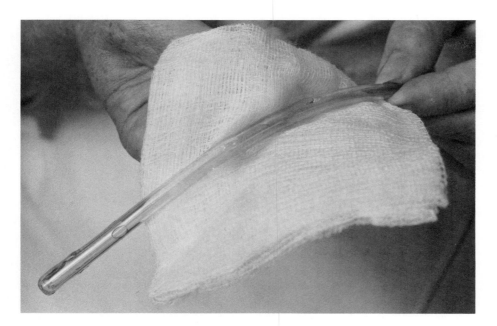

8 Lubricate the first 15–20 cm (6–8 in.) of the tube with water-soluble lubricant to facilitate insertion. *Caution: Never use an oil-based lubricant because it will not dissolve, and respiratory complications could result if the tube is mistakenly inserted into the trachea.*

Implementing

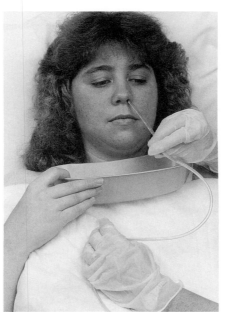

9 Drape the client with a bed-saver pad, and ask her to remove her glasses and dentures, if she has them. Give her an emesis basin and explain that the tube could activate her gag reflex as it enters her throat. Provide her with tissues for excessive tearing, which can occur as the tube passes the nasopharynx. Fowler's position is advised because it will lessen the potential for aspiration, making swallowing easier, and enhance the tube's movement into the stomach via gravity. If this position is contraindicated, a right side-lying position is also acceptable. Because there is the risk of activating the gag reflex and causing vomiting, apply clean gloves at this time. Insert the tube into the naris and gently advance it along the floor of the nasal passage. Slight pressure is sometimes necessary to pass the nasopharynx. *Caution: Never force the tube. If you meet resistance, remove the tube, relubricate it, and intubate the other naris if it is patent.*

(Continues)

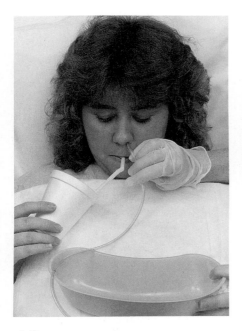

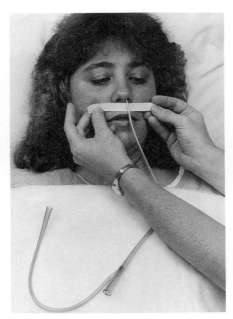

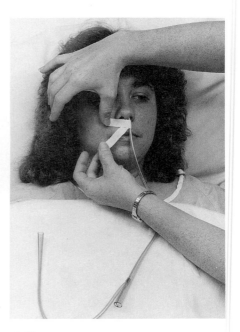

10 When the tube enters the oropharynx, pause briefly to minimize the potential for emesis. Ask the client to flex her head forward and sip water (or dry swallow if fluids are contraindicated). This will ease the tube's insertion into the esophagus. *Caution: Never have the client hyperextend her neck at this point. Doing so opens the airway and could permit the tube to enter the trachea.* Advance the tube 5–10 cm (2–4 in.) with each swallow. If the client starts to cough or gasp for air, remove the tube immediately because you may have inserted the tube into the airway.

11 When the predesignated mark on the tube is at the level of the client's nostril, secure the tube to the client's nose. To do this, cut a strip of tape 10 cm (4 in.) in length. Slide it sticky-side up under the tube between the client's nose and mouth.

12 Next, grasp one end of the tape and transfer it around and to the opposite side of the tube, adhering the sticky side to the tube and the client's face.

13 Finally, do the same with the remaining tape end and adhere it to the tube and the client's face.

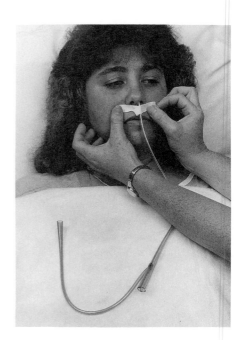

Evaluating

14 Check the back of your client's mouth with a penlight to ensure that the tube is not curled at the oropharynx.

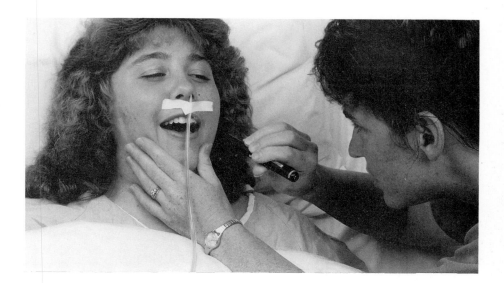

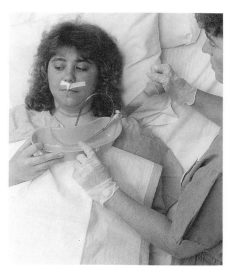

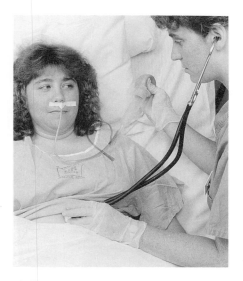

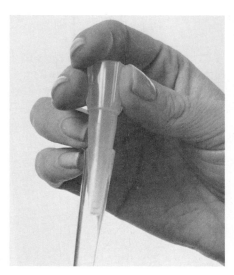

15 To ensure that the tube is correctly positioned in the stomach, aspirate for stomach contents by attaching a 50-ml bulb or piston syringe to the open end of the tube. If the tube is positioned correctly, gastric contents will return after you have squeezed the bulb or pulled back on the piston. Unless the stomach contents appear to contain blood, reinstill the aspirate to maintain the electrolyte balance. Hold the syringe barrel 30–45 cm (12–18 in.) above the client's abdomen and allow the aspirate to return via gravity flow.

16 To perform another test for correct stomach placement, inject approximately 5–10 ml of air into the open end of the tube ($\frac{1}{2}$–1 ml for premature and small neonates and up to 5 ml for the larger child) as you auscultate the epigastric area with your stethoscope. With a properly positioned tube, you will hear a "whoosh" as air enters the stomach. If the client eructates instead, the tube may be in the esophagus. You also can ask the client to hum or speak. If the tube is in the trachea, she will be unable to do so. *Caution: Always perform these tests to confirm correct stomach placement of the tube before instilling anything into the tube.*

17 Either connect the tube to suction or insert a tube plug (as shown).

(Continues)

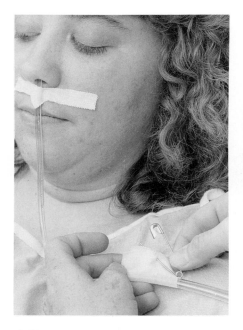

18 Attach the tube to the client's gown by inserting a safety pin through a tape tab. Document the procedure.

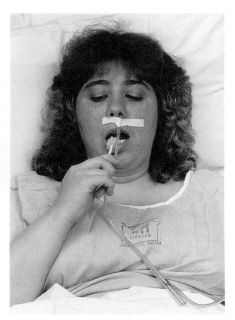

19 *Providing Oral and Nasal Hygiene:* Clean and refresh the client's mouth after inserting the nasogastric tube. A Toothette is being used here. Lip balm also can be applied to the lips for moisture and comfort.

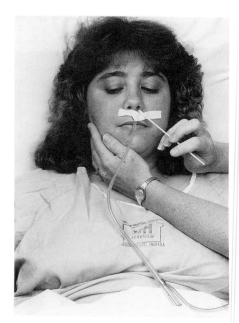

20 The cotton-tipped swab has been moistened with a water-soluble lubricant to clean and help protect the naris from potential skin irritation. Frequently assess the client for the need for oral and nasal hygiene. If possible, keep lip balm and Toothettes at the bedside.

INSERTING A SMALL-BORE FEEDING TUBE

Note: Follow the guidelines for inserting a nasogastric tube, with the following variations.

Assessing and Planning

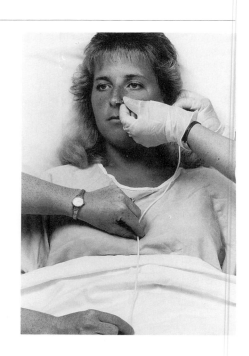

1 If inserting the small-bore feeding tube into the stomach, measure the distance as described on p. 258, and mark. If the tube will be inserted into the intestine, add approximately another 9 inches (as shown) for the adult, and mark accordingly.

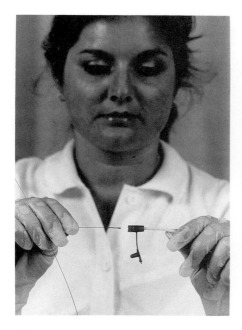

2 To facilitate ease of insertion through the nasal passageway and into the stomach, the stylet that is packaged with the feeding tube can be introduced into the proximal end of the tube and threaded through the length of the tube. First, irrigate the tube with 10 ml of water by attaching a 30-ml syringe to the proximal end of the tube. This will activate the internal Hydromer lubricant and facilitate insertion of the stylet. Insert the stylet until it reaches the weighted tip and its Luer connector firmly attaches to the feeding tube's Luer connector at the proximal tip.

3 For most small-bore feeding tubes, external lubrication at the tip's distal end is not necessary. Instead, insert the distal (weighted) end of the tube into a small amount of water, as shown, to activate the Hydromer lubricant.

Implementing

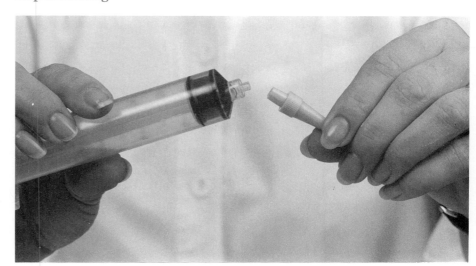

4 Always use syringes ≥30 ml when aspirating or instilling anything into the small-bore feeding tube. Syringes smaller in size could generate too much pressure in the small-bore tube, damaging the tube. Use 5–10 ml water to flush this tube. *Caution: Before instilling anything into the tube, ensure that proper stomach position has been confirmed by radiography. Small-bore tubes become displaced relatively easily, and there is risk of instilling fluid into the client's respiratory tract.* After confirming proper position of the feeding tube, remove the stylet, if it was used, by applying gentle traction. NEVER reinsert the stylet into the tube once the tube has been inserted into the client.

INSERTING AN OROGASTRIC TUBE

Note: Follow the guidelines for inserting nasogastric tubes, with the following variations for assessing and implementing.

Assessing

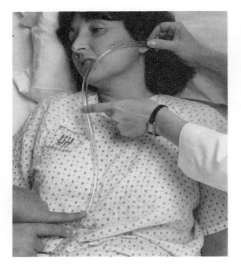

1 If nasal intubation is contraindicated, you may be required to insert the tube through your client's mouth. Measure the distance from the tragus of the ear to the mouth to the tip of the xiphoid process to determine the approximate distance to the stomach. Mark the site with indelible ink.

Implementing

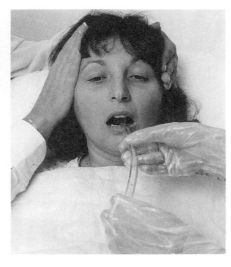

2 Ask the client to open her mouth, and then glide the tube toward the back of her throat. If necessary depress the tongue with a tongue depressor.

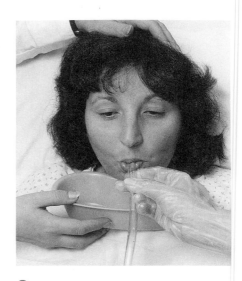

3 At the oropharynx, pause briefly to minimize the potential for emesis. Then instruct the client to flex her head forward and begin swallowing. She may, at this point, guide the tube with her lips and teeth, as if it were a spaghetti noodle. *Note: Alert clients who require frequent oral intubations should be taught to insert their own tubes.*

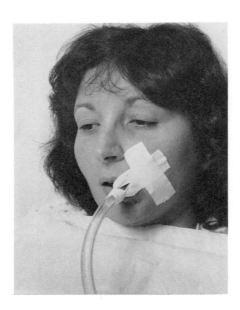

4 When you have determined correct stomach placement, tape the tube to the client's cheek.

REMOVING A NASOGASTRIC TUBE

ice ske

Caution: Nurses never insert or remove nasogastric tubes for postoperative clients with gastric or esophageal resections. Hemorrhage could result from an injury to the suture line.

Assessing and Planning

1 Before removing the nasogastric tube, assess the client's abdomen by auscultating for bowel sounds and inspecting and palpating for distention. If you do not hear bowel sounds, or if the abdomen is quite distended, check with the physician to make sure the tube should be removed. Assess the client's knowledge of the procedure, and explain why the tube will be removed. If the tube is connected to suction, disconnect it at this time. Because there is the risk of stimulating the gag reflex and causing vomiting, apply gloves.

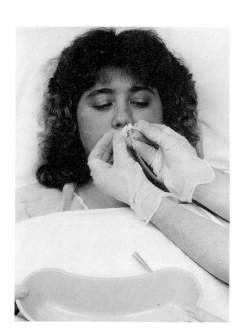

2 Remove the tape from the client's nose and rotate the tubing back and forth to ensure that it is mobile.

Cover the client's gown with

Implementing

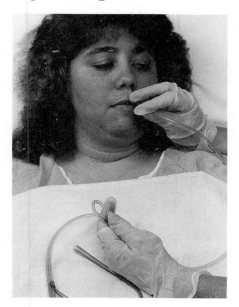

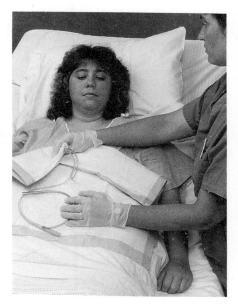

3 Clamp the tube or squeeze it firmly between your fingers. Ask the client to take a deep breath and to exhale slowly as you withdraw the tube. This will relax the pharynx and prevent aspiration as well. Then remove the tube in one continuous movement.

a bed-saver pad to protect her from drainage of gastric contents. Place her in Fowler's position to prevent aspiration of the gastric contents as the tube is removed.

4 Cover the tube with the bed-saver pad and remove it from the bedside; remove your gloves. Wash your hands. Provide the client with materials for oral and nasal hygiene, and document the procedure.

Evaluating

5 Continue to monitor the client for distention, alterations in nutrition, nausea, or any of the symptoms that necessitated the tube's insertion.

a) irrigate tube c̄ 30cc top
to clean out gastric secretions

b) 30cc air

IRRIGATING A NASOGASTRIC TUBE

Caution: Irrigation is contraindicated for clients with gastric resections without a specific physician's order to do so.

Assessing and Planning

1 If you have determined that the nasogastric tube is no longer patent, obtain a physician's order for an irrigation. Wash your hands and assemble the following materials: normal saline (or the prescribed irrigant), usually 60–90 ml; an irrigation set with a 50- or 60-ml bulb or piston syringe; a bed-saver pad; stethoscope for confirming correct stomach placement; and an emesis basin for the return of the irrigant. In addition, you will need a pair of clean gloves.

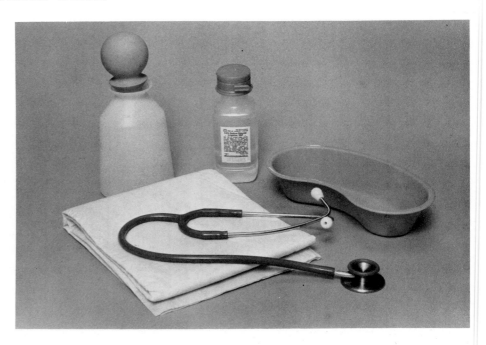

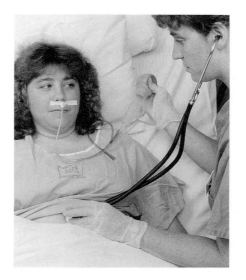

2 Assess your client's knowledge of the procedure, and explain why it has been prescribed. Place her in semi-Fowler's or Fowler's position, put on clean gloves, and disconnect the tube from suction or unclamp it and confirm the tube's correct stomach placement. If the client can speak and if you are able to hear the "whoosh" of air over the epigastric area as you inject 5–10 ml of air into the tube as shown ($\frac{1}{2}$ to 1 ml for premature and small neonates and up to 5 ml for larger children), you can assume that the tube is correctly positioned in the stomach. Be sure to drape the client's gown for the procedure.

Implementing

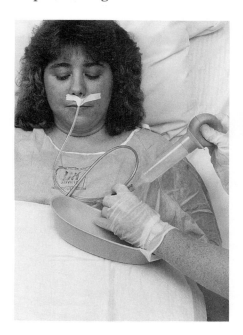

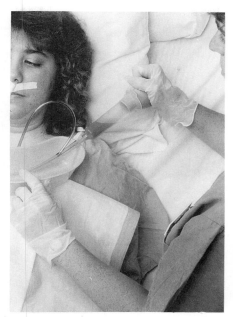

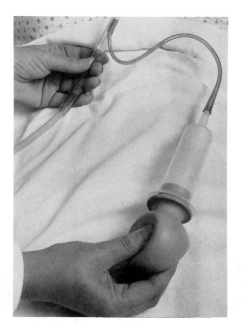

3 Draw up 20–30 ml of the irrigant into the syringe (see physician's order for the amount of irrigant for the pediatric population), attach it to the open end of the tube, and apply gentle pressure as you inject it into the tube. To prevent injury to the tissues, do not force the irrigant through the tube. If you cannot instill the irrigant, check the tubing for kinks, have the client turn from side to side, or pull back slightly on the tube to change its position at the distal end. Remember to recheck for stomach placement if you have altered the position of the tube.

4 After instilling the irrigant, gently pull back on the piston or decompress the bulb to get an equal return, and empty the return into the emesis basin. *Note: If you are unable to get a return, or if the return is less than the instilled amount, be sure to note this on the intake and output record.* Instill and withdraw the irrigant two more times or until the returns become clear. Then reclamp the tube or reconnect to suction, as indicated. Document the procedure and the results.

5 *Note: If the client has a double-lumen sump tube, you will need to instill 15–20 ml of air into the pigtail port after you have reconnected the larger lumen to suction. Never instill liquid into this port because doing so could result in tube malfunction.*

Evaluating

6 Periodically, assess the patency of the tube and irrigate if indicated, provided you have a physician's order.

ADMINISTERING NASOGASTRIC TUBE FEEDINGS

GIVING AN INTERMITTENT TUBE FEEDING

Assessing and Planning

1 If tube feedings have been prescribed for your client, determine the problems the client may have regarding food allergies or medically related problems of nutrition. If the client has had a previous feeding, determine if alterations in bowel elimination, nausea, and flatulence have occurred. These are indications that there may be an intolerance to the feeding solution. Inspect and palpate her abdomen for distention, which would suggest nonabsorption of the previous feeding.

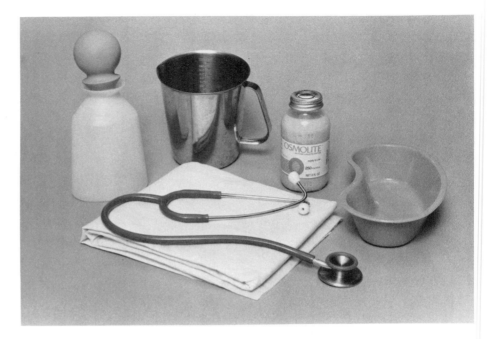

2 For an intermittent tube feeding, assemble the following equipment: irrigation set with a 50-ml piston or bulb syringe, emesis basin, measured container, the prescribed feeding solution, bed-saver pads, stethoscope for testing correct stomach placement, and 30–50 ml of water. In addition, you will need clean gloves. A refrigerated feeding solution should be warmed to room temperature to prevent vasoconstriction and cramping. Check the date on the solution to make sure it is fresh, and ensure that the feeding apparatus is clean because residual solution can be a medium for bacterial growth.

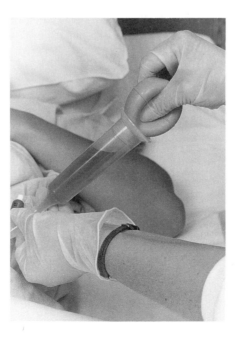

3 Explain the procedure to the client; place her in Fowler's position to enhance the solution's gravitational flow and to prevent aspiration. If a sitting position is contraindicated, a slightly elevated right side-lying position is acceptable. Apply clean gloves, remove the tube plug, and attach the syringe to the opened end of the tube. Aspirate all the stomach contents (as shown), and measure the amount to evaluate the absorption of the last feeding. Check your agency's aspiration precaution rule to determine whether or not to withhold this feeding. The standard protocol for whether to withhold the feeding is a residual of 75–100 ml.

Implementing

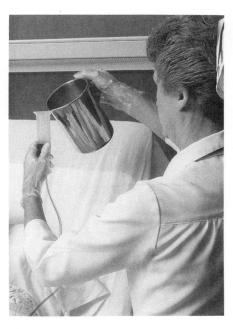
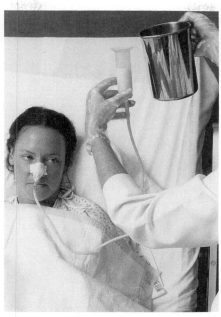
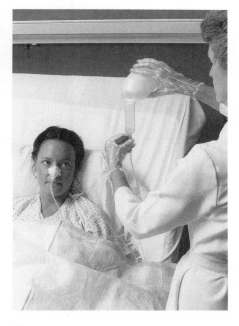

4 Remove the bulb or piston, and reinstill the measured aspirate via the syringe barrel to prevent loss of electrolytes and gastric juices. For effective gravity flow, hold the syringe 30–45 cm (12–18 in.) above the client's abdomen. To make this feeding as pleasant as possible, try to avoid instilling the gastric contents directly in front of the client.

5 Before the aspirate drains from the neck of the syringe, begin pouring the feeding solution into the syringe barrel. This will prevent the instillation of air into the client's stomach. Raise or lower the syringe if you need to adjust the flow to ensure a slow instillation of the feeding.

6 When the desired amount of feeding has been poured, flush the tubing with 30–50 ml of water, unless contraindicated. For the pediatric population, flush with 1–2 ml of water for small tubes and approximately 5 ml for larger tubes, or as prescribed. Be sure to add the water before the feeding solution has drained from the neck of the syringe. Clamp the tube before removing the syringe to prevent reflux of the feeding.

(Continues)

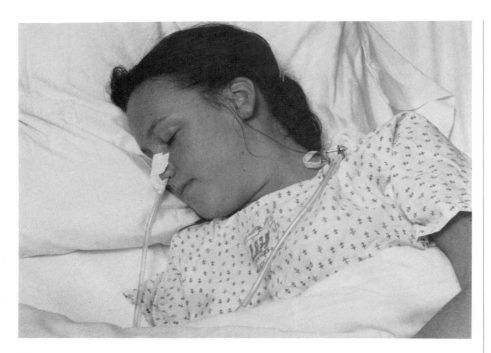

7   For better absorption, have your client remain in Fowler's position for 45–60 minutes after the solution has been infused. If this is uncomfortable, she may be positioned in a slightly elevated right side-lying position (as shown) so that the solution can flow by gravity from the greater stomach curve to the pylorus. Wash and dry the syringe and the other feeding containers, and return them to the bedside stand. Document the feeding in the chart and on the intake and output record.

Evaluating

8   Assess for alterations in fluid volume, nutrition, and bowel elimination. If these occur, the rate of infusion or the concentration of the feeding solution may need altering. Monitor the fluid and electrolyte status by checking laboratory values, and assess the client's vital signs, skin turgor, intake and output balance, and mucous membranes. Query the client about the presence of thirst, the primary indicator of dehydration. Tube feedings that are high in protein content tend to increase the risk of osmotic diuresis, which can result in depletion of extracellular and cellular water. To help prevent this, periodically instill water into the nasogastric tube, basing the amount and frequency on your assessment and the tube-feeding guidelines. Perform urine glucose tests every 6–8 hours to assess for glycosuria, which can be caused by the high osmolarity of the feeding solution. Administer nasal and oral hygiene after each feeding, and weigh the client daily, if prescribed.

GIVING A CONTINUOUS-DRIP TUBE FEEDING

Note: *Review the guidelines for giving an intermittent tube feeding, and make the following variations.*

Planning

There are several ways to administer a continuous-drip tube feeding. One simple method is to obtain the commercial screw-on drip chamber and tubing apparatus available for your client's bottled feeding solution.

1   Place the plastic bag over the bottle containing the feeding solution so that the hole in the bag is centered over the bottle's neck.

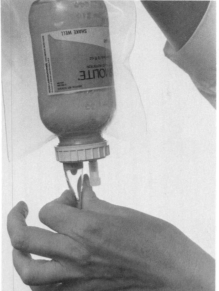

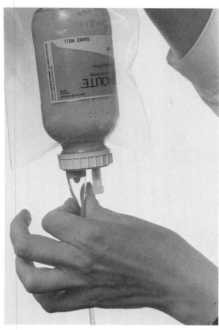

Implementing

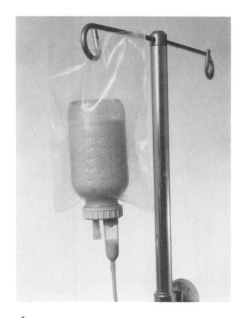

2 Remove the bottle cap and screw on the drip chamber and tubing apparatus.

3 Turn the bottle upside down and squeeze the drip chamber to fill it to one third to one half of its capacity. Then allow the solution to flow to the end of the tubing, and clamp it off.

4 Hang the solution on an IV pole that has been adjusted to 30–45 cm (12–18 in.) above the client's abdomen. After you have aspirated and measured residual gastric contents, connect the feeding tube to the gastric tube, and reinforce the connection with a piece of tape. Adjust the drip rate to deliver the feeding over the desired length of time.

5 As an alternative, pour the prescribed feeding solution into a feeding container, as shown.

(Continues)

MANAGING FEEDING PUMPS

Evaluating

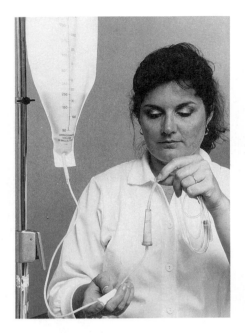

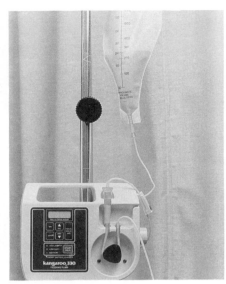

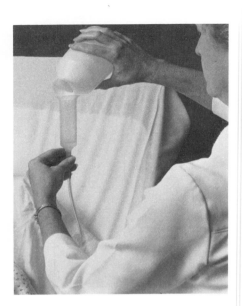

6 Hang the feeding container and prime the tubing to remove the air. Attach the primed tubing to the client's gastric tube.

7 Feeding pumps are often used for clients who have either smaller-bore gastric tubes or intestinal tubes for which gravity flow or drip-regulated methods of infusion are inadequate. Pumps are also indicated for clients who require careful monitoring of their intake or who need a specific amount of formula infused over a specified period of time. Familiarize yourself with the types of feeding pumps your agency uses, and follow the operating instructions for those pumps.

8 To ensure adequate absorption of any continuous-drip feeding and to verify correct stomach placement, discontinue the feedings every 6 hours, or as indicated, and aspirate and measure gastric contents. The protocol for most agencies is to withhold the feeding if more than 75–100 ml of gastric contents is measured. Then, flush the tubing with 30–50 ml of water to ensure patency as well as to increase fluid intake. *Note: To prevent spoilage, the same solution should not be hung for longer than 3–4 hours at a time (or the manufacturer's recommended time).*

ADMINISTERING GASTRIC LAVAGE

Assessing and Planning

1 Take the client's vital signs to establish a baseline for subsequent assessment, and inspect and palpate the abdomen to assess the degree of distention. Explain the procedure, tell the client why it is being done, and reassure her or him. Insert a nasogastric tube if one is not already in place (see steps, pp. 256–262).

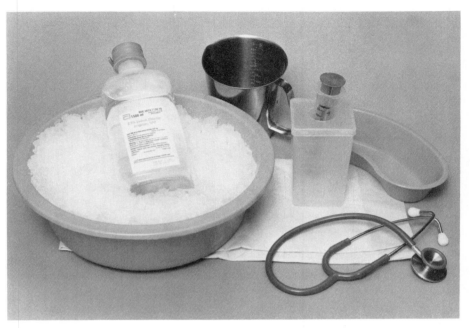

2 Assemble the following: the prescribed irrigant (either tap water or normal saline), usually 1,000–1,500 ml (500 ml for the pediatric population) iced or at room temperature; a measuring container for evaluating the amount of aspirate; an irrigation set with a 50-ml piston syringe (20 ml for the pediatric population); bed-saver pads; an emesis basin; and a stethoscope. You also should have blood pressure monitoring equipment, a rectal or axillary thermometer, and blankets at the bedside. *Note: If iced lavage has been prescribed you may pour the irrigant into a metal container for faster chilling, but do not pour the solution directly over ice because you would dilute the irrigant and make it difficult to keep accurate intake and output records.*

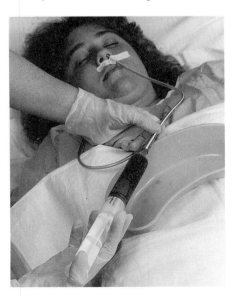

3 Place the client in a semi-Fowler's or Fowler's position. If this position is contraindicated because of hypovolemia or other conditions, lower the head of the bed (as shown). Drape the client with a bed-saver pad, apply clean gloves, and confirm correct stomach placement of the nasogastric tube by aspirating gastric contents with the syringe. Rather than reinstill the aspirate, inject it into a measuring container for later disposal.

(Continues)

Implementing

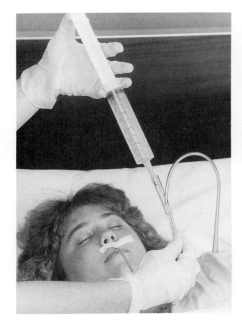

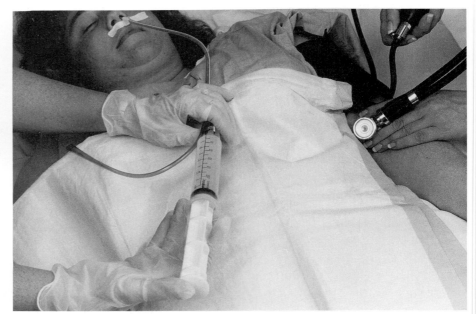

4 Draw up approximately 50 ml of the irrigation solution into the syringe and instill it into the tube using gentle pressure. Do not use force. Aspirate and inject the return into the measuring container. Continue to instill and aspirate until the returns are clear or pink-tinged.

5 Have a co-worker monitor vital signs as you perform the lavage. If a decrease in blood pressure occurs, lower the head of the bed. Cover the client with blankets if her temperature drops because of the icy lavage. After 20–30 minutes (or the prescribed amount of time) if the aspirate has not become clear or pink-tinged, the physician should be notified for medical intervention.

Evaluating

6 Accurately record the amounts of both the irrigant and return to evaluate the quantity of blood loss. Continue to monitor the variations in blood pressure and pulse rates as an assessment for hypovolemia and potential shock. Provide materials for oral and nasal hygiene; document the procedure describing the type and amount of irrigant, the amount and character of the return, and your assessment of the client's condition and tolerance of the procedure.

ASPIRATING STOMACH CONTENTS FOR GASTRIC ANALYSIS

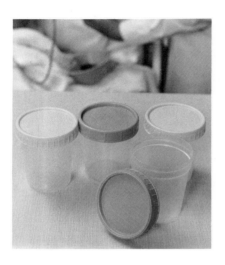

If possible, explain the procedure to the client at least a day ahead of time because he or she must fast for at least 8 hours before the test. A gastric analysis evaluates the amount of acid produced by the parietal cells when the stomach is in a state of rest. Therefore fluids, smoking, and anticholinergics are also contraindicated because they will affect the gastric contents. At the prescribed time, insert a nasogastric tube (see steps, pp. 256–262) and aspirate the residual stomach contents with a 50-ml syringe. Usually, you will discard the first aspirate unless the physician wants to test the residual. After waiting the prescribed amount of time, aspirate all the stomach contents again and place them in a specimen container that has been properly labeled, dated, and numbered. Send the container to the laboratory. You will probably do this three or four more times at 15-minute intervals. Depending on the type of test ordered, you may be required to repeat the procedure after administering subcutaneous histamine to the client. Histamine not only stimulates acid secretion, it rapidly dilates capillaries as well, resulting in a potential drop in blood pressure, increased pulse rate, and headache. Assess and document the client's pulse and blood pressure immediately after the histamine administration.

GIVING GASTROSTOMY TUBE FEEDINGS

Assessing and Planning

1 If tube feedings have been prescribed for your client who has a gastrostomy tube, determine whether the client has a history of food allergies or medically related alterations in nutrition. If the client has already received a tube feeding, inspect and palpate the abdomen to assess for gastric distention. If the abdomen is distended, the previous feeding may not have been adequately absorbed. Monitor the client for indications of intolerance to the previous feeding: alterations in bowel elimination, flatulence, and nausea. Assess the client's understanding of the procedure and intervene accordingly.

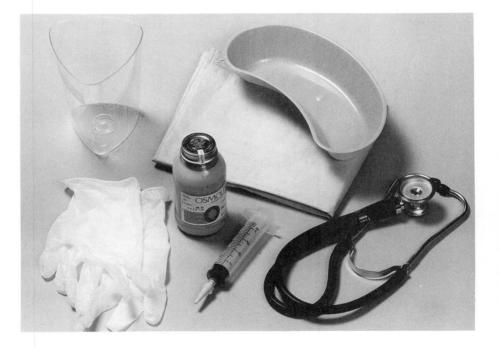

Assemble the following materials and equipment for an intermittent feeding: a 50-ml bulb or piston syringe (10–20 ml syringe for the pediatric population); a stethoscope; 30–50 ml of water; a measured container; emesis basin; a bed-saver pad; and the prescribed solution for tube feeding, which should be warmed to room temperature to minimize the potential for cramping and vasoconstriction. ***Note:*** *To administer feedings via continuous drip, follow procedure, pp. 270–272.*

(Continues)

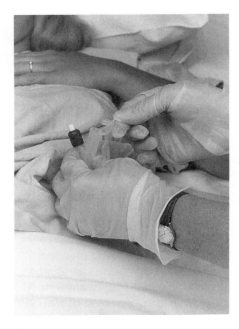

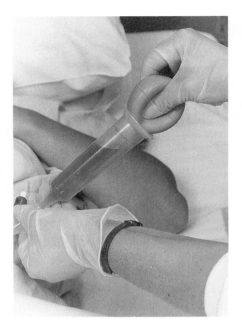

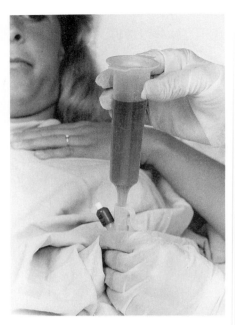

2 Place the client in semi-Fowler's or a right side-lying position. Protect the client's gown and bed linen with a bed-saver pad, apply clean gloves, and detach the feeding port plug from the tube's lumen.

3 Insert the syringe into the open end of the tube and aspirate the residual stomach contents to evaluate the absorption of the previous feeding. Follow your agency's aspiration precaution rule to determine whether to give this feeding. The usual protocol for withholding a feeding is a residual amount of 75–100 ml of gastric contents. *Note: If this is the client's first tube feeding, ensure patency of the tube by instilling 10–20 ml of water first (1–2 ml for small children and 5 ml for larger children).*

Implementing

5 Pour in the premeasured formula, instilling it before the aspirate has drained from the neck of the syringe barrel to avoid introducing air into the client's stomach. If the client complains of discomfort or cramping during the feeding, lower the syringe barrel and pause for a few moments. If the solution oozes around the abdominal exit site, the balloon at the distal end of the tube may not be flush with the gastric wall. Applying slight tension on the tube may correct this problem.

4 Remove the bulb or piston and reinstill the measured aspirate via the syringe barrel, allowing it to flow into the stomach by gravity.

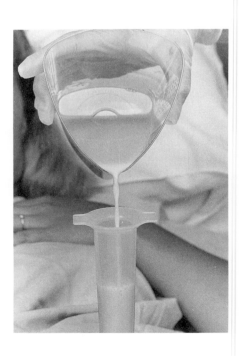

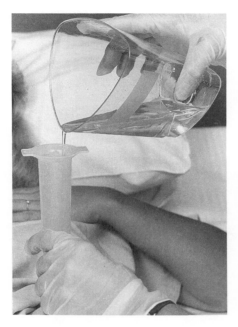

6 Flush the tubing with 30–50 ml of water, unless otherwise prescribed, to help maintain tubal patency, as well as increase the fluid intake and aid in the excretion of waste products. Pour the water into the syringe barrel before the formula has drained from the barrel neck.

7 When the feeding has been completed, reinsert the plug into the feeding port. If the client complains of abdominal discomfort, nausea, fever, or distention, detach the feeding port plug, and place the tube's open end over an emesis basin to release the gastric contents. Document the procedure in the chart and on the intake and output record.

Evaluating

8 Assess the client for alterations in fluid volume, bowel elimination, and nutrition; observe for indicators of fluid and electrolyte imbalance: thirst, change in vital signs, and alterations in skin and mucous membrane moisture. Tube feedings that are high in protein content tend to increase the risk of osmotic diuresis, which can result in depletion of extracellular and cellular water. To help prevent this, periodically instill water into the tube, basing the amount and frequency on your assessment and the tube-feeding guidelines. Monitor laboratory values as well. Every 6–8 hours, test the urine for increased glucose levels, potentially caused by the high osmolarity of the feeding solution. Change the dressing as prescribed, and observe for leaking gastric contents that could cause skin excoriation. Cleanse the area thoroughly and use skin barriers if they are indicated (see procedures, Managing Stoma Care, pp. 289–305). Evaluate the patency of the tube, and if you have an order for irrigation, do so when it becomes necessary.

Managing Intestinal Tubes

Nursing Guidelines for Managing Intestinal Tubes

SINGLE-LUMEN TUBES

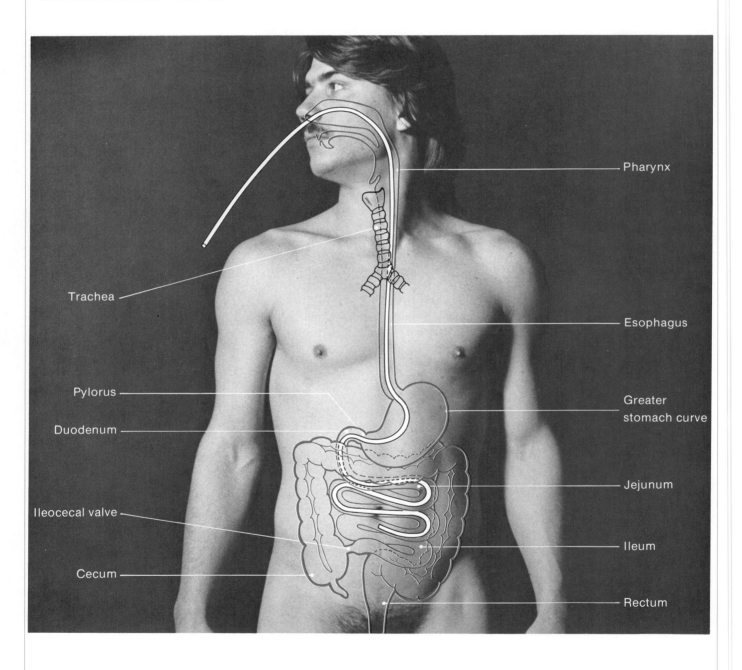

Description	91–300 cm (36 in.–10 ft); made of silicone, rubber, or polyurethane. Most are mercury-weighted at the distal end and have centimeter markings at 25, 50, and 75.
Sizes	Decompression tubes usually 16–18F Feeders usually 8–16F
Uses	Gavage, decompression, medication instillation, splinting of the small bowel after anastomosis
Nursing Considerations	■ The tubes are usually inserted by the physician. ■ The insertion of the tube into the stomach is similar to that of the nasogastric tube. ■ For decompression, connect the tube to intermittent suction. ■ Ensure intestinal placement by checking pH of aspirate: a reading greater than 7 indicates intestinal contents; one less than 7 indicates gastric contents. ■ Tube feedings are usually begun with water, advanced to half-strength of the formula, and finally to full strength, according to client tolerance. ■ Reposition the client frequently when the tube is in position to facilitate drainage. ■ Use infusion pumps to deliver feedings if continuous feedings are prescribed. ■ Provide oral and nasal hygiene at least three to four times daily.

(Continues)

DOUBLE-LUMEN TUBES

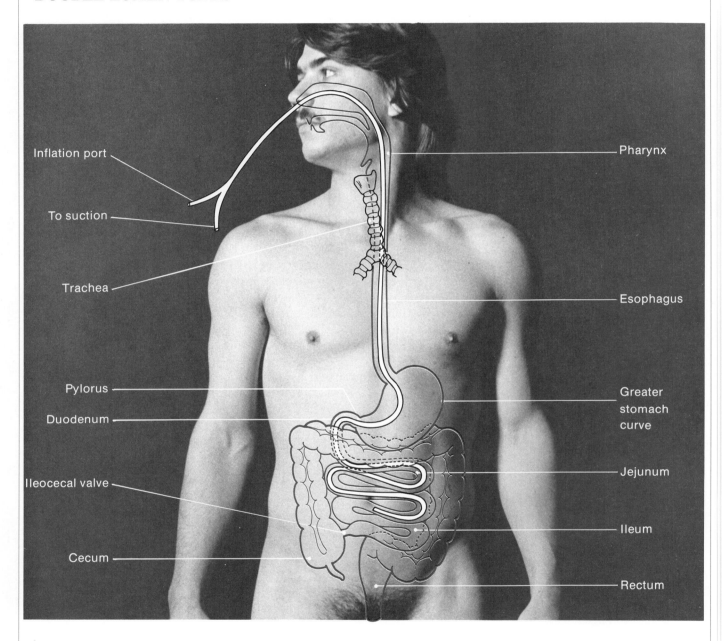

Inflation port

To suction

Trachea

Pylorus

Duodenum

Ileocecal valve

Cecum

Pharynx

Esophagus

Greater stomach curve

Jejunum

Ileum

Rectum

Description

180–300 cm (72 in.–10 ft) in length; rubber or plastic material; one outlet is for suction, and the other is for balloon inflation with air, water, saline, or mercury.

Size

12–18F

Uses

Decompression, gavage, diagnostic testing

Nursing Considerations

- The tube is usually inserted by the physician.
- The insertion to the stomach is similar to the insertion of a naso-gastric tube.
- This tube is most often used for clients with bowel obstructions.
- It is usually attached to intermittent suction.
- In the Hodge tube, only air is injected into the pigtail port.
- Assess the client frequently for the need for oral and nasal hygiene.
- Frequently reposition the client to facilitate drainage.
- Ensure correct intestinal placement by checking pH of aspirated intestinal contents: a reading greater than 7 indicates intestinal contents; one less than 7 indicates gastric contents.

(Continues)

JEJUNOSTOMY TUBES

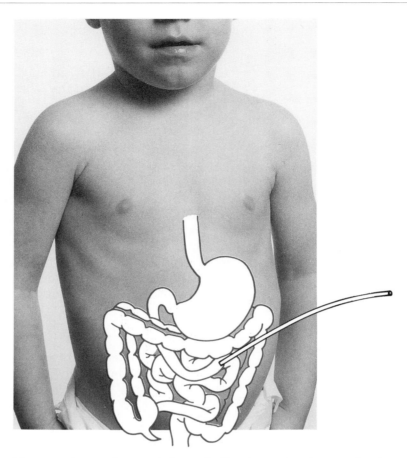

Description	May use larger-lumen tubes, similar to gastrostomy tube (see description, p. 253); or smaller-lumen tubes, 35 cm (14 in.), made of silicone or plastic; 8F.
Use	Usually gavage only

Nursing Considerations

- The tube is surgically inserted into the jejunum and sutured into place; after 2 weeks, it usually can be removed and reinserted as necessary for feedings.
- It is often inserted to feed clients after upper gastrointestinal and abdominal surgery because the jejunum can accommodate larger-volume feedings.
- The feedings are begun with water or weak concentrations of formula, advancing to full strength usually after 24 hours.
- Assess for "dumping syndrome" and diarrhea due to high osmolarity of formula.
- Perform tests for urine glucose every 6–8 hours when giving high-carbohydrate formulas.
- Frequently inspect abdominal exit site for indications of skin breakdown potentially caused by leaking intestinal contents.
- If necessary, use skin barriers to protect the skin from the highly caustic intestinal contents (see procedures, Managing Stoma Care).
- Change postoperative dressing as ordered, using aseptic technique.
- Involve parents in their children's tube feedings.
- Infants should be given nipples to satisfy sucking needs.

ASSISTING WITH THE INSERTION OF AN INTESTINAL TUBE

Assessing and Planning

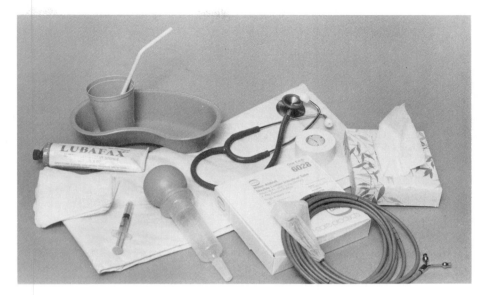

1 Because the insertion of an intestinal tube as far as the stomach is similar to that of the nasogastric tube, familiarize yourself with the insertion of a nasogastric tube, pp. 256–262. Assemble the following materials: the prescribed intestinal tube (a Miller-Abbott is shown); tissues; 50-ml bulb or piston syringe; hypoallergenic tape, 2.5 cm in width; 4 × 4 gauze pads; drinking glass with a straw; 5-ml syringe; emesis basin; bed-saver pad; water-soluble lubricant; and a stethoscope. In addition, you will need to obtain mercury if it will be used for balloon inflation.

2 Flush water through the tube to test its patency.

(Continues)

3 Attach the 5-ml syringe to the inflation lumen of the intestinal tube and inflate the balloon with air until it is just less than fully distended. Submerge the balloon in water and test it for leaks as evidenced by bubbles in the water. Then deflate the balloon.

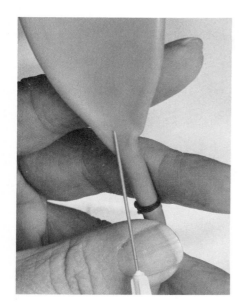

4 *Note: If you are using a single-lumen Cantor tube, inject the bag at the distal end of the tube with the prescribed amount (usually 1–2 ml) of mercury prior to its insertion.*

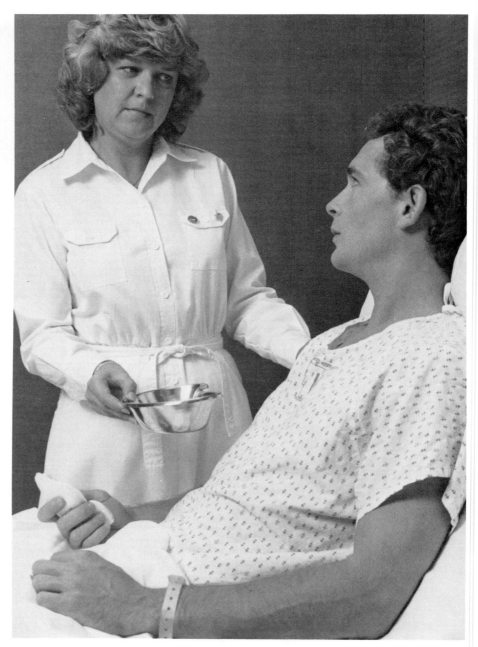

5 After testing the equipment, bring it into the client's room and explain the procedure, carefully outlining the steps during which his assistance and cooperation will facilitate the tube's insertion. Assist the client into semi-Fowler's or Fowler's position, or into a slightly elevated right side-lying position if Fowler's position is contraindicated. Either position will facilitate the tube's insertion by gravity and reduce the risk of aspiration. If appropriate, have him remove his glasses and dentures, and provide him with an emesis basin because emesis can occur if the gag reflex is activated. Together, agree on a signal he can use, such as tapping your arm, to alert you or the physician to stop momentarily if the procedure becomes too uncomfortable. Protect the client's gown and bed linen with a bed-saver pad.

6 The tube is measured from the nostril to the ear.

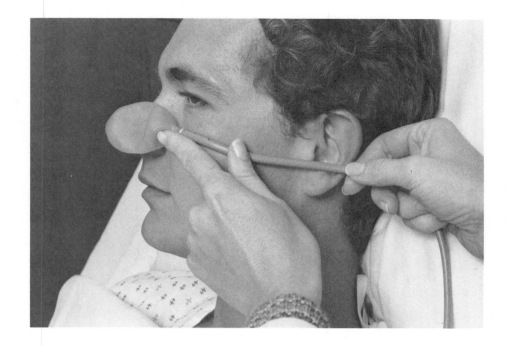

Implementing

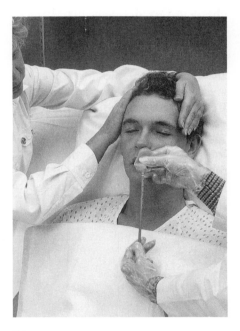

7 It is then measured from the ear to the tip of the xiphoid process. The total NEX (nose-ear-xiphoid) measurement is then marked on the tube with indelible ink or remembered if the measurement equals the centimeter markings on the tube.

8 Generously lubricate the first 15 cm (6 in.) of the tube with water-soluble lubricant for ease of insertion.

9 As the physician begins to insert the tube, help the client hold his head in an erect or slightly flexed position.

(Continues)

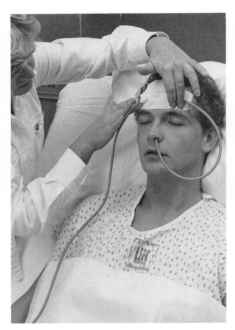

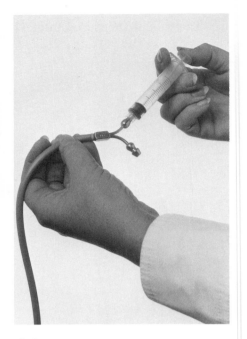

10 After the tube has been inserted 15 cm (6 in.), instruct the client to flex his head forward. This will lessen the chance of activating the gag reflex and prevent the insertion of the tube into the trachea. He should then take sips of water (or dry swallow if fluids are contraindicated). The physician will advance the tube 5–10 cm (2–4 in.) with each swallow. When the predesignated mark is at the level of the client's nostril, confirm correct stomach placement (see procedure, p. 261).

11 After confirming stomach placement, prepare a gauze sling for the tubing by folding a gauze pad in half and inserting the tubing into the fold. Tape the sling to the client's forehead. This will keep the tube stabilized as it advances into the intestine. Do not tape the tube to the client's nose because doing so could hamper the tube's advancement and the tension on the tube could injure the client's nose.

12 For double-lumen tubes the physician will then inject 3–10 ml of mercury, air, water, or saline (depending on the type of tube) into the balloon port. Any one of these substances will act as a bolus for easier advancement past the pylorus. The syringe is then often taped to the balloon port to prevent accidental instillation or aspiration. Tape can instead be placed over the balloon port.

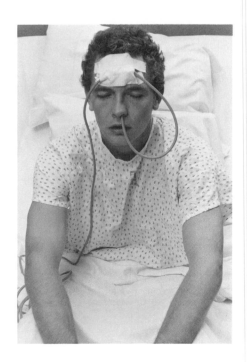

13 If the client is able, instruct him to lean forward with his arms extended to help advance the tube to the duodenum.

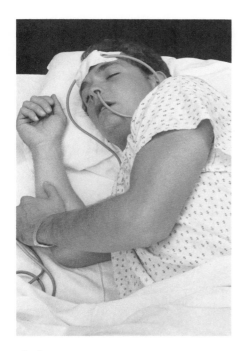

14 If the client cannot sit up, the following maneuver might enhance tube movement into the intestine. Throughout the procedure, the head of the bed is elevated slightly (as shown). First, the client rests on his right side so that the tube can pass into the duodenum. After the prescribed time has passed, the client lies supine. Then, to advance the tube to the opposite arm of the duodenum, the client lies on his left side. If you have been asked to insert the tube a prescribed distance, lubricate the tubing with water-soluble lubricant and gradually advance the tube 5–10 cm (2–4 in.) every 2 hours. Do not force the tube if you meet resistance. A peristaltic wave could be preventing its advancement. Wait a few minutes and try again. Provide oral and nasal hygiene at regular intervals. When an x-ray film has confirmed the tube's proper position, attach the excess tubing to the client's gown. Then attach the open lumen to intermittent suction, or as prescribed by the physician. Document the procedure.

Evaluating

15 Prior to tube feedings or instillations, or as a means of assessing for correct intestinal position, aspirate intestinal contents through the open lumen to confirm alkalinity. A pH greater than 7 (or a test strip that turns blue) indicates intestinal placement; a pH less than 7 indicates gastric placement.

If the tube is connected to suction, assess the character and amount of drainage and change the suction container (or empty it) according to agency protocol. Reposition the client frequently to facilitate drainage. Monitor and record the client's intake and output, and assess for the presence of peristalsis by auscultating the abdomen for bowel sounds. Continue to provide materials for oral and nasal hygiene.

REMOVING AN INTESTINAL TUBE

Assessing and Planning

1 Before removing the intestinal tube, assess the client's abdomen by auscultating for bowel sounds and inspecting and palpating for distention. If you do not hear bowel sounds or if the abdomen is quite distended, check with the physician to make sure the tube should be removed. Assess the client's knowledge of the procedure and explain why the tube will be removed. Familiarize yourself with the steps for the removal of a nasogastric tube, p. 265. Because the client may become nauseated during the procedure, you should check to see if an antiemetic has been prescribed. *Note: If the tube has passed through the ileocecal valve, the physician may allow it to pass through the rectum rather than removing it through the nose.*

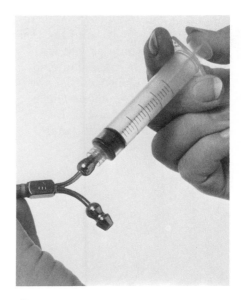

2 If you are removing a Miller-Abbott tube, attach a syringe to the balloon part (as shown), and aspirate the mercury or balloon-inflating substance.

(Continues)

Implementing

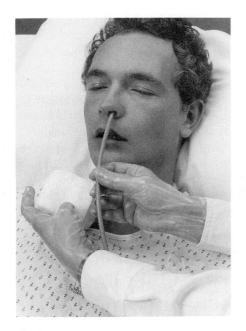

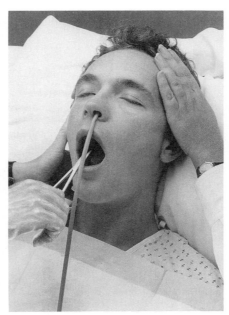

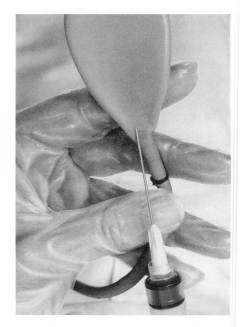

3 Protect the client's gown with a bed-saver pad. Assist him into a semi-Fowler's or Fowler's position to help prevent aspiration of the drainage. If the tube is connected to suction, turn off the suction machine, apply gloves, and detach the tube from the client's nose. Pinch or clamp the tubing as you withdraw 5–10 cm (2–4 in.) every 5–10 minutes. Ask the client to exhale as you withdraw the tube because doing so will relax the pharynx. Blot the tube with a gauze pad or paper towel as you withdraw it, to remove gastric and intestinal drainage.

4 If the intestinal tube is disposable, you may wish to grasp the balloon with a hemostat when it reaches the client's oropharynx and snip it off with scissors, removing the balloon through the client's mouth to avoid passing it through the nose. If the tube is not disposable, gently pull it through the client's nose. Remove the tube from the client's bedside, and provide materials for oral and nasal hygiene. Document the procedure.

5 If you have removed a Cantor tube, aspirate the mercury from the bag at the distal end of the tube. Dispose of the mercury or return it to the central supply area, according to agency protocol for disposal of hazardous materials.

Evaluating

6 To evaluate his tolerance to the tube's removal, continue to assess the client for distention, nausea, vomiting, or ileus.

Managing Stoma Care

Nursing Guidelines for Managing Ostomies

ASCENDING COLOSTOMY

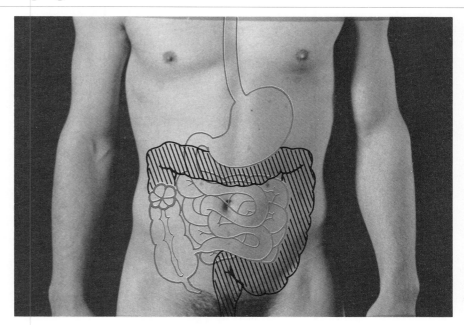

Surgical Indications

Perforating diverticulitis, Hirschsprung's disease, obstructed colon, trauma (for example, gunshot or stab wounds), rectovaginal fistula, and inoperable tumors in the colon.

Nursing Considerations

- This is the least common colostomy.
- The surgery is performed on clients of all ages.
- The stoma location is on the right upper quadrant or right lumbar area of the abdomen, and it usually protrudes.
- This ostomy is managed as if it were an ileostomy (see p. 295).
- The client will have liquid or pasty stools that flow almost continually.
- The effluent contains digestive enzymes that are damaging to the skin.
- Peristomal skin assessment, skin care, and a properly fitting appliance are essential for preventing skin breakdown.
- Full-time use of an appliance (usually a drainable pouch) with a skin barrier is necessary.
- Irrigation is contraindicated.
- Odor control is usually not a major problem because most appliances are odorproof.

(Continues)

TRANSVERSE COLOSTOMIES

Surgical Indications

Same as ascending colostomies. These ostomies are usually temporary and are the most frequently performed fecal diversions for relief of bowel obstruction and colon perforation secondary to trauma.

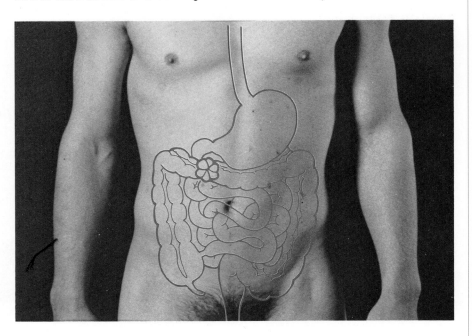

Nursing Considerations for the Single-Barrel Colostomy

- The surgery is performed on clients of all ages.
- The stoma location is usually high on the abdomen, at waist level. and near the midline. It usually protrudes.
- The stools are usually semisolid, although formed stools are possible.
- A drainable pouch is recommended.
- The enzymatic, watery stools can lead to peristomal skin irritation.
- The rectum is not removed, so the client occasionally may defecate from the rectum.
- Although this ostomy is not controllable, it is more predictable than an ascending colostomy as to when it will function.

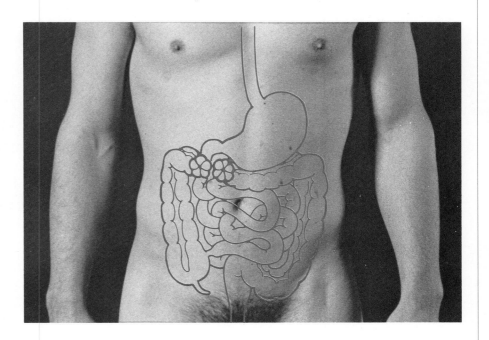

Nursing Considerations for the Double-Barrel Colostomy

- This is often a temporary intervention for resting the colon, with a possible anastomosis at a later date.
- The client has two stomas: the proximal stoma is active and discharges feces; the distal stoma is inactive and discharges mucus. The inactive stoma may be covered eventually with a gauze pad to absorb mucus.
- Postoperatively, the client may use a loop ostomy appliance or an open-end drain with a skin barrier.
- The client may experience occasional rectal drainage of stool or mucus.

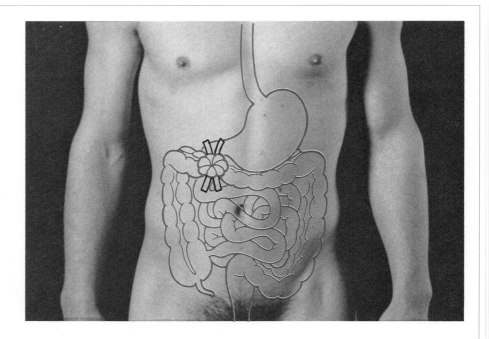

Nursing Considerations for the Loop Colostomy

- An intact segment of the colon is looped through the abdomen rather than severed.
- The loop is held exterior to the body and stabilized with a plastic bridge or glass rod for 7–10 days postoperatively.
- Fecal material is released through an incision on the anterior section of the loop.
- This type of fecal diversion is usually performed in emergency situations; therefore the client is often ill-prepared both physiologically and psychologically.

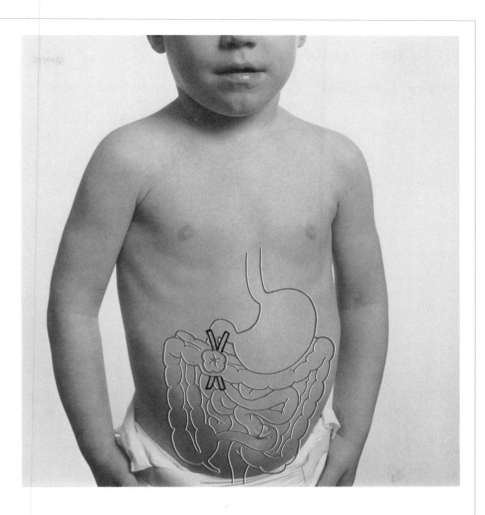

Nursing Considerations for the Pediatric Colostomate

- For the child, a pediatric postoperative pouch and skin barrier are used during the first 3–5 postoperative days. Thereafter pediatric drainable pouches are frequently used.
- The use of skin barriers and close observation of peristomal skin is crucial because of the watery, enzymatic feces.
- For the infant, a diaper alone might be used until discharge from the hospital. Follow agency protocol.
- Closely monitor the infant and child for weight loss and indications of dehydration.

(Continues)

DESCENDING OR SIGMOID COLOSTOMY

Surgical Indications   Cancer of the sigmoid colon or rectum, chronic diverticulitis, congenital anomaly, or trauma.

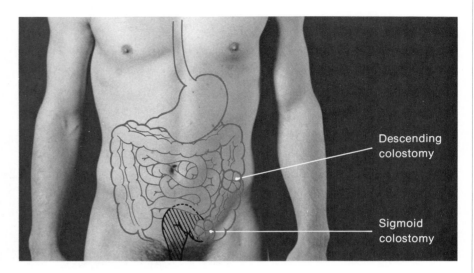

Descending colostomy

Sigmoid colostomy

Nursing Considerations

- This is the most commonly performed fecal diversion.
- The surgery may be performed on clients of all ages, but most clients are 40 years of age or older.
- The stoma is located in the left lower quadrant, and it might be either flush or protruded.
- After recovery, clients may wear either a closed nondrainable pouch or an open drainable pouch, depending on whether or not they will be irrigating their colostomies.
- After the initial postoperative period, the stools may be pasty to semisolid.
- Elimination may be regulated by irrigation and diet.
- Teach the client how to manage elimination by increasing intake of foods high in bulk and decreasing intake of foods known to give the individual loose stools, flatus, and odor. Increase the intake of fluids as well.
- Encourage the intake of parsley, yogurt, and cranberry juice to decrease fecal odor.

ILEOSTOMY

Surgical Indications   Ulcerative colitis (80%), Crohn's disease, cancer, trauma, familial polyposis.

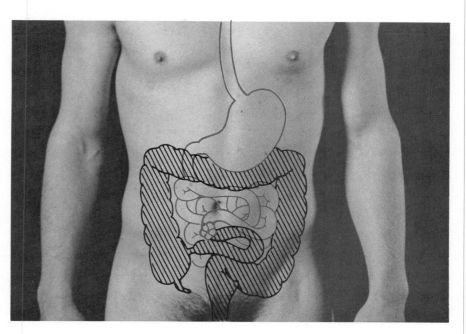

Nursing Considerations for the Brooke Ileostomy

- This procedure is performed most frequently on young adults, including adolescents, with 40 years as the average age.
- The stoma is located in the right lower quadrant, and it usually protrudes.
- The pouch must fit properly to prevent skin breakdown caused by the enzymatic effluent.
- Change the pouch immediately if leakage occurs at the peristomal area or if the client complains of itching or burning around the stoma.
- Because of a potential fluid volume deficit from colon loss, encourage a fluid intake of 2–3 L/day.
- Because of electrolyte loss, increase the client's intake of sodium and potassium through foods, fluids, and supplements.
- Instruct the client to decrease roughage in the diet, which can cause a blockage, and to chew food thoroughly.
- Change the appliance when the ileostomy is more quiescent, for example, in the morning before eating or 2–4 hours after meals.
- The maximum wearing time for the pouch is 7 days, although some clients change their pouches as frequently as every 3 days, and others change them every 5 days.

(Continues)

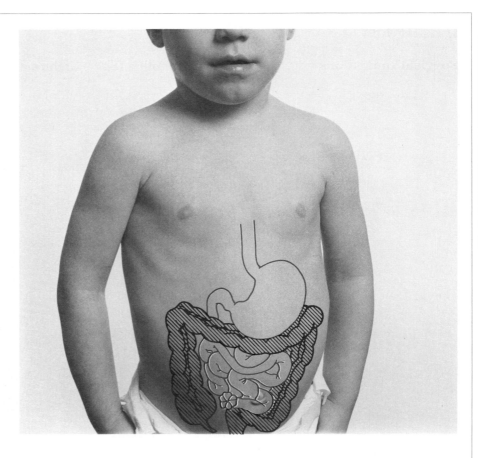

Nursing Considerations for the Pediatric Ileostomate

- Care of these children is similar to that given to children with pediatric transverse loops.
- The fecal output is high in digestive enzymes, and therefore the use of skin barriers and close observation of the peristomal skin are essential.

CONTINENT ILEOSTOMY (KOCK POUCH)

Surgical Indications

Ulcerative colitis and familial polyposis. It is often contraindicated for clients with Crohn's disease because of the potential for recurrence of the disease, which could necessitate pouch removal.

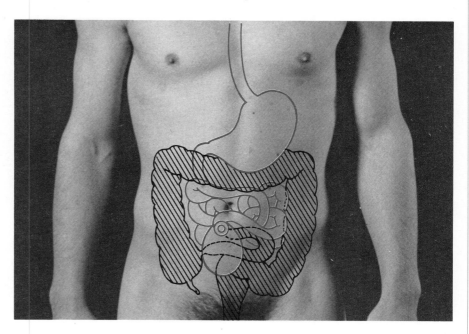

Nursing Considerations

- The age group involved is the same as that for the ileostomy.
- The stoma is located on the right lower quadrant, and it is flush with the skin.
- The intra-abdominal pouch (reservoir) is created from the looped ileum. It collects feces, making external collection pouches unnecessary.
- A gastrostomy tube is often sutured into the stomach during surgery for decompression.
- A 28F catheter is inserted into the reservoir and sutured to the client's skin during surgery; it remains in place for 14–21 days to provide pouch decompression. It is irrigated with normal saline every 4–6 hours, or as prescribed.
- At 14–21 days postoperatively, the reservoir is intubated and drained every 3–4 hours with a lubricated silastic catheter. This is decreased to every 6 hours by week 8 or 9.
- The stoma is covered with a bandage or a gauze pad between intubations to absorb leaks or mucus.
- Instruct the client to avoid gas-forming foods, decrease roughage, and chew the food thoroughly to prevent clogging the silastic catheter.
- The adjustment to the body change is usually less traumatic for these clients than for those with conventional ileostomies.
- The reservoir gradually increases in size and may attain a capacity of 500 ml.

(Continues)

ILEOANAL RESERVOIR

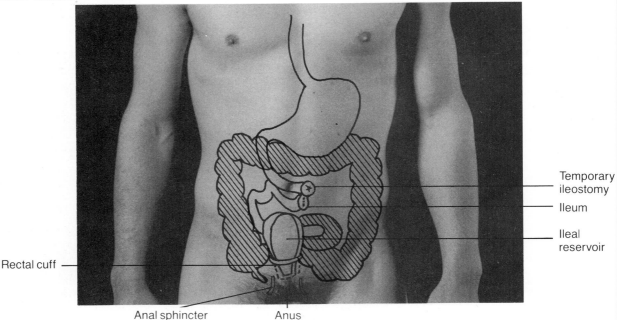

Temporary ileostomy

Ileum

Ileal reservoir

Rectal cuff

Anal sphincter   Anus

Surgical Indications

Clients with ulcerative colitis or familial polyposis who normally would require a total colectomy have an option for preserving fecal continence by having an ileoanal reservoir. It is done in two stages. The first stage, which follows total colectomy and removal of the anal lining (with preservation of the anal sphincter), involves construction of an ileal reservoir from the small bowel. The reservoir's ileal outlet is brought down through the cuff of the rectal muscle and anastomosed to the anal canal. The reservoir stores the feces. A temporary ileostomy is performed to enable healing of the anastomosis. During the second stage (after 2–3 months), the temporary ileostomy is taken down, and fecal continence is restored.

Nursing Considerations

- The ideal client for this procedure is 20–40 years of age, has good sphincter control, is physically fit enough to endure a full year of recovery, and is very motivated not to have a permanent ileostomy.
- For care of the temporary ileostomy during the first stage of this procedure, see discussion, p. 295, for nursing care considerations for the client with an ileostomy.
- There are more surgical complications with this procedure than with a permanent ileostomy.
- To prevent fluid and electrolyte imbalance caused by the colectomy, encourage clients to increase their fluid intake to 8–10 glasses/day.
- Following the first stage of this procedure the client will experience mucus production through the anus. The ileostomy takedown is scheduled following a normal healing process.
- During the period of mucus incontinence, irrigate the mucus out of the reservoir daily using 60 ml water. Cleanse the perianal area with water and cotton balls, avoiding soap and toilet paper, which can cause irritation and itching.

- Following the second stage of this procedure, the client may experience incontinence of feces and 10 or more bowel movements per day. This will decrease in frequency after 3–6 months as the reservoir expands and absorbs fluids, with 4–8 bowel movements per day and increased ability to control stool. Suggest that the client wear a small pad to protect clothing. Antidiarrheals, bulk-forming diet, and dietary changes may be necessary to control this problem.
- Suggest that the client avoid foods that cause liquid stools, such as spinach, highly seasoned foods, raw fruit, and broccoli, and to increase intake of the foods that cause thickened stools, such as bananas, jello, pasta, cheese, and apples.
- Although this procedure enables evacuation of feces through the anus and appears to restore normal functioning, it is important to note that anatomic structure of the colon and rectum has changed.
- Perianal skin care is essential following the second stage of this procedure because of irritation caused by enzymes in the stool. Cleansing gently with a soft tissue or spraying water with a squirt bottle will help protect the skin. Following cleansing and drying, apply an occlusive protective skin sealant or ointment to nonirritated skin. Sitz baths may be recommended for clients whose skin irritation worsens or fails to heal.
- Teach the client that the following foods may promote perianal irritation: nuts, popcorn, oriental vegetables, and raw fruits and vegetables (e.g., oranges, corn, and celery).
- Some clients may benefit from exercising the anal sphincter and deep pelvic muscles to promote bowel function control. These exercises are not begun until a minimum of 2 weeks following surgery. As appropriate, teach the client the following:

  —Anal sphincter toning: Squeeze and hold the anal muscles to a slow count of three; release. Repeat this exercise 10–20 times a day.
  —Deep pelvic muscle toning: Pull in your abdomen as though you are flattening your stomach. Hold for a slow count of 3; release. Repeat this exercise 10–20 times a day.

PATCH TESTING YOUR CLIENT'S SKIN

At least 24 hours prior to ostomy surgery, perform skin patch testing to assess for allergies your client potentially may have to tape that may be used to adhere the ostomy appliance to the abdominal skin. Test the abdomen on the nonoperative side, rather than testing the inner arm. The inner arm is not as sensitive as the abdomen, and the test results may not be as accurate.

Test at least four different types of tape that are used by your agency. This will provide you with more options should the client prove to be allergic to more than one type. The photo depicts the testing of foam, silk, and two types of paper tape on the client's abdomen. If you are patch testing skin on a client with abdominal hair, clip the hair with scissors as

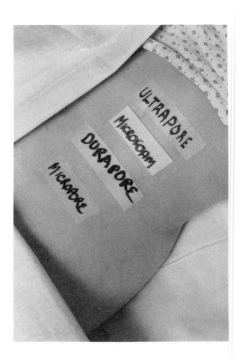

close to the follicle as possible before applying the tape. Unless the client complains of itching and burning before the 24-hour period has elapsed, remove the tape at the scheduled time, using a tape solvent if necessary. Thoroughly cleanse the area with water and a gentle soap or skin cleanser; assess for redness, swelling, and other indicators of an allergic reaction. Document the test's results in the chart. If your client does have an allergic reaction to any of the tapes, note the type(s) on the front of the chart, stating "Allergic to _____ Tape." This will alert both the surgical team before their application of the postoperative pouch and the nursing staff during follow-up care.

APPLYING A DRAINABLE POUCH

A drainable pouch is typically worn during the early part of the client's hospital stay. It is usually clear to facilitate observation of fecal drainage.

Assessing and Planning

1 To apply a drainable pouch, assemble the following materials: the postoperative pouch, a pectin wafer skin barrier, straight scissors, curved scissors (optional), a pouch closure clip, skin cleanser (optional), stomal measurement guide, skin barrier paste, 4 × 4 gauze pads, and skin preparation wipes (optional, for protecting the skin if you plan to reinforce the seal of the pouch to the client's skin with tape). In addition, keep a supply of bed-saver pads and gloves at the client's bedside.

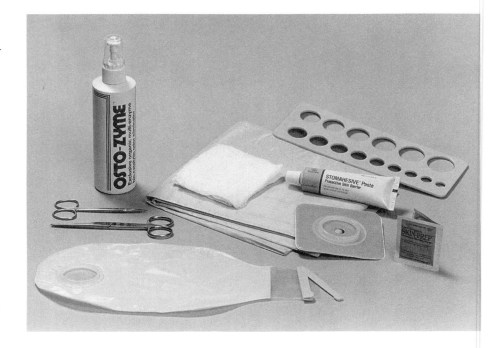

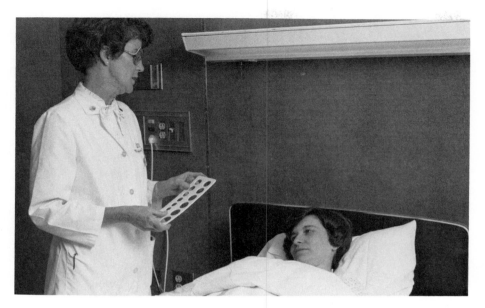

2 Explain the procedure to the client, and lower the head of the bed to decrease the angle at the peristomal area. Assess the client's reaction to her stoma, and let her know that you have as much time as she needs for answering her questions and assisting her with future pouch applications. If she is psychologically ready, encourage her to inspect and touch her stoma so that she can begin to develop a realistic appraisal of her altered appearance and body function. It is essential that you project a positive reaction to the client's ostomy.

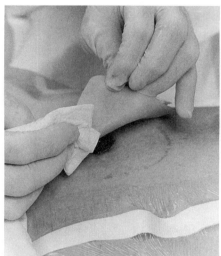

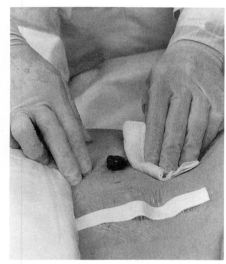

3 To protect the client's gown and bed from fecal drainage, place a bed-saver pad under the pouch. Then, apply gloves and moisten a 4 × 4 gauze pad or cloth with warm water and lift up the uppermost inside corner of the skin barrier. Position the moistened gauze pad at the loosened corner, and gently depress the skin as you peel back the adhesive material. This method will facilitate the removal of the appliance as quickly and painlessly as possible.

4 After removing the appliance, assess the color of the stoma. It should be a healthy red, similar in color to the mucosal lining of the inner cheek. Report immediately a darker, purplish cast or a very pale stoma, which would suggest impaired blood circulation to the area. Also assess for impaired peristomal skin integrity potentially caused by leakage of fecal effluent, an allergic reaction to the tape or skin barrier, or infected hair follicles (folliculitis). Plan skin care and/or appliance changes accordingly.

(Continues)

Implementing

5   Cleanse the peristomal area with warm water and a skin cleanser (as shown) or a nonoily soap such as Ivory. Be sure to avoid using soaps that contain creams or lanolin because the residue left on the skin could prevent the appliance from adhering properly. Rinse and dry the skin thoroughly.

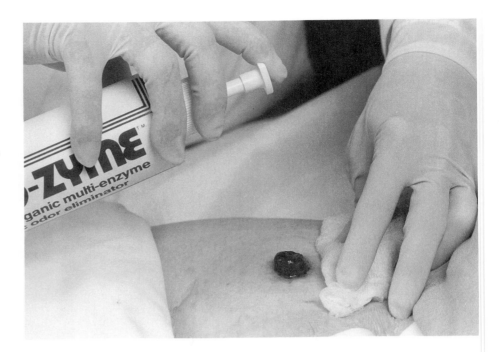

6   A pectin wafer skin barrier protects the client's peristomal skin from contact with the effluent and pouch adhesive. If you are using a pectin wafer with squared edges, curve the edges (as shown) to prevent them from jabbing your client's skin. Set the skin barrier aside.

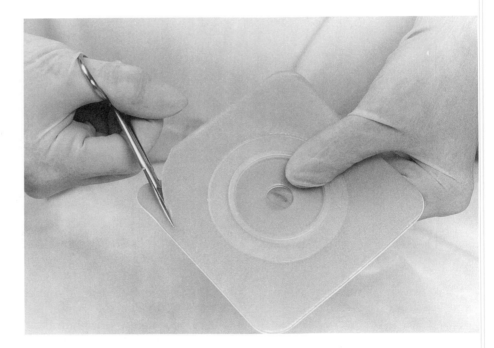

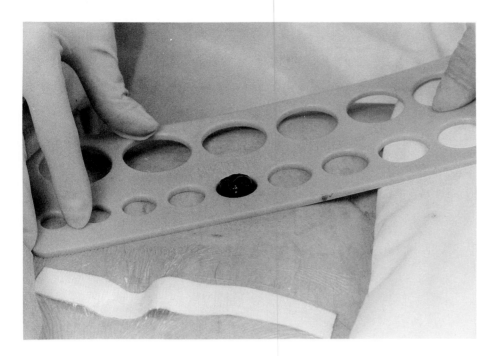

7 Measure the stoma with a stomal measuring guide. You will need to measure the stoma frequently during the postoperative period because the stoma will continue to shrink in size, with the majority of the shrinkage occurring during the first 2–3 months.

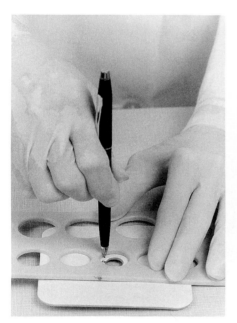

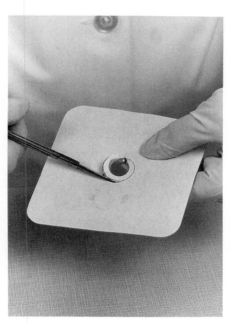

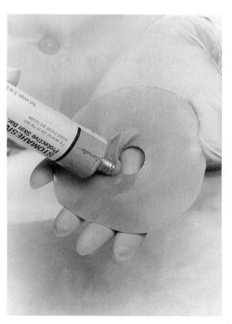

8 Trace the exact measurement of the stoma on the back and in the center of the skin barrier.

9 Cut out the circle from the skin barrier.

10 Remove the adhesive backing from the pectin wafer skin barrier. After removing the adhesive backing, apply protective skin barrier paste to the adhesive side of the pectin wafer along the periphery of the circle you cut out (as shown). This will help protect the client's peristomal skin from effluent drainage.

(Continues)

11 Apply the pectin wafer, adhesive side down, over the client's stoma. Then attach the pouch to the pectin wafer by gently snapping the back of the pouch onto the lip of the pectin wafer, as shown.

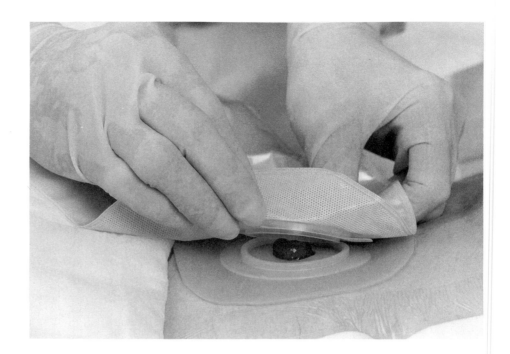

12 Continue snapping the pouch to the pectin wafer in a circular fashion. Note that the pouch angles toward the side of the bed. This facilitates emptying the pouch into a basin or bed pan during the early postoperative period. It should be angled in this manner only during the period of time the client is on bed rest. If you will be taping the pouch to the client's skin to reinforce the seal, see procedure in Chapter 8.

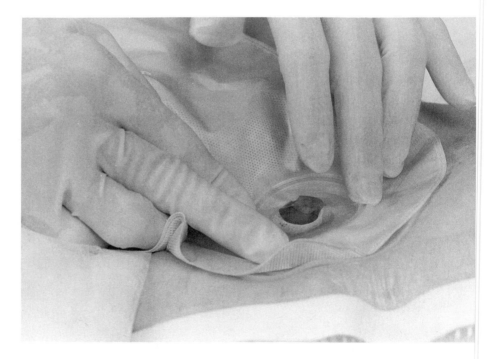

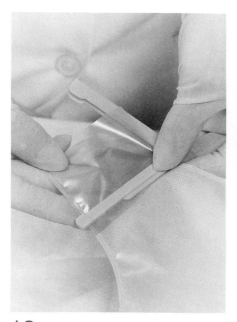

13 Open and position the tail closure device (clamp) 1½ inch from the bottom of the pouch tail.

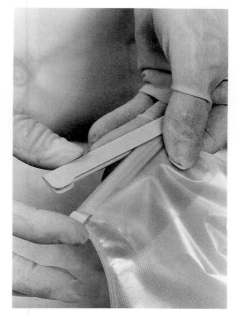

14 Fold the end of the pouch tail over the clamp, as shown. Then, snap the clamp together. You will hear or feel it snap.

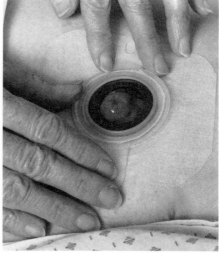

16 The top portion of a disposable pouch has been cut away to show you a correct fit.

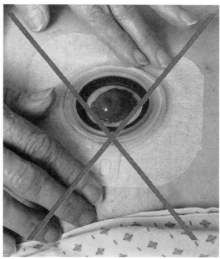

17 The top portion of a disposable pouch that no longer fits because of typical stomal shrinkage occurring during the postoperative period has been cut away. Because the exposed peristomal skin can readily become excoriated after contact with caustic fecal effluent, it is essential that the appliance be changed as soon as stomal shrinkage occurs and the skin is exposed. Similarly, if your client has an irregularly shaped stoma, you should use karaya paste to fill in the exposed area, or cut a pectin wafer skin barrier to fit the stoma.

Evaluating

15 Continue to monitor the client for alterations in fluid and electrolyte balance, impairment of stomal and peristomal skin, alterations in nutrition, and daily changes in body weight. In addition, it is especially important in the early postoperative period to be alert to indications of paralytic ileus or peritonitis. Inspect and palpate the abdomen for the presence of distention or rigidity, and auscultate the abdomen to ensure that there are bowel sounds. Although an absence of fecal output is one indicator of ileus, an ileostomy usually does not function until the first 12–24 hours; a lack of fecal output during the first 24–36 hours is often normal for a colostomy. Keep accurate daily records of the amount, color, and consistency of fecal output, and compare the output to the client's intake.

When the pouch becomes one-third full, detach the closure clip and empty the pouch into a basin or bed pan. If the pouch is allowed to become full of effluent, its seal with the skin can break, resulting in leakage of effluent onto the client's abdomen.

DILATING A STOMA

Stoma dilation is performed to stretch and relax the stomal sphincter and to assess the direction of the proximal colon prior to a colostomy irrigation. Check for a physician's order before dilating a client's stoma, because the procedure is not done for all colostomates.

Assessing and Planning

1 Assemble the following materials: gauze pads, water-soluble lubricant, and a disposable glove. Be sure that you also have bed-saver pads on hand. Then ask the client to remove her appliance.

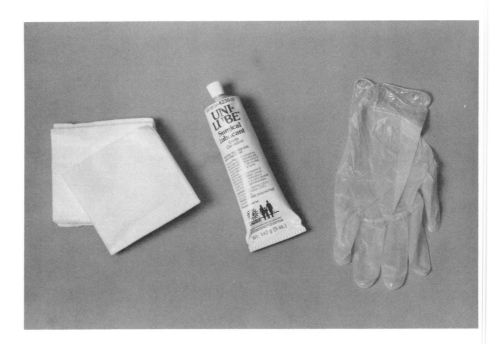

2 Instruct the client to put on the disposable glove and generously lubricate the small and index fingers of her gloved hand with the water-soluble lubricant.

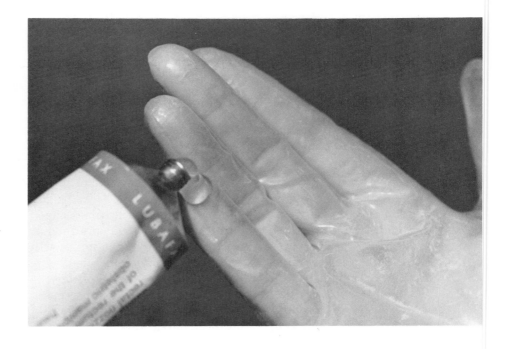

Implementing

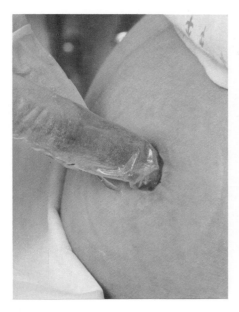 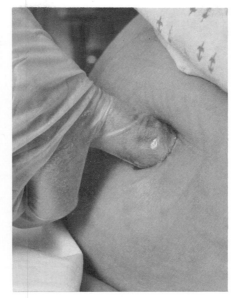

3 Drape the client's lap with a bed-saver pad, and position a gauze pad under the stoma to collect drainage. Instruct the client to introduce her small finger gently into the stoma and to maintain the position for 1 minute to relax the sphincter.

4 She may then insert her index finger, gently rotating the finger to midknuckle or 5 cm (2 in.) to assess the direction of the proximal colon. This assessment will enable her to position the tip of the irrigation cone correctly.

Evaluating

5 Because the stoma comprises a vast number of capillaries, there may be slight bleeding from this procedure; however, copious bleeding is abnormal and should be reported immediately. Document the procedure and your client's performance.

IRRIGATING A COLOSTOMY

Colostomy irrigations are performed to evacuate the bowel of stored fecal content, potentially enabling clients to regulate their fecal elimination. They are most appropriate for clients with ostomies of the descending or sigmoid colon. Check for a physician's order before performing this procedure. Irrigations are not performed for all colostomates; and they are contraindicated for infants, for clients with diarrhea, or for those receiving radiation therapy.

Assessing

1 To ensure that your client does not have an obstruction or paralytic ileus, assess the client's abdomen before initiating the procedure by palpating for distention and auscultating to determine the presence of bowel sounds.

Planning

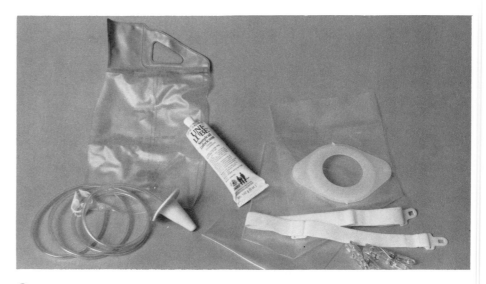

2 Assemble the following equipment: an irrigation bag with tubing and a cone, irrigation sleeve and belt, water-soluble lubricant, and closure clamps. You will also need an IV pole or a bathroom hook and the prescribed amount of irrigant, which is usually warm tap water. Unless otherwise prescribed, the amount of the first postoperative irrigation is 500 ml, and it is gradually increased by 250 ml up to 1000 ml until the effective amount is determined by a complete and comfortable evacuation.

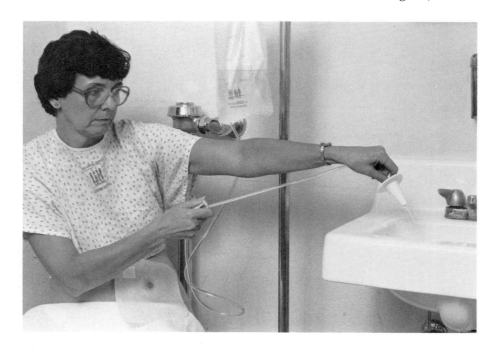

3 Although the procedure can be performed in bed, if the client is ambulatory set up the equipment in the bathroom. Ideally, at this stage in the client's recovery, she should perform as much self-care as possible, with your assistance. This photo shows 750 ml of warm tap water hung on an IV pole. The bottom of the irrigation bag should be positioned at shoulder level to ensure an effective rate of flow. Instruct the client to open the clamp on the irrigation tubing, and allow the irrigant to flow through the tubing and irrigation cone to remove the air from the irrigation set (as shown). She should then remove her used appliance and perform stomal dilation (if prescribed) to relax the sphincter and to assess the direction of the proximal colon (see steps in preceding procedure).

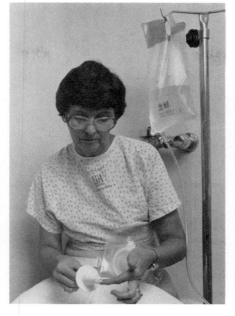

Implementing

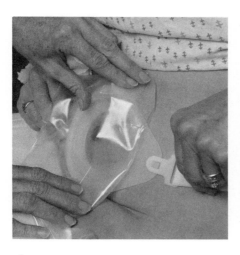

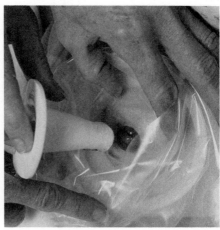

4 Assist the client with applying the irrigation sleeve and belt, and instruct her to place the tail of the sleeve between her legs so that the irrigation return can drain directly into the toilet. If the client is in bed, the tail of the sleeve can be placed into a bed pan.

5 Squeeze some water-soluble lubricant onto a paper towel and have the client generously lubricate the tip of the irrigation cone. An irrigation cone is preferred to a straight catheter as a means of delivering the irrigant because the latter has a greater potential for perforating the bowel.

6 Assist the client with placing the cone into the proximal end of the irrigation sleeve and gently centering the tip of the cone into the stoma until it fits snugly, facing the direction of the proximal colon.

7 Control the speed of the irrigational flow by adjusting the regulator. Instruct the client to stop the flow if she begins cramping. Once the cramps have subsided, she can slowly restart the flow. However, if the cramps continue, the irrigation should be discontinued.

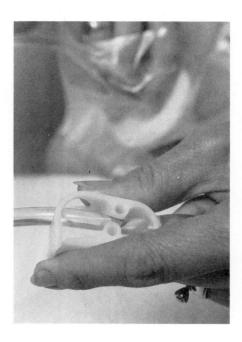

(Continues)

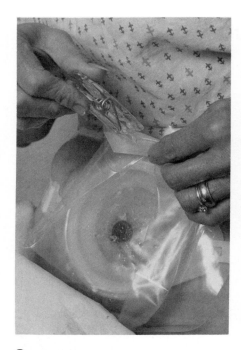
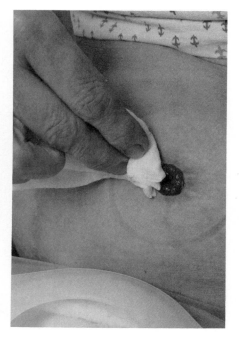

8 When the irrigant has finished draining, instruct the client to fold the top end of the irrigation sleeve twice and to secure it with a closure clamp. This will protect her from the forceful rush of the return. It will usually take around 45 minutes for a complete evacuation, with the initial return occurring within the first 15–20 minutes. During the final 15–20 minutes, the client should be encouraged to ambulate to facilitate evacuation. If there is no return, instruct the client to massage her abdomen or drink warm fluids to stimulate peristalsis. *Note: If you are keeping output records, you will need to measure the return. To do this, either fold up the tail of the irrigation sleeve and secure it with the other closure clamp or allow the return to flow directly into a bed pan. Subtract the amount of irrigant from the return.*

9 When a complete evacuation has been achieved, the client should remove the irrigation equipment and clean the peristomal skin with water and cleanser or a gentle soap. The stoma may be lightly patted with a soft cloth. When the peristomal skin has been rinsed and dried, the client may then apply a drainable pouch or the appliance appropriate for her needs.

Evaluating

10 Inspect and palpate the client's abdomen to assess for gastric distention, which can be indicative of an incomplete evacuation. Assess the stoma and peristomal skin for color and integrity. Document the procedure, noting the amount of irrigant and the character and amount of the return. If client teaching took place, document the client's performance.

DRAINING A CONTINENT ILEOSTOMY (KOCK POUCH)

Assessing

1 To assess the need for draining the internal pouch, inspect the client's abdomen and gently palpate the abdomen exterior to the pouch to determine the amount of fecal content. Assess the client's knowledge of the procedure, and explain why it is performed.

Planning

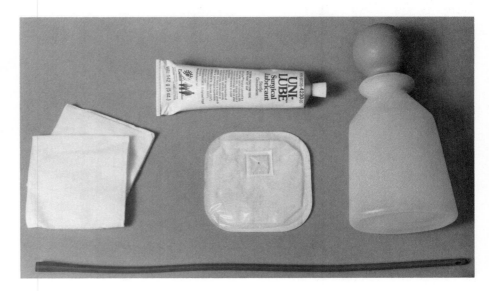

2 Assemble the following materials and equipment: an irrigation set with a 50-ml syringe; 30–40 ml of warm water; a number 28 silastic or teflon-coated catheter; water-soluble lubricant; and a stoma cap (as shown) or a bandage, depending on your client's need for drainage absorption. If the client is ambulatory, perform the procedure in the bathroom.

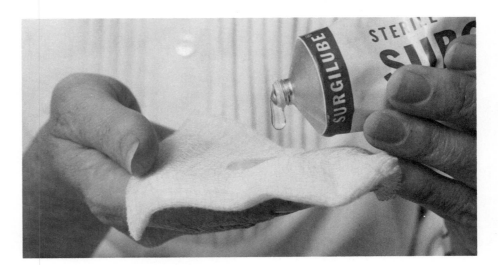

3 Squeeze some water-soluble lubricant onto a gauze pad or paper towel, and instruct the client to lubricate 7.5 cm (3 in.) of the catheter's tip.

(Continues)

Implementing

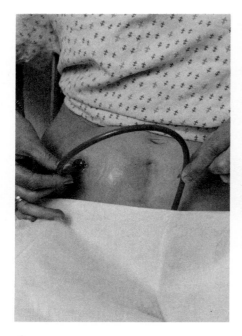

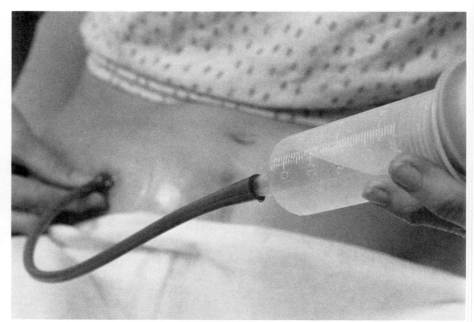

4 The client should next place the draining end of the catheter between her legs so that the fecal material can empty into the toilet (or into a 500-ml bed pan if she is performing the procedure in bed). She should then carefully insert the catheter's lubricated tip into the stoma, angling downward so that it can enter the nipple valve that leads into the internal pouch (reservoir). At approximately 5–7.5 cm (2–3 in.) when the client feels resistance, the catheter has entered the nipple valve. Instruct her to use gentle pressure as she enters the reservoir via the nipple valve. If the client has difficulty entering the reservoir, she should take deep breaths and press gently with the catheter during exhalations.

5 If fecal contents do not drain easily through the catheter after the reservoir has been intubated, instill 30–50 ml of warm water through the catheter with a 50-ml syringe, and try again. The client also may try bearing down with her abdominal muscles,

pressing gently on the abdomen exterior to the pouch, or moving the catheter gently in and out of the pouch. *Note: The pouch should be flushed with water on a daily basis to remove the fecal residue.*

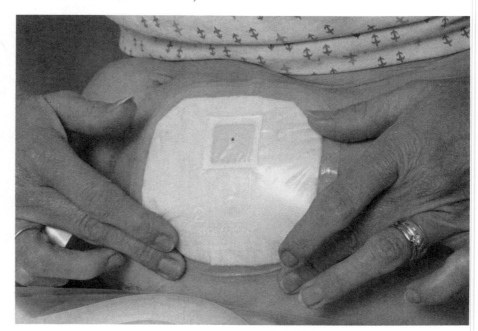

6 When the ileostomy has been drained, have the client remove the catheter, clean the peristomal skin, and apply a stoma cap (as shown) or a bandage.

Evaluating

7 Observe for stomal bleeding. Slight bleeding is normal, but report large amounts immediately. Monitor the client for indications of fluid volume deficit, and increase the fluid intake to 8 to 10 glasses per day if indicated. Also, continue to assess the client for the following indicators of peritonitis, the most frequently occurring complication of this surgery in the early postoperative stage: fever, abdominal tenderness, elevated pulse, and an absence of bowel sounds. Document the procedure and your observations.

Managing Rectal Elimination and Distention

ADMINISTERING A NONRETENTION ENEMA

Assessing and Planning

1 Describe the procedure to the client and explain why it has been prescribed. Gather the following information: the time, amount, and character of the last stool; an evaluation of sphincter control; and the ability to ambulate to the bathroom. This information will assist you in your evaluation of the return and enable you to assemble the appropriate equipment.

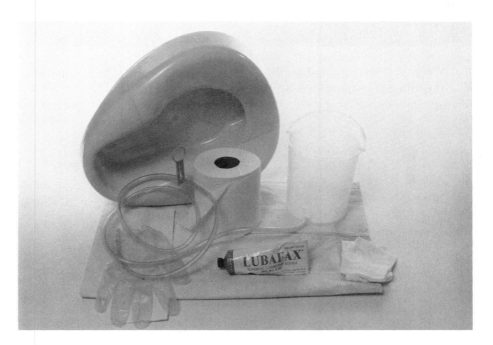

2 Assemble the following equipment: a container and tubing with a clamp for delivering the enema solution, a bed-saver pad, water-soluble lubricant, toilet paper, disposable gloves, 4 × 4 gauze pads, and a bed pan if the client has limited sphincter control or is nonambulatory. Prepare the prescribed amount of enema solution and warm it to 40.5° C (105° F) or as prescribed. You can either hang the solution container on an IV pole or place it on a bedside stand elevated 30–45 cm (12–18 in.) above the client's abdomen.

(Continues)

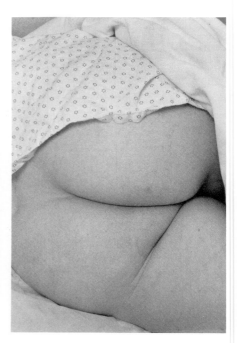

3 Flush air from the tubing by opening the tube clamp and allowing the solution to flow to the end of the tubing. Then reclamp the tube.

5 Pull the curtain to ensure privacy, and assist the client into a left side-lying position with the right knee flexed (Sim's position). This position will enhance the flow of enema solution into the client's sigmoid colon. Place a bed-saver pad under the hips and expose the buttocks. For optimal hydrostatic pressure, suspend the enema solution 30–45 cm (12–18 in.) above the client's abdomen. If the client has poor sphincter tone, place her on a bed pan in a supine position.

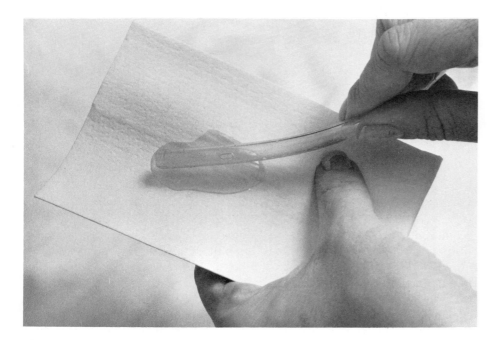

4 Lubricate the tip of the tube with water-soluble lubricant, usually around 5 cm (2 in.) for the adult and 2.5 cm (1 in.) for the child.

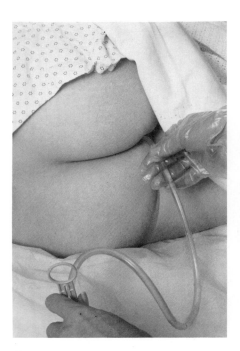

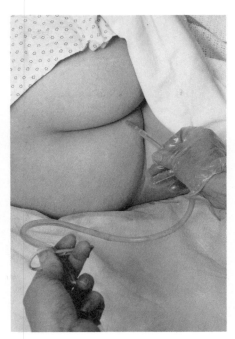

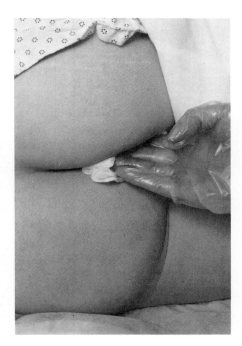

6 Apply a clean glove and separate the client's buttocks. Insert the tube 5–10 cm (2–4 in.) toward the umbilicus, past both the external and internal sphincters. For infants and small children, insert the tube 2.5–7.5 cm (1–3 in.). Be sure to avoid external hemorrhoids, and be very gentle if the client has internal hemorrhoids. Let the solution flow slowly to prevent cramping. Advise the client to breathe in deeply through her mouth if she experiences discomfort. If cramps occur, stop the flow until the cramps subside; then start the flow again, slowly.

7 When the solution has been instilled, clamp and then gently remove the tube.

8 If the client has difficulty retaining the solution for the usual 5- to 10-minute period, press the anus firmly with tissues or gauze, and encourage her to keep her upper body flat until she is allowed to expel the solution. Then either assist the client into the bathroom or, if she cannot ambulate, assist her onto a bed pan in Fowler's position. If indicated, instruct the client not to flush the toilet so that you can inspect the returns. Provide her with materials for perianal cleansing after the solution has been expelled, as well as a washcloth for handwashing if she is on bed rest.

Evaluating

9 Evaluate the return, and document the procedure.

ADMINISTERING A RETENTION ENEMA

Assessing and Planning

1 Familiarize yourself with the steps for giving a nonretention enema in the preceding procedure. Explain the procedure and position the client accordingly.

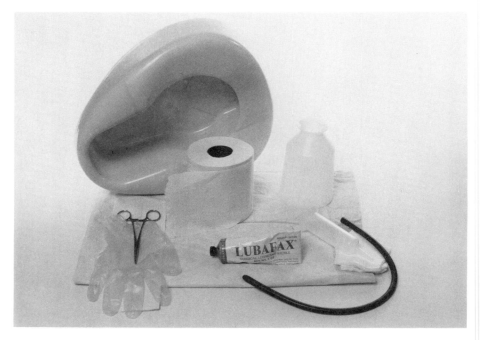

2 Assemble the following materials: a 50-ml syringe barrel; rectal tube or a catheter, 20–22F for an adult, 12–18F for a child; tubing clamp or hemostat; water-soluble lubricant; toilet paper; 4 × 4 gauze pads; bed-saver pad; bed pan (optional, depending on the client's sphincter tone and ability to ambulate to the bathroom); and the prescribed enema solution warmed to no more than 40.5° C (105° F) to minimize the stimulation of peristalsis (or obtain a commercially prepared enema such as a Fleets).

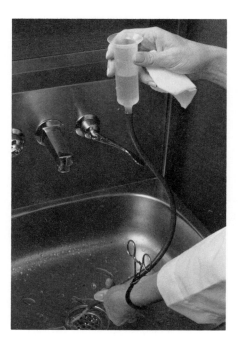

3 To avoid instilling air into the client's rectum, pour a small amount of solution into the syringe barrel and slowly flush the solution through the tubing just until it begins to drain out the distal end. When the solution reaches the end of the tube, pinch the tubing or clamp it. Do not allow the solution to drain out of the tubing because a loss of solution could diminish its desired therapeutic effect.

4 Lubricate the tip of the tubing with a water-soluble lubricant.

Implementing

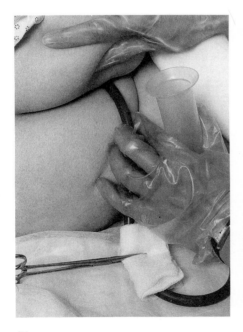

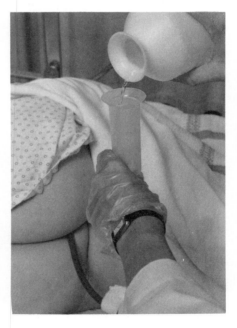

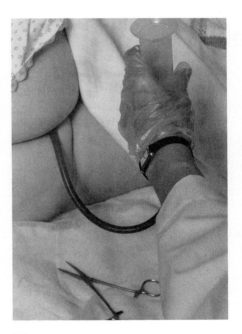

5 Apply gloves. Then separate the client's buttocks, and gently insert the tube toward the umbilicus, past both the external and internal sphincters. Use care to avoid traumatizing external and internal hemorrhoids if they are present.

6 Fill the barrel of the syringe with the remaining solution.

7 Then unclamp the tubing and raise the level of the barrel to achieve adequate hydrostatic pressure. The solution should be instilled slowly to avoid stimulating peristalsis because the client will need to retain the enema for at least 1 hour.

(Continues)

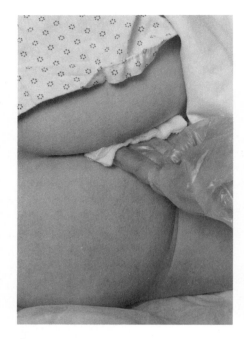

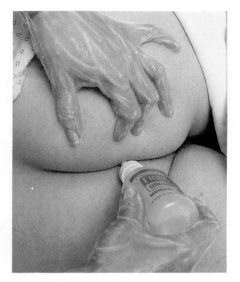

8 When the solution has been instilled, gently remove the tube and press firmly on the client's anus for a few moments, using a gauze pad or toilet paper (or the client may wish to do this herself). Advise the client to lie flat for 30 minutes to help prevent the stimulation of peristalsis. Before leaving the room, be sure a call light and bed pan are within reach in case she is unable to retain the solution. When the prescribed retention time has elapsed, assist the client into the bathroom or onto a bed pan as indicated. *Note: If the client is unable to retain an enema solution, a Foley catheter can be inserted, following the steps for inserting a rectal tube in the next procedure. After insertion past the external and internal sphincters, inflate the balloon with the designated amount of air. Then pull the balloon gently against the anal sphincter to seal the rectum.*

9 If a Fleets enema has been prescribed, separate the client's buttocks, and gently insert the prelubricated tip into the anus. Then raise the base of the container to avoid instilling air into the rectum, and squeeze the container to instill the solution.

Evaluating

10 If the procedure necessitates your observation of the return, do so at this time. If an oil-based retention enema was instilled, determine whether a cleansing enema needs to be instilled next. Document the procedure.

INSERTING A RECTAL TUBE

Assessing and Planning

1 A rectal tube can be inserted to relieve gastric distention when the distention is caused by flatus. However, you should first auscultate the client's abdomen for bowel sounds. An absence of bowel sounds in a rigid abdomen can mean that an obstruction or paralytic ileus, rather than flatus, is causing the distention; either condition necessitates immediate medical intervention.

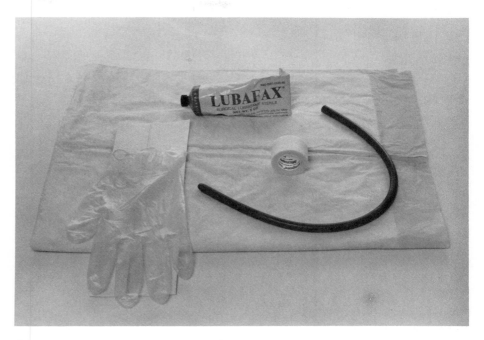

2 Assemble the following materials: a rectal tube or a catheter, 22–24F for adults or 12–18F for children; water-soluble lubricant; hypoallergenic tape; a bed-saver pad; and disposable gloves. You will also need a flatus bag or a receptacle to collect potential fecal discharge, such as a stool specimen container. Or wrap the draining end of the tube or catheter with gauze and tape. Explain the procedure to the client and provide privacy.

Implementing

3 Assist the client into a Sim's position, and place a bed-saver pad under the buttocks. Lubricate the tip of the tube with water-soluble lubricant, apply gloves, and insert the tube into the rectum 7.5–10 cm (3–4 in.), past both the external and internal sphincters. (For a child, insert the tube 2.5–7.5 cm [1–3 in.].)

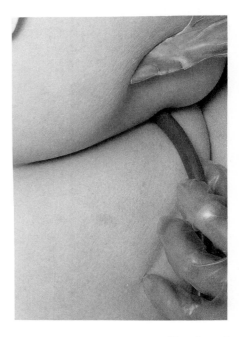

(Continues)

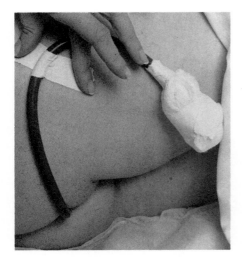

4 If relief from distention is not immediate, tape the tube to the thigh so that the client can have mobility without dislodging the tube. *Caution: To minimize the potential for rectal irritation or a loss in sphincter tone, do not leave the tube indwelling for longer than 20–30 minutes.* At the appropriate time, remove the tube and clean or discard it, depending on agency policy. Wash your hands, and document the procedure.

Evaluating

5 Continue to assess the client for distention, and intervene accordingly.

TESTING STOOL FOR OCCULT BLOOD

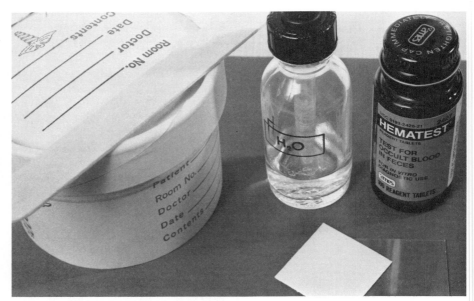

If possible, advise the client not to eat red meat for 24 hours prior to testing. Obtain a stool specimen, using gloves while handling the feces. If the client is unable to defecate, you might need to obtain the specimen during a digital rectal exam. Note the presence of hemorrhoids, which if present, may give a false-positive reading.

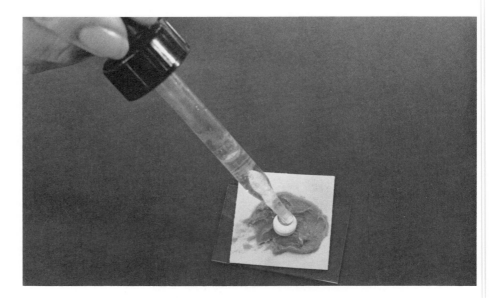

Smear the stool onto the filter paper with a tongue blade or with your gloved finger if you have performed a digital exam. Place the filter paper on a glass or procelain plate, and add the prescribed reagent. In this photo, the reagent is a tablet that is moistened with drops of water.

The type of reagent will vary, however, depending on the type of test performed. Finally, observe the filter paper for color changes. In many tests, the filter paper will turn blue if the feces contain blood. Wash your hands and record the procedure and the results.

References

Adrian L: Intestinal neoplasms and inflammatory processes. In: *Manual of Nursing Therapeutics: Applying Nursing Diagnoses to Medical Disorders,* 2d ed. Swearingen PL. St. Louis: Mosby, 1990.

Bard Interventional Products: *Care of a Percutaneous Endoscopic Gastrostomy (PEG) and the Button Replacement Gastrostomy.* Billerica, MA: CR Bard, 1987.

Bowers AC, Thompson JM: *Clinical Manual of Health Assessment,* 3d ed. St. Louis: Mosby, 1988.

Broadwell DC, Jackson BS: *Principles of Ostomy Care.* St. Louis: Mosby, 1982.

Brown PA: Gastrointestinal disorders. In: *Manual of Nursing Therapeutics,* 2d ed. Swearingen PL. St. Louis: Mosby, 1990.

Given BA, Simmons SJ: *Gastroenterology in Clinical Nursing,* 4th ed. St. Louis: Mosby, 1984.

Huth MM, O'Brien ME: The gastrostomy feeding button. *Pediatr Nurs* 1987; 13(4):241–245.

Keen J: Gastrointestinal dysfunctions. In: *Manual of Critical Care: Applying Nursing Diagnoses to Adult Critical Illness,* 2d ed. Swearingen PL et al. St. Louis: Mosby, 1991.

Keen J: Gastrointestinal disorders. In: *Manual of Nursing Therapeutics: Applying Nursing Diagnoses to Medical Disorders,* 2d ed. Swearingen PL. St. Louis: Mosby, 1990.

Kneisl CR, Ames SW: *Adult Health Nursing: A Biopsychosocial Approach.* Redwood City, CA: Addison-Wesley, 1986.

McConnell EA: Meeting the challenge of intestinal obstruction. *Nursing 87* (July) 1987; 34–42.

Metheny N: Measures to test placement of nasogastric and nasointestinal feeding tubes: A review. *Nurs Res* 1988; 37(6):324–329.

Patras AZ et al: Managing GI bleeding: It takes a two-track mind. *Nursing 88* (April) 1988; 68–74.

Petrillo MH: Enterostomal therapy. *Nurs Clin North Am* 1987; 22: 253–356.

Spence A, Mason E: *Human Anatomy and Physiology,* 3d ed. Redwood City, CA: Benjamin/Cummings, 1987.

Thompson JM et al: *Mosby's Manual of Clinical Nursing,* 2d ed. St. Louis: Mosby, 1989.

Wicks LJ: Treatment modalities for colorectal cancer. *Semin Oncol Nurs* 1986; 2:242–248.

Chapter 6

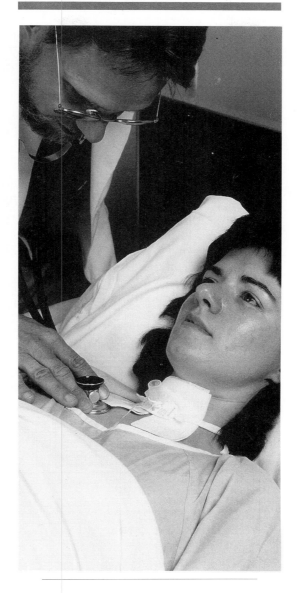

Managing
Respiratory
Procedures

CHAPTER OUTLINE

ASSESSING THE RESPIRATORY SYSTEM

The Respiratory System

Nursing Assessment Guideline

Examining the Thorax

Inspecting
Palpating for Thoracic Expansion
Palpating for Fremitus and Crepitation (Subcutaneous Emphysema)
Percussing
Auscultating

MAINTAINING PATENT AIRWAYS

Nursing Guidelines to Artificial Airways

Oropharyngeal Tube
Nasopharyngeal Tube
Endotracheal Tube
Tracheostomy Tube
Tracheostomy Button

Inserting Artificial Airways

Inserting an Oropharyngeal Airway
Inserting a Nasopharyngeal Airway

Performing Mouth-to-Mask Ventilation

Managing Routine Tracheostomy Care

Suctioning the Client with a Tracheostomy
Managing Tracheostomy Cuffs
Providing Tracheostomy Hygiene

MANAGING RESPIRATORY THERAPY

Administering Oxygen, Humidity, and Aerosol Therapy

Nursing Guidelines to Devices Used in the Delivery of Oxygen, Humidity, and Aerosols

Low-Flow System
High-Flow System
Simple Face Mask (Low-Flow System)
Nasal Cannula (Low-Flow System)
Partial Rebreathing Mask (Low-Flow System)
Nonrebreathing Mask (Low-Flow/High-Flow System)
Venturi (Air-Entrainment) Mask (High-Flow System)
CPAP Mask
Oxygen Hood
Incubator (Isolette)
Croupette
Oxygen Analyzers
Aerosol Face Mask
Tracheostomy Collar
T-Piece

Converting a Nonrebreathing Mask to a Partial Rebreathing Mask
Assembling a Venturi Delivery System
Setting Up an Oxygen System with Humidification
Delivering Heated Humidity
Assembling a Nebulizer

Employing Techniques for Lung Inflation

Instructing Clients in Deep-Breathing Exercises
Assisting with Coughing
Using Incentive Spirometers
Assisting with IPPB

Performing Chest Physiotherapy

Percussing, Vibrating, and Draining the Adult
Percussing, Vibrating, and Draining the Infant or Small Child

MANAGING THE CLIENT WITH A CHEST TUBE

Nursing Guidelines to a Disposable Closed Chest Drainage System

Suction Control Chamber
Water Seal Chamber
Collection Chamber

Monitoring the Client with a Chest Tube

Assisting with the Removal of a Chest Tube

Assessing the Respiratory System

THE RESPIRATORY SYSTEM

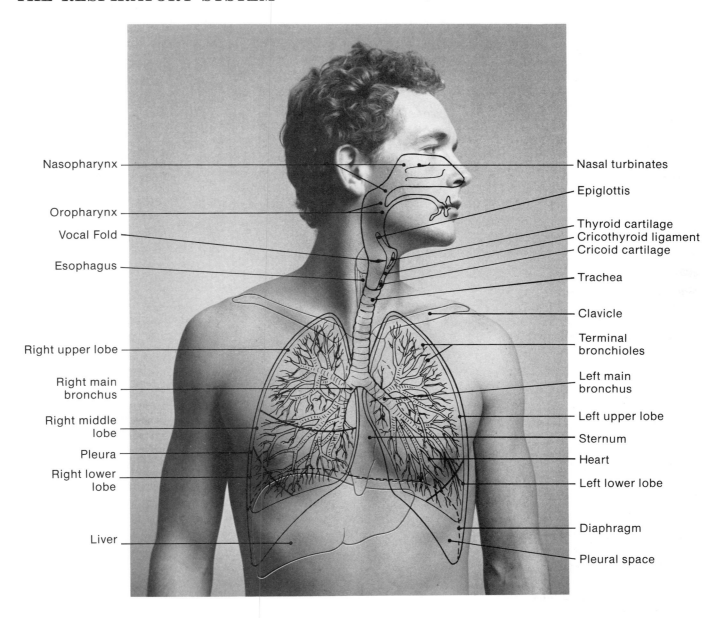

Nasopharynx

Oropharynx

Vocal Fold

Esophagus

Right upper lobe

Right main bronchus

Right middle lobe

Pleura

Right lower lobe

Liver

Nasal turbinates

Epiglottis

Thyroid cartilage
Cricothyroid ligament
Cricoid cartilage

Trachea

Clavicle

Terminal bronchioles

Left main bronchus

Left upper lobe

Sternum

Heart

Left lower lobe

Diaphragm

Pleural space

Nursing Assessment Guideline

To assess your client's respiratory system, you need to interview him or her for subjective data, take vital signs, and examine the thorax. A comprehensive nursing care plan includes a complete evaluation for the following subjective data:

Personal factors: age, occupation—for example, coal mining or history of working with chemicals or other toxins; geographic history

History or family history of: bronchitis, tuberculosis, pneumonia, lung cancer, emphysema, asthma, allergies, surgery for lung or breathing disorders

Smoking: history, past and present; amount; live or work with smokers

Pollutants: environmental and/or occupational

Psychologic stressors

History or presence of: colds, respiratory infections, cough; frequency of same

Medications: for example, flu vaccine, pneumococcal pneumonia vaccine, dates of same; over-the-counter or prescription; use of vaporizer or nebulizer; oxygen

Chest x-ray film: frequency, date of most recent

Pulmonary function test: frequency, date of most recent

Presence of: fever/chills, diaphoresis, fatigue, postnasal drip, chest pain

Activity intolerance

Recent weight loss/gain

Peripheral edema

Alterations in breathing: painful, labored, oral, noisy, wheezing, shortness of breath, paroxysmal nocturnal dyspnea, relation to activity

Cough: duration, frequency, character, productive or nonproductive, activated by which factors

Sputum: color, frequency, odor, amount, consistency, hemoptysis

EXAMINING THE THORAX

INSPECTING

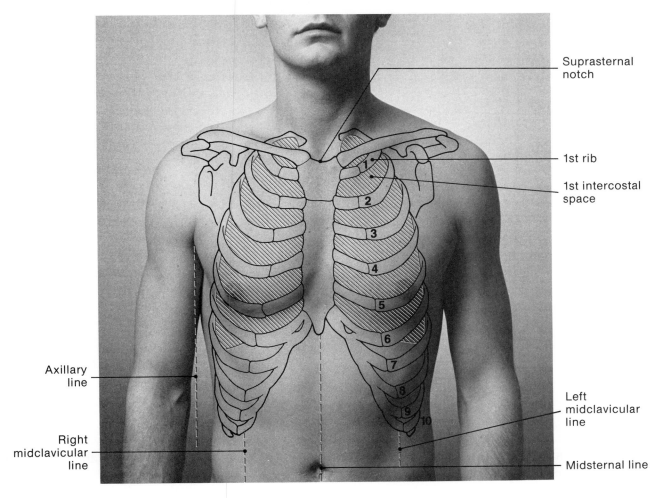

Familiarize yourself with these overlays so that you can identify thoracic locations by intercostal space and anatomic landmark. Explain the assessment procedure to the client and ask him to lower his gown to the waist. Be sure to provide the client with a towel or a bath blanket for warmth and privacy. If possible, the client should sit on the edge of the bed and dangle his legs to promote optimal chest excursion. Inspect the anterior, lateral, and posterior chest, noting anteroposterior diameter and the symmetry of chest movement. An increased anteroposterior diameter, "barrel

chest," is often found in clients with emphysema. The client also might have deformities, such as scoliosis or kyphosis, that can alter aeration. Observe for scarring from trauma or previous thoracic surgeries. Also inspect the extremities and note the temperature and texture of the skin. Does the client have digital clubbing, a swelling or "drumstick" appearance of the extremity tips frequently found in clients with pulmonary disease? Also observe for the presence of cyanosis in the distal extremities, nail beds, conjunctiva, lips, tips of the ears, or nose. Assess the rate, depth, and

rhythm of the respirations while the client is unaware that you are doing so and therefore will be less likely to alter them. The healthy adult will have a rate of 12–20 even and moderate breaths per minute; the young child will have 20–25; and the infant can have 40 or more. Children younger than age 6 or 7 breathe using their abdominal muscles. Individuals older than age 6 or 7 who use their abdominal muscles for respirations may have thoracic problems. Note the client's ratio of inspiration to expiration, which normally is 1:1–1:2. With chronic obstructive pulmonary

(Continues)

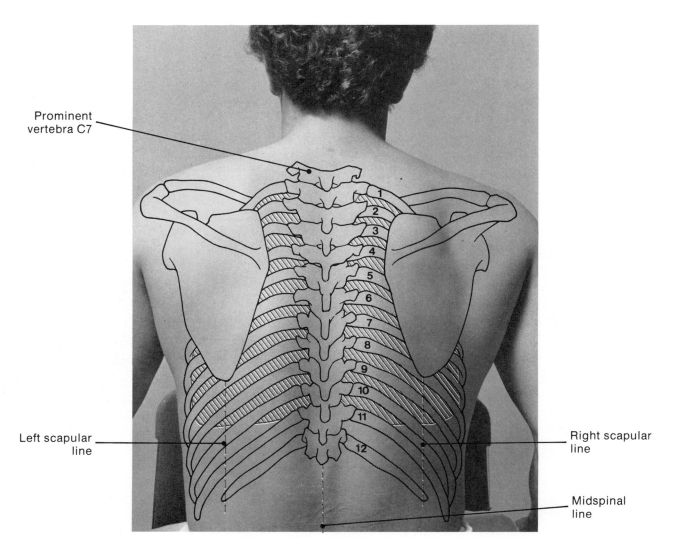

Prominent vertebra C7

Left scapular line

Right scapular line

Midspinal line

disease (COPD), the expiration is prolonged, for example, 1:3–1:4. Also listen to the respirations to detect labored breathing (increased work of breathing) or congestion. Observe for indications of labored breathing, such as the use of accessory muscles while breathing (for example, neck or shoulder muscles), flared nostrils, or bulging of intercostal spaces during expiration. Clients with breathing difficulties might sit up and lean forward to facilitate respirations. Finally, note the position of the trachea, which is normally at the midline. Record any deviation and the side to which it deviates. With pneumothorax and pleural effusion, it might deviate away from the affected side; with atelectasis, it can deviate toward the affected side.

PALPATING FOR THORACIC EXPANSION

Place your hands together at the base of the sternum so that your thumbs meet (as shown).

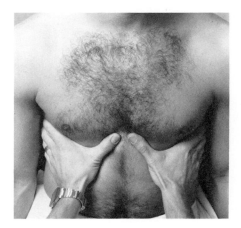

Instruct the client to inhale deeply. Observe the quality and symmetry of the expansion. If one side moves more than the other, there might be a lung pathology, pneumothorax, an obstruction of a major bronchus, or the client might be protecting a fractured rib or avoiding discomfort. In the healthy adult, your thumbs should separate 5.0–7.5 cm (2–3 in.). Repeat the assessment posteriorly.

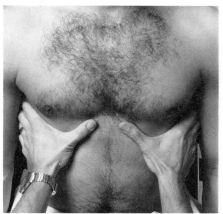

PALPATING FOR FREMITUS AND CREPITATION (SUBCUTANEOUS EMPHYSEMA)

Fremitus is the vibration of the thoracic wall that is felt over the chest when a person speaks. Position your hand over a lung segment (right photo), and instruct the client to say "ninety-nine" so that you can feel the vibration on the palmar surface. Continue the assessment over the lung segments, progressing from right to left (or vice versa), and from the top of the chest to the bottom, repeating the assessment on the posterior chest. The response normally should be equal when comparing one side of the chest to the symmetric area on the opposite side. An increase in fremitus is often found in clients with lung abscesses or with consolidation, as in the case of pneumonia, because the density of the tissues will increase the transmission of the vibrations. A decrease or absence in fremitus will be found in clients with COPD, pneumothorax, or pleural effusion when additional air or fluid or a fibrous thickening creates an additional layer through which the vibrations must be transmitted. Fremitus is normally greater at parasternal or intrascapular areas.

Palpation also can be performed to assess for crepitation (subcutaneous emphysema), a crackling sound or sensation felt in the subcutaneous tissues. It is usually caused by the presence of a foreign body, such as a tracheostomy tube or chest tube, and it is located in the area around the foreign body.

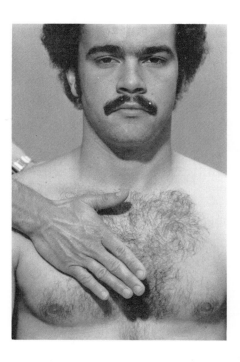

PERCUSSING

Percussion will help you determine whether underlying structures are solid or filled with air or fluid. Percussion of the thorax is performed by placing a middle finger over an intercostal space and sharply striking that finger with the opposite middle finger to elicit sounds. Hollow sounds, referred to as resonance, mostly will be heard over the greater portions of the healthy lung. Hyperresonance, which is booming and low in pitch, normally may be heard in children with thin chest walls. It also will be found in clients with hyperinflated lungs or where there is an increase in pleural air, for example in clients with emphysema or a pneumothorax. Dullness will be elicited over dense lung areas in clients with pneumonia or atelectasis, but it is normally heard over the heart and liver. When percussing, you can follow the same pattern used for auscultating (see p. 332). The assessment should progress down one side of the chest, going from right to left (or vice versa) so that each side is checked against the symmetrical area on the opposite side, and repeated on the posterior (or anterior) chest.

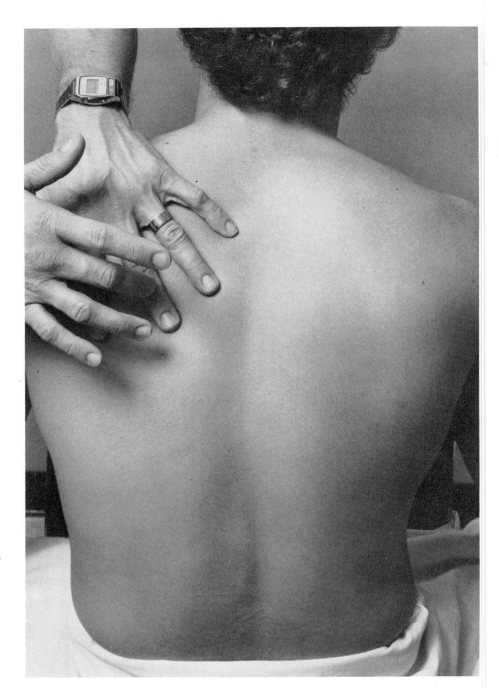

AUSCULTATING

Warm the diaphragm of the stethoscope between your hands before placing it on the client's skin. Instruct the client to breathe through his mouth, more slowly and deeply than usual. Listen to at least one full breath in each position, comparing one side of the chest to the symmetrical area on the opposite side of the chest. (See next page for auscultation patterns.)

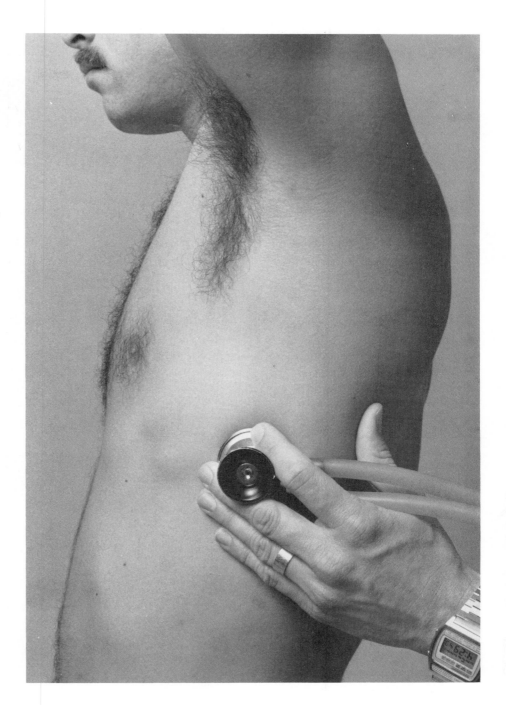

Follow the pattern in these photos for auscultating your client's chest. Listen for normal breath sounds (see Table 6-1), which include vesicular, bronchial, and bronchovesicular sounds; note their intensity, decrease in intensity, or absence from one auscultation site when compared to its symmetrical opposite. Vesicular sounds are soft and swishing and are considered normal when heard over the peripheral lung, but they are abnormal when heard over the large airways. A decrease in their sound over a segment of the peripheral lung might be found with emphysema, in the presence of pleural fluid, or with a pneumothorax. Bronchial sounds are louder, coarser, and of longer duration, and they can be heard over the trachea and bronchi during inhalation and exhalation. They should not be heard over the normal peripheral lung, but they may be elicited over lungs of clients with some type of consolidation, such as a lung tumor or atelectasis. Bronchovesicular sounds are moderate in both pitch and intensity and are heard at the sternal borders of the major bronchi. Assume there is an abnormality if they are heard over the peripheral lung, which can occur with consolidation.

Review Table 6-2 to help you identify adventitious (added or abnormal) breath sounds. Regardless of the terminology used in your agency to describe adventitious sounds, it is important that you determine whether the added sounds you hear are continuous or discontinuous, low or high in pitch, fine or coarse, and whether they are heard during inhalation or exhalation. Coarse crackles (rales), associated with resolving pneumonia or pulmonary edema, are often heard during inhalation and may be eliminated by cough-

[handwritten in left margin: Do breath sounds clear with cough]

[handwritten in center margin: State location]

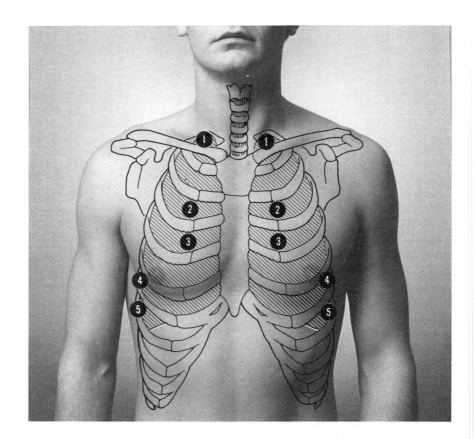

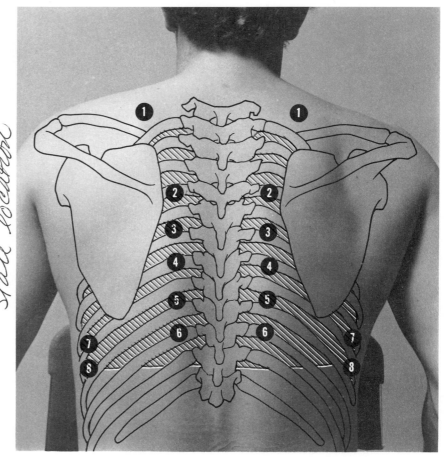

Table 6-1   Assessing Normal Breath Sounds

Type	Normal site	Duration	Characteristics
Vesicular	Peripheral lung	I > E	Soft and swishing sounds. Abnormal when heard over the large airways.
Bronchial	Trachea and bronchi	E > I	Louder, coarser, and of longer duration than vesicular. Abnormal if heard over peripheral lung.
Bronchovesicular	Sternal border of the major bronchi	E = I	Moderate in pitch and intensity. Abnormal if heard over peripheral lung.

I = inspiration; E = expiration.

SOURCE: Swearingen PL: *Manual of Critical Care: Applying Nursing Diagnoses to Adult Critical Illness,* 2d ed. St. Louis: Mosby, 1991.

ing when they are caused by secretions in the airway. Fine crackles, found in interstitial lung disease or heart failure, are heard late during inspiration, usually over lung bases, and are rarely cleared by coughing. Wheezes (sibilant rhonchi) are musical and high in pitch and are most often associated with bronchial asthma or COPD. They are best heard over the larynx during exhalation; however, wheezes of different pitches and sounds might at times be heard simultaneously over all lung fields. Rhonchi occur with increased sputum production and are usually heard during exhalation as air passes through passages narrowed by mucosal swelling or secretions. They are usually cleared or lessened by coughing.

A pleural friction rub sounds like two pieces of sand paper rubbing together, and it is caused by the loss of normal pleural lubrication. It is typically heard over the anterolateral chest, and it can be caused, for example, by pleurisy.

Table 6-2   Adventitious Sounds*

Acoustic characteristics	Time-expanded waveform	ATS recommended term†	ACCP report‡	A current British usage	Other term(s)	Some common clinical associations
Discontinuous, interrupted, explosive sounds—loud, duration of about 10 msec. Low in pitch initial deflection width§ averaging 1.5 msec.		Coarse crackle	Rale	Crackle	Bubbling rales Coarse crepitations	Pulmonary edema Resolving pneumonia
Discontinuous, interrupted, explosive sounds—less loud than above and of shorter duration. They average less than 5 msec in duration and are lower in pitch. Initial deflection width§ averages about 0.7 msec.		Fine crackle	Rale	Crackle	Fine crepitations	Interstitial fibrosis
Continuous sounds—longer than 250 msec, high-pitched, dominant frequency of 400 Hz or more; a hissing sound.		Wheeze	Sibilant rhonchus	High-pitched wheeze	Sibilant rale Musical rale	Airway narrowing
Continuous sounds—longer than 250 msec, low-pitched, dominant frequency about 200 Hz or less; a snoring sound.		Rhonchus	Sonorous rhonchus	Low-pitched wheeze		Sputum production

*Used with permission from American Thoracic Society.

†From 1977, American Thoracic Society (ATS) ad Hoc Committee on pulmonary nomenclature.

‡From 1974 ATS/American College of Chest Physicians (ACCP) committee on pulmonary nomenclature.

§Time in msec from the onset of the crackle until the first deflection returns to the baseline.

Maintaining Patent Airways

Nursing Guidelines to Artificial Airways

**OROPHARYNGEAL
TUBE**

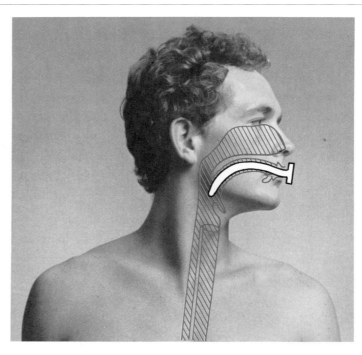

Description	S-shaped, plastic device that fits over the tongue and extends into the posterior pharynx. Available in infant, child, and adult sizes.
Uses	For clients requiring an assisted airway immediately postanesthesia, or for those who are semiconscious and in danger of obstructing their own airways with a displaced tongue. It also can be used when suctioning is required on a short-term basis, or as a bite blocker when used with an endotracheal tube.

Nursing Considerations

- To facilitate insertion and to keep the client's tongue from falling back into the pharynx, the client should be supine with a hyperextended neck unless it is contraindicated by head and neck injuries.
- After insertion, keep the client's head turned to the side to prevent aspiration from vomitus and secretions.
- Remove the airway every 4 hours and provide oral hygiene.
- The airway should not be discontinued until the client is conscious, can swallow on his own, and his gag and cough reflexes have returned.
- This airway is contraindicated in the conscious client because it stimulates the gag reflex.

NASOPHARYNGEAL TUBE

Description

Rubber or latex tube (also called trumpet) that extends from the naris to the hypopharynx. Large variation in sizes accommodates the infant to the adult.

Uses

For clients requiring short-term airway management when the oral route is contraindicated, or for those with a sensitive gag reflex. Also inserted to protect the nasal mucosa during nasopharyngeal or nasotracheal suctioning.

Nursing Considerations

- Prior to insertion, lubricate the tube with water-soluble lubricant, or topical anesthetic, if prescribed.
- For optimal fit, the diameter of the tube should be only slightly smaller than the diameter of the naris.
- To prevent pressure areas, rotate the tube to the alternate naris at least every 8 hours.
- Provide nasal hygiene to both nares.
- Nasotracheal suctioning should be done only when necessary because it can stimulate the vagus nerve and potentially may lead to bradycardia and cardiac arrest.

(Continues)

ENDOTRACHEAL TUBE

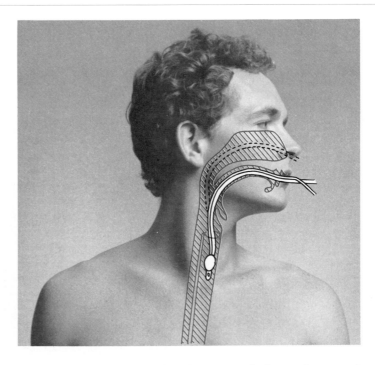

Description

Polyvinyl chloride curved tube that extends from the mouth or nose to just above the bifurcation of the trachea (carina). Inner and outer diameters of the tube are measured in millimeters, the length in centimeters. Sized to accommodate the newborn to the adult, with cuffed tubes available in adolescent and adult sizes. Has universal adaptors for use with mechanical ventilation.

Uses

Most commonly for clients receiving general anesthesia or in short-term emergency situations to provide a patent airway, facilitate suctioning, or provide a means for mechanical ventilation.

Nursing Considerations

- Turn the client to the side to prevent aspiration from vomitus and secretions.
- Keep the airway taped securely in place. Accidental extubation can be life threatening.
- To monitor tube slippage, mark the tube at the nose or mouth with indelible ink.
- Provide frequent oral and nasal hygiene.
- Oral tubes should be repositioned to the opposite side of the mouth every 8 hours to prevent pressure areas in the mouth. With nasal tubes, the nares should be evaluated frequently for breakdown.
- Hyperinflate the client's lungs with high concentrations of oxygen before, during, and after suctioning (see p. 345) to minimize hypoxemia.
- Because there is the risk of this tube slipping into the right main stem bronchus, monitor for symmetry of respiratory movement and the presence of bilateral breath sounds.
- To prevent unconscious clients from biting down on oral tubes, an oropharyngeal airway or a bite block can be inserted to keep the jaws apart.

- Provide means for communication; keep the call light within the client's reach.
- Frequently monitor cuff pressure to prevent tracheal necrosis. It should not be greater than 25 mm Hg.
- Continuous humidification or aerosol therapy via a T-piece is necessary to prevent drying of membranes and respiratory complications.
- Review Nursing Considerations for the tracheostomy tube. The nursing care plan is basically the same.

TRACHEOSTOMY TUBE

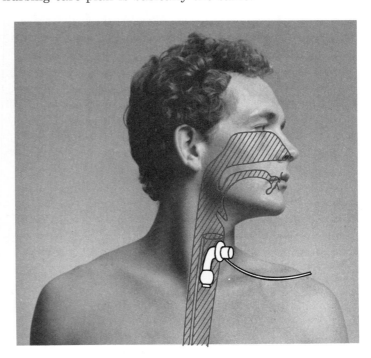

Description

Plastic, metal, or foam tube that extends from an incision in the anterior neck directly into the trachea. Available in infant to adult sizes, but smaller sizes generally come without cuffs. Single-cannula tubes indicated for short-term use; tubes with both inner and outer cannulas are most often used in long-term care. Can attach to mechanical ventilator with an adaptor.

Nursing Considerations

- To assess need for suctioning and patency of airway, frequently auscultate lung fields and trachea for breath sounds.
- To minimize the potential for infection and for client comfort, change the dressing around the tracheostomy as soon as blood and secretions collect.
- Hyperinflate the client's lungs with high concentrations of oxygen before, during, and after suctioning to minimize hypoxemia.
- Encourage turning, coughing, deep breathing, and range of motion exercises to help mobilize secretions.
- Continuous humidification or aerosol therapy via T-piece or tracheostomy collar is necessary to prevent drying of membranes and respiratory complications.
- If heated humidity is delivered, monitor the temperature frequently to prevent injury to the trachea. Keep it within 34°–36° C.

(Continues)

- Inflate cuffed tracheostomy tubes during eating, intermittent positive pressure breathing (IPPB), and mechanical ventilation.
- Provide a means for communication, and keep the call light within reach.
- Secure the tube carefully to prevent accidental dislodgement.
- Keep an identical, spare tracheostomy tube and obturator at the client's bedside.

TRACHEOSTOMY BUTTON

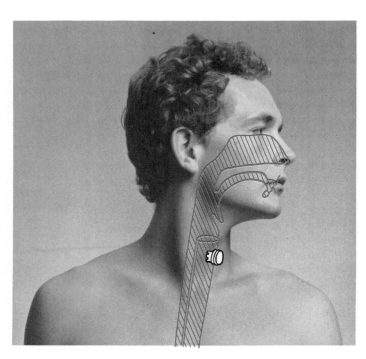

Description

Short tube that extends from the tracheal stoma to just inside the tracheal wall. Most come with adaptors for use with IPPB and manual resuscitator, and plugs for closing the button.

Uses

Maintains stoma for emergency airway management after the tracheostomy tube has been removed. It also can be used to wean client from ventilatory support.

Nursing Considerations

- The button allows the client to cough and breathe more easily than does a tracheostomy tube.
- Remove closure plug for suctioning and/or ventilating.
- Insert IPPB adaptor plug for ventilating.
- The client can speak when the button is plugged.
- To prevent skin irritation, keep stomal area clean with hydrogen peroxide. Dry thoroughly after rinsing with sterile water.
- Clean the cannula often, according to agency protocol, by immersing in hydrogen peroxide solution and rinsing with sterile water.

INSERTING ARTIFICIAL AIRWAYS

INSERTING AN OROPHARYNGEAL AIRWAY

Assessing and Planning

1   Choose the correct airway size. Generally, they are available in infant, child, and adult sizes. Wash your hands and explain the procedure to the client, even though she is semiconscious. Position her so that her neck is hyperextended, unless this position is contraindicated by a head or neck injury. You also can roll a large towel or small pillow and place it under the client's shoulders to increase the angle of the head tilt. Positioning her in this manner will open her airway and help keep the tongue away from the pharynx. Push up on the client's mandible (as shown) to prevent obstruction of the oral pharynx by her tongue.

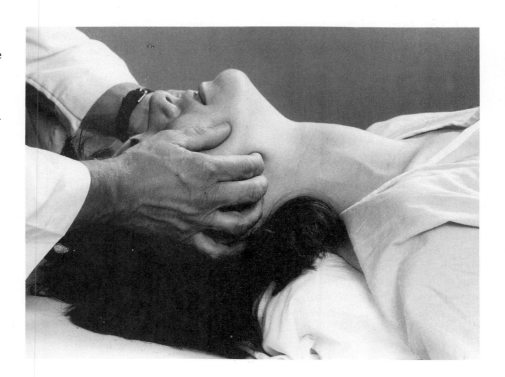

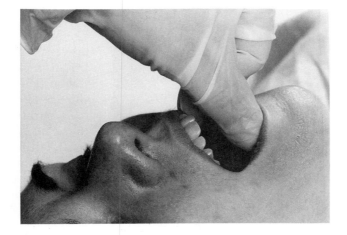

2   To open her mouth, apply gloves and employ the crossed-finger technique (as shown). In this position, your fingers will pop out of her mouth should she have a seizure or clamp down with her teeth. *Note: If you use a tongue blade instead, depress the tongue and place the airway directly over the tongue and into the back of the mouth.* Before inserting the artificial airway, make sure the client's airway is clear of obstructions.

(Continues)

Implementing

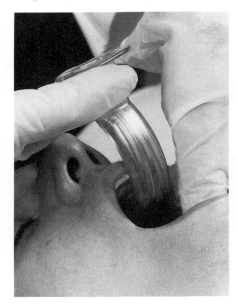

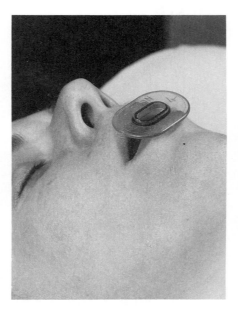

Evaluating

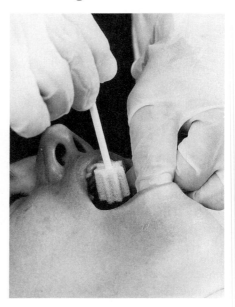

3 With your other hand, position the airway so that it is upside down, with the tip pointing upward toward the roof of the mouth. Insert it into the back of the mouth. Positioning it in this manner will depress the tongue and prevent tongue displacement into the posterior pharynx.

4 Turn the airway another 180 degrees so that its curve fits over the tongue. Turn the client to her side to prevent aspiration from vomitus and secretions. Wash your hands and document the procedure.

5 At least every 4 hours, remove the airway by gently pulling it downward and outward following the natural curve of the mouth. Use a gauze-covered tongue depressor or employ the crossed-finger technique to keep the client's mouth open while assessing the oral cavity and providing hygiene. The photo illustrates swabbing the mouth with a Toothette.

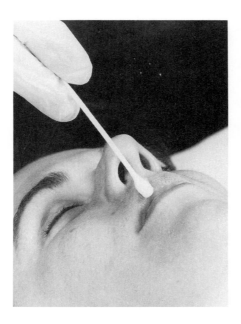

6 Moisturize the client's lips to prevent cracking and breakdown from the pressure of the airway's flange. The photograph illustrates the use of a cotton-tipped applicator saturated with a water-soluble lubricant. Following mouth care, reinsert the airway following the steps outlined above. Before discontinuing the airway, ensure that the client is at least semiconscious, that she can swallow on her own, and that gag and cough reflexes have returned.

INSERTING A NASOPHARYNGEAL AIRWAY

Assessing and Planning

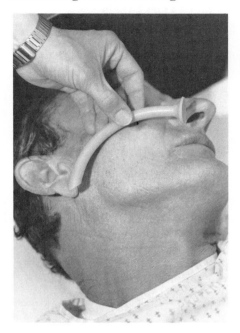

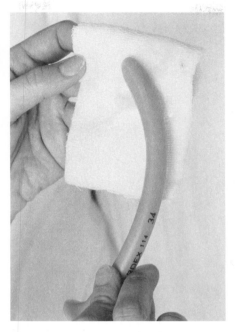

Implementing

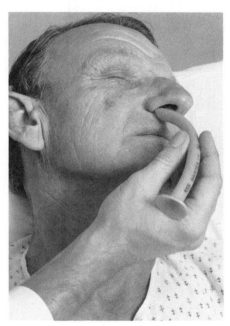

1 Explain the procedure to your client. Place him in semi-Fowler's to high-Fowler's position to enhance his respirations unless this position is contraindicated. Select an airway that extends from the earlobe to the naris. For optimal fit, the outer diameter of the airway should be only slightly smaller than that of the naris.

2 If you have an order for an anesthetic jelly, lubricate the entire length of the airway with the topical anesthetic. Otherwise, lubricate the airway with a water-soluble lubricant to facilitate its insertion.

3 Select the naris that looks more patent; gently insert the airway while pushing up the tip of the nose so that the tube follows the curve of the nasopharynx. If the naris you selected proves to be obstructed, intubate the other.

4 When the flange of the airway reaches the naris, the distal end of the airway should be correctly positioned in the hypopharynx.

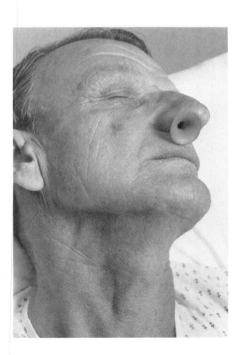

(Continues)

Evaluating

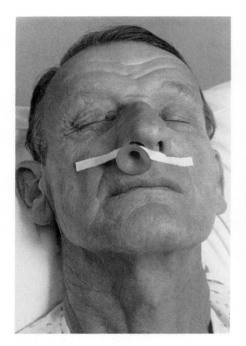

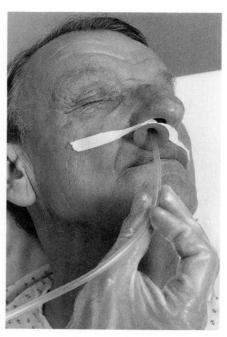

5 To prevent its expulsion, tape the airway in place by looping 1.25 cm (½ in.) of hypoallergenic tape over the area of the airway that is distal to the flange and adhering the rest of the tape to the skin above the client's upper lip. Use a skin preparation first if your client has sensitive skin. Wash your hands and document the procedure.

6 Prior to its removal, suction down the airway (see guidelines, p. 343) to remove the secretions. Be sure to rotate the airway to the other naris at least every 8 hours. Assess the naris for breakdown and provide materials for cleansing the naris and moisturizing the nasal mucosa.

PERFORMING MOUTH-TO-MASK VENTILATION

When a mask is available, mouth-to-mask ventilation replaces mouth-to-mouth ventilation to prevent the health care worker's mouth from coming into direct contact with the client's oral secretions. To position the client's head and neck appropriately, see photo and review the procedure, p. 339. Position the mask over the client's mouth, keeping the mask in place with your index finger and thumb and extending your other fingers over the client's jawline. Take a deep breath and position your mouth over the mouthpiece. Exhale and watch the client's chest rise and fall or listen for breath sounds. Continue until one of the following occurs:

- The client's spontaneous ventilations return.
- You are relieved by an individual trained in the procedure.
- Adjunct equipment arrives (e.g., mask and self-inflating bag or endotracheal tube).
- The attending physician arrives and requests that you stop.

MANAGING ROUTINE TRACHEOSTOMY CARE

SUCTIONING THE CLIENT WITH A TRACHEOSTOMY

Assessing and Planning

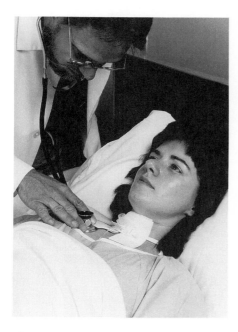

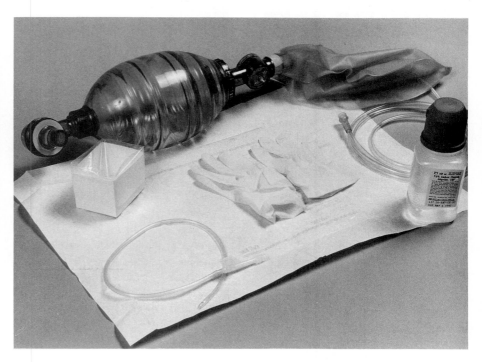

1 Evaluate the client's need for suctioning by bilaterally auscultating the lung fields to identify and locate secretions. If suctioning is needed, explain the procedure to the client and place her in Fowler's position unless it is contraindicated. Remember that suctioning is always done as needed rather than as a standard order; therefore frequent client assessment is crucial. Frequent suctioning may cause airway irritation, resulting in more secretions.

2 Assemble the following materials: sterile solution (usually normal saline), a sterile suction kit containing a suction catheter of the appropriate size, gloves, and basin; suction tubing; and a manual resuscitator, such as the Ambu or Laerdal, with a tracheostomy adaptor and an attached oxygen reservoir (optional) for delivering higher oxygen concentrations. The use of two gloves (one designated sterile to protect the client and one designated clean to protect the nurse's other hand) is recommended because of the potential for infection from the herpetic virus found in the oral secretions of some clients. *Note: To minimize the potential for hypoxia, make sure the outer diameter of the suction catheter is no greater than half of the inner diameter of the tracheostomy tube.*

(Continues)

3 Attach the resuscitator to source oxygen (as shown). When hyperinflating the client (using the "sigh maneuver") you will need to adjust the oxygen flowmeter to deliver 12–15 L/min or enough to ensure that the reservoir bag remains inflated during manual ventilation, which will provide the necessary oxygen concentration.

4 Wash your hands and loosen the cap on the sterile solution bottle. Open the sterile suction kit on a clean surface using the internal wrapping as a sterile field, and fill the sterile basin with the sterile solution.

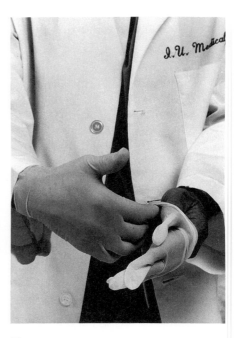

5 Put on sterile gloves, following the procedure in Chapter 1.

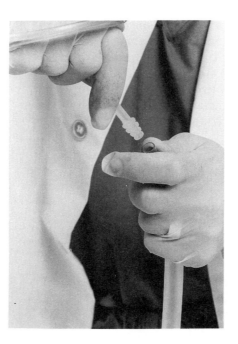

6 Attach the suction catheter to the suction tubing, holding the sterile catheter in your dominant hand and the suction tubing in your nondominant hand. *Note: The same catheter can be used during the entire procedure provided it does not become contaminated, and it is not used to suction the oropharynx or nasopharynx before suctioning or resuctioning the trachea. If either of these situations occurs, replace the contaminated catheter with a sterile one to prevent contaminating the respiratory tract.*

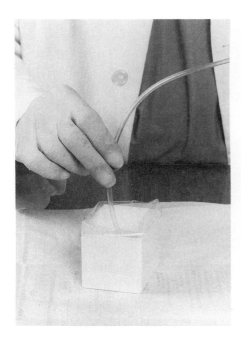

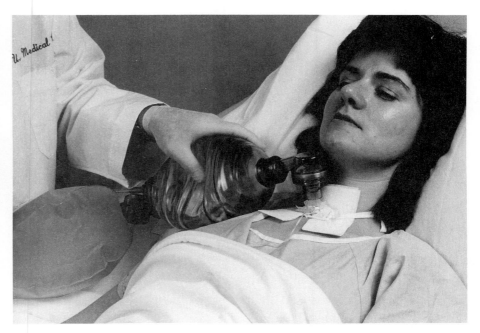

7 Set the suction regulator dial at 80–120 mm Hg. Submerge the tip of the catheter into the sterile solution, and briefly place your nondominant thumb over the suction port to produce suction. This not only tests the efficiency of the suction apparatus but also lubricates the catheter to facilitate its insertion into the trachea. In addition, it lubricates the inside of the catheter, which helps to prevent tenacious secretions from sticking to the tubing.

8 Using your nondominant hand, oxygenate your client with three to five deep lung inflations to help compensate for the oxygen you will remove during the suctioning process. To do this, turn the oxygen on, position the tracheostomy adaptor of the resuscitator directly over the tracheostomy tube, and compress the bag to deliver the oxygen. Wait for the client to exhale before administering each successive ventilation. Ideally, a second person should "sigh" the client. Because the second person can place both hands firmly around the resuscitation bag, there is less potential for trauma from manipulation of the bag. In addition, the second person can provide greater volume with two hands than that which can be provided with one hand.

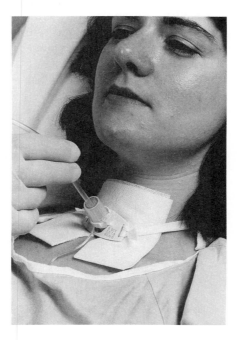

Implementing

9 Remove the oxygen device and position it on the bed or on the client's chest, with the tracheostomy adaptor facing up. With your dominant (sterile) hand, gently insert the catheter into the tracheostomy, keeping your nondominant thumb off the suction port. Insert the catheter as far as it will go, but do not use force. When you reach the carina or bronchial wall, withdraw the catheter 1–2 cm to prevent damaging the area.

(Continues)

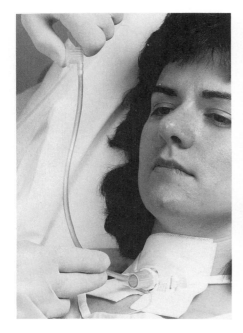

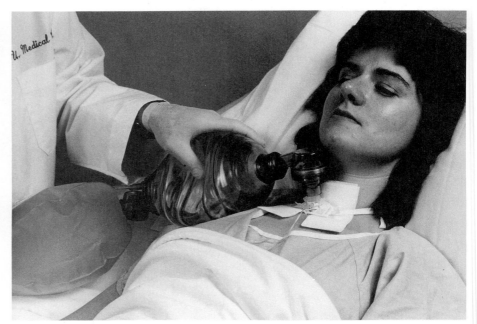

10 Place your nondominant thumb over the suction port to produce suction. Rotate the catheter between your dominant thumb and forefinger, gradually withdrawing the catheter as you apply intermittent suction by moving your nondominant thumb up and down on the suction port. This should prevent the catheter from adhering to the mucosa and damaging the bronchial wall. To minimize hypoxemia, do not suction for longer than 10–15 seconds during each suction attempt. Some experts suggest having the client turn the head to the right while you attempt to suction the left tracheobronchial tree, and the head to the left while you attempt to suction the right tracheobronchial tree. Although this technique is recommended, its efficacy has not been proved.

11 To prevent suction-induced hypoxemia, reoxygenate the client after every suction attempt, following the technique outlined in step 8.

12 If your client has a tracheostomy tube with an inflated cuff, before deflating the cuff (see p. 348), you will need to suction above the cuff to ensure removal of the secretions in the upper respiratory tract. First reoxygenate the client and rinse the catheter in the sterile solution. Suction the mouth and pharynx by employing the same technique used for suctioning the tracheostomy. When suctioning the pharynx, instruct the client to extend her tongue so that you can suction the area more readily.

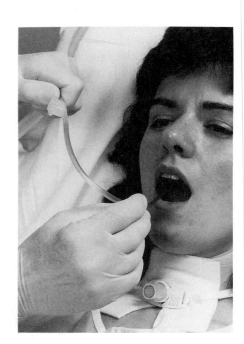

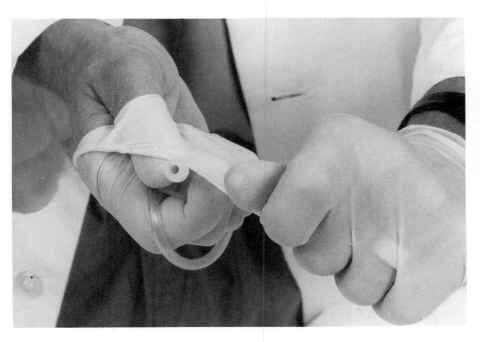

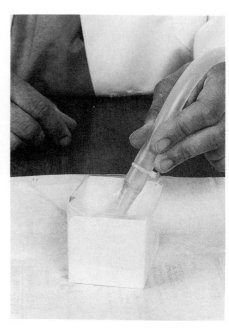

13 Dispose of the contaminated catheter by pulling your glove inside out over the catheter and depositing both into a waste container. Again, reoxygenate the client or attach her or his own delivery system, increasing the liter flow for a few minutes. Remember to turn the oxygen flow back to the regular prescribed rate.

14 Flush the suction tubing by applying suction while submerging the tubing in the same solution you used to rinse the sterile catheter.

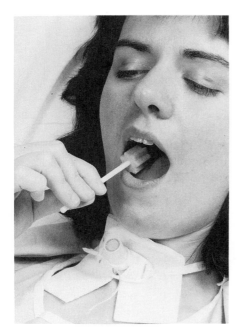

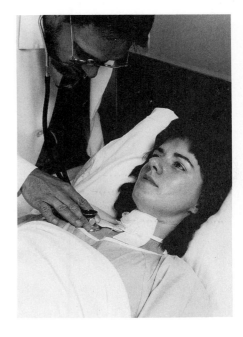

15 Provide your client with materials for oral hygiene. A Toothette, for example, is a convenient way to refresh the mouth.

Evaluating

16 Again auscultate the lung fields to evaluate the results of the suctioning. Optimally, the client will have absent or greatly diminished adventitious sounds and should exhibit nonlabored respirations. In addition, the apical pulse will be within her normal rate, indicating that suctioning has not stimulated the vagus nerve and slowed the heart rate. Document the procedure: Note the amount, color, odor, and consistency of the secretions and your client's response to the procedure. If secretions are tenacious, the physician might prescribe continuous aerosol or humidity via a T-piece or tracheostomy mask. Augment fluid intake unless it is medically contraindicated.

MANAGING TRACHEOSTOMY CUFFS

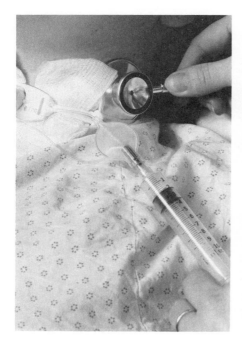

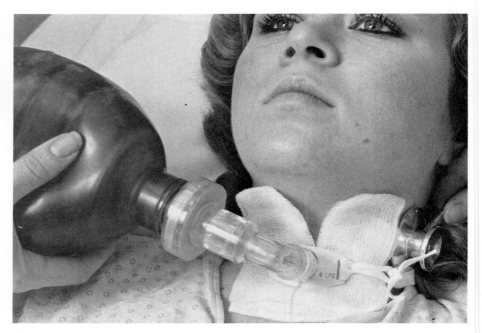

1   When properly using a high-volume/low-pressure (floppy) cuff, it is not necessary to deflate the cuff hourly, but it is important to inflate the cuff correctly when necessary, for example, when the client receives IPPB or if mechanical ventilation is used. With the aid of an assistant you can easily inflate the cuff. Attach a calibrated 10-cc syringe to the distal end of the cuff (the inflating balloon).

2   Have your assistant hyperinflate the client with a manual resuscitator as you slowly inject air into the cuff. At the point air movement is no longer heard when auscultating next to the cli-

ent's trachea, the cuff is inflated to the "just seal" point. In most situations, the inflating balloon will seal when the syringe is removed.

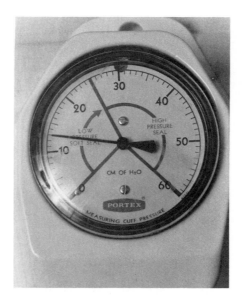

3   When a manometer (such as the one shown) is available, you can inflate the cuff on your own. In addition to the calibrated syringe, you will also need a three-way stopcock.

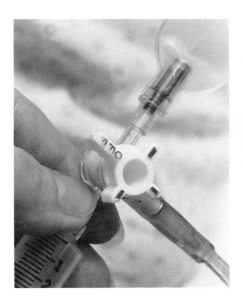

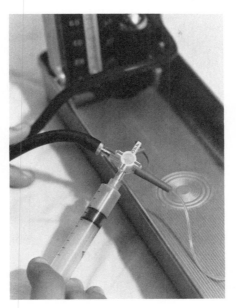

4 Attach the three ends of the stopcock to the inflating balloon, the manometer tubing, and the syringe. Open the stopcock to all ports (as shown). Inject air into the inflating balloon until the manometer reads 25 cm H_2O, or until it reaches the prescribed pressure. The cuff should now be properly inflated.

5 You also may use a blood pressure manometer in the same way. Inject air into the inflating balloon until the manometer reads 15 mm Hg or the prescribed pressure.

6 *Variation for Foam Cuffs:* If your client has a foam cuff, you will not inject air into the cuff to inflate it. Instead, when the port is open, ambient air will enter the balloon and conform it to the client's trachea.

7 The physician will aspirate air from the foam cuff prior to intubation or extubation, but it might be your responsibility to assess the cuff's proper functioning prior to the procedure.

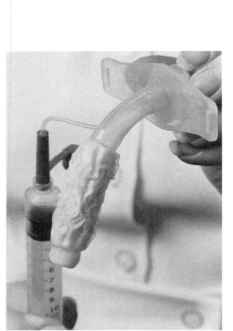

PROVIDING TRACHEOSTOMY HYGIENE

1 Wash your hands and obtain a sterile tracheostomy tray that contains the following: two soaking trays (bowls), gloves, plastic forceps, gauze sponges, unfilled gauze tracheostomy dressing, pipe cleaner, twill tape, cotton-tipped applicators, and overwrap; impervious plastic bag for disposal of used dressing and supplies; and sterile normal saline and hydrogen peroxide. Pour the hydrogen peroxide and normal saline into each of the sterile bowls. Apply the sterile gloves and remove the soiled tracheostomy dressing using the forceps. Avoid touching the dressing with your gloved hands. Deposit the dressing into the impervious plastic bag.

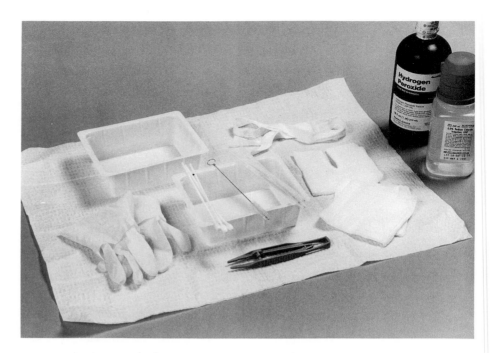

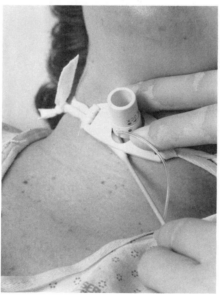

2 *Cleansing the Stoma Site:* Cleanse the stoma with a sterile cotton-tipped applicator that has been moistened with hydrogen peroxide. After you have cleansed the stomal site, swab the tube's flange. Rinse the stomal site with another sterile cotton-tipped applicator that has been moistened with sterile normal saline, and dry the area with sterile gauze pads. Be sure to record the condition of the stoma at least once a shift.

3 *Cleaning the Inner Cannula:* **Note:** *Not all tracheostomy tubes have an inner cannula.* During each suctioning and as necessary (or at least once during each shift), remove the inner cannula and immerse it in a solution of hydrogen peroxide.

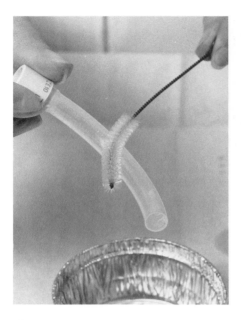

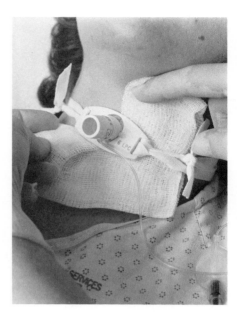

4 With a sterile test-tube brush, clean the cannula on both the outside and the inside, being certain to remove all the encrustations.

5 Rinse the cannula thoroughly with sterile saline. Suction the outer cannula and reinsert the inner cannula and lock it into position. *Caution: To prevent the formation of crusts in the outer cannula, the inner cannula should not be removed for longer than 5 minutes; if the client is on oxygen therapy or a respirator, the inner cannula must be replaced as soon as possible. Always have a sterile spare available.*

6 *Changing the Tracheostomy Dressing:* Insert the tracheostomy dressing so that the slit encircles the tracheostomy tube (as shown). If the client has a copious amount of drainage, it is a good idea to position the dressing with the slit side up, which will provide more surface area on the lower portion of the dressing to absorb the moisture. Although the dressing should be changed at least once a shift, more frequent changes are necessary if blood and secretions collect at the site.

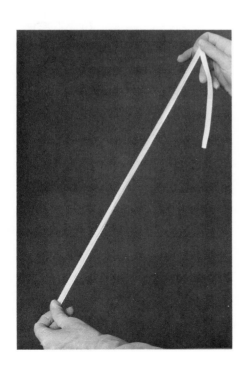

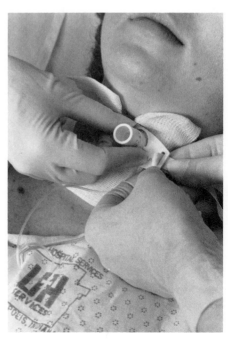

7 *Changing Tracheostomy Ties:* For your client's safety, ask another nurse to assist you by holding the tracheostomy tube in place as you change the ties. Begin by cutting two pieces of twill tape, each approximately 45 cm (18 in.) in length. Fold over a quarter of each tape and pinch the creases to facilitate their insertion into the flange of the tube.

8 Insert the folded end of one of the twill tapes through the slot in the flange.

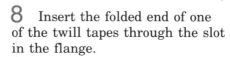

(Continues)

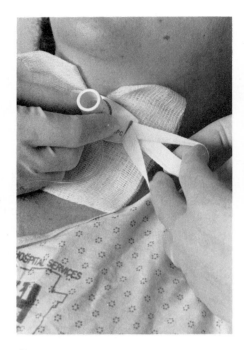

9 Tie a slip knot by pulling the folded end through the slot approximately 5 cm (2 in.) and forming a loop. Pull the longer end of the tape through the center of the loop (as shown).

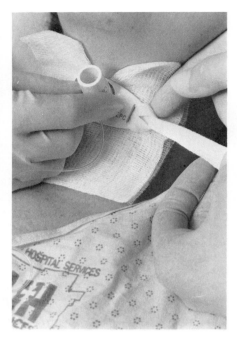

10 Pull the longer end snugly to complete the slip knot. Do the same on the other side, or ask your assistant to do this as you hold the tracheostomy tube in place.

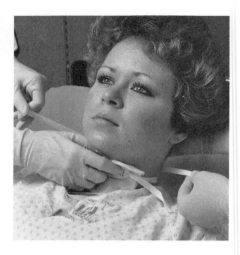

11 Pass the long end of the tape behind the client's head as your assistant does the same; exchange the ends.

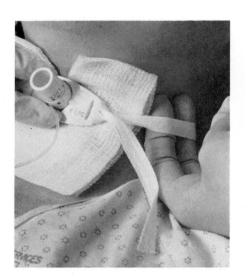

12 Before tying a square knot, ensure that one or two fingers can fit between the tape and the client's neck. The tape should fit snugly enough to prevent the tracheostomy tube's expulsion, but not so tightly that it is uncomfortable for the client.

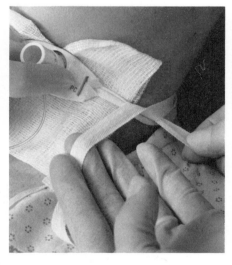

13 Tie the two ends of the tape together.

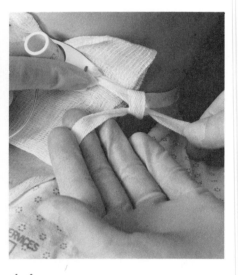

14 Make a square knot, tying the knot on the side of the client's neck to prevent pressure to areas on the back of the neck. As an extra precaution, tie another square knot over the original to make a double square knot. Repeat on the other side.

Managing Respiratory Therapy

ADMINISTERING OXYGEN, HUMIDITY, AND AEROSOL THERAPY

Nursing Guidelines to Devices Used in the Delivery of Oxygen, Humidity, and Aerosols

LOW-FLOW SYSTEM

A method of oxygen delivery that does not supply all of the inspired gas needs; thus, room air will be inhaled along with oxygen. The fraction of inspired oxygen (FiO_2) will vary, depending on respiratory rate, tidal volume, and liter flow. It is contraindicated for clients requiring carefully gauged concentrations of oxygen.

HIGH-FLOW SYSTEM

A method of oxygen delivery that supplies all of the inspired gas needs regardless of the client's respiratory status. This system is a precise and consistent method for controlling the client's FiO_2.

Both high-flow and low-flow systems can deliver a variety of oxygen concentrations.

Devices Used in the Administration of Supplemental and Environmental Therapy

SIMPLE FACE MASK (LOW-FLOW SYSTEM)

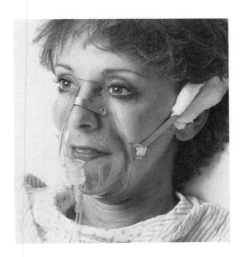

Description

Clear, plastic device with exhalation ports, which covers the nose and mouth. It can deliver 35%–60% oxygen concentrations.

Uses

Short-term therapy when moderate concentrations of oxygen are desired, but it must be used cautiously on clients who potentially may vomit and aspirate.

Nursing Considerations

- The recommended liter flow is 5–8 L/min.
- Use with a humidifier prevents drying of nasal and oral mucosa.
- To prevent skin irritation, keep the face as dry as possible.
- Ensure a tight fit so that the mask will yield maximum oxygen concentration.
- Pad behind ears and over bony prominences to prevent skin breakdown.
- Frequently monitor client's vital signs, arterial blood gas (ABG) values, breath sounds, and level of consciousness to evaluate respiratory status.

(Continues)

NASAL CANNULA (LOW-FLOW SYSTEM)

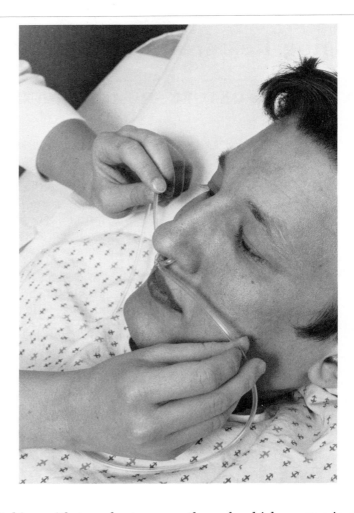

Description

Plastic tubing with two short prongs through which oxygen is administered into the nares. It can achieve up to a 50% oxygen concentration.

Uses

Clients without nasal obstructions for whom simple, comfortable, long-term therapy is desired. For example, it is frequently used for clients with myocardial infarctions and to deliver maintenance oxygen to clients with COPD.

Nursing Considerations

- The recommended liter flow is 1–6 L/min. Increased rates can cause client discomfort, such as headaches.
- It is more comfortable and convenient than most other oxygen administration devices, especially the nasal catheter.
- Some cannulas are adjusted and tightened under the chin; others are secured with an elastic strap at the back of the head.
- Pad behind ears and over bony prominences to prevent skin breakdown.
- Use with a humidifier will prevent drying of nasal mucosa.
- For client comfort, frequently provide nasal and oral hygiene.
- When administering oxygen to clients with COPD, observe for signs of oxygen-induced hypoventilation: shallow respirations, dyspnea, confusion/restlessness, tremors.
- Monitor the client's vital signs, breath sounds, ABG values, and level of consciousness to evaluate respiratory status.

PARTIAL REBREATHING MASK (LOW-FLOW SYSTEM)

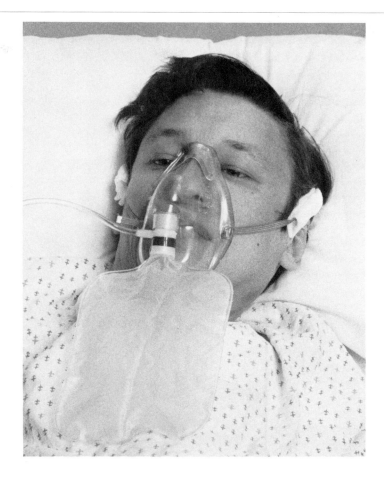

Description

Clear, plastic face mask with exhalation ports, which attaches to a reservoir bag, allowing client to rebreathe one third of his exhaled air in conjunction with source oxygen. This increases FiO_2 by recycling expired oxygen. It can deliver oxygen concentrations up to 60%.

Uses

Short-term treatment for clients having increased FiO_2 demands in such conditions as cardiac or pulmonary disease. It is usually contraindicated for clients with COPD.

Nursing Considerations

- Occlude reservoir bag at the bedside to test for leaks and patency before applying to client.
- To prevent carbon dioxide buildup, the liter flow must be adequate (greater than 6 L/min) to ensure that the reservoir bag does not totally deflate during inspiration. Increase the liter flow as needed.
- When delivering higher oxygen concentrations, observe for signs of oxygen toxicity: cough, dyspnea, substernal pain and burning, nausea.
- Mask requires tight fit to deliver prescribed oxygen concentrations.
- To prevent skin irritation, pad behind ears and over bony prominences.
- Monitor the client's vital signs, ABG values, breath sounds, and level of consciousness to evaluate respiratory status.
- Mask can easily convert to nonrebreathing mask by inserting rubber disks at the port between reservoir bag and mask, and at one of the exhalation ports.

(Continues)

NONREBREATHING MASK (LOW-FLOW/ HIGH-FLOW SYSTEM)

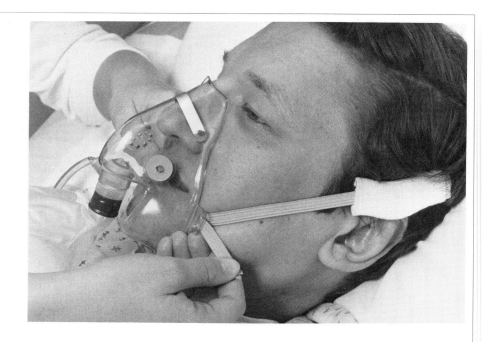

Description

Similar to partial rebreathing mask, except that it has two rubber disks. One disk occludes the port between the reservoir bag and the mask, and the other disk occludes one of the exhalation ports. To achieve higher concentrations of oxygen, this system allows exhaled gas to leave the mask while at the same time preventing inhalation of room air. It can deliver up to 80%–95% oxygen concentrations.

Uses

To increase client's FiO_2 on a short-term basis in such conditions as cardiac failure or pulmonary disease. It is usually contraindicated for clients with COPD.

Nursing Considerations

- Occlude reservoir bag at the bedside to test for leaks and patency before applying to client.
- To prevent carbon dioxide buildup, liter flow must be adequate (greater than 6 L/min) so that reservoir bag does not totally deflate during inspiration. Increase the liter flow as needed.
- Use with humidifier will prevent drying of nasal and oral mucosa.
- To function properly, mask should fit client's face snugly with no audible leaks.
- Pad behind ears and over bony prominences to prevent skin breakdown.
- When delivering high oxygen concentrations, observe for signs of oxygen toxicity: coughing, substernal pain and burning, dyspnea, and nausea.
- The mask can convert to a partial rebreather (see procedure, p. 367) or simple face mask.
- Frequently monitor the client's vital signs, ABG values, breath sounds, and level of consciousness to evaluate respiratory status.
- If the oxygen is turned off, the client has only one small exhalation port through which to breathe.

Managing Respiratory Therapy

VENTURI (AIR-ENTRAINMENT) MASK (HIGH-FLOW SYSTEM)

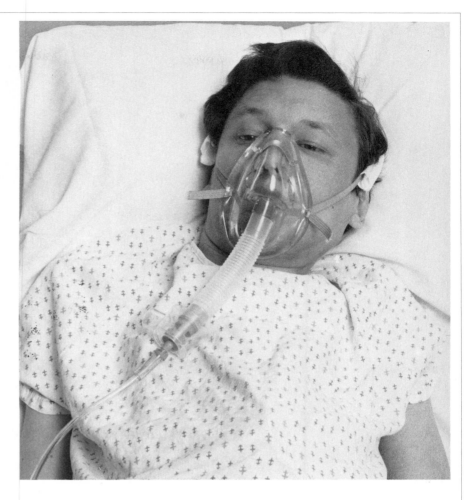

Description

Different brands of masks may vary in design, but it is the size of the opening in the adaptor or jet that determines the delivered percentage of oxygen concentration. It can deliver 24%–50% oxygen concentration.

Uses

For clients requiring reliable, precise, and controlled concentrations of oxygen, for example, those with COPD.

Nursing Considerations

- Explain to client that if his oxygen concentrations are increased, the total liter flow delivered to him will decrease, resulting in a reduced gas flow (velocity).
- To function properly, the mask should fit snugly with no audible leaks.
- Pad areas behind ears and over bony prominences to prevent skin breakdown.
- When administering oxygen to clients with COPD, observe for signs of oxygen-induced hypoventilation: shallow respirations, dyspnea, confusion/restlessness, tremors.
- When using mask without humidity, keep humidity adaptor attached to prevent air entrainment ports from being occluded by blanket or body weight.
- For humidity, each mask comes with special humidity adaptors that can be attached to appropriate humidification devices.

(Continues)

CPAP MASK

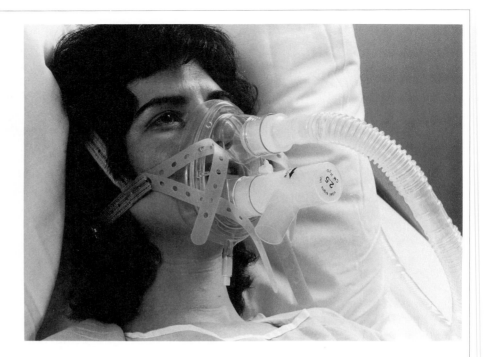

Description

Cushioned mask with harness-type headgear that can be used to create a seal on the client's face, enabling exhalation against pressure, which maintains alveolar patency during exhalation.

Uses

For clients requiring constant positive airway pressure (CPAP) in the treatment of oxygen deficiencies, such as in preventing or treating atelectasis. Clients in critical care areas with signs of early adult respiratory distress syndrome (ARDS) also may benefit from this mask.

Nursing Considerations

- This mask is indicated for clients who are severely hypoxemic (Pao_2 <60 mm Hg).
- This mask is contraindicated for clients with COPD and hypotension caused by hypovolemia.
- Potential side effects of positive end expiratory pressure can include fluid retention, decreased cardiac output, pneumothorax, and gastric distention.
- Benefits of this mask are lost after 1 hour following every removal because the alveoli will collapse in the susceptible client after this amount of time has lapsed. Do not discontinue this mask for anything less than an urgent matter (e.g., removal of sputum or vomitus).
- Careful monitoring of the client's arterial blood gases (ABGs) is critical for clients who are treated with CPAP.

  —This client's $Paco_2$ must remain in the "normal" range (30–50 mm Hg), and the pH must remain in the "normal" range (7.30–7.50).

  —If the client's $Paco_2$ is greater than "normal" and the pH is less than "normal," mechanical ventilation may be necessary due to acute ventilatory failure.

- The client's risk of aspiration is markedly enhanced should vomiting occur with this mask in place. Monitor the client at frequent intervals.
- Clients who cough spontaneously may experience difficulty handling secretions. Remove the mask, as necessary, to facilitate sputum removal.
- The necessary snug fit of the mask to the face is uncomfortable for most clients.
- Provide writing materials for this client, whose verbal communication will be impaired by this mask.
- A humidifier chamber can be used to deliver warmed gas to the CPAP mask. Attach wide-bore tubing to the outlet port of the humidifier reservoir, as shown in the photo on p. 370, to deliver the gas to the mask. Fill the reservoir with sterile water.
- Adjust the head strap, as needed, to ensure that the two latex straps remain positioned $\frac{1}{2}$ inch in front of the ears, level with the earlobes.

OXYGEN HOOD

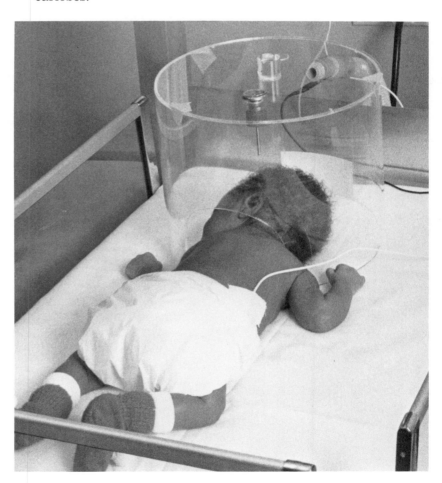

Description

Clear, plastic, rigid dome with inlet ports through which low or high concentrations of oxygen can be delivered. It covers just the head of the infant, and it is similar to the oxygen hut, which is cubic in shape, and designed for the older child.

(Continues)

Uses

For infants in cribs or incubators, or under radiant warmers when controlled concentrations of oxygen, temperature, and humidity are desired.

Nursing Considerations

- When removing hood during suctioning or feeding, direct oxygen source toward child's airway to prevent a drastic reduction of his FiO_2.
- Keep neck opening from being obstructed with towels, toys, and blankets so that the gas flow can flush carbon dioxide from the hood.
- When an outside heating source is not used, the temperature is usually kept at 29°–34° C, and this range produces a small amount of condensation.
- Observe for buildup of condensation in the delivery tubing and empty as needed.
- To prevent an increase in oxygen consumption, the gas should be warmed and humidified when it is delivered to the neonate.
- When a heated humidifier is used with the hood, check the hood temperature frequently and maintain the range between 34° and 36° C, or as prescribed. For premature infants, keep the hood as close to body temperature as possible.
- Add sterile solution to the humidifier or nebulizer as necessary.
- Keep tubing free of condensation buildup.
- Use an oxygen analyzer (see p. 363) to ensure that oxygen concentrations are within the prescribed range.

INCUBATOR (ISOLETTE)

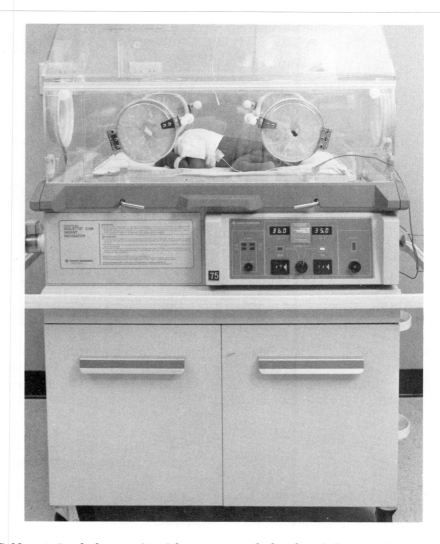

Description

Self-contained clear unit with access portholes for giving nursing care. Can deliver 40%–60% concentrations of oxygen.

Uses

For newborn, especially premature, infants for whom oxygen therapy, controlled temperature, and humidity are desired. Can also provide infant isolation.

Nursing Considerations

- When portholes are open, oxygen concentration can drop drastically. Open portholes only as necessary.
- Use oxygen analyzer (see p. 363) to assess concentrations of oxygen.
- To be assured of delivering oxygen concentrations greater than 40%, oxygen hoods must be used in conjunction with the unit.
- When humidity is used, change sheets often. Dampness contributes to respiratory complications and bacterial growth.
- Monitor incubator temperature to keep within 34°–36° C, or as prescribed. Attach temperature probe to infant with hypoallergenic tape.
- When the incubator is unplugged (e.g., for transport), keep the portholes open to prevent buildup of carbon dioxide, and provide external oxygen. If the move requires more than 5–10 minutes, use a special transport incubator instead.

(Continues)

CROUPETTE

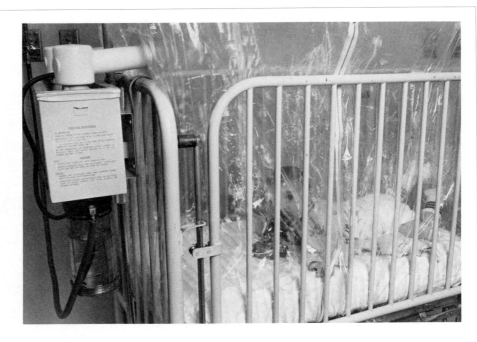

Description

Pneumatically powered system, used in conjunction with a vinyl canopy for the delivery of aerosol or humidity, temperature, and oxygen. Can be used either with crushed ice for aerosol delivery and to maintain body temperature or with heated humidifiers. It can maintain oxygen concentrations of 30%–50%.

Uses

For the child who is larger than an infant and who needs high humidity, oxygen, and a temperature-controlled environment.

Nursing Considerations

- Keep oxygen at 10–12 L/min or as prescribed.
- Verify that the nebulizer is working by observing for mist in the tent.
- For cool mist aerosol, maintain adequate levels of crushed ice in the tank.
- If heated humidity is prescribed, keep temperatures between 34° and 36° C, or as prescribed.
- To maintain adequate oxygen concentrations, keep zippers closed and the canopy tucked securely under mattress.
- Use oxygen analyzers (see p. 363) to monitor oxygen concentrations.
- To minimize potentials for both respiratory complications and bacterial growth, change bed clothes and sheets frequently.
- Spend as much time with child as possible to keep him from feeling isolated.
- Monitor child frequently for signs of chilling or need for suctioning.
- Observe for skin maceration from mist, and occasionally remove child from mist, unless contraindicated.

OXYGEN ANALYZERS

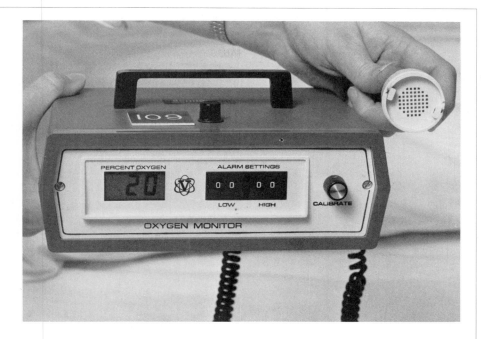

Description

Although there are many types of units that vary in design and operational principle, each is portable and used at the bedside to draw in the client's environmental oxygen via a sampling tube.

Use

Each unit measures the concentration of oxygen being delivered in such devices as tents, hoods, and incubators to ensure that the client is receiving the prescribed FiO_2.

Nursing Considerations

- Before monitoring the client's oxygen concentration, measure the room air to ensure that the unit calibrates to 0.21 (21%). Adjust the dial, if necessary, to achieve this reading.
- When measuring oxygen concentrations with the device described in this section, position the sampling tube next to the client's nose.
- If necessary, adjust the flow rate to achieve the prescribed FiO_2.
- When the unit is used from client to client, clean the sampling tube with an alcohol swab.

(Continues)

**Attachments and Devices
Used to Administer
Aerosol Therapy**

AEROSOL FACE MASK

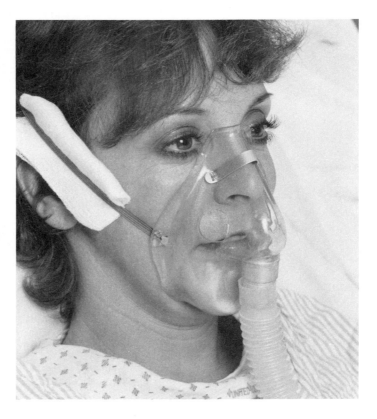

Description

Plastic face mask with two large exhalation ports, which connects the client to a humidifier or nebulizer.

Uses

Supplies client with warmed and moistened room air or oxygen, which prevents drying of tracheal secretions and liquefies thickened secretions.

Nursing Considerations

- Observe for visible and constant mist or vapor, which indicates adequate humidification is being delivered. Increase the flow rate if mist disappears during inspiration.
- Observe for condensation buildup in the tubing and empty as necessary.
- Keep nebulizer or humidifier supplied with adequate levels of sterile solution. Discard residual solution before replenishing the fluid reservoir.
- If using heated humidity, check the temperature frequently to prevent injury to the respiratory tract. Keep within 34°–36° C, or as prescribed.
- Assess for increased secretion production and encourage coughing. Suction as necessary.
- Pad bony prominences and behind ears to prevent skin breakdown.
- To ensure adequate delivery of aerosol, mask should fit snugly.

TRACHEOSTOMY COLLAR

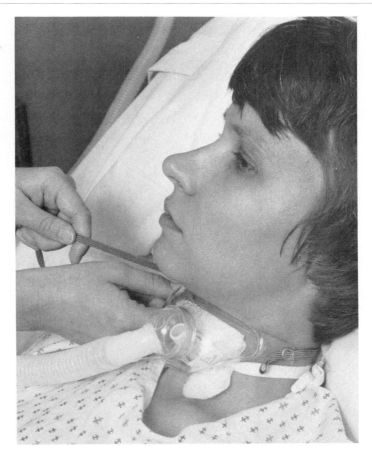

Description

Lightweight, plastic device that connects the client's tracheostomy to a humidification source. It is positioned directly over the tracheostomy and secured in place with an elastic strap.

Uses

Supplies client with warmed and moistened room air or oxygen, which prevents drying of tracheal secretions and liquefies thickened secretions. It also can be used to deliver aerosolized medications.

Nursing Considerations

- Observe for visible and constant mist or vapor, which indicates adequate humidification is being delivered.
- Observe for condensation buildup in tubing and empty at least q2h and as necessary, especially before turning the client.
- The trachea can be suctioned directly through the frontal port.
- Keep humidification source supplied with adequate levels of sterile solution. Discard residual fluid before replenishing the fluid reservoir.
- When using heated humidity, check the temperature frequently to prevent injury to the trachea. Keep within range of 34°–36° C, or as prescribed.
- Assess for increased secretion production and encourage coughing. Suction as necessary.

(Continues)

T-PIECE

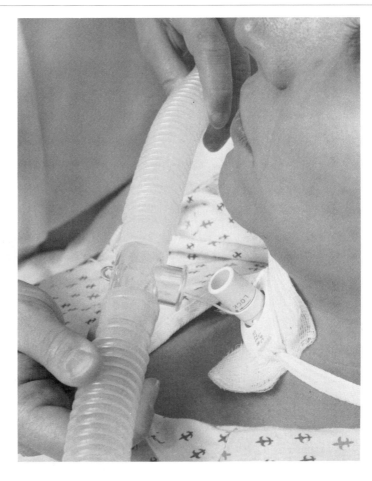

Description

Lightweight plastic tube that connects the client's tracheostomy or endotracheal tube to a humidification source via a center connection.

Uses

Same as tracheostomy collar, but also can be connected to an endotracheal tube.

Nursing Considerations

■ The reservoir tube on both sides of the T-piece allows for the accumulation of oxygen so that the client receives a consistent oxygen concentration with each inspiration.

■ Keep T-piece in proper alignment to prevent undue pressure on the stoma.

■ Keep exhalation ends of tube unobstructed.

■ Visible and constant vapor or mist produced in the device indicates adequate humidification.

■ Observe for condensation buildup in tubing and empty frequently, especially before turning the client.

■ If attached to a venturi, it can function as high-flow system.

■ Clean the center connection as necessary with hydrogen peroxide to prevent it from sticking to the tracheostomy.

■ Keep humidification source supplied with a sterile solution. Discard residual fluid before replenishing fluid reservoir.

■ When using heated humidity, monitor temperature frequently to prevent damage to trachea. Keep within 34°–36° C, or as prescribed.

■ Assess for increased secretion production and encourage coughing. Suction as necessary.

CONVERTING A NONREBREATHING MASK TO A PARTIAL REBREATHING MASK

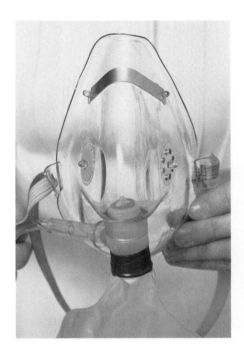 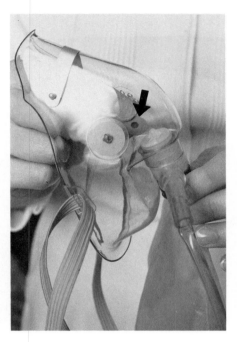 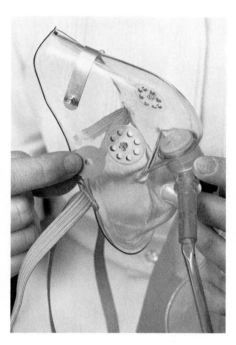

The difference between a nonrebreathing mask and a partial rebreathing mask is that the former has two rubber disks. One disk occludes one of the exhalation ports, and the other occludes the port between the mask and the reservoir bag. These disks allow for the exhalation of gas while also minimizing inhalation of room air. When it is no longer necessary for the client to receive the higher concentration of oxygen that is provided by the nonrebreathing mask, the physician might prescribe a partial rebreathing mask. You can easily convert the client's existing mask to a partial rebreather.

1 Begin by removing the rubber disk at the port between the mask and the reservoir bag.

2 Remove the rubber disk at the exhalation port. Save the disks in the event your client might again need the higher oxygen concentrations that require reconversion to a nonrebreathing mask.

ASSEMBLING A VENTURI DELIVERY SYSTEM

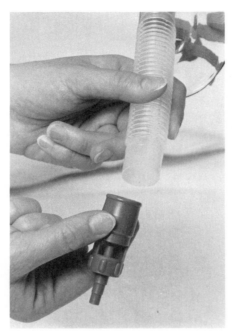

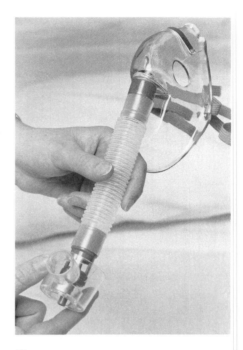

1   A venturi mask comes prepackaged with a 15- to 20-cm (6- to 8-in.) wide-bore tube, a humidification adaptor, and a variety of jets or adaptors that are usually color coded to coincide with the prescribed concentration of oxygen. To assemble a venturi mask, attach the wide-bore tubing to the mask's adaptor.

2   The lower hand in the photograph holds the jet adaptor. The size of the jet's opening determines the delivered concentration of oxygen. Slide the jet into the open end of the wide-bore tubing. Keep the remaining jets at your client's bedside in case the physician prescribes a different oxygen concentration at a later time. Most manufacturers imprint the adaptors with concentration and recommended liter flow, for example, 24% (4–6 L/min).

3   Attach the humidity adaptor to the jet, regardless of whether or not humidity has been prescribed. The adaptor will prevent the jet adaptor's air entrainment ports from becoming occluded by blankets or the client's body.

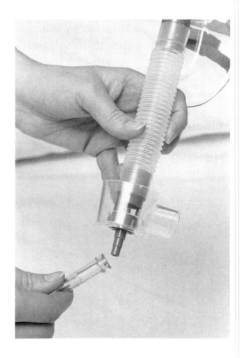

4   Attach the oxygen tubing to the jet's nipple, and the other end of the tubing to the oxygen flowmeter. Adjust the flowmeter to the level prescribed on the nipple.

SETTING UP AN OXYGEN SYSTEM WITH HUMIDIFICATION

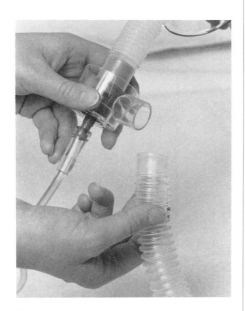

5 If humidification has been prescribed, attach one end of the wide-bore tubing to the humidity adaptor, and the other end to the humidifier or nebulizer.

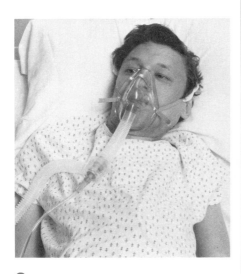

6 Apply the venturi mask to your client. The client in this photograph is wearing a venturi mask that is attached to humidity. The system also can attach to a T-piece for a client with a tracheostomy.

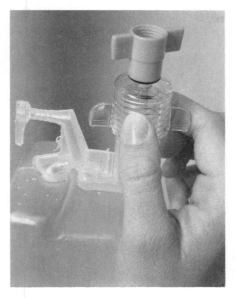

1 Follow these steps to deliver humidified oxygen to your client. A disposable humidifier is used here, but the principles are basically the same if you are using a reusable humidifier. Attach the adaptor to the humidifier. The adaptor is usually packaged with the disposable humidifier.

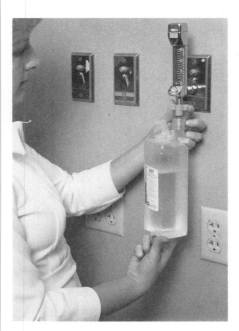

3 Connect the humidifier to the flowmeter via the adaptor.

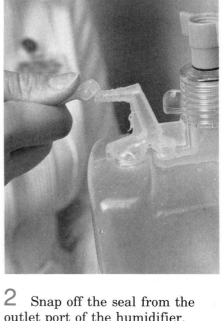

2 Snap off the seal from the outlet port of the humidifier.

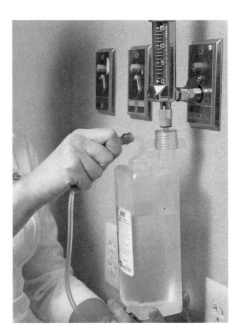

4 Connect small-bore oxygen tubing to the outlet port of the humidifier bottle.

(Continues)

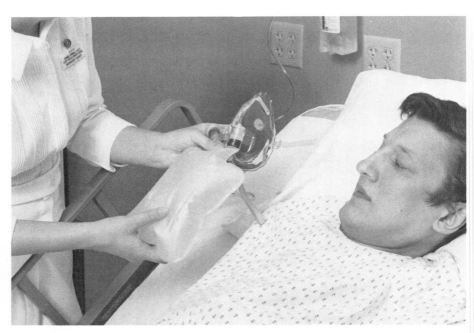

5 Adjust the flowmeter to the prescribed number of liters of oxygen per minute.

6 You are now ready to attach the distal end of the oxygen tubing to one of the following: simple oxygen mask, nasal cannula, partial rebreathing mask, or to a nonrebreathing mask as shown here.

DELIVERING HEATED HUMIDITY

1 A heated servo-controlled cascade humidifier can be used to deliver either warmed oxygen or humidity. In this photo, wide-bore tubing is attached to deliver the humidity. In addition, the reservoir is filled with sterile water. If oxygen also has been prescribed for your client, you will need to attach one end of the small-bore oxygen tubing to the oxygen flowmeter and the other end to the oxygen port of the system. Remember to adjust the flowmeter to achieve the prescribed FiO_2.

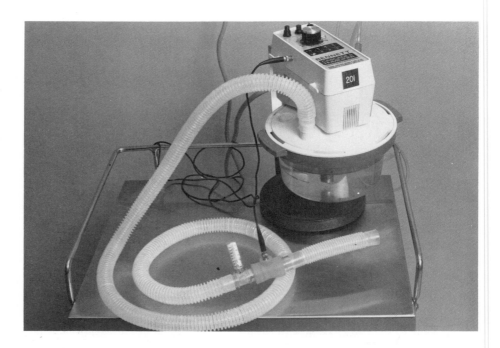

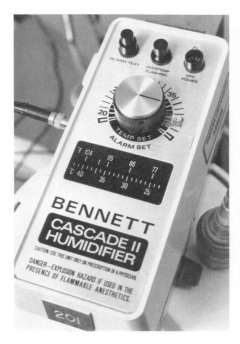

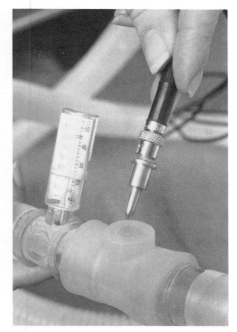

2 Set the temperature control dial to the prescribed temperature (usually as close to body temperature as possible). The unit pictured shows the connection of the temperature probe on the left side.

3 The other end of the probe attaches to a rubber adaptor, as close to the client's airway as is feasible. The unit will automatically heat and turn off, as needed, to maintain the preset temperature. If the heat surpasses that which you have set on the temperature-control dial, or in the event of an equipment malfunction, an alarm will sound.

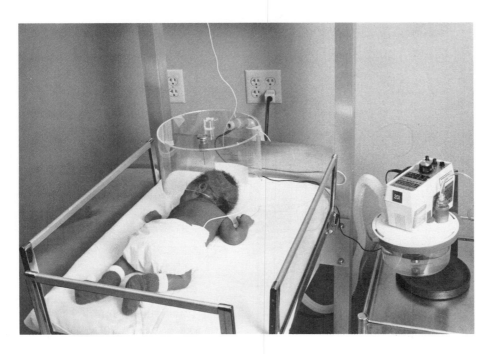

4 You can now attach the free end of the wide-bore tubing to an oxygen hood.

(Continues)

5 Or attach the tubing to a tracheostomy collar or to a T-piece (as shown).

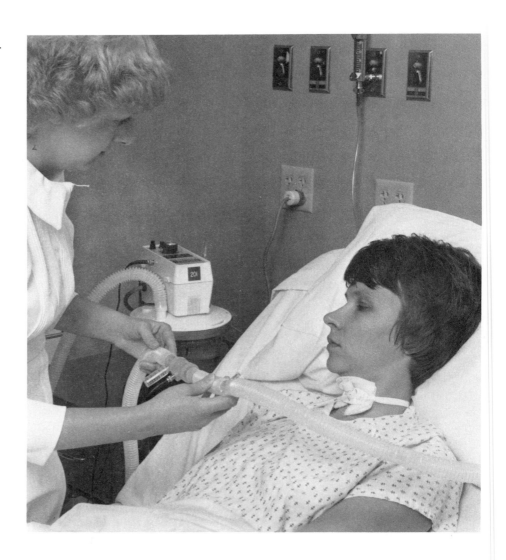

ASSEMBLING A NEBULIZER

1 A common method for the delivery of aerosol therapy is the use of a pneumatic (jet) nebulizer as outlined in these steps. The first step is to attach a venturi adaptor to the nebulizer bottle.

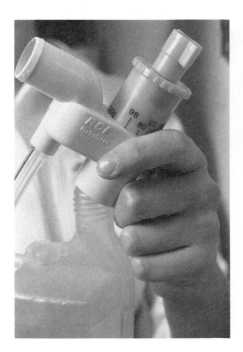

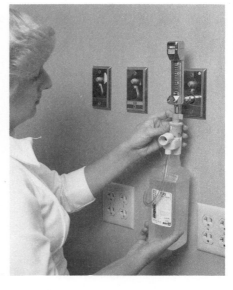

2 Attach the assembled nebulizer to the flowmeter.

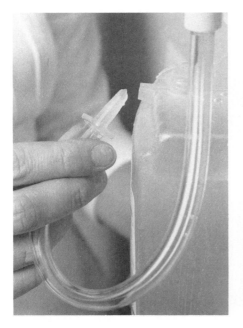

3 This venturi adaptor has a small tube that collects condensate. Connect it to the small outlet on the front of the nebulizer, after first snapping off the outlet's seal.

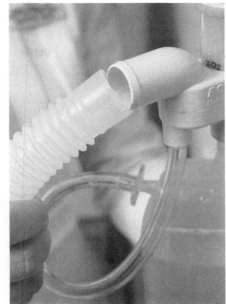

4 Attach wide-bore tubing to the outlet of the venturi adaptor.

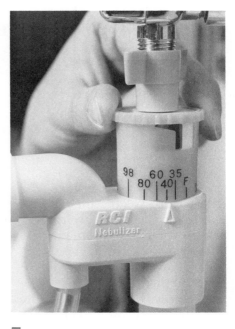

5 If you also will be delivering oxygen, adjust the venturi dial to the prescribed oxygen concentration. If oxygen has not been prescribed, set the dial to "F" (for Full).

6 Adjust the flowmeter until a visible mist is produced at the distal end of the tubing. The flowmeter is usually turned to its maximum level to ensure adequate gas flow to the client.

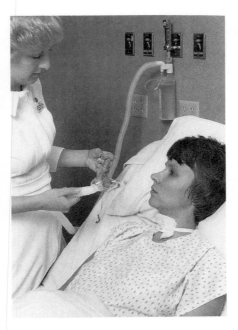

7 Connect the distal end of the tubing to an aerosol mask, to a T-piece, or to a tracheostomy collar (as shown).

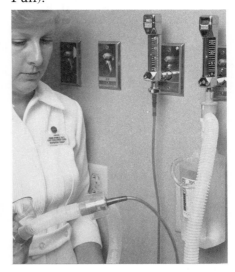

8 The tubing also can be connected to the high humidity adaptor of a venturi mask. Check to make sure the client is receiving adequate gas flow from the nebulizer. Mist should be visible from the delivery device during inspiration and exhalation. If mist is not visible, increase the liter flow by adjusting the flowmeter.

EMPLOYING TECHNIQUES FOR LUNG INFLATION

INSTRUCTING CLIENTS IN DEEP-BREATHING EXERCISES

Teaching Apical Expansion Exercises: Clients who will benefit from this exercise are those who might be restricting their upper chest movement because of splinting from pain—for example, clients who have had a lobectomy, mastectomy, or gross pleural effusion. Position your fingers below the clavicles and apply moderate pressure (top photo). Instruct the client to inhale while pushing his chest upward and forward, expanding against your finger pressure. Encourage him to retain the expansion for a few moments and then exhale quietly and passively. Once you have taught him the technique, he can perform the exercise on his own by positioning his fingers over the same area. When done correctly and frequently, apical expansion will help reexpand remaining lung tissue, eliminate secretions, and minimize flattening of the upper chest wall.

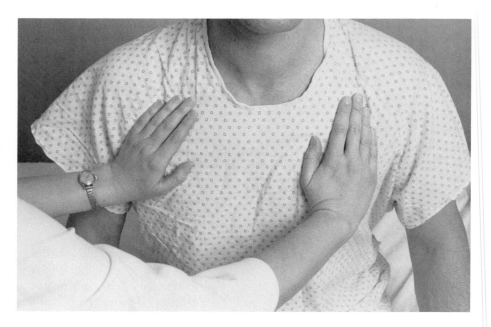

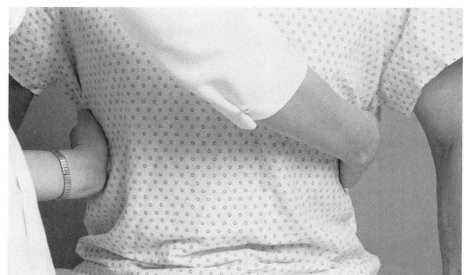

Teaching Basal Expansion Exercises: Lower thoracic exercises are frequently indicated for clients recovering from chest surgery, for whom pain on the affected side inhibits bilateral chest movement. Position your hands on the midaxillary lines in the area of the eighth ribs, and apply moderate pressure as the client inhales (bottom photo). Instruct the client to attempt to move your hands outward as he expands his lower ribs. He should retain his maximum inhalation for 1 or 2 seconds to help promote aeration of his alveoli, and then exhale in a relaxed, passive manner. Clients with COPD, especially, should be closely observed for both a slow, relaxed exhalation and a relaxed upper chest. Encourage clients to perform the exercise on their own by using the palms of their hands. When practiced frequently and correctly, this technique will promote and maintain lower chest wall mobility.

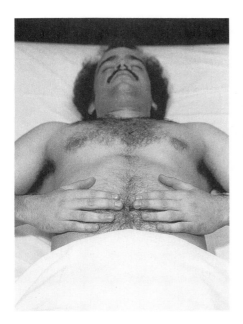

Teaching Diaphragmatic Breathing: Your clients will breathe more efficiently and obtain better lung function when correctly using their abdominal muscles and diaphragms.

To instruct the client in diaphragmatic breathing, have him assume a supine position and flex his knees to relax the abdominal wall. He should then place his hands over his abdomen and breathe in deeply and slowly through his nose as he pushes his abdomen outward. If he does this correctly, his hands will rise during the inspiration. The exhalation should be quiet and passive, with the lower ribs and abdomen sinking downward as the abdomen relaxes. Once the client has been taught diaphragmatic breathing while supine, he may then assume other positions for practicing this technique. Emphasize the need for frequent and regular practice until breathing in this manner becomes automatic and no longer requires a conscious effort. *Note: Clients with COPD should be taught to inhale through the nose and exhale slowly through pursed (puckered) lips. This will help to minimize small airway collapse.*

ASSISTING WITH COUGHING

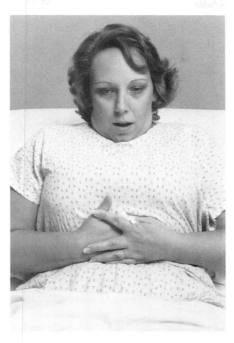

Teaching clients an effective, controlled cough is essential in the management of bronchial secretions, and it should be taught to all clients *before* surgery. Instruct the client to sit with her upper body flexed slightly forward. If this position is contraindicated, she can assume a lateral position, with flexed knees and hips. Either position will promote a forceful cough, while also minimizing strain in the lower back. First, instruct the client to take two or three deep breaths with passive exhalation. She should then take a deep breath, hold it briefly, and cough forcefully.

An alternative method is the "double cough" technique, which is especially recommended for clients with COPD in whom one very forceful cough could cause small airway collapse. The client is instructed to cough from the midinspiratory point rather than from the point of deep inspiration. The client exhales in a rapid succession of two or more abrupt, sharp coughs. The first cough

loosens secretions, and the following cough(s) facilitates the movement of the secretions toward the upper airway.

To minimize pain, a postoperative client will require splinting over her incisional area during the coughing process. A pillow can be pressed over the affected area (below), or you can show the client how to splint her own incision by pressing the arm and hand of the unaffected side against the site (left).

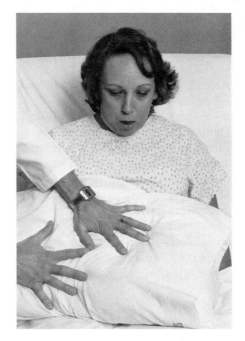

USING INCENTIVE SPIROMETERS

Assessing

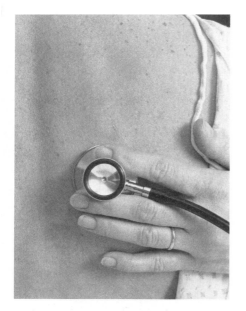

1 Auscultate the client's lung fields to establish a baseline for postexercise comparison. Explain the procedure in detail. Many clients incorrectly *exhale* rather than inhale during the exercise. Incentive spirometry is a goal-oriented and measurable breathing exercise that helps clients increase their inspiratory volume while also inflating their alveoli.

Planning and Implementing

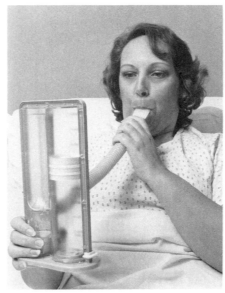

2 Many disposable flow-incentive spirometers have pointers that you can slide to the prescribed inspiratory volume level. Check the operating instructions on the unit used by your agency. Instruct the client to hold the unit upright because tilting it will make the exercise less challenging. She should complete a normal exhalation and then seal her lips tightly around the mouthpiece while inhaling slowly and deeply. Encourage the client to sustain the inspiration long enough to elevate the disk for at least 3 seconds.

Evaluating

3 Auscultate the client's lung fields for postexercise breath sounds, and compare them to your earlier assessment. Document the procedure and the client's response.

ASSISTING WITH IPPB

Assessing and Planning

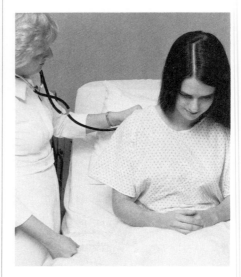

1 If IPPB has been prescribed for your client, explain to the client that this treatment will assist her in achieving deep lung inflation while also promoting expectoration of secretions. To facilitate lung expansion, assist her into Fowler's position, unless it is contraindicated. If a pain medication has been prescribed to precede the therapy, begin the procedure 30 minutes after administering the drug. Assess the baseline status of the client's respiratory system before initiating the therapy.

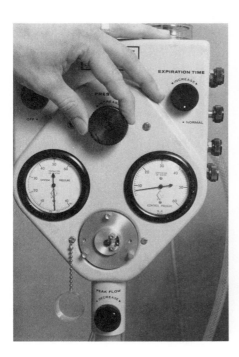

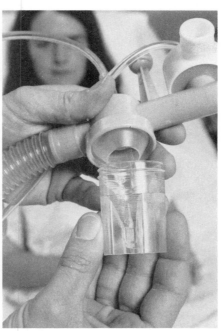

Implementing

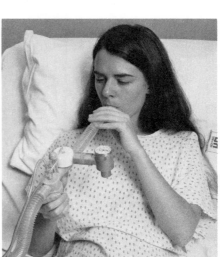

2 Turn the pressure control knob to achieve the prescribed amount of tidal volume or pressure.

3 Fill the nebulizer with sterile water, saline, or the prescribed medication with diluent, and reattach it. *Note: Some bronchodilators, such as metaproterenol, significantly alter the heart rate. Monitor the client's pulse rate frequently throughout the therapy and record the pretreatment and posttreatment measurements. Stay with the client throughout the treatment.*

4 Instruct the client to place her lips tightly around the mouth piece and inhale as the unit cycles on. Observe for adequate chest expansion with each inhalation, and make sure the exhalations are relaxed and passive. Forced exhalations can further increase small airway obstruction. Encourage both diaphragmatic breathing and coughing during the treatment.

5 To determine whether your client is receiving adequate deep lung inflations during the therapy, a measuring device such as the Wright respirometer will measure the index of her expired tidal volume. It connects to the expiratory port of the IPPB manifold. (See its attachment to the manifold in the preceding photograph.)

(Continues)

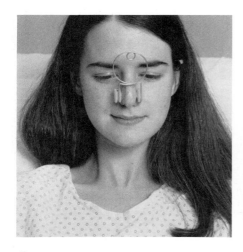

6 If your client cannot avoid breathing through her nose during the treatment, provide her with nose clips. However, once she becomes accustomed to the therapy and no longer breathes through her nose, she might no longer need them.

Evaluating

7 When the treatment has been completed, auscultate the lung fields to assess for improved aeration and absent or diminished adventitious sounds. Document the procedure, noting the client's response to the therapy, as well as the amount and character of the expectorated secretions.

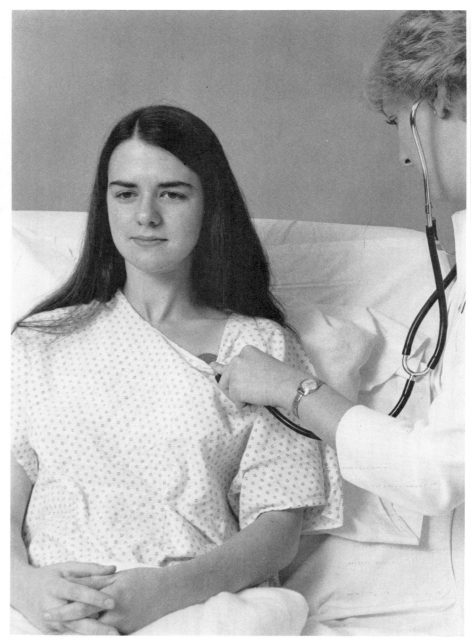

PERFORMING CHEST PHYSIOTHERAPY

PERCUSSING, VIBRATING, AND DRAINING THE ADULT

Assessing and Planning

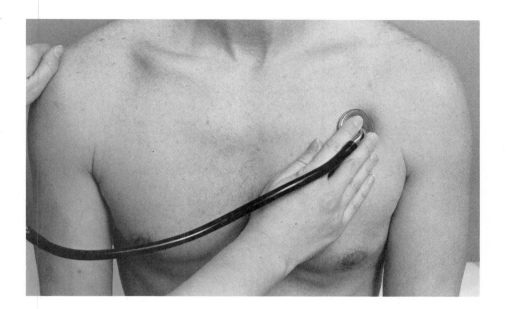

1 Auscultate your client's lung fields to assess breath sounds and monitor the rate and depth of the respirations to provide a baseline for posttreatment assessment. Note the presence and location of retained secretions. Be especially alert to diminished, absent, or bronchial breath sounds, which are indicative of obstructed airways and reduced airflow. Then palpate for bilateral thoracic expansion and percuss for areas of dullness. Thoroughly explain each step, and demonstrate the techniques you will use during the procedure. Clients with chronic lung diseases may need to perform the procedure on their own after discharge. Therefore, they should be able to demonstrate the process to you within 2–3 days prior to discharge. Provide an emesis basin and tissues for expectoration of secretions. To minimize the potential for vomiting and discomfort, the procedure should be performed either before meals or at least 1 hour after eating. Ensure that you percuss and vibrate over a thin layer of clothing or a towel to avoid traumatizing the skin.

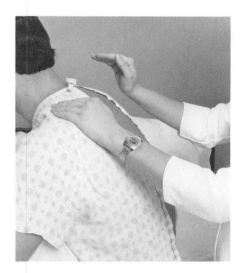

2 *Understanding Percussion (Clapping):* Percussion is performed by clapping cupped hands alternately and in rapid sequence over a lung segment. Cupping the hand provides a trapped pocket of air that will transmit vibrations through the chest wall to the secretions, thereby loosening or dislodging them. Your elbows should be flexed and the wrist relaxed to achieve a rapid, popping action. Although percussion is a noisy procedure, it should not be painful to the client. It is performed during inhalation and exhalation while the client deep breathes.

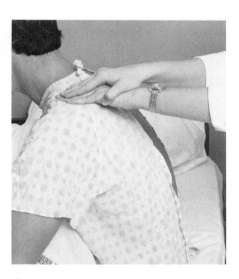

3 *Understanding Vibration:* Vibration or shaking is often performed in conjunction with percussion as an aid to segmental drainage by loosening secretions and propelling them into the larger bronchi. Flatten your hands, and position them one on top of the other over a lung segment. With straight arms, lean into the client's chest, using moderate pressure. Alternately contract and relax your shoulder and upper arm muscles to produce a vibratory shaking. Vibrate for approximately 10 seconds per exhalation as the client exhales slowly and completely.

(Continues)

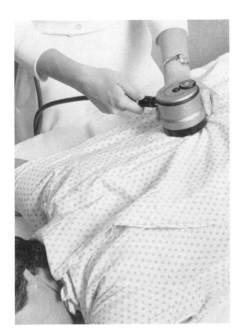

Implementing

Positioning Your Client for Segmental Bronchial Drainage: The physician might prescribe some or all of the following positions, with or without percussion and vibration, to drain the loosened secretions out of the client's lung, preventing them from repooling or draining into healthy lung segments. Many of the positions will need modification for clients with compromised cardiac, neurologic, or pulmonary conditions. A complete sequence for percussion, vibration, and drainage, however, will consist of the following: (1) Have the client assume the prescribed position(s) for 5–15 minutes, or until secretions can be expectorated; (2) percuss the involved lung segments for 2–3 minutes each; (3) vibrate for at least two or three exhalations, depending on the client's secretion viscosity; (4) encourage coughing and expectoration or suction as needed; (5) change to the next position, if others have been prescribed.

4 *Using Mechanical Percussors/Vibrators:* The use of a mechanical percussor is often indicated for clients in critical care areas, who are connected to external equipment. They help to lessen operator fatigue, as well.

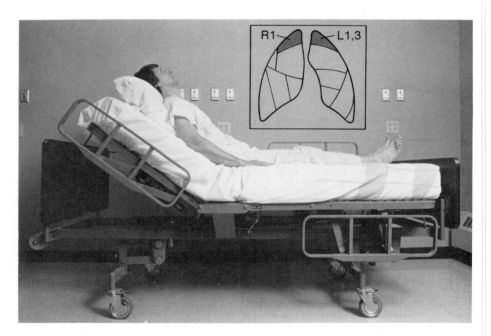

5 *To drain the apical segments of the upper lobes,* position your client so that he is reclining at a 30-degree angle. Percuss and vibrate the segments between the clavicles and the scapulae.

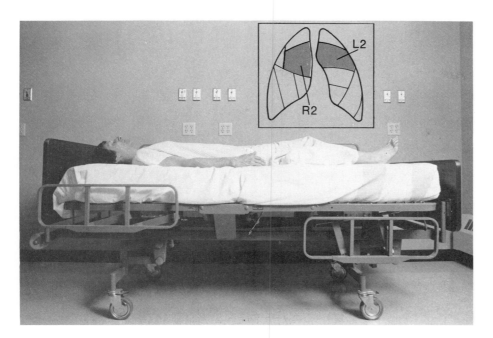

6 *To drain the anterior segments of the upper lobes,* the client should be supine, with knees flexed for comfort and effective breathing. Percuss and vibrate the segments between the clavicles and nipples.

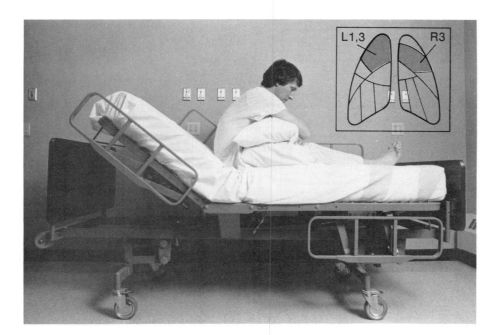

7 *To drain the posterior segments of the upper lobes,* instruct the client to lean forward over two pillows to achieve a 30-degree angle. Percuss and vibrate over the upper back, near but not over the scapulae.

(Continues)

8 *To drain the lateral and medial segments of the right middle lobe,* raise the foot of the bed around 15 degrees. The client should lie on his left side and then rotate a quarter turn toward his back. Place a pillow under his back to support his position. Percuss and vibrate over the uppermost nipple. If your client is a female, cup your hand under the axilla and extend your fingers forward, beneath her breast. Repeat after having the client lie on the right side and rotate a quarter turn toward the back (as shown). *This drains the lingular segments of the left upper lobe.* *Caution: A head-down position is usually contraindicated for clients with increased intracranial pressure, known intracranial disease, hypertension, and hemodynamic instability.*

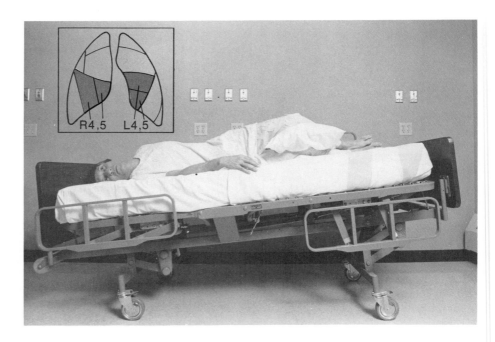

9 *To drain the superior segments of both lower lobes,* the client should assume a prone position, with two pillows under the hips. Percuss and vibrate over the middle of his back at the tips of the scapulae.

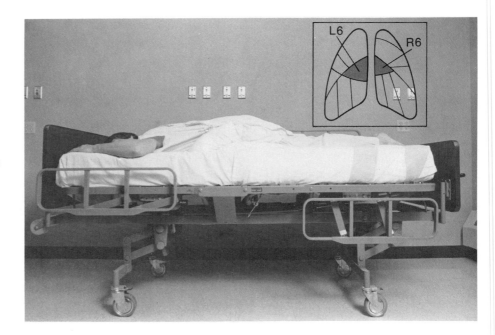

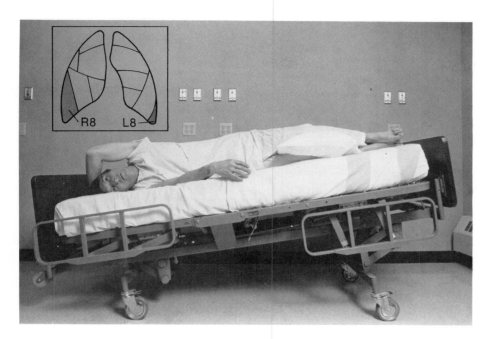

10 *To drain the anterior basal segments of the lower lobes,* raise the foot of the bed approximately 30 degrees. Instruct the client to lie on his side with a pillow between his knees and to place his upper arm over his head. Percuss and vibrate under the axillae over the lower ribs. The photograph depicts the position for draining the left anterior basal segment.

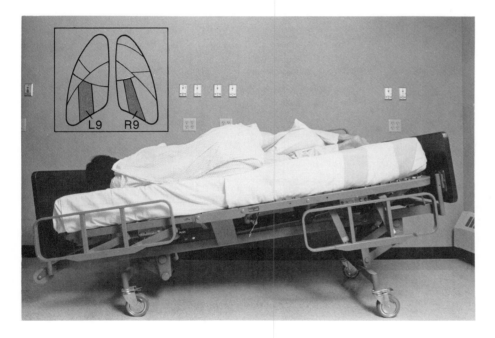

11 *To drain the lateral basal segments of the lower lobes,* raise the foot of the bed approximately 30 degrees. Have the client lie on his abdomen and rotate the upper half of his body a quarter turn toward his side. Percuss and vibrate over the lower ribs on his lateral chest. After he assumes the corresponding position on his opposite side, percuss and vibrate that segment. The photograph depicts the position for draining the right lateral segment.

(Continues)

12 *To drain the posterior basal segments of the lower lobes,* raise the foot of the bed around 30 degrees. Have the client lie on his abdomen with two pillows under his hips. Percuss and vibrate the segment over the lower ribs on both sides of his spine, but avoid the area over the kidneys.

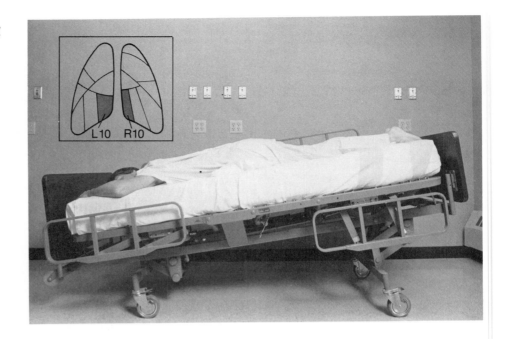

Evaluating

13 Auscultate the client's lung fields and monitor the rate and depth of his respirations to evaluate the results of the treatment. Optimally, improved aeration will result in improved breath sounds and a respiratory rate within normal limits. Document the procedure and the client's response. Note the amount, color, and character of his expectoration. Provide him with mouthwash or other oral hygiene.

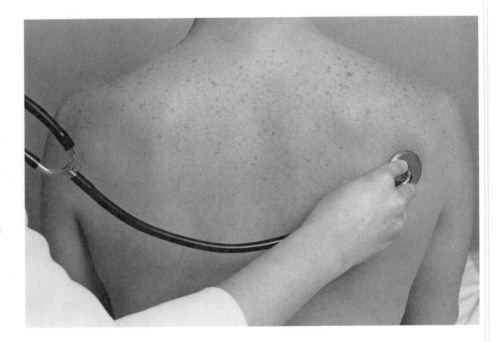

PERCUSSING, VIBRATING, AND DRAINING THE INFANT OR SMALL CHILD

Assessing and Planning

Implementing

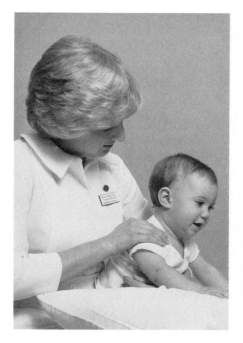

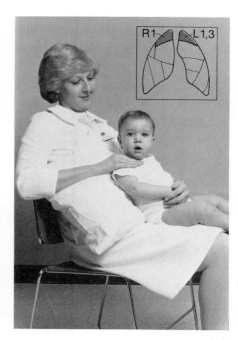

1 Review the process for percussing, vibrating, and draining the adult, but follow these variations for the infant or small child. Infants will better tolerate the procedure just prior to feeding. Before initiating the therapy, hold and comfort the infant for a while. At all times, speak reassuringly to help minimize the fear and anxiety he or she will experience, especially during percussion and while in head-down positions. Develop a rapport with the small child, and if possible, first demonstrate the procedure on one of his favorite dolls or stuffed animals. Percussion and vibration, if prescribed, should be less forceful and vigorous for infants and children than for adults.

2 If a child is too small for hand percussion, consider cutting a bulb syringe in half, dissecting as if you were slicing a globe at the equator, and taping the cut surfaces to make it smooth (shown). Percuss while holding onto the nozzle. To make an infant's vibrator, remove the toothbrush from a portable electric toothbrush and tape padding over its vibrating surface.

3 *To drain the apical segments of the upper lobes,* position the child so that he is reclining at a 30-degree angle, and place a pillow between the two of you. Percuss and vibrate the segments between the clavicles and scapulae.

(Continues)

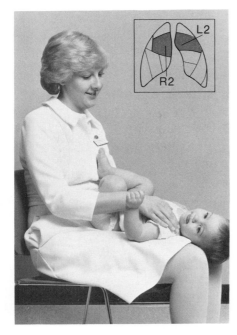

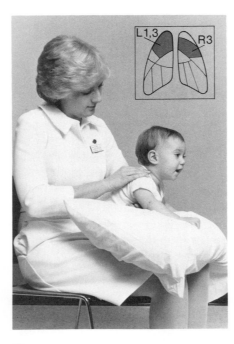

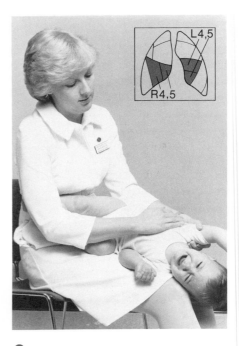

4 *To drain the anterior segments of the upper lobes,* position the child so that he is supine. Then percuss and vibrate the segments between the clavicles and nipples. If you have determined the need for suctioning, use a bulb syringe as demonstrated on p. 236.

5 *To drain the posterior segments of the upper lobes,* lean the child forward at about a 30-degree angle; percuss and vibrate the upper back on both sides.

6 *To drain the lateral and medial segments of the right middle lobe,* position the child as shown so that he is on the left side, with the head down at a 15-degree angle. Then rotate the child toward his back a quarter turn and percuss and vibrate over the uppermost nipple. Turn the child to the corresponding position on the opposite side *to drain the lingular segments of the left upper lobe.*

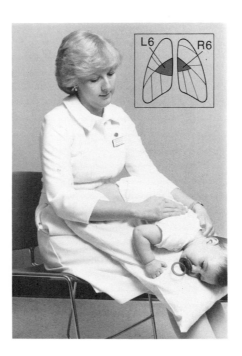

7 *To drain the superior segments of the lower lobes,* position the child on his abdomen, over a pillow. Percuss and vibrate on each side of the spine, below the tips of the scapulae.

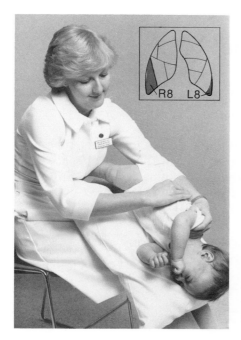

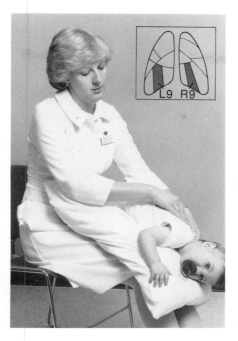

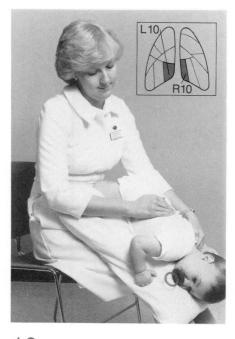

8 *To drain the anterior basal segments of the lower lobes,* extend your legs and position the child on a pillow so that the head is down approximately 30 degrees and he is on his side. Percuss and vibrate the segments over the lower ribs beneath the axillae. Turn the child to the opposite side, and repeat the procedure.

9 *To drain the lateral basal segments of the lower lobes,* place the child in a prone position, with his head down approximately 30 degrees. Rotate the upper half of the body a quarter turn toward the side. Percuss and vibrate over the lower ribs. Repeat the procedure after rotating the child to the opposite side.

10 *To drain the posterior basal segments of the lower lobes,* position the child so that he is prone, with the head lowered 30 degrees. Percuss and vibrate over the lower ribs on each side of the spine, avoiding the area over the kidneys.

11 *Evaluating:* See step 13, p. 384.

Managing the Client with a Chest Tube

Nursing Guidelines to a Disposable Closed Chest Drainage System

A disposable closed chest drainage system attaches to a chest tube to relieve pressure from a buildup of air or fluid in the pleural space. For example, clients who have had thoracic trauma with concomitant pleural tears, a spontaneous pneumothorax, or a hemothorax will require a chest tube and closed chest drainage.

Tube for connection to chest tube

Collection chamber

Water seal chamber

Suction control chamber

SUCTION CONTROL CHAMBER

- If the system is attached to suction, monitor the water level at least every 8 hours by pinching off the short tube to stop bubbling in the chamber. This will enable you to check the true water level.
- The amount of suction is determined by the water level in this chamber rather than by the suction control gauge. The physician will specify the amount of water, usually 20–25 cm for the adult and 10–20 cm for the pediatric population.
- Maintain only gentle bubbling in this chamber when suction is being used. More vigorous bubbling causes evaporation of the fluid.
- Cessation of bubbling when connected to suction could mean that the suction control gauge is set too low or that sterile solution needs to be added to the appropriate level. If increasing the suction or adding solution do not elicit bubbling, check for air leaks in the tubing or at the insertion site.
- If the system is providing closed water seal for gravity drainage, or if suction needs to be discontinued during client transport, keep the short tube unclamped so that it can act as an air vent, maintaining negative or equal pressure within the system.

WATER SEAL CHAMBER

- Fluctuations (tidaling) in this chamber occur normally during inhalation and exhalation until the lung reexpands and the client no longer requires chest drainage.
- Fluctuations in water level greater than 6 cm per respiration could mean the client has copious secretions or increased work of breathing due to low compliance. Assess the client for indicators of increased work breathing and auscultate the lung fields for breath sounds. If congestion is noted, encourage coughing, turning, and deep breathing to facilitate secretion expectoration, and suction if necessary.
- A cessation in water level fluctuations prior to lung reexpansion could mean the tubing is either kinked or occluded, or that one of the connection sites is loose. Ask the client to cough and change positions. Check for kinks, and check the connection sites for integrity.
- Bubbling in this chamber is normal if the client has an air leak, for example, from a pneumothorax. However, once the tear in the client's lung tissue begins to seal over, the bubbling should lessen. If continuous bubbling occurs in the chamber after it has had only occasional bubbling, assess the client's respiratory status. If the client's respirations and lung sounds are normal for the client, follow these steps to find the leak:

  1. Squeeze the chest tube at the insertion site, but for no longer than a second or two to prevent pressure buildup in the chest. If the bubbling stops, air may be entering the chest from the insertion site. Palpate around the insertion site, and if leakage is noted, apply tape to the area to reinforce the air-occlusive seal.
  2. If the bubbling continues as you squeeze the chest tube, the leak is in the tubing or within the drainage system itself. Squeeze the connection between the chest tube and the long rubber tube. If the bubbling stops, reinforce the juncture with tape or replace the tubing.

(Continues)

COLLECTION CHAMBER

3. Bubbling that continues means the fault is within the drainage system itself, and it should be replaced with a new system.

- Monitor the drainage every 30 minutes for the first 2 hours after chest tube insertion, then hourly for the next 24 hours, and every
- 2 hours thereafter.
  Mark the level of drainage directly on the chamber every 8 hours
- with the time and date.
  Drainage greater than 100 ml/hour is considered excessive, and the physician should be alerted immediately.
- Cessation in drainage can mean either the client's lung has reexpanded or the tubing is kinked or occluded with tissue and/or blood.

MONITORING THE CLIENT WITH A CHEST TUBE

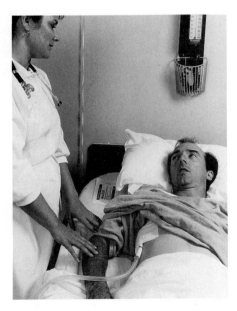

1 Assess the client for comfort, and administer pain medications as prescribed. Keep a petrolatum gauze pad within easy reach so that you can apply pressure with an air-occlusive material in case the chest tube becomes dislodged from the client's chest. Unless contraindicated, keep the client in semi-Fowler's position for his comfort and to facilitate drainage. Monitor the closed chest drainage system by following the guidelines on pp. 389–390.

Know your agency's policy regarding clamping a chest tube. Some specialists say the chest tube should not be clamped for any reason until the client's condition has improved enough for the tube to be removed; others believe there are special indications for clamping, such as a disconnection between the chest tube and the drainage tubing to prevent tension pneumothorax.

2 Auscultate your client's lung fields for breath sounds and monitor the vital signs to assess for signs of respiratory distress. Recognize the indications of acute pneumothorax: sharp, stabbing pain on the affected side; shortness of breath; and cyanosis. A physical assessment during pneumothorax might reveal diminished or absent breath sounds on the affected side, as well as a decrease in chest expansion and tactile fremitus. You might also note hyperresonance in the affected lung while percussing over that area. Deviation of the trachea toward the unaffected side indicates a tension pneumothorax. This is life threatening and requires immediate treatment.

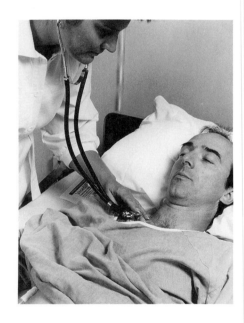

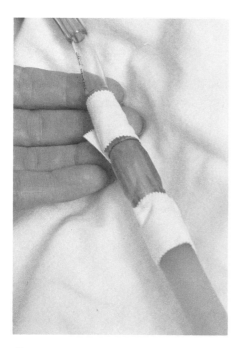

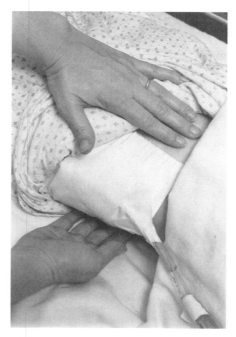

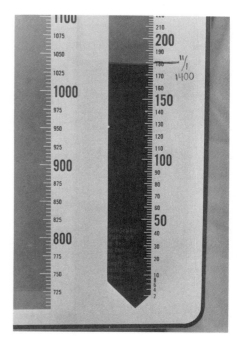

3 Ensure that the system is air tight by checking to see that the chest tube is securely connected to the drainage chamber and that all connection sites are secure.

4 Palpate around the dressing site to assess for crepitation (subcutaneous emphysema). Also, inspect the dressing for abnormal drainage. Any sudden change in amount, odor, or appearance of the drainage should be documented, and the physician should be notified.

5 Check the amount, color, and character of the drainage in the drainage collection chamber at least every 30 minutes during the first 2 hours after chest tube insertion. Do this hourly during the next 24 hours and every 2 hours thereafter. Every 8 hours, mark the time and date directly on the chamber at the level of the drainage.

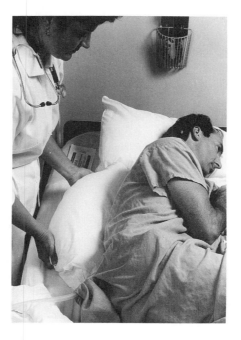

6 Unless it is contraindicated, reposition the client every 2 hours to provide comfort and to facilitate drainage. Place a pillow at the back to support his position. Also, assist the client with range of motion exercises on the affected shoulder. These should be performed a minimum of three times per day.

(Continues)

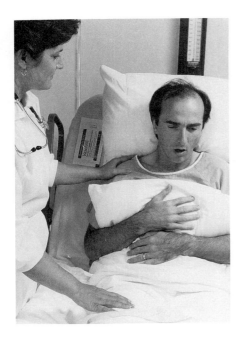

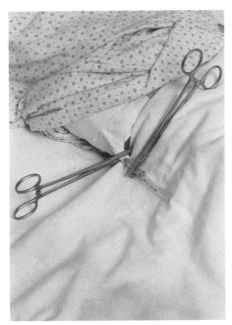

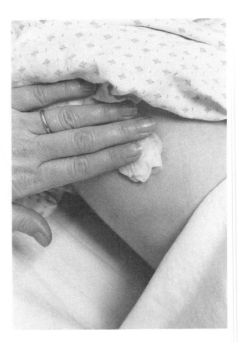

7 Encourage deep breathing and coughing exercises to facilitate drainage and help remove accumulations from the pleural space and tracheobronchial tree. This will help the lung to reexpand. Splint the insertion site with a pillow or with your hand to minimize discomfort. *Note: To ensure that the client is achieving adequate thoracic expansion, palpate for thoracic expansion, following the procedure, p. 329. Your thumbs should separate at least 2.5–5 cm (1–2 in.) as the client inhales.*

8 If your client *does not* have an air leak, if chest tube clamping is approved by your agency, and if the chest tube becomes accidentally disconnected from the drainage system but you are unable to reconnect it immediately, clamp the chest tube close to the insertion site with a rubber-shod clamp. Immediate action is necessary to prevent a pneumothorax. Be certain to have the client exhale fully before clamping the tube to prevent an air buildup in the pleural space. Attach a second clamp distal to the first as a precautionary measure. *Caution: To prevent a tension pneumothorax, the tube should not be clamped for longer than a minute or two while you change the drainage system or reattach the chest tube to the rubber tubing of the drainage system.*

9 If the chest tube should be accidentally pulled out from the insertion site, remove the dressing and immediately apply pressure with the petrolatum gauze to prevent a pneumothorax. If petrolatum gauze is not available, apply pressure with a towel or a gloved hand. Have a co-worker notify a physician immediately. If the client already has a pneumothorax, this is a life-threatening situation.

10 Most closed chest drainage systems have drainage collection chambers that can be removed and replaced without disrupting the closed system. Follow agency and system manufacturer's guidelines for changing the collection chamber.

ASSISTING WITH THE REMOVAL OF A CHEST TUBE

Assessing

1 Assess your client's respiratory status by auscultating the lung fields for the presence of normal breath sounds and palpating to ensure that improved bilateral chest expansion has occurred. Determine the need for a pain medication. If one has been prescribed, administer it 30 minutes prior to the removal of the chest tube. In many instances, the chest tube will have been clamped for a period of time (1–2 days prior to removal) to evaluate the client's tolerance.

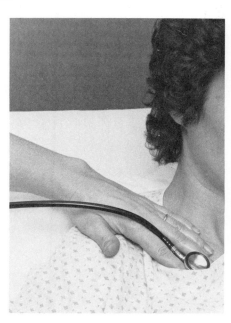

(Continues)

Planning

2   You will need to assemble a suture-removal kit, sterile 4 × 4 gauze pads, 3-in. tape, a petrolatum gauze pad, and tincture of benzoin for tape adherence. An impervious drape should be placed under the client's chest to protect the bed from drainage.

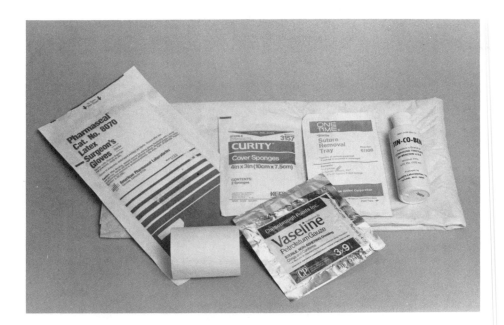

3   Explain the procedure to your client. Instruct her in the Valsalva maneuver so that she can hold her breath and bear down as the physician removes the tube. This will increase intrathoracic pressure, thereby lessening the potential for air to enter the pleural space.

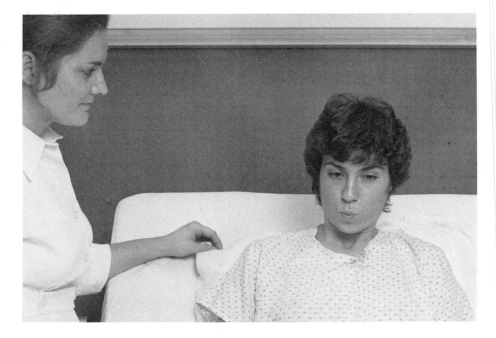

Implementing

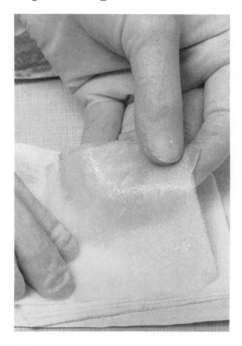

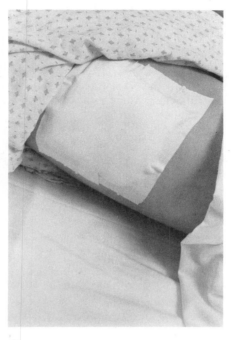

4 Prior to the chest tube removal, prepare the sterile dressing using aseptic technique. After opening the packages, put on sterile gloves and place the petrolatum gauze pad on top of the sterile 4 × 4. The physician will then apply the dressing to the insertion site immediately after removing the chest tube. This will minimize the potential for air to enter the chest wall.

5 Tape the dressing in place. To seal the site from inrushing air, cover the entire dressing with wide strips of air-occlusive tape.

Evaluating

6 Continue to monitor your client's respiratory status. Observe for indications of a pneumothorax and/or for the condition that necessitated the chest tube's insertion. Assess the dressing for copious drainage, and document the procedure and your assessments.

References

American Heart Association: Standards and guidelines for cardiopulmonary resuscitation (CPR) and emergency cardiac care (ECC). *JAMA* 1986; 255(21):2841–3044.

Barnes TA: *Respiratory Care Practice.* Chicago: Yearbook Medical Publishers, 1988.

Bates B: *A Guide to Physical Examination and History Taking,* 4th ed. Philadelphia: Lippincott, 1987.

Bowers AC, Thompson JM: *Clinical Manual of Health Assessment,* 3d ed. St. Louis: Mosby, 1988.

Burton G et al: *Respiratory Care: A Guide to Clinical Practice,* 2d ed. Philadelphia: Lippincott, 1984.

Carroll PF: The ins and outs of chest drainage systems. *Nursing 86* 1986; 16(12):26–33.

Carroll PF: Lowering the risks of endotracheal suctioning. *Nursing 88* 1988; 18(5):46–50.

Cystic Fibrosis Foundation: Segmental drainage. Rockville, MD: Cystic Fibrosis Foundation, 1980.

Duncan CR et al: Effect of chest tube management on drainage after cardiac surgery. *Heart Lung* 1987; 16(1):1–9.

Farley J: About chest tubes. *Nursing 88* 1988; 18(6):16.

Gaskell DV, Webber BA: *The Brompton Hospital Guide to Chest Physiotherapy,* 4th ed. Oxford, England: Blackwell Scientific Publications, 1980.

Heitz U, Howard C: Respiratory dysfunctions. In: *Manual of Critical Care: Applying Nursing Diagnoses to Adult Critical Illness,* 2d ed. Swearingen PL. St. Louis: Mosby, 1991.

Hoffman LA et al: Fine tuning your chest PT. *Am J Nurs* 1987; 87(12): 1566–1572.

Howard C: Respiratory disorders. In: *Manual of Nursing Therapeutics: Applying Nursing Diagnoses to Medical Disorders,* 2d ed. Swearingen PL. St. Louis: Mosby, 1990.

Kacmarek RM, Stoller JK: *Current Respiratory Care.* Toronto: BC Decker, 1988.

Kacmarek RM et al: *Essentials of Respiratory Therapy,* 2d ed. Chicago: Yearbook Medical Publishers, 1985.

Mapp CS: Trach care: Are you aware of all the dangers? *Nursing 88* 1988; 18(7):34–42.

McHugh J: Perfecting the 3 steps of chest physiotherapy. *Nursing 87* 1987; 17(11):54–57.

McPherson S: *Respiratory Therapy Equipment,* 3d ed. St. Louis: Mosby, 1985.

Palau D, Jones S: Test your skill at troubleshooting chest tubes. *RN* (Oct) 1986; 43–45.

Reports of the ATS AdHoc Committee on Pulmonary Nomenclature: Updated nomenclature for membership reaction, *Am Thor Soc News* 1977; 3:5.

Seidel H et al: *Mosby's Guide to Physical Examination.* St. Louis: Mosby, 1987.

Shapiro BA et al: *Clinical Application of Respiratory Care,* 3d ed. Chicago: Yearbook Medical Publishers, 1985.

Spence A, Mason E: *Human Anatomy and Physiology,* 3d ed. Redwood City, CA: Benjamin/Cummings, 1989.

Stevens SA, Becker KL: How to perform a picture perfect respiratory assessment. *Nursing 88* 1988; 18(1): 58–63.

Swearingen PL: Breath sounds. In: *Manual of Critical Care.* Swearingen PL. St. Louis: Mosby, 1991.

Thompson JM et al: *Mosby's Manual of Clinical Nursing,* 2d ed. St. Louis: Mosby, 1989.

Wilkins RL et al: *Clinical Assessment of Respiratory Care,* 2d ed. St. Louis: Mosby, 1990.

Chapter 7

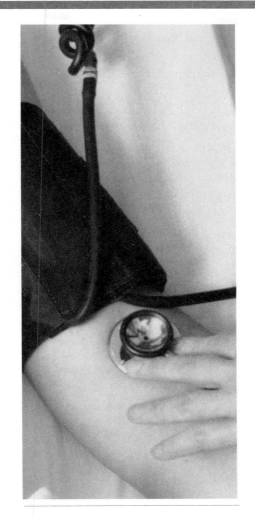

Managing Cardiovascular Procedures

CHAPTER OUTLINE

ASSESSING THE CARDIOVASCULAR SYSTEM

The Cardiovascular System

Nursing Assessment Guideline

Examining the Cardiac Area

Inspecting and Palpating
Auscultating

Palpating Arterial Pulses

MONITORING THE CARDIOVASCULAR SYSTEM

Inspecting the Jugular Vein

Measuring Arterial Blood Pressure

Obtaining the Ankle-Brachial Pressure Ratio (A/B Ratio)

Measuring Paradoxical Pulse

Nursing Guidelines for Identifying Common Telemetry Lead Sites

Applying Disposable Electrodes for Telemetry Monitoring

Positioning Electrodes for a 12-Lead EKG

Assessing the Postcardiac Catheterization Client

Measuring Central Venous Pressure (CVP)

CARING FOR CLIENTS WITH VASCULAR DISORDERS

Applying Elastic (Antiembolic) Stockings

Employing Buerger-Allen Exercises

Assessing the Cardiovascular System

THE CARDIOVASCULAR SYSTEM

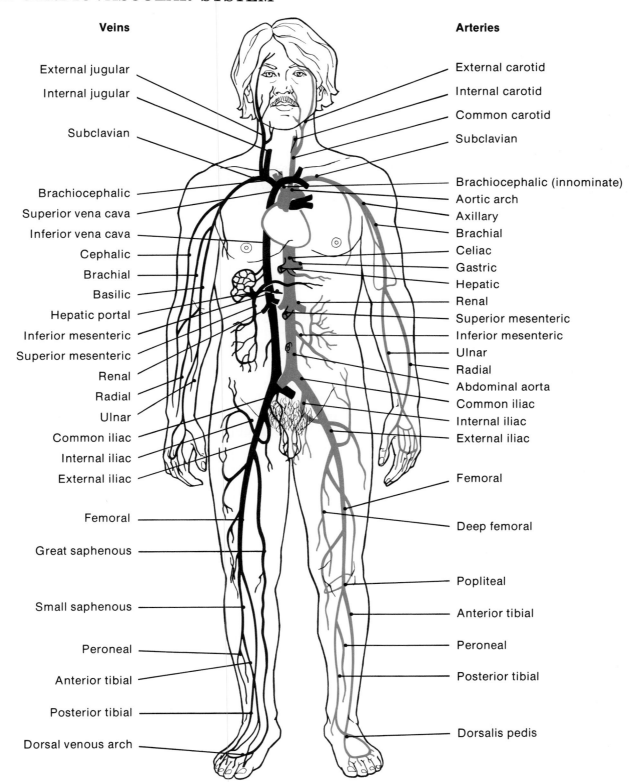

Veins

External jugular
Internal jugular
Subclavian
Brachiocephalic
Superior vena cava
Inferior vena cava
Cephalic
Brachial
Basilic
Hepatic portal
Inferior mesenteric
Superior mesenteric
Renal
Radial
Ulnar
Common iliac
Internal iliac
External iliac
Femoral
Great saphenous
Small saphenous
Peroneal
Anterior tibial
Posterior tibial
Dorsal venous arch

Arteries

External carotid
Internal carotid
Common carotid
Subclavian
Brachiocephalic (innominate)
Aortic arch
Axillary
Brachial
Celiac
Gastric
Hepatic
Renal
Superior mesenteric
Inferior mesenteric
Ulnar
Radial
Abdominal aorta
Common iliac
Internal iliac
External iliac
Femoral
Deep femoral
Popliteal
Anterior tibial
Peroneal
Posterior tibial
Dorsalis pedis

Nursing Assessment Guideline

To assess your client's cardiovascular system, you need to interview him or her for subjective data, take vital signs, examine the cardiac area, and monitor pulses. A comprehensive nursing care plan includes a complete evaluation for the following subjective data:

Personal factors: age, sex, race, nationality, occupation, marital status

History or family history of: cardiac or coronary artery disease (especially prior to the age of 60), myocardial infarction (MI), diabetes mellitus, gout, hypertension, cerebrovascular accident (CVA), congenital heart defects, rheumatic heart disease, angina, congestive heart failure

Risk factors: smoking, type-A personality, major life change units, excessive stress, obesity, lack of exercise

Dietary habits: intake in approximate amounts of calories, cholesterol, sodium, fluids, "fast foods," alcohol; food allergies

Medications: for example, nitroglycerin, diuretics, cardiotonics (such as digoxin), quinidine, antiarrhythmics, beta blockers, antihypertensives, calcium channel blockers; over-the-counter; drug allergies

Pain: location, intensity, duration, character, precipitating factors, methods of alleviation

Cyanosis: precipitating factors, sites

Peripheral vascular alterations: coldness, numbness, discolorations, blanching, edema, sites

Limitations of activities: exercise intolerance, dyspnea on exertion, precipitating factors

Sleep patterns: need for pillows, nocturia, night sweats

Miscellaneous: diaphoresis, syncope, dizziness, palpitations, nausea, vomiting, edema, digital clubbing, headaches

EXAMINING THE CARDIAC AREA

Explain the procedure to your client and examine him in a warm, quiet, and private environment. Assist the client into a supine position, with his head slightly elevated. Ask him to uncover his chest, but provide a robe or blanket for warmth and privacy. For optimal inspection and to facilitate palpation of the cardiac area, approach the client on his right side.

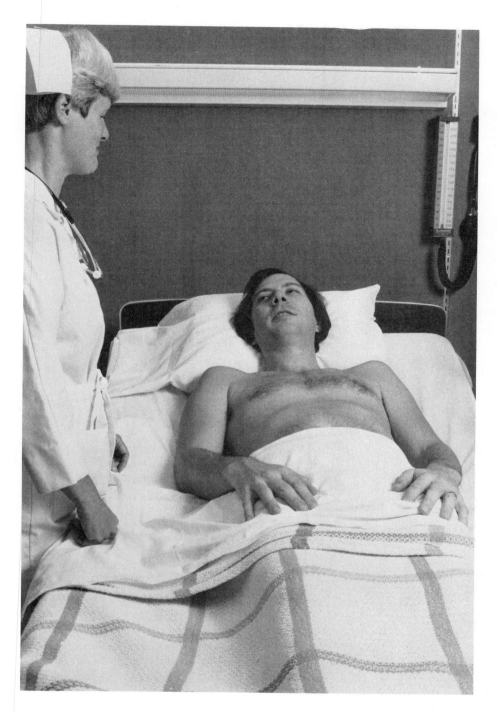

(Continues)

To assist you with your examination and documentation of sites, familiarize yourself with these anatomic landmarks.

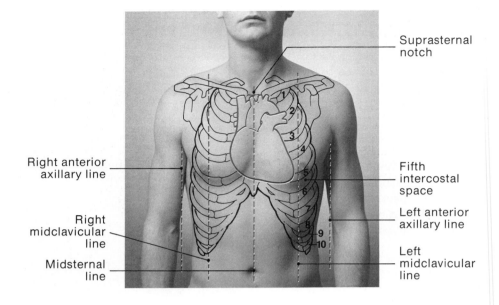

Right anterior axillary line

Right midclavicular line

Midsternal line

Suprasternal notch

Fifth intercostal space

Left anterior axillary line

Left midclavicular line

INSPECTING AND PALPATING

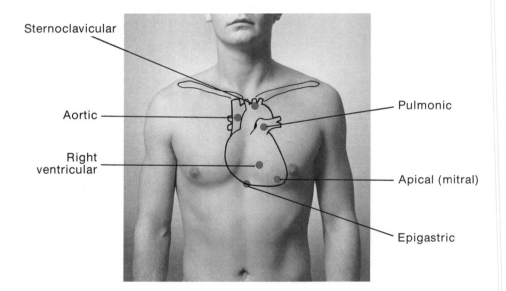

Sternoclavicular

Aortic

Right ventricular

Pulmonic

Apical (mitral)

Epigastric

Identify these areas for cardiac palpation on your client's chest. Begin by inspecting the apical area for the point of maximal impulse (PMI) at the fifth intercostal space, near the left midclavicular line. Normally, it is seen in the male client as a pulsation covering an area no greater than 2 cm. If the PMI is not observable, for example, in clients with barrel chests, in obese males, and in females, you may need to palpate for it. A pulsation that covers a larger area may indicate left ventricular hypertrophy, a recent MI, or an aneurysm.

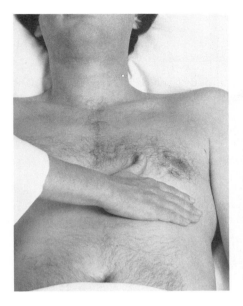

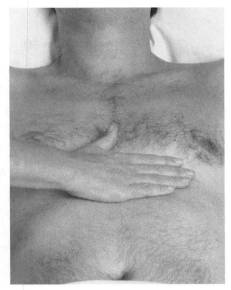

Palpate the apical area to assess duration and strength of the beat. An abnormally strong and sustained pulsation is often found in clients with left ventricular hypertrophy. However, anemia, fever, or hyperthyroidism can produce moderately strong pulsations. Also, palpate for thrills by using the palmar surface of your hand (as shown). Thrills give the sensation of water running through a hose. They are most often indicative of ventricular or atrial septal defects. If you are able to palpate a thrill, you will probably also detect a murmur over the same area during auscultation.

Palpate these areas using the palmar surface of your hand and the fat pads of your fingers: right ventricular, aortic, pulmonic, sternoclavicular, and epigastric (as shown). Note the presence or absence of pulsations. In addition to the apical area, they may be felt over the aortic and right ventricular areas; you might detect a light pulsation at the sternoclavicular area. Bounding pulsations at the epigastric or sternoclavicular areas, however, could be indicative of an aortic aneurysm.

AUSCULTATING

Familiarize yourself with these areas for cardiac auscultation. Remember that a valve's sound is heard better in the direction of its blood flow rather than directly over the valve itself. Use this guideline as you develop your own pattern for cardiac auscultation.

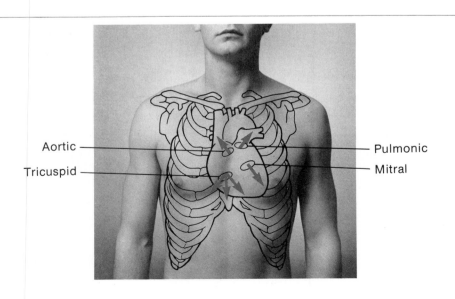

Aortic —
Tricuspid —
Pulmonic —
Mitral —

Table 7-1 Assessing Heart Sounds

Sound	Auscultation site	Timing	Pitch	Clinical occurrence	End-piece/patient position
S_1 (M_1 T_1)	Apex	Beginning of systole	High	Closing of mitral and tricuspid valves. Normal sound.	Diaphragm/patient supine
S_1 split	Apex	Beginning of systole	High	Ventricles contracting at different times due to electrical or mechanical problems. For example, a longer time span between M_1 T_1 caused by right bundle-branch heart block, or reversal (T_1 M_1) caused by mitral stenosis.	Same as S_1
S_2 (A_2 P_2)	A_2 at 2nd ICS, RSB; P_2 at 2nd ICS, LSB	End of systole	High	Closing of aortic and pulmonic valves. Normal sound.	Diaphragm/patient supine
S_2 Physiologic split	2nd ICS, LSB	End of systole	High	Accentuated by inspiration; disappears on expiration. Sound that corresponds with the respiratory cycle due to normal delay in closure of pulmonic valve during inspiration. It is accentuated during exercise or in individuals with thin chest walls; heard most often in children and young adults.	Same as S_2
S_2 Persistent (wide) split	2nd ICS, LSB	End of systole	High	Heard throughout the respiratory cycle; caused by late closure of pulmonic valve or early closure of aortic valve. Occurs in atrial septal defect, right ventricular failure, pulmonic stenosis, hypertension, or right bundle-branch heart block.	Same as S_2
S_2 Paradoxic (reversed) split (P_2 A_2)	2nd ICS, LSB	End of systole	High	Because of delayed left ventricular systole, the aortic valve closes after the pulmonic valve rather than before it. (Normally during expiration the two sounds merge.) Causes may include left bundle-branch heart block, aortic stenosis, severe left ventricular failure, MI, and severe hypertension.	Same as S_2
S_2 Fixed split	2nd ICS, LSB	End of systole	High	Heard with equal intensity during inspiration and expiration due to split of pulmonic and aortic components, which are unaffected by blood volume or respiratory changes. May be heard in pulmonary stenosis or atrial septal defect.	Same as S_2

Table 7-1, *Continued*

Sound	Auscultation site	Timing	Pitch	Clinical occurrence	End-piece/patient position
S_3 (ventricular gallop)	Apex	Early diastole just after S_2	Dull, low	Early and rapid filling of ventricle, as in early ventricular failure, CHF; common in children, during last trimester of pregnancy, and possibly in healthy adults over age 50.	Bell/patient in left lateral or supine position
S_4 (atrial gallop)	Apex	Late in diastole just before S_1	Low	Atrium filling against increased resistance of stiff ventricle, as in CHF, coronary artery disease, cardiomyopathy, pulmonary artery hypertension, ventricular failure. May be normal in infants, children, and athletes.	Same as S_3

ICS = intercostal space; RSB = right sternal border; LSB = left sternal border.

SOURCE: Swearingen PL: *Manual of Critical Care: Applying Nursing Diagnoses to Adult Critical Illness,* 2d ed. St. Louis: Mosby, 1991.

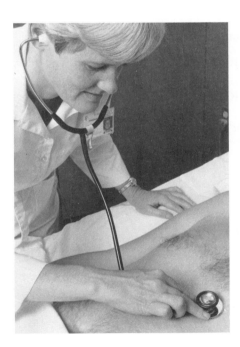

Review Table 7-1. Use the diaphragm of the stethoscope to auscultate normal heart sounds, S_1 and S_2. S_1 ("lub") is heard best over mitral and tricuspid areas, and S_2 ("dub") is heard best over aortic and pulmonic areas. Both sounds are more easily heard when the client is supine. If the heart sounds are distant, for example, in clients who are obese or who have large thoraxes, ask the client to turn slightly toward his left side so the heart is closer to the chest wall.

(Continues)

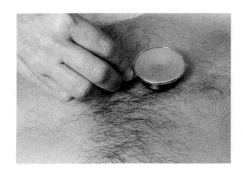

Lightly position the bell side of the stethoscope against the client's chest to detect adventitious heart sounds such as murmurs and gallops (see Table 7-2). Follow the guideline, p. 404, for auscultating normal heart sounds. Murmurs may be heard during systole (between S_1 and S_2) at the pulmonic and mitral area, or during diastole (between S_2 and S_1)

over most of the cardiac area, but the latter are more often pathologic and are found in heart disease or congenital defects. Murmurs may be palpated as thrills over the same area. Note the timing, location, intensity, and pitch of murmurs when recording your findings. S_3 (ventricular gallop) is a dull and low-pitched sound, "lub-dub-dee" (S_1-S_2-S_3), and it is best heard over the apical and right ventricular areas during exhalation when the client lies on his left side. In this position, gravity enhances ventricular filling and thereby exaggerates the sound. Because a ventricular gallop is one of the first clinical signs of congestive heart failure, early detection can avert advancing cardiac failure. Normally it

may be heard in children and in young adults. S_4 (atrial gallop) has a higher pitch, and if present, it is elicited in the mitral area (apex). It sounds like "dee-lub-dub" (S_4-S_1-S_2). Clients with congestive heart failure might have both S_3 and S_4 (sounding like a galloping horse in the chest), as well as an increased heart rate. A pericardial friction rub might be heard in postmyocardial infarction clients when they lean forward and exhale deeply. It sounds like two pieces of sandpaper rubbing against each other. Whereas a pericardial rub is heard when the client exhales, a pleural rub (see p. 333) is heard only when the client holds his breath.

Table 7-2   Commonly Occurring Heart Murmurs

Type	Timing	Pitch	Quality	Auscultation site	Radiation
Pulmonic stenosis	Systolic ejection	Medium-high	Harsh	2nd ICS, LSB	Toward left shoulder, back
Aortic stenosis	Midsystolic	Medium-high	Harsh	2nd ICS, RSB	Toward carotid arteries
Ventricular septal defect	Late systolic	High	Blowing	4th ICS, LSB	Toward right sternal border
Mitral insufficiency	Holosystolic	High	Blowing	5–6th ICS, left MCL	Toward left axilla
Tricuspid insufficiency	Holosystolic	High	Blowing	4th ICS, LSB	Toward apex
Aortic insufficiency	Early diastolic	High	Blowing	2nd ICS, RSB	Toward sternum
Pulmonary insufficiency	Early diastolic	High	Blowing	2nd ICS, LSB	Toward sternum
Mitral stenosis	Mid-late diastolic	Low	Rumbling	5th ICS, left MCL	Toward axilla
Tricuspid stenosis	Mid-late diastolic	Low	Rumbling	4th ICS, LSB	Usually none

ICS = intercostal space; RSB = right sternal border; LSB = left sternal border; MCL = midclavicular line.

SOURCE: From Swearingen PL: *Manual of Critical Care: Applying Nursing Diagnoses to Adult Critical Illness*, 2d ed. St. Louis: Mosby, 1991.

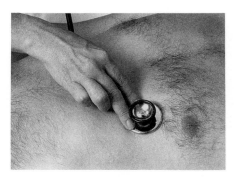

Auscultate the chest for the apical pulse (as shown) for 1 minute to determine the rate and rhythm of the heart. Irregular rhythms, bradycardia (less than 60 beats per minute) in nonathletes, or tachycardia (greater than 100 beats per minute) are considered abnormal in adults. Palpate the brachial or radial pulse as you auscultate the apical pulse to assess for a potential pulse deficit in the peripheral artery. A peripheral pulse deficit occurs when the cardiac systole is not strong enough to produce a palpable arterial pulse. It can occur with atrial fibrillation. If a pulse deficit is found, ask an associate to count peripheral pulsations while you auscultate the apical pulse. Document both pulse rates.

PALPATING ARTERIAL PULSES

Review these anatomic landmarks to assist you in locating the arterial pulse points. For infants, pulses can range between 80 and 180 beats per minute. At 4 years old, children can have pulses ranging from 80 to 120, and at age 10, pulses range from 70 to 110. From 14 years on, pulses can range from 50 to 100, with women averaging a slightly faster pulse than men.

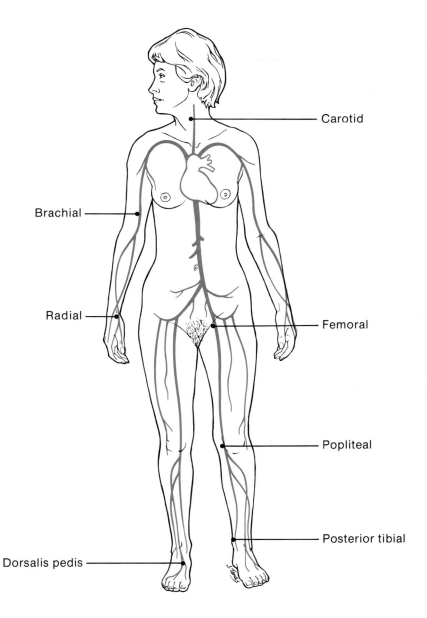

(Continues)

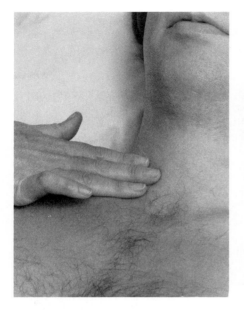

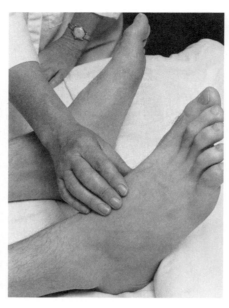

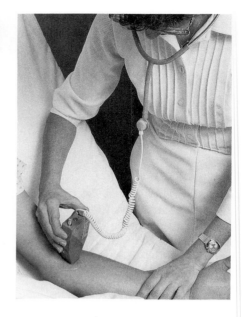

Begin your assessment of the arterial pulses by palpating the carotid artery to evaluate rate, rhythm, and amplitude of the pulse. Use a light touch to avoid arterial occlusion and the precipitation of bradycardia by carotid sinus massage. Palpate *only* one artery at a time to ensure adequate cerebral blood flow. The artery should feel soft and pliant to the touch, but clients with atherosclerosis may have cordlike arteries. Palpate the opposite artery and compare the two pulses. An abrupt cessation of one pulse with accompanying chest or back pain suggests an aortic aneurysm.

Palpate the peripheral pulses for rate, rhythm, and amplitude; compare each pulse to its corresponding pulse on the opposite side. Begin by palpating the brachial arteries, and then palpate the radial arteries. Palpate the femoral and popliteal arteries and complete the assessment with the arteries farthest from the heart: posterior tibial and dorsalis pedis (as shown). The posterior tibial pulse can be palpated behind and slightly inferior to the medial malleolus; the dorsalis pedis pulse is best palpated over the dorsum of the foot, with the foot slightly dorsiflexed.

Using a Doppler Ultrasonic Probe: If you are unable to palpate peripheral arterial pulses, a Doppler ultrasonic probe may be used to elicit sounds that will identify the flow of arterial blood. In this photo, the nurse has positioned the probe's transducer over the client's brachial pulse site, which she has lubricated with a conducting gel. The earphones enable her to hear wavelike "whooshing" sounds, which are produced by the reflection of red blood cells as they flow through the artery. The Doppler also can be used to evaluate the patency of veins and arteries for clients with a potential for thrombus or embolus, or for those who have undergone vein grafts. After using the Doppler, record either the presence or the absence of pulsations. Be sure to describe the rate and character of the sound you hear, including its intensity and frequency.

Monitoring the Cardiovascular System

INSPECTING THE JUGULAR VEIN

To inspect the jugular vein, elevate the head of the client's bed to a 45-degree angle. Assess and record the highest level of distention and pulsation in the interior jugular vein in centimeters, using the sternal angle (the point at which the clavicles meet) as a reference point. If you find the level to be 3 cm above the sternal angle, the client's central venous pressure is probably elevated. The client in the photo does not have a distended jugular vein. Normal findings are as follows: When the client is lying flat, the jugular vein will be slightly distended; when the client is in Fowler's position, the vein will be flat.

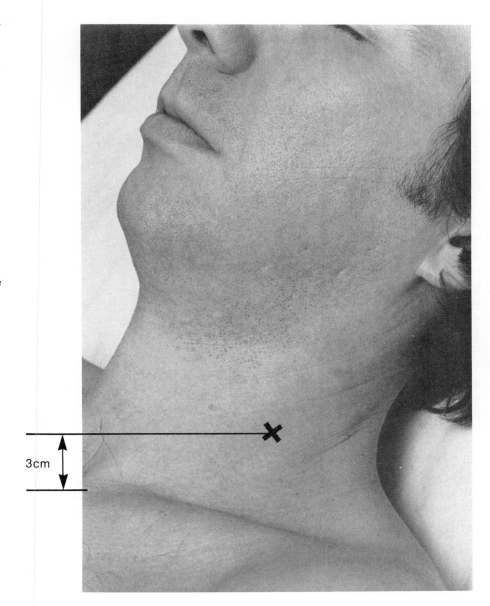

3cm

MEASURING ARTERIAL BLOOD PRESSURE

Assessing and Planning

1 Assess your client's knowledge of the procedure and follow up accordingly, stressing the importance of regular blood pressure monitoring. Determine whether the client has exercised, eaten, drunk, or smoked within the last 30 minutes. These activities, in addition to pain, urinary bladder distention, or merely having the blood pressure measured, can alter the reading. It is also important that you have the correct bladder and cuff size. The bladder from an adult-sized cuff has been removed here to help you envision its width and length. To ensure an accurate reading, the width of the bladder should be 40% of the circumference of the midpoint of the limb on which it is used (or approximately 20% wider than the diameter of the same site). The length of the bladder should be equal to 80% of the limb's midpoint circumference. For the average adult arm, bladder widths of 12–14 cm are recommended, but remember, it is the circumference of the limb, not the client's age, that determines cuff size.

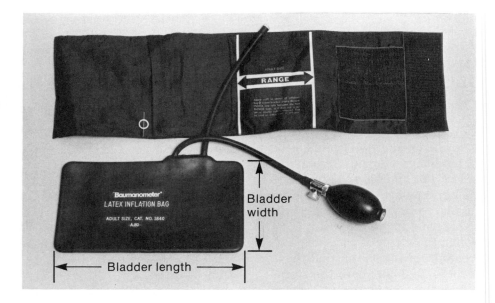

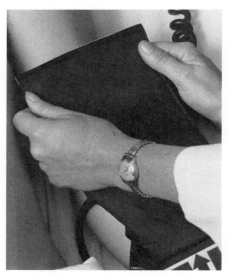

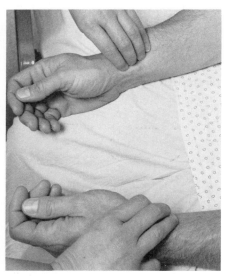

2 For example, in this photo the width of the cuff is being compared to the diameter of the client's upper arm to ensure that the cuff's bladder is 20% wider than the arm's diameter. If the bladder is too narrow, the blood pressure reading may be falsely high; if it is too wide, the reading may be falsely low.

3 If this is an initial screening, you should measure the blood pressure in both arms; if it is a routine assessment, first compare the quality of the pulses in both arms by palpating both radial pulses simultaneously (as shown). Measure the blood pressure in the arm with the stronger pulse if the pulses are unequal; if they are equal, measure the pressure on the right arm if you are right-handed or on the left arm if you are left-handed. This is recommended for your comfort and convenience to facilitate the procedure.

Implementing

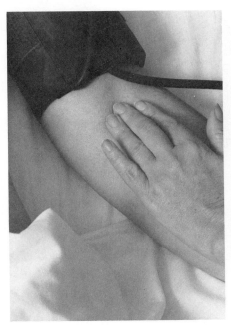

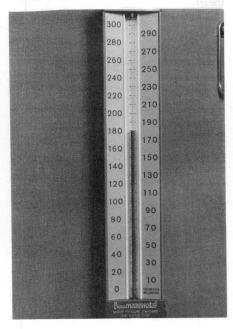

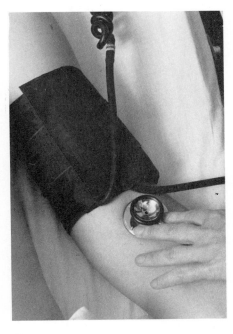

4 Support and position the client's arm at his heart level, and place the center of the cuff's bladder over the brachial artery. Wrap the cuff snugly around the upper arm 2.5 cm (1 in.) above the antecubital space to allow room for the diaphragm of the stethoscope. While you palpate the brachial (or radial) artery, inflate the cuff until you feel the pulse disappear.

5 When you feel the pulse disappear, immediately note the reading on the manometer. This is the palpated systolic blood pressure. Read the gauge at eye level to ensure a correct reading. Then rapidly deflate the cuff and wait 30 seconds to allow for a decrease in venous congestion. A failure to do so could cause an alteration in the reading.

6 Place the stethoscope over the brachial artery, and rapidly reinflate the cuff to a point 30 mm Hg above the palpated systolic pressure, which is referred to as the point of maximum inflation. You must inflate to this point to ensure that the first sound (systolic pressure or Korotkoff I) is heard and that you have inflated above the auscultatory gap that occasionally occurs in hypertensive clients. *Note: To minimize extraneous sounds, the diaphragm of the stethoscope should contact neither the cuff nor any clothing.*

(Continues)

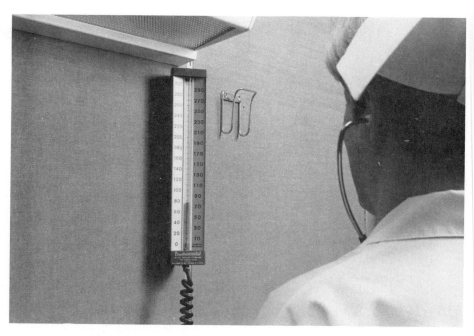

7   Slowly deflate the cuff at a rate of 2–4 mm Hg per heart beat, and note the systolic pressure when the first sound is heard (Korotkoff I) for both adults and children. To be sure that the first sound you hear is not an extraneous noise, make sure the initial sound is accompanied by at least one other consecutive beat. The diastolic pressure is recorded for children when the sound muffles (Korotkoff IV), and for both children and adults when the sound disappears and silence begins (Korotkoff V). Thus, for children, three numbers should be recorded: Korotkoff I, Korotkoff IV, and Korotkoff V; for adults, only Korotkoff I and Korotkoff V are recorded, unless sounds are heard all the way down to zero. If this occurs, record three numbers: systolic, muffled sound, and the disappearance (zero); for example, 100/40/0. After completely deflating the cuff, wait 2 minutes for venous congestion to decrease and repeat the procedure in the same arm to verify the reading. If this is the initial screening, measure the blood pressure three times in both arms, averaging each of the last two readings.

Evaluating

8 Document your client's blood pressure, noting the limb(s) on which the blood pressure was taken, the client's position during the reading, and the cuff size. If you have been the first to detect hypertension or related significant findings, refer the client for further evaluation. Based on two or more readings on two or more occasions for the adult (ages 18 and over), diastolic pressure <85 mm Hg is considered normal; 85–89 mm Hg is considered high normal; 90–104 mm Hg is considered mildly hypertensive; 105–114 mm Hg is considered moderately hypertensive; and ≥115 mm Hg is considered severely hypertensive. Systolic pressure <140 mm Hg is considered normal; 140–159 mm Hg is considered borderline isolated systolic hypertension; and ≥160 mm Hg is considered isolated systolic hypertension. The classification of borderline/isolated systolic or isolated systolic pressure takes precedence over high normal diastolic pressure when both occur in the same client. High normal diastolic pressure takes precedence over a classification of normal systolic pressure when both occur in the same person (Chobanian AM et al, 1988).

For children, the following systolic/diastolic blood pressure values are considered significantly hypertensive (Report of the second task force on blood pressure control in children—1987).

- ages 3–5 ≥116/76 mm Hg
- ages 6–9 ≥122/78 mm Hg
- ages 10–12 ≥126/82 mm Hg

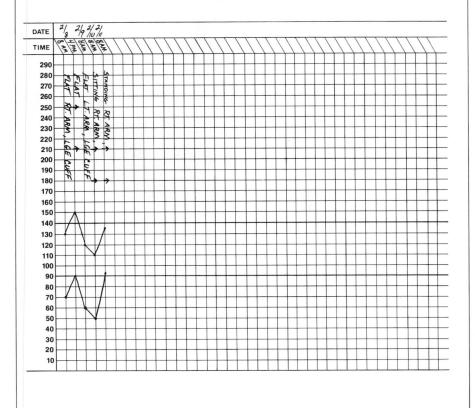

- ages 13–15 ≥136/86 mm Hg
- ages 16–18 ≥142/92 mm Hg.

Clients with systolic pressures less than 90 mm Hg and diastolic pressures less than 60 mm Hg may be considered hypotensive if illness or medications are the cause, and you should evaluate and follow up accordingly. However, if it is your client's typical pattern, low pressure readings are considered to be both normal and desirable. Establish your client's baseline blood pressure status early on admission so that you will have an adequate database from which to evaluate the integrity of each body system.

OBTAINING THE ANKLE-BRACHIAL PRESSURE RATIO (A/B RATIO)

A/B ratios are obtained to evaluate the patency of the vascular system in the lower extremities following vascular surgery or in the presence of vascular insufficiency.

Assessing and Planning

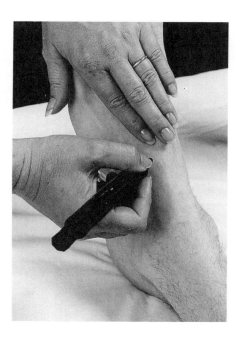

1 Explain the procedure to the client. Review anatomic landmarks of pedal pulses (dorsalis pedis and posterior tibial), p. 407. Locate and mark sites of pedal pulses with indelible ink.

Implementing

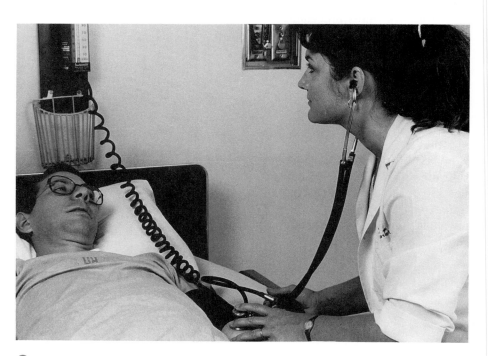

2 Measure the systolic brachial pressure on the client's operative or involved side and record.

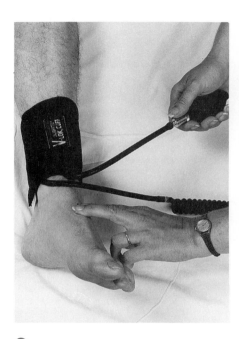

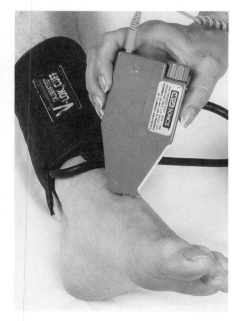

3 With the client maintaining the same position to prevent a false reading, wrap an appropriately sized blood pressure cuff around the client's ankle above the malleolus. If possible, avoid placing the cuff on any new incisions, lesions, or skin grafts. If pedal pulses were palpable, position your finger over the marked site as shown.

4 If pulses are not palpable, assess pulses with a Doppler probe (review procedure, p. 408). Regardless of the method used to assess the pulse, inflate the cuff until the pulse is no longer palpable (or audible if using a Doppler probe), and then continue to inflate 20 mm Hg higher than this number. Slowly deflate the cuff until the pulse returns. Record this measurement. Next, measure the pressure over the site of the other pedal pulse (for example, the posterior tibial if you already have palpated the dorsalis pedis). Repeat on the opposite extremity if measurements are to be obtained on both sides.

Evaluating

5 Divide the highest of the two ankle (pedal) pressures on one foot by the brachial systolic pressure:

$$\frac{\text{ankle pressure}}{\text{brachial pressure}} = \text{A/B ratio.}$$

Repeat for the opposite foot, if applicable, and record.

Notify physician of a ratio less than that specified on physician's orders. Clinical significance for ankle/brachial ratio is as follows (Cudworth-Bergin, 1984).

Ankle/brachial ratio	Clinical significance
1 to 0.75	Mild vascular insufficiency
0.75 to 0.5	Claudication
0.5 to 0.25	Pain at rest
0.25 to 0	Pregangrene

MEASURING PARADOXICAL PULSE

A paradoxical pulse refers to a decrease of ≥10 mm Hg in the systolic blood pressure during inspiration. If present, paradoxical pulse can signal pericardial disease, such as cardiac tamponade.

Assessing, Planning, and Implementing

1   Explain the procedure to the client. Measure the client's systolic blood pressure (see procedure, p. 410) with him inhaling and holding a deep breath. Record the client's systolic pressure, noting that it was measured with the client holding his breath.

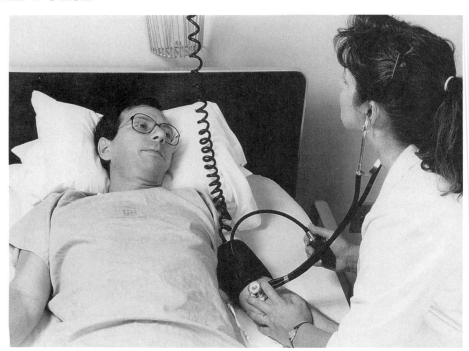

2   Have the client take a deep breath and then exhale. As the client exhales, measure his systolic blood pressure and record, noting that it was measured with the client exhaling his breath.

Evaluating

3   Compare the systolic blood pressure readings from steps 1 and 2, noting the difference in mm Hg. If the difference is ≥10 mm Hg, the client has a paradoxical pulse (pulsus paradoxus). Record the readings, and notify the physician accordingly.

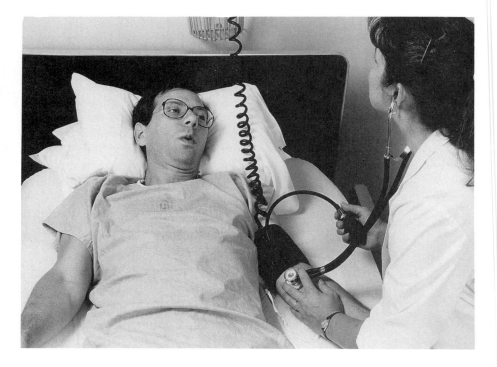

Nursing Guidelines for Identifying Common Telemetry Lead Sites

If your agency uses telemetry monitoring, it will employ either a two-electrode or a three-electrode monitor. Review these common lead sites to assist you with electrode placement. Negative, positive, and ground lead positions will vary, depending on the telemetry unit you will use; however, the electrode placement will be the same, regardless of the telemetry unit. Position the upper electrodes just under the clavicular hollows at the midclavicular line. This will minimize artifact from muscles and arm movement. Lower electrodes are placed at the intercostal spaces, either at the right sternal border, fourth or fifth intercostal space, or at the left midclavicular line, sixth or seventh intercostal space. If necessary, vary the electrode placement slightly to accommodate your client's anatomy. For example, obese clients may require electrode placement over bony surfaces to decrease artifact from adipose tissue.

two-electrode monitor

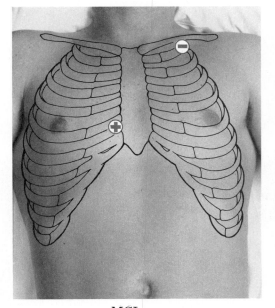

MCL₁

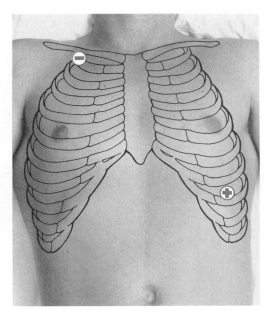

Lead II

three-electrode monitor

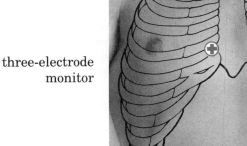

MCL₁

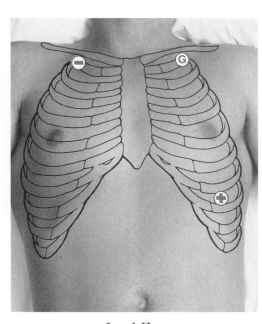

Lead II

APPLYING DISPOSABLE ELECTRODES FOR TELEMETRY MONITORING

Assessing and Planning

1 The procedure for applying disposable electrodes is the same, regardless of the type of cardiac monitoring equipment that is used. In these photos the steps for initiating telemetry monitoring are also included. If the physician prescribes telemetry for your client, study the operational guidelines for the telemetry unit your agency employs. Determine the prescribed lead site position, and familiarize yourself with the guidelines for identifying common telemetry lead sites, p. 417. Assemble scissors for clipping hair (optional), an alcohol pad to remove skin oils (optional), electrodes, electrode wires, the telemetry unit, tincture of benzoin, gauze pads, and a telemetry carrying pouch.

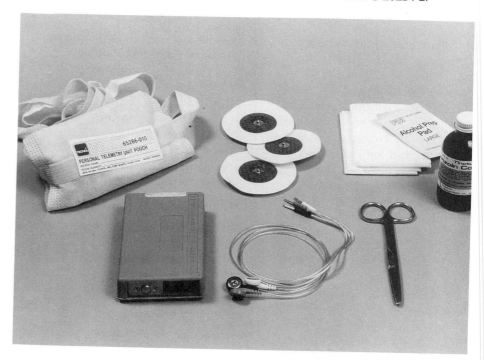

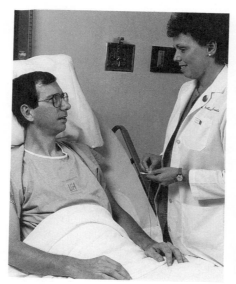

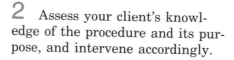

2 Assess your client's knowledge of the procedure and its purpose, and intervene accordingly.

3 Insert the battery into the transmitter. *Note: Many transmitters have a test light on the back that lights up when pressed if the battery is functioning.*

Implementing

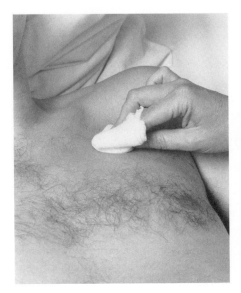

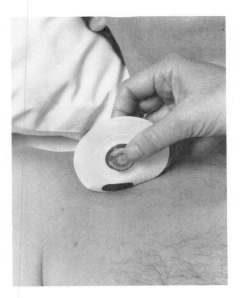

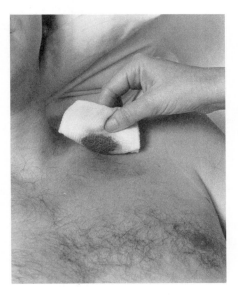

4   If necessary, and with your client's permission, shave or clip his chest hair at the lead sites to allow for better conductivity. Briskly rub the sites with a dry 4 x 4 gauze pad to produce erythema and to remove the skin oils that can interfere with electrical conductivity. A gauze pad saturated with alcohol also can be used to remove the skin oils.

5   To enhance electrical conductivity, some disposable electrodes have rough patches for slightly abrading the skin at the lead site. If your client's electrode does not have this feature, you may instead lightly scrape the skin with a tongue blade.

6   If your client is not allergic to tincture of benzoin, apply a small amount to the lead sites with a clean gauze pad. This will facilitate electrode adherence and inhibit skin breakdown. Let it dry thoroughly.

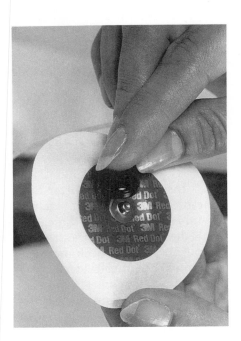

7   Attach lead wires to the appropriate electrodes. The monitoring system your agency employs will identify the positive, negative, and lead sites. The lead wires will be coded by color, by symbols, or by initials.

(Continues)

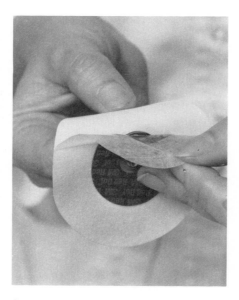

8 Ensure that the lead wires are securely connected to the telemetry transmitter.

9 Remove the electrode's paper backing, but touch the adhesive surface only minimally.

10 Inspect the spongy center of the electrode's adhesive surface. If it is not covered with a moist gel, replace the electrode with a new one.

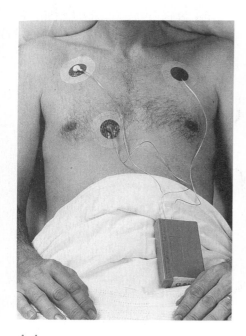

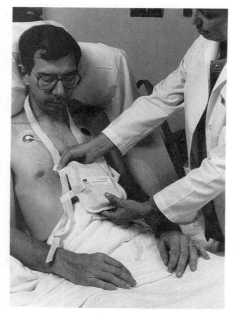

11 Position the electrodes to form the desired pattern. Electrodes should be placed near but not over bony surfaces unless the client is obese. In that case, you may place them over bones to minimize artifact from adipose tissue. And, to minimize artifact from muscles or arm movement, position the upper electrodes just below the clavicular hollows at the midclavicular line.

12 Insert the transmitter into a cloth carrying pouch. Attach the telemetry pouch to the client, either by wrapping both straps around the client's neck or by wrapping the interior strap around the client's neck and the exterior strap around the client's abdomen. Secure the straps to the pouch with Velcro™ if it is used by the pouch manufacturer. Another option is to place the telemetry pouch in a pajama top pocket. Make sure the pouch is in a comfortable position for the client and that it does not obstruct the electrodes.

Evaluating

13 At the central console, press the recorder button on the unit reserved for your client. When the waveform has been printed, tear off the printout sheet. Evaluate the waveform, and file a 6-second printout in your client's chart as a baseline for future readings. Set the alarm's limits to those prescribed by the physician—for example, at a low of 50 and a high of 120.

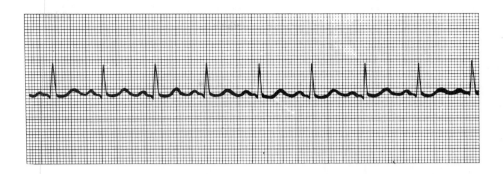

POSITIONING ELECTRODES FOR A 12-LEAD EKG

Assessing and Planning

Implementing

1 Assemble the appropriate electrodes, indelible pen to mark anatomic sites (optional), and scissors for clipping hair (optional). Plug in the EKG machine, and turn it on to allow it to warm up, if this is appropriate for the machine used by your agency. *Note: For our purposes, we will demonstrate placement of the electrodes only. Refer to specialized texts for evaluation of lead tracings or interpretation of EKG strips.* Place the client no higher than semi-Fowler's position to ensure proper heart position.

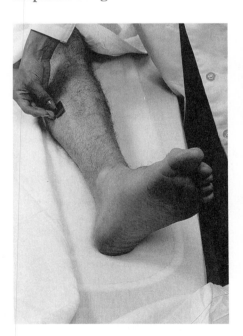

2 Attach the appropriate electrode to the client's medial calf, as shown. Repeat on the opposite limb. Place the electrodes on a smooth and fleshy part of each extremity to ensure optimal conduction.

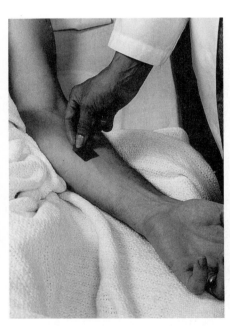

3 Attach the appropriate electrode to the inner aspect of the forearm, as shown. Repeat on the opposite limb.

(Continues)

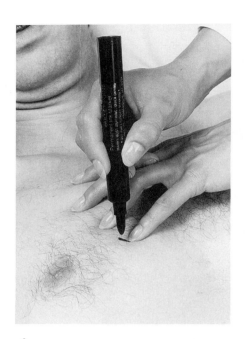

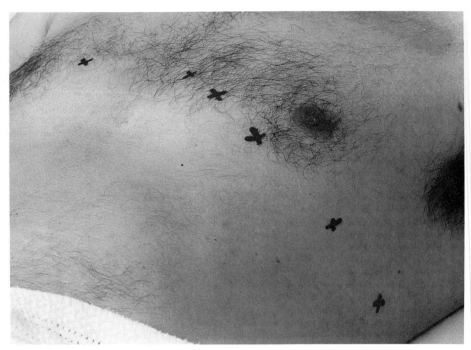

4 Begin to identify chest lead sites, using indelible ink to mark the sites. First, position your fingers to identify the fourth intercostal space at the right sternal border for V-1.

5 Continue to mark the remaining chest sites, as shown. As necessary, review anatomic landmarks on p. 402. V-2: fourth intercostal space at the left sternal border; V-3: site midway between V-2 and V-4; V-4: fifth intercostal space at the midclavicular line; V-5: fifth intercostal space at the anterior axillary line (horizontal with V-4); V-6: fifth intercostal space at the midaxillary line.

Evaluating

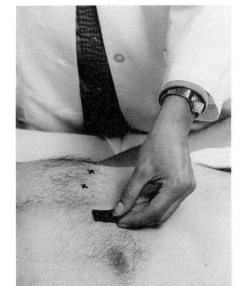

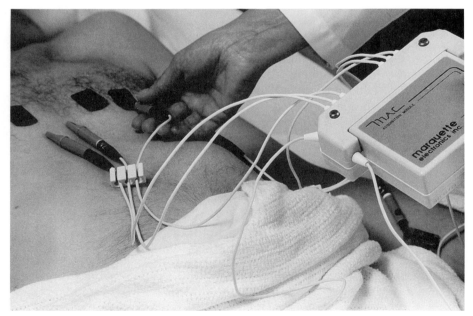

6 Attach electrodes to the lead sites, as shown.

7 Next, attach the appropriate lead wires to the electrodes. Lead wires are usually labeled with an identifying landmark, for example, "RL" (right leg), V-6, and so on. Follow agency and manufacturer's guidelines for running the EKG machine and recording the limb and chest lead tracings.

ASSESSING THE POSTCARDIAC CATHETERIZATION CLIENT

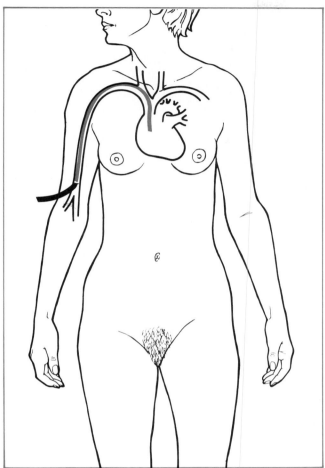

Antecubital site

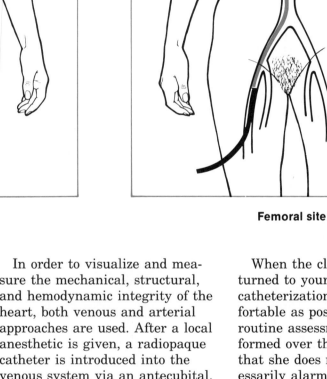

Femoral site

A cardiac catheterization is an invasive procedure performed to assess cardiac anatomy and function. It frequently is performed for clients with chest pain of unknown origin, congenital heart disease, pulmonary hypertension, dysrhythmias, congestive heart failure, and postmyocardial infarction to determine ventricular function. It is a valuable diagnostic tool for the preoperative cardiac client, and it is performed postoperatively, as well, to assess the results of cardiac surgery. It is usually performed in conjunction with angiography, during which a contrast medium is injected for envisioning the ventricle, aorta, and coronary arteries.

In order to visualize and measure the mechanical, structural, and hemodynamic integrity of the heart, both venous and arterial approaches are used. After a local anesthetic is given, a radiopaque catheter is introduced into the venous system via an antecubital, basilic, or femoral approach. Measurements of right atrial, right ventricular, and pulmonary arterial vasculature may be obtained. To visualize the coronary arteries and identify location and severity of any stenotic lesions, another catheter is introduced into the arterial system and fed through the aorta into the coronary arteries. The entire procedure usually lasts 2–4 hours.

When the client has been returned to your care after cardiac catheterization, make her as comfortable as possible; explain that routine assessments will be performed over the next 24 hours so that she does not become unnecessarily alarmed, thinking her condition has deteriorated. The protocol for assessment will vary from agency to agency. The following are general procedures for assessment and its frequency. Be sure to follow the protocol outlined by your agency.

(Continues)

1 Measure and record the blood pressure every 15 minutes until it is stable on at least three successive checks. Once it is stable, measure it every 2 hours for the next 12 hours, and every 4 hours thereafter. *Caution: If the catheterization site was the antecubital area, be sure to measure the blood pressure in the opposite arm.* Notify the physician and lower the head of the bed if the client's systolic pressure drops 20 mm Hg lower than that already recorded. Hypotension can be a result of cardiac tamponade, vagal response, hematoma at the catheterization site, or hypovolemia. The hypertonic dye used during the catheterization can cause osmotic diuresis, so be sure to monitor the urinary output carefully. In addition to diuresis, also be alert to hypotension and bradycardia, which occur with dye reaction. If you suspect that the client is having a dye reaction, place her in Trendelenburg position, administer fluid boluses per agency protocol, and notify the cardiologist immediately. In clients with heart disease, the hypotension caused by a dye reaction can precipitate angina and even myocardial infarction. With fluid replacement this situation usually resolves quickly.

If the client is not being monitored continuously on a cardiac monitor, auscultate the apical pulse with each blood pressure check. Be alert to an irregular pulse rate, which could be indicative of dysrhythmias. Remember that an acute myocardial infarction can occur as a complication of cardiac catheterization; therefore, you must monitor the client closely for dysrhythmias, as well as for diaphoresis, a thready pulse, and complaints of chest pain.

Encourage increased fluid in-

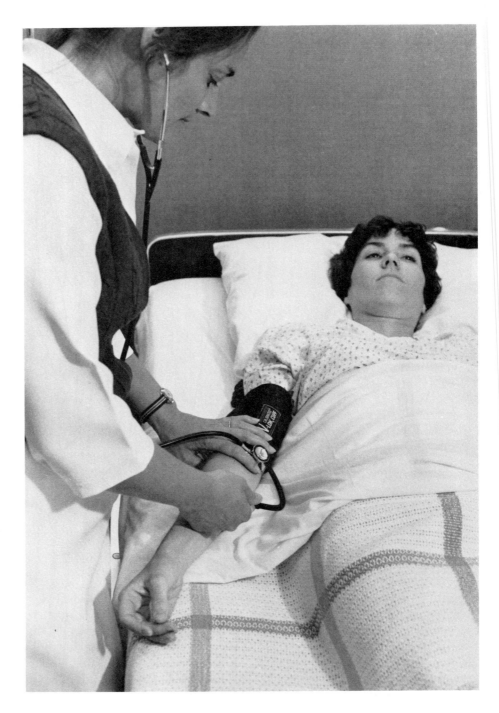

take (or increase IV drip rates as prescribed) to assist in washing the dye from the client's system. Be alert to signs of fluid overload, which can occur in response to the increased intake: tachypnea, tachycardia, shortness of breath, crackles, rhonchi, increased CVP, gallop rhythm, and increased BP.

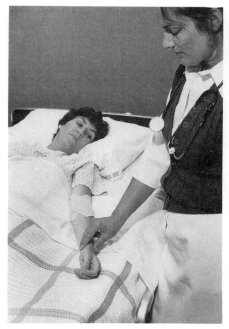 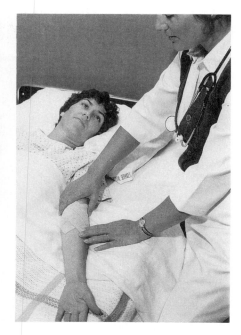

2 Assess the limb distal to the catheterization site to ensure that the color, temperature, sensation, capillary refill, and pulse(s) are adequate. Compare these assessments to the uninvolved limb. If the catheterization site was in the upper extremities, palpate the radial pulse. Palpate the popliteal, dorsalis pedis, and posterior tibial pulses if the site was in the lower extremities. In addition, the client should be able to move her fingers or toes easily. A faint pulse; pain at the catheterization site; or coolness, numbness, or tingling at the distal extremity can be indicative of an embolus, thrombus, or arterial insufficiency in the involved limb and should be reported to the attending physician immediately. Instruct the client to alert you if any of these conditions occur.

3 Inspect the pressure dressing over the catheterization site for the presence of bleeding. Ask the client about pain or tenderness at the site, which could be indicative of a hematoma formation. If bleeding occurs, apply pressure to the site. Then recheck vital signs and notify the cardiologist. Be especially alert to (and palpate for) hematoma formation in the anatomic sites that were catheterized. The arterial catheterization site is more vulnerable to bleeding than the venous catheterization site because of the higher pressures that are present in the arterial system. Bleeding at the femoral arterial site may place the patient at risk for hemodynamic demise because significant blood loss into the peritoneum and abdominal cavity may occur. The peritoneum and abdominal cavity can hold significant blood volume, thus masking the true extent of blood loss until significant bleeding has occurred. Monitor for signs of bleeding (hematoma) when the client returns

from the catheterization laboratory, and reassess frequently per agency protocol or as prescribed. If there are signs of bleeding (hematoma), mark the borders. If the hematoma enlarges, mark the new borders and inform the cardiologist promptly.

Keep the limb in extension to prevent bleeding, and encourage the client to keep it immobile for approximately 6 hours or per agency protocol. Movement may cause the clot to dislodge and bleeding to occur. Use sand bags, as necessary, to keep the limb immobile and in extension. Some agencies apply sand bags directly to the insertion site to provide pressure as a further deterrent against bleeding. Instruct the client to apply pressure to the site and alert you immediately if she detects bleeding. In many instances, the client will be on bed rest until the next morning. Check the orders for ambulation and follow through accordingly. Carefully document every assessment.

MEASURING CENTRAL VENOUS PRESSURE (CVP)

Assessing and Planning

1 Explain the procedure to your client. Check the intake and output record, measure his pulse and blood pressure, and auscultate his cardiac area for heart sounds. This assessment will provide you with a baseline from which to evaluate his CVP. Normal CVP values are as follows: 2–6 mm Hg or 5–12 cm H_2O.

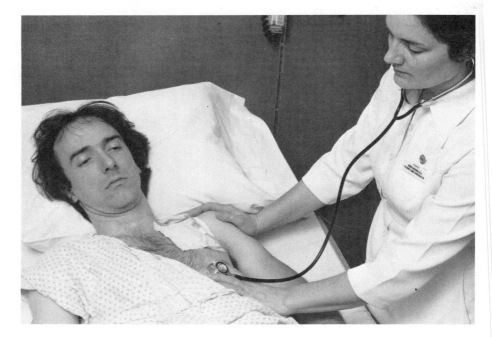

2 To minimize inaccuracies, the client should neither cough nor strain, and he must be in the same position for every reading. If the supine position is not contraindicated (and if previous readings were taken with the client in this position), place him flat in bed and remove his pillow. This will increase intrathoracic venous pressure and minimize the risk of an air embolism during the negative phase of inspiration. Make sure the IV solution is running well, and, to minimize the potential for an air embolism, ensure that all IV connections are securely attached.

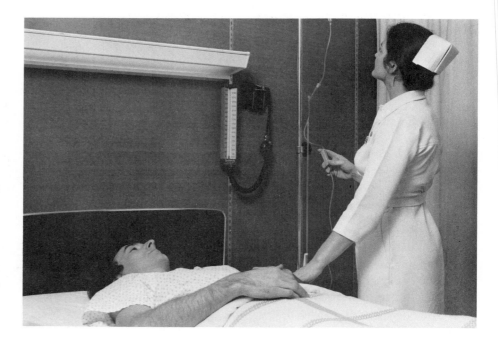

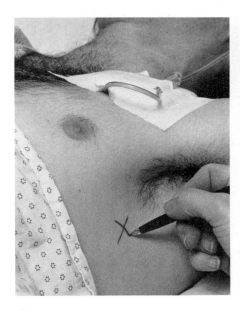

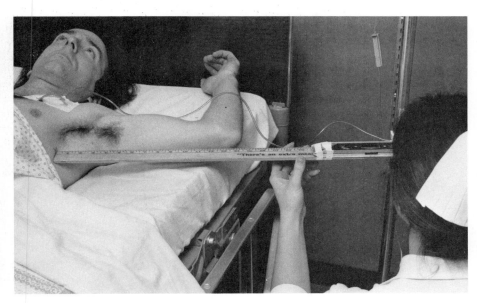

3 Locate the level of the client's right atrium at the fourth or fifth intercostal space of his midaxillary line. Mark the site with indelible ink to ensure that the pressure is always measured from this point.

4 A reusable manometer may have an attached arm that lines up the client's marked midaxillary site to the exact level of 0 point on the manometer scale. However, most disposable manometers, such as the one in this photo, will require the use of a yardstick and a carpenter's level to accomplish the same goal. Po-

sition one end of the yardstick against the marked midaxillary site and the other end against the 0 point on the manometer scale. Adjust the manometer scale until the gauge on the carpenter's level is plumb (when the bubble is centered). This will ensure a CVP measurement from the exact level of the right atrium.

Implementing

5 If your client's IV connects to an infusion pump, turn the pump off at this time. Rotate the stopcock so that the solution is off to the client, open to the manometer, and open to the solution to allow the solution to enter the manometer. Let the manometer fill slowly to the 25-cm mark, or 10–20 cm above the expected pressure reading. Because a CVP normally will calibrate between 5 and 15 cm H_2O, filling the scale to at least 10 cm above the expected norm will ensure calibration of most readings.

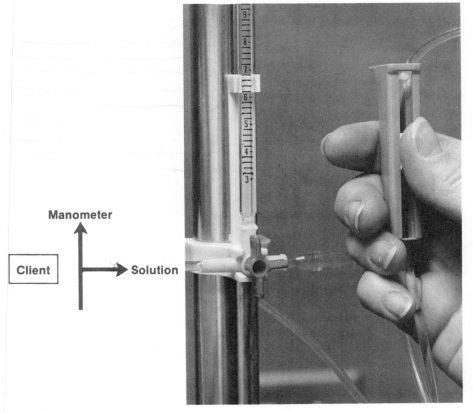

(Continues)

6 Rotate the stopcock so that it is open to the manometer, open to the client, and off to the solution. This will allow the solution to enter the client.

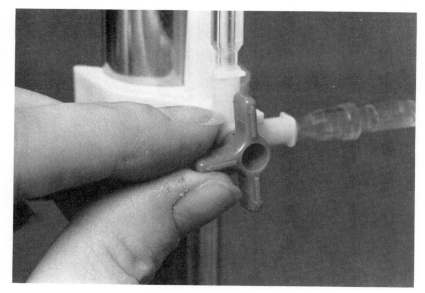

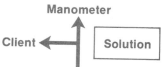

7 Observe the height of the fluid in the manometer at eye level to make sure the reading is not distorted. The level should fall as the solution flows into the client and adjusts to the pressure level of the right atrium. It will then fluctuate in response to the client's respirations. Record the measurement when the level is at the lowest point.

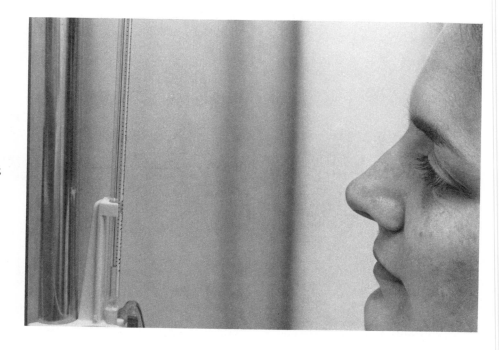

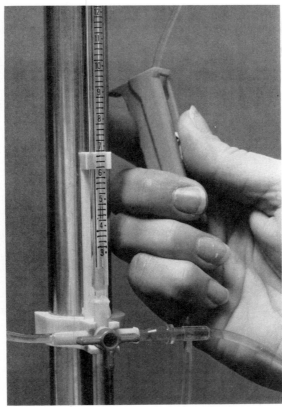

Manometer

Client ⟷ Solution

8 Adjust the stopcock so that it is open to the solution, open to the client, and off to the manometer. Adjust the flow rate to the prescribed rate, and return the client to a comfortable position.

Evaluating

9 Compare the client's CVP to his baseline to ensure that it is within his norm. Consider also his cardiac assessment, blood pressure, level of consciousness, skin turgor, diagnosis, fluid intake, and hourly urine output. Review the parameters the physician has ordered for reporting CVP readings, and follow up accordingly. Rates near zero may indicate hypovolemic shock, and rates above 15 cm H_2O may indicate hypervolemia or poor cardiac contractility. Both extremes necessitate further assessment and evaluation. Document the procedure, the CVP reading, and the client's position during the procedure.

Caring for Clients with Vascular Disorders

APPLYING ELASTIC (ANTIEMBOLIC) STOCKINGS

Assessing and Planning

1 The best time for applying elastic stockings is early in the morning before swelling has occurred in your client's legs and feet. Determine the type of stocking the physician has prescribed, either thigh-high stockings or below-the-knee stockings. Explain the procedure to your client. Drape his thighs as you remove the top linen. Assess both legs and feet for ulcers or infections,

the absence of peripheral pulses below the femoral artery, or unequal pulses. These conditions, in addition to peripheral edema secondary to congestive heart failure, are contraindications for applying these hose. Also, evaluate the color and temperature of both extremities. If you find them cool or cyanotic, alert the physician. *Note: The stockings can be applied easily if talc or corn starch is sprinkled on the legs and feet first to absorb perspiration.*

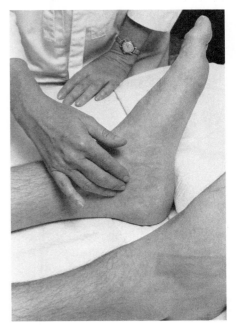

(Continues)

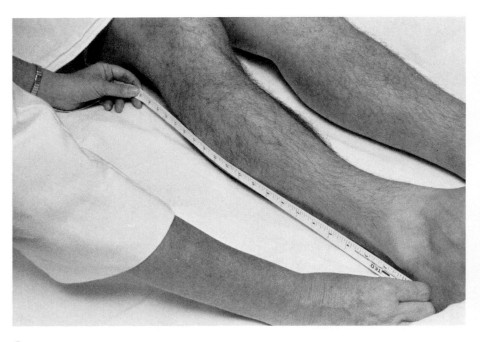

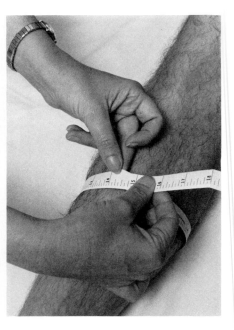

2 To ensure a correct fit, measure the leg from the Achilles tendon to the popliteal fold (as shown) for the below-the-knee stockings, or from the Achilles tendon to the gluteal furrow for the thigh-high stockings. A tape measure is usually included with each package.

3 Measure the circumference of the midcalf (and the midthigh for the thigh-high stocking). Compare your measurements to the manufacturer's guidelines to make sure you have the correct size.

Implementing

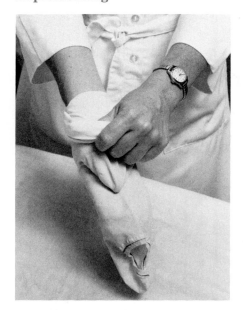

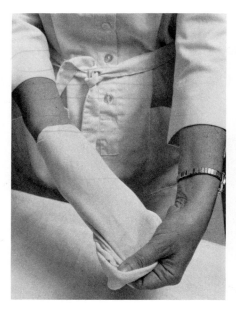

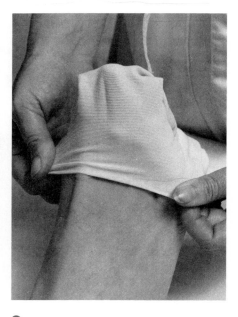

4 Make sure the stockings are "inside out." The manufacturer often packages them that way. Insert your hand through the top of the stocking deeply enough to grasp the stocking's toe.

5 With your free hand, invert the stocking to its heel by pulling the stocking over the hand that is inside the stocking. Remove your hand from the inside of the stocking.

6 Grasp each side of the stocking and pull the inverted stocking foot over your client's toes.

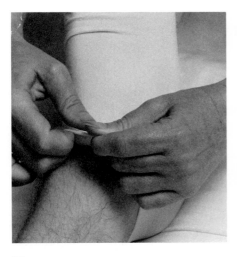

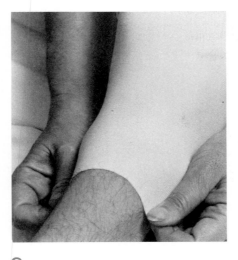

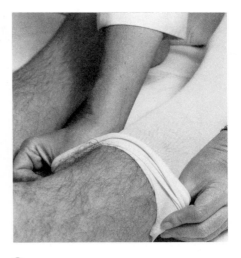

7   In one motion, pull the stocking past the client's heel so that the stocking will be anchored and not slip back.

8   Grasp the fabric by the sides as you pull it up past the ankle.

9   In increments of 2 inches at a time, continue to pull the stocking up in this manner until you reach the premeasured area. Apply the other stocking in the same way. Because wrinkles can cause pressure areas, both stockings must fit smoothly.

Evaluating

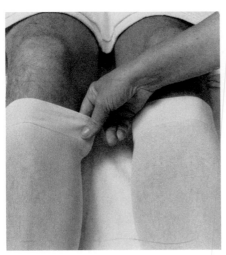

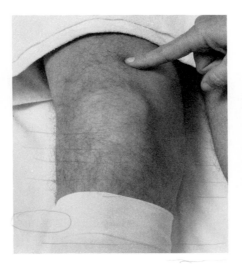

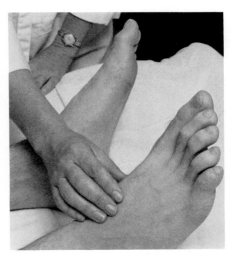

10   Periodically, check that the stocking does not roll at the top. Alert your client to watch for this, if he is able, explaining that rolling can produce a tourniquet effect. This can cause stasis to occur, predisposing thrombus formation and increasing edema.

11   Monitor the client frequently for swelling proximal to the stocking top. To do this, press a finger into the flesh above the stocking. If you can see a dent after removing your finger, swelling has occurred and the stockings should be removed.

12   To minimize swelling proximal to the hose, and for client comfort, remove the stockings at least twice a day for 30 minutes at a time. Wash and dry the legs (or provide the client with the materials to do so), and reapply talc or corn starch. Always palpate peripheral pulses in the legs and feet before reapplying the hose, and observe for improvement or for an alteration in his circulatory system, such as swelling and color changes. Wash the hose with detergent and water.

EMPLOYING BUERGER-ALLEN EXERCISES

Assessing and Planning

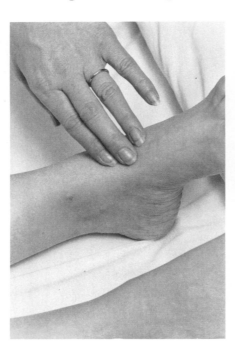

Implementing

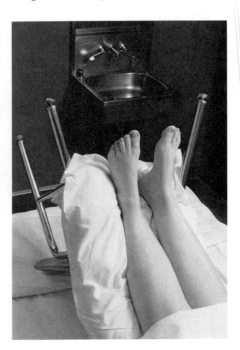

1 The physician may prescribe Buerger-Allen exercises for clients with occlusive arterial disorders—for example, arteriosclerosis obliterans, Buerger's disease, or Raynaud's disease. Explain to your client that these exercises will promote circulation in the lower extremities by the gravitational filling and emptying of the blood vessels. To evaluate the effectiveness of the exercises, you must first perform a baseline assessment of your client's legs and feet. While your client lies flat, palpate the femoral, popliteal, posterior tibial, and pedal pulses. Then assess for the presence or absence of pain and ulcerations and the temperature and color of the extremities.

2 Initially, the client should recline with her legs elevated above the level of her heart for a minute, or until blanching occurs in the legs and feet. You may raise the foot of the hospital bed, but it is a good idea to show the client how to implement the procedure at home. In this photo, the back of a straight-back chair is cushioned with a pillow so that the chair's back supports the client's legs. Make sure you keep the client warm because chilling will further diminish arterial circulation.

3 Once blanching has occurred, have the client sit on the side of the bed and plantarflex her feet. This is the first of six leg-stretching positions that are employed to promote blood flow and minimize stasis. This and the following five positions should be maintained for 30 seconds each. ***Note:*** *Instead of the six leg-stretching positions, the physician may prescribe one in which the client's legs dangle over the side of the bed for 3 minutes, or until they are pink.*

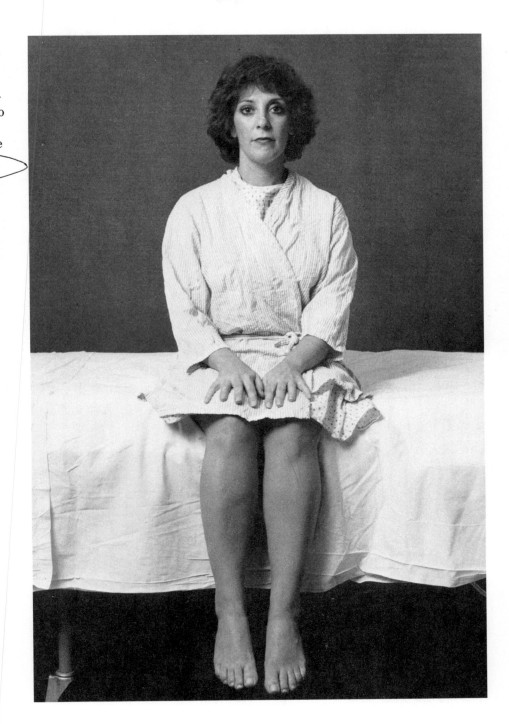

(Continues)

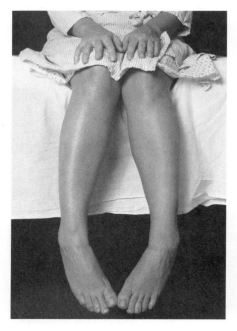

4 For the second position, the client plantarflexes and inverts her feet.

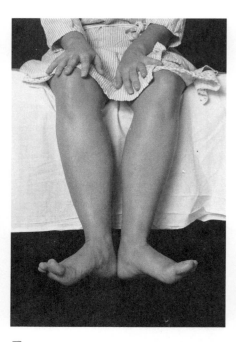

5 For the third position, the client dorsiflexes and everts her feet.

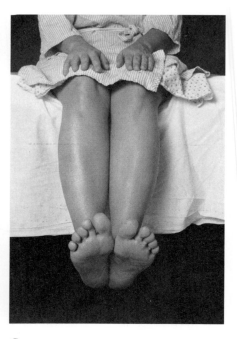

6 For the fourth position, the client dorsiflexes her feet.

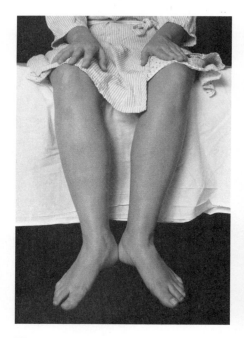

7 For the fifth position, the client plantarflexes and everts her feet.

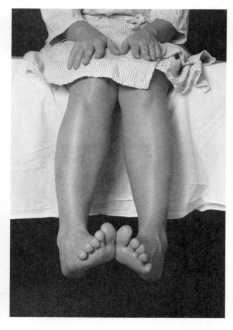

8 For the sixth position, she dorsiflexes and inverts her feet. Observe her feet and legs at this time. Optimally, they will be red or pink to indicate that adequate circulation has occurred.

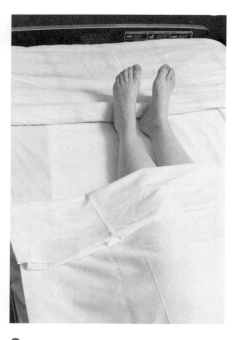

9 Finally the client should lie flat in a supine position. Usually, this position is maintained for 3–5 minutes. Depending on the physician's orders, the set may be repeated another four or five times. Buerger-Allen exercises are usually prescribed for three or four times daily.

Evaluating

10 When the exercise has been completed, evaluate its effectiveness by comparing the color, temperature, and pulsations of the legs and feet to your initial assessment; document accordingly. Note whether the skin is mottled, blanched, red, black, gray, or blue. Determine whether a foot cradle is needed to keep the bed covers off the affected skin. To enhance arterial circulation, ensure that the client and the environment are kept warm.

References

American Heart Association: Standards and guidelines for cardiopulmonary resuscitation (CPR) and emergency cardiac care (ECC). *JAMA* 1986; 255(21):2841–3044.

Andreoli KG: *Comprehensive Cardiac Care*, 6th ed. St. Louis: Mosby, 1987.

Baas LS: Cardiovascular dysfunctions. In: *Manual of Critical Care: Applying Nursing Diagnoses to Adult Critical Illness*, 2d ed. Swearingen PL. St. Louis: Mosby, 1991.

Bowers AC, Thompson JM: *Clinical Manual of Health Assessment*, 3d ed. St. Louis: Mosby, 1988.

Canobbrio M: *Nursing Care of Patients with Cardiovascular Disorders*. St. Louis: Mosby, 1989.

Chobanian AM et al: 1988 report of the joint national committee on detection, evaluation, and treatment of high blood pressure. Bethesda, MD, May 1988, NIH Publication No. 88-1088.

Cudworth-Bergin K: Detecting arterial problems with a Doppler probe. *RN* 1984; 47(1):38–41.

Holloway NM: *Nursing the Critically Ill Adult*, 3d ed. Redwood City, CA: Addison-Wesley, 1988.

Keen JH: Coronary Artery Thrombolysis. In: *Manual of Critical Care:*

Applying Nursing Diagnoses to Adult Critical Illness, 2d ed. Swearingen PL. St. Louis: Mosby, 1991.

Report of the second task force on blood pressure control in children—1987. *Pediatrics* 1987; 79:1–25.

Roderick B: How to manage CVP lines. *RN* 1985; 48(8):22–25.

Sommers MS: Cardiac tamponade. In: *Manual of Critical Care: Applying Nursing Diagnoses to Adult Critical Illness*, 2d ed. Swearingen PL. St. Louis: Mosby, 1991.

Spence A, Mason E: *Human Anatomy and Physiology*, 3d ed. Redwood City, CA: Benjamin/Cummings, 1987.

Steuble BT: Cardiovascular disorders. In: *Manual of Nursing Therapeutics: Applying Nursing Diagnoses to Medical Disorders*, 2d ed. Swearingen PL. St. Louis: Mosby, 1990.

Steuble BT: Cardiovascular dysfunctions. In: *Manual of Critical Care: Applying Nursing Diagnoses to Adult Critical Illness*, 2d ed. Swearingen PL. St. Louis: Mosby, 1991.

Swearingen PL: Heart sounds. In: *Manual of Critical Care*, 2d ed. St. Louis: Mosby, 1991.

Thompson JM et al: *Mosby's Manual of Clinical Nursing*, 2d ed. St. Louis: Mosby, 1989.

1 Down
2 planterflex & inverts
3 dorsiflex & everts
4 dorsiflex
5 planter flex & everts
6 dorsiflex & inverts
7 Lay flat 3-5 minutes
  Repeat set 4-5 x
  3 x 5 day

Chapter 8

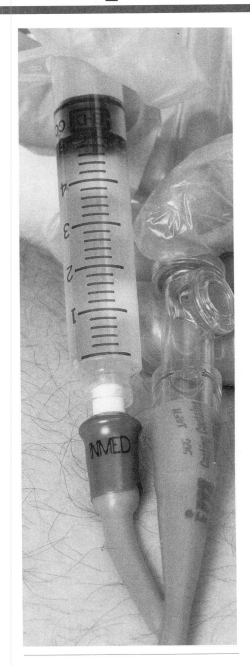

Managing
Renal-Urinary
Procedures

CHAPTER OUTLINE

ASSESSING THE RENAL-URINARY SYSTEM

The Renal-Urinary System

Nursing Assessment Guideline

Assessing the Bladder

Inspecting
Palpating
Percussing

Palpating the Kidneys

Assessing Skin Turgor

Weighing the Client on a Bed Scale

Collecting a 24-Hour Urine Specimen

CATHETERIZING AND MANAGING CATHETER CARE

Performing Intermittent Catheterization

Inserting a Robinson (Straight) Catheter into a Female
Inserting a Robinson (Straight) Catheter into a Male

Managing a Foley Catheter

Performing a Catheterization with a Foley (Indwelling) Catheter

General Guidelines for Foley Catheter Management

Making a Catheter Strap
Obtaining a Urine Specimen
Emptying the Drainage Bag
Using a Urine Meter
Irrigating the Catheter
Removing a Foley Catheter

CARING FOR CLIENTS WITH RENAL-URINARY DISORDERS

Applying an External Urinary Device (with a Leg Drainage System)

Monitoring the Client Receiving Continuous Bladder Irrigation (CBI)

Establishing CBI

Nursing Guidelines for the Care of Clients with CBI

Nursing Guidelines for the Care of the Client with a Suprapubic Catheter

Nursing Guidelines for the Care of the Client with a Nephrostomy Tube and Ureteral Stents

Administering a Sodium Polystyrene Sulfonate (Kayexalate) Enema

Performing the Credé Maneuver

CARING FOR CLIENTS WITH URINARY DIVERSIONS

Nursing Guidelines to Common Types of Urinary Diversions

Ileal Conduit
Cutaneous Ureterostomy
Continent Urinary Diversion

Performing a Postoperative Assessment

Managing Appliance Care

Applying a Postoperative (Disposable) Pouch
Picture Framing the Pouch
Connecting the Pouch to a Urinary Drainage System

Assessing the Renal-Urinary System

THE RENAL-URINARY SYSTEM

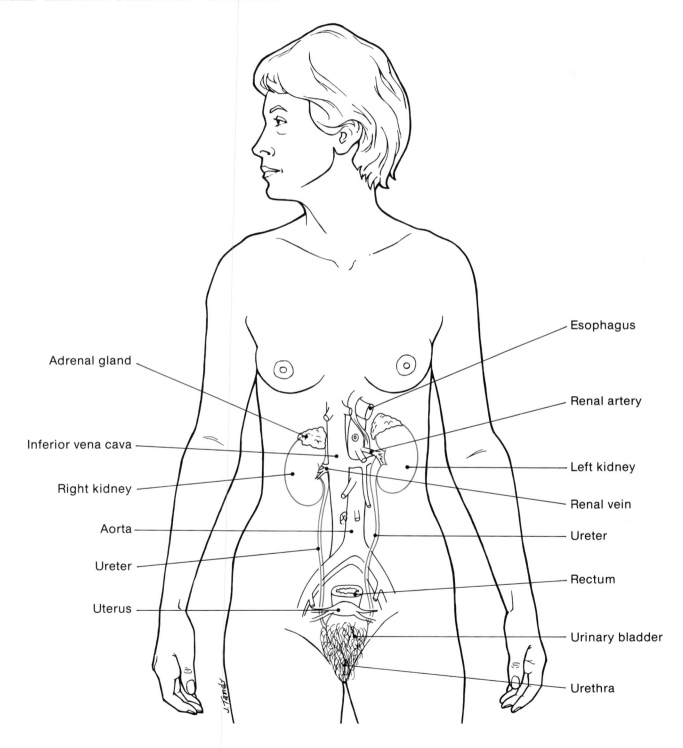

Adrenal gland

Inferior vena cava

Right kidney

Aorta

Ureter

Uterus

Esophagus

Renal artery

Left kidney

Renal vein

Ureter

Rectum

Urinary bladder

Urethra

J. Tandy

(Continues)

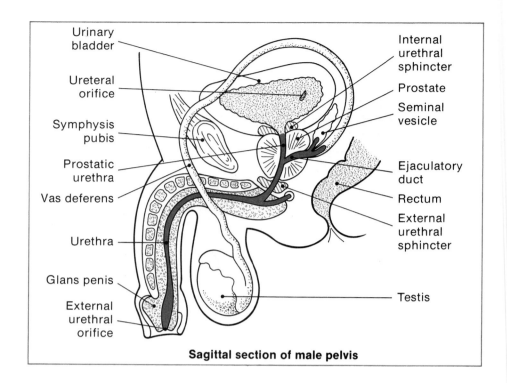

Urinary bladder

Ureteral orifice

Symphysis pubis

Prostatic urethra

Vas deferens

Urethra

Glans penis

External urethral orifice

Internal urethral sphincter

Prostate

Seminal vesicle

Ejaculatory duct

Rectum

External urethral sphincter

Testis

Sagittal section of male pelvis

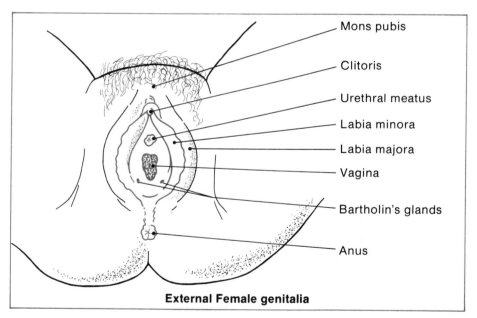

Mons pubis

Clitoris

Urethral meatus

Labia minora

Labia majora

Vagina

Bartholin's glands

Anus

External Female genitalia

Nursing Assessment Guideline

To assess your client's renal-urinary system, you need to interview him or her for subjective data, take vital signs, assess the bladder and kidneys, and obtain a urine specimen. A comprehensive nursing care plan includes a complete evaluation for the following subjective data:

Personal factors: for example, age, marital status, occupation, continued exposure to nephrotoxic substances such as carbon tetrachloride, use of recreational drugs

History or family history of: renal calculi, strictures, urinary tract disease and/or infections, polyuria, incontinence, diabetes mellitus, renal transplant, dialysis, cardiac disease, or endocrine disorders such as diabetes insipidus

History of: renal/urinary trauma or surgery, blood transfusions, glomerulonephritis, autoimmune diseases

Dietary habits: intake in approximate amounts of sodium, calcium, protein, purines, potassium, phosphates, or acids; amounts consumed of coffee, tea, or alcoholic beverages; presence or history of polydipsia and polyphagia; food allergies

Risk factors: psychologic stressors, hypertension, pregnancy, smoking

Medications: diuretics, antispasmotics, anticholinergics, aspirin or acetaminophen; presence of drug allergies

Alterations in urinary elimination: frequency, urgency, retention, nocturia, dysuria, residual urine, hesitancy, burning during voiding, stress incontinence, presence of an ostomy

Amount and character of urine: polyuria, oliguria, anuria; changes in color, odor, clarity

Flow of urinary stream: high/low pressure, change in size

Fluid status: fluid volume deficit or excess, thirst, presence of peripheral or periorbital edema

Pain: location—for example, lower back, flank, perineum, testicular area, suprapubic area, inner thigh, groin; intensity; relieved by; intensified by

Urethral discharge: amount and character

Presence of genital sores or ulcers

ASSESSING THE BLADDER

INSPECTING

Routine assessment of the bladder is essential when you are caring for clients with urinary tract disorders, as well as for those who have indwelling catheters. Be sure that you provide warmth and privacy for your client, and that you have washed your hands and explained the reason for the assessment. To facilitate the procedure, the client's gown should be raised to the umbilicus and the sheet or drape lowered to the symphysis pubis. Unless your client is obese, a distended bladder usually can be assessed visually while you are at eye level to the lower abdomen. Often you will be able to see a swollen mound just proximal to the symphysis pubis.

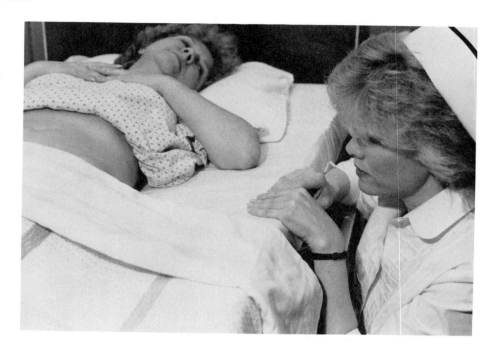

PALPATING

If your client is oliguric or anuric and you need to assess for bladder retention to ensure that catheterization is indicated; if you are assessing your client for a potential catheter obstruction; or if you are assessing for residual urine in clients with neurogenic bladders, light palpation of the bladder can be employed to help determine bladder size. Palpate at the midline, approximately 5 cm (2 in.) above the symphysis pubis. If the bladder is distended, you should be able to feel its firm, rounded contour. *Note: For routine assessment, the client should void prior to bladder palpation to minimize the potential for discomfort.*

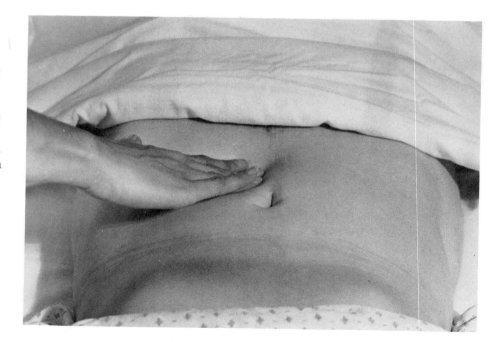

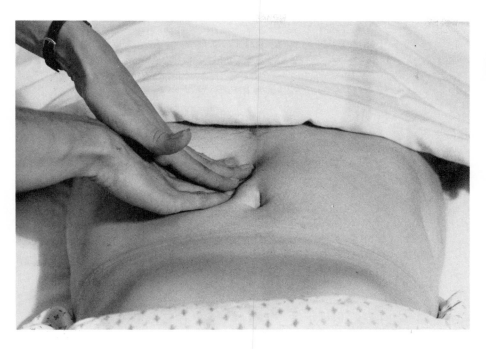

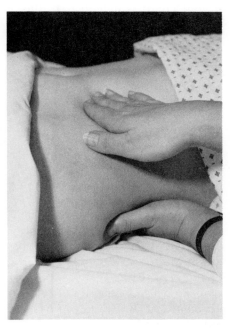

PALPATING THE KIDNEYS

Deep Palpation: When the bladder is not distended, it may be necessary to palpate deeply to assess for location and size. To do this, press with the fingertips of both hands approximately 2.5–5 cm (1–2 in.) proximal to the symphysis pubis, near the midline. Assess for size and location of the bladder and for the presence of any masses. Be sure to note indications of client discomfort, as well.

PERCUSSING

Percussion is another assessment tool that will help you determine whether the bladder is empty or if it contains urine. Place a middle finger at the midline, approximately 5 cm (2 in.) above the symphysis pubis. To elicit sounds, sharply strike that finger with the opposite middle finger. If the bladder contains urine, you should hear dull sounds as you continue to percuss downward toward the symphysis pubis. However, an empty bladder should produce tympanic (hollow) sounds.

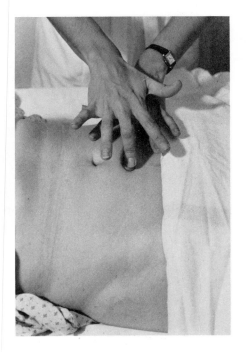

Although not always a routine assessment for the hospitalized urologic client, kidney palpation can be incorporated into a comprehensive assessment. Position your hands on both sides of the client's flank at the area between the iliac crest and lower costal margins (as shown). Instruct the client to inhale, and increase the pressure between your hands with each inhalation until you feel you have achieved the maximum depth. As the client inhales deeply a final time, you should be able to feel the lower edge of the kidney between your hands. This will be more difficult if your client is obese. Compare your assessment of the left kidney to that of the right kidney. Assess and document differences in size, absence of a kidney, masses, nodules, and discomfort from the assessment. *Caution: Kidney palpation is contraindicated in clients in whom neuroblastoma or Wilm's tumor is suspected.*

ASSESSING SKIN TURGOR

If your client is dehydrated, the suppleness of the skin will be diminished because of moisture loss. To assess skin turgor, lift a section of skin along an area in which there is adequate subcutaneous tissue—for example, the forearm, lower abdomen, or calf. Release the skin (far right) and observe its return to the original position. If the client has good turgor, the skin will return quickly to its original position. For clients with poor turgor, the skin will remain in the lifted position (tenting) and return slowly to the original position.

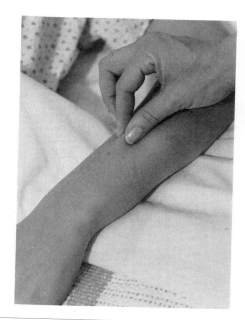 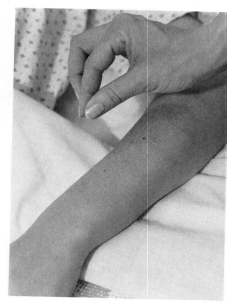

WEIGHING THE CLIENT ON A BED SCALE

To monitor hydration status more precisely, for example in clients with nephrotic syndrome, it may be necessary to weigh your clients at the same time every day. If your client is immobile or restricted to bed rest, an order for a bed scale should be obtained to facilitate the process.

Be certain to balance the scale first, by following manufacturer's instructions. Lock the attached weighing platform securely in place, and then lock the wheels on the bed. To provide warmth and to prevent the potential for cross-contamination, cover the platform with a drape before moving the client. It is important that the same type of drape be used consistently with each weighing to prevent miscalculations of the client's weight. If your client is immobile, follow the procedure in Chapter 2 for transferring the immobile client. Weigh the client, return her to her bed, and document the weight on the appropriate records.

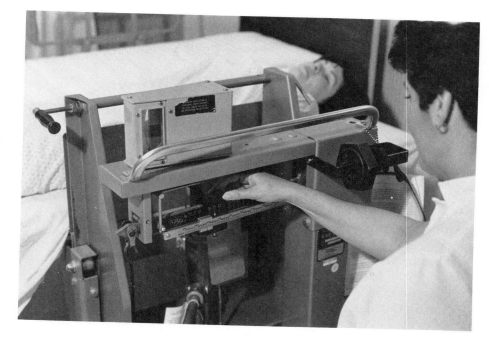

COLLECTING A 24-HOUR URINE SPECIMEN

If a 24-hour urine specimen has been ordered for your client, explain the procedure and point out the proper container and storage area for the urine. Some agencies require the refrigeration of all specimens; others advocate that the urine container be kept on ice. For some collection procedures, such as the creatinine clearance test, refrigeration may not be necessary.

To begin the test, have the client void. *Discard* the urine, and record the time. This is the starting time for the collection. *All* urine must be collected during the next 24 hours, and the final specimen should be obtained as close as possible to the termination of the collection period.

During the collection period, post signs on the client's door, bathroom door, and near the bed to remind personnel and the client about the need to save all

urine. After obtaining the final specimen, record the time again on the laboratory slip (and on other appropriate records) and arrange for its delivery to the laboratory. If the client is menstruating, be sure to note it on the laboratory slip.

Catheterizing and Managing Catheter Care

PERFORMING INTERMITTENT CATHETERIZATION

INSERTING A ROBINSON (STRAIGHT) CATHETER INTO A FEMALE

Unless catheterization has been specifically ordered, avoid this procedure if other measures can be taken to achieve the same outcome. For example, many experts believe that a midstream urine catch is as dependable a specimen as that obtained via an invasive catheterization. Often, clients who have urine retention can void after the stimulus of hearing running water or submerging their hands in a basin of warm water. Other clients respond to the sensation of warm water being poured over their perineums.

(Continues)

Assessing

Planning

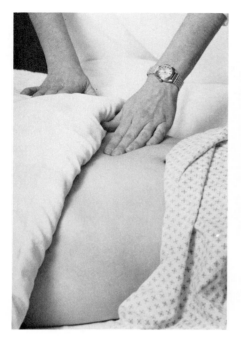

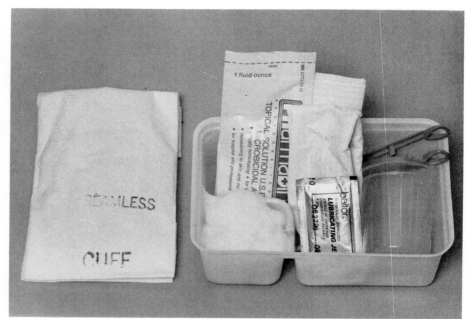

1   Inspect the lower abdomen and palpate or percuss the bladder to determine the need for catheterization or the degree of distention. If intermittent catheterization is indicated, explain the procedure to your client and arrange for a private and warm environment.

2   Obtain a urethral catheterization kit or assemble the following sterile materials for urethral catheterization: an underpad and a fenestrated drape, rayon or cotton balls, gloves, forceps, specimen container, water-soluble lubricant, and an antimicrobial solution.

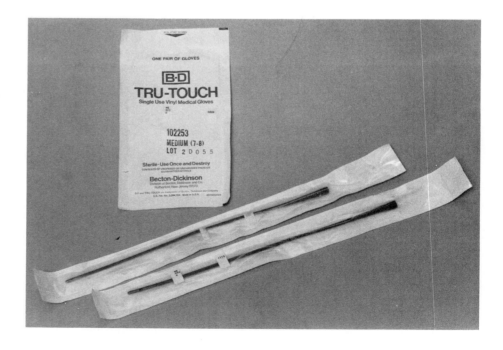

3   In addition, assemble an extra pair of sterile gloves and two straight Robinson catheters of a size appropriate for your client (from 16 to 22F). Although the extra gloves and catheter may not be necessary during the procedure, they will be readily available at the bedside in the event of contamination of the original catheter or gloves.

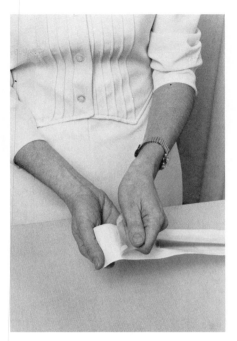

4 Wash your hands and open the catheter kit on a clean, dry surface, using aseptic technique.

5 Using aseptic technique, open an end of one of the catheter packages and drop the catheter into the opened catheterization kit.

Implementing

6 Assist your client into a dorsal recumbent position, and instruct her to flex her knees. To ensure her warmth and protect her privacy, place a folded bath blanket, sheet, or towel over her abdomen and upper thighs until it is time to cover the perineum with a sterile drape. Grasp the sterile underpad, which is the uppermost drape in the catheterization kit. Hold it by a small section at two corners and wrap the undersurface around your hands (as shown) so that you can insert it under the client's buttocks with minimal contamination. Instruct the client to raise her buttocks so that you can position the underpad (far right).

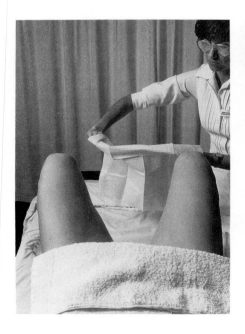

(Continues)

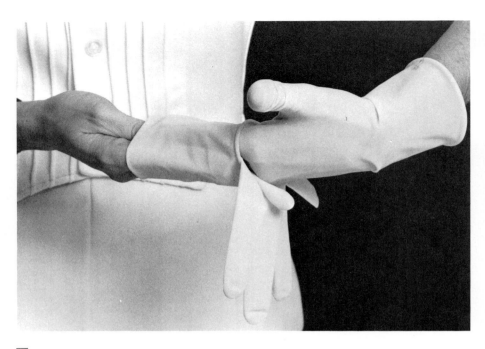

7 Put on sterile gloves, following aseptic technique as detailed in Chapter 1.

9 Set one or two of the cotton balls aside, and pour the antimicrobial solution over the others.

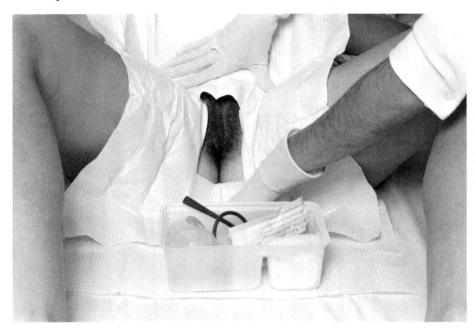

8 Instruct the client to abduct her legs and pull up on the sheet or towel as you place the fenestrated sterile drape over her perineum. Move the sterile catheterization kit to the sterile field between her legs.

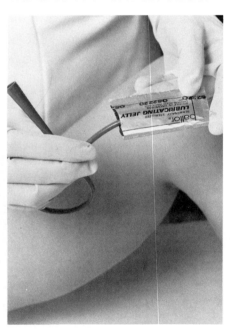

10 Open the sterile lubricant and either place the catheter's tip into the package (as shown) or squeeze the lubricant onto the sterile field and generously lubricate the tip of the catheter.

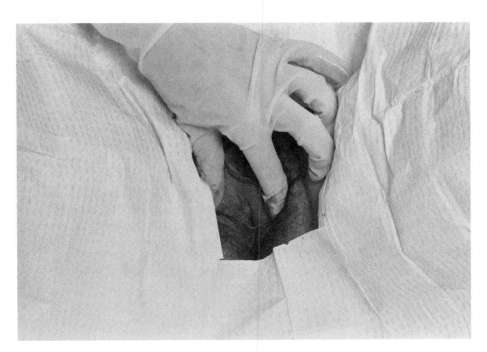

11 You are ready to prepare the urethral meatus and its surrounding area. With your non-dominant hand, separate the labia to expose the urethral mea- tus. Use your thumb and index finger to apply slight upward and backward tension. This hand is now considered contaminated.

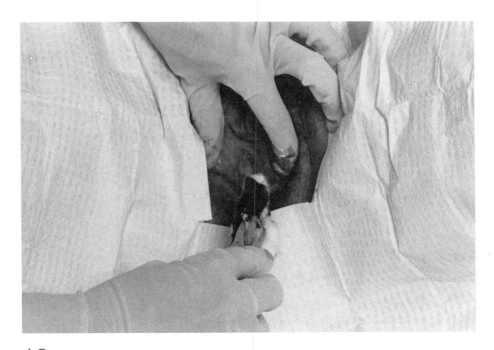

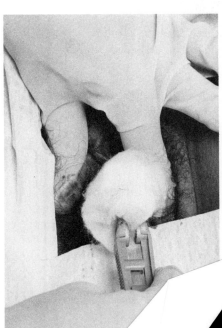

12 With your dominant hand, grasp a saturated cotton ball with the sterile forceps. With one downward stroke per cotton ball, cleanse on each side of the mea- tus. After each stroke, discard the used cotton ball into a waste con- tainer. Cleanse the meatus (as shown) with one downward stroke. Continue to separate the labia until you have completed the catheterization. *Note:* If the labia are allowed to fall together, repeat the cleansing process.

13 After pre wipe the mea*s)* ton ball, u stroke. D

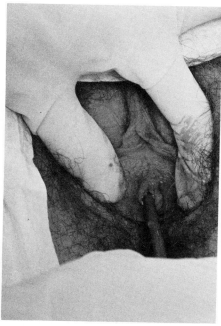

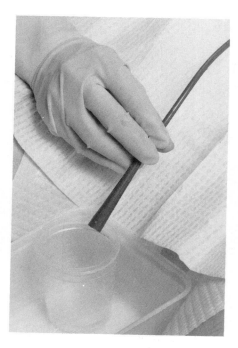

15   When you have catheterized the client successfully, obtain a urine specimen if one has been ordered. Place the sterile specimen cup at the distal end of the catheter. After obtaining the specimen, allow the urine to drain into the empty catheterization tray. Follow agency policy regarding the amount of urine you should allow to drain. Rapid decompression of the bladder, resulting from a quick release of large amounts of urine (quantities greater than 800–1,000 ml), can lead to shock.

14   Gently insert the catheter into the meatus, and ask the client to breathe deeply and slowly and to bear down with per pelvic muscles. If you meet resistance, slightly angle the catheter toward her symphysis pubis, but do not force the catheter. If urine has not returned after you have inserted the catheter 7.5–10 cm (3–4 in.) (adjust the insertion length accordingly in the pediatric population), it is possible that your client is dehydrated or has recently voided. It is more likely, however, that you have inserted the catheter into the vagina, rather than into the urethra. Use the extra pair of sterile gloves and a new catheter and repeat the catheterization. Keep the original catheter in place to avoid making the same mistake.

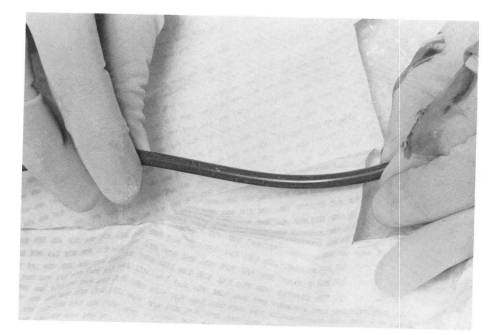

16   After emptying the bladder, squeeze the catheter between your thumb and index finger to prevent urine from filling the urethra. Gently remove the catheter. Remove the catheterization materials from the bedside, and assist your client into a comfortable position.

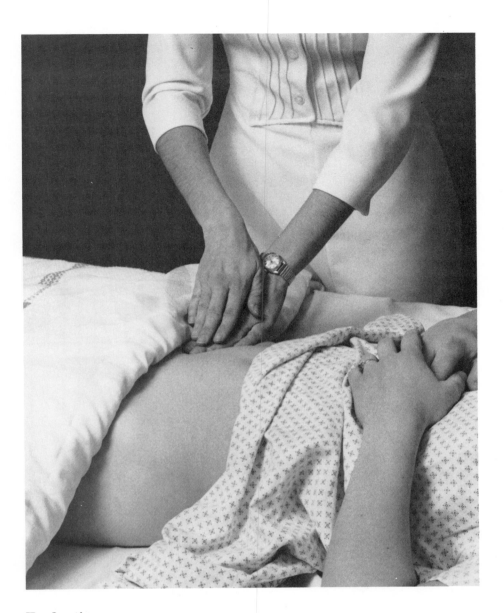

Evaluating

17 Measure the urine; document the procedure, noting the amount, color, and character of the urine. If the catheterization was ordered for urinary retention, assess your client periodically for her ability to void and for a distended bladder.

INSERTING A ROBINSON (STRAIGHT) CATHETER INTO A MALE

Implementing

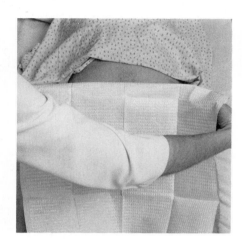

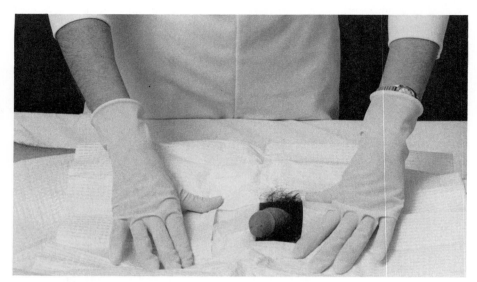

1   Follow steps 1–5 for catheterizing a female in the preceding technique. The male client should assume a dorsal recumbent position with his legs extended. Hold the sterile underpad so that the undersurface of the two corners encircles your hands. Ask the client to raise his gown as you position the pad over his thighs and under his penis.

2   After putting on sterile gloves, position the fenestrated drape so that its open surface encircles the penis.

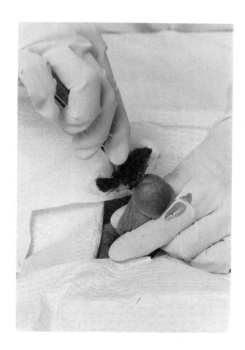

3   Prepare the cotton balls with the antimicrobial solution, following step 9 in the preceding technique. Hold the penis upright with your nondominant hand, and prepare the glans and meatus with your dominant hand, being certain to keep this hand sterile. Hold the cotton balls with the sterile forceps, and cleanse the penis from the meatus toward the shaft, using a circular motion. If your client is uncircumcised, maintain a gentle retraction on the foreskin throughout the procedure. Use fresh cotton balls and repeat the cleansing process at least three more times, disposing of each used cotton ball outside of the sterile field.

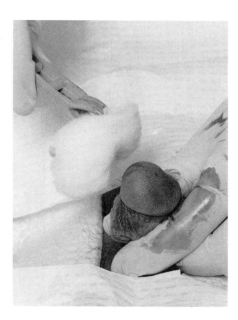

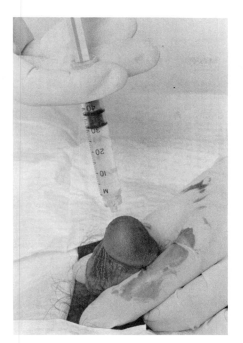

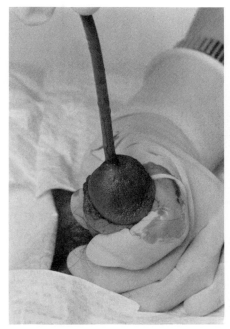

4 After a thorough cleansing, wipe the glans with a dry cotton ball.

5 If the catheterization kit contains a premeasured, lubricant-filled syringe, you can inject the lubricant directly into the urethra of an adult. Otherwise, lubricate the tip of the catheter at least 17.5 cm (7 in.), following step 10 in the preceding technique. Adjust the insertion length accordingly in the pediatric population.

6 Continue to hold the shaft of the penis at a 90-degree angle to the client's abdomen. Apply gentle traction to straighten the urethra, and ask the client to bear down as if to urinate (ask the pediatric client to blow out air) so that the sphincters will relax and allow an easier entry into the urethra. Gently insert the catheter approximately 15–20 cm (6–8 in.) until the tip enters the bladder and urine is returned. Adjust the insertion length accordingly in the pediatric population. If you feel resistance, increase the traction on the penis and apply a little more pressure with the catheter, but do not use force. This will enable you to advance the catheter beyond the many folds in the urethra.

(Continues)

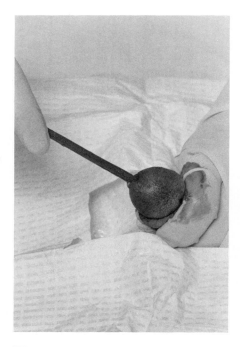

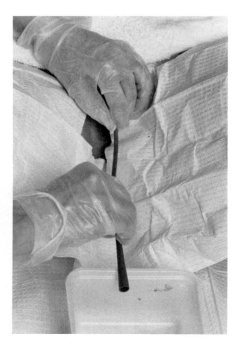

7 If you continue to feel resistance, change the angle of the penis, and use short, rotating movements as you advance the catheter. Continue the insertion until urine begins to flow. Once the catheter has entered the bladder, reposition the foreskin for clients who are uncircumcised. *Caution: For clients with prostatic hypertrophy, it may be difficult to pass the catheter beyond the prostatic gland. In that situation you may need a special urologic Coudé catheter (12–16F) for the adult client. For the pediatric client, notify the physician for insertion.*

8 Obtain a urine specimen and/or empty the bladder, following steps 15–17 in the preceding technique.

MANAGING A FOLEY CATHETER

PERFORMING A CATHETERIZATION WITH A FOLEY (INDWELLING) CATHETER

Assessing and Planning

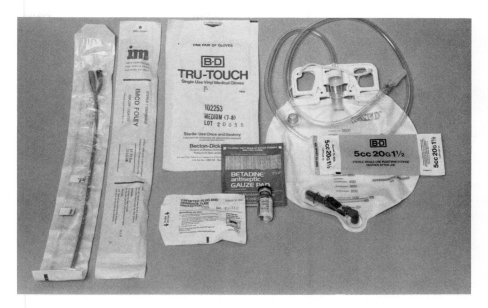

1 Follow the steps for assessing and planning in the procedure, pp. 446–447, for performing intermittent catheterization. In addition to the catheterization kit, you also will need the following sterile supplies: a drainage collection bag with tubing, a syringe and sterile water for inflating the catheter balloon, and two Foley catheters and an extra pair of sterile gloves in the event either becomes contaminated during the procedure. In addition, you might wish to keep an extra drainage tubing protector and an antimicrobial wipe at the bedside to help prevent contamination of the opened system during subsequent interventions, such as an irrigation or instillation.

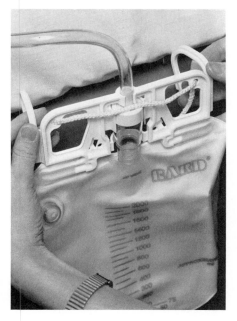

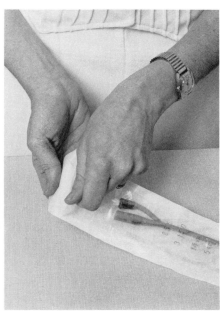

2 Attach the drainage collection bag to the bed frame, and bring the drainage tubing up onto the bed so that it will be readily accessible. Make sure the end of the tubing remains covered by the drainage tubing protector.

3 After opening the sterile catheterization kit, aseptically open one of the sterile packages containing the Foley and drop the catheter onto the sterile field. Do the same for the sterile syringe if it is not prepackaged with the catheterization kit. Cleanse the urethral meatus and surrounding area, following the appropriate steps for preparing the female or the male. These steps were described in the preceding procedures.

(Continues)

Implementing

4 Following the steps in the previous two procedures for intermittent catheterization of the male or the female, insert the catheter.

To make sure the catheter is in the bladder, advance it another 2.5 cm (1 in.) beyond the distance at which urine begins to flow. For the adult female, the total distance of the insertion will be approximately 7.5–10 cm (3–4 in.). The total distance for the adult male, however, can be as much as 25 cm (10 in.), and the bifurcation of the catheter might be quite close to the urethral meatus. If the syringe for balloon inflation does not already contain the sterile water, aspirate the appropriate amount. The usual amount is 5 ml, but this can vary depending on the brand and size of catheter used. The appropriate amount is always stamped on the lumen of the balloon portal. Slowly inject the water as you assess the client for discomfort. If the client complains of pain, immediately aspirate the water

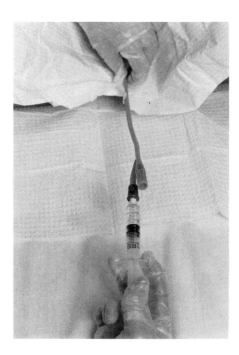

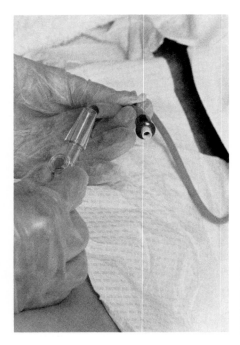

because the balloon may be incorrectly positioned in the urethra. After inflating the balloon, pull back gently on the catheter to check for resistance, a sign that the balloon is correctly positioned against the proximal wall of the bladder.

5 Remove the drainage tubing protector and connect the drainage tubing to the open lumen of the catheter. This often requires manipulation, and because your gloves no longer can be considered sterile, it might be necessary to use the antimicrobial wipe at the connection site. Secure the tubing to the bed linen with the attached clip (bottom photo). Be certain to keep the tubing looped on the bed rather than hanging on the floor.

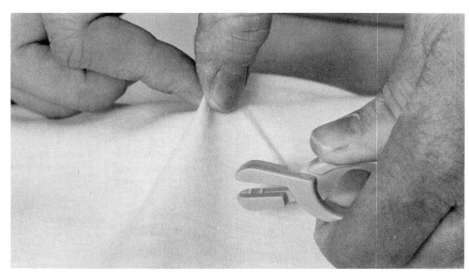

Evaluating

 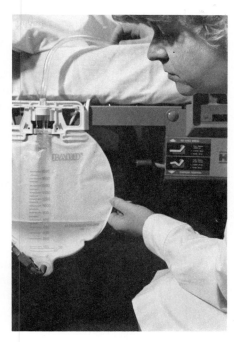 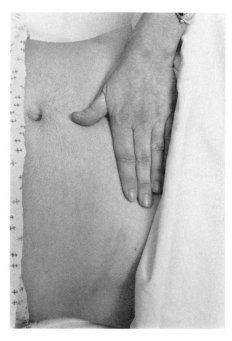

6 Tape the drainage tubing to your client to help prevent it from becoming dislodged. For female clients, tape the tubing to the medial thigh. For the male client, tape the tubing either to the anterior thigh or to the lower abdomen. It is believed that the latter position especially minimizes urethral pressure that would occur at the normal penoscrotal angle. For more secure taping, place a strip of tape on your client's skin; then tape the catheter to the tape (as shown). Allow some slack in the tubing. If the catheter will be left indwelling for an extended period of time, protect your client's skin by making a dressing similar to a Montgomery strap (see the next procedure). Label the drainage bag with the time and date so that it can be changed periodically according to agency protocol.

7 Document the procedure, noting the time and date of catheterization as well as the size and type of catheter used. Periodically check the drainage tubing for patency and ensure that the output of urine is adequate when compared to the client's intake. Assess the urine for the presence of blood, cloudiness, or a foul odor, which are indications that the client may have a urinary tract infection.

8 If the client has a diminished urinary output, inspect the lower abdomen and palpate or percuss the bladder to assess for urine retention, which can occur with an occluded catheter. Obtain an order for an irrigation, if indicated. Also, assess the client for the presence of fever, chills, or discomfort, which are indicators of a urinary tract infection. Ensure that the perineum is washed daily.

General Guidelines for Foley Catheter Management

- Coil and secure the drainage tubing to the bed linen to prevent looping below the drainage bag, which can promote urine stasis and bacterial growth.
- To prevent urinary tract infections caused by urinary reflux, always keep the drainage bag below the level of the client's bladder: Instruct ambulatory clients to carry the drainage bag below the level of their bladders.
  Instruct transport personnel to keep the drainage bag below the client's bladder.
- To reduce the risk of transferring organisms from one client's urinary drainage container to another client's urinary drainage container, the Centers for Disease Control recommends that no more than one client in a room have an indwelling urethral catheter.
- Unless it is contraindicated, as, for example, in cardiac and renal failure clients, encourage a fluid intake of at least 2–3 L/day to dilute the urine and maximize urinary flow. It is believed that this will help reduce the risk of urinary tract infections.
- Unless it has been specifically ordered, hand irrigate the catheter *only* when it is obstructed.
- Assess for indications of a urinary tract infection: chills, increased temperature, flank/suprapubic pain, hematuria, and cloudy or foul-smelling urine.
- Inspect and cleanse the perineal area during the client's daily bath.
- Be alert to meatal swelling, discharge, and erythema, which are indicators of infection. For clients performing self-care, remind them of the importance of daily perineal cleansing.
- Evaluate the need for an indwelling drainage device on a daily basis. Collaborate with the physician to remove the device as soon as possible to reduce the risk of the client developing a urinary tract infection. The longer the catheter remains in the bladder, the greater the risk of urinary tract infection to the client.
- Label and keep a separate graduated drainage container for each client with a urinary drainage device. Use this container only for emptying the client's urinary drainage bag; rinse it and allow it to dry between uses. This practice reduces the risk of transferring organisms from one client's drainage bag to another client's drainage bag via a shared graduate that may be contaminated.

MAKING A CATHETER STRAP

Instead of using tape to anchor your client's Foley catheter, consider making a catheter strap, which is similar to a Montgomery strap. This will eliminate the need for repeated removal and reapplication of tape when frequent repositioning of the Foley is necessary. To make the catheter strap, you will need two pieces of tape 10 × 10 cm (4 × 4 in.) and a 25-cm (10-in.) piece of twill tape.

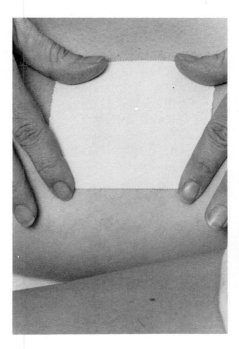

1 For a female client, adhere one of the tape squares to the medial thigh. Attach the tape to the anterior thigh or lower abdomen for male clients. Shave the site first, if necessary.

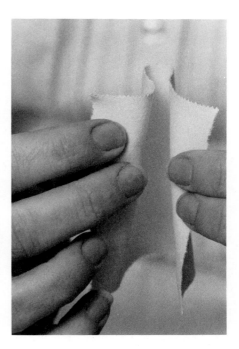

2 Fold the other square in half, so that the nonadhering surfaces face one another.

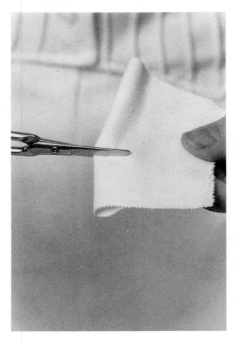

3 Cut two slits along the folded edge, 6 mm ($\frac{1}{4}$ in.) in width and approximately 2.5 cm (1 in.) apart.

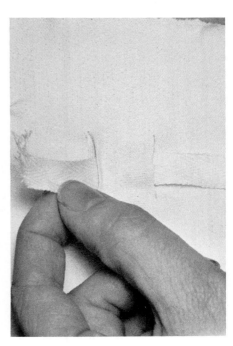

4 Unfold the tape and pull the twill tape through the slits.

(Continues)

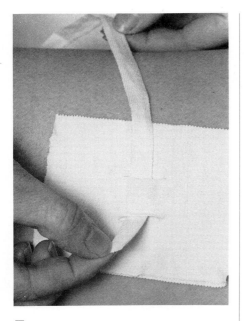

5 Adhere the second tape to the first, and pull the twill tape until it is at equal lengths on each side.

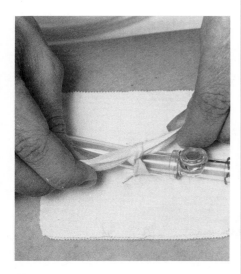

6 Position the drainage tubing over the twill tape, and tie the tape around the tubing. When the outer tape square becomes soiled, you can easily replace it without removing the inner square, thus saving your client discomfort.

OBTAINING A URINE SPECIMEN

As you know, urine in the drainage bag is considered contaminated; and disconnecting the catheter from the drainage tubing opens the system and increases the potential for infection. Therefore, urine samples for diagnostic testing must be obtained through a closed system, either through a sampling port or directly through the urinary catheter.

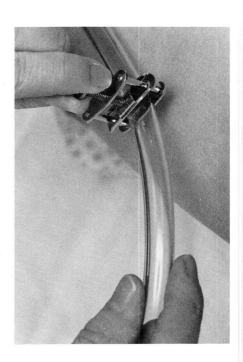

1 To obtain the specimen, you will need to clamp the drainage tubing for a few minutes (usually around 15) to allow the urine to collect in the catheter.

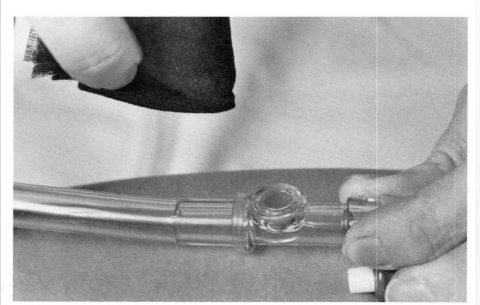

2 Wash your hands and cleanse the sampling port with an antimicrobial wipe. Allow it to dry.

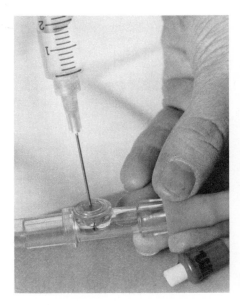

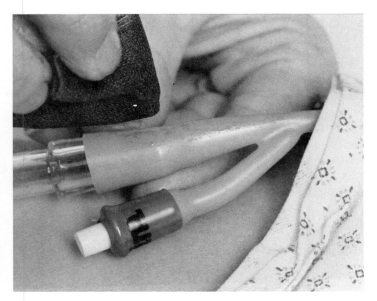

3 Aspirate the urine directly through the port, using a sterile needle and syringe. Usually, 2–3 ml will be adequate for a diagnostic test. Cleanse the sampling port again with an antimicrobial wipe.

4 If the catheter does not have a sampling port, cleanse the catheter just distal to the bifurcation.

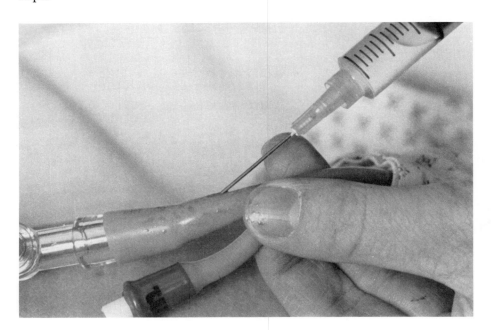

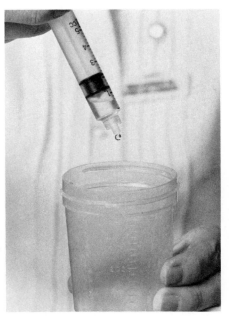

5 Using a 21- to 25-gauge needle and a sterile syringe, aspirate the urine through the catheter wall. Point the needle away from the bifurcation to prevent puncturing the balloon port and aspirating the balloon's contents. Remove the needle and cleanse the site again.

6 Inject the urine into a sterile specimen cup unless the syringe itself is to be sent to the laboratory. Label the specimen with the client's name, the time and date of collection, and note that it was obtained from the catheter. If you cannot send the specimen to the laboratory immediately, refrigerate it. Be sure that you have unclamped the catheter.

EMPTYING THE DRAINAGE BAG

The urinary drainage bag should be emptied every 8 hours, or more frequently during periods of large urinary output. This is essential in reducing the infection risk because urine that is allowed to stagnate is an excellent medium for bacterial growth.

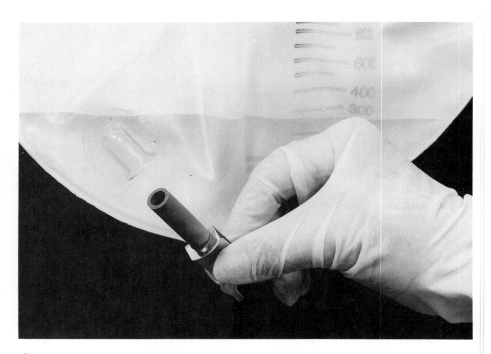

1 To empty the bag, wash your hands and apply clean gloves; then position the client's measuring container under the spout. Detach the spout from its protective sleeve.

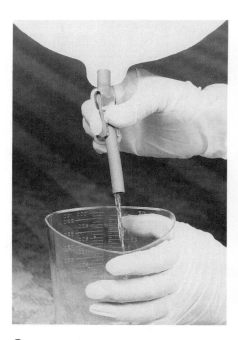

2 Open the clamp, allowing the entire contents to drain into the measuring container. To prevent contamination, do not allow the spout to touch the measuring container.

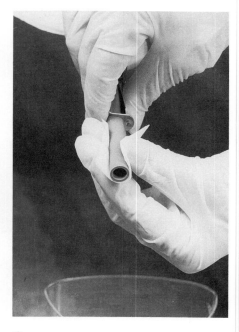

3 After emptying the drainage bag, clean the spout with an antiseptic wipe and reinsert it into its sleeve on the drainage bag. Measure and record the amount of urine. Empty and wash the measuring container. Remove your gloves and wash your hands.

USING A URINE METER

When accurate monitoring of urinary output is necessary, for example, for clients in acute renal failure, obtain a urine meter with a drainage bag and attach it to your client's Foley catheter. The urine meter will enable you to measure minute quantities of urine, either hourly or during specified time intervals.

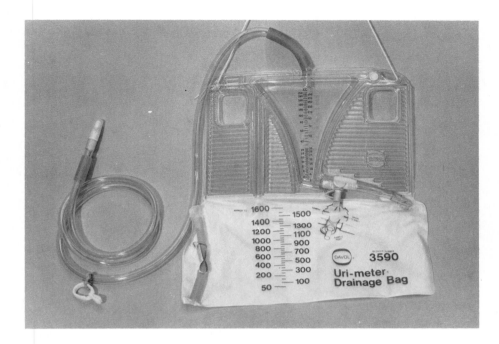

1   Wash your hands and explain the procedure to your client. Place a bed-saver pad under the catheter, and attach the urine meter to the bedside frame next to the Foley drainage bag. Secure the drainage tubing to the bed linen so that it will be readily accessible.

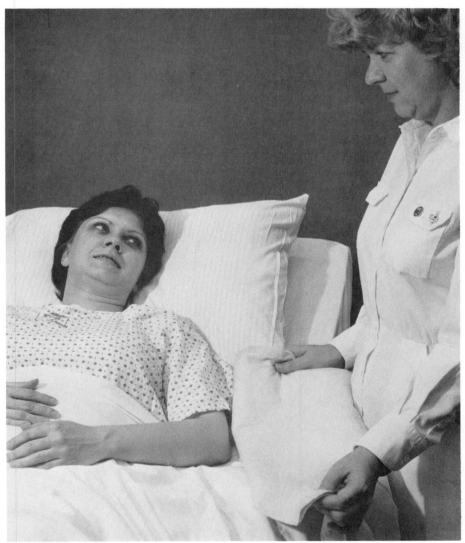

(Continues)

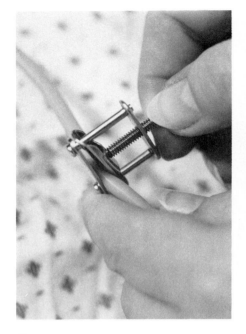

2 Straighten the drainage tubing to drain the urine into the drainage bag, and then clamp the catheter.

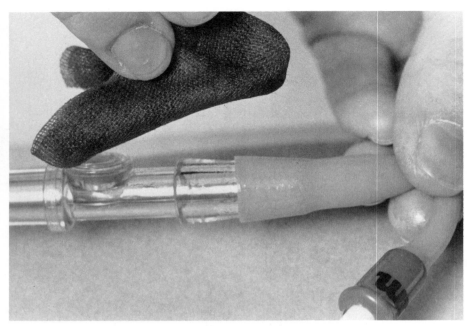

3 Thoroughly cleanse the connection site of the catheter and drainage tubing with an antiseptic wipe. Because it is sometimes difficult to manipulate the tubing without touching the ends, it may be a good idea to apply sterile gloves.

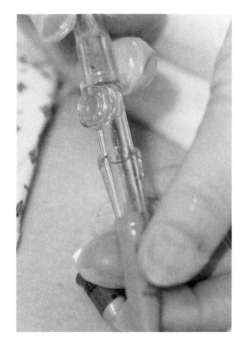

4 Aseptically detach the Foley drainage tubing from the catheter.

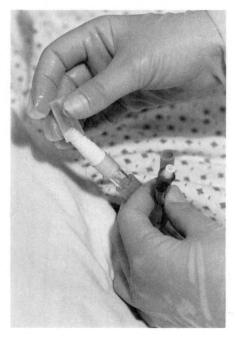

5 Remove the protective cap on the end of the urine meter drainage tubing, and aseptically insert the tubing into the catheter lumen. Unclamp the catheter and tape the drainage tubing to your client's thigh or abdomen. After measuring the output, discard the Foley drainage system.

6 Hourly, or during specified time intervals, straighten the drainage tubing and inspect the collection chamber to assess the amount of urine that has collected. Record the amount and open the stopcock to allow the urine to drain into the drainage bag. When the client no longer requires hourly urine checks, just keep the stopcock open to allow the urine to drain into the drainage bag. This will prevent re-opening the system to attach a regular drainage bag, which potentially could contaminate both the system and the client's urinary tract.

IRRIGATING THE CATHETER

Assessing

1 Because irrigating a catheter can greatly increase the risk of infection by opening a closed system, irrigation should not be performed unless you are certain the catheter is obstructed. Diminished urinary output is an unacceptable rationale for irrigation, unless it is accompanied by additional indications of obstruction (see step 2, below). Evaluate the integrity of the collection system by inspecting the drainage tubing for kinks or exterior obstructions. Evaluate your client's intake and compare it to the output. If you assess that your client might be dehydrated, increase the fluid intake and reevaluate the output after 30–45 minutes. Because hypotension also can reduce urinary output, be sure to check the client's blood pressure.

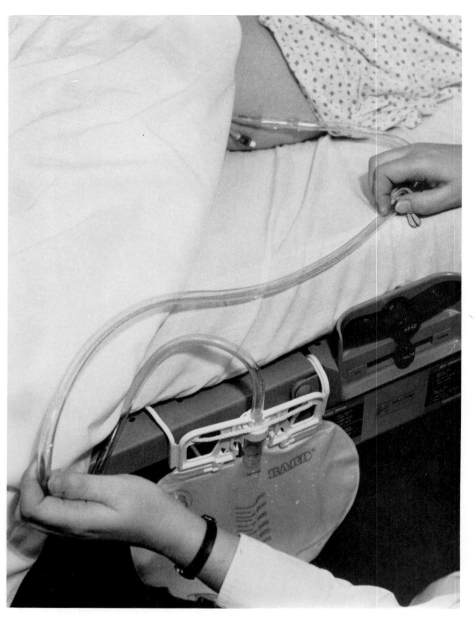

2 Inspect the suprapubic area and palpate or percuss your client's bladder. If the bladder is distended, the urinary output is minimal (less than 30 ml/hr or 0.5 ml/kg/hr), blood clots are noted, urine is leaking around the catheter, or the client is experiencing bladder spasms, obtain an order for an irrigation.

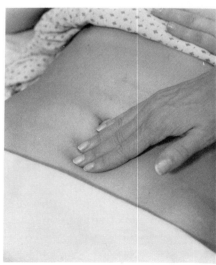

Planning

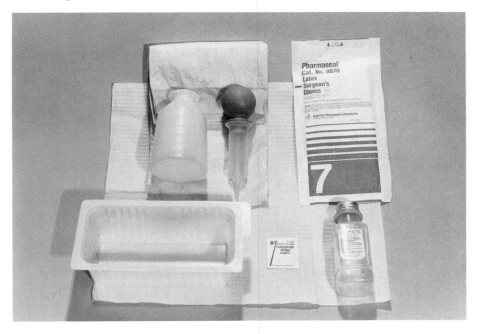

3 Obtain a catheter irrigation kit or assemble the following *sterile* materials: underpad, for use as a sterile field and bed protector; drainage tray; graduated container; 50- to 60-ml bulb (*not* piston) syringe; gloves; an antiseptic wipe; and normal saline or the prescribed irrigant warmed to room temperature. You also will need a bed-saver pad. Remember to keep the following items sterile at all times: the open ends of both the drainage tubing and the catheter, the irrigant, and the syringe.

4 Wash your hands and explain the procedure to your client. After the client assumes a dorsal recumbent position, place a bed-saver pad under the Foley catheter. Aseptically open the irrigation tray, and place the underpad over a clean, dry surface to make a sterile field. Pour the sterile irrigant into the graduated container, and position the empty tray close to the client's perineum.

Implementing

5 Clean the connection of the drainage tubing and catheter with an antiseptic wipe.

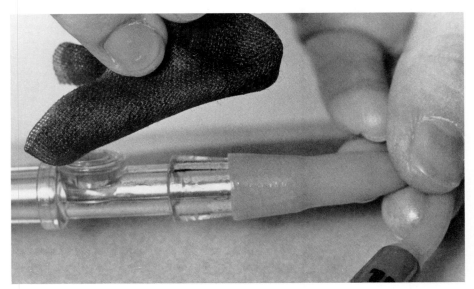

(Continues)

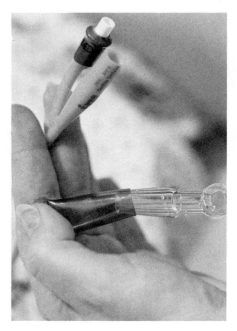

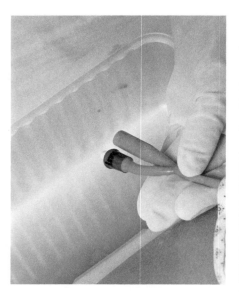

6   Disconnect the drainage tubing from the Foley. Keep the end of the drainage tubing sterile by capping it with a tube protector (as shown) or by attaching a sterile gauze pad and securing it with a rubber band. To keep the end of the catheter sterile, place it over the drainage tray so that it will be protected as you apply sterile gloves.

7   Put on sterile gloves and aspirate 30–50 ml of the sterile irrigant into the bulb syringe. Attach the syringe to the end of the catheter, and inject the irrigant gently by slowly squeezing the bulb of the syringe.

8   Remove the syringe and allow the irrigant to return into the drainage tray by gravity. After the irrigant has returned, and if it is indicated, repeat the irrigation process until the returns are clear. If the fluid fails to return, gently rotate the catheter between your fingers, press gently on the suprapubic area, or ask the client to perform a Valsalva maneuver or turn from side to side. If these measures fail to return the irrigant, apply gentle suction with the bulb. This might be necessary if blood clots are obstructing the catheter. Unless absolutely necessary, avoid aspiration with a piston syringe because vigorous suctioning can damage the bladder wall. Follow agency protocol for further intervention if you still are unable to return the irrigant. It may be necessary to reconnect the drainage tubing and observe the client closely for the next hour or two, assessing for continued indications of obstruction as well as for eventual gravity drainage, which may occur once bladder spasms cease. If the obstruction continues, notify the physician for further intervention, such as changing the catheter.

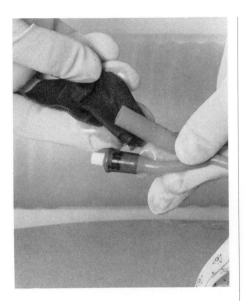

9 After completing the irrigation, clean the open end of the catheter with an antiseptic wipe.

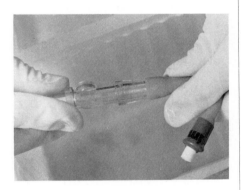

10 Grasp the drainage tubing, remove the protective cover, and aseptically connect the drainage tubing to the open end of the catheter. Assist the client into a comfortable position, and remove the used equipment from the bedside. Measure the amount of the return and compare it to the amount that was instilled. Document the procedure, noting the amount and character of the return. Be certain to note the amount of residual irrigant on the intake and output record, as well. Continue to assess the client to ensure that there are no indications of bladder distention, spasms, or diminished urinary output.

REMOVING A FOLEY CATHETER

When the physician has requested the discontinuation of your client's Foley catheter, you first will need to deflate the balloon to allow the catheter to pass through the urethra.

1 Apply clean gloves. Place a bed-saver pad under your client's catheter, and cleanse the balloon port with an antiseptic wipe. Untape the catheter from your client's thigh or abdomen.

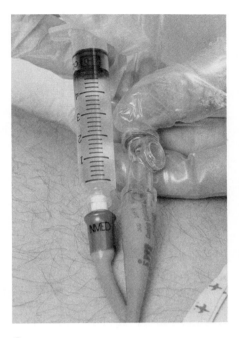

2 Depending on the type of catheter used, either cut the balloon port or attach a sterile syringe to the balloon port (some catheters may require both a syringe and a needle), and aspirate the water. The amount required to inflate the balloon should be imprinted on the lumen of the balloon port. Be certain to aspirate the same amount of water that was injected after the catheter's insertion. When the water has been aspirated, pinch the catheter between your thumb and index finger to prevent urine from filling the urethra during the removal. Gently pull on the catheter to remove it from your client's bladder and urethra. If you are unable to withdraw the catheter, do not use force. Notify the physician, instead, for further intervention. Remove the catheter and drainage bag from the bedside, and provide your client with soap and water for cleansing the meatus and perineum. Measure and document the output and record the procedure. During the first 24 hours following the removal of the Foley catheter, or according to agency protocol, document the time, amount, and character of each voiding.

Caring for Clients with Renal-Urinary Disorders

APPLYING AN EXTERNAL URINARY DEVICE (WITH A LEG DRAINAGE SYSTEM)

Assessing and Planning

When caring for male clients for whom the prolonged use of indwelling catheters may be contraindicated, you might assess the need for an external collection device such as the Hollister™ Male Urinary Collection System. Exdwelling catheters, also known as condom and Texas catheters, usually require a physician's order. Be sure to read manufacturer's instructions carefully before applying the exdwelling catheter used by your agency.

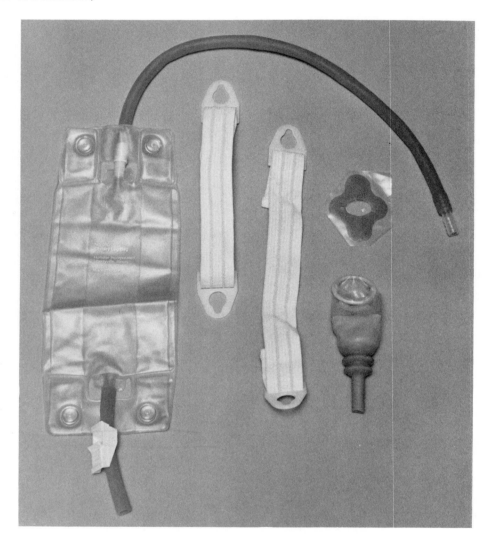

1 If an external urinary device has been prescribed for your client, explain the procedure and, if appropriate, prepare to instruct him in the application technique.

Assemble the following equipment: leg drainage bag, extension tubing, leg straps, skin protector, and the exdwelling (condom) catheter.

Implementing

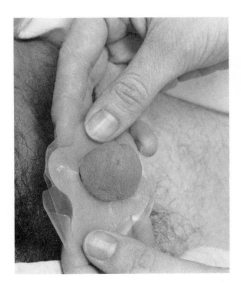

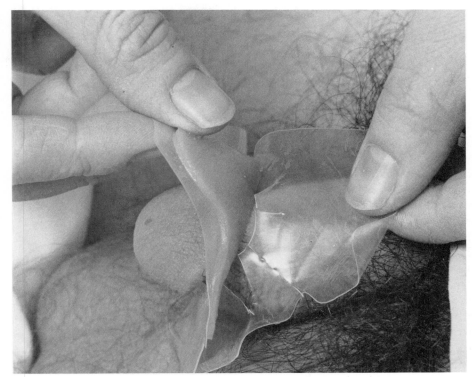

2 Wash your hands and begin the procedure by trimming or pushing the pubic hair away from the penis. It is seldom necessary to shave the hair because hair that adheres to the sticky surface of the adhesive skin protector can be pulled away carefully. Gently pull the glans penis through the opening of the skin protector. The skin protector will stretch and yet rapidly return to its original shape without constricting the penis or losing its elasticity.

3 Pull off the protective film on the underside of the skin protector. Adhere the posterior surface of the skin protector to the shaft of the penis. Be certain that the pubic hair is pushed away first.

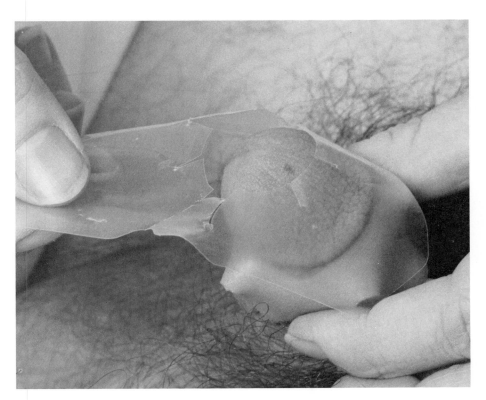

4 Remove the protective film from the anterior surface of the skin protector.

(Continues)

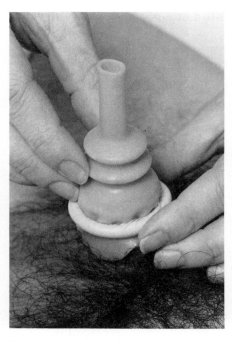

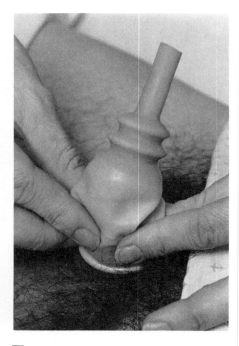

5   Roll the catheter until the inner flap is exposed. This is important because it is this flap that prevents the reflux of urine.

6   Position the catheter over the glans penis so that the opening of the inner flap surrounds the urethral meatus.

7   Carefully unroll the catheter with as little wrinkling as possible until it covers the skin protector. Gently press along the exterior of the catheter to adhere it to the skin protector. If more than a few wrinkles occur, do not attempt to reposition the catheter on the skin protector. See step 11 for removal instructions.

Assembling the Leg Drainage Bag

8   After removing the drainage bag from its container, close the drain clamp at the bottom of the bag.

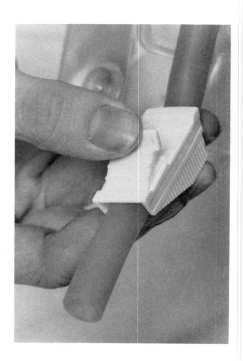

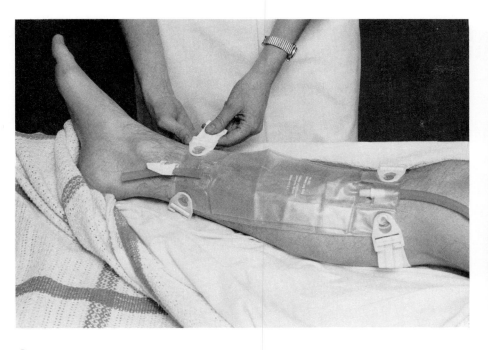

9 Position the bag at the medial aspect of the lower leg, and bring each strap around the leg, attaching them to the buttons on the drainage bag. Adjust each strap so that it securely attaches the drainage bag to the leg yet does not constrict circulation.

10 Attach the extension tubing to the external urinary device via the connector. The tubing should have enough slack so that it does not tug on the external catheter. For shorter clients, the tubing can be cut to ensure a good fit. Explain to the client that the drainage bag can be emptied by opening the drain clamp. Wash your hands and document the procedure. *Note: For nonambulatory clients, a closed drainage collection bag can be used instead.*

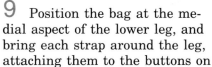

Evaluating

11 Periodically assess the skin under the straps for pressure areas or irritation, and ensure that the straps are not too tight by placing two fingers between the client's skin and the straps (as shown). Alert, mobile clients should be shown how to adjust the straps and to assess for the presence of leakage or irritation.

It is recommended that the catheter be changed daily. To remove the catheter, roll it off the penis together with the skin protector. After removal, warm water can be used to remove any residue left by the skin protector.

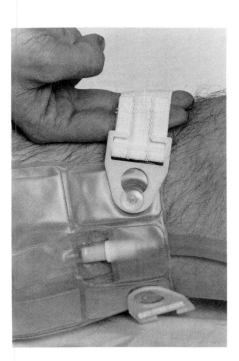

MONITORING THE CLIENT RECEIVING CONTINUOUS BLADDER IRRIGATION (CBI)

ESTABLISHING CBI

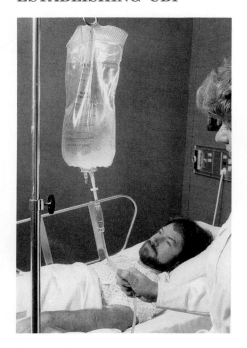

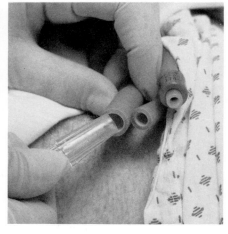

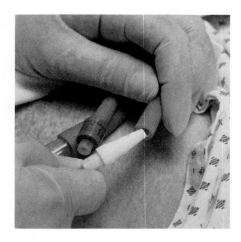

1   If your client has had a transurethral prostatectomy, he might return from surgery with a three-way Foley catheter, which allows closed continuous bladder irrigation. The irrigation is usually performed for a 24-hour period, during which the client remains on bed rest. If the irrigation solution and drainage bag were not already connected in surgery, it might be your responsibility to assemble the equipment and establish the irrigation. Explain the procedure to your client, and wash your hands. Obtain the prescribed irrigation solution (usually a glycine preparation), its special irrigation tubing, and a large (3,000–4,000 ml) collection bag (optional). Spike the solution container, hang it on an IV pole, and prime the tubing as you would an intravenous infusion set. Be certain to flush out all the air, and then clamp off the tubing.

2   If the three-way catheter is not already attached to a large collection bag, you may need to detach the regular-sized collection bag and replace it with the large bag. To do this, briefly clamp the catheter, apply sterile gloves, cleanse the large outflow lumen with an antiseptic wipe, and aseptically attach the tubing for the large collection bag (as shown). Unclamp the catheter.

3   Cleanse the inflow lumen with an antiseptic wipe, and aseptically insert the connector for the primed infusion tubing. Establish the prescribed flow rate and refer to the following guidelines for client care. Document the procedure.

Nursing Guidelines for the Care of Clients with CBI

- Unless otherwise prescribed, keep the client on bed rest during CBI (usually 24 hours).
- Moderate bleeding (pink to deep-pink returns) is normal. Bright red returns containing numerous blood clots are indicative of hemorrhage, and the physician should be alerted immediately.
- With normal hematuria, maintain the infusion rate of the irrigant at 40–60 drops/min. Increase the rate if the returns are a brighter red, and decrease the rate when the returns become clearer.
- Monitor vital signs at least every 4 hours during the irrigation (every 15 minutes if they are unstable). Assess for these indicators of impending shock if the returns are bright red: hypotension, pallor, diaphoresis, and rapid pulse and respirations.
- To ensure that there is no obstruction, which can occur with blood clots, inspect the catheter for patency and assess the client's suprapubic area for distention. In addition, question the client regarding the presence of severe discomfort or recurring bladder spasms.
- Keep careful records of intake and output, subtracting the amount of irrigation solution from the total output to determine the true amount of urine production.
- Irrigate *only* if the catheter is obstructed and if you have a physician's order to do so.
- If the physician orders traction on the balloon portion of the catheter, maintain traction with tape or a gauze strip. The traction will keep the balloon wedged against the prostatic fossa to minimize bleeding.
- If it is not contraindicated, encourage a fluid intake of 2–3 L/day. Dilute urine has less potential for the growth of bacteria and the formation of encrustations.
- When a glycine irrigating solution is used, assess for these signs of hyponatremia: muscle twitching, confusion, convulsions.

Nursing Guidelines for the Care of the Client with a Suprapubic Catheter

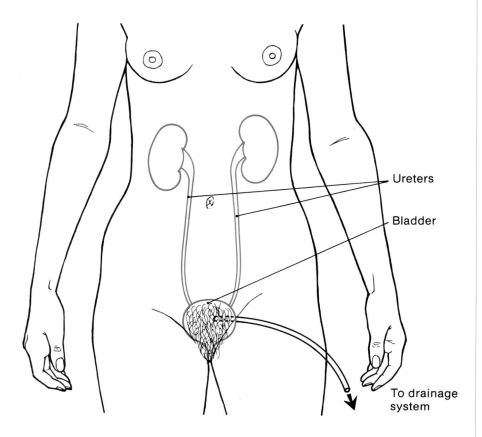

Ureters

Bladder

To drainage system

If your client is having bladder or prostatic surgery or a vaginal hysterectomy, or if the urethra is impassable, the physician might drain the bladder via an incision through the suprapubic area into the bladder. The catheter is then attached to a closed drainage collection container.

- To prevent dislodging, tape the tubing securely to the lateral abdomen.
- Should the catheter become dislodged, cover the site with a sterile dressing, and inform the physician at once for immediate replacement.
- To prevent contamination from the backflow of urine, keep the drainage collection container below the level of the client's bladder.
- Slight hematuria is normal during the first 24–48 hours postinsertion. Bright red drainage is abnormal and should be reported immediately. Be sure to document the character and amount of drainage. It should have a characteristic urine odor. Foul-smelling, cloudy urine or drainage is indicative of an infection.
- Keep drainage records from the suprapubic catheter separate from those of other indwelling catheters or tubes.

■ Inspect the catheter for patency, and prevent external obstruction. Irrigate only if an internal obstruction is noted, following the procedure, pp. 466–469.

■ Assess the dressing for drainage, and change it as soon as it becomes wet, using aseptic technique. Because it contains urine, a saturated dressing can lead to skin breakdown. Consider applying a pectin wafer skin barrier around the catheter insertion site to protect the skin.

■ Encourage a fluid intake of at least 2–3 L/day. Dilute urine minimizes the potential for infection and encrustations.

■ Prior to removal, the physician will order the catheter clamped for 3–4 hours at a time to test the client's ability to void spontaneously. After the client has voided, unclamp the catheter and measure the residual urine in the collection container. Notify the physician for removal when the residual urine is less than 100 ml after each of two successive voidings. Usually the catheter can be removed safely at that time.

Nursing Guidelines for the Care of the Client with a Nephrostomy Tube and Ureteral Stents

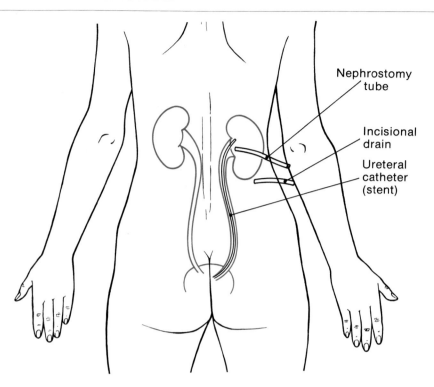

A percutaneous nephrostomy tube might be inserted for the client who has a ureteral obstruction, such as nephrolithiasis. The tube is inserted directly into the renal pelvis via an incision in the flank (below the posterior ribs and above the ilium) and anchored in place with one or more sutures or an inflated balloon. The tube is then connected to a closed drainage collection container. Ureteral catheters (stents) and drains also might be inserted (as shown).

- To prevent the nephrostomy tube from becoming dislodged, tape it securely to the client's flank. Elastic tape works especially well. Unless otherwise prescribed, keep the client on bed rest.
- Should the tube become dislodged, cover the site with a sterile dressing and notify the physician at once for immediate replacement.
- To prevent infection from reflux, keep the drainage collection container below the level of the client's kidney at all times.
- Clients also will have an indwelling bladder catheter to measure urine from the functioning kidney.
- A ureteral stent may be placed for a client with nephrolithiasis to help locate the stones.
- Monitor and record the character and amount of drainage in the collection container every hour. Some hematuria is normal during the first and second day postinsertion; bright red drainage is abnormal and should be reported to the physician immediately. An abrupt cessation in urine is often indicative of a dislodged or obstructed catheter. Copious amounts of drainage, however (e.g.,

2,000 ml or more during an 8-hour period), can signal postobstructive diuresis, which can cause fluid and electrolyte disturbances. Differentiate and record the amounts for each tube or catheter, and add the total together for total output.

■ During the first 24 hours postinsertion, monitor the client for indications of hemorrhage: decrease in blood pressure, rapid pulse and respirations, and copious amounts of bright red drainage. Also be alert to swelling or bruising in the affected flank, which can signal internal bleeding. Also assess for these indicators of infection: increase in temperature, chills, and foul-smelling and cloudy urine in the collection container. Also monitor the insertion site for erythema, swelling, and purulent drainage.

■ To reduce the risk of infection, keep the drainage system closed at all times unless you have a physician's *specific* order for irrigation.

■ If irrigation has been prescribed, instill a maximum of 5 ml of irrigant at one time into the nephrostomy tube. Greater amounts, resulting in overdistention, can damage the kidney. To instill the irrigant into the tube, it may be necessary to attach a male adaptor to a 5-ml syringe (as shown).

■ Assess the dressing for excessive drainage and the insertion site for leakage around the tube. Either problem is indicative of a tube that is dislodged or obstructed. To prevent skin breakdown from the highly irritating urine, change the dressing before it becomes saturated.

■ Because pyelonephritis can result from an infection, *always* use aseptic technique for dressing changes and irrigation.

■ To minimize the potential for infection and the formation of calculi, encourage a fluid intake of at least 2–3 L/day.

■ Once ureteral patency has been determined, the physician might order the nephrostomy tube clamped before removal to ensure client tolerance. During the clamping period, assess the client for the presence of flank pain or fever, or for a diminished urinary output. These are indications of ureteral obstruction.

ADMINISTERING A SODIUM POLYSTYRENE SULFONATE (KAYEXALATE) ENEMA

Sodium polystyrene sulfonate is a sodium resin, which exchanges sodium for potassium in the gastrointestinal tract for clients with hyperkalemia. It frequently is given with sorbitol, which because of its hypertonicity induces diarrhea. This facilitates expulsion and prevents reabsorption of the potassium.

Assessing and Planning

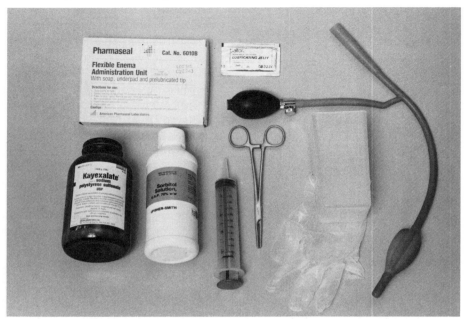

1 If your client has hyperkalemia, which could be caused by a diminished urinary output, acid-base imbalance, or cellular breakdown, the physician might prescribe sodium polystyrene sulfonate. However, if the client is unable to tolerate it orally because of nausea and vomiting or diminished bowel sounds, it will be necessary to administer it rectally. Assemble the following materials to administer the enema: the prescribed amounts of sodium polystyrene sulfonate and sorbitol; one or more 50-ml piston syringes, depending on the prescribed amounts to be administered; water-soluble lubricant; a hemostat or tubing clamp; clean glove; a container for mixing the enema solution; a rectal tube with an inflatable balloon; a device for inflating the balloon, such as a sphygmomanometer bulb; and a kit for administering a cleansing tap water enema after the client has expelled the sodium polystyrene sulfonate. In addition, you will need a bed-saver pad and a bed pan at the client's bedside, unless your client is able to walk to the bathroom. Mix the prescribed amounts of sodium polystyrene sulfonate with the sorbitol and aspirate or pour the solution into the piston syringe(s). If it is too thick for an easy administration, dilute it slightly with water.

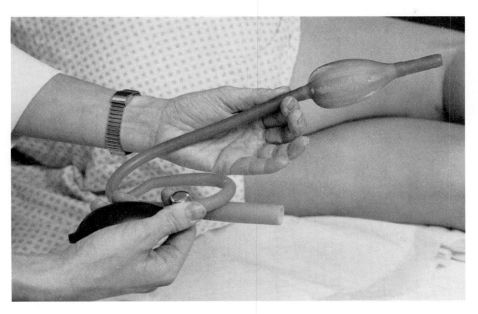

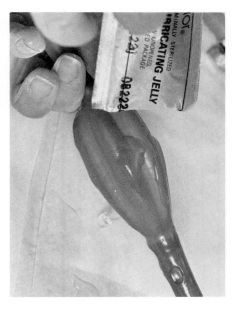

2 Review the procedure in Chapter 5 for administering a retention enema. Wash your hands and explain the procedure to the client. Assist her into a left side-lying (Sim's) position, and place a bed-saver pad under the buttocks. Assess the integrity of the balloon at the end of the rectal tube: compress the inflating bulb and count the number of compressions that are needed to inflate the balloon to two thirds of its capacity (make appropriate modifications for the pediatric population). Make a note of that number. *Caution:* *To prevent injury to the rectal tissue, never inflate the balloon more than two thirds of its capacity once it is in the rectum.*

3 Generously lubricate the tip and balloon of the rectal tube with water-soluble lubricant. Be sure that the balloon is completely collapsed.

(Continues)

Implementing

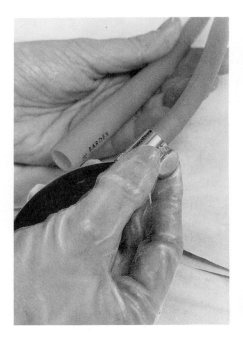

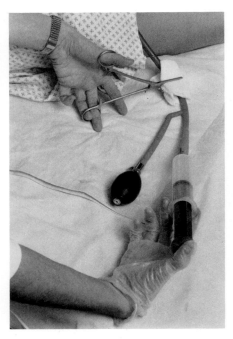

Evaluating

6 When the retention time has expired, unclamp the tubing, deflate the balloon, and remove the tube from the client's rectum. The client may then expel the solution. If the client is ambulatory, ask to see the returns in the toilet. Otherwise, assist the client onto the bed pan. After the expulsion, administer cleansing tap water enemas until the returns are clear and no longer brown. Provide materials for cleansing the rectal area, and assist the client into a position of comfort. Document the procedure and its results. Continue to assess the client for indications of hyperkalemia: weakness, cramps, twitching, diarrhea.

4 Put on a clean glove and insert the deflated balloon into the client's rectum past the external and internal sphincters. Inflate the balloon, compressing the bulb the same number of times required to inflate it to two thirds of its capacity (see step 2, p. 481). Inflating the balloon will help the client retain the solution. Pull back gently on the rectal tube to ensure that the balloon is properly inflated and cannot be pulled past the sphincters.

5 Attach the piston syringe containing the solution to the open end of the rectal tube. Position the opened hemostat around the area you will later clamp. Administer the medication in a bolus, clamp the tubing, and remove the empty syringe. Either attach another syringe containing the solution or maintain the clamped tubing for 30–45 minutes, or the prescribed amount of time, until the client is allowed to expel the solution. Be reassuring and periodically advise the client of the time remaining until the solution can be expelled.

PERFORMING THE CREDÉ MANEUVER

Manual pressure applied to the bladder, the Credé maneuver, can be employed to facilitate the removal of urine for clients whose bladders are flaccid, for example clients with hypotonic neurogenic bladders. The procedure should not be performed without a physician's order. It is contraindicated for clients with especially strong sphincter resistance because the high intravesical pressure it produces potentially can result in ureteral reflux and infection. The Credé maneuver is also contraindicated for clients with spinal cord injury at or above T-6 because of the potential for autonomic dysreflexia caused by this stimulus.

Assessing and Planning

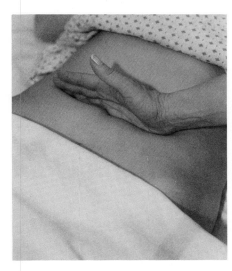

1 Usually the procedure is performed every 4–6 hours to prevent the bladder from becoming overly distended. However, you should periodically assess your client's bladder for distention during the interim periods. When the bladder is full, provide privacy and assist a female client onto a bed pan or provide a urinal for your male client. Clients with arm and hand strength and mobility should be taught to use the maneuver as an alternative to self-catheterization. When the client is in a comfortable position, place the ulnar surface of your hand at the umbilicus.

Evaluating

3 Percuss the client's bladder to ensure that all the urine has been removed. If you elicit dull sounds, you must repeat the procedure until all urine has been expressed. This will help prevent urinary tract infections caused by residual urine. If you elicit tympanic, hollow sounds, assume that the bladder is empty. Remove the

Implementing

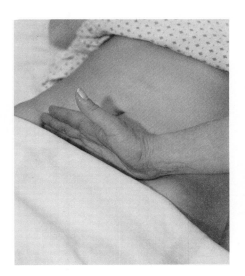

2 Instruct the client to bear down with the abdominal muscles, if possible. Press downward and sweep your hand onto the suprapubic area, using a kneading motion to initiate urination. Continue the maneuver every 30 seconds until urination ceases.

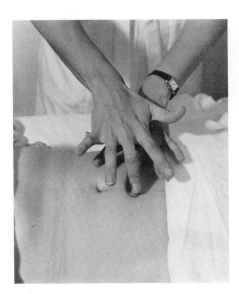

urinal or bed pan and assist the client into a comfortable position. Document the procedure.

Caring for Clients with Urinary Diversions

Nursing Guidelines to Common Types of Urinary Diversions

ILEAL CONDUIT (ALSO CALLED ILEAL LOOP, BRICKER'S LOOP, ILEAL BLADDER)

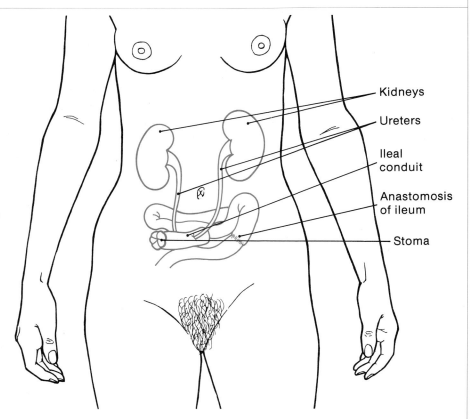

Kidneys

Ureters

Ileal conduit

Anastomosis of ileum

Stoma

Description

A 15- to 20-cm (6- to 8-in.) segment of the ileum is removed to function as a pipeline for the urine. The ureters are then detached from the bladder, shortened, and anastomosed to the ileum. The ileal segment is brought out through the abdomen, where it forms a stoma. Urine then flows from the kidneys through the ureters and out through the ileal conduit and stoma. The intestine is anastomosed, and it continues to function normally.

Indications

Bladder malignancy, congenital anomalies, intractable incontinence, chronic urinary tract infections, neurogenic bladder.

Nursing Considerations

Note: You can also follow these guidelines for clients who have had colon conduits.

- The continuous flow of urine requires the constant use of an appliance.
- Mucus may be present in the urine because of the nature of the ileal segment that is used.

- If the client has had bladder cancer, a cystectomy also will have been performed, as well as a prostatectomy for the male client.
- An indwelling urethral catheter (drain) might be inserted to drain mucus and to minimize the potential for infection. When the client has had a cystectomy, do *not* irrigate the catheter because doing so could result in peritonitis.
- Ureteral stents also might be inserted temporarily to anchor the ureteral-ileal attachment and to prevent the leakage of urine. These stents also drain into the appliance (pouch) and are usually removed on the fifth to seventh postoperative day.
- Inspect the incisional dressing at least every 4 hours, and change it as soon as it is wet, using aseptic technique. Change the dressing carefully to prevent disruption of the drains.
- Assess for indications of a urinary tract infection: chills, increased temperature, flank pain, hematuria.
- Be alert to the following signs of hyperchloremic metabolic acidosis and hypokalemia caused by the reabsorption of sodium and chloride from the urine in the ileal segment, resulting in compensatory loss of potassium and bicarbonate: nausea, changes in level of consciousness (from sleepy to combative), changes in heart rate, and changes in muscle tone (from convulsions to flaccidity).
- Encourage increased oral intake of fluids as directed and, if the client is hypokalemic, the increased intake of foods high in potassium content, such as bananas, apricots, and cantaloupes.
- Encourage ambulation by the second or third postoperative day to help prevent urinary stasis, which would increase the risk of electrolyte and acid-base imbalance.
- Monitor intake and output, differentiating and recording the total amount of output from all drains, stents, and catheters. Notify the physician if the total urinary output is less than 60 ml over a 2-hour period. In the presence of an adequate intake, this can signal ureteral obstruction, a leak in the urinary diversion, or impending renal failure. Other signs of ureteral obstruction include nausea, vomiting, and flank pain.
- Teach the client the importance of weekly monitoring of urinary pH following hospital discharge to ensure that it is 6.0 or less. Individuals with urinary diversions have a higher rate of urinary tract infection than the general population, and thus it is important to keep their urine acidic to minimize the risk of infection. Encourage clients whose urine tests at a pH of greater than 6.0 to increase their fluid intake and, with physician approval, to consume 500–1,000 mg of vitamin C/day to increase their urine acidity.

(Continues)

CUTANEOUS URETEROSTOMY

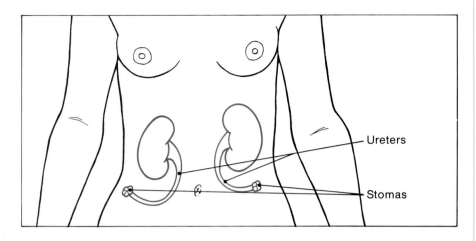

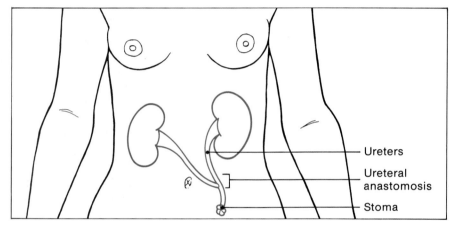

Description

The ureters are resected from the bladder, and one or both then are brought directly through the abdominal wall. Although it is more common for the client to have two stomas requiring the use of two appliances, one ureter might be joined to the other inside the body, resulting in one stoma. Usually the ureters are sutured flush with the skin without a protruding stoma.

Indications

This is an older method of urinary diversion and one that is employed less frequently than the ileal conduit. It is indicated for clients with intractable incontinence, bladder malignancies, and other urinary conditions in which the more complicated surgeries involving intestinal resections are contraindicated. This is often a temporary procedure, for example, for the child for whom later reversal is intended, or it is employed for clients whose life expectancy is minimal.

Nursing Considerations

(Also see the guidelines for the ileal conduit.)

- Because the stoma is small and flush with the skin, fitting the appliance will be challenging. Extra care must be taken to prevent urine leakage and skin breakdown.
- Mucus particles in the collection system are abnormal because an intestinal segment is not used.
- If the client has an indwelling urethral catheter for draining blood and mucus from the diseased bladder, hand irrigate *only* if ordered.
- Carefully assess the client for these indicators of ureteral and stomal stenosis: oliguria, anuria, and/or a stomal retraction. If stenosis does occur, irreversible damage to the urinary tract may result.
- Monitor the functioning of the ureteral stents, which exit from the stoma. Their purpose is to maintain patency of the ureters and promote healing of the anastomosis. Each stent can be expected to produce approximately the same amount of urine. Urine draining from these stents should be pink during the first 24 hours, becoming amber-colored by the third postoperative day. Diminished or absent drainage may signal mucus blockage or ureteral problems.
- Monitor intake and output, differentiating and recording the total amount of output from all drains, stents, and catheters. Notify the physician if the total urinary output is less than 60 ml over a 2-hour period. In the presence of an adequate intake, this can signal ureteral obstruction, a leak in the urinary diversion, or impending renal failure. Other signs of ureteral obstruction include nausea, vomiting, and flank pain.
- Teach the client the importance of weekly monitoring of urinary pH following hospital discharge to ensure that it is 6.0 or less. Individuals with urinary diversions have a higher rate of urinary tract infection than the general population, and thus it is important to keep their urine acidic to minimize the risk of infection. For clients whose urine tests at a pH of greater than 6.0, encourage them to increase their fluid intake and, with physician approval, to consume 500–1,000 mg of vitamin C/day to increase their urine acidity.

(Continues)

CONTINENT URINARY DIVERSION

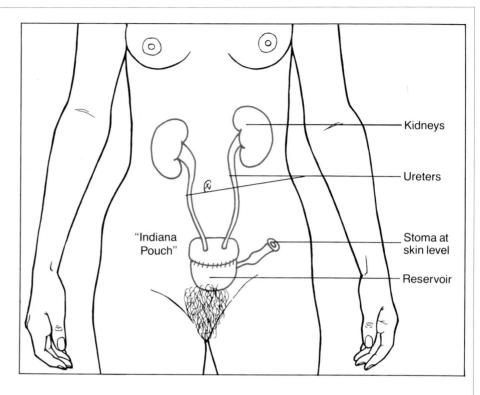

Kidneys

Ureters

"Indiana Pouch"

Stoma at skin level

Reservoir

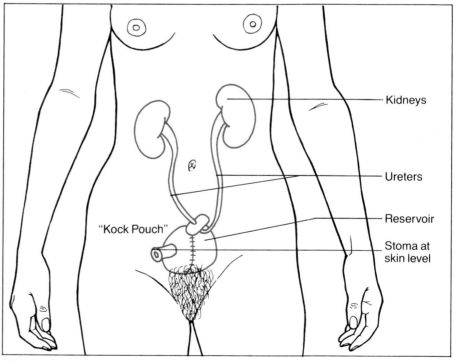

Kidneys

Ureters

Reservoir

"Kock Pouch"

Stoma at skin level

Description	There are several different types of continent urinary diversions, but the two that are most common are the Kock continent urostomy and the Indiana (ileocecal) reservoir. Continent urinary diversions have three components in common: a reservoir, a continence mechanism, and an antireflux mechanism. With the Kock continent urostomy, for example, the reservoir is formed with a 70- to 90-cm segment of ileum, with the center section arranged in a "U" position. The antireflux and continence mechanisms are created via the intussusception of a portion of the bowel segment at each end of the reservoir to form one-way passages. The distal (nipple) valve is in the reservoir, and the proximal (stoma) end is at the skin level. The ureters are attached to the proximal, closed end of the ileum. The Indiana reservoir is constructed from the cecum, the ascending colon, and a portion of the ileum. The ileum is decreased in size and brought out to the cutaneous surface to form a stoma. These diversions do not require external appliances for urine collection and are minimally disfiguring to the client.
Indications	Urinary tract trauma, congenital birth defects, spinal cord injury, bladder and pelvic malignancies, and for clients with other urinary diversions who desire conversion to a diversion that obviates the need for an external appliance.

Nursing Considerations

- Clients must meet the following selection criteria before surgery: positive prognosis, age and life-style needs conducive to the benefits afforded by this procedure, positive motivation toward self-care, strong compliance, physical dexterity with ability to learn and manage self-catheterization every 3–6 hours, and adequate renal functioning.
- Contraindications *may* include the following: compromised renal functioning, physical or psychologic instability, obesity, extensive preoperative radiation therapy, and inability to tolerate a lengthy surgical procedure.
- Be alert to the following early postoperative complications:

  —mucus accumulation with resultant reservoir obstruction.

  —pelvic abscess.

  —fistula formation between the reservoir and cutaneous tissue or adjacent bowel.

  —small-bowel obstruction.

  —pyelonephritis.

- Be alert to the following late complications:

  —incontinence.

  —calculus formation.

  —problems with pouch catheterization.

  —stricture formation at the site of anastomosis of the ureter or bowel.

  —development of hyperchloremic metabolic acidosis (usually mild, see discussion with ileal conduit, p. 485).

- No external appliance is used.

(Continues)

- Urine is drained at prescribed intervals by intubating (catheterizing) the reservoir via the external stoma.
- Clients with a Kock continent urostomy usually have urine draining from the reservoir catheter (Medina) and ureteral stents.
- Clients with an Indiana reservoir usually have ureteral stents that exit from the stoma and through which most of their urine drains. In addition, they may have a reservoir catheter that exits from a stab wound and that serves as an overflow catheter.
- Be alert to the following signs of intra-abdominal urine leakage or anastomosis breakdown: flank pain, increased abdominal girth, increased drainage from Penrose drains, and decreased urinary output from the stoma and stents.
- For clients with the Kock continent urostomy, monitor for functioning of the Medina catheter, which is present to prevent reservoir distention and promote healing of the suture lines. Large amounts of mucus will drain from this catheter in the early postoperative period, necessitating irrigation with 30–50 ml normal saline, which is instilled gently and allowed to drain via gravity drainage. Mucus drainage will continue for several months postoperatively but should lessen in amount.
- Monitor intake and output, differentiating and recording the total amount of output from all drains, stents, and catheters, Notify the physician if the total urinary output is less than 60 ml over a 2-hour period. In the presence of an adequate intake, this can signal ureteral obstruction, a leak in the urinary diversion, or impending renal failure. Other signs of ureteral obstruction include nausea, vomiting, and flank pain.

Following hospital discharge
- Encourage the client to drink 8–10 glasses of water a day (unless contraindicated by an underlying medical condition) to thin the mucus that forms in the reservoir. Thick mucus is often the result of not drinking enough water.
- Teach client to avoid drinking after 7–8 P.M. and therefore minimize pouch leakage at night.
- Teach client to cut one of the following to the appropriate size and use to cover the stoma: panty liner, sanitary napkin, disposable diaper, bed-saver pad, or an incontinence product.
- Encourage the client to catheterize the pouch on a regularly scheduled basis to ensure steady and progressive enlargement of the pouch.
- Teach the client to relax the abdominal muscles rather than bear down when catheterizing the pouch to facilitate catheter insertion. Changing positions also may help, as will rolling the catheter between the fingers on insertion.
- Teach the client the importance of weekly monitoring of urinary pH following hospital discharge to ensure that it is 6.0 or less. Individuals with urinary diversions have a higher rate of urinary tract infection than the general population, and thus it is important to keep their urine acidic to minimize the risk of infection. For clients whose urine tests at a pH of greater than 6.0, encourage them to increase their fluid intake and, with physician approval, to consume 500–1,000 mg of vitamin C/day to increase their urine acidity.

PERFORMING A POSTOPERATIVE ASSESSMENT

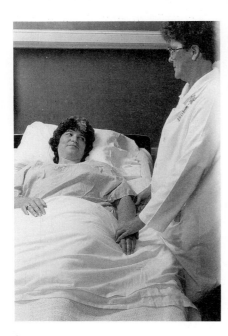

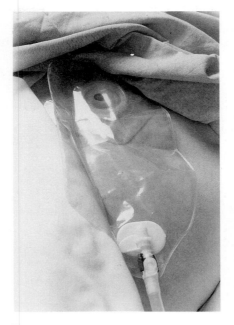

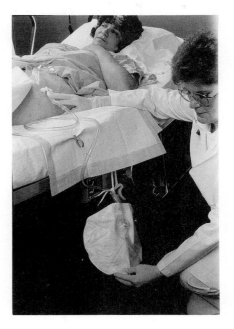

1 Regardless of the type of urinary diversion surgery that was performed, the postoperative assessment of your urostomy client will be basically the same. Explain to the client that you will be assessing her stoma and the area surrounding it (the peristomal area), the amount and character of the urine, and the integrity of the stomal sutures. Remember that your positive and reassuring attitude is crucial both the client's acceptance of the surgery and to her altered body appearance and function.

2 Apply clean gloves. Then raise the client's gown to expose the pouch, and place a bed-saver pad under the involved flank to protect the bed linen. As you do this, place your hand under the client's back to check for dampness, which could indicate that the pouch is leaking urine. Note that the postoperative pouch angles toward the side of the bed. This makes it accessible to the nurse and enterostomal therapist and facilitates its connection to a urinary drainage bag while the client is on bed rest. Inspect the area around the pouch's attachment to the faceplate to ensure that leakage has not occurred. Ask the client if she is experiencing itching or burning, which are signs of leakage. If either has occurred, the pouch must be changed and replaced with one that fits correctly. Otherwise, your client can continue to wear the same pouch for 3–4 days.

3 Inspect the drainage bag to ensure that urine is flowing adequately and that the output is comparable to the client's intake of fluids. Optimally, the output will be around 1,500 ml/day. A diminished production of urine might be caused by reduced intake, urinary blockage, or kidney failure. An absence of urine can be indicative of a leak in the conduit system or a blockage of the ureters, and could necessitate a return to surgery. Also note the character of the urine. If your client has an ileal conduit, the urine might contain mucus because of the nature of the intestine that was used to form the conduit. This is normal. The urine may be dark in color if the client is taking antibiotics, is dehydrated, or has impaired liver function. Be sure to report immediately abnormal quantities of blood. Some postoperative hematuria is not unusual, but it should decrease gradually.

(Continues)

4 To inspect the stoma, position your fingers around the faceplate to anchor it in place, and grasp the tab on the pouch with your other hand. Detach the pouch from the faceplate by lifting up on the tab. Be sure to have a clean cloth or gauze pad available to absorb the urine after the pouch has been opened.

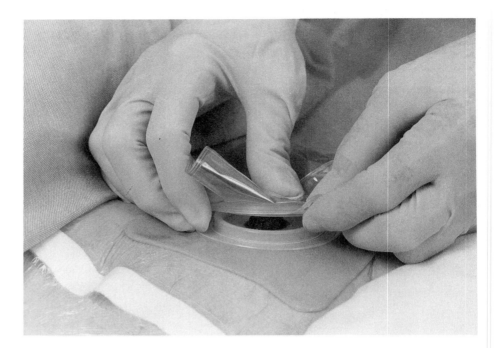

5 To detach the pouch from the faceplate, lift up on the tab. When the area has been dried, assess the stoma. It should be pink or red, similar in color to the mucosal lining of the mouth. Slight bleeding may be normal because of the large number of capillaries in the area. Note whether the stoma is flush with the skin or protruding; assess the degree of edema, if present. Explain to the client that the stoma will continue to decrease in size over the next 6–8 weeks, and this will necessitate frequent stomal measurements to ensure a properly fitting pouch and skin barrier. Make sure the opening in the skin barrier is the exact measurement of the stoma. It should touch the stoma on all sides. Finally, inspect the sutures to make sure they are intact. Replace the pouch, wash your hands, and document your observations.

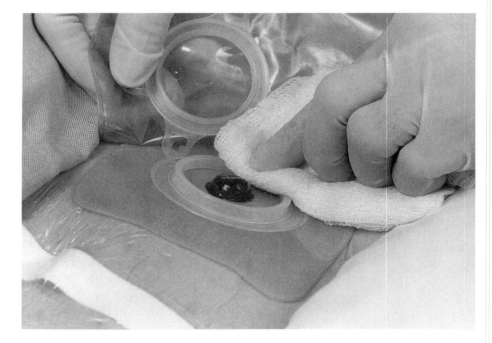

MANAGING APPLIANCE CARE

APPLYING A POSTOPERATIVE (DISPOSABLE) POUCH

Assessing and Planning

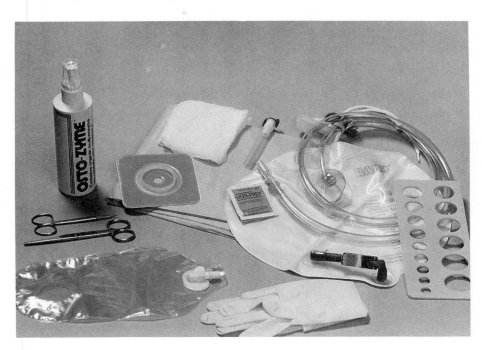

1 A disposable pouch is usually applied on the client's third or fourth postoperative day. Many clients choose to wear disposable pouches after their discharge rather than change to reusable (permanent) pouches. The materials used for disposable pouches will vary from agency to agency. The following is a general procedure for pouch application, and it should include these materials or a variation of the same: a measuring guide, a disposable pouch, tape (optional), a skin barrier such as a pectin wafer, skin cleanser (optional), a skin preparation to protect the skin from a reaction to the tape if it is used, and scissors. In addition, a urine collection bag should be used during the night, or while the client is on bed rest. Be sure to stock the client's bedside stand with plenty of clean cloths or gauze pads, gloves, and bed-saver pads. If you will use tape to reinforce the seal of the pouch, cut four strips approximately 10 cm (4 in.) in length.

(Continues)

2 Explain the procedure to the client and lower the head of the bed to decrease the angle at the peristomal area, but do encourage the client to inspect the stoma and ask questions during the procedure. This procedure also can be used for client teaching. Place a bed-saver pad under the involved flank to protect the bed linen, and have clean cloths, gauze pads, toilet paper, or tampons accessible for absorbing the urine. To remove the pouch, moisten a cloth with warm water and lift up the inside corner of the skin barrier. Place the moist cloth at the loosened corner and gently depress sections of the skin as you peel back the adhesive material. The moist cloth will help loosen the adhesive and facilitate its removal as quickly and painlessly as possible.

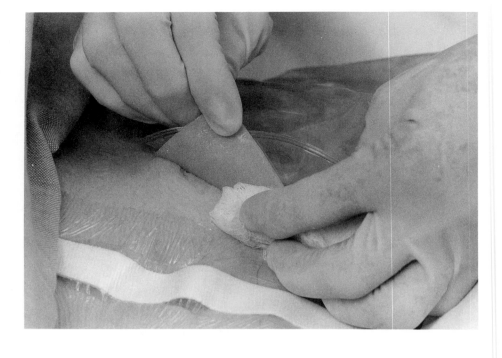

3 When you have removed the skin barrier and pouch, inspect the stoma and peristomal area. Assess for irritation, allergic reactions to the tape or adhesive, weeping, or inflamed hair follicles (folliculitis). If the opening of the skin barrier is too large and allows seepage of urine onto the peristomal area, you might see an alkaline encrustation that consists of white crystalline deposits. Hyperplasia, which is a very tender area of thickened skin, can also result from prolonged exposure to urine, especially if the urine is alkaline.

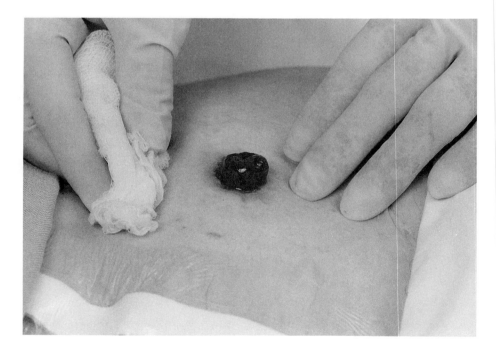

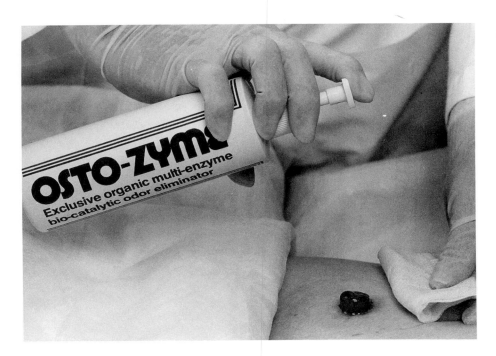

4 Clean the skin with a warm, wet cloth. If you use soap, it must be nonoily (for example, Ivory) because oily soaps will leave a residue, which can prevent the proper adherence of the pouch. Another option is to cleanse the peristomal skin with a skin cleanser/deodorizer (as shown), which also helps remove adhesive residual.

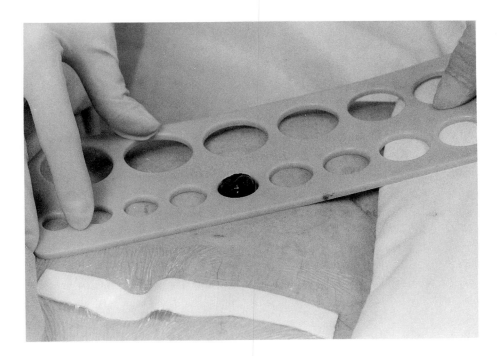

5 Measure the stoma with the measuring guide.

(Continues)

Implementing

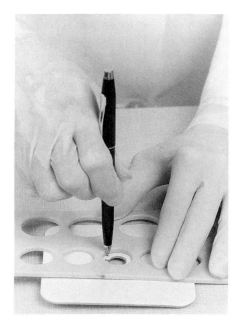

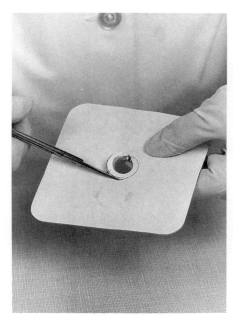

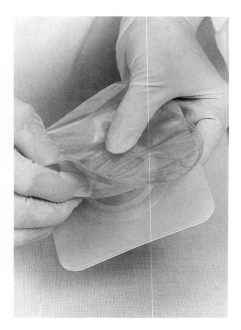

6 Trace the outline of the measured stoma on the back of the pectin wafer skin barrier. If the stoma is irregular in shape, you will need to customize the pattern to fit the shape of the stoma.

7 Cut out the circle (or shape) you have traced.

8 Snap the pouch onto the pectin wafer at an angle, as shown.

9 Remove the protective paper backing from the pectin wafer. Set the pouch aside, with the adhesive side up.

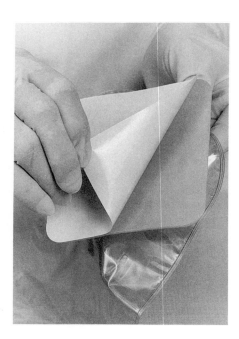

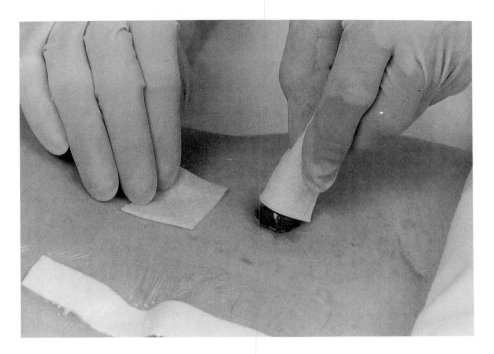

10 If you plan to reinforce the pouch with tape, prepare the periphery of the peristomal skin with a skin preparation before applying the skin barrier and pouch. This will help to prevent a skin reaction to the tape. Be sure to let the skin dry thoroughly before applying the skin barrier and pouch. *Caution: Do not apply a skin protector to skin that is broken or irritated.* To prevent the client's stoma from draining onto the peristomal area, hold a gauze pad or tampon over the stoma (as shown).

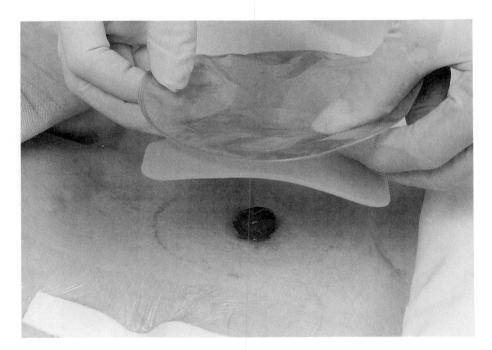

11 Position the pouch so that the opening is directly over the stoma. While the client is on bed rest, angle the tail of the pouch toward the side of the bed (as shown).

(Continues)

12 Then adhere the barrier and pouch to the client's skin by gently pressing around the periphery with your fingertips. The warmth of your hands will enhance the seal.

Evaluating

13 Document the procedure, noting your assessment of the stoma and peristomal skin, the amount and character of the urine, and the type of equipment and materials you used.

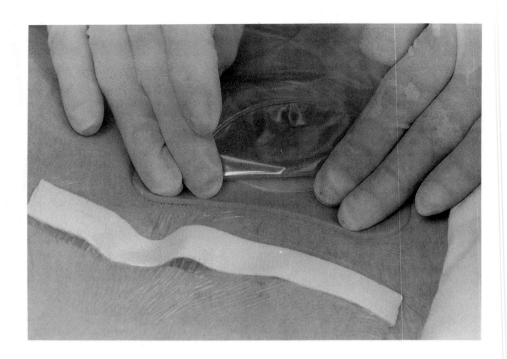

PICTURE FRAMING THE POUCH

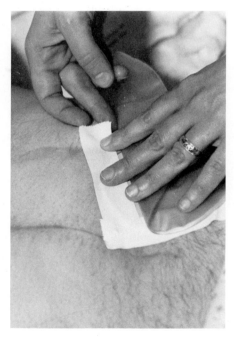

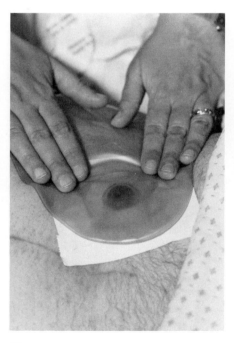

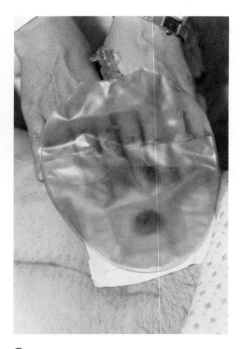

1 If desired, reinforce the seal by "picture framing" the pouch and skin barrier to the client's skin. Attach four strips of tape to form a square around the pouch and skin barrier.

2 Press around the exterior of the pouch.

3 Lift up the tail of the pouch and press along the underside. If you will attach the pouch to a drainage bag at this time, see procedure, p. 499. Return the client to a position of comfort, and wash your hands.

CONNECTING THE POUCH TO A URINARY DRAINAGE SYSTEM

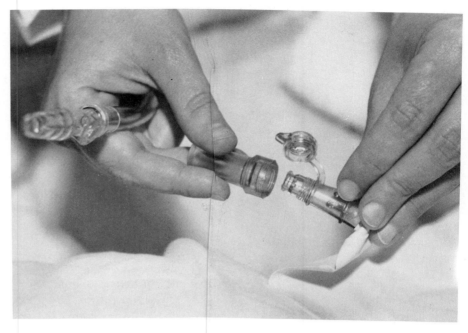

1 During the night, or while your client is on bed rest, ensure that the urinary pouch is attached to a urinary drainage system. A pouch that becomes too full of urine can break the seal of the appliance to the skin. In addition, urine that stagnates in a pouch becomes an excellent medium for bacterial growth, which can lead to urinary tract infections. In the hospital, the client has the option of attaching the pouch to a urinary collection bag and tubing, or to a leg bag (see procedure, pp. 472–473). Most pouches are packaged with an adaptor (as shown). Remove the plug from the drain on the pouch, and snap on the adaptor. *Note: If the urine drainage system is not fresh from its package, wear gloves to prevent contact of your hands with urine.*

2 Insert the drainage system tubing directly into the adaptor.

References

Bellinger MF: The history of urinary diversion and undiversion. *J Enterostomal Ther* 1989; 16(1):395–401.

Bowers AC, Thompson JM: *Clinical Manual of Health Assessment,* 3d ed. St. Louis: Mosby, 1988.

Broadwell DC, Jackson BS: *Principles of Ostomy Care.* St. Louis: Mosby, 1982.

Centers for Disease Control: Guidelines for the prevention and control of nosocomial infections, Atlanta, 1981–1984. US Department of Health and Human Services.

Ghiotto DL: A full range of care for nephrostomy patients. *RN* 1988; 51(5):72–77.

Hass N, Dalton J: Perioperative management of the continent urinary pouch: an experience with five cases. *J Enterostomal Ther* 1987; 14(5):188–193.

Horne M: Renal disorders. In: *Manual of Nursing Therapeutics: Applying Nursing Diagnoses to Medical Disorders,* 2d ed. Swearingen PL. St. Louis: Mosby, 1990.

Horne M, Swearingen PL: *Pocket Guide to Fluid and Electrolytes.* St. Louis: Mosby, 1989.

Jansen PR: Urinary disorders. In: *Manual of Nursing Therapeutics,* 2d ed. Swearingen PL. St. Louis: Mosby, 1990.

Spence A, Mason E: *Human Anatomy and Physiology,* 3d ed. Redwood City, CA: Benjamin/Cummings, 1987.

Spencer MB, Floruta C: Nursing implications for managing urinary diversions. *Ostomy/Wound Management* (winter) 1986; 48–54.

Swift CM: Spinal cord injuries. In: *Manual of Nursing Therapeutics: Applying Nursing Diagnoses to Medical Disorders,* 2d ed. Swearingen PL. St. Louis: Mosby, 1990.

Thompson JM et al: *Mosby's Manual of Clinical Nursing,* 2d ed. St. Louis: Mosby, 1989.

Weiskittel PD: Renal-urinary dysfunctions. In: *Manual of Critical Care: Applying Nursing Diagnoses to Adult Critical Illness,* 2d ed. Swearingen PL. St. Louis: Mosby, 1991.

Chapter 9

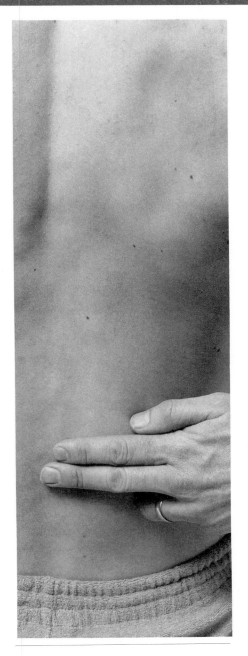

Managing Musculoskeletal Procedures

CHAPTER OUTLINE

Assessing the Musculoskeletal System

THE MUSCULOSKELETAL SYSTEM

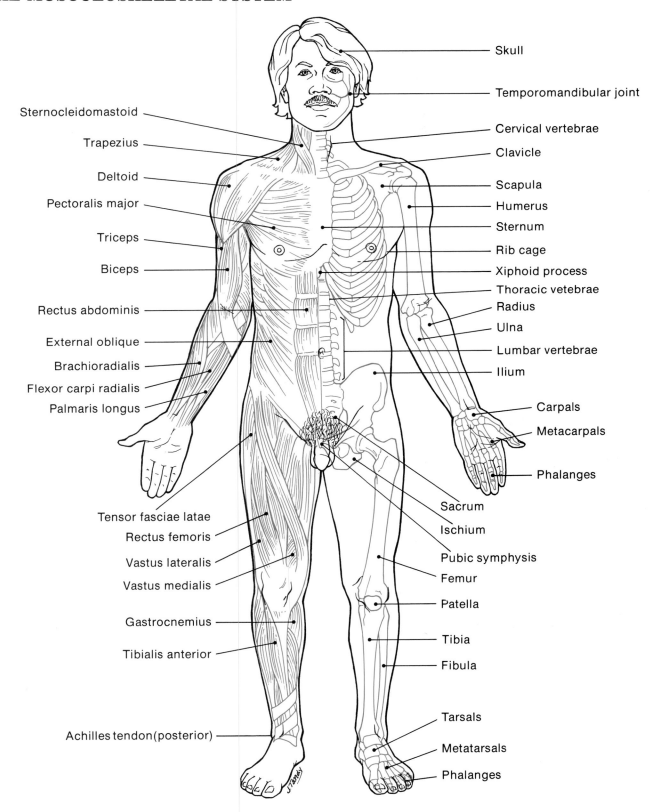

Skull

Temporomandibular joint

Cervical vertebrae

Clavicle

Scapula

Humerus

Sternum

Rib cage

Xiphoid process

Thoracic vetebrae

Radius

Ulna

Lumbar vertebrae

Ilium

Carpals

Metacarpals

Phalanges

Sacrum

Ischium

Pubic symphysis

Femur

Patella

Tibia

Fibula

Tarsals

Metatarsals

Phalanges

Sternocleidomastoid

Trapezius

Deltoid

Pectoralis major

Triceps

Biceps

Rectus abdominis

External oblique

Brachioradialis

Flexor carpi radialis

Palmaris longus

Tensor fasciae latae

Rectus femoris

Vastus lateralis

Vastus medialis

Gastrocnemius

Tibialis anterior

Achilles tendon(posterior)

Nursing Assessment Guideline

To assess your client's musculoskeletal system, you need to interview him or her for subjective data; take vital signs; evaluate range of motion (ROM), muscular strength, and activities of daily living; and assess neurovascular integrity. A comprehensive nursing care plan includes a complete evaluation for the following subjective data:

Personal factors: for example, age, marital status, recreational activities; description of home environment—levels, stairways, throw rugs

History or family history of: arthritis, gout, rickets, or other musculoskeletal and joint disorders

Occupation: past and present, type of work, accident potential, safety precautions employed

Activities of daily living: abilities/alterations in the performance of eating, getting dressed, writing, moving, or caring for personal hygiene

Exercise: type, frequency, tolerance/intolerance to

Use of assistive devices: for example, crutches, cane, walker, wheelchair

History of injuries: what, when, how occurred, degree of recovery

History of musculoskeletal surgery: what, when, results

Medications: for example, use of aspirin and other nonsteroidal anti-inflammatory agents, steroids, antispasmodics

Allergies: for example, to foods, medications, cast materials, adhesives

Pain: location, onset, duration, character, radiation, relieved by, intensified by, effect of weather

Gait disorders: weakness, clumsiness, discomfort, stiffness

Muscular disorders: weakness, fatigue, atrophy, hypertrophy, paralysis, pain, tremors, tics, spasms, aching

Skeletal disorders: history and/or presence of fractures, crepitus, pain, ecchymosis, hematoma

Joint disorders: history and/or presence of injury, swelling, erythema, enlargement, stiffness, limitation of movement, aching, crepitus

PERFORMING A GENERAL ASSESSMENT OF THE MUSCULOSKELETAL SYSTEM

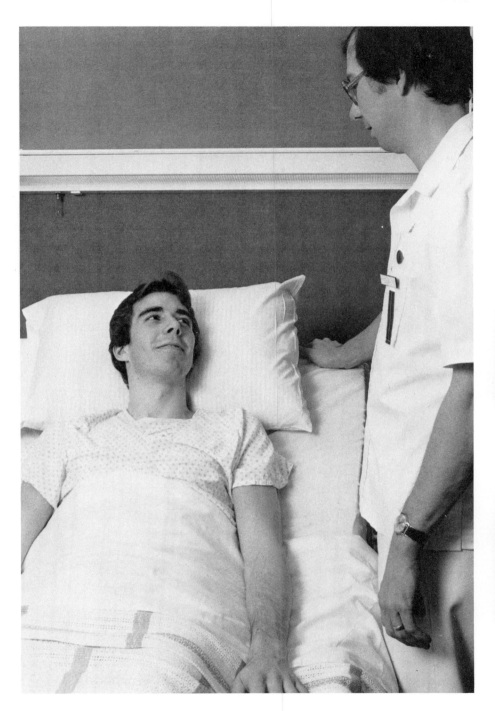

Provide a warm and private environment for your client, and explain the assessment procedure. For a full inspection, the client should wear only underwear so that you can more accurately assess posture, alignment, and body build.

INSPECTING

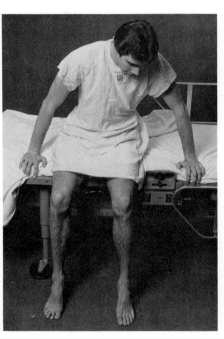

1 If it is not contraindicated, ask the client to get out of bed so that you can evaluate posture, gait, and ROM. Assess his ability to get out of bed. Does he appear to have discomfort, and does he require the use of an assistive device?

(Continues)

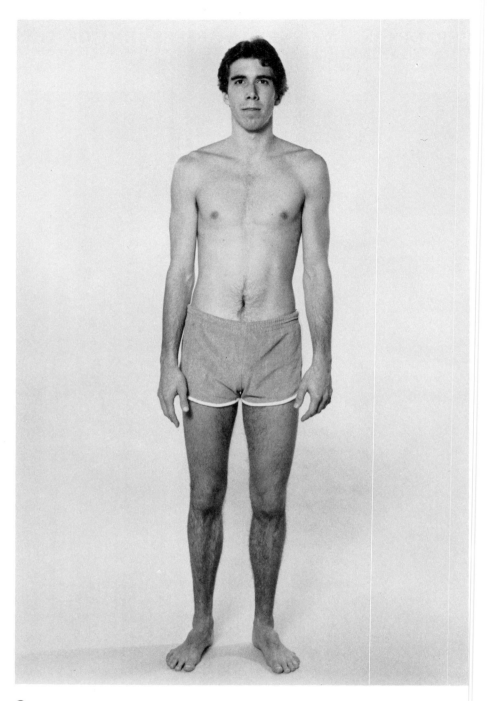

2 Once he is out of bed, ask him to stand facing you, with his hands hanging loosely at his sides and his head level. Inspect his body build, and compare one side to the other. Observe for the presence of masses, atrophy, absence of body parts, or gross abnormalities, such as one limb shorter than the other. As a check for scoliosis, assess for asymmetry of the shoulders, the clavicles, and the nipple line.

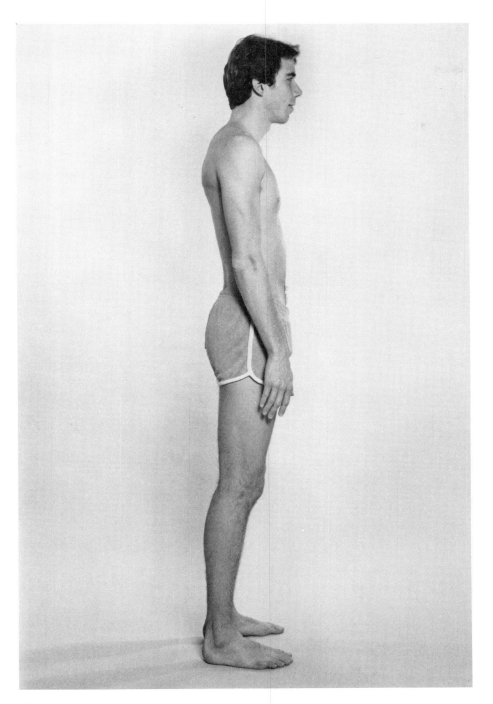

3 Inspect the client laterally to assess spine curvature. Normally in adults, the cervical and lumbar areas will appear moderately concave, whereas the thorax will appear convex. Note an exaggerated inward curve of the lumbar area, called lordosis (swayback), or an abnormal roundness of the thorax, referred to as kyphosis (hunchback). Gibbus is an angular deformity of collapsed vertebrae, which can occur with osteoarthritis or Pott's disease (tuberculosis of the spinal column). Also assess for displacement of the scapulae (winging), which is typically found with scoliosis. A lateral inspection also aids in identifying ankylosing spondylitis because the client will have a stooped appearance.

(Continues)

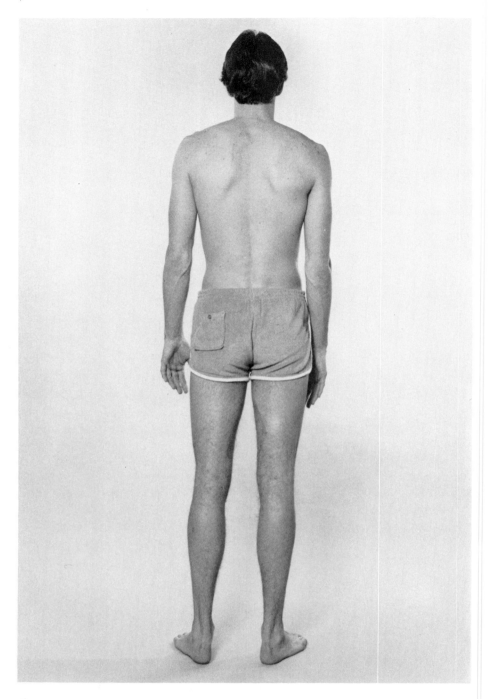

4   When you inspect the client posteriorly, note the alignment of the spine. If the spine deviates laterally, for example with scoliosis, document the area of deviation; record it as either a "C" or "S" curve. Again, be alert to asymmetry of the shoulders, scapulae, and posterior iliac crests.

With advanced structural (non-functional) scoliosis, one scapula is usually flattened, whereas the other is elevated. In Sprengel's deformity, the scapula(e) is usually small and located in the lower cervical and upper thoracic area, causing the shoulder(s) to be elevated.

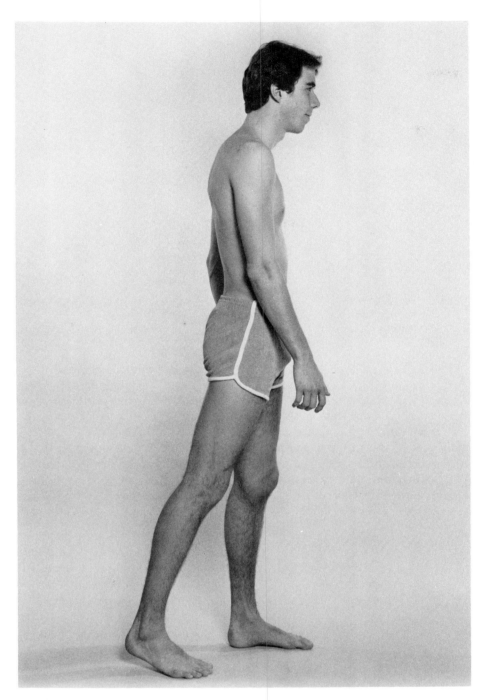

5 If it is not contraindicated, instruct the client to walk; as he does, observe his gait. Are you able to hear dragging, which occurs with spasticity or footdrop? Does he limp, have a distorted gait, or use assistive devices? His weight should be evenly distributed as he steps first onto the heels and then onto the balls of his feet. His toes should point forward, and his arms should swing slightly in opposition to his gait. Be alert to genu varum (bowed legs) or genu valgum (knock-knee). Moderate genu varum is normal in the newborn, possibly due to the intrauterine position. It should become mild by 6 months of age and resolve by 18 months. Mild genu valgum is common between 2 and 3 years of age but should resolve between the ages of 4 and 10. Document your assessment, being certain to note any alterations from the norm.

PALPATING THE SPINE

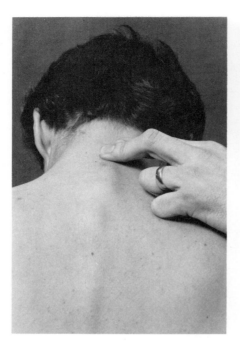 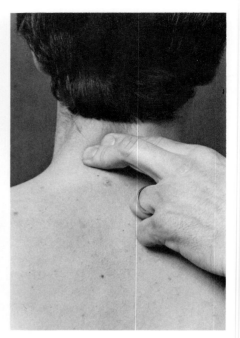

1   *Caution: If the client has a neck injury, all neck movements are contraindicated.* Palpate the cervical spinous processes with the client's neck in a flexed position. Assess the range of motion and question him about the presence of any discomfort. Then instruct the client to return his head to the neutral position (above) so that you can assess for crepitus, a grating sound or sensation that can be heard or felt by the examiner during joint movement. Crepitus is usually not significant unless it is accompanied by pain or compromised circulation.

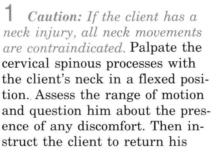

2   Continue to palpate the entire vertebral column, noting any deviations in alignment, areas of discomfort, or the presence of spasms.

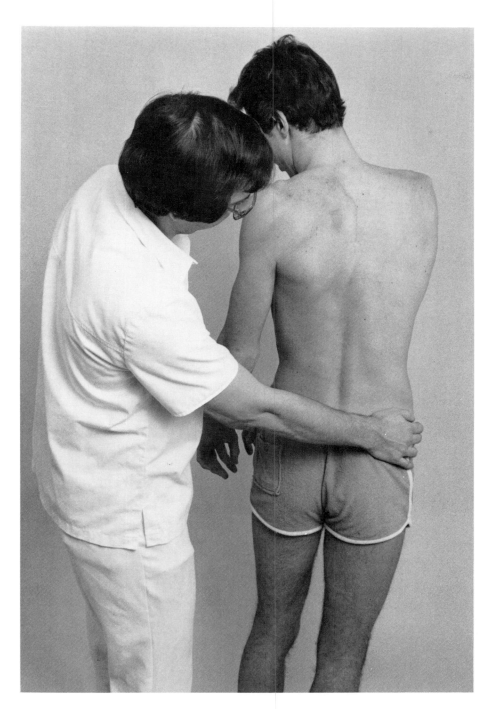

3 To assess the rotation of the lower vertebral column, stabilize the client's hips (as shown) as he rotates his trunk to the right and then to the left. Optimally, the trunk rotation will be bilaterally equal and approximately 30 degrees to either side. Continue to evaluate the client's ROM as he bends forward, backward, and laterally. Clients with some forms of muscular dystrophy will exhibit marked weakness of the trunk muscles.

If you suspect that your client has scoliosis, as evidenced by a lateral curvature of the spine, closely observe him as he bends forward at the waist. If the curvature does not resolve as he bends forward, his condition is considered to be nonfunctional. With this type of scoliosis, structural changes occur in the spinal column, making the disorder especially difficult to correct. If your client is an infant, check for congenital hip dislocation by performing the Ortolani click test (see procedure, p. 232–233); watch for waddling in the toddler.

EVALUATING JOINT RANGE OF MOTION (ROM) AND MUSCULAR STRENGTH

A general assessment of your client's joints and muscles will involve either one or three phases. In phase one, the examiner demonstrates active ROM on his or her own joints and the client returns the demonstration. Review Chapter 2 to assist you with movement components involved with the ROM of each joint. If the client has independent ROM without discomfort, further assessment is usually unnecessary. However, if the client has limited ROM or ROM with discomfort, it will be necessary for you to perform passive ROM on the involved joints to evaluate the degree of motion (phase two), followed by resistive exercises to assess the strength of the involved muscle groups (phase three). During ROM, assess the joints for bilateral symmetry of motion. Also note any dislocation, subluxation (a partial dislocation), ankylosis, swelling, and crepitus. Assess the muscles for strength, bulk, tone, and bilateral symmetry. Key areas for assessment are presented in the following steps. If you desire greater detail, including the average degrees of motion for each joint, be sure to consult any assessment text. To ensure your client's relaxation and cooperation, assess painful joints and extremities last. *Caution: Never put a fractured extremity through ROM or resistive exercises.*

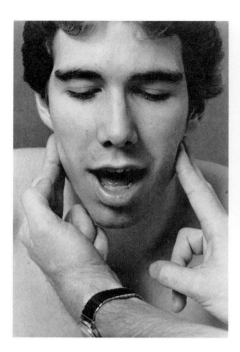

1   Assess your client from head to toe, beginning at the temporomandibular joint (TMJ). Place your fingers on the joints (as shown), and instruct the client to move his mandible from side to side and then up and down. Assess for ROM and discomfort or crepitus. *Note: If you have difficulty palpating the joint as depicted here, place your little fingers into the external auditory canals, instead. You should be able to palpate both the mandible and temporal bones as the client performs ROM on the joint.*

2   If the client experiences either discomfort or limited ROM with the neck movements, perform passive ROM on his cervical joints followed by resistive exercises to evaluate key muscle groups. To evaluate the strength of the neck rotator muscles, restrain the client's head at the mandible as the client attempts to turn his head to each side. *Caution: If the client has a neck injury or a neurologic pathology of the upper extremity, cervical muscle resistive exercises are contraindicated.*

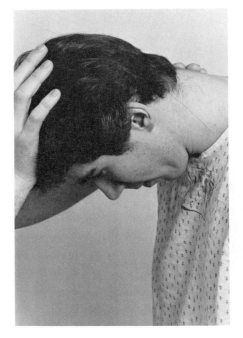

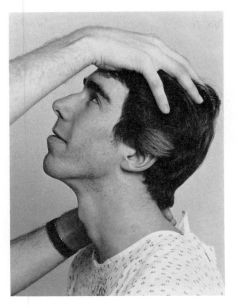

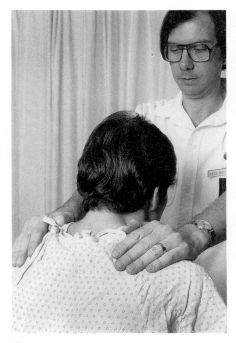

3 To evaluate the neck flexors, ask the client to maintain his neck in a flexed position as you attempt to extend his head.

4 With the client's neck extended, attempt to flex his head toward his chest as he tries to maintain his neck in extension. This will evaluate the strength of the neck extensors.

5 If the client experiences discomfort or limited ROM with the shoulder movements, perform passive ROM on the shoulder joints. Assess the strength of the shoulder elevators by pressing down on the client's acromioclavicular joints as he attempts to raise his shoulders.

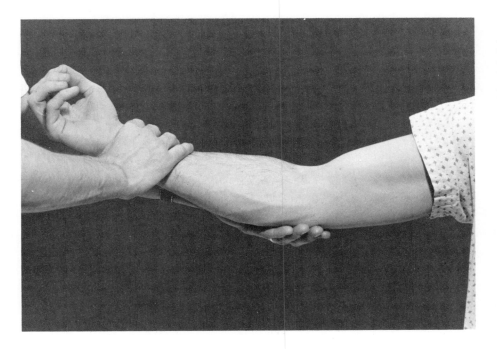

6 Evaluate the client's active ROM of the elbow joints. If he experiences either discomfort or limited ROM, perform passive ROM and then evaluate the strength of the following key muscle groups. Assess the strength of the elbow flexors by holding the client's forearm as he attempts to flex his elbow. Repeat the assessment on the opposite arm. Remember, the dominant arm is normally stronger than the nondominant arm.

(Continues)

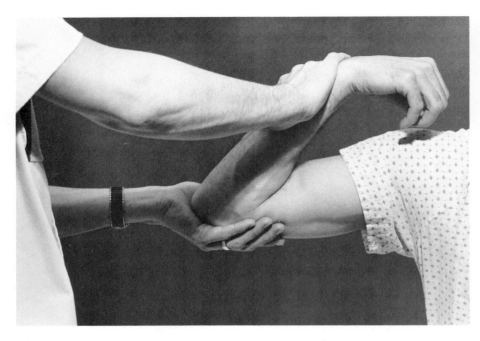

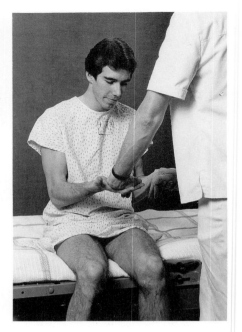

7 Test the strength of the elbow extensors by holding the client's forearm with the elbow in a flexed position as he attempts to extend the elbow. Repeat the assessment on the opposite arm. Again, the dominant arm is normally stronger than the opposite arm.

8 If the client experiences discomfort or limited ROM while performing active ROM on each wrist, perform passive ROM and then evaluate the strength of the wrist flexors. Place your hands against the client's palms and instruct him to push up against your resistance.

9 Another exercise for evaluating both wrist and hand flexors is to have the client tightly grip your index and middle fingers. Assess the strength of both hands and compare the strength of one to the other. The dominant hand is normally stronger.

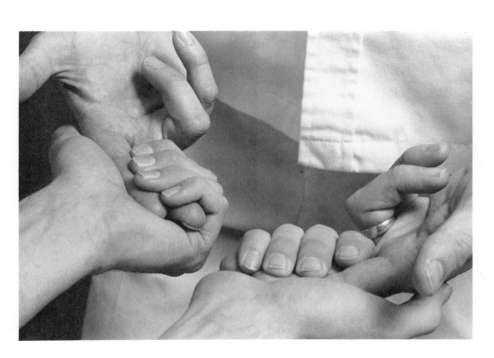

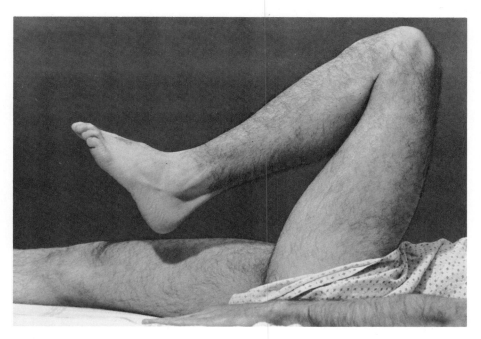

10   When the client has assumed a supine position, closely observe his ability to flex each hip. Instruct him to pull each bent knee alternately in toward his chest. Optimally, the opposite hip will remain extended as the other flexes.

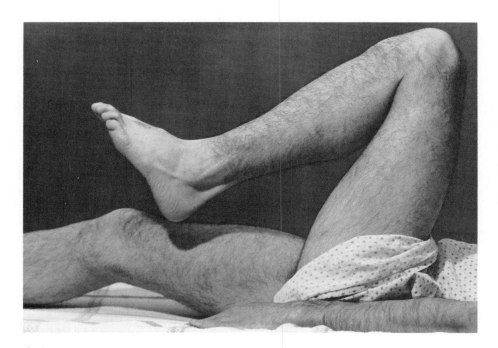

11   If the opposite hip also flexes (as shown) the client has a positive Thomas test, which is indicative of a flexion contracture of that hip. *Note: With the client in this position, you can easily test the strength of the knee extensors (quadriceps) by holding the client's knee into his chest as he attempts to extend his hip.* Repeat the assessment on the client's opposite side.

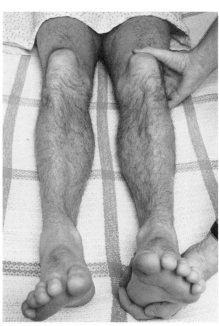

12   If it has been necessary for you to perform passive ROM on the hip joints, evaluate the strength of the hip abductor muscles by holding the client's leg at the midline as he attempts to abduct it.

(Continues)

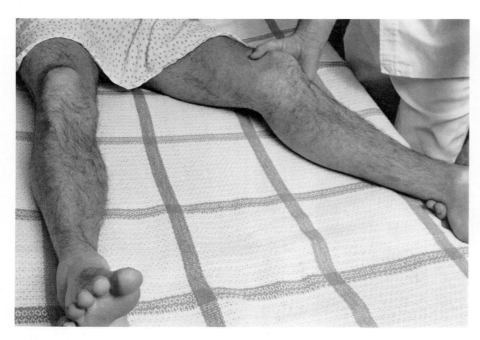

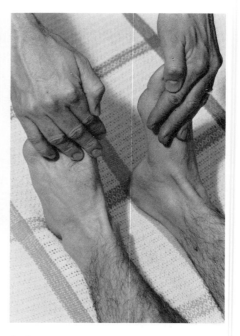

13 Evaluate the hip adductor muscles by holding the client's leg in the abducted position as he attempts to adduct the leg back to the midline.

14 If the client has limited ROM or discomfort during the ankle movements, perform passive ROM on both ankles. Then evaluate the strength of the ankle flexors by applying resistance at the dorsum of each foot (as shown) as the client attempts to dorsiflex each foot. Compare the strength bilaterally.

Test the strength of the ankle extensors by pushing against the soles of the feet as the client attempts to plantarflex the feet. Again, compare the strength bilaterally. Document the results of the assessment, being certain to describe in detail any alterations from the norm.

MEASURING
MUSCLE GIRTH

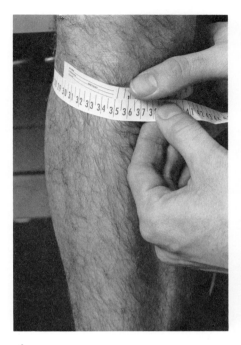
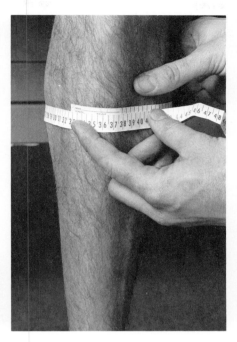
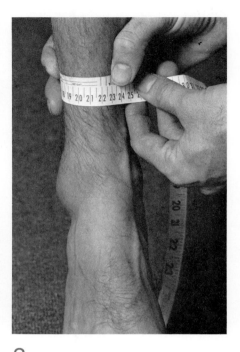

1 When comparing one extremity to the other to assess for unilateral atrophy or hypertrophy, measure the circumference of the proximal, medial, and distal areas of the involved extremity, and compare each measurement to the exact corresponding areas on the opposite extremity. For example, to assess for atrophied or hypertrophied muscles in the lower leg, wrap a nonstretchable tape measure around the leg just below the knee. Measure and document the circumference, and then lightly mark the site you just measured with washable ink.

2 Measure the circumference of the extremity at the area of greatest bulk. After measuring and documenting the circumference, mark the measurement site with the ink.

3 Measure the circumference of the distal end. For example, when measuring the lower leg, position the tape measure just above the medial and lateral malleoli. Mark the circumference site with ink, and then measure the distances between each landmark. Repeat the assessment on the opposite extremity by first measuring and marking the distances from the corresponding landmarks and then measuring the proximal, medial, and distal circumferences. A marked difference in circumference between the extremities often occurs with either disuse atrophy of one extremity or hypertrophy due to overuse of the opposite extremity. When comparing the upper extremities, remember that a slight difference in circumference may be normal because of the preference of the dominant hand.

EVALUATING ACTIVITIES OF DAILY LIVING

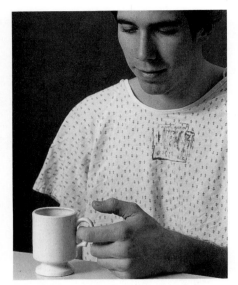

A complete evaluation of the client's musculoskeletal system should include an ongoing assessment of his ability to perform activities of daily living. Observe his ability to eat, write, perform functions of daily hygiene, and get dressed. For example, evaluate his ability to grasp a cup (as shown) or cut his meat, count coins, dial a telephone, write his name, or button or zip his clothing. Determine whether he has full functioning capacity and is therefore independent. If he is slow and tires easily, requires assistance, or is incapable of doing most things for himself, determine the degree of his dependence.

PERFORMING NEUROVASCULAR ASSESSMENTS

EVALUATING NEUROVASCULAR INTEGRITY

Clients with musculoskeletal injuries will require frequent neurovascular assessments of the involved extremities. It is essential that you establish your client's "normal" integrity or baseline prior to the application of an immobilization device because he or she normally may exhibit neurovascular differences when one extremity is compared to the opposite extremity. Therefore, you cannot always rely on a bilateral comparison alone. The areas of assessment should include evaluations for the following: capillary refill, color, temperature, pulse, sensation, pain, edema, and motion. Be sure to instruct your clients so that they can recognize these indicators of impairment and alert you immediately should they occur.

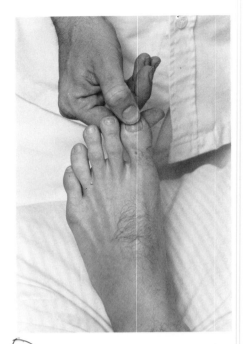

1 *Capillary Refill, Color, and Temperature:* Assess the extremity distal to the injury. Is it warm, cool, or cold? Do the nail beds of the fingers or toes appear pink, pale, or cyanotic? To assess for adequate circulation, depress the nail bed (as shown) of each toe or finger until it blanches, and then release the pressure. Evaluate the speed at which the blood returns. Is the return sluggish or rapid? Optimally, the color will change from white to pink rapidly (<3 seconds). If this does not occur, the toes or fingers will require close observation and further evaluation.

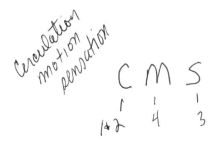

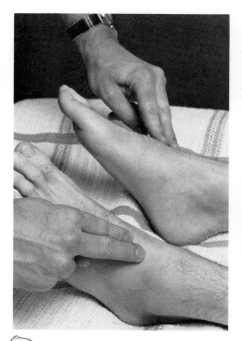

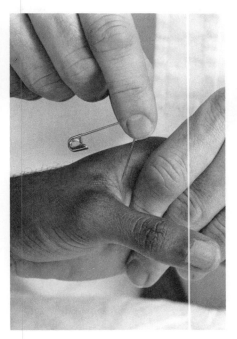

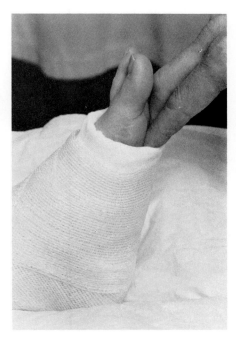

② *Pulsations:* Bilaterally palpate peripheral pulses distal to the injury, and compare the regularity and strength of each. If they are unequal, or if the pulse in the involved extremity does not correspond to the client's baseline, close observation and further assessments are again warranted.

3 *Sensations or Pain:* Touch, lightly pinch, or gently prick the involved extremity with a sterile pin to assess sensation. Question the client about the presence of numbness or tingling. Constant pain with concomitant numbness is significant because it could be caused by a compressed nerve, which if left untreated could result in paralysis of the involved extremity.

4 *Edema and Motion:* Note any swelling distal to the injury. If the client is wearing a cast, ensure that you can fit two fingertips into the cast opening. Usually, the involved extremity is elevated above the level of the heart immediately after the application of the cast, and it is maintained in this position until edema is no longer a problem. Ice packs can also be applied to the surgical or injury site to help minimize swelling.

Ask the client to move all the involved fingers or toes. Moving all the digits is important because different nerves innervate different digits. Assess for the presence of pain with the movement.

ASSESSING NERVE FUNCTION

The following five assessments of nerve function each have two components. The first element evaluates sensation, and the second evaluates motion. Loss of sensation and movement necessitates an immediate intervention, for example, removing the cast or immobilization device to prevent irreversible damage. Impaired sensation and/or movement requires an immediate notification of the physician and close observation. Frequently the involved extremity can be elevated higher than its present level to reduce the edema that potentially could be causing the problem.

Assessing the Radial Nerve

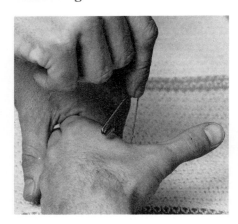

1 Prick the web between the client's thumb and index finger.

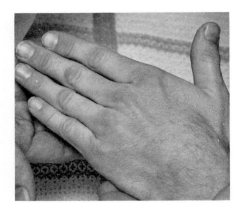

2 Instruct the client to hyperextend his thumb and then to extend all four fingers.

Assessing the Ulnar Nerve

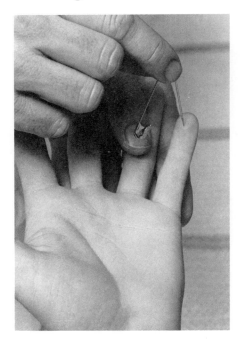

1 Prick the distal fat pad of the small finger.

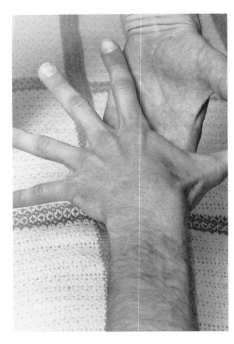

2 Instruct the client to abduct all fingers.

Assessing the Median Nerve

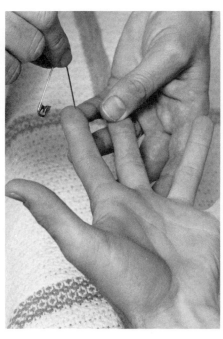

1 Prick the distal fat pad of the index finger.

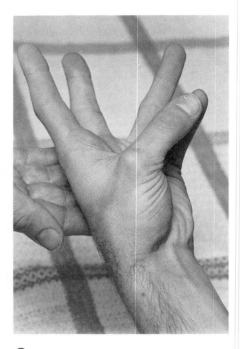

2 Instruct the client to oppose the thumb to the little finger and/or to flex the wrist.

Assessing the Peroneal Nerve

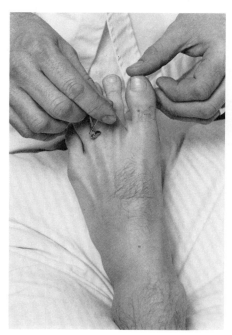

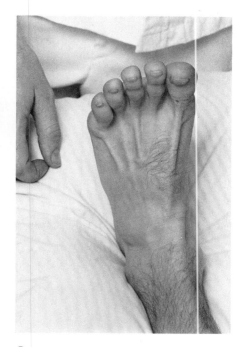

1 Prick the web between the great toe and the second toe.

2 Instruct the client to dorsiflex the ankle and extend the toes.

Assessing the Tibial Nerve

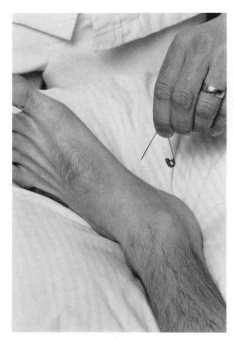

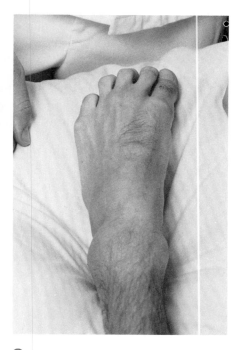

1 Prick both the lateral surface and the medial surface (as shown) of the sole of the foot.

2 Instruct the client to plantarflex the ankle and flex the toes.

Using Immobilization and Comfort Devices

Nursing Guidelines to the Care of Clients in Immobilization Devices

SOFT CERVICAL
COLLAR

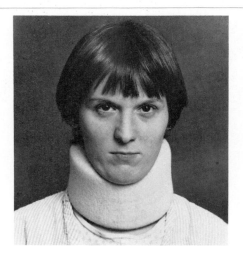

Description   Felt or foam collar, usually covered with stockinette material. Can be hooked in position or secured in place with Velcro™ strips.

Nursing Considerations
- It is used intermittently and/or on a short-term basis for the relief of muscle spasms or for cervical immobilization after a cervical injury. Because it provides gentle support only, it should not be used when complete neck immobilization is desired.
- Ensure that the collar fits snugly enough to provide proper immobilization, yet not so tightly that the airway can become obstructed.
- If the physician requests that the neck be kept in slight flexion, position the tapered end of the collar anteriorally.
- If slight extension is desired, place the wide end of the collar anteriorally.
- These collars should be hand-washed and allowed to drip dry.
- Provide the client with oral and written instructions for appliance care, application, and removal.

HARD CERVICAL COLLAR

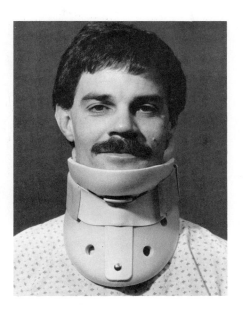

Description

Rigid plastic collar, contoured to fit the chin and neck. Frequently, it is fitted to the client by the orthopedic supply company.

Nursing Considerations

- This type of collar is applied more frequently for long-term use, or in instances when more rigid support is desired, for example after cervical fractures or fusions.
- Ensure that the collar is not so tight that the airway is in danger of obstruction.
- Assess the client for discomfort and/or skin irritation around the jaw, clavicle, and spinous processes. Pad the bony prominences to prevent this problem.
- Cleanse the collar by sponging it with warm soapy water.
- Provide the client with oral and written instructions prior to discharge regarding appliance care, application, and removal.

(Continues)

CLAVICLE SPLINT

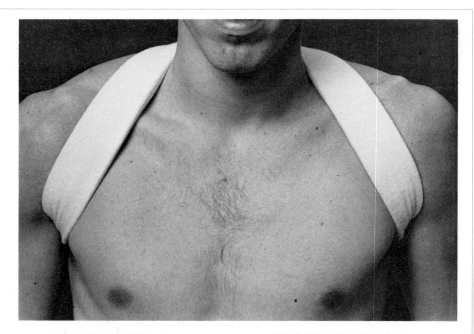

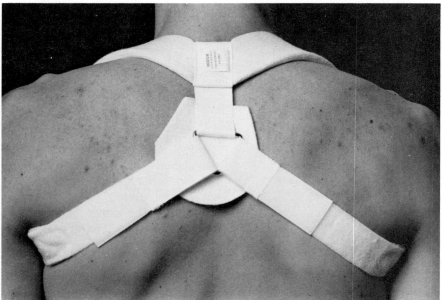

Description

Has padded straps that encircle the anterior axillae to provide compression at the clavicular area. Each strap adjusts in size and closes in the back with catch or Velcro™ closures (bottom photo).

Nursing Considerations

- This splint is frequently applied after a clavicular fracture.
- Prior to application, obtain a baseline neurovascular assessment in the upper extremities, and obtain follow-up assessments thereafter, at least every 4 hours.
- Evaluate the tension of the straps with each position change to ensure that the splint provides proper immobilization without excessive pressure at the axillae.
- Assess for discomfort and/or skin irritation, especially at the axillary areas, and provide skin care as indicated.

ARM/SHOULDER IMMOBILIZER

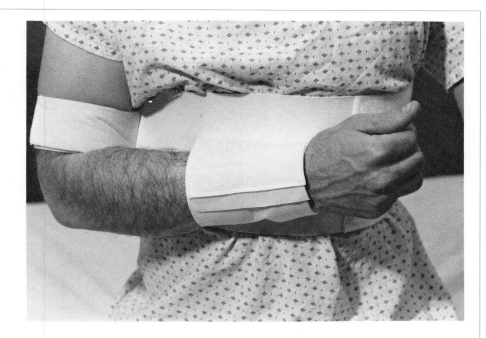

Description

Elasticized fabric has a chest band and a humeral cuff to keep the shoulder immobilized. The wristband provides elbow flexion while supporting the lower arm across the abdomen for comfort.

Nursing Considerations

- This device can be used after a shoulder dislocation, clavicular or humeral fracture, shoulder surgery, or acromioclavicular separation.
- Perform a baseline neurovascular assessment prior to application of the immobilizer, and obtain subsequent assessments thereafter, at least every 4 hours.
- Also evaluate respiratory status to ensure that the chest band is not too tight.
- Assess for areas of discomfort and/or skin breakdown, and provide skin care as indicated.

(Continues)

WRIST/FOREARM SPLINT

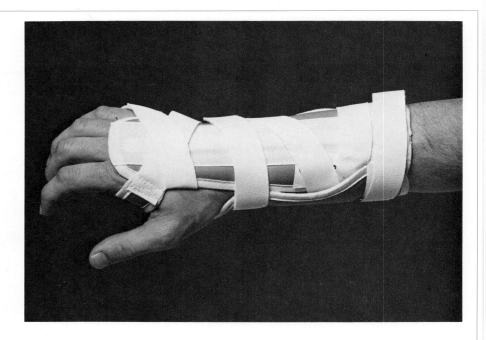

Description

Foam or vinyl splint with elasticized straps, extending from the palm to the midforearm. It attaches with hooks or Velcro™ strips.

Nursing Considerations

- This splint provides immobilization to the wrist following wrist sprain or wrist surgery, and it prevents ulnar deviation for clients with rheumatoid arthritis.
- Obtain baseline neurovascular status prior to initial application, and at least every 4 hours thereafter.
- Unless it is contraindicated, remove the splint every 8 hours or as prescribed, and assess the skin for breakdown, especially around the splint edges.

ABDUCTION PILLOW

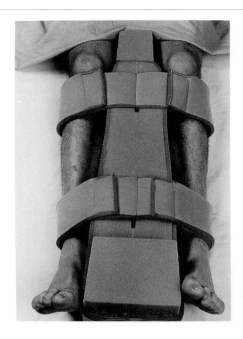

Description

An A-shaped pillow, usually of foam construction, with foam straps that wrap around the client's legs.

Nursing Considerations

- The pillow keeps the hips in abduction after a surgical hip repair or replacement to help prevent hip dislocation.
- Assess postoperative neurovascular status hourly until stable, and every 4 hours thereafter.
- Ensure that two fingers can fit between the pillow straps and the client's skin.
- Remove the straps every 4 hours and assess the skin for irritation.
- Massage the skin, and sprinkle cornstarch on the client's legs if perspiration is a problem because of the pillow's foam construction.
- When transferring the client to the chair or wheelchair, the physician may request that you keep the pillow in place to prevent hip adduction during the move (see procedure, p. 580).
- Watch for signs of skin breakdown, especially around the heels and coccyx, and provide skin care as indicated.
- To keep the client's heels off the bed and thus prevent skin breakdown, position a folded towel or narrow pillow just proximal to the client's heels.

(Continues)

DENIS-BROWNE SPLINT

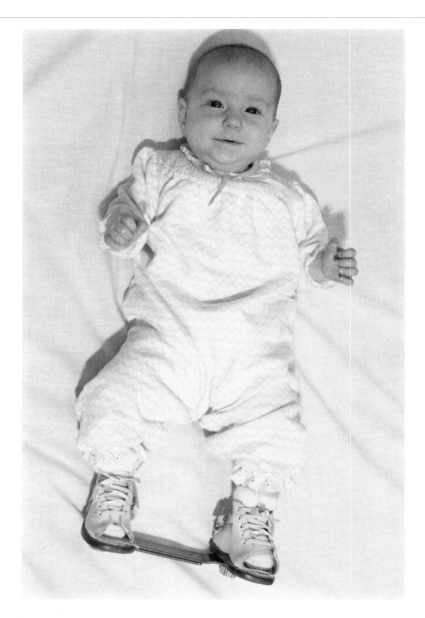

Description

Two foot plates are attached to a metal crossbar. If oxford-type shoes are not already attached to the crossbar, the feet are strapped to the plates with adhesive tape. The shoes are usually open-toed to accommodate the child's growth.

Nursing Considerations

- This splint is used to apply mild external rotation to the feet for the child with talipes deformities (clubfoot).
- The splint is usually indicated for the infant under 1 year of age, and it is worn at nighttime and during naps.
- Demonstrate removal and application to the parents. Show them skin assessment techniques, especially around the shoe edges. Also show them how to perform neurovascular assessments and observe for impaired circulation in the feet.
- Expect frustration and irritability from an infant who cannot kick her feet in the manner in which she is accustomed. Provide hugs and comfort measures when these splints are worn.

APPLYING ELASTIC BANDAGES

Elastic bandages are applied to provide immobilization and support and to minimize swelling. They are wrapped from the limb's most distal part toward the trunk. Fingers or toes should be left unwrapped to provide access for neurovascular assessments. The bandage should be applied firmly but never tightly, with each turn positioned at equal distances from the others to provide even pressure. Always take baseline neurovascular assessments (see pp. 518–519) before wrapping the bandage, and repeat the assessments 15 minutes after the application and every 4 hours thereafter for as long as the bandage is worn. Obtain a bandage of the appropriate width to accommodate the client's affected limb or injured area, for example, a 4-in. bandage for the lower leg, a 6-in. bandage for the thigh, a 3-in. bandage for the hand and forearm, and a 2-in. bandage for a child. Unless otherwise indicated, remove the bandage at least every 8 hours to assess for excess pressure or irritation and to provide skin care.

WRAPPING A LONG, CYLINDRICAL BODY PART

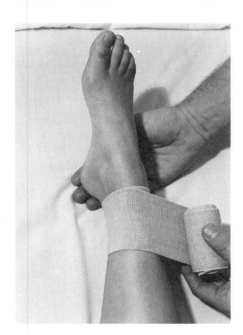

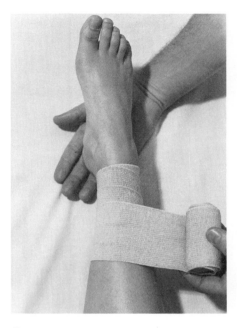

1 A spiral turn is used over a long, cylindrical body part or one of increasing circumference such as the calf. Beginning at the distal end of the limb, make a circular turn by wrapping the bandage once, and then repeating the previous turn to anchor the bandage in place.

2 Spiral turns are made next, overlapping each previous turn by one half to two thirds of the width of the roll.

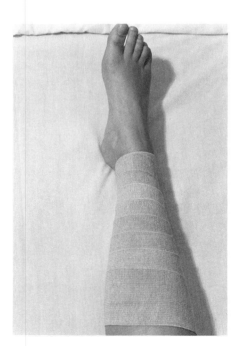

3 Continue to wrap the limb, making sure the completed wrap is evenly spaced and wrinkle-free, and that it is comfortable for the client. Either tape or clip the end of the bandage to secure it in place.

WRAPPING A JOINT

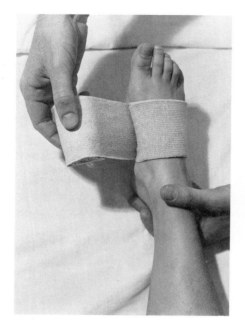

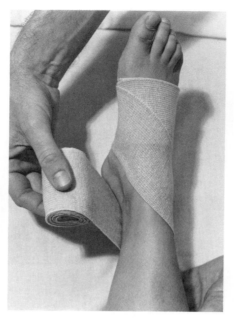

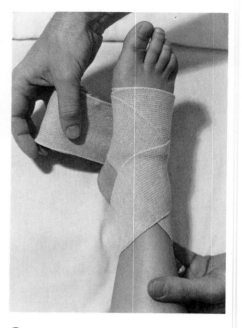

1   Some joints can be properly immobilized or supported with a figure-eight turn. First, anchor the bandage in place by making a double circular turn on the area of the limb distal to the joint.

2   Begin a figure-eight turn by making an ascending turn and wrapping the bandage around the joint.

3   Finish the figure-eight turn by making a descending turn.

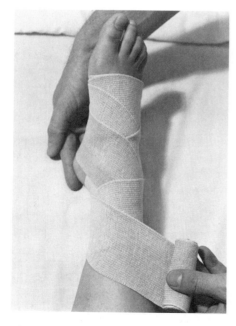

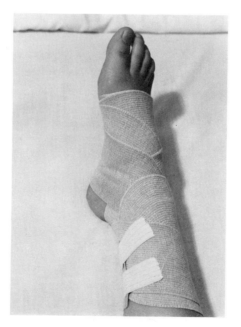

5   When the joint has been wrapped in an even and wrinkle-free manner, secure the end of the bandage to the rest of the wrapped surface with tape or clips. *Caution: If the bandage is to be applied to decrease edema rather than to support the joint, it is essential that the heel also be wrapped or fluid will collect in the heel, potentially resulting in pressure necrosis.*

4   Continue the turns by overlapping the bandage in an alternately ascending and descending fashion.

WRAPPING A RESIDUAL LIMB (STUMP)

Postoperatively, a residual limb may be wrapped with an elastic bandage or limb shrinker to reduce swelling and to mold the stump for eventual prosthetic fitting. One effective way to wrap a residual limb if an elastic limb shrinker is unavailable is to employ a modified figure-eight turn using an elastic bandage. Be sure to include client teaching in this procedure.

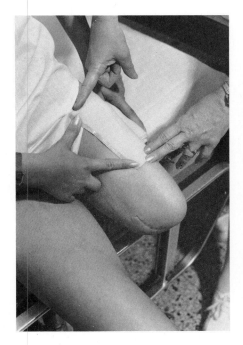

1   It is essential that you position the end of the elastic bandage high on the groin and that this area is properly wrapped without bulging fatty tissue. If the fatty tissue is not contained by the wrapped bandage, the prosthesis will not fit properly.

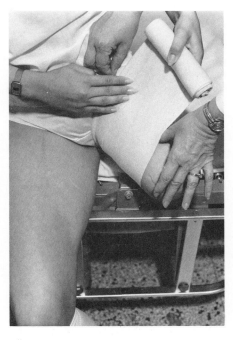

2   Make a circular turn to anchor the bandage in place.

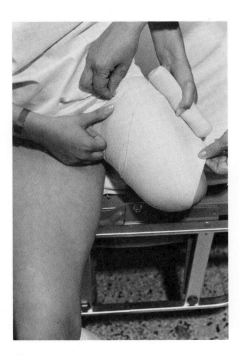

3   Make a spiral turn that overlaps the circular turn, and wrap the distal end of the residual limb.

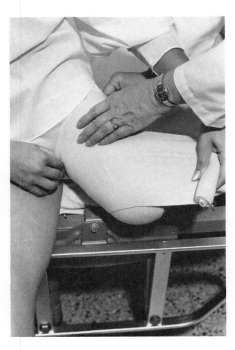

4   Make alternately descending turns (above) and ascending turns

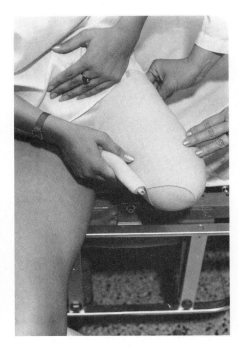

until the residual limb has been completely wrapped.

(Continues)

APPLYING A TRIANGULAR ARM SLING

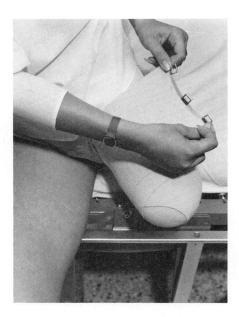

5 Once the residual limb has been wrapped, use tape or clips to secure the end of the bandage to the rest of the wrap.

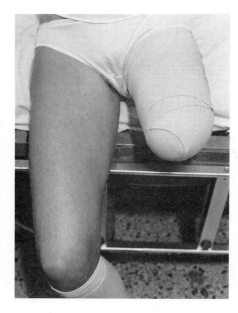

6 Ensure that the bandage is wrinkle-free and that the client does not complain of discomfort from tightness. Be certain that rolls of fatty tissue do not protrude from the bandage, especially along the groin area. Prior to discharge, your client should be proficient in wrapping the residual limb independently.

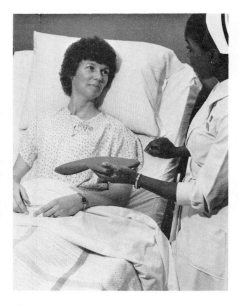

1 A triangle bandage is a versatile and sturdy cloth that can be used in a variety of situations to provide support and immobilization to the hand, elbow, and shoulder. Explain the procedure to the client and position her so that she is sitting comfortably.

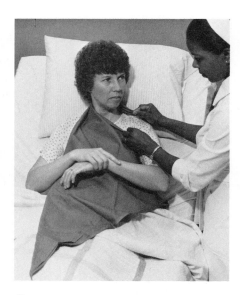

3 Bring the proximal tail up and around the neck so that it hangs over the involved shoulder.

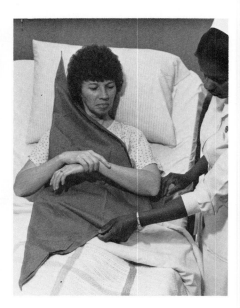

2 Have the client flex and support the involved elbow. Then place the triangle bandage on the client so that it is positioned between the involved arm and chest, with the apex of the triangle under the involved elbow.

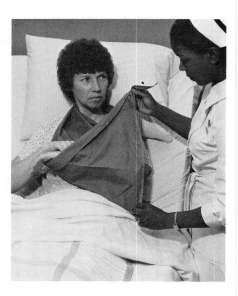

4 The distal tail should then be brought up and over the forearm and chest and positioned on the shoulder.

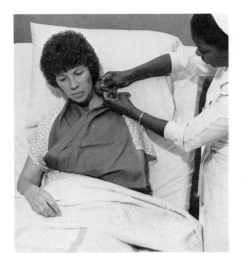

5 Tie the two tails together at the side of the neck (on the involved side). Avoid tying the tails over the vertebral column because doing so can result in skin irritation or pressure over the bony prominences. Tie the ends into a square knot by following the movements left-over-right and under, and right-over-left and under.

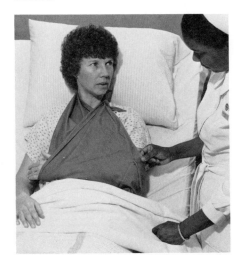

6 Finally, fold the apex of the triangle at the elbow, and either tape or pin the fold in place. If the sling has been applied to minimize swelling of the hand, ensure that the hand is elevated above the level of the elbow. Remove the sling as prescribed, and inspect the skin for indications of irritation, especially around the site of the knot.

MANAGING ROUTINE CAST CARE

ASSISTING WITH CAST APPLICATION

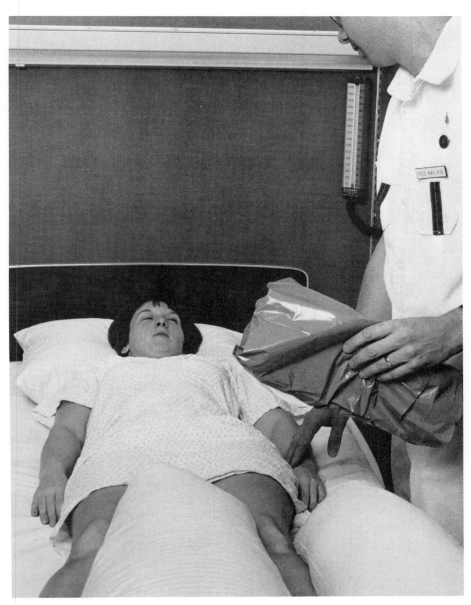

1 Prior to cast application, explain the procedure to the client. For example, depending on the type of cast material used, inform her that she might feel heat as the cast is applied and drying, but that the cast might feel cold and damp after that. Assess the skin on the involved extremity (or area to be casted) for impaired vascular supply, abrasions, ecchymotic areas, and lacerations. Any of these disorders should be carefully documented. The client should also be assessed for potential contraindications to casting, such as diabetes mellitus with peripheral vascular disease (PVD), arteriosclerotic vascular disease, or a peripheral neuropathy. Question the client about allergies to any of the cast materials. Use large plastic bags or bed-saver pads to protect the bed linen or cast application site.

(Continues)

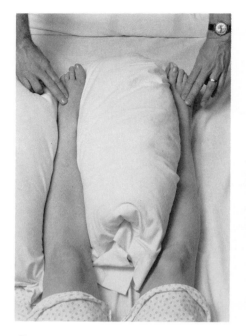

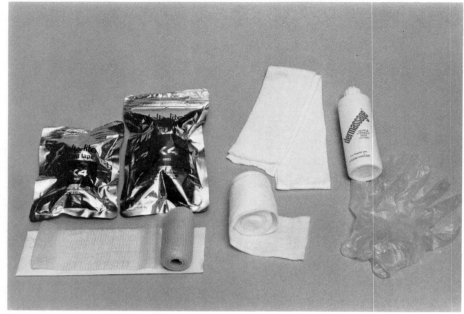

2   Assess the client's neurovascular status by following the procedures, p. 518. Establish the client's baseline in both extremities prior to cast application. Evaluate and record color, temperature, sensation, edema, capillary refill, and pulsations.

3   The materials used for cast application will vary, depending on whether a plaster or synthetic cast will be applied. The following are materials that are typically used when a synthetic cast is applied: rolls of cast material; stockinette, padding, or sheet wadding; a lubricant, either massage cream or one that is water-soluble; and two pairs of disposable gloves. In addition, you will need a plastic-lined bucket filled with fresh water. The water temperature will be determined by the brand of synthetic cast material used. Use a water thermometer to attain the desired temperature. Generally, lukewarm water is used when a plaster cast is applied.

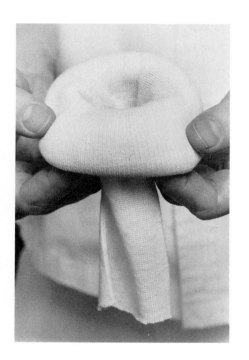

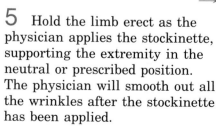

←

4   After the stockinette has been measured and cut to fit the extremity, ensure that it is rolled to facilitate its application onto the extremity.

→

5   Hold the limb erect as the physician applies the stockinette, supporting the extremity in the neutral or prescribed position. The physician will smooth out all the wrinkles after the stockinette has been applied.

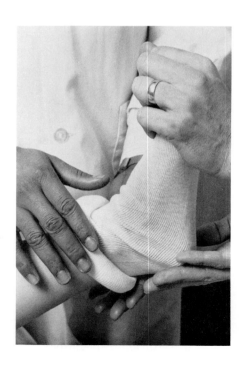

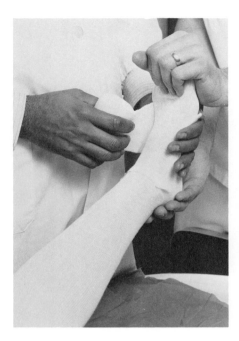 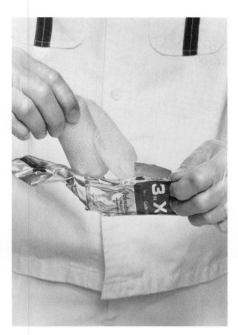 

6 Continue to support the limb in the neutral or desired position as the physician wraps padding around the extremity. One to three layers of padding will be used, and extra padding may be applied over bony prominences or the injured area. It should not, however, cover the edges of the stockinette. Be certain to maintain the extremity in the same prescribed position throughout the entire procedure. Failure to do so could produce wrinkles inside the cast, potentially resulting in pressure areas that can lead to neurovascular impairment.

7 When a synthetic cast is applied, usually both the physician and the assistant apply gloves, and the synthetic casting material is then removed from its package. Opening the package earlier could affect the chemical composition of the cast material.

8 The roll of cast material is then immersed in water for the required amount of time, usually 7–12 seconds, but this will vary depending on the type of cast material that is used. Typically, the roll is then gently squeezed to remove the excess water.
Note: Some synthetic cast materials are activated by compression or by special lights and might not require water.

(Continues)

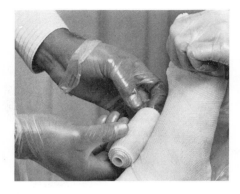

9 Support the limb by grasping the client's toes (or fingers for arm casts) as the physician applies the cast material. If possible, you should also support the limb in areas on which the physician has not yet applied the cast material. Depending on the size and desired thickness of the cast, one to several rolls of cast material may be applied. The physician takes tucks or twists the cast material to ensure conformity to the limb. The stockinette is then pulled over the cast material to cover proximal and distal opening edges, and it is secured in place by another layer or two of the cast material.

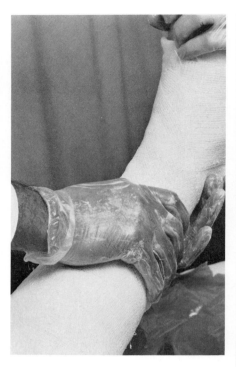

10 To lessen the tack on the gloves and to facilitate the cast molding process, the physician may request that a generous amount of cream or water-soluble lubricant be squeezed onto the gloves. The physician then molds the cast to conform it to the extremity.

PERFORMING ROUTINE ASSESSMENTS AND INTERVENTIONS FOR CLIENTS IN CASTS

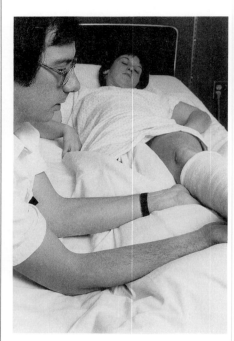

1 After a cast has been applied, elevate the entire extremity above the level of the client's heart by using pillows, suspension, or bed gatch. If your client has had surgery or has sustained trauma, place ice packs along the sides of the cast during the first 48 hours to minimize the potential for edema. When handling the cast, extend your fingers and ensure that only your palms come in contact with the cast. Fingerprints on a damp cast could dent or flatten the cast material, causing pressure areas that could result in client discomfort and neurovascular impairment. To enhance drying of the cast, keep sheets and blankets off the cast and reposition the client every 2–3 hours during the first 24–48 hours, the time required for the average-sized plaster cast to dry. A synthetic cast will dry much more quickly. Check under the cast to assess for flattened areas or indentations.

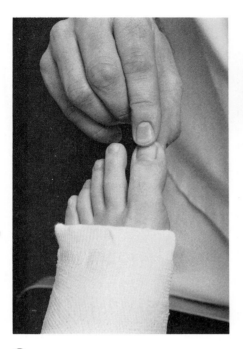

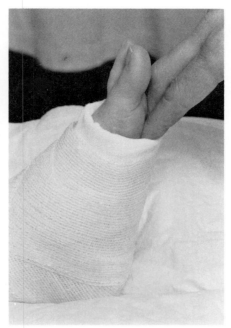

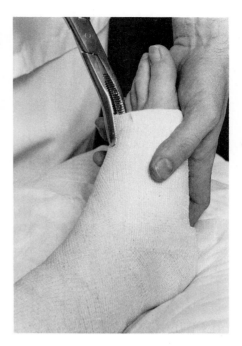

2 Perform neurovascular assessments every 30 minutes for several hours after cast application, and then hourly during the first 24 hours. Compare the assessments to the client's baseline. If they are normal after the first 24 hours, the assessments can be performed every 4 hours during the first few days after cast application. Assess circulation by evaluating the speed of capillary refill, color, and temperature of the toes or fingers. (Review procedures, p. 518.)

3 If possible, monitor the pulses distal to the fracture or injury, and assess for edema by inserting two fingers into the proximal and distal cast openings. Review the procedures, p. 520, to assist you with your evaluation of your client's nerve function. Describe alterations in neurovascular status to the client so that she can notify you in the event they occur. Explain to the client, significant other, parents, or family members that constant or increasing pain, numbness or tingling, impaired movement of the involved fingers or toes, or pain on passive movement require immediate attention. Parents of infants or small children should be shown a basic neurovascular assessment and told to be alert to irritability and/or constant crying of their child.

4 Feel along the cast edges to check for rough edges, for plaster crumbs, or for areas that press into the client's skin. It may be necessary to bend the cast edge slightly with a duckbilled cast bender (as shown). Extensive bending and trimming should be done by the physician. When the cast has dried, you can petal the rough edges (see the technique for cast petaling in the next procedure).

(Continues)

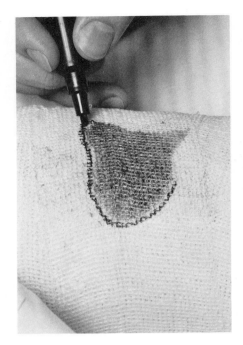

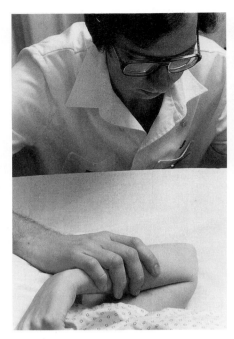

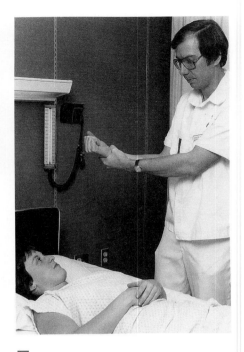

5 Monitor postsurgical or post-traumatic drainage by inspecting the entire cast. Encircle—or simply measure—the drainage stain after every shift (depending on agency policy) to provide a baseline for subsequent evaluation of the amount of exudate. Inform the physician of daily amounts and/or changes. It is also essential that you inspect both the sheet and the underside of the cast to ensure that drainage has not seeped into these areas. A foul-smelling odor from the cast or cast openings should be noted and promptly reported because it can be indicative of an infection. *Caution: Wear gloves if you will come into direct contact with the drainage.*

6 Because your client might be immobilized for several hours or even days, assess the skin integrity on an ongoing basis, especially around bony prominences and cast edges, which have greater potential for skin irritation or breakdown. Massage these sites with alcohol (to toughen the skin) or with a lotion, depending on agency protocol. Before using alcohol, make sure the skin is unbroken.

7 Ensure that the client receives full ROM exercises on the unaffected extremities, as well as on the joints distal and proximal to the cast unless it is medically contraindicated. Teach your client active ROM exercises for the unaffected extremities, and assisted ROM for the casted extremity, which can be implemented with physician approval once healing has occurred. Also, explain that moving the fingers or toes of the casted extremity will enhance peripheral circulation to minimize edema and pain. With physician approval, isometric exercises can be taught to the client to minimize muscle atrophy in the affected limb. Teach the isometric (muscle-setting) exercises on the unaffected limb so that the client can adapt the exercise to the casted limb. Demonstrate muscle palpation so that the client can feel the changes that occur with muscle contraction and relaxation.

Nursing Guidelines for the Care of Clients in Casts

- Instruct the client not to insert any object into the cast.
- Observe for indicators of pressure areas under the cast: client complaints of burning or pain, drainage on the cast surface, odor from the cast openings.
- If your client has an open wound under the cast, assess for indications of infection: increased temperature and pulse rates; increase in drainage, pain, erythema, and swelling; foul-smelling exudate; restlessness; and an increased white blood cell count.
- Especially during the first 3 days after a fracture, observe the client for indications of a fat embolus (particularly if the client has sustained multiple trauma or a fracture of the hip and femur): increased temperature and pulse rate; precordial chest pain, dyspnea, and cough; and agitation or disorientation. Petechiae at buccal membranes, chest, and hard palate might appear later. Monitor blood gases for respiratory acidosis ($Paco_2$ >40 mm Hg; ph <7.40), and serum and urine values for the presence of fat and lipase. Treatment may include the administration of oxygen, diuretics, and anti-inflammatory agents.
- Be alert to indications of compartment syndrome, which can occur when blood or drainage collect under the tissue of the injured extremity, resulting in swelling and diminished blood flow: client complaints of severe pain, which is usually unrelieved by the usual dosage of analgesic; and neurovascular impairment (increasing circumference of the extremity and capillary return >3 seconds). Later neurovascular findings include **pain** that is increased with pressure applied over the involved compartment and passive movement of the digits, **polar (coolness), pulselessness, paresthesias, and paralysis.** This is a medical emergency: The physician must be notified at once, and the extremity must be elevated above its present position. Typically, the cast is bivalved, and occasionally surgical intervention is required to relieve the problem.
- For comfort and to prevent skin breakdown, a sheepskin pad or pressure-relief mattress should be used under the immobilized client (see Chapter 2).
- A slightly damp cloth with cleanser can be used to clean soiled areas on a plaster cast. Excess moisture must be wiped away after the cleansing. Most synthetic casts can be cleaned with mild soap and water, followed by a thorough rinsing. The synthetic cast should be blotted with towels and then dried with a handheld hair dryer using a cool setting.

PETALING A CAST

Once the cast has dried and the client's swelling has subsided, rough cast edges can be covered with strips of moleskin or adhesive waterproof tape.

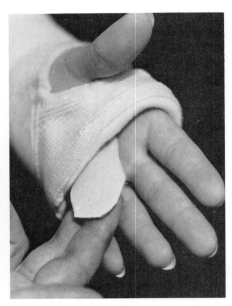

1 Cut several 5.0- to 7.5-cm (2- to 3-in.) strips of tape that is 2.5 cm (1 in.) in width. The number of strips will be determined by the size of the involved cast area. Then, curve the corners of each strip (as shown).

2 Insert the sticky side of the tape into the cast edge. Ensure that the petal is securely adhered and unwrinkled to prevent unrolling and client discomfort.

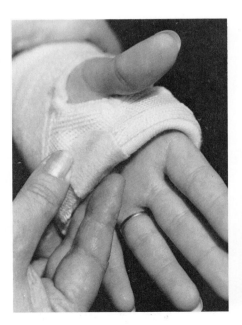

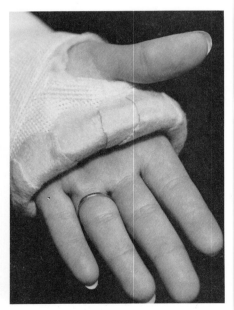

3 Lap the tape over the cast edge and adhere it to the front surface of the cast.

4 Continue the process, overlapping the edges of the tape strips until the rough cast surface has been completely covered by the tape. Teach the procedure to the client so that the tape can be replaced after it becomes soiled or begins to peel.

Managing Routine Traction Care

MAKING A BOWLINE TRACTION KNOT

There are several types of knots that are used for traction. The bowline knot is one that will not slip, and we therefore recommend its use over others.

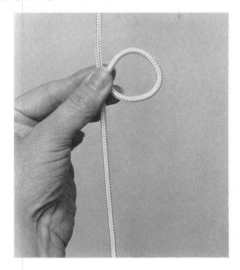

1 Make a loop in a traction rope that is both intact and unfrayed.

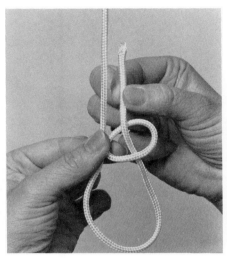

2 Bring the end of the rope up through the loop.

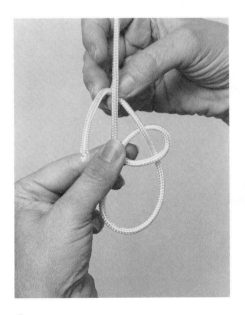

3 Wrap the end behind and around the rope that is proximal to the loop.

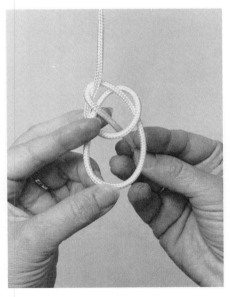

4 Thread the end down through the original loop.

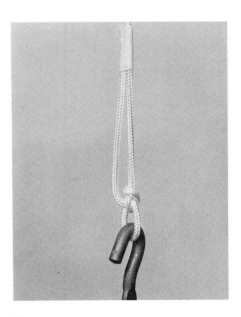

5 Tighten the knot and attach the weight to the loop that is below the knot. To prevent the end from fraying, wrap it with a small strip of tape. It is also a good idea to tape the end to the rope to discourage others from tampering with the knot.

General Guidelines for the Care of the Client in Traction

- Perform and document neurovascular assessments (see pp. 518–519) prior to application of the traction apparatus to provide a baseline for subsequent assessments. For nonadhesive skin traction (for example, Buck's boot, cervical collar, or pelvic belt) perform a neurovascular assessment every 4 hours, and 30–45 minutes after every reapplication of the traction. For adhesive skin traction (for example, Buck's with adhesive straps or Bryant's) and skeletal traction, perform the assessments hourly during the first 24 hours, and every 4 hours thereafter if they are normal for the client and remain stable. Assessments should be repeated 30–45 minutes after the extremities are rewrapped with adhesive skin traction.

- Unless the traction involves the neck or upper extremities, provide the client with a trapeze and instruct her or him in its use. ***Note: It may be necessary to obtain a physician's order for a trapeze for the pediatric population.***

- For clients receiving continuous traction, the use of sheepskin pads or pressure-relief mattresses is essential to the integrity of the skin. Inspect the skin, especially that over bony prominences, and perform skin care at frequent intervals.

- To provide the prescribed line of pull, ensure that the client maintains proper alignment and that the ropes and pulleys are in alignment, as well. Ensure that the weights are hanging freely and that the rope is centered over the pulley track.

- Because the immobilized client is at risk for the development of thrombi secondary to venous stasis, secure an order for antiembolic stockings and apply them following the procedure in Chapter 7.

- Make sure the client exercises the uninvolved extremities and joints, using ROM, ankle circling, and isometric (muscle-setting) exercises. Unless contraindicated, isometric exercises should be employed on the involved extremity as well.

- For the immobilized client, monitor and document bowel status and evaluate the diet. Increase roughage and obtain an order for a stool softener or cathartic if indicated. Ensure an adequate fluid intake (at least 2–3 L/day) to prevent urinary tract infections, retention, and renal calculi.

- To prevent respiratory complications, encourage coughing and deep-breathing exercises and/or the use of incentive spirometry; auscultate the chest for lung sounds daily to identify and avert the development of hypostatic pneumonia or atelectasis. For further detail, see Chapter 6.

CARING FOR CLIENTS IN SKIN TRACTION

Skin traction works by exerting a force directly to the body surface, which in turn indirectly affects the underlying muscles and bones. It can be applied to the spine, long bones of the extremities, and pelvis.

APPLYING CERVICAL TRACTION

Cervical traction is applied for clients with cervical spine disorders, "whiplash," muscle spasms in the neck, or neck pain. Generally, nurses can apply cervical traction for the client who does not have a significant fracture or subluxation.

Assessing and Planning

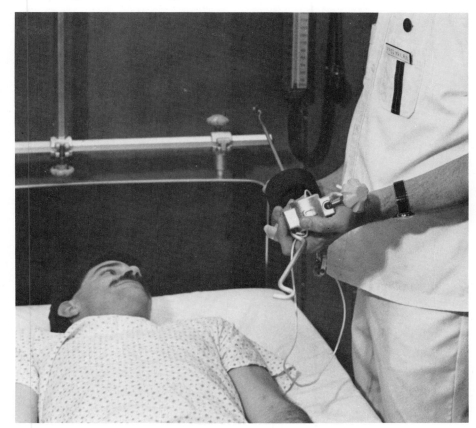

1 Review a traction manual before entering the client's room so that you are familiar with the setup, and then assemble the cervical traction apparatus. Explain the procedure to the client and perform a baseline neurologic assessment on the upper extremities. It is essential that the client and family members be informed about the importance of maintaining the prescribed position; avoiding the adjustment or removal of the traction apparatus unless it is approved; and reporting the presence of pressure, pain, paresthesias, or weakness in the neck or upper extremities immediately. The client should remain supine for this therapy, with the shoulders relaxed and level, and the back flattened against the bed.

(Continues)

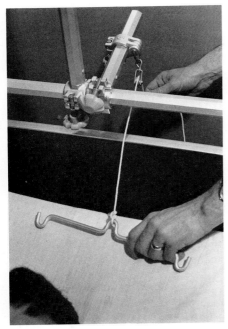

Implementing

3 Insert the cervical collar carefully under the client's neck; then buckle the straps (bottom photo).

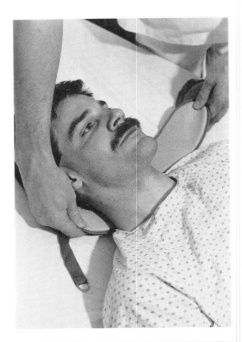

2 Attach the prescribed traction frame to the bed. Ensure that the spreader bar is of an appropriate size. It should be wide enough so that once the cervical collar is attached, the straps will neither touch the sides of the client's head nor pinch his ears. The client should also be positioned far enough down in bed so that there is ample room for the spreader bar and rope. The rope should then be tied to the spreader bar and threaded through the pulley, with the prescribed weight (usually no greater than 5 pounds) attached to the opposite end.

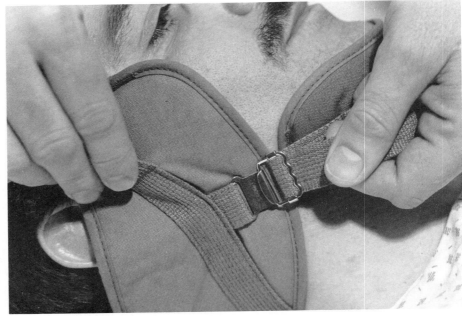

4   Adjust the collar if the strap is not centered over the chin, and make sure that the strap does not touch the client's throat. When the client is comfortable in the collar, attach the ends of the spreader bar through each of the collar rings (right). Use slow, even motions to avoid jerking the weights and injuring the client. When the weights are connected, make sure that the traction pull is over the occiput rather than the chin, and that it is bilaterally equal. Ask the client if it pulls more on one side than the other, and adjust it accordingly. Document the procedure.

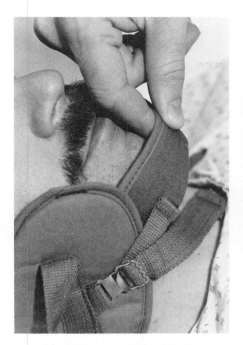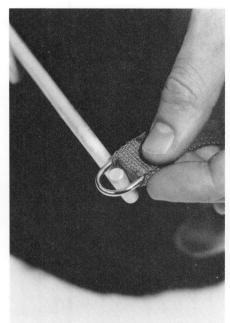

5   The physician may request that the head of the bed be elevated to provide countertraction. If this is the case, ensure that the pulley system can be raised and lowered independent of the bed so that the direction of the traction force can be altered to accommodate the client's position.

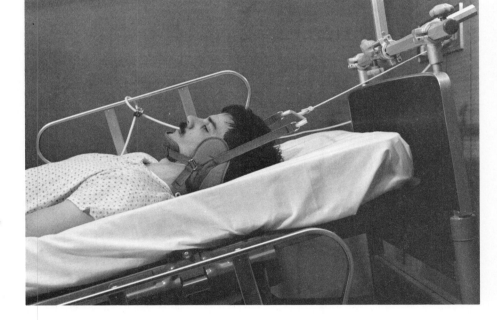

(Continues)

Evaluating

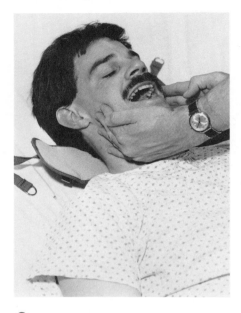

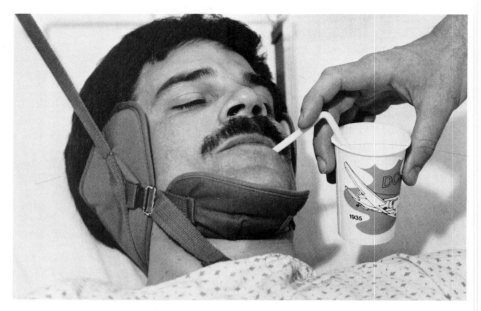

6   If intermittent rather than continuous traction has been prescribed, perform thorough client assessments after removing the collar and discontinuing the traction. Palpate the client's temporomandibular joint (see p. 512) to assess for discomfort or limited range of motion. Pain in this area, headaches, and neck pain are indications that the weight might be too much for the client's tolerance, and the physician should be informed of the problem. Also, evaluate skin integrity at this time by inspecting the ears, chin, and occipital areas for the presence of skin irritation or pressure from the collar. Inspect and massage the skin over the elbows, heels, sacrum, and other bony prominences as well, to enhance local circulation. Remember to perform neurologic assessments on the upper extremities 30 minutes after the traction has been reapplied.

7   Evaluate the client's oral intake. If continuous traction is prescribed, it may be necessary to modify the diet to one that is soft or liquid to facilitate the client's chewing and swallowing. If the client must be immobile for pro-

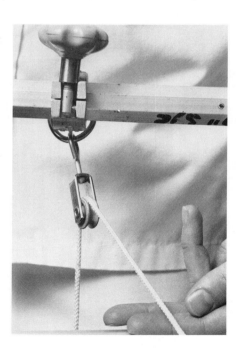

longed periods of time, encourage a fluid intake of 2–3 L/day to minimize the potential for a urinary tract infection, retention, and renal calculi. Be sure to keep a glass containing fluids and a straw within the client's reach.

8   During routine assessment of the client, also evaluate the traction apparatus. The weights should hang freely, and the ropes must be unfrayed and centered over the pulley tracks. Check the client's alignment in relation to the traction apparatus to ensure that he receives a direct line of pull.

APPLYING A PELVIC BELT

Pelvic traction is applied for clients with sciatica, low back pain, and muscle spasms in the lower back.

Assessing and Planning

1   Obtain the prescribed traction apparatus and a pelvic belt sized to fit your client. Review a traction manual to assist you with assembling the traction apparatus used by your agency. Explain the procedure to your client, and obtain and record the client's baseline neurologic assessments. In addition, evaluate the strength of both legs by instructing the client to press her feet against both your hands (see step 12, p. 550). Explain the importance of maintaining the prescribed position, keeping the traction uninterrupted, and reporting immediately any prolonged discomfort, weakness, or paresthesia of the lower extremities.

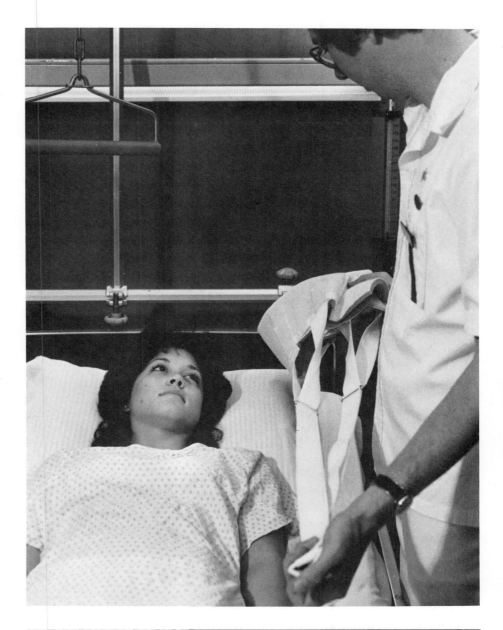

2   For countertraction and comfort, the physician may prescribe the Williams' position in which the client's hips and knees are flexed to approximately 45 degrees and the head of the bed is elevated 20–30 degrees.

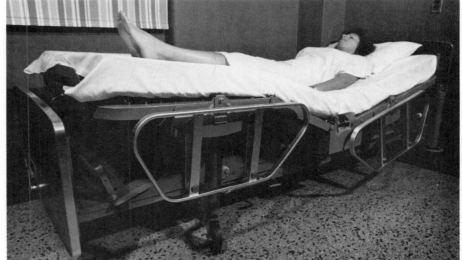

(Continues)

Implementing

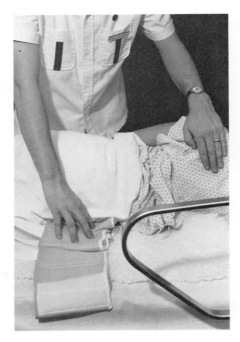

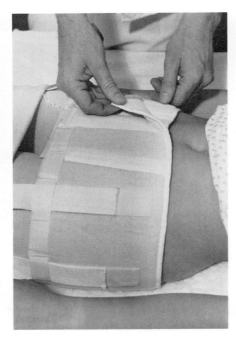

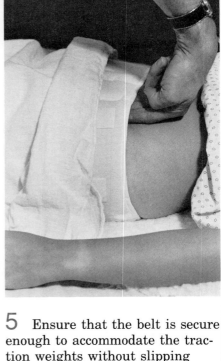

3 To position the belt around the client, assist her into a side-lying position, fan-fold half the belt, and tuck it under her hips. As you assist her onto her other side, pull the fan-folded section from underneath her. As she returns to the supine position, ensure that the belt is evenly centered under her hips.

4 The belt should encircle the pelvis rather than the waistline, with the top of the belt positioned just proximal to the iliac crests. Close the belt by attaching the Velcro™ strips together (as shown).

5 Ensure that the belt is secure enough to accommodate the traction weights without slipping downward. However, it should not be so tight that it causes discomfort and skin irritation or impairs bowel and/or bladder function. You should be able to fit two fingers between the client's skin and the belt.

6 Position the straps of the belt along the lower legs, making certain they are equal in length to provide even traction. Adjust the straps if they are not the same length. Attach the prescribed weight, which is usually 8–10 pounds.

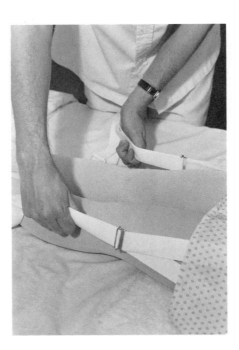

Evaluating

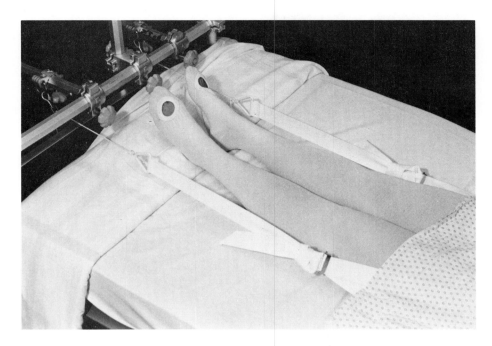

7 Assess the client for proper alignment, and make sure the ropes and pulleys are properly aligned. Ensure that the traction knots are secure and taped at the ends to prevent fraying.

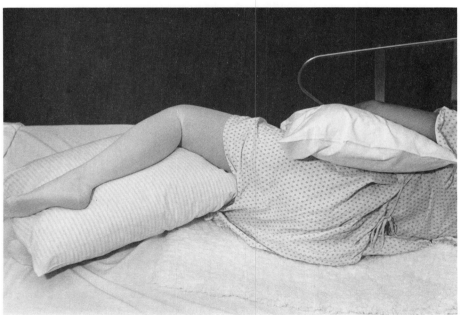

8 If intermittent traction has been prescribed for your client, encourage side-lying positions when she is out of traction. The bed should be flat. Her knees and hips should be flexed; pillows should be placed under the head and upper arm and between the knees to take the pressure off the lower back.

(Continues)

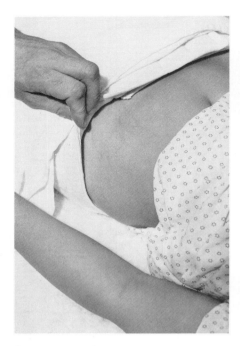

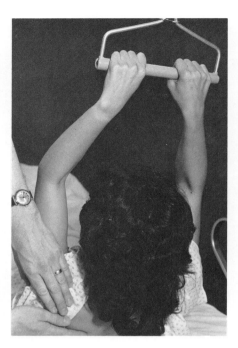

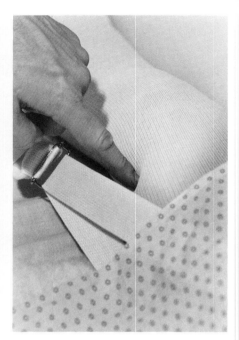

9 At least every 4 hours, assess and massage all skin areas that are prone to breakdown, especially the skin over the iliac crests, sacrum, and greater trochanters.

10 Unless it is contraindicated, instruct the client to elevate her upper body by flexing her knees and lifting up on a trapeze. As she does, inspect and massage the back, especially the scapular and sacral areas.

11 Evaluate neurologic status at least every 4 hours, as well as 30–45 minutes after the traction has been reapplied. In addition, be sure to assess for sciatic nerve constriction by evaluating sensation along the lateral thighs, just proximal to the patellae (as shown) as well as the lower leg proximal to the malleoli. Report a lack of sensation or tingling to the physician and remove the client from traction unless otherwise directed.

12 Evaluate the strength of both legs by asking the client to press her feet against your hands. Compare this assessment to the baseline assessment you made prior to the initial application of traction.

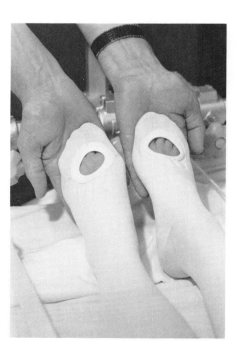

APPLYING A BUCK'S BOOT FOR EXTENSION TRACTION

Buck's extension is provided for the client either by adhesive straps or by a sponge rubber boot, such as that shown. It is indicated for clients who require presurgical immobilization of a fractured hip, or for clients with fractured femurs, pelvic injuries, sciatica, muscle spasms, degenerative arthritis of the knees, or knee injuries requiring minimal immobilization.

Assessing and Planning

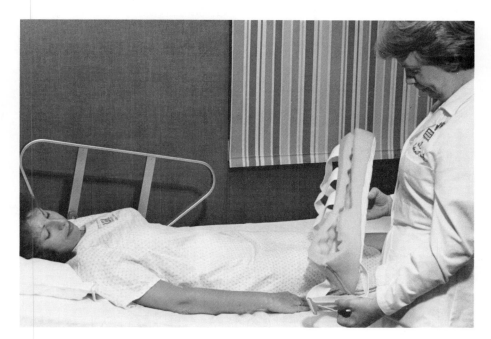

1 Obtain a traction boot of the proper size for your client, as well as the prescribed traction apparatus. Review a traction manual to familiarize yourself with the traction setup prior to entering the client's room. Explain the procedure to the client, and inform the client and family members of the importance of maintaining the prescribed position throughout the therapy; keeping the traction uninterrupted; and immediately reporting prolonged discomfort, weakness, or paresthesias in the lower extremity.

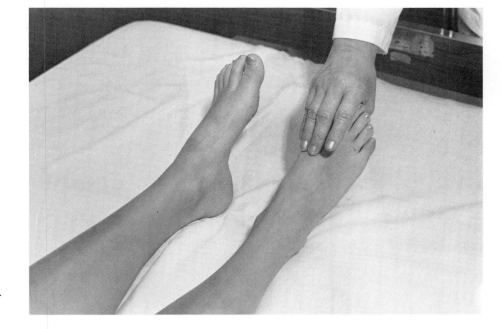

2 Perform and record a baseline neurovascular assessment of the lower extremities prior to applying the traction boot. Also, assess the client's normal ability to dorsiflex her foot because footdrop caused from peroneal nerve compression is an occasional complication of this therapy.

(Continues)

Implementing

3 Gently position the boot under the client's involved foot and calf, and fasten the Velcro™ straps.

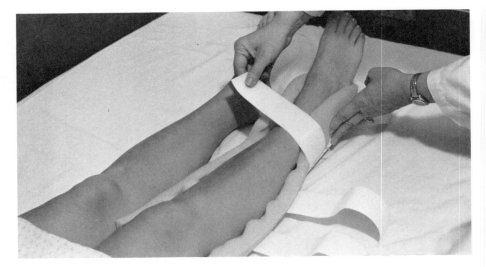

4 Although the boot should fit the client's leg securely, it should not be so tight that it produces pressure areas on the skin. Ensure that two fingertips can fit between the client's leg and each strap. This is especially important for the strap closest to the client's patella. Because it encircles the area in which the peroneal nerve lies close to the fibular head, it can potentially compress the nerve, resulting in peroneal nerve palsy (footdrop).

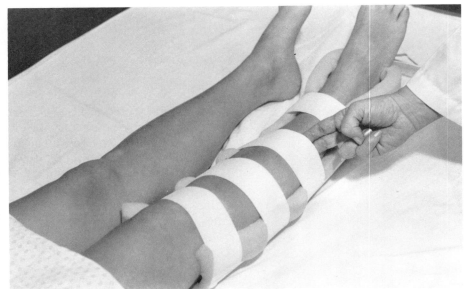

5 Attach the boot to the traction apparatus. Be sure to tape the free end of the knot to prevent it from fraying.

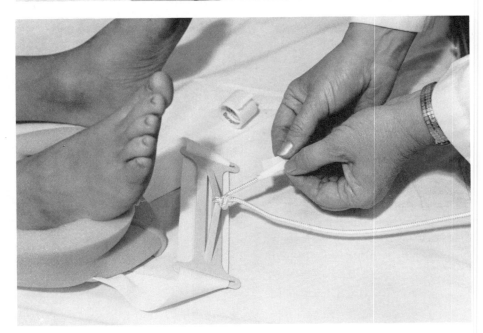

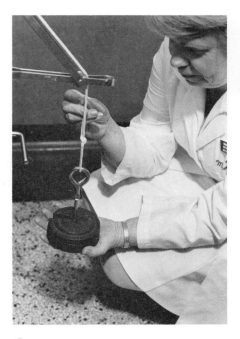

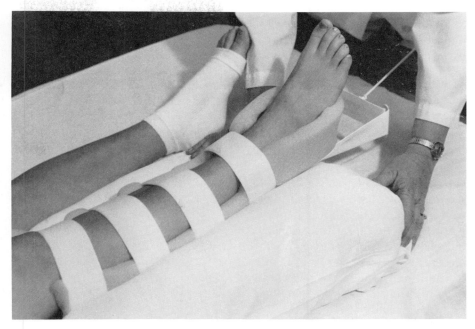

6 If it is prescribed, apply countertraction by elevating the foot of the bed approximately 15 cm (6 in.). *Note: If the physician does not want the foot of the bed elevated, the client's position in bed will require close observation to ensure that she does not slide to the end of the bed.* Attach the prescribed weight, which is usually no greater than 8–10 pounds.

7 Place a narrow pillow or folded blanket under the involved calf to keep the heel off the bed. This will prevent irritation and breakdown caused by mattress pressure on the heel. The pillow should not occlude the popliteal space nor press on the Achilles tendon. Protect the uninvolved heel by applying a heel protector. Document the procedure.

Evaluating

8 Assess the integrity of the client's skin on the involved heel by pulling the boot down and away from the heel (as shown). Remove the heel protector on the uninvolved foot, and inspect and massage the skin. Perform neurovascular assessments every 4 hours, as well as 30–45 minutes after reapplication of the traction boot. Review the procedure, p. 521, to assist you in assessing the integrity of the peroneal nerve. Client complaints of tingling on the anterior leg or dorsum of the foot may signal peroneal nerve impairment.

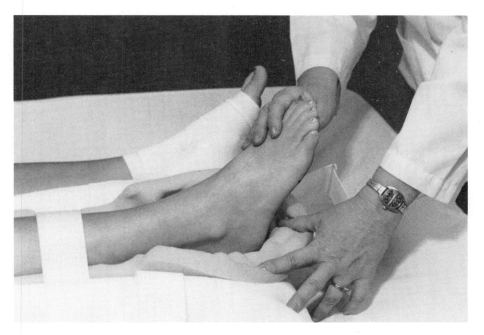

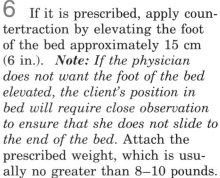

(Continues)

9 Unless it is contraindicated (for example, because of a fracture), remove the traction boot at least every 8 hours and cleanse and dry the leg. The sponge boot can cause increased perspiration, which can lead to skin maceration. Inspect the entire leg at that time to assess for pressure areas or breakdown, especially the dorsum of the foot, both malleoli, Achilles tendon area, anterior tibia, and the fibular head. Encourage the client to exercise her uninvolved extremities actively, as well as the joints distal to the injury if it is not contraindicated. Muscle setting (isometrics) is especially good for the involved leg.

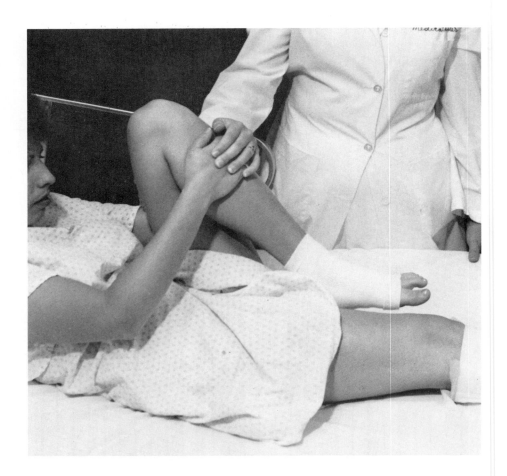

ASSISTING THE CLIENT WITH COTREL DYNAMIC TRACTION

Cotrel traction may be prescribed for the preoperative management of clients with scoliosis to enhance soft tissue stretching prior to spinal fusion. This will minimize the amount of pressure required to correct the curvature when the client is in the postoperative cast. In addition, it is a method of therapy that allows clients active participation in their own treatment.

Assessing and Planning

1 Assemble the Cotrel traction apparatus, and review the traction manual for its setup prior to entering the client's room. Plan to instruct the client in the step-by-step performance of the exercise routine. The head gear should be applied in front of the mirror (as shown) so that the client can become familiar with both the exact position of the head halter (see top photo p. 555) and the proper tension. It should be tightened securely but not be so tight that it causes too much pressure over the occiput. Depending on agency policy, children and adolescents can be encouraged to wear their own clothing during the exercise to provide extra padding for the pelvic halter.

Implementing

2 Instruct the client to get up onto the center of the bed, with her feet positioned at the edge of the mattress. This will ensure that she starts from the same position each time she initiates the exercise. Be sure that the traction apparatus is centered over the client's body.

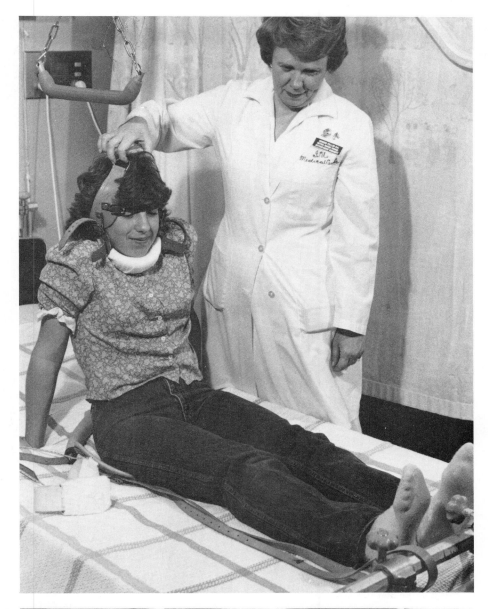

3 Show the client how to apply the pelvic halter so that the leather plates are centered over the trochanters, with the horizontal straps criss-crossing over each iliac crest. The vertical straps are extended from the trochanters to the end of the bed to provide countertraction.

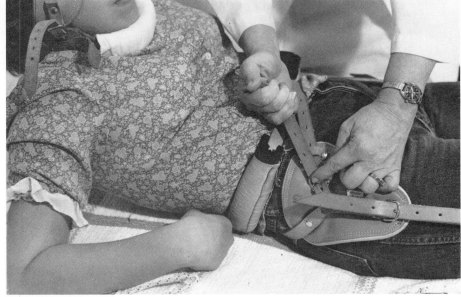

(Continues)

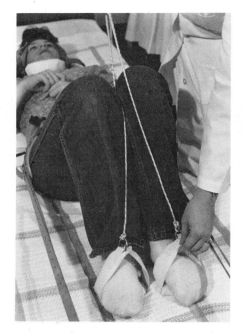

4 Instruct the client to flex her knees and hips so that the foot stirrups can be applied next. The foot stirrups connect to the head halter through the traction cord.

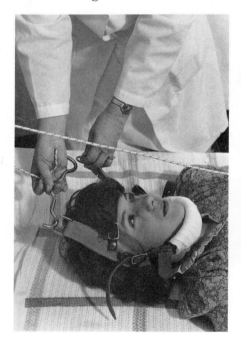

5 Attach the spreader bar to the rings on each side of the head halter.

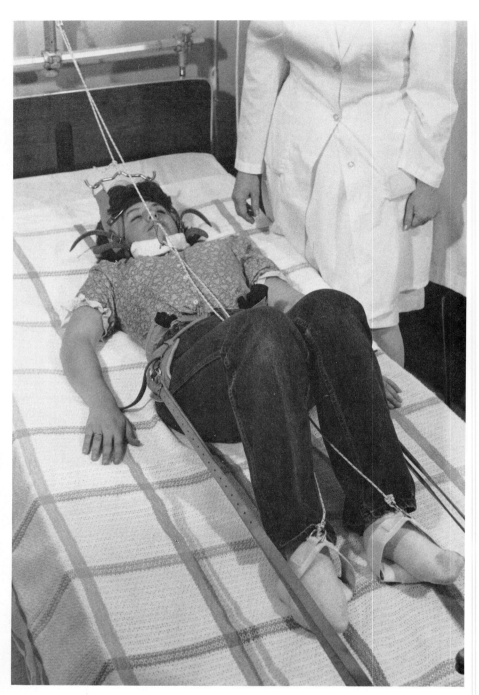

6 While the client's hips and knees remain in a flexed position, assess her for comfort and proper alignment, and ensure that all the straps and halters are secure.

7 Instruct the client to extend the lower extremities by pushing her feet against the stirrups. This action produces a force at the occiput and pelvis, which promotes elongation of the spine. Encourage the client to relax the muscles in her trunk during the exercise. To ensure that the force is transmitted to the occiput rather than to the chin, instruct the client to open and close her mouth. If she cannot do this during the extension phase, the angle of the pulley at the head of the bed must be repositioned to attain a 45-degree angle to the plane of the client's body. Instruct the client to maintain the extension for 15 seconds and then to relax for 15 seconds by flexing her knees and hips.

Evaluating

The exercise should be performed for 10 minutes out of every hour on a daily basis, usually from the hours of 9 AM to 9 PM. Keep a traction schedule at the client's bedside, and initial it each time the exercise is performed. Assess for pressure areas over the occiput, chin, iliac crests, and buttocks. The application of alcohol to the iliac crests will toughen the skin and help to minimize breakdown. Explain to the client that bruising may occur initially, but this is a temporary condition. As the client becomes more accustomed to the treatment, encourage her to tighten the cinch progressively on the head halter to reduce the slack in the system and enhance the force of the traction.

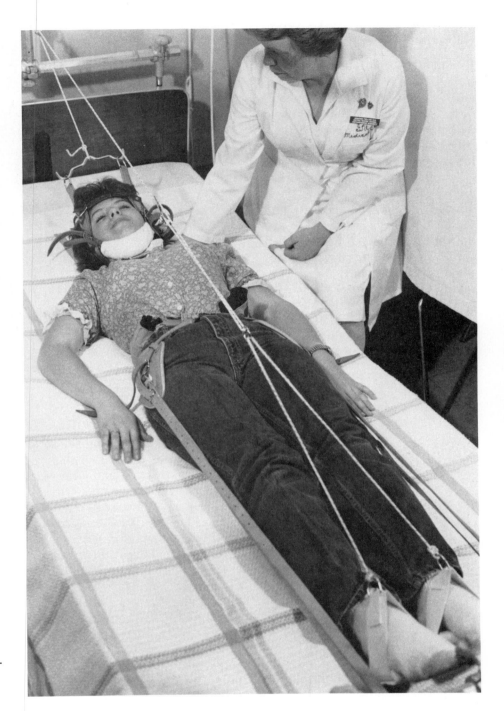

CARING FOR CHILDREN IN BRYANT'S TRACTION

Bryant's traction is employed for infants with fractured femurs, and, in a modified form (as shown in the following photos), for those with congenital dislocated hips (CDH). The traction is always bilateral to provide effective immobilization for both legs. For children with fractured femurs, the hips are flexed at 90 degrees, and the legs and feet are together at the child's midline. Children with CDH begin their treatment in the same position, usually for a period of 3–5 days. After this initial period, the hip abduction process begins, with the degree of abduction gradually increasing over a period of time, to the tolerance of the child.

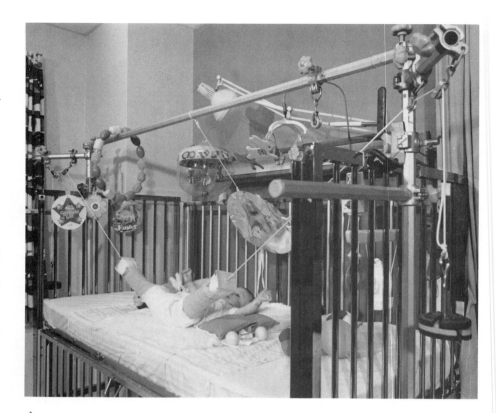

1   Perform neurovascular assessments hourly during the first 24 hours after the initial application of the traction and on a regular basis thereafter once the assessment results prove to be normal for the child. Assessments should also be performed 30 minutes after reapplication of the traction and/or rewrapping of the elastic bandages (for children with CDH). Review the procedure, pp. 518–521, to assist you with neurovascular and nerve function assessments. Be especially alert to indicators of peroneal nerve palsy (footdrop), including the infant's inability to dorsiflex his feet and extend his toes. Make sure the elastic bandages are not too tight around the fibular heads (in the area just distal to the patellae on the lateral legs), and ensure that the child's alignment is correct so that the traction does not promote external rotation. Either situation increases the risk of footdrop or paralysis. Notify the physician immediately if you detect any neurovascular deficit. Also, demonstrate the assessments to the parents or caregivers, stressing their importance. Instruct them to alert you immediately in the event of any compromise, including prolonged irritability of the child.

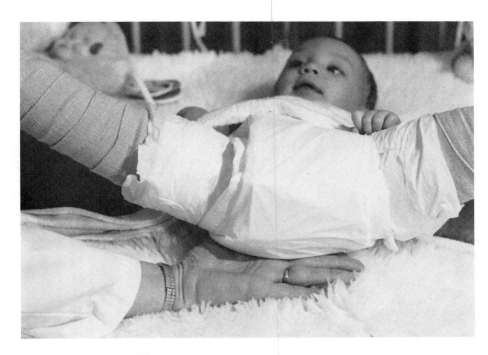

2 Assess the position of the child's buttocks in relationship to the mattress. The traction weight is appropriate if the infant's buttocks just clear the mattress (as shown); you should be able to place a flattened hand under the buttocks. Notify the physician if the buttocks are either too high or too low. He or she may wish to alter the weights.

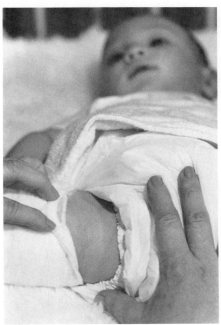

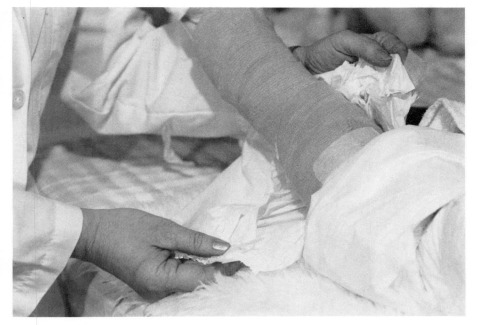

3 Every 2–4 hours, inspect the infant's skin to evaluate its integrity, especially that over the malleoli, dorsum of the feet, and the groin (as shown).

4 For children with CDH who are in modified Bryant's traction, rewrap the elastic bandages every 8 hours, with physician approval, to enable you to inspect and massage the infant's skin. Then wrap the groin area with waterproof material, such as the plastic from a disposable diaper, to protect the elastic bandages from urine and feces. Ensure that the elastic bandages do not slip down toward the feet because this will alter the traction. *Caution: Do not unwrap the bandages if the child has a fractured femur.*

(Continues)

5 To prevent urinary tract infections, you will need to increase the infant's fluid intake. To ensure that the diaper provides total absorption of the urine, you may pad the diaper with a sanitary pad (as shown). This will minimize the potential for saturation of the elastic bandages, which could promote skin maceration. Assess the infant for indications of a urinary tract infection by evaluating the urine for foul-smelling odor and the infant for increased temperature and irritability. Obtain an order for urine tests if appropriate.

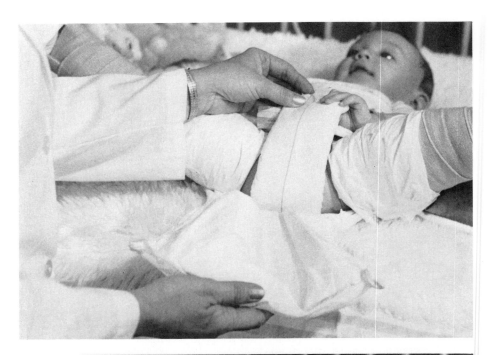

6 Unless the infant has a rash or areas of broken skin, massage the skin over the bony prominences with alcohol (to toughen the skin) or with lotion to minimize the potential for breakdown. Provide a sheepskin or small pressure-alleviation mattress to protect his skin.

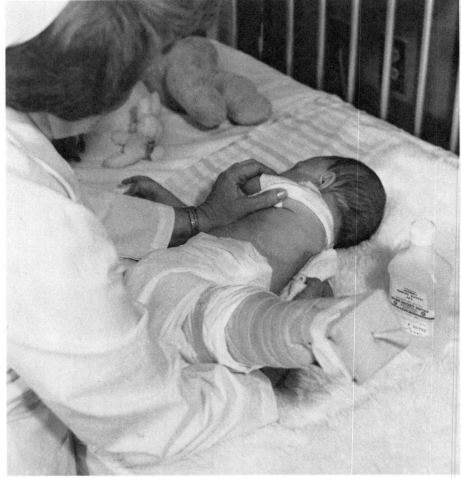

7 For feedings, the infant with CDH can be placed in an infant seat so that his head can be elevated for 30 minutes during and after feedings. This will enhance the passage of the food through the pylorus and minimize the potential for aspiration of vomitus. Make sure the infant seat can accommodate the child's hip abduction without altering the angle or causing excess pressure on the lateral thighs.

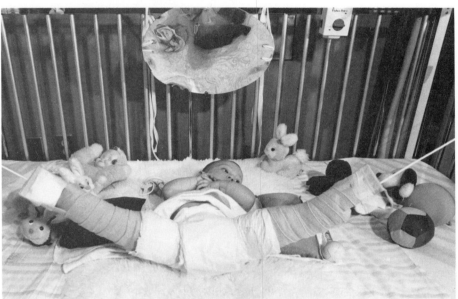

8 Provide the infant with the stimulation of social, emotional, and motor development during his prolonged period of immobility by keeping bright-colored, noise-making toys, mobiles, pictures, and an unbreakable mirror within his eye level. Be sure to put toys within reach, and rearrange the toys daily to provide the infant with a fresh environment. Encourage family members or caretakers to have frequent interaction with the child. Explain that passive ROM exercises on the uninvolved extremities can be incorporated into pat-a-cake and peek-a-boo games.

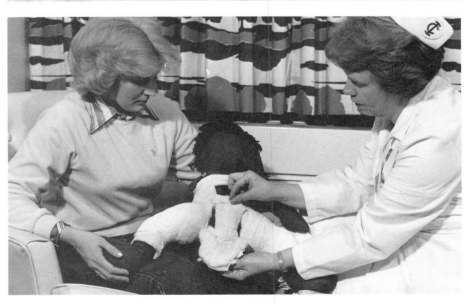

9 Frequent interaction between yourself and the parents or caretakers is essential to ensure that all the needs of the infant are met. Demonstrate procedures such as neurovascular assessments and ROM exercises; assist them as necessary during their first attempts. If possible, provide them with written materials about the care of the infant with a fractured femur or CDH. If a hip spica cast will be applied once the Bryant's traction is removed, do preliminary teaching by demonstrating cast care on a demonstrator doll (as shown).

CARING FOR CLIENTS IN SKELETAL TRACTION

PERFORMING ROUTINE CARE OF CLIENTS IN SKELETAL TRACTION

With skeletal traction, pins or wires are inserted directly into or through the bone to provide a direct longitudinal pull as a means of reducing a fracture. Typical sites for skeletal traction on the extremities are the distal femur, the proximal tibia, and the proximal ulna. Casts are occasionally applied to the extremity in conjunction with the skeletal traction to help immobilize the extremity and stabilize the pin. Review and incorporate the general guidelines for the care of the client in traction, p. 542.

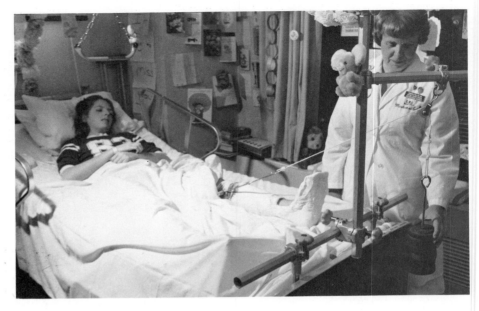

1 At least every 2 hours, inspect the client's alignment with the traction apparatus to ensure that there is a direct line of pull and that it is in a straight line with the fractured bone. Also make sure that the prescribed amount of weight hangs freely and that the rope is intact and centered over the pulley track. Remember that you never should lift or remove the weights. Releasing the traction could result in pain, muscle spasms, and injury to nerves and blood vessels in the involved extremity.

2 Perform neurovascular and nerve function assessments hourly during the first 24 hours after traction application, and at least every 4 hours thereafter as long as the assessment results are normal for that client (review the procedure, pp. 518–521).

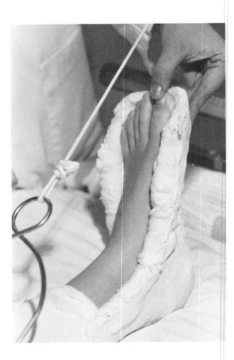

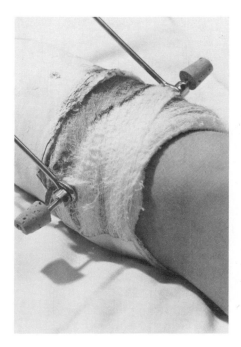

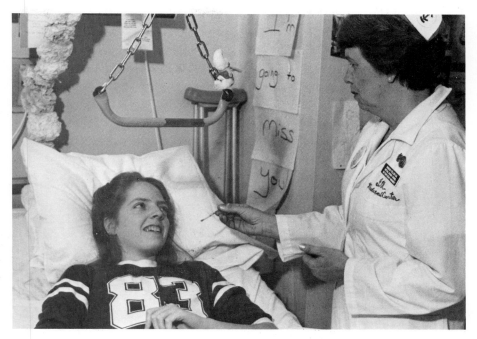

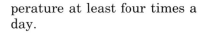

3 Inspect the pin or wire at least once every 4 hours to assess for migration. Assess the insertion site for indications of infection: erythema; edema; foul-smelling, purulent drainage; or gross bleeding. Report any of these conditions to the physician. Note that the corks are placed on either side of the pin to protect the client and staff members from injury (see procedure, p. 570, for appropriate pin care).

4 Because an elevated temperature is another indication of infection, monitor your client's temperature at least four times a day.

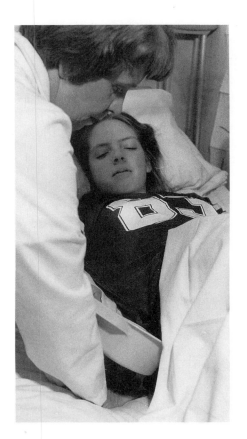

5 Your client in traction might require the use of a fracture bed pan. To position the fracture bed pan, instruct the client to flex the uninvolved knee and to press down with the foot to lift the buttocks. A trapeze also can be used to elevate the body. Slide the bed pan under the buttocks from the client's unaffected side, with the narrow end inserted first. Be sure to monitor both bowel and urinary function. Immobility can result in constipation, urinary tract infections, and retention. Encourage the intake of foods containing roughage, and ensure an intake of 2–3 L/day of fluid. If indicated, obtain an order for a stool softener.

(Continues)

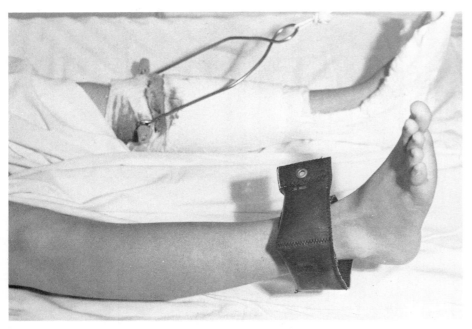

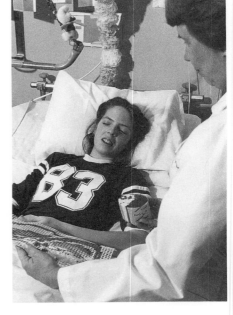

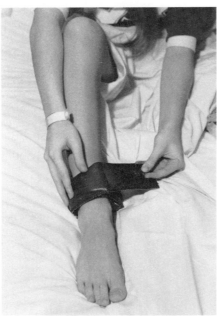

6   Encourage ROM on the uninvolved extremities and isometric (muscle-setting) exercises on both uninvolved and involved extremities. Teach the client how to apply weights (2–5 pounds) to the uninvolved ankle (bottom right). Lifting the leg up and down with the resistance of the added weight will enhance the development of the quadriceps muscle in preparation for weight bearing if crutches will be prescribed when the client becomes ambulatory.

7   Minimizing your client's boredom will require the occasional initiation of bedside projects, as well as provision of newspapers, books, magazines, handicrafts, and puzzles. Always take the time to provide empathy, reassurance, and emotional comfort for the immobilized client.

PERFORMING ROUTINE CARE AND ASSESSMENTS FOR CLIENTS IN HALO VESTS

Halo traction is frequently used for clients with scoliosis, cervical fractures and fusions, torticollus, and rheumatoid arthritis. A metal ring (the halo) surrounding the head attaches to the skull with four pins, each penetrating through the skin and into the skull approximately 30 mm (⅛ in.). The traction headpiece attaches to either a plaster or plastic vest to provide head and neck immobilization. The main advantage of halo traction is the early mobility it allows, which reduces the potential for circulatory, respiratory, and neurologic complications.

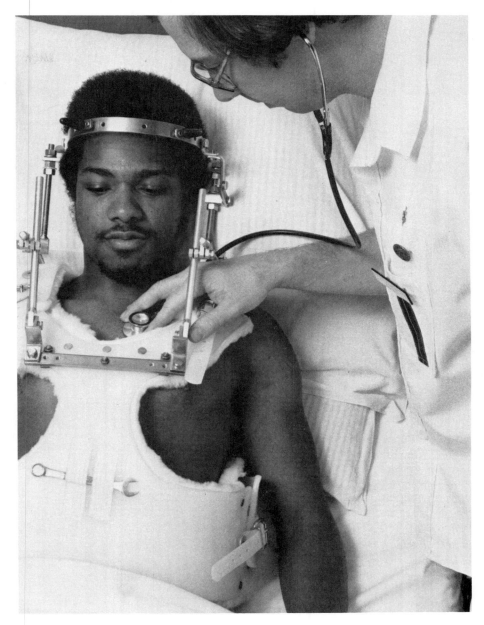

1 Assess the client's respiratory status (see Chapter 6) at least every 4 hours to ensure that the lungs are clear and that the vest does not press on the diaphragm, compromising chest expansion. Pulmonary emboli can occur in clients with spinal cord injuries, yet some clients with neurologic impairment due to a cervical cord injury are unable to feel the pain associated with this disorder.

Close assessment of these clients is especially critical. Keep an incentive spirometer at the bedside and instruct the client in its use. Note that an open-end wrench is taped to the client's vest. This wrench provides immediate release of the bolts to remove the vest in the event the client requires external cardiac compression.

(Continues)

2   In addition, a torque screwdriver should be kept available for the physician for tightening the pins to adjust the degree of tension on the anterior metal bars. The traction is correctly adjusted when there is neither flexion nor extension of the neck. The neck always should be kept in a neutral position.

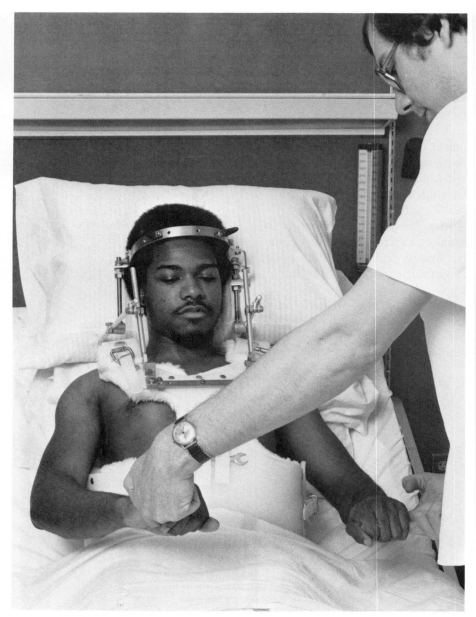

3   After the vest has been applied, assess the client's neurologic status hourly for a minimum of 24 hours until it is stable, and every 4 hours thereafter. Evaluate strength, sensation, and movement of the upper extremities; assess cranial nerve function to ensure that the pins in the skull are not impinging on the cranial nerve (see procedures for assessment in Chapter 10).

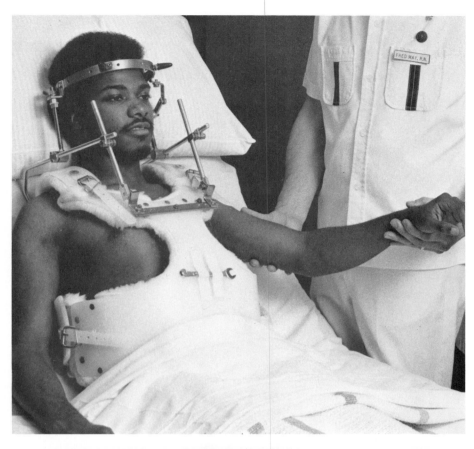

4 Instruct the client to perform active or assisted ROM exercises at least three times a day unless it is contraindicated by the client's disorder, for example a cervical fracture.

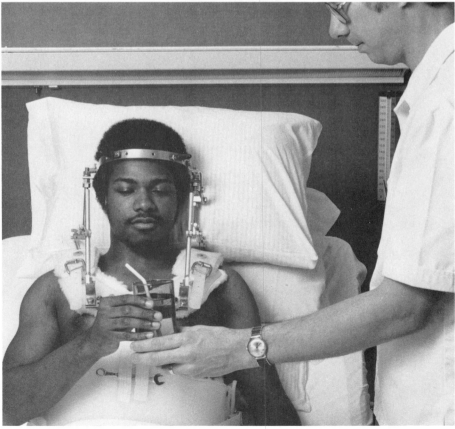

5 Keep careful intake and output records, and encourage fluids to maintain a fluid intake of 2–3 L/day. This will minimize the potential for renal calculi, urinary tract infections, and retention. Evaluate the urine for indications of infection: cloudiness, foul odor, and hematuria. Assess the client for the presence of chills and fever.

(Continues)

6   At least every 4 hours, inspect and massage the client's
skin, especially around the vest
edges. Skin irritation and pressure areas are a potential problem of wearing the vest. An air,
eggcrate, or water mattress or a
sheepskin pad should be used on
the bed to help protect the client's skin.

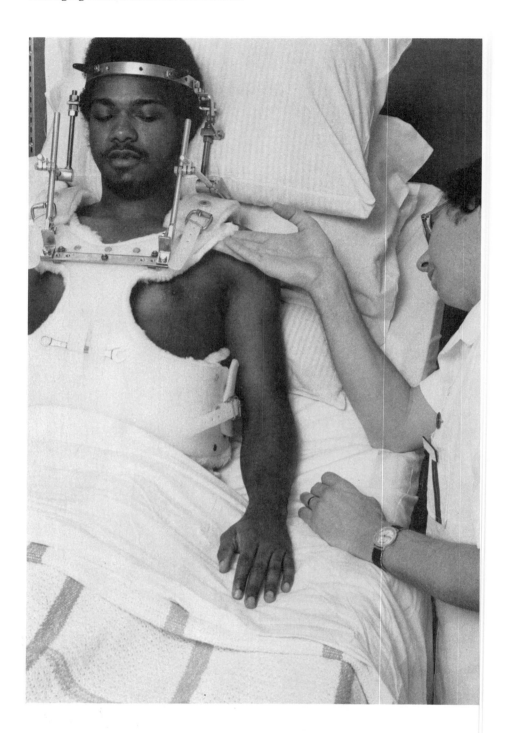

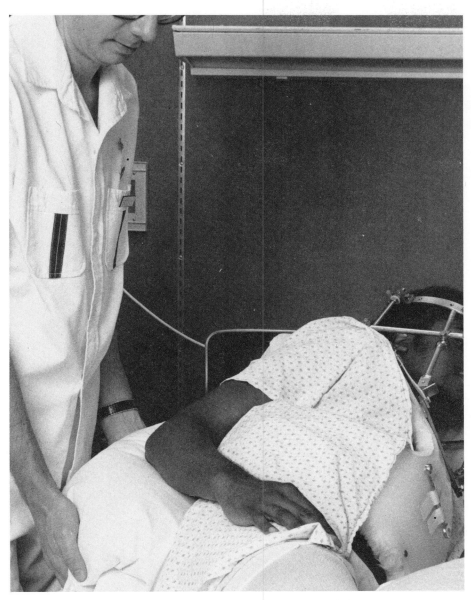

7 Assist the client with position changes every 2 hours to enhance circulation, prevent contractures, and maintain skin integrity. Follow the procedures in Chapter 2 for proper client positioning.

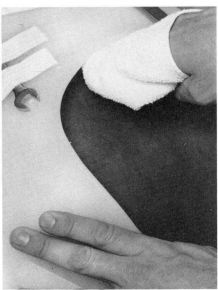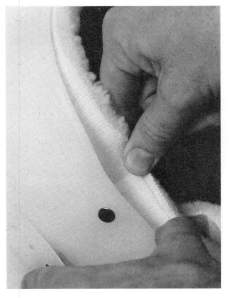

8 The sheepskin that lines the plastic vest should be removed at least weekly for washing and drying. Remove the sheepskin by detaching it from the Velcro™ strips that hold it in place (right). The client's skin should be bathed, rinsed, and dried daily. Specially trained personnel can open the vest at the sides for a more total cleansing and skin inspection.

(Continues)

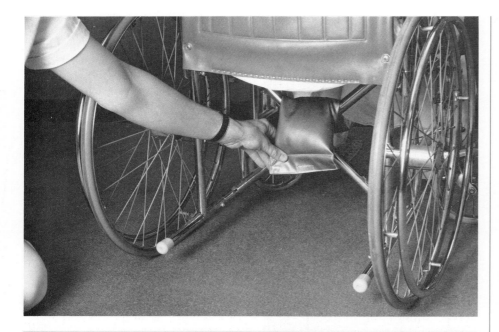

PROVIDING PIN CARE

The frequency and type of pin care will vary, according to physician preference. Many experts do agree, however, that iodine solutions should not be used because it is believed that they corrode the pins. If pin care has been ordered, the site is usually cleansed with hydrogen peroxide, leaving intact any superficial crust, followed by application of an antibiotic ointment. Both solutions are applied with sterile cotton-tipped applicators, following aseptic technique. In some instances, sterile 2×2 gauze sponges are split to the center and coated with antibiotic ointment, and then centered around the pins.

During pin care, assess for indications of infection: erythema, edema, tenderness, and/or purulent drainage. In addition, the position of each pin should be evaluated to ensure that it has not migrated. If a pin appears to be loose, the physician should be notified and the client instructed to remain immobile until the pin is secured.

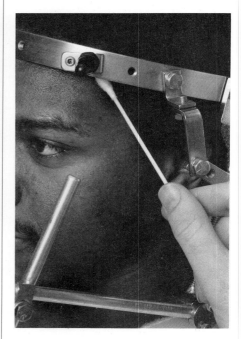

9 At least three times a day, assist the immobile client into a high-backed wheelchair that will support his shoulders. Place a 10-pound weight at the wheelchair crossbar to prevent the chair from tipping backward (top photo). Be sure to provide the client with a hand mirror or prism glasses because his visual field is greatly impaired by his head and neck immobility.

Providing Special Care for Clients with Musculoskeletal Disorders

MAKING A TRACTION BED

If your client is in continuous rather than intermittent traction, it may be necessary for you to change the linen by making the bed from its head to its foot to avoid interfering with the client's alignment and traction apparatus. This procedure is contraindicated for clients in cervical traction for whom logrolling should be employed, instead.

1 Explain the procedure to the client and then raise the bed to an optimal working level. Loosen the linen at the top of the bed.

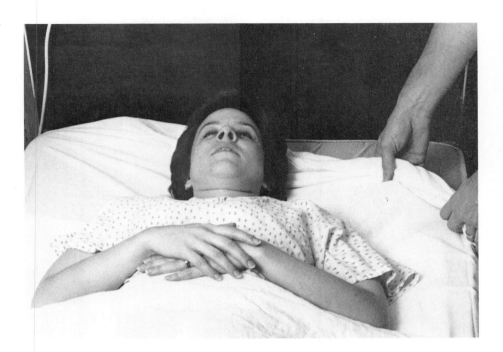

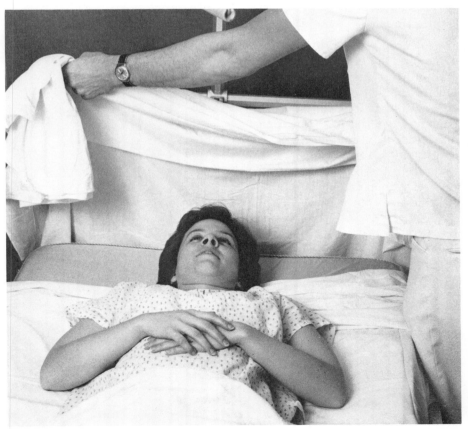

2 Fan-fold and place the fresh linen along the top of the bed.

(Continues)

3   Instruct the client to raise her upper body on the trapeze as you begin to remove the used bottom linen. Then, ease the used linen past the client's buttocks.

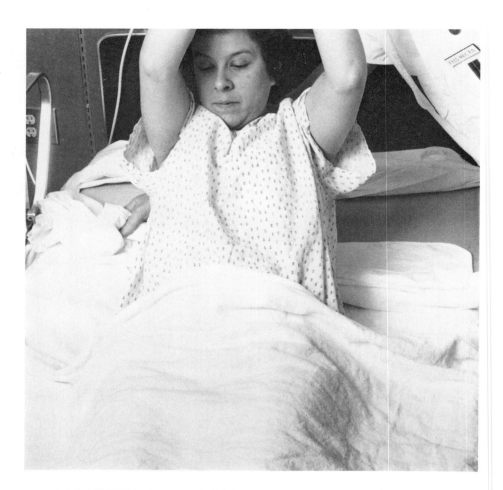

4   Secure the fresh linen to the corners at the head of the bed and pull the linen from the top toward the foot of the bed as the client lifts her upper body on the trapeze. Ease the fresh linen past her buttocks. Complete the bed making after removing the used linen from the bed. Make sure the fresh linen is taut and wrinkle-free.

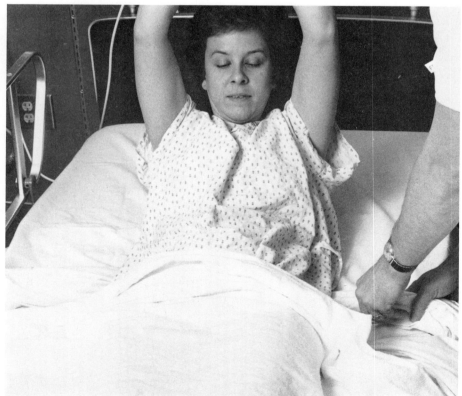

MAINTAINING A PORTABLE WOUND-DRAINAGE SYSTEM

Assessing and Planning

1 If your client has a postsurgical indwelling drain that connects to a portable vacuum container, you will need to inspect the tubing and container for patency; empty the container every shift, or as necessary; and ensure constant suction. The vacuum container should be attached to the bed linen to keep it off the floor.

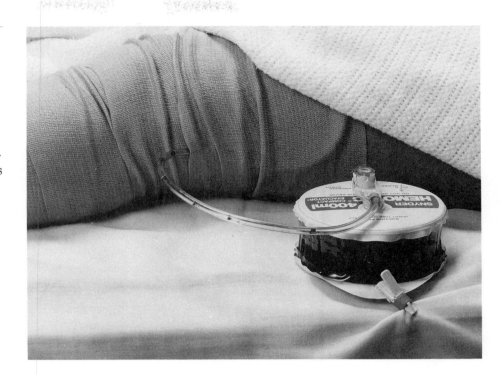

Implementing

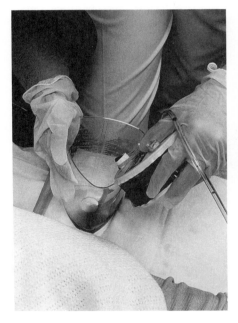

2 To empty the vacuum container, obtain the client's measuring container and place a bedsaver pad under your working area to protect the bed linen. Wash your hands, apply gloves, and aseptically pull the drain plug to open the container. Pour the contents into the container without touching the drain port or spout with your hands or the measuring container.

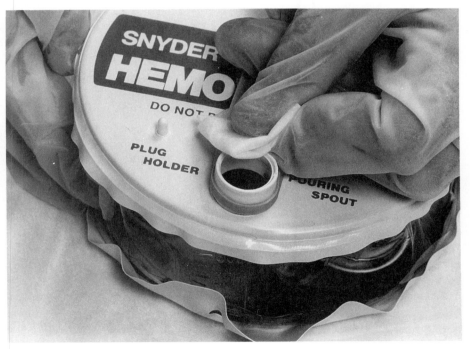

3 When the vacuum container has been emptied, wipe the drain port and plug with an antiseptic wipe.

(Continues)

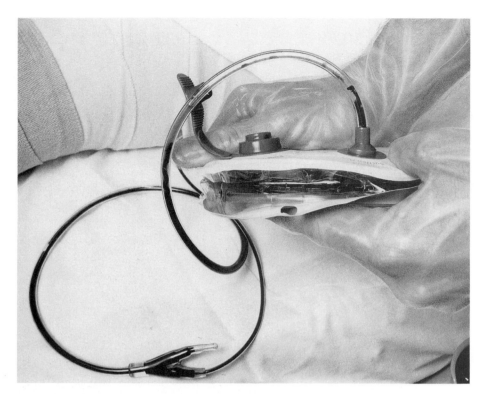

4   Compress the container (as shown), and aseptically reinsert the drain plug as you hold the container compressed. This will reestablish the low-pressure suction. Measure and document the drainage, noting its color, odor, amount, and consistency. Discard the drainage according to agency policy, remove the gloves, and wash your hands again.

Evaluating

5   Continue to monitor the container and tubing for proper drainage and patency, and ensure that suction is maintained. At least every 4 hours, or as necessary, apply gloves, remove the drainage plug, compress the container, and reinsert the plug to reestablish suction.

APPLYING A HYDROCULATOR PACK (MOIST HEAT) TO ARTHRITIC JOINTS

A hydroculator pack can be applied to your client's arthritic joints to relieve discomfort and reduce joint stiffness and muscle spasms. Moist heat provides greater relief than dry heat does at the same temperature because it penetrates more deeply and holds the temperature for a longer period of time. Moist heat packs are usually contraindicated for clients with impaired circulation and sensation, skin infections, or complications from previous heat applications, for example blisters or rashes.

Assessing and Planning

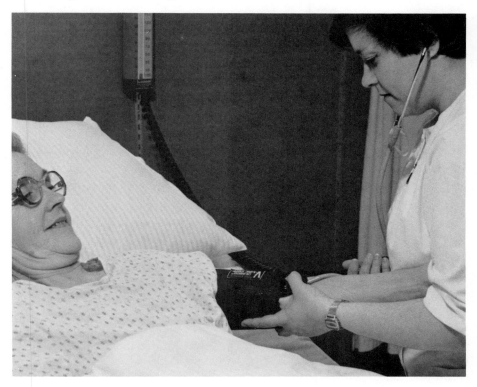

1 Take the client's baseline vital signs. This is especially important with the older adult for whom heat may aggravate an already impaired cardiac condition.

Inspect the application site for indications of complications from previous heat applications, and explain the procedure to the client.

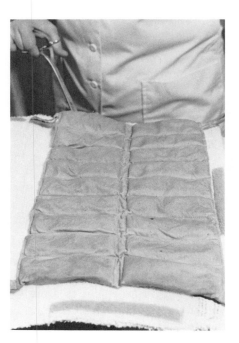

2 Heat the pack in the steam machine or heating device used by your agency. In many agencies, the temperature is controlled so that it never exceeds 48.9° C. Place the heated pack on its terrycloth cover or on a double thickness of terrycloth towels if the cover is unavailable.

(Continues)

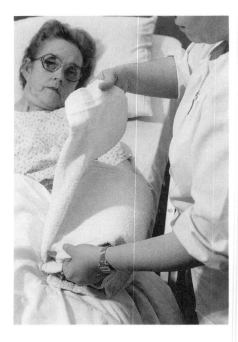

3   Wrap the pack in the double thickness of terrycloth towels or terrycloth hydroculator pack cover.

Implementing

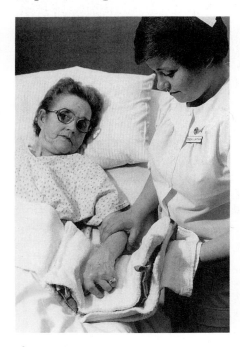

4   Place the covered pack under the client's involved area, and position a folded terrycloth towel under the pack (as shown). The extra towel will protect the bed linen from moisture and help to secure the hydroculator pack in position once it is wrapped around the joints (above). Keep the call light within the client's reach, and instruct her to alert you if the temperature becomes too uncomfortable.

Evaluating

5   Unless the client alerts you sooner, assess the client and evaluate the temperature of the pack after approximately 10 minutes. Assess the client for potential complications such as diaphoresis, hypotension, and tachycardia. Unwrap the pack and inspect the skin for excess erythema, and then rewrap the pack. Question the client about her comfort level. When the treatment time has elapsed (usually after a total of 20 minutes), remove the pack, evaluate the client's skin, and obtain posttreatment vital signs. Document the procedure and the client's response.

MANAGING THE CLIENT WITH A BLOOD REINFUSION SYSTEM

Assessing and Planning

1 A reinfusion (blood conservation) system, such as the Stryker, is a closed operation that collects, filters, and enables reinfusion of the client's whole blood. Clients who may benefit from this procedure include those with hip and knee replacements, as well as other populations with large draining incisions. The duration of the collection time and reinfusion is established by the physician and system manufacturer's protocol. Because infection is a potential contraindication to reinfusion, monitor the client for the presence of fever; white blood cell count $\geq 11,000 \, \mu l$; and signs of local infection, including warmth, erythema, tenderness, and purulent drainage at the wound site.

Monitor the amount of drainage in the reservoir. The shed blood should be reinfused within a 6-hour period of initiating the collection or when drainage accumulates to approximately 400 ml, whichever comes first (Standards Committee, American Association of Blood Banks, 1989). If the client does not already have an IV infusion of normal saline, establish one at this time (see section "Administering Blood and Blood Components," p. 149, for details) with 500 ml normal saline, if it is prescribed. Obtain a standard blood administration set with a 40-micron microaggregate filter and tubing with a three-way stopcock.

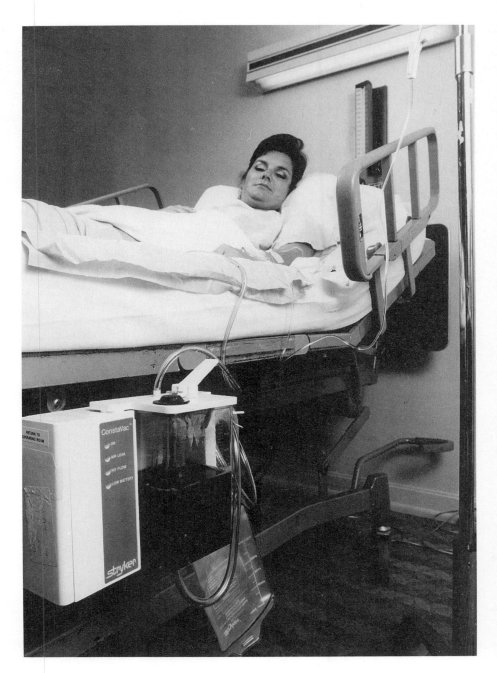

(Continues)

Implementing

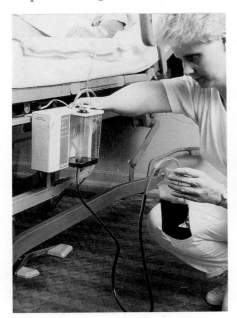

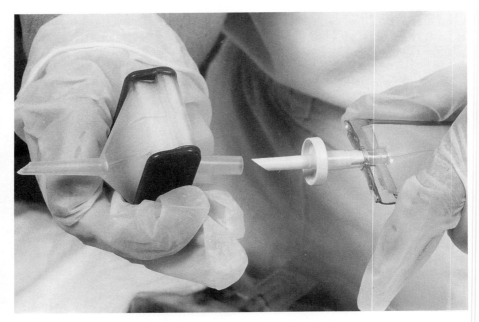

2 When it is time to reinfuse the blood, uncoil the blood bag tubing (this will facilitate blood flow), and press the valve lever on top of the reservoir to transfer the blood from the reservoir to the blood bag. If using the Stryker system, some blood will remain at the bottom of the reservoir. Some manufacturers recommend that this fluid not be reinfused because it may contain fats that have risen to the top of the collected fluid. When the blood has been transferred to the blood bag, clamp off the blood bag tubing as close to the blood bag as possible.

3 Put on clean gloves to prevent contact with the client's blood. Attach the 40-micron filter to the spiked end of the standard blood infusion tubing.

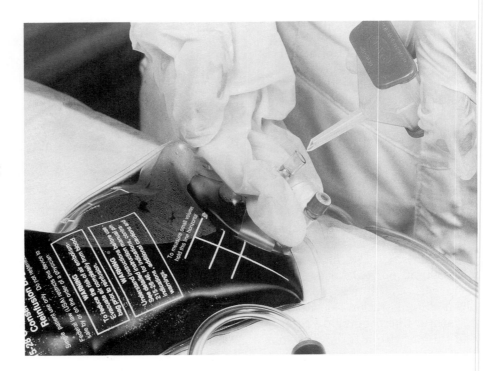

4 Next, remove the protective cover from the port of entry into the blood bag and insert the blood filter into the blood bag (as shown).

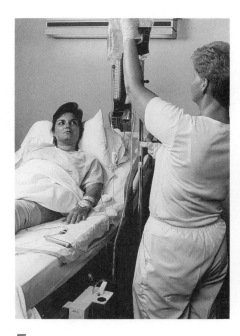

5 Hang the blood bag as shown and prime the tubing to ensure that all air has been expelled from the tubing.

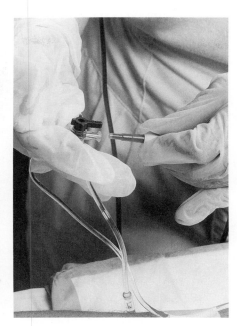

6 Using a twisting motion, attach the distal end of the primed blood infusion set to the three-way stopcock that is attached to the saline infusion.

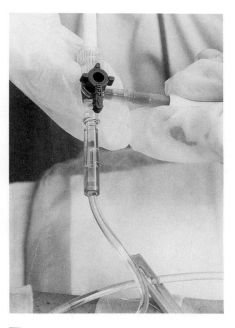

7 Turn the stopcock so that it is off to the saline and open to the blood.

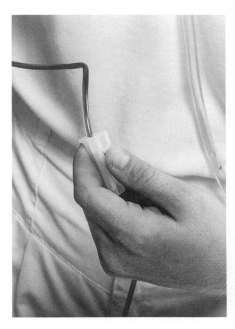

8 Unclamp the blood and let it run in over a 1- to 2-hour period or as prescribed.

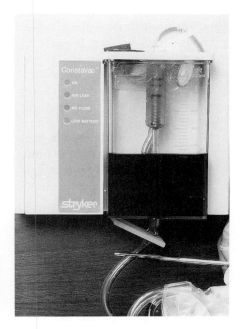

Evaluating

9 Monitor the client at frequent intervals to ensure that the blood is infusing appropriately. When the blood has infused into the client, clamp the tubing between the reinfusion system and the blood bag. If this is the last infusion, you may snip off the blood bag tubing (as shown) if desired. Wipe the exposed tubing with a dry gauze pad to prevent blood from dripping onto the floor, or cap the tubing with a cap supplied by the manufacturer.

MONITORING THE CLIENT UNDERGOING CONTINUOUS PASSIVE MOTION (CPM)

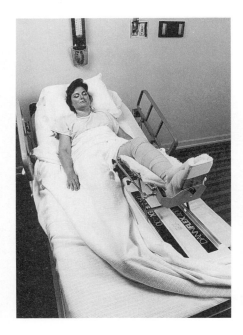
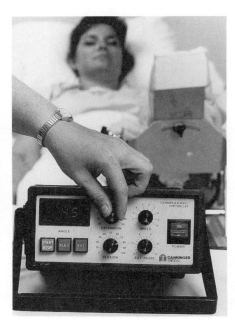

Clients with the following disorders or surgeries may benefit from CPM: total knee or hip replacement, synovectomy, tibial plateau fracture, open menisectomy, hip fracture, or femoral shaft fracture fixation. Benefits of CPM include more flexion, which results in greater joint range of motion, and less postoperative pain and joint swelling.

The following are nursing considerations when managing the client in knee CPM:

- Ensure that the machine is anchored securely to the bedframe.
- Place a pillowcase over the sheepskin (under the client's lower leg) to keep it clean.
- Adjust the machine so that it is in a flat (0-degree) position when putting the client on and taking the client off the machine.
- Set the foot pedal in a neutral position and make sure it touches the bottom of the client's foot lightly.

- Position the client's knee over the point at which the machine bends.
- Stay with the client through one complete cycle when first putting her on the machine to ensure that she can tolerate the movement.
- Keep the hand control for the machine within the client's reach, and teach her how to turn the machine on and off.
- For optimal results, try to keep the machine in continuous motion for at least 20 hours/day.
- Remove ace bandages or elastic stockings every 8 hours (or as policy permits) for skin care and assessment of tissue and skin integrity.
- The goal of therapy is 90-degree knee flexion prior to the client's hospital discharge.

The physician prescribes the amount of flexion, usually 45 degrees. Adjust as prescribed.

TRANSFERRING THE CLIENT WITH A TOTAL HIP REPLACEMENT

When hip adduction and hip flexion are contraindicated, for example for a client with a total hip replacement, follow these steps to transfer the client from the bed to the wheelchair. Be sure that the client has enough upper body strength and mobility in the uninvolved leg to assist you with this procedure. Explain the procedure to the client and ensure that he understands each step and his role during the transfer.

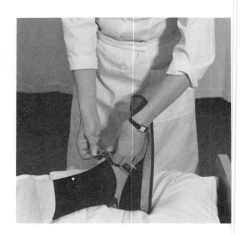

1   Put a sturdy rubber-soled shoe on the client's uninvolved foot so that he can safely pivot during the transfer.

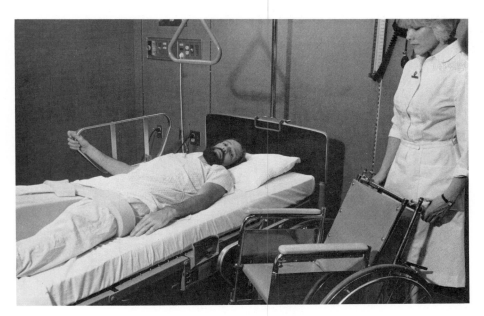

2 Position a wheelchair at a 45-degree angle to the head of the bed on the side opposite the client's involved hip. Lock both the wheelchair and the bed to keep them stable during the move. Either swing away or remove the foot rests so that they will not obstruct the move. If the wheelchair has an adjustable backrest, tilt it back to minimize the hip flexion for the client once he sits in the chair. However, if the chairback does not recline, place a pillow in the seat to help keep the client's hip in as much extension as possible.

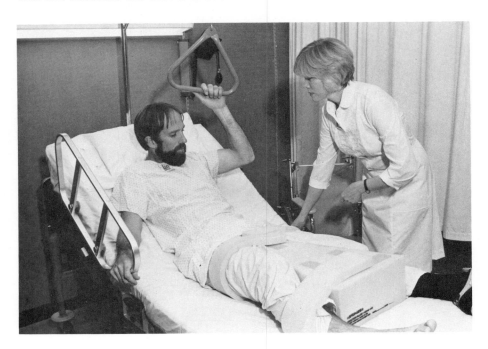

3 Raise the head of the bed to a level the client can tolerate, but no greater than 45 degrees. Remember to keep the client's hips in minimal flexion to prevent dislocation of the involved hip. Although it is not possible to keep the client's hips in full extension during this procedure, by keeping them constantly abducted with an abduction pillow, the potential for dislocation is minimized. ***Note:*** *Whereas many surgeons request that the client be moved with the abduction pillow in place, others request that it be removed for the transfer and replaced once the client is sitting in the chair. Follow the surgeon's preference accordingly.*

(Continues)

4 To begin the transfer, grasp both the client's involved leg and the abduction pillow, and ask the client to lift his upper body into a slight sitting position as you do. Remember to bend your knees, keep your back straight, and separate your feet to provide a wide base of support.

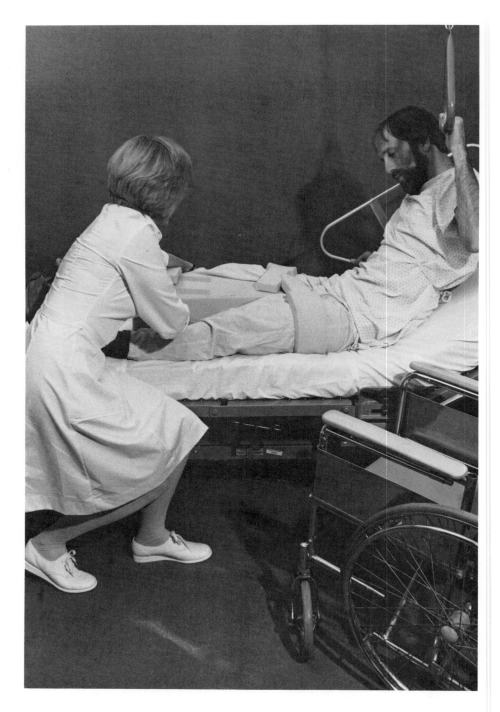

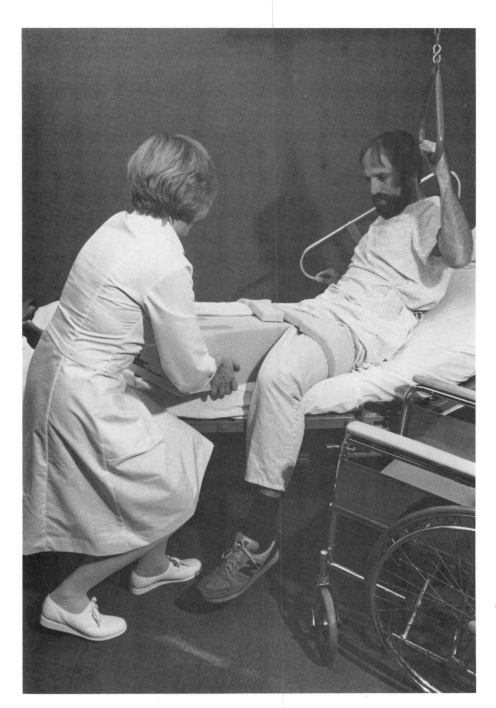

5 Pivot onto your forward foot as you move the client's involved leg and abduction pillow to the side of the bed.

(Continues)

6 Shift your weight onto your back foot as you move the pillow and leg off the bed. At the same time, instruct the client to slide his buttocks toward the edge of the bed.

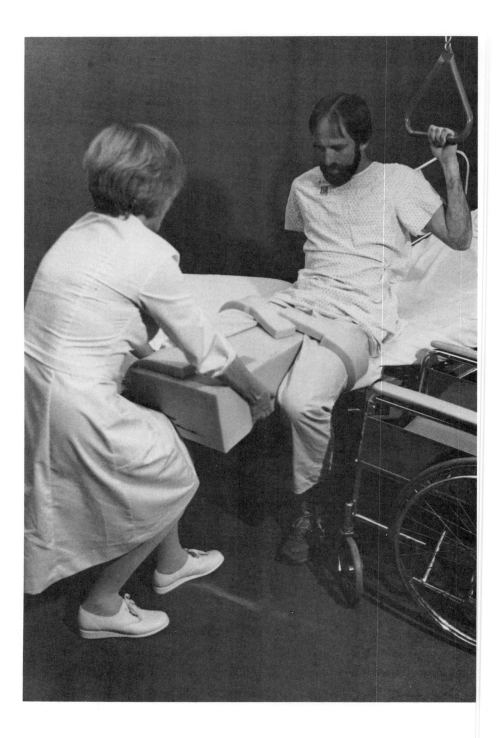

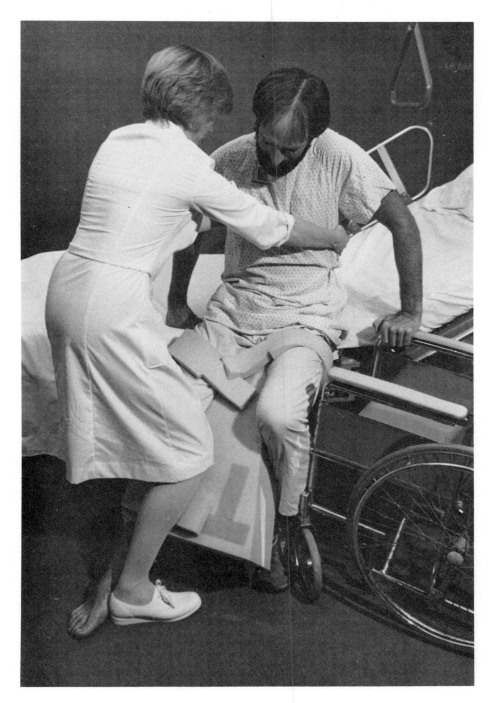

7 Once both of the client's legs are off the bed, instruct him to grasp the wheelchair armrest that is closer to him, and to stand and bear weight on his uninvolved leg unless the physician has allowed weight bearing on the involved extremity also. Position your hands under his axillae as you guide him into a standing position. *Note: If the client is more dependent, place a transfer belt around his waist and grasp him at waist level by holding onto the belt.*

(Continues)

8 Once the client is standing, instruct him to grasp the opposite armrest and to pivot on his uninvolved foot until the backs of his legs are positioned against the seat of the wheelchair.

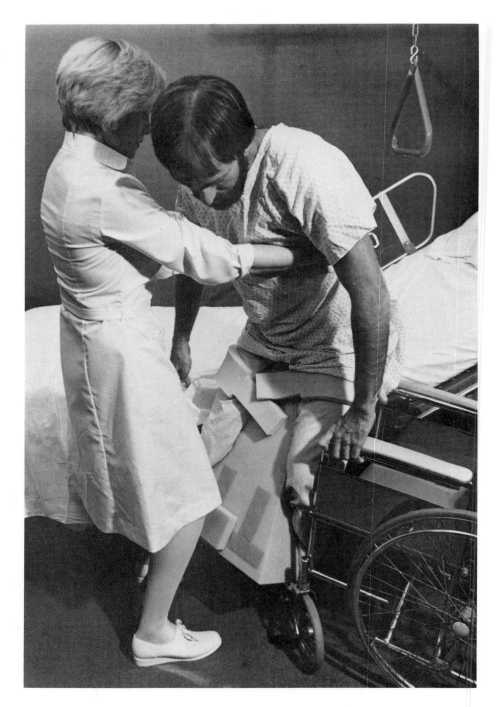

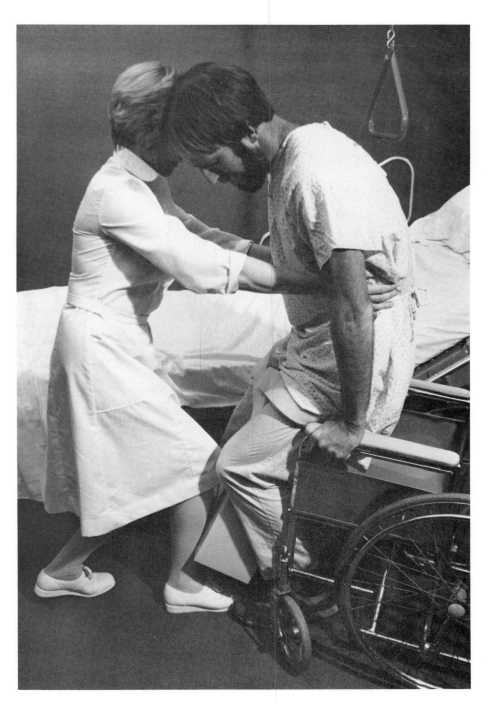

9   When the client attains the position described on the facing page, instruct him to grasp both armrests and prepare to sit, avoiding bending over at the waist as he begins his descent. Although the abduction pillow will prevent you from keeping your body close to the client's, you should position your forward knee against the client's uninvolved knee to help keep him stabilized.

(Continues)

10 As the client lowers his body into the wheelchair, bend your knees and lower your body as you continue to guide him.

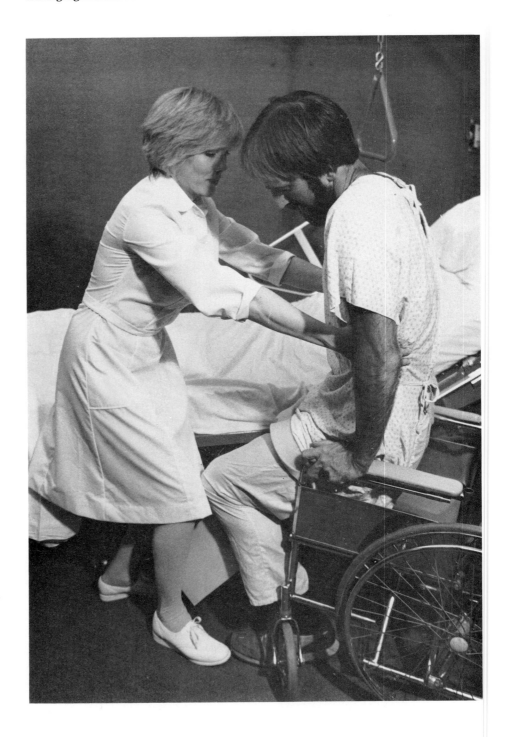

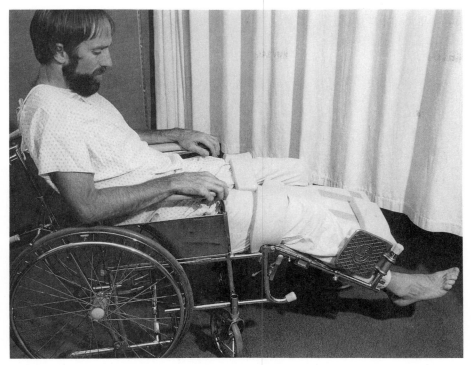

11 Support the client's involved leg with his knee in slight flexion by repositioning the legrest. Ensure that his hips are minimally flexed and that they remain in abduction. To return the client to the bed, reverse these steps.

References

Bowers AC, Thompson JM: *Clinical Manual of Health Assessment,* 3d ed. St. Louis: Mosby, 1988.

Dunn B: Components of a musculoskeletal examination. *Orthop Nurs* 1982; 1:33–36.

Gamron RB: Taking the pressure out of compartment syndrome. *Am J Nurs* 1988; 88(8):1076–1080.

Hensinger RN, MacEwen GD: Evaluation of the Cotrel dynamic spine traction in the treatment of scoliosis. *Orthop Rev* 1974; 111:27–34.

Horne M, Swearingen PL: *Pocket Guide to Fluids and Electrolytes.* St. Louis: Mosby, 1989.

Jobes R: Cranial nerve assessment with halo traction. *Orthop Nurs* 1982; 1:11–15.

Kozier B, Erb G: *Techniques in Clinical Nursing,* 3d ed. Redwood City, CA: Addison-Wesley, 1989.

Linley JF: Screening children for common orthopaedic problems. *Am J Nurs* 1987; 87(10):1312–1316.

Morris L et al: Nursing the patient in traction. *RN* (Jan) 1988; 26–31.

Morris L et al: Special care for skeletal traction. *RN* (Feb) 1988; 24–29.

Ross D: Compartment syndrome. In: *Manual of Critical Care: Applying Nursing Diagnoses to Adult Critical Illness,* 2d ed. Swearingen PL. St. Louis: Mosby, 1991.

Ross D: Musculoskeletal disorders. In: *Manual of Nursing Therapeutics: Applying Nursing Diagnoses to Medical Disorders,* 2d ed. Swearingen PL. St. Louis: Mosby, 1990.

Spence A, Mason E: *Human Anatomy and Physiology,* 3d ed. Redwood City, CA: Benjamin/Cummings, 1987.

Standards Committee, American Association for Blood Banks and Transfusion Services, 13th ed. Arlington, VA: American Association of Blood Banks, 1989.

Thompson JM et al: *Mosby's Manual of Clinical Nursing,* 2d ed. St. Louis: Mosby, 1989.

Chapter 10

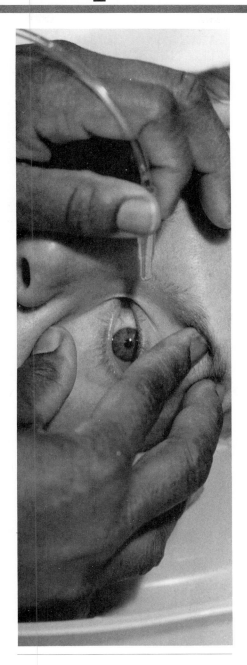

Managing
Neurosensory
Procedures

CHAPTER OUTLINE

ASSESSING THE NEUROLOGIC SYSTEM

The Neurologic System

Nursing Assessment Guideline

Monitoring the Status of a Neurologically Impaired Client

Performing a Neurologic Check
Testing Cerebellar and Motor Function
Assessing Sensory Function Using a Dermatome Chart
Evaluating Deep Tendon Reflexes

Assessing Cranial Drainage for the Presence of Cerebrospinal Fluid

CARING FOR CLIENTS WITH NEUROLOGIC DISORDERS

Assisting the Client with a Transcutaneous Electrical Nerve Stimulator Device

Applying Intermittent Pneumatic Compression (Antiembolic) Cuffs

Providing Care During a Seizure

Using a Hyperthermia or Hypothermia System

Assessing Clients with Subarachnoid Drains

Nursing Guidelines for the Care of Clients on Special Beds and Frames

Roto Rest Kinetic Treatment Table
Clinitron Air Fluidized Therapy
Therapulse Pulsating Air Suspension Therapy

CARING FOR CLIENTS WITH DISORDERS OF THE SENSORY SYSTEM

Assessing Auditory Function

Performing the Watch Test
Performing the Weber and Rinne Tests

Irrigating the External Auditory Canal

Irrigating the Eye

Using Op-Site on Decubitus Ulcers

Assessing the Neurologic System

THE NEUROLOGIC SYSTEM

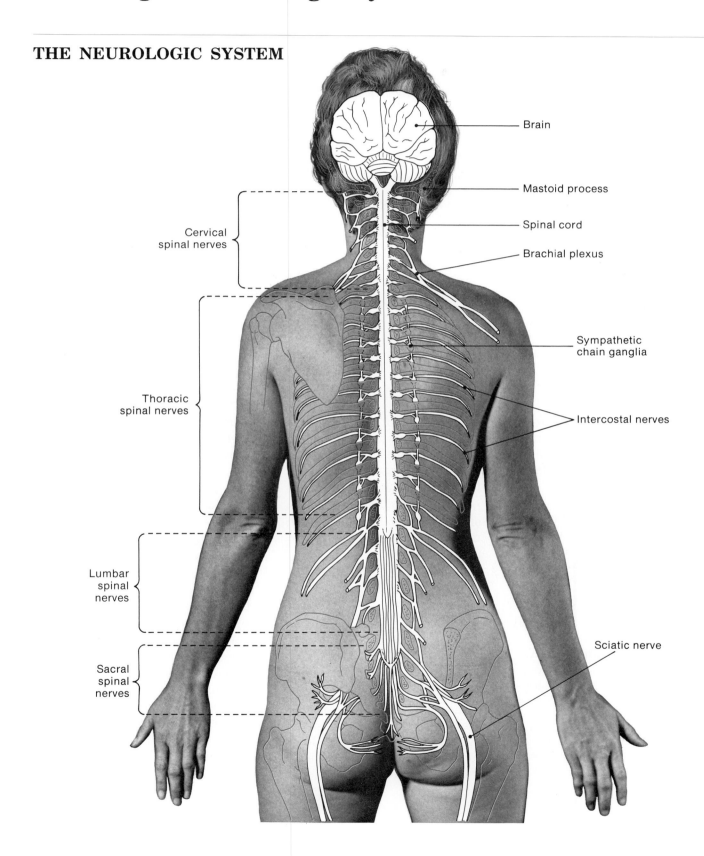

Cervical spinal nerves

Thoracic spinal nerves

Lumbar spinal nerves

Sacral spinal nerves

Brain

Mastoid process

Spinal cord

Brachial plexus

Sympathetic chain ganglia

Intercostal nerves

Sciatic nerve

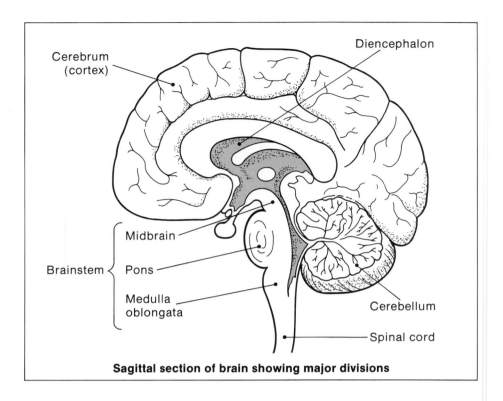

Sagittal section of brain showing major divisions

Nursing Assessment Guideline

To assess your client's neurologic system, you need to interview the client, family members, or significant others for subjective data; take vital signs; and perform a basic assessment of neurologic function. A comprehensive nursing care plan includes a complete evaluation for the following subjective data:

Personal factors: for example, age, marital status, educational level, environmental/employment description, amounts of alcoholic beverages consumed, exercise patterns, leisure activities, stress level

History or family history of: diabetes mellitus, hypertension, seizures, neurologic disorders, cardiac disease

History of: fainting, weakness, paralysis, tics, tremors, coordination impairment, nervousness, dizziness, neurologic trauma or surgery

Integrity of integration: periods of confusion or loss of memory; impairment of emotions, judgment, speech

Activities of daily living: independent, requires assistance, dependent

Use of assistive devices: for example, cane, walker, wheelchair

Medications: for example, antispasmodics, antiepilepsy drugs, sedatives, depressants, antidepressants, anti-inflammatory agents, antiemetics, over-the-counter drugs; history of medication allergies

Balance problems: frequency, precipitating factors, position, time of day, relation to activity

Pain: location, onset, duration, character, radiation, relieved/intensified by, paresthesias, anesthesia (loss of sensation)

Headaches: history, frequency, onset, duration, character, precipitating factors, location, presence of photophobia, relieved/intensified by

Seizures: frequency, presence of aura or other prodomal symptoms, duration, clinical presentation during and after, necessity for oxygen or medication during or after (for example, with status epilepticus)

MONITORING THE STATUS OF A NEUROLOGICALLY IMPAIRED CLIENT

PERFORMING A NEUROLOGIC CHECK

A neurologic check is a part of an ongoing assessment of the neurologically impaired client. It should be performed at specific intervals to evaluate the client's level of consciousness, pupillary reflexes, and motor and sensory function. A neurologic check is not as extensive as a complete neurologic examination, and we suggest that you consult an assessment text if you desire greater detail. The components of a neurologic check may vary, depending on agency protocol or the client's condition, so be sure to follow the guidelines established by your agency or those prescribed by the physician.

Once a complete baseline check has been performed, the neurologic check should then be performed every 1–2 hours, or as frequently as every 15 minutes for clients who are unstable. Document each assessment, comparing the results to previous checks, and notify the physician of changes in the client's condition. Even subtle deterioration is significant, and it can alert you to the need for immediate medical intervention.

Familiarize yourself with the following terms and definitions for levels of consciousness. Terminology may vary from agency to agency.

Alert/Awake: responds promptly and appropriately to verbal and tactile stimuli

Lethargic: drowsy, responds slowly yet appropriately

Obtunded: somnolent, may be disoriented when awake

Stuporous: arouses with difficulty, may be combative, might respond to simple commands

Semicomatose: responds to painful stimuli only

Comatose: unresponsive even to painful stimuli, hypotonic

1 Evaluate your client's level of consciousness using the Glasgow Coma Scale (see Table 10-1) or some other objective means for the rapid evaluation of consciousness and detection of changes and trends. Take vital signs and assess the client for a slowed or rapid pulse rate, a rising systolic blood pressure, and a widening pulse pressure, which can occur with increasing intracranial pressure. Count the respirations, noting the rate, depth, and rhythm. Be especially alert to Cheyne-Stokes respirations, which are distinguished by periods of hyperventilation followed by periods of apnea. This is one type of breathing pattern that can occur with a brain dysfunction. Biot's is another type of respiration pattern that can occur with neurologic impairment, such as increased intracranial pressure and meningitis. Biot's respirations are characterized by slow and deep or rapid and shallow breaths, followed by periods of apnea. For more information, see Table 10-2, "Assessing Respiratory Patterns." Because wide fluctuations in temperature can occur with the neurologically impaired client, monitor the client's temperature closely.

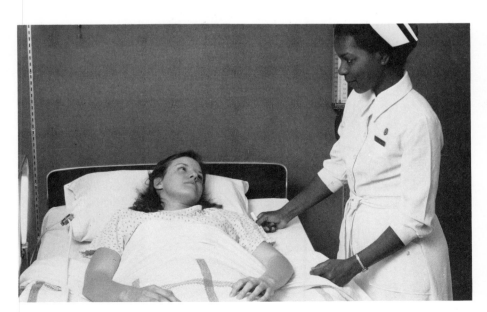

(Continues)

Table 10-1   Glasgow Coma Scale

Response	Rating	
Best eye-opening response (Record "C" if eyes closed due to swelling)	Spontaneously	4
	To speech	3
	To pain	2
	No response	1
Best motor response (Record best upper-limb response to painful stimuli)	Obeys verbal command	6
	Localizes pain	5
	Flexion—withdrawal	4
	Flexion—abnormal	3
	Extension—abnormal	2
	No response	1
Best verbal response (Record "E" if endotracheal tube is in place or "T" if tracheostomy tube is in place)	Conversation—oriented x3	5
	Conversation—confused	4
	Speech—inappropriate	3
	Sounds—incomprehensible	2
	No response	1
Total score:	15 = normal	
	13–15 = minor head injury	
	9–12 = moderate head injury	
	3–8 = severe head injury	
	≤7 = coma	
	3 = deep coma or brain death	

SOURCE: Swift CM: Neurologic disorders. In: *Manual of Nursing Therapeutics: Applying Nursing Diagnoses to Medical Disorders,* 2d ed. Swearingen PL. St. Louis: Mosby, 1990.

If your client does not awaken easily to your voice or touch, press on the nail beds, or if this is ineffective, *cautiously* apply painful stimuli. For example, exert pressure with your knuckles on the sternum or pinch the sternocleidomastoid muscle, being certain to avoid causing any harm to the client. Either stimulus should elicit a response. If the client is comatose, observe the posture after a painful stimulus has been applied. Posturing can be indicative of neurologic damage or disease. *Decerebrate* posturing (left photo), which can occur with upper brainstem injury, is the extension of the extremities after a stimulus. *Decorticate* posturing (right photo) is upper extremity flexion with lower extremity extension, and it can occur with an injury to the cortex.

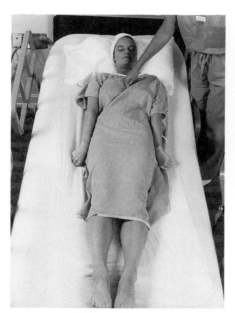

Decerebrate

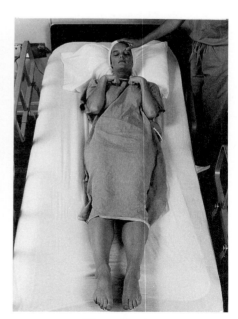

Decorticate

Table 10-2   Assessing Respiratory Patterns

Type	Waveform	Characteristics	Possible clinical condition
Eupnea		Normal rate and rhythm for adults and teenagers (12–20 breaths/min).	Normal pattern while awake.
Bradypnea		Decreased rate (<12 breaths/min); regular rhythm.	Normal sleep pattern; opiate or alcohol use; tumor; metabolic disorder.
Tachypnea		Rapid rate (>20 breaths/min); hypo- or hyperventilation.	Fever; restrictive respiratory disorders; pulmonary emboli.
Hyperpnea		Depth of respirations greater than normal.	Meeting increased metabolic demand (e.g., exercise).
Apnea		Cessation of breathing; may be intermittent.	Intermittent with central nervous system (CNS) disturbances or drug intoxication; obstructed airway; respiratory arrest if it persists.
Cheyne-Stokes		Alternating patterns of apnea (10–20 seconds) with periods of deep and rapid breathing.	Congestive heart failure (CHF), narcotic or hypnotic overdose, thyrotoxicosis, dissecting aneurysm, subarachnoid hemorrhage, increased intracranial pressure [ICP], and aortic valve disorders; may be normal in elderly during sleep.
Biot's		Irregular (can be slow and deep or rapid and shallow) followed by periods of apnea.	CNS abnormalities (e.g., meningitis, increased ICP).
Kussmaul's		Deep, rapid (>20 breaths/min), sighing, labored.	Renal failure, DKA, sepsis, shock.
Apneustic		Prolonged inspiration followed by short expirations.	Anoxia, meningitis.

SOURCE: Swearingen PL: *Manual of Critical Care: Applying Nursing Diagnoses to Adult Critical Illness,* 2d ed., St. Louis: Mosby, 1991.

Observe and test the client's orientation to time, person, and place; behavior; mood; knowledge; memory; and speech patterns. Are the responses prompt and appropriate to the questions asked, and does she respond correctly to simple commands? Note the facial expression and the ability to maintain eye contact with you, and assess whether her mood is appropriate to the situation. One way to test abstract reasoning is to ask the client to interpret a simple proverb. Long-term and short-term memory can be evaluated during a health history. Finally, note whether the client's speech patterns are appropriate for her educational, socioeconomic, and ethnic background. It is wise to avoid asking questions that can be responded to with "yes" or "no" answers.

As you evaluate mental status, inspect the client's eyes. They should open spontaneously, and both eyes should move together in unison. Evaluate the size and shape of the pupils and note whether they are bilaterally equal. Use a pupil gauge (at right) to assist you with documenting their size. Be alert to dilatation of one pupil, which occurs with head injuries resulting in epidural and subdural hematoma or uncal herniation. Dilatation of the pupil on the affected (injured) side is termed *ipsilateral dilatation.* Dilatation of the pupil on the opposite side is termed *contralateral dilatation.*

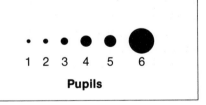

1 2 3 4 5 6
Pupils

(Continues)

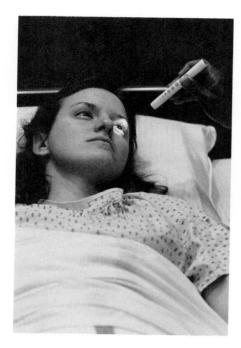

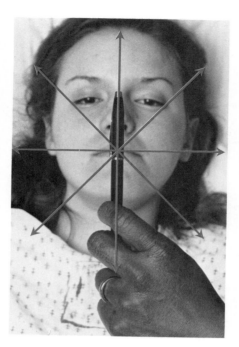

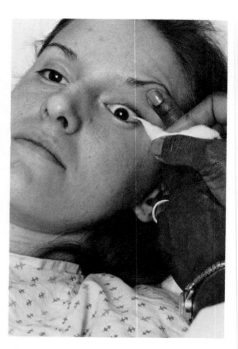

2 Check the pupillary response to light. Dim the lights and instruct the client to focus her gaze on an object in her direct line of vision. Move your penlight from outside the client's field of vision toward the pupil and shine the light into the left eye, observing for a pupillary reaction. Repeat the test on the right eye. Optimally, both pupils will react equally (and at the same rapid rate) and constrict to the same size. Evaluate the client's consensual light reflex by observing each pupil as the light is shined into the opposite eye. The right pupil should constrict as the light is shined into the left eye, and vice versa. If this response does not occur, the client might have brainstem dysfunction.

3 In some clinical situations, the physician may request that you test the client's extraocular eye movements during the neurologic check. To do this, position a pen 30–37.5 cm (12–15 in.) from the client's nose. Instruct the client to focus her eyes on the pen but to avoid moving her head. Slowly move the pen up and down, to each side, and then on the diagonals, as depicted by the arrows in the photo. If her third (oculomotor), fourth (trochlear), and sixth (abducens) cranial nerves are intact, she should be able to follow the movements of the pen with her eyes moving in unison. Describe any deficit, if present. Observe for involuntary, rapid movements of the eyeball (nystagmus), which can occur with neurologic impairments such as a cerebrovascular accident (CVA), cerebellar tumor, or multiple sclerosis. Nystagmus also can occur with phenytoin (Dilantin) toxicity.

4 To assess the alert client's blink (corneal) reflex, lightly brush your fingertips across the eyelashes. If this reflex is normal, the client will respond by blinking. If the client is not alert, gently touch the outer aspect of each cornea with a wisp of cotton (as shown). If the client neither blinks nor tears, the fifth cranial (trigeminal) nerve might be compromised. ***Note: If the client is a contact lens wearer, a diminished reflex might occur normally.***

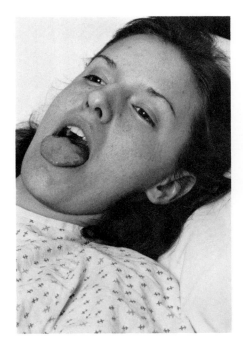

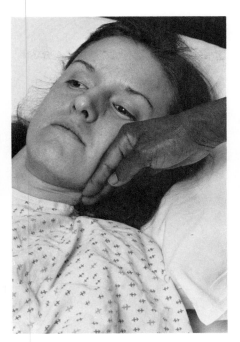

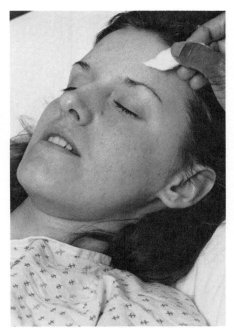

5 Evaluate the ability of the client to extend her tongue. Note whether the tongue quivers excessively or deviates to one side, and document accordingly. Your client's inability to perform this task, or excessive quivering or a weakness on one side of the tongue, suggests an impairment of the 12th cranial (hypoglossal) nerve, which can occur with a CVA.

6 The 11th cranial (spinal accessory) nerve mediates the sternocleidomastoid and upper trapezius muscles. To test its integrity, place your hand against the client's cheek and instruct her to turn her head toward your hand. Repeat the assessment on the opposite side. With a neurologic impairment, such as a CVA or a brain tumor, the client may have a unilateral deficit in strength.

7 Test the client's nerve sensory function next. Explain that she is to describe both the sensation and the location of the sensation while her eyes are closed. Be sure to show her the cotton wisp so that she does not become alarmed, expecting a painful process. Touch the client's forehead.

(Continues)

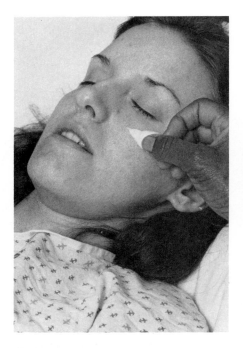

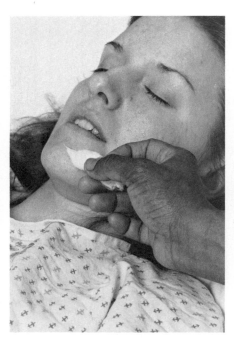

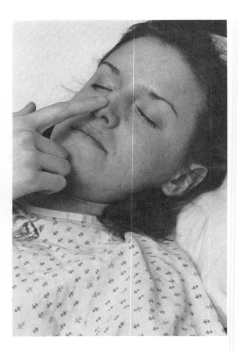

8   Touch her cheek and then her chin (center photo). Repeat the test on the opposite side of the client's face. She should describe a tickling sensation on all three areas of the face, and the sensations should be felt equally on both sides. If the response is abnormal, you can use a sterile pin to assess other areas of the body. However, a pin should be used judiciously, and never on the face. See the procedure, pp. 604–606, for assessing sensory function using a dermatome chart.

9   To test coordination (cerebellar function), instruct the client to close her eyes and to touch her nose alternately with the index fingers of her right hand and then her left hand, gradually increasing the speed of the movements. With a normal response, the movements will be smooth and accurate.

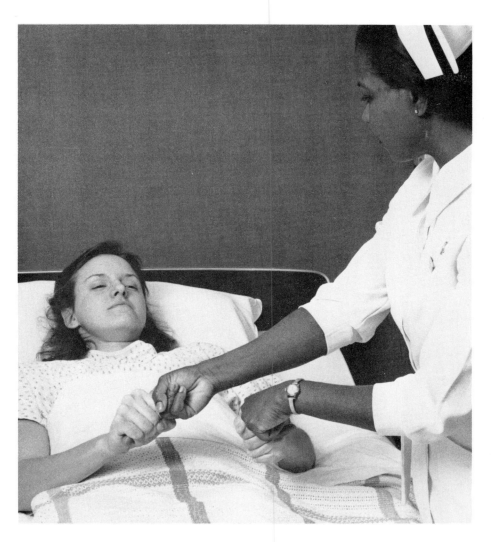

10 To evaluate the motor function of the client's upper extremities, ask her to grip and squeeze your index and middle fingers. Document the strength of each hand, noting whether the grip is bilaterally equal or unequal. Remember, however, the client's dominant hand normally may be stronger than the nondominant hand. *Note: To recall quickly which of the client's hands is stronger, cross your hands so that your right hand is grasped by the client's right hand and your left hand by the client's left hand. By recalling which of your hands was gripped more tightly, you can readily document which of your client's hands is stronger.* Other tests for upper extremity motor function are found in Chapter 9.

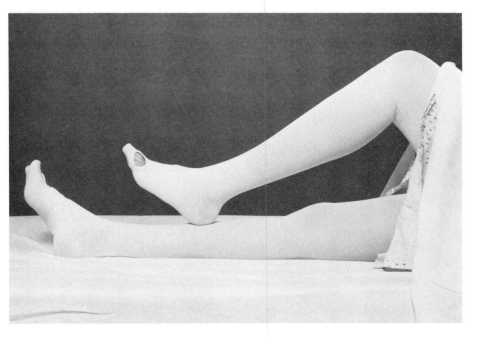

11 To evaluate the coordination (cerebellar function) of the lower extremities, instruct the client to slide her left heel down her right shin and to repeat the procedure on her left shin using her right heel. She should be able to do this smoothly and accurately. Document any deficit.

(Continues)

12 To evaluate the motor function of the lower extremities, push your hands against the soles of the client's feet. Instruct her to resist the pressure. Document the response, noting whether it is bilaterally equal or unequal. Note also whether the tone of the muscles is normal, hypotonic, or hypertonic. Other tests for lower extremity motor function are found in Chapter 9.

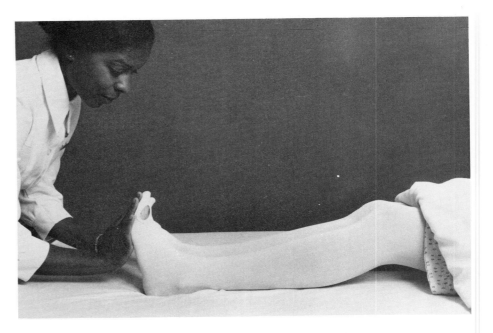

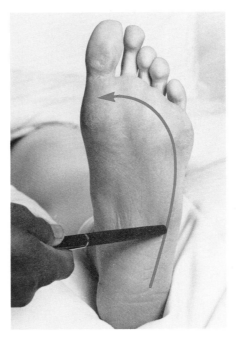

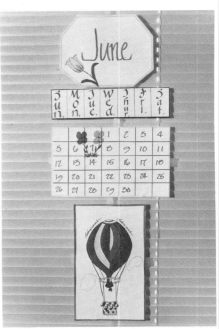

13 To test the client's plantar reflex, stroke along the lateral surface of the sole of each foot, as shown by the arrow on the photograph. If the toes curl downward, her response is normal. However, if the smaller toes fan apart and the large toe dorsiflexes toward the client's head, this is called the Babinski reflex. A positive Babinski is considered normal in the infant under 12–18 months, but it is a sign of motor nerve dysfunction in the adult.

14 To help orient the neurologically impaired client to the month and date, keep a brightly colored calendar within sight. Also, photographs of family and friends are important constants in the client's life and should be used in the hospital environment whenever possible.

TESTING CEREBELLAR AND MOTOR FUNCTION

If your client is ambulatory, you can perform gross motor and balance testing to evaluate cerebellar function. See steps 9–12 in the preceding procedure for motor and cerebellar testing for the client who is on bed rest.

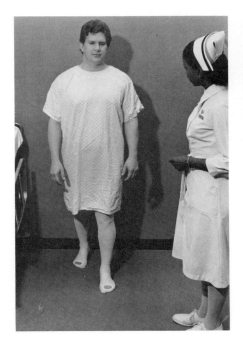

1 Instruct the client to walk across the room in a straight line. Observe the gait and posture. Normally, movements will be smooth and even, and the arms will swing slightly in opposition to the gait. Be alert to an unsteady gait, rigid or flaccid arm movements, and swaying, which can occur with a cerebellar dysfunction.

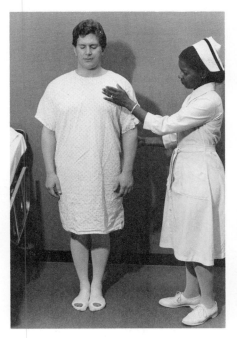

2 Evaluate the client for a positive Romberg's sign. Instruct him to stand still, with his arms at his sides and his feet together. He should first perform the test with his eyes shut, maintaining the stance for a full minute, and then repeat the test with his eyes open. Without touching him, guard him with your hands as you observe him in this position. Normally, you can expect to see slight swaying. Excessive swaying or an inability to maintain the stance without widening his foot base (whether the client's eyes are open or shut) occurs with a positive Romberg's sign. If he has trouble maintaining his balance only when his eyes are shut, he has a loss of position sense referred to as *sensory ataxia*. If he cannot maintain his balance whether or not his eyes are open or shut, the condition is referred to as *cerebellar ataxia*.

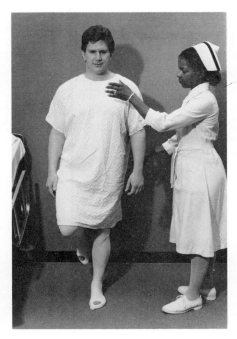

3 Instruct the client to stand first on one foot and then on the other. Guard him as you observe his stance. Normally, the stance can be maintained for at least 5 seconds. An inability to maintain the stance occurs when the equilibrium is disturbed. Document the results of the testing.

ASSESSING SENSORY FUNCTION USING A DERMATOME CHART

If you are assessing a neurologically impaired client who is alert and cooperative, you can evaluate sensory function by testing dermatome zones. Dermatome zones, which are divided into segmental skin bands as depicted by these overlays, compare anatomically to the innervation by a dorsal root to a cutaneous nerve. These nerves deliver the sensations of pain, temperature, touch, and vibration to the spinal cord and, ultimately, to the brain. The *spinothalmic* tract transmits the sensations of pain, temperature, and crude touch; the *dorsal column* tract transmits the perceptions of light touch and vibra-

tions. Even though there is usually a great deal of overlap in nerve distribution, a knowledge of the dermatome zones can help you locate the approximate level of the neurologic lesion or injury. For example, a diminished or heightened response at the client's thumb can alert you to a potential disorder at level C6 of the spinal cord.

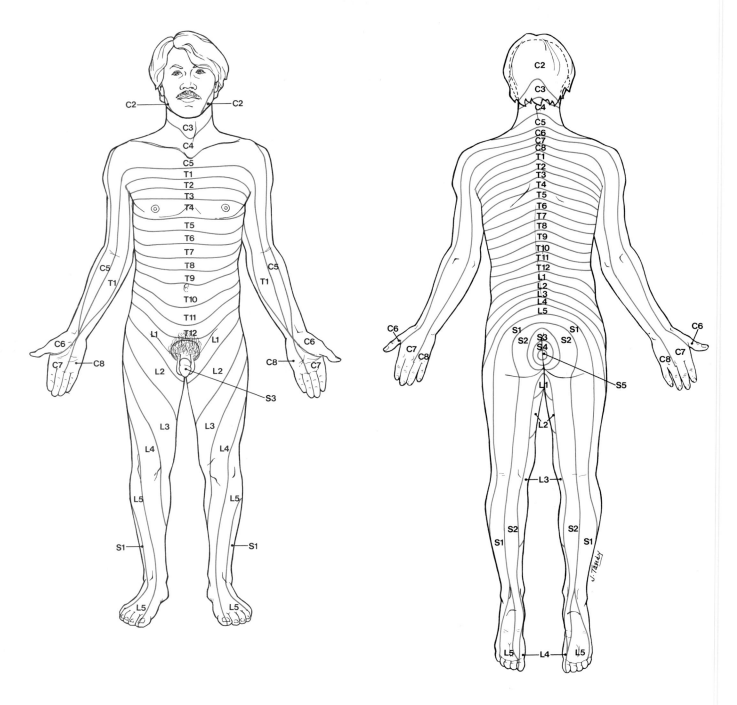

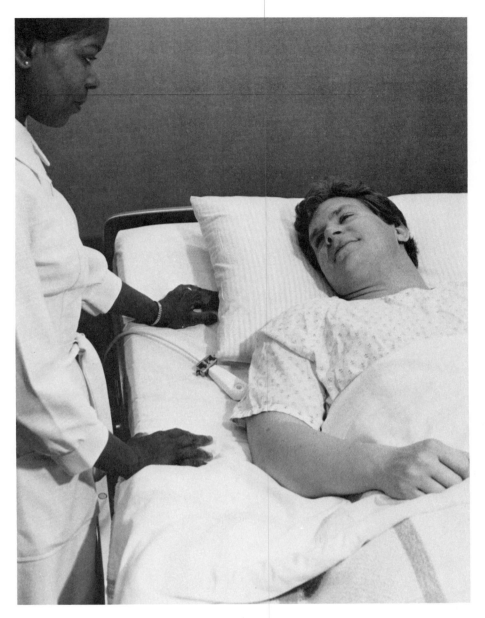

1 Explain the procedure to the client, and display the instruments that will be used during the assessment. A sterile safety pin and cotton wisp are commonly used to test sensation.

(Continues)

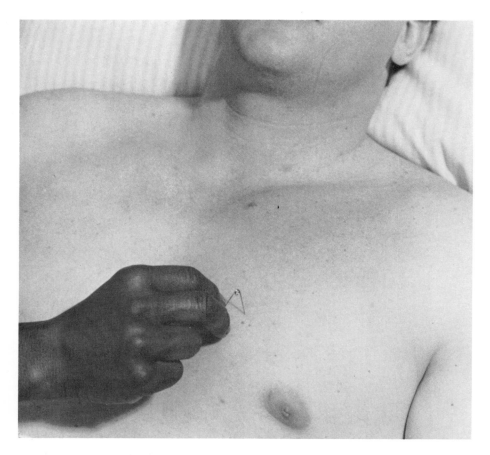

2 To test the spinothalmic tract, you can use both the pointed and blunt (bottom left) ends of a safety pin. Instruct the client to keep his eyes closed, and then stimulate anatomic locations at random, using both ends of the pin. Ask the client whether he feels a sharp or dull sensation. An abnormal response necessitates a more thorough assessment. Record the dermatome zone(s) in which the client has a diminished, heightened, or absent sensation. *Note: Because the spinothalmic tract transmits both pain and temperature, you can assess sensory function with warmth and coolness, for example by using test tubes filled with warm and cool water. The use of both testing modalities is rarely necessary, however.*

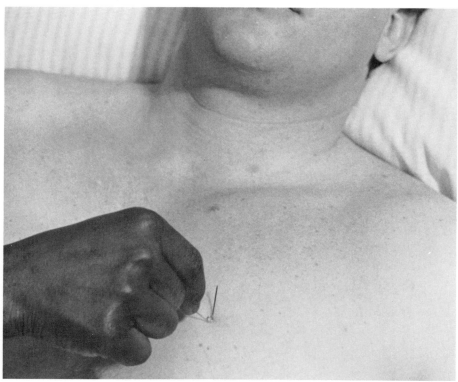

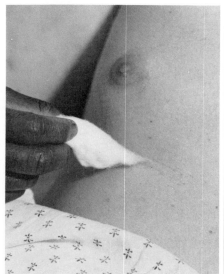

3 The dorsal column tract is assessed for light touch perception by brushing a cotton wisp against the client's skin. Again, test random areas and ask the client to alert you as soon as the sensation is felt. Record the dermatome zone(s) in which the client has diminished, heightened, or absent sensations.

EVALUATING DEEP TENDON REFLEXES

Deep tendon reflexes (DTRs) are present in all normal adults. An absence of or heightened reflexes denote a pathology associated with an interruption of an impulse at the associated anatomic site in the spinal cord. Evaluate your client's DTRs according to the following scale:

0 Nonreflexive
1 Hyporeflexive—diminished response, can occur normally in the older client
2 Normal
3 Brisk—not always associated with a pathology
4 Hyperreflexive

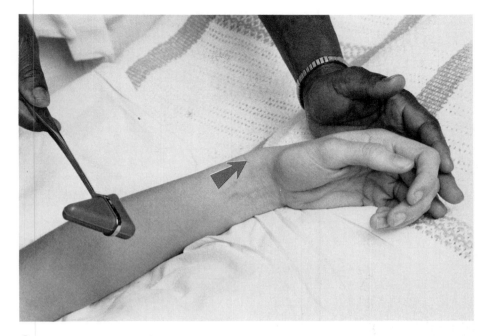

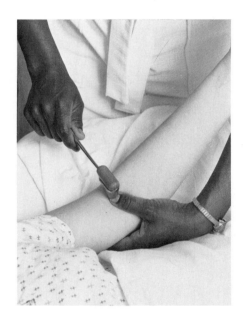

1 To test the biceps reflex (C5–C6 innervation), place your thumb over the client's biceps tendon at the antecubital fossa. Flex the client's elbow slightly, and then percuss your thumb with the pointed end of the reflex hammer. In a normal response, the client's elbow will flex and you should feel the tendon contract. Repeat the test on the tendon in the opposite extremity, noting the tone and symmetry of the reflex.

2 To test the brachioradialis (supinator) reflex (C5–C6 innervation), rest the client's forearm on a flat surface such as the bed or the client's lap, maintaining the hand in a moderate curve. Using the blunt end of the reflex hammer, percuss the brachioradialis tendon, which is located 2.5– 5.0 cm (1–2 in.) above the wrist over the radius (see arrow). In a normal response, the client's elbow will flex and the forearm will rotate laterally. Test the reflex of the tendon in the opposite extremity, noting the tone and symmetry of the response.

3 To test the triceps reflex (C6–C7–C8 innervation), flex the client's elbow. Using the pointed end of the reflex hammer, percuss the triceps tendon just proximal to the olecranon between the epicondyles (see arrow). The elbow should extend as the triceps tendon contracts. Repeat the test on the tendon in the opposite extremity, noting the tone and symmetry of the reflex.

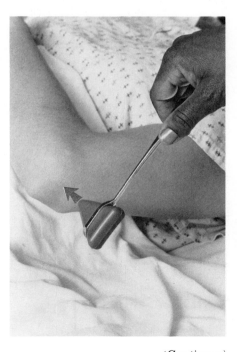

(Continues)

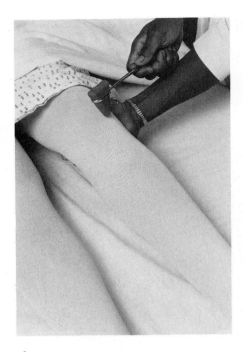

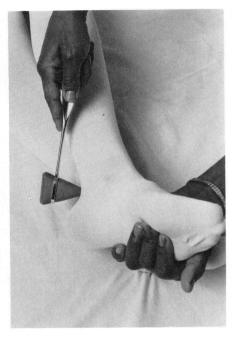

4 To test the patellar reflex (L2–L3–L4 innervation), have the client sit on the edge of the bed. If the client is unable to sit, flex and support the knee at the popliteal space (as shown) and percuss the patellar tendon just distal to the patella. Use the pointed end of the reflex hammer and tap the site lightly. The knee should extend, and the quadriceps muscle should contract. Test the reflex on the tendon in the opposite extremity, noting the tone and symmetry of the reflex. *Note: In the older adult, the response may be normally hyporeflexive.*

5 To test the ankle reflex (S1–S2 innervation), place the knee in slight flexion and then externally rotate and dorsiflex the ankle. Percuss the Achilles tendon with the pointed end of the reflex hammer. The client's ankle should plantarflex as the tendon contracts. Repeat the test on the tendon in the opposite extremity, noting the tone and symmetry of the reflex. Document the results of the assessment procedure.

ASSESSING CRANIAL DRAINAGE FOR THE PRESENCE OF CEREBROSPINAL FLUID

If your client has sustained a craniocerebral injury or is recovering from a craniotomy, careful observation of any drainage from the eyes, ears, nose, or traumatic area is critical. Cerebrospinal fluid is colorless and generally nonpurulent, and its presence is indicative of a serious breach of cranial integrity. Because the risk of bacteria entering into the brain is very high if a tract exists, *any* suspicious drainage should be reported immediately. Because cerebrospinal fluid contains glucose, you can test clear, nonsanguineous drainage with a glucose reagent stick and compare the results to the back of the reagent container. The test results will be positive for the presence of glucose if the drainage contains cerebrospinal fluid.

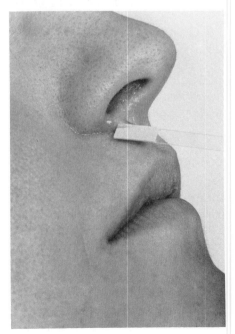

Caring for Clients with Neurologic Disorders

ASSISTING THE CLIENT WITH A TRANSCUTANEOUS ELECTRICAL NERVE STIMULATOR DEVICE

A transcutaneous electrical nerve stimulator (TENS) device is battery operated, and it is used to deliver electrical impulses to the body to relieve pain. A client experiencing acute or chronic pain, for whom narcotics are contraindicated or ineffective, will especially benefit from this device. It is used most frequently for chronic back pain or headaches. It should not be used, however, for clients with cardiac pacemakers because the electrical impulses it generates can interrupt pacing. In addition, it should be avoided for clients who are pregnant, or who have dysrhythmias or myocardial ischemia.

Assessing and Planning

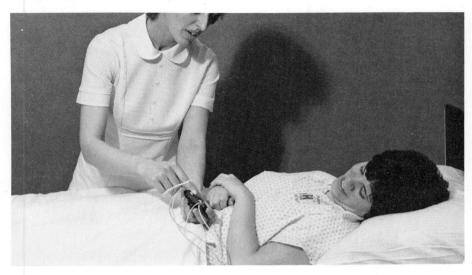

1 If your client has been using a TENS device, chances are she has already been trained in its use and application by a TENS specialist. Consult with the TENS specialist or read the manufacturer's instructions for operating the device before explaining it to your client.

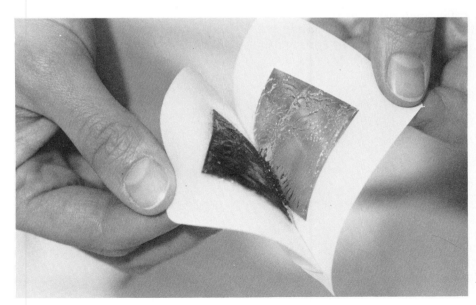

2 The electrodes are either reusable or disposable. Either they require the use of a conducting gel, or they are water conductive and will need moistening with water. Many disposable electrodes, such as that in the photo, already contain the conducting gel and are self-adhering.

(Continues)

Implementing

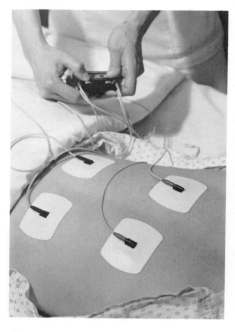

Evaluating

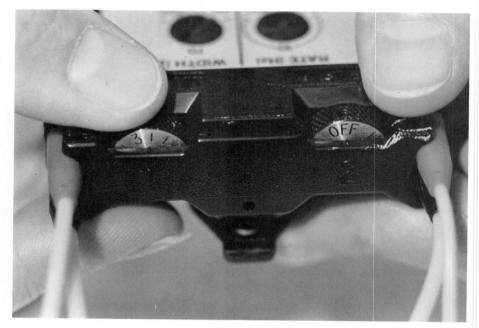

3   Attach the electrodes to the client's skin according to the pattern designed for your client. For example, for postoperative clients, place the electrodes on both sides of the incision. For clients with radiating pain, place the electrodes over the involved nerve roots along the spine. Attach the lead wires, making sure they are securely connected at both ends.

4   Many TENS devices have two dials that are labeled "intensity," "energy," or "amplitude," and each operates a set of two electrodes. In addition, most devices have a rate (frequency) dial that can be adjusted to deliver the desired number of electrical impulses per second, as well as a pulse-width dial that adjusts the impulse duration. If the client experiences a burning or itching sensation, lower the pulse-width dial. If the sensation is too intense, lower both the amplitude dial and the pulse-width dial and adjust the rate accordingly. A mild to moderate sensation is the goal with this therapy. A sensation that is too intense can result in muscle spasms caused by overstimulation of the nerve.

APPLYING INTERMITTENT PNEUMATIC COMPRESSION (ANTIEMBOLIC) CUFFS

Clients who are immobile for an extended period of time are at risk of developing deep venous thrombosis due to stasis in the lower extremities. Intermittent calf compression via sequential pressure cuffs can be employed to empty the calf veins, thereby minimizing venous stasis. By allowing better drainage of the veins, the fibrinolytic (anticlotting) system is improved, as well. Because the cuffs work on the principle of compression, they are contraindicated in disorders associated with venous thrombosis or arterial insufficiency.

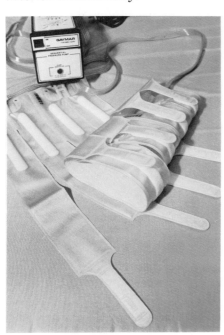

Assessing and Planning

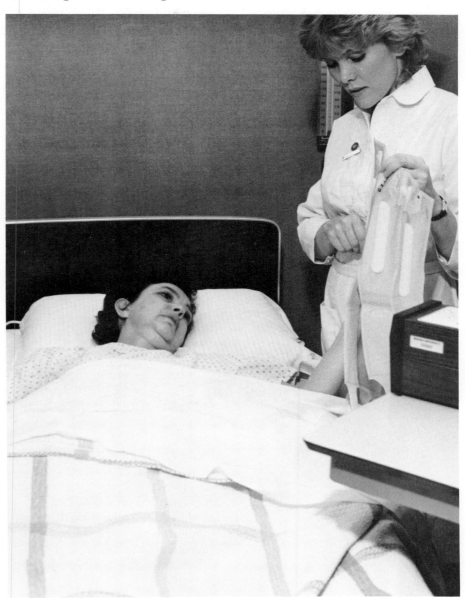

1 Assemble the equipment and explain the procedure to your client. Let her know that the cuffs are quite comfortable and that they will be worn during the period of time she is on bed rest.

(Continues)

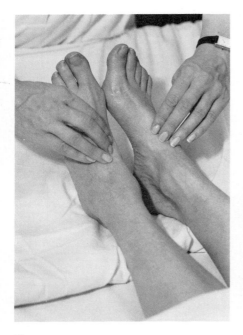

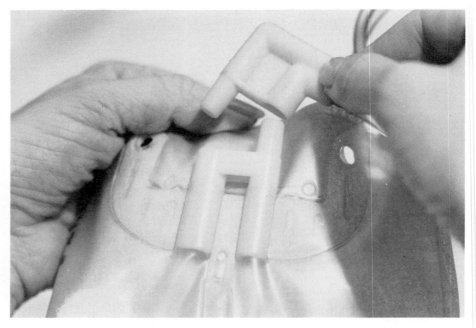

2 Palpate both pedal pulses (as shown) and popliteal pulses, and perform baseline neurovascular assessments in both feet (review the procedure in Chapter 9) before applying the cuffs. If the client shows evidence of marked arterial insufficiency (see Chapter 7), notify the physician because the application of the cuffs might be contraindicated.

3 Attach the tubing to each cuff. The unit in these photos is marked "ankle" or "knee" at the appropriate connector cell to ensure that the tubing is connected to the proper ankle or knee plug.

Implementing

4 Place one of the cuffs over the client's lower leg, with the tubing positioned at the medial aspect. Position the padded side against the client's leg so that the Velcro™ is on the exterior of the cuff. Note that with the Thrombogard device, the end tabs are identified as either "ankle" (as shown) or "knee." With other brands the narrower straps are placed over the ankle, and the wider straps are positioned over the calf.

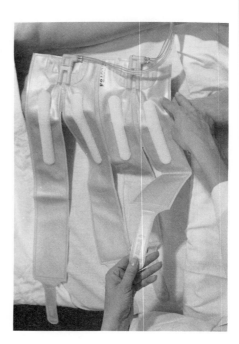

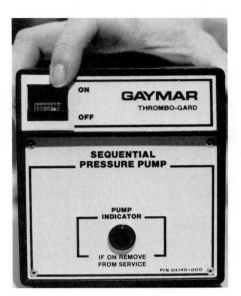

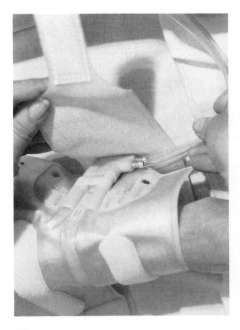

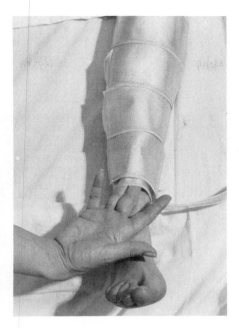

5   Wrap the cuff around the client's leg and the connector cell (as shown). Place two fingers over the cell before attaching the Velcro™ strip to ensure proper slack in the cuff.

6   Once the straps have been attached to the cuff, again ensure that two fingers fit between the client's skin and the cuff at both the ankle and the knee before turning on the unit.

7   Plug the unit into a grounded outlet and press the switch to "on" to activate the device. Observe each cuff for at least two cycles to evaluate its functioning. Be sure that only one cuff is filled at a time. The ankle cell should fill first, followed by the inflation of the second, third, and knee cells. All the cells will remain inflated until the system vents, at which time all the cells should deflate. The cuff on the opposite leg should then begin its sequential filling in the same manner. If the sequence is reversed, remove the cuff and correct the problem. Document the procedure, being certain to note the client's baseline neurovascular assessment and the condition of the skin on both legs.

8   At prescribed intervals, unplug the unit and remove the cuffs after they have deflated. Inspect the skin and provide skin care. However, avoid massaging the skin because vigorous rubbing can dislodge a thrombus. Perform a neurovascular assessment (see Chapter 9) to evaluate the color, temperature, sensation, pulses, and capillary refill of the distal extremities, and compare the assessment to the baseline assessment.

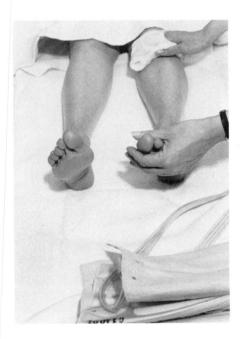

PROVIDING CARE DURING A SEIZURE

Assessing and Planning

1　A client history of seizure disorders or the potential for a seizure should alert you to the need for protective measures. These include an oral airway of an appropriate size at the bedside table or taped to the headboard, raised and padded side rails, and a padded headboard. Children with seizure disorders can wear soft seizure helmets (as shown) when they are ambulatory.

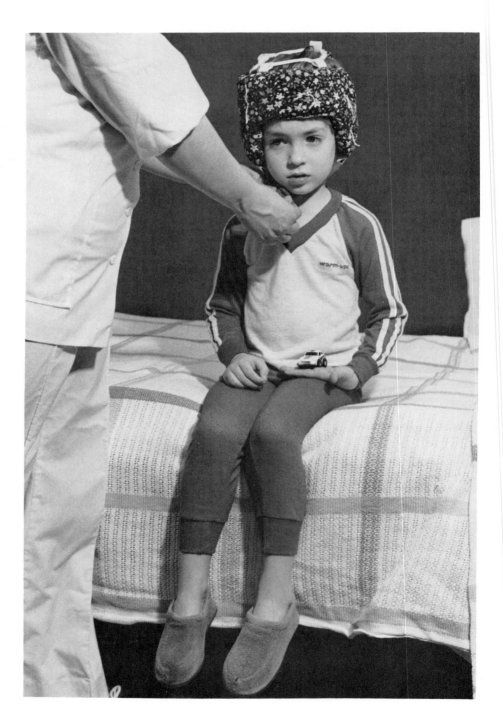

Implementing

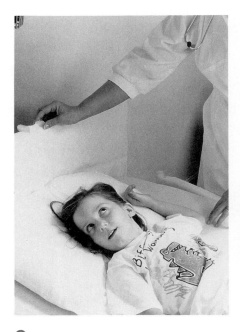

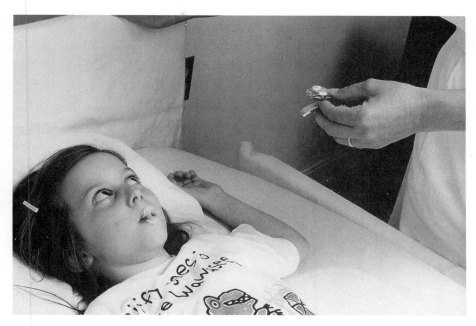

2   If your client has a seizure, position her head to the side to promote drainage of secretions and prevent aspiration into the lungs. If your client's tongue is obstructing her airway, remove the oral airway from the bedside table or headboard and insert it cautiously (see procedure, Chapter 6).

3   A single seizure can last from 2 to 5 minutes. Always stay with the client, noting the onset, duration, and type of seizure. Do not attempt to restrain her, since this can increase the risk of injury. Observe the client's posture, pupillary changes, skin color, and the extremities involved. When the seizure has ceased, comfort and reorient the client, noting any cyanosis or difficult respiratory patterns. If the cyanosis persists, be sure to have oxygen available.

Evaluating
Document the seizure carefully, using descriptive terminology, the time of onset and duration, and any information about possible precipitating events.

USING A HYPERTHERMIA OR HYPOTHERMIA SYSTEM

Many neurologic disorders involve the hypothalamus, the part of the brain that regulates body temperature. When vast fluctuations in body temperature occur, a hyperthermia or hypothermia system such as the Blanketrol® in these photos can be used to help keep your client's temperature within normal range, thereby minimizing the risk of irreversible brain damage.

Assessing and Planning

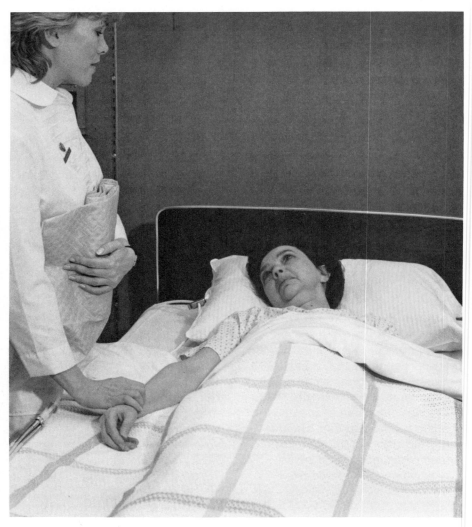

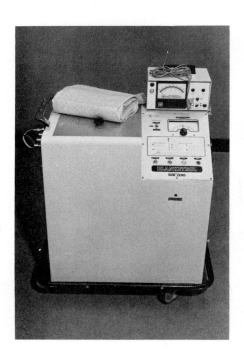

1 Explain the procedure to the client and inform her that she will feel either warmth or coolness. Instruct her to alert you if the temperature becomes too extreme. Perform and record baseline assessments of the client's vital signs and neurologic status.

Note the integrity of the skin and document its condition before initiating the treatment. *Note: If the client's temperature will be greatly decreased, coat the skin with a thin layer of lanolin ointment to help prevent cold burns.*

2 Ensure that the fluid level in the Blanketrol® unit is at least 1.25–2.50 cm (½–1 in.) above the coils in the reservoir. Add distilled water if necessary.

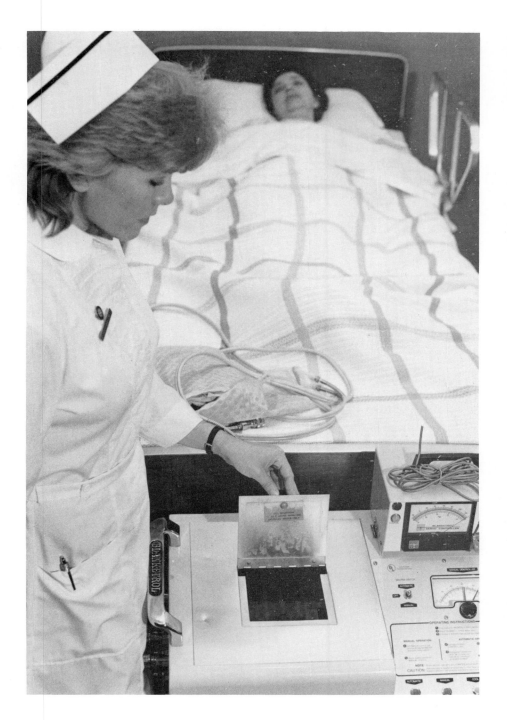

(Continues)

Implementing

3 Cover the blanket with either a blanket cover or a sheet. With the client in a side-lying position, fan-fold and lay the blanket along the client's side, with the hose end of the blanket at the foot of the bed. Tuck the blanket under the client's buttocks and shoulders.

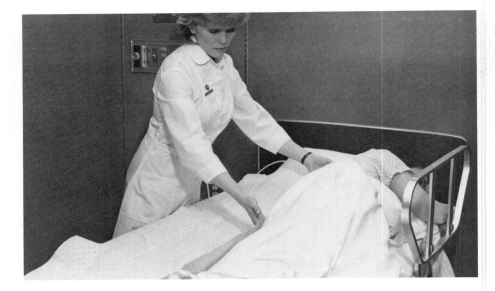

4 While the client is still on her side, apply a glove, coat the rectal probe (thermometer) with a water-soluble lubricant, and insert it approximately 7.5–10 cm (3–4 in.) into the rectum (adjust the insertion length accordingly for the pediatric population). Tape it to the buttocks with hypoallergenic tape (for the neonate, tape the unlubricated probe to the axilla). Then assist her onto the opposite side so that you can straighten the blanket, and return her to her back so that the maximum amount of skin surface is in contact with the blanket. *Note: If a rapid increase or decrease in your client's temperature is needed, a second blanket can be used to cover the client.*

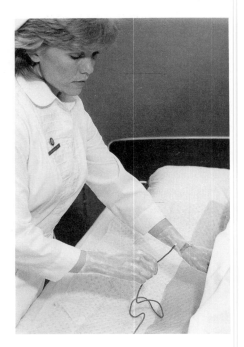

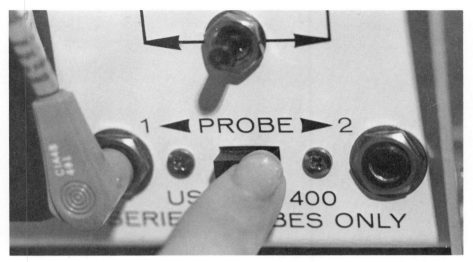

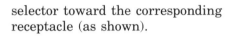

5 To connect the blanket hose to the Blanketrol®, locate the connectors on the side of the machine. Grasp the collar on the female connector that is directly above the attached hose. Push the collar back and insert the male fitting. Release the collar and push the male fitting until it locks in place. Make sure the master switch is in the "off" position, and connect the three-pronged plug to the outlet. Ensure that the servo-controller is plugged into the receptacle on the Blanketrol®.

6 Insert the rectal probe plug (shown on the left in the above photo) into one of the probe receptacles. Then turn the probe selector toward the corresponding receptacle (as shown).

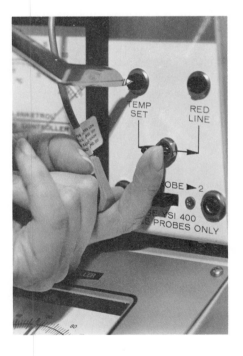

7 Set the prescribed temperature by pushing the temperature set switch to the left and turning the temperature set control screw with your scissors to the prescribed temperature (as shown). When the switch is released, the needle pointer will show the core temperature. This is the same switch you will push to check the calibrations by adjusting the needle to the red line.

(Continues)

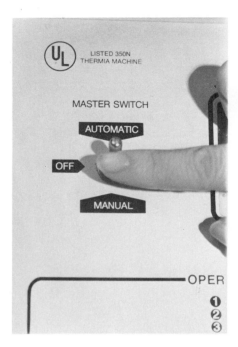

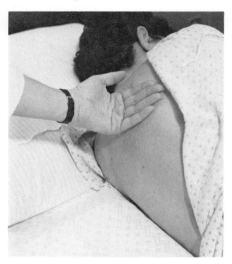

Evaluating

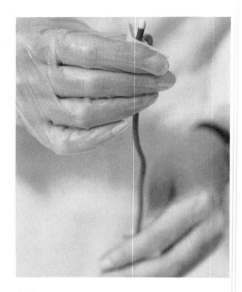

8 Move the master control switch on the Blanketrol® to "automatic." Document the procedure, the client's baseline assessment, and the response and tolerance to the treatment.

9 Perform and document neurologic checks and vital signs, and compare them to the client's baseline. Assess the client's skin integrity and temperature, and be alert to alterations such as swelling or color changes that could indicate frostbite or burns. Check the servo-controller reading to ensure that the client's temperature is reaching the desired level.

10 Periodically remove the rectal probe and assess the client's body temperature with a rectal thermometer to ensure that the probe is accurately recording the client's actual body temperature. Clean and reinsert the probe.

ASSESSING CLIENTS WITH SUBARACHNOID DRAINS

Subarachnoid/lumbar drains are small catheters that are placed in the lumbar cistern of the spinal column via lumbar puncture. Most often, these drains are placed after cranial or ear, nose, or throat (ENT) surgery in which there is the risk of cerebrospinal fluid (CSF) leak. By having a means to drain off a specific amount of CSF, thus reducing the circulating CSF, pressure on the dural incision is minimized.

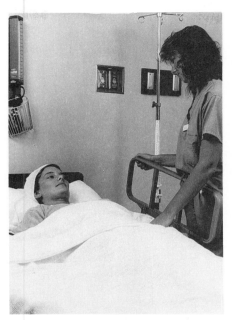

1 Monitor the client to ensure that the head of the bed is in the correct prescribed position with the zero point of the drainage pressure scale, which is attached to a support such as an IV pole. Usually, the zero point of the subarachnoid/lumbar drainage system is positioned on the same plane as the client's earlobe.

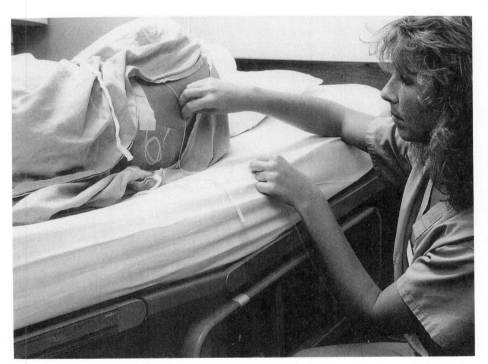

2 Assess the insertion site for the presence of infection, including erythema, warmth, purulent drainage; cerebrospinal fluid leakage, which would appear as a clear fluid; and the integrity of the attachment of the subarachnoid catheter to the drainage tubing.

(Continues)

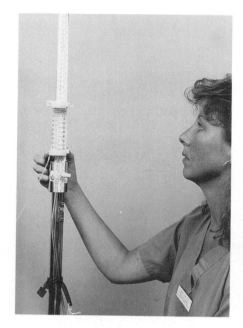

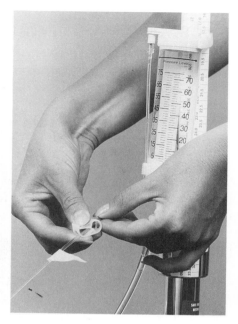

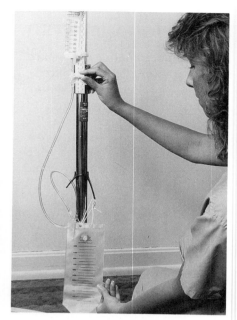

3   The position of the drip chamber on the IV pole is determined by the amount of cerebrospinal fluid drainage: the greater the amount of drainage, the higher the prescribed position of the drip chamber to slow the release of the CSF. Monitor the client for severe headache and nausea, early signs of too rapid drainage of the CSF. If this condition were allowed to continue, signs of neurologic deterioration would occur owing to downward shifting of intracranial contents: decreased LOC, irritability, confusion, weakness, paresis, and changes in pupillary reactivity and size (see pp. 595–597). The grid along the pole is measured in centimeters. The physician will specify the amount in centimeters to move the drip chamber in relationship to the client's clinical condition.

4   Be aware that if you must change the client's position, clamp the drain first (unless otherwise directed) to prevent a rapid change in the circulating volume of CSF that could result in a change in the client's neurologic status. Ensure that a tape tab is positioned between the tubing clamp and the drip chamber (and as close to the drip chamber as possible) to keep the clamp out of contact with the client. This will prevent the client from inadvertently rolling over onto the clamp and stopping the flow of CSF.

5   Every 2–4 hours (or as prescribed), note and document the amount of drainage in the drip chamber, and adjust the stopcock to empty the CSF into the drainage bag. Change the drainage bag every 24 hours (or per agency protocol), using sterile technique. Be sure to clamp the drainage tubing first to prevent rapid outflow of large amounts of CSF.

Nursing Guidelines for the Care of Clients on Special Beds and Frames

Complications of immobility such as atelectasis, pneumonia, decubitus ulcers, and renal calculi are frequent occurrences in clients with neurologic disorders. Because many of these clients are unable to participate actively in their own turning, and yet may require frequent turning without the interruption of their alignment, special beds are often indicated to facilitate nursing care and to prevent or minimize the complications of prolonged bed rest. The Roto Rest Kinetic Treatment Table, Clinitron Air Fluidized Therapy, and Therapulse Pulsating Air Suspension Therapy are three types of beds or frames that may be used by your agency. Follow manufacturer's instructions carefully to ensure the proper care and/or safe turning for your clients.

ROTO REST KINETIC TREATMENT TABLE

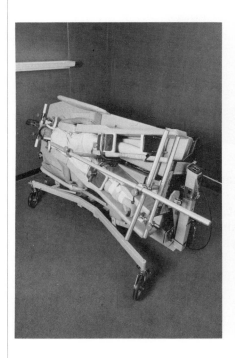

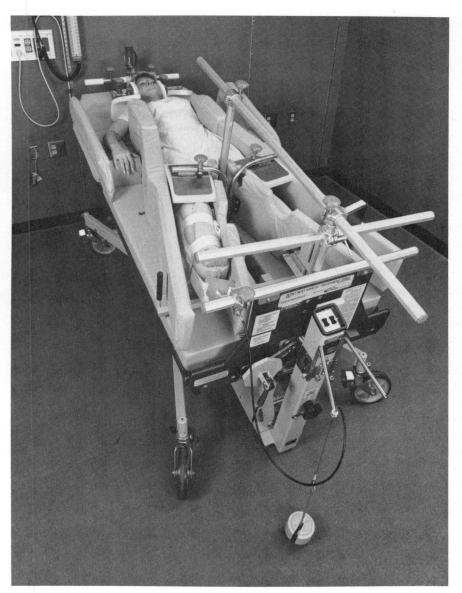

The Roto Rest is an automatic turning table that continuously rotates the client from side to side every 3.5 minutes, achieving a 62-degree lateral angle (see left). This continuous lateral rotation can enhance

(Continues)

the distribution of pulmonary blood flow. The client is secured to the table via closely fitting pads that conform to the extremities and trunk. When the table achieves its most lateral position, the padded knee and shoulder braces give added security. Safety straps are also available for confused or combative clients. In addition to cervical traction, the table also allows the application of traction to all extremities.

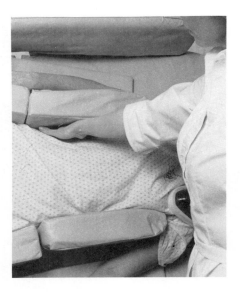

- To minimize the risk of skin irritation or inhibited chest excursion, ensure that a hand's breadth can comfortably fit between the client and the padded side packs. Adjust the packs if the space is greater than a hand's breadth because skin irritation can result from the client sliding against the side packs during the table's lateral rotation.

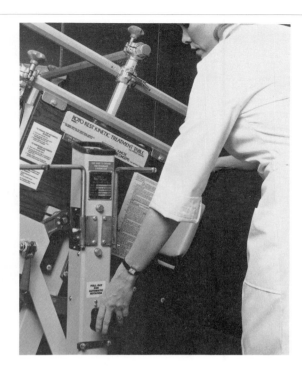

■ The Roto Rest can be changed from automatic to manual by pushing in the knob at the posterior end of the table (as shown). In addition, a constant horizontal surface or lesser turning angles can be achieved with the degree-adjustment dial, which is also at the posterior end of the table.

 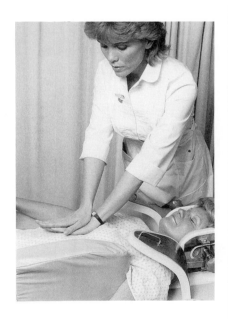

■ In an emergency situation in which your client requires chest compressions for cardiopulmonary resuscitation (CPR), level the table's surface, remove the padded thoracic pack (left), and stand on the frame of the table if you are not tall enough to deliver the compressions from floor level. Because of the table's firm surface, it is not necessary to use a cardiac board.

(Continues)

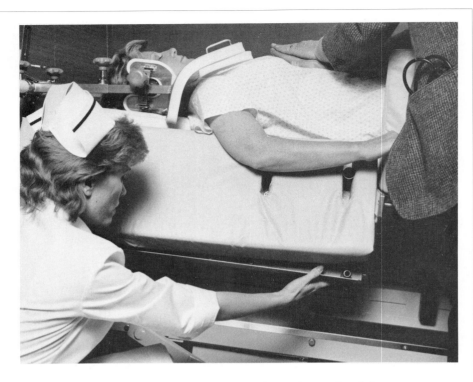

Once you are assisted by another member of your health team, you can take the time to lower the level of the table, and then lower the side arm to provide closer access to the client's chest.

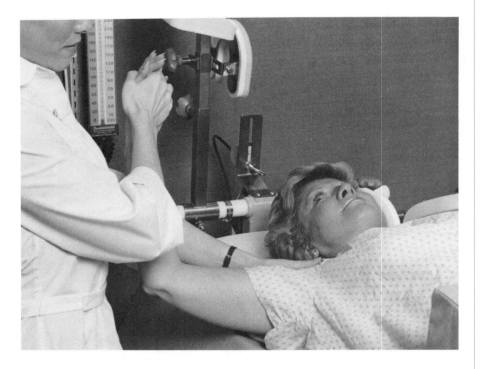

■ In nonemergency situations, the lowered side arm also allows you access to the client's upper extremities for full range of motion exercises.

 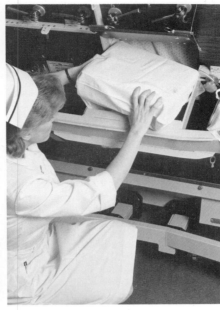 

- When the client needs to use a bed pan, first lock the table in its most lateral position, and then open the rectal hatch (left). Remove the rectal pack (center).

  Insert a full-sized bed pan (right), close the rectal hatch, place the client in a horizontal position, and lock the table in that position.

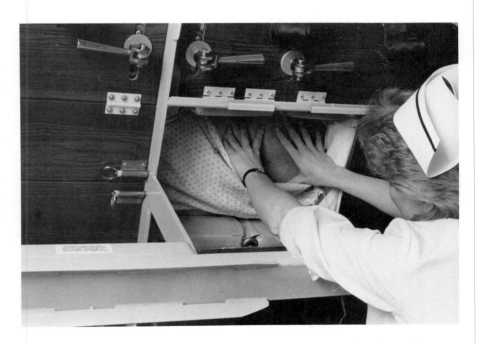

- Other openings such as the cervical and thoracic hatches allow accessibility to the client for bathing, skin care, and inspection.

(Continues)

CLINITRON AIR FLUIDIZED THERAPY

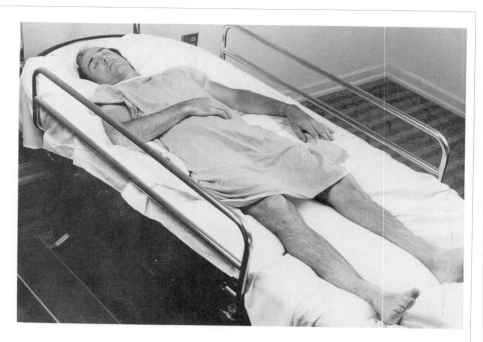

Clients with altered tissue and skin integrity (e.g., those with burns, grafts, or pressure ulcers) and those at risk for pressure ulcers (e.g., clients on strict bed rest or with impaired sensation or limited mobility) may benefit from air fluidized therapy, which gives the benefits of flotation and yet achieves this end in a completely dry environment. When the system is turned on, room air is drawn into the system, filtered, cooled or heated, and forced upward through the "beads," which sets them in motion and creates the effect of fluid and flotation.

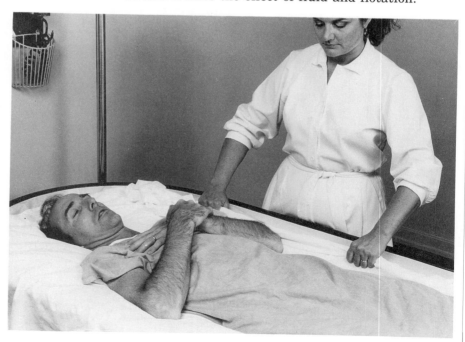

■ To turn the client into a side-lying position, first have him cross his arms. Then roll the sheet toward his body, with your hands positioned at his hips and shoulder. Pull him toward you and turn him to the side as you lift up on the sheet.

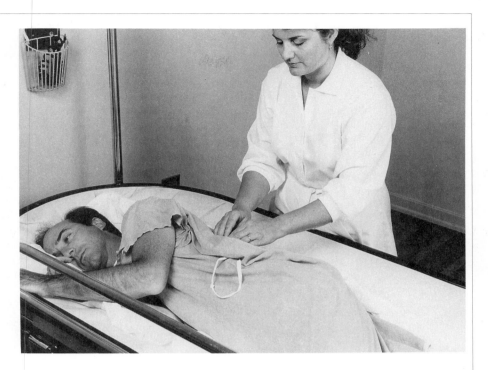

■ If you have turned the client into a side-lying position to perform a procedure that necessitates the client's being still, such as a dressing change, turn the bed off (see p. 632) before implementing the procedure to ensure client immobilization.

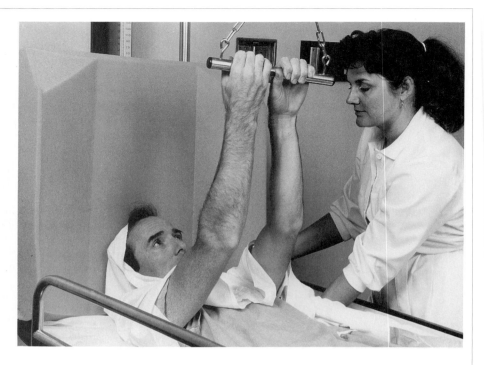

■ To raise the head of the bed, for example, for meals or insertion of a nasogastric (NG) tube, it will be necessary to insert a foam wedge. To do this, position the foam wedge contoured side out at the head of the bed. Then wrap a sheet around the client's head and shoulders and ask him to grasp a trapeze (or get a helper if the bed is not equipped with a trapeze).

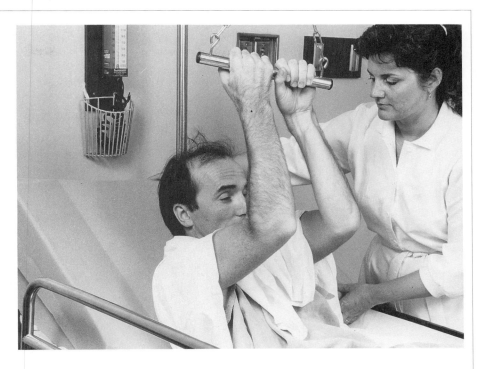

As the client raises his upper body, slide the wedge down and under his upper body.

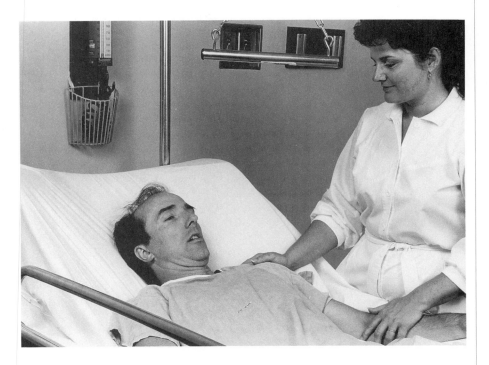

Then, straighten the sheet around the foam wedge.

(Continues)

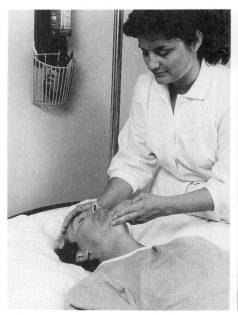

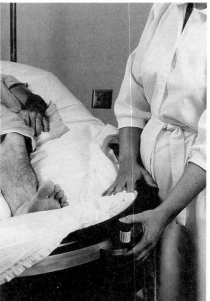

Note: If the client requires CPR, it will be necessary to perform the head tilt maneuver before turning the system off. Turning the system off before tilting the client's head back would make it difficult to position the head in the hardened bed surface.

After performing the head tilt maneuver, turn the system off by pressing the button at the end of the bed (as shown).

Once you have turned off the system, you then can perform chest compressions on the hardened surface (as shown).

THERAPULSE PULSATING AIR SUSPENSION THERAPY

The Therapulse system adds continuous pulsating action to the benefits of a static low-air-loss system for clients with the same needs as those on an air fluidized system. Suspension on the air cushions, which alternate inflation with deflation, helps keep skin pressure below the point of capillary closure and thus helps minimize the risk of tissue breakdown. The system also provides a temperature-controlled, dry environment.

■ Cover the cushions only with the cover sheet provided by the manufacturer. If your client is incontinent, use special pads under the client's buttocks (as shown) to protect the cover sheet and help keep the client dry and comfortable. To ensure that the client is getting maximum pressure relief to all tissue, inspect the client's degree of sinking into the cushions when in the supine position. Optimally, the client sinks approximately 40% into the cushions. If this is not occurring, check with the manufacturer's representative for adjustment.

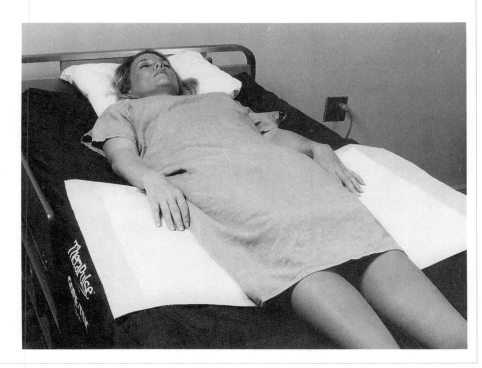

(Continues)

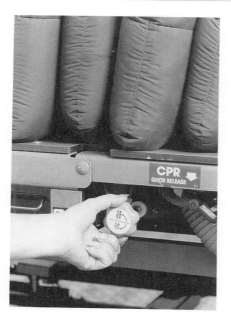

- To turn the client from side to side and perform other nursing procedures, turn the adjuster dial to "instaflate," which will stop the pulsations from occurring and provide a firm surface for client care. To return the client to the pulsation mode following completion of nursing care, turn the dial back to "memory return."

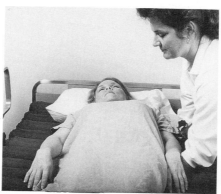

- Post a turning schedule and turn the client from side to side to help prevent respiratory problems caused by immobility. After turning the adjuster dial to "instaflate," position your arms under the client's trunk and turn her onto her side (see Chapter 2 for turning guidelines).

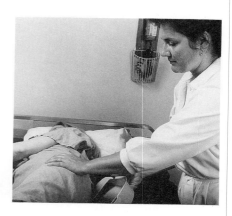

- Once the client is on her side, you can perform routine assessment and nursing care, such as providing a bed pan. To position the bed pan, you must first press the seat deflation button. Then slide the bed pan under the client's hips, as shown, and press the button again to reinflate that area of the bed. If it is not contraindicated, raise the head of the bed.

■ If CPR is indicated, depress the CPR quick-release lever. This will deflate the bed in seconds.

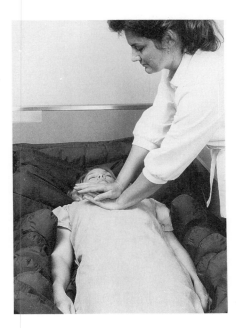

■ Deflating the bed will enable you to initiate CPR promptly, without the necessity of a crashboard.

Caring for Clients with Disorders of the Sensory System

ASSESSING AUDITORY FUNCTION

There are several methods for assessing your client's hearing acuity. The simplest method is to stand approximately 60 cm (2 ft) from the client and out of his or her vision. Instruct the client to cover one ear as you whisper two-syllable words such as *base-ball* or *armchair*. With normal hearing, the client should be able to hear and repeat at least 50% of your words at this distance. If the client is unable to hear the whispered word, gradually increase the intensity of your voice until your words are heard and repeated. Perform the same test on the client's opposite ear, using different words.

PERFORMING THE WATCH TEST

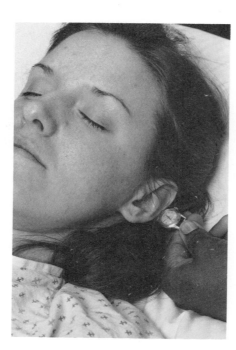

Another method for testing hearing acuity is the watch test, whereby the client covers one ear as you position a ticking watch approximately 2.5–5.0 cm (1–2 in.) from her uncovered ear. Instruct the client to alert you when she no longer can hear the watch, and slowly move the watch away from the ear. With normal hearing, the client should be able to hear the ticking 5 cm from her ear, provided she is in a quiet room. Repeat the test on the opposite ear, and record the farthest distance at which the client was able to hear the ticking for both ears.

PERFORMING THE WEBER AND RINNE TESTS

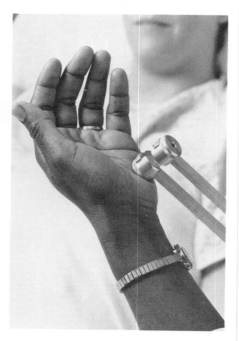

1 The Weber and Rinne tests are more sophisticated assessments of your client's auditory function. A combination of the two tests can help categorize an auditory dysfunction as either conductive or sensorineural (perceptive). With conductive hearing loss, there is a physical obstruction of the sound, such as a fusion of the stapes or a foreign body in the external canal. With a sensorineural hearing loss, the dysfunction can occur with the eighth cranial nerve, or in the cortex itself. To perform either the Weber or the Rinne test, first activate a tuning fork by holding it by its base and gently striking the prongs against the palmar surface of your hand (as shown). This will cause the prongs to vibrate.

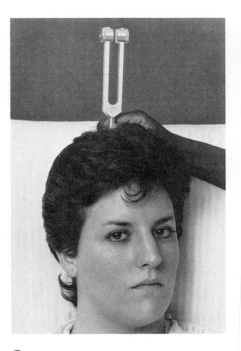

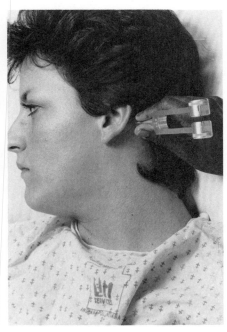

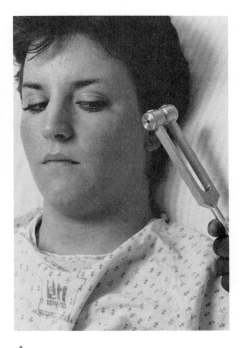

2 To perform the Weber test, activate the tuning fork, and position the base of the fork on the top of the client's head (as shown) or at the top of the forehead. Normally, the client will hear the sound equally in both ears. This is recorded as Weber negative. With conductive loss the sound will lateralize to the poorer ear. This occurs because the normal ear is penetrated by ordinary room noise, masking hearing in that ear. The poorer ear, on the other hand, is not penetrated by ordinary room noise and thus can hear the bone-conducted sound. Document the results as either "Weber negative" or "Lateralization Right" (or "Left").

3 To perform the Rinne test, instruct the client to cover one ear. After activating the tuning fork, position its base on the mastoid process of the uncovered ear. Instruct the client to alert you once she no longer can hear the sound. As soon as she alerts you, make a mental note of the amount of time during which she heard the sound.

4 Immediately move the prongs of the tuning fork in front of the uncovered ear, approximately 1.25–2.5 cm ($\frac{1}{2}$–1 in.) Because air conduction lasts at least twice as long as bone conduction, the client should be able to hear the sound twice as long in this position. The reverse is true if the client has conductive hearing loss. Repeat the test in the opposite ear. Document the results as positive if the client has normal hearing, or negative if the results are reversed.

IRRIGATING THE EXTERNAL AUDITORY CANAL

Assessing

1 The physician may prescribe external auditory canal irrigation to remove cerumen or debris. Before irrigating the ear, explain the procedure to the client and inspect the external auditory canal with an otoscope to assess the location and amount of cerumen or debris and to ensure that the tympanic membrane is intact. For an adult, lift the pinna up and back to straighten the canal; for a child, pull the earlobe down and back. Instruct the client to tilt her head toward the unaffected ear. Insert the speculum of the otoscope slowly and carefully. Be sure that you have selected a speculum that will comfortably fit the external canal. Smaller specula have a greater potential for damaging the ear.

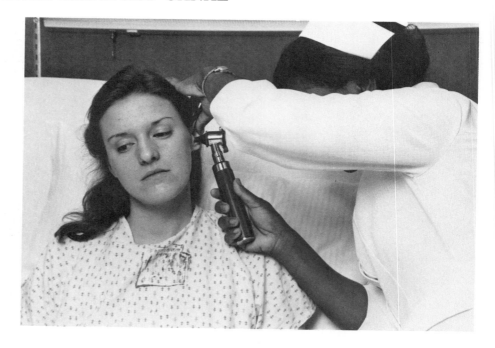

Planning

2 After inspecting the client's ear, prepare the prescribed irrigating solution, making sure it is warmed to room temperature. For an adult, use either a 50-ml asepto or a Pomeroy ear syringe. For a child, obtain a 20- to 30-ml syringe with a rubber tip. If you use a Pomeroy syringe, first oil the plunger with one to two drops of lubricant (as shown) to minimize the friction of the plunger against the barrel.

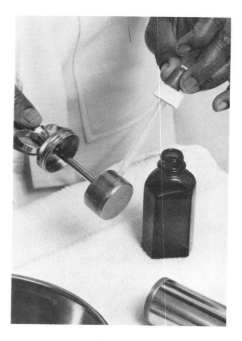

Implementing

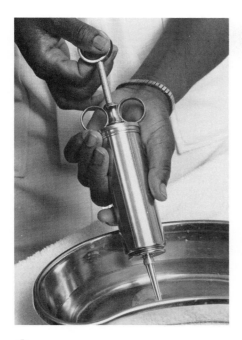

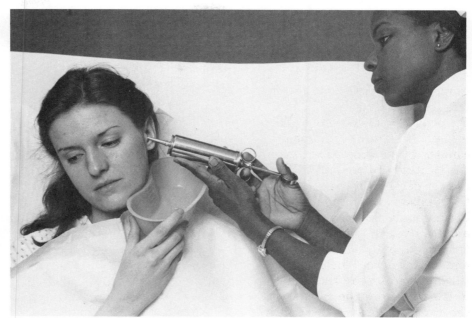

3 Aspirate approximately 50 ml of the irrigant into the syringe.

4 Drape the client with a bed-saver pad, and ask her to hold an emesis basin under her affected ear. Position the tip of the syringe very carefully into the external canal so that it angles either upward (as shown) or toward the wall of the canal to avoid injecting the irrigant onto the tympanic membrane. Make sure the client tilts her head toward the unaffected ear.

After correctly positioning the syringe, lift the pinna up and back and slowly inject the irrigant until you have administered the prescribed amount. *Caution: Stop the procedure immediately and notify the physician if the client complains of a sudden pain in her ear. This is an indication that the tympanic membrane may have been perforated.*

Evaluating

5 Observe the return as it drains into the emesis basin. When the procedure has been completed, dry the outer ear with cotton balls and inspect the external auditory canal once more with the otoscope to evaluate the effectiveness of the irrigation. Document the procedure, noting the amount and type of irrigant, the character of the return, and your final evaluation of the external auditory canal.

IRRIGATING THE EYE

Assessing and Planning

Implementing

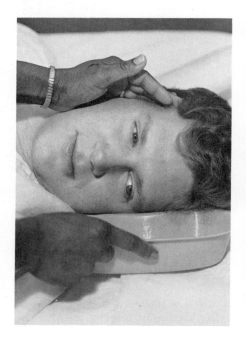

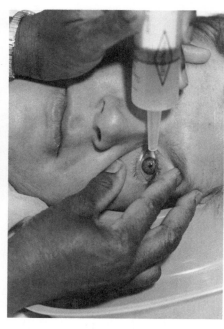

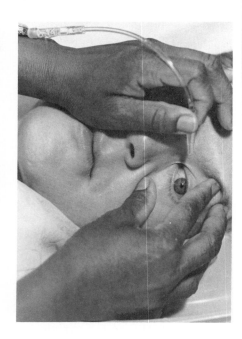

1 If an eye irrigation has been prescribed for your client, assemble the sterile irrigating solution warmed to room temperature, a sterile 50-ml syringe (or sterile infusion tubing if larger amounts of irrigant are to be used), sterile gauze pads, bed-saver pads, and an emesis basin. Fill the syringe with the irrigant. Explain the procedure to your client and position him so that he is on his side with his affected eye lowermost. Position the emesis basin underneath the affected eye, and drape the client's gown and bed with the bed-saver pads. Then wash your hands.

2 Retract the upper and lower eyelids with your thumb and index finger, and administer the irrigant so that it flows from the inner to the outer canthus.

Evaluating

3 After completing the procedure, blot the client's eye gently with a sterile gauze pad, wiping from the inner to the outer canthus. Document the procedure, noting the type and amount of irrigant and the client's tolerance to the irrigation.

Note: Follow the same procedure if you are using infusion tubing to deliver the irrigant.

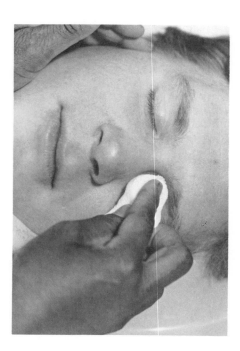

USING OP-SITE ON DECUBITUS ULCERS

Op-Site is a transparent polyure-thane self-adhering dressing. Because it prevents the escape of fluid, it provides a moist environment that is believed to enhance granulation and epithelization for optimal wound healing.

Assessing and Planning

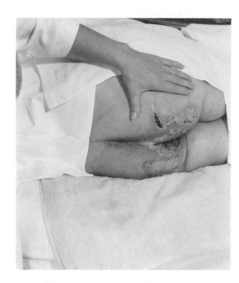

1 Wash your hands and position and drape the client so that you have good visualization of and access to the decubitus ulcer. Determine the size of dressing that will effectively cover the wound and yet provide at least a 5-cm (2-in.) border around the site, if possible. Op-Site dressings are available in a variety of sizes, ranging from 5 × 7.5 cm to 28 × 30 cm.

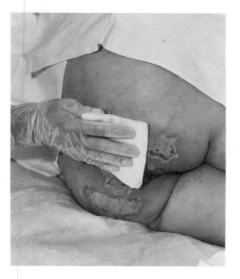

2 Apply clean gloves and thoroughly cleanse the wound. Rinse it well with normal saline. To ensure complete adherence of the dressing, you must be sure to dry the site completely. If the wound is on the buttocks of a client with frequent episodes of diarrhea, it may be necessary to apply a thin layer of liquid skin barrier around the periphery of the area to improve dressing adherence.

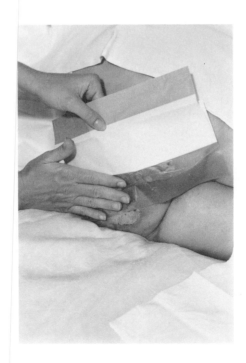

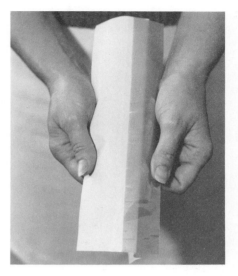

3 Peel the protective paper backing from the Op-Site sheet, just enough to adhere a small section of the dressing to the client's skin. Avoid peeling back more than 2.5 cm (1 in.).

Implementing

4 Position the sticky side of the dressing over the interior border of the wound site, allowing a 5-cm (2-in.) border to extend beyond the wound site, if possible. If the wound is on the buttocks, it may help to place the Op-Site sheet slightly on the diagonal, with a second sheet crossing it at the sacral area. Adhere the exposed section of the dressing to the client's skin. *Note: It is challenging to apply a transparent dressing with gloves on. However, if you cannot avoid touching the client's wound, apply gloves. The nurse in these photos is touching only the transparent dressing, and therefore gloves are unnecessary.*

(Continues)

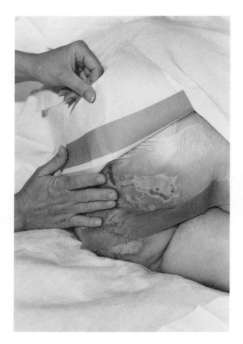

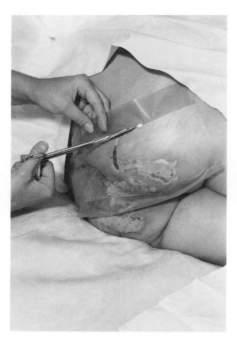

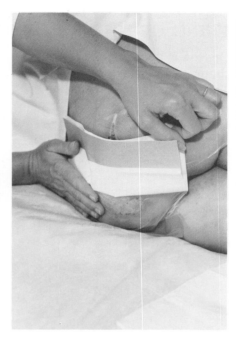

5 Gradually peel away the protective paper as you smooth the dressing over the wound and surrounding area. Although you should avoid stretching the dressing, gentle tension will help prevent wrinkling. If a wrinkle does appear, however, pinch it together.

6 Once the dressing has been smoothed on the client's skin, use bandage scissors to cut off the green tabs. *Note: After use, it is always a good idea to clean the scissor blades with an alcohol wipe.*

7 In the same manner, apply a second sheet if needed, and cut away the green tabs. If the dressing is on the buttocks, be sure to trim the dressing, as necessary, to accommodate the anus.

Evaluating

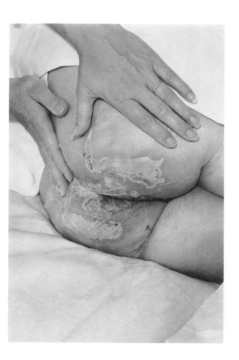

8 Ensure that the entire wound site is covered; then wash your hands and document the procedure. Be sure to note the size and character of the decubitus ulcer. It is not necessary to cover Op-Site with gauze or tape. Leaving the dressing uncovered allows observation of the wound without disruption of the dressing. Expect to see exudate forming under the dressing. This is normal, and it is the mechanism for moist wound healing. Leave the dressing on until it begins to slough away. This usually takes 4–5 days. If you need to remove the dressing prior to this time, apply gloves, soak the dressing with a solution of soap and water, and peel back the edges.

References

Bay-Monk H, Steinmetz CG: *Nursing Care of the Eye*. San Mateo, CA and Norwalk, CT: Appleton & Lange, 1988.

Bickford ME: Patient teaching tools in the ophthalmic unit. *J Ophthalm Nurs Technol* 1988; 7(2):50–55.

Bowers AC, Thompson JM: *Clinical Manual of Health Assessment*, 3d ed. St. Louis: Mosby, 1988.

Callanan M: Neurologic dysfunctions. In: *Manual of Critical Care: Applying Nursing Diagnoses to Adult Critical Illness,* 2d ed. Swearingen PL et al. St. Louis: Mosby, 1991.

Cuzzell JZ, Willey T: Pressure relief perennials. *Am J Nurs* 1987; 87(9):1157–1160.

Deveau BJ: Sensory disorders. In: *Manual of Nursing Therapeutics: Applying Nursing Diagnoses to Medical Disorders,* 2d ed. Swearingen PL. St. Louis: Mosby, 1990.

Hannley M: *Basic Principles of Auditory Assessment*. San Diego: College-Hill Press, 1986.

Hickey J: *Neurological and Neurosurgical Nursing*. Philadelphia: Lippincott, 1986.

Kozier B, Erb G: *Techniques in Clinical Nursing,* 3d ed. Redwood City, CA: Addison-Wesley, 1989.

Rudy EB: *Advanced Neurological and Neurosurgical Nursing*. St. Louis: Mosby, 1984.

Spence A, Mason E: *Human Anatomy and Physiology,* 3d ed. Redwood City, CA: Benjamin/Cummings, 1987.

Stevens SA, Becker KL: A simple, step-by-step approach to neurologic assessment. *Nursing 88:* (Sept) 1988; 53–61.

Stotts NA: Pressure ulcers. In: *Manual of Nursing Therapeutics,* 2d ed. Swearingen PL. St. Louis: Mosby, 1990.

Stowe AC: Neurologic dysfunctions. In: *Manual of Critical Care: Applying Nursing Diagnoses to Adult Critical Illness,* 2d ed. Swearingen PL. St. Louis: Mosby, 1991.

Swearingen PL: Assessing respiratory patterns. In: *Manual of Critical Care: Applying Nursing Diagnoses to Adult Critical Illness,* 2d ed. Swearingen PL. St. Louis: Mosby, 1991.

Swift CM: Neurologic disorders. In: *Manual of Nursing Therapeutics: Applying Nursing Diagnoses to Medical Disorders,* 2d ed. Swearingen PL. St. Louis: Mosby, 1990.

Thompson JM et al: *Mosby's Manual of Clinical Nursing,* 2d ed. St. Louis: Mosby, 1989.

INDEX